D0948290

GENERAL HISTORY OF AFRICA · VII

Africa under Colonial Domination 1880-1935

Unesco General History of Africa

UNESCO International Scientific Committee for the Drafting of a General History of Africa

GENERAL HISTORY OF AFRICA · VII

Africa under Colonial Domination 1880-1935

EDITOR A. ADU BOAHEN

HEINEMANN · CALIFORNIA · UNESCO

First published 1985 by the
United Nations Educational, Scientific
and Cultural Organization,
7 Place de Fontenoy, 75700 Paris

and

Heinemann Educational Books Ltd
22 Bedford Square, London WCIB 3HH
P.M.B. 5205, Ibadan P.O. Box 45314, Nairobi
EDINBURGH   MELBOURNE   AUCKLAND
HONG KONG   SINGAPORE   KUALA LUMPUR
NEW DELHI   KINGSTON   PORT OF SPAIN

First published 1985
in the United States of America by the
University of California Press
2120 Berkeley Way, Berkeley
California 94720, United States of America

© Unesco 1985

Heinemann Educational Books ISBN 0 435 94813 X

Unesco   ISBN 92–3–101–713–6
University of California Press ISBN 0–520–03918–1
                                LCN 78–57321

Filmset in 11 pt Monophoto Ehrhardt by
Northumberland Press Ltd, Gateshead, Tyne and Wear
Printed and bound in Great Britain by
Richard Clay (The Chaucer Press) Ltd, Bungay, Suffolk

Contents

Contents

N.B.   Y. KWARTENG worked as editorial assistant to the volume editor.

List of figures

List of plates

List of tables

Acknowledgements for plates

Akpan, M. B., 11.2, 28.2
Alan Hutchison Library, 29.5
Asare Opoku, K., 20.7
BBC Hulton Picture Library, 2.2(e), 4.3, 4.4, 6.4, 13.1(c), 13.1(d), 16.1, 17.1, 17.2
Clarendon Press, Oxford, 25.2
East African Publishing House, Nairobi, 7.2, 26.1, 26.2
Edinburgh University Press, 20.5
Foreign and Commonwealth Office, London, 19.4
Frank Cass and Co., 19.1
Garyounis University, Benghazi, Central Library, 5.1, 5.2
Harlingue-Viollet, 2.2(f), 5.4, 6.1, 6.5(a), 6.5(b), 10.2, 10.3, 11.1, 23.1, 23.2, 24.1, 28.2
Hopson, Susan, 6.2
Illustrated London News Picture Library, 13.3
Imperial War Museum, London, 2.2(d), 12.1, 12.2, 12.3, 12.4, 12.5, 13.4
International African Institute, London, 27.1
Keystone Press Agency, 16.3, 25.3
Lapi Viollet, 10.1
Longman, 2.2(c), 6.3, 9.2, 16.2, 24.2, 25.1
Mary Evans Picture Library, 2.1, 4.1, 13.1(a)
Methodist Missionary Society, London, 20.4
Musée de l'Homme, Paris, front cover photograph
Museum of Mankind, London, 1.1
National Army Museum, London, 2.2(a), 9.1
Popperfoto, 21.3, 26.2
Roger-Viollet, 13.1(b), 13.2, 24.3
Royal Commonwealth Society, London, 2.2(b), 4.2, 4.5, 7.1, 7.3, 9.3, 19.2, 19.3, 20.2, 29.1, 29.2, 29.3
Spillman, G. 1968 (see Bibliography), 5.4
Stanford University Press, 18.1
Sudanese Ministry of Social Affairs, Khartoum, 23.3
Tshibangu, Mgr T., 20.6
University of Washington, Seattle, 20.3
Verger, Pierre, 29.4(a)–(d)
Werner Forman Archives, 21.1, 21.2
Zambia National Tourist Board, 20.1
Zimbabwe National Archives, Harare, 8.3

Preface

AMADOU-MAHTAR M'BOW
Director-General of Unesco

For a long time, all kinds of myths and prejudices concealed the true history of Africa from the world at large. African societies were looked upon as societies that could have no history. In spite of important work done by such pioneers as Leo Frobenius, Maurice Delafosse and Arturo Labriola, as early as the first decades of this century, a great many non-African experts could not rid themselves of certain preconceptions and argued that the lack of written sources and documents made it impossible to engage in any scientific study of such societies.

Although the *Iliad* and *Odyssey* were rightly regarded as essential sources for the history of ancient Greece, African oral tradition, the collective memory of peoples which holds the thread of many events marking their lives, was rejected as worthless. In writing the history of a large part of Africa, the only sources used were from outside the continent, and the final product gave a picture not so much of the paths actually taken by the African peoples as of those that the authors thought they must have taken. Since the European Middle Ages were often used as a yardstick, modes of production, social relations and political institutions were visualized only by reference to the European past.

In fact, there was a refusal to see Africans as the creators of original cultures which flowered and survived over the centuries in patterns of their own making and which historians are unable to grasp unless they forgo their prejudices and rethink their approach.

Furthermore, the continent of Africa was hardly ever looked upon as a historical entity. On the contrary, emphasis was laid on everything likely to lend credence to the idea that a split had existed, from time immemorial, between a 'white Africa' and a 'black Africa', each unaware of the other's existence. The Sahara was often presented as an impenetrable space preventing any intermingling of ethnic groups and peoples or any exchange of goods, beliefs, customs and ideas between the societies that had grown up on either side of the desert. Hermetic frontiers were drawn between the civilizations of Ancient Egypt and Nubia and those of the peoples south of the Sahara.

It is true that the history of Africa north of the Sahara has been more closely linked with that of the Mediterranean basin than has the history of sub-Saharan Africa, but it is now widely recognized that the various civilizations of the African continent, for all their differing languages and cultures, represent, to a greater or lesser degree, the historical offshoots of a set of peoples and societies united by bonds centuries old.

Another phenomenon which did great disservice to the objective study of the African past was the appearance, with the slave trade and colonization, of racial stereotypes which bred contempt and lack of understanding and became so deep-rooted that they distorted even the basic concepts of historiography. From the time when the notions of 'white' and 'black' were used as generic labels by the colonialists, who were regarded as superior, the colonized Africans had to struggle against both economic and psychological enslavement. Africans were identifiable by the colour of their skin, they had become a kind of merchandise, they were earmarked for hard labour and eventually, in the minds of those dominating them, they came to symbolize an imaginary and allegedly inferior *Negro* race. This pattern of spurious identification relegated the history of the African peoples in many minds to the rank of ethno-history, in which appreciation of the historical and cultural facts was bound to be warped.

The situation has changed significantly since the end of the Second World War and in particular since the African countries became independent and began to take an active part in the life of the international community and in the mutual exchanges that are its *raison d'être*. An increasing number of historians has endeavoured to tackle the study of Africa with a more rigorous, objective and open-minded outlook by using – with all due precautions – actual African sources. In exercising their right to take the historical initiative, Africans themselves have felt a deep-seated need to re-establish the historical authenticity of their societies on solid foundations.

In this context, the importance of the eight-volume *General History of Africa*, which Unesco is publishing, speaks for itself.

The experts from many countries working on this project began by laying down the theoretical and methodological basis for the *History*. They have been at pains to call in question the over-simplifications arising from a linear and restrictive conception of world history and to re-establish the true facts wherever necessary and possible. They have endeavoured to highlight the historical data that give a clearer picture of the evolution of the different peoples of Africa in their specific socio-cultural setting.

To tackle this huge task, made all the more complex and difficult by the vast range of sources and the fact that documents were widely scattered, Unesco has had to proceed by stages. The first stage, from 1965 to 1969, was devoted to gathering documentation and planning the work. Operational assignments were conducted in the field and included campaigns to collect oral traditions, the creation of regional documentation centres for oral traditions, the collection of unpublished manuscripts in Arabic and Ajami (African languages written in Arabic script), the compilation of archival inventories and the preparation of a *Guide to the Sources of the History of Africa*, culled from the archives and libraries of the countries of Europe and later published in eleven volumes. In addition, meetings were organized to enable experts from Africa and other continents to discuss questions of methodology and lay down the broad lines for the project after careful examination of the available sources.

The second stage, which lasted from 1969 to 1971, was devoted to shaping the *History* and linking its different parts. The purpose of the international meetings of experts held in Paris in 1969 and Addis Ababa in 1970 was to study and define the problems involved in drafting and publishing the *History*: presentation in eight volumes, the principal edition in English, French and Arabic, translation into African languages such as Kiswahili, Hausa, Fulani, Yoruba or Lingala, prospective versions in German, Russian, Portuguese, Spanish and Chinese, as well as abridged editions designed for a wide African and international public.[1]

The third stage has involved actual drafting and publication. This began with the appointment of the 39-member International Scientific Committee, two-thirds African and one-third non-African, which assumes intellectual responsibility for the *History*.

The method used is interdisciplinary and is based on a multi-faceted approach and a wide variety of sources. The first among these is archaeology, which holds many of the keys to the history of African cultures and civilizations. Thanks to archaeology, it is now acknowledged that Africa was very probably the cradle of mankind and the scene – in the neolithic period – of one of the first technological revolutions in history. Archaeology has also shown that Egypt was the setting for one of the most brilliant ancient civilizations of the world. But another very important source is oral tradition, which, after being long despised, has now emerged as an invaluable instrument for discovering the history of Africa, making it possible to follow the movements of its different peoples in both space and time, to understand the African vision of the world from the inside and to grasp the original features of the values on which the cultures and institutions of the continent are based.

We are indebted to the International Scientific Committee in charge of this *General History of Africa*, and to its Rapporteur and the editors and authors of the various volumes and chapters, for having shed a new light on the African past in its authentic and all-encompassing form and for having avoided any dogmatism in the study of essential issues. Among these issues we might cite: the slave trade, that 'endlessly bleeding wound', which was responsible for one of the cruellest mass deportations in the history of mankind, which sapped the African continent of its life-blood while contributing significantly to the economic and commercial expansion

1. Volumes I and II have been published in Portuguese and Spanish, and Volume I in Arabic.

of Europe; colonization, with all the effects it had on population, economics, psychology and culture; relations between Africa south of the Sahara and the Arab world; and, finally, the process of decolonization and nation-building which mobilized the intelligence and passion of people still alive and sometimes still active today. All these issues have been broached with a concern for honesty and rigour which is not the least of the *History*'s merits. By taking stock of our knowledge of Africa, putting forward a variety of viewpoints on African cultures and offering a new reading of history, the *History* has the signal advantage of showing up the light and shade and of openly portraying the differences of opinion that may exist between scholars.

By demonstrating the inadequacy of the methodological approaches which have long been used in research on Africa, this *History* calls for a new and careful study of the twofold problem areas of historiography and cultural identity, which are united by links of reciprocity. Like any historical work of value, the *History* paves the way for a great deal of further research on a variety of topics.

It is for this reason that the International Scientific Committee, in close collaboration with Unesco, decided to embark on additional studies in an attempt to go deeper into a number of issues which will permit a clearer understanding of certain aspects of the African past. The findings being published in the series 'Unesco Studies and Documents – General History of Africa'[2] will prove a useful supplement to the *History*, as will the works planned on aspects of national or subregional history.

The *General History* sheds light both on the historical unity of Africa and also its relations with the other continents, particularly the Americas and the Caribbean. For a long time, the creative manifestations of the descendants of Africans in the Americas were lumped together by some historians as a heterogeneous collection of *Africanisms*. Needless to say, this is not the attitude of the authors of the *History*, in which the resistance of the slaves shipped to America, the constant and massive participation of the descendants of Africans in the struggles for the initial independence of America and in national liberation movements, are rightly perceived for what they were: vigorous assertions of identity, which helped forge the universal concept of mankind. Although the phenomenon may vary in different places, it is now quite clear that ways of feeling, thinking, dreaming and acting in certain nations of the western hemisphere have

2. The following eight volumes have already been published in this series: *The peopling of ancient Egypt and the deciphering of Meroitic script*; *The African slave trade from the fifteenth to the nineteenth century*; *Historical relations across the Indian Ocean*; *The historiography of Southern Africa*; *The decolonization of Africa: Southern Africa and the Horn of Africa*; *African ethnonyms and toponyms*; *Historical and socio-cultural relations between black Africa and the Arab world from 1935 to the present* and *The methodology of contemporary African history*.

been marked by their African heritage. The cultural inheritance of Africa is visible everywhere, from the southern United States to northern Brazil, across the Caribbean and on the Pacific seaboard. In certain places it even underpins the cultural identity of some of the most important elements of the population.

The *History* also clearly brings out Africa's relations with southern Asia across the Indian Ocean and the African contributions to other civilizations through mutual exchanges.

I am convinced that the efforts of the peoples of Africa to conquer or strengthen their independence, secure their development and assert their cultural characteristics, must be rooted in historical awareness renewed, keenly felt and taken up by each succeeding generation.

My own background, the experience I gained as a teacher and as chairman, from the early days of independence, of the first commission set up to reform history and geography curricula in some of the countries of West and Central Africa, taught me how necessary it was for the education of young people and for the information of the public at large to have a history book produced by scholars with inside knowledge of the problems and hopes of Africa and with the ability to apprehend the continent in its entirety.

For all these reasons, Unesco's goal will be to ensure that this *General History of Africa* is widely disseminated in a large number of languages and is used as a basis for producing children's books, school textbooks and radio and television programmes. Young people, whether schoolchildren or students, and adults in Africa and elsewhere will thus be able to form a truer picture of the African continent's past and the factors that explain it, as well as a fairer understanding of its cultural heritage and its contribution to the general progress of mankind. The *History* should thus contribute to improved international cooperation and stronger solidarity among peoples in their aspirations to justice, progress and peace. This is, at least, my most cherished hope.

It remains for me to express my deep gratitude to the members of the International Scientific Committee, the Rapporteur, the different volume editors, the authors and all those who have collaborated in this tremendous undertaking. The work they have accomplished and the contribution they have made plainly go to show how people from different backgrounds but all imbued with the same spirit of goodwill and enthusiasm in the service of universal truth can, within the international framework provided by Unesco, bring to fruition a project of considerable scientific and cultural import. My thanks also go to the organizations and governments whose generosity has made it possible for Unesco to publish this *History* in different languages and thus ensure that it will have the worldwide impact it deserves and thereby serve the international community as a whole.

Description of the Project

B. A. OGOT

*Former President, International Scientific Committee
for the Drafting of a General History of Africa*

The General Conference of Unesco at its 16th Session instructed the
Director-General to undertake the drafting of a *General History of Africa*.
The enormous task of implementing the project was entrusted to an International Scientific Committee which was established by the Executive
Board in 1970. This Committee, under the Statutes adopted by the Executive Board of Unesco in 1971, is composed of thirty-nine members (two-
thirds of whom are African and one-third non-African) serving in their
personal capacity and appointed by the Director-General of Unesco for
the duration of the Committee's mandate.

The first task of the Committee was to define the principal characteristics
of the work. These were defined at the first session of the Committee
as follows:

(a) Although aiming at the highest possible scientific level, the history
does not seek to be exhaustive and is a work of synthesis avoiding dogmatism. In many respects, it is a statement of problems showing the present
state of knowledge and the main trends in research, and it does not hesitate
to show divergencies of views where these exist. In this way, it prepares
the ground for future work.

(b) Africa is considered in this work as a totality. The aim is to show
the historical relationships between the various parts of the continent, too
frequently subdivided in works published to date. Africa's historical connections with the other continents receive due attention, these connections
being analysed in terms of mutual exchanges and multilateral influences,
bringing out, in its appropriate light, Africa's contribution to the history
of mankind.

(c) *The General History of Africa* is, in particular, a history of ideas and
civilizations, societies and institutions. It is based on a wide variety of
sources, including oral tradition and art forms.

(d) The *History* is viewed essentially from the inside. Although a scholarly
work, it is also, in large measure, a faithful reflection of the way in which
African authors view their own civilization. While prepared in an international framework and drawing to the full on the present stock of scientific
knowledge, it should also be a vitally important element in the recognition

of the African heritage and should bring out the factors making for unity in the continent. This effort to view things from within is the novel feature of the project and should, in addition to its scientific quality, give it great topical significance. By showing the true face of Africa, the *History* could, in an era absorbed in economic and technical struggles, offer a particular conception of human values.

The Committee has decided to present the work covering over three million years of African history in eight volumes, each containing about eight hundred pages of text with illustrations, photographs, maps and line drawings.

A chief editor, assisted if necessary by one or two co-editors, is responsible for the preparation of each volume. The editors are elected by the Committee either from among its members or from outside by a two-thirds majority. They are responsible for preparing the volumes in accordance with the decisions and plans adopted by the Committee. On scientific matters, they are accountable to the Committee or, between two sessions of the Committee, to its Bureau for the contents of the volumes, the final version of the texts, the illustrations and, in general, for all scientific and technical aspects of the *History*. The Bureau ultimately approves the final manuscript. When it considers the manuscript ready for publication, it transmits it to the Director-General of Unesco. Thus the Committee, or the Bureau between committee sessions, remains fully in charge of the project.

Each volume consists of some thirty chapters. Each chapter is the work of a principal author assisted, if necessary, by one or two collaborators. The authors are selected by the Committee on the basis of their *curricula vitae*. Preference is given to African authors, provided they have requisite qualifications. Special effort is also made to ensure, as far as possible, that all regions of the continent, as well as other regions having historical or cultural ties with Africa, are equitably represented among the authors.

When the editor of a volume has approved texts of chapters, they are then sent to all members of the Committee for criticism. In addition, the text of the volume editor is submitted for examination to a Reading Committee, set up within the International Scientific Committee on the basis of the members' fields of competence. The Reading Committee analyses the chapters from the standpoint of both substance and form. The Bureau then gives final approval to the manuscripts.

Such a seemingly long and involved procedure has proved necessary, since it provides the best possible guarantee of the scientific objectivity of the *General History of Africa*. There have, in fact, been instances when the Bureau has rejected manuscripts or insisted on major revisions or even reassigned the drafting of a chapter to another author. Occasionally, specialists in a particular period of history or in a particular question are consulted to put the finishing touches to a volume.

The work will be published first in a hard-cover edition in English, French and Arabic, and later in paperback editions in the same languages. An abridged version in English and French will serve as a basis for translation into African languages. The Committee has chosen Kiswahili and Hausa as the first African languages into which the work will be translated.

Also, every effort will be made to ensure publication of the *General History of Africa* in other languages of wide international currency such as Chinese, Portuguese, Russian, German, Italian, Spanish, Japanese, etc.

It is thus evident that this is a gigantic task which constitutes an immense challenge to African historians and to the scholarly community at large, as well as to Unesco under whose auspices the work is being done. For the writing of a continental history of Africa, covering the last three million years, using the highest canons of scholarship and involving, as it must do, scholars drawn from diverse countries, cultures, ideologies and historical traditions, is surely a complex undertaking. It constitutes a continental, international and interdisciplinary project of great proportions.

In conclusion, I would like to underline the significance of this work for Africa and for the world. At a time when the peoples of Africa are striving towards unity and greater cooperation in shaping their individual destinies, a proper understanding of Africa's past, with an awareness of common ties among Africans and between Africa and other continents, should not only be a major contribution towards mutual understanding among the people of the earth, but also a source of knowledge of a cultural heritage that belongs to all mankind.

Note on chronology

It has been agreed to adopt the following method for writing dates. With regard to prehistory, dates may be written in two different ways.

One way is by reference to the present era, that is, dates BP (before present), the reference year being $+1950$; all dates are negative in relation to $+1950$.

The other way is by reference to the beginning of the Christian era. Dates are represented in relation to the Christian era by a simple $+$ or $-$ sign before the date. When referring to centuries, the terms BC and AD are replaced by 'before our era' and 'of our era'.

Some examples are as follows:

(i) 2300 BP $= -350$
(ii) 2900 BC $= -2900$
 AD 1800 $= +1800$
(iii) 5th century BC $=$ 5th century before our era
 3rd century AD $=$ 3rd century of our era

1

Africa and the colonial challenge

A. ADU BOAHEN

Never in the history of Africa did so many changes occur and with such speed as they did between 1880 and 1935. Indeed, the most fundamental and dramatic – though tragic – of these changes took place in the much shorter period from 1890 to 1910, the period that saw the conquest and occupation of virtually the whole continent of Africa by the imperial powers and the establishment of the colonial system. The period after 1910 was essentially one of consolidation and exploitation of the system. The pace of this drama was truly astonishing, for as late as 1880 only very limited areas of Africa had come under the direct rule of Europeans. In the whole of West Africa, only the island and coastal areas of Senegal, the town of Freetown and its environs (now in Sierra Leone), the southern parts of the Gold Coast (now Ghana), the coastal areas of Abidjan in Ivory Coast and Porto Novo in Dahomey (now Benin) and the island of Lagos (in what is now Nigeria) had come under the direct rule of Europeans. In North Africa, it was only Algeria that had by 1880 been colonized by the French. Not an inch of the whole of East Africa had come under the control of any European power, while only the coastal stretches of Mozambique and Angola of the whole of Central Africa were being ruled by the Portuguese. It was only in Southern Africa that foreign rule had not only been firmly implanted but had even been extended a considerable distance inland (see Fig. 1.1). In short, by as late as 1880, about as much as 80% of the continent of Africa was being ruled by her own kings, queens, clan and lineage heads, in empires, kingdoms, communities and polities of various sizes and shapes.

However, within the next thirty years, this situation underwent a phenomenal and indeed a revolutionary change. By 1914, with the sole exception of Ethiopia and Liberia, the whole of Africa had been subjected to the rule of European powers in colonies of various sizes which were generally much larger physically but often bore little or no relationship to the pre-existing polities. But it was not African sovereignty and independence alone that had been lost at that time. It represented also an assault on established cultures. As Ferhat Abbas pointed out in 1930 in reference to the French colonization of Algeria, for the French, colonization was 'simply a military

[handwritten margin note: Libya was ruled by the Italians]

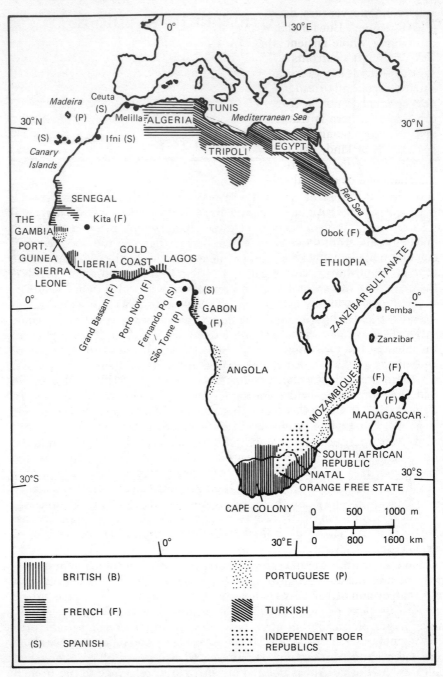

FIG. 1.1 *Africa on the eve of partition showing extent of conquest by 1880*

and economic venture defended thereafter by the appropriate ad
trative regime'. But for the Algerians, it was 'a veritable revolution, \
throwing a whole ancient world of beliefs and ideas and an immemo.
way of life. It confronts a whole people with sudden change. An enti\
nation, without any preparation, finds itself forced to adapt or perish. This
situation is bound to lead to a moral and physical disequilibrium, the barrenness of which is not far from total disintegration.'[1] The nature of colonialism depicted here is true not only of French colonialism in Algeria but
of European colonialism throughout Africa; the difference being one of
degree not of kind, one of style not of substance. In other words, then,
during the period 1880 to 1935, Africa did face a very serious challenge,
the challenge of colonialism.

The state of African preparedness

What was the attitude of the Africans themselves to the establishment of
colonialism, involving as it did such a fundamental change in the nature
of the relationships that had existed between them and the Europeans over
the preceding three hundred years? This is a question that has so far not
been seriously considered by historians, African or European, but it needs
to be answered. The answer is quite clear and unequivocal: an overwhelming
majority of African authorities and leaders were vehemently opposed to
this change and expressed their determination to maintain the status quo
and, above all, to retain their sovereignty and independence, an issue on
which virtually all of them were not in any way prepared to compromise.
This answer can be documented from the very words of the contemporary
African leaders themselves. In 1891, when the British offered protection
to Prempeh I of Asante in the Gold Coast, he replied:

> The suggestion that Asante in its present state should come and enjoy
> the protection of Her Majesty the Queen and Empress of India I
> may say is a matter of very serious consideration, and which I am
> happy to say we have arrived at this conclusion, that my kingdom
> of Asante will never commit itself to any such policy. Asante must
> remain as of old at the same time to remain friendly with all white
> men. I do not write this in a boastful spirit but in the clear sense
> of its meaning ... the cause of Asante is progressing and there is
> no reason for any Asante man to feel alarm at the prospects or to
> believe for a single instant that our cause has been driven back by
> the events of the past hostilities.[2]

In 1895, Wobogo, the Moro Naba, or King of the Mossi (in modern
Upper Volta), told the French officer, Captain Destenave:

1. F. Abbās, 1931, p. 9; quoted by J. Berque in Chapter 24 below.
2. Quoted by J. Fynn in M. Crowder (ed.), 1971, pp. 43–4.

3

I know that the whites wish to kill me in order to take my country, and yet you claim that they will help me to organize my country. But I find my country good just as it is. I have no need of them. I know what is necessary for me and what I want: I have my own merchants: also, consider yourself fortunate that I do not order your head to be cut off. Go away now, and above all, never come back.[3]

Similar sentiments were expressed by Lat Dior, the Damel of Cayor (in modern Senegal) in 1883 (quoted in Chapter 6 below), by King Machemba of the Yao in what is now mainland Tanzania in 1890 (quoted in Chapter 3 below) and by Hendrik Wittboi, a king in what is now Namibia (quoted in Chapter 3 below). But the last and most fascinating piece of evidence I would like to cite here is the moving appeal addressed by Menelik of Ethiopia to Queen Victoria of Great Britain in April 1891. Similar letters were sent to the heads of state of France, Germany, Italy and Russia. In this appeal, Menelik first defined the then boundaries of Ethiopia, and – expressing personal expansionist ambitions – declared his intention to re-establish 'the former boundaries of Ethiopia as far as Khartoum and the Niza Lake, including all of the territories of the Gallas', and added:

> *I have no intention at all of being an indifferent spectator, if the distant Powers hold the idea of dividing up Africa, Ethiopia having been for the past fourteen centuries, an island of Christians in a sea of Pagans.*
>
> Since the All-Powerful has protected Ethiopia up until now, I am hopeful that He will keep and enlarge it also in the future, and I do not think for a moment that He will divide Ethiopia among the other Powers.
>
> Formerly the boundary of Ethiopia was the sea. Failing the use of force and failing the aid of the Christians, our boundary on the sea fell into the hands of the Muslims. Today we do not pretend to be able to recover our sea coast by force; but we hope that the Christian Powers, advised by our Saviour, Jesus Christ, will restore our seacoast boundary to us, or that they will give us at least a few points along the coast.[4]

When in spite of this appeal, the Italians launched their campaign against Ethiopia with the connivance of Britain and France, Menelik issued a mobilization proclamation on 17 September 1895 in which he stated:

Enemies have now come upon us to ruin our country and to change our religion ... Our enemies have begun the affair by advancing and digging into the country like moles. With the help of God I will not

3. Quoted by M. Crowder, 1968, p. 97.
4. Archives of the Ministero degli Affari Esteri (Rome), ASMAI, Ethiopia Pos. 36/13–109 Menelik to Queen Victoria, Addis Ababa, 14 Miazia, 1883, encl. in Tarnielli to MAE, London, 6 August 1891.

deliver up my country to them ... Today, you who are strong, give me of your strength, and you who are weak, help me by prayer.[5]

These are the very words of the men who were facing the colonial challenge and they prove beyond any doubt the strength of their determination to oppose the Europeans and to defend their sovereignty, religion and traditional way of life.

It is equally clear from all these quotations that these rulers were confident of their preparedness to face the European invaders, as well might they have been. First, they were fully confident that their magic, their ancestors and certainly their gods or god would come to their aid, and many of them on the eve of the actual physical confrontation either resorted to prayers or sacrifices or to herbs and incantations. As Elliot P. Skinner has recorded:

> It is generally believed by the Mossi that when the French attacked Ouagadougou, the deposed Mogho Naba Wobogo made sacrifices to earth shrines. Tradition has it that he sacrificed a black cock, a black ram, a black donkey, and a black slave on a large hill near the White Volta River, beseeching the earth goddess to drive the French away and to destroy the traitor Mazi whom they had placed upon the throne.[6]

And as will be seen in many of the following chapters, religion was indeed one of the weapons used against colonialism. Moreover, many African rulers had been able to build empires of varying size only a couple of decades back, and some were still in the process of expanding or reviving their kingdoms. Many of them had been able to defend their sovereignties with the support of their people using traditional weapons and tactics. Some of them, like Samori Ture of the Mandinka empire in West Africa, and Menelik of Ethiopia, had even been able to modernize their armies. Because of this, the African rulers saw no reason why they could not maintain their sovereignty at that time. Furthermore, some thought they could stave off the invaders through diplomacy. As we shall see below, in 1889, while Cecil Rhodes was preparing to occupy the land of the Ndebele, their king, Lobengula, dispatched a delegation to London to see Queen Victoria; and while the British invading army was marching towards Kumasi in 1896 to seize Prempeh five years after he had turned down the British offer of protection, he dispatched a powerful diplomatic mission to Queen Victoria. As seen above, Menelik addressed a similar appeal to the same monarch as well as to other European heads of state.

It is also obvious from some of the quotations above that many African rulers did in fact welcome the new changes that were steadily being introduced from the third decade of the nineteenth century since these changes had hitherto posed no threat to their sovereignty and independence. In

5. Quoted in H. Marcus, 1975, p. 160.
6. E. P. Skinner, 1964, p. 133. See also E. Isichei, 1977, p. 181.

West Africa, for instance, thanks to the activities of the missionaries, Fourah Bay College had been founded as early as 1827 in Sierra Leone, while elementary schools and a secondary school each in the Gold Coast and Nigeria had been established by the 1870s. Indeed, a call for the establishment of a university in West Africa by the Caribbean-born pan-Africanist, Edward Wilmot Blyden had already gone out. As early as 1887 some of the wealthy Africans had even begun to send their children to Europe for further education and professional training and some of them had returned to the Gold Coast as fully qualified barristers and doctors.

Above all, following the abolition of the hideous and inhuman traffic in slaves, the Africans had been able to change over to an economy based on the exportation of cash crops – palm oil in Nigeria, groundnuts in Senegal and The Gambia – all before 1880 and cocoa had just been re-introduced into the Gold Coast by Tetteh Quashie from Fernando Po in 1879. And all this had occurred without the establishment of any direct European rule except in small pockets on the coast. Indeed, the relatively small group of West Africans who had benefited from European-style education were – by 1880 – doing extremely well. They were dominating the few civil service posts offered by European administrations; on the coast, some of them were running their own import–export businesses and were monopolizing the internal distribution of imported goods. It was in East Africa that European influences were still minimal, although after the epoch-making journeys of Livingstone and Stanley and the subsequent propaganda by missionary societies, it was only a matter of time before churches and schools, and with them roads and railways, would make their appearance.

As far as Africans were concerned, then, they did not see any need for any radical change in their centuries-old relations with Europe, and they were confident that if the Europeans wanted to force any changes on them and push their way inland, they would be able to stop them as they had been able to do for the last two or three hundred years. Hence the note of confidence, if not of defiance, that rings through the words quoted above.

But what the Africans did not realize was that by 1880, thanks to the diffusion of the industrial revolution in Europe, and the subsequent technological progress signified by the steamship, the railway, the telegraph, and, above all, the first machine gun – the Maxim gun – the Europeans whom they were about to face now had new political ambitions, economic needs and a relatively advanced technology. That is, they did not know that the old era of free trade and informal political control had given way to, to borrow Basil Davidson's words, 'the era of the new imperialism and rival capitalist monopolies'[7] and therefore that it was not only trade that the Europeans now wanted but also direct political control. Secondly, the African leaders were not aware of the fact that the guns that they had used hitherto and stockpiled, the muzzle-loading muskets – the French

7. B. Davidson, 1978(a), p. 19.

captured 21 365 muskets from the Baule of Ivory Coast after the suppression of their final revolt in 1911[8] – were totally outmoded and no match for the new breech-loading rifles used by the Europeans, which had about ten times the rate of fire at six times the charge, and the new ultra-rapid-fire Maxims (see Plate 1.1). The English poet Hilaire Belloc summed up the situation aptly:

> Whatever happens we have got
> The maxim-gun and they have not[9]

It is here that African rulers miscalculated, in many cases with tragic consequences. As will be seen later, all the chiefs quoted above, except one, were defeated and lost their sovereignty. Lat Dior, moreover, was killed; Prempeh, Behazin and Cetshwayo of the Zulu were exiled and Lobengula of the Ndebele died in flight. Only Menelik, as will be seen in a later chapter, defeated the Italian invaders and thereby maintained his sovereignty and independence.

The structure of Volume VII

It is evident, then, that relations between Africans and Europeans did undergo a revolutionary change and Africa was faced with a serious colonial challenge between 1880 and 1935. What then were the origins of this phenomenal challenge, the challenge of colonialism? Or put differently, how and why did the three-centuries-old relations between Africa and Europe undergo such drastic and fundamental change during this period? How was the colonial system established in Africa and what measures, political, economic, psychological and ideological, were adopted to underpin the system? How prepared was Africa to face and how did she face this challenge and with what success? Which of the new changes were accepted and which were rejected? What of the old was retained and what was destroyed? What adaptations and accommodations were made? How many institutions were undermined, or how many disintegrated? What were the effects of all this on Africa, its peoples and their political, social and economic structures and institutions? Finally, what is the significance of colonialism for Africa and her history? These are the questions that this volume will attempt to answer.

For the purpose of answering these questions, and explaining African initiatives and responses in the face of the colonial challenge, this volume has been divided, apart from the first two chapters, into three main sections. Each section is preceded by a chapter (3, 13, 22) in which the theme of the section is surveyed in a general way and from a continental perspective, and the subsequent chapters are dealt with on a regional basis. The introductory section comprising this and the next chapter discusses African

8. T. C. Weiskel, 1980, p. 203.
9. Quoted by M. Perham, 1961, p. 32.

PLATE 1.1 *The Asante War of 1896 (Gold Coast): some of the British invaders with a Maxim gun*

attitudes and preparedness on the eve of this fundamental change in the relations between Africa and the Europeans, and the reasons for the partition, conquest and occupation of Africa by the European imperial powers. It should be pointed out, since this is often ignored, that the phase of actual conquest was preceded by years of negotiation and treaty-making between the imperial powers and African rulers. This phase of negotiation shows that the European powers originally accepted their African counterparts as their equals, and, secondly, that the former did recognize the sovereignty and independence of the African states and polities.

The second section deals with a theme that had until the 1960s either been grossly misrepresented or entirely ignored by the colonial school of African historiography, namely, African initiatives and reactions in the face of the conquest and occupation of Africa. To the members of this school such as H. H. Johnston, Sir Alan Burns and, more recently, Margery Perham, Lewis H. Gann and Peter Duignan,[10] Africans in fact welcomed the establishment of colonial rule since not only did it save them from anarchy and internecine warfare but it also brought them some concrete benefits. Thus Margery Perham:

> most of the tribes quickly accepted European rule as part of an irresistible order, one which brought many benefits, above all peace, and exciting novelties, railways and roads, lamps, bicycles, ploughs, new foods and crops, and all that could be acquired and experienced in town and city. For the ruling classes, traditional or created, it brought a new strength and security of status and new forms of wealth and power. For many years after annexation, though there was much bewilderment, revolts were very few, and there does not *appear* to have been much sense of indignity at being ruled.[11]

Such ideas are also reflected in the use of such Eurocentric terms as 'pacification', *Pax Britannica* and *Pax Gallica* used to describe what amounted to the conquest and occupation of Africa between 1890 and 1914.

Those historians who did pay some attention to this subject mentioned it almost accidentally or casually. In their *A Short History of Africa* which first appeared in 1962, one of the very first modern professional surveys of the history of Africa, the English historians, Roland Oliver and J. D. Fage, devoted only a single paragraph to what they termed 'bitter resistance' by Africans in a chapter of fourteen pages dealing with what has become known as the European Scramble for African colonies. It is to correct this wrong interpretation of the colonial school and to redress the balance and highlight the African perspective that we have devoted as many as seven chapters to this theme of African initiatives and reactions.

It will be seen from these chapters that the view that Africans received

10. H. H. Johnston, 1899, 1913; A. C. Burns, 1957; M. Perham, 1960(a); L. H. Gann and P. Duignan, 1967.
11. M. Perham, 1960(a), p. 28.

the invading soldiers with elation and quickly accepted colonial rule is not borne out by the available evidence. In fact, African reactions were the very reverse. It is quite evident that Africans were faced with only two options, either to readily surrender their sovereignty and independence, or to defend them at all costs. It is most significant that the great majority of them, as will be amply demonstrated in this volume, irrespective of the political and socio-economic structures of their states and in the face of all the odds against them, did decide to defend their sovereignty and independence. The weight of the odds against them on the one hand and the strength of the determination to resist at any price on the other are both captured by the relief reproduced on the jacket of this volume. This relief, painted on one of the walls of the palace of the kings of Dahomey in Abomey, depicts an African armed with only a bow and arrow defiantly and squarely facing a European armed with a gun.

John D. Hargreaves, for instance, poses this interesting question. Given the:

> range of possible attitudes on the part of the European invaders, a number of options might be open to African rulers. Among the short-term advantages obtainable from treaties or from collaboration with Europeans were not merely access to fire-arms and consumer goods, but opportunities to enlist powerful allies in external or internal disputes. Why then did so many African states reject such opportunities, choosing to resist the Europeans in battle?[12]

This may sound enigmatic, but only so to somebody looking at the whole issue from a Eurocentric point of view. To the African, the issue at stake was not short-term or long-term advantages but rather the fundamental question of his land and his sovereignty, and it is precisely because of this that virtually all African polities, centralized and non-centralized alike, sooner or later chose to maintain or defend or try to regain their sovereignty. To them, there could be no compromise on that, and indeed many of the leaders of these states chose to die on the battlefield, go into voluntary flight or face exile rather than surrender their sovereignty without a struggle.

A great majority of African rulers, then, did opt for the defence of their sovereignty and independence. It is in the strategies and the tactics that they adopted to achieve this universal objective that they differed. Most African rulers chose the strategy of confrontation, using either diplomatic or military weapons or both. As will be seen below, Samori Ture, and Kabarega of Bunyoro resorted to both weapons while Prempeh I and Mwanga of Buganda relied on diplomacy. Others such as Tofa of Porto Novo (in what is now Benin) chose the strategy of alliance or co-operation, *not* of collaboration.

This question of strategy should be highlighted here because it has been

12. J. D. Hargreaves in L. H. Gann and P. Duignan (eds), 1969, pp. 205–6.

grossly misunderstood hitherto and this has led to the classification of some of the African rulers as collaborators and their action as that of collaboration. We are opposed to the use of this term collaboration not only because it is inaccurate but also because it is derogatory and Eurocentric. As we have seen above, the fundamental issue at stake between the 1880s and the 1900s as far as the African rulers were concerned, was that of sovereignty, and on this, it was quite clear that nobody was prepared to compromise. Those African rulers who have been mistakenly termed collaborators were those who thought that the best way of safeguarding their sovereignty or even regaining the sovereignty that they might have lost to some African power previous to the arrival of the Europeans was *not* to collaborate but rather to *ally* with the European invaders. A collaborator is surely one who betrays the national cause by colluding with the enemy to pursue the goals and objectives of the enemy rather than the interests of his own nation. But as we have seen, the Africans were all faced with the question of surrendering, retaining or regaining their sovereignty. Those who threw in their lot with the Europeans therefore had their own objective, and it is therefore totally wrong to call them collaborators.

In any case, since the Second World War, the term collaborator has assumed very pejorative connotations and the interesting thing is that some of the historians who use it are aware of this. R. Robinson, for example, stated: 'It should be stressed that the term [collaborator] is used in no pejorative sense'.[13] The question then is if it *can* be so used, why use it at all, especially in the African case where it is so inaccurate? Why not use the word ally which is indeed the more appropriate term? Tofa, the king of the Gun kingdom of Porto Novo has always been cited as a typical example of a collaborator. But was he? As Hargreaves has clearly shown,[14] Tofa was facing three different enemies at the time of the arrival of the French – the Yoruba to the north-east, the Fon kings of Dahomey to the north and the British on the coast – and he must have seen the arrival of the French as a god-sent opportunity for him not only to protect his sovereignty but even to make some gains at the expense of his enemies. He naturally chose, therefore, not to *collaborate* but to *ally* with the French. Surely only those historians who are not aware of the problems with which Tofa was confronted at that time, or who deny the African any initiative or an awareness of his own interests, or who see the whole issue from a Eurocentric viewpoint, would describe Tofa as a collaborator. Moreover, the fallacy of this term is further demonstrated by the fact that the so-called collaborators who at some points were prepared to ally with Europeans often later became the opposers or resisters of the Europeans: Wobogo, the king of Mossi, Lat Dior, the Damel of Gayor, and even the great Samori Ture himself are examples of such rulers. This makes the classification quite absurd.

13. R. Robinson in R. Owen and B. Sutcliffe (eds), 1972, p. 120.
14. J. D. Hargreaves, in L. H. Gann and P. Duignan (eds), 1969, pp. 214–16.

Finally, only those historians who are really ignorant of or hold very simplistic views about the political and ethno-cultural situation in Africa on the eve of the European partition and conquest would use that term. They assume that all African countries, like many European countries, are inhabited by the same ethno-cultural group or nation, and therefore that any section of that group that allied with an invader could be termed a collaborator. But no African country or colony or empire was made up of any such single ethnic group. Each country or empire was populated by numerous ethno-cultural groups or nations who were as different from each other as, say, the Italians are from the Germans or the French. Moreover, prior to the arrival of the European invaders, relations between these different groups were often hostile while some might even have been subjugated by others. To label such subjugated or hostile groups who chose to join the invading European group against their former foreign enemies or rulers as collaborators is to miss the point. Indeed, as will be demonstrated in some of the chapters of this volume, the nature of African reactions and responses to colonialism was determined not only by the ethno-cultural and political situation with which the Africans were confronted but also by the very nature of the socio-economic forces at work in the particular society at the time of the confrontation, and the nature of its political organization.

Many European historians have condemned the opposers as being romantic and short-sighted and have praised the so-called collaborators as being far-sighted and progressive. As Oliver and Fage put it in 1962:

> If these [African rulers] were far-sighted and well-informed, and more particularly if they had had access to foreign advisers such as missionaries or traders they might well understand that nothing was to be gained by resistance, and much by negotiation. If they were less far-sighted, less fortunate or less well-advised, they would see their traditional enemies siding with the invader and would themselves assume an attitude of resistance, which could all too easily end in military defeat, the deposition of chiefs, the loss of land to the native allies of the occupying power, possibly even to the political fragmentation of the society or state ... As with the slave trade in earlier times, there were gainers as well as losers, and both were to be found within the confines of every colonial territory.[15]

Ronald E. Robinson and John Gallagher have also described opposition or resistance as consisting of 'romantic reactionary struggles against the facts, the passionate protests of societies which were shocked by the new age of change and would not be comforted'.[16] But these views are highly questionable and the dichotomy between resisters and so-called collaborators is not only mechanistic but simply unconvincing. There were certainly

15. R. Oliver and J. D. Fage, 1962, p. 203.
16. R. E. Robinson and J. Gallagher in F. H. Hinsley (ed.), 1962, pp. 639–40.

losers and gainers in the slave trade, but there were no gainers this time. Both resisters and so-called collaborators lost in the end, and what is interesting is that it is the so-called romantic leaders and diehards who are still remembered, and have become a source of inspiration to the nationalist leaders of today.[17] I entirely agree with the conclusion of Robert I. Rotberg and Ali A. Mazrui that 'there is no gainsaying that the introduction of western norms and power, and accompanying controls and constraints, was everywhere in Africa questioned by the peoples affected'.[18]

However, whatever strategy the Africans adopted, all of them – with the sole exception of the Liberians and Ethiopians – failed, for reasons that will be discussed below, to maintain their sovereignty, and by the beginning of the First World War, the cut-off date for the first section of this volume, Africa had been subjected to colonial rule. How and why the Liberians and Ethiopians managed to survive in the face of this colonial onslaught is treated in Chapter 11.

What then did these colonial powers do with their new colonies in the political, social and economic fields after the interlude of the First World War? It is this question which is answered in the second section of this volume. Here, since the various political mechanisms devised for the administration of their colonies, and the ideologies behind them, are well covered in many of the existing works surveying colonialism in Africa,[19] only a single chapter has been devoted to this theme. Instead, much more attention is given to the economic and social aspects of the colonial system and its impact on Africa so as to redress the balance. It will be seen from these chapters that the period after the First World War and up to 1935, the period which has been described by some recent historians as the high noon of colonialism, did see the building of an infrastructure of roads and railways and the introduction of some social changes such as primary and secondary schools. However, the colonial rulers had one principal end in view, namely, the exploitation of the resources of Africa, 'animal, vegetable and mineral', for the sole benefit of the colonial powers and their mercantile, mining and financial companies in the metropolitan countries. One of the chapters in this section to which particular attention should be drawn is the one dealing with the demographic aspects of colonial rule, a theme which is not normally found in existing surveys of colonialism in Africa.

What were African initiatives and reactions in the face of this consolidation of colonialism and the exploitation of their continent? This is the

17. For further developments of this point see A. A. Boahen, 'Towards a new categorization and periodization of African responses and reactions to colonialism' (unpublished) on which parts of this chapter are based.

18. R. I. Rotberg and A. A. Mazrui (eds), 1970, p. xviii.

19. See S. H. Roberts, 1929; Lord Hailey, 1938 and 1957; S. C. Easton, 1964; L. H. Gann and P. Duignan (eds), 1969 and 1970; P. Gifford and W. R. Louis (eds), 1967 and 1971; J. Suret-Canale, 1971.

question which is answered in the third section of this volume and a great deal of attention is paid to this question in conformity with the philosophy underlying this work, that is, to view the story from an African standpoint and to highlight African initiatives and reactions. African attitudes in this period were certainly not characterized by indifference or passivity or ready acceptance. If the period has been described as the classic era of colonialism, it is also the classic era of the strategy of resistance or protest in Africa. As will be shown both in the general survey as well as in the subsequent regional surveys, Africans did resort to a number of devices and measures – and indeed a whole variety of these were devised – to resist colonialism.

It should be emphasized that the objectives at this time were, with the exception of those of the North African leaders, not to overthrow the colonial system but rather to seek its amelioration and an accommodation within it. The main objectives were to render the colonial system less oppressive, less dehumanizing and to make it beneficial to the Africans as well as the Europeans. African leaders sought the correction of such specific measures and abuses as forced labour, high taxation, compulsory cultivation of crops, land alienation, pass laws, low prices of agricultural products and high prices of imported goods, racial discrimination and segregation, and to improve inadequate facilities such as hospitals, pipe-borne water and schools.

These grievances against the colonial system were felt, it should be emphasized, among all classes of society, the educated as well as the illiterate and the urban as well as the rural dwellers, and generated a common consciousness among them as Africans and black men as opposed to their oppressors, the colonial rulers and the white men. It is during this period that we see the strengthening of African political nationalism which had its beginnings immediately after the completion of the establishment of the colonial system in the 1910s.

The articulation of this feeling and the leadership of the movement, which during the period up to the 1910s was the responsibility of the traditional authorities and developed within the framework of the pre-colonial political structures, was now assumed by the new educated elite groups or members of the new middle class. Those new leaders were, rather paradoxically, the products of the colonial system itself, created and sustained through the schools and the administrative, mining, financial and commercial institutions that it introduced. It is the concentration of the leadership of the nationalist and anti-colonialist activities in the hands of the educated Africans who lived mainly in the new urban centres which has led to the incorrect identification of African nationalism in the inter-war period exclusively with that class and its characterization as primarily an urban phenomenon.

Numerous groups and associations were formed for the articulation of these nationalist aspirations. As is evident in the chapters in this section, the strategies and tactics that were devised during this period in order to give expression to these aspirations were equally diverse. As B. O. Oloruntimehin and E. S. Atiento-Odhiambo have shown (Chapters 22 and 26 below), these groups included youth associations, ethnic associations, old boys' associations, political parties, political movements of both a territorial and inter-territorial nature and inside as well as outside the continent, trade unions, literary clubs, civil servants' clubs, improvement associations, and various religious sects or movements. Some of these had been formed in the period before the First World War but there is no doubt that they proliferated during the period under review, as the chapters show.

The weapons or tactics adopted during the period, unlike those of the pre-First World War period when rebellions and so-called riots were more prevalent, were petitions and delegations to the metropolitan and local governments, strikes, boycotts, above all the press and international congresses. The inter-war period was easily the hey-day of journalism in Africa in general and in West Africa in particular, while pan-African congresses also became a typical feature of the anti-colonial movement. These congresses were calculated to give nationalist and anti-colonial movements in Africa an international flavour; they hoped also to draw the attention of the metropolitan powers to events in the colonies, and it was for this reason that the pan-African congresses organized by the American black, Dr W. E. B. Du Bois were held in Paris, London, Brussels and even Lisbon. This theme is taken up in greater detail in Chapter 29, which deals with the interactions between the blacks of Africa and the blacks of the diaspora in the Americas during the entire period under review.

However, despite the diversity of associations and the complexity of the tactics they developed, with the sole exception of Egypt, very little real impact had been made on the colonial system by the early 1930s. And when in 1935, the imperial forces of Fascist Italy under Mussolini seized and occupied Ethiopia, one of the two remaining bastions of hope and the main symbol of Africa's future revival and rejuvenation, it looked as if the continent of Africa was doomed to be for ever under the yoke of colonialism. But this was not to be. The resilience of the African people, the occupation of Ethiopia itself, the intensification of African nationalism and anti-colonialist sentiment after the Second World War, coupled with the emergence of new mass political parties and a new radical leadership dedicated not to the amelioration but rather the complete uprooting of colonialism – all these factors combined, as Volume VIII of this work will show, to bring about the liquidation of colonial rule from the continent at a rate as quick, and within about the same twenty-year period, as it took to establish it. However, between 1880 and 1935, colonialism appeared to be firmly imprinted on Africa. What marks then did it leave on Africa? This is the question that is answered in the last chapter of the volume.

Sources for the writing of Volume VII

Two final topics should be considered in this introductory chapter. These are the sources for the study of, and the periodization for, the history of colonialism in Africa. As far as sources are concerned, the authors and research students enjoy some advantages as well as disadvantages over those of the other volumes. To take the latter first, this volume and Volume VIII cover periods in which, unlike those of the other volumes, part of the archival materials is still inaccessible to scholars. Indeed, some archival material in several metropolitan countries such as that in France for the period up to 1930 was opened to scholars only after some of these chapters had already been completed. Moreover, with the partition and the entry of so many different European powers into Africa, the problem of language that faces research students becomes a difficult one.

To compensate for this, more journals and periodicals become available and published parliamentary papers, debates, commissions of inquiries, papers of private companies and associations, and published annual reports become more numerous than in the periods before; all of these are available. Above all, some of the actors in the colonial drama themselves are still alive and can be and have been interviewed. Others, both African and European, have also begun to publish their memoirs and autobiographies or to recall them in novels, plays and learned treatises. In all these respects, the authors of this volume enjoy some advantages over most of the authors of the other volumes.

Finally, it appears far more research has been and is still being done on the subject of colonialism and far more has been published and is still being published on it than on any other theme in African history. Indeed, within the last ten years, a five-volume history of colonialism in Africa edited by L. H. Gann and Peter Duignan and published by the Cambridge University Press has appeared. The theme has also attracted far more attention in the Eastern European countries than probably any other theme. This of course makes the work of synthesis relatively easier as far as sources are concerned but rather more exacting with respect to the mass of material to be absorbed by authors.

Periodization of colonialism in Africa

The question of the periodization of the history of colonialism in Africa, which has been ignored by many historians but was raised by A. B. Davidson and Michael Crowder in the 1960s, should be briefly looked at.

Some historians have proposed 1870 as the date for the beginning of the European Scramble for Africa and the imposition of colonial rule. This date, however, seems to be too early. As G. N. Uzoigwe shows in Chapter 2, it was the activities of the French in the Senegambia region, of King Leopold of the Belgians represented by H. M. Stanley, and the French represented by Pierre Savorgnan de Brazza in the Congo region, and of the Portuguese in Central Africa that touched off the Scramble and all these activities surely did not commence until the late 1870s and early 1880s. It seems, therefore, that 1880 would be a more appropriate date than 1870.[20] From 1880 to the collapse of colonialism in the 1960s and 1970s, therefore, the study of colonial rule and African initiatives and reactions should be divided into three eras: 1880–1919 (subdivided into 1880–1900 and 1900–19, the periods of conquest and occupation respectively), which we would term the era of the defence of African sovereignty and independence using the strategy of confrontation or alliance or temporary submission; the period 1919–35 which we would call the period of accommodation using the strategy of protest or resistance; and the period since 1935 which is the period of the independence movements using the strategy of positive action.[21]

It is our contention that the period from 1880 to about 1919, the so-called era of pacification in the view of some historians, was the period which, from the European perspective, saw the completion of the partition on paper, the deployment of troops to effect the partition on the ground, and the effective occupation of the conquered areas, signified by the introduction of various administrative measures and an infrastructure of roads, railways and the telegraph for the exploitation of the resources of the colonies.

From the African perspective, as we have seen already, this period saw African kings, queens, lineage and clan heads all dominated by one overriding consideration, that of maintaining or regaining their sovereignty, patrimony and culture by the strategy of confrontation or alliance or submission. By 1919, in practically the whole of Africa, with the conspicuous exception of Libya and some parts of the Sahara, and Liberia and Ethiopia, the confrontation had been resolved in favour of the Europeans, and all Africans, the so-called resisters and the so-called collaborators alike, had lost their sovereignty.

The second phase is from 1919 to 1935, and this is the phase in which we can properly categorize African reactions in terms of resistance, or as we would prefer to call it, of protest. We have chosen 1919 not only because it succeeds influential events such as the end of the First World War, the October Revolution in the Russian empire and the calling of the first Pan-African Congress by Du Bois – all of which had a revolutionary impact on the course of world history – but also because by that date

20. See M. Crowder, 1968, pp. 17–19.
21. For different periodizations, see A. B. Davidson, in T. O. Ranger (ed.), 1968(c), pp. 177–88. Also M. Crowder, 1968, pp. 17–19.

opposition to the European occupation of Africa as such had ended in most parts of the continent.

We also chose 1935 rather than 1945 as the terminal date of the volume because that was the year of the invasion and occupation of Ethiopia by the Fascist forces of Mussolini. That crises shocked and outraged Africans, especially the educated Africans, and blacks the world over. It also awakened them more dramatically to the inhuman, racist and oppressive nature of colonialism far more than the Second World War did. As Kwame Nkrumah, later first President of Ghana, described his reactions on hearing the news of that invasion, 'At that moment it was almost as if the whole of London had declared war on me personally';[22] and as he confessed, that crisis exacerbated his hatred for colonialism. Indeed, it seems most likely that the struggle for the liberation of Africa from colonialism would have been launched in the late 1930s but for the outbreak of the Second World War.

The final period from 1935 to the era of the independence revolution belongs properly to the next and final volume of this work and should not be discussed here.

22. K. Nkrumah, 1957, p. 27.

European partition and conquest of Africa: an overview

G. N. UZOIGWE

Introduction: a generation of war and revolutionary change

The generation following 1880 witnessed one of the most significant historical movements of modern times. During this period Africa, a continent of over 28 million square kilometres, was partitioned, conquered and occupied effectively by the industrialized nations of Europe. Historians have not yet come to grips with the deleterious impact of this generation of continuous war on both the colonized and the colonizer. But that it was a generation of revolutionary change of a fundamental nature is generally stressed.

The great significance of our period, however, goes beyond the war and the change that it witnessed. Empires have risen and fallen in the past, conquests and usurpations are as old as history itself, and models of colonial administration and integration have been tried and tested in days gone by. Africa was the last continent to be subdued by Europe. What is most remarkable about our period is the co-ordinated manner, speed and comparative ease – from the European point of view – with which the occupation and subjugation of so vast a continent was accomplished. Nothing like it had happened before.

What gave rise to such a phenomenon? Or, to put it another way, why was Africa partitioned politically and systematically occupied in the period that it was? And why were Africans unable to keep their adversaries at bay? These questions have exercised the skills of historians of the partition and of the new imperialism since the 1880s. No generally acceptable explanation exists; on the contrary, the historiography of the partition has become one of the most controversial and emotive issues of our time. It presents the historian with the awesome task of making sense of an extraordinary phantasmagoria of conflicting interpretations.

The partition of Africa and the new imperialism: a review

There is need, therefore, to bring sanity to the jumble of theories regarding this crucial movement in African history. They may be conveniently categorized as follows: economic, psychological, diplomatic, and the African dimension.

The economic theory

The popularity of this theory has changed, like fashion, with the times. Before communism became a threat to the capitalist system of the West, no one seriously questioned the economic basis of imperial expansion. It was no accident, therefore, that Joseph Schumpeter's attack upon the notion of capitalist imperialism[1] was extremely popular among non-Marxist scholars. The onslaught against this theory which he initiated has been pressed home so devastatingly that, today, it has reached the point of diminishing returns. Consequently, the theory of economic imperialism, in modified form, has begun increasingly nowadays to win acceptance.

What is the meaning of economic imperialism? Its theoretical roots can be traced back to 1900 when the German Social Democrats placed the subject of *Weltpolitik*, that is, the policy of imperial expansion on a global scale, on the agenda of their annual party congress held at Mainz. It was here that Rosa Luxemburg first pointed out that imperialism was the final stage of capitalism. It was here also that George Ledebour noted that 'the central point of the *Weltpolitik*' was 'an upsurge of all capitalism towards a policy of plunder, which takes European and American capitalism into all parts of the world'.[2] The classic and clearest statement of this theory, however, was provided by John Atkinson Hobson. He argued that overproduction, surplus capital, and under-consumption in industrialized nations led them 'to place larger and larger portions of their economic resources outside the area of their present political domain, and to stimulate a policy of political expansion so as to take in new areas'. This he saw as the 'economic taproot of imperialism'. Admitting that non-economic forces did play a part in imperial expansion, he was nevertheless convinced that although 'An ambitious statesman, a pushing trader, may suggest or even initiate a step of imperial expansion, may assist in educating patriotic public opinion of the urgent need of some fresh advance ... the final determination rests with the financial power'.[3]

Borrowing freely from the central arguments of the German Social Democrats as well as from those of Hobson, V. I. Lenin emphasized that the new imperialism was characterized by the transition of capitalism from a 'pre-monopolist' orientation 'in which free competition was predominant ... to the stage of monopoly capitalism to finance capital' which '*is connected* with the intensification of the struggle for the partition of the world'.[4] Just as competitive capitalism thrived on the export of commodi-

1. J. Schumpeter, 1955.
2. Quoted in L. Basso, in N. Chomsky, *et al.*, 1972, p. 114.
3. J. A. Hobson, 1902, pp. 59, 80–1.
4. V. I. Lenin, 1916, p. 92 (emphasis in original).

ties, so monopoly capitalism thrived on the export of capital derived from the super-profits amassed by the cartel of banks and industry. This development, according to Lenin, was the highest stage of capitalism. Following Luxemburg, and in opposition to Hobson, Lenin believed that capitalism was doomed to self-destruction because having finally partitioned the world, the capitalists, now rentiers and parasites living on incomes from their investments, would be threatened by the growing nations who would demand a repartition of the world. The capitalists, greedy as ever, would refuse to comply. The issue, therefore, would be settled by war which they would inevitably lose. War, then, is the inevitable consequence of imperialism, the violent death of capitalism.

It is not surprising that this rousing propaganda has been accepted by many Marxist scholars. 'Third World' nationalists and radicals also accepted the views of Hobson and Lenin as a matter of course. And in alliance with radical western scholars, they portray imperialism and colonialism as the outcome of blatant economic exploitation.[5]

Although Hobson and Lenin were not particularly concerned with Africa, it is obvious that their analyses have fundamental implications for its partition. Consequently, a disparate army of non-Marxist scholars has, more or less, demolished the Marxist economic imperialism theory as it relates to Africa.[6] A typical reaction of Marxist scholars to this apparent victory is that although the criticisms of Hobson and Lenin are basically correct, they are nevertheless misdirected. 'The target', writes Bob Sutcliffe, 'is often a mirage and the weapons inappropriate' because imperialism, conceived as a general phenomenon, views the value of empire as a totality, and therefore 'a national balance sheet has very little meaning'.[7] A more compelling argument, however, is that even a thorough demolition of the classic theory of economic imperialism does not necessarily refute the conclusion that imperialism was essentially economic in its fundamental impulses. To belittle other economic views of imperialism and then to jubilantly hang their proponents because of their suspected association with Hobson and Lenin is rather unscholarly. It is now clear from more serious investigations of African history in this period that those who persist in trivializing the economic dimension of the partition do so at their own peril.[8]

The psychological theories

I discuss these theories – usually classified as *Social Darwinism, evangelical*

5. W. Rodney, 1972; also Chinweizu, 1975, especially Chapter 3.
6. Representative of these criticisms are D. K. Fieldhouse, 1961; M. Blaug, 1961; B. Sutcliffe in R. Owen and B. Sutcliffe (eds), 1972, pp. 316–20.
7. B. Sutcliffe in R. Owen and B. Sutcliffe (eds), 1972, p. 318; *cf. idem*, pp. 312–23.
8. See, for example, A. G. Hopkins, 1968, 1973; C. W. Newbury and A. S. Kanya-Forstner, 1969; J. Stengers, 1962.

Christianity, and *social atavism* – in psychological terms because of their proponents' common belief in the primacy of the 'white race'.

Social Darwinism

The appearance in November 1859 of Charles Darwin's *The Origin of Species by Means of Natural Selection or the Preservation of Favoured Races in the Struggle for Life*[9] seemed to some to provide scientific backing for the belief in the primacy of the European race, a theme that has figured continuously, in various guises, in European writing since the seventeenth century. The later Darwinians, therefore, were elated to be able to justify the conquest of what they called 'subject races' or 'backward races' by the 'master race' as the inevitable process of 'natural selection' by which the stronger dominates the weaker in the struggle for existence. They preached, therefore, that might was right. The partition of Africa was consequently seen by them as part of this inevitable, natural process. The interesting aspect of this flagrant racial jingoism which has been described appropriately as 'Albinism' is its affirmation of imperial responsibility.[10] The fact remains, however, that Social Darwinism, applied to the conquest of Africa, was more a rationalization after the event than its originator.

Evangelical Christianity

Evangelical Christianity, in whose eyes the *Origin of Species* was damnable heresy, had no qualms, nevertheless, in accepting its racial implications. The racial content of evangelical Christianity was, however, tempered with a generous dose of humanitarian and philanthropic zeal – sentiments widespread among European policy-makers during the conquest of Africa. It has been argued, therefore, that the partition of Africa was due, in no small measure, to a 'broader missionary' and humanitarian impulse which aimed at the regeneration of African peoples.[11] It has been asserted, moreover, that it was the missionaries who prepared the ground for the imposition of colonialism in East and Central Africa as well as in Madagascar.[12] Although it is true that missionaries did not resist the conquest of Africa, and that they did, in some areas, actively pursue that conquest, the missionary factor cannot be sustained as a general theory of imperialism because of its limited application.

Social atavism

It was Joseph Schumpeter who first explained the new imperialism in

9. C. Darwin, 1859.
10. For more details of these views see R. Maunier, trans. and ed. by E. O. Lorimer, 1949; and G. Himmelfarb, 1960.
11. See J. S. Galbraith, 1961, pp. 34–48; G. Bennett, (ed.), 1953; C. P. Groves in L. H. Gann and P. Duignan (eds), 1969, for surveys of the missionary impulse towards imperial expansion.
12. R. Oliver, 1965; R. I. Rotberg, 1965; P. M. Mutibwa, 1974.

sociological terms. To him, imperialism was the consequence of certain imponderable, psychological elements and not of economic pressures. His argument, couched in humanistic rather than in European racial terms, is based on what he saw as the natural desire of man to dominate his fellow men for the sake of dominating them. This native impulse to aggression is governed by man's universal thirst for usurpation. Imperialism, therefore, is a collective national egotism: 'the objectless disposition on the part of a state to unlimited forcible expansion'.[13] The new imperialism, he argued, was also atavistic in character,[14] that is, it was a reversion to earlier primitive political and social instincts in man which may have been justified in pre-modern times but were certainly not in the modern world. He then demonstrated how capitalism was, by its nature, 'anti-imperialistic' and benign. Presided over by innovative entrepreneurs, it was opposed entirely to the aggressive, imperialistic motivations of the ancient monarchies and warrior classes, whose ambitions had no clear objects. Capitalism, on the contrary, had clear objects and was, therefore, opposed completely to this atavistic behaviour characteristic of ancient regimes. Thus he concluded that the economic explanation of the new imperialism, based as it was on the logical development of capitalism, was invalid. In spite of the attraction of this argument, its major weakness is its nebulous and ahistorical quality. While the psychological theories may have an element of truth in them as an explanation of the partition, they do not explain why the partition occurred when it did. They do suggest, however, why it was possible and considered desirable.

The diplomatic theories

These constitute the purely political, and perhaps the most popular, explanations of the partition. But in an interesting way they provide specific and concrete backing to the psychological theories. In these diplomatic theories we see the national egotism of European states either in conflict with one another, or acting in concert to ensure self-preservation, or reacting decisively against the forces of primordial African nationalisms. It is proposed, therefore, to treat these theories in the following terms: *national prestige*; *balance of power*; and *global strategy*.

National prestige

The greatest exponent of this theory is Carlton Hayes. In a perceptive passage he contends:

> France sought compensation for European loss in overseas gain. England would offset her European isolation by enlarging and glorifying the British empire. Russia, halted in the Balkans, would turn anew

13. J. Schumpeter, 1955, p. 6.
14. ibid., p. 65.

to Asia, and Germany and Italy would show the world that the prestige they had won by might inside Europe they were entitled to enhance by imperial exploits outside. The lesser powers, with no great prestige at stake, managed to get on without any new imperialism, though Portugal and Holland displayed a revived pride in the empires they already possessed and the latter's was administered with renewed vigor.[15]

Hayes concludes therefore that 'the new imperialism' was basically 'a nationalistic phenomenon' and that its proponents hankered after national prestige. European leaders, in short, having consolidated their nations and realigned their diplomatic forces at home, were propelled by a nebulous or atavistic force which expressed itself in a 'psychological reaction, an ardent desire to maintain or recover national prestige'. Thus, he concludes, the partition of Africa was not an economic phenomenon.[16]

Balance of power

F. H. Hinsley,[17] on the other hand, emphasizes Europe's need for peace and stability at home as the primary cause of the partition. According to him, the decisive date for the shift towards an extra-European age – an age of imperialism – was 1878. From that year, at the Congress of Berlin, Russian and British rivalries in the Balkans and the Ottoman Empire brought the nations of Europe to the very verge of conflagration. European statesmen averted this crisis in power politics and drew back. Power politics from that point on to the Bosnian crisis of 1908 were removed from Europe and played out in Africa and Asia. When conflicting interests in Africa threatened to destroy European peace, the European powers had no choice but to carve up Africa in order to preserve the European diplomatic balance that had stabilized itself by the 1880s.

Global strategy

There is a third school which maintains that the European interest in Africa which gave rise to the Scramble was a matter of global strategy, not economics. The foremost exponents of this view, Ronald Robinson and John Gallagher, who stress the strategic importance of Africa to India for Britain, blame the partition of Africa on the impact of atavistic 'proto-nationalist' movements in Africa which threatened the global strategic interests of European nations. These 'romantic, reactionary struggles' – gallant anachronisms in their view – compelled reluctant European statesmen, hitherto content to exercise informal paramountcy and moral suasion in Africa, to partition and conquer the continent. Africa was occupied,

15. C. J. H. Hayes, 1941, p. 220.
16. ibid.
17. F. H. Hinsley, 1959(a), 1959(b) in E. A. Benians, J. Butler and C. E. Carrington (eds), 1959.

therefore, not because of what it could offer materially to the Europeans – for it was economically worthless – but because it was threatening European interests elsewhere.[18]

One primary aim of the psychological theories as well as of their cousins, the diplomatic theories, has been to debunk the notion that the partition of Africa was motivated by economic impulses. But the prestige argument only appears unconvincing when its economic concomitant is eliminated or unduly played down. Hayes, for example, has documented in detail the tariff war which took place between the European nations during the crucial period of the partition.[19] He even concedes that, 'What actually started the economic push into the "Dark Continent" and the sun-baked islands of the Pacific was not so much an overproduction of factory goods in Europe as an under-supply of raw materials';[20] and that therefore 'to prevent too much of the world from being ... monopolized by France, Germany, Italy, or any other protectionist power, Great Britain moved mightily to gather the lion's share into her own free-trade empire'. In other words, neo-mercantilism, once established, had very important consequences for the emergence of imperial rivalries.[21] And yet, on the very next page, Hayes sets out to argue confidently, as we have seen, against the economic under-pinnings of the new imperialism. H. Brunschwig, too, while positing a non-economic interpretation of French imperialism was faced with the stark economic dimension of empire, and was thus compelled to assign it some role. Thus, while he sees Anglo-Saxon imperialism as economic and philanthropic, that of France is seen as being motivated by prestige.[22] With respect to the global strategy thesis, informed reactions have been largely negative. Its attraction, however, for non-Africanist historians – or for the lay reader – has been simply overwhelming. Yet we know that this thesis, developed from the more eclectic assumptions of Langer[23] and the more considered analysis of Hinsley, is too neat and too circumstantial to be acceptable. It has been tested in West, Central, Southern and East Africa and found wanting.[24] And with respect to Egypt and North Africa, it has been shown that there were strong reasons unconnected with Britain's Indian imperial strategy necessitating a British presence.[25] It is gratifying to note that Robinson, at any rate, has begun to de-emphasize the exagger-

18. See J. Gallagher and R. Robinson, 1953; R. E. Robinson and J. Gallagher in F. H. Hinsley (ed.), 1962. R. E. Robinson and J. Gallagher, 1961.

19. C. J. H. Hayes, 1941, pp. 205–8.

20. ibid., p. 218.

21. ibid., p. 219.

22. H. Brunschwig, 1966, pp. 4–13.

23. W. L. Langer, 1935.

24. See J. Stengers, 1962; C. W. Newbury and A. S. Kanya-Forstner, 1969; G. N. Uzoigwe, 1974 and 1977; W. R. Louis (ed.), 1976.

25. G. N. Uzoigwe, 1974.

epercussions of the *baton Egyptien* on the Scramble elsewhere in
a.[26]

e African dimension theory

Thus far, the theories of the partition have treated Africa in the context
of European history. Clearly, this is a major flaw. Even the 'proto-
nationalist' atavism approach of Robinson and Gallagher is not fully
developed precisely because the focus of their interest is Europe and Asia.

The need, therefore, to look at the partition from the African historical
perspective becomes crucial. Contrary to general belief, such an approach
is no ingenious discovery of the 'new' African historiography. J. S. Keltie's
remarkable book, *The Partition of Africa*,[27] published in 1893, *does* note
perceptively that the Scramble of the 1880s was the logical consequence
of the nibbling at the continent which started some 300 years ago. It
also gives a nodding acceptance to the view that the partition was economically motivated although that is not its central argument. In the 1930s,
George Hardy, the prolific French colonial historian, also demonstrated
the local African dimensions of the partition, and he treated Africa very
much as a historical unity. Like Keltie, he argues that although the
immediate cause of partition was the economic rivalry of the countries
of industrial Europe, it was at the same time an important phase in the
longstanding contact between Europe and Africa. He suggests that African
resistance to increasing European influence precipitated the actual conquest
just as the increasing commercial rivalry of the industrialized nations led
to the partition.[28]

For a long time such views of the partition were ignored. But with the
publication in 1956 of K. Onwuka Dike's classic *Trade and Politics in the
Niger Delta*,[29] the African dimension of the partition was resurrected.
Although Dike's book is limited in its time span and geographical range,
it nevertheless encouraged a generation of historians to begin to treat the
partition in the context of a long period of contact of different races and
cultures. Unfortunately, while Roland Oliver and J. D. Fage demonstrate
this extended relationship in their very popular *Short History of Africa*,[30]
they still emphasize the European rather than the African dimension of
the partition. It is therefore refreshing that A. G. Hopkins' important
study,[31] although limited in its geographical scope, should attempt an
African-oriented reinterpretation of imperialism in West Africa. His conclusion is worth quoting:

26. R. Robinson in R. Owen and B. Sutcliffe (eds), 1972.
27. J. S. Keltie, 1893.
28. G. Hardy, 1930, pp. 124–37.
29. K. O. Dike, 1956.
30. R. Oliver and J. D. Fage, 1970.
31. A. G. Hopkins, 1973.

26

At one extreme it is possible to conceive of areas where the transition from the slave trade was made successfully, where incomes were maintained, and where internal tensions were controlled. In these cases an explanation of partition will need to emphasise external pressures, such as mercantile demands and Anglo-French rivalries. At the other extreme, it is possible to envisage cases where the indigenous rulers adopted reactionary attitudes, where attempts were made to maintain incomes by predatory means, and where internal conflicts were pronounced. In these cases an explanation of imperialism will need to place more weight on disintegrative forces on the African side of the frontier, though without neglecting external factors.[32]

The present writer agrees with most of the views of members of this school.[33] Like them, he explains the partition in both African and European terms, and therefore sees the African dimension theory as supplementing the Eurocentric theories already discussed. He sees the partition and conquest as the logical consequence of European nibbling at Africa which started well before the nineteenth century; he accepts that the essentially economic impulse that necessitated that nibbling changed drastically during the last quarter of the nineteenth century; that the change was caused by the transition from slave to legitimate trade and the subsequent decline in both the export and import trade during that period, and that it was this economic change in Africa and the consequent African resistance to increasing European influence that precipitated the actual military conquest. It would appear, indeed, that the African dimension theory provides a better rounded, more historically focused theory of the partition than any of the purely Eurocentric theories.

The beginnings of the Scramble

Although by the end of the third quarter of the nineteenth century, the European powers of France, Britain, Portugal and Germany had acquired commercial interests and were exercising considerable influence in different parts of Africa, their direct political control there was extremely limited. Both Germany and, especially, Britain were able to wield all the influence they wanted, and no statesmen in their right senses would have freely elected to incur the costs, and court the unforeseen contingencies of formal annexation when they could derive the same advantages from informal control. 'Refusals to annex', it has been remarked perceptively, 'are no proof of reluctance to control'.[34] This explains both the attitudes of

---

32. ibid., pp. 165–6.
33. The African dimension theory is more fully developed in A. G. Hopkins, 1973 and in G. N. Uzoigwe, 1973.
34. J. Gallagher and R. Robinson, 1953, p. 3.

Salisbury and Bismarck and indeed of most of the major actors in the partition.

But this attitude began to change as a result of three major events which occurred between 1876 and 1880. The first was the new interest which the Duke of Brabant, crowned a constitutional king (Leopold I) of the Belgians in 1865, proclaimed in Africa. This was signified by the so-called Brussels Geographical Conference which he convened in 1876 and which resulted in the setting up of the African International Association and the employment of H. M. Stanley in 1879 to explore the Congos in the name of the Association. These moves culminated in the creation of the Congo Free State, whose recognition by all the great European nations Leopold managed to obtain before the Berlin West African conference had ended its deliberations.[35]

The second significant series of events was the activities of Portugal from 1876 onwards. Piqued by the fact that it was invited to the Brussels conference only as an afterthought, Portugal sent out a flurry of expeditions which by 1880 had resulted in the annexation to the Portuguese crown of the practically independent estates of the Afro-Portuguese rulers in Mozambique. So far as the Portuguese and King Leopold were concerned, then, the Scramble was under way by 1876.

The third and final factor which helped to set the partition in motion was undoubtedly the expansionist mood which characterized French colonial policy between 1879 and 1880. This was signified by her participation with Britain in the dual control of Egypt (1879), the dispatch of Savorgnan de Brazza into the Congo and the ratification of his treaties with Chief Makoko of the Bateke, and the revival of French colonial initiative in both Tunisia and Madagascar.[36]

These moves on the part of these powers between 1876 and 1880 gave a clear indication that they were all now committed to colonial expansion and the establishment of formal control in Africa, and it was this that finally compelled both Britain and Germany to abandon their preference for informal control and influence in favour of a formal policy leading to their annexations in Southern, East and West Africa from the end of 1883 onwards.[37] The German initiative, for instance, resulted in the annexation of South West Africa, Togoland, the Cameroons, and German East Africa, which in turn further accelerated the pace of the Scramble.

By the early 1880s, the Scramble was well under way, and it was out of fear of being pushed out of Africa altogether that Portugal proposed the calling of an international conference to sort out the territorial disputes in the area of Central Africa. It seems evident from the above, then, that

35. PRO FO 403/192, 'Memorandum by Sir E. Hertslet on the most important Political and Territorial changes which have taken place in central and East Africa since 1883 (with Additional Notes by Sir P. Anderson)', February, 1893. Confidential.

36. P. M. Mutibwa, 1974, Chapters 6 and 7.

37. See G. Cecil, 1932, pp. 225–6; F. D. Lugard, 1929, p. 13.

it was not the British occupation of Egypt in 1882 that triggered off the Scramble, as has been argued by Robinson and Gallagher,[38] but rather the events of the period 1876 to 1880 in different parts of Africa.

The Berlin West Africa Conference, 1884–5

The idea of an international conference to settle the territorial disputes arising from European activities in the Congo region, first suggested by Portugal, was later taken up by Bismarck who, after sounding the opinions of the other powers, was encouraged to bring it about. The conference was held at Berlin between 15 November 1884 and 26 November 1885. The news that such a conference was to be held increased the intensity of the Scramble. The conference did not discuss seriously either the slave trade or the lofty humanitarian idealism that was supposed to have inspired it. It nevertheless passed empty resolutions regarding the abolition of the slave trade and the welfare of Africans.

It was not, ostensibly, the initial intention of the conference to attempt a general partition of Africa. It nevertheless ended up disposing of territory, passing resolutions pertaining to the free navigation of the Niger, the Benue, and their affluents; and laying down 'the rules to be observed in future with regard to the occupation of territory on the coasts of Africa'.[39] According to Article 34 of the Berlin Act, the document signed by the participants in the conference, any European nation which, in the future, took possession of an African coast or declared a 'protectorate' there, had to notify such action to the signatory powers of the Berlin Act in order to have its claims ratified. This was the so-called doctrine of *spheres of influence* to which was linked the absurd concept of the hinterland, which came to be interpreted to mean that possession of a coast also implied ownership of its hinterland to an almost unlimited distance. Article 35 stipulated that an occupier of any such coastal possessions had also to demonstrate that it possessed sufficient 'authority' there 'to protect existing rights, and, as the case may be, freedom of trade and of transit under the conditions agreed upon'. This was the so-called doctrine of *effective occupation* that was to make the conquest of Africa such a murderous business.

In recognizing the Congo Free State, permitting territorial negotiations, and by laying down rules and regulations for the 'legal' appropriation of African territory, the European powers had arrogated to themselves the right of sanctioning the principle of sharing out and conquering another continent. There is no precedent in world history where a group of states in one continent felt justified in talking about the sharing and occupation of the territory of another continent in such a bold manner. This is the major significance of the conference for African history. The argument

38. R. Robinson and J. Gallagher, 1961.
39. PRO FO 403/192, Memo by Sir E. Hertslet, February 1893, p. 1.

PLATE 2.1 *A session of the Berlin West African Conference, 1884–5*

that the conference, contrary to popular opinion, did not partition Africa[40] is correct only in the most technical sense. To all intents and purposes the appropriation of territory did take place at the conference and the question of future appropriation is clearly implied in its decisions. By 1885, in fact, the broad lines of the final partition of Africa had already been drawn.

Treaty-making 1885–1902

Prior to the Berlin Act, European powers had acquired spheres of influence in Africa in a variety of ways – through settlement, exploration, the establishment of commercial posts, missionary settlements, the occupation of strategic areas, and by making treaties with African rulers.[41] Following the conference, influence by means of treaty became the most important method of effecting the paper partition of the continent. These treaties took two forms – those between Africans and Europeans, and bilateral agreements between the Europeans themselves. The African–European treaties were basically of two kinds. Firstly, there were the slave trade and the commercial treaties; these had generated friction, which in turn led to European political interference in African affairs. Secondly, there were the political treaties by which African rulers either purportedly surrendered sovereignty in return for protection, or undertook not to enter into treaty obligations with other European nations.

These political treaties were in vogue during our period. They were made either by representatives of European governments or by those of private organizations who later transferred them to their respective governments. If a metropolitan government accepted them, the territories in question were usually annexed or declared a protectorate; if, on the other hand, it suspected their authenticity, or if it felt constrained by the vicissitudes of *Weltpolitik* to exercise caution, these treaties were used for bargaining purposes during the bilateral European negotiations. Africans, on the other hand, entered into these arrangements for a variety of motives, but particularly because of the interests of their people. In some cases, they desired treaty relations with Europeans because they hoped that the prestige of such a relationship would endow them with certain political advantages in dealing with their neighbours. Sometimes a weak African state would desire a treaty with a European power in the hope of using it to renounce allegiance to another African state that claimed sovereignty over it. An African sovereign would also desire a treaty in the hope of using it to keep recalcitrant subject states in line. And sometimes a treaty with one European nation was seen by some African states as a means of preserving their independence which was being threatened by

40. S. E. Crowe, 1942, pp. 152–75.
41. G. N. Uzoigwe, 1976(a), pp. 189–93.

31

other European nations.[42] Whatever was the case, the African–European political treaties played an important role in the final partition of Africa.

The treaties between the Imperial British East Africa Company (IBEAC) and Buganda represent an instance when an African sovereign sought the help of the representative of a European company in his dispute with his own subjects. Kabaka Mwanga II had written to the company asking that it should 'be good enough to come and put me on my throne' and had promised to repay the company with 'plenty of ivory and you may do any trade in Uganda and all *you like* in the country under me'.[43] When he received no reply to this request, he sent two ambassadors, Samuel Mwemba and Victor Senkezi, to Zanzibar to request the assistance of the British, French, and German consuls. 'If they want to help us', he instructed his ambassadors to ask, 'what repayment should we make them? Because I do not want to give them (or you) my land. I want all Europeans of all nations to come to Uganda, to build and to trade as they like.'[44] It is clear that in making a treaty, Mwanga did not mean to give up his sovereignty. Later, he was to discover, to his cost, that the Europeans thought otherwise. Captain F. D. Lugard's treaties with Mwanga in December 1890 and March 1892, which offered Mwanga 'protection', were imposed upon him rather than negotiated with him. It is true that the IBEAC did help to restore him to his throne but the victory of the Baganda Protestants (decided by Lugard's Maxim gun) over the Baganda Catholics at the Battle of Mengo (24 January 1892) had left the Kabaka in a very weak position. When the company ceased operations in Buganda (31 March 1893) it then transferred these treaties to the British government. Colonel H. E. Colvile's final treaty with Mwanga (27 August 1894) confirmed all the previous treaties. But it went further than them. Colvile demanded and secured for his country 'control of Foreign affairs and revenue and taxes' which passed from Mwanga 'to H.M.Govt., whose representative should also be the supreme court of appeal on all civil cases'.[45] In the same year Britain declared a protectorate over Buganda.

It is revealing that Lugard should later on write in his diaries with respect to treaties offering company protection as follows:

> No man if he understood would sign it, and to say that a savage chief has been told that he cedes all rights to the company in exchange for nothing is an obvious untruth. If he has been told that the company will protect him against his enemies, and share in his wars as an ally, he has been told a lie, for the company have no idea of doing any such thing and no force to do it with if they wished.[46]

42. S. Touval, 1966, p. 286.
43. PRO FO 84/2061, Mwanga to Jackson, 15 June 1889 (emphasis added).
44. PRO FO 84/2064, Mwanga to Euam-Smith, 25 April 1890.
45. PRO FO 2/72, Colvile to Hardinge, 28 Aug., 1894 (encl.) contains text of this treaty.
46. M. Perham and M. Bull (eds), 1963, Vol. I, p. 318.

Lugard was saying, in essence, that his own treaties were fraudulently obtained! We do not have space to discuss the numerous other African–European treaties. But a passing mention may be made of the requests made by the Emir of Nupe in what is now Nigeria to Lieutenant L. A. A. Mizon to form an alliance with him against the Royal Niger Company, with whom he had quarrelled,[47] as an example of an African sovereign's desire to seek the help of one European power against another European power threatening his independence.

The bilateral European partition treaties

The acquisition of a sphere of influence by treaty was usually the first stage in the occupation of an African state by a European power. If such a treaty was not contested by any other European power, the incumbent power gradually turned its treaty rights into sovereign rights. A sphere of influence arose, therefore, in the first instance, by a unilateral declaration; it became a reality only when it was accepted or not contested by other European powers. Often spheres of influences were contested, but these territorial difficulties and boundary disputes were eventually settled and ratified as a result of mutual agreements between two or more imperialist powers operating in the same region. The limits of these territorial settlements were determined, as closely as possible, by a natural boundary, or, where no such boundary existed, by longitude and latitude. Occasionally they took account of indigenous political boundaries.

The Anglo–German Treaty of 29 April (and 7 May) 1885 which defined the 'spheres of action' of the two countries in certain parts of Africa is regarded as perhaps the first serious application of the spheres of influence theory in modern times.[48] By a series of similar treaties, agreements and conventions, the paper partition of Africa was virtually concluded by the end of the century. We can deal only briefly here with the most significant of them.

The Anglo–German delimitation treaty of 1 November 1886, to take one example, is particularly significant. It placed Zanzibar and most of its dependencies within Britain's sphere of influence; on the other hand, it assured Germany's political influence in East Africa, thereby providing official recognition of the breach of Britain's monopoly in the area.[49] In effect the treaty thus partitioned the Omani empire. By the terms of the subsequent clarificatory agreement of 1887, Britain undertook 'to discourage British annexations in the rear of the German Sphere of Influence, on the understanding that the German Government will equally discourage German annexations in the rear of the British Sphere'. It was further agreed

47. For details see R. A. Adeleye, 1971, pp. 136–9.
48. S. Touval, 1966, p. 286.
49. PRO FO 403/192, Memo by Sir E. Hertslet, February 1893.

that if either country occupied the coast, 'the other could not, without consent, occupy unclaimed regions in the rear'.[50] The vagueness of these hinterland arrangements regarding the westward 'sphere of influence' of both countries led to the famous Heligoland Treaty of 1890 which concluded comprehensively the partition of East Africa. Most significantly, it reserved Uganda for Britain; but it also destroyed Britain's grand illusion of a Cape-to-Cairo route, surrendered Heligoland to Germany and put an end to the independence of Zanzibar.

The Anglo-German Treaties of 1890 and 1893 and the Anglo-Italian Treaty of 1891, taken together, recognized the Upper Nile as falling within the British sphere of influence. To the south, the Franco-Portuguese Treaty (1886), the German-Portuguese Treaty (1886), and the Anglo-Portuguese Treaty (1891) both recognized Portugal's influence in Angola and Mozambique as well as delimiting the British sphere in Central Africa. The Anglo–Congo Free State Treaty (1894) is equally significant because it settled the limits of the Congo Free State in such a way that it acted as a buffer between French territories and the Nile valley and provided for the British a Cape-to-Cairo corridor from Uganda via Lake Tanganyika (withdrawn in June because of German protest). In West Africa, the most important arrangements were the Say–Barruwa Agreement (1890) and the Niger Convention (1898)[51] by which Britain and France concluded the partition of that region. Finally, the Anglo-French Convention of 21 March 1899 settled the Egyptian question while the Peace of Vereeniging (1902) – which ended the Anglo-Boer war – confirmed, temporarily, at any rate, British supremacy in South Africa.

How legitimate were the political treaties with African rulers, and the bilateral European agreements on which were based the partition and conquest of Africa? An examination of the political treaties suggests the conclusion that some of them were legally indefensible, some morally bankrupt, while others were procured legally. Nevertheless, they were essentially political acts defensible only in the context of European positive law which saw force as the basis of all law. Even where Africans openly sought treaty arrangements with Europeans, their decisions were invariably based on their perceptions of European strength. There were occasions, too, when Africans who suspected the Europeans' motives for seeking treaties and refused to enter into such a relationship, were induced, through unbearable pressures, none the less to do so. There were also numerous instances in which the Africans and the Europeans disagreed on the interpretation of the arrangements between them. In such cases, as far as the African rulers were concerned, these political treaties did not imply any loss of sovereignty. They tended to regard them as co-operative arrangements, forced or un-forced, which might prove to be of mutual advantage to the parties con-

50. PRO FO 403/142, Salisbury to Malet, 14 June 1890.

51. For the most detailed account of the Niger Convention see G. N. Uzoigwe, 1974, Chapters 5 and 6; *cf.* B. I. Obichere, 1971, Chapter 8.

cerned. European views on the question of the legitimacy of these treaties varied. While some regarded them as legitimate, others, like Lugard, were convinced that nearly all of them were fraudulently obtained, some were outright forgeries, some were plainly bogus, and most were illegally executed.[52] And yet, in most cases, these absurd treaties were accorded recognition in terms of European diplomatic convention – including, for example, Karl Peters' bogus East African treaties and the IBEAC treaties which Lugard himself dismissed as 'utter fraud'.[53] There were only very few instances when, on closer scrutiny, such treaties were found wanting and – as was the case with Lugard's treaties with Nikki – were invalidated at the conference table.

The idea, too, that the European bilateral treaties, which disposed of African territory in some European capital without the presence or approval of those whose future was being determined, could be held to be valid, was explained in terms of European positive law. The European leaders were quite aware that a sphere of influence by treaty between two European nations did not affect the rights of the African sovereigns within that sphere. But because a sphere of influence was a political rather than a legal notion, a friendly power might choose to respect this fact while an unfriendly power might choose to ignore it. The same was true of the hinterland doctrine, notorious for its evocation of the principle of 'manifest destiny' and the wild claims made on its behalf. Both doctrines, in short, had no legitimacy in international law.[54] 'The modern doctrine of Hinterland', Salisbury observed in 1896, 'with its inevitable contradictions, indicates the un-informed and unstable condition of international law as applied to territorial claims resting on constructive occupation or control.'[55] In other words, 'a claim of sovereignty in Africa can only be maintained by real occupation of the territory claimed'.[56] And since the notion of effective occupation – with which the vast majority of the African states were unfamiliar – and the African notion of the real meaning of these treaty relations with Euro-peans were in fundamental contradiction with one another, the situation of conflict was bound to be intensified. Thus the stage was set for the systematic military occupation of the hinterland by the European powers.

Military conquest, 1885–1902

For whatever reason, the French were the most active in pursuing this policy of military conquest. Advancing from the upper to the lower Niger, they promptly defeated the Damel of Cayor, Lat Dior, who fought to the

52. See F. D. Lugard, 1893, II, p. 580; M. Perham and M. Bull (eds), 1963, Vol. I, p. 318; J. M. Gray, 1948.
53. M. Perham and M. Bull, 1963, Vol. I, p. 318.
54. M. F. Lindley, 1926, pp. 234–5.
55. Quoted in G. N. Uzoigwe, 1976(a), pp. 196–7.
56. Quoted in F. D. Lugard, 1929, p. 13.

death in 1886; they beat Mamadou Lamine at the battle of Touba-Kouta (1887), thus ending the Soninke empire he had founded in Senegambia; they succeeded in breaking the prolonged and celebrated resistance of the great Samori Ture when they finally captured him (1898) and exiled him to Gabon (1900); and by a series of victories – Koundian (1889), Segu (1890), and Youri (1891) – Major Louis Archinard brought to an end the Segu Tukulor empire although its ruler, Ahmadu, continued a stubborn resistance until his death in Sokoto in 1898. Elsewhere in West Africa the French conquered the Ivory Coast and the future French Guinea where they set up colonies in 1893. And between 1890 and 1894 the conquest and occupation of the kingdom of Dahomey was accomplished. By the late 1890s, the French had completed the conquest of Gabon, consolidated their position in North Africa, completed the conquest of Madagascar (exiling Queen Ranavalona III in 1897 to Algiers), and in the eastern Sahara-Sahel borderlands ended the obstinate resistance of Rabih of Sennar when he was killed in battle in 1900.

Britain's military imperialism was equally spectacular and bloody; the African response, as will be seen in the following chapters, was also resolute and often prolonged. Operating from its coastal possessions on the Gold Coast (now Ghana) and in Nigeria, Britain halted effectively French expansion towards the lower Niger and into the Asante hinterland. The last Kumasi expedition (1900) was followed up in 1901 by the annexation of Asante, and Nana Prempeh was exiled to the Seychelles. The Northern Territories to the north of Asante were also formally annexed in 1901, having been occupied between 1896 and 1898. From the Lagos colony, Britain launched its conquest of Nigeria. By 1893 most of Yorubaland had been proclaimed a protectorate; the conquest of Itsekiriland was accomplished in 1894, and Nana Olomu, its resourceful 'merchant prince', was exiled to Accra; and while apparently unable to challenge King Jaja of Opobo in open battle, Harry Johnston, the British Consul, tricked him into attending a meeting aboard a British warship, where he was made prisoner and shipped to the West Indies in 1887. Both Brass and Bini were duly conquered by the end of the century. By 1900, British supremacy in southern Nigeria was more or less assured. The effective occupation of Igboland and some other areas of the eastern hinterland, however, were not accomplished until the first two decades of this century. To the north, British conquest was accomplished from Nupe, where – by 1895 – George Goldie's Royal Niger Company exercised influence from Lokoja to the sea. Ilorin was occupied in 1897; and after the establishment of the West African Frontier Force in 1898 the Sokoto sultanate was conquered by Lugard in 1902.

In North Africa, Britain, already in a commanding position in Egypt, waited until 1896 when the reconquest of the Sudan was authorized. This was achieved in 1898 with savage and unnecessary bloodshed. Over 20000 Sudanese, including their leader, Khalifa 'Abdallāh, died in battle. France's occupation of Fashoda in the south of the Sudan (1898) was understandably not countenanced by Lord Salisbury, and the French were forced to withdraw.

The formal declaration of a British protectorate over Zanzibar in November 1890, and the efforts then made to abolish the institution of slavery, led to revolts which were easily crushed. It was from Zanzibar that the rest of British East Africa was conquered. The major prize sought by Britain in this region was Uganda, where the battle of Mengo (1892) – in Buganda, the centre of operations – led eventually to the formal declaration of the Uganda Protectorate (1894). The way was thus cleared for the conquest of the rest of Uganda which was accomplished with the capture of King Kabarega and King Mwanga and their exile to the Seychelles in 1899. In Kenya, however, it took Britain some ten years before it established effective rule among the Nandi.

In Central and Southern Africa, Cecil Rhodes's British South Africa Company (BSAC) undertook the occupation of Mashonaland without Lobengula's sanction. In 1893 the king was forced to flee from his capital, and he died the following year. His kingdom was not conquered finally, however, until the bloody suppression of the Ndebele–Mashona revolt of 1896–7. The conquest of what is now Zambia was less eventful and was completed in 1901. The last of Britain's partition wars was fought against the Boers in South Africa. The particular interest of the Anglo–Boer war (1899–1902) is that it was fought between the Europeans themselves.

The other European powers found effective occupation equally arduous. The Germans, for example, were able to establish their rule effectively in South West Africa by the end of the century, primarily because of the more than one hundred years of hostility that had prevented the Nama and the Maherero from working together. In Togoland, the Germans allied themselves with the small kingdoms of the Kotokoli and the Chakossi to facilitate the crushing of the resistance of the non-centralized Konkomba (1897–8) and Kabre (1890). In the Cameroons, the German commander, Major Hans Dominik, encountered the greatest difficulty in the north, but by 1902 he had managed to subdue the Fula principalities. The conquest of German East Africa, however, proved to be the fiercest and most prolonged of all these effective wars of occupation. It lasted from 1888 to 1907. The most notable expeditions were those sent against the celebrated Abushiri, the lion-hearted (1888–9); the Wahehe (1889–8); and the leaders of the Majī Majī resistance (1905–7).

Portugal's military occupation of its territories, which started in the 1880s, was not completed until well into the twentieth century. For the Portuguese it was a particularly arduous enterprise but it nevertheless led eventually to the consolidation of Portuguese authority in Mozambique, Angola and Guinea (now Guinea-Bissau). The Congo Free State, too, faced very grave problems before it was able to accomplish a military occupation of its sphere of influence. It started by allying with the Congo Arabs who were particularly hostile to it. When the futility of this alliance became obvious, Leopold ordered an expedition against them. It took some three years (1892–5) before they were subdued. But the conquest of Katanga, initiated in 1891, was not completed until early in this century.

Italy fared worst in its wars of effective occupation. In 1883 it had managed to occupy a part of Eritrea. It also obtained the eastern coast of Somalia during the first partition of the Omani empire in 1886. The Treaty of Wuchale (or Uccialli) (1889), signed with Emperor Menelik II of Ethiopia, later defined the Ethiopian–Eritrean boundary. It was a result of a curious interpretation placed upon this treaty that Italy informed the other European powers that Ethiopia was an Italian protectorate. Although Italy's attempt to occupy its fictitious protectorate ended in ignominious defeat at Adowa (1896), it managed, nevertheless, to retain its portion of Eritrea and Somalia. In North Africa, it was not until 1911 that Italy was able to occupy the coastal areas of Cyrenaica and Tripolitania (Libya). Morocco managed to preserve its independence until Spain and France ended it in 1912. By 1914, therefore, only Liberia and Ethiopia remained – at least nominally – independent.

Why were European powers able to conquer Africa?

European powers were able to conquer Africa with such relative ease because in virtually every respect the dice was so heavily loaded in their favour. In the first place, thanks to the activities of European explorers and missionaries, Europeans were by 1880 far more knowledgeable about Africa and its interior – its physical appearance, terrain, economy and other resources and the strength and weakness of its states and societies – than Africans were about Europe.

Secondly, owing to the revolutionary changes in medical technology and in particular the discovery of the prophylactic use of quinine against malaria, Europeans became far less fearful of Africa than they had been before the middle of the nineteenth century.[57]

Thirdly, as a result of the uneven nature of the trade between Europe and Africa up to the 1870s, and even after, as well as the increasing pace of the industrial revolution, the material and financial resources available to Europe were overwhelming in comparison with those of Africa. Thus while European powers could afford to spend millions of pounds on overseas campaigns, African states were unable to sustain any protracted military confrontation against them.

Fourthly, while the period after the Russo-Turkish war of 1877–8 was marked, according to J. Holland Rose, by 'a state of political equilibrium which made for peace and stagnation in Europe',[58] the same period in

57. P. Curtin, S. Feierman, L. Thompson and J. Vansina, 1978, p. 445; J. H. Rose, 1905, pp. 508–72.
58. J. H. Rose, 1905.

Africa was marked by inter-state and intra-state conflict and rivalry – the Mandingo against the Tukulor, the Asante against the Fante, the Baganda against the Banyoro, the Batoro against the Banyoro, the Mashona against the Ndebele, etc. Thus, while Europe could focus her attention militarily almost exclusively on her imperial activities overseas without any distraction at home, African states and countries had their attention divided. Moreover, in addition to enjoying peace at home, however divided the European powers were on imperial and colonial issues, throughout the era of partition and up to 1914 they always managed to resolve these questions without resort to war. Thus, in spite of the intense competition and the numerous crises in Africa, the European powers involved in the partition displayed a remarkable spirit of solidarity which not only eliminated wars among them but also prevented the African rulers and communities from effectively playing one European power against the other. Throughout the period under review, various European powers took on the African states one at a time, and on no occasion was an African state assisted by one European power against another.

By contrast, the behaviour of the African states was not only marked by lack of solidarity, unity or co-operation but some of them did not hesitate to ally with the invading European forces against their neighbours, only to be vanquished later themselves. The Baganda allied with the British against the Banyoro, and the Barotse with the British against the Ndebele, while the Bambara teamed up with the French against the Tukulor.[59] As a result of all this, the heroic and memorable stands which the Africans took against the European invaders were – as will be seen in subsequent chapters[60] – more often than not, isolated forms of uncoordinated resistance, even at the regional level.

The final and easily the most decisive factor was, of course, the overwhelming logistic and military superiority that Europe enjoyed over Africa. While Europe was using professional and well-drilled armies, very few African states had established standing armies and fewer still had professional armies. Most African states recruited and mobilized individuals on an *ad hoc* basis for either defence or offence. Besides, in addition to their own armies, the European powers could always, as A. Isaacman and J. Vansina have contended, rely on African mercenaries and levies which gave them the numerical superiority they needed.[61] In fact, as A. Laroui puts it, most of the armies were African in recruitment and only European in command. Above all, by the terms of the Brussels Convention of 1890, the imperial powers agreed not to sell arms to Africans. This meant that most African armies were armed with completely outmoded, old and often unserviceable guns, mainly flint-locks or muzzle-loading muskets, and had

59. M. Crowder, 1968, pp. 81, 85; R. Oliver and G. Mathew (eds), 1971; V. Harlow and E. M. Chilver (eds), 1965.
60. See Chapters 3–9 below.
61. See Chapter 8 below.

PLATES 2.2(a)–(f) *Weapons used by Africans and their European opponents during the wars between 1880 and 1935*

PLATE 2.2(c) *A nineteenth-century Yoruba (Nigeria) oba (king) with his generals armed with outmoded flintlock Dane guns*

PLATE 2.2(a) *The Asante War of 1896 (Gold Coast): throwing axes and knives*

PLATE 2.2(b) *Kavirondo warriors (Kenya) with spears and shields*

PLATE 2.2(d) *Soldiers of the King's African Rifles with a Maxim gun*

PLATE 2.2(e) *A Gatling gun*

(*for Plate 2.2(f) see next page*)

PLATE 2.2(f) *Aeroplanes used in the colonial wars of the 1920s*

no heavy artillery or naval power whatsoever. The European armies, on the other hand, were armed with the most up-to-date heavy artillery, and guns such as the repeater rifle, and above all the Gatling and the Maxim guns. They also used the heavy artillery of naval forces. As Laroui has pointed out, even motor vehicles and aeroplanes[62] were used in the later campaigns. It is significant that the two African leaders who were able to inflict some defeats on the Europeans, Samori and Menelik, managed to obtain some of these up-to-date weapons. But in the end even Samori too was overpowered by the French. The overwhelming superiority that Europe enjoyed over Africa is summed up succinctly in Hilaire Belloc's famous couplet already quoted in Chapter 1.

In view of these economic, political and above all military and technological advantages enjoyed by European powers over African polities, the contest was a most uneven one and it is not at all surprising that the former could vanquish the latter with such relative ease. Indeed, for Europe, the timing of the conquest could not have been better; for Africa it could not have been worse.

The map of Africa after partition and occupation

The new geopolitical map of Africa that evolved after about a generation of systematic boundary-making and military occupation was quite different from what it had been in 1879 (see Fig. 1.1). The European powers had partitioned the continent into some forty political units. The new boundaries have been regarded by some scholars as unacceptable because they were deemed to be arbitrary, artificial, precipitate and haphazard and to have distorted the national pre-European political order. Others, such as Joseph Anene and Saadia Touval, have regarded them as making more sense than they did by 1879.[63]

There is some truth in both points of view. Some 30% of the total

62. See Chapter 5 below.
63. J. C. Anene, 1970.

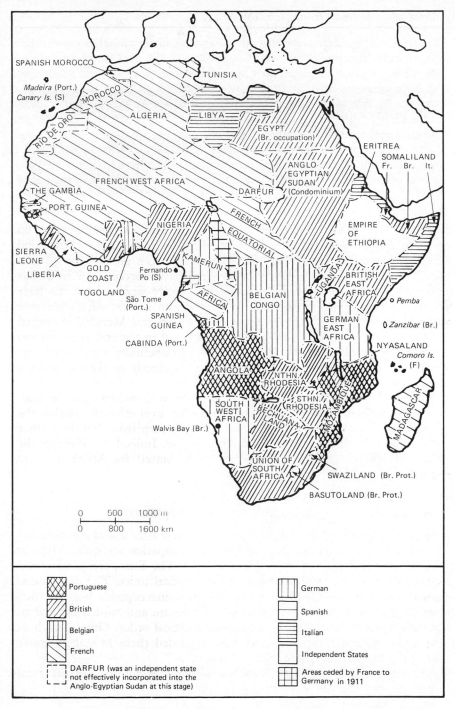

SPANISH MOROCCO

Madeira (Port.)
Canary Is. (S)

MOROCCO

TUNISIA

ALGERIA

LIBYA

RIO DE ORO

EGYPT
(Br. occupation)

ERITREA
SOMALILAND
Fr. Br. It.

FRENCH WEST AFRICA

ANGLO-
EGYPTIAN
SUDAN
(Condominium)

DARFUR

THE GAMBIA

PORT. GUINEA

NIGERIA

FRENCH

EQUATORIAL

EMPIRE
OF
ETHIOPIA

SIERRA
LEONE

LIBERIA

GOLD
COAST

TOGOLAND

Fernando
Po (S)

KAMERUN

AFRICA

UGANDA

BRITISH
EAST
AFRICA

São Tome
(Port.)

SPANISH
GUINEA

BELGIAN
CONGO

GERMAN
EAST
AFRICA

○ Pemba

CABINDA (Port.)

ANGOLA

NTHN.
RHODESIA

STHN.
RHODESIA

NYASALAND

Ò Zanzibar (Br.)

Comoro Is.
(F)

SOUTH
WEST
AFRICA

BECHUANA-
LAND

MOZAMBIQUE

MADAGASCAR

Walvis Bay (Br.)

UNION OF
SOUTH
AFRICA

SWAZILAND (Br. Prot.)

BASUTOLAND (Br. Prot.)

0   500   1000 m
0   800   1600 km

Portuguese

British

Belgian

French

DARFUR (was an independent state
not effectively incorporated into the
Anglo-Egyptian Sudan at this stage)

German

Spanish

Italian

Independent States

Areas ceded by France to
Germany in 1911

FIG. 2.1 *Africa in 1914 (after R. Oliver and J. D. Fage, 1962)*

43

length of the borders were drawn as straight lines, and these and others often cut right across ethnic and linguistic boundaries. On the other hand, the remaining borders did follow national boundaries and cannot therefore be considered as arbitrary or as ill-considered as the criticisms would suggest. Moreover, African political units evolving as a result, for example, of the Oyo–Dahomey conflict, the Fulani *djihāds*, the Mfecane in Southern Africa, or the internal struggle for power in both Ethiopia and Uganda during the second half of the nineteenth century, testify to the fluidity of African boundaries, frontiers and enclaves prior to the partition. What is not often realized is the extent to which the partition solidified these fluid boundaries, or the extent of the efforts made by the boundary commissioners to rectify anomalies, where politically possible, during the numerous boundary delimitations. On balance, then, although the map of Africa in 1914 (see Fig. 2.1), compared to what it was in 1879, may have looked very confusing, the delimitation had nevertheless been a remarkably efficient job, thanks to the new advances in cartography. And although the partition must be condemned as illegal and immoral, and it must be recognized that some of the boundaries were indeed artificial and arbitrary, it would be undesirable – indeed dangerous – to continue to advocate a return to the fluid, pre-European international boundaries – except after a very close scrutiny – because of the 'mess' said to have been created by the partition.

By 1902 the conquest of Africa was all but concluded. It had been a particularly bloody business. The devastating power of the Maxim gun and the relative sophistication of European technology must have been a sobering experience for the Africans. But though the conquest of Africa by Europe was accomplished with such relative ease, the occupation and the establishment of European administration in Africa – as the following chapters will demonstrate – were not.

3 African initiatives and resistance in the face of partition and conquest

T. O. RANGER

In tropical Africa the twenty years between 1880 and 1900 presented a strange and brutal paradox. The process of European conquest and occupation was clearly irreversible. But it was also eminently resistible. It was irreversible because of the revolution in technology. For the first time the whites had a decisive advantage in weapons, and for the first time the railway, the cable and the steamship enabled them to offer some answer to the problem of communication within Africa and between Africa and Europe. It was resistible because of the size of Africa; because of the strengths of its peoples; and because in the event Europe did not deploy very many men or very much technology. True, the whites made up for their shortage of men by recruiting African auxiliaries. But they were not diabolically clever manipulators of divided and outmatched blacks. The Europeans were merely running through the repertoire of old imperial devices. In detail they often knew much less about a situation than African rulers did. The implementation of the strategy of advance was very haphazard and clumsy. Europeans bumped into, provoked and even invented through ignorance and alarm, a multitude of African resistances.

The Europeans were 'bound to win in the end', and after they had won they tidied up the untidy process. Books were written about what was called 'pacification'; the impression was given that most Africans had thankfully accepted the so-called *Pax Colonica*; and the facts of African resistance were glossed over. But the victory of the Europeans does not mean that African resistance was unimportant at the time or undeserving of study now. And in fact it has been studied a good deal in the last twenty years.

Most of this research of the last two decades has been sober, detailed, scholarly, not avoiding the ambiguities of many of the resistances. But most of it has been based upon, or used to demonstrate, three dogmatic assumptions, which I believe still to be essentially true, even though each has been modified by recent research and analysis. It has been argued, first, that the fact of African resistance is significant because it proves that Africans did not acquiesce placidly in a European 'pacification'. It has been argued, secondly, that this resistance was neither despairing nor irrational, but that it was often powered by rational and innovative ideologies. It has been argued, thirdly, that these resistances were not futile; that they had significant consequences in their time and still have significant resonances today. These three arguments are worth restating here, together with the modifications proposed to them.

The generality of resistance

In 1965 the Soviet historian, A. B. Davidson, called upon scholars to refute 'the traditional European historiographical view' in which 'the African people apprehended the coming of the colonialists as good fortune; as deliverance from fratricidal internecine wars, from the tyranny of neighbouring tribes, from epidemics, and periodic starvations'; in which peoples who did not resist were described as 'peace-loving' and those who did resist were described as 'blood-thirsty'. Davidson remarked that 'protectors of colonial rule refused to consider rebellion a regular phenomenon'. They explained it in terms of 'primitive and irrational' responses, or in terms of the agitation of the 'blood-thirsty' minority. 'They rejected the only correct explanation which regards rebellions as just wars for liberation, which is why they were supported by the overwhelming majority of Africans.'[1]

In 1965 Davidson emphasized that 'many rebellions are not yet known . . . Often we do not have concrete information about those rebellions that are considered an established fact'. Since then, the job of 'discovering' resistances has gone on apace. Historians have begun to classify revolts more rigorously, distinguishing 'social banditry' from 'peasant rebellion', and guerrilla warfare from the clash of armies. In some cases episodes trumpeted by the colonialists as rebellions have been shown to have been forced upon the people by ignorance and fear on the part of the whites.[2] In many more cases considerable and significant resistances have been rescued from obscurity. We now possess detailed studies for most of the 'major' uprisings and in some cases a vigorous argument about how best to explain and interpret them has been taking place. From all this it is quite clear that Davidson was right to think that resistance was a 'regular phenomenon'.

It is clear also that the old attempts to distinguish naturally warlike from naturally peaceful African societies are beside the point. I have argued myself in a number of articles that so far as large-scale African polities are concerned it makes no sense to discriminate between so-called warlike, raiding states, and so-called peaceful, trading and cultivating ones, since virtually all states made some attempt to find a basis on which to manipulate the Europeans without recourse to arms; virtually all of them had some crucial interests or values which they were prepared to defend, if necessary

1. A. B. Davidson in T. O. Ranger (ed.), 1968(c), pp. 181–3.
2. S. Marks, 1970.

by armed resistance.[3] But I was myself mistaken to go on to argue that the foremost among the societies engaged in either resistance or manipulation had more in common with each other 'than with those small-scale societies that could neither resist nor exploit colonial rule'.[4] Among others, Shula Marks has shown in her study of Khoisan resistance in South Africa that non-centralized peoples are just as capable of putting up a determined fight against white advance as centralized ones. John Thornton has contrasted the resistance potential of states and of stateless societies much to the advantage of the latter:

> States are often praised for their role in resistance to the European invasion ... actually ... their role was ambiguous. Some, it is true, resisted fairly well ... But many other state societies collapsed on impact with the Europeans ... On the other hand the resistance of stateless societies was often long-lived and heroic ... it was the stateless societies – Igbo, Baule, Agni and others – that carried on the guerrilla wars.[5]

In short, virtually every sort of African society resisted, and there was resistance in virtually every region of European advance. We can now accept this as a fact which no longer needs elaboration. What we need to do now is to move from cataloguing to interpretation; from merely demonstrating resistance to assessing and explaining its degrees of intensity. Historians of particular national territories have been concerned to demonstrate that there was resistance in their area and to claim it as part of the local protest tradition; and it is always possible to do this since there was some resistance virtually everywhere. But this piecemeal approach can obscure the fact that there were striking differences in the intensity of resistance from one region to another. There were armed resistance in Northern Rhodesia (now Zambia) but on nothing like the scale and for nothing like the duration of those in Southern Rhodesia (now Zimbabwe), which in turn cannot be compared for 'regularity' with resistances against the Portuguese in the Zambezi valley. It is plain that we need rigorous comparative regional studies. The chapters which follow suggest further patterns of contrast and some of the explanations and consequences of them.

The ideology of resistance

Colonial apologists stressed the irrationality and desperation of armed resistance. They claimed that it was often the result of 'superstition' and that peoples otherwise content to accept colonial rule had been worked upon by 'witch-doctors'. Many European critics of colonialism, sympathetic to African protest, nevertheless also accepted that Africans had little in

3. T. O. Ranger in L. H. Gann and P. Duignan (eds), 1969, pp. 293–304.
4. S. Marks, 1972, pp. 55–80.
5. J. Thornton, 1973, pp. 119–20.

their 'traditional' patterns of thought which helped them to come to an effective or practical response to attacks on their way of life. The ideologies of revolt were thought of as 'the magic of despair', bound to fail and incapable of pointing to the future. In such a view the resistances, however heroic, were tragic dead ends.[6]

Over the last decade or so historians of resistance have sought to combat this sort of interpretation. They have done this in two ways, by asserting strictly secular ideologies of revolt, and by 'disinfecting' religious ideologies.

The chief secular ideology which has been proposed is the concept of 'sovereignty'. Jacob Ajayi has written that 'the most fundamental aspect of the European impact was the loss of sovereignty ... once a people lose their sovereignty, and they are exposed to another culture, they lose at least a little of their self-confidence and self-respect; they lose their right of self-steering, their freedom of choice as to what to change in their own culture or what to copy or reject from the other culture.'[7]

A similar point is made with more emphasis by Walter Rodney:

> The decisiveness of the short period of colonialism ... springs mainly from the fact that Africa lost power ... During the centuries of pre-colonial trade some control over social, political and economic life was retained in Africa, in spite of the disadvantageous commerce with Europeans. That little control over internal matters disappeared under colonialism ... The power to act independently is the guarantee to participate actively and *consciously* in history. To be colonised is to be removed from history ... Overnight, African political states lost their power, independence and meaning.[8]

That Ajayi and Rodney can see the decisive importance of the loss of sovereignty is far from demonstrating, of course, that African resisters conceived of sovereignty in this way. Rodney himself deplores the 'partial and inadequate view of the world' which prevented African leaders from fully understanding what was at stake in the encounter with Europe. Ajayi asserts, however, that the rulers of African states 'as guardians of the sovereignty of the people' were 'hostile to whatever powers challenged this sovereignty'.[9] And historians have recovered some striking explicit statements of sovereignty.

There are statements of simple autonomy like the retort of chief Machemba of the Yao to the German commander, Hermann von Wissman, in 1890:

> I have listened to your words but can find no reason why I should obey you – I would rather die first ... I do not fall at your feet, for you are God's creature just as I am ... I am Sultan here in my

6. M. Gluckman, 1963, pp. 137–45.
7. J. F. A. Ajayi in T. O. Ranger (ed.), 1968(c), pp. 196–7.
8. W. Rodney, 1972, pp. 245–6. Emphasis in original.
9. J. F. A. Ajayi in L. H. Gann and P. Duignan (eds), 1969, p. 506.

land. You are Sultan there in yours. Yet listen, I do not say to you that you should obey me; for I know that you are a free man ... As for me, I will not come to you, and if you are strong enough, then come and fetch me.[10]

There are statements which express the desire to modernize but not at the expense of sovereignty, as in the case of chief Makombe Hanga, ruler of Barue in central Mozambique, who told a white visitor in 1895: 'I see how you white men advance more and more in Africa, on all sides of my country companies are at work ... My country will also have to take up these reforms and I am quite prepared to open it up ... I should also like to have good roads and railways ... *But I will remain the Makombe my fathers have been.*'[11]

And there are also striking expressions of a wider philosophy of sovereignty. The most striking come from South West Africa. The Nama leader, Hendrik Wittboi, confided to his diary that: 'By colour and mode of life we belong together and this Africa is in general the land of the Red Captains [i.e. Africans]. That we form different kingdoms and regions reflects only a trivial subdivision of Africa.' Wittboi told the German administrator, Theodor Leutwein, in 1894, that 'the Lord God has established various kingdoms in the world. Therefore I know and believe that it is no sin or crime that I should wish to remain the independent chief of my land and people.'[12]

In any case, whatever problems people may have found in understanding the initial impact of European advance, there was no doubt about the consequences of loss of sovereignty once European rule was established. Wittboi's old enemy, chief Maherero, leader of the Herero rising, wrote to him appealing for joint action in 1904: 'It is my wish that we weak nations should rise up against the Germans ... Let the whole of Africa fight against the Germans, and let us rather die together than through maltreatment, prison or in any other way.'[13] The elders of the noncentralized and fiercely independent Matumbi of eastern Tanganyika (now Tanzania), among whom the Majī Majī rising broke out in 1905, said of the German regime: 'This has now become an absolute ruler. Destroy him.'[14]

The idea of sovereignty clearly did provide an ideology for resistance. Nevertheless, important modifications must be made. Rulers were not always very clearly 'guardians of the sovereignty of the people'. In nineteenth-century Africa – in the west, east and south – new states had

10. Quoted by B. Davidson, 1964(a), pp. 357–8.
11. Quoted by A. Isaacman, 1976, pp. 128–9.
12. Among studies of South West African resistance are: H. Dreschler, 1966; H. Bley, 1968 and 1971. The quotation here is from J. Iliffe in G. Kibodya (ed.), 1968.
13. Iliffe in Kibodya (ed.), 1968.
14. Mzee Ndundule Mangaya quoted in G. C. K. Gwassa and J. Iliffe (eds), 1968, p. 5.

arisen, based on 'the military technology of Europe'.[15] Such states often
resisted the direct extension of European power but their resistance was
undermined by the disaffection of many of their subjects. Thornton tells
us of West African states like those of Samori Ture or of Shehu Ahmadu
that 'they were burdened by constant revolts caused mainly by their high-
handed and exploitative state structures ... by and large the leadership
of the states, exploitative and tyrannical as they were, did not possess the
legitimacy to go to the country and carry on the wars'.[16] Allen Isaacman
writes of the 'secondary states' of the Zambezi valley that their 'imposition
of the alien rule of the *mestizos* generated African opposition, as did the
forced mobilization of labour'; their history 'was marred by numerous
revolts ... resistance to this form of alien rule as well as to predatory slave
raiding activities. Such a situation obviously did not lend itself to an ongoing
and unified effort' against the whites.[17]

States such as these may be contrasted with longer-established polities
in which the rulers had achieved 'legitimacy'. But even here it would be
over-romantic to suppose that all ancient aristocracies enjoyed popular trust
and support. The ruling groups among some long-established peoples took
their own advantage of the opportunities offered by nineteenth-century
weapons and commerce to develop an arbitrary power, with the result that
they could not count on popular support in a confrontation with the whites.
This partly accounts for the ineffectiveness of resistance in Northern
Rhodesia, where the Bemba chiefs faced what Henry S. Meebelo has called
'a popular revulsion against the ruling class', and where the aristocracy
of Barotseland feared a slave uprising if they attempted to oppose the
extension of British influence.[18]

A number of historians, indeed, have stressed the importance of discriminating between resistances which were motivated by the desire of
a ruling group to retain its exploitative power, and resistances on a much
wider scale, which were often directed as much against the authoritarianism
of African rulers as against colonial oppression. Edward Steinhart urges
that

> protest and resistance can be and are directed ... against domestic
> forms of oppression ... Protest must be viewed as something other
> than the expression of national aspirations ... by focusing on leader-
> ship we have accepted the interpretation of anti-colonialism as 'African
> nationalism', a movement to expel aliens and to restore 'national'
> independence. If instead we look within the protest movements ...
> we are apt to discover that the impulses which the leaders organize
> and interpret are profoundly anti-authoritarian and revolutionary
> rather than anti-foreign and 'nationalist'.[19]

15. P. Bohannan and P. Curtin, 1971, p. 271.
16. J. Thornton, 1973, pp. 120–1.
17. A. Isaacman, 1976, pp. 103–4.
18. H. S. Meebelo, 1971, p. 68.
19. E. Steinhart, unpublished paper.

Even where a long-established polity enjoyed a leadership with recognized legitimacy and was able to mobilize the majority of its population
into resistance, recent historians have been inclined to criticize 'the narrow
sense of primordial loyalty' and the 'parochialism' which did no more than
to focus on sovereignty as previously understood. Such historians have
emphasized instead the significance of those resistances in which the idea
of sovereignty was redefined. Thus Isaacman argues that the 1917 revolt
in the Zambezi valley was unlike previous resistances there, 'which were
designed to regain the independence of a historical polity or a group of
related peoples'. The 1917 revolt 'sought to liberate all the peoples of the
Zambezi from colonial oppression', appealing especially to the oppressed
peasantry of whatever ethnicity. 'The shift in primordial loyalties represented a new level of political consciousness in which the Portuguese were
perceived for the first time as the common oppressor.'[20]

The role of religious ideas

Meanwhile historians have been re-examining the role of religious ideas
in the resistances. What they have found bears little resemblance either
to the 'fanatical witch-doctors' of colonial reports, or to 'the magic of
despair'. They have found, to begin with, that religious teachings and
symbols often bore very directly on the question of sovereignty and
legitimacy. Rulers were legitimized through ritual recognition, and when
a ruler and his people determined to defend their sovereignty they naturally
drew heavily on religious symbols and ideas. Rodney, in a paper on
Ovimbundu resistance in Angola, remarks that 'a great deal of attention
has been paid to spiritual resistance in a later stage of the African struggle –
notably in cases like the Maji Maji wars ... but for "primary resistances"
there is a tendency to under-emphasize the fact that African peoples everywhere automatically resisted not only in material terms but also with their
own metaphysical religious weapons.'[21]

In another paper, this time on the resistance of the Gaza state to the
Portuguese in southern Mozambique, Rodney writes of the possible
traumatic consequences of the commitment of spiritual resources to the
struggle. 'The Ngoni of Gaza suffered not only the destruction of their
political capital but also the defilement of their principal shrine'; after
military defeat in 1895 the royal ritual objects were lost; diviners threw
away their divining bones after the incomprehensible event of defeat; the
'high priestess' was dismissed and executed. 'Awareness of crisis at a deep
spiritual level was quite widespread.'[22]

It was out of crises of legitimacy of this sort that the great movements
which attempted to redefine sovereignty often emerged. Such movements

20. A. Isaacman, 1976, pp. 343, 345, 370.
21. W. Rodney, 1971(b).
22. W. Rodney, 1971(a).

almost invariably had the advantage of spiritual leaders, enunciating the message of wider unity. Sometimes this sort of development took place in the context of Islam – and Islamic ideologies of millennialism and resistance spread right across the Sudanic belt from east to west. Sometimes it happened because of the influence of Christian ideas – and Hendrik Wittboi drew upon Protestant Christianity for his doctrine of sovereignty, while an African independent Christian prophet was active among the Nama at the time of their rising against the Germans. Very often it happened in the context of African religion.

I have argued myself that this happened in Southern Rhodesia and that the risings of 1896 were inspired and co-ordinated by religious leaders. Isaacman argues that the 1917 rising in the Zambezi valley was given moral fervour by the teachings of the spirit medium, Mbuya, who did not call for the restoration of her own Barue state but preached instead the gospel of the brotherhood and oppression of all Africans, and of the concern for their welfare and for the redress of their wrongs on the part of the high god, Mwari.[23] In the case of the Majī Majī rising of 1905 the ideology of revolt was powered by both Islamic and African millennial enthusiasm. The great Tanganyikan coastal resistances of 1888 to 1891 had been led by members of the Swahili commercial and urban elite; there had been no development of a religious ideology of protest, either Islamic or 'traditional'; resistance depended upon the idea of defending established sovereignties.[24] But after the defeat of this coastal opposition and the co-option of many of the Swahili elite into German service, the basis of protest changed and widened. Majī Majī was inspired by a combination of a new prophetic message, emerging from the African cult centres of the hinterland, and populist enthusiastic Islam.[25]

The prophetic teaching which underlay some of the great resistances is slowly being rescued from the garbled accounts of their adversaries. Gilbert Gwassa's account of the development and character of Kinjikitile's Majī Majī ideology is a classic example of this sort of rescue work. Another striking, and as yet unpublished, reconstruction has been made by Mongameli Mabona for the teachings of the great militant Xhosa prophet, Makana, whose message, enunciated in the early nineteenth century, 'lost its force only in 1890, when Xhosa national resistance finally collapsed'. As Mabona remarks, his teaching has usually been seen as 'a salmagundi of incompatible or unrelated religious concepts'. Mabona shows instead that it was 'a skilfully tailored pattern of Khoisan, Xhosa and Christian elements', put together with very great creative imagination.

Makana made brilliant word coinages to express his concepts of divinity – concepts of space and of the scattering of light. 'His powerful mind and religious genius ... moulded a body of doctrine which was to serve as

23. T. O. Ranger, 1967; A. Isaacman, 1976, pp. 304–5, 307, 310, 313, 316, 326.
24. R. D. Jackson in R. I. Rotberg and A. Mazrui (eds), 1970.
25. G. Gwassa in T. O. Ranger and I. Kimambo (eds), 1972.

an ideological dynamo for the Xhosa nation.' In some ways Makana's teaching was an African version of the Protestant Christian ideology of sovereignty, which later gave Wittboi confidence in the divine right of the Red Captains. Makana explored the fundamental differences between black and white – different customs, different divinities, different destinies. The creator was Dali'dephu, great ancestor of the Xhosa, who had made Uthixo to be the god of the white men. Uthixo was an inferior to Dali'dephu, and the white men were morally the inferior of the Xhosa – continually vexed with the idea of sin. But this difference did not matter until the two moral universes came into contact and into conflict; then Dali'dephu would assert himself to ensure that his own particular children, the Xhosa, and their own particular and superior way of life triumphed over the superficial powers of the whites. Makana appealed for pan-Xhosa unity; for confidence in their moral universe. Dali'dephu would sweep the whites away; the Xhosa dead would return; 'a new era would begin'.[26]

Conceptual and symbolic innovations such as Makana's had a relevance which long outlasted the particular resistance with which they were first associated. So far from being desperate nonsense, prophetic messages of this kind were a systematic attempt to widen and redefine the idea of deity and its relation to the moral order, and involved wide-ranging changes in Xhosa internal assumptions and relationships as well as providing the 'bedrock of ideology for resistance'. Peter Rigby has argued strongly against the idea that African prophetism was 'merely the result of exogenous forces of disruption during the colonial period' or sprang 'from a breakdown of African religions'. Prophetism was certainly, in his view, very much a matter of protest, and had played 'a major part in *most* protest movements in Africa', but the prophet emerged 'not merely as a reaction to exogenous experience but upon the grounds of the viability and adaptability of African religions'.[27] With this view of African religious systems regularly able to throw up prophetic leadership out of their own tensions and potentialities, and of prophetic leaders able to create new syntheses which simultaneously revalidated the old and allowed for the new, we have moved a long way from the idea of prophetic ideologies of resistance as 'the magic of despair'.

Valuable as all this work has been, the emphasis upon religious ideology in resistance has been challenged from two sides. On the one hand some scholars argue that the role of religion in resistance has been overstated; on the other hand some scholars argue that the role of resistance in religion has been exaggerated.

Thus colonial writers spoke of a 'witch' as leading the Giriama rising in the coastal hinterland of Kenya; more recent historians have reinterpreted her as a 'prophetess'. But Cynthia Brantley Smith, in her admirable and exhaustive account of the Giriama, establishes that she was no sort of

26. M. A. Mabona, 1974.
27. P. Rigby, 1974.

religious leader: merely a respected and assertive woman.[28] This is a case in which a retranslation of colonialist terms like 'witch' and 'witch-doctor' is not enough to correct the distortion of official accounts. It has been suggested by two researchers on Ndebele and Shona history that the same is true of my own account of the 1896 risings in Southern Rhodesia; the British South Africa Company said the risings were fomented by 'witch-doctors'; I argued that they were powered by a profound prophetic ideology; Julian Cobbing and David Beach assert that the spirit mediums were of much more restricted influence than I allowed and that the priests of Mwari participated in the risings hardly at all.[29] It will perhaps not be found surprising that I am unready for such drastic revisions. But it certainly *is* true that recent work on African religion in Southern Rhodesia shows that its relationship to resistance cannot have been so straightforward as I had supposed. It is plain that neither the Mwari cult nor the system of spirit mediums was capable of committing itself wholly to resistance or wholly to anything; both were based on constant and intense competition between and within shrines; the astonishing survival of the cults depended upon the fact that priests or mediums who had backed a mistaken or defeated cause could rapidly be replaced by rivals waiting in the wings, and upon the fact that some important cult centres would always adopt positions different from others. Some Mwari shrines backed the rising and others did not, and at the shrines which did support it the families in charge were replaced after its suppression. I was wrong to suppose that the *total* religious leadership of the Shona would commit itself wholly to the risings; the risings *were* crucially important but not so important that they could – or should – disrupt the long-term patterns of persistence and effectiveness of the cults.[30]

All this is relevant to the argument over the centrality of protest to prophetic movements. A prophet emerges in response to a popular sense that there is need for radical and innovative action, but such a popular sense need not arise only because of external threat. A prophet can be thrown up because of deep anxiety over internal tensions or transformations, or even because of a general desire to accelerate the pace of change and to seize on new opportunities. Thus a prophetic leader often directs his teaching to the internal morality of African societies – sometimes leading a protest movement against internal authoritarianism, sometimes 'protesting' more against the facts of human nature. It emerges clearly from the work that is now being done on the remarkable number of prophetic leaders in nineteenth-century Africa that many of them were not concerned with resistance to the whites, or even directly with the whites at all.

Even those prophetic leaders who were primarily concerned to find a

28. C. B. Smith, 1973.
29. J. Cobbing, 1974 and 1977; D. Beach, 1971 and 1979.
30. M. Schoffeleers in Schoffeleers (ed.), forthcoming.

restatement which would help to define the relations of their people to the Europeans were by no means unanimous in recommending rejection or resistance. As Mabona remarks, Xhosa prophetism produced both an 'ideology for resistance' and an ideology 'for a process of controlled accommodation'. The prophet of resistance was Makana; the prophet of 'controlled accommodation' was Ntsikana. Ntsikana was a creative religious genius of the same order as Makana; the debates between them on the nature of divinity had very immediate practical consequences and divided the Xhosa into factions, but they were conducted in profound theological terms. And in fact Ntsikana was not primarily concerned with the problems of relationships to the whites, his intention was rather to bring about changes in Xhosa society by means of accepting some of the dynamics of Christian thought, while at the same time repudiating many of the cultural assumptions of the whites. As O. P. Raum tells us, among many Xhosa today 'the beginning of Christianity is not credited to the missionaries but rather to a Christian forerunner in the person of Ntsikana'.[31]

Though no other case presents us with so dramatic and direct a prophetic clash as the debate between Makana and Ntsikana, the same range of prophetic possibilities comes out clearly even in areas of very determined resistance, like the areas in which Majī Majī took place, or the Shona areas of Rhodesia. After the defeat of Majī Majī the cluster of symbols and claims to spiritual power which Kinjikitile had made use of was drawn upon by a succession of prophetic figures who were concerned with the internal purification of African societies, and who led what have been called 'witchcraft eradication movements'.

As for the Shona, Elleck Mashingaidze has written a fascinating paper on the sequence of prophetic advice given to the Shona people of the Mazoe valley area. The most influential mediums first advised the people to listen carefully to missionary teaching; then advised them to take part in the risings and drive out the whites; and then advised them once more to send their children to mission schools to gain what they could of white 'wisdom'. Mashingaidze does not see this as a sequence of confusion or betrayal. He writes:

> Military defeat in 1897 ... did not result in an abandonment of the traditional world as the whites had naïvely anticipated ... The Shona began to try to understand the whites ... Traditional religion, as represented by Nehanda and other mediums, was not opposed to the Christian faith as such. The role of traditional religion from the beginning of the encounter of the two systems was to moderate change ... It kept on reminding the people that in spite of the military outcome ... they should not lose their cultural identity. In fact, traditional religion remained the source of Shona constructive and creative response to Christianity and the Western culture as a whole.

31. O. P. Raum in E. Benz (ed.), 1965, pp. 47–70.

It reminded people that there was still room for accepting or rejecting certain aspects of the new order.[32]

One might say that the Shona prophets were seeking to mitigate the effects of the loss of political sovereignty by preserving a certain spiritual autonomy. Yet the potentialities of Shona prophetism for producing an ideology of resistance were not lost and in the 1970s some mediums were deeply involved in the nationalist and guerrilla struggle.

Seen from the perspective of the history of resistance the inward-turning focus of much prophetism, which identifies the source of evil as internal sin rather than external oppression, may seem like 'false consciousness'. Seen from the perspective of the history of African religion the interest of these movements lies precisely in the extent to which they succeed in answering the inner-directed anxieties of African societies. Thus Professor B. A. Ogot has taken issue with those who interpret Kenyan prophetic movements as essentially anti-colonial. He writes of one such prophet, Simeo Ondeto, that he was indeed 'revolutionary' but that his revolution was in the moral rather than the political sphere and was to take place within the individual. The essence of prophetic movements, writes Ogot, is that they are 'transforming spiritual and social agencies creating new communities capable of facing the challenges of the modern world'.[33] The great prophetic ideologies of resistance thus fall into place as part of a larger attempt to redefine the moral basis of society.

The consequences and relevance of African resistance

Up to about twenty years ago it was generally accepted that resistances had been dead ends, leading nowhere. Since then it has been strongly argued that resistances looked in all kinds of ways to the future. In so far as they were concerned with sovereignty they can be seen as anticipating the recovery of sovereignty and the triumphs of African nationalism; in so far as they possessed prophetic ideologies they can be seen as contributing to new communities of concept. Some of them resulted in improving the position of the peoples who had revolted. Others threw up an alternative leadership to the officially recognized chiefs. I have argued myself that the resistances were 'connected' to mass nationalism by virtue of having been movements of mass commitment; by means of a continuity of atmosphere and symbol which ran through other mass movements in the intermediary period; and finally by reason of the explicit inspiration which the nationalist movements drew from the memory of the heroic past.[34]

These arguments have been developed by other writers and the contemporary relevance of the resistances became an axiom of nationalist and

32. E. Mashingaidze, 1974.
33. B. A. Ogot, 1974(a).
34. T. O. Ranger, 1968(a).

guerrilla theorists. Thus Rodney, at the end of his examination of the Ovimbundu resistance to the Portuguese, wrote:

> The resurgence of armed resistance on the Benguela plateau has taken place within the past few years. How it came about and what links it owes to earlier epochs are such major questions that no attempts will be made here to provide any answers, which would inevitably be inadequate. It is enough to note that *Angolan freedom fighters themselves affirm a connexion between their wars of national liberation and previous resistances, and that (on their authority) the mass of the people are said to recall positively the spirit of such events as the Bailundu war.* Idle academicians are in no position to challenge this.[35]

Academicians – whether idle or not – *have* challenged the postulated connection between the resistances and the subsequent freedom struggle. Such challenges have come both from the 'right' and from the 'left'.

Writing from a position somewhere on the 'right', Henri Brunschwig has denied that there is any clear line of descent from the resistances to modern nationalist movements. In Brunschwig's view there has been over many centuries in Africa a struggle between the adaptation of, and the resistance to, externally derived ideas. The 'adaptors' created the great Sudanic empires: the resisters endeavoured to repudiate them. The adaptors made use of the enlarging principles of Islam and Christianity: the resisters drew upon what Brunschwig calls 'animism' and 'ethnicity'. Long before colonialism there had been 'innumerable revolts' against African innovators; most of the resistance to colonialism sprang from the same 'animist' and 'ethnic' roots. Modern African nationalism and pan-Africanism, on the other hand, are manifestations of the tendency towards centralizing innovation and the adoption of 'large' ideas, and thus stand in a tradition quite opposite to that of resistance.[36]

Writing from the 'left' a number of other historians have challenged the postulated link between resistance and nationalism on the grounds that this is an intellectual device to allow the ruling, and sometimes selfish, minorities of the new states to claim revolutionary legitimacy. Steinhart has made the most explicit statement of this challenge: 'Instead of examining anti-colonial resistance through the distorting lens of nationalist mythology, we must create a better "myth", one better suited to interpreting the reality of African protest ... A "myth" of revolutionary upsurge may lead us further and deeper in our understanding of twentieth-century movements of protest and liberation than the failing "myth of nationalism" has brought us.' In this way Steinhart seeks to claim the heritage of the resistances for radical anti-authoritarian protest within the new national states of Africa.[37]

35. W. Rodney, 1971(b), p. 9.
36. H. Brunschwig, 1974, pp. 63–4.
37. E. Steinhart, unpublished paper.

A more recent full-length study of resistance – Isaacman's book on African revolt in the Zambezi valley – implicitly seeks to deal with both Brunschwig's and Steinhart's objections. Isaacman deals with Brunschwig by placing his emphasis not on the 'parochialisms' of ethnic revolts but on the redefinitions of sovereignty which he claims to have taken place in the 1917 rising. He deals with Steinhart by linking up this sort of enlarged resistance not with an elite nationalism but with the radical Mozambican liberation movement, FRELIMO. In Isaacman's restatement the idea of a link between earlier resistance and contemporary freedom movements assumes this form: 'the nature of the appeal, which was phrased in broad anti-colonial terms and the scope of the alliance which this appeal made possible suggest that the 1917 rebellion occupied a transitional position between earlier African forms of resistance and the wars of liberation of the mid-twentieth century ... The 1917 rebellion constituted both the culmination of the long tradition of Zambezian resistance and simultaneously became the progenitor of the current liberation struggle.' In 1917, as in FRELIMO's struggle, 'the issue was oppression and not race'. Moreover, 'the links with FRELIMO extended beyond a shared ideological commitment' since the tradition of resistance 'served both as a source of pride and a model for future activity'.[38]

The periodization of resistance: the economic interpretation

I began this chapter by describing the situation in the last twenty years of the nineteenth century. Yet it has proved extremely difficult in practice to discuss resistance within this chronological limitation. At one extreme I have discussed Makana, the Xhosa prophet of the early nineteenth century. At the other extreme I have discussed the Zambezi rising of 1917 and its links with FRELIMO. But at least I have so far limited discussion to armed resistance to white invasion or to armed uprisings against colonial rule as it began to 'bite'; the chronological extensions arise from the uneven nature of white advance into Africa and from the still more uneven establishment of effective colonial control. Using this essentially political definition the period between 1880 and 1900 emerges as a crucial period of resistance, even if many of the great attempts to redefine sovereignty through protest took place later.

If we now turn in conclusion to the developing emphasis on *economic* resistance, the chronological limits become even less clearly defined. Perhaps the most radical reinterpretation is that of Samir Amin. Amin argues that the really crucial West African resistances to Europe came in the late seventeenth and eighteenth centuries, and he dismisses the resistances of the Scramble period itself as the half-hearted, rearguard actions

38. A. Isaacman, 1976, pp. 344, 345, 375.

of an already compromised ruling class. In Amin's eyes what was essentially at stake in the confrontation between Africa and Europe was not formal political control but Europe's attempts at economic manipulation. The truly significant African resistance was directed against such economic manipulation.

Amin argues that the trade across the Sahara had 'strengthened state centralization and stimulated progress'. The European-controlled Atlantic trade, on the other hand, 'did not give rise to any productive forces: on the contrary, this caused a disintegration of society ... African societies obviously opposed this worsening of their situation, and Islam served as the basis for their resistance ... The Muslim priests tried to organize a resistance movement; their aim was to stop the slave trade, i.e. the export of the labour force, but not to end internal slavery ... Islam changed its character from being a religion of a minority group of traders, it became a popular movement of resistance.'

Amin identifies three important resistances of this kind – the wars of 1673 to 1677; the Torodo revolution of 1776, which 'overthrew the military aristocracy and ended the slave trade'; and the movement of the prophet Diile in 1830 in the kingdom of Waalo, which failed 'in the face of French military intervention'. Amin is here describing resistances which were directed against an African aristocracy, but which were also a response to French economic aggression.

As the nineteenth century developed, Amin goes on to argue, the French ceased to demand slaves and came to demand raw materials and agricultural produce instead. In Waalo they began to experiment with agricultural plantations but these failed because of 'the resistance of the village communities'. The French could not succeed in overcoming resistance to proletarianization until they had occupied the whole area and were able to use continuous force. But this colonial conquest came so late in the progression that resistance to it was not very effective. By this time Islam had ceased to be an ideology of resistance and had become the spiritual solace of the defeated aristocracy, who used it to discipline peasant cultivators and to ensure that they produced whatever the French demanded from them.[39]

If Amin argues that the really important resistances came before the Scramble, other historians employing the economic perspective seem to be arguing that the really important resistances to formal colonial rule came only in the twentieth century. Certainly there was plenty of economic resistance during the Scramble. In particular, the Europeans broke away from their old alliance with African traders and middlemen and used force to set up a monopoly of commerce. The result was fierce resistance on the part of African traders – whether it was led by chief Nana Olomu of Itsekiri in the Niger delta (Nigeria), whom A. G. Hopkins describes as

39. S. Amin, 1972.

the very type of the *homo economicus*, or by the African and Swahili chiefs who had dominated the slave trade in northern Mozambique, or by the great trader, Rumaliza, who fought against both the Belgians and the Germans in East Africa.

Immanuel Wallerstein has seen this war of the traders as one of the decisive events of early colonialism: 'Many parts of sub-Saharan Africa ... [had been] engaged in a process of relatively autonomous development, tied to the European world in a limited but important manner through the intermediary of merchants or state trading agents on each side ... Yet in 1879 this whole structure began to crumble, and by 1900 it had ceased to exist.' With the imposition of colonial rule, 'the characteristic link between Africans and Europeans was no longer that between trading partners ... The most immediate effect of colonial rule was its impact on African traders ... by the end of World War I the radical decline of the relative importance of the African, as well as of the Arab, trading class had become an accomplished fact.'[40]

But in general recent historians have been unsympathetic to trader resistance. Hopkins warns us not to imagine that Niger delta traders like Nana Olomu were forerunners of nationalism or spokesmen for popular grievances, pointing out that their 'vision of social justice did not include the emancipation of their own slaves'. Nancy Hafkin stresses the purely selfish interests of the resistant chiefs of northern Mozambique: 'In no sense', she concludes, 'was their resistance popular or progressive.'[41]

The capacity of the great traders to resist, like that of the rulers of the secondary states, was undercut because they had generated too many African grievances. When the British Imperial East Africa Company wanted to break the power of Arab, Swahili and African traders it was able to build a new trade route inland from Malindi 'supported by stockades built by communities of slaves who had run away from their Arab masters on the coastal plantations'.[42] The 'important entrepreneurs' of the Lagos hinterland found it hard to offer effective resistance to the advance of the British because of the unrest of their 'large labour force consisting mainly of slaves and serfs'.[43] The conditions of international trade, which had brought about the rise of powerful African traders, had also ensured that their success would have to be brought at the price of much internal tension and resentment.

There were exceptions to this situation of tension between the powerful traders and the general populace. Thus in the Bailundu kingdom in Angola 'everyone was engaged in commerce'; during the 1870s 'Umbundu entrepreneurs discovered and developed a new type of root rubber' and 'during the next decade an unprecedented number of Bailundu moved into private

40. I. Wallerstein in L. H. Gann and P. Duignan (eds), 1970, pp. 402–7.
41. A. G. Hopkins, 1973, p. 147; N. Hafkin, 1971.
42. C. B. Smith, 1973, pp. 112, 113.
43. A. G. Hopkins, 1966(a), p. 141.

trade'. This widespread commercial prosperity came to an end with the drop of rubber prices in 1899–1902. 'The problem was intensified after 1899 in Bailundu by the intrusion of European traders ... When rubber prices plummetted, both Portuguese merchants and a new wave of poor whites ... arrived to establish themselves in commerce.' In the opinion of the most recent study of the Bailundu war of 1902, resentment at this European trade aggression had a great deal to do with the massive popular uprising which broke out against the Portuguese.[44]

But in general historians of resistance who work from the economic perspective associate mass revolt not with resentment at the European attack on trade, but with the more slowly developing realization on the part of African populations that the whites were determined to obtain cheap labour. Many Africans might at first welcome the Europeans as protectors against over-demanding chiefs, or rapacious Swahili traders, or slave-masters. But they very soon discovered that European demands upon them were equally, if not more, intolerable. At first many African slave-owners, chiefs and traders might respond to the Europeans with fear and hatred, but many of them found that in the longer run the interest of black and white holders of power often coincided. In this way a profound transformation of the pattern of resistance took place.

Donald Denoon has put the point neatly:

> When we speak of the Scramble for Africa, we generally mean the European division of African territory and sovereignty. There was another aspect to this phenomenon – the scramble for African resources. Diamonds and gold were among these, but perhaps the most valuable resource, and that for which the colonial authorities scrambled passionately, was African labour. Just as the old European and Arab traders had bought slaves elsewhere in Africa, so the new labour-recruiting agencies scrambled for unskilled labour to work in the mining fields ... In Angola and Zambezi and Katanga (by the turn of the century) recruiting agents from the mines of the south were competing with agents from the Portuguese forced labour plantations in the Bight of Benin.[45]

Just as the first Scramble for territory and sovereignty was resisted so was this second Scramble for labour. It was resisted in arms, and much of the support given to the great revolts of the early twentieth century which tried to redefine sovereignty came from men who hated forced labour. It was also resisted by desertion and strikes, by refusal to work underground, by compound riots. In the work of scholars like Charles van Onselen we have a new dimension for studies of resistance – no longer the dimension of 'Zambian resistance' or of 'Bemba resistance' but the dimension of resist-

44. D. L. Wheeler and C. D. Christensen in F.-W. Heimer (ed.), 1973, pp. 54–92.
45. D. Denoon, 1972, p. 74.

ance along the whole early colonial inter-territorial network of labour migration.[46]

Conclusion

It can be seen, then, that the historiography of resistance is a lively and argumentative one. Yet the modifications and new perspectives enlarge rather than controvert the three basic propositions I have been discussing. The 'regularity' and 'generality' of resistance emerges yet more clearly when we add to our catalogue of armed opposition and revolt during the Scramble the earlier indirect resistances to European economic aggression. Exploration of the ideological basis of resistance gains a new richness when we add the first manifestations of 'consciousness' on the part of workers or peasants to the idea of sovereignty and to the search for a new moral order. And the exploration of the links between resistance and the present situation of Africa gains a new resonance from the idea of economic resistance. The last word may rest not with a historian but with a political scientist, Colin Leys, who has called for a more dynamic and historically founded theory of 'underdevelopment':

> in one critical respect underdevelopment theory tends to resemble 'development theory' – it concentrates on what happens *to* the under-developed countries at the hands of imperialism and colonialism rather than on the total historical process involved, including the various forms of struggle against imperialism and colonialism which grow out of the conditions of underdevelopment ... what is needed is not a theory of underdevelopment but a theory of underdevelopment and its liquidation ... a theory of this kind implies nothing less than a theory of world history from the standpoint of the underdeveloped countries, a theory of the oppression and liberation of these countries; something ... in a fairly rudimentary stage of development, however keenly the need for it may be felt.[47]

The study of the resistances is not a romantic dwelling upon the futile glories of the past but can make its own contribution to a theory of oppression and liberation.

46. C. van Onselen, 1973, pp. 237–55.
47. C. Leys, 1975, pp. 20–1.

African initiatives and resistance in North-East Africa

H. A. IBRAHIM
based on a contribution by the late ABBAS I. ALI

Nowhere in Africa were African initiatives and resistance in the face of European partition and occupation of Africa as determined and protracted as in the modern states of Egypt, Sudan and Somalia. These reactions started in 1881 with the military uprising in Egypt, and continued in some parts of the area until as late as the 1920s. Never in the history of Africa did a people put up such a strong fight in defence of their freedom, their sovereignty and above all their culture and religion. In this chapter, a survey of these initiatives and reactions will be attempted, beginning first with those in Egypt, then Sudan and finally Somaliland.

Egypt

The Urabist revolution

The financial maladministration of Khedive Ismāʿīl (1863–79) and the huge loans that he borrowed from Europe had, by 1880, placed Egypt on the verge of bankruptcy. While half of Egypt's revenue had been strictly allocated to the service of these debts, heavy taxes were imposed on the Egyptian people and the *fallaḥīn* (sing. *fallāḥ*: 'peasant') majority who could not afford to pay them were mercilessly flogged. This economic hardship and humiliation created widespread discontent and bitter opposition to Khedive Tawfīḳ (1879–92) and his corrupt government. Tawfīḳ was further despised for his total subservience to the European powers who took advantage of his weakness and Egypt's indebtedness to control the country's finance and government. It soon became virtually impossible for any Egyptian government to initiate any administrative or economic reform without the prior and unanimous approval of fourteen European powers. While the Egyptians were suffering all this misery, resident foreigners were leading a comfortable life. They were not even subject to the law of the land, but had their own laws and courts. Foreigners had, furthermore, exploited this privileged position to enrich themselves at the expense of the Egyptian masses; often through corrupt and immoral

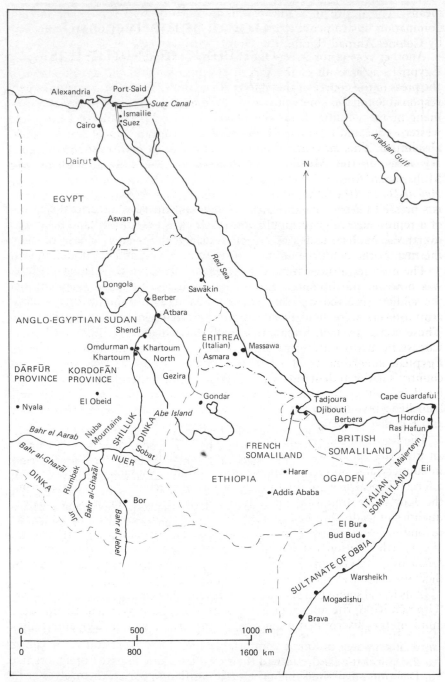

FIG. 4.1 *Politics and nationalism in North-East Africa*

means. The desire to eradicate this humiliating and repugnant foreign domination was to prove a major reason for the outbreak of resistance led by Colonel Aḥmad ʿUrābī: the Urabist revolution.[1]

Another reason for it was the maturity of liberal political ideas among Egyptians as a result of the spread of education and the development of the press in the course of the nineteenth century. This maturity was largely responsible for the emergence and development of a constitutional movement in the country from the 1860s onwards, particularly among the western-educated Egyptians who opposed European control and Khedival absolutism. This movement found considerable support in the revolutionary ideas of the Muslim reformers, Djamāl al-Dīn al-Afghānī and Muḥammad ʿAbduh. Led by Muḥammad Sharīf Pasha, who was nicknamed *Abū al-Dastūr* (the father of the constitution), these constitutional nationalists pressed for the enactment of a liberal constitution and the formation of a representative government.[2] Some of them may even have hoped to overthrow Muḥammad ʿAlī's dynasty, which had ruled the nation since the turn of the century.

The most important immediate factor in the outbreak of the revolution was, however, the discontent and frustration of the Egyptian military. While the soldiers received very low salaries – 20 piasters a month[3] – Egyptian army officers were not allowed promotion to higher ranks in the army. These were, in fact, exclusively monopolized by the foreign Turco-Circassian aristocratic army officers who despised and ill-treated their Egyptian subordinates. To end this inferior status and to achieve the country's national demands, the Egyptian military therefore actively interfered in politics for the first time in the modern history of Egypt and launched a revolution early in February 1881 against European colonialism and Khedive Tawfīḳ.

The leader of the revolution – Colonel Aḥmad ʿUrābī (1839–1911) was an attractive person with a strong *fallāh* origin. Though 'simple and lacking in subtlety and political refinement',[4] ʿUrābī was a courageous man and a forceful speaker who often interspersed his speeches with passages from the Ḳurʾān, 'a trait that made him popular among the masses'. These qualities of leadership had soon made ʿUrābī the undisputed leader of the revolution, and he was instrumental in the formation of *al-Ḥizb al-Waṭanī* (the Nationalist Party). Its members were a mixture of men of *fallāh* origin and some of the Turkish notables who were all united in their discontent at the autocracy of Tawfīḳ's rule.

In its initial stages the revolution achieved a remarkable degree of success. ʿUthmān Rifḳī, the notorious Circassian Minister of War and the mastermind of the discriminatory policy in the army, was sacked and a dis-

1. A. al-Rāfʿī, 1966, pp. 82–5.
2. P. J. Vatikiotis, 1969, pp. 126–30.
3. Public Record Office, Kew, FO 141/168, Dufferin's report, p. 4.
4. A. L. al-Sayyid, 1968, p. 9.

PLATE 4.1 *Colonel Ahmad ʿUrābī (ʿArabi Pasha') (1839–1911)*

tinguished poet and revolutionary politician – Maḥmūd Sāmī al-Barūdī –
replaced him. Subsequently a full-fledged Urabist Cabinet was formed in
which Aḥmad 'Urābī himself became the Minister of War.[5] Tawfīḳ was
so scared that he ordered the formation of a People's Assembly and enacted –
on 7 February 1882 – a relatively liberal constitution. Knowing that this
gesture to constitutionalism was not genuine, the Urabists remained intent
on overthrowing Tawfīḳ and might even have planned to declare Egypt
a republic. This development threatened foreign privileges and interests
and consequently brought the revolution into direct confrontation with
European powers.

Meanwhile the Khedive was conspiring behind the scenes to crush the
revolution. To provide a pretext for foreign intervention – some Egyptian
historians maintain – the Khedive and the British organized the Alexandria
massacre of 12 June 1882 in which many foreigners were killed and a great
deal of property was damaged.[6] Whether this accusation is true or not
is irrelevant as the Khedive had in fact invited the British to intervene
and they responded enthusiastically and quickly. But the Egyptian Cabinet
unanimously decided to repel the invasion and rejected the British ultimatum to desist from fortifying shore defences, and to dismantle gun
emplacements around Alexandria. This gave the British fleet a further
pretext to bombard Alexandria on 11 July 1882. The Egyptian army and
people put up a gallant resistance against the invaders, but they were
defeated by superior arms. About two thousand Egyptians were killed in
this battle.

After the fall of Alexandria the Egyptian army withdrew to Kafr
al-Dawār, a few miles away. By then, 'Urābī had declared a *djihād* against
the British in a proclamation that was distributed to the Egyptian people.
Fighting around Kafr al-Dawār broke out several times during August
1882. The solid resistance of the Egyptian army and people made it very
difficult for the invaders to occupy Cairo from this direction. They therefore decided to occupy the Suez Canal and launch a major attack against
the capital from there.

The Egyptian masses readily sent financial support to their army and
thousands of young people offered to join as conscripts. Nevertheless, all
the odds were against the Egyptian resistance movement. 'Urābī could
not muster more than 16 000 trained troops, and even this small number
was dispersed around Kafr al-Dawār, Dimyāṭ (Damietta) and the Suez
Canal area. Moreover, the Egyptian army lacked training, modern arms
and ammunition, and efficient means of transport. A modern army of 20 000
men under the command of Sir Garnet Wolseley quickly crossed the Canal,
occupied Ismailie, broke the backbone of the revolution in the battle of
al-Tall al-Kabīr on 13 September 1882,[7] and occupied the country. Though

5. M. Shibayka, 1965, p. 604.
6. M. al-Murshidi, 1958, p. 58.
7. A. al-Rafʿī, 1966, pp. 487–96.

PLATE 4.2 *Alexandria after bombardment in 1882 by the British fleet*

the British had deceitfully promised speedy evacuation, the British occupation of Egypt was to last seventy-two years.

The failure of the Urabist revolution to rid the country of European influence and to end the arbitrary rule of the Turks in Egypt can easily be explained. Although supported by the bulk of the Egyptian people, the revolution did not have sufficient time to mobilize this support. Moreover, a serious rift soon occurred in the united nationalist front as a result of a growing conflict between the military party and the constitutional nationalists. While the latter opposed on principle the involvement of the army in politics, the former insisted that their control of the government would be the best safeguard for the revolution. The revolution, furthermore, suffered from internal intrigues from the Khedive and his Circassian supporters who betrayed the revolution and aided the British occupation.

'Urābī himself made a number of mistakes. His reluctance to depose the Khedive at the beginning of the revolution on the grounds that this would invite foreign intervention and cause chaos inside the country gave Tawfīk valuable time in which to intrigue and conspire against the revolution. Another fatal mistake was 'Urābī's refusal to listen to the advice of some of his military advisers to block the Suez Canal, his own view being – mistaken as it proved – that France would not allow Britain to use the Canal to invade Egypt. Ultimately, however, the Urabist revolution was defeated by British military superiority.

Egyptian initiatives and reaction to British conquest 1882–1914

The military defeat of the Urabist revolution broke the national spirit and created an atmosphere of despair and disillusionment during the first decade of the British occupation of Egypt (1882–92). Within Egypt itself there was no effective resistance to the occupation during this decade, and the most important nationalist voices were those of the nationalists in exile. Djamāl al-Dīn al-Afghānī and Muḥammad 'Abduh began the publication of a pan-Islamic magazine in 1883 – al-'Urwa al-Wuthḳā (the indissoluble bond) – which aimed to free Egypt from the British occupation by stirring up public opinion in Egypt. Though this magazine closed down after publishing only eighteen issues, it had a profound influence on the few groups of Egyptians who read it – students, 'ulamā' (Muslim scholars), and intellectuals. Al-'Urwa provided a source of opposition to the British and kept alive the spirit of self-determination.[8] Its anti-British message was taken up in the 1890s by a group of political pan-Islamist writers. The most prominent of them was Shaykh 'Alī Yūsuf, who published a newspaper, al-Mu'ayyad in 1900, and in 1907 he formed Ḥizb al-Iṣlāḥ al-Dustūrī (the Constitutional Reformers) an organization which forcefully attacked British hegemony in Egypt.

8. A. L. al-Sayyid, 1968, pp. 87–90.

In 1893 the Egyptian nationalist movement began to emerge from this quiescent phase when certain Egyptian elements started to criticize and resist the British occupation of Egypt. First among them was the ambitious new Khedive 'Abbās Ḥilmī ('Abbās II, 1892–1914), who encouraged the development of a nationalist movement demanding the immediate evacuation of the British. His financial assistance to the press, which enabled the movement to become articulate, was of particular importance. During the first three years of his reign, 'Abbās placed himself at the forefront of this movement and he became a very real challenge to the autocratic rule of Lord Cromer, the British Agent and Consul-General, and succeeded in forcing the pro-British prime minister to resign on 15 January 1893. Although he was unable after that to act so openly owing to pressure from the British, Ḥilmī nevertheless attracted some dedicated recruits who were willing to carry on the struggle against the British occupation. They were a group of young intellectuals, who were familiar with the ideas of the French revolution and with modern social and political theories. The old Egyptian society with its strict code and religious restrictions was, in fact, gradually breaking up, a development that led to considerable instability. The educated Egyptians were particularly alarmed by the British domination of the civil service, the only area of advancement that remained open to them. By 1905, 42% of the higher posts were occupied by the British, 30% by Armenians and Syrians, and only 28% by Egyptians.[10]

The most vehement opponents of British rule at that time were Muṣṭafā Kāmil, a charismatic leader and eloquent orator, and his Nationalist Party. Kāmil had at first concentrated his efforts on winning European support for the cause of Egypt's independence. He had apparently felt that other European states were so jealous of the British occupation of Egypt that they would actively support any attempts to remove them. With generous funds supplied by the Khedive, Kāmil toured European capitals during the period 1895–8 where he addressed meetings, gave interviews to newspapers, and wrote articles and pamphlets.[11] These activities aroused a great deal of interest in Europe, but that was as far as it went. Kāmil's optimistic belief that Europe in general, and France in particular, would support the Egyptian cause was wholly unjustified. Since France had her own colonies in North Africa, it is not surprising that she was not won over by Kāmil's arguments in favour of self-rule. Nor was she ready to go to war with England over Egypt, as the Fashoda incident had shown in 1898. The most urgent task facing the young nationalists was to disprove Cromer's biased claim that the Egyptians were incapable of ruling themselves on civilized principles, and to convince the Egyptians themselves that they formed a nation capable and indeed deserving of self-rule. Kāmil

9. ibid., pp. 99–136.
10. Milner report, p. 30 (Egypt, No. 1, (1921), Cmd 1131, Report of Milner Mission to Egypt).
11. P. M. Holt (ed.), 1968, pp. 308–19.

PLATE 4.3 *'Abbās Ḥilmī ('Abbās II, 1892–1914) Khedive of Egypt*

was preoccupied with this task from 1898 onwards. Until 1906 his views were expressed in numerous speeches and articles in the newspapers of the day, particularly in *al-Liwā* (The Flag) which he founded in 1900. He stressed Egypt's past to combat defeatism and to show that the Egyptians were capable of great things. 'Had I not been born an Egyptian, I would have wished to become one', and 'there is no sense in life when it is coupled with despair, and no sense in despair as long as there is life'[12] – such were the slogans he devised. Kāmil's speeches and articles aimed to break down local rivalries and unite all the population in a nationalist front, and to develop national education in order to strengthen patriotic sentiment. His political activities began to bear fruit as he was able to organize a strike of law students in February 1906.

The Dinshāway incident of May 1906 profoundly boosted Kāmil's campaign in Egypt. Briefly, a group of British officers came to Dinshāway village on a pigeon-shooting trip, which the villagers objected to since pigeons were their means of livelihood. A clash followed in which one of the British officers was fatally wounded. The British authorities over-reacted to this incident and passed very severe sentences on the villagers. Four were sentenced to be hanged and many others were sentenced to long terms of imprisonment. Although public executions had been stopped two years previously, the hangings were carried out in public, and the whole village of Dinshāway was forced to watch the executions.[13] This barbaric behaviour had, in Kāmil's view, done more to awaken people's feelings against the occupation than the passage of ten years of occupation.[14] The incident certainly caused an upsurge of Egyptian nationalism and for the first time since 1882, the British became aware of the insecurity of their position in Egypt. It was this which forced the British to reconsider their oppressive policy and to declare their intention of preparing the country for self-government. Cromer retired in 1907 to make way for a new Consul-General, Eldon Gorst, to implement the new policy. This represented a great triumph for Kāmil and his Nationalist Party, which was inaugurated publicly in 1907.

After the premature death of Kāmil in February 1908 Muḥammad Farīd succeeded him as president of the Nationalist Party. Farīd lacked many of the qualities of leadership that Kāmil had possessed, but he continued to write, and to address public meetings demanding the evacuation of British troops. His nationalist activities earned him six months' imprisonment in 1911, after which he went into exile.[15]

By 1907 some prominent Egyptian intellectuals had come to believe that Britain was too strong to be expelled from Egypt by revolutionary action. Moreover, they felt that there were real signs of a change in British policy

12. A. L. al-Sayyid, 1968, p. 161.
13. M. G. al-Masada, 1974, pp. 84–91.
14. M. H. Haykal, n.d., p. 148.
15. A. Ṣabrī, 1969, pp. 81–109.

after the Dinshāway incident. Consequently they saw no harm in co-operating with the British in Egypt in order to secure such concessions as could be extracted until such time as full independence could be achieved. This group formed a new political party called the *Umma* Party (the Peoples' Party) in October 1907, which had its own newspaper, *al-Djarīda*. Led by the prominent journalist and educationalist, Aḥmad Luṭfī al-Sayyid, who was referred to by educated Egyptians as *Faylasūf al-Djīl* (the philosopher of the generation), the *Djarīda-Umma* group urged the Egyptians to modernize their Islamic tradition by adopting such European ideas and institutions as they considered necessary for progress.[16] The programme of the *Umma* Party called for the creation of an Egyptian personality, for without it, it was felt that Egypt could not achieve real independence. It stressed the importance of agricultural reform and asked for an increase in the powers of the provincial councils and the assembly in preparation for eventual constitutional rule. Most important of all, the party emphasized the need for education as an essential means for training capable administrators and attaining national independence. But the *Umma* Party was not very popular among the Egyptian nationalists because of its co-operation with the British authorities. Its secular liberalism had, furthermore, failed to take root among a great number of Egyptians because of their instinctive adherence to their Islamic traditions.[17]

Before the First World War the Egyptian nationalist movement was thus a disunited and a predominantly elitist movement unable to command popular following. Consequently it was too weak to wrest any significant concessions from the British authorities and made little progress along the path of self-government. The nationalists had to wait until 1919 before coming out in open revolt against the British occupation.

The Sudan

The Mahdist revolution

From 1821 the Sudan was governed by the Ottoman government of Egypt, and by 1880 the people of the Sudan – like the people of Egypt – were also fighting to rid themselves of an alien ruling aristocracy. The themes of the *djihād* and Islamic resistance to alien rule, propagated by 'Urābī in Egypt, were also evident in the militant revolutionary movement under the leadership of Muḥammad Aḥmad al-Mahdī in the Sudan. His movement, the *Mahdiyya*, was essentially a *djihād* – a holy war – and as such claimed the support of all Muslims. Its fundamental objective, as stated repeatedly in the Mahdī's letters and proclamations,[18] was to revive and return to the pure and primitive faith of Islam, 'purged of heresies and

16. P. J. Vatikiotis, 1969, pp. 229–30.
17. ibid., p. 234.
18. For a good collection of those letters and proclamations see M. I. Abū Salīm, 1969.

73

accretions',[19] and to spread it to the whole world, by force if deemed necessary. The genuine spiritual fervour of the Mahdist revolution was expressed in the *bay'a*, the oath of allegiance that the supporters of the Mahdī – whom he styled the *Anṣār* following the example of the Prophet[20] – had to give to the Mahdī or his representative before being admitted to the Mahdiyya. In this *bay'a*, the *Anṣār* swore allegiance to the Mahdī in 'renouncing this world and abandoning it, and being content with what is with God, desiring what is with God and the world to come, and we will not flee from the *jihād*'.[21]

To say that the Mahdist revolution was religious does not mean that religion was the sole factor in its generation. For there were also other, secondary, factors – all arising from the faults of the corrupt Turco-Egyptian administration – that caused general discontent in the Sudan. The violence that accompanied the original conquest in 1820–1 had created a strong desire for revenge, while the heavy taxes that the Turks imposed and levied by force led to widespread discontent. In addition, the attempts of the government to suppress the slave trade had alienated some northern Sudanese as they struck at an important source of wealth and the basis of the domestic and agrarian economy of the country. Finally, the government's partiality to the Shaykiyya people and the Khatmīyya sect seems to have aroused the jealousy of other local and religious groups, and stimulated them to support the Mahdī.[22]

The leader of the Mahdist revolution, Muḥammad Aḥmad Ibn 'Abdallāh was a pious man whose ideal was the Prophet Muḥammad himself. Just as the Prophet before him had assumed leadership of his community at the age of 40, so Muḥammad Aḥmad assumed the Mahdī-ship at the same age, secretly communicated it to a group of trusty followers, and then declared it openly to the general public. This brought him into direct military confrontation with the Anglo-Egyptian government, a struggle which lasted for four years (1881–5). The government at first underestimated the Mahdī and dismissed him as a mere *darwīsh* (a mendicant) – an attitude reflected in the weak and disorganized expedition that was sent to deal with him in Abā Island. A brief skirmish followed in which the *Anṣār* achieved a quick and easy victory, and the administration was thrown into utter confusion. The Mahdī and his followers considered their victory to have been a miracle.[23]

The Mahdī's political foresight and his military genius was clearly reflected in his decision to 'emigrate' after this encounter from Abā to *Djabal Ḳadīr* in the Nuba mountains. Apart from being another parallel

19. P. M. Holt, 1970, p. 19.
20. *Anṣār* ('helpers') was the name originally given to the supporters of the Prophet Muḥammad in Medina.
21. P. M. Holt, 1970, p. 117.
22. N. Shouqair, 1967, pp. 631–6.
23. M. Shibayka, 1978, pp. 39–44.

PLATE 4.4 *Muḥammad Aḥmad Ibn ʿAbdallāh, the Mahdī (1844–85)*

75

with the life of the Prophet, this *hidjra* moved the revolution from an open and defenceless area that was within reach of the government's forces to a remote and strategically fortified region. This *hidjra* was indeed a turning-point in the history of the Mahdiyya. Its main significance was that in moving the revolution from the riverain regions to the western Sudan, the westerners thenceforward became its key administrators and military commanders, while the riverain people in the movement declined in significance.[24]

Another turning-point in the history of the Mahdist revolution was the battle at Shaykān on 5 November 1883. By that time Khedive Tawfīk and his government were determined to crush the Mahdī, now in control of the key towns of Kordofān province. Consequently, the Egyptian government organized an expedition that was composed of the remnants of 'Urābī's soldiers and commanded by a British army officer, Hicks Pasha. The *Anṣār* completely annihilated their enemy at Shaykān's forest in the neighbourhood of al-'Obeid.[25] The victory was a great boost for the Mahdī and his revolution. While many Sudanese joined the revolution, delegates from some Muslim countries came to congratulate the Mahdī on his victory against the 'infidels'. However, the immediate consequence of the triumph at Shaykān was the total collapse of the Turco-Egyptian administration in the western Sudan and the establishment of Mahdist rule in the provinces of Kordofān, Dārfūr and Bahr al-Ghazāl. The Mahdī was now ready to turn to his next objective, to gain control of Khartoum and end Turco-Egyptian rule in the Sudan.[26]

The Mahdists struck next in the eastern Sudan under the able leadership of 'Uthmān Digna. Digna won many victories against government forces and posed a threat to the Red Sea ports which Britain had pledged to defend. The British then attempted to intervene militarily, but to very little effect. Except for Sawākin, the *Anṣār* controlled the whole of the eastern Sudan and prevented any supplies and reinforcements from Egypt reaching Khartoum through the Berber–Sawākin route.

Meanwhile, British policy towards the Sudan question had undergone a significant change after the battle at Shaykān. While previously maintaining that it was an exclusively Egyptian concern, after Shaykān the British government felt that its imperial interests necessitated Egypt's immediate withdrawal from the Sudan.[27] Hence it ordered the Egyptian government to abandon the Sudan and sent General Charles Gordon to see that this was done. As the Mahdī advanced towards Khartoum Gordon found himself in a very dangerous situation. After a long siege, the Mahdist forces

24. M. I. Abū Salīm, 1970, pp. 21–2.
25. I. Zulfu, 1976, pp. 203–29.
26. M. A. Al-Ḥasan, 1964, p. 4.
27. M. Shibeika, 1952, pp. 107–9.

attacked the town, killed Gordon on 26 January 1885, and put an end
to Turco-Egyptian rule in the Sudan.[28]

During its first four years (1881–5), the Mahdiyya developed from a
movement of religious protest into a powerful and militant state that dominated the Sudan for fourteen years. Its administrative, financial and judicial
institutions, and its legislation, were based strictly upon the dual foundations of the Ḳur'ān and the Sunna, though the Mahdī occasionally passed
new forms of legislation on such pressing problems as the status of women
and landownership.[29]

The relations of the Mahdist state with the outside world were strictly
governed by the *djihād*. Both the Mahdī and his Khalīfa, 'Abdullāh Ibn
al-Sayyid Muḥammad, had written letters of warning (*indhārāt*) – virtually
ultimatums – to some leaders of the world, such as the Khedive of Egypt,
the Ottoman emperor and the emperor of Abyssinia, to accept the Mahdī's
mission, or be faced with an immediate *djihād* if they they did not respond
positively.[30]

While the Mahdī did not live long enough to pursue such a policy –
he died in June 1885 – the *djihād* became the cornerstone of the foreign
policy of his successor, Khalīfa 'Abdullāh. In spite of the tremendous
administrative and economic problems facing him, Khalīfa 'Abdullāh
pressed forward with the *djihād* on two fronts: against Egypt and Ethiopia.
Under the leadership of 'Abd al-Raḥmān al-Nudjūmī, the Mahdist forces
invaded Egypt, but they were defeated at the battle of Tushki in 1889.
The Mahdists' advance on the eastern front was also checked and the
Anṣar lost Tokar and Kassala respectively in 1891 and 1894. The ideological
commitment of the Khalīfa to the *djihād* had frustrated the attempts of
the Ethiopian emperor to conclude an African alliance between the Sudan
and Ethiopia against European imperialism. For, as a prerequisite to this
alliance, the Khalīfa insisted that the emperor should accept and believe
in Mahdism and Islam. The outcome of this dogmatism was a long military
confrontation that weakened both states and made them an easier prey
for European imperialism.[31]

By March 1896 the British imperial government had decided to invade
the Sudan and an Anglo-Egyptian force was formed for this purpose under
the command of General H. H. Kitchener. During the first phase of this
invasion – March to September 1896 – the enemy forces occupied the
whole of Dongola province without encountering any serious resistance
from the Sudanese people, partly because of their technical superiority
and partly because they took the Khalīfa by surprise.

As the Khalīfa had rightly surmised, the occupation of Dongola was
no more than a prelude to a full-scale invasion of the Mahdist state. While

28. M. M. Hamza, 1972, pp. 159–83.
29. P. M. Holt, 1970, p. 128.
30. N. Shouqair, 1967, pp. 921–9.
31. M. S. Al-Ḳaddāl, 1973, pp. 105–7.

Kitchener was advancing southwards, the Khalīfa mobilized his forces, determined to resist the invaders. Commanded by Emir Maḥmūd Aḥmad, the *Anṣār* tried unsuccessfully to repel the enemy attack at the battle of Atbara on 8 April 1898.[32] Three thousand Sudanese were killed, and over 4000 were wounded. Maḥmūd himself was captured and put in prison at Rosetta in Egypt, where he died some years later.

After the defeat at Atbara the Khalīfa decided to meet the enemy in the vicinity of his capital, Omdurman, because he understood that the difficulties of supply and transport would prohibit the movement of any large force of troops. Hence the Sudanese fought the enemy with magnificent courage at the battle of Karari on 2 September 1898.[33] Once again they were defeated by superior armaments. Nearly 11 000 Sudanese were killed and about 16 000 wounded. When he saw that the day was lost, the Khalīfa withdrew to the east of Kordofān where he hoped to gather his supporters and make a fresh attack on the invaders in the capital. He continued to be a problem for the new administration for a whole year, but was finally defeated at the battle of Umm Diwaykrāt on 24 November 1899. After the battle, the Khalīfa was found dead upon his sheepskin prayer-rug,[34] all the other Mahdist generals and leaders having been either killed or imprisoned. This marked the collapse of the Mahdist state, although the Mahdiyya as a religious and political sentiment never died.

The Mahdist risings

Although under British colonial rule the Mahdist sect was outlawed, a sizeable section of the Sudanese community remained Mahdist at heart. The majority expressed their resentment of British rule by continuing to read the *ratīb* (the Mahdī's prayer-book) and to practise other Mahdist rituals. But a dedicated Mahdist minority repeatedly tried to topple the 'infidel' rule by force. Hardly a year passed between 1900 and 1914 without a Mahdist rising in the northern Sudan. The main source of inspiration and strength for these risings was the Muslim doctrine of *Nabī 'Īsā* (Prophet Jesus). It was generally believed among Muslims that the Mahdī would reappear in order to bring justice to the world after it had been filled with injustice. But his mission would be temporarily halted by *al-masīḥ al-dadjdjāl* (the anti-Christ). *Nabī 'Īsā* would, however, soon appear in order to secure the permanence of the glorious Mahdiyya. The *Anṣār* had apparently identified the British with *al-dadjdjāl* and many of them assumed the *'isāship* to expel them from the country.[35]

32. M. A. Ibrāhīm, 1969, pp. 196–237.
33. For information about the imprisoned Mahdist emirs, see H. 'A. Ibrāhīm, 1974, pp. 33–45.
34. P. M. Holt, 1970, p. 243.
35. H. 'A. Ibrāhīm, 1979, p. 440.

PLATE 4.5 *Maḥmūd Aḥmad, one of the commenders of the Anṣār (the Mahdist army), after his capture by Anglo-Egyptian forces*

79

Mahdist uprisings occurred in February 1900, in 1902–3 and in 1904. But the most important of these Mahdist risings was organized and led in 1908 by a distinguished Mahdist, 'Abd al-Ḳādir Muḥammad Imām, usually called Wad Ḥabūba. Wad Ḥabūba preached Mahdism in the Djazīra and defied the government from his camp in Tuḳūr village near Kamlīn. A government force advanced towards him, but it was resisted and two government officials were killed in this encounter. While the authorities were shocked by this incident, Wad Ḥabūba launched a surprise attack in May on the enemy at the village of Katfīya.

The Mahdists fought bravely, but within a few days the backbone of the revolt had been broken. In the manner of the Mahdī, however, Wad Ḥabūba had 'emigrated', presumably to find asylum in Omdurman where he apparently hoped to secretly continue to propagate the Mahdist cause. But he was arrested *en route* and publicly hanged on 17 May 1908, while many of his followers were sentenced to death or to long terms of imprisonment.[36] During an unfair trial, Wad Ḥabūba defied the British imperialists by telling the court trying him:

> My desire is that the Sudan should be governed by Muslims according to Mohammadan law and the Mahdī's doctrines and precepts. I know the people of the Sudan better than the government does. I have no hesitation in saying that their friendliness and flattery is nothing but hypocrisy and lies. I am ready to swear that the people prefer Mahdism to the present government.[37]

Though uncoordinated and unable to command any large following, these numerous messianic risings provided an element of continuity with the era of the Mahdist state, and proved that Mahdism was still alive as a vital religious and political force in the Sudan. The risings had, furthermore, demonstrated that the mood of resistance to colonial rule remained entrenched in the hearts of many northern Sudanese.

Protest movements in the Nuba mountains and the southern Sudan

The struggle of the Sudanese people in the Nuba mountains and the southern Sudan was one of the most serious challenges that the British colonialists faced before the First World War. The numerous risings and revolts that broke out in these parts of the country were, however, essentially local in character. They were, furthermore, direct responses to the changes that colonialism introduced into the social fabric of those diversified communities, a product of the destruction by the British of social and political institutions of those communities and their replacement by new structures of their own.

36. ibid., p. 448.
37. Sudan Intelligence Report, May 1908.

In spite of the ruthlessness of the colonial forces, various Nuba communities had actively opposed British domination. While Aḥmad al-Nuʿmān, *mek* of Kitra, declared his open hostility, in 1906 the population of Talodi launched an uprising in which a number of government officials and soldiers were slaughtered. A more serious revolt was that of *mek* Fakī ʿAlī of the Miri hills. ʿAlī harassed government forces for two years, but he was arrested in 1916 and imprisoned in Wādī Halfa.[38]

In the southern region of the Sudan, resistance was led and sustained by the Nuer people living in the lands adjoining the river Sobat and the White Nile. Under previous administrations, the Nuer were accustomed to managing their own affairs, since these administrations did not exercise effective control over them. But now the Nuer refused to recognize the supremacy of the new government and continued to show hostility towards it. Two of their leaders, Dengkur and Diu, were particularly active in this respect. Though these two influential leaders died in 1906 and 1907 respectively, Nuer activism never died, and in 1914 another Nuer leader, Dowl Diu, attacked a government post. In spite of the numerous indiscriminate punitive measures, the Nuer resistance continued to gain momentum until it broke out in the popular and widespread Nuer revolt of 1927.

The Azande under the leadership of Yambio, their chief, were determined not to allow any foreign troops to enter their land. They faced the danger of invasion from both the Belgians and the Condominium government. The Belgians were increasing their activities on the southern borders of Zandeland. Yambio seemed to have feared Belgian invasion more than the British. He therefore thought that the best policy open to him was to neutralize the British with signs of friendship and thereby gain a free hand to deal with the imminent Belgian danger. He invited the British to establish a trading post in his kingdom. The invitation was made in the belief that the British would not be able to come, but that if they did he would fight them. His true intention seems to have been to play the British off against the Belgians, for he had apparently become convinced that British interests in his country would make the Belgians think twice before attacking him.[39]

But the British took up the invitation and in January 1903 a patrol left Wau for Yambio's territory. While on the march it was attacked by the Azande. The patrol escaped to Rumbek. In January 1904 the government in Khartoum sent another patrol, which was also attacked by the Azande, and ultimately it was forced to retreat to Tonj.

While the Belgians were preparing an attack on Yambio's territory, the latter mobilized a force of 10 000 Azande and launched a daring attack on the Belgian post at Mayawa. The Azande courageously harassed the intruders, but they could not stand up to the Belgian rifle fire with spears alone. This battle seriously weakened Zande military power and morale.

38. A. S. Cudsi, 1969, pp. 112–16.
39. ibid., p. 220.

With his military power broken, Yambio had to meet a government expeditionary force in January 1905. He was ultimately defeated and imprisoned, and died soon afterwards, on 10 February 1905. His people, however, continued the struggle. In 1908 some of Yambio's warriors attempted to stir up a rising while others fought the British during the First World War.[40]

Somaliland

The Somali reaction to partition 1884–97

From the middle of the nineteenth century the Somali peninsula was drawn into the theatre of European colonial competition between Italy, Britain and France. With their interests in India and other parts of Asia in the early 1880s, Britain and France sought to establish themselves on the Somali coast because of its strategic and commercial importance. Eventually, with Italy joining in, they extended their influence in the interior and each of them established a protectorate in Somaliland. While the activities of the French had led them to establish a protectorate in 1885, the British government did not declare its protectorate until two years later – this was on the Somali coast from Djibuti eastwards, and included the Bender Ziadeh. Through the good offices of the British East Africa Company and the British government, Italy was also able to acquire control of the towns of Brava, Merca, Mogadishu and Warsheikh in November 1888. The Italian government declared a protectorate over those portions of the coast connecting the towns, and this was subsequently extended to include Obbia and the Majerteyn Somali in the north (see Figure 4.1).

Ethiopia had also expanded into Somali-inhabited territories, and had managed to establish a tentative administration in the Haud and Ogaden. One view suggests that while the European invasion of Somalia was motivated by imperialist and capitalist considerations, the Ethiopian expansion there was essentially 'a defensive reaction to the establishment of European colonies in the vicinity'. Since Italy, Britain and France were pushing inland from their respective coastal possessions – this interpretation argues – the Ethiopian emperor, Menelik, 'endeavoured to keep them as far as possible from the centre of his power in the highlands, through the expedient of extending his own frontiers'.[41] Yet it should be noted that Shoan expansion under Menelik had begun before the Europeans had become involved in the area, first against the Oromo and later against the Somali.

The partition of Somaliland, formally virtually completed by 1897, ignored the legitimate interests of the Somali people and deprived them of their freedom and independence. Hence it was bound to awaken their

40. ibid., pp. 238–54.
41. S. Touval, 1963, p. 74.

suspicions and stimulate them to resent and resist this alien conquest. The Somali chiefs and sultans were particularly disturbed by this encroachment because of its effect upon their political influence. They never willingly gave up their sovereignty and it was they who provided the leadership for the numerous local risings against European and Ethiopian rulers during the era of partition.

Being aware of the rivalry between European powers in the field of colonial expansion, the Somali chiefs tried to play them off one against the other. They did this by concluding treaties with one or other of the European powers in the hope that the exercise of diplomacy would counter the growing menace to their independence. The Somali chiefs, for example, signed many treaties with the British. Little was really conceded to Britain by those treaties. The preamble to each treaty explained that they were entered into, on the Somali side, 'for the maintenance of our independence, the preservation of order, and other good and sufficient reasons'. Nor did the clans concerned expressly cede their land to Britain; they specifically pledged themselves 'never to cede, sell, mortgage, or otherwise give for occupation, save to the British Government, any portion of the territory presently inhabited by them or being under their control'.[42] Ultimately these treaties failed in their objective as the European powers and Ethiopia managed to settle their mutual colonial disputes in this area peacefully.

Besides this diplomatic effort, some of the Somali clans took up arms to try to preserve their sovereignty. The British were obliged to send four expeditions: in 1886 and 1890, against the Isa; in 1893, against the Habar Gerhajis; and in 1895, against the Habar Awal.[43] The Italians also suffered heavy losses of life. In 1887 a party of Italians was massacred at Harar and in 1896 a party of fourteen Italians was killed by the Bimal people. The frequent clashes between the Ethiopian forces and the Somali clans did not permit the former to complete their occupation of the Ogaden nor to extend their authority far beyond scattered military posts established throughout the region.[44]

It must, however, be remembered that the Somali, in spite of their cultural identity, did not then constitute a single political unity. Foreign aggression thus encountered not a single nation, but congeries of disunited and often mutually hostile clans.[45] Moreover, the Somali peoples were still armed with spears and bows and arrows, and were not immediately able to import firearms and ammunition in any quantity. Nevertheless, the Somali resistance during the partition era kept alive the nationalist spirit, and consequently stimulated the subsequent *djihād* of Sayyid Muḥammad Abdille Ḥasan against the European and Ethiopian occupation. To this we now turn.

42. I. M. Lewis, 1965, pp. 46–7.
43. A. Hamilton, 1911, p. 47.
44. S. Touval, 1963, p. 74.
45. I. M. Lewis, 1965, p. 43.

The Somali fight for freedom 1897–1914

Sayyid Muḥammad was born in 1864. He mastered the Ḳu'rān at the age of 7. At 19 he left his home to acquire learning in the major centres of Islam in eastern Africa, Harar and Mogadishu. It is also believed that he travelled as far afield as the Sudanese Mahdist strongholds in Kordofān.[46] In 1895 the Sayyid set out on a pilgrimage to Mecca, and spent a year in Arabia, also visiting Hejaz and Palestine. While in Mecca, he studied under Shaykh Muḥammad Ṣālih, and joined his sect, the Ṣāliḥīyya order. Possibly this extensive travel and periods spent abroad in different parts of the Muslim world had brought the Sayyid into contact with the then current ideas of Islamic revivalism.[47] On his return home, he settled for a time in Berbera where he taught and preached to his countrymen, urging them to return to the strict path of Muslim devotion.

Sayyid Muḥammad was conscious that the Christian (European and Ethiopian) incursions had threatened the social and economic foundation of Somali society. As early as July 1899, he wrote to a Somali clan and gave them this warning: 'Do you not see that the infidels have destroyed our religion and have made our children their own?' By this, he was apparently referring to the establishment of Christian schools in Somalia which he considered a threat to the Ḳu'rānic schools. Al-Sayyid felt that the effectiveness of Christian proselytization could also be seen in the adoption of Christian names such as 'John 'Abdullāhī'. All this confirmed al-Sayyid's belief that Christian colonization sought to destroy the Muslim faith.

The Mahdist movement in the Sudan had strong repercussions in Somaliland, and the Sayyid, like other religious leaders, was inspired by the brilliant career of the Mahdī. The awareness on the part of the Somali of the earlier revolution in the Sudan and their sympathy for adherents of a common faith were indeed a contributory factor in the rise of Sayyid Muḥammad.[48] In one of his speeches, the Sayyid accused the British military authorities of exporting animals for the war against the Mahdī – the holy man of the Sudan – to whom God had given victory.[49] But the extent to which Sayyid Muḥammad viewed his *djihād* in the general context of Islamic revival, and how far he was inspired and influenced by the Mahdist revolution in the Sudan, remains unclear. Even the assumption that he conferred with the Mahdist emir of the eastern Sudan, 'Uthmān Digna, during his visit to the Sudan cannot be amply substantiated, though some Somali traditions claim that the guerrilla tactics

46. A. Sheikh-Abdi, 1978, pp. 61–2.
47. M. O. Abd al-Halim, 1975, p. 339.
48. I. M. Lewis, 1965, p. 69.
49. L. Silberman, n.d., p. 47.

employed by the Somali in the course of the *djihād* were copied from the Mahdists of the eastern Sudan.[50]

One of the more serious factors hampering unity among the nomadic Somali was the traditional lineage system with its sectional loyalties. But through his personal charisma and brilliant leadership, al-Sayyid managed to command a heterogeneous following, consisting of various Somali clans, and to create a standing army which was estimated at 12000 men.[51] In this successful mobilization against alien colonial rule, al-Sayyid appealed to the religious sentiments of the Somali as Muslims irrespective of clan allegiances. He had, furthermore, composed a large number of poems, of which many are still well known throughout Somalia, by means of which he 'successfully rallied a host of contentious clansmen behind the twin banners of Islam and homeland'.[52]

Al-Sayyid started his *djihād* at Berbera where between 1895 and 1897 he tried to arouse the people against the imperialists. But his first revolutionary action was the occupation of Burao in the centre of British Somaliland in August 1899. The British were so harassed by this that between the years 1900 and 1904 they sent four expeditions to repel al-Sayyid's attacks. Though the British were helped in these operations by the Italians, al-Sayyid's exceptional military skills and his successful use of cavalry and guerrilla tactics won his warriors a number of victories. One of these was at Gamburu hill in April 1903 in which nine British officers were killed.

By the end of 1904, however, the Sayyid's force had been greatly weakened. He therefore withdrew to the Italian Majerteyn Protectorate where, on 5 March 1905, he signed the Treaty of Illing with the Italians in which he dictated his own terms. By 1908 al-Sayyid had mobilized his forces for a new round of fighting that forced the British to withdraw from the interior in November 1909, and concentrate on the coast. But al-Sayyid threatened to attack the coastal towns as well. In August 1913 he gained a major victory by annihilating the newly established camel constabulary. This disaster forced the British to ally with the Ethiopian Governor of Harar and to mount joint expeditions against al-Sayyid until his death at Imi in Ethiopia in November 1920.

Under the able leadership of Sayyid Muḥammad, the Somali people had thus continued to harass the European imperialists and the Ethiopians for twenty years. They were able to win military, political and even diplomatic victories. Though this Somali *djihād* ultimately failed to rid the country of alien rule, it encouraged a strong nationalist feeling. The Somali people had come to see themselves as a single whole fighting against foreign incursions. Besides that, Sayyid Muḥammad's struggle left in the Somali

50. M. O. Abd al-Halim, 1975, pp. 369–70.
51. D. Jardine, 1923, p. 69.
52. A. Sheikh-Abdi, 1978, p. 62.

national consciousness an ideal of patriotism which could never be effaced, and which was to inspire later generations of his countrymen.[53]

Conclusion

Perhaps no part of Africa resisted European conquest and occupation in the period 1880–1914 so forcefully as the north-eastern part of the continent. This is shown by the thousands of Egyptians, Sudanese and Somali who lost their lives in the battles and skirmishes fought between them and the colonial forces. The strength of this resistance was due to the fact that besides the patriotic sentiment which inspired it, there was an even more fundamental sentiment at work, namely an intense religious faith. The peoples of Egypt, the Sudan and Somaliland were not fighting in defence of home alone, but also in defence of religion. Muslims there, like their fellow adherents in other parts of the Islamic world, were conscious of the social and religious disruption that would be caused by alien encroachment on hitherto Muslim territories. It was also against the spirit of Islam that a Muslim population should accept a position of political subordination to a Christian power. The revolutionary movements of ʿUrābī, the Mahdī and Sayyid Muḥammad should therefore be understood in the context of the numerous reforming movements that spread and profoundly affected the Muslim world during the eighteenth and nineteenth centuries.

53. I. M. Lewis, 1965, p. 91.

African initiatives and resistance in North Africa and the Sahara

A. LAROUI

The subject of this chapter is highly complex, not so much because of the facts, which are on the whole fairly well known, but when it comes to interpreting them. Our task is to study the initiatives taken by the people of the Maghrib and the Sahara to counter the colonial thrust, and their reactions to the conquest in progress. To give a preliminary idea of the complexity of the situation, let us examine the situation in 1907 (see Fig. 5.1).

In the west, Morocco was having a revolution, which was to overthrow Sultan 'Abd al-'Azīz (1894–1908), because he had ratified the French conquest of Tuāt province and agreed to the reforms imposed by the European powers at the Algeciras Conference in April 1906. The protagonists of this revolution were members of the *Makhzen*[1] and were connected with the *zawāyā* (sing. *zāwiya*), the local centres of Sufi religious brotherhoods (*tarīqa*), and with local chieftaincies.

In the east, Tunisia was seeing the birth of a nationalist movement in the true sense of the term. Associations of the first graduates turned out by modern education were being set up, while opposition newspapers were appearing in the language of the colonial power. A new elite was making itself conspicuous by taking unprecedented initiatives.

In the south, the western Sahara was the scene of a large-scale French operation aimed at encircling and strangling independent Morocco. Spain was soon to follow the French example in Morocco itself, and Italy in Tripolitania, in this case at the expense of the Sultan in Constantinople.

Thus, in our period and area, we need to distinguish between three levels:

> (1) that of the organized state,[2] Moroccan in the west and Ottoman in the east of North Africa. That is where we must look for initiative properly so called.

---

1. The Government of Morocco, and more broadly the political and religious elite of the country.

2. The structure of this state must not be interpreted in terms of that of European liberal states; this would be falling into the trap of colonial ideology.

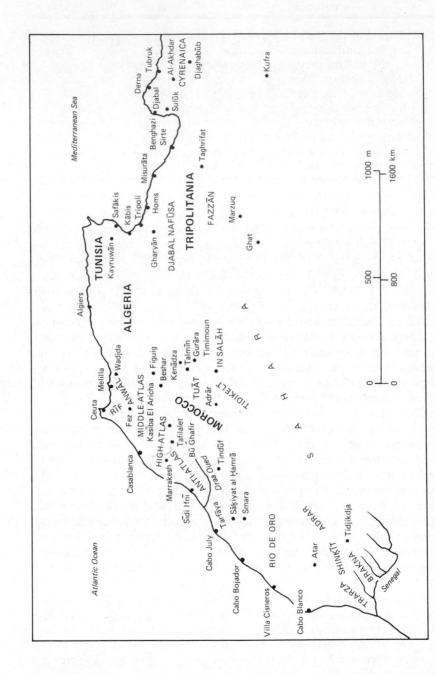

FIG. 5.1 *The major regions of the Maghrib and the Sahara*

(2) the level of the Sufi brotherhoods, no doubt religious in inspiration but unquestionably political in function. In North Africa and the Sahara they were always defensive organizations against external threats. When the state was strong the brotherhoods were part of its mechanism; when it became weak or broke up they became independent and took the initiative. Thus, when Constantinople gave up its sovereignty the Sanūsī brotherhood became the core of the resistance to the Italians in Cyrenaica, and when the Moroccan state was powerless to do anything, that of the Kettānīs rallied the anti-French forces at Shinkīt and in the Shawiya.

(3) the level of the *djema'a*,[3] which only came out into the open when the other levels had been put out of action by armed force. The *djema'a* began by refusing all contact with the colonial authorities, despite their tempting offers. When it eventually gave in, it had only one limited move left: it would only react to colonial policy, which in a way was what set it up as an independent force.

Colonial historians knowingly distort the facts when they ignore the level of the organized state, reduce brotherhoods to some kind of super-ethnic group and see nothing in Maghribi society but ethnic groups. These, moreover, they interpret according to anthropological models of kinship which are more theoretical than real. By this skewed approach, they break the resistance up into a sporadic set of disorganized reactions to a policy of conquest that seems eminently rational by contrast.

When speaking of the state or the brotherhoods, we shall use the word 'initiatives'; at the local level the word 'reactions'. Although both ideas coexist in the history of the Maghrib, each can nevertheless be used separately to define the characteristics of a given period (before and after 1912 in Morocco, before and after 1922 in Libya).

Our source material for Maghribian initiatives to resist colonial ambitions is political and diplomatic. It is familiar material, and the problem for historians today is to assemble and preserve it. The evidence for local reactions is mainly written statements and oral accounts. Obviously, the accounts must be recorded and the handwritten statements assembled before they get lost; but the serious problem is to evaluate them, that is to know what we may legitimately expect of them.

Here two points must be made. First, as regards statements by educated townspeople, we must remember that the military conquest was preceded by lengthy psychological and political preparation. Meanwhile, the urban elite had lost all their will to resist. Those of its members who have left memoirs were not members of the resistance at the time, whatever may be said of them today. Secondly, as regards the oral accounts, we

3. An assembly representing *one* of the various levels of ethnic division.

must not forget that the witnesses were bound to have been exposed to two sorts of influences. The first was European. Accounts of engagements seen from the colonial standpoint were published almost immediately in the specialist press;[4] it was also colonial policy to send the sons of subject chiefs to French schools in the hope of turning them into faithful allies. Barely ten years after the event, for example, a son might give details of his father's battles which the latter knew nothing about, though, from then on, he would knit them into his account in all good faith. The colonial version, though contemporaneous with the events, is not perfect; it is tainted with the hostility that existed in the armies of the colonial powers between metropolitan and colonial regiments. The officers of the latter did not hesitate to portray their campaigns in Africa in such a way as to make them look comparable to the battles waged in Europe by the former.[5]

The second influence was nationalist. Operations for conquest were contemporaneous with reformist and nationalist activity in the towns. Even when they were taking place far from the towns, the townspeople eagerly followed their ups and downs and immediately used them for ideological ends. It was often the militant townsman who got the old highland warrior to dictate his recollections.

For the two reasons given, the statements we now have cannot transform the colonial account or the nationalist version: but they can throw a different light on them, always provided we go beyond their strictly local setting.

The Maghrib states and the Europeans

The nineteenth-century colonialist drive in North Africa was unusual in being a sequel to earlier campaigns (see Fig. 5.2).

The Moroccan government had for four centuries been resisting the Spaniards who had established themselves at Ceuta and Melilla. It always forbade the inhabitants to have anything to do with them; and it was to break this blockade that Spain launched the 1859–60 war that was so disastrous for Morocco. She was forced to pay a heavy fine, to agree to the enlargement of the fortified part of Melilla and to cede a port on the Atlantic coast as a refuge for fishermen from the Canary Islands.[6] With the acquisition of the bay of Rio de Oro – whose occupation was notified on 26 December 1884, to the signatories to the Berlin Act on

4. The chronicle of the pacification was published monthly from 1898 onwards in *Afrique française*, journal of the *Comité de l'Afrique française*.

5. General Guillaume wrote of the conquest of the Middle Atlas, 'But it was not so unusual as to be exempt from the general principles of the art of war': A. Guillaume, 1946, p. 457.

6. After years of argument agreement was reached on the port of Sīdī Ifnī, but it was not occupied until 1934.

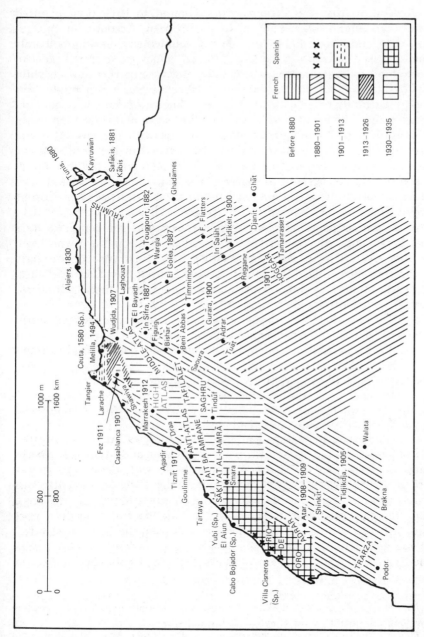

FIG. 5.2 *The European campaigns in the Maghrib*

the division of Africa into zones of influence – Spain by the end of the century had three bridgeheads on the North African coast.

In 1880 and 1881, when the Madrid Conference on the protection of individuals in Morocco met in two sessions, the Makhzen made a last attempt to get its independence and sovereignty over a clearly defined territory accepted at the international level. Despite English support, the attempt failed in the face of the selfish alliance of France, Spain and Italy. France, which had briefly thought all was lost in Morocco, raised the Tuāt problem immediately after the end of this conference. Indeed, there was much talk in Paris at the time about the plan for a trans-Saharan railway line, which would open up Central Africa to French trade. But the plan ran up against a serious obstacle: the oases of the central Sahara were politically dependent on Morocco. France tried to convert the Sultan to her view, but buttressed by English support, he rejected the French demands while at the same time strengthening his administrative and political presence in Tuāt.

In the east of the Maghrib, the Tunisians had for centuries been fighting the Italians as the Moroccans had been fighting the Spanish. United Italy certainly had designs on the Regency of Tunis: it sent immigrants there, invested capital there and propagated its culture there. But the real danger threatening Tunisia came from France, which had already been established in Algeria for over half a century.

The Sultan in Constantinople had taken advantage of his misfortunes in Algeria to bring Tripolitania and Cyrenaica back under his direct administration and regain his political influence in Tunisia.[7] There is no doubt that there was considerable pro-Ottoman feeling among the elite in the Regency of Tunis. The Bey, who saw this as a threat to his prerogatives, thought he would do best to rely on Italy and France. This more or less deliberate course of action was fatal for him. When the French government took advantage of a favourable diplomatic situation to attack the country, the Bey found himself isolated at home and abroad, and on 12 May 1881 was constrained to sign a treaty putting him under the protectorate of France. But the inhabitants of the Sahel and of the religious capital, Kayruwān, at once revolted, hoping for a rapid Ottoman intervention. A second French expedition was then raised, and was to meet strong resistance in the mountainous areas of the north-west, the centre and the south. Safākis and Kābis were bombarded by naval units; Kayruwān withstood a long siege in the autumn of 1881; and the southern territories near Tripolitania for long remained an insecure area.

Italy maintained her claims to the country; but the Tunisians obviously could not play that card. On the other hand, they remained faithful to

7. See E. Kuran, 1970.

Islamic sovereignty; the link with Constantinople was never completely broken, and this was to be one of the foundations of early Tunisian nationalism.

We need not concern ourselves here with the intense diplomatic activity that enabled the various European states to define their respective spheres of influence. This preparatory period ended with the general agreement of April 1904 between France and England. Until that date each power interested in the Maghrib was content to keep its claims alive, and on occasion took some territory as security.

Thus, at the end of Hassan I's reign, Morocco sustained a defeat in the 1893 war, which allowed Spain to consolidate her 1860 gains in the neighbourhood of Melilla. Seven years later, at the end of the regency of the vizier Bā Aḥmad, France judged that the time was ripe to settle the Tuāt problems to her advantage once and for all. On the pretext of scientific exploration a strong expedition gradually approached the coveted oases, and in December 1899 appeared before In Ṣalāḥ and demanded immediate surrender. The local chief, appointed by the Sultan of Morocco, surrounded by soldiers of the Makhzen and assisted by the sherifs of In Ṣalāḥ, resisted fiercely. After bloody battles, such as that of In Ghār on 27 December 1899, where the outcome was not in doubt given the disparity between the two sides, the whole oasis region was conquered; the last battle took place at Talmīn in March 1901. England and Germany, warned by the young Sultan 'Abd al-'Azīz, advised him to accept the *fait accompli*; and this he did, signing under duress the draft treaty of 20 April 1902. In return for this major concession, however, he tried to have the line of demarcation in the south and east between Morocco and the French possessions clearly defined; but to no effect, for France preferred the vagueness which offered her the prospect of further conquests.

The loss of Tuāt was one of the main reasons for the break-up of the Sultan's authority, which got worse and worse until 1911. The members of the Makhzen were aware that France planned to encircle Morocco in order to isolate and subjugate it; they also knew that England no longer opposed French designs. The domestic reforms the Makhzen had introduced to strengthen the army and administration had not had the desired results. From Germany it no longer counted on anything but diplomatic help; and Germany did indeed uphold Moroccan independence until November 1911, when she signed an agreement with France giving the latter a free hand in Morocco in exchange for compensations in equatorial Africa.

After 1905 France decided to precipitate matters and occupy the so-called *bilād al-sibā*.[8] These were poor, underpopulated desert areas which because

8. Colonial ideology represented the *bilād al-sibā* as independent territories, in which the Sultan's sovereignty was purely nominal and amounted only to religious influence.

of their character the Sultan had left to be administered by local chiefs, though without giving up his sovereign rights. He was regularly kept informed of colonial intrigues, and when the French threat took definite shape, he sent a duly authorized representative to direct the resistance. This is what happened in the Kenādza area and at Shinķīt.

Having always refused to define the frontier with Morocco beyond Figuig, France pursued a policy of slowly nibbling away at territory. Working their way up the valley of the Sawra, her forces gradually occupied the territory between Wādī Gīr and Wādī Zūsfānā, on the pretext of ending lawlessness and insecurity and allowing frontier trade to expand. The French government also suggested to the Makhzen that it should share customs receipts with it, and obtained satisfaction in March 1910.

Further south, France had imposed the protectorate on the emirs of the Trarza and the Brakna. Then, in 1905, a specialist in the affairs of the Islamic clerisy, Xavier Coppolani, came from Algeria to introduce the policy of 'peaceful penetration' which took the form of making direct contact with chiefs and the leaders of religious brotherhoods with a view to winning them over to French influence. He found himself up against a worthy opponent in Shaykh Mā' al-'Aynayn who for more than thirty years had acted as the Sultan of Morocco's representative. Mulāy 'Abd al-'Azīz was informed, and sent his uncle Mulāy Idrīs, who galvanized the resistance forces. Meanwhile, Coppolani's camp at Tidjikdja was attacked in April 1905 and the apostle of peaceful penetration was killed. Taking advantage of the internal crisis racking Morocco, France demanded the recall of Mulāy Idrīs, and obtained it in January 1907; but resistance continued none the less. A strong expedition led by Colonel Gouraud moved northwards; it suffered a serious reverse at al-Muynām on 16 June 1908, but succeeded in entering Atar on 9 January 1909. Shaykh Mā' al-'Aynayn withdrew with his followers into the Sāķiyat al-Ḥamrā, whence his forces continued to harass the French and the Spaniards until 1933.

During the same period Spain advanced on France's coat-tails. When France occupied Shinķīt, Spain moved out of her settlement on the bay of Rio de Oro and in 1906 organized the Saharan intervention force which penetrated 30 km inland. In the north, the Spaniards waited until the French entered Wadjda in 1907 before mounting a 45 000-strong expedition which in September 1909 set out to conquer the Rīf. In response, the local population, inspired by Shaykh Ameriyān's call to *djihād*, mounted a fierce resistance which was only to die out in 1926.

At the other end of North Africa, Ottoman Tripolitania came under attack from Italy in 1911 (see Fig. 5.3). The Young Turk revolution had greatly weakened the Ottoman state; and meanwhile Italy had been given the green light by England and France. On 28 September 1911 Italy presented an ultimatum to Constantinople complaining of Ottoman

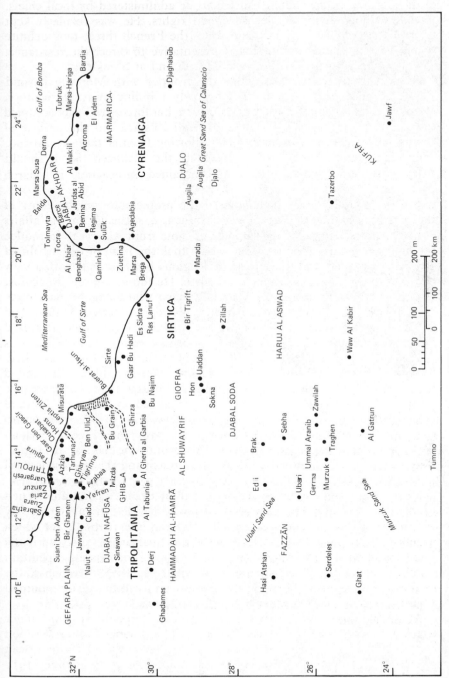

FIG. 5.3 *Ottoman Tripolitania, Sirtica and Cyrenaica (after J. Wright, 1969)*

95

PLATE 5.1 *Sayyid Aḥmad al-Sharīf al-Sanūsī, the spiritual leader of the Sanūsiyya, 1902–33*

negligence and the prevailing anarchy in the country, and then, without taking any notice of the Turkish Government's conciliatory reply, landed armies at Tripoli, Benghazi, Homs and Tubruk in October which easily captured the cities. However, when the Italians ventured outside the city limits, they faced fierce resistance. A series of battles took place on the outskirts of the cities among which was al-Hāni on 23 October 1911 outside Tripoli. The Italians suffered a humiliating defeat and committed great atrocities against the population of the city of Tripoli.[9] Outside Benghazi, the Italians fought three major battles at Djulianā, al-Kuwayfiya, and al-Hawwārī, on 28 November 1911. They were defeated and forced to retreat to Benghazi. At al-Khumṣ the Italians and the Turkish-Arab forces fought desperately from 23 October 1911 to 2 May 1912 for control of the strategic point of al-Markib, before the Italians succeeded in driving the defenders out.[10]

9. P. Maltese, 1968, pp. 210–24.
10. K. al-Tillīsī, 1973, pp. 463–7. The sections on Libya in this chapter were based on contributions by I. El-Hareir and Jan Vansina (Editor).

In Derna, the small Turkish force withdrew to the mountains overlooking the town and, with the help of the indigenous population, clashed with Italians. The resistance in Derna was buttressed by the arrival of a group of Turkish officers under the command of Anwar Pasha (Enver), and Mustafā Kamal (later Atatürk). With the help of Ahmad al-Sharīf, the spiritual leader of the Sanūsiyya, Anwar and his group mobilized the Arabs of the hinterland and succeeded in recruiting a formidable army.

Anwar led this army in two battles against the Italians at al-Karkaf and Sīdī 'Abdallāh on 8 October 1912 and 3 March 1912.[11] At Tubruk the Arabs met the Italians in two major encounters: al-Nādūra on 3 March 1912, and al-Mudawwar on 17 July 1912, in which the Italian commander, General Salsa, was killed.[12] It is difficult to cover all the battles fought against the Italians in Libya in a survey history; however, it is sufficient to say that in and around every city, town and valley, there was an encounter against the Italians. It was because of this fierce resistance that the Italians gained little more than the five towns in the first six months of the war.

By the end of 1911, many Italians had begun to show signs of disappointment about the duration of the war in Libya. In order to pressure Turkey to withdraw from Libya, the Italian government attacked the Turkish Straits, the Dodecanese Islands, and the Dardanelles. Italy's new action in the heart of the Turkish land threatened world peace and the revival of the 'Eastern Question', an issue no European power wanted raised because of its complications. The major European powers therefore put pressure on Turkey and Italy to come to a peaceful agreement, and succeeded in inducing, if not forcing Turkey to sign the Lausanne Agreement with Italy on 18 October 1912. According to this treaty, Turkey – to save her face before the Islamic world – granted independence to the Libyan people, and, in return, Italy promised to withdraw from Turkish waters.[13]

The reaction of the Libyans to the peace treaty – on which they were not consulted – was divided. Some wanted to negotiate with the Italians, while others wanted to fight to the end. The people of Cyrenaica under the spiritual leader, Ahmad al-Sharīf, belonged to the former camp.

Seizing the opportunity of the Turkish withdrawal from Libya, the Italians launched an attack on Ahmad al-Sharīf's forces south of Derna, but suffered a stunning defeat at the battle of Yawm al-Djumā' on 16 May 1913.[14] This battle was very important because it was the first large-scale encounter between the Arabs and the Italians after the Turkish withdrawal. Citing the decree issued by the Turkish Sultan which granted

11. ibid., p. 27.
12. ibid., pp. 344–6.
13. Al-Zāwī, 1973, pp. 140–56.
14. Al-Tillīsī, 1973, pp. 321–2.

the Libyans independence, Aḥmad al-Sharīf declared the formation of a government called 'al-Ḥukūma al-Sanūsiyya', the Sanūsī government.[15]

In Tripolitania, the Italians launched a similar attack directed at the major force in the Western Mountains where they defeated the Libyans at the battle of Djandūba on 23 March 1913. This victory opened the way to the Fazzān region for the Italians. They formed an expedition commanded by Colonel Miani who succeeded in defeating the Libyan warriors in three consecutive battles and occupied Ṣabhā in February 1913.[16]

Until the eve of the First World War, resistance in North Africa[17] was the work of an organized state. The invading forces were met by contingents of regular soldiers although there were fewer of them than of local warriors. When the state found itself compelled to accept the *fait accompli*, given the relative strengths of the two sides, it implicitly delegated its duty to resist to a leader of a brotherhood who never broke off relations with the political leader of the Muslim community.[18] Thus what was happening in this first period was a *political war* waged explicitly in the name of Islamic sovereignty.

By 1914 resistance organized by a centralized indigenous political authority had come to an end except in Libya. But the situation created by the First World War prevented the colonial powers from moving on to the phase of effective occupation. French, Spaniards and Italians sought only to maintain what they had already gained. But they suffered serious reverses; and this led General Lyautey, the French Resident in Morocco, to remark that: 'He who does not advance retreats'. The Germans and Turks called on the people of North Africa to throw off the colonial yoke; pan-Islamic leaders such as the Tunisian Bach Hamba and the Moroccan al-Aṭṭābī were received in Berlin, and took part in propaganda tours in neutral countries; emissaries were sent into the Rīf and to the Wādī Nūn area; and arms were shipped to the Tripolitanian resistance fighters through the port of Misurāta. There is no doubt that some of the people believed that the colonizers could be driven back into the sea. The fragility of the occupation in the territories conquered immediately before the war is shown by the extreme nervousness of the proconsuls of this period and the 'liberalism' they had to parade. Lyautey went so far as to behave like a mere minister of foreign affairs to the Sultan of Morocco.

This waiting period came to an end in 1921. In Tripolitania the new proconsul, Volpi, carried away by the tide of nationalism that was to

15. Aḥmad al-Sharīf documents at the University of Kār Yūnis, Benghazi, Libya.
16. Al-Tillīsī, 1973, pp. 46–7.
17. For the resistance of the Libyans during the First World War, see Chapter 12.
18. Note that the position of the two Sultans, Moroccan and Ottoman, was only comparable until 1919, when the Sultan in Constantinople renounced sovereignty over several Arab territories. Moreover in 1925 the Ottoman caliphate was abolished.

allow Mussolini to march on Rome, put an end to an allegedly liberal policy and denounced all earlier agreements reached during and after the First World War. This was followed by the launching of a number of invasions for a 'reconquista'. A large army under the command of General Graziani marched on Gharyān, capital of Tripolitania, which was captured on 7 November 1922. Another attacked Misurāta and took it on 20 February 1923.[19] The central committee of the United Republic set up on January 1922,[20] torn by disputes among its members as well as the civil war between Misurāta and Warfallāh on the one hand, and the civil strife between the Arabs and the Berbers of the Western Mountains on the other, could not mobilize sufficient force to stop the Italians. Consequently, the central committee collapsed and its members fled the country to Egypt, the Sudan and Tunisia.

To worsen the situation even further, on 21 December 1922, Emir Idrīs al-Sanūsī, the Union's spiritual leader and supreme commander, went into voluntary exile to Egypt. His unexplained and sudden departure, which is still being debated among historians, completely demoralized the people and caused many of the warriors either to leave the country or surrender to the Italians. However, before leaving, al-Sanūsī appointed his brother Al-Riḍā as his deputy, and 'Umar al-Mukhtār as commander of the National Forces in the Green Mountains, and it was under his leadership and because of the efficient guerrilla warfare that he developed that the resistance continued until 1931. He divided his forces into three major mobile companies (*adwār*) and camped in the mountainous area south of al-Mardj at Jardas. The series of attacks launched against him in the summer of 1923 were all repelled. Another army sent against his camp in March was routed.

It was Tripolitania that fell first. By June 1924, all arable land was occupied. But aware of their weakness as long as they did not control the desert, the Italians began a long campaign to control the desert and finally Fazzān. This was not marked by success despite the use of aerial bombing and poison gas. Several Italian advances were stopped. As late as 1928 the Libyans blocked the main Italian force at Faqhrift south of Surt. But by the end of 1929 and the beginning of 1930, Fazzān was finally occupied and the Libyan resistance in the west and south collapsed.

Meanwhile, the resistance in Cyrenaica continued and succeeded in inflicting heavy defeats on the Italians. When the Fascists failed to suppress the revolution of 'Umar al-Mukhtār in Cyrenaica through direct military attack, they resorted to some measures unprecedented in the history of colonial wars in Africa. They first erected a 300 km-long wire fence along the Tripoli–Egyptian border to prevent any aid coming from Egypt.

19. Al-Tillīsī, 1973, pp. 63–76; see also R. Graziani, 1976, pp. 98–104, 161–71, 339–67.
20. See Chapter 12.

Secondly, continually enforced, they occupied the oases of Djalo, Djaghabūb and Kufra to encircle and isolate the warriors in Cyrenaica. Finally, they evacuated all the rural population of Cyrenaica to the desert of Sirt where they kept them in fenced concentration camps. This measure was meant to deprive al-Mukhtār's forces of any local assistance. Other mass prisons and concentration camps were established at al-Makrūn, Sulūk, al-Aghayla and al-Barayka. Conditions in these camps were so bad that it is believed that more than a hundred thousand people died of starvation and diseases, not to mention their animals which were confiscated. In al-Barayka prison camp alone, there were 80 000 persons of whom 30 000 are said to have died between 1930 and 1932, according to the Italians' own statistics.[21]

Despite these wicked measures, the revolt continued and hit-and-run tactics were resorted to. The Italians again offered to negotiate with al-Mukhtār. A series of meetings were held between the two sides. Among them was the one held near al-Mardj on 19 July 1929, attended by Governor Badoglio. At this meeting, the Italians offered to bribe al-Mukhtār who turned down the offer and insisted on liberating his country.[22] Later, when al-Mukhtār discovered that the Italians were trying to apply the policy of 'divide and rule' among his followers, he broke the talks with the Italians and resumed his tactics of guerrilla warfare which included skirmishes, raids, ambushes, surprise attacks and incursions spread all over the country. In the last twenty-one months before his capture, he fought 277 battles with the Italians as Graziani himself admits.[23] In September 1931, however, al-Mukhtār was captured and taken to Benghazi. He was then court-martialed and executed before thousands of Libyans at the town of Sulūk on 16 September 1931.

After the capture of al-Mukhtār, his followers elected Yūsuf Abū Rāhil, his deputy, as commander. He continued the struggle for six months and then decided to suspend and withdraw to Egypt. He was killed in his attempt to cross the Libya–Egyptian border. On 24 January 1932, Badoglio announced the conquest and occupation of Libya and one of the longest resistances to European imperialism thus came to its more or less inevitable end. It is worth remembering that at this very time northern Morocco was the scene of an equally fierce war and an equally heroic resistance.[24]

Until 1931 enormous areas of the Atlas and the Sahara, regarded as economically unprofitable, existed outside any colonial control; and this was where those who did not wish to surrender to the French or Spanish armies took refuge. But the inhabitants did not remain entirely isolated;

21. M. T. al-Ashhāb, 1947, p. 482.
22. I. El-Hareir, 1981.
23. R. Graziani, 1980, p. 296.
24. The Rīf war is dealt with in Chapter 24 below.

PLATE 5.2 'Umar al-Mukhtār (b. c. 1862), a leader of Sanūsī resistance to Italian colonization until his execution in 1931

they were in touch with the subjugated areas, whose markets and dispensaries they visited. This was the period of peaceful penetration and a policy of contact; an ambiguous period, from which we must be careful not to draw general conclusions.

In 1931 a change took place in French colonial policy. Worried at Germany's rebuilding of her strength, the French Minister of War, Messimy, set the year 1935 as the *terminus ad quem* for conquest and occupation. All necessary means were given to the army in Africa, and arrangements were made to co-ordinate operations with the Spaniards; the advent of a republic in Madrid made this co-ordination easy. Thus every spring an expedition was mounted to put down one of the 'dissident spots'.

To understand fully what was about to happen we must remember that the conquest was carried out in the name of the Sultan;[25] that the army of pacification was mainly indigenous; that the policy of contact had enabled the colonial authorities to understand the contradictions within communities encircled for years; and that every community contained both indigenous people and refugees who had sometimes come from a great distance. Above all we must consider why on earth people should fight to the death for customs which the colonial power was obviously prepared to preserve and strengthen.

Yet despite that final conquest was nowhere easy.[26] The Middle Atlas was reduced in two campaigns in 1931 and 1932; from 12 July to 16 September of the latter year the bloody battle of Tazĭkzaūt took place. The French army surrounded 3000 families who had been retreating before the colonial advance since 1922. The battle lasted from 22 August to 11 September. Neither massive bombardment nor blockade could break the resistance led by al-Wakki Amhouch and his brothers. The shelters had to be cleared by grenades. After the battle, they counted 500 killed among the Moroccans. This battle clearly demonstrated the limits of the policy of contact with the ethnic groups. In 1933 it was the turn of the Djabal Saghrū, where the battle of Bū Ghāfir (13 February to 25 March) was equally bloody. In 1934 the last resistance fighters were surrounded in the Anti-Atlas; after which the French could enter Tindūf in March. A week later, on 6 April 1934, the Spaniards were at last able to take possession of Sīdī Ifnī.

In 1930 and 1931, when the colonial powers might reasonably have supposed that the conquest was nearing its end, the Italian leaders were talking about *Pax Romana* and the French were ceremonially celebrating the centenary of the capture of Algiers and the fiftieth anniversary of

25. 'It thus took 22 years of continuous effort to reach the heart of the Berber mountains and bring the last rebels under the authority of the sovereign of Morocco', A. Guillaume, 1946, p. 456.
26. 'Not one tribe came over to us without first being defeated', ibid., p. 9.

PLATE 5.3 *Amghar Hassū ū Bāsallām of the Ilemchan (the Aït Atta of the Sahara), leader of the resistance fighters at Bū Ghāfir (Saghrū) in Algeria in 1933*

the protectorate over Tunisia. Theoreticians of colonization saw this as the revenge of Rome over Islam and the West over the East. But at that time nationalism, already established in the towns, was preparing to spread into the country areas. For those involved, the last battles were not so much the end of an era as a sign of the rejection of any voluntary submission.[27]

Stages of resistance

Two phases can thus be distinguished in Maghribi resistance to the colonial drive: one from 1880 to about 1912, the other from 1921 to 1935 (the intervening period being the ambiguous one of the First World War). Let us now, over and above the chronicle of military events and subjective reports, consider some questions that might pave the way to thinking and research.

During the first phase the campaigns always followed a pattern that had been developed by France during the conquest of Algeria, and had then been taken up by Spain and Italy. Before invading a coveted territory a colonial power took good care to obtain its competitors' consent, either through a bilateral convention or in the lobbies of an international conference.[28] Once this had been done, the following stages in the conquest took place:

(1) An incident was identified and used as a justification for intervention: hence the usual stories of raids and plundering groups (the case of the Krumirs on the Tunisian–Algerian frontier has remained famous). Thus the Tidikelt was annexed on the pretext that it had served as a refuge for Bū Shūsha, who fought the French from 1869 to 1874, the Gurāra because Ḳaddūr b. Hamza found help and succour there during his struggle from 1872 to 1879, and Shinḳīt because the Moors often crossed the River Senegal.[29]

(2) The objections of the Powers and the Sultan, the sovereign of the coveted territory, were disposed of by stressing the administrative sloppiness and insecurity rife in the said territory.

(3) Territorial pawns were taken at the first opportunity, for example during a period of national tension or a change of ruler. Thus France unexpectedly occupied In Ṣalāḥ in January 1900. The

27. This is a fundamental point in modernist Islam. Total submission to God, which is what the word *islam* means in Arabic, implies non-submission to anyone except God.

28. France was given *carte blanche* in Tunisia in the lobbies of the 1878 Congress of Berlin, and in Morocco at the 1906 Algeciras conference.

29. South-east of Morocco the French complained endlessly about the depredations of the Awlād Dzārīr and Dawī Maniya. This was the excuse for taking Bechar which (in order to deceive French public opinion itself) was given the name Colomb.

inhabitants called for help and the Sultan of Morocco protested; but France refused to discuss the matter on the grounds that inability to maintain law and order amounted to a loss of sovereignty.[30] When sovereignty was undeniable, as at Wudjida and Casablanca (occupied in March and August 1907 respectively), the French made evacuation of their forces contingent on restoration of order (which their very presence made impossible).

(4) Through a series of pressures and promises, delegated sovereignty (*tawfīd*) was obtained, which legalized the occupation. This was the effect of the protectorate treaties.

(5) The next stage was true conquest, known in the typically Eurocentric way as pacification. Its speed depended from now on solely on the order of priorities drawn up by the colonial power.

As we have already noted, this first phase was marked by political and diplomatic activity that makes it part and parcel of international history; it thus poses no new problems for the historian.

This is not the case for the second phase, that of total conquest or the so-called pacification. For obvious reasons, resistance in the towns and in the plains was always short-lived. The mountains, initially regarded as economically valueless,[31] were sealed off by a security belt, and this was to be tightened over the years. The desert areas were watched over from strong points on the Atlantic coast.[32] This policy was imposed on the colonial power by force of circumstance, for it reflected ecological and socio-political facts.[33] It is important to grasp the reality of this situation which has been masked by the ideological distortions introduced by colonial historians. At this stage in our knowledge all we can do is to raise some questions that seem relevant to us:

(1) Why was it necessary to obtain a formal treaty from the Sultan of Morocco or Constantinople to legalize the conquest and turn it into mere 'pacification'?

(2) Why were the inhabitants taken by surprise at every colonial attack?

(3) Why was the army so North Africanized that it could be said to have European officers in command of indigenous troops?

30. But France still insisted that the Sultan should recognize the *fait accompli*.

31. Until indications of mineral wealth were discovered there, as in the Rīf. This was what impelled the Spaniards to speed up their conquest.

32. Hence the role delegated by the French and Spaniards to the Rakībat, because their nomadic life took them from the Adrar to the Anti-Atlas and the *Hammāda Darʿa*.

33. The colonial leaders were aware of this, and were keen to appear to be continuing their predecessors' work. General Guillaume, after describing the pacification campaigns in the Middle Atlas, appended an account of the battles of the great Moroccan ruler Mulāy Ismāʿīl (1672–1727) in the same area.

(4) Why was there division in the resistance movement which could not be overcome even at times of the greatest danger?

These questions among others help to bring out the reactions of the inhabitants during the so-called pacification phase.

The failure of African initiatives and resistance

In spite of the strong determination of the people of the Maghrib to maintain their sovereignty and way of life, and despite the protracted nature of the resistance, the whole of the Maghrib had fallen to the imperial powers of France, Spain and Italy by 1935. The final question to be considered then is why the Maghribians failed.

Contrary to what might be supposed the demographic, ecological and economic circumstances were for most of the time against the North African resistance fighter.

We now know that the population of North Africa was overestimated in the nineteenth century. Men old enough to carry arms were limited in number and also available only for a very short period because of the requirements of agriculture and stock-rearing; and this left the initiative in the hands of the enemy. Tidikelt was conquered by a column of 1000 men, having a population not exceeding 20000. At Tīt on 7 May 1902, when the Tawārik of the Ahaggar were defeated, they numbered 300 as against 130; but that was the most they could muster, and the loss of 93 dead was a blow from which they did not easily recover. The supposedly overpopulated highland areas were little better off; in every decisive engagement the assailants had the advantage of numbers. The people of the Rīf were attacked by 300000 French soldiers (not counting the Spaniards) – i.e. the equivalent of the whole population of northern Morocco. At the height of the resistance in the Middle Atlas, a total number of 10000, including women and children, had to face an army of 80000 men. In the Djabal Saghrū 7000 fighting soldiers were assailed by 34000 men equipped with the latest weapons.[34] Admittedly not all the colonial troops were combatants; but it is undeniable that in terms of sheer numbers, the advantage always lay with the colonial army, which set out to strike 'the natives with terror and despondency'.[35]

Much is often made of the indigenous fighters' mobility and knowledge of the terrain; but these were tactical advantages that counted for less and less as the war went on. The exploit at Tidjikdja in June 1905, in which the apostle of peaceful penetration, Xavier Coppolani, was killed and which delayed the conquest of the Adrār until 1909; the battle of Kasība, from 8 to 10 June 1913, in which the French lost 100 dead

34. E. F. Gautier, 1910, pp. 12 and 129; A. Guillaume, 1946, pp. 114 and 414; A. Ayache, 1956, p. 332.
35. A. Bernard and L. N. E. Lacroix, 1921, p. 332.

and 140 wounded; the even bloodier one at al-Harī on 13 November 1914, when they left behind 510 dead and 176 wounded; the battle of Anwāl, from 22 to 26 July 1921, in which the Spaniards lost 15000 dead, 700 prisoners, 20000 rifles, 400 machine guns and 150 field guns; all these heroic feats of arms (showing admirable knowledge of the terrain, and decisively influenced by mobility and ruthlessness in battle) stopped the colonial advance for a few years but did not help to regain lost territory. Neither the desert dwellers nor the highlanders could take much time off from their orchard farming and stock-rearing; and this allowed the invader to launch real economic warfare against them. During the Adrār campaign in 1909 the French soldiers occupied the oases at the time of the date harvest and waited for the men to be compelled by hunger to come and surrender (admittedly not for long). In areas where seasonal migration with stock took place, they closed off the winter pastures and relied on cold and hunger to bring the inhabitants to terms. When operations began, a total blockade was imposed, as against the Zayyān in 1917–18 and the people of the Rīf in 1925–6. In 1928–9 the Italians, as has been pointed out above, deported the people of Cyrenaica to the north and concentrated them in camps surrounded by barbed wire. One consequence of the nagging hunger created by such policies, harder on the livestock than the people, was that the colonial army found volunteers immediately after the end of operations.

The resistance fighters' great asset, mobility, soon became only relative. From 1901 onwards the French army began to use racing camels, to such good effect that the conquest of the Sahara has been described as due to Sha'amba camel-riders.[36] The railway also preceded conquest almost everywhere: it reached 'Ayn Sifrā in 1887, Bishār in 1905 and Zīz in 1930. In 1915 motor vehicles were tried for the first time, and Epinat lorries[37] drove up and down the roads of the Atlas in anticipation of the 1931–3 campaigns. Lastly, aircraft were used from 1920 onwards, for aerial photography in preparation for the campaigns and to demoralize the inhabitants during operations.[38]

This brings us to the problem of weapons, which not being produced locally had to be taken from the enemy. France had always made an international issue out of arms smuggling to the Maghrib, accusing Germany and Turkey of being suppliers, and Spain and even England of tolerating arms traffic on the coasts of the Rīf and the Atlantic coast in the case of Morocco and via the Libyan oases for Tunisia and the central Sahara. It is true that this traffic had always existed; but never-

36. The Sha'amba are nomads of the Algerian Tell.
37. Named after a French businessman at Marrakesh with interests in the mines.
38. Italy was actually the first to use aircraft in a colonial war, in 1911. In the 1921–6 campaigns, aircraft under the command of the future Marshal Badoglio played a decisive role in defeating the resistance fighters in Tripolitania and the Fezzān.

PLATE 5.4 *Morocco, the Rif War: spotter aircraft dropping instructions for artillery range adjustment*

theless, the fact remains that the French authorities themselves admitted that they found hardly any German weapons in the Middle Atlas or Anti-Atlas. As each large clan grouping was forced to surrender, it passed its rifles on to its neighbours who were still free; so that it was at the end of operations in March 1934 that the French recovered the largest number of rifles, namely 25 000. We must remember that these weapons were often useless because of lack of ammunition, and above all that they were of doubtful effectiveness against the aircraft, long-range heavy artillery and armour with which the invading armies were equipped after the First World War. It was this that made the French generals say that the 1931–4 campaigns were 'real manoeuvres with a live enemy'.[39]

The final adverse factor was a political and ideological one. The people of North Africa and the Sahara are all Muslim, and Islam lays down strict rules for people's wars. Contrary to the idea common in the West, the *djihād* as understood in recent centuries is defensive: that is, military service and the taxes that flow from it are only compulsory for everyone if the country is the victim of aggression. In the case of an offensive war (and there have been none in North Africa for centuries), contributions and service are only voluntary. In the circumstances of the nineteenth century, this left the military initiative to the invader. Defence of the realm was traditionally one of the provisions of the *bay'a* (sovereign's investiture contract). In the event of attack, were Muslims supposed to organize resistance themselves immediately, or ought they to await the sultan's instructions? The question has been discussed at length by the doctors of law, and the view that prevailed was that responsibility should be left to the sovereign so as to stop demagogy and extravagant promises. This explains why, when French or Spanish soldiers appeared in a district, as they did in Tuāt in 1864 and 1890 or Tarfāya in 1885, the inhabitants sent a delegation to the Sultan and then awaited his orders. Responsibility was thus left with the sovereign; and he was in a dilemma, for if he held aloof, he jeopardized the legitimacy of his authority, and if he replied favourably to the request, the powers would hold him responsible for anything that happened. Usually he advised calm, delegated a chief to maintain order, and allowed those involved to hope that the problem was being solved through diplomatic means (which many of those on the spot were all too ready to believe).[40] Here we come to the heart of the matter. When the Sultan failed,[41] and a religious or lay leader

39. A. Guillaume, 1946, p. 398.
40. The situation of the Sultan in Constantinople in the nineteenth century was little different.
41. He sometimes succeeded either in delaying the conquest, as at Tuāt in 1890, or in winning back a district as in the case of Tarfāya, which the English gave back in 1898.

felt obliged to take up the banner of the *djihād* in his stead but without his blessing, he would certainly not get unanimous support. The colonial powers could then play on all kinds of rivalries and hostilities.

Within the framework of a society which had become *de facto* leaderless, the colonial army could easily take advantage of a divided opposition. Fully to appreciate how this worked, we must remember that the sultan's administration was often indirect, being delegated to local chiefs, Islamic clerics or shaykhs. When the sultan was unable to lead the resistance himself, every individual thought of safeguarding his own privileges, or 'climbing on the bandwagon' as one specialist in native affairs put it.[42] France had no difficulty in obtaining help to conquer Tuāt from the Sherif of Wazzān (who could take up *ziyāra* (collections) among his followers in Algeria only with the permission of the French governor), at Shinkīt from Shaykhs Sīdiya and Sa'd Būḥ, in the Tafilālet from the leader of the *Nāṣiriyya zāwiya*, and lastly in the Rīf from the chief of the Darḳāwa. In Tripolitania, the Italians won over to their side the Ibādites of the Djabal Nafūsa, who were opposed to the Sunnī majority in the country. Where a great chief had built up a principality, the colonial authorities waited for a succession dispute to arise and then offered their support to each of the claimants in turn; this is what happened with the Trarza between 1901 and 1904 and among the Zayyān between 1917 and 1919. But the impact of this 'native policy' must not be exaggerated. Whenever a chief favoured the French, he immediately lost his prestige and was no longer of any use: so much so that in the end the authorities no longer sought public submissions.

The tendency of leaders of *zawāyā* and the great chiefs to compromise and play a double game thus resulted not so much from ethnic divisions and rivalries as from the disappearance of the supreme political power, whose successive defeats exposed its military weakness.

History has handed down to us the names of some thirty chiefs who led the resistance against the French, Spaniards and Italians during the period 1900–35, not counting Muḥammad Ibn 'Abd al-Karīm and 'Abd al-Malik.[43] The others can be divided into two quite distinct groups regardless of their success or failure.

One group was in continual touch with the Sultan, served him and appealed to him when the colonial threat loomed; the others acted under the influence of the local *djema'a*. The former were more far-seeing but were handicapped by the military weakness of the Sultan; the latter were more tenacious in their actions, but their influence was limited to the narrow boundaries of their commands.

42. L. V. Justinard, 1951, p. 105.
43. 'Abd al-Karīm is not discussed here because his story is to be dealt with elsewhere. As for 'Abd al-Malik, grandson of the emir 'Abd al-Kāder of Algeria and an officer in the Ottoman army, he seems to have been an adventurer who served the interests of Turkey, Spain and France in turn.

When Mulāy 'Abd al-Ḥafiẓ rose against his brother Mulāy 'Abd al-Azīz and tried to restore Moroccan sovereignty over the whole area recognized as belonging to it at the end of the nineteenth century, his chief supporters were the following: Shaykh Mā' al-'Aynayn and his sons Hassana and al-Aḳdāf (who led the resistance at Shinḳīt), his other sons al-Ḥibā, Murābbih Rabbuh and al-Ni'mat (who retreated before the French advance from Marrakesh in 1912 to Tiznīt in 1917, and then to Kerdūs and Widjdjān in 1934) and the great Azaghar chiefs Muhā Ū Sa'īd and Muhā Ū Ḥammū (who held up the French thrust into the Atlas until 1922). When the attempt failed, mainly because of their geographical isolation, they did not surrender, like other southern chiefs who had long been in contact with the French. But, deprived of the Sultan's support, they could no longer operate effectively. Al-Ḥibā proclaimed himself sultan in 1912, but found no support in the towns or among the great chiefs. The others shut themselves up within their commands, defending themselves against all comers and each hoping to die before seeing 'the face of the French', as chief al-Madanī of the Akhās put it so well.[44]

In contrast to these were the local chiefs. Some were extempore ones, like Muḥammad al-Ḥadjdjamī in the neighbourhood of Fez in 1911 and Nafrūtan al-Samladī and his disciple al-Naḳḳādī in the Tafilālet between 1919 and 1934. Others were traditionally acknowledged ones, like 'Alī Amhawūsh, his sons al-Makkī and al-Murtaḍā and his disciples Ibn al-Tayyibī and Muhand Ū al-Ḥādjdj (who successively led the struggle in the Middle Atlas from 1919 to 1934), or Ḥassū ū Bāsallām, leader of the resistance at Bū Ghāfir in February and March 1933. The latter group refused to compromise; when defeated they moved on until they were hemmed in in mountain or desert retreats and subjected to a barrage of fire. How are we to understand such dogged tenaciousness when in complete isolation?

We must remember that throughout the nineteenth century, a popular movement was growing up which advocated war to the death; it was disparaged by the *'ulamā'* and the members of the Makhzen because it was accompanied by an appeal to the supernatural and belief in the millennium. There is an account of al-Ḥibā and his brother Murābbih Rabbuh, on the eve of the battle of Bū 'Uthmān on 6 September 1912, calling on the angels to help the resistance fighters. At the time of the battle of 26 June 1922 there is mention of the *Kerkūr* of Tafesaset, a rock at whose foot the colonial advance would supposedly stop on pain of a cosmic cataclysm.[45] This was a natural belief on the part of sherifs and clerics leading mostly unlettered peoples; but it was also an attitude

44. M. al-Sūsī, 1961, Vol. 20, p. 202.
45. A. Guillaume, 1946, pp. 219–20. On al-Ḥibā see Ibn Ibrāhīm, *Al-Ḥamla al-Faransiyya 'alā Marrākush*, manuscript K.320, Archives of Rabat, p. 16.

which the urban elite was bound to regard as dangerous because it was archaic and unrealistic. Abū Shuʿayb al-Dukkālī, one of the pioneers of the reformist movement, well expressed this critical attitude to this sort of resistance by saying of al-Ḥibā's action: 'I am against resistance fighters who give the Europeans excuses to occupy Muslim land, like Bū Amāma, the chiefs of the Shāwiya and the Banī Matīr, and many more whose number is countless in the East and the West'.[46]

Just as there were two stages in colonial policy and two kinds of resistance, so likewise there were two quite distinct groups of resistance leader. Concentrating on the phase of conquest and occupation, the phase of stubborn scattered resistance led by chiefs and Islamic clerics with millenarian ideas little to the taste of the urban elite, we find the following characteristics:

(1) they had broken with the historic elite, which understood the real relative strengths of the colonial army and the indigenous fighters;

(2) they expected a miracle to stave off the conquest;

(3) they were disunited and scattered by exile, hunger and distrust;

(4) they refused to accept what seemed inevitable after the event.

These characteristics differentiate this stage fundamentally from the resistance during the first stage, i.e. from the *political war* waged by an organized state whose purposes the nationalists were to make their own. Hence the difficult question of whether this scattered, localized resistance can be regarded as an early form of nationalism.

In the event, it was considered archaic and ineffectual and was left to its fate by the historic leaders. But immediately after its final failure it was selectively taken up again for the purposes of the cause. The point was that the nationalists celebrated successful attacks, remembered the names of chiefs who died without surrendering, but forgot those who survived to become the pawns of European officers even when they too had put up a fierce resistance before submitting.

This resistance served at least to some extent as a legend to galvanize others. The battles of Tazīkzaūt and Bū Ghafīr and the figures of Muhā Ū Ḥammū, al-Nakkādī, and so on, allowed the nationalists to ask the embarrassing question whether a surrender obtained by overwhelming force was a real surrender. The colonial generals, who spoke of peaceful penetration when conquest was easy, reverted after 1926 to Bugeaud's

---

46. Ibn Ibrāhīm, *Al-Ḥamla*, pp. 13 and 30–5. Bū Amāma fought the French around Figuig between 1880 and 1885; Bū Ḥimāra rose against Sultan Mulāy ʿAbd al-ʿAzīz, who was accused of being pro-European, and led a revolt which lasted from 1902 to 1909; in Shāwiya Muḥammad Bū ʿAzzawī led the resistance fighters from 1907 to 1909; and among the Banī Matīr, Akkā Bū Bidmānī made a stand against the invading army from 1911 to 1913.

ideas that the enemy must be destroyed and that as many troops were needed to hold North Africa as to conquer it.[47]

This is as good as saying that the 'conquest of men's hearts and minds' never took place.

47. G. Spillmann reports Lyautey as saying at the end of 1924, 'Some people apparently venture to argue that a tribe is only really subjugated when it has been given a bloody thrashing.' G. Spillman, 1968, p. 60. The Spanish attitude always smacked unpleasantly of the Crusades, a mixture of hate and fear. In Tripolitania in 1921 Volpi spoke of a policy of blood.

African initiatives and resistance in West Africa, 1880–1914

M'BAYE GUEYE and A. ADU BOAHEN

During the period 1880 to 1914, the whole of West Africa, with the sole exception of Liberia (see Chapter 2), was brought under colonial rule. This phenomenon which meant essentially the loss of African sovereignty and independence as well as land, was accomplished in two phases. The first phase lasted from 1880 to the early 1900s, and the second from the early 1900s to the outbreak of the First World War in 1914. Each of these phases saw different European activities which produced different initiatives and reactions on the part of the Africans. It should be emphasized that these reactions were very much determined by the local African situation. Variables included the nature of the polity (whether or not centralized, whether or not dominated by another African power, and whether or not on the upswing or settled and declining),[1] the nature of the leadership provided, the extent of the penetration of European political, religious and economic influences by the 1870s and the experiences gained from this. Another equally important variable was the method adopted by the European imperialists in the establishment of their control over the area between 1880 and 1914.

The first phase saw either the use of diplomacy or military invasion, or both, by the Europeans. This was the classical era of treaty-making in practically every nook and corner of West Africa followed in most cases by military invasions, conquests and occupation by armies of varying sizes and discipline. The period from 1880 to 1900 was the high-water mark of European conquest and occupation of West Africa. Never in the known history of the continent has so much military action been seen and so many invasions and campaigns launched against African states and communities (see Fig. 6.1). Particularly memorable were the French campaigns in the Western Sudan, Ivory Coast and Dahomey (now Benin) between 1880 and 1898, and the British campaigns in Asante (in what is now Ghana), the Niger Delta region (Nigeria) and in Northern Nigeria between 1895 and 1903 (see Fig. 6.2).

During this first phase, practically all Africans had the same objectives,

1. A. S. Kanya-Forstner in M. Crowder (ed.), 1971, p. 75.

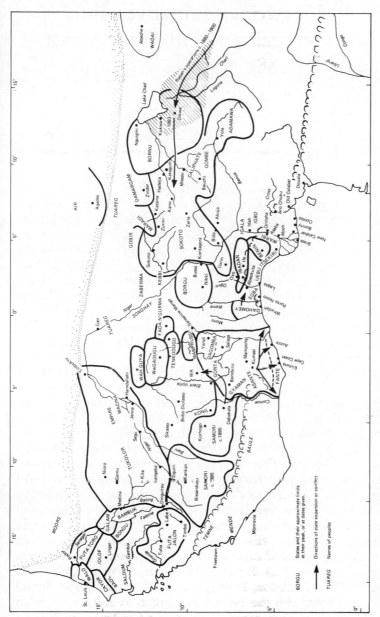

FIG. 6.1 *States and peoples of West Africa at the outset of European partition (after J. D. Fage, 1978)*

BORGU   States and their approximate limits
         at their peak, or at dates given.

→   Directions of state expansion or conflict

TUAREG   Names of peoples

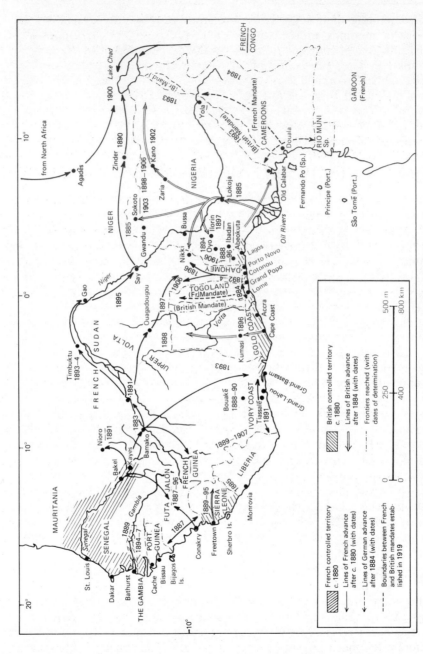

FIG. 6.2 *The European advance into West Africa, c. 1880–1919 (after J. D. Fage, 1978)*

that of defending their sovereignty and traditional way of life. It is the strategies or methods adopted that varied. Three options were open to the Africans, that of confrontation, that of alliance and that of acquiescence or submission. The strategy of confrontation involved open warfare, sieges, guerrilla tactics, scorched earth policies as well as diplomacy. As will be seen below, all three options were resorted to. Though three main European powers were involved in the conquest and occupation of West Africa, we shall confine ourselves in this chapter to the two principal ones, namely, Britain and France.

Conquest and reaction in French West Africa, 1880–1900

It is quite clear from the available evidence that the French – from 1880 onwards – adopted a policy of extending their control over the whole region from the Senegal first to the Niger and then Chad and linking these areas with their posts on the Guinea coast in Ivory Coast and Dahomey. The execution of this policy was entrusted to officers of the Senegalese area. As one would expect, therefore, in their occupation of West Africa, the French resorted almost exclusively to the method of military conquest rather than the conclusion of treaties of protectorate as the British did. In terms of African reactions, all the options open to them were resorted to, namely, submission, alliance and confrontation. However, as will be seen below, far more of the rulers opted for the strategy of militant confrontation than those of submission and alliance while opposition here was far more protracted than anywhere else in West Africa for two main reasons. The first, as pointed out already, was that the French used the method of military conquest almost exclusively, which consequently evoked militant reaction. The second was that the people were far more Islamized than those of the other areas of West Africa, and as Michael Crowder has pointed out, since 'for Muslim societies of West Africa the imposition of white rule meant submission to the infidel which was intolerable to any good Muslim',[2] they tended to resist the Europeans with added fervour and tenacity often lacking among non-Muslims. Let us illustrate these general conclusions by a study of the events in Senegambia, the Tukulor and Mandingo empires, in the Baule areas of Ivory Coast and finally in Dahomey.

Senegambia

In Senegal, where the conquest had been going on since 1854, France had by 1880 obtained firm bases of operations with the annexation of Walo, the northern part of Cayor and Diander. Since 1860, a French protectorate had been imposed on the states of Upper Senegal. However meagre these results were, they had not been obtained without difficulties.

2. M. Crowder, 1968, p. 72; see also A. S. Kanya-Forstner in M. Crowder (ed.), 1971, pp. 53–4.

Although expelled from Cayor in 1864 by France, Lat Dior Diop, the Damel of Cayor, nevertheless chose the strategy of confrontation by continuing the struggle against the French. In 1871, with the defeat of the French by Prussia, the Governor of Senegal abandoned the annexation of Cayor and recognized Lat Dior once again as Damel. Consequently, friendly relations were established between him and the French administration in Senegal.

In 1879, the governor, Brière de l'Isle, obtained permission from the Damel to build a road connecting Dakar with Saint-Louis. But when Lat Dior learned in 1881 that a railway was what was actually involved, he declared his opposition to the project. He realized that the railway would bring the independence of Cayor to an end. In 1881, informed that construction was about to begin, he took steps to prevent it. Orders were issued to all the chiefs to punish severely any Cayor subject who supplied anything whatsoever to the French workmen.[3] Thereafter, emissaries were dispatched to Ely, the emir of Trarza, Abdul Bokar Kane of Futa Toro and Alboury N'Diaye of Djoloff. Lat Dior invited them to join a holy alliance and to synchronize their struggle in order to facilitate the eviction of the French from the land of their forefathers.[4]

On 17 November 1882 he sent a letter to Governor Servatius, forbidding him to begin construction even in the suburbs of the territory that was an integral part of Cayor. 'As long as I live, be well assured', he wrote, 'I shall oppose with all my might the construction of this railway ... The sight of sabres and lances is pleasing to our eyes. That is why every time I receive a letter from you concerning the railway, I will always answer no, no and I will never make you any other reply. Even were I to go to rest, my horse Malay would give you the same answer.'[5] Nothing could better refute those who regard Lat Dior's position in this matter as merely the caprice of a feudal chieftain without regard for the welfare of his people than these sentiments. Be that as it may, noting the persistency of the governor in carrying out his project, Lat Dior forbade his subjects to cultivate groundnuts. He was convinced that if the French could not obtain groundnuts, they would return home. He also ordered those of his subjects living near the French posts to resettle in the Cayor heartland. The villages of those who disobeyed these orders were burnt down and their possessions confiscated.

In December 1882, Colonel Wendling invaded Cayor at the head of an expeditionary column composed chiefly of African riflemen and auxiliaries from the annexed territories. Having fought the French since 1861, Lat Dior knew that he had little chance of defeating them in conventional warfare. He withdrew at Wendling's approach and went to settle in Djoloff. In Cayor, Wendling invested Lat Dior's cousin, Samba Yaya Fall, with

3. ANSOM – Governor Lanneau to the Minister – Senegal I, 466, 24 May 1881.
4. ANSOM – Governor Vallon to the Minister – Senegal I, 67b, 23 July 1882.
5. ASAOF – Lat Dior to the Governor – Senegal I, 68b, 8 January 1883.

power. In August 1883, he was dismissed and replaced by Samba Laobe Fall, Lat Dior's nephew. The governor was convinced that Lat Dior would never make war on his nephew. He was not mistaken: Lat Dior contrived a compromise with his kinsman who, in 1885, authorized him to return to Cayor.

In October 1886, Samba Laobe Fall was killed at Tivaouane by a detachment of *spahis*. Governor Genouille thereupon decided to abolish the title of Damel. He divided Cayor into six provinces which were entrusted to former captives of the crown.[6] A decree was also passed expelling Lat Dior from Cayor. When he was notified of this measure, Lat Dior went into a towering rage. He mobilized the 300 partisans who had remained faithful but released from oath all those who were not resolved to die with him, and took to the field against the French and their allies, his former subjects. Lat Dior was firmly resolved to sell his life dearly. He therefore feigned compliance with the expulsion order by heading for Djoloff. By one of his bold counter-marches, he managed to slip undetected into a position between his enemies and the railway. On 27 October 1886, at about 11 a.m., he surprised the French and their allies at the well of Dekhle and inflicted heavy losses on them. He fell there, as did his two sons and eighty of his partisans.[7] The death of Lat Dior naturally spelled the end of Cayor's independence and facilitated French seizure of the rest of the country.

Tukulor empire

In the Tukulor empire (see Fig. 6.1), Ahmadu, who succeeded his father, Al Hadj 'Umar, the founder of the empire, was, like most African rulers, determined to ensure the survival of his state and maintain its independence and sovereignty. To achieve these objectives, he chose the strategies of alliance and militant confrontation. However, unlike most of the rulers of the region, he relied more on the former rather than on the latter. Indeed, as will be seen below, from his accession until as late as 1890, he still stuck to his policy of alliance or co-operation with the French and it was only in the last two years that he resorted to warfare.

But that Ahmadu should have chosen these strategies should not surprise us since the political and economic realities facing him left him no other alternatives. Politically, right from the beginning of his reign, Ahmadu was forced to fight on three fronts: against his brothers who contested his authority, his subjects – the Bambara, Mandinka, Fulani and others – who deeply detested their new Tukulor masters and sought to recover their independence by force, and against the French. To worsen his plight, not only had the army which his father had used to establish the empire become weakened numerically, numbering only 4000 *talibés*

6. ANSOM – Genouille to the Minister – Senegal I, 86a, 13 November 1886.
7. ibid.

(i.e. students of religion who formed the backbone of 'Umar's army) and 11 000 *sofas* (infantry) by 1866,[8] but he did not have the same sort of control over it nor could he inspire it to the same extent as his father had been able to do. As one would expect, Ahmadu's immediate concerns, then, were first and foremost to consolidate his own position by dealing with his brothers – indeed in 1872 some of his brothers had tried to overthrow him, and then ensuring the survival of the empire by suppressing the rebellions raging among the subject groups, especially the Bambara. To do this, he needed arms and ammunition as well as financial resources through trade, both of which necessitated friendly relations with the French. Furthermore, most of the *talibés* were recruited from Futa Toro, the homeland of his father, and, as this area was under the French, he had to win their co-operation. Confronted with all these internal problems as he was, is it surprising that soon after his accession he agreed to negotiate with the French? The negotiations took place between him and Lieutenant Mage, the representative of the French. Both agreed that in return for the supply of cannon and for the recognition of his authority, Ahmadu was to allow French traders to operate in his empire.[9]

Though this treaty was not ratified by the French administration nor did Ahmadu receive any cannon, and though the French continued to assist the rebels and in 1878 even attacked Saboucire, the Tukulor fortress in Kuasso, Ahmadu continued his friendly attitude towards the French. This served him well for it enabled him to quell the rebellions of his brothers in 1874, and those in the Bambara territories of Segu and Kaarta by the late 1870s. He therefore readily agreed when the French who, in their preparation to conquer the area between the Senegal and the Niger needed the co-operation of Ahmadu, renewed their request for the reopening of negotiations in 1880. These negotiations, concluded by Captain Gallieni, led to the treaty of Mango between him and the French. Under the terms of this treaty, Ahmadu undertook to allow the French to build and maintain trade routes through his empire and granted them permission to build and sail steamboats on the Niger. In return, the French recognized the sovereign existence of his empire, agreed to grant him free access to Futa, and promised not to invade his territory or build any fortifications in it. Above all, the French agreed to give in payment four field guns and 1000 rifles, and to pay a yearly rent of 200 rifles, 200 barrels of gunpowder, 200 artillery shells and 50 000 flints.[10]

This treaty was obviously a great diplomatic victory for Ahmadu, and had the French ratified it and sincerely implemented its terms, there is no doubt that Ahmadu's empire would have survived. But of course even Gallieni himself had no intention of implementing the treaty and in any case his government did not ratify it. Under the new Upper Senegal

8. A. S. Kanya-Forstner in M. Crowder (ed.), 1971, p. 61.
9. ibid., pp. 63–4.
10. ibid., p. 65.

military command headed by Lt.-Colonel Borgnis-Desbordes, the French began their invasion of the empire in 1881 and by February 1883 they had occupied Bamako on the Niger without any opposition. Nor did the Tukulor attack the gunboats launched on the Niger in 1884. Ahmadu's only reaction was to forbid the sale of any item whatsoever to the French.[11] In 1884, at the head of an imposing army, Ahmadu went up the Niger towards Bamako. However, contrary to all expectations, he suddenly headed for Kaarta not to attack or threaten the fragile lines of communication of the French but rather to besiege Nioro, the capital of Kaarta with a view to deposing his brother Moutaga, its king whom he considered as too independent of the central authority.[12]

It is obvious from Ahmadu's attack on his brother rather than on the French, and the fact that the Bambara of the district of Beledugu near Bamako were still in rebellion, that he was still not fully in control in his own territory and that he still needed the support of the French. This surely must account for his reaction to the French invasions between 1881 and 1883. His need for French co-operation was further strengthened by the fact that the siege of Nioro further depleted his military resources. The French, on their part, were also desperate for an alliance with Ahmadu. Between 1885 and 1888, they were engaged in the suppression of the rebellion of the Soninke leader Mamadou Lamine and they were most anxious therefore to prevent any alliance between him and Ahmadu. Hence, although Ahmadu was aware that the French were still aiding the Bambara rebels, he nevertheless agreed to conclude another treaty, the Treaty of Gori, on 12 May 1887. Under its terms, Ahmadu agreed to place his empire under the nominal protection of the French while the French in turn pledged not to invade his territories and to remove the ban that they had placed on the purchase of arms by Ahmadu.

However, by 1888, the French had suppressed Lamine's rebellion and, as will be seen later, concluded another treaty with Samori and therefore did not need an alliance with Ahmadu any longer. This together with the aggressiveness of the French military command led to the assumption of the offensive against Ahmadu signified by their attack on the Tukulor fortress – of Kundian – 'that troublesome obstacle on the road to Siguiri and Dinguiray' in February 1889.[13] The operation was not concluded with all the speed desired. The 'tata' was very solidly built with double walls of masonry while the garrison had removed the thatch roofing to prevent the rapid spread of fire. It took an intensive bombardment of eight hours' duration by Archinard's 80-mm mountain guns to breach the walls. The Tukulor, who had held fast under this deluge, put up a fierce resistance to the French, meeting their bombardment with con-

11. Y. Saint-Martin, 1972, p. 301.
12. ibid., p. 316.
13. ibid., p. 379.

tinued musket fire followed by a house-to-house fight. Many of them perished with their weapons in their hands.[14]

Ahmadu, at grips with his internal difficulties, thereupon transferred the struggle to the religious plane. He appealed to all the Muslims of the empire to take up arms in defence of the faith. Letters requesting help were dispatched to Djoloff, Mauritania and Futa.[15] These steps failed to produce satisfactory results, and Archinard, after careful preparation and the acquisition of adequate arms including 'two 95 mm field-guns with 100 of the latest melinite shells',[16] seized the capital of the empire in April 1890. From there he marched against the fortress of Ouessebougou, defended by the Bambara loyal to Ahmadu. All of them were slain in battle though not without inflicting heavy losses on their assailants. Two of the twenty-seven Europeans were killed and eight of them were wounded while thirteen African soldiers were killed and 876 wounded. From there, Archinard captured Koniakary after having beaten the Tukulor resistance put up against him. Faced with the stubborn resistance of the Tukulor garrisons, Archinard called a halt and requested Ahmadu to capitulate and to go and settle in a Dinguiray village as a mere private individual.

It was not until this point that Ahmadu abandoned his weapon of diplomacy in favour of a military one. In June 1890, his soldiers attacked the railway at Talaari and engaged the French in numerous skirmishes between Kayes and Bafulabe. In one of them, the French lost forty-three killed and wounded out of a force of 125. In September, taking advantage of the isolation of Koniakary by flood, they attempted but failed to reconquer it.[17]

Ahmadu was, however, also preparing to defend Nioro. He divided his troops into four groups with the main body concentrating around Nioro under the command of the Bambara general Bafi and the former king of Djoloff, Alboury N'Diaye.[18] On 23 December 1890, Bassiru's army was routed by the French using their 80-mm and 95-mm guns, and on 1 January 1891, Archinard entered Nioro. Alboury's attempt to retake Nioro on 3 January 1891 failed after the Tukulor army had been routed. The Sultan lost more than 3000 killed or taken prisoner. He retreated to Macina, which he left after the hard-fought battle of Kori-Kori. Even in exile in Hausa territory, he maintained an attitude of 'uncompromising independence' toward the French.[19]

14. ibid., p. 381.
15. ibid., p. 390.
16. A. S. Kanya-Forstner in M. Crowder (ed.), 1971, p. 69.
17. ibid., p. 70.
18. ibid., p. 73.
19. Y. Saint-Martin, 1972, p. 427.

Samori and the French

Unlike Ahmadu, Samori Ture chose the strategy of confrontation, not of alliance, though he used the weapons of both diplomacy and warfare but with the emphasis on the latter. By 1881, Samori had already moulded 'the southern part of the Sudanese savannas all along the great West African forest' between the northern parts of modern Sierra Leone to the Sassandra River in the Ivory Coast, into a single empire under his unquestioned authority[20] (see Fig. 6.1). Unlike the Tukulor empire, the Mandingo empire was still in the ascendant by 1882 when the first encounter between Samori and the French occurred. The conquest of the area had also enabled Samori to build a powerful army relatively well equipped with European arms. This army was divided into two wings, the infantry wing (the *sofa*) which by 1887 numbered between 30 000 and 35 000 men, and the cavalry wing numbering no more than 3000 by 1887. The infantry was divided into permanent units of ten to twenty men known as the *sé* (feet) or *kulu* (heaps) commanded by a *kuntigi* (chief), and ten *sé* formed a *bolo* (arm) under the command of a *bolokuntigi*.[21] The cavalry was divided into bands of fifty called *sèrè*. The *bolo* formed the main striking force while a *sèrè* rode alongside each *bolo*. Since each of these units was permanent, its members developed feelings of friendship first among themselves and of loyalty first to their local leader and then to Samori. Thus the army soon assumed 'a quasi-national character because it achieved a very remarkable homogeneity'.[22] But the unique features of Samori's army were its weapons and training. Unlike most of the armies of West Africa, not only was this army virtually professional, but it was armed by Samori himself. Up to 1876, he armed them with old guns which the local blacksmiths could repair themselves. But from 1876 onwards he also began to order more modern European weapons, mainly from Sierra Leone, and carefully studied them to find those that were most suitable for his area. Thus from 1885, he replaced the Chassepot rifles, whose large cartridges soon rotted in humid conditions, with the more suitable Gras rifles with lighter cartridges, and Kropatscheks which were Gras repeater rifles. He continued to rely on these types until the 1880s since he was able to train a group of blacksmiths who could effectively manufacture copies. From 1888, he also added to his stock some of the new quick-firing rifles and by 1893 he had about 6000 of them which he used until his defeat in 1898. However, he never acquired any artillery which was a great handicap in his campaigns against the French. Arms purchases were financed from the sale of ivory and gold mined from the old medieval goldfields of Bure in the south and from the exchange of slaves for horses in the Sahel and Mossi regions. The army was, however, not only well

20. For a detailed study of the life and activities of Samori, see Y. Person, 1968–75.
21. Y. Person in M. Crowder (ed.), 1971, pp. 121–6.
22. ibid., pp. 121–2.

PLATE 6.1 *Samori Ture (c. 1830–1900) after his capture by the forces of Captain Gouraud (right) in September 1898*

armed but also well trained and disciplined and it developed a high level of *esprit de corps* and homogeneity.

It is evident, then, that Samori was virtually at the height of his power when he first came into contact with the French in 1882. In February of that year he was called upon by Lieutenant Alakamessa who notified him of the order from the Upper Senegal-Niger high command to withdraw from Kenyeran, an important market centre barring Samori's way to the Mandingo areas. As one would expect, Samori refused. This led to a surprise attack on his army by Borgnis-Desbordes who was however forced to beat a hasty retreat. Samori's brother, Kémé-Brema, attacked the French at Wenyako near Bamako in April. Though he won the battle on 2 April, he was defeated on 12 April by a much smaller French army. Samori thereupon tried to avoid conflict with the French and directed his action towards Kenedugu.

In 1885, when Combes occupied Bure, the gold of which was important to the economy of Samori's empire, Samori realized how great was the threat that hung over his state. He resolved to expel the French from the area by force. Three armies, his own and those of Kémé and Masara-Mamadi, were charged with this operation. By a vast pincer movement, Bure was easily recaptured and the French were forced to decamp for fear of being encircled. Samori thereupon decided to cultivate his relations with the British in Sierra Leone. After having occupied Falaba in 1884, he dispatched emissaries to Freetown, to propose to the governor that he place his entire country under the protection of the British government. The offer was a mere manoeuvre on the part of Samori, whose intention was in no way to relinquish his sovereignty but to make the French respect it by allying himself with a powerful government.[23]

When that move failed, Samori turned to the French and signed a treaty with them on 28 March 1886. He agreed to withdraw his troops to the right bank of the Niger, but maintained his rights over Bure and the Mandingo of Kangaba.[24] In another treaty with the French on 25 March 1887 which amended that of the previous year, Samori ceded the left bank of the river to the French and even agreed to place his country under French protection.

Samori had perhaps signed the second document in the hope that the French would help him against Tieba, the Faama of Sikasso whom he attacked in April 1887 with a 12000-strong army, while the French had signed it because they needed to prevent any alliance between Samori and Mamadou Lamine whom they were then fighting. When he saw that instead of behaving as allies and assisting him, the French were rather encouraging dissidence and rebellion in the areas recently subdued and were attempting to prevent him from obtaining supplies of weapons

23. J. D. Hargreaves in L. H. Gann and P. Duignan (eds), 1969, pp. 207–8.
24. ibid., p. 208.

from Sierra Leone, he raised the siege in August 1888 and prepared to take up arms against the invader.[25] He reorganized the army, concluded a treaty with the British in Sierra Leone in May 1890 which enabled him to buy modern weapons for the next three years in increasing quantities, and trained his troops in the European manner. Platoons and companies were activated. He adopted defence as his military tactic. Of course, there could be no question of using the 'tatas' for shelter, as there was no chance that they could hold out against artillery. His strategy consisted of endowing his troops with great mobility, so that they could surprise the enemy, inflict heavy losses upon him, and then disappear.[26]

In March 1890, Archinard captured Segu and in his attempt to defeat Samori before ceding the Upper Senegal-Niger command to Humbert, attacked him in March 1891. Archinard thought that Samori's empire would collapse at the first onslaught. Though that attack resulted in the capturing of Kankan on 7 April and the burning of Bissandugu, its effect was quite the opposite since it not only provided Samori with a salutary warning but it also enabled him to continue the attacks on the French at Kankan and to defeat them at the battle of Dabadugu on 3 September 1891.

The major confrontation between the French and Samori, however, took place in 1892. Bent on defeating Samori, Humbert launched an attack on the central part of the Empire in January 1892 with 1300 carefully picked riflemen and 3000 porters. Samori took personal command of his carefully chosen army of 2500 men to meet Humbert. Though these men 'fighting like demons, clung fiercely to every defensive point on the way', to quote Yves Person's words,[27] they were defeated and Humbert succeeded in capturing Bissandugu, Sanankoro and Kerwane. It is important to note, however, that Humbert himself admitted that the results were very meagre in comparison to the heavy losses that he had sustained. Furthermore, Samori had ordered the civilian population to withdraw at the approach of the French troops.

However, Samori had no illusions. After the violent encounters with the Humbert column in which he lost over a thousand men of his elite units as compared with only about a hundred lost by the French, he became convinced of the futility of confronting the French. There were then two options open to him: either to surrender or to withdraw. He ruled out the former and decided to abandon his homeland and move to the east to create a new empire out of the reach of the Europeans. Still continuing his scorched-earth policy, he began his move eastwards towards the Bandama and Comoe rivers. Though in 1894 he lost the last route supplying him with modern weapons – the one to Monrovia – he nevertheless fought on. At the beginning of 1895, he encountered

25. ibid., p. 209.
26. Y. Person in M. Crowder (ed.), 1971, p. 134.
27. ibid., p. 135.

126

and beat back a French column coming from the Baule country under the command of Monteil, and between July 1895 and January 1896 went on to conquer the Abron (Gyaman) kingdom and the western part of Gonja. By that time, he had succeeded in creating a new empire in the hinterland of the Ivory Coast and Asante (see Fig. 6.1).[28] In March 1897, his son Sarankenyi-Mori met and defeated a British column under the command of Henderson near Wa while Samori himself attacked and destroyed Kong in May 1897 and pushed on to Bobo where he encountered a French column under the command of Caudrelier.

Caught between the French and the British and having vainly attempted to sow discord between the British and the French by returning to the latter the territory of Bouna coveted by the former, Samori decided to return to his Toma allies in Liberia. On the way, he was captured in a surprise attack at Guelemou by Gouraud on 29 September 1898 and deported to Gabon where he died in 1900. His capture brought to an end what a recent scholar has described as 'the longest series of campaigns against a single enemy in the history of French Sudanese conquest'.[29]

Dahomey

Behanzin, the king of Dahomey (Abomey), like Samori, chose the strategy of confrontation in defence of the sovereignty and independence of his state.[30] Direct conflict occurred during the last decade of the nineteenth century when France declared a protectorate over Porto Novo, a vassal of Abomey. This move constituted a serious blow to the economic interests of Abomey. In 1889, the heir to the throne, Prince Kondo, informed the governor of the Rivières de Sud, Bayol, that the Fon people would never accept such a situation. In February 1890, Bayol ordered the occupation of Cotonou and the arrest of all the Fon notables in the town. Prince Kondo, who had begun his reign in December 1889 under the name of Behanzin, reacted by mobilizing his troops. At the time, Abomey had a permanent army which, in peacetime, numbered 4000 men and women. In wartime military service was compulsory for all males, supported by the Amazons, who were dreaded female warriors.

The French garrison was attacked at dusk, at the same time as part of the army dispatched to the region of Porto Novo set about destroying the palm trees. According to Behanzin, those economic counter-measures quickly induced the French to sue for peace. On 3 October, Father Dorgère presented himself in Abomey with proposals for peace. In return for the recognition of Cotonou as a French possession and the right of the French to levy custom duties and station a garrison of troops there, the French were to pay Behanzin an annuity of 20 000 francs. The king accepted these terms and the treaty was signed on 3 October 1890. However, to

28. ibid., p. 138.
29. T. C. Weiskel, 1980, pp. 99–102.
30. D. Ross in M. Crowder (ed.), 1971, p. 144.

defend the rest of his state, the king started to modernize his army. Between January 1891 and August 1892 he purchased, '1,700 rapid-firing rifles, six Krupp cannon of various bore, five machine-guns, 400,000 assorted cartridges and a large quantity of shell'[31] from German firms operating in Lome.

However the French were determined to conquer Dahomey and obtained the necessary excuse when the Resident of Porto Novo, who was making a trip up the Weme River in the gunboat *Topaz*, was fired upon on 27 March 1892 by some Fon soldiers. Colonel Dodds, a Senegalese mulatto, was placed in charge of this mission and arrived at Cotonou in May 1892. Porto Novo, where the French assembled 2000 men, became the centre of operations. Dodds moved his men up the Weme river and, on 4 October, began his march to Abomey. The Fon united all the three divisions of their army of about 12000 strong and moved it against the invading French army between the river and Abomey. However, all the efforts of the Fon soldiers using their traditional methods of surprise dawn attacks, unexpected strikes, defensive stands, harrying invading forces and other guerrilla tactics, failed to halt the French let alone beat them back and they suffered heavy casualties. The losses of the Fon were estimated at 2000 dead (including virtually all the Amazons) and 3000 wounded, while that of the French was only 10 officers and 67 men.[32] But what upset the Fon military plan most was the destruction of the harvest by the Yoruba slaves released by Dodds' army. Abomey was faced with an acute problem of provisions. To avoid starvation, some soldiers went home to search for food and to defend their villages which were being pillaged by the liberated slaves.

With the disintegration of the Fon army, the only solution, needless to say, was peace. Dodds encamped at Cana, accepted the proposals of Behanzin, but demanded payment of a heavy war indemnity and the surrender of all weapons. Such conditions were obviously unacceptable to the very dignity of the Fon people. In November 1892, Dodds, continuing his inexorable advance, entered Abomey, which Behanzin had set on fire before heading to the northern part of his kingdom where he settled. Instead of submitting or being deposed by his people as the French had expected, he rather set about reorganizing his army for which he had the full support of his people. In March 1893, he was able to regroup 2000 men who carried out numerous raids in the areas held by the French. In April 1893, the notables made new proposals for peace. They were prepared to cede the southern part of the kingdom to France but could not accept the deposition of Behanzin, in whom they saw the incarnation of the values of their people and the symbol of the independent existence of their state. The French therefore launched another expeditionary force

31. ibid., p. 158.
32. ibid., p. 160.

in September, again under the command of Dodds, now a general, which succeeded in conquering northern Dahomey. Goutchilli was appointed and crowned king on 15 January 1894 and Behanzin was arrested following a betrayal on 29 January 1894.[33]

The Baule and the French

It used to be thought that opposition to the French in the forest regions of Guinea and Ivory Coast did not begin until after 1900.[34] However, recent research especially among the Lagoon people and the Baule of Ivory Coast has revealed that this view is erroneous and that French penetration from the coast inland evoked hostile reactions from the people right from the beginning.[35] The first French missions into the Baule country from the coast were launched by two expeditions, the military expedition of Lieutenants Armand and de Tavernost in February 1891 and the commercial one of Voituret and Papillon in March 1891. Etien Komenan, the chief of the Baule of Tiassalé, was determined to stop this penetration and refused to give Armand and de Tavernost an interpreter to accompany them to the north. They were therefore obliged to return to the coast; meanwhile, Etien Komenan had Voituret and Papillon assassinated before they could ever reach Tiassalé.[36] To punish the Baule, the French launched a military expedition under the command of Lt Staup but this was attacked by Etien Komenan's forces on 11 May 1891 and forced to beat an ignominious retreat to the coast. When force failed, the French resorted to diplomacy and succeeded in concluding a treaty with the Baule of Tiassalé and Niamwé on 29 December 1892 under which they agreed to pay a tribute of 100 oz of gold in exchange for free trade with the Africans and Europeans on the coast. It was in the light of this treaty that the French sent their second exploratory mission into Baule country in March 1893 under the command of Jean-Baptiste Marchand who was already well known for his military exploits in the Western Sudan. Halfway up the Bandama *en route* to Tiassalé, Marchand encountered the opposition of Etien Komenan who had resolved that 'no white man would pass through Tiassalé'.[37] Marchand therefore returned to Grand Lahou and having collected a force of about 120 men, embarked on an invasion of Tiassalé on 18 May 1893 which he occupied a week later after Etien Komenan had fled. From there, Marchand resumed his march northwards and in November 1893 entered Gbuékékro which was later to be renamed Bouaké by the French. Here, he was opposed by the chief of the town, Kouassi Gbuèké, who was then in alliance

33. ibid., p. 166.
34. M. Crowder, 1968, p. 95; J. Bony, 1980, pp. 14–15.
35. T. C. Weiskel, 1980, pp. 33–141; S. Koffi, 1976, pp. 120–89.
36. T. C. Weiskel, 1980, pp. 38–9.
37. ibid., p. 44.

with Samori. Marchand had therefore to press on to Kong from where he sent a strong appeal to Paris to dispatch an expedition to occupy Kong with a view to forestalling both Samori and the British as well as signing a treaty with the Dyula of Kong. It was in response to this appeal that the expedition under Monteil was launched in September 1894, which entered Tiassalé in December 1894.

Monteil's expedition encountered an even more determined resistance from the Baule who revolted and attacked them at Ouossou north of Tiassalé, at Ahuakro and at Moronou between 25 and 28 December. It was because of this determined Baule opposition that Monteil was ordered to return to the coast in February 1895.

The period from 1895 to 1898 was one of peace in Baule territory. However, after defeating and capturing Samori in September 1898, the French decided to begin an effective occupation of Baule territory, and therefore began to build a permanent military post at Bouaké without consulting the Baule. They also began to free slaves and they captured and executed Katia Kofi, the chief of Katiakofikro, for fomenting anti-French feelings in that area. Mainly as a result of these provocations, the Baule groups in that area once again rose up in rebellion and on 22 December 1898 launched an all-out attack on the French garrisons in that area, led by Kouadio Okou, chief of Lomo; Yao Guié, a Ngban chief; Kasso, the brother of the murdered chief of Katiakofikro; Akafou Bulare, another Ngban chief; and Kouamé Dié, the paramount chief of the Warebo Baule. In reply, the French declared the Baule area a military territory and launched a series of campaigns. These resulted in the capture of the Baule gold-mining centre of Kokumbo from a Baule defence force of 1500 to 2000 men in June 1901, in the capturing and shooting of the great Kouamé Dié in February 1902 and the capture of Akafou Bulare (Akafou, the Man of Iron) who was beaten to death in his cell in July 1902. But, resorting to guerrilla tactics, the Baule continued to harass the French forces and peace was not restored until François-Joseph Clozel, who became the acting governor of the colony in November 1902, realized the futility of force and ordered a halt to military operations.[38]

Conquest and reaction in British West Africa, 1880–1900

While the French resorted mainly to warfare in their occupation of French West Africa during the period 1880 to 1900, the British, by contrast, used a combination of peaceful diplomacy and warfare. Using the former approach, they concluded a number of treaties of protection with African states as they did in the northern parts of Sierra Leone, the northern

38. For details of all these campaigns and the guerrilla and other methods that the Baule used, see T. C. Weiskel, 1980, pp. 98–141.

parts of the Gold Coast (now Ghana) and in some parts of Yorubaland. In other parts, as in Asante, Ijebu in Yorubaland, in the Niger Delta areas and especially in Northern Nigeria, however, the British by and large used force. In reacting to the British, the peoples of the area in question, like those in French West Africa, resorted to all the options open to them, those of confrontation, alliance and submission or a combination of any of these options. Let us analyse what happened in Asante, Southern Nigeria and in Northern Nigeria as cases in point.

Asante (Gold Coast)

Nowhere in West Africa had there been a longer tradition of confrontation between Africans and Europeans than in the Gold Coast between the Asante and the British. This started in the 1760s and culminated in a military engagement in 1824 in which the Asante defeated the British forces and their allies and killed their commander, Sir Charles MacCarthy, the then Governor of the Gold Coast.[39] Two years later, the British avenged this defeat at the battle of Dodowa. In 1850 and 1863 war was narrowly averted but between 1869 and 1872, the Asante launched a three-pronged attack which resulted in the occupation of virtually all the southern and coastal states of the Gold Coast. To beat back the Asante, the British government launched one of the best organized campaigns of the period under the command of one of the most famous British officers of the day, General Garnet Wolseley. Armed with the latest weapons, this army succeeded in pushing the Asante army across the Pra river and entered and sacked Kumasi in February 1874 after a very fierce last-ditch stand by the Asante army at Amoafo near Bekwai.[40]

This decisive defeat of the Asante by the British in 1874 had very far-reaching consequences and was to influence, to a great extent, the reactions of the Asante during the period 1880–1900. The first obvious effect was the disintegration of the Asante empire. By the Treaty of Fomena, Asante recognized the independence of all the vassal states south of the Pra. Taking advantage of the weakening of the military power of Asante, the vassal states to the north of the Volta river also broke away. Even the core of the empire that remained began to break up. Anxious to see that the Asante empire was never revived, the British instigated some of the member states of the Asante Union to assert their independence, and Dwaben, Kokofu, Bekwai and Nsuta began to defy the Asantehene.[41] The conflict between Kumasi and Dwaben in fact led to a civil war which ended in the defeat of the former and the mass migration of the

39. For details about the rise of Asante, see J. K. Fynn in M. Crowder (ed.), 1971, pp. 19–33; A. A. Boahen, 1966; A. A. Boahen in J. F. A. Ajayi and M. Crowder (eds), 1974.
40. J. K. Fynn in M. Crowder (ed.), 1971, pp. 36–42.
41. ibid., p. 43.

people into the recently proclaimed British Protectorate and Colony of the Gold Coast. Above all, the Asantehene was deposed partly as a result of the outcome of the 1874 war. On the death of his successor only seven years later, a civil war broke out over the succession and it was not until 1888 that Prempeh I emerged as the new Asantehene.

Fortunately, Prempeh proved equal to the crisis with which he was confronted. Within three years of his succession, he was able to reunite the member states of the Asante Union (or Confederacy) and even to persuade the Dwaben to return home. Alarmed partly by this revival of Asante and partly by the possibility of either the French or the Germans taking over Asante, the British offered to place Asante under their protection. Prempeh's firm but polite rejection of this offer is quoted elsewhere.[42] Prempeh followed up this rejection with an invasion and defeat of the Nkoransa, the Mo and the Abease in 1892. In reaction, the British offered to station a British Resident at Kumasi in return for the payment of annual stipends to the Asantehene and his other leading kings. Not only did the Asantehene reject this offer but dispatched a high-powered mission to the Queen of England 'to lay before your Majesty divers matters affecting the good estate of our kingdom'.[43] This diplomatic mission left Kumasi in November 1894 attended by over three hundred retainers. It entered Cape Coast on 10 December and left for England on 3 April 1895. Not only did the British government refuse to see the Asante mission but, while it was still there, instructed the governor on the coast to issue an ultimatum to the Asantehene to receive a British Resident and pay the war indemnity of 50000 oz of gold imposed on Asante in 1874. Of course, the Asantehene refused to comply with these requests, all the more so since he was awaiting the outcome of the mission to London.

Using this as an excuse, the British launched a full-scale expedition against Asante under the command of Sir Francis Scott. This expedition entered Kumasi in January 1896 without firing a shot since Prempeh and his advisors had decided not to fight the British but to accept British protection. In spite of this, Prempeh, his mother who was also then the Queen, his uncles and some of the war chiefs were arrested and deported first to Sierra Leone and thence to the Seychelles Islands in 1900.[44] (See Plate 6.2.)

Why did the Asante decide not to fight the British on this occasion? Fortunately, we have Prempeh's own answer to this question while he was in exile on the Seychelles Islands. When his chiefs demanded war with the British, Prempeh first recalled the days of the civil war in Kumasi and the role the British had played in bringing about peace as well as his enstoolment and then added: 'through this favour received in the hands of the English Government, I am not prepared to fight the British troops in spite [sic] I am to be captured by them – secondly, I would

42. See Chapter 1 above.
43. I. Wilks, 1975, pp. 637–41.
44. A. A. Boahen, 1977.

PLATE 6.2 *Nana Prempeh I of Asante (c. 1872–1931) during his exile in the Seychelles (c. 1908). Seated on his right is Nana Yaa Asantewaa, Queen of Edweso and leader of the 1900 Asante rebellion, and, on his left, his mother and father*

133

rather surrender to secure the lives and tranquillity of my people and country men.'[45]

The unfortunate Prempeh thought that he could break with tradition and use the weapon of diplomacy instead of military confrontation in an age of bitter imperial rivalry. But in view of the experiences of 1874 and the undoubted military superiority enjoyed by the British over Asante, Prempeh's decision was most realistic, sensible and dignified.

Southern Nigeria

The agencies and methods that the British adopted to bring the whole of modern Nigeria under their control varied, as did the initiatives and reactions on the part of the Nigerians. Yorubaland was won by the missionaries and the Lagos government; the Oil Rivers by the missionaries and the consuls; and Northern Nigeria by both the National African Company (from 1886 the Royal Niger Company) and the British government. The main weapons used by the British were diplomacy and military confrontation. Nigerian reactions therefore varied from open military confrontation to temporary alliances and submission.

Mainly as a result of the activities of the missionaries, British influence and trade had penetrated from Lagos, occupied in 1851, to most parts of Yorubaland, and a number of anti-slave trade, and trade and protection treaties had been concluded between the British and many Yoruba rulers by 1884. In 1886, the British administration was also able to convince Ibadan and the Ekitiparapo (comprising the Ekiti, Ijesha and Egba), who had been at war since 1879, to sign a peace treaty. That the British had accomplished so much in Yorubaland by 1886 should not surprise us. Apart from the activities of the European traders and missionaries, which had preceded the wars, after fighting among themselves since the 1850s, the Yoruba were themselves war-weary and needed peace; hence their acceptance of the intervention by the British. The only state in Yorubaland that had effectively resisted the missionaries, the British traders, and the Lagos administration, until the 1880s was Ijebu. Bent on occupying Yorubaland from the early 1890s, the British decided to teach Ijebu a lesson and at the same time demonstrate to the remaining Yoruba states the futility of opposing them.[46] Using an alleged insult to Governor Denton in 1892 as a pretext, the British launched a well-prepared expedition of about 1000 men armed with rifles, machine guns and a Maxim gun. The Ijebu courageously raised an army of between 7000 and 10000 men but in spite of this huge numerical superiority and in spite of the fact that some of them were armed with firearms, they were routed by the invaders.[47] It would appear that all the remaining

45. Quoted in ibid.
46. M. Crowder, 1968, pp. 126–7.
47. R. Smith in M. Crowder (ed.), 1971, p. 180.

Yoruba states learnt a lesson from this invasion, and it is not surprising that between 1893 and 1899 Abeokuta, Ibadan, Ekiti-Ijesa and Oyo readily agreed to negotiate treaties and accepted British residents. It was merely to ensure the total submission of the Alafin that the British bombarded Oyo in 1895. Abeokuta remained nominally independent until 1914.

While the Yoruba, by and large, chose the strategy of submission, the rulers of the kingdom of Benin and some of the rulers of the states of the Niger Delta chose that of confrontation. Though Benin had signed a treaty of protection with the British in 1892, she none the less guarded her sovereignty with determination. This, of course, would not be tolerated in that age, and using the killing of the British acting consul-general and five other Englishmen on their way to Benin as an excuse, the British launched a punitive expedition of 1500 men against Benin in 1897. Though the Oba himself would have liked to submit, a majority of his chiefs raised an army to beat back the invasion. They were, however, defeated and the capital was looted of its precious bronze treasures and then burnt.[48]

In the Niger Delta, as in many other areas of Nigeria, the British had signed treaties of protection with most of the chiefs by 1884. However, while some, like Calabar and Bonny, had allowed missionaries to operate in their states, others had not. Moreover, all of them were insisting on their sovereign rights to regulate trade and to levy duties on British traders. This, the new British consuls, such as Hewett and Johnston, would not tolerate. A typical example of the rulers who stood up to the British consuls and missionaries was Jaja of Opobo (see Plate 6.3). He insisted on payment of duties by British traders and ordered a complete stoppage of trade in the river until one British firm agreed to pay duties. The consul, Johnston, ordered him to stop levying duties on English traders. But instead of doing so, Jaja dispatched a mission to the Foreign Office to protest against the order. When Jaja still refused to comply in spite of Johnston's threats to bombard his town with British gunboats, Johnston enticed Jaja on board a ship in 1887 under a promise of safe-conduct but arrested him and sent him to Accra[49] where he was tried and deported to the West Indies. The other Delta states – Old Calabar, New Calabar, Brass and Bonny – stunned by this treatment of one of the most powerful and wealthy rulers of the Delta states and divided internally, surrendered and accepted governing councils imposed on them by Johnston.

Another ruler who defied the British was Nana, the governor of the river in the Itsekiri kingdom. Like Jaja, he insisted on controlling the trade on the Benin river and therefore the British raised an army to seize his capital. The first attempt in April 1894 was repulsed but the second, in September, succeeded. Nana escaped to Lagos where he sur-

48. J. B. Webster and A. A. Boahen, 1967, pp. 247–9.
49. M. Crowder, 1968, pp. 119–23; O. Ikime, 1973, p. 10.

PLATE 6.3 *Jaja* (c. *1821–91*), *ruler of the Niger delta state of Opobo* (*1869–87*)

rendered himself to the British governor who promptly tried him and deported him first to Calabar and then to the Gold Coast.[50]

Conquest and Reaction in Northern Nigeria

If the conquest and occupation of Southern Nigeria was the work of the British government with the assistance of the traders and the missionaries, that of Northern Nigeria was accomplished by the National African Company (from 1886 the Royal Niger Company – RNC) and the British government, and the main method used, like that of the French in the Western Sudan, was military conquest. This had been preceded by a series of treaties between the rulers of Northern Nigeria and the RNC. These treaties were calculated to secure the area for the British rather than the French or the Germans who were encroaching from the west and east respectively.

Following the establishment of the principle of effective occupation at the Berlin Conference and to forestall the French and the Germans, the RNC felt compelled to move in. The doors to the north lay through Ilorin and Nupe, both of which were determined to maintain their independence and sovereignty. Nupe was therefore invaded in 1897. The RNC's force, according to D. J. M. Muffett, 'consisted of Major A. R. Arnold, commanding thirty-one officers and other Europeans, including Sir George Goldie himself, and 507 rank and file formed in seven companies, supported by 565 carriers and one 12-pounder B.L. gun and one 9-pounder B.L. gun (both Whitworth's), five R.M.L. (rifled muzzle loading) 7-pounder guns and six .45 Maxims'.[51] It was supported by a flotilla consisting of eleven vessels. The Etsu of Nupe and his huge army, estimated at 25 000–30 000 cavalry and infantry men and armed mainly with the traditional weapons of bows, arrows, spears and swords, put up a spirited fight. Nevertheless, the RNC came out victorious in the end, deposed the Etsu and installed a more pliable one. Nupe was defeated because, as Crowder has pointed out, it failed to realize that 'head-on cavalry charges against rapid-firing rifles, artillery and maxim guns was the worst military strategy possible'.[52] A similar invasion was launched against Ilorin in the same year. After meeting another spirited defence, the RNC brought Ilorin into subjection.

Surprisingly, other rulers of the north were not intimidated by these victories. On the contrary, apart from that of Zaria, all the other emirs, spurred on by their implacable hatred for the infidel, were determined to die rather than surrender their land and faith. As the Sultan of Sokoto informed Lugard in May 1902, 'Between us and you there are no dealings except as between musulmans and unbelievers ... War as God Almighty

50. O. Ikime in M. Crowder (ed.), 1971, pp. 227–8.
51. D. J. M. Muffett in M. Crowder (ed.), 1971, pp. 283–4.
52. M. Crowder, 1968, p. 131.

has enjoined on us'.[53] The British therefore had to launch a series of campaigns – against Kontagora in 1900, Adamawa in 1901, Bauchi in 1902, Kano, Sokoto and Burwuri in 1903.[54] The rulers of all these emirates rose to the occasion but they had no effective answer to their enemies' Maxim guns, rifles and muzzle-loading 7-pounder cannon and therefore suffered defeat.

African Reactions and Responses in West Africa,

1900–14

As is evident from the above, by 1900, the efforts of the Africans to maintain their sovereignty and independence had been frustrated and the period from 1900 to the outbreak of the First World War saw the introduction of various kinds of machinery for the administration and above all, for the exploitation of the newly acquired estates. As Angoulvant, who was appointed Governor of the Ivory Coast in August 1908, put it:

> What has to be established above all is the indisputable principle of our authority ... On the part of the natives, the acceptance of this principle must be expressed in a deferential welcome and absolute respect for our representatives whoever they may be, in the full payment of taxes at a uniform rate of 2.50 francs, in serious co-operation in the construction of tracks and roads, in the acceptance of paid porterage, in the following of our advice [sic] in regard to labour, in recourse to our justice ... Signs of impatience or disrespect towards our authority, and the deliberate lack of goodwill are to be repressed without delay.[55]

In all the newly acquired colonies, the objectives outlined here were pursued and the methods were applied. District commissioners and travelling commissioners were appointed, new courts were established, new codes and new laws were introduced, chiefs were confirmed or deposed and new ones appointed, direct and indirect taxation was introduced, and forced labour was demanded for the construction of roads and railways. All these measures naturally generated various reactions.

During this second phase, while there were differences in the objectives in view, the strategy adopted for the attainment of these objectives by West Africans was the same. The main objectives were three: to regain their independence and sovereignty, which implied expelling the colonial

53. D. J. M. Muffett in M. Crowder (ed), 1971, pp. 284–7.

54. The British campaigns in Northern Nigeria and the brave resistance of the rulers are too well known to be discussed here. For details, see D. J. M. Muffett in M. Crowder (ed.), 1971; R. A. Adeleye, 1971; M. Last, 1967.

55. Quoted by J. Suret-Canale, 1971, pp. 97–8.

rulers altogether; to seek to correct or redress certain specific abuses or oppressive aspects of the colonial system; or to seek accommodation within it. The strategy that was adopted during this phase was neither submission nor alliance but that of resistance and this took many forms: revolts or rebellions, migrations, strikes, boycotts, petitions and delegations and finally ideological protest. The leadership during this period also remained virtually the same as that between 1880 and 1900, that is mainly that of the traditional rulers. Briefly let us illustrate each of these strategies.

The most popular weapon used by West Africans during this period was rebellion or revolt. Notable among rebellions was that led by Mamadou Lamine in Senegal between 1885 and 1887; that led by Fode Silla, the marabout king of Kombo; and Fode Kabba, the Muslim ruler of Niamina and the Casamance districts in The Gambia between 1898 and 1901; the Hut Tax rebellion of 1898 in Sierra Leone led by Bai Bureh; the Asante rebellion of 1900 in the Gold Coast led by Yaa Asantewaa, the queen of Edweso; the Ekumeku rebellion of 1898–1900 and the Aro rising between 1898 and 1902 in eastern Nigeria; the rebellions of the Bariba of Borgu and the Somba of Atacora in Dahomey between 1913 and 1914; the Mossi rebellions in Koudougou and Fada N'Gurma in Upper Volta from 1908 to 1914; that of the Gurunsi in 1915–16; that of the Lobi and the Djoula in French Sudan between 1908 and 1909; the uprising in Porto Novo in Dahomey; the revolts of the Baule, Akouse, Sassandra and the Guro in Ivory Coast between 1900 and 1914; and the numerous uprisings in several parts of Guinea between 1908 and 1914. It is interesting to note that these rebellions increased in intensity during the First World War.[56] Three typical examples which must be looked at in a little detail to illustrate the nature and motives of these revolts are the rebellion led by Mamadou Lamine, the Hut Tax rebellion, and the Yaa Asantewaa rebellion.

The rebellion of Mamadou Lamine

The rebellion of Mamadou Lamine was directed against foreign domination. The Soninke population was scattered among the various states comprising the territory of Upper Senegal. Some of them were by 1880 more or less subjected to French authority, the others to that of Ahmadu. Construction work on the telegraph line and the Kayes–Niger railway line required large numbers of workers, recruited principally among the Soninke. The exhausting labour and the precarious living conditions which were their lot caused a high death rate among them. As a result, a movement of protest arose directly not only against the daily humiliations but

56. For details of all these revolts, see O. Ikime, 1973; A. E. Afigbo, 1973; B. O. Oloruntimehin, 1973(b); J. Osuntokun, 1977; M. Crowder, 1977(c); J. Suret-Canale, 1971, pp. 93–107; M. Crowder, 1968; (ed.), 1971; A. Duperray, 1978; I. Kimba, 1979; G. Yapé, 1977; M. Michel, 1982; T. C. Weiskel, 1980; S. Koffi, 1976. See also Chapter 12.

especially against foreign presence in the region.[57] Mamadou Lamine acted as a catalyst to this movement by grouping around him all the past or present victims of the new socio-political order. It was with the envied title of pilgrim that he returned, in 1885, to his homeland, then in the throes of a triple crisis, at once political, economic and social. In his first public sermons, he applied himself to transferring the crisis to a religious plane, favouring the strict Sanūsiyya doctrine, which refused to permit Muslims to live under any non-Islamic authority. That was enough to bring about the spontaneous adherence of the Soninke to his programme. His travels in Khasso, Guoy, Bambuck and Bondu daily saw new numbers of his countrymen rally to the cause. By the end of 1885, he had imposing forces at his disposal, ready to go to battle for freedom.

The death of Boubacar Saada, the Almamy of Bondu and a French protégé, provided him with the opportunity to launch his offensive. Omar Penda, imposed by France as the late Almamy's successor, refused to grant Mamadou Lamine permission to pass through Bondu on his way to The Gambia. The Soninke chief thereupon invaded Bondu in January 1886. Frey, who was on the Niger, dispatched contingents to Kayes and Bakel to secure his rear. Mamadou Lamine then gave his movement a radical turn. His sermons thereafter concerned only total war against Christians.[58] The Soninke condemned the French as well as their African allies such as Omar Penda of Bondu, Sambala of Medina and the farmers established in Bakel, Medina and Kayes. Some Soninke in French service joined Mamadou Lamine's camp while others established in the French posts furnished him with information concerning French troop movements.

Against the superior weaponry of the enemy, Mamadou Lamine could count on the numerical superiority and fanaticism of his soldiers, who were convinced they were fighting for God and their country. After his defeat at Bakel, he resorted to guerrilla warfare. In March 1886, Mamadou Lamine decided to attack Bakel, which symbolized the French presence in the area and the humiliation of the Soninke people. He established a blockade of the city, occupying all its approaches with troops. When Captain Jolly attempted to loosen his grip by attacking the Soninke based at Koungani, he was forced to beat a hasty retreat, leaving ten dead and a cannon on the scene. Mamadou Lamine thereupon stormed the city with his 10 000 men. The assault failed. With victory but a hair's breadth away, the Soninke headquarters was wiped out by a shell. In the confusion which followed, Mamadou Lamine's warriors fled.[59] Nevertheless, on his orders, the telegraph line between Bakel and Kayes was cut.

The experience at Bakel taught Lamine that with the weapons at his

57. A. K. Tandia, 1973, p. 83.
58. ibid., p. 89.
59. ibid., p. 92.

disposal, he would never be able to seize fortified French posts. He therefore took to guerrilla warfare. Frey, who had returned from Niger, terrorized the populations of Guidimakha to wean them away from Mamadou Lamine's cause. Their villages were burned, their crops and livestock confiscated. That policy only strengthened the Soninke in their determination to rid their country of the French. Mamadou Lamine devoted the rainy season of 1886 to reorganizing his forces. He set up his headquarters at Diana in Upper Gambia, where he erected a fortress that became a centre of propaganda and a base of operations. In July, the Soninke attacked Senoudebou, reconquered Boulebane and executed Omar Penda, the French protégé of Bondu.[60] After 1887, the alliance between Gallieni and Ahmadu against the Soninke precipitated the failure of the uprising. Souaibou, Mamadou Lamine's son, attacked by Ahmadu's army, was forced to surrender Diafounou and Guidimakha to the son of Al Hadj 'Umar. While attempting to rejoin his father, he was captured and executed. In December 1887, Lamine was finally defeated at Touba-Kouta by the French with the help of the auxiliaries furnished by Moussa Molo of the Upper Casamance.

The Hut Tax rebellion

The Hut Tax rebellion of 1898 was the response of the Temne and the Mende of Sierra Leone to the consolidation of British rule over them by the appointment of district commissioners, the expansion of the frontier police, the abolition of the slave trade and slavery, the implementation of the Protectorate Ordinance of 1896 which empowered the government to dispose of waste land and, finally, the imposition of a tax of 5s a year on all two-roomed houses and 10s on all larger houses in the Protectorate.[61] All the Temne chiefs unanimously decided not to pay the tax and rose up in rebellion under the leadership of one of them, Bai Bureh (see Plate 6.4). They were joined by the Mende people thereby involving almost three-quarters of the Protectorate. The rebel forces attacked and looted trading stations and killed British officials and troops and all those suspected of assisting the colonial government. As one district commissioner reported in April 1898, 'The object appears to be the massacre of all Sierra Leoneans (i.e. the Creoles of Freetown) and Europeans and thoroughly it is being done. The country is destroyed as regards Trade – several traders being killed and places burnt'.[62] By May 1898, the rebel armies were within about 40 km of Freetown and two companies of troops had to be hastily brought in from Lagos to defend the town.

What was the true nature of this revolt? The British governor of Sierra

60. ibid., p. 95.
61. This section is based on J. A. Langley, n.d.
62. ibid.

PLATE 6.4 *Bai Bureh* (c. *1845*–c. *1908*), *leader of the 1898 Hut Tax rebellion in Sierra Leone, pictured after his arrest*

Leone, who was stunned by the rebellion, attributed not only that rebellion but the general resistance to colonial rule that was raging at the time to 'the growing political consciousness of the African, and his increasing sense of his worth and autonomy'. As he put it, 'the native is beginning to feel his strength from the value that is set on him for the products of his country and his labour by the white man and in future the latter will not be able to trade so much on his simplicity and ignorance of the world as in the past'.[63] Governor Cardew's analysis cannot be faulted and is equally true of most of the rebellions and guerrilla wars that occurred in West Africa between the late 1890s and 1914.

The Yaa Asantewaa War

Like the Hut Tax rebellion of 1898, the Asante uprising of 1900 was precipitated by the attempts of the British to consolidate their rule by the deposition of some of the anti-British chiefs and the appointment to replace them of people who were not traditionally qualified, and by the imposition of a tax, in this case 4s per head, as a war indemnity in 1897. But the last straw that really precipitated action was the demand of the British governor, Arnold Hodgson, for the Golden Stool to be sent to him so that he could sit on it. The Golden Stool was the most sacred object of the Asante, which they considered as the embodiment of their soul and a symbol of their survival as a nation. That demand, therefore, could not but touch off an instantaneous rebellion of nearly all the principal states under the leadership of the Queen of Edweso, Nana Yaa Asantewaa (see Plate 6.2).[64]

The Asante forces attacked the Governor and his party who had to seek refuge in the fort at Kumasi which the Asante then besieged. When the governor and his party escaped from the fort, the Asante fought several pitched battles with the British which lasted from April to November 1900 when Yaa Asantewaa was arrested and deported with other Asante generals to the Seychelles.

Similar revolts, pitched battles and guerrilla warfare raged in the Ivory Coast in response to the brutal methods including forced labour and high taxation used by that cruel Governor, Angoulvant, for the consolidation of French rule and the exploitation of the colony. This resistance by the Baule which broke out in 1908 continued until 1910 when, using the notorious search and destroy tactics, the French suppressed all remaining opposition with a brutality and wickedness unparalleled in the annals of African resistance (see Plate 6.5a). At the end of this, the population of the Baule had dropped from about 1.5 million in 1900 to about 260000

---

63. ibid.
64. For details, see J. K. Fynn in M. Crowder (ed.), 1971, pp. 46–9.

PLATE 6.5(a) *French officers display the head of an African during the suppression of resistance in the Ivory Coast in the early 1900s*

PLATE 6.5(b) *Chiefs surrender to Lieutenant Boudet after resisting the French conquest of the Ivory Coast*

144

by 1911.[65] The neighbours of the Baule, the Guro, the Dan and the Bete held out till 1919.

Mass Migration

But revolts and rebellions were not the only strategy of resistance adopted by West Africans from 1900 to 1914. One widespread method of resistance was mass migration in protest against the harshness of colonial rule. This was particularly common in the French colonies where, unable to resort to armed revolt owing to the stationing of military control units in the annexed sector, the Africans resorted to fleeing, in order to elude the measures that they found so oppressive and humiliating. Thus between 1882 and 1889, the Fulani population of the suburbs of Saint-Louis migrated in large numbers towards Ahmadu's empire. Of the 30 000 Fulani living in the suburbs in 1882, only 10 000 remained in 1889. In 1916 and 1917 more than 12 000 people left the Ivory Coast for the Gold Coast. Large numbers also left Senegal for The Gambia, Upper Volta for the Gold Coast, and Dahomey for Nigeria during the period.[66] It should be pointed out that these rebellions and protest migrations were resorted to, by and large, by the rural folk and in the inland parts of those colonies whose direct contact with the Europeans dated only from the 1880s and 1890s. In the coastal areas and new urban centres where the educated elite lived and where a working class was emerging, less violent options were resorted to. These included strikes, boycotts, ideological protest, the use of newspapers and, above all, the dispatch of petitions and delegations to the local as well as the metropolitan colonial governments by various societies and movements.

Strikes

Strikes as a weapon of protest became more common after the First World War, but there were a few in the period before. A strike by railway workers on the Dakar–Saint-Louis line occurred as early as 1890; in 1891 there was the strike of Dahomey women who were employed in the Cameroons; labourers went on strike for higher pay in Lagos in 1897, an action described by Basil Davidson as 'the first major colonial strike';[67] in 1918–19 occurred a strike of the Cotonou and Grand Popo paddlers in Dahomey; and in 1919 the first strike of dockers at the Conakry port in Guinea.[68]

65. J. Suret-Canale, 1971, pp. 95–103. For details of the final phase of Baule resistance, see T. C. Weiskel, 1980, pp. 172–210; J. Bony, 1980, pp. 17–29.
66. A. I. Asiwaju, 1976(b).
67. B. Davidson, 1978(b), p. 173; A. G. Hopkins, 1966(b).
68. J. Suret-Canale, 1977, pp. 46–50.

Ideological protest

Ideological protest was seen during the period under review mainly in the religious field: among Christians, Muslims and Traditionalists. Thus, as B. O. Oloruntimehin has shown, the adherents of the traditional religion among the Mossi of Upper Volta, the Lobi and the Bambara of French Sudan banded together against the spread of French culture as well as the Christian and Muslim religions. The adherents of the Islamic religion especially in the Western Sudan belt also revived Mahdism or founded movements such as Mouridiyya led by Shaikh Ahmadu Bamba and the Hamalliyya led by Shaikh Hamallah to protest against the French presence.[69] The African Christians, especially in the British West African colonies, also rebelled against the European domination of the churches and the imposition of European culture and liturgy. This resulted in the breakaway of these members to form their own messianic or millenarian or Ethiopian churches with distinctively African liturgies and doctrines. Such, for example, was the Native Baptist Church, the first African church formed in Nigeria in April 1888.[70]

Elite associations

Many clubs and associations were also formed by the educated Africans mainly in the urban centres as vehicles for protest against the abuse and iniquities of colonial systems during this period. These associations used newspapers, plays, tracts and pamphlets as their main weapons.[71] Examples of such bodies, which acted as watch dogs of colonial rule, were the Aborigines Rights Protection Society (ARPS) formed in the Gold Coast in 1897, the Young Senegalese Club founded in 1910, and the Peoples Union and the Anti-Slavery and Aborigines Protection Society formed in Nigeria in 1908 and 1912 respectively. The ARPS was easily the most active. It was formed to protest against the Land Bill of 1896 which was to give control of all so-called waste or unoccupied lands to the government. As a result of a delegation it dispatched to London in 1898 which met the Secretary of State for Colonies, this obnoxious Bill was withdrawn. From then on, the ARPS sent a series of petitions to the local administration as well as the Colonial Office protesting against various projected Bills. It sent two delegations to England, one in 1906 to demand the repeal of the 1894 Towns Ordinance and the second in 1911 to oppose the Forestry Bill of 1910. It was certainly the most successful of the mouthpieces of the elite and traditional rulers of West Africa and the greatest opponent of colonialism until the formation of the National Congress of British West Africa after the First World War. In French

69. B. O. Oloruntimehin, 1973(b), pp. 32–3.
70. E. A. Ayandele, 1966, pp. 194–8.
71. F. Omu, 1978.

West Africa, the Young Senegalese Club formed in 1910 also actively campaigned for equal rights.

It should be evident from this discussion that the peoples of West Africa devised all kinds of strategies and tactics first to oppose the establishment of the colonial system and second, after the failure of their early efforts, to resist certain specific measures and institutions of the system. These various strategies and measures proved on the whole unsuccessful, and by the end of the period under review, colonialism had become firmly entrenched in the whole of West Africa.

The causes of failure

Every case of resistance and armed insurrection went down to defeat, at least if one considers only the results at the scene of action. And yet the West Africans lacked neither courage nor military science. But they were at a heavy disadvantage in the face of the invaders. Apart from the technical superiority of their enemies' weapons, they had no real compensatory advantage over the conquerors. To be sure, they had a better knowledge of their country, and the severity of the climate, which forced the Europeans to suspend operations during certain periods of the year, occasionally provided them with some respite. But the bulk of the conquering troops were Africans officered by Europeans. Hence these riflemen were not out of their element. Frequently the West Africans, like the Maghribians (see Chapter 5) did not even have the advantage of greater numbers. Often behind the regular troops of the invaders, there marched thousands of African auxiliaries from annexed or protected territories whose chief function was systematically to pillage the country in conflict with their protector so as to disrupt its internal organization. Moreover, the West African states never succeeded in setting up an organic alliance that would compel their enemies to do battle simultaneously on several fronts. Certain states clearly perceived the necessity for this, but their attempts to bring it about came to naught. Most of the resisters resorted to guerrilla warfare too late, when they had learned through defeat that neither conventional warfare nor the defensive systems of the 'tatas' left them any chance of success in the face of enemies possessing weapons capable of greater destruction. To all that must be added the fact, already pointed out above, that in 1890 the imperialists, by the Brussels Convention, reached an agreement that no further arms should be sold to Africans. Thereafter, the Africans encountered severe logistic problems. Finally, like Africans elsewhere, those of West Africa, except Samori, had to use outmoded weapons such as dane guns and bows and arrows in the face of cannon and the Maxim gun. In the combination of all these factors lay the source of the African defeat.

Looking back over this heroic period of African history, the question obviously suggests itself whether resistance was not 'heroic madness' or a criminal attitude. These authors do not believe so. It matters little, from their standpoint, that the African armies should have suffered defeat at the hands of better equipped enemies, so long as the cause for which the resisters laid down their lives continues to haunt the minds of their descendants.

African initiatives and resistance in East Africa, 1880–1914

7

H. A. MWANZI

Much has been written about the African response to foreign penetration and eventual rule towards the end of the last century and the beginning of the present. Most of the discussion, if not all of it, has been centred on the dichotomy between resisters, who by implication are to be praised as heroes, and so-called collaborators, who also by implication are to be condemned as traitors. This classification came about as a result of the nationalist struggle for independence in Africa, as elsewhere in the world. Those involved in the movement tended to see themselves as heirs to a long tradition of struggle whose roots go back to the beginning of this century, if not earlier. It was assumed that independence was a good thing and to strive for it was natural. Consequently, all those who had resisted European penetration of Africa, in order to preserve its independence, were heroes to be emulated and given an honourable place in the histories of the countries that had gained their independence through resistance to colonial rule. Put in these terms, this view is an attempt to use the standards of the present, with the aid of hindsight, to interpret the events of the past. In the colonial situation, those who resisted were described by colonial officials as short-sighted while those who collaborated were seen as far-sighted. Today, nationalist historians in East Africa condemn so-called collaborators, especially chiefs, and praise resisters.[1]

Among the resisters, there were also divisions. There were those who took to armed confrontation with the intruders – active resistance. Then there were those who, though they did not take to arms, refused to co-operate with the intruders. This form of resistance is referred to as passive resistance. There has not been a similar treatment of the so-called collaborators. They are often put together as simply one undifferentiated group.

However, as Professor Adu Boahen has correctly pointed out, it is a distortion of African history to see it in terms of heroes and villains. This approach fails to consider the prevailing circumstances under which various groups or individuals operated. The options available to them

1. G. Muriuki, 1974, p. 233.

and their interpretations of these options may have been different from those imposed on them by politicians and scholars alike. It makes sense, as Boahen has suggested, to see the events of the time and their key actors in terms of diplomacy, pursued independently or backed by force. To appreciate the extent to which diplomacy could go, it is necessary to understand the socio-economic forces operating in a particular society at the time of the encounter. For East Africa, a survey of such factors in the 1890s will be an appropriate setting for the events that followed. But, as R. I. Rotberg and Ali Mazrui state: 'There is no gainsaying that the introduction of Western norms and power and accompanying controls was everywhere in Africa questioned by the people affected'.[2] This questioning, however, took various forms. 'The response to the invasion was determined by the structure of each society at the time. Though all societies were determined to preserve their sovereignty, the reaction to invasion was not uniform.'[3] Variations occurred in accordance with the social cohesion or otherwise of a given society.

In the 1890s – the period that preceded European occupation of East Africa – the societies of the region had achieved differing stages of social organization.[4] Some, such as the Baganda and the Banyoro in Uganda, the Banyambo in Tanganyika (now Tanzania) and the Wanga in Kenya, had achieved a high degree of centralized government (see Fig. 7.1). In such societies, response to foreign penetration tended to be dictated by the king or the leadership as a whole. What had existed in Europe at one time – 'The religion of the king is my religion' – sums up the attitude well. Other societies, such as the Nyamwezi in Tanganyika or the Nandi in Kenya were in the process of forming centralized governments. This process is often referred to as state formation. However, the vast majority of societies in this region did not have centralized governments. But lack of central governments does not imply lack of government, a mistake which some foreigners commenting on African societies have made in the past.

Again various societies had had different levels of contact with Europeans or Arabs, the two external forces impinging on East Africa at this time. On the whole, coastal areas had had a longer contact with Europeans and Arabs than the interior areas. Of the interior peoples, three or four groups had had longer contact with the Arabs than the rest. The Akamba in Kenya and the Nyamwezi in Tanganyika were involved in the caravan trade from the interior to the coast – a phenomenon often referred to as long-distance trade.[5] The Baganda as well as the Wanga in Kenya had also had contact with Arabs trading in ivory and slaves prior to

2. R. I. Rotberg and A. A. Mazrui (eds), 1970, p. xviii.
3. M. H. Y. Kaniki in M. H. Y. Kaniki (ed.), 1980, p. 6.
4. For a detailed discussion of Tanzanian societies before the advent of colonialism, see A. M. H. Sheriff in M. H. Y. Kaniki (ed.), 1980.
5. See I. Kimambo, 1970.

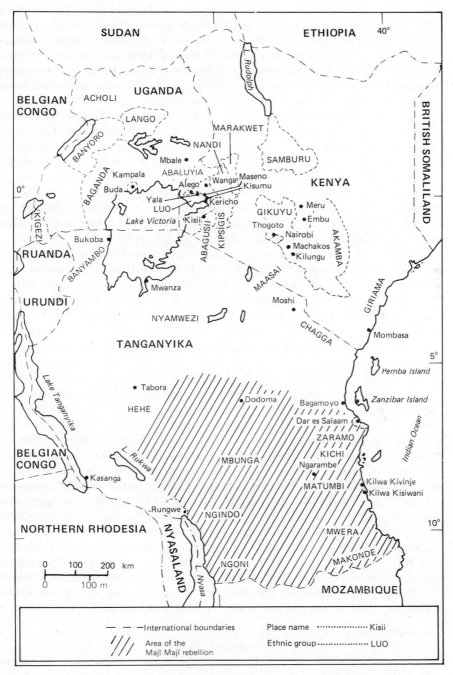

FIG. 7.1 *People and polities of East Africa, showing areas of the Majī Majī rebellion*

the 1890s. Again the degree of exposure to these outside influences determined the type and extent of resistance put up by various societies.

Apart from these human influences, there were ecological changes taking place in East Africa in the 1890s, which also affected response to foreign penetration. The whole region underwent ecological stress resulting in drought with consequent famines. Rinderpest epidemics also occurred.[6] Again, some societies were affected by these natural calamities more deeply than others. Pastoral societies, such as the Maasai of Kenya, seem to have been hit worst of all. A number of Maasai families such as the Waiyaki and Njonjo families took refuge among the neighbouring Gikuyu where they were to play a different role both in relation to their response to colonial advance and in relation to the colonial system that was consequently set up, as well as to the post-colonial society.[7] Others took refuge among the Nandi.[8] Still others were to offer their services as soldiers, first to King Mumia of Wanga among the Abaluyia as mercenaries, and, second, to British imperial agents as part of the expeditionary force that was used to conquer the country that is now called Kenya. This was especially the case against the Nandi.[9] The Maasai example serves to illustrate the kind of dislocation that had taken place among the economies of various societies in this general area. Thus, colonialism came to an area already suffering from an economic crisis with all its attendant effects.

The European Scramble for East Africa and the patterns of African resistance

The colonialist Scramble for East Africa involved three competing powers: the Sultanate of Zanzibar, Germany and Britain. The first on the scene were the Arabs who operated from Zanzibar. Their interests both on the coast and in the interior were largely commercial, revolving around the trade in slaves and ivory. Before the 1880s and 1890s, these Arabs and Swahili traders were content to operate from the coast. But during the closing decades of the last century, Arab interests in the interior of East Africa began to be threatened by German and British interests that had been steadily penetrating the area. In the face of this, the Arabs attempted to take political control of some areas in order to protect their commercial concessions. Thus, they set up a colony at Ujiji on the shores of Lake Tanganyika; and in Buganda, they staged a coup at the expense of the Christians after co-operating with them to remove Mwanga from the throne.[10] The Europeans in the interior included traders and missionaries, all of whom wanted the occupation of East Africa by their home

6. W. Rodney, n.d., p. 4.
7. G. H. Mungeam, 1970, p. 137; K. J. King, 1971(a).
8. H. A. Mwanzi, 1977.
9. K. J. King, 1971(a).
10. R. Oliver, 1951, p. 54.

PLATE 7.1 *The construction of the Uganda Railway: a platelaying gang shifts camp*

153

governments in order to provide them with security as well as a free hand to carry out their enterprises without hindrance.

The methods of European advance varied from place to place. But, on the whole, they were characterized by the use of force combined with, where it was possible, diplomatic alliances with one group against another. Force took the form of invasions which were often also looting exercises. To facilitate advance inland, railways were constructed. The Uganda railway, linking the interior of Uganda and Kenya with the coast, reached the Lake Victoria basin in 1901. The Germans likewise started the construction of railways and road networks. The first railway was started on the coast at Tanga after 1891 and reached the foothills of the Usambara mountains in 1905.

The response in Kenya

African response to all this was, as already indicated, both military and diplomatic, though at times there was withdrawal, non-co-operation or passivity. The Nandi in Kenya, for instance, resisted militarily the construction of the railway through their territory. Of all the peoples of Kenya, they put up the strongest and longest military resistance to British imperialism; it began in the 1890s and did not end until their leader was murdered by the British commanders in 1905, on his way to the negotiations which had been treacherously arranged. That event weakened Nandi resistance and eventually led to the British occupation of their territory.

That the Nandi resisted the British for over seven years was due to the nature of their society. Nandi society was divided into territorial units called *pororiet*. Warriors from each unit were responsible for the defence of the territory. For this reason, the warriors slept in a common hut. This was the nearest thing to a standing army. These territorial armies came together under the leadership of an *orgoiyot*, or traditional leader. It was he who decided when the army would go on a raid. The armies were linked to him through a personal representative who sat at each territorial council. Because territory rather than clan was the centre of Nandi social life, this meant that clan rivalry was absent. The result was a cohesive society, and it was this cohesion that gave the society military superiority over its neighbours. Matson writes that 'It is surprising that so small a tribe as the Nandi was able to terrorize much larger peoples and to continue to do so almost with impunity for several decades.'[11] Given the social cohesion of the society as well as the confidence of the warriors both in themselves and in their leaders, it is not surprising that they became a military power to reckon with. Their military successes led them to believe that they were superior to other people, white men included. As G. W. B. Huntingford noted, 'The Nandi thinks himself at least the equal, if not the superior of the whiteman; and any estimate

11. A. T. Matson, 1970, p. 72.

of the changes brought about by the impact of our civilization must be considered in the light of this fact'.[12] The Nandi successfully resisted this occupation for over seven years, then, because of the success with which the society had been knit together as a fighting force.

This contrasts with the response of some other communities in Kenya. In central Kenya, for instance, each leader or group or clan reacted separately to this foreign intrusion.[13] A typical example was the reaction of Waiyaki among the Gikuyu. His parents were originally Maasai who, because of the upheavals that took place in Maasailand in the nineteenth century, had moved to settle in southern Gikuyuland. Here, Waiyaki had gained influence partly because of his contact with caravan traders. The Imperial British East Africa Company (IBEAC) regarded him as the paramount Chief of all the Gikuyu people. But his conduct, as Muriuki has pointed out, 'right from the beginning demonstrated that he was genuinely interested in friendship with the whiteman'.[14] He ensured the safe passage of Count Teleki's expedition through southern Gikuyu and entered into a blood brotherhood treaty with Frederick Lugard who was then a company agent. The blood brotherhood ceremony was the highest expression of trust among the Gikuyu. After this treaty, Waiyaki allowed Lugard to build a fort on his land. But when later Waiyaki's requests, such as the possession of firearms were turned down by these agents of British imperialism, he turned against them and stormed the company's station at Dagoretti. Subsequently, he again changed his tactics and made an alliance with the foreigners in a diplomatic effort to safeguard his position, but he was deported. Waiyaki's behaviour illustrates the point, sometimes missed, that no one was a resister or a so-called collaborator all his life. People changed their tactics in accordance with the prevailing situation and probably as their understanding of the forces surrounding them deepened. The colonial situation was dynamic, not static, and so were the reactions of the Africans.

Lenana of the Maasai similarly allied himself with the British by contrast with another section of the Maasai who were opposed to a foreign presence in their area. Often those who made an alliance with the British were rewarded with posts such as chiefships in the colonial system. So Lenana, like many others, was made a paramount chief of the Maasai in Kenya. African resistance varied in accordance with the nature of the society and in accordance with how each community perceived the external threat to its sovereignty.[15] What differed was the extent or otherwise of resistance. As Ochieng puts it, 'practically everywhere in Kenya the imposition of colonial rule was resisted. Better armed and employing groups of

12. Quoted by S. K. Arap Ng'eny, 1970, p. 109.
13. See G. Muriuki, 1974. See also G. H. Mungeam, 1970.
14. G. Muriuki, 1974, p. 152.
15. R. I. Rotberg and A. A. Mazrui (eds), 1970, p. xviii.

mercenaries, the British imposed their authority only by violence'.[16]

On the coast, the Mazrui family resisted the take-over by the IBEAC. This resistance was led by Mbaruk bin Rashid who organized hit-and-run warfare against the superior weapons of the British forces. It took reinforcements of Indian troops brought in by the British to defeat him. He fled Tanganyika, only to fall into the hands of the Germans. The Mazrui resistance came about as a result of British attempts to interfere in the internal affairs of the coastal societies. After the Mazrui family had settled in Takarungu on the Kenya coast, they had gradually begun to extend their influence to many parts of the coast. They acquired, for example, the monopoly of buying grain from the Mijikenda people along the coast and had thus come to control the sale of food crops on the coast. The monopoly was resisted by the Giriama between 1877 and 1883 when war broke out between the two groups. The Mazrui were defeated. Thereafter, they had come to some understanding with the Giriama whereupon the two communities became trading partners. The coming of the British interfered with this arrangement as well as the internal organization of the Mazrui society, providing one reason why the Mazrui resisted the imposition of British rule.

When in 1895, the Wali Takarungu died, the IBEAC chose their local friend to succeed him instead of Mbaruk who had a better claim to the throne but was known not to favour the British presence.[17] It was for this reason that Mbaruk sought to drive the British away from the coast by force.

Further inland, the Akamba did not like British interference in their affairs. The founding of Machakos station by the Company in 1889 led to hostilities between the IBEAC and the local community. Company agents looted the surrounding areas of food and property – mainly goats and cattle. They also interfered with religious shrines which people regarded as sacred. In response to this, the local population under Msiba Mwea organized a boycott of the IBEAC station in 1890,[18] refusing to sell it food. Peace only prevailed when F. D. Lugard, a company agent, arrived to make a peace treaty which involved the signing of a 'blood-brotherhood' accord with the local population.

In northern Kenya, behind Kisimayu hinterland, the Ogaden Somali, the Mazrui family and the Akamba resisted British intrusion. Again it took Indian reinforcements to defeat them in 1899. The Taita who had refused to provide porters and who had resisted caravan traders' interference in their country were besieged in 1897 by IBEAC troops under the command of Captain Nelson, who reported that they 'made a most determined attack ... coming up to the guns. The fight lasted about twenty minutes and at last the enemy fled in all directions, leaving a

16. W. R. Ochieng, 1977, p. 89.
17. ibid., p. 90.
18. ibid., p. 91.

large number of dead on the ground including Mwangeka.'[19] Captain Nelson himself and eleven of his men were wounded by Taita poisoned arrows.

Elsewhere in western Kenya, among the Abaluyia, the pattern of response was the same, involving military encounter as well as diplomatic alliance. King Mumia of the Wanga was particularly adept at the use of diplomacy. He saw the British as an ally whom he could use to extend his influence over the whole of western Kenya, by helping him to defeat his neighbouring adversaries such as the Iteso and the Luo with whom he had been at loggerheads for quite some time. Wanga kings had a tradition of employing mercenaries to fight for their cause. Thus, in Mumia's thinking, the British were simply another group of mercenaries to be used. Likewise, the British saw in Mumia a willing agent to help them to extend their control over the whole area. Indeed, the British occupation of western Kenya was accomplished largely through his help. This debt was freely acknowledged by British officials, among whom was Sir Harry Johnston who noted that 'he [Mumia] from the very first regarded British officials and the idea of a British Protectorate with hearty good-will. His influence through all the troubled times of Uganda had done much to ensure the safety of British communications with the east coast'.[20] The same sentiments were echoed by another colonial official on the occasion of Mumia's death in 1949. The then district commissioner who, with other high government officials, attended the burial service, concluded his speech at the ceremony by saying, 'so passed a great figure in the early history of East Africa'.[21]

The response in Tanganyika

The pattern of response in Tanganyika was similar to that obtaining in Kenya as described above, that is, it involved the use of force as well as diplomatic alliances.[22] Mbunga clashed with German forces in 1891 and in 1893 while the hinterland behind Kilwa had its armed resistance organized behind Haoan bin Omari. The Makonde defied German penetration till 1899.[23] The Hehe, under their leader Mkwawa, clashed with German forces in 1891, killing about 290.[24] The Germans set out to avenge this loss. In 1894, they stormed the Hehe region and captured its capital. But the leader, Mkwawa, escaped. After being hunted for four years by his enemies, he committed suicide in order to avoid capture.

19. Quoted in ibid., p. 24.
20. Quoted in W. J. Eggeling, 1948, p. 199. Eggeling adds: 'Uganda has much for which to thank Mumia'.
21. Quoted in W. J. Eggeling, 1950, p. 105.
22. For a detailed discussion of the responses of Tanzanian societies to colonial invasion see: A. J. Temu, in M. H. Y. Kaniki (ed.), 1980.
23. J. Iliffe, 1967, p. 499.
24. J. Iliffe, 1969, p. 17; see also G. C. K. Gwassa in B. A. Ogot (ed.), 1972(a).

The coastal people of Tanganyika organized their resistance around the person and leadership of Abushiri.[25] Socially, the coast of Tanganyika, like that of Kenya, had been dominated for centuries by Swahili and Islamic culture. Here a mixed population of Arabs and Africans intermarried freely, and carried out local trade. Then, in the nineteenth century, coastal Arabs significantly increased their activities in the interior because of the demand for ivory and slaves. The result of this flourishing trade was the establishment of numerous new towns along the coast. The coming of the Germans threatened this trade as they sought to supplant it with their own. The local populations, especially the Arabs, resented this and organized a resistance.

Abushiri, the leader of this resistance, was born in 1845 of an Arab father and an Oromo ('Galla') mother. He was a descendant of one of the first Arab settlers on the coast, a member of a group who had come to regard themselves as local people. Like many others, he opposed the influence of the Sultanate of Zanzibar on the coast and even advocated independence. As a young man, he had organized expeditions into the interior to trade in ivory. From the profits made, he bought himself a farm and planted sugar cane. He was also engaged in a campaign against the Nyamwezi. This had enabled him to assemble warriors who were later to be used against the Germans. Under his leadership, the coastal people fired on a German warship at Tanga in September 1888 and then gave the Germans two days to leave the coast. They later attacked Kilwa, killed the two Germans there, and then Bagamoyo with 8000 men on 22 September. But the Germans, who termed this 'the Arab revolt' sent out Hermann von Wissman. He reached Zanzibar in April 1889, attacked Abushiri in his fortress near Bagamoyo and drove him out. Abushiri escaped northwards to Uzigua where he was betrayed and handed over to the Germans who hanged him at Pangani on 15 December 1889. The coastal resistance finally collapsed when Kilwa was bombarded and taken by the Germans in May 1890.[26]

These were among those who took to arms in Tanganyika in an effort to defend their independence. But the Germans, like the British in Kenya, were practised in the art of divide and rule by allying with one group against another. There were many such allies. The Marealle and the Kibanga near the Tanganyikan mountains of Kilimanjaro and Usambara were, to name but two examples, among those who saw in the Germans an opportunity to make friends in order to defeat their enemies. These people, like others such as the Wanga in Kenya, believed that they were using the Germans even though in the process they were made use of much more by the Germans than perhaps they realized. The Arabs on

25. A. J. Temu in M. H. Y. Kaniki (ed.), 1980, pp. 92–9; for further discussion of the resistance of Abushiri, see R. D. Jackson in R. I. Rotberg and A. A. Mazrui (eds), 1970.

26. J. Iliffe, 1979, pp. 92–7.

PLATE 7.2 *Chief Abushiri (c. 1845–89), a leader of coastal resistance to German and British colonization in East Africa, 1888–9*

the coast, however, were firmly in the employ of the Germans as they were in that of the British and they provided the first local personnel in the service of imperialism.

The response in Uganda

A similar pattern of response to British colonialism took place in Uganda (see Fig. 7.1). The period between 1891 and 1899 saw a clash between the forces of Kabarega, the King of Bunyoro and those of Lugard and other British agents. After some clashes in which Kabarega's forces were defeated, Kabarega turned to diplomacy. Twice he attempted to come to terms with Lugard, but the latter would not countenance these gestures.[27] Mwanga, the Kabaka of Buganda, at times tried to intercede on behalf of the Bunyoro king but to no avail. Eventually, Kabarega resorted to guerrilla warfare, probably the first of its kind in East Africa. He withdrew from Bunyoro to the Lango country in the north from where he harassed British forces time and again. One of the British officials occupying Bunyoro at the time, Thurston, commented: 'Kabarega was at his old tricks – giving every possible trouble but never standing up for a fair fight, preferring to pursue his favourite methods of assassination. Kabarega caused poison to be given to a friendly chief and he died, but I have had the poisoner killed.'[28] Thurston's description is a perfect example of the guerrilla tactic of withdrawing to a neighbouring country in order to harass occupying forces in one's own country. Kabarega was later joined in Lango by Mwanga, but their hide-out was stormed in 1899 and both kings were captured and taken to Kisimayu where Mwanga died in 1903. In this episode, we have both military confrontation and diplomatic initiative by Kabarega and Mwanga as will be shown in the sequel.

Probably the greatest diplomat of all those who had to deal with the advent of imperialism in East Africa in the last decade of the nineteenth century was Mwanga, the Kabaka of Buganda, which had been declared a British Protectorate in 1894. When he ascended the throne in 1894, he seemed to be suspicious of Europeans, mostly missionaries at that time, so he sought to restrict his people's interactions with them. Those among the Baganda who had embraced the Christian faith and who would not obey his orders were put to death as traitors.[29] Today, Christians regard them as martyrs. Mwanga was, however, violently resisting attempts by British agents to take over his country even though disguised as missionaries. But his diplomatic ability also became apparent in the way he handled various, often warring religious sects. At one time, he would play the two Christian sects, Catholics and Protestants, against Muslims when he thought the latter were becoming too powerful and therefore threatening

27. A. R. Dunbar, 1965, p. 82.
28. Quoted by A. R. Dunbar, 1965, p. 93.
29. R. Oliver, 1951, p. 54; see also R. P. Ashe, 1894, pp. 55–82.

PLATE 7.3 *Mwanga* (c. *1866–1903*), *ex-King of Buganda, and Kabarega* (c. *1850–1923*), *ex-King of Bunyoro, on their way to the coast and exile in the Seychelles*

his control of the country. At another time, he would ally with Muslims against Catholics or Protestants or both depending on who he thought was dangerous to his rule. Thus, Mwanga was adept at the diplomatic game of divide and rule, a tactic which the colonizing powers were able to use so effectively in controlling Africa. When it was necessary, Mwanga resorted to a revival of some old tradition in an attempt to drive out all foreigners as happened in 1888.[30] On this occasion, he intended to entice all foreigners and their Baganda followers to a naval parade on an island on Lake Victoria. There he would leave them to starve to death. It seems to have been a tradition of Baganda kings to carry out naval exercises on the lake. Mwanga sought to do this as a trick to drive out foreigners. However, the plan was leaked to the foreigners who then staged a coup, deposed Mwanga and put his brother on the throne as a kind of a puppet ruler. Later, however, in 1889, Mwanga managed to regain his throne only to be exiled to Kisimayu, as already indicated, in 1899, where he died in 1903.

There were, however, those among the Baganda who allied themselves firmly with British imperialism in what has come to be known as Baganda sub-imperialism with regard to the rest of Uganda. It was Baganda agents, especially after the 1900 Agreement, who were responsible for spreading British colonialism to the rest of the country. Notable among them was Kakunguru, a Muganda general, who largely spearheaded the spread of British control to eastern and northern Uganda. It was he, for instance, who captured Kabarega when the British decided to storm his hide-out in Lango country.[31] The 1900 Agreement made the Baganda partners with the British in the advance of British imperialism in the area. Buganda became such a staging-point that many of the early colonial administrators in Uganda were Baganda. Hatred for colonialism consequently came to be directed at the Baganda rather than at the colonial masters themselves. Many of the political problems that later plagued Uganda stem from this early partnership between the British and the Baganda.

East Africa under colonial rule

Having thus suppressed all opposition and resistance by the East Africans and having established firm control over their spheres of influence, the colonial powers set out to transform the region both politically, and, even more importantly, economically. One of the first economic activities was, as already indicated, to build railway lines both in Tanganyika to the Usambara and Kilimanjaro areas, and in Kenya to link the coast with the Lake Victoria basin.

With the railways came European settlers. The aim was to orient East African economies towards export by making the area dependent on

30. R. Oliver, 1951, p. 55.
31. A. R. Dunbar, 1965, p. 96.

economic arrangements in Europe. In this regard, it was to be a source for raw materials rather than an area for industrialization.

The attitude among some colonial officials as well as among white settlers, was that the region was there for the taking. As the British Commissioner of the East Africa Protectorate, Sir Charles Eliot put it: 'We have in East Africa the rare experience of dealing with a tabula rasa, an almost untouched and sparsely inhabited country, where we can do as we wish, to regulate immigration and open or close the door as seems best'.[32] It is not, therefore, surprising that as commissioner, he encouraged European settlers to grab as much land in the highlands of Kenya as possible. Ukambani was the first area in Kenya to be occupied by white settlers in the late 1890s. But of all the peoples of Kenya, the Maasai lost more land to white settlement than any other community. Twice land was taken from them,[33] first in 1904 when they were removed to a reserve in Laikipia, and then in 1911, when they were again removed to give room to white settlement. On both occasions, the Maasai were said by the colonial government to have entered into an agreement to surrender their land. However, on the last occasion, the Maasai challenged the decision in a British court which, not surprisingly, ruled against them. These so-called agreements ignored the nature of authority in Maasai land. Authority lay in the reigning age-group. Since age-groups were not involved in the negotiations, the agreements were not acceptable to the Maasai. At the same time, white settlement was also taking place in Tanganyika. By 1905, there were 284 white settlers in Tanganyika,[34] mainly in the Usambara and Kilimanjaro areas.

From the beginning, the settlers sought to dominate these colonies. In Kenya, for instance, they had by 1902 formed a Planters and Farmers Association to press for their demand to have the highlands of Kenya reserved for them.[35] Though Indians had been used to construct the Uganda railway, they were excluded from this area. Eliot agreed with this demand and confined Indian settlement to land immediately along the railway. The policy of excluding Indians from the highlands was eventually adopted by every protectorate commissioner and colonial governor after Eliot. The response of the Indians to this was to form their own association to press for a share of the highlands. In 1907, they presented their case to the Secretary of State for the Colonies, Winston Churchill, when he visited East Africa. However, the conflict between these two groups was not resolved until the 1920s. By the beginning of the First World War, cash crops or the plantation economy in Kenya were firmly in the hands of white settlers who excluded both Africans and Indians from participation. This state of affairs influenced the African response to the white presence in Kenya.

32. C. Eliot, 1905, p. 103.
33. M. P. K. Sorrenson, 1968, p. 276.
34. W. Rodney, n.d., p. 5.
35. R. K. Tangri, 1967.

The position in Tanganyika and Uganda was different. In Tanganyika, beginning in the southern part of the country, Africans were encouraged, first by missionaries, then by colonial officials, to take to peasant production of cash crops, basically cotton and coffee. In addition, collective farms for cotton were introduced. By 1908 Africans were producing two-thirds of Tanganyika's cotton exports, while by 1912, the African contribution accounted for over 70%.[36] During the same period, African coffee production around the Kilimanjaro area had caught up with that of the settlers. The extent to which changes had taken place in Tanganyika can be seen in the amount of wage labour employed. It has been estimated that by 1931, the African wage-earning population in Tanganyika was 172000,[37] or about one-fifth of the able-bodied male population at the time. On the whole, 'economic activity in German East Africa was at a higher level than in British East Africa on the eve of the First World War. It was also more varied, with a mining sector and several manufacturing sectors making consumer goods'.[38] Thus by 1914, the organization and utilization of labour in Tanganyika had been redirected towards the creation of surplus which was expropriated by the colonial state and European commerce. As in Kenya, settlers in Tanganyika sought to control the colony and assumed a dominant role during this period.

Probably the most far-reaching economic reorganization, in comparison with Kenya and Tanganyika, took place in Uganda. The 1900 Agreement distributed land in Buganda in an attempt to create a landed class that would be loyal to the colonial system. This land distribution led to the development of different class and property relations since landlords and tenants came into existence. In addition, it was understood that Uganda was to be a country where African agricultural production predominated. This was one of the factors that acted as a barrier to large-scale white settlement, such as took place in Kenya and Tanganyika. Unlike in Kenya, but as was more the case in Tanganyika, efforts were made by the colonial regime to place the export-oriented economy into the hands of the indigenous people. The peasant production of cash crops was to become the mainstay of the economy of Uganda. What started in Buganda was eventually extended to other parts of the colony, notably in the west where the climate, as in Buganda, was favourable. By 1907, cotton produced in this manner accounted for 35% of all exports from Uganda.[39] Generally speaking, cash transactions were well entrenched in Uganda, as in the rest of East Africa, on the eve of the First World War. Peasants sold their produce to Asian and European traders. A monetary economy had set in and the grounds for further incorporation into the capitalist system had been laid.

36. W. Rodney, n.d., p. 9.
37. ibid., p. 10.
38. ibid., p. 14.
39. C. Ehrlich, 1957, p. 169.

The demands of the system brought Africans face to face with what had happened and was happening among them. These included introduction of a hut tax, labour requirements, loss of further land, lack of political freedom and corrosion of their culture. Various kinds of responses and reactions were elicited against or in acceptance according to the way each of these measures was experienced.

Taxes were introduced not so much as, or not entirely as a means of raising revenue, but as a way of forcing Africans away from their homes into the labour market and into the monetary economy. Labour was required for settler farms and for public works such as road construction. The conditions under which Africans worked were often harsh. There were other influences introduced by more subtle agents of imperialism such as missionaries and traders.

Anti-colonial movements in East Africa to 1914

In these early days of colonialism, each locality responded differently, except in a few cases where there was co-ordinated action over a wider area. In Kenya, as elsewhere in East Africa, the early responses by such people as the Mazruis and the Nandi, were meant to protect their independence against foreign threats. The subsequent responses in the interior of the country were meant to rid people of oppression and colonial domination. Although this was not a period of nationalist struggle in a modern sense, there are signs of the beginnings of it. Among the Luo in western Kenya, protest against mission domination led to the establishment of an independent Church in 1910 under John Owalo.[40] He had started as a Roman Catholic, then joined the Scottish Mission at Kikuyu only to change again and join the (Anglican) Church Missionary Society at Maseno. It was while at Maseno that he claimed to have received a call from God to start his own religion. As B. A. Ogot puts it:

> After much controversy, the P. C. Nyanza authorized him to start his own mission, since his teaching was not subversive of good order and morality. So in 1910 Owalo founded his Nomia Luo Mission ... proclaimed himself a Prophet, and denied the Divinity of Christ. Within the next few years, he had more than 10,000 adherents in the District, had built his own primary schools, and demanded ... a secondary school free from 'undue missionary influence'.[41]

Then in 1913 came the Mumbo cult, a movement which was against white domination but which used religion as an ideology. From Luoland, it spread to the Gusii, thus showing that it had the potential of spreading to other parts of Kenya. The political content of the movement was not disguised. As the founder, Onyango Dande explained: 'The Christian

40. M. P. K. Sorrenson, 1968, p. 280.
41. See Chapter 26 below; see also B. A. Ogot, 1963, p. 256.

religion is rotten and so is its practice of making its believers wear clothes. My followers must let their hair grow ... All Europeans are your enemies, but the time is shortly coming when they will disappear from our country.'[42] The reaction of the colonial regime was to suppress this movement, as indeed they did to every other movement that challenged their domination.

A similar movement to the one described above was taking place among the Akamba in eastern Kenya. Again, religion was used. It started in 1911 when a certain woman by the name of Siotume was said to be possessed with a spirit. However, the movement was soon taken over by a young man named Kiamba who turned it into a political protest against colonialism in Kenya.[43] He formed some kind of police force to help him carry out his threat. He was, however, arrested and banished. This event was a protest against the way in which settlers in Ukambani were treating their African labour force.

On the whole, early anti-colonial movements in Kenya, in the period before the First World War, took place in western and eastern Kenya. The Giriama on the coast took the opportunity offered by the war to revolt against colonial rule in 1914. They refused to be moved to provide land for white settlement on the coast. The Giriama had several times been involved in conflicts with the British. During the Mazrui resistance against the British, the former sought allies among the Giriama – their trading partners in the past – who supplied them with food. Late in the nineteenth century, the Giriama came into conflict with the British over the latter's ban on ivory hunting.[44] Again in 1913, the Giriama resisted attempts to take away young men to work on European farms. They also resisted attempts to replace their traditional council of elders with colonial headmen. The 1914 rising was therefore a culmination of a series of resistances. The British reaction was to burn down houses and confiscate property. The Giriama like the Mazruis and others resorted to a form of guerrilla warfare, but were eventually defeated.

Uganda was calmer than Kenya. But in 1911, the Acholi in northern Uganda revolted against British colonial rule.[45] It was a reaction against labour recruitment as well as against an effort to disarm them. One of the chief concerns of colonialism was to make sure that the colonized were rendered helpless in the face of cruel exploitation. For this reason, it was important that they did not possess firearms; hence the campaign to collect arms and to disarm the colonized population. The Acholi refused to surrender their guns voluntarily. However, they lost the fight in the ensuing contest.

The most serious challenge to colonial rule in East Africa during this

42. Quoted by M. P. K. Sorrenson, 1968, p. 280. For a full discussion of the Mumbo cult, see B. A. Ogot and W. Ochieng in B. A. Ogot (ed.), 1972.
43. M. P. K. Sorrenson, 1968, p. 281.
44. C. B. Smith, 1973, p. 118.
45. A. B. Adimola, 1954.

period – the Majī Majī uprising – occurred in Tanganyika and it was one in which both religion and magic were resorted to (see Fig. 7.1). Dr Townsend has accurately summed up the situation which characterized German colonial history; pointing out that 'during the first twenty years of Germany's colonial history ... the native had been most cruelly treated and unjustly exploited ... Robbed of his lands, his home, his freedom and often wantonly and cruelly of his life by the colonial adventurer, official or trading company, his continuous and fierce revolts were but the tragic witnesses to his wretchedness and helplessness.'[46] The state of affairs was not confined to German colonies. It was typical of colonialism in its entire period in Africa. Forced labour, taxation, harassment and conditions of work all combined to cause the Majī Majī uprising. However, the immediate cause was the introduction of a communal cotton scheme. People were required to work on this scheme for twenty-eight days in a year. But the proceeds did not go to the workers. They were paid such low sums that some refused to take them. This African response was not against growing cotton as such, which they had willingly started growing as a cash crop. It was a reaction against this particular scheme which exploited their labour and threatened the African economy by forcing people to leave their own farms to work on public ones.

To unite the people of Tanganyika in their challenge to the Germans, the leader of the movement, the prophet, Kinjikitile Ngwale, who lived at Ngarambe, made use of their religious beliefs. He taught them that the unity and freedom of all Africans was a fundamental principle and therefore that they were to unite and fight for their freedom against the Germans in a war which had been ordained by God, and that they would be assisted by their ancestors who would return to life. To underscore and give concrete expression to the unity of the African people, Kinjikitile Ngwale built a large shrine, which he called the 'House of God' and prepared medicinal water (*majī*), which, he said, could make his followers who drank it immune to European bullets. The movement, which lasted from July 1905 to August 1907, spread over an area of 26 000 sq km of the southern third of Tanganyika. According to G. C. K. Gwassa:

> It [Majī Majī] involved over twenty differing ethnic groups. In its organizational scale and ethnic variety, Majī Majī was a movement both different from and more complex than earlier reactions and resistance to the imposition of colonial rule, for the latter had usually been confined within ethnic boundaries. By comparison with the past, Majī Majī was a revolutionary movement creating fundamental changes in traditional organizational scale.[47]

The war broke out in the last week of July 1905 and the first victims were the founder himself and his assistant who were hanged on 4 August

46. Quoted by J. Iliffe, 1969, p. 3.
47. G. C. K. Gwassa in T. O. Ranger and I. Kimambo (eds), 1972, p. 202.

1905. His brother picked up his mantle and assumed the title of 'Nyamguni', one of the three divinities in the area, and continued to administer the *maji* but it was ineffective. The ancestors did not return as promised and the movement was brutally suppressed by the German colonial authorities.

The Majī Majī uprising was the first large-scale movement of resistance to colonial rule in East Africa. In the words of John Iliffe it was 'a final attempt by Tanganyika's old societies to destroy the colonial order by force',[48] and it was truly a mass movement of peasants against colonial exploitation. It shook the German regime in Tanganyika whose response was not just the suppression of the movement, but also the abandonment of the communal cotton scheme. There were also some reforms in the colonial structure, especially with regard to labour recruitment and utilization, which were designed to make colonialism palatable to Africans. But the rebellion failed and this failure did indeed make 'the passing of the old societies inevitable'.[49]

On the whole, between 1890 and 1914 dramatic changes took place in East Africa. Colonialism was imposed on the people, violently in most cases, even if the violence was sometimes disguised in the form of law. African responses to the initial impact combined military confrontation with diplomatic efforts in a vain attempt to preserve their independence. Where Africans did not engage in military or diplomatic activity, they acquiesced or remained indifferent, except where direct demands were made on them. The establishment of colonialism meant the reorganization of the political and economic life of the people. Taxes were introduced. Forced labour and general deprivation of political rights were practised. Some Africans responded to these changes violently. Others acquiesced. In Tanganyika and Uganda, some Africans had moved to peasant production of cash crops, particularly cotton and coffee. In Kenya, Africans were denied the production of cash crops. The economy there was settler-based. Various African responses to this position have been outlined. More were to follow in the period after the First World War.

48. J. Iliffe, 1979, p. 168.
49. ibid.

African initiatives and resistance in Central Africa, 1880–1914

A. ISAACMAN and J. VANSINA

This chapter[1] examines the changing nature of resistance to European
rule in Central Africa from 1880 to 1914. Central Africa is defined as
the area included in the states of Belgian Congo (now Zaire), Northern
Rhodesia (now Zambia), Nyasaland (now Malawi), Angola and Mozambique. Like most regions of Africa on the eve of the Scramble, this zone
was occupied by a host of peoples organized either in state or centralized
political systems or in small-scale political units.[2] Among the first category
were the Lunda and Luba kingdoms of the Belgian Congo, the Humbe
and Chokwe states of Angola, the Mozambican kingdom of the Mwenemutapa, the Undi kingdom in Nyasaland, and the numerous states founded
by the Nguni and the Kololo in the Zambezi-Limpopo basins. Among
the latter were the Yao and lakeside Tonga of Nyasaland, the Bisa and
Lala of Northern Rhodesia, the Sena, Tonga and Chopi of Mozambique,
the Kisama, Bakongo and Loango of Angola, and the Loga, Mongo,
Ngombem Budja and Bowa of the Belgian Congo (see Fig. 8.1). Although
historians may have overestimated the degree of turmoil and stress within
these societies, political fragmentation, ethnic and regional particularism
and internal conflicts between competing strata[3] placed serious limitations
on the capacity of the peoples of Central Africa to react to the Europeans.
Despite these divisive tendencies, however, confrontation and resistance
remained the dominant reaction to European imperialist conquest and
occupation.

1. This chapter was commissioned in 1975 and completed in 1976.
2. For details, see Volume VI of this History.
3. We use the term 'strata' to indicate a socio-economic differentiation which existed
in most pre-colonial Central African societies. Because of the absence of extensive field-
work analysing the organization of pre-capitalist economies and the related process of class
formation, delineating with any certainty the actual degree of stratification in these societies
is often impossible. There is no doubt that by the middle of the nineteenth century class
had replaced kinship as the dominant social variable in a number of commercial societies,
but in many other cases insufficient data are available to enable one to make this distinction.
The works of Catherine Coquery-Vidrovitch, Claude Meillassoux, Emmanuel Terray and
Maurice Godelier, though not in total agreement, represent an important theoretical breakthrough for an analysis of class formation in pre-capitalist African societies.

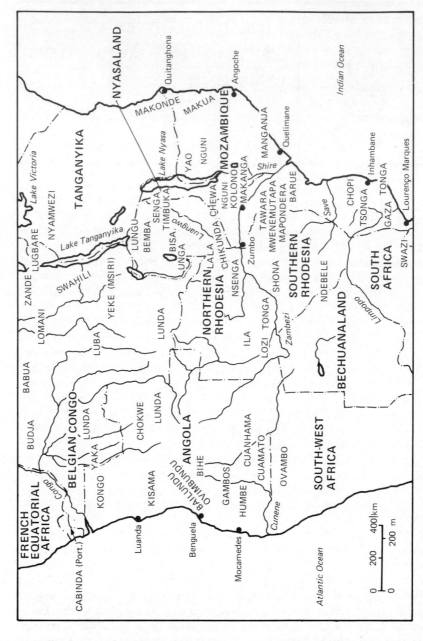

FIG. 8.1 *Peoples and polities of Central Africa, c. 1900*

Rather than merely describing the anti-colonial activity from country to country, we have focused on the patterns of opposition which characterized the region as a whole. By analysing African reactions in terms of the goals of the participants, three broad categories can be identified:

(1) opposition or confrontation which attempted to maintain the sovereignty of the indigenous societies;
(2) localized resistance which sought to ameliorate specific abuses imposed by the colonial regime;
(3) rebellions which aimed to destroy the alien system which had generated these abuses. Although localized resistance and rebellions are treated as discrete analytical categories, it is important to emphasize that resisters tended to adjust their goals to the contemporary military and political realities.

The struggle to maintain independence: the era of confrontation and alliance

In the period after 1880 intensified imperialist competition among European nations precipitated an unprecedented invasion of Africa. The emphasis on conquest and occupation was most clearly articulated at the Congress of Berlin in which effective control became the accepted prerequisite for international recognition of European territorial holdings. Faced with this new threat to their sovereignty, the peoples of Central Africa reacted in a variety of ways. Some, such as the Lozi, engaged in a diplomatic delaying action while others, like the Inhambane Tonga and Sena, allied with Europeans in an effort to free themselves from the oppressive rule of an alien African aristocracy. Many Central African states and smaller chieftaincies instead took up arms to protect their autonomy. Although sharing a common goal, the opponents differed substantially in their short-term strategy, ethnic composition, scale and the degree of success which they achieved.

The strategies of confrontation adopted by the Central Africans shared a common *raison d'être* – to drive out the Europeans and protect their homelands, way of life and means of livelihood. While the goal of political independence remained paramount, many African states were prepared to mobilize their forces to prevent any infringement on their cultural autonomy or economic sovereignty. In Nyasaland, for example, the Nguni of Gomani attacked missionary stations in 1896, in part to protest against the debilitating effect of Christianity, while in Mozambique the Barue frustrated Lisbon's efforts to incorporate them into its informal empire by using the Catholic Church to convert the royal family.[4] Economic

4. For a discussion of the Portuguese efforts to use Catholicism as a mechanism for social control, see A. Isaacman, 1973: this uses oral data to reinterpret the meaning of what was assumed to be a Catholic ritual.

encroachments also motivated a number of polities to adopt a hostile posture towards the European imperialists. A principal source of friction was the effort by European governments and their trading and missionary agents to undercut the middlemen position of several interior states and to terminate the slave trade which was no longer compatible with the desire of the capitalist powers for 'stable' markets and raw materials. During the last two decades of the century, the Yao, Makua, Yeke, Chikunda, Ovimbundu and Chokwe, among others, forcefully resisted these alien pressures. Simultaneously many peasants and agriculturalists fought to maintain control over the means of production and prevent the expropriation of their land, cattle, labour and women.

African leaders recognized the necessity of neutralizing the European arms advantage if they were to survive. Many societies already participating in international trade benefited from access to the weapons market and had acquired vast arsenals in exchange for captives. The Chokwe, Ovimbundu and Chikunda were so successful that their forces were often better armed than the respective Congo Free State and Portuguese troops who sought to conquer them. Other Central African peoples, previously not involved in extensive commercial ventures, increased their exports to obtain modern guns and ammunition. During the last quarter of the century, for example, the Ovambo, Shangaan, and even several conservative Nguni offshoots acquired modern rifles in anticipation of a clash with the Europeans.[5] Wherever possible, they expanded their arsenals through skilful diplomacy. Gaza leaders were able to play off the British against the Portuguese and acquire arms from the former, while Bemba (Plate 8.1) militants acquired arms from the Arabs who feared Britain's growing presence.[6] Other states such as Quitanghona in northern Mozambique and the Chikunda polities of the Zambezi valley even agreed to recognize Portugal's nominal rule in exchange for large caches of weapons which were ultimately used against Lisbon's forces.[7]

A number of African societies also expanded their defensive capabilities through internal military innovations. The Barue developed munitions plants which produced powder, rifles and even components for their

5. W. G. Clarence-Smith and R. Moorsom, 1975, pp. 372–3: examines the impact and response of the Ovambo to Portuguese and South African colonialism; I. Linden, in B. Pachai (ed.), 1972, pp. 246–7: some interesting information on initial patterns of interaction between the Maseko Nguni and the British; D. L. Wheeler, 1968, pp. 585–602: an analysis of Gungunyane's unsuccessful efforts to maintain Shangaan independence through diplomacy.

6. D. L. Wheeler, 1968, p. 591; A. D. Roberts, 1974, pp. 202–3: the best study on the Bemba published to date.

7. N. Hafkin, 1973, pp. 375–7: an important analysis of the slave trade and conservative resistance to the Portuguese; A. Isaacman, 1976, pp. 22–49: an analysis of the various types of resistance movements with a special emphasis on the growing political consciousness of the anti-colonial forces.

PLATE 8.1 *Bemba chief among his people receiving a European, 1883*

artillery.[8] New and expansive defensive structures such as the fortified town of Jumbe of Kota and the *aringas* of the Zambezi and Luangwa valley were built to withstand European siege.[9] Other Africans, among them the Makua, Lunda and the disparate bands who operated in the Gambo region of southern Angola, developed guerrilla tactics that stifled the first imperialist advances. Around the turn of the century Barue, Tawara, Tonga and other Shona religious spirit mediums (*svikiro*) (see Fig. 8.1) provided divinely inspired medicines to neutralize the European weapons and turn their bullets into water.[10]

Despite the common commitment of some of the Africans to prevent foreign rule and to acquire modern weapons, the immediate tactics they employed varied substantially. In several cases African states reacted violently to the first European encroachments despite the overwhelming military advantage which the enemy enjoyed. Thus, the Chewa leader Mwase Kasungu led his people in a futile effort against the British, ultimately committing suicide in 1896 rather than capitulating.[11] At about the same time the Bihe of Angola ambushed a colonial force seeking to establish interior posts which would cut through their homelands, and the Humbe, to the south, attacked a Portuguese force after Lisbon refused to pay rent for the right to maintain a small fort within its borders.[12]

Other African leaders sought to avoid initial confrontations in the hope that they could either strengthen their military capacity or negotiate a 'just' treaty in which the sovereignty of their state would be recognized. For almost a decade Gungunyane (Plate 8.2) negotiated with both the British and Portuguese and was prepared to make a variety of concessions short of renouncing Shangaan independence.[13] The Barue royal family pursued a similar policy seeking to enlist the support of Karl Peters, a German adventurer, whom they thought had close ties to Bismarck's government, while sporadic Bemba resistance at the end of the century occurred only after fifteen years of diplomatic manoeuvring with Great

8. J. de Azevedo Coutinho, 1904, pp. 46–7: description of Portuguese wars with the Barue at the turn of the twentieth century.

9. M. D. D. Newitt, 1973, pp. 226–9: an important analysis of the powerful *prazero* families and their relations with Lisbon. The author has also published extensively on related matters in *Race* and the *Journal of African History*.

10. J. Vansina, 1969, pp. 21–2. See also A. Isaacman, 1976, pp. 49–74, 126–56: Shona uses of medicine to neutralize European weapons.

11. R. Tangri, 1968, pp. 2–4: a summary of the initial protest patterns among Malawians.

12. R. Pélissier, 1969, p. 67: a thoroughly documented account of the numerous wars which occurred in southern Angola. The author is currently completing a general military history of Angola. D. L. Wheeler, 1963, p. 334: a thorough examination of Portuguese colonial policy during the nineteenth century.

13. J. J. T. Botelho, 1934, Vol. II, pp. 419–33: the standard military history of Mozambique. Volume II is of particular importance for the late nineteenth-century conflicts. D. L. Wheeler, 1968.

PLATE 8.2 *Gunguyane and his warriors*

Britain.[14] In the most extreme cases, states like Quitanghona in northern Mozambique and the Chikunda empires of the Zambezi valley willingly acknowledged the nominal authority of the Portuguese so long as no serious effort was made to impose colonial rule.[15] This strategy, however, invariably led to confrontation, since the Congress of Berlin explicitly demanded effective control as a pre-condition for international recognition of a claim to colonial possession.

Many Central African societies that were unable to offer effective opposition or that failed to comprehend the implications of colonial rule submitted peacefully in the first instance but soon after rose up in an effort to regain their independence. This pattern of delayed confrontation occurred with great regularity in the Congo where the indigenous population initially considered the agents of the Congo Free State trading partners and allies against the alien slavers. Only when Free State officials sought to impose taxes and conscript labour did the local societies recognize they had inadvertently yielded their autonomy. During the period between 1885 and 1905 more than a dozen nominally 'subjugated' groups revolted in the lower and central Congo.[16] Of these, the most successful were the Yaka who effectively fought the Europeans for more than a decade before they were finally conquered in 1906, and the Budja and Bowa who revolted at the end of the century against forced labour on the rubber plantations. At their high point the rebels had mobilized more than 5000 workers who fought a protracted guerrilla war from their bases deep in the forest region.[17]

In addition to the variety of initial reactions, the resisters differed in their degree of parochialism and ethnic particularism. At one extreme were a number of societies, both large and small, that confronted the invaders without any effort to create broader alliances. In Angola the Bihe, Humbe and Ganguela initially fought the aliens without the assistance of their neighbours who shared a common hatred of the Portuguese,[18] while Lisbon benefited in Mozambique from the intense competition between the Chikunda conquest states which precluded any effective alliance. Even the related Ngoni states were unable or unwilling to co-operate in the face of British expansion in Nyasaland. In the 1890s the Maseko,

14. A. Isaacman, 1976, pp. 49–74; A. D. Roberts, 1974, pp. 229–92: for a fascinating contemporary account of Barue efforts to get German assistance, see C. [K.] Peters, 1902, p. 116.

15. N. Hafkin, 1973, pp. 375–7; A. Isaacman, 1976, pp. 22–48; M. D. D. Newitt, 1973, pp. 295–311.

16. C. Young, 1965, p. 283 (Map 5); F. Flament *et al.*, 1952, pp. 106–531; A. Lejeune-Choquet, 1906, gives details about some of the smaller insurrections and a little more about primary resistance. See also R. Harms, 1975, pp. 73–88.

17. F. Flament *et al*, 1952, pp. 162–4, 499. The territory remained under military occupation until 1908. Cf. M. Plancquaert, 1932, pp. 134, 138.

18. R. Pélissier, 1969, pp. 67–72; D. L. Wheeler, 1963, p. 334.

Gomani and Mpeseni individually fought the undermanned British colonial force and were overwhelmed, enabling Britain to establish the Nyasaland colony.[19] The failure of competing factions within a given state to unify in the face of European incursions represented the logical extension of their short-sighted particularism. There are many examples in which rivals actually assisted the imperialist powers in the hope of enhancing their internal position. Such divisive tendencies undercut the efforts of the Luba and Barue to remain autonomous.[20] In the case of the latter, Lisbon, through its imperial agent, the Mozambican Company, forced a secret alliance with Chipitura, a dissident member of the Barue aristocracy. The latter agreed to recognize Portuguese sovereignty in exchange for assistance against his internal rival Hanga.

Other African polities sought to overcome their limited military capacity by organizing broad-based multi-ethnic, anti-colonial alliances. The powerful Gaza ruler Gungunyane, for example, appealed to the Swazi to join the struggle against the Portuguese, while the Barue created a multi-ethnic network which included Tonga, Tawara and a variety of Shona peoples living in Southern Rhodesia (now Zimbabwe).[21] As in the case of the Barue, such temporary unions occurred most often where economic, kinship or religious alliances had previously existed. The formation of the Yao confederation under Makanjuira and the Makua–Swahili alliance combined all three elements, while financial considerations underpinned the ill-fated Bemba–Arab efforts at the end of the nineteenth century.[22] Occasionally, historic rivals cast aside their animosity in an effort to survive, which explains the alliance of the central Lunda and Chokwe against the Congo Free State's forces despite a mutual enmity which dated back over a generation. Similar considerations also motivated the Mburuma Nsenga and Tawara to aid the Chikunda at the turn of the century and the Cuanhama–Cuamato alliance in southern Angola.

Not surprisingly, a high correlation existed between the degree of ethnic particularism and the scale of the resistance movements. Where African societies fought alone, the size of their army and their potential to resist were generally limited. The rapid demise of the Nguni states and the Chewa of Mwase Kasungu reflect the inherent disadvantage faced by isolated polities. The broad-based alliances were often able to field large, well-equipped armies and generally put up sustained resistance. Thus, the forces of Makanjuira and his Yao compatriots were estimated at 25 000

19. J. McCracken in B. Pachai (ed.), 1972: discusses differential Nguni reaction to European penetration. I Linden in B. Pachai (ed.), 1972, pp. 241–4.
20. J. Vansina, 1966, pp. 242–4: a comprehensive study of pre-colonial Central Africa with an emphasis on Zaire. A. Isaacman, 1976, pp. 49–74.
21. P. Warhurst, 1962, p. 59.
22. A. D. Roberts, 1974, pp. 242, 271.

men, which was about the size of both the Cuanhama–Cuamato army and that of the Barue.[23]

Because the resistance movements did not achieve their ultimate political goals, there has been a tendency to minimize or ignore their immediate military accomplishments and to brand them all as failures. In fact, variations in scale, access to modern weapons, and the size and preparation of the imperialist forces yielded a wide range of situations. While many African polities were defeated quickly, an equally large number contained the initial European incursions and inflicted heavy losses on the enemy. In southern Angola, the Humbe and Cuamato repulsed several Portuguese attacks and in the battle of 1904 killed more than 300 of the 500-man contingent.[24] The Chikunda states repeatedly defeated Lisbon's disorganized army during the last decade of the nineteenth century while to the north, in Nyasaland, the Yao kept the British colonial army at bay for almost five years.[25] A similar situation occurred in the Congo where the Chokwe inflicted heavy losses on the Force Publique for twenty years before finally succumbing.[26] Perhaps most successful were the Swahili–Makua alliance which remained outside the sphere of Portuguese rule until 1910, and the Cuamato and Cuanhama who were not finally defeated until 1915.[27]

Despite these hard-won successes, all wars of independence in Central Africa ultimately failed. A combination of several factors, most antedating the Scramble, help explain the African inability to thwart European advances. These include the conquest origin of many of the most powerful states, ethnic particularism, and internal cleavages among the ruling strata or class and occasionally, between it and their subject population. Their net effect was to limit the likelihood of large-scale, broad-based and coordinated anti-colonial efforts necessary to counteract the distinct advantage in firepower and military technology which the European imperialist forces enjoyed.

African rivalries, moreover, facilitated a strategy of divide and rule which Harry Johnston and other colonial officials employed with consummate skill. The annals of the struggle for the retention of the African's independence and sovereignty are replete with examples of Africans who not only submitted but aided the colonial powers in an effort to avenge

23. E. Stokes (1966a) in E. Stokes and R. Brown (eds), 1966, pp. 267–8: examines survival strategy of Lozi under Lewanika; R. Pélissier, 1969, p. 103; J. de Azevedo Coutinho, 1904, p. 43.

24. R. Pélissier, 1969, p. 79.

25. A. Isaacman, 1976, pp. 22–48; E. Stokes (1966b) in E. Stokes and R. Brown (eds), 1966, pp. 366–8: examines strategy of British and reaction of various Malawian peoples.

26. J. Vansina, 1966, pp. 226–7.

27. N. Hafkin, 1973, p. 384; M. D. D. Newitt, 1972(b), pp. 670–1: a discussion of the conflicting interests of the Portuguese and the African slave trading elite and the ultimate conquest of the region of Angoche. R. Pélissier, 1969, pp. 102–8.

past abuses perpetrated by their neighbours. The Inhambane Tonga and the Sena helped the Portuguese against their respective Shangaan and Barue overlords, while in the Congo a number of subject people co-operated with the Belgians to free themselves from Yeke and Arab rule or from the slave raiders. In addition, several African leaders recognized that alliances with the Europeans could fulfil their expansionist aspirations and simultaneously strengthen their own internal position. Such considerations, for example, motivated Tippu Tib and the sons of Msiri to aid the Congo Free State.[28] Other African societies, including some which initially opposed the invaders, later allied[29] with them in exchange for material benefits and promises of improved status in the new colonial order. Thus, once the Yao were defeated, they helped to conquer the Mpeseni Nguni who, in turn, were used by the Portuguese to defeat the Barue.

Without African allies and mercenaries, it would not have been possible for the Europeans to impose their rule at such a minimal cost in manpower. More than 90% of the Portuguese armies which finally 'conquered' the Zambezi valley in 1902, for example, were African levies.[30] Although not as extreme, a similar pattern existed in Angola. To the north, the Congo Free State army consisted of African levies with some Zanzibari and Hausa mercenaries. Only the officers were Europeans. The success of Harry Johnston's policy of divide and rule is also demonstrated by the large number of Africans who participated in the British occupation of Nyasaland and Northern Rhodesia.

Early localized resistance against colonial rule and capitalism

Unlike pre-colonial resistance, the major aim of which was to maintain independence, resistance by peasants and workers during the early twentieth century was directly motivated by the efforts of the colonial regimes to reinforce their hegemony and impose capitalist relationships designed to exploit the human and natural resources of Central Africa. Although a detailed examination and comparison of the Portuguese, British and Belgian colonial systems falls outside the scope of this study, it is

28. L. Farrant, 1975, pp. 108–11; R. Slade, 1962, pp. 94–102. On Mukunda Bantu, Msiri's son, see A. Munongo, 1948; L. Bittremieux, 1936, pp. 69–83. He was about to be swept completely aside by the Sanga.

29. J. McCracken in B. Pachai (ed.), 1972, p. 227; A. J. Dachs, 1972, in *idem*, pp. 288–9; A. Isaacman, 1976, pp. 49–74: one of the few articles which examines the motive and impact of collaborators.

30. Instead of alliance, some historians would prefer the term collaboration and for a theoretical analysis of collaboration, see A. Isaacman and B. Isaacman, 1977, pp. 55–61. For the volume editor's reasons for objecting to that term, see Introduction, above.

useful to examine their inherent abuses, which generated recurring patterns of localized resistance.[31]

The most immediate concern of the colonial officials was to institutionalize an administrative system to control the activities of the subject peoples. Towards this end they removed a substantial number of uncooperative 'traditional' rulers, thereby violating the religious and cultural sanctity of kingship. To reinforce their tenuous rule, they dispatched African police, drawn from the ranks of mercenaries and allies, to oversee the activities of 'colonial chiefs' and to intimidate the local population. Given their desire for self-aggrandizement and their monopoly of power, it is hardly surprising that members of the Force Publique of the Congo, the 'Guerras Pretas' of Angola, the Sepais of Mozambique, and the British Native Police of Northern Rhodesia and Nyasaland engaged in predatory activities and repeatedly abused their authority.

To provide a pool of cheap labour for government projects and European capitalist interests, the colonial powers resorted to forced labour practices coupled with repressive taxation. In the Congo, Africans were compelled to collect rubber and to work on the railways and in the mines, while in Mozambique a variety of multi-national concessionary companies were the principal beneficiaries of the forced labour. Other Mozambicans were exported to Southern Rhodesia, South Africa and São Tomé. In São Tomé, on the cocoa plantations, they were joined by thousands of Angolans. Although the details differed, this pattern of coercion and intimidation was repeated in recruiting Africans to work on the European plantations of Nyasaland and subsequently in the mines of Northern Rhodesia.[32]

The peasants who remained at home were not exempted from conscription. Many members of the rural population were required by law to provide several weeks of free labour on public works projects or face immediate imprisonment. They were also subject to the capricious demands of local officials and were often compelled to sell their produce at deflated prices.

In short, Africans incurred heavy social and economic costs under colonial rule. Families were separated either temporarily or permanently, and the local peasantry lived in fear of the abuses which the Europeans and African mercenaries perpetrated. In the economic sphere, the export of an appreciable part of the labour force in many areas intensified the

31. For a discussion of the policies of the respective colonial regimes, see T. O. Ranger in L. H. Gann and P. Duignan (eds), 1969; J. Stengers in *idem*; R. J. Hammond in *idem*; G. J. Bender, 1978; E. Mondlane, 1969, pp. 23–58; H. Mebeelo, 1971, pp. 71–90; B. S. Krishnamurty in B. Pachai (ed.), 1972, pp. 384–405; A. A. Boavida, 1967; a broad overview of Portuguese exploitation in Angola.

32. For a discussion of forced labour, see J. Duffy, 1967; H. W. Nevinson, 1906; C. Coquery-Vidrovitch, 1972.

existing manpower shortages, resulting in rural stagnation and under-development.

These abuses generated recurring protests by peasants and workers aimed at ameliorating specific grievances rather than eliminating the repressive system which created them. Because of its sporadic nature, much of this local opposition has been ignored by contemporaries and historians alike. Nevertheless, 'day-to-day resistance', withdrawal, 'social banditry'[33] and peasant revolts constituted an important chapter in the anti-colonial legacy of Central Africa.

Like the slaves in the American South, many African peasants covertly retaliated against the repressive system. Because both groups lacked any significant power, direct confrontation was often not a viable strategy. Instead, they expressed their hostility through tax evasion, work slowdowns and surreptitious destruction of property. The dominant European population, as in the United States, perceived these forms of 'day-to-day resistance' as *prima facie* evidence of the docility and ignorance of their subordinates rather than as expressions of discontent.[34]

Tax evasion occurred with great frequency throughout all of Central Africa. Just before the arrival of the tax collector, all or part of a village would flee into an inaccessible region until the state official departed. In Northern Rhodesia, the Gwemba Tonga were notoriously successful evaders, as were their Bisa and Unga neighbours who fled into the Bagwelu swamps.[35] This practice was so common in Mozambique that one official noted in disgust, 'It remains unknown how many times six or more adults will flee from their kraal leaving only a blind, ill or elderly individual who is exempt from taxes'.[36] Those Africans fortunate enough to live along international borders could slide back and forth across the frontier avoiding the tax collectors of both colonies. The Yaka periodically fled across the Kwango River which separated Angola and the Congo, while their compatriots took advantage of the unpatrolled frontier to cross into the French Congo where they remained until harassed by local tax officials.[37]

33. This term is being retained on the insistence of the authors. The volume editor would have preferred 'commando activities'.

34. For a pioneering discussion of this question, see R. A. Bauer and A. H. Bauer, 1942, pp. 388–419. More recently this theme has been discussed by such scholars as John W. Blasingame, Eugene Genovese and Peter Kolchin.

35. R. I. Rotberg, 1966, p. 75: a political history of both countries with some information on early localized resistance to colonialism. H. S. Meebelo, 1971, pp. 97–8: an important study of resistance movements including localized forms rarely discussed.

36. A. A. C. Xavier, 1889, p. 25–6: an important contemporary account of Portuguese rule. Includes examples of localized resistance.

37. G. Moulaert, 1945, pp. 28–43: tells how in Manyanga the local population resisted attempts in 1885 and 1893 to delimit the border with French Congo so that the population could flee from porterage. A new incident in 1902 led to a diplomatic confrontation and the border was finally settled in 1908. Along all the borders inhabitants fled tax collectors or appeals for forced labour, going now to one side of the border, now to the other. Remarks to this effect abound in the literature and in the traditions.

A similar strategy was employed by disenchanted members of the rural populations living in the Milanje region along the Nyasaland–Mozambique border and in the Gaerezi Valley separating Rhodesia and Mozambique.

The peasants also developed a number of techniques to avoid or minimize the discomforts of forced labour. In the most extreme situations, as in the case of the Namwhana and Lungu of Northern Rhodesia, they took up arms and drove the recruiters off their land.[38] Labour grievances also precipitated the 1893–4 Manjanga insurrection in the lower Congo and countless uprisings in the rubber collecting areas.[39] Other less dangerous tactics included feigned illness, work slowdowns, strikes and fleeing. In the Abercorn District of Northern Rhodesia colonial officials repeatedly complained that the Africans 'loafed and systematically had to be driven'. Ultimately, the workers ceased their labour entirely until they were guaranteed a salary.[40] The lack of co-operation and the high rate of absenteeism convinced European officials of the inherently slothful nature of the Africans. One Portuguese administrator noted that 'None of them flee on account of bad treatment, nor do they have the slightest other justifiable reason ... Thus, I am left to conclude that the great reluctance which almost all of them exhibit towards work has been the sole cause of their fleeing the services in question.'[41]

Other disgruntled workers sabotaged agricultural equipment, burned warehouses and robbed stores belonging to the concessionary companies and local traders, and destroyed transportation and communication lines.

Flight across international borders was yet another common expression of discontent. Although the clandestine nature of the exodus precludes any accurate assessment they appear to have been rather large in scale. Official British records indicate that more than 50000 Africans living in the Zambezi valley fled into Southern Rhodesia and Nyasaland between 1895 and 1907 in the misguided hope that British colonialism would be more benign.[42] The existence of a common or related ethnic group on either side of the frontier facilitated the withdrawal of the Ovambo and Bakongo from Angola and the Shona and Chewa from Mozambique (see Fig. 8.1). In Nyasaland large numbers of lakeside Tonga and Tumbuka migrated from the Rukuru watershed to outside the sphere of British control to avoid paying taxes.[43]

Creation of refugee communities in desolate areas constituted a variant of the withdrawal strategy. Rather than crossing international boundaries, the peasants, many of whom had refused to satisfy their 'legal' responsi-

38. H. S. Meebelo, 1971, pp. 90–1.
39. F. Flament *et al.*, 1952, pp. 498–9.
40. H. S. Meebelo, 1971, pp. 95–7.
41. Arquivo Histórico de Moçambique, Fundo do Século XX, Cx. 4–185, m. 37: António Gomes to Sub-intendente do Governi em Macequece, 18 November 1916.
42. C. Wiese, 1891, p. 241.
43. J. McCracken in B. Pachai (ed.), 1972, pp. 227–8.

bilities, created autonomous enclaves. This phenomenon occurred with some regularity among Bemba dissidents who fled into the interior. 'Out of reach, the mitanda dwellers attained a kind of independence which they fiercely and jealously guarded'.[44] A similar pattern occurred in the Gambo region of southern Angola which became a hide-out for outlaws and the disenchanted, in the rugged Gaerezi mountains separating Mozambique from Southern Rhodesia, and in the forest and mountainous areas of the Congo.[45] Although little is known about the internal organization of these communities, their commitment to remain free and their location in harsh backwater areas is strikingly similar to that of the maroon communities of escaped slaves in the Americas.[46]

Other fugitive communities, not content just to remain outside the sphere of European control, adopted an aggressive posture towards the colonial regimes. They attacked specific symbols of rural oppression – the plantations, labour recruiters, tax collectors and African police – in an effort to protect their natal villages and kinship groups from continued harassment and exploitation. Like the 'social bandits' of Sicily or north-eastern Brazil, analysed by Eric Hobsbawm,[47] the attacks were led by individuals who were not regarded as criminals by their own society, although they had violated the laws of the colonial regime. The best known of 'social bandit' leaders was Mapóndera who successfully battled Southern Rhodesian and Portuguese colonial forces from 1892 to 1903 while protecting the local peasantry from tax collectors, labour recruiters, exploitative company officials and abusive administrators (see Plate 8.3). Mapondera and his band of followers repeatedly attacked the warehouses of the Companhia de Zambésia and the shops of rural merchants, both of which were symbols of economic exploitation. The rebels were able to survive against overwhelming odds because they received the constant support of the rural population which regularly provided them with food, ammunition and strategic information.[48] A number of other 'social bandits' operated in Mozambique, including Mapondera's successor, Dambakushamba, Moave, and Samakungu as well as in the Huila Highlands of southern Angola, suggesting that this form of resistance was not uncommon and needs to be explored for other parts of Central Africa as well.[49] Preliminary research suggests that a similar pattern occurred with some regularity in the Congo. The actions of Kasongo Niembo in Shaba province, the raids of Kiamfu and his Yaka followers and the Luba support of the rebel Kwilu all seem to conform to the 'social bandit' model.

On occasion, the African levies recruited to quash local dissidents them-

44. H. S. Meebelo, 1971, pp. 102–3.
45. R. Pélissier, 1969, p. 76.
46. See R. S. Price, 1973, pp. 1–30.
47. E. J. Hobsbawm, 1969.
48. A. Isaacman, 1977.
49. A. Isaacman, 1976, pp. 97–125; W. G. Clarence-Smith, 1979, pp. 82–8.

PLATE 8.3 *Mapondera (d. 1904), a leader of guerrilla resistance to British and Portuguese rule in Southern Rhodesia and Mozambique, 1894–1903*

selves revolted to protest against the colonial abuses from which they were not entirely immune. Low wages, harsh punishment and the capricious actions of their European officers generally precipitated the insurrections. The most famous mutinies occurred in the Congo Free State where the entire Luluabourg garrison revolted in 1895. Led by dissident non-commissioned officers, the soldiers killed the commandant of the post in retaliation for his abusive rule. For more than six months the rebels controlled most of Kasai province but they were ultimately defeated by loyalist troops.[50] Two years later the bulk of the field army revolted.[51] While documentation about the alienation of African elements in the Portuguese colonial army remains extremely sketchy, several instances of defections to anti-colonial forces, and the 1917 Tete mutiny suggest, at a minimum, an undercurrent of hostility.[52]

During the early colonial period, there were also numerous peasant revolts which tended to be relatively localized and of short duration. Rarely did the peasants seek to solidify their initial gains or to shift their goals from an attack on the symbols of their oppression to an attack on the colonial system as a whole. As a rule, increased or more strictly enforced taxation and labour demands precipitated the uprisings. In the Zambezi valley between 1890 and 1905 at least sixteen different uprisings occurred. Most of these revolts were directed against the Companhia de Moçambique and the Companhia de Zambésia to which Lisbon ceded most of central Mozambique. Both of these undercapitalized firms sought to maximize profits by imposing a heavy hut tax and exporting forced labour, policies which precipitated the uprisings.[53] During this period there were also several small-scale uprisings in Angola. Peasant revolts among the Ila, Gwemba Tonga and Western Lunda during the first decade of this century concerned British officials in Northern Rhodesia, while in the Congo conservative estimates place the number of localized rural uprisings at more than ten per year.[54]

Although most of these uprisings were amorphous, kaleidoscopic and parochial, in several instances participation raised the political consciousness of the peasants to such a level that they subsequently joined broader-

50. The best account so far is M. Storme, 1961, which is but the first part of a much longer projected study. Elements of this mutiny fought until 1908.

51. F. Flament *et al.*, 1952, pp. 383–460. A doctoral dissertation by Bimanyu dealing with this topic is expected.

52. Rhodesian National Archives, N3/26/2/2, R.N.L.B.: Kanyemba to Managing Director, R.N.L.B., 12 May 1917.

53. A. Isaacman, 1976, pp. 97–125.

54. Before 1909 scattered indications are available in *Le Mouvement géographique* and *La Belgique coloniale*. From 1909 to 1959 more precise data can be found in Chambre des Représentants: F. Flament *et al.*, 1952, p. 530, mentions twelve major operations in Kasai alone from 1893 to 1911. Kasai, however, was the area where large-scale resistance, fuelled by armaments from Angola, was the most pronounced. The Rapport gives the number of police operations per year. See also R. I. Rotberg, 1966, pp. 73–5; H. S. Meebelo, 1971, pp. 97–8.

based anti-colonial movements. This was the case in southern Mozambique where the Tonga joined Gungunyane after the tax revolt of 1894 had been quashed and in the Zambezi valley where Sena and Tonga peasants joined Cambuemba in the 1898 rebellion.[55] Two decades later Tulante Alavaro Buta, an alienated convert to Christianity, was able to organize a mass movement of alienated Bakongo who opposed Portuguese demands for additional labour recruits. Ultimately, his alliance included peasants not only in the Catholic north but those Bakongo recently converted to Protestantism in the south.[56]

Buta's efforts were part of an emerging pattern of protest by disenchanted converts to Christianity. Where Africans were either unable effectively to express their hostility to colonialism or resented the discrimination within the European-dominated Protestant churches, they often formed independent or separatist churches to remedy their grievances. A proliferation of these autonomous religious bodies occurred in Nyasaland and Northern Rhodesia during the first decade of the twentieth century. Perhaps the most famous was the Ethiopian Church founded by Willie Mokalapa. Mokalapa and his disciples repeatedly protested against discrimination by European missionaries and the existence of a promotion bar which limited the upward mobility of skilled Africans. Their long-term goal was to demonstrate that Africans could direct their own religious and secular activities independently of the Europeans.[57] Other church groups such as the Watchtower movement in Northern Rhodesia and the AME in Mozambique pursued similar programmes.

In addition to this localized resistance in the rural areas, reformist agitation was beginning to take place in the urban centres where educated Africans and mulattoes quickly learned that their training and the egalitarian doctrines preached by the missionaries did not preclude social, economic and political discrimination. The mulatto intellectuals of Angola, such as José de Fontes Pereira were among the first to vent their frustration and hostility. Having adopted Portuguese culture *in toto*, they were dismayed at the growing racism that accompanied the influex of European immigrants at the end of the nineteenth century. In an effort to protect their privileged status, they published long editorials and essays bemoaning their declining position, while simultaneously urging Lisbon to guarantee their rights and to end the flagrant exploitation of the Africans. These expressions of discontent proved futile and in 1906 they organized the first mulatto association to lobby for their rights. Four years later, a union of mulatto intellectuals throughout the Portuguese colonies was formed.[58]

55. J. de Azevedo Coutinho, 1904, pp. 28–30; A. Isaacman, 1976, pp. 126–56.
56. D. L. Wheeler and R. Pélissier, 1971, pp. 89–90; J. Marcum, 1969, pp. 53–4.
57. T. O. Ranger, 1965; R. I. Rotberg, 1966, pp. 58–60.
58. D. L. Wheeler and R. Pélissier, 1971, pp. 84–6, 93–8; D. Wheeler in R. Chilcote (ed.) 1972, pp. 67–87; J. Marcum, 1969, pp. 16–22.

At about the same time a small number of reformist intellectual organizations emerged in Mozambique. Among the most important was the Associação African which published the newspaper *Brado Africano*, Mozambique's first protest journal. Like their Angolan counterpart, these writers were part of an emerging mulatto and African bourgeoisie which sought to protect their limited economic privileges and reaffirm their racial and cultural equality.[59]

At about the same period in neighbouring Nyasaland and Northern Rhodesia civil servants, teachers and other African professionals were organizing associations to protect their relatively privileged class position and to agitate for reforms within the existing colonial order. Between 1912 and 1918 a number of such organizations, including the North Nyasa Native Association and the West Nyasa Association, were founded.[60] These groups were to become a prominent force in Central African politics in the inter-war period.

Colonial insurrections to 1918

Colonial insurrections can be differentiated from localized forms of resistance in terms of both their scale and goals. Unlike the sporadic protests which tended to be atomized and highly particularistic, the rebellions were based on mass mobilization and ethnic pluralism. The increased involvement of an oppressed peasantry, at least in some of the uprisings, suggests that class considerations were also becoming an important factor. Inextricably related to this broader base of support was a redefinition and expansion of goals. Protests against a particular set of grievances were rejected in favour of a strategy designed to destroy the repressive system which had generated them.

While colonial insurrections reflected both a higher level of political consciousness and greater alienation, they were not entirely distinct analytically from the atomized opposition which generally antedated them. Like the fugitive communities, they rejected reform from within, seeking independence rather than amelioration. Their similarity to peasant revolts and 'social banditry' lay in their adoption of an offensive, or confrontationist, strategy. Participation in localized protests, moreover, often heightened the level of political consciousness, motivating many Africans to engage in more radical anti-colonial activity.

From 1885, when the first areas of Central Africa were conquered, until 1918, there were more than twenty insurrections.[61] None of the five

59. E. Mondlane, 1969, pp. 104–6: written by the deceased founder of Frelimo, this book attempts to place the recent liberation struggle within a broader historical framework.
60. R. Tangri, 1968, p. 5; J. Van Velsen in E. Stokes and R. Brown (eds), 1966, pp. 376–7: discusses formation of associations to protect the position of the subaltern elite and their efforts to seek reforms within the colonial system.
61. This represents a minimum figure which will undoubtedly be revised as further research is done in this subject.

colonies – Angola, Mozambique, Nyasaland, Northern Rhodesia or the Congo – were spared, although the overwhelming preponderance of insurrections occurred in the Portuguese colonies and the Congo, where the combination of extremely oppressive rule and a weak administrative and military structure precipitated recurring revolutionary activity.

These insurrections, although differing in detail, all faced similar organizational problems which, in turn, generated common characteristics and placed serious constraints on their capacity to succeed. Among the fundamental problems which had to be resolved were: finding a leader with the prestige, commitment and expertise to mobilize and direct a mass movement; determining the principles around which to organize a broad anti-colonial movement; and locating a source of arms and munitions.

The initial unsuccessful struggles to remain independent just before the imposition of colonial rule had resulted in the death or removal of many of the most respected and militant leaders. Among those killed were the Chewa leader Mwase Kasungu and the Yeke ruler Msiri. Others were either exiled like Gungunyane, and Mwenemutapa Chioco, the royal family of the Barue, or were replaced by more pliable members of the royal family as was the fate of the Humbe ruler Tehuango and the Quitanghona leader Shaikh Mahmud. The destruction or co-option of the historic leadership convinced colonial officials that they had effectively 'occupied' their respective territories which, in turn, dramatically reduced the possibility of subsequent uprisings. They failed, however, to recognize the continued legitimacy and viability of indigenous political institutions, the availability of alternative sources of leadership, and the commitment of many Central African peoples to be free.

The prominent role played by a number of royal families in the insurrections challenged the generally held assumption that pronounced military setbacks at the time of the Scramble had undercut the position of the indigenous authorities. The sacred power inherent in the position of kingship and the strong anti-Portuguese sentiment among the masses enabled the exiled Mwenemutapa ruler Chioco to organize the rebellion of 1897, a pattern repeated twenty years later when Nongwe-Nongwe returned from Southern Rhodesia to lead the Barue and neighbouring Zambezi peoples in the 1917 insurrection.[62] Similarly, the Bailundu ruler Muta-ya-Kavela, despite his nominal acceptance of Portuguese authority, forged an anti-colonial coalition during the 1902 rebellion and to the north the Dembo ruler Cazuangonongo rose up with his supporters in 1908.[63] In southern Angola the displaced Cuamato leader (*soba*) Sihetekela reasserted his authority and led his people into an anti-Portuguese alliance with the

62. T. O. Ranger, 1968b, pp. 1–2; A. Isaacman, 1976, pp. 156–85.

63. D. L. Wheeler and C. D. Christensen in F.-W. Heimer (ed.), 1973, pp. 75–6; J. Marcum, 1969, p. 16: a very important work which includes the early twentieth-century antecedents of the recent war of liberation.

Cuanhama, setting the stage for the 1915 war.[64] Similarly, Congo Free
State officials were dismayed to find their nominal subject the Lunda king,
Mushidi, organizing a major rebellion which lasted from 1905 to 1909.[65]

Just as the colonial authorities failed to comprehend the resiliency of
kingship, they also overestimated the power of their newly co-opted rulers
– the 'colonial' chiefs – to impose requirements which violated the values
and interests of their constituents. The Quitanghona rebellion of 1904,
for example, was directed at both the Portuguese and their puppet ruler
Said bin Amissi, who was overthrown in favour of the legitimate leader
Shaikh Mahmud.[66] A similar usurpation of power by a co-opted member of
the royal family precipitated the Humbe rebellion of 1891.[67] In other cases,
such as in Makanga, the council of elders, reflecting the prevailing sentiment of their constituents, demanded that the 'colonial' chief Chinsinga
renounce Portuguese rule or be deposed. He reluctantly agreed to declare
Makanga independent which led to a violent confrontation with Lisbon's
forces.[68]

Even where the legitimate leadership had been effectively removed or
co-opted, other potential leaders emerged that enjoyed popular support.
Often these men had played a prominent role in the wars of independence.
Gungunyane's principal lieutenant and war leader Maguiguana organized
the Shangaan insurrection of 1897.[69] The famous *mestizo* soldier Cambuemba, whose anti-Portuguese exploits had become legendary, played
a similar role in the Sena-Tonga rebellion which embroiled the entire lower
Zambezi valley two years later.[70] In several insurrections in the Congo
the leadership came from commoners who were able to mobilize mass
support. Kandolo, a disaffected sergeant in the Force Publique, for
example, led a military revolt in 1897, which, unlike other mutinies, sought
to drive out the Europeans and liberate the Congo Free State.[71]

Cult priests and spirit mediums organized and sanctified a number of
insurrections. This involvement, which antedated the colonial period, was
a logical extension of their historic role as spiritual guardians of the homelands. In 1909 the Tonga priest Maluma called for the immediate ousting
of the colonial overlords in Nyasaland. 'The time has come for us to fight
the white people, we will start now and fight through the rainy season.
The black people [will] rise and drive all the white people out of the

---

64. R. Pélissier, 1969, pp. 100–1.
65. E. Bustin, 1975, p. 48.
66. N. Hafkin, 1973, p. 378.
67. R. Pélissier, 1969, p. 73.
68. A. Isaacman, 1972, pp. 132–3: an examination of the operation of the Zambezi *prazos*
and the resistance of the Afro-Portuguese *prazeros* to Portuguese rule.
69. T. Coelho, 1898, p. 83; J. J. T. Botelho, 1934, II, pp. 533–47.
70. J. de Azevedo Coutinho, 1904, pp. 26–8; J. J. T. Botelho, 1921, Vol. II, pp. 549–57.
71. F. Flament *et al.*, 1952, p. 411. At the least, they sought to occupy the former Arab
zone, i.e. about half of the state.

country'.[72] Maluma subsequently led the Tonga into battle. Similarly, the Mbona cult priests played an important leadership role in the Massingire rebellion of 1884, and there are suggestions that the Kandundu cult officials were actively involved in the Bailundu rebellion of 1904.[73] In the Congo, the cult priestess Maria Nkoie prophesied her war charms would neutralize European guns. With this assurance her followers began a five-year campaign which lasted until 1921. At its high point the Ikaya rebellion, named after the famous war charms, had spread throughout a vast region of the Congo.[74] Nowhere was religious leadership so significant as in the Zambezi valley. Shona spirit mediums mobilized public support behind the abortive rebellions of 1897, 1901 and 1904, claiming at various times that the divinely inspired drought, famines and cattle disease which threatened their economic survival, would end once the alien intruders had been driven away. In 1917 the spirit medium Mbuya threatened to withhold divine recognition from the Barue leader Nongwe-Nongwe unless he reversed his unpopular position and agreed to participate in an anti-colonial rebellion. Reluctantly, he agreed.[75]

As the influence of Protestant missionaries increased, several alienated African converts attempted to build anti-colonial movements phrased in revolutionary millennial doctrine. The most famous of these early leaders were Kamwana and John Chilembwe, both of Nyasaland. The former, a member of the Watchtower, prophesied that a new order of divinely sanctioned African states would begin in 1914. During the interim, Kamwana urged his 10 000 followers to purify themselves and specifically eschewed any violent resistance to British rule.[76] While there is some uncertainty as to Chilembwe's ultimate goal, he also envisioned a divinely inspired African state but, unlike Kamwana, he led his followers in an abortive and perhaps symbolic insurrection in 1915.[77] In death he became an anti-colonial martyr whose significance exceeded his earthly accomplishments.

Like Chilembwe, almost all the leaders recognized the need to create alliances which transcended their local base of support. The unsuccessful wars of opposition had demonstrated that individual polities lacked the requisite resources to prevent European penetration. This fact was accurately foreseen by the leader of the Mozambican state of Makanga just before the 1899 rebellion. 'The Africans of all tribes must unite in good faith, in a coordinated effort to acquire large supplies of arms and

72. Cited in R. I. Rotberg, 1966, pp. 75–6.

73. W. Montagu-Kerr, 1886, pp. 275–6; D. L. Wheeler and C. D. Christensen in F.-W. Heimer (ed.), 1973, p. 75.

74. G. Moulaert, 1945, pp. 187–8.

75. A. Isaacman, 1976, pp. 126–85.

76. G. Shepperson, and T. Price, 1958, p. 156.

77. For the classic work about Chilembwe, see G. Shepperson and T. Price, 1958. This seminal study also includes important information on Kamwana.

ammunition and when we have achieved this we must expel all the Portuguese'.[78]

Efforts to build broad-based revolutionary movements followed three general patterns. The first was an attempt to reactivate historical links with culturally related peoples in order to recruit entire polities into the camp of the insurgents. The rebels also sought to secure the assistance of powerful groups, which by virtue of their relative distance or past differences, had not been previously considered allies. Finally, the leaders directed economic appeals specifically at alienated peasants. All three organizing principles were used at various times and in different combinations to increase the scale of the rebellion and mobilize public support against a common oppressor.

Historic relations based on shared ancestry were often invoked to broaden the base of support. Muta-ya-Kavela benefited from the assistance of a number of related Umbundu kingdoms during the 1904 Bailundu rebellion in Angola, while to the south several Ovambo chieftaincies joined with Cuamato groups in an insurrection three years later.[79] In Mozambique, Mwenemutapa Chioco received the aid of a number of independent Tawara polities on the basis of his prestigious position as patrilineal descendant of Mtota, first king of the Tawara, and the Barue benefited from recurring marital unions with the Tonga.[80] A common ancestry, symbolized by the hierarchical network of spirit mediums, also helped to unify the disparate Shona chieftaincies in their uprisings of 1901, 1904 and 1917,[81] while the spread of the Ikaya rebellion in the Congo was based on a shared system which facilitated the incorporation of the disparate peoples living along the bend of the Zaire river.[82]

In search of additional allies, the leaders of the various insurrections often appealed to former adversaries who shared a common hatred of the colonial system. The Bailundu were able to gain the support of a number of former subject people including the Kasongi, Civanda and Ngalanga, while the Shangaan benefited from the assistance of chieftaincies that they had alienated during their expansionist phase prior to the Scramble.[83] In a number of cases, reconciliation occurred only after the leaders of a pro-European group recognized the full implications of their act. The Lunda, under Mushidi, first aided the Congo Free State against the Chokwe but, in a dramatic reversal in 1905, joined with their former enemies in a struggle

78. J. Fernandes Júnior, 1955, p. 50.

79. D. L. Wheeler and C. D. Christensen in F.-W. Heimer (ed.), 1973, p. 76; R. Pélissier, 1969, pp. 85–7.

80. T. O. Ranger, 1968b, pp. 1–2; A. Isaacman, 1973, pp. 395–400.

81. A. Isaacman, 1976, pp. 126–85.

82. F. Flament *et al.*, 1952, p. 411.

83. D. L. Wheeler and C. D. Christensen, in F.-W. Heimer (ed.), 1973, p. 76; J. J. T. Botelho, 1934, Vol. II, pp. 433–67.

which was not crushed until the famine of 1910–12.[84] (See Fig. 8.1.) In Mozambique the strategically located Sena, who fought on the side of the Portuguese in the 1901 Barue war, enthusiastically supported the Barue sixteen years later as part of a pan-Zambezian movement to destroy the repressive colonial system.[85]

The insurgents also increased their numbers by incorporating alienated peasants and rural workers who individually opposed the continued demands of the colonial authorities and their capitalist allies. The appeal was not made in ethnic or cultural terms nor was it necessarily directed at the chiefs, many of whom had been co-opted. Instead, the rebels urged the economically oppressed to join the insurrection in order to eliminate both the abusive taxation and labour practices and the system which had spawned them. The Kamwana movement in Nyasaland was initially based on the support of the Lakeside Tonga but rapidly grew to include alienated Nguni, Senga and Tumbuka peasants.[86] Similarly, Chilembwe's appeal to the rural masses lacked ethnic overtones, addressing instead the need to end exploitation and create a divinely sanctioned African nation.[87] The Bailundu gained adherents from among non-Umbundu peasants who suffered from forced labour and economic exploitation. In the Zambezi valley many of the peasants who had previously expressed their animosity through localized resistance joined the recurring insurrections.[88] A similar pattern occurred in the Congo where exploited rubber farmers precipitated the Kuba rebellion of 1904.[89]

The question of arms acquisition need not be examined at length. It suffices to say that the rebels obtained modern weapons through surreptitious trade agreements with European, Asian and African merchants, raids on European stockades, acquisitions from defecting African police and mercenaries, alliances with neighbouring peoples who were still independent and, in some cases, construction of arms and munitions plants. While some of the rebels, such as the Barue and Cuamato, were able to build up relatively large arsenals, the insurgents rarely possessed the firepower that earlier resisters had amassed.

Given the extremely unfavourable balance of military power and the expanded size of the African police and mercenary forces, it is little wonder that the insurrections all ultimately failed. Nevertheless, a number of them scored significant, though short-term, successes, challenging the commonly held belief in African docility. The Bailundu, for example, drove the

84. E. Bustin, 1975, p. 48.

85. This shift in allegiance is documented at great length in the Arquivos da Companhia de Mozambique, File 1633.

86. G. Shepperson and T. Price, 1958, p. 156.

87. See G. Shepperson and T. Price, 1958; G. S. Mwase, 1967.

88. D. L. Wheeler and C. D. Christensen in F.-W. Heimer (ed.), 1973, pp. 76–7; A. Isaacman, 1976, pp. 126–85.

89. The rubber farmers triggered the rebellion. J. Vansina, 1969, pp. 21–2.

Portuguese off the Ovimbundu highlands in 1904. Three years later the Portuguese suffered a similar defeat at the hands of the Cuamato in southern Angola. Perhaps the greatest military accomplishment was achieved by the Barue and their allies who during the 1917 rebellion liberated the entire Zambezi valley for a fleeting moment. Had it not been for the intercession of 30 000 Nguni mercenaries, the rebellion would probably have spread to other parts of Mozambique.

Conclusion

This study has examined the early forms of African initiatives and resistance in the face of European rule. Throughout the essay we have attempted to document the frequency and vigour of this anti-colonial activity. The desire of most Africans to be free was matched by the ambitions of a smaller group of mercenaries and allies without whom it would have been impossible for the Europeans to have imposed their rule so thoroughly. Thus, there existed both a tradition of confrontation and resistance and a tradition of co-operation. Although the political context had changed, the struggle between these two competing forces was to remain a vital factor in Central and Southern Africa during the struggle for independence in the 1960s and 1970s.

African initiatives and resistance in Southern Africa

D. CHANAIWA

Southern Africa on the eve of colonial rule

When discussing African respones to the European colonization of Southern Africa in the nineteenth century, it is important to understand the wider cultural and social environment in which they occurred. The major historical forces were expansionist settler colonialism, missionary Christianity and education, and finally, the Zulu revolution and its by-products – the Mfecane and Nguni migrations. By the time of the Berlin West African Conference (1884–5) with its feverish competition among European nations for colonial possessions in Africa, the Scramble between the British and the Afrikaners for Southern African territories had been going on for over seventy years. Terms such as 'treaty', 'sphere of influence', 'effective occupation', 'annexation' and 'frontier force', which became common throughout the rest of Africa after the Berlin Conference, had been in widespread use in Southern Africa since 1815. European settlers in Southern Africa, unlike their counterparts in the rest of Africa, were from the beginning interested in establishing permanent homes in their new environment, attracted by its temperate climate, fertile agricultural land, cheap African labour and an abundance of minerals.

By 1880 there were a total of four white polities in South Africa: the Cape Colony and Natal, with their predominantly English-speaking white population of 185 000 and 20 000 respectively, and the South African Republic and Orange Free State, each with over 50 000 Dutch-speaking whites. Then, on 12 September 1890, a further British colony, Mashonaland, was established. In these five settler colonies, vast majorities of indigenous Africans were dominated by white minorities. For the San and Khoikhoi this domination had been going on for over two hundred years while others, such as the Xhosa, Mfengu, Thembu and Mpondo peoples, had been subjugated to varying forms of colonial rule for nearly a century (see Fig. 9.1).[1]

1. For African responses before the 1880s see W. M. Macmillan, 1963; C. W. De Kiewiet, 1965; J. Phillip, 1828; J. S. Marais, 1957.

FIG. 9.1 *Peoples and polities of Southern Africa, showing the Nguni migrations and the area of the Chimurenga*

Under the Sand River Convention (1852), the British and Afrikaners had agreed not to sell firearms to Africans throughout Southern Africa. The Convention deprived the Africans of the means they needed for effective resistance and self-defence.

Thus, by the time the European nations adopted the Brussels General Act of 1890, forbidding the sale of firearms to Africans, whites in Southern Africa had for some time been attempting to implement a policy of disarming the Africans, although during the 1870s and 1880s some groups were able to purchase firearms with wages earned on the diamond fields. Additionally, the Afrikaners, English colonists and the British government maintained an aura of racial identity that transcended their political and economic differences. They felt it was in their common interest to conquer, rule and exploit the Africans. Thus, they not only acted to prevent firearms from passing into African hands, but generally refrained from using local Africans as allies in their battles against one another. All this considerably conditioned African initiatives and reactions and limited the options open to them.

The Zulu revolution and its aftermath

Added to this were the epoch-making events which had erupted throughout Southern Africa during the early nineteenth century. These included the Zulu revolution, and the Mfecane in South Africa; the Nguni migrations of the Ndebele into Southern Rhodesia (now Zombabwe), the Kololo into Northern Rhodesia (now Zambia) and the Nguni into Nyasaland (now Malawi) and Tanganyika (now Tanzania); the Bemba activities in Northern Zambia; the Yao–Swahili alliance; and the slave trade in Malawi (see Fig. 9.1). Some of these events spread with explosive speed and caused sudden changes in the political, economic, social and military systems of numerous African societies throughout Southern Africa. This was a period of nation-building and political expansion which saw the strongest and most centralized states establish domains or spheres of influence over the weaker and less united ones. While countless contemporary European statesmen and observers regarded these far-reaching changes as mere outbursts of African barbarity, blood-thirstiness and heathenism, they should be seen rather as manifestations of political creativity which led to the emergence of new, inter-ethnic institutions and loyalties, the legacies of which are still visible today.

Though creative, these far-reaching changes caused immeasurable destruction to human and natural resources. Natural disasters such as drought, epidemics and famine also often accompanied the violence and magnified the extent of the ensuing destruction. This continuing incidence of conflict and disasters created a perpetual sense of insecurity and despair among the small, unaggressive tributary communities, many of whom were forced to adapt to living in caves or crude hilltop dwellings to avoid further attacks by raiders. There arose ruling aristocracies, class distinctions and taxation without political representation or consultation. As a result, there soon emerged rulers and ruled, oppressors and underdogs, and haves and have-nots.

The missionary factor

Both missionary Christianity and education were also important factors which determined the course and nature of African responses to colonial conquest. The missionaries had created an African class of evangelists, teachers, journalists, businessmen, lawyers and clerks who often seemed to accept the supposed cultural inferiority of the Africans, to accept settler colonialism as a fact of life and who admired the white man for his power, wealth and technology.[2] Examples of these individuals were Tiyo Soga (1829–71), the first African missionary to be ordained by the United Presbyterian Church in Britain, founder of the Mgwali mission where he preached to both Africans and Europeans, and translator of John Bunyan's *Pilgrim's Progress* into Xhosa as *U-Hambo Lom-Hambi*, the first book written by an African to be published by the Lovedale Press, in 1867; John Langalibalele Dube, a Methodist minister, an ardent follower of the black American educationalist, Booker T. Washington, founder-president of the Zulu Christian Industrial School, the Natal Bantu Business League and the first president of the African National Congress; John Tengo Jabavu (1859–1921), a devout Methodist, founder-editor of the English/ Xhosa weekly *Imvo Zabantsundu*; and Walter Rubusana, a Congregationalist minister and the only African ever elected to the Cape Provincial Council.

Ideologically, these mission-educated Africans shared the universalism, utopianism and non-racialism of the missionaries and of the Aborigines' Protection Society. They were committed to constitutionalism, gradualism, and cultural assimilation as advocated by a few white liberals among the settlers. But they also were disciples of Booker T. Washington's doctrine of black economic self-determination and of his conservative politics of accommodation.

Like the missionaries, they often categorized the African masses as 'benighted people' and 'noble savages' and then assumed the responsibility of overhauling traditional Africa through introducing Christianity, education, capitalism, industrialization, and the Protestant work ethic. They generally acquiesced in colonial expansion and conquest, partly because, like the missionaries, they associated colonialism with Christianity and 'civilization', and partly because they respected the 'overwhelming superiority' of European weapons and warfare.

Thus, to Tiyo Soga, the Xhosa cattle-killing episode of 1857 was a

2. For details, see D. Chanaiwa in A. Mugomba and M. Nyaggah (eds), 1980.

national suicide by his 'poor infatuated countrymen' who had become 'dupes of designing impostors'. He hoped, however, that 'this affliction will, in the providence of God, be productive of much spiritual benefit to the Kaffirs'. He claimed that: 'It is by terrible things that God sometimes accomplished His purposes. In the present calamities I think I see the future salvation of my countrymen, both in a physical and moral point of view.'[3] Dube condemned the Bambata rebellion (1906–8) in his newspaper, *Ilanga lase Natal*, and instead advised the Zulu to accept Christianity and education. Part of the reason why Jabavu boycotted the African National Congress was because he felt that the elite still needed the guiding leadership of white liberals.

The elite was torn between its utopian world of missionaries, humanitarians and white liberals, the traditionalist world of the African masses which it sometimes despised, and the colonialist world of settler racism, exploitation and oppression which determined the real life and status of its members. These created a moralist world of their own to which they attempted to lead both the African and settler worlds.

Their mistake was to associate colonial conquest with the spread of Christianity, education and technology and then to despise African resistance as heathenism and backwardness. Their condemnation of traditional Africa only bolstered and upheld the colonialist ideology which they opposed. On the other hand, by their own sermons, lifestyles and beliefs, they helped to undermine psychologically the African's capacity to resist missionary-settler propaganda and in a way hindered the development of a truly African historical, racial and liberationist consciousness. They and their fellow African Christian followers either stood on the sidelines and watched, or took refuge in mission stations rather than join the armed resistance against colonial conquest and occupation.

Models of African initiatives and reactions

The above-mentioned factors significantly affected the nature and intensity of African responses to the encroaching European imperialism and colonization. Generally, there were three distinct models of initiatives and responses: (1) that of violent confrontation as exhibited by the Zulu, Ndebele, Changanana, Bemba, Yao and Nguni; and the Mangwende, Makoni and Mutasa paramountcies; (2) that of protectorate or wardship chosen by the Sotho, Swazi, Ngwato, Tswana and Lozi, all independent, non-tributary states who sought protection from the British against the Zulu, Ndebele, Bemba, the Nguni and the Boers; and (3) that of alliance adopted by the numerous small tributaries, raid victims and refugees such as the Khoikhoi, Xhosa, Mpondo, Thembu, Mfengu and Hlubi in South Africa; the Bisa, Lungu, Iwa and Senga in Northern Rhodesia; and the

3. J. A. Chalmers, 1877, p. 140.

Cewa, Njanja, Nkonde and Tonga in Nyasaland, in the hope of securing 'protection, peace and security'. Thus, there existed historical rivalries among the nascent and expansionist kingdoms, as well as conflicts of interest amid the different cultural segments and dynasties within them. Each ruler, society and individual responded to the growing European intrusion in the context of pre-colonial, inter-regional relations and realities.

The European colonizers did not fail to exploit the situation they found. Their study of contemporary African political systems enabled them to predict the forms of African reaction and resistance. The Zulu, Ndebele, Yao and Nguni expansionism, for example, could only function smoothly, they found, when the aristocracies were powerful and supreme, and when the tributary chiefs were weak and disunited, or at least felt the need for military protection and were confident that the ruling aristocracy could provide it.

War-weariness and insecurity contributed greatly to the acceptance of British wardship or alliance on the part of several African polities and individuals. They also provided pretexts for British interference in African affairs through offers of 'liberation' and 'protection' to the underdogs, 'alliances' with less powerful kingdoms, and invasion of the militaristic ones. The British employed a deliberate tactic of 'divide and conquer'. As a result, they exploited African rivalries, fears and weaknesses to their fullest advantage.

The Zulu, Ndebele, Bemba and Yao: the politics of confrontation

Violent confrontation, conquest and destruction were virtually inevitable for the Zulu, Ndebele, Bemba and Yao because they and the European colonizers sought to rule the same territories and the same peoples. As a group, they occupied or dominated the most densely populated, fertile and mineral-rich lands of Southern Africa. Their interests made it impossible for them to compromise or coexist with the Europeans. Only the superior power would survive.

The Zulu were the most powerful African nation south of the Limpopo, the Ndebele between the Limpopo and the Zambezi, the Bemba in Northern Rhodesia and the Yao in southern and northern Nyasaland respectively. But from the very beginning, the Zulu, Ndebele, Changana, Kololo and Nguni kingdoms found themselves surrounded by powerful and hostile neighbours: in the case of the Zulu, the Boers, British Sotho and Swazi; and for the Ndebele, the Boers, Portuguese, Lozi, Changan and Ngwato – each of these hostile neighbours capable of conquering and evicting them. The Boers and the Portuguese were uncompromising in their conduct of external affairs, pursuing a policy of raid and conquest.

Up to the early 1870s, the Zulu, Ndebele, Bemba and Yao had been able to maintain their sovereignty, independence and security. They had also successfully resisted the intrusion of the missionaries, the European traders, concessionaires and labour recruiters who had by then reached the conclusion that the conquest and dismantling of these resistant African states was essential. They deluded themselves that Africans were yearning for Christianity, trade and western culture, but that the raids, tyranny and heathenism of their kings, administrators and soldiers were ruthlessly crushing 'their ambition, enterprise and desire for salvation'. Consequently, these outsiders adopted an attitude of conquest before Christianity and trade.

The Zulu

The Zulu under Cetshwayo and the Ndebele under Lobengula therefore decided on the strategy of confrontation using first the tactics of diplomacy and later those of armed resistance. In accordance with this strategy, Cetshwayo at first continued the isolationist, pacifist foreign policies of his predecessor Mpande. His inveterate enemies being the Transvaal Boers, he maintained an effective alliance with the English colonists of the Natal and he developed friendly relations with Theophilus Shepstone, the famous Secretary for Native Affairs in Natal. But when the British annexed the Transvaal in 1877 and made Shepstone the Administrator, Cetshwayo's alliance system quickly collapsed. Shepstone then supported the Boers, who had crossed the Buffalo river into Zululand, pegged out farms and were claiming land titles. The new British High Commissioner for South Africa, Sir Bartle Frere, was also intent on achieving the federation of settler colonies.[4] Shepstone convinced him that such a federation could not be achieved in South Africa until the military power of the Zulu nation had been broken, and that the very existence of the Zulu nation threatened the security and economic development of Natal. He also argued that with the destruction of the Zulu, the Boers would be impressed that the British government had a sound view of race relations and the strength needed to enforce its decisions.

Meanwhile, Cetshwayo had appealed to Sir Henry Bulwer, the Lieutenant-Governor of Natal, to settle the Zulu–Boer border dispute. Sir Henry appointed a boundary commission, which reviewed the dispute, declared that the Boers' claims were illegal and recommended that they return to the Transvaal side of the river. Frere, however, was determined to break the power of the Zulu nation in order to achieve federation. So he concealed the report and recommendations of the commission until he had secured the pretext for invasion and received military reinforcements. The pretext came on 28 July 1878, when Mehlokazulu, Kuzulu and Tshekwana, chief Sirayo's sons and their uncle, Zuluhlenga, crossed the

4. C. F. Goodfellow, 1966.

PLATE 9.1 *Site of the battle of Isandhlwana, 1879, a Zulu victory over British forces*

Buffalo river and brought back the wives of the chief, who had crossed into Natal. Frere and Shepstone exploited this incident to the fullest advantage. Soon, South Africa and the Colonial Office were flooded with rumours of an imminent Zulu invasion of Natal. Missionaries were advised to leave Zululand. At this point, Shepstone and Frere began to misrepresent the Zulu army as a raiding and menacing force, and Cetshwayo as a blood-thirsty tyrant.

Frere then ordered Cetshwayo to surrender Sirayo's sons and brother to Sir Henry Bulwer for trial though the Zulu had never been conquered nor made to submit to British rule. Cetshwayo proposed instead to pay £50 sterling and to apologize for the incident. On 11 December 1878 Frere sent Cetshwayo an ultimatum. Among its demands were the delivery of the accused along with 500 head of cattle, the disbanding of the Zulu army within thirty days, the admission of missionaries and the stationing of a British Resident in Zululand. Frere knew that no independent and self-respecting ruler would comply with such extreme demands.

Then, on 11 January 1879, under the command of Lord Chelmsford, a British army of over 7000 soldiers with some 1000 white volunteers and 7000 African auxiliaries invaded Zululand from three points. On 22 January the Zulu army achieved a memorable victory at the battle of Isandhlwana, when it killed 1600 of the invaders and turned back the assault. But on 4 July the British forces returned and overran the Zulu nation. Cetshwayo was banished to Cape Town, and Zululand was divided into thirteen separate chiefdoms, which were placed under the supervision of puppet chiefs. These chiefs included Cetshwayo's rival, Zibhebhu, his cousin, Hamu, who had deserted to join the British forces during the war and John Dunn, a white man. The division of Zululand was a classic case of the systematic destruction of a nation achieved by the policy of divide and conquer. To perpetuate this, the new chiefs were instructed to disband all existing military organization, prohibit the importation of arms and accept arbitration by the British Resident.

The degree of rivalry among the chiefs was so great, however, and the threat of anarchy increasing so rapidly that, in an effort to 'restore order' within the most unstable areas of the former Zulu nation, Cetshwayo had to be brought back. Zibhebhu was allowed to keep his chiefdom. But soon civil war broke out between the forces of Cetshwayo and Zibhebhu. Cetshwayo died in flight at the height of the battle in 1884. The diminished Zulu nation was then placed under the leadership of Dinizulu, Cetshwayo's 15-year-old son, whose power and authority was dependent on white support. The Zulu had at last succumbed to British control.

The Ndebele

From 1870 to 1890 Lobengula, like Cetshwayo of the Zulu, consistently and successfully pursued a well-formulated diplomatic strategy to protect

PLATE 9.2 *Lobengula* (c. *1836–94*), *King of the Ndebele, 1870–94*

203

the vital interest of the Ndebele nation. He restricted immigration and informed alien whites that he was not interested in opening his country to them for mining or hunting. Added to this, he had developed several tactics, such as constantly moving from one town to another, pitting one European nation, company or individual against another, and postponing decisions to frustrate impatient concessionaires. As a longer-range strategy, he sought either military alliance or protectorate status with the British government to counter the Germans, Portuguese and Afrikaners, and so prevent uncontrolled South African colonial expansion.

These forms of diplomatic resistance apparently worked effectively until 1888, when the South African financier, Cecil John Rhodes, convinced Sir Hercules Robinson, the High Commissioner, and Sir Sidney Shippard, the Deputy Commissioner for Bechuanaland, to enlist the help of the Reverend John Smith Moffat. Moffat had left Matabeleland in 1865 after totally failing to convert the Ndebele. He had ultimately become Shippard's assistant commissioner. Moffat was eager to effect the colonization of the Ndebele to vindicate himself for his past failure. Moreover, he resented Mzilikazi, Lobengula and the Ndebele rulers generally for their successful resistance to Christianity. Thus motivated by a combination of vengeance, arrogance and racism, he was keen to pave the way for the destruction of the Ndebele state.[5]

Moffat chose to support Rhodes and the Chartered Company because, as he noted, the Company would inevitably bring about the conquest and the dismantling of the Ndebele nation 'unless history here should be different from history elsewhere in South Africa'. At first, Moffat posed as a spiritual adviser, interested not in gold, game or conquest, but in giving 'friendly advice' to an 'old friend'. The 'advice' was that Lobengula should 'ally' with the British, rather than with the Afrikaners, Portuguese or Germans. Moffat also led Lobengula to believe that he was doing no more than simply renewing the old Anglo-Ndebele treaty, enacted in 1836 between his father, Mzilikazi, and Sir Benjamin D'Urban, the former British Governor of South Africa. So on 11 February 1888 Lobengula signed what has since been canonized as 'the Moffat treaty'. Under its terms, he promised to refrain from entering into any correspondence or treaty with any foreign state or power to sell, alienate, or cede, or permit or countenance any sale, alienation, or cession of the whole or any part of the said land he controlled, or upon any other subject, without the previous knowledge and sanction of Her Majesty's High Commissioner for South Africa.[6] With this treaty in force, the British occupation of Rhodesia began. Moffat had put both Matabeleland and Mashonaland squarely under the British sphere of influence.

Under the European international convention of the late nineteenth

5. R. U. Moffat, 1969, p. 233.
6. ibid., p. 370.

century, Lobengula had commended himself to British colonialism. The Ndebele thereafter could deal only with the British. Thus, their diplomatic options for playing European nations against one another had been terminated. Soon, hordes of British concessionaires and syndicates descended on Lobengula seeking mineral and land rights in Matabeleland and Mashonaland. In mercenary fashion, these zealous speculators readily offered him stores of guns, ammunition, money, clothing, utensils and ornaments and performed all manner of services to gain his favour.

Noting this, Rhodes dispatched Rudd, Thompson and Maguire[7] to seek a monopolistic agreement with Lobengula, which would be used to apply for a royal charter to shut out other British concessionaires and syndicates. Rhodes wanted 'not merely local rights, shared with every casual adventurer, but the sole command of the mineral resources of the whole country'. On the strength of the Rudd Concession, as the agreement is called, Rhodes's company occupied Mashonaland on 12 September 1890.

The controversial Rudd Concession was obtained primarily by the conspiratorial deception of Lobengula by both British imperial officials and missionaries. Moffat had been sent to Matabeleland for a second time to condition Lobengula for the arrival of Rhodes's agents. Feigning friendship and neutrality as a minister of God, Moffat introduced Rudd, Thompson and Maguire as 'honourable and upright men' and endorsed Shippard highly. He pleaded vigorously on their behalf during the four-week negotiations that ensued. Thereafter, Shippard arrived with Major Guild-Adams and sixteen mounted policemen. After nine days of negotiations with Lobengula, he departed, just six days before the concession was signed. According to Rudd's diary, by then 'almost all political matters had been talked out in a most friendly spirit'.

The Rudd Concession consisted of two distinct and interrelated segments: the written segment, which was both important and advantageous to the concessionaires; and the verbal, which was advantageous to Lobengula. Under the written agreement – that is, the original draft of the proposals presented to Lobengula – the king granted to the concessionaires complete and exclusive domain over all the metal and mineral resources in his kingdoms, principalities and dominions, together with full power to do all they deemed necessary to procure these resources. The grantees also were empowered 'to take all necessary and lawful steps' to exclude from competition all other persons seeking land, minerals or mining rights. Lobengula further agreed not to grant concessions of land or mining rights to any other persons or interests without the prior consent and concurrence of the grantees.

In return, the concessionaires agreed to pay Lobengula and his heirs £100 sterling per month in perpetuity. They also agreed to give him 1000 Martini-Henry breech-loading rifles and 100 000 rounds of suitable ball cartridges. The draft stipulated that 500 of the rifles and 50 000 of the

7. For more details, see P. Mason, 1958; C. Palley, 1966; S. Samkange, 1967.

cartridges were to be delivered to Lobengula before the start of mining operations in the territory. The concessionaires also agreed 'to deliver on the Zambezi River a steamboat with guns suitable for defensive purposes upon the said river'.

During the course of the negotiations, however, the king verbally set forth certain conditions which he apparently regarded *prima facie* as being thereafter an integral part of the agreement. According to Helm, Lobengula thus stipulated and the concessionaires consented that: (1) the grantees would bring no more than ten white men at a time to perform mining work in his territories; (2) the miners would not dig in or near the towns; (3) the whites would 'abide by the laws of his country and in fact be as his people', and (4) the miners would fight in defence of the country under Ndebele command, if needed. The concessionaires also verbally clarified that by 'full power to do all things that they may deem necessary to win and procure minerals', they meant erection of dwellings to house their overseers, bringing and erecting the machinery they needed, and the use of wood and water. Unfortunately, these verbal conditions were not written into the final agreement, and thus, under European contractual law, were not enforceable parts of the agreement.

From disappointed rival concessionaires and especially from two literate Africans, John Kumalo and John Makunga, who sympathetically interpreted the concession, Lobengula and his *indunas* (councillors) learned that they had been cheated; that the concession had already been published in European newspapers and that Rhodes had already formed the company to occupy both Matabeleland and Mashonaland. Shock, fear and confusion took over the Ndebele nation as the people became aware of the full meaning and ramifications of the concession, and, especially, the dreadful inevitability of a great monarch and great nation moving towards catastrophe. Several of the *indunas* and warriors were furious, and Lobengula was terribly embarrassed and fearful of losing power.

He published notice of repudiation of the concession in the *Bechuanaland News* of February 1889. At his orders, the pro-British *induna*, Lotshe, was killed by the Mbesu regiment, together with his wives, children and livestock. Once he was aware of the collusion between Rhodes, the missionaries and the imperial officials in South Africa, he decided to appeal directly to the British government in England. Through letters and a delegation, he appealed to Queen Victoria to repudiate the treaty or to declare a protectorate over Matabeleland and Mashonaland. In January 1889 he sent an official delegation to London consisting of *indunas* Motshede and Babiyance, who had audience with Queen Victoria and some leading members of the Aborigines' Protection Society. The *indunas* returned with royal greetings but no repudiation. Rhodes obtained his monopolist royal charter to colonize the area. In early 1890 his pioneers marched from South Africa, through Matabeleland into Mashonaland and hoisted the Union Jack at Salisbury on 12 September 1890.

From September 1890 to October 1893 the Ndebele nation and settler colony of Mashonaland kept a wary eye on each other. As had happened between the settlers and the Xhosa in the Cape as well as the settlers and the Zulu in Natal, it was a matter of time before the inevitable military showdown occurred.

The whole scenario of the Anglo-Ndebele war of 1893 was virtually a carbon copy of the Anglo-Zulu war of 1879, with Rhodes in place of Sir Bartle Frere, Dr Leander Starr Jameson – the Company Administrator of Mashonaland – in place of Shepstone, and the Victoria incident (August 1893) for the Sirayo incident. Lobengula, like Cetshwayo, tried in vain to prevent the war by appealing to Jameson, Rhodes and the British government. But by then he had no white nor African friends anywhere. The total force that invaded Matabeleland consisted of 1200 white soldiers from Mashonaland and South Africa – including 200 imperial troops of the Bechuanaland Border Police. Then there were 1000 African auxiliaries made up of Shona, Mfengu, Khoikhoi, coloureds and 600 mounted Ngwato under the command of Kgama.

Rather than throw his estimated 20000 soldiers in a suicidal attack against the well-armed settlers and their African auxiliaries, Lobengula and his people evacuated Matabeleland and fled northwards towards Northern Rhodesia. He, like Cetshwayo, died in flight, either of smallpox or a heart attack. Now leaderless, the Ndebele nation fell apart. One by one Ndebele *indunas* came to surrender to Jameson at the *indaba* (meeting) tree. The settlers immediately went about staking their new farms and mineral claims. The Company expropriated 280000 Ndebele cattle, kept 240000 and distributed the rest to the white troopers and some of the African 'friendlies'.

After the conquest of Matabeleland, Britain granted the Company the Matabele order-in-council, dated 18 July 1894, which empowered it to impose the hut tax and establish a 'Native Department' to control the whole colony of Southern Rhodesia. By the end of 1895, the Company had instituted an African administration modelled on those of the Cape Colony and Natal, including the hut tax, reservations, and passes, for the purposes of dispossessing the Africans of their land, livestock and minerals, as well as forcing them to work for the whites.

The Ngwato, Lozi, Sotho, Tswana and Swazi initiatives and reaction: the model of protectorate or wardship

Unlike the Zulu and the Ndebele, the Ngwato, Lozi, Sotho, Tswana and Swazi had in common their alliances with strong humanitarian-imperialist missionaries of the 'government-from-London school'. These clerics were particularly opposed to 'the hammer-and-tongs policy of certain classes of colonial politicians – the conquest, spoliation and unending degradation of all coloured people'.[8] Among these were Mackenzie for Kgama, Setshele and Caseitsiwe, Casalis for Moshoeshoe and Coillard for Lewanika. These humanitarian missionaries were, however, only opposed to uncontrolled expansion by the white colonists of South Africa, especially on the part of the Boers and Rhodes, and to the accompanying instances of frontier violence and exploitation, which disrupted their earnest and successful work. They believed in the unquestionable superiority of the white race, culture and religion, and they viewed colonization, commerce and Christianity as inseparable allies. At the same time they also emphasized the need for imperial responsibility (paternal guardianship) over the Africans. They sought to smooth cultural contact between the colonizer and the colonized and to 'protect' and 'civilize' the African in an effort to make him a more useful member of the new colonial community. Through letters, delegations and personal appearances, they lobbied relentlessly with the High Commissioner, the Colonial Office and humanitarian groups in England to assure this 'protection'. Nyasaland became a British protectorate largely because of effective lobbying by the Scottish missionaries in their zealous efforts to defend their Christian Africans and mission stations at Blantyre, Bandawe and Ibanda against the encroachment of Rhodes's frontier men.

A dominant characteristic of the pro-missionary rulers was their general political and military weakness. Their kingships had grown largely out of *coups d'état*. In 1875 Kgama drove out Sekgoma, his father, and Kgamane, his brother, and named himself king. Kgamane fled with his followers and established his kingdom on the Transvaal side of the Limpopo river. The loyalist and conservative segments of the Ngwato, however, still remained loyal to the deposed Sekgoma. Thereafter, in 1884, Lewanika was also deposed and forced into exile at Kgama's capital. He returned in 1885 and ousted the usurper, Tatila Akufuna. Thus these pro-missionary kings had insecure positions, and were constantly faced with the imminent dangers of civil wars and unrest.

Added to this, their states had barely survived the Zulu revolution and the Nguni subjection. None the less, the Sotho and Swazi continued to be perennial targets of Zulu raids, while the Ngwato, Tswana, Kwena and Lozi suffered the raids and invasions of the Ndebele. They were also the victims of land-hungry, often trigger-happy Boer 'filibusters', who launched commando raids on their villages, capturing livestock and seizing captive labourers, making frequent 'treaties of friendship' with neighbouring sub-chiefs, then claiming land rights and spheres of influence. Through such infringements, the Zulu, Ndebele and Boers became inveterate enemies.

Much as these kings may have abhorred the principles of westernization and colonialism, they none the less were in desperate need of foreign support to assure their survival. Thus, they ultimately adopted missionary alliance

8. W. Howitt, 1969, p. 501.

PLATE 9.3 *King Moshoeshoe I of the Basuto* (c. *1785–1870*)

and British (metropolitan) protection as essential instruments of policy. For the same reason, they turned to the missionaries for advice and spiritual guidance in matters relating to Europeans, and attempted to manipulate them to enhance their shaky internal situations. Coillard, Mackenzie and Casalis were the closest European friends, confidants and foreign ministers, of Lewanika, Kgama and Moshoeshoe, respectively.

Out of necessity, these kings acquiesced readily in Christianity and accepted protectorate status. Kgama and Lewanika became practising Christians, and, like most converted doctrinaires, they occasionally proved to be more devout even than the missionaries. They not only abandoned their ancestral traditions, beliefs and rituals, but used their political offices to impose the tenets of western, Christian civilization on their people. Their spirited efforts to banish the public use of alcoholic beverages were near-obsessive. They imposed stringent liquor laws which included a ban on the brewing of African beer. The more they alienated their people by the enforcement of such measures, the more they were forced to rely on missionaries.

In fact the connection these kings had with the missionaries lay at the heart of their resistance through diplomacy to those who sought to dispossess them of their lands. Through alliance with anti-Boer, anti-Zulu and anti-Ndebele missionaries, they were able to maintain their independent existence up to the eve of the Scramble and subsequently won imperial protection at the expense of local, settler colonialism. These monarchs actively sought protectorate status, though it necessitated some restrictions upon their sovereignty, land rights and civil liberties. Under protectorate status they retained a nominal degree of self-government and enjoyed the defence provided by a permanent resident British police force, while their people were accorded the right to possess firearms provided they registered them. Thus, those smaller African kingdoms which had been unable to prevent white settlement and economic development owing to their geographical location and modes of living, were granted protectorate status and survived, while the superior states, politically and militarily geared to withstand the threats of colonization, were invaded, conquered and dismantled.

The Tswana

The cases of the Tswana and the Swazi clearly illustrate this model. There were three major contending forces in the Scramble for Bechuanaland (now Botswana). These were the four Bechuanaland rulers (the rulers of the Kwena, the Ngwato, the Ngwaketse and the Tswana) and their missionary allies who wanted British imperial protection and trusteeship; the Transvaal Boers who looked upon Bechuanaland as their natural hinterland for land, livestock, minerals and labour; and the Cape colonists, represented by Rhodes, who wanted to forestall Boer expansion and alliance with the

Germans in South West Africa (now Namibia). The African rulers, like Moshoeshoe, sought to forestall settler colonial rule by acquiring protectorate status. When alarmed by a dissident sect of the Dutch Reformed Church in the Transvaal – the Doppers – who wanted to cross through Tswana territories to Damaraland in 1876, Kgama, king of the Ngwato section of the Tswana, had written to the 'Great Queen of the English People' requesting protection. He wanted to know the conditions for protection and he emphasized that the relationship would be guided by 'Christian morality'. Furthermore, his rival brother, Kgamane, had settled in the Transvaal with his followers and was fighting with the Boers in the hope of gaining the Ngwato throne (see Fig. 9.1).

The British were bitterly divided over Bechuanaland. The Rhodes–Robinson group wanted to eliminate the imperial factor in favour of settler colonialism – including joint annexation by the Cape and the Transvaal, which only failed because the Transvaal refused. But the Mackenzie–Warren humanitarian-imperialist groups, like the African rulers, wanted to forestall settler colonialsim, because they were opposed to the brutality and destructiveness of settler colonialism over their Tswana Christian converts and church schools. Mackenzie in particular waged a very effective and successful campaign in South Africa and England.[9]

The Transvaal, on the other hand, was practising the policy of expansion by infiltration and incorporation which Moshoeshoe was implementing among the southern Sotho. Individual Boers had signed bogus treaties with The Tlhaping and the Rolong of southern Bechuanaland and subsequently had declared the 'republics' of Stellaland at Vryburg under William Van Niekerk, and of Goshen at Rooigrond under Gey Van Pitius. The Transvaal's strategy was first to unite the 'sister republics' and then annex them. The accompanying misunderstandings over the bogus treaties exacerbated old African rivalries and led to wars between chiefs Mankurwane and Mashauw (Tlhaping) and between Montshiwa and Moshette (Rolong) in which the Boers were recruited as volunteers and assistants. Consequently, southern Bechuanaland was – as Mackenzie described it – 'the abode of anarchy, filibustering and outrage'.

Then, in 1884, Britain sent Sir Charles Warren to restore law and order. Warren declared the southern part of Bechuanaland as a British crown colony, and Sir Hercules Robinson, the British High Commissioner for South Africa and Governor of the Cape Colony, appointed Mackenzie as the new Deputy Commissioner, although he was soon replaced by Rhodes because Cape colonial public opinion objected to his 'pro-native, anti-Boer policy'. Then, after discussions with a number of Tswana chiefs, Britain declared a protectorate over northern Bechuanaland in 1885. Under the charter of Rhodes's British South Africa Company, the Bechuanaland Protectorate was supposed to be annexed to Southern Rhodesia, but the

9. J. Mackenzie, 1887.

Tswana rulers and their missionary allies prevented that. In 1895, these rulers, Kgama and Sebele, who had succeeded Sechele in 1892, and Bathoen (Ngwaketse) went to England, accompanied by London Missionary Society missionary, Rev. W. C. Willoughby, and through their audiences with Queen Victoria, the Colonial Secretary and leaders of philanthropic societies, they succeeded in retaining their protectorate status.

The Swazi

The Swazi did not have to deal with settler colonialism until the Great Trek and the founding of Natal and the Transvaal republic. By then the kingdom was under Mswati. The society consisted of a dominant immigrant Nguni group to which the royal Nkosi-Dlamini dynasty belonged, and the indigenous Sotho people. The Nguni had established their rule over the Sotho by conquest and marriage alliance and had created a centralized, unified kingdom based on common loyalty to the crown, on friendships and intermarriages. Like the southern Sotho and the Tswana, they had survived the ravages of the Zulu revolution, but were occasionally victims of Zulu raids. Their foreign policy was designed to secure defensive alliance against the Zulu. Thus initially Mswati regarded the settlers of Natal and the Transvaal as well as the British government as potential allies against his traditional African enemies.[10]

The settlers, on the other hand, were interested only in the land, live-stock, labour and minerals of the Swazi. The Transvaal was particularly interested in the annexation of Swaziland in order to gain access to the sea through Kosi Bay. At the same time, Natal and Britain were particularly afraid of a German–Transvaal partnership in promoting a railway to Kosi Bay. But neither of them was willing to assume direct responsibility over Swaziland, a small area that was isolated from the larger colonies and the lines of communications, and where no substantial mineral discoveries had been made. Mswati was caught between this Boer–British Scramble. Furthermore, individual Boer and British settlers, traders and prospectors began to exert pressure upon Mswati for all kinds of concessions involving private ownership of land, leaseholds, trade monopolies, mining rights and even rights to collect revenue and customs.

Mswati granted several concessions before his death in 1868. There was a succession crisis in Swaziland in which the Boers and the British intervened for the purposes of placing their own puppet in power. The Boers sent a force to defeat the other contenders and installed Mbandzeni, the youngest son of Mswati by his second wife, and a weak ruler who was much addicted to the white man's liquor. Mbandzeni unwittingly granted all sorts of concessions 'of the most amazing scope, variety and intricacy', including some cases of land, mineral and trading monopolies

10. J. S. M. Matsebula, 1972; R. P. Stevens, 1967.

which were granted to different individuals over the same area. By 1890 there were 364 registered concessions covering almost every square yard of the small Swazi territory of under 10 000 square miles. By then the royal family was earning around £12 000 sterling annually in concession fees.

The granting of concessions, however, provided the Boers and the British with the pretext to undermine Swazi sovereignty. By the 1880s, Mbandzeni was overwhelmed by the problems of law and order, of concession disputes between himself and the white concessionaires and among the concessionaires themselves. At first he requested British protection and a British Resident, but the British refused. Then he turned to Theophilus Shepstone, the Secretary for Native Affairs in Natal, who appointed his own son, also called Theophilus, in 1886 as a resident adviser to Mbandzeni in matters involving whites. Unwittingly, Mbandzeni authorized Shepstone to head a committee of fifteen elected whites and five appointed whites and in 1888 he gave the committee a charter of rights which conferred the power of self-government. Most of the concessions were granted during Shepstone's term as resident adviser (1886–9). But the white committee also failed to settle the concession disputes before Mbandzeni's death in 1889, which was followed by the establishment of dual Boer–British rule in 1890. Under the Swaziland Convention of 1890, the two powers established a dual provisional government committee to govern Swaziland, and a chief court to inquire into the validity of concessions, which confirmed 352 of the 364 concessions. The committee installed Ngwane, a 16-year-old son of Mbandzeni, and declared the mother, Gwamile Mduli, the queen regent.

Dual rule did not work well because of the growing Boer–British rivalry in South Africa. Under the Convention of 1894 Britain pawned Swaziland to the Transvaal by conferring 'all rights of protection, legislation, jurisdiction, and administration over Swaziland' provided the Transvaal would not annex Swaziland. The queen regent and her council strongly protested and even sent a delegation to England, but to no avail. The Transvaal appointed a resident special commissioner in 1895, thereby supplanting Swazi sovereignty by settler colonialism. Then, under the Treaty of Vereeniging (1902) which ended the Anglo-Boer war of 1899–1902, Swaziland was taken over by Britain. The Swaziland order-in-council, proclaiming the country a 'protectorate' was issued on 25 June 1903, and the South Africa Act of 1909 stipulated the conditions for the future transfer of Swaziland, Basutoland (now Lesotho) and Bechuanaland, together known as High Commission Territories, to the Union of South Africa. The transfer never materialized because of African opposition.

The Hlubi, Mpondomise, Bhaca, Senga, Njanja, Shona, Tonga, Tawara, etc., initiatives and reactions: the model of alliance

Internally, each of these groups lacked the political unity and military strength to withstand the increasing threat of white colonialism. They were also without diplomatic and military alliances with their neighbours. Instead, they frequently raided, fought and generally distrusted each other. Their compositions ranged from autonomous chieftaincies to bands of nomadic refugees, captive slaves, and wards of either the colonialists or missionaries. Most were tributaries or raid victims of the Zulu, Ndebele, Bemba, Yao or Nguni.

While some of these small groups, like the Barwe, Mangwende, Makoni and Mutasa paramountcies, chose armed resistance against the threat of colonialism as did the Xhosa, many others such as the Hlubi, Mpondomise, Bhaca, Senga and Njanja allied themselves with the whites in the misguided hope of thereby assuring their protection and security. On the whole, these small societies were accustomed to the diplomatic practice of switching allegiances and gravitating towards the stronger prevailing power, or of feigning non-alignment while manipulating the dominant powers to their own advantage. The Shona, Tonga, Tawara, Venda and Ndau had frequently employed these strategies throughout the eighteenth and nineteenth centuries, during the rivalry between the Changamire and Mwenemutapa dynasties, while the Sotho, Mpondo, Mfengu, Thembu and Tonga had utilized similar strategies to exploit the rivalry between the Mtetwa and Ndwande confederacies. Thus many of these peoples readily aligned themselves with the British against the Zulu, Ndebele, Bemba, Nguni and Yao. Added to this, several of the small groups, such as the Mfengu, Thembu, Njanja, Cewa and Tawara, had for some time existed under strong military influence. As a result, they had among their people significant segments of Christianized, sometimes educated Africans, who not only rejected the traditional culture, but challenged the traditional leadership to the advantage of the colonizer.

Thus, by offering alliance, protection and/or liberation, the British were easily able to divide and conquer them. They then established permanent white settlement in these areas.

African initiatives and reactions, 1895–1914

By the late 1890s practically all the peoples of Southern Africa had been either fully or partly colonized and were everywhere being subjected to various forms of pressures, economic, political and religious.

Before long, the hut tax, forced labour, severe suppression of traditional beliefs and customs and especially land alienation were introduced. This foreign interference intensified in proportion to the settlers' increasing need for cheap indigenous labour to work on the farms and in the mines, and for the hut tax to meet at least part of the administrative expenses. Africans were compelled to vacate their homelands to make room for white settlers and to serve as army 'volunteers'. In Rhodesia (Northern and Southern) and Nyasaland, the Chartered Company administrators simply transplanted the 'Native Laws' of South Africa. In Rhodesia, where white settlement was the heaviest, the administration tolerated no obstacles to its economic ventures, even if these obstacles were Shona lives and rights. It readily commandeered Shona lands, livestock, crops and stores of food and subjected the Shona to forced labour to serve the interest of the settlers, who had been drawn to Mashonaland with promises of a better, easier and richer way of life. Above all, the colonial justice introduced was characterized by arbitrariness and irregularities. Coupled with all this was a succession of natural disasters, including epidemics of smallpox and rinderpest, drought and even a plague of locusts.[11]

The Africans did not of course watch these events unconcerned. In this atmosphere of colonialism, landlessness, destitution, oppression and westernization, most of them came to believe, like the Xhosa, that the white man was the cause of all their troubles. Resentment against alien rule engendered – during the 1890s and early 1900s – a growing attitude of resistance towards whites and a strong sense of unity among political leaders, followers, priests and even formerly hostile groups. Examples of such responses aimed at overthrowing the colonial system because of its unbearable oppression and exploitation were the Ndebele–Shona *Chimurenga* of 1896–7, the Herero revolt of 1904 and the Bambata or Zulu rebellion of 1906.

The Ndebele–Shona *Chimurenga*

The *Chimurenga*, as the Shona termed their form of armed resistance, began in Matabeleland in March 1896, and in June 1896 in Mashonaland. The first casualty was an African policeman employed by the British South Africa Company, killed on 20 March.[12] The first attack upon Europeans occurred in the town of Essexvale on 22 March, when seven whites and two Africans were killed. The *Chimurenga* then swiftly spread throughout Matabeleland and Mashonaland (see Fig. 9.1). Within a week, 130 whites had been killed in Matabeleland.

Africans were armed with Martini-Henry rifles, Lee Metfords, elephant guns, muskets, and blunderbusses, as well as with the traditional spears,

11. D. Chanaiwa, 1974; R. E. R. Martin, 1897; T. O. Ranger, 1967.
12. For eyewitness account of the *Chimurenga*, mostly by European settlers, soldiers and reporters, see R. S. S. Baden-Powell, 1897; F. C. Selous, 1896; R. E. R. Martin, 1897.

axes, knobkerries, and bows and arrows, and they initiated the *Chimurenga* when the majority of the Company's troopers were in South Africa involved in mounting the Jameson Raid against the Boers. Furthermore, African policemen deserted the Company with their guns and ammunition and joined their African comrades in such great numbers that, as a precaution, the remaining 'loyals' had to be disarmed.

The Company hurriedly mobilized the Europeans into the Matabeleland Relief Force, which consisted of imperial troops and the Rhodesia Horse Volunteers (settlers), as well as Africans. At its peak the force consisted of 2000 Europeans, 250 Ngwato sent by Kgama, 200 'Colonial [South African] Natives', and about 150 Rhodesian Africans, under the supreme command of Sir Frederick Carrington, a veteran of the Xhosa–settler wars. Essentially, the *Chimurenga* was conducted as guerrilla warfare. The troopers relied on the siege and dynamite. They also destroyed crops and appropriated African cattle, goats, sheep, fowl and grain to starve the resisters, and to enrich themselves.

In Matabeleland, the *Chimurenga* lasted from March to December 1896, and proved very costly for the Company. On 15 July the Company was forced to issue a proclamation of clemency for Africans who would surrender themselves and their arms. After the battle of Ntaba zika Mambo (5 July 1896), Cecil Rhodes was 'determined to seize the first chance of negotiation, or to manufacture a chance if none arose'. By then he had given up any hope of achieving a 'total and unconditional victory', because a prolonged *Chimurenga* or a military stalemate would have caused bankruptcy, or forced the British imperial government to turn the colony into a protectorate. In August the Ndebele found themselves besieged at the Matopo hills and, after a protracted battle and generous peace offers by Rhodes, they finally chose to negotiate. What followed was a series of peace talks between Rhodes and the Ndebele *indunas* that lasted from August 1897 to 5 January 1898, when Rhodes included six of the *Chimurenga* chiefs (*indunas* Dhliso, Somabulana, Mlugulu, Sikombo, Khomo and Nyamanda) among the ten Company appointees. He assigned them land for settlement, donated 2 300 000 kg of grain, and promised to redress their grievances against the Company.

With victory and peace in Matabeleland, the Company then concentrated upon the Shona *Chimurenga* that had been raging simultaneously since June 1896 and continued, intermittently, to 1903. The leading centres of the *Chimurenga* were the paramountcies of Mashayamombe in western, of Makoni in central, and of Mangwende in north-eastern Mashonaland. But several smaller paramountcies such as Nyandoro, Seke, Whata, Chiota, Chikmakwa, Swoswe, Zwimba, Mashanganyika, and Masembura, either took the initiative for a *Chimurenga* themselves or allied with others.

The *Chimurenga*, like the Xhosa cattle-killing episode, has been labelled by Eurocentric historians as atavistic and millenarian because of the important role of the traditional prophets and priests, known as the *svikiro*.[13] The leading *svikiro* were Mukwati in Matabeleland, Kagubi in western Mashonaland and Nehanda (a female *svikiro*) in central and northern Mashonaland, together with a host of local junior prophets. The *svikiro* told the Ndebele and Shona that the white man had brought all their sufferings, namely forced labour, the hut tax and flogging, as well as natural disasters of locusts, rinderpest and drought. They convinced many Africans that the Shona God, Mwari (Mlimo in Sindebele), having been moved by the suffering of his people, had decreed that the white men were to be driven out of the country; and that the Africans had nothing to fear because Mwari, being on their side, would turn the white man's bullets into harmless water. Generally speaking, many Africans believed that the *svikiro* were announcing Mwari's commandments and that failure to obey would bring more sufferings to the paramountcies and personal misfortunes to individuals.

The *svikiro* were primarily revolutionary prophets who articulated the real causes of the *Chimurenga* and the general consensus of the people without which they would have had relatively little credibility and influence. Furthermore, as the custodians of Shona traditions and acknowledged authorities on many aspects of Shona life, they feared that their role was being usurped by the European missionaries. More importantly, the apparently leading role of the *svikiro* was a function of the politico-military segmentation of the Ndebele and, especially, the Shona people. The *svikiro* were the only authorities whose influence extended across paramountcies. The spiritual provinces of Mukwati, Nehanda and Kagubi covered more than one paramountcy. Unlike the paramount chiefs, the *svikiro* had an elaborate but secret network of communication through which they exchanged numerous messages and co-ordinated their efforts adeptly. They even revived the old Rozvi dynasty and confederacy by proclaiming Mudzinganyama Jiri Muteveri, the great-grandson of a former Rozvi king, as the new king. Many Africans accepted the proclamation and pledged allegiance to Mudzinganyama, but the confederacy was short-lived because Mudzinganyama was soon arrested and imprisoned by the settlers. Simultaneously, Mukwati was assassinated, reportedly by a disillusioned follower.

Kagubi and Nehanda were most influential over the young and militant princes of the paramountcies, such as Muchemwa of Mangwende, Mhiripiri of Makoni and Panashe of Nyandoro. But Kagubi was captured

13. The word *svikiro* is derived from the verb *kusvika* meaning to arrive at or reach a place. *Svikiro* literally means the person, vehicle or instrument or medium through which gods and spirits communicate with the people. Thus, a priest, rabbi and prophet in western culture and a caliph and mallam in Muslim culture could be a *svikiro* in the Shona society. The *svikiro* should not be confused with a medical practitioner, *nganga* (so-called witch-doctor in Europe) or with a fortune teller. The *svikiro* was a priest, an intellectual, an educator, and a leader wrapped into one person. Here we are using the translation *prophets* for the convenience of non-Shona readers.

in October 1897 and Nehanda two months later. On 2 March 1898 they were charged with murder and condemned to death by hanging. The two were buried in a secret place, 'so that no natives would take away their bodies and claim that their spirits had descended to any other prophetess or witch-doctors'.

Without a highly centralized politico-military machinery, without guns and ammunition, and, more significantly, without the *svikiro*, Shona paramounts were defeated one by one in 1897. On 4 September Makoni was handcuffed, blindfolded, and shot in the presence of the troopers, 'friendlies', and his own subjects. As reported by an eyewitness correspondent of *The Times* (London), Makoni stood and died 'with a courage and dignity that extorted an unwilling admiration from all who were present'. Similarly, Mashayamombe, who had nearly paralysed communications between Salisbury and Bulawayo, was defeated and killed on 25 July. Between July and September the settlers successfully carried out sieges against the paramountcies in central Mashonaland. Mangwende was conquered in September but his son, Muchemwa, together with a few councillors, continued the resistance until 1903 when the *Chimurenga* was finally contained.

The toll of the *Chimurenga* has been estimated at 450 dead and 188 wounded Europeans, and 8 000 African deaths. Of the 450 Europeans, 372 were resident settlers, representing one-tenth of the white population in the colony. The remainder were imperial troopers and mercenaries. But some of the most intransigent Shona continued the *Chimurenga* and even formed alliances with other Africans in Mozambique who were also resisting Portuguese colonialism. The most celebrated post-*Chimurenga* resistance was that of Kadungure Mapondera, the ruler of the Rozvi paramountcy, located in the Mazoe area, which previously had retained its independence against both the Ndebele and the Portuguese. Mapondera did not take part in the *Chimurenga* because, after refusing to pay the hut tax, he and his closest followers had emigrated to northern Mozambique in 1894 and joined the Barwe in their war against the Portuguese. He returned to Rhodesia in 1900 and recruited a Shona army consisting of the Korekore, Tavara, and several young militants from the paramountcies of north-eastern and central Mashonaland, including Mangwende and Makoni. He allied with the titular Mutapa, Chioco, and thus with the Mwari *svikiro*. Until June 1902 he waged guerrilla warfare against settlers and loyalist paramountcies in northern Mashonaland. He again emigrated to Mozambique to join the on-going Barwe *Chimurenga*, but the allied forces were soon overwhelmed by the Portuguese, due primarily to the latter's superiority in firearms. Mapondera returned to Rhodesia, and on 30 August 1903 he surrendered and was sentenced to seven years' hard labour for murder and sedition. He died in prison from hunger strike.

The Herero

In 1904 the Herero, feeling the cumulative and bitter effects of colonial rule in South West Africa, took advantage of the withdrawal of German troops from Hereroland to put down an uprising among the Bondelswarts, and revolted in January 1904, killing 100 Germans, destroying several farms and capturing cattle. Theodor Leutwein, the German commander, was replaced by General von Trotha, who decided upon total military victory and complete destruction of the Herero people by ruthless tactics and massacres. Between 75 and 80% of an estimated Herero population of 60 000–80 000 were slaughtered; 14 000 were put in prison camps; and 2000 fled to South Africa. Samuel Maherero and 1000 followers fled across the Kalahari desert to Bechuanaland.

All land and livestock were confiscated, and the Africans were forbidden to form ethnic organizations and practise traditional ceremonies. They had no means of existence other than employment by white settlers. Their own gods and priests having been defeated and, thus, proved inferior, they submitted to Christianity in mass conversions. Then, in 1915, South African troops occupied South West Africa and kept it under martial law until 1921. By that date, 10 673 white South Africans had joined those German settlers who had not been repatriated to Germany. The Africans were allowed to resume subsistence-level agriculture in barren reserves and were therefore forced to depend on migrant employment.

Despite this fate, the Herero nevertheless left a legacy of resistance to colonial rule, of cross-ethnic allegiances and of cultural, historical, racial and nationalist consciousness that was inherited by later generations of freedom fighters throughout Southern Africa.

Conclusion

By the first decade of the twentieth century there were practically no indigenous sovereign states in Southern Africa. The vast majority of the Africans had by then entered the third level of resistance characterized by the struggle to obtain a favourable *modus vivendi* under colonial rule, economy and culture. In reality it was a different form of response to the struggles against colonial conquest and occupation, and it belongs to a different chapter in African history. For by then both the political and religious leadership of the traditional societies had been conquered, colonized and humiliated. The traditional kings had been supplanted by an alien Secretary for Native Affairs such as Theophilus Shepstone in Natal, or the so-called 'Native Commissioners' and 'Native Departments' elsewhere. The African masses were primarily recognized as the 'black problem' and were, as Jabavu described them, 'landless, voteless, helots, pariahs, social outcasts in their fatherland with no future in any path of life'.[14] Further-

14. D. D. T. Jabavu, 1920, p. 16.

more, these were the first Africans to face the crisis in identity[15] created by new artificial colonial boundaries which partitioned cultural-linguistic-historical groups, by cultural shock in mining and farming compounds, the homes of the whites, and in Christian churches and schools throughout the settler-dominated world.

The thrust of African thoughts and actions now centred on the individualist acquisition of the knowledge, technology and material goods of the white world, and on exposing – and hopefully correcting – the 'native disabilities'[16] within the framework of colonial domination. This led to the beginning of the non-violent civil rights protests epitomized, as will be seen later, by the South African Native National Congress formed in 1912, by the Southern Rhodesia Native Welfare Association, by the trade unionism of Clements Kadalie and by religious separatism and Ethiopian-ism. The new leadership vacuum was filled by the mission-educated Christian elites who were committed not only to universalism, non-racialism and capitalist materialism, but also to non-ethnicity, and thus were the first to undermine ethnic and sectional co-operation by African chiefs, groups and individuals. The new course of African responses to colonial rule as opposed to colonial conquest came to be determined mostly by the urban masses under the leadership of the educated elites. The rural masses either lived by subsistence-oriented production in the reserves or drifted into the market-oriented capitalist economy as low-paid wage-earners in European mines, fields, kitchens or factories.

15. R. F. Betts (ed.), 1972.
16. See, for example, S. T. Plaatje, 1916; S. M. Molema, 1920.

Madagascar, 1880s–1930s: African initiatives and reaction to colonial conquest and domination

M. ESOAVELOMANDROSO

The Anglo–Merina Treaty,[1] which was signed on 23 October 1817 and ratified in 1820, conferred on Radama I the title of 'King of Madagascar' and on 14 February 1822 he went on to proclaim his sovereignty over the entire island (see Fig. 10.1). A kingdom which had the backing of the leading world power of the time accordingly made its appearance on the diplomatic scene. But it was a kingdom whose sovereignty France initially contested, denied and fought against. It was not until 1862 that the government of Napoleon III signed a treaty with Radama II recognizing him as king of Madagascar. This, in the eyes of the authorities in Antananarivo, sanctioned the kingdom's existence and signified the abandonment of France's territorial demands, even though the preamble to the treaty reserved 'France's rights', in other words, its specific claims to its former trading posts and establishments and to the Sakalava and Antakarana protectorates.

A new situation was created by the assassination in 1863 of Radama II by the ruling oligarchy, which regarded him as too liberal-minded and unduly favourable to the Europeans. Rainilaiarivony, who was prime minister from 1864 to 1895, adopted a fairly flexible policy in a bid to ensure that the independence of the kingdom would be respected. Thus it was that, although unable to unify the territory completely, he set about organizing the government, administration and army. He succeeded after a fashion in consolidating his power and in holding the conquered regions together, in spite of his rivals' plots, and the discontent and, at times, open rebellion of the masses. At the same time, however, colonialist imperialism was growing in Europe, and France again sought to dominate Madagascar. The diplomatic efforts which Rainilaiarivony deployed in an endeavour to steer clear of this danger were unsuccessful and the two wars waged by France – from 1883 to 1885, and from 1894 to 1895 – terminated in

1. The Merina are the inhabitants of the Imerina, a region in the Central Highlands of Madagascar, with its capital at Antananarivo. The Merina kingdom set itself the task of unifying the entire island.

FIG. 10.1 *Madagascar around 1900*

PLATE 10.2 *Ranavalona III, Queen of Madagascar (1883–97) in full court dress*

PLATE 10.1 *Rainilaiarivony, Prime Minister of Madagascar (1864–95), husband of Ranavalona II and III*

the eviction of the prime minister and the dismantling of the royal government. Although they gained control of Antananarivo, the French very soon encountered armed resistance in some of the rural areas of the Imerina and in its subject provinces. In the independent regions, they found themselves having to contend with kings and military leaders who put up spirited opposition to them. Eventually, however, French technical superiority put an end to these uncoordinated pockets of resistance. Even so, all over the island, people rose up and organized themselves, first to combat the abuses of the colonial regime and subsequently to recover independence for their country.

A country divided in the face of the imperialist threat

In the last quarter of the nineteenth century, France reverted to a policy of colonial expansion. In the first place, between 1870 and 1880, following its defeat at the hands of Prussia, the country went through a period of introspection while it nursed its forces within its national borders. Then, between 1880 and 1890, a number of republican figures, like Léon Gambetta and Jules Ferry, felt that colonial conquests would restore their country to its place among the great powers. Hostile public opinion compelled them to adopt a policy of 'small doses', but they were nevertheless able to impose a protectorate over Tunisia in 1881 and, despite the absence of an overall plan and limited resources, to dispatch expeditions to mainland Africa, Tonkin and Madagascar. From 1890 onwards, France's ambitions came into sharper focus, as public opinion was largely won over by imperialist thinking and business circles began to display an increasing interest in colonial ventures.[2] Thus Madagascar, which was embellished by colonial propaganda as being a vast consumer market, a land of untold riches, and an island coveted by the British, became the target for a host of ambitions and designs. The government of Queen Ranavalona accordingly had to contend with this foreign threat while simultaneously trying to smooth over the latent or overt tensions that were rife among the Imerina and throughout the entire island.

The situation on the eve of the first Franco–Merina war[3]

France's renewed interest in Madagascar stemmed from the propaganda which was deliberately orchestrated by the French parliamentarians of the island of Réunion, kept alive by right-wing Catholic circles and later supported by the colonial faction. These different movements joined forces to recall and defend France's 'historic rights' over Madagascar. That claim, which had its roots in the memory of the annexation proclaimed under Louis XIV and of the fruitless attempts made in the eighteenth century to set up a prosperous *France Orientale*, based on the trading posts established in the eighteenth century and under the Restoration, was developed throughout the nineteenth century in a large number of written documents before being put to the French parliament officially in 1884. The Réunion lobby demanded the complete conquest of the island, so that the overflow of Réunion's Creole population could be settled there and the abundant resources which the British seemed likely to exploit could be reserved for their own use. French Catholic missionaries in Madagascar, for their part, were reduced to evangelizing the lower social classes since most of the noble families and the rich and powerful commoners had been converted to Protestantism. Consequently they demanded official support from France in their bid to overcome the competition of the Protestants, whom they portrayed as being a product of the innumerable 'underhand dealings' of the British. This 'perfidious Albion' theory found a favourable echo in certain business circles which, in an endeavour to conquer the Malagasy market at the expense of the British and Americans, sought to debar the latter by annexing the island rather than by reducing the prices of their own goods. Colonial propaganda appealed to people's chauvinistic sentiments and the belief in France's humanitarian and civilizing mission. In order to prime public opinion for the conquest, the 'Kingdom of

2. G. Jacob, 1966, pp. 2–3.
3. C. R. Ageron, 1978(a), pp. 114–18.

Madagascar' was presented, in blatant bad faith, as being a 'barbarous state', headed by a 'foreign tribe' which had exalted 'tyranny as a system of government' and still engaged in the slave trade.

There was scarcely any foundation for all these arguments devised by the advocates of the colonization of the island. The royal government, which was accused of being pro-British, displayed in its attitude to foreign powers a subtlety dictated by its determination to defend the independence of the kingdom. It attempted to elicit from each of the powers the support which they were capable of giving to its own ambitions.[4] Madagascar was not, it was argued, the vassal of Great Britain: the trust that existed between the two countries was solid solely because the British, unlike the French, were not intent on colonizing the island. That purportedly 'barbarous' kingdom, where the 'forces of darkness' predominated, was, in fact, ruled by a queen and a prime minister who had been converts to Christianity since 21 February 1869. It is true that they had been baptized as Protestants and that the majority of the leaders and the population had followed their example, but they had not prevented people from embracing Catholicism nor had they thwarted the activities of the French missionaries. This liberal attitude goes to show the separation that existed between the churches and the state, even though 'around the chapel in the queen's palace, the Prime Minister may have tried to form a national Church, the Palace Church, composed of Malagasy churchmen and evangelists in his service'.[5] These attempts gave rise to lingering fears among the Jesuits and to an 'incorrigible mistrust' among the representatives of the London Missionary Society (LMS).

In 1877, the royal government freed the *Masombika* slaves imported from the African mainland and arranged for them to be settled on lands allocated to them. In 1878, it recast the legal system, which was henceforward entrusted to three courts whose task it was to conduct investigations, while decision-making lay with the prime minister. The 'Code of 305 Articles, a legislative innovation embracing civil law, criminal law and legal procedure'[6] was promulgated in 1881. All these measures, and others besides, illustrate the determination of Rainilaiarivony to 'modernize' his country and to turn it into a 'civilized state' in its dealings with Europe.

All these endeavours would have disarmed people moved by a genuine desire to civilize Madagascar and to spread the Gospel there. However, the elected representatives of Réunion, backed by the Catholic parliamentarians and the colonial lobby, were unbending in their demands for the conquest of Madagascar. They took advantage of three pretexts to pressure the French government into embarking on military action in Madagascar in 1882.

In 1878, Jean Laborde – who had initially been a business partner of

4. F. Esoavelomandroso, 1979.
5. H. Vidal, 1970, p. 6, n. 20.
6. H. Deschamps, 1960, p. 181.

the leading dignitaries of the kingdom under Ranavalona I in the manufacture of arms and munitions and landed property, and who subsequently became French consul on the accession of Radama II – died in Antananarivo, leaving real estate which his nephews, Edouard Laborde and Campan, claimed without success. The demand for this inheritance emanating from Paris was founded on the treaty of 1868, which empowered French nationals to acquire landed property in Madagascar, while the refusal of the authorities in Antananarivo to countenance it rested on the law stipulating that land belonged exclusively to the sovereign. The 'Laborde inheritance' case posed a problem of land ownership that was of direct concern to the settlers and traders living on the island. The issue at stake was whether they were entitled to own the land they worked or could at least expect to obtain a long-term leasehold on it.[7]

In April 1881, relations between France and Madagascar became even more acrimonious over the *Toalé* affair. The *Toalé* was a dhow whose owner – an Arab but a French subject – together with three other Muslim members of the crew, were murdered by the men of the Sakalava king, Bakary, in the bay of Marambitsy, an area outside the control of the Merina authorities. These people, who were gunrunners, had been verbally challenged and ordered to hand over their cargo; instead, they opened fire on the Sakalava, who fired back and killed them. The French claimed reparation from the Queen of Madagascar for this smuggling incident.[8]

In the course of the same year, two English missionaries, on a tour of the Sambirano coast on the north-west of the island, persuaded the Sakalava chiefs of the region to raise the Merina flag. France protested on the grounds of the protectorate treaties it had signed with the sovereigns of the region in 1840 and 1841. Rainilaiarivony, in response, reminded the French of the treaty of 1868 which the Government of Napoleon III had signed with the 'Queen of Madagascar'.

The lack of sincerity evidenced in this exchange convinced Rainilaiarivony that the French were acting in bad faith and prompted him to adopt a policy for paying the reparations and purchasing arms and munitions. These activities proved unpopular on account of the heavy burden which they placed on the people. The difficulties with France did not give him time to assimilate the conquests made by Radama II, still less to pursue the unification of the country. Hence it was a prime minister beset by domestic problems who had to negotiate with Baudais, the French consul, who was suddenly to break off diplomatic relations and to leave Antananarivo on 21 March 1882.

The isolation of the Malagasy rulers, 1882–94

In June 1882, Captain Le Timbre had the Merina flags removed from

7. G. Jacob, 1966, p. 5.
8. P. Boiteau, 1958, p. 172.

the bay of Ampasindava without meeting any resistance. Rainilaiarivony still thought that it was possible to avoid a conflict and to settle the differences by peaceful means. He accordingly sent an embassy led by his nephew, Ravoninahitriniarivo, the Minister of Foreign Affairs, to Europe and the United States from October 1882 to August 1883, in a bid to come to an understanding with France and to seek the support of the other powers.[9] However, apart from the trade agreements signed with London, Washington and Berlin, and Britain's relinquishment of its nationals' right to land ownership in exchange for leases whose length would be determined by mutual agreement, the Malagasy plenipotentiaries achieved very little. The French, humoured by the British who wanted a free hand in Egypt, refused to come to any arrangement, although the envoys of Ranavalona II had agreed to remove their flags and garrisons from the bay of Ampasindava and had accepted long leaseholds for foreigners. The embassy was still in Europe when the French navy bombarded Majunga in May 1883 and thereby sparked off the first Franco–Merina war (1883–5). Diplomatic action had been unable to prevent war, therefore, and the authorities in Antananarivo were bitterly surprised to find that the leading powers were primarily concerned with their own interests and sometimes, indeed often, reached agreement among themselves at the expense of the small nations. The attitude of Great Britain, which had been looked upon as a faithful ally, was a disappointment, and is said to have prompted the prime minister to speak, with disillusion, of 'pretending to quarrel, like the French and the British'.

The French thus attacked a kingdom that was diplomatically isolated. A small squadron, commanded by Admiral Pierre, bombarded the ports in the north-west and east of the island, and occupied Tamatave. France demanded that Rainilaiarivony cede the portion of Madagascar situated to the north of the 16th parallel of latitude and that he recognize the right of French people settled on the island to own land. The prime minister continued to hold out against the pressures on him, while leaving the door open to negotiations. During this 'bogus' war, in which negotiations were conducted with greater alacrity than military operations, the object of France's demands underwent a change: the issue was no longer one of recognizing France's historic rights in north-western Madagascar but of imposing a protectorate over the entire island. Rainilaiarivony maintained his original stand and refused to sacrifice the independence of his country. However, while the French and Malagasy leaders adopted two seemingly irreconcilable attitudes, their subjects were yielding to a growing sense of lassitude. On the Malagasy side, the blockade and the war effort had brought on an economic crisis and had created quite serious political unrest. As for the French, the Tonkin expedition had prevented the reinforcement of the troops engaged in Madagascar. Furthermore, the views of the

9. P. M. Mutibwa, 1974, pp. 218–46.

minister, Freycinet, who was inclined to be conciliatory, overruled those held by the advocates of a march on Antananarivo. The course of events, therefore, prompted the two governments to sign a peace treaty or, in other words, to be content with a compromise.

The somewhat obscure treaty of 17 December 1885 put an end to a war in which there were neither victors nor vanquished. It was so vague and ambiguous that it was interpreted by both parties as each saw fit. The treaty granted France the right to 'represent Madagascar in all its foreign relations' and to maintain a resident-general with a military escort at Antananarivo. It granted French nationals the right to obtain long-term leases of up to ninety-nine years and the French navy the right to occupy Diego Suarez, while the French government was awarded an indemnity of ten million francs. This treaty, in which there is no mention of the word 'protectorate', recognized Queen Ranavalona as sovereign of the entire island and as sole owner of land. The 'Appendix' or explanatory letter which the prime minister demanded and secured from the French negotiators on 9 January 1886, before agreeing to ratify the treaty, laid down the powers of the resident-general, fixed the size of his military escort at fifty men, and described the limits of the territory of Diego Suarez as being one nautical mile to the south and west and four miles to the north. These terms were meant to limit the scope of the treaty. The French administration, on the other hand, attached no significance to the 'Appendix' and interpreted the agreement concluded on 17 December 1885 as being a protectorate treaty. By contrast, the Malagasy government, which was dominated by Rainilaiarivony, refused to consider the document as a treaty establishing a protectorate over the island and put forward a quite different interpretation of the document, in opposition to the French schemes. This interpretation was based on constant references to the 'Appendix', which had limited the scope of the clauses that were regarded as being prejudicial to the independence of the kingdom. The rulers in Antananarivo accordingly attempted to prevent the protectorate from coming into being by playing on the differences between the French and the Malagasy texts and the clarifications spelt out in the additional protocol.[10]

Thus, a war of attrition came to be waged between the prime minister and successive residents-general as misunderstandings continued to multiply. Without waiting for the outcome of the endless negotiations on the demarcation of the French zone around Diego Suarez, the French navy occupied a broad strip of land to the south of the port. A second conflict, over the 'exequatur' ('a written official recognition and authorization of a consular officer issued by the government to which he is accredited'), dominated the ten years of the 'phantom protectorate' from 1885 to 1895. The resident-general demanded that he be granted the 'exequatur' in order

10. F. Esoavelomandroso, 1977(b).

to prove that Madagascar was a protectorate, but Rainilaiarivony refused to grant it so as to assert the kingdom's independence. Until the signature of the Anglo-French agreement of 1890, whereby the French recognized the British protectorate over Zanzibar, in exchange for which Britain accepted 'the French protectorate over Madagascar with its consequences', the prime minister managed not to depart from the stand he had taken. These diplomatic difficulties were exacerbated by the economic problems which the kingdom experienced.

In order to settle the indemnity due to France, the Malagasy government contracted a loan with the Comptoir National d'Escompte de Paris (CNEP), the guarantee for which consisted of the customs receipts of the island's six main ports: Tamatave, Majunga, Fenerive, Vohemar, Vatomandry and Mananjary. Agents – who were appointed by the French bank but paid by the royal authorities – supervised the tax collection, which deprived the Malagasy state of a substantial source of revenue.

This need for funds, and the pressures exerted by Le Myre de Vilers, the first French resident-general in Antananarivo, compelled the prime minister to grant vast concessions to the Europeans both for mining – of copper in the Betsileo and gold in the Boina – and timber exploitation. The Suberbie gold-deposit concession in the Maevatanana region, notorious for its use of forced labour in the mines, brought in very little income to the government. On the other hand, it contributed to the weakening of authority on account of the number of workers who fled and swelled the ranks of the *fahavalo* or irregulars who created an atmosphere of insecurity in the north-west of the island. At the same period, twelve forestry concessions were granted to foreigners on the east coast. The limited resources of the concession-holders and the attitude of Rainilaiarivony who, in spite of appearances, was disinclined to make their task any easier, meant that the attempts to exploit the Malagasy forests were not altogether successful. These concessions did not enrich the royal government or benefit the local population, nor did they produce as good a return as the foreign capitalists would have liked.[11]

The proceeds of the customs duties were not sufficient to cover the six-monthly payments due to the CNEP since the concessions granted to foreigners had not produced the results expected, and thus, in order to replenish the coffers of the state, the royal government increased the number of taxes and stepped up forced labour. In addition to the burden which they habitually had to bear, the inhabitants were required to pay an income tax of one piastre per person and the *fitia tsy mba hetra*, a sort of general contribution that was theoretically 'voluntary'. Some people refused to perform the tasks required of them under the *fanompoana* or forced labour system, while others took to banditry, and the gangs of

---

11. M. Esoavelomandroso, 1979, pp. 186–93.

plunderers were bold enough to attack the holy city of Ambohimanga in 1888 and even the capital in 1890.[12]

These disturbances, which threatened the interests of the privileged classes and the expatriates, alarmed the resident-general and revealed a grave crisis of authority in the 'Kingdom of Madagascar'. The French parliament made the most of this situation and dispatched Le Myre de Vilers, who had been resident-general from 1886 to 1889, with a plan for setting up a real protectorate. When Rainilaiarivony rejected this plan, the French parliament voted by a large majority to go to war, and the Merina government, in its bid to preserve independence, could only acquiesce. But the royal authorities embarked on this war in 1894 in circumstances that were not at all favourable to them.

The 'Kingdom of Madagascar' in 1894: weakness and disarray

On the eve of the French conquest, the 'Kingdom of Madagascar' was sapped by serious internal tensions. At the official level at least, the baptism of Ranavalona II marked the beginning of the decline in ancestor worship and the disappearance of the royal and even local *sampy* or shrines which formed the political and religious foundations of traditional Imerina; it was also responsible for the often forced conversion of thousands of subjects, the destruction of a number of long-established hierarchies through the dismissal of the *sampy* guardians, and the rise of a Christianized elite. Political, economic and religious affairs were all intertwined. The supporters of the Eglise du Palais (the Palace Church) not only handled the affairs of state, such as censuses, education and recruitment for the army and forced labour, but also took advantage of their positions and the economic system to enrich themselves through trade and moneylending. Guardians of *sampy* and local dignitaries who had been deprived of their traditional powers and privileges opposed the island's leaders by taking flight or by refusing to build churches or setting fire to them.[13] Moreover, the Christianized Merina were by no means unanimous in their support for the official Church. Those who were not integrated into the Church and who practised a sort of popular Christianity drawing its inspiration from the Bible and from local history and folklore, formed an educated elite which could lay claim to political leadership.

They engaged in trade and made a practice of preaching their ideas on market days. Other Christians reacted against the overbearing tutelage of the official Church by turning to Catholicism or placing themselves under the protection of a dignitary. Others struggled for the independence and freedom of their religious life, like the dissidents of Ambatonakanga who, in 1893, created their own church, which they baptized *Tranozozoro*, the

12. F. Esoavelomandroso, 1977(b), p. 50.
13. F. Esoavelomandroso, 1980.

house or church of reeds.[14] This dissident movement took shape in the very heart of the capital, which was a bastion of Christianity, and bore witness to the sense of unease felt by some of the faithful.

These tensions added to the decline of the Imerina, which further exacerbated by foreign, and especially French, pressures and by the archaic nature of the economic domination wielded by the leading figures in Antananarivo, made it impossible for them to fulfil their ambition of creating a nation-state. The officer merchants recouped their losses by exploiting the forced labour system to the full, now that it had lost its former connotation as a ritual obligation, by investing in land and by engaging in moneylending. Opposing these magnates of the capital and devotees of the Palace Church were the host of small farmers and day-labourers who were in debt to them and on whom the *fanompoana* bore down most heavily.

All this laid bare 'the disintegration of the social fabric and the machinery of government'[15] and revealed the existence of a deep-seated crisis within the 'Kingdom of Madagascar', which was thus incapable of resisting the French expedition. But there was more to Madagascar than the mere trappings of state. The ordinary folk among the Merina who did not identify with their leaders, the subject population who endeavoured, as best it could, to escape the oppression of the oligarchy, and the independent kingdoms of Antananarivo, each in turn, were to resist French penetration and conquest.

A country offering uncoordinated resistance to colonial conquest

The breakdown of society within the 'Kingdom of Madagascar', the collapse of the old order, the domination of the oligarchy, the economic crisis and the imperialist threat were all factors that gave rise to a profound moral and spiritual malaise among the mass of the people, who began to hark back to an idealized vision of the past and to advocate a return to traditional ways. It was not very long, therefore, before the leaders had to face a barrage of criticism. The colonial conquest, in 1894 and 1895, provided the opponents of the regime with an opportunity to give vent to their opinions and hastened the fall of the government, which was already under fire in both Merina and the subject provinces and was ignored or contested by the independent peoples.

The failure of leadership

Public opinion and parliament in France had decided to back the expedition to the hilt: the army had ample resources and a large number of troops

14. S. Ayache and C. Richard, 1978, pp. 133–82.
15. G. Jacob, 1977, p. 213.

at its disposal and the terrain had been thoroughly reconnoitred by explorers and military personnel and was therefore well known. On the Malagasy side, however, the state was much less firmly established than in 1883. The ageing and dictatorial Rainilaiarivony had become unpopular. Faced with having to put down a whole series of plots involving his close associates, and even his own children, he could have complete confidence in neither the leading dignitaries of the regime, who coveted his high office and hoped one day to replace him, nor the army, which was disorganized by the increasing number of desertions and was demoralized by rampant corruption and greed. His strategy had not evolved with the times. In spite of his piecemeal and badly organized efforts to purchase arms and munitions and attempts to effectively mobilize the forces of the kingdom, the only allies he really trusted were 'General *Tazo* (fever) and General *Ala* (the forest)'. As in 1883, he hoped that the lack of a road through the virtually impenetrable forest and the debilitating effect of the climate on the Europeans would prevent an expeditionary corps from marching on Antananarivo.

Indeed, the campaign did take a heavy toll of the French, but this was due to the lack of foresight of certain departments in the Ministry of War. The troops had disembarked at Majunga and were to use the celebrated 'Lefèbvre carts' in their advance on the capital. They were therefore compelled to build a road. Fever and dysentery broke out while they were laying the earthworks in the swamplands, and the expeditionary corps was turned into an 'endlessly straggling column caught up in its baggage trains and its dead and dying'.[16]

The royal army did not mount any guerrilla attacks on the flanks or at the rear of the sorely tried French troops. Ranavalona's forces were dispersed at the various ports. Those who were sent to head off the French erected fortifications which they evacuated as soon as they were bombarded or circumvented. Neither the soldiers nor their officers had received any proper military training and they were bewildered rather than motivated. Rajestera, an officer at the front, recalled the dissension and strife in the army when he wrote: 'There was a feeling of discouragement on all sides, as much among the ranks as among their chiefs, especially when it was learnt that, although the Prime Minister's relatives and friends, and especially his grandson, Ratsimanisa, had discreetly remained behind in Imerina, they were sharing in the honours which ought rightly to have been bestowed on those who had to suffer the fatigue and dangers of the war'. The announcement that Ratsimanisa, of whom the officers disparagingly spoke as being 'a mere boy who no sooner wakes up than he falls asleep again and is just about fit to grill sweet potatoes', had been elevated to the rank of the 'Fifteen Honours', one of the highest in

16. H. Deschamps, 1960, p. 230; M. Brown, 1978, pp. 236–56.

the hierarchy, was the last straw that sapped morale and blunted the resistance.[17]

In view of this situation, General Duchesne, commander-in-chief of the French expeditionary corps, detached a light column from the main body of the army, which was bogged down by its sick and its carts and equipment. This column drove the queen's regular troops before it and put them to flight before taking Antananarivo on 30 September 1895. By then, however, the *foloalindahy*, or royal army, was only a pale shadow of Radama's former army. Rainilaiarivony had succeeded in humbling the *Mainty* and excluding the *Andriana*, who had formed the backbone of the armies of the eighteenth and early nineteenth centuries, but he did not manage to forge a large, well-trained army properly commanded by men who were loyal to him, who respected the property of the state and who were intent on preserving their country's independence. The prime minister was surrounded by a bevy of courtiers who were willing to flatter him and quick to fill their pockets by every possible means, but who were incapable of giving him the slightest piece of useful advice on how to conduct the affairs of state and were determined to serve whomever held all the reins of power. Most of these people, who had been incapable of defending the kingdom's independence, became the often zealous allies of the colonizers. They disowned and at times fought the mass of the people who, seeing the ignominious flight of the royal army and the 'treason' of the island's leaders, rose up to combat the French.

The *Menalamba* movements in Imerina

The behaviour of the Merina population under the conquest can be accounted for by the nature of the relations it maintained with the government, which was monopolized by the *Andafiavaratra*, in other words, the family and hangers-on of the prime minister, Rainilaiarivony.[18]

The relations of the six *toko*, or districts, of Imerina with the reigning oligarchy were not all the same. For instance, the Vakinisisaony, the ancestral land of the Imerina kings and the initial region of adoption of *sampy* such as Ikelimalaza, held the privilege of conferring legitimacy on the sovereign. However, throughout the nineteenth century, the inhabitants of the Vakinisisaony, who had a reputation for toughness, suffered under the burden of forced labour and felt the full weight of the power of the Avaradrano, the people who had supported Andrianampoinimerina. Many of the *Andriana*, or nobles, of the Vakinisisaony were eliminated, as in the case of the guardians of Ikelimalaza, which was first confiscated by Andrianampoinimerina and then burnt down in 1869. From that time onwards, opposition to the Christian government crystallized round the worship of this *sampy* in the southern part of Vakinisisaony. In the northern

17. Quoted by M. Esoavelomandroso, 1975, p. 62, n. 67.
18. S. Ellis, 1980(a), 1980(b).

part of the *toko*, groups that continued to respect the traditional religion, and Christians existed side by side. However, splits occurred among the Christians in the villages, as in the case of Ambohimalaza, where the nobles and slaves were predominantly Catholic and the commoners were Protestants. The same contrast between advocates of the traditional cults and Christians was to be found in other districts. In the Ambodirano, Ramainandro, a locality with a large Christian population allied to a *foko* or township in the Avaradrano, stood opposite Amboanana, which remained committed to the worship of the *sampy*.

The capture of Antananarivo, which spelt the downfall of the urban Christian world, sparked off the mobilization of the rural areas in defence of the ancestral heritage. The uprising at Amboanana, which broke out in November 1895 on the day of the *Fandroana* (see Fig. 10.2), the queen's birthday and a public holiday, marked the beginning of the population's opposition to the French conquest. This big rebellion was known as *Menalamba* (or the 'Red Plaids'), because the rebels 'coloured their garments with the red soil of the country in order that they might not easily be recognized at a distance'. The insurgents seized Aribonimano, killed the governor and an English missionary and his family, and demanded the abolition of Christian worship, schools, military service and forced labour. In March 1896, other movements broke out in the north and south of Imerina, with demands for a return to the ancient beliefs and a purge of the governing class and with the aim of compelling the French to withdraw.

The *Menalamba* took over the weapons of the soldiers who had deserted from the *foloalindahy* or purchased them from Indian or Creole traders, which suggests that communication with the coast was relatively easy. They were organized after the manner of the royal troops, complete with a table of honours and a division into regiments. They attacked the representatives of the oligarchy, whom they regarded as holding power illegally and as being responsible for the defeat, as well as foreign missionaries and Malagasy evangelists, who were the proponents of Christianity and hence the enemies of the traditional beliefs. They accordingly set about burning down churches and schools and restoring the ancestral religion to a place of honour. The cult of the Ravololona *sampy* was fostered and ancient rites, such as the *valirano* and the *sotrovakaka* – two types of oath – were again practised.

However, some of the actions of the *Menalamba* alienated part of the population. Their strategy included attacks on market-places, in a bid to make an impression on people's imaginations, cause panic, and undermine an institution that was a symbol of the constraints and order imposed by the oligarchy. But these attacks also enabled them to replenish their supplies. These assaults on markets and the raids they made to seize the crops of villages which had not come over to their side made it easier to sow confusion in the minds of the sedentary population, which failed to

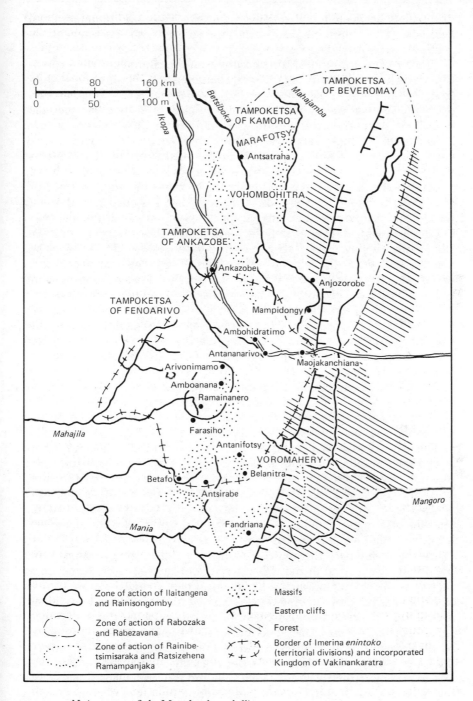

FIG. 10.2 *Major zones of the* **Menalamba** *rebellions*

Zone of action of Ilaitangena and Rainisongomby

Zone of action of Rabozaka and Rabezavana

Zone of action of Rainibe-tsimisaraka and Ratsizehena Ramampanjaka

Massifs

Eastern cliffs

Forest

Border of Imerina *enintoko* (territorial divisions) and incorporated Kingdom of Vakinankaratra

distinguish between the *Menalamba* and the *jirika*, or plunderers and brigands. The colonizers and their local allies took advantage of this confusion to isolate the insurgents.

These *Menalamba* movements occurred on the confines of the Imerina, in areas where insecurity was a permanent feature. Since they were far from Antananarivo, they became the hiding places of irregulars and deserters. Contact was established with the Sakalava in the north-west and with the Betsimisaraka in the south-east, and this made it easier to procure arms. Access to these areas was difficult, bordered as they were by the bare and desolate Tampoketsa range in the north-west and by the forest to the east. They were inhabited by herdsmen who were employed by the leaders in the capital and who enjoyed a measure of freedom from the central authority. They were also the areas that provided forced labour for the gold mines, which accounted for the population's displeasure with the government. Hence, local dignitaries and the governors of small administrative posts like Rabazavana and Rabozaka in the north of the Imerina had little difficulty in setting these irregulars and malcontents against the foreigners and their allies whom they looked upon as being responsible for the economic, social, political and religious upheavals that had shaken the *tanindrazana*, the land of their forefathers. In fact, the attitudes of the emancipated slaves varied from one region to another, and even within the same region. In central Imerina, where slaves represented a high proportion of the population, they quite frequently reacted with enthusiasm to the conquest, converting to Catholicism, which was represented as being an act of allegiance to France, and returned to the regions from which they had originated. By contrast, on the less populated edges of the Imerina, the freed slaves had to contend with material problems and joined the insurgents.

The *Menalamba* were composed of an assortment of groups whose attitude to a number of issues appeared to be tinged with ambiguity. For instance, they despised the capital and yet, at the same time, they venerated it. Although it was a bastion of Christianity and the seat of the authority which they challenged, the capital was nevertheless the symbol of the kingdom and was still, in the popular mind, the capital of Andrianampoin-imerina. Its fall was a forewarning of the chaos that had to be warded off. When the *Menalamba* threatened Antananarivo, they were demonstrating both their disapproval of the urban world and their anxiety to remain in contact with the 'capital of the kingdom'. Their attitude was even more ambiguous when they attempted to draw a distinction between Ranavalona, in their view the rightful monarch, and Rainilaiarivony, the prime minister and a usurper, when, in fact, the former had been chosen and appointed by the latter. The same can be said of their attempts to entice some of the leaders away from the rest of the oligarchy. Thus, while there was a clear-cut enmity between the *Menalamba* and foreigners, hostility towards the oligarchy was less pronounced and more a matter of degree.

Popular resistance in Imerina failed because of the severity of the repressive measures taken, but above all because of the lack of co-ordination between the different movements and the failure to join up with the insurrections which broke out in the other regions of Madagascar.

Popular opposition in the regions subject to the royal authority

In some regions, the population's reaction to the French conquest stemmed from the influence wielded by the *Menalamba*. In 1896, in the Mampikony region in the north-west, Rainitavy, a former Merina governor, recruited a motley crew of Merina deserters and Sakalava herdsmen and replenished the *Menalamba* of Rabozaka with arms purchased in the region. The uprising he organized was the only *Menalamba* movement in which commercial considerations played a fundamental part: the aim was to take control of regional trade, of which the Indians and Creoles had a virtual monopoly, which is why they were attacked. In the nearby regions of the Imerina, the relations of the *Menalamba* leaders maintained with local kings and dignitaries were instrumental in the spread of some of their ideas. The Tanala Rainimangoro, for instance, declared that he had received orders from Antananarivo to drive out the French.[19]

Elsewhere, such relations were non-existent. In the provinces that were most firmly controlled and hence most heavily exploited, the fall of Antananarivo in September 1895 was the signal for attacks on the Manamboninahitra, who were chiefly officer merchants, and on Merina immigrants and foreigners. In the eastern province, for example,[20] the revolt of the 'Vorimo', a clan living on the lower Mangoro, triggered off a series of uprisings which created a climate of insecurity in the region throughout 1896. In the first instance, these revolts were directed exclusively against the Merina oligarchy. Until October 1895, when the governor-general of the province, Rainandriamampandry, was recalled to Antananarivo, members of the Betsimisaraka tended to destroy the soldiers' rice fields, refused to feed the royal army, or else merely deserted. From December of the same year, they openly attacked military posts and took the initiative of mounting sorties or organized raids against Merina plantations. The insurgents spared the lives of foreigners because they mistakenly thought that the French had come to save them from their oppressors. However, the very harsh measures which detachments of the army of occupation took to put down the revolts came as a surprise to the Betsimisaraka and later inclined them to believe that the French were not so much their friends as the allies of the Merina. From then on, the insurgents stepped up their offensive, and attacked the French as well as the Merina. The movement did not start to die down until December 1896, but then disappeared altogether with the introduction of the measures taken

19. S. Ellis, 1980(b), p. 212.
20. M. Esoavelomandroso, 1979, pp. 346–52.

by General Galliéni to replace the representatives of the oligarchy by local chiefs.

The population in the regions subject to the French conquests can accordingly be said to have expressed their opposition in a variety of ways.

The resistance of the independent peoples

At the outset, the French thought that by capturing Antananarivo they had gained control over the entire island. However, after putting down the *Menalamba* movements and thereby having occupied Imerina, they discovered that they also had to conquer the independent regions. The peoples who had not been subject to the royal authority took up arms and repelled the French attempts at penetration.

In the Ambongo – an example of a region whose principal feature was its political division into a host of small units – the French employed several stratagems to gain control. While seeking to reach an understanding with the main chiefs or kings both on the seaboard and in the interior, from 1897 onwards they installed military posts in the large villages so as to keep order in the region.[21] Early in 1899, however, disturbances stemming from the same determination to reject colonial domination and to uphold the region's independence broke out under the leadership of the main chiefs. One by one and in haphazard order, these groups of insurgents clashed with the locally recruited infantrymen led by the French, who never had to contend with two opponents at the same time. On the contrary, they were free to strike whomever and wherever they wished. The bands of resisters were isolated from one another and were incapable of uniting in the face of the common enemy. The chiefs were primarily responsible for this state of affairs and, through lack of foresight and selfishness, were unable to foster the growth of a popular struggle in defence of Sakalava independence.

The conquest of Menabe, a large and well-organized kingdom, began in 1897, and was to be the practical illustration of the policy devised by Galliéni with the threefold aim of isolating and wearing down the main enemy, the centralized Merina authority; of fostering the political autonomy of the main regions of the island against Imerina, in accordance with the 'divide and rule' principle; and of taking advantage of that autonomy to bring about colonization at the least possible cost.[22] King Toera and his principal chiefs, who were assembled at Ambiky, were said to be making ready to lay down their arms, but Major Gérard, who was in charge of the operation, preferred to invest the capital rather than accept their submission and to 'massacre all the Sakalava who could not escape, including King Toera'. This cruel and underhand act strengthened the resolve of the Sakalava, and a well-organized resistance movement, led by

21. M. Esoavelomandroso, 1981.
22. B. Schlemmer, 1980, p. 109.

Ingereza, the brother and successor of Toera, spread throughout the Menabe and lasted until 1902. The peoples of Antandroy and Mahafale in the south also opposed French attempts at penetration and only submitted in 1904.

As a result of his policy of gradual annexation and after a long period of colonial penetration, Galliéni was able to claim in 1904 or thereabouts that the unification of the island was complete. There was not a single part of the island that escaped the authority of Antananarivo and all the regions acknowledged the power of the colonizers. However, that unity in common submission to France created a new situation which accounts for the different forms of action taken by the Malagasy to improve their lot and indeed to recover their independence.

A country united by its submission to France and its opposition to colonial domination

Malagasy reactions to the conquest and colonial penetration which had come to an end in 1904 had all come to nothing. Officially, the military operations were over and the different administrative, economic and cultural cogs of colonization set in place by Galliéni were henceforward able to function and to allow France to establish its ascendancy once and for all.

Yet, that same year of 1904 saw the beginning of a new period that was to be marked by the struggles of the Malagasy people against colonial oppression.

From colonization to the dawning of the national movement

For the Malagasy people, the colonial situation meant that they had lost their freedom and dignity. While they sometimes still found a measure of continuity between the nineteenth and twentieth centuries, they felt the perpetual strain in their everyday lives of a foreign presence which, after having snatched power from them and turned them into a subject people, now exploited and oppressed them. France decided to 'civilize' the Malagasy people and 'assimilate' them, and hence to compel them to become something else or, in other words, to alienate them. This attempt to destroy the national personality and to change the way of life of the island's inhabitants sparked off a variety of reactions.

From the administrative standpoint, the colonial venture broke down the long-established political framework. In Imerina, Galliéni abolished the monarchy on 28 February 1897 and the privileges of the aristocracy on 17 April. Elsewhere, however, he did not abolish the different dynasties, at least not *de jure*. On the contrary, he started out by attempting, as the Minister had instructed him to do, to combat the Merina hegemony and to embark on the '*politique des races*' which had earlier been tried out in the Soudan (French West Africa) and Indochina. Former sovereigns or their sons were accordingly brought into the administration as 'native governors', while 'internal protectorates' were created among the extensive kingdoms in the west and south-west. This system did not prove satisfactory, however, and from 1905 onwards the number of Merina assistants was increased to a disproportionate degree, since the Merina were regarded as being more suitable material for 'progress and adaptation' than the other peoples. Finally, Galliéni introduced French settlers (*colons*) and Asian immigrant workers into the new colony which greatly alienated the indigenous people. Galliéni's 'Franco-Merina synthesis' was extended to cover the entire island, its key features being the *fokonolona*, the village communities, considered as having collective responsibility for their affairs, and the corvée or forced labour system, which was legally designated as the 'provision of services' in 1907 and was brought into general use between 1908 and 1915.[23] This entailed the *de facto* abandonment of the '*politique des races*', the abolition in 1909 of the two regional schools on the coast, one at Analalava on the north-west coast and the other at Mahanoro on the east coast (the third was in Antananarivo) which had been set up by Galliéni as breeding-grounds for potential civil servants, and the phasing-out of the 'internal protectorates'. The finishing touches were put to the territorial unification of Madagascar with three measures. The first was the standardization of the administration (between 1927 and 1932, three attempts were made to define the boundaries of administrative districts). The second was the widespread introduction of administrative *fokonolona* as the medium for the exercise of authority. The third was the setting up of a restrictive body of law with the institution, in 1901, of the 'native code' (*indigénat*), forming the basis for dispensing administrative justice in which the judiciary and the executive were merged. While, in the case of the Merina, these measures descended in a direct line from the reforms introduced by Rainilaiarivony and pointed to a degree of continuity between the nineteenth and twentieth centuries, in other regions they represented a complete break with the past and entailed far-reaching changes that were not always understood by the Malagasy and were consequently often resisted.

For the Malagasy, colonization also meant the economic exploitation of the island by the expatriate minority. Very early on, this so-called 'development' of the colony came up against the problem of manpower resources. After Galliéni had reintroduced the Merina royal *fanompoana* and had decided to extend it to the whole of the island in 1896 and 1897, thereby compelling every able-bodied Malagasy male between the ages of 16 and 60 to furnish fifty days of unpaid labour a year, the Office Central du Travail was established in 1900 and was charged with the task of

23. J. Fremigacci, 1980, p. 2.

PLATE 10.3 *Madagascar: workers employed in the construction of the Antananarivo–Tamatave railway*

facilitating the recruitment of workers for private firms. Faced with the resistance of the Malagasy to any form of recruitment, the administration took over and, in 1926, established the Service de la Main d'Oeuvre pour les Travaux d'Intérêt Général (SMOTIG), which required conscripts not actually called up for military service to work for three years – subsequently reduced to two years – on the colony's construction sites. The SMOTIG, which was regarded by the Malagasy as being 'slavery in disguise', was deeply resented not only by the people who were commandeered but also by 'voluntary' wage labourers who lost their jobs as a result.

The colonial oppression was further aggravated by the forcible takeover of land, which was then distributed to *colon* settlers. Under a decree promulgated in 1926, the state was declared owner of 'all vacant and ownerless land not developed, enclosed or granted by way of a concession as of the date of promulgation of the decree'.[24] Thenceforth, the good land was monopolized by the administration and the settlers encroached on the native reserves, while the Malagasy no longer had any title to ownership over their ancestral lands. The areas most affected by this land takeover, which was greatly resented by the Malagasy, were the north-western and eastern seaboards.

These economic changes and the political upheavals they engendered inevitably caused social and cultural transformations. The very way of life of the clan societies of the coastal regions was undermined and they were threatened with progressive decay or structural breakdown. Confiscation of the most fertile land; the heavy tax burden which compelled whole populations – like the Atandroy in 1921 – to emigrate to the plantations of Réunion and the north-west of the island; the forced redeployment of workers; the dissemination of formal schooling and Christianity; the departure of Malagasy soldiers to France to take part in the First World War; the abolition of slavery; the humiliation of the noble faction – all these factors brought about drastic changes in the social structures, caused the break up of a number of clans, and debased ancestral values and practices. In Imerina, the vastly increased number of schools and the wholesale recruitment of junior civil servants gave rise to dismay both in the ranks of the former oligarchy which had been deprived of its power by the conquest and among the new elite trained in the colonial schools, who gained the impression that they had been 'deliberately debarred from positions of responsibility by the colonial system'.[25]

Thus, colonial oppression affected all the different levels of Malagasy society, even though its forms differed in the different regions, and it provoked different reactions.

24. L. Rabearimanana, 1980, p. 58.
25. A. Spacensky, 1970, p. 24.

The first reactions in opposition to the colonial system

In 1904, at a time when effective occupation was regarded as being over, the colonizers were nevertheless aware of just how precarious the situation was. Their apprehensions were confirmed by the insurrection of 1904–5 in the south-east of the island. The uprising which broke out in November 1904 in the province of Farafangana spread very quickly westwards, as a result of the traditional contacts that had existed in historical times between the eastern peoples and the Bara (see Fig. 10.3). The solidarity of the clans in the face of the common enemy accounted for the speed at which the movement spread, while the geographical setting, with its forests and escarpments, offered an explanation for the difficulties encountered by the forces sent to put down the rebellion. The insurgents – led by chiefs belonging both to the Bara clans (such as Befanoha) and to the south-eastern clans (such as Mahavelo and the Masianaka group and Resohiry from the Vangaindrano region), or by dissident militiamen like Corporal Kotavy – attacked military posts at Amparihy, Begogo and Esira, and concessions, including the *Emeraude*, where they killed the owner, Lieutenant Conchon. Locally recruited infantrymen deserted their posts at Tsivory and Bekitro, or joined the rebellion, as in the case of Antanimora.

Galliéni explained away the insurrection by claiming that it was due to the mentality of the local people 'with their warlike disposition' and 'their attractive conception of disorder and plunder'. Victor Augagneur, his successor, saw the reasons as lying in the 'surfeit of administration' (increased taxation, abuses in tax collection, and the tyrannical attitude of heads of military posts or isolated settlers). These explanations were inadequate, since they overlooked an essential aspect of the insurrection (the struggle for the recovery of freedom) and the organizational ability of the insurgents, who attacked all those who personified the colonial administration, whether they were French occupying forces or Malagasy civil servants or schoolteachers. By way of conclusion to his study of the 1904 rebellion, G. Jacob states that it undoubtedly had a twofold significance: 'it was a fight for independence and a struggle against colonial exploitation'.[26] The suppression of this first revolt against the oppression of the administration forced the Malagasy to seek other forms of struggle.

One of the most widespread forms of anti-colonial response was passive resistance: a refusal to comply with orders; the rejection of everything that was regarded as a sign of 'civilization' but was closely bound up with colonization and the foreign presence; keeping children away from school, which was looked upon in some circles as merely being a form of 'colonial forced labour'; and abandonment of the villages created along the roads in the south in an attempt to keep the population together. These refusals

26. G. Jacob, 1979, p. 17.

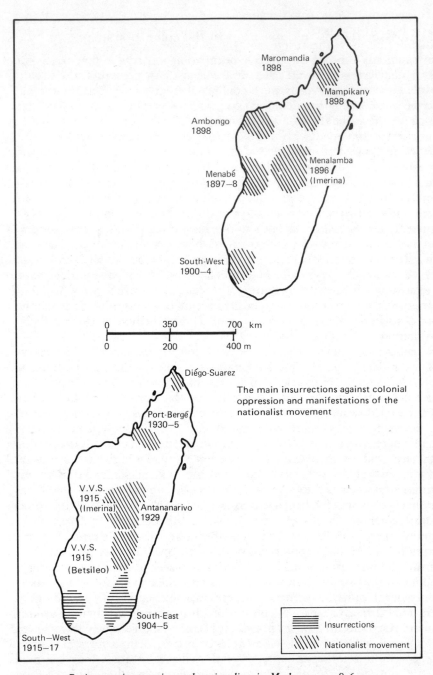

Maromandia
1898

Mampikany
1898

Ambongo
1898

Menalamba
1896
(Imerina)

Menabé
1897–8

South-West
1900–4

0   350   700 km

0   200   400 m

Diégo-Suarez

Port-Bergé
1930–5

The main insurrections against colonial
oppression and manifestations of the
nationalist movement

V.V.S.
1915
(Imerina)

Antananarivo
1929

V.V.S.
1915
(Betsileo)

South-East
1904–5

South—West
1915–17

Insurrections

Nationalist movement

FIG. 10.3 *Resistance, insurrection and nationalism in Madagascar, 1896–1935*

to co-operate did not seem dangerous to the colonizers, who believed that peace had finally been established in Madagascar in 1905. But then, suddenly, in 1915, the revolt of the *Sadiavahe* – the nickname given to the insurgents – broke out in the south-west, while in Antananarivo the police discovered the existence of a secret society known as *Vy Vato Sakelika* or VVS – 'strong and hard like stone and iron' (see Fig. 10.3).

The *Sadiavahe* movement (1915–17) was an armed peasant uprising which first began on the left bank of the river Menarandra in early February 1915 and spread very quickly to the districts of Ampanihy and Tsihombe.[27] The *Sadiavahe* stole cattle, attacked villages, cut telegraph wires, and withdrew into hiding-places well away from the posts controlled by the administration. They formed bands ranging in number from ten to forty members at most, were extremely mobile, and scoured wide areas of the south. Among the reasons why entire villages gave open or clandestine support to the *Sadiavahe* were the virtually chronic poverty of the population as a result of the very infrequent but violent rainfall, the imposition of a cattle tax, and the far-reaching effects of the First World War which had led to the mobilization of reservists, tax increases, food shortages and insufficient cash earnings to pay taxes.

In Antananarivo, seven students from the capital's medical school, which was the only institution providing tuition for the highest degree then open to Malagasy nationals, created the VVS in July 1913, just after the publication of a series of articles written by the Protestant minister Ravelojaona under the title of 'Japan and the Japanese'.[28] These articles called on the Malagasy to model themselves on Japan, where modernism and tradition had been so skilfully blended. The students were joined by clerks and office workers and primary-school teachers. The anticlericalism of Augagneur, the governor-general from 1905 to 1910, and the campaign conducted against the missions, gave a fresh lease of life to the *Tranozozoro*, whose ministers demanded a 'free church in a free country',[29] both in their sermons and in their writings. As they campaigned against 'French atheism' and the adoption of 'false French ways', the intelligentsia stressed the national tradition of the Protestant faith whose democratic structures could become a refuge for the resistance.[30] They also drew attention to and fostered Malagasy cultural nationalism, through a literary renaissance, the restoration to prominence of certain periods in the country's past, and the revival of ancient rites for gaining admission into the secret society. Although the VVS was a clandestine organization, it expressed its opinions openly in the press by calling on the Malagasy to sacrifice themselves for their homeland, so that its people could advance and live in freedom and dignity. As the bearer of a national message, this secret society was an

27. F. Esoavelomandroso, 1975, pp. 135–69.
28. F. Esoavelomandroso, 1981, pp. 100–11.
29. S. Ayache and C. Richard, 1978, p. 176.
30. J. Fremigacci, 1980, p. 11.

intolerable challenge to the administration, especially in wartime. The very harsh sentences meted out in the form of hard labour, deportation to the camp at Nosy Lava, banning of the newspaper whose editors were implicated in the affair, and dismissal from the civil service; the changes made in school curricula in order to delete the teaching of history – a subject regarded as a vehicle for ideas about freedom and equality that offered too much scope for speculation – the increased importance attached to the French language; the greater prominence given to local dialects in an attempt to belittle the Merina dialect, which had been imposed as a national language some years earlier – all these were measures which showed how conscious the colonizers had become of the nascent nationalism within the elite and how much they feared its consequences. The outcome of these repressive measures was that the Malagasy were prompted to abandon their clandestine action and, from then onwards, to switch openly to channelling their political demands through press campaigns, the establishment of trade unions, and so on.

Struggles to recover dignity

The decade following the First World War was an important period because of the growing awareness displayed throughout the country in the preparation and consolidation of a national movement. The beginning of this decisive turning-point in Malagasy history can be dated from the return of the ex-servicemen to Madagascar.

Basking in glory, these war veterans, who were convinced that they had served France in the same way as any Frenchman, demanded the same rights as those the French enjoyed, and they were supported in this by a large number of their compatriots. Faced with the attitude of the press and the chamber of commerce, which were opposed to wholesale naturalization, they gradually drew a distinction between two images of France: the one far-off but generous and the other close at hand and unjust. Under the leadership of Ralaimongo, therefore, they embarked on a long-drawn-out struggle to obtain French citizenship.

Ralaimongo (1884–1942), who had been successively a Protestant primary-school teacher, a clerk, and a student in Paris, and who was an ex-serviceman, a socialist and a freemason, was the true founder of the national movement. The circles he had frequented in Paris, which had consisted of pacifists, socialists and radicals, and especially the members of the Ligue des Droits de l'Homme, had a profound influence on him. When he returned to Madagascar in 1922, he settled in Diego Suarez, which was an ideal environment for spreading propaganda because of the presence of the workers at the naval arsenal and the complexity of the land-tenure problems in the Mahavavy plain and the Antalaha region. Until May 1929, it was Diego Suarez rather than Antananarivo that was the focal point of the national movement which, besides agitating for equal rights, denounced the intolerable abuses of the colonial system, such as the land expropriations in the north-west and around Lake Alaotra, the absence of liberties, the despotism and high-handedness of the administration, and the racial segregation displayed in the attempts to check the outbreak of plague at Tamatave and in the highlands in 1921. The originality of Ralaimongo's approach can be seen from the novel methods he used. The watchwords of the campaign set in motion against the colonial system were legality and legitimacy, on the grounds that Madagascar had been declared a French colony by the law of 6 August 1896 annexing the island, and that all French laws should accordingly be applied there. Successful representations were made to the business community, which showed more drive than the members of the civil service who were afraid of administrative sanctions, and the movement was, in fact, financed by traders, especially those in the capital.

The Ralaimongo group, which was strengthened by the support of Ravoahangy, a former member of the VVS; Emmanuel Razafindrakoto; Abraham Razafy, secretary of the Antananarivo branch of the French SFIO trade union; and Jules Ranaivo, was joined by several left-wing Europeans, including Albertini, a lawyer, Dussac, Planque and Vittori. In an endeavour to present and defend their demands, from 1927 onwards they published two newspapers – *L'Opinion* in Diego Suarez, and *L'Aurore Malgache* in Antananarivo – which had to contend with all sorts of petty reprisals on the part of the administration. At the political level, the group demanded 'the management of the overall interests of the country by a Council-General with extended powers', the abolition of the Government-General and the representation of Madagascar in the French government.[31]

In parallel with the action of the Ralaimongo group, religious agitation flared up again in the *Tranozozoro* cult. Renewed controversy between the Malagasy congregation and the European Protestant ministers only ended in 1929, with the judgement handed down by the Conseil du Contentieux recognizing the *Tranozozoro* as an indigenous mission. From then onwards, the sect agitated for self government under cover of a movement preaching religious autonomy, whose leaders were followers of Ralaimongo and Dussac.

Having organized, with Ralaimongo and Ravoahangy, the 'Pétition des Indigènes de Madagascar', demanding French citizenship, the abolition of the *indigénat* judicial regime and the application of the social and cultural benefits introduced under the Third Republic, Dussac arrived in Antananarivo in May 1929 to explain the petition's aims. A conference, which was planned for 19 May but which 'Malagasy subjects' were barred from attending, turned into a vast procession in the streets of the capital, in which thousands of demonstrators chanted rebellious slogans such as 'Long live freedom and the right of assembly!' and 'Down with the

31. A. Spacensky, 1970, p. 30.

indigénat!' This first mass demonstration marked a decisive stage in the growth of the nationalist movement (see Fig. 10.3). The events of 19 May 1929 represented both the culmination of the struggle for equality and the starting-point of the demands for independence. They also marked the beginning of authentic political militancy, in the shape of propaganda campaigns, the creation of political cells and parties, and the emergence of a broad-based and varied press. Ralaimongo, who had been exiled to Port Bergé, encouraged the peasants to engage in the type of resistance practised by Gandhi in India. In 1931, he openly mooted the idea of independence in response to a speech by Paul Reynaud, the Minister of the Colonies, which rejected the case for wholesale naturalization. In *L'Opinion* of 20 July 1934, Ravoahangy evoked 'the natural and inalienable right to form a free and independent nation'. From 1935 onwards, other newspapers that were openly nationalistic in outlook began to appear. Both *Ny Fierenena malagasy* ('The Malagasy Nation') and *Ny Rariny* ('Justice') constantly urged that Madagascar must become free. The movement was losing momentum, however. In fact, 'the business community had been hard-hit by the economic crisis and withdrew its support ... Civil servants were afraid of compromising themselves and of losing their jobs. The Protestant ministers were embarrassed at the political turn taken by developments and retreated into their churches. The Malagasy middle class was terribly prone to adopt a wait-and-see attitude and preferred the direct and personal benefits accruing from French citizenship.'[32] It would take the Popular Front to give the movement fresh impetus.

Conclusion

The armed, but scattered and uncoordinated resistance of the people of Madagascar to the French conquest did not prevent the colonial system from being established. But the logic of colonialism and the traumatic shock suffered by the Malagasy, threatened as they were with the loss of their identity, prompted them to take up several forms of combat in a bid to recover their dignity. The struggles against colonial oppression fostered the birth and vigorous growth of the national movement, even though, in 1935 as in 1940, too many regional, religious and social dissensions prevented a clear-cut awareness of all that colonialism implied and accounted for the apparently unshakeable position of the administration.

32. F. Koerner, 1968, p. 18.

Liberia and Ethiopia, 1880–1914: the survival of two African states

M. B. AKPAN
based on contributions from A. B. Jones and R. Pankhurst

'Ethiopia shall stretch forth her hands unto God'. Blessed, glorious promise! Our trust is not to be in chariots or horses ... [but in] the Lord. And surely, in reviewing our [African] history as a people, whether we consider our preservation in the lands of our exile or the preservation of our fatherland from invasion, we are compelled to exclaim: Hitherto hath the Lord helped us.[1]
(Edward W. Blyden, Liberian scholar, 1862).

Ethiopia has need of no one; she stretches out her hands unto God.[2]
(Menelik II, Emperor of Ethiopia, 1893).

We have realized as never before that this is an era of a New Diplomacy, a diplomacy which is not bound by the cardinal principles of international law or even of natural justice or equity, where small nations are concerned ... Great states meet and partition small states without any consultation of the latter; and they are helpless as they have no adequate army or navy to meet force with force.[4]
(Arthur Barclay, President of Liberia, 1907).

The quotations above show the bond, however tenuous, that bound Liberia and Ethiopia, and particularly the common predicament that derived from aggression committed against both states by European powers engaged in the Scramble for the partition of Africa (1880–1914). This chapter is therefore a comparative study of historical developments in the two states particularly during the crucial period of the Scramble and partition when European powers imposed colonial rule on most of Africa. After introducing their territories, peoples, and governments, the chapter examines how Liberia and Ethiopia were challenged and affected by, or responded to, the strategies and processes whereby Europeans imposed their rule on Africa;

1. E. W. Blyden, 1864, p. 358.
2. R. Pankhurst, 1976.
3. A. Barclay, F. E. R. Johnson and T. M. Stewart, 'Report of Liberian Commission to Europe *in re* Franco-Liberian Frontier', in Liberian National Archives (LNA), file entitled *Executive President: Presidential Commissions* (EPPC).

why both states escaped European rule; and the major political, economic and social changes that occurred in them.

Liberia and Ethiopia on the eve of the Scramble for Africa

Liberia

Liberia was technically a colony of the American Colonization Society (ACS) which founded it in 1822 with the assistance of the United States government for settling 'free' Afro-Americans willing to flee the oppression of slavery and white racism, and recaptured Africans ('Recaptives') rescued on the Atlantic waters from slave ships by American naval vessels.

Monrovia, established in 1822 by the pioneer Afro-American emigrants, formed Liberia's nucleus. Thereafter, up to about 1906, over 18 000 New World Africans mostly aided by the ACS settled, annually, in Liberia in congeries of over thirty towns close to the Atlantic littoral on land obtained by the ACS or the Liberian government from the African chiefs of the region. Almost all of them were Afro-Americans, but at least 400 were Afro-West Indians from Barbados who emigrated in 1865 and settled together at Crozierville, 13 km inland from Monrovia. Over 5000 Recaptives – mostly from the Congo region – were also settled, particularly between 1844 and 1863, initially in the care of the Americo-Liberians – as the New World African settlers and their descendants were collectively designated.[4]

Needing land for farming, trade, and for building a great nation, and faced with some competition from the British and the French seeking land to build trading factories and military stations, the Americo-Liberians greatly expanded Liberia's territory from the few isolated points on the coast initially leased to them by African chiefs. By December 1875, when the expansion virtually ceased, Liberia allegedly stretched for 960 km along the Atlantic coast and between 320 and 400 km inland and hypothetically as far as the River Niger (see Fig. 11.1). It embraced the Americo-Liberian and Recaptive settlements and peoples and the indigenous African ethnic groups and their territories. These groups included the Vai, Dei, Bassa, Kru and Grebo near the coast; and the Gola, Kissi, Bandi, Kpele, Loma, and Mandingo further inland.[5]

The Americo-Liberians practised an essentially western culture in their life style, political institutions, through the use of the English language, individual ownership and perpetual alienation of land, and their adherence to Christianity and monogamy. The indigenous Africans were Traditionalists or Muslims, spoke their own languages, and held land communally. Their villages were governed by chiefs and elders assisted by age-grade or socio-political organizations like the *poro* (for men) and *sande* (for

4. M. B. Akpan, 1973(b), pp. 217–23.
5. M. B. Akpan, 1976, pp. 72–5.

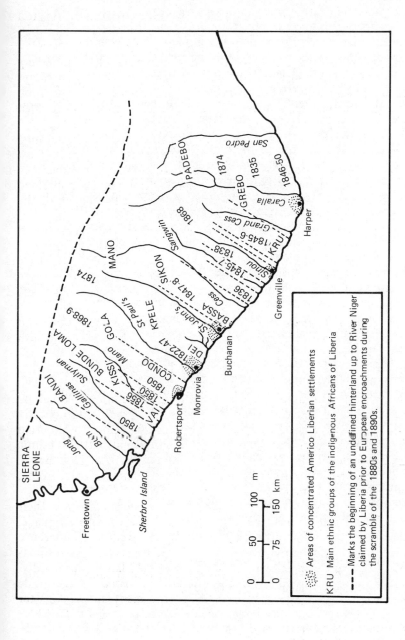

FIG. 11.1 *Liberia: territory annexed by the Americo-Liberians, 1822–74 (after W. B. Morgan and J. C. Pugh, 1969)*

women). Although they appreciated western education brought by the Americo-Liberians and white missionaries, some of their elders opposed the propagation of Christianity and other interference with their laws and customs.

Lacking effective military might, trained administrative personnel, and funds, the Liberian government could not implement its plans for effective occupation of Liberian territory by building roads, railways, military and administrative posts and Americo-Liberian settlements across its length and breadth, or by co-operating with interior chiefs by paying them regular stipends and inviting them to 'represent' their people in the Liberian legislature as 'referees'. Hence when the Europeans commenced their Scramble in about 1880 (culminating in the Berlin Conference of 1884–5), Liberia seemed likely to lose to them vast stretches of the territory she already claimed.[6] The Liberian government was therefore concerned during the Scramble primarily to preserve territory it had already acquired.

On the eve of the Scramble, the internal development of Liberia had not undergone much change since it had gained its independence from the American Colonization Society in 1847. The Legislature, modelled after the American Congress, consisted of a House of Representatives and a Senate. The Executive comprised the President and Vice-President elected biennially by the people, and cabinet members appointed by the President with the consent of the Senate. The Executive was represented in the county – the unit of local administration – by a county superintendent who headed the county's administration. In spite of the President's theoretically vast powers, owing to inadequate means of enforcing executive authority outside Monrovia, considerable political power was wielded by certain Americo-Liberian families at the county level, sometimes extending over several generations, during the Republican and True Whig regimes. Such families, described sarcastically by a Liberian critic as 'the lords and noblemen' of Liberia, included the Hoffs, Shermans and Watsons of Cape Mount; the Barclays, Colemans, Coopers, Dennises, Grimeses, Howards, Johnsons, Kings and Morrises of Montserrado; the Harmons and Horaces of Grand Bassa; the Birches, Greenes, Grigsbys, Rosses and Witherspoons of Sinoe; and the Brewers, Dossens, Gibsons, Tubmans and Yancys of Maryland. These families constituted the political (and invariably the economic) elite.[7]

Serious social cleavages, however, undermined Liberia's national unity. For example, the Republic's two political parties formed around independence in 1847 (the Republican, dominated by the mulatto settlers; and the

6. R. W. Shufeldt, *World Cruise: Liberia and the Liberian Boundary Dispute* (Naval Historical Foundation Collection, Manuscript Division, Library of Congress, Washington, DC), Shufeldt to Coppinger, Fernando Po, 8 May 1879.

7. LNA, *Executive Department: Correspondence General 1887–1899*, Ross to Cheeseman, Greenville, 12 July 1892 (EDCG 1887–1899); *Liberian Letters*, 15, Dennis to Coppinger, Monrovia, 22 August 1871; *Sierra Leone Weekly News*, 3 June 1899; LNA, Liberian Legislature, *Minutes of the Senate*, 1848–1900.

True Whig, dominated by the black settlers, the Congos and the educated indigenous Africans) lacked fundamental ideological or political differences and therefore tended to engage in sterile, acrimonious, biennial electioneering for political ascendancy to control the Republic's vast patronage system. The Republicans ruled Liberia from Independence to 1870, when they were overthrown by the True Whigs, but they regained power in 1871 only to lose it again to the True Whigs in 1877. The True Whigs then ruled Liberia continuously until 1980 when they were overthrown in a coup led by Master-Sergeant (now General) Samuel Doe.

More fundamental has been the cleavage between the Americo-Liberians and Liberia's indigenous Africans. Throughout the nineteenth century, Americo-Liberians' policy was to assimilate the indigenous Africans culturally and politically by 'civilizing' and Christianizing them, and giving them equal rights with the settlers. Although this was achieved to some extent with the Recaptives (who were much less numerous than the settlers), the Americo-Liberians, mindful of their own privileged position, maintained tight political control over Liberia by restricting political participation of even those indigenous Africans who were educated. Only very few of them were given the franchise on an equal footing with the Americo-Liberians (although these might themselves be illiterate and poor). The main indigenous African representation (mostly of the coastal Africans) in the Liberian Legislature as from 1875 consisted of African chiefs designated 'referees' (or 'delegates'), after their chiefdoms had paid an annual 'delegate fee' of $100 to the Liberian government. As the delegates 'spoke' through an interpreter solely on ethnic matters and could not vote, they had very little influence on government policy.[8] Hence both the educated Africans and the chiefs resented their restricted representation.

Furthermore the Liberian government sought to maximize its import and export duties and other levies on trade and shipping which constituted its main sources of revenue. To facilitate collection and control of the external trade by Americo-Liberian merchants, from 1839 the government restricted foreign merchants to trade at only six Americo Liberian ports of-entry. The restrictions and levies alienated both the foreign merchants who resented them, and the indigenous African chiefs who had formerly controlled the external trade and levied the dues. Often, the foreign merchants and chiefs combined to resist or defy the trade restrictions and levies, or to appeal to European states to intervene on their behalf. Thus, at various times during the nineteenth century, the Vai, Kru and Grebo

8. Only during the presidency of William V. S. Tubman (1944–71) were reforms introduced to give the Africans almost equal rights with Americo-Liberians and indigenous African elites assimilated to their way of life. The rights included extension in 1944 of the franchise to all adult indigenous African males who paid a hut tax of $2, which did away with the 'delegate' system; and the extension of the county system of the Americo-Liberian communities to all parts of Liberia, which abolished the colonial-type system of 'indirect rule'.

of the Liberian coast put up an armed resistance to Liberian government impositions on their trade.[9]

Ethiopia

After over a hundred years of disunity, the ancient Ethiopian empire was revived by Emperor Tewodros II (1855–68). By defeating the powerful, frequently warring feudal rulers (or *rases*) of Ethiopia's Tigre, Begemdir, Gojjam, Simien, Wello and Shoa provinces, over which the puppet emperor at Gondar had hardly any control, Tewodros reunited the empire during the early years of his reign under his strong rule (see Fig. 11.2).[10] These provinces, located mostly on the high Ethiopian plateau from Eritrea to the Awash valley, were peopled predominantly by the Agaws, Amharas and Tigreans. These peoples professed the dominant Amhara–Tigrean culture characterized partly by Monophysite Christianity of the Ethiopian Orthodox Church, the closely related Amharic and Tigrean languages, a socio-political structure comprising 'a hierarchy of superior–inferior relations held together by powerful authority figures', and an agriculture-based economy that generated 'a strong attachment to land' and 'a corresponding network of land-based rights and services' usually associated with feudalism.[11]

Reunited under Tewodros, the Amhara–Tigre core formed, as did Monrovia and other Americo-Liberian settlements in Liberia, the spring-board for Ethiopia's further expansion during the second half of the nineteenth century into the lands of the surrounding, mostly lowland populations over some of whom the imperial government had at various earlier times occasionally exercised a 'shifting and often uneasy' relationship or jurisdiction.[12] The Amhara–Tigre core was, however, not monolithic but was divided politically by regional rivalries, and physically by ravines and highlands which hindered communication and transportation.

Tewodros's subjugation of the *rases* with superior imported arms, and his own eventual defeat in April 1867 by a British punitive force dramatized to Ethiopian leaders the significance of modern weapons for controlling the empire and containing political rivals or external aggression.

As Tewodros's successor, Emperor Yohannes IV (1871–89), was, as will be seen below, preoccupied with repelling Egyptian and Sudanese Mahdist aggression. Further Ethiopian expansion – over Ethiopia's so-called 'historic lands', to over twice Ethiopia's size – occurred mostly under Emperor Menelik II (1889–1913) whose reign coincided with the European Scramble for Africa.[13]

9. J. D. Hargreaves, 1963, p. 243.
10. R. Greenfield, 1965, p. 70; P. Gilkes, 1975, pp. 9–10.
11. C. Clapham in R. Lemarchand (ed.), 1977, pp. 36, 37.
12. H. G. Marcus, 1975, p. 140.
13. R. Greenfield, 1965, p. 96.

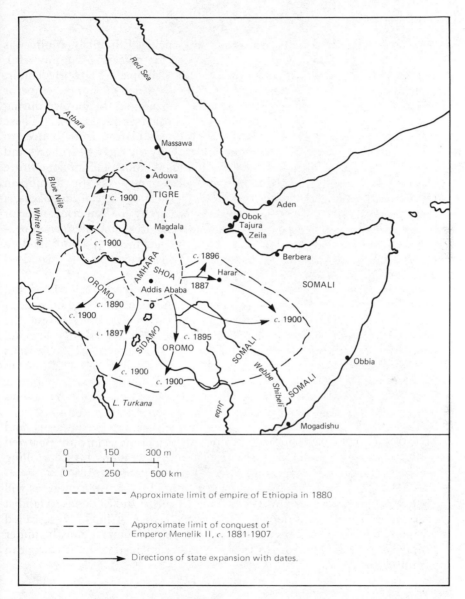

Red Sea

Atbara

Blue Nile

White Nile

Massawa

● Adowa

c. 1900   TIGRE

Aden

c. 1900

Magdala

Obok
Tajura
Zeila

c. 1896

Berbera

AMHARA   SHOA

Harar

OROMO

Addis Ababa   1887

SOMALI

c. 1890

c. 1900

c. 1900

c. 1897

SIDAMO

c. 1895

OROMO

SOMALI

Webbe Shibeli

SOMALI

Obbia

c. 1900

c. 1900

L. Turkana

Juba

Mogadishu

0   150   300 m

0   250   500 km

- - - - - - - Approximate limit of empire of Ethiopia in 1880

— — — Approximate limit of conquest of
Emperor Menelik II, *c.* 1881-1907

⟶ Directions of state expansion with dates.

FIG. 11.2 *The expansion of Ethiopian territory under Emperor Menelik II (after J. D. Fage,
1978)*

255

PLATE 11.1 *Menelik, King of Shoa, 1865–89; Emperor of Ethiopia, 1889–1913*

By the time of Menelik's reign, the political culture of Ethiopia had already crystallized. The Ethiopian imperial system was organized at three basic levels: district or *seignorey*, province, and nation; and on three separate axes: the economic, political and religious. The lord, governor and emperor, ruling respectively over the district, province and empire and related to one another in a 'hierarchy of superior–inferior relations' constituted the pillars of the system since each was 'at once governor, judge, military leader and courtier'. As a rule the emperor appointed the provincial governors who in turn appointed the lords or sub-governors over the districts into which his province was divided.

The lord possessed certain rights known as *gult*: essentially the right to collect tribute in kind from each household in the district and to appropriate labour for work on his farms or on other projects he might designate. Part of the tribute was retained for his own use, and the remainder was transmitted to his overlord – the provincial governor. He adjudicated cases and disputes in the district, mobilized and commanded the local militia, and organized public works to develop the district (besides ensuring that his 'parish', often coterminous with the district, discharged its obligations to the local Ethiopian Orthodox church).[14] As a rule, the obligations due to the lord or church from the district's population, based primarily on their attachment to land for livelihood, were comparatively light in the Amhara–Tigre core provinces. There, land was owned and controlled by the *rist* system, that is, mostly by individual lineages; it was practically inalienable and was therefore unavailable for distribution by the emperor or governor for patronage purposes. The obligations were heavy in the regions in the south and west conquered by Menelik, where the lords and *naftanyas* (literally 'gunbearers': settlers from the Abyssinian highlands) greatly exploited the people partly through *gult* rights and obligations.[15]

The provincial governors performed functions similar to those of the lords but on a larger scale. Those in the Amhara–Tigre core were recruited mostly from the emperor's close relatives or from local noblemen presumed loyal to the emperor. Governors of the newly conquered regions in the south and west where alienable land was available, were predominantly Amhara, Shoan, Tigrean or other northern noble or military men who received *gult* rights (or *rist-gult* land in lieu of governorship) for their services to the emperor. Thus continued loyalty to the governor or emperor greatly depended on the availability of *gult* for rewards, and of military power to enforce authority.[16]

The emperor was the most important single factor in the imperial system. He performed institutionalized executive, legislative, and judicial functions

14. D. N. Levine, 1974, pp. 114–20; P. Gilkes, 1975, pp. 13–14.
15. ibid.
16. C. Clapham in R. Lemarchand (ed.), 1977; P. Gilkes, 1975, pp. 28–9; D. N. Levine, 1974, pp. 120–1.

which have been classified by Christopher Clapham as 'protective', 'extractive and distributive', 'regulative', and 'symbolic'. The emperor personally led his army, managed imperial affairs, and dispensed justice and patronage. More importantly perhaps, the emperor symbolized national unity and independence by virtue of his alleged descent from the Biblical King Solomon and his coronation and anointment by the *abuna*, the Egyptian head of the Ethiopian Orthodox Church.[17]

The imperial system inherited by Tewodros lacked a notable 'historic bureaucracy'.[18] Excepting comparatively few offices with well-defined functions like the *Tsahafe T'ezaz* (Imperial Secretary) and the *Afa-Negus* (Chief Justice), the imperial administration was largely personalized in the emperor and his regional representatives: the governors and lords.[19] Tewodros himself attempted to create a bureaucracy by often replacing existing governors of aristocratic stock by paid army generals of humble birth, loyal to, and dependent on him. But the new governors were overthrown and replaced by pre-existing dynasties during widespread revolts against his increasingly harsh rule.[20]

The similarities between Liberia's and Ethiopia's political systems were too obvious from the analysis thus far to belabour. Besides possessing a core and periphery, and a central government, each had sub-political systems centred on local chiefdoms (or villages) like those of the Gola in Liberia or the Oromo ('Galla') in Ethiopia not discussed in this chapter, with political cultures more or less different from the dominant political culture at the centre. Both systems were solidly based on privilege at the core, and extensively utilized patronage and assimilation techniques. Nevertheless, whereas Ethiopia's imperial system was largely 'African', lacking political parties or parliament – Tewodros, Yohannes and Menelik became Emperor by virtue of their superior military power over their rivals, and not through the ballot box – Liberia's central government was thoroughly western. At any rate, each system possessed or developed the mechanisms and instruments necessary for containing European aggression unleashed by the Scramble and partition.

European aggression on Liberian and Ethiopian territory, 1880–1914

Both Liberia and Ethiopia had enjoyed more or less amicable relations with the European powers up to 1879. During the period of the Scramble from the 1880s onwards, these relations began to change and both of them were subjected to varying degrees of European imperialist pressures and aggression with contrasting results and consequences.

17. C. Clapham in R. Lemarchand (ed.), 1977, pp. 44–5.
18. D. Crummey, 1969, p. 465.
19. R. Pankhurst, 1967, p. 12.
20. C. Clapham in R. Lemarchand (ed.), 1977, p. 47.

PLATE 11.2 *E. J. Barclay, Secretary of State, Liberia*

Liberia

Neither invited to, nor represented at, the Berlin Conference, Liberia at first refused to be bound by its decisions such as the principle of 'effective occupation' on the ground. As Liberia's Secretary of State, Edwin J. Barclay stated in June 1887, the Liberian view was that the Berlin decisions 'refer to further acquisitions of African territory by European powers and not to the present possessions or future acquisition of an African state'.[21] The Liberians insisted, correctly, that being an African government and country, Liberia required no 'effective occupation' since all the inhabitants were Liberians.

In the end, to avoid losing Liberia's entire hinterland, the Liberian government commenced measures from the late 1890s for effective occupation. Liberia's President from 1904 to 1911, Arthur Barclay, aptly stated the issues at stake, arguing in December 1906 that:

> Liberia was a recognized state long before the Berlin Conference ... and there might be ground on its part to question some of the *dicta* laid down at that Conference. But it is a fact that the great powers really settle the principles of international law. Small states must conform. It results, therefore, that we are compelled to occupy our frontiers with a frontier guard, suitable officials, and give to the frontier district an organized government on civilized lines.[22]

European imperialism in Liberia during the Scramble and partition occurred in three main forms: (1) expropriation of Liberian territory by European powers; (2) gross interference in Liberia's internal affairs by them and; (3) control of Liberia's economy by European merchants, financiers, concessionaires and entrepreneurs who enjoyed the confidence and patronage of these powers. European imperialist activities in Liberia further weakened and destabilized her.

Heeding invitations by the Vai of north-western Liberia, and Sierra Leonean and British merchants stationed on the Vai coast, and mindful of Sierra Leone's commerce and revenue, Britain intervened from 1860 allegedly to protect the Vai and the merchants from Liberian impositions. After fruitless, intermittent discussions between British, Liberian and Vai representatives, Britain annexed most of the Vai chiefdoms to Sierra Leone in March 1882, although the Vai chiefs never desired British rule (save British intervention) (see Fig. 11.3).[23] Liberians, stunned by the British action, but helpless, issued an emotional, ineffective 'Memorandum and Protest' against the action, copies of which were sent to all nations with

21. Quoted in M. B. Akpan, 1973(b), p. 223.
22. A. Barclay, Annual Message, 11 December 1906, in *Liberia Bulletin*, No. 30, February 1907, p. 69 (hereafter, *Bulletin*).
23. Public Record Office, Kew (PRO), FO 84/1699, Derby to Havelock, 2 March 1883; Granville to Lowell, 10 March 1883.

PLATE 11.3 *Arthur Barclay, President of Liberia, 1904–11*

261

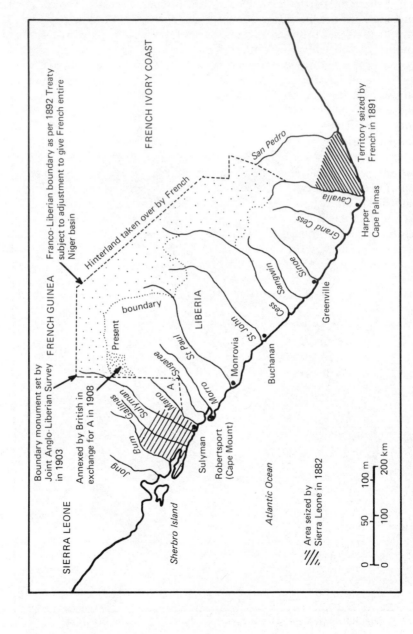

FIG. 11.3 *British and French encroachments on territory claimed by Liberia, 1882–1914 (after R. E. Anderson, 1952)*

Labels within the map:

SIERRA LEONE

FRENCH GUINEA

Boundary monument set by Joint Anglo-Liberian Survey in 1903

Annexed by British in exchange for A in 1908

Franco-Liberian boundary as per 1892 Treaty subject to adjustment to give French entire Niger basin

FRENCH IVORY COAST

Hinterland taken over by French

Present boundary

LIBERIA

Territory seized by French in 1891

Jong
Bum
Galinas
Sulyman
Mano
Sugaree
A
Morro
St Paul
St John
Cess
Sangwin
Sinoe
Grand Cess
Cavalla
San Pedro

Sherbro Island
Sulyman
Robertsport (Cape Mount)
Monrovia
Buchanan
Greenville
Harper
Cape Palmas

Atlantic Ocean

Area seized by Sierra Leone in 1882

0   50   100 m
0   100   200 km

which Liberia had treaty relations. It implored these nations to aid Liberia and to mediate 'to arrest a course of events which threaten her destruction'. Among the few governments to reply was that of the United States, to which Liberians particularly looked for intervention to secure 'a just arrangement' of the boundary question. But the United States government promptly advised Liberia to acquiesce at the British action, which dimmed the hopes of the Liberians entirely. Most of the other nations appealed to were European and were themselves intensifying existing expansionism or about to seek territorial aggrandizement in Africa. Hence Liberia's appeal fell mostly on deaf or unsympathetic ears.[24] In November 1885 Liberia signed an agreement with Britain which fixed the boundary with Sierra Leone at the River Mano to Liberia's disadvantage.

Similarly, the French annexed south-eastern Liberia between the Cavalla and San Pedro rivers in May 1891, taking advantage of its inhabitants' discontent with Liberia's trade policies and Liberia's lack of effective occupation of the district[25] (see Fig. 11.3). Once again, the Liberians issued an emotional appeal to the 'civilized Christian nations of the world' to intercede on their behalf, but in vain.[26] Helpless and powerless, Liberia concluded an agreement with France in December 1892 which fixed Liberia's boundary with the Ivory Coast at the Cavalla river and thereby gave France the Cavalla–San Pedro district and a large slice of Liberia's hitherto undefined hinterland, purportedly in return for France relinquishing her vague claims to Garraway, Buchanan and Butaw on the Liberian coast.[27]

To prevent further encroachments on Liberia, the Liberian government sent envoys to Washington and London in 1890 and 1892 respectively to obtain their commitment to the preservation of Liberia's territorial integrity; but neither would be committed.[28]

Liberia lost further territory to Britain and France between 1892 and 1914 as those powers advanced competitively to occupy Africa's heartland and subsequently demarcated their territories' boundaries with Liberia.

Britain, hitherto confined to the Sierra Leone coast, annexed its hinterland in 1896 and imposed a colonial or 'native administration' over

24. G. W. Gibson and A. F. Russell, 1883.

25. African Colonization Society, *Seventy-Seventh Annual Report*, January 1894, pp. 9–10; E. Hertslet, 1909, Vol. III, pp. 1132–3.

26. Maryland County, 'France versus Liberia: a document adopted by citizens of Maryland County against the Franco-Liberian Treaty now before the Liberian Senate – urging the Senate to reject it, and praying France to refrain; and affirming by reference to Liberian deeds Liberia's right to the San Pedro Region' (February 1893) in LNA, Executive, Department of State, Domestic Correspondence (EDSDC), 1855–1898. Also see United States National Archives (USNA) Despatches of United States Ministers at Monrovia (DUSM) 11/70, McCoy to Gresham, Monrovia, 27 April 1893.

27. Archives Nationales, Paris: Franco-Liberian Boundary Agreement, 1892, M.12. 8972; USNA, DUSM 11/52, McCoy to Foster, Monrovia, 1 February 1893.

28. H. R. Lynch, 1967, p. 185.

it. The territory annexed included Kanre-Lahun, the principal town of the Luawa chiefdom, with whose chief, Kai Lundu, T. J. Alldridge had concluded a treaty in 1890 on behalf of the British government. By 1902, following some civil commotion, a British force had occupied Kanre-Lahun.

To forestall the British in Kanre-Lahun district, the Liberian government established a 'native administration' by posting administrative and customs officials and a military unit there in February 1907. But the British force would not withdraw, even though the Governor of Sierra Leone, G. B. Haddon-Smith, who visited Kanre-Lahun that month and was escorted into it by the Liberian military unit, recognized the district as Liberian territory held by Britain 'temporarily' for Liberia.[29] Rather, in June 1907, Liberia's Consul-General in London, Henry Hayman, informed President Barclay that the French and British governments were 'contemplating very serious measures' which might almost 'impair the independence of Liberia' unless Liberia's boundary with France's Ivory Coast and Guinea was settled.[30]

Moved by this threat, President Barclay visited London and Paris in September 1907 to seek guarantees for Liberia's sovereignty and territorial integrity. However, not only did both governments refuse to give any guarantees but the French government rather drew up, almost unilaterally, a boundary 'agreement' which gave France a further slice of Liberian territory beyond the Makona river, and committed Liberia to establish military posts on the Franco–Liberian frontier 'which the French authorities would be allowed to occupy [temporarily] if the resources of the Liberian Government do not allow her at the time to keep up a garrison there herself'.[31] Barclay, understandably, initially refused to sign the 'agreement' but was compelled to do so after the United States government, to which he had strongly appealed to intervene, advised him to sign on the grounds that 'if we rejected it, the French would likely make further encroachments and we would eventually suffer material loss of territory'.[32] This one-sided treaty settled part of the Franco–Liberian boundary problem. The solution of the rest was started in July 1908 when a joint Franco–Liberian commission began boundary limitation work.[33] However,

29. A. Barclay, *Annual Message*, December 1908; US Department of State, *Report of the Commission of the United States of America to the Republic of Liberia* (Washington DC, October 1909); PRO, FO 267/65, H. H. Johnston, 'Memo respecting the Americo-Liberian Occupation of North-West Liberia', 19 April 1907; FO 267/75, Haddon-Smith to Elgin, Freetown, 28 March 1907.

30. Barclay to Lyon, Monrovia, 9 August 1907 enclosed in USNA, DUSM 326/202, Lyon to Secretary, Monrovia, 9 August 1907; EPCG 1905–1912, Barclay to Lyon, 9 August 1907.

31. E. Hertslet, 1909, Vol. III, pp. 1140–1; R. L. Buell, 1928, Vol. II, p. 790.

32. A. Barclay, F. E. R. Johnson and T. M. Stewart, 'Report of Liberia Commission to Europe in Re Franco-Liberian Matters, September 1907', in LNA, EPCEPG; USNA, DUSM (NF), 326/345, Ellis to Secretary, Monrovia, 12 January 1910.

33. *Cabinet Minutes*, for 6 August 1909.

up to the mid 1920s the French still occasionally threatened to seize Liberia's territory.

Apparently envious of the French gain of Liberian territory in 1907, Britain also insisted on acquiring the Kanre-Lahun district and in September 1908, instructed Major Le Mesurier, the Briton commanding the British troops stationed at Kanre-Lahun, to forbid the Liberian commissioners in the Kanre-Lahun district to perform administrative functions other than the collection of customs duties. A month later, Le Mesurier ordered them to remove their customs posts and to leave Kanre-Lahun altogether, as according to him, the new Liberian frontier with Sierra Leone was to be marked by the natural boundaries of the Moa and Mafissa rivers.[34]

Between November 1909 and early 1910, the Liberian government tried in vain to secure the Kanre-Lahun district from the British by persuasion.[35] The matter was finally settled in January 1911 by an Anglo–Liberian treaty, by which Britain retained the Kanre-Lahun district but ceded to Liberia the much less desirable territory between the Morro and Mano rivers and paid £4000 'compensation' to the Liberian government with which to develop the territory ceded (see Fig. 11.3). (Liberia also won the right to free navigation of the Mano river.) The final delimitation of the new Liberian–Sierra Leone boundary occurred in 1915. Thus Liberia survived the British aggression but was mutilated and anguished.[36]

Ethiopia

European imperial designs against Ethiopia's territory and independence were no less diabolical than those directed against Liberia (see Fig. 11.4). Their beginnings could be traced to 1869 when an Italian Lazarist missionary, Giuseppe Sapeto, purchased the Red Sea port of Assab from a local sultan for 6000 Maria Theresa dollars. The port became the property of a private Italian shipping company, the Societa Rubattino, and in 1882 was declared an Italian colony.[37]

Emperor Yohannes, though a notable patriot and a staunch adherent of the Ethiopian Orthodox Church, was less immediately concerned with the advent of Italy than with the departure of Egypt.[38] The latter then ruled much of the Red Sea and Gulf of Aden coasts of Africa, and their

34. USNA, DUSM (NF) 326/–, Lemadine to Barclay, 30 September 1908; PRO, FO 367/209; Cooper to Le Mesurier, Gbonibu, 25 November 1909.

35. R. L. Buell, 1928, Vol. II, pp. 784–9; USNA, DUSM (NF), 326/339, Ellis to Secretary, Monrovia, 6 January 1910.

36. PRO, FO 367/233, Baldwin, 'Annual Report', 30 September 1911; A. Barclay, *Annual Message*, 12 December 1911.

37. Italy, Ministero dell'Affari Esteri, *Trattati, convensioni, accordi protocolli ed altri documenti relativi all'Africa* (Roma, 1906). 1–25–6.

38. For a brief Ethiopian chronicle of the reign of Yohannes see M. Chaine, 1913.

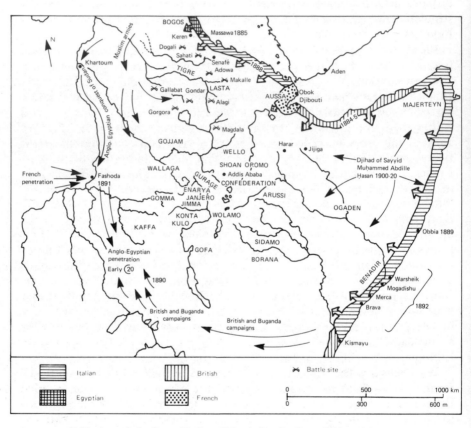

Map labels:

BOGOS
Keren
Massawa 1885
Dogali
Sahati
Khartoum
Senafé
Adowa
Aden
TIGRE
Makalle
Gallabat Gondar
LASTA
Alagi
AUSSA
Obok
Djibouti
Gorgora
MAJERTEYN
Magdala
GOJJAM
WELLO
Harar
Jijiga
Djihad of Sayyid
Muhammed Abdille
Hasan 1900-20
WALLAGA
SHOAN OROMO
French
penetration
Fashoda
1891
GURAGE
Addis Ababa
CONFEDERATION
ENARYA
ARUSSI
GOMMA
JANJERO
JIMMA
OGADEN
KONTA
WOLAMO
KULO
KAFFA
SIDAMO
Obbia 1889
GOFA
BORANA
Anglo-Egyptian
penetration
Early 20
1890
BENADIR
Warsheik
Mogadishu
Merca
1892
Brava
British and Buganda
campaigns
British and Buganda
campaigns
Kismayu
Muslim armies
Conquest of Sudan
Anglo-Egyptian
1884-5

Legend:
Italian
British
Egyptian
French
Battle site

Scale:
0   500   1000 km
0   300   600 m

FIG. 11.4 *Ethiopia and the Scramble for Africa (after R. Greenfield, 1965)*

266

immediate hinterlands, including the port of Massawa and the city of Harar. Egypt, which had come under British occupation in 1882, was faced with the rebellion of the Sudanese Mahdī, Muḥammad Aḥmad, which caused Britain to decide in 1883 that the Sudan would have to be evacuated of Egyptian and British troops. Egyptian rule thereupon collapsed in the whole Red Sea and Gulf of Aden area bordering Ethiopia. Since several Sudanese towns with Egyptian garrisons and European inhabitants were besieged by the Mahdists, Britain decided on enlisting Yohannes's help in their evacuation. A British officer, Rear-Admiral Sir William Hewett, was dispatched to negotiate with Yohannes who agreed to assist, but he also stipulated that territories on the Sudanese frontier recently occupied by Egypt should be returned to him. He also asked for control of Massawa. His first demand was accepted, but, as for the port, Britain merely promised free transit 'under British protection' for Ethiopian goods, including arms and ammunition.[39] A treaty embodying these principles was signed on 3 June 1884, after which the notable Ethiopian warrior Ras Alula relieved six garrisons in the Sudan.[40]

The value of the agreement was, however, short-lived, for on 3 February 1885, the Italians seized Massawa. They did so with the consent of the British who favoured Italian expansion in the hope of curbing that of France, their principal rival in the Scramble for Africa. The Italian officer in charge of the occupation, Rear-Admiral Caimi, proclaimed to the inhabitants that this action was taken in agreement with the British and Egyptians, and promised: 'No obstacle shall be put by me on your trade; on the contrary, all my exertions shall aim at facilitating it.'[41] This profession, however, rapidly proved worthless, for the Italians soon stopped the supply of arms to Yohannes, and penetrated inland as far as the villages of Sahati and Wia. Ras Alula protested against this infiltration, but the Italians replied by fortifying the disputed areas, and by sending more troops which were intercepted by Ras Alula at Dogali in January 1887. The invaders thereupon evacuated Sahati and Wia, but, complaining of a 'massacre' at Dogali, blockaded all shipping bringing supplies to Ethiopia.[42]

War between the Italians and Yohannes seemed imminent, but the former, anxious to avoid a difficult mountainous campaign, persuaded Britain to mediate. A British diplomat, Sir Gerald Portal, was dispatched to the Emperor to ask him to agree to an Italian occupation of Sahati and Wia, and of the Senahit or Bogos area which the Egyptians had ceded in 1884. When these proposals were read out, Yohannes bluntly answered 'I can do nothing with all this. By the Treaty made by Admiral Hewett,

39. A. B. Wylde, 1901, pp. 472–4.
40. ibid., p. 35.
41. E. Hertslet, 1909, Vol. I, p. 8.
42. On contemporary Italian attitudes to the battle of Dogali and other events in the history of Italian expansion see A. Dejaco, 1972.

all the country evacuated by the Egyptians on my frontier was ceded to me at the instigation of England, and now you come to ask me to give it up again.' Angered that Britain had thus departed from the treaty, he wrote to Queen Victoria, protesting that if she wished to make peace it should be when the Italians were in their country and the Ethiopians in theirs.[43]

Yohannes, faced with the growing threat from Italy, strengthened his defences by moving up a garrison stationed on the Sudan frontier. Finding the area unguarded, the Mahdists attacked there. The emperor hastened to Matamma to resist them, but at the close of a victorious battle on 10 March 1889, was mortally wounded by a stray bullet. News of his death caused his army to disintegrate. There was great confusion throughout northern Ethiopia, the more so as the country was suffering from a serious cattle plague and famine followed by epidemics of smallpox and cholera.[44] During this period of difficulty the Italians advanced rapidly inland. By the end of 1889 they had occupied a stretch of the northern plateau where they established their colony of Eritrea with its capital at Asmara.[45]

During much of Emperor Yohannes's grim resistance against Egyptian and Italian aggression, Menelik, Shoa's ruler and nominally subordinated to the emperor, maintained cordial relations with Italy (see Plate 11.1). Contact with Italy was valuable to Menelik, for the Italian envoy, Count Antonelli, the only foreign diplomat more or less permanently at his court, provided convenient access to Europe and her technology; besides, the Italians supplied him with several physicians as well as numerous firearms. As a consequence of this friendship with Italy, Menelik was able as King of Shoa (1865–89) to forcibly acquire the rich regions of Arussi, Harar, Kulo and Konta to the south and south-east, and Gurage and Wallaga to the south-west.[46] Italy for its part regarded Menelik's co-operation as a useful, if in the long run dispensable, asset in its expansionist ambitions. This friendship culminated on 2 May 1889 – less than two months after the death of Emperor Yohannes – in a Treaty of Peace and Amity signed between Menelik and Italy at the Ethiopian village of Wuchale.

The Wuchale (Italian: Uccialli) treaty, which was to constitute a turning-point in the relations between the two countries, contained articles of benefit to both. In it Menelik recognized Italian sovereignty over the greater part of the Eritrean plateau, including Asmara, while Italy recognized him as emperor – the first such recognition he had been accorded – and promised that he could import arms and ammunition through Italian territory. The most important section of the treaty, however, was Article XVII which was soon in dispute. The quarrel arose from the fact that the treaty had

43. G. L. Portal, 1892, p. 158.
44. R. Pankhurst, 1966.
45. A. B. Wylde, 1901, p. 49.
46. H. G. Marcus in L. H. Gann and P. Duignan (eds), 1969, pp. 422–4; R. Greenfield, 1965, pp. 98–9.

two texts, one in Amharic and the other in Italian. The sense of Article XVII differed materially between the two versions. The Amharic version stated that Menelik could avail himself of the services of the Italian authorities for all communications he might wish to have with other powers; the Italian text made this obligatory.[47]

Though the Italian text of this article was soon used by Italy to claim a protectorate over Ethiopia, relations between the two countries remained cordial for several months.[48] Menelik dispatched his cousin, Ras Makonnen, the governor of Harar, to Italy in July 1889 to negotiate implementation of the agreement, while General Baldissera, the officer in charge of Italian expansion, advanced further into the Eritrean plateau in accordance with the Wuchale treaty. On 2 August he issued a proclamation for the occupation of Asmara, while on 1 October Ras Makonnen signed an additional convention to the Wuchale treaty in Rome. In it Italy again recognized Menelik as emperor, while the latter recognized Italy's sovereignty over the Red Sea colony on the basis of the frontiers in existence at the time. Provision was also made for an Italian bank loan of 4 000 000 lire.[49]

Ideas of co-operation were, however, almost immediately dashed, for on 11 October the Italian Foreign Minister Crispi announced that 'in conformity with article XXXIV of the perpetual treaty between Italy and Ethiopia ... His Majesty the King of Ethiopia consents to avail himself of the Government of His Majesty the King of Italy for the conduct of all matters which he may have with other Powers or Governments.'[50]

Crispi's announcement, though phrased in a roundabout manner, thus constituted an unequivocal Italian claim to a protectorate over Ethiopia. Italy's claim was duly recognized by the European powers. Cartographers in Europe described the country on their maps as 'Italian Abyssinia', and when Menelik informed the powers of his coronation as emperor, scheduled for 3 November 1889, they replied, to his chagrin, that since Ethiopia was a protectorate they could not deal with him directly but only through Italy. Britain later entered into three protocols with Italy, on 24 March and 14 April 1891 and 5 May 1894, defining the frontiers between British colonial territory and the alleged protectorate.[51]

The Italians in support of their claim meanwhile advanced from Eritrea into Tigre, in northern Ethiopia. Passing the limits earlier agreed to, they crossed the Mareb river and occupied the town of Adowa in January 1890. They then informed Ras Mangasha, the son of Yohannes and the ruler

47. C. Rossetti, 1910, pp. 41–4; E. Work, 1936, pp. 84–6; S. Rubenson, 1964; C. Giglio, 1968.
48. On the history of Italo–Ethiopian relations between the treaty of Wuchale and the battle of Adowa, see C. C. Rossini, 1935; J. L. Niege, 1968.
49. C. Rossetti, 1910, pp. 45–7.
50. E. Hertslet, 1909, Vol. I, pp. 1, 17.
51. E. Work, 1936, pp. 128–33, 138–9.

of Tigre province, that they would not withdraw until Menelik recognized their interpretation of the Wuchale treaty.[52]

Menelik refused to accept this interpretation. On 27 September 1890, he wrote to King Umberto I of Italy pointing out that he had discovered that the two texts of Article XVII did not agree and declared:

> When I made that treaty of friendship with Italy, in order that our secrets be guarded and that our understanding should not be spoiled, I said that because of our friendship our affairs in Europe might be carried on with the aid of the Sovereign of Italy, but I have not made any treaty which obliges me to do so, and today, I am not the man to accept it. That one independent power does not seek the aid of another to carry on its affairs your Majesty understands very well.[53]

Determined not to become further dependent on the Italian loan, he began paying it back. Relations between Italy and Ethiopia reached a deadlock. During the resultant discussions the Italian envoy, Antonelli, informed Menelik that, 'Italy cannot notify the other Powers that she was mistaken in Article XVII, because she must maintain her dignity'. Menelik's consort, Empress Taytu, replied, 'We also have made known to the Powers that the said Article, as it is written in our language, has another meaning. As you, we also ought to respect our dignity. You wish Ethiopia to be represented before the other Powers as your protectorate, but this shall never be'.[54]

After several years' delay, which Menelik turned to advantage by importing large quantities of firearms, especially from France and Russia, and by acquiring Kaffa, Wolamo, Sidamo, Bale, parts of the Ogaden, Gofa, Beni, Shangul and the lands of the eastern and western Boran Oromo ('Galla') mostly through conquest, he finally denounced the Wuchale treaty on 12 February 1893. On 27 February he informed the European powers, and, referring to Italy's claims, alluded to the biblical phrase, declaring that 'Ethiopia has need of no one; she stretches out her hands unto God'. He spoke from a position of strength, for he was by then in possession of 82 000 rifles and twenty-eight cannon.[55]

Fighting between the Italians and Ethiopians broke out in December 1894 when Batha Hagos, an Eritrean chief, rebelled against the rule of Italy. Early in January 1895 the Italians attacked Ras Mangasha in Tigre and occupied much of that province. Menelik thereupon ordered the mobilization of his army on 17 September, and marched north with a large force which won significant victories at Amba Alagi on 7 December and Makalle at the end of the year. The Italians then fell back on Adowa where, after a period of inaction, the final confrontation took place (see Plate 11.4).

52. A. B. Wylde, 1901, p. 51.
53. E. Work, 1936, p. 107.
54. Quoted in ibid., p. 118.
55. Quoted in ibid., pp. 134–5.

PLATE 11.4 *The battle of Adowa: a drawing after a painting in Addis Ababa University*

Menelik was in a relatively strong position. He had the support of the local population, whose patriotism had been intensified by the fact that the Italians had been expropriating Eritrean land for the settlement of their colonists.[56] The inhabitants were therefore willing to show his troops good paths and report on enemy movements. The Italians, on the other hand, had to face the enmity of the local people, and had no accurate maps; they therefore moved in confusion in an almost unknown country. Menelik's army, moreover, was much larger. It was composed of over 100 000 men with modern rifles, besides others with antique firearms and spears, whereas the invaders had only about 17 000 men of whom 10 596 were Italian and the rest were Eritrean levies. The Italians had some superiority in cannon, but with fifty-six pieces as against Menelik's forty this was by no means decisive.

The outcome of the day's fighting at Adowa was a remarkable victory for Menelik, and a complete defeat for his enemies. During the battle, 261 Italian officers, 2918 Italian non-commissioned officers and men, and about 2000 *askaris* or local troops, were killed; in addition 954 Italian soldiers were permanently missing; and 470 Italians and 958 *askaris* were wounded. Total Italian casualties amounted to over 40 per cent of the fighting force which was almost completely routed, and lost all its artillery, besides 11 000 rifles.[57]

As a result of Menelik's victory, on 26 October the Italians agreed to the Peace Treaty of Addis Ababa which annulled the Treaty of Wuchale, and recognized the absolute independence of Ethiopia.[58] Menelik, on the other hand, for reasons not divulged, did not demand an Italian withdrawal from Eritrea, though he had often expressed a desire for access to the sea. The southern frontier of the Italian colony was thus confirmed on the Mareb river.

The Adowa campaign gave Menelik considerable international prestige. The French and British dispatched diplomatic missions to sign treaties with him, while other embassies arrived from the Sudanese Mahdists, the Sultan of the Ottoman empire and the Tsar of Russia.[59]

The outcome of the battle, the greatest victory of an African over a European army since the time of Hannibal, was of major significance in the history of Europe's relations with Africa. The Ethiopians acquired prestige throughout the Red Sea area, as noted by the Polish traveller, Count Potocki, who remarked that the Somali displayed 'race-pride on the victory of their neighbours over a great European power'.[60]

Increasing interest in Ethiopia, the last indigenous independent state

56. R. Pankhurst, 1964, pp. 119–56.
57. G. F. H. Berkeley, 1902, p. 345.
58. C. Rossetti, 1910, pp. 181–3.
59. On the diplomatic missions to Menelik at this time see E. Gleichen, 1898; J. R. Rodd, 1923; H. P. M. d'Orléans, 1898; R. P. Skinner, 1906; F. Rosen, 1907.
60. J. Potocki, 1900, p. 88.

in black Africa, was also evinced by black intellectuals in the New World. The Haitian, Benito Sylvain, one of the first apostles of pan-Africanism, travelled to Ethiopia four times between 1889 and 1906, carrying letters to and from President Alexis of Haiti,[61] while William H. Ellis, a black American of Cuban descent, visited the country twice in 1903 and 1904 with various plans for economic development and the settlement of black Americans.[62]

An Ethiopian impact was also felt in South Africa where the biblical prophecy about Ethiopia stretching forth her hands unto God had aroused interest some years earlier. An Ethiopian Church had been established in South Africa by 1900.[63] Increasing awareness of Ethiopia was later manifested by the appearance in 1911 of the Gold Coast intellectual J. E. Casely Hayford's book, *Ethiopia Unbound*, which was dedicated 'to the sons of Ethiopia the World Wide Over'.

Economic and social developments and European intervention in Liberia's and Ethiopia's internal affairs, 1880–1914

Liberia

Side by side with European encroachments, Liberia faced serious internal economic and social problems. The Scramble and partition forced the Liberian government to advance into the Liberian hinterland to subjugate the indigenous ethnic groups and establish a colonial-type administration over them.[64] Each administrative unit or district was governed 'indirectly' through its principal chiefs in collaboration with a government-appointed district commissioner. Up to 1914 most of the commissioners were Americo-Liberian or educated indigenous Liberian military officers. The administration was largely oppressive and corrupt. Most of the district commissioners, their aides, and troops, being poorly and irregularly paid, and seldom supervised from Monrovia, lived off their districts by extorting food, labour for their private farms, and excessive fines and taxes (above the official one dollar poll-tax on adult males, and labour required for public buildings and roads).[65]

61. A. Bervin, 1969.
62. R. Pankhurst, 1972.
63. G. Shepperson, 1968, pp. 251–3.
64. At least two Liberian presidents have openly admitted that Americo–Liberian rule over the indigenous Liberians was colonial in nature; namely Arthur Barclay (1904–12), and William V. S. Tubman (1944–71) – the latter in his Annual Message to the Liberian Legislature in November 1960. See *The Liberian Age*, 25 November 1960, p. 9.
65. Liberian Department of the Treasury, *Report of the Secretary of the Treasury to the Senate and House of Representatives of the Republic of Liberia, December 1921* (Monrovia, December 1921), pp. 13–14.

Not surprisingly, the indigenous Africans resisted not only their military subjugation to Liberian government authority – just as Africans elsewhere resisted subjugation to European rule – but also the excesses of the Liberian administration. Until subjugated by the Liberian militia, the Liberian Frontier Force and American naval ships, the Kru resisted intermittently, and particularly in 1915–16; the Grebo resisted in 1910; the Kissi in 1913; the Kpele and Bandi, 1911–14; the Gio and Mano, 1913–18; the Gbolobo Grebo, 1916–18; the Gola and Bandi, 1918–19; the Joquelle Kpele, 1916–20; and the Sikon in 1921. These protracted wars on different fronts and the cost and inefficiency of the 'native administration' encouraged foreign intervention and strained the government's human and material resources.[66]

The government's revenues were never adequate. Foreign aid was meagre. Most Americo-Liberians preferred trade to agriculture and were seriously hurt by the worldwide depression of the late nineteenth century. By 1890 resident German, British and Dutch merchants dominated Liberia's external trade. Coffee, Liberia's major export commodity since the 1860s, was produced mostly by Americo-Liberian planters and entrepreneurs using both Recaptive and indigenous African labour. Owing to the depression and adverse competition in the world market with better-prepared Brazilian coffee, the price of Liberian coffee drastically fell from 1898 onwards.[67] The consequent cuts in Liberian coffee output and exports and the general contraction of the volume and value of Liberia's external trade drastically reduced government revenues which consisted mostly of customs dues and other levies on trade and shipping. Besides, the government lacked the means to collect effectively from reluctant Liberian and foreign merchants or to stop smuggling.

To avoid bankruptcy, the government borrowed frequently and heavily from Liberian and resident foreign merchants 'to carry out its most ordinary operations': $10000 in November 1896 at 9% interest from the German trading firm, A. Woermann and Company, 'to meet the current expenses of the Government';[68] $15 000 in February 1898 from the Dutch firm, Oost Afrikaansche Cie, to pay the expenses of the Liberian Legislature;[69] and an unspecified amount in June 1900 from the German firm, Wiechers and Helm, 'to meet quarterly payments of the civil list' – to mention a few examples.[70] Furthermore, the Liberian government borrowed £100000 in 1871, £100000 in 1906 and $1700000 in 1912 from British and European financiers on harsh terms. For repayment it hypothecated its customs revenue. This was administered by British officers as from

---

66. M. B. Akpan, forthcoming.
67. M. B. Akpan, 1975, pp. 136–7.
68. LNA, *Cabinet Minutes*, Meeting of 19 November 1896.
69. LNA, *Cabinet Minutes*, Meeting of 11 February 1898.
70. LNA, *Cabinet Minutes*, Meeting of 13 June 1900.

1906, and by an 'International Receivership' as from 1912, to ensure and facilitate repayment to creditors.[71]

Left with meagre funds after debt payments, and lacking skilled manpower, Liberia could not develop her human or natural resources to any extent or build an infrastructure. American missionary and philanthropic bodies bore the brunt of providing and funding most of Liberia's elementary and high schools, and Liberia's university established in Monrovia in 1862. They also sponsored most of the missionary work in Liberia, for which they employed mostly Liberian and white American missionaries and teachers.

The decline of Liberian trade and agriculture and of foreign aid as from the late nineteenth century increased the Liberian government's exploitation of the indigenous Liberians through the corvée, poll tax and other levies; and Liberians' dependence on their government for jobs. Competition to control these jobs or the social surplus increased between political parties and interest groups like the 'founding fathers' (or Americo-Liberians who had settled in Liberia before Independence) and the 'sons of the soil' (or Americo-Liberians born in Liberia).

Some social and economic developments did nevertheless occur. In 1900 the Liberian government reopened the Liberia College (which it had closed down in 1895 for lack of funds and progress) and thereafter more or less subsidized it to greater productivity. The following year, an Americo-Liberian engineer, T. J. R. Faulkner, installed Liberia's first telephone linking Monrovia with several neighbouring Liberian towns.[72] In 1900 a cable station in Monrovia built by a German firm was opened and linked Liberia with the outside world. During 1906–7 a British firm, the Liberia Development Company, built several motor roads from Monrovia inland, using a part of the loan of 1906. Furthermore, several foreign firms obtained and exploited rubber, mineral and other concessions in Liberia from the Liberian government.[73]

Ethiopia

Like Liberia, Ethiopia underwent significant economic changes from the last decades of the nineteenth century on.

Menelik was desirous of modernizing his age-old country, and displayed keen interest in innovations of all kinds. This interest caused de Castro, an Italian physician, to describe him as 'a progressive sovereign in the true sense of the word', and to add, with humour, that if an adventurer

71. M. B. Akpan, 1975, p. 159.
72. G. W. Gibson, *Annual Message*, 10 December 1901.
73. A. Barclay, *Annual Message*, 11 December 1911; D. B. Howard, *Annual Message*, 12 December 1912; *Cabinet Minutes*, meeting of 18 July 1912.

PLATE 11.5 *Teaching staff and students of Liberia College, 1900*

proposed to erect an escalator to the moon the emperor would ask him to build it 'if only to see if it could be done'.[74] Menelik's reign witnessed numerous innovations without precedent in Ethiopia's history. The first, and one of the most important, was the foundation in the mid 1880s of the capital, Addis Ababa, literally 'New Flower', which by 1910 had a population of some 100000 inhabitants.[75] The construction of the first modern bridges was also effected at this time, and improved the country's difficult communications. In 1892 the taxes were reorganized and a tithe instituted for the army, thereby ostensibly ending the soldiers' traditional practice of looting from the peasants. In 1894, the first national currency was issued 'in order', a proclamation declared, 'that our country may increase in honour and our commerce prosper'. A postal system was also being brought into existence in the 1890s. Postage stamps, ordered like the coins from France, were put on sale in 1893, and a decree establishing post offices was issued in 1894. French advisers were used in developing the service, and entry into the International Postal Union was effected in 1908. A concession for a railway from Addis Ababa to the French Somaliland port of Djibuti was granted in 1894, but technical, financial and political difficulties were so great that the line, largely constructed with French capital, did not reach the railway town of Dire Dawa until 1902 and Akaki, 23 km from Addis Ababa, until 1915. Two telegraph lines had, meanwhile, been established at the turn of the century. One, constructed by the French engineers working on the railway, followed its track, while the other, erected by Italian technicians, linked the capital with Eritrea and the south and west. Early in the twentieth century, the first modern roads were constructed between Addis Ababa and Addis Alem, and between Harar and Dire Dawa, with the assistance of Italian and French engineers respectively, while the capital's wood supply was improved by the introduction, probably by a Frenchman, of eucalyptus trees from Australia.

The later years of the reign saw the establishment of various modern institutions. The Bank of Abyssinia was founded in 1905, as an affiliate of the British-owned National Bank of Egypt. The first modern hotel in Addis Ababa, the Etege, was established by Empress Taytu in 1907. The Menelik II School was set up with the help of Coptic teachers from Egypt in 1908, Menelik having already shown his interest in modern education by sending several students to Switzerland and Russia. The Menelik II Hospital, founded to replace an earlier Russian Red Cross establishment set up during the Adowa war, was erected in 1910, while a state printing press came into existence in 1911.[76] Failing health, and the increasing complexity of government, had meanwhile caused Menelik in 1907 to establish his country's first Cabinet, which, according to his chronicler

74. L. de Castro, 1915, Vol. I, p. 162.
75. ibid., pp. 189–246; E. Mérab, 1921–9, II, pp. 13–193; R. Pankhurst, 1962(a), pp. 33–61.
76. G. Sellassie, 1930–2, Vol. II, pp. 527–8.

Gabre Sellassie, stemmed from a 'desire of implanting European customs'. Ethiopia by the end of Menelik's reign had thus been placed on the road of modernization.[77]

The outcome of the Scramble and partition for Liberia and Ethiopia

The European Scramble for and partition of Africa did have some interesting but contrasting impacts on Liberia and Ethiopia. For one thing, they were the only two states in the whole of the continent that survived the imperialist onslaught and retained their sovereignty and independence. But while, as indicated above, Ethiopia not merely survived but in fact greatly expanded her southern and eastern frontiers during that period, Liberia lost a great deal of her territory to both Britain and France. The last question to be considered is how these contrasting impacts on Ethiopia and Liberia can be accounted for. In other words, why did both of them survive while one lost and the other gained territory?

Both Liberia and Ethiopia survived for three main common reasons: the determination of the peoples of both states to remain independent, the diplomatic dexterity displayed by the leaders of both countries at the time, and finally, the rivalry among the imperial powers which prevented any one of them from occupying either of these states. To all this must be added, in the case of Ethiopia, her military strength. On the other hand, Ethiopia gained further territories while Liberia lost part of hers mainly because of the internal conditions – political, economic and military – in each of the states and of course the degree of the interference of the Europeans in these internal affairs.

One of the main reasons for the survival of both Liberia and Ethiopia was the very strong belief of the peoples of both countries that they were destined by the Almighty God to survive, a belief which very much strengthened their determination to resist all European encroachments and aggression. Growing largely out of the experience of involuntary servitude in the New World, there was imbedded within the Liberian consciousness a firm faith in a Divine Being as controller of the destiny of the Nation. Several Liberian presidents were ministers of the gospel. Indeed, Liberians have always viewed each major event in their history as the result of divine intervention. It is this same belief that underlies the much-quoted expression of Emperor Menelik of Ethiopia in 1893 that 'Ethiopia has need of no one; she stretches out her hands unto God', as well as the passage from his letter to Queen Victoria in August 1891 and his proclamation of September 1895 on the eve of the battle of Adowa quoted in the first chapter of this volume.[78] There is no doubt that this firm belief on the part of the

77. L. de Castro, 1915, Vol. I, p. 162.
78. See p. 4 above.

peoples of these countries filled them with a determination that should go some way to explaining their successful opposition to all the European onslaughts.

The second main reason for the survival of Ethiopia and Liberia was diplomatic. On the one hand, both were able to play one European power against the other and were able to resist by diplomacy the more indirect pressures of the colonial powers. Menelik certainly succeeded in playing Italy, France and Britain off against each other. Having relied on French arms to defend himself against the Italians in 1896, he made use of the British in 1902 when the French attempted to obtain excessive control over the Djibuti railway. Menelik's objective, de Castro states, was simply to make use of the technological achievements of Europe without succumbing to it politically. 'If Europeans came into our house to bring us civilization', the Emperor is said to have reasoned, 'we thank them very much, but they must bring it without us losing our sovereignty. We know how to profit from whatever aspects of their civilization are most helpful to us'.[79] Liberia also constantly played off France against Britain, and Britain against Germany, while she did not hesitate, whenever the going was tough, to bring in the United States to make the necessary threatening noises to ward off any of these powers.

On the other hand, there is no doubt that the determination of the imperial powers to prevent any one of them gaining control of either of those states was a crucial factor in the survival of those states. For mainly economic reasons, Germany, France and Britain were not prepared to see any one of them in sole control of Liberia since the traders of each of these countries were active there. For sentimental reasons, the United States was bent on ensuring the survival of Liberia. Thus, from October 1862 when a formal Treaty of Commerce and Navigation was signed and ratified by the United States Congress, United States military gunboats continued to appear periodically in Liberian waters to put an end to the resistance of the indigenous peoples to Liberian rule and at the same time to moderate French and British ambitions to carve up Liberia on the pretext that Liberia was unable to police her borders.[80] At other times, the United States employed diplomatic means to warn Britain and France of the moral judgement of history should either of them make any attempt to end the independence of Liberia. Thus in 1879 and 1898, the United States warned France and Germany not to annex or establish a protectorate over Liberia.[81] In the same way, for mainly strategic reasons, Britain, France and Italy were not prepared to see any one of them in sole control of Ethiopia. It is significant that when in 1906 the imperial powers of Britain, France and Italy felt that Menelik's failing health would be followed by the disintegration of his empire, all three of them came together to secretly sign

79. C. Rossetti, 1910, pp. 319–25.
80. C. H. Huberich, 1947, Vol. I, p. 213.
81. E. W. Chester, 1974, p. 133.

a tripartite Convention in which Ethiopia was divided among them, a move which was exposed by Menelik even before his death.[82]

However, in the case of Ethiopia, there is one unique and crucial factor that should be cited in explanation of her survival, and which also explains the fact that she was able to extend her territorial limits during the period under review, and that is her military strength. Had Menelik lost the battle of Adowa, Ethiopia would undoubtedly have become an Italian colony in 1896. But as shown above, thanks to her military strength which was far superior to that of Italy in Africa, Ethiopia won that battle and thereby maintained her independence. Even after the battle of Adowa, Menelik persisted in stockpiling arms, a fact confirmed by a British traveller, John Boyes, who noted, early in the twentieth century, that 'practically all the Abyssinians' were 'armed with rifles', and that 'the Abyssinians are the best armed native race in Africa' and 'could not easily be brought under subjection by any foreign Power'.[83] At a military parade held in Addis Ababa in 1902 to commemorate Ethiopia's victory at Adowa, an estimated 600000 Ethiopian troops – about 100000 short of the empire's total military strength – were present, 90000 of whom were men of the imperial standing army.[84] All the troops were armed with modern weapons, including rifles, machine guns, and cannon. Most of the artillery and rapid-fire weapons were stored at Addis Ababa and significantly boosted the emperor's power *vis-à-vis* that of the provincial governors.[85] And it was this army that enabled Menelik to extend the frontiers of Ethiopia in the late 1880s and throughout the 1890s.

But if Liberia and Ethiopia did survive, the former did so mutilated and emaciated, and this was the outcome of her military weakness and the hopeless internal conditions of the state. Liberia's navy in any year consisted of one or two gunboats (including those presented by Britain). Her army was the Americo-Liberian militia up to 1908 when the Liberian Frontier Force (LFF) was organized to complement it. The militia numbered under 2000 men in any year up to 1914 and was mostly poorly trained, paid and equipped.[86] It was mustered mostly during wars with the indigenous Africans when invariably it was assisted by 'auxiliary' indigenous Liberian 'warriors'. It lacked the means of quick transportation to the scene of war. By 1880 it was divided into four regiments – one stationed in each county – each under an Americo-Liberian commander subordinated to the Liberian president, the army's commander-in-chief.[87] The typical condition of the militia was portrayed in President Barclay's description of its Fifth Regiment in May 1906 as: 'unsatisfactory: Colonel

82. C. Rossetti, 1910, p. 331.
83. J. Boyes, n.d. p. 22.
84. H. G. Marcus, 1975, pp. 217–18.
85. ibid.
86. A. Barclay, *Inaugural Address*, 4 January 1904.
87. USNA, DUSM 10/22, Enclosure, Barclay to Taylor, Monrovia, 27 August 1887.

Carter, its commander, being also a preacher and absent constantly; the Lieutenant Colonel being illiterate; the major being deaf; the Regiment is rapidly going down and must be reconstructed'.[88] The LFF, no less inefficient than the militia, comprised in December 1913 three American and seven Liberian officers and over 600 enlisted men stationed in over a dozen detachments in the Liberian hinterland. Up to 1914, the officer commanding each detachment performed both military and administrative duties in his district. Consequently he received instructions from, and reported to both the Department of War and the Department of Interior (neither of which co-ordinated with the other). Liberia's military weakness markedly contrasted with Ethiopia's military might and largely accounted for Liberia's inability to defend her territory from encroachment by Europeans during the Scramble.

No less hopeless was the internal situation. As indicated above, and for reasons already given above, the Liberian government was perennially near-bankrupt and owed huge debts to local and foreign creditors. By January 1908 Liberia's indebtedness to Britain comprised, according to the British Consul-General at Monrovia, £60 000 a year 'for several years' while her indebtedness to German merchants in Liberia amounted to $120 000 by September 1905. This indebtedness enabled the imperial powers to constantly interfere in the internal affairs of Liberia during the period under review in a way that they never did in Ethiopia where they were never provided with the cause nor the excuse so to do. Throughout the last three decades of the nineteenth century, the imperial powers sent mission upon mission to Liberia to offer aid to her to pay her debts if she would come under their protection. France did this in 1879, Germany in 1887 and Spain in 1886, and each power offered to regulate Liberia's finances, organize her defence, and establish and control her Frontier Force. At the same time, their resident ambassadors and representatives treated the Liberians with contempt and frequently imposed on her by denouncing her trade, customs and citizenship laws or bullying her to redress their nationals' grievances as Britain did in September 1869, August 1870, April 1871, February and June 1882, November 1886 and finally January 1909.[89] Germany similarly brought in her gunboats to intimidate Liberia in February and October 1881, in August 1897, January and September 1898 and December 1912. On each occasion, the German government demanded financial indemnity ranging between $3000 and $60 000 from the Liberian government on mostly trivial grounds, particularly alleged 'insults' by Liberian officials to the German consul or German merchants in Liberia who invited the German intervention.

The three years 1907–9 witnessed an unprecedented escalation of this interference by Britain, France and Germany culminating in the famous

88. LNA, *Cabinet Minutes*, of the Meeting of 3 May 1906.

89. *Liberian Letters*, 15, Dennis to Coppinger, Monrovia, September 1870; *Repository*, LVIII, July 1882, pp. 90–1, 123–5; *Bulletin*, 10 February 1897, pp. 51–4.

'Cadell Incident' of 11 and 12 February 1909. The issues involved included the obvious deplorable economic, social and political conditions in Liberia, the rivalry among European powers for influence and territory in Liberia at Liberia's expense and Liberians' indebtedness to these powers or their nationals.

Such European intervention in Liberia had far-reaching effects on Liberian politics and society. First, it divided the Liberians into pro-British and pro-American factions[90] who staged massive anti-Barclay and pro-Barclay demonstrations in Monrovia in January 1909.[91] Moreover, the employment of Europeans at high salaries to implement the reforms demanded by the powers also greatly strained the Liberian government's already depleted revenues. But for the active intervention of the United States, thanks to the activities of the American Minister Resident in Monrovia, Ernest Lyon, an Afro-American thoroughly in sympathy with Liberia and her leaders' anxiety to obtain American support from 1909 onwards, there is no doubt that Liberia would have fallen victim to the other imperial powers.

Never at any time was Ethiopia subjected to such persistent intervention by the European imperial powers in her internal affairs. On the contrary, thanks to the Adowa victory, she was accorded every respect and accepted into the comity of nations more or less as an equal during the period that Liberia was virtually under the siege of the imperial powers. Granted the military weakness of Liberia, and, above all, her internal dislocation, due partly to her own economic weakness and the active interference of Europeans in her internal affairs, the surprising fact is not that Liberia survived anguished and emaciated, but that she survived at all.

90. USNA, DUSM 405/238, Lyon to Secretary, Monrovia, 14 August 1908; London. USNA, Records of the Department of State relating to the internal affairs of Liberia (RDSL), 1909–1929. Reid to Secretary, London, 14 February 1909.

91. PRO FO 369/596, Wallis to Grey, Monrovia, 11 March 1909.

The First World War and its consequences

M. CROWDER

The First World War was essentially a quarrel between European powers which involved Africa, both directly and indirectly, because at the outbreak of hostilities the greater part of it was ruled by the European belligerents. Campaigns were fought on African soil which – though they only marginally affected the overall course of war – had significant implications for Africa. More than a million African soldiers were involved in these campaigns or campaigns in Europe. Even more men, as well as women and children, were recruited, often forcibly, as carriers to support armies whose supplies could not be moved by conventional methods such as road, rail or pack-animal. Over 150 000 soldiers and carriers lost their lives during the war. Many more were wounded and disabled. By the time the war ended, every country in Africa, with the exception of the small Spanish territories – which remained neutral – had been formally committed to one side or the other. Belgian, British, French, Italian and Portuguese administrations were allied – more or less actively – against German colonies (see Fig. 2.1). Even the last remaining independent states on the continent – Liberia, Ethiopia and Dārfūr – became involved. Liberia declared for the Allies on the entry of the United States into the war in 1917. The pro-Muslim boy-Emperor of Ethiopia, Lij Iyasu, proclaimed his country's allegiance to Turkey, thereby causing considerable concern among the Allies that he would inspire a *djihād* among the Muslims of the Horn of Africa where Sayyid Muḥammad Abdille Ḥasan's forces were still giving trouble to the British. British, French and Italian troops moved to Berbera, Djibuti and Massawa, but the intervention proved unnecessary since shocked Christian nobles overthrew the Emperor in September 1916. Similarly, Sultan 'Alī Dīnār of Dārfūr, nominally tributary to, but effectively independent of, the Anglo-Egyptian Sudan, responded to the Turkish call to *djihād* and raided French Chad, threatened British Borno (Northern Nigeria) and tried to stir up revolt in Kordofān (Sudan). Not until February 1916 was he defeated and killed in battle and Dārfūr fully incorporated into Sudan.

Whether directly involved in the fighting or not, nearly every African territory was affected by the exclusion of the Germans from the African trade, the wartime shortages of imports caused by scarcity of shipping space, or, on the brighter side, sudden booms in demands for strategic resources.

A great deal has been written about the European campaigns in Africa during the First World War,[1] and the consequent distribution of German territory among the victorious Allied powers[2] – the last chapter in the Scramble for Africa. Much less has been written about the impact of the war on Africans and on the administrative structures recently imposed on them by their European conquerors.[3] How far did these fragile structures withstand the exodus of European administrative personnel, the spectacle of white conqueror fighting white conqueror, the exactions on recently subdued Africans in terms of men and material, and the widespread revolts that took place on the occasion, though not always directly, or even indirectly as a result of the war? What were the social, political and economic consequences of involving Africans in the European war? It is with these broad questions that this chapter will be principally concerned. However a brief account of the military campaigns is essential if we are fully to understand the implications of the war for Africa.

The War on African soil

The immediate consequence for Africa of the declaration of war in Europe was the invasion by the Allies of Germany's colonies. Neither side had prepared for war in sub-Saharan Africa. Indeed there was short-lived hope that it might be isolated from the war. Governor Doering of Togo suggested to his neighbours in British Gold Coast (now Ghana) and French Dahomey (now Benin) that Togo should be neutralized so that the spectacle of Europeans fighting each other would not be witnessed by their African subjects.[4] In German East Africa (now Tanzania) the Governor, Dr Schnee, was intent on avoiding hostilities so he could pursue his energetic programme of development, and when the British bombarded Dar es Salaam shortly after the declaration of war, he subscribed to a short-lived

1. For the Togo and Cameroon campaigns, see F. J. Moberly (ed.), 1931; for the German South West Africa campaign see Union of South Africa, 1924; W. K. Hancock, 1962, pp. 394–400; for German East Africa, see R. C. Hordern, 1941, Vol. I, and, for the German point of view, P. E. von Lettow-Vorbeck, n.d. There is a good summary of the complexities of this campaign in L. Mosley, 1963.

2. See in particular G. L. Beer, 1923; and W. R. Louis, 1963(a).

3. There are a number of doctoral theses relating to the First World War in Africa which have as yet not been published, but see J. Osuntokun, 1978. Since writing this chapter in 1977, an issue of the *Journal of African History*, Volume XIX, 1978, has been devoted to 'World War I and Africa' and is primarily concerned with the impact of the war on Africans. It has been possible to take note of some of the points made in this important symposium.

4. R. Cornevin, 1962, p. 208.

truce that would neutralize German East Africa.[5] There was even optimism in some quarters that the articles of the Berlin Act of 1885 covering the neutrality of the conventional basin of the Congo would avert war in east-central Africa.[6]

The forces in favour of involving Germany's African possessions in the war were, however, more pressing. From the point of view of Britain, given her naval supremacy, the strategy as laid down by the Committee for Imperial Defence was to carry war to her enemy's colonies. To maintain this naval supremacy, Germany's African communications system and principal ports had to be put out of action. For the Allies, successful campaigns in Germany's colonial possessions might result in their being shared by the victors as spoils of war. This was certainly a major consideration in the decision of the Commandant-General of the South African forces, General Louis Botha, and the Minister of Defence, J. C. Smuts, in the face of real opposition from Afrikaner irreconcilables, to commit South African forces to the Allied side and invade German South West Africa (now Namibia), and later participate in the East African campaign.[7] Not only did Botha and Smuts covet South West Africa as a potential fifth province but they hoped that if they assisted a British victory in German East Africa, parts of conquered German territory might be offered to the Portuguese in exchange for Delagoa Bay – the natural port for the Transvaal – going to South Africa.[8] In Britain, it was considered that the involvement of South Africa and her loyalty would be ensured by the prospect of South West Africa becoming hers.[9] For the French, invasion of Cameroon would retrieve the territory reluctantly ceded in 1911 to Germany in the aftermath of the Agadir crisis (see Fig. 12.1b). Even Belgium, which had immediately invoked the perpetual neutrality of the Congo (now Zaire) under Article X of the Berlin Act, eagerly joined in the invasion of German African territory once her own neutrality had been violated by the Germans, in the hope that successful participation would give her a bargaining position in the eventual peace settlement.[10]

Germany's colonies were not easily defensible given Allied naval supremacy and her much smaller colonial forces. There was early optimism that the anticipated speedy German victory in Europe would avoid direct colonial involvement while achieving Germany's ambition of a *Mittelafrika* linking Cameroon and German East Africa and thwarting once and for

---

5. P. E. von Lettow-Vorbeck, n.d., pp. 27–8. See also W. R. Louis, 1963(b), p. 209 citing H. Schnee, 1919, p. 28.

6. W. R. Louis, 1963(b) pp. 209–10 for a brief discussion of the implications of the neutrality of the Congo Basin for German and British East Africa.

7. D. Denoon, 1972, p. 121.

8. R. Hyam, 1972, p. 28.

9. ibid., p. 26.

10. W. R. Louis, 1963(b), Chapter XIX.

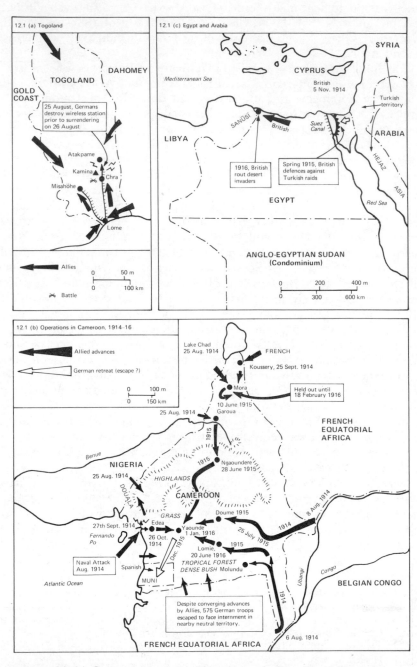

12.1 (a) Togoland

DAHOMEY

TOGOLAND

GOLD
COAST

25 August, Germans
destroy wireless station
prior to surrendering
on 26 August

Atakpame
Kamina
Misahöhe
Chra
Lome

Allies

0   50 m
0   100 km

Battle

12.1 (c) Egypt and Arabia

SYRIA

CYPRUS

Mediterranean Sea

British
5 Nov. 1914

Turkish
territory

SANDSI

British

Suez
Canal

ARABIA

LIBYA

HEJAZ

ASIA

1916, British
rout desert
invaders

Spring 1915, British
defences against
Turkish raids

Red Sea

EGYPT

ANGLO-EGYPTIAN SUDAN
(Condominium)

0   200   400 m
0   300   600 km

12.1 (b) Operations in Cameroon, 1914–16

Allied advances

German retreat (escape ?)

0   100 m
0   150 km

Lake Chad
25 Aug. 1914

FRENCH

Koussery, 25 Sept. 1914

Mora

Held out until
18 February 1916

10 June 1915
Garoua

25 Aug. 1914

1915

FRENCH
EQUATORIAL
AFRICA

Benue

NIGERIA

25 Aug. 1914

HIGHLANDS

1915

Ngaoundere
28 June 1915

DOUALA

CAMEROON

GRASS

Doume 1915

8 Aug. 1914

27th Sept. 1914

Edea

Fernando
Po

26 Oct.
1914

Yaounde
1 Jan. 1916

25 July 1915

1914

Dec. 1915

Lomie,
20 June 1916

1915

Naval Attack
Aug. 1914

Spanish

MUNI

TROPICAL FOREST
DENSE BUSH Molundu

Ubangi

Congo

BELGIAN CONGO

Atlantic Ocean

1914

Despite converging advances
by Allies, 575 German troops
escaped to face internment in
nearby neutral territory.

FRENCH EQUATORIAL AFRICA

6 Aug. 1914

FIG. 12.1(a)–(e) *Campaigns fought in Africa during the First World War (after A. Banks, 1975)*

286

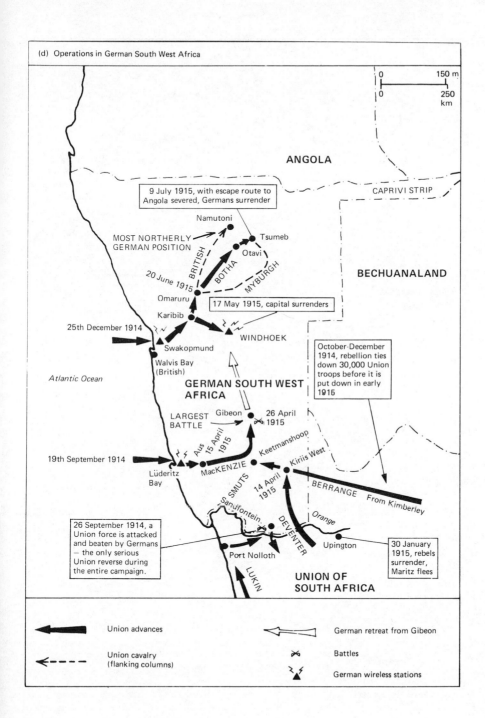

(d) Operations in German South West Africa

ANGOLA

CAPRIVI STRIP

9 July 1915, with escape route to
Angola severed, Germans surrender

Namutoni

Tsumeb

MOST NORTHERLY
GERMAN POSITION

BRITISH

BOTHA

Otavi

MYBURGH

BECHUANALAND

20 June 1915

Omaruru

Karibib

17 May 1915, capital surrenders

25th December 1914

Swakopmund

WINDHOEK

Walvis Bay
(British)

Atlantic Ocean

GERMAN SOUTH WEST
AFRICA

October-December
1914, rebellion ties
down 30,000 Union
troops before it is
put down in early
1915

LARGEST
BATTLE

Gibeon

26 April
1915

Aus 15 April
1915

Keetmanshoop

19th September 1914

Lüderitz
Bay

MacKENZIE

Kiriis West

14 April
1915

BERRANGE

From Kimberley

SMUTS

Sandfontein

Orange

26 September 1914, a
Union force is attacked
and beaten by Germans
— the only serious
Union reverse during
the entire campaign.

DEVENTER

Upington

30 January
1915, rebels
surrender,
Maritz flees

Port Nolloth

LUKIN

UNION OF
SOUTH AFRICA

⬅	Union advances	
⬸ (dashed)	Union cavalry (flanking columns)	
⇦ (open)	German retreat from Gibeon	
✕	Battles	
⚡▲	German wireless stations	

150 m

250 km

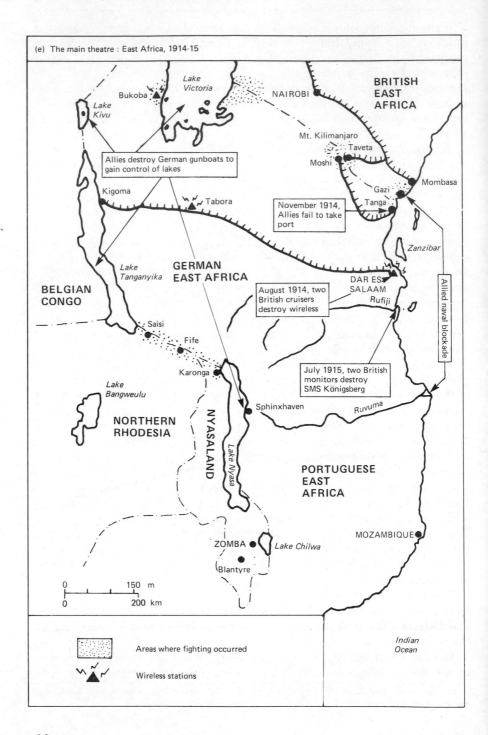

(e) The main theatre : East Africa, 1914-15

BRITISH EAST AFRICA

Lake Victoria

Bukoba

Lake Kivu

NAIROBI

Allies destroy German gunboats to gain control of lakes

Mt. Kilimanjaro

Taveta

Moshi

Gazi

Mombasa

Kigoma

Tabora

November 1914, Allies fail to take port

Tanga

GERMAN EAST AFRICA

Zanzibar

BELGIAN CONGO

Lake Tanganyika

August 1914, two British cruisers destroy wireless

DAR ES SALAAM

Rufiji

Allied naval blockade

Saisi

Fife

Karonga

Lake Bangweulu

NORTHERN RHODESIA

July 1915, two British monitors destroy SMS Königsberg

Sphinxhaven

Ruvuma

NYASALAND

Lake Nyasa

PORTUGUESE EAST AFRICA

ZOMBA

Lake Chilwa

MOZAMBIQUE

Blantyre

| 0 | | 150 m |
| 0 | | 200 km |

Indian Ocean

Areas where fighting occurred

Wireless stations

288

all Britain's longed-for Cape to Cairo route.[11] But once it was clear that quick victory would not be achieved, it was perceived that protracted campaigns in Africa would tie down Allied colonial troops who might otherwise be sent to the European front. This strategy was brilliantly pursued by General P. E. von Lettow-Vorbeck, the German commander in East Africa who engaged a combined Allied force – at one time over ten times greater than his own – for the duration of the war (see Fig. 12.1e).

The campaigns in Africa can be divided into two distinct phases. During the first, which lasted only a few weeks, the Allies were concerned to knock out Germany's offensive capability and ensure that her fleet could not use her African ports. Thus Lomé in Togo, Duala in Cameroon, and Swakopmund and Lüderitz Bay in South West Africa were occupied soon after the outbreak of war. In German East Africa, British cruisers bombarded Dar es Salaam and Tanga in August, and though neither port was taken until later in the war, they could not be used by German warships. In Egypt, on the entry of Turkey into the war on Germany's side, the British defences of the Suez Canal were strengthened and a Turkish expedition repulsed in February 1915. Thereafter Egypt served as the major base for Britain's operations against Turkey and her Middle Eastern provinces, and became the fulcrum of British power in Africa and the Middle East for the next three decades.

The campaigns of the first phase of the war in Africa were vital to its global strategy. The campaigns of the second phase, with the exception of those mounted from Egypt against the Turkish empire, were of marginal significance to the outcome of the world struggle. Nevertheless the Allies were determined to conquer the German colonies both to prevent them being used as bases for the subversion of their often tenuous authority in their own colonies, and to share them among themselves in the event of an overall Allied victory. Thus once the South African government had put down the Afrikaner rebellion which had received support from the Germans in South West Africa, it mounted an invasion of the territory which took six months to complete. The South West Africa campaign (see Fig. 12.1d) was the only one in which African troops were not involved, since the Union generals were reluctant to arm their African population, while the Germans dared not, after having so brutally put down the Herero and Nama risings.

The protracted Cameroon campaign (see Fig. 12.1b) was largely fought by African troops. Despite their superiority in numbers, the French, British and Belgian allies took over fifteen months to complete their conquest of the territory.

In East Africa von Lettow-Vorbeck, appreciating that he could not hope to win the battle against forces which outnumbered his own by more than

11. For a discussion of the German plans for the establishment of a *Mittelafrika* in the event of victory see F. Fischer, 1967, pp. 102–3 and map on p. 596.

PLATE 12.1 General Count von Lettow-Vorbeck (second from right), German Commander-in-Chief in East Africa during the First World War, and colleagues

ten to one, determined at least to tie them down as long as possible by resorting to guerrilla tactics.[12] Right up to the end of hostilities he remained undefeated, leading his bedraggled column through Portuguese East Africa (now Mozambique) and then on its last march into Northern Rhodesia (now Zambia) where he learnt of the armistice in Europe. At a conservative estimate, some 160000 Allied troops were engaged by von Lettow-Vorbeck's force which never exceeded a strength of 15000. As in Cameroon, African troops proved vital to both sides, many of them fighting with great bravery, and proving much more effective fighters than the white South African troops who were decimated by disease. At times the ration for Nigerian foot soldiers was half-a-pound of rice a day with nothing to go with it.[13] The carriers suffered particular hardships and it was estimated that at least 45000 died from disease in the campaign.[14]

The European exodus

The war saw a large-scale exodus of European administrative and commercial personnel from the Allied colonies in Africa, as they left for the Western Front or enlisted in locally based regiments for campaigns elsewhere in Africa. In some parts the European presence, already thinly spread, was diminished by more than half. In Northern Nigeria, many political officers on secondment from the army were recalled to their regiments while others voluntarily enlisted, with the result that Northern Nigeria was denuded of administrators.[15] Some divisions in Northern Nigeria, like Borgu, were without any European administrator for much of the war.[16] In Northern Rhodesia, as much as 40% of the adult European population was on active service.[17] In French Black Africa there was general mobilization of Europeans of military age, while in British East Africa, Europeans were registered for war work. In some parts, particularly the countryside, it was rumoured that the white man was leaving for ever.[18] In Morocco, where the Resident-General, Louis Lyautey, had to withdraw so many of his troops for the European front, German prisoners of war were used on public works to persuade the Moroccans that the French were winning the war.[19]

12. The British *Official History* comments that von Lettow-Vorbeck 'had successfully contained in Africa for over four years a force considerably larger than Lord Roberts' whole army in the South African War'.
13. W. D. Downes, 1919, p. 90.
14. L. Mosley, 1963, p. 234.
15. A. M. Fika, 1978.
16. See M. Crowder, 1973.
17. L. H. Gann, 1964, p. 163.
18. In Nigeria the British administration reported that the various 'petty risings were due to unrest caused by the war and rumours of the withdrawal of government', *Nigeria Annual Report for 1915*, 1917, p. 23.
19. R. Bidwell, 1973, p. 23.

The result of this exodus was a slowdown, if not a complete stoppage, of many essential services manned by Europeans. In certain instances Africans were specially trained, as in Senegal, to fill the vacancies thus created.[20] In British West Africa, others jobs hitherto reserved for whites were filled by educated Africans which, as Richard Rathbone has pointed out, goes some way towards explaining the loyalty of the elites during the war.[21] In French West Africa, the governor-general complained that the British, who were not subjected to general mobilization in their colonies, were taking advantage of the fact that their French allies were, by filling the trading vacuum left by the departure of French commercial agents to the front.[22] Only in Egypt was there a net increase in the European presence, since there was an enormous influx of British troops using Egypt as a base for the Allied offensive in the Middle East.

From the African point of view, perhaps even more remarkable than the apparent exodus of Europeans was the spectacle of white people fighting each other, a thing they had never done during the colonial occupation. What is more they encouraged their subjects in uniform to kill the 'enemy' white man, who hitherto had belonged to a clan who, by virtue of the colour of his skin, was held to be sacrosanct and desecration of whose person had hitherto been visited with the direst retribution.[23]

The African involvement in the War

Except in the German South West African campaign, African troops were a major factor in the Allied successes in their African campaigns. African troops were called on during the war not only to fight on African soil, but also to reinforce European armies on the Western and Middle Eastern fronts. Further, they were instrumental in putting down the various revolts against colonial authority, just as they had been instrumental in the European conquest of Africa.

Over a million troops were actually recruited during the war to supplement the generally small forces maintained by the colonial authorities. Only France had substantial armies on the ground in her various African colonies on the outbreak of war and though subsequently Germany was accused of militarizing her colonies, it was really France alone against whom this accusation could be levelled with accuracy. In addition to troops, carriers

20. Gouvernement Général de l'AOF, Textes relatifs à la formation et la réorganisation des cadres indigènes en AOF, 1916: 'Circulaire relative à la formation du personnel des cadres indigènes', Dakar, 1 October 1916, pp. 3–4. Also 'Circulaire relative à la réorganisation des cadres des agents indigènes de l'AOF', Dakar, 1 October 1916, pp. 27–8.

21. R. Rathbone, 1978, p. 6.

22. Archives du Sénégal, Dakar, Série D, 4D73, Recrutement indigène (1918). Rapport et Correspondance du Ministre des Colonies et du Ministre de Guerre. Reprise de recrutement: Mission Diagne. 1917–18: 'Projet de Recrutement'.

23. Letter from Sir Frederick Lugard to his wife dated 19 June 1918, cited in M. Perham, 1960(b), p. 549.

were recruited on a massive scale – some three carriers were necessary to keep each fighting soldier in the field. Further, North Africans were recruited to work at factory benches vacated by Frenchmen conscripted into the army. The subsequent voluntary migration of Algerian labour to France has its origin in the First World War. All in all over 2.5 million Africans, or well over 1% of the population of the continent, were involved in war work of some kind.

Recruits for both fighting and carrier service were raised by three methods. The first was on a purely volunteer basis where Africans offered their services freely without any outside pressure. Thus, in the early stages of the war on the Palestine and Syrian fronts, large numbers of impoverished *fallāḥīn* (peasants) in Egypt offered their services in return for what were comparatively attractive wages. There is no doubt that in most African countries there were volunteers for the army who knew exactly what enlistment entailed. The Senegalese *citoyens* of the Four Communes of Senegal were quite prepared to accept the full obligations of compulsory military service exacted from Metropolitan Frenchmen if it would guarantee their own status as citizens. And to this end their Deputy, Blaise Diagne, secured the passage of a Law of 29 September 1916 which stated that 'the natives of the *communes de plein exercice* of Senegal are and remain French citizens as provided for by the law of 15 October 1915'. In Madagascar all 45 000 recruits into the French army were said to have been volunteers,[24] but the great majority of African recruits went into the various armies against their will, either as forced 'volunteers' or as conscripts.

A great deal of recruitment was undertaken through chiefs who were expected to deliver up the numbers required of them by the political officers. In some areas they had no difficulty in obtaining genuine volunteers; in others, men were impressed by the chiefs and presented to the political officers as volunteers. Much of the unpopularity of chiefs in Northern Rhodesia after the war can be attributed to their role in recruitment of soldiers and carriers.[25]

Large numbers of soldiers and carriers, however, were formally conscripted. In French Black Africa, a Decree of 1912 aimed at creating a permanent black army made military service for four years compulsory for all African males between the ages of 20 and 28. The aim was to replace garrison troops in Algeria with black African troops so that the former would be available for service in Europe in the eventuality of war. If such a war were prolonged, General Mangin wrote, 'Our African forces would constitute an almost indefinite reserve, the source of which is beyond the reach of the adversary.' After the outbreak of war, with 14 785 African troops in West Africa alone, it was decided to recruit 50 000 more during the 1915–16 recruitment campaign. Thus began in French

24. H. Deschamps, 1962; G. S. Chapus, 1961.
25. L. H. Gann, 1964, p. 164.

PLATE 12.2 *German East African campaign: troops of the Nigerian Brigade disembarking at Lindi, December 1917*

Africa an exercise called by Governor Angoulvant a *véritable chasse à l'homme*[26] and recently described by Jide Osuntokun as a new slave trade.[27] Chiefs were given quotas of men to fill, and rounded up strangers and former slaves to avoid enlisting their immediate dependants or kinsmen. Since births were not registered, many men above and below military age were recruited. But, as we shall see, the recruitment campaign provoked widespread revolts and the insurgent areas were impossible to recruit in. Desperate for more men and in the hope that an African of high standing might succeed where Frenchmen had not, the French Government resorted to the appointment in 1918 of Blaise Diagne as High Commissioner for the Recruitment of Black Troops. Set the target of recruiting 40 000 men, his teams actually enlisted 63 378, few of whom, however, saw the front since the war ended in November 1918.

Compulsory recruitment was also used to raise troops and carriers in British East Africa, under the compulsory service order of 1915, which made all males aged between 18 and 45 liable for military service. This was extended to the Uganda Protectorate in April 1917. Forced recruitment of porters in all districts in Northern Rhodesia meant that for a large part of the war over a third of the adult males of the territory were involved in carrier service.[28] After 1917, the heavy demands of the Syrian front forced the British Protectorate government in Egypt to introduce conscription and requisition of animals despite its earlier promise that it would bear the full burden of the war. Village *'umdas* 'paid off old scores as they shepherded their enemies into the arms of the recruiting agents or swept animals into the insatiable Syrian caravan'.[29] In Algeria, Tunisia and even Morocco, which was still being conquered, colonial subjects were pressed into the war. Over 483 000 colonial soldiers from all over Africa are estimated to have served in the French army during the war, most of them compulsorily recruited. The Belgians in the Congo impressed up to 260 000 porters during the East African campaign.[30] The sheer numbers involved are mind-boggling, especially as this was so soon after the European conquest. The slave trade at its height never reached a tenth of the numbers involved in any one year.

While the war directly took an enormous toll in dead and wounded in Africa, it further accounted for innumerable indirect deaths in the Africa-wide influenza epidemic of 1918–19 whose spread was facilitated by the movement of troops and carriers returning home.

26. Archives du Sénégal, Dakar, Série D, File 4D45, Lt. Governor, Ivory Coast to Governor-General, French West Africa, 18 December 1915.
27. J. Osuntokun, 1977.
28. R. Hall, 1965, p. 102.
29. T. Little, 1958, p. 128.
30. C. Young, 1965, p. 219.

PLATE 12.3 *Men of the Egyptian Labour Corps embarking for service overseas. The corps served in Egypt, France, Mesopotamia and Salonika*

PLATE 12.4 *German East African campaign: wounded of the Nigerian Brigade ready to be moved from Nyangao after the battle of Mahiwa, 15–19 October 1917*

PLATE 12.5 *German East African campaign: Belgian African troops at Ndanda, January 1918, en route to the coast after German forces had crossed the Rovuma river, January 1918*

The African challenge to European authority

At a time when the Allied colonial regimes in Africa could least afford trouble in their own backyards, their authority – still only tenuously established in places like southern Ivory Coast, much of Libya, or Karamoja in Uganda – was widely challenged by armed risings and other forms of protest by their subjects. As a result the Allied powers had to divert scarce military resources, needed for fighting the Germans in Africa as well as on the Western Front, to dealing with local revolts. So scarce were these resources, and so widespread the revolts in certain areas such as French West Africa and Libya that the reimposition of European control over the revolted areas had to be delayed until troops became available. Large areas of Haut-Sénégal-Niger and Dahomey remained out of French control for as long as a year for lack of troops. Thus the French were initially unable to deal with the revolt of 1916 in Dahomeyan Borgu because neighbouring groups – the Somba of Atacora, the Pila Pila of Semere and the Ohori among others – were also in revolt. In Morocco Lyautey, its conquistador, feared that metropolitan instructions to return half his 70000 troops to France and withdraw to the Atlantic coast might lead to revolt. Though he had to release the men, he did not withdraw and managed to avert challenge to his authority. As it was, France had to keep the other 35 000 troops in Morocco throughout the war. In Portuguese East Africa the German invasion inspired Portuguese subjects to take the occasion to overthrow their hated overlords.[31]

The causes of the widespread revolts and protest movements that took place during the war varied considerably and were not all directly connected with the war itself. In some cases what were described as revolts were, in effect, as in Libya, just the continuation of primary resistance to European occupation. In many cases the motives for revolt or protest were mixed. There can be no doubt that the visual evidence of the apparent weakening of European authority as represented by the exodus of Europeans encouraged those contemplating revolt just as the influx of Europeans, in particular British troops, discouraged it in Egypt.

A number of themes run through the wartime risings: the desire to regain a lost independence; resentment against wartime measures, in particular compulsory recruitment and forced labour; religious, and in particular pan-Islamic, opposition to the war; reaction to economic hardships occasioned by the war; and discontent with particular aspects of the colonial dispensation, full realization of the nature of which in many areas coincided with the wartime years. There is a final theme, particularly significant in South Africa, that of pro-German sentiment among the subjects of the Allied powers.

31. C. P. Fendall, 1921, p. 120. Also J. Duffy, 1959, p. 367.

The desire to return to a life independent of white rule, that is a return to the *status quo ante*, comes out clearly in the revolts of the Borgawa and Ohori-Ije in French Dahomey and of various Igbo groups in Owerri province of Nigeria.[32] To a greater or lesser extent the desire to get rid of the white overlord runs through the majority of revolts against French authority in West Africa. Certainly one of the exacerbating factors in the rising of the Egba in 1918 in Southern Nigeria was the very recent loss of their semi-independent status at the outbreak of the war. In Egypt, the Wafd riots which took place immediately after the war were largely inspired by a desire to shake off the recently imposed British protectorate, which, in its short wartime life of four years, had proved itself excessively obnoxious to nationalists and *fallāḥīn* alike. In Madagascar 500 Malagasy, mainly intellectuals, were arrested at the end of 1915 and accused of 'forming a well-organised secret society with the aim of expelling the French and restoring a Malagasy government'.[33]

A major concern of the Allied powers during the war was that Turkey's entry on the German side might encourage dissidence among their Muslim subjects. While Turkey's call to *djihād* evoked less response among the subject Muslim populations of Africa than the Allied colonial authorities feared, they were constantly on the alert in case of disaffection among their Muslim subjects and were at great pains to reassure Muslim chiefs and leaders that the Allies were not hostile to Islam. The imposition of martial law and the imprisonment of nationalists in Egypt was partly inspired by fear of a sympathetic response to the Turkish call for *djihād* among the Egyptians. The British in Northern Nigeria, which was predominantly Muslim, were very sensitive to the possible impact of Islamic propaganda there, but the community of interest established between the Sultan and emirs of the Sokoto Caliphate and the British ensured the loyalty of the bulk of Northern Nigerian Muslims.

There were some nervous moments for the British when the Sanūsī Sufi brotherhood in Libya, still resisting the Italian occupation of its country, responded to the Turkish call to *djihād* and invaded western Egypt in November 1915. The Sanūsī force took the Egyptian port of al-Sallūm with three-quarters of the Egyptian garrison going over to its side, while the British escaped by sea. It then advanced on Sīdī Barrānī and Marsā Matrūh. Thereafter the British seized the initiative and drove the Sanūsīs back into Libya.[34] Though defeated in Egypt, members of the brotherhood as well as other Libyans inflicted a decisive defeat on the Italians at the battle of al-Karadābiyya, the worst defeat suffered by the Italians since Adowa in 1896. They then drove the Italians, who had to divert the bulk of their troops to the Austrian front, to the coast, so that by 1917 Italy

32. See J. Osuntokun, 1977.
33. N. Heseltine, 1971, p. 158.
34. E. E. Evans-Pritchard, 1949, pp. 127–8.

was on the verge of losing Libya altogether.[35] These victories led to the establishment of the Tripolitanian Republic (al-Djumhūriyya al-Ṭarābulusiyya) on 16 November 1918 in western Libya and the Emirate of Cyrenaica in eastern Libya. Italy recognized these states in 1919 and granted each one its own parliament. Further rights were granted by Italy under the Treaty of al-Radjma in 1920. In January 1922, these two states agreed to form a political union and elected Idrīs al-Sanūsī, the leader of the Sanūsiyya, as the head of the union and set up a central committee with its headquarters at Gharyān.

The Libyan risings found a sympathetic response in southern Tunisia, where 15000 French troops were needed to suppress the revolt,[36] and among the Tawārik and other Muslims in French Niger and Chad, where Islamic abhorrence of infidel rule, the drought of 1914 and intensive recruitment for the army had provoked considerable discontent. In December 1916 Sanūsī's forces invaded Niger, where they gained the support of Kaossen, leader of the Tarkī Tawārik, Firhūn, chief of the Oullimiden Tawārik, and the Sultan of Agades. They took Agades and a combined French and British force was needed to defeat them.[37]

Not only Islamic risings threatened the Allied powers in their colonies. John Chilembwe's rising in Nyasaland (now Malawi) of January 1915 had strong Christian undertones, while the Kitawala Watchtower movement in the Rhodesias preached the imminence of the end of the world and disobedience to constituted authority. It capitalized on the disruption caused in Northern Rhodesia by von Lettow-Vorbeck's invasion at the end of the war. Similarly apocalyptic was the widespread movement in the Niger delta area of Nigeria, led by Garrick Braide, otherwise known as Elijah II, who preached the imminent demise of the British administration. In Ivory Coast, the Prophet Harris was deported in December 1914 because 'the events in Europe demand more than ever the maintenance of tranquillity among the people of the Colony'.[38] In Kenya, in Nyanza, the Mumbo cult which grew rapidly during the war years, rejected the Christian religion, and declared: 'All Europeans are your enemies, but the time is shortly coming when they will disappear from our country.'[39]

Perhaps the most important cause of revolt was the forced recruitment of men for service as soldiers and carriers. Such was the hatred of forced recruitment that it was a major inspiration for nearly all the revolts that

35. N. Barbour (ed.), 1959; al-Tillisi, 1973, pp. 25–6, 46–7, 274–5, 405–10; A. M. Barbar, 1980.
36. D. L. Ling, 1967.
37. See A. Salifou, 1973; J. Osuntokun, 1975.
38. Confidential Memorandum from the Lieutenant-Governor of the Ivory Coast to Administratuers of the Cercles, 16 December 1914, quoted in G. M. Haliburton, 1971, p. 139.
39. Quoted by B. A. Ogot in B. A. Ogot (ed.), 1974, p. 264. For further details on the risings in this section, see Chapters 20, 26, 27 and 29.

took place in French Black Africa, and evoked some resistance in the otherwise peaceful Gold Coast colony.[40]

John Chilembwe's rising was precipitated by the enlistment of Nyasas and their large death toll in the first weeks of the war in battle with the Germans. In his memorable censored letter to the *Nyasaland Times* of 26 November 1914 he protested: 'We understand that we have been invited to shed our innocent blood in this world's war ... we are imposed upon more than any other nationality under the sun'.[41]

Economic hardship caused by the war certainly underlay and even provoked resistance against the colonial authorities. The risings in the midwest of Nigeria and the Niger delta during the early stages of the war cannot be understood except in the context of falling prices for palm products, and the drop in trade due to the exclusion of the producers' main customers, the Germans.[42] Indeed, pro-German sympathy among Allied subjects, where it was found, derived largely from the fact that Germans had in many parts of Africa been the principal traders; and their exclusion by the Allies was associated with the economic depression that attended the first year of the war.

In South Africa the Afrikaner revolt of late 1914 against the government's decision to support the Allies was due both to pro-German sympathy and hatred of Britain. The Germans themselves did their best to provoke disaffection among the African subjects of the Allies, being particularly active along the north-eastern border of Nigeria and in Libya. In Uganda, shortly after the commencement of hostilities, Nyindo, Paramount Chief of Kigezi, was persuaded by his half-brother, the Mwami of Ruanda, to revolt against the British on behalf of the Germans.[43]

In many cases, and notably Nigeria, wartime revolts were not directly attributable to specific wartime measures. Rather they were directed against obnoxious features of colonial rule such as taxation, which was introduced into Yorubaland for the first time in 1916 and together with the increased powers given to traditional rulers under the policy of 'indirect rule', provoked the Iseyin riots.[44] In French West Africa the impositions of the *indigénat* (a discriminatory judicial code), the reorganization of administrative boundaries, the suppression of chiefs or the exactions of chiefs without traditional authority were all major causes of the revolts that broke out in every colony of the federation.

These revolts were, whatever their cause, put down ruthlessly by the colonial authorities. 'Rebels' were impressed into the army, flogged or even hanged, chiefs exiled or imprisoned, and villages razed to the ground to serve as a warning. But not all protests were violent in character. Many

40. See D. Killingray, 1978, p. 46; R. G. Thomas, 1975.
41. Quoted in R. I. Rotberg, 1965, p. 82.
42. J. Osuntokun, 1977.
43. W. R. Louis, 1963(b), p. 213.
44. J. A. Atanda, 1969.

people tried to avoid the source of their grievances by emigration or other forms of evasive action. Thus large numbers of French subjects in Senegal, Guinea, Haut-Sénégal-Niger and Ivory Coast undertook what A. I. Asiwaju has termed 'protest migrations' to the neighbouring British territories.[45] To avoid recruitment teams, inhabitants of whole villages fled to the bush. Young men mutilated themselves rather than serve in the colonial army. The protest migrations were of such magnitude that it was estimated that French West Africa lost some 62000 subjects as a result of them.[46] In Zanzibar, too, men hid all day and slept in trees at night to avoid being impressed as carriers.[47]

The economic consequences of the War

The declaration of war brought considerable economic disruption to Africa. Generally there followed a depression in the prices paid for Africa's primary products, while knowledge that henceforth imported goods would be in short supply led to a rise in their prices. In Uganda there was an overnight increase of 50% in the price of imports.[48] The pattern of African trade with Europe was radically changed by the exclusion of the Germans from the Allied territories, where in certain cases, like Sierra Leone, they had accounted for 80% of the import–export trade. Germany's own colonies, even before they were occupied by the Allies, were cut off from trade with the metropole because of Allied dominion over the seas. Germany, from being tropical Africa's major overseas trading partner, was now almost entirely excluded from trading activities in the continent, for once the Allies completed their occupation of the German colonies, all German nationals were interned and their plantations, commercial houses and industries were taken over by the occupying powers. Even in the case of the French African territories, where the French groundnut-milling industry would normally have been able to absorb the oil-seeds hitherto imported by the Germans, it was unable to do so, as it was located in the German-occupied part of north-east France. Thus where France had been the major importer of the Gambian groundnut crop, she was now replaced by Britain whose share of the crop rose from 4% in 1912 to 48% in 1916.[49] Indeed the dramatic substitution of British for German traders would almost suggest that the war, as far as the African colonies were concerned, was seen by Britain, (like Germany, a free-trade nation) as an opportunity for economic aggrandizement. While generally the excluded German traders were replaced by nationals of the governing power of the colonies in which they

45. I. A. Asiwaju, 1976(b).
46. See M. Crowder in J. F. A. Ajayi and M. Crowder (eds), 1974, p. 506.
47. H. M. Smith, 1926, p. 191.
48. K. Ingham, 1958, p. 191.
49. P. H. S. Hatton, 1966.

had traded, in French West Africa, the British made headway against the French because of the mobilization of French traders.[50]

The depression that followed the outbreak of war soon gave way to a boom in those products needed to boost the Allied war effort. Thus Egyptian cotton rose from £E3 a quintal in 1914 to £E8 in 1916–18.[51] But increased demand was not always reflected by increased prices, for often the colonial governments controlled the prices paid to the producers. Certain countries suffered badly throughout the war. To take the example of the Gold Coast, its major export crop of cocoa was not nearly in such demand as, for instance, oil-seeds. Furthermore the buying capacity of the African-based import–export houses was severely hampered by the enlistment, voluntary or obligatory, of so many of the European personnel; in French West Africa some 75% of the European traders had left for the war by 1917.[52]

While prices of exports did not always reflect the increased demand for them, because of controlled prices, and while demand for labour, too, was not always reflected in increased wages, the prices of imports, where they were obtainable, rose throughout the war. While the vast majority of Africans in the subsistence sector were not affected by this inflation, those in the wage-earning or export crop-producing sectors were. Thus the Egyptian peasant producing cotton found that the benefit he received from increased prices for his product did not offset the steep rise in the cost of fuel, clothing and cereals.[53]

The war witnessed an increased level of state intervention in the economies of the African colonies, whether in the form of price control, requisition of food crops, compulsory cultivation of crops, recruitment of labour for essential projects or allocation of shipping space. Generally such intervention tended to favour the import–export houses of the colonial power controlling the colony concerned. Thus in Nigeria, companies like John Holt and the United Africa Company were used as buying agents and had both priority in shipping space and easier access to loans from the banks, with the result that smaller import–export companies, in particular Nigerian-controlled ones, suffered.[54]

Demands for traditionally subsistence crops, including yams, manioc and beans, for the feeding of the Allies in Europe and for the armies in Africa or the Middle Eastern front, added to the hardship of those outside the subsistence sector. And where subsistence crops were requisitioned – as they widely were – or paid for at prices below the free-market price, the producers themselves suffered. Thus by the end of the war the Egyptian

50. M. Crowder in J. F. A. Ajayi and M. Crowder (eds), 1974, p. 506.
51. G. Baer, 1962.
52. M. Crowder in J. F. A. Ajayi and M. Crowder (eds), 1974, p. 506.
53. M. Y. Zayid, 1965, p. 76. During the war overall production fell sharply, see P. O'Brien in P. M. Holt (ed.), 1968, pp. 188–90.
54. J. Osuntokun, 1978.

fallāḥīn were hard put to keep body and soul together, what with inflation, and the requisition of their cereals and animals.[55] In French West Africa the demands for men for the war conflicted with demands for sorghum, millet, maize, etc. which they would normally have produced. By 1916 France was in a desperate situation for food, for her crop in terms of wheat had suffered a shortfall of 30 million quintals, 60 million as against the 90 million required. The following year, with a world shortfall in the wheat crop, her own crop was only 40 million quintals.[56] Thus in both these years wheat or substitutes had to be found overseas. North Africa, so close to France, was an obvious source of supply and even recently conquered Morocco was enlisted in her *ravitaillement*. But demands were made even as far afield as Madagascar. In addition to such demands, the subsistence farmer in territories in which campaigns were fought, particularly in East Africa, was subject to the exactions of armies which, because of supply problems, could not but live off the land.

Demands for troops and carriers as well as for increased production of both export and subsistence crops resulted in shortages of labour in many parts of the continent during the war. Recruitment of carriers in Northern Rhodesia for the East Africa campaign cut off Southern Rhodesia (now Zimbabwe) and Katanga from their traditional source of labour[57] and the Belgian administration in the Congo had to conduct forced recruitment of labour for the country's mines. The influenza epidemic at the end of the war in East and Central Africa particularly affected the returning carriers and created acute shortages of labour in Kenya and the Rhodesias. This shortage occurred among European as well as African personnel; and in Southern Rhodesia, where white railway workers had hitherto been laid off at will by their employers because of the availability of replacements, they were now at such a premium that they were able to form unions,[58] previously resisted by employers and Government.

The shortage of imports may have led to a fall in production where agriculture, as in Egypt, was dependent on imports of fertilizers, farm implements and irrigation machinery, but it also encouraged the development of import substitution industries in some countries, particularly South Africa where the potentialities of overseas markets for local products came to be realized at this time.[59] In the Belgian Congo, cut off from the occupied metropolis, the war was a great stimulus to increased self-sufficiency, as it was in the early years of the war in German East Africa. The influx of British troops into Egypt and the injection of some £200 million into the economy during the war period was an important stimulus to industrial growth.

55. T. Little, 1958, p. 128.
56. H. C. Cosnier, 1922.
57. L. H. Gann, 1964, p. 164.
58. ibid., p. 172.
59. F. Wilson in M. Wilson and L. Thompson (eds), 1971, p. 135.

The war introduced the internal combustion engine and, with it, motorable roads to many parts of Africa. In East Africa, the protracted campaign against the Germans and the problem of moving supplies led to the construction of a number of motorable roads, such as that from Dodoma in German East Africa to Tukuyu at the north end of Lake Nyasa, which reduced to two to three days a journey that hitherto had taken two to three weeks.[60] In those areas where there was sustained military activity, or where transit facilities were required, ports developed rapidly. Mombasa, Bizerta, Port Harcourt and Dakar are cases in point. In Nigeria, the Enugu coal mines were opened up during the war to provide the railways with a local source of fuel.

Generally government revenues diminished during the war, since they were largely dependent on duties on imported goods. The colonies nevertheless bore a large part of the burden of the cost of local campaigns, apart from making grants to the metropolitan powers to help the war effort. Except where military exigencies necessitated them, public works came to a halt and development plans were shelved until after the war.

The socio-political consequences of the War

The social consequences of the war for Africa varied considerably from territory to territory and depended on the extent of their involvement, in particular the degree of recruitment or military activity in them. Unfortunately, until recently relatively little attention has been given to the social impact of the war. This is somewhat surprising, since for some areas like eastern Africa, the First World War, as Ranger has put it, was 'the most awe-inspiring, destructive and capricious demonstration of European "absolute power" that eastern Africa ever experienced. The scale of the forces involved, the massiveness of the fire-power, the extent of devastation and disease, the number of African lives lost – all these dwarfed the original campaigns of colonial conquest, and even the suppression of the Majī Majī rising.'[61] Writing in the 1930s Dr H. R. A. Philip remarked that the 'experiences of the years from 1914 to 1918 were such as to effectively awaken the Kenya native from the sleep of the centuries'.[62] Compared with the research conducted on the political consequences of the war for Africa, comparatively little has been undertaken on its social consequences. Yet its impact on soldiers, carriers and labourers who were uprooted from the circumscribed worlds of their villages and sent thousands of miles away and their impact on their societies on their return[63] forms a major theme in colonial history.

60. P. Mitchell, 1954, p. 38.
61. T. O. Ranger, 1975, p. 45.
62. Quoted by B. A. Ogot in B. A. Ogot (ed.), 1974, p. 265.
63. See for example M. J. Echenberg, 1975; Y. Person, 1960, pp. 106–7 refers to the dominant role played by old soldiers in Kissi society after the First World War, particularly as agents for modernization.

There is no doubt that the war opened up new windows for many Africans, particularly the educated elite groups. Margery Perham has written that it is 'difficult to overestimate the effect upon Africans, who had been largely enclosed within a bilateral relationship with their European rulers, of looking outside this enclosure and seeing themselves as part of a continent and of a world'.[64] In many parts of Africa the war gave a boost, if not always to nationalist activity, at least to the development of a more critical approach by the educated elites towards their colonial masters. Bethwell Ogot has suggested that the shared wartime experience of African and European soldiers had a similar effect for the less-educated:

> The African soldier soon discovered the weaknesses and the strength of the European, who up to that time had been regarded by the majority of Africans as a superman. In fact, the warrant and non-commissioned African officers were instructing European volunteers in the technique of modern warfare. It was becoming evident that the European did not know everything. The returning porters and soldiers spread the new views of the white man; and much of the self-confidence and assertiveness that the Africans in Kenya displayed in the 1920s had a lot to do with this new knowledge.[65]

He also points out that, significantly, several African political leaders in Kenya had either fought or served in the East African campaign. In Guinea the return of the *anciens combattants* heralded strikes, riots in the de-mobilization camps and attacks on the authority of chiefs.[66]

If the war saw an end of attempts by Africans to regain the lost sovereignty of their pre-colonial polities, it also saw a rise in demands for participation in the process of government of the new polities imposed on them by the Europeans. These demands – inspired by President Woodrow Wilson's Fourteen Points which were made in reaction to the Soviet proposals put forward in October 1917 for the immediate conclusion of peace without annexation or indemnity – even extended to the right to self-determination. In the case of the Arab countries of North Africa the joint announcement by Britain and France in November 1918 that the Allies were contemplating the enfranchisement of peoples oppressed by the Turks presented the spectacle of one group of Arabs being offered independence, while another, ruled by those very powers who were offering freedom to the Turkish provinces, was denied it.

Sa'd Zaghlūl's Wafd Party in Egypt took its name from the delegation (*Wafd*) he tried to send to the Versailles Peace Conference to negotiate Egypt's return to independence.[67] Similarly in Tunisia, though the wartime Resident, Alapetite, had kept as firm a grip on the nationalists as the British

64. M. Perham, 1961, p. 45.
65. B. A. Ogot in B. A. Ogot (ed.), 1974, p. 265.
66. A. Summers and R. W. Johnson, 1978.
67. M. Zayid in P. M. Holt (ed.), 1968, pp. 341–2; for the activities of the Wafd Party, see Chapter 23.

had in Egypt, after the war their leaders sent a telegram to President Wilson of the United States to enlist his assistance in their demands for self-determination.[68]

While Wilson's Fourteen Points did not inspire demands for immediate independence in Africa south of the Sahara, his liberal sentiments encouraged West African nationalists to hope that they could influence the Versailles Peace Conference and also encouraged them to demand a greater say in their own affairs.[69] As the Sierra Leonean, F. W. Dove, a delegate to the National Congress of British West Africa put it, the time had 'passed when the African peoples should be coerced against their will to do things that are not in accordance with their best interests'.[70] In the Sudan, Wilson's Fourteen Points, coupled with the inspiration of the Arab revolt of 1916, proved a turning-point in Sudanese nationalism, informing the attitudes of a new generation of politically conscious young men who had passed through government schools and had acquired some modern, western skills.[71]

In many territories where heavy contributions had been made in terms of men and material to the war effort, there was hope that these would be rewarded at least by social and political reform. In some cases the colonial governments specifically promised reform in return for increased assistance from their subject populations. Blaise Diagne was promised a package of post-war reforms in French Black Africa if he could recruit the additional men France required for the European front. This he did, but the reforms were never put into effect.[72] The Algerian contribution to the war effort was rewarded by economic and political improvements in the status of Algerians which were, however, opposed by the settlers and perceived as too limited by the Emir Khālid, grandson of 'Abd al-Kādir, who strongly criticized the French administration and was deported in 1924. He has justly been described as the founder of the Algerian nationalist movement.[73] In Tunisia a delegation of thirty men representative of the Arab community called on the Bey to initiate political reform, reminding him of the sacrifices Tunisia had made in the war.[74] Certainly much of the impetus behind the foundation of the Destūr or Constitution Party in 1920 came from returned soldiers and labourers who were dissatisfied with their subordinate position in their own country.[75] In British West Africa, the press, while generally extremely loyal to the British and critical of the

68. N. A. Ziadeh, 1962, p. 60.

69. J. A. Langley, 1973, p. 107 and *passim*.

70. *Memorandum of the National Congress of British West Africa*, 1920, F. W. Dove, delegate of Sierra Leone.

71. M. 'Abd Al-Rahim, 1969, p. 94.

72. M. Crowder, 1977(d), in M. Crowder, 1977(a), p. 117.

73. C. V. Confer, 1966, p. 113.

74. N. A. Ziadeh, 1962, p. 88.

75. ibid., p. 123. For the activities of the Destūr, see Chapter 24.

Germans, believed that the reward for this loyalty would be a more significant role for the educated elite in the colonial decision-making process.[76]

The war acted not only as a stimulus to African nationalism but also to white nationalism, particularly in South Africa. There, though the Afrikaner rebellion was speedily put down, the spirit which informed it was not. As William Henry Vatcher has put it:

> The rebellion reconfirmed what the Boer War had taught, that force was not the answer, that battle must be pitched in the political arena. Thus, in a real sense, modern Afrikaner nationalism, conceived in the Boer War, was born in the 1914 rebellion. If the first world war had not taken place, the Boers might have been better able to adjust to the conciliatory policy of Botha and Smuts. The war forced on them the decision to organize, first covertly in the form of the Afrikaner Broederbond, then in the form of the 'purified' National Party.[77]

In Kenya, the white settlers used the war to make major political advances *vis-à-vis* the colonial government. They secured the right of whites to elect representatives to the Legislative Council, where after 1918 they formed a majority. This, coupled with the Crown Lands Ordinance, which made racial segregation in the White Highlands possible, the Native Registration Ordinance, which introduced a pseudo-pass law for Africans, and the Soldier Settlement Scheme which allocated large portions of the Nandi reserve for settlement of white soldiers after the war, entrenched the white minority in a dominant position in Kenya up to the 1950s.[78]

A major stimulus to Kenya nationalism was the reaction against such privileges gained by the white community, in particular with regard to land. Thus the Kikuyu Association, consisting mainly of chiefs, was founded in 1920 to defend Kikuyu land interests while Harry Thuku's Young Kikuyu Association, founded a year later, aimed at defence of both land and labour.[79]

In South Africa, the rise of Afrikaner nationalism and Republican agitation during the war gave serious concern to African leaders in Swaziland and Basutoland (now Lesotho). They feared that their countries might be integrated into the Union, which with its increasingly racist policies, exemplified by the provisions of the Native Land Act of 1913, might, under Afrikaner pressure, gain independence, and that thereafter there would be no protection for their interests. As Simon Phamote of the Sotho National Council declared, his people feared 'the Union because we know that ... the Boers will one day get their independence from the

76. F. Omu, 1968, pp. 44–9.
77. W. H. Vatcher, 1965, p. 46.
78. G. Bennett, 1963, pp. 35–45.
79. ibid., p. 45. For further details, see Chapter 26.

British.'[80] Within the Union, the South African Native National Congress (later to become the African National Congress) presented a memorandum after the war to King George V of Britain, citing the African contribution to the war in both the South West African and East African campaigns as well as in France, and recalling that the war had been fought to liberate oppressed peoples and to grant to every nation the right to determine its sovereign destiny.[81] The Congress was informed by the British Colonial Office that Britain could not interfere in the internal affairs of South Africa and the Congress appeal was not presented to the Peace Conference.

Conclusion

The war saw a major change in the climate of international opinion with regard to colonialism. Prior to the war, the European colonial powers had been accountable only to themselves. After the war, at the Versailles Peace Conference, the colonial record of one of them, Germany, was examined and found wanting, according to newly conceived standards of morality concerning the governance of colonial peoples.[82] Undoubtedly, most of the other colonial powers would have been found equally wanting if their own record had been similarly scrutinized.[83] The idea of administering so-called backward peoples as a 'sacred trust', though evident in the 1890s in the prohibition, for example, of the sale of alcohol to Africans, was now enshrined in the Mandates where the victorious Allies took over the administration of Germany's colonies on behalf of the League of Nations – 'responsible for the ... promotion to the utmost of the material and moral well-being and the social progress of [their] inhabitants'.[84] Theoretically the principle of international accountability had been underlined, though, because of the weakness of the League of Nations, little could be done, for instance, about the deplorable conditions of the indigenous inhabitants of South West Africa administered under Mandate by the Union.[85] The right of self-determination, first enunciated at the Congress of the Socialist Second International held in London in 1896, had also been enunciated by the leader of a major world power, Woodrow Wilson, whilst the newly-emerged Soviet Union was to attack all forms of colonialism in Africa.

Even if the lot of the subject peoples did not change much for the better in the years following the war, when even willing attempts at reform were

80. R. Hyam, 1972, p. 80.
81. L. Kuper in M. Wilson and L. M. Thompson (eds), 1971, p. 439.
82. See for example *German Colonization Handbooks* prepared under the direction of the Historical Section of the Foreign Office, No. 36, London, 1919 and C. Fidel, 1926. On Germany's colonial record in Togo see M. Crowder, 1968, pp. 241–8.
83. L. H. Gann and P. Duignan, 1967, p. 79.
84. This is the standard wording for the African mandates.
85. See R. Segal and R. First, 1967.

aborted by the depression,[86] searching questions about the morality of colonialism had begun to be asked. And it was in this climate that the nationalist movement gestated that was eventually to obtain independence for many African countries. For example, leaders of the National Congress of British West Africa like J. E. Casely Hayford and H. C. Bankole-Bright were able to gain an international hearing through the League of Nations Union, concerning themselves with the administration of Togoland and appealing to the Covenant of the League as a charter for 'just treatment towards our people'. And at long range, the idea of the Mandate evolved into the post-Second World War concept of Trusteeship, which incorporated the explicit goal of eventual independence for the Trust Territories which were to be visited by 'neutral' missions of inspection.

The First World War, then, represented a turning-point in African history, not as dramatic as the Second World War, but nevertheless important in many areas. One of its most important legacies was the re-ordering of the map of Africa roughly as it is today (see Fig. 12.2). Germany was eliminated as a colonial power, and replaced by France and Britain in the Cameroon and Togo, by the Union of South Africa in South West Africa and by Britain and Belgium in German East Africa, the latter gaining the small but densely populated provinces of Ruanda and Urundi (now Rwanda and Burundi).[87]

The intricate negotiations that took place at Versailles over the re-allocation of these territories to the Allied victors belongs properly to the history of Europe, though the way in which Cameroon and Togo were divided, with little reference to historical and ethnic considerations, was to create considerable bitterness among certain sections of the population in these territories and their immediate neighbours, in particular the Ewe of Togo and the Gold Coast. As far as the African inhabitants of the former German colonies were concerned, their lot was not noticeably improved by the change of masters. Indeed some Africans compared their former masters favourably with their new ones, and in Cameroon and Togo, a certain nostalgia for the earlier regime grew as the French introduced their forced labour and the British proved less energetic than their Teutonic cousins in developing their territories.[88] Because France and Britain saw themselves as temporary stewards in the Mandate territories, the two Togolands remained less developed than say Ivory Coast and Gold Coast, and Tanganyika less developed than Kenya or Uganda. And if South West Africa developed spectacularly under South African 'stewardship', it was to the benefit of the fast-growing settler population; as far as the indigenous inhabitants were concerned, the brutal experience of German rule was

86. An example is A. Sarraut, 1923.
87. See W. R. Louis, 1963(b), for an account of the negotiations leading up to the decision of the Peace Conference to allocate Ruanda and Urundi to the Belgians.
88. See C. E. Welch, 1966, p. 58.

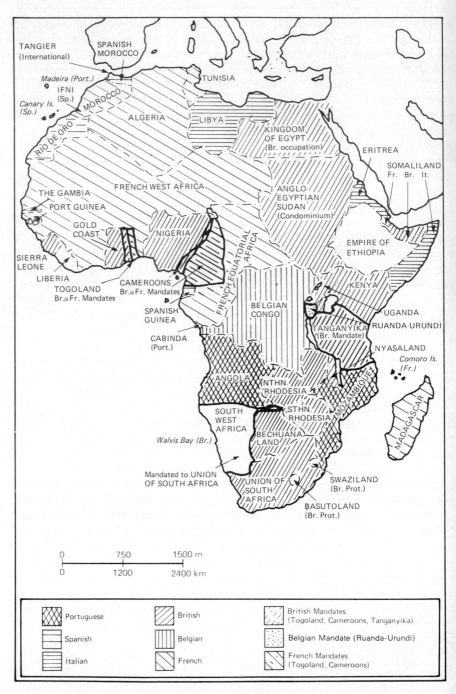

TANGIER
(International)

SPANISH
MOROCCO

Madeira (Port.)
IFNI
(Sp.)
Canary Is.
(Sp.)

MOROCCO

RIO DE ORO

TUNISIA

ALGERIA

LIBYA

KINGDOM
OF EGYPT
(Br. occupation)

ERITREA

SOMALILAND
Fr. Br. It.

FRENCH WEST AFRICA

ANGLO-
EGYPTIAN
SUDAN
(Condominium)

THE GAMBIA
PORT. GUINEA
GOLD
COAST

SIERRA
LEONE
LIBERIA
TOGOLAND
Br.α Fr. Mandates

NIGERIA

CAMEROONS
Br.α Fr. Mandates

SPANISH
GUINEA

CABINDA
(Port.)

FRENCH EQUATORIAL AFRICA

EMPIRE OF
ETHIOPIA

KENYA

BELGIAN
CONGO

UGANDA
RUANDA-URUNDI

TANGANYIKA
(Br. Mandate)

NYASALAND

Comoro Is.
(Fr.)

ANGOLA

NTHN.
RHODESIA

SOUTH
WEST
AFRICA

STHN.
RHODESIA

Walvis Bay (Br.)

BECHUANA-
LAND

MOZAMBIQUE

MADAGASCAR

Mandated to UNION
OF SOUTH AFRICA

UNION OF
SOUTH
AFRICA

SWAZILAND
(Br. Prot.)

BASUTOLAND
(Br. Prot.)

| 0 | 750 | 1500 m |
| 0 | 1200 | 2400 km |

Portuguese

Spanish

Italian

British

Belgian

French

British Mandates
(Togoland, Cameroons, Tanganyika)

Belgian Mandate (Ruanda-Urundi)

French Mandates
(Togoland, Cameroons)

FIG. 12.2 *The changed map of Africa after the First World War (after J. D. Fage, 1978)*

exchanged for that of a government committed to racist policies and the settlement and exploitation of the country by and for whites.

The First World War, though essentially a European war, involved Africa intimately. It marked both the end of the partition of Africa and of attempts by Africans to regain independence based on their pre-partition polities. Though it represented a period of immense social and economic upheaval for many African countries, it ushered in a twenty-year period of tranquillity for the European administrations, except in places like the French and Spanish Rīf, French Mauritania and Italian Libya.

However, ideas concerning the self-determination of peoples and the accountability of colonial powers had been sown during this war. These ideas were to influence profoundly the development of the incipient nationalist movements during the ensuing period of peace. But it was to take a second world war to provide the cataclysm which translated the requests of the nationalists for greater participation in the process of government, into demands for full control of it.

Methods and institutions of European domination

R. F. BETTS
revised by M. ASIWAJU

'Native policy'

Shortly after or concurrently with the military conquest and occupation of Africa by the imperial powers of Europe, Africa was overlaid with a colonial administrative grid which, while neither uniform nor simple, was welded out of a few commonly held ideas and beliefs. As at no other time or in any other continent subjected to European domination, colonial policy came to be referred to as 'native policy'. Granted that the term supported a variety of definitions in the administration of 'natives', the word generally employed in describing Africans, there was general agreement both in theory and in practice that colonial rule could only be effectively secured through the use of indigenous personnel and institutions in some complementary or supportive function.

This realization was the result of the colonial situation already determined by those nineteenth-century Europeans who had been operating in Africa. With Algeria and Southern Africa listed as the notable exceptions, the vast land mass of the continent was considered climatically inhospitable to intensive white settlement, while the local populations appeared to be insufficiently concentrated geographically to allow for effective direct administration by European personnel. Essentially, Africa was deemed to be a congeries of tropical estates whose populations were to be both enlisted and directed by the Europeans for externally defined purposes. What Sir Frederick (later Lord) Lugard would define as a 'dual mandate' in his famous book of that name first published in 1922, was generally accepted as the theoretical justification for the European presence: social and economic development as much for the sake of the rest of the world as for Africa.

In contemporary imperialist ideology, therefore, the purpose of the European presence was defined in terms of a responsibility or trust. The British government's White Paper on Kenya issued in 1923, which established the principle of 'native paramountcy', included the statement that 'His Majesty's Government regard themselves as exercising a trust on behalf of the African populations . . . the object of which may be defined

PLATES 13.1(a)–(d) *Colonial governors and administrators*

PLATE 13.1(a) *Frederick, Lord Lugard (1858–1945), High Commissioner, then Governor of Northern Nigeria, 1900–7, 1912–14; Governor of Nigeria, 1914–19*

PLATE 13.1(b) *Louis-Gabriel Angoulvant, Lieutenant-Governor of Ivory Coast, 1908–16*

PLATE 13.1(c) *General Joseph Simon Gallieni (1849–1916), Commandant-Supérieur of French Soudan, 1886–8; Governor-General of Madagascar, 1896–1905*

PLATE 13.1(d) *Albert Heinrich Schnee (1871–1949), Governor of German East Africa, 1912–18*

as the protection and advancement of the native races ...'[1] The French Minister of Colonies, Albert Sarraut, argued in his well-known study, *La mise en valeur des colonies françaises*, that the 'sole right which should be recognized is that of the strong to protect the weak'. France, he continued, was guaranteeing 'the economic growth and human development' of its colonies.[2]

Both statements suggest that paternalistic attitude which had thoroughly permeated European thought about colonial Africa and which was both internationalized and institutionalized with the mandates system that emerged from the League of Nations after the First World War. In the language of Article 22 of the League of Nations Covenant, the colonial effort, particularly in Africa, was now proclaimed to be a responsibility undertaken in the name of higher civilization, with 'the tutelage of such peoples [the colonial populations] ... entrusted to advanced nations'.[3] Behind such rhetoric still stood an attitude of cultural and racial superiority, formed in the eighteenth and nineteenth centuries, and regularly given expression in descriptions of the African as childlike or 'non-adult'. The European domination which such an imagined social condition required was thought to be of long duration, which meant that the colonial hold on Africa would last into some unforeseeable future.

As for those few areas which already had large residential white minorities and were receiving still more such immigrants at this time, the anticipated future condition was one of permanency of settlement and of the continuance of European primacy in all matters relating to politics and property. Yet even in such territories – except South Africa where a policy of severely unequal segregation had already been imposed – notions of co-operative development were frequently expressed, and the African populations were at least officially enjoined to accept and follow European guidance.

Beyond such considerations, colonial policy was without clear, final objectives. More short-range process than well-defined system, it vaguely included notions of self-government in its British form, and of political integration in its French and Portuguese forms. Broadly poised between these policies of 'differentiation' and 'identity', colonial administration of the inter-war era was described by its practitioners as necessarily empirical, an exercise in cultural and political accommodation.

Yet what seminal thought and experimentation that did occur were pre-war in origin. Following upon the 'paper occupation' of Africa in the 1880s and 1890s, the process of military conquest and domination occurred, and

1. *Indians in Kenya*, Cmd 1922 (1923).
2. A. Sarraut, 1923, p. 19.
3. While becoming a member of the League of Nations, the Soviet Union did express reservations about certain articles of the League Covenant. In particular the Soviet Union disapproved of Article 22 and accordingly refused to assign a representative to the Mandates Commission.

this gave rise to many of the methods of administrative control to be employed even before the century ended. As a result, the inter-war years were those in which many of these earlier practices were structured into official policy and in which administrative expediency was elevated to the status of well-articulated theory. In retrospect, the period can clearly be seen as the one in which the bureaucratization of colonial administration occurred.

Although there was initially no universally accepted approach to colonial administration in Africa, most lines of thought converged on what might be called conjunctive administration (usually termed indirect rule); that which joined African authorities, in traditionally-held or European-imposed political roles, to the colonial government, but in an obviously subordinate capacity. The reasons for general concurrence on this broad principle of rule are varied. First, the historical pattern of late nineteenth-century colonial acquisition was a formative factor, as size alone added a new dimension to the problem of colonial rule. Secondly the internal penetration of Africa rapidly outpaced the numbers of European personnel available to administer the newly possessed lands. Furthermore, since such penetration extended into many regions yet untouched by European cultural contact, direct rule of any kind would have been an entirely new experience and therefore immediately unworkable. Primarily as a result of these conditions, previously noted by several critics,[4] the direct rule characteristic of the smaller possessions on the coast gave way to the indirect rule of the larger possessions in the interior. Furthermore, at the turn of the century, the collapse of rule by chartered companies necessitated the establishment of national control over weakly held extensive territories. Yet this condition was in turn met (except in German East Africa) with a type of informal rule similar to the loose methods employed previously by the companies, as was most evident in Italian Somaliland.

There were also reasons which sprang from European cultural perceptions and announced political intentions. Not only was there widespread acceptance of the principle of empire 'on the cheap', with little or no direct cost to the metropolitan state, but there was also general agreement that the least social dislocation would assure the most indigenous co-operation. Speaking of British policy in Africa, Lugard asserted that 'institutions and methods, in order to command success and promote the happiness and welfare of the people must be deep-rooted in their traditions and prejudices'.[5] Likewise the French Minister of Colonies, Georges Léyguès, had stated in 1906: 'The fundamental principle of our colonial policy must be scrupulous respect for the beliefs, habits and traditions of the conquered or protected peoples'.[6]

4. See M. Perham, 1960(b), pp. 140–1; J. D. Fage in P. Gifford and W. R. Louis (eds), 1967, p. 703.
5. F. D. Lugard, 1929, p. 211.
6. *La Depêche Coloniale*, 12 July 1906, p. 1.

These explanations and arguments in respect of shortage of personnel and the need to reduce cost to the barest minimum are themselves directly related to a more fundamental problem which dictated the adoption of the conjunctive system of administration by all the colonial governments in the twentieth century. This was the failure of the assimilationist or direct administration policy which was the vogue in the nineteenth century. Whether in respect of the French in the Four Communes of Senegal or of the British with regards to the Crown colonies of Sierra Leone, Gold Coast (now Ghana) and Lagos (in what is now Nigeria), assimilation had, by the end of the nineteenth century, been frustrated not only by the cultural resistance of the African peoples concerned. There was also a loss of enthusiasm on the part of the French and the British colonial officials themselves, due to the emergent trend of conflict and friction between the European colonial elite and the locally produced western-educated Africans. In both the French and British colonies, the end of the nineteenth century was marked by a systematic frustration of westernized Africans' expectations. As A. E. Afigbo has correctly observed,[7] the end of the nineteenth century in the colonies of British West Africa witnessed not just the systematic removal of educated Africans who had held positions of responsibility in the earlier decades: the same period also saw the systematic tightening of conditions under which Africans could become French citizens in Senegal and elsewhere. It was, indeed, this loss of fellowship between the European colonialist and the educated Africans at the end of the century, which created the artificial scarcity of administrative personnel, as the new regimes began to exercise restriction on the recruitment of highly skilled Africans into the administrations.

In the light of these considerations, no colonial power immediately sought to dispose completely of the socio-political structures already in place. However, policy ran a long gamut, from reluctant acceptance and forced adaptation of such structures as in Portuguese Angola and German East Africa, to considered efforts at institutional preservation as in British Northern Nigeria or French Morocco. Nevertheless, the basic demands of the colonial system everywhere had the effect of modifying the purposes, hence of distorting the functions of and weakening basic African institutions. The very fact that most African states were acquired by conquest and the exile or deposition of some ruling chiefs in itself brought the whole business of chieftaincy, for instance, into disrepute. The universal imposition of European-planned taxes was certainly another disruptive colonial measure, but even the modest efforts made in the direction of what is today called modernization also remoulded local institutions. If the vast majority of the African population was not regularly affected by the European presence, basic political institutions were.

7. A. E. Afigbo in J. F. A. Ajayi and M. Crowder (eds), 1974, p. 443.

Colonial rule and structure

From the palace of the Sultan of Morocco to the kraal of the East and Southern African chief, European colonial administrators sought and employed 'native authorities' as allies or agents through whom the demands of alien rule might effectively be made on the African populations at large. The arrangement of such authority was asymmetrical, no matter how little existing institutions were modified or subsumed to European needs. At the pinnacle of the administrative system stood the governor or resident-general who, while ultimately responsible to his national government, frequently enjoyed the powers of a sovereign.

The institutional framework within which he acted varied considerably in size and complexity, but he was usually assisted in the inter-war period by some form of consultative council or commercial interests. The centralized nature of colonial administration in the French, Portuguese and Belgian systems assured the retention of legislative authority in the metropolis. In the British African possessions, however, colonial councils did emerge as proto-parliamentary bodies with appointed or elected membership, or both, and with functions varying from the advisory to the legislative, thus unintentionally but logically preparing the way for political devolution. While the Africans began to make their appearance in the colonial conciliar system, and most particularly in the British version, their number and the means by which they were appointed effectively guaranteed that they would have no noticeable impact on the mode of European domination in the inter-war period.

The crucial institution of all colonial organization was the district or provincial unit, called a *cercle* in French West Africa. The continued use of this military term was a reminder of the nature of colonial acquisitions. Over the *cercle*, a European administrator exercised colonial authority and directed both the activities of his European subordinates and the African authorities enlisted in the colonial administration.

The most important and most discussed African component was the local chief. Indeed, every colonial power in Black Africa depended on the chief, whether traditional or warrant in authority, as the basic element of the administrative structure. The French colonial administrator, Robert Delavignette, explained the nature of the system succinctly, and in a way applicable to more than the French West African situation, when he wrote: 'There is no colonization without native policy; no native policy without a territorial command; and no territorial command without native chiefs who serve as links between the colonial authority and the population.'[8]

Although no observer or critic has doubted that chiefly activities were integral to the colonial system throughout the continent, there has been a considerable academic debate about the uses to which the various

8. R. Delavignette, 1946, p. 121.

European powers put these chiefs.[9] The major question has centred on the difference between direct and indirect rule, between delegation of European authority to the African rulers and European mediation of traditional authority enjoyed by these rulers. While most scholarly interest has been directed to the distinction between the British and French modes of control in sub-Saharan Africa, where procedures, if not ultimate effects, were distinctive, the issue is perhaps best placed in historical perspective by a general review of continental policy, but with special attention still given to the activities of the British and French.

The most famous explanation of the importance of the 'native authority' to the colonial order was that of Lugard, who encased in theory the most discussed and imitated method of domination: indirect rule. As with so many administrators in the colonial realm, he made virtue of a widespread necessity, but few wrote so persuasively of that virtue.

Confronted with the large territory of Northern Nigeria to administer after the transfer of the Royal Niger Company's authority to the state, and then faced with a shortage of men and funds, Lugard realized that any suggestion of direct control was out of the question. But such a conclusion was also supported by his belief, which had already been formed during his earlier service in Uganda, that the use of existing indigenous institutions was the best method of colonial administration. In his service as high commissioner for Northern Nigeria between 1900 and 1907, Lugard therefore developed his general practice and offered a detailed explanation of it in his many instructions to administrators, which were published as *Political Memoranda*.

The best résumé of his policy is found in a set of instructions he issued to his officers in 1906, in which he argues for 'a single Government in which the Native Chiefs have well-defined duties and an acknowledged status equally with the British officials'.[10] The basis of what was to become the system of indirect rule was therefore one of co-operation, not subordination, with the British Resident acting primarily in an advisory, not an executive capacity, and with the African 'chief' – in this instance, the Fulani emir – continuing in a traditional role which was now carefully guided, not rigidly fixed by the imposed colonial administration. In this attempt to integrate the emirs into the colonial system, Lugard wished to leave to them most of their old responsibilities, functions, and perquisites of office so that they would continue to appear in the eyes of the local populations as the legitimate rulers.

If, then, the essential of Lugard's rule was the use of existing authorities in existing capacities, something more was intended. Modifications along

9. See H. Deschamps, 1963; M. Crowder, 1964; M. Crowder and O. Ikime (eds), 1970; A. I. Asiwaju, 1976(a).
10. F. D. Lugard, 1919, p. 298.

European lines were expected in matters such as justice and taxation.[11] 'The great task of indirect rule,' wrote Lugard's biographer in an article defending his policy, 'is to hold the ring, to preserve a fair field within which Africans can strike their own balance between conservatism and adaptation.'[12] That task depended in large measure on the knowledge that European administrators had of local customs and institutions – and, of course, on the willingness of the native authorities to make such adjustments towards modernization within the context of their own institutions.

This broad sketch of indirect rule in Northern Nigeria can be aligned with another which, like Lugard's, met most success in regions overlaid with Muslim political institutions. Reaching beyond Africa in scope, this form of indirect administration was primarily given theoretical definition by the French. What they labelled a *politique d'association* received considerable recognition at the turn of the century and was enthusiastically contrasted with the older ideal of political assimilation. The conservative colonial theorist, Jules Harmand, offered one of the best explanations of this policy in a long section of his influential work, *Domination et colonisation*, published in 1910. Association, he therein stated, is 'indirect administration, with the preservation but improved governance of the institutions of the conquered peoples, and with respect for their past'.[13] With the publication in 1923 of Sarraut's *La mise en valeur des colonies françaises*, the policy was given the aura of official sanctity.

Originally suggested for Indochina and later extended as policy to Africa, 'association' was none the less geographically limited as a colonial practice. Only in Morocco did the French seriously consider it, and there primarily because of the attention given to indigenous affairs by the Resident-General, Louis-Hubert Lyautey, who, in the initial years of the protectorate, ruled with few restrictions from the metropolitan government. Throughout Morocco the forms of the Sherifian state were preserved, while at the local level administrative activities were strikingly similar to those proposed by Lugard. The French *contrôleur civil* was to perform in an advisory not a supervisory capacity with respect to the *cadi*, a Muslim official fulfilling magisterial functions in accordance with the *shari'a*. A comparable arrangement existed in the Spanish-dominated portion of Morocco where the *cadi* was guided in his role by the *Inventore*, the Spanish counterpart of the *contrôleur civil*. The *cadi* was also administratively retained as before in Italian Somaliland, but there he was joined in the responsibilities of local government by assigned warrant chiefs.

In theory such indirect administration also applied to French colonial activities south of the Sahara, but in fact practice was at severe variance with it. In a statement frequently referred to as most descriptive of the

11. In Nigeria, the modifications brought about by indirect rule in practice have been carefully documented in O. Ikime (ed.), 1980, Chapters 25, 26, 27.

12. M. Perham, 1934, p. 331.

13. J. Harmand, 1910, p. 163.

PLATE 13.2 *Louis-Hubert Lyautey (1859–1935), French Resident-General in Morocco, 1912–25*

methods which the French actually pursued in this region between the wars, the Governor-General of French West Africa, Joost Van Vollenhoven, remarked in 1917: The chiefs 'have no power of their own, for there are not two authorities in the *cercle* . . . ; there is only one! Only the *commandant du cercle* commands; only he is responsible. The native chief is but an instrument, an auxiliary'.[14] Despite official pronouncements, therefore, the French used indigenous authorities not indirectly, but directly and subordinately in their colonial administration. And in like manner so did the Portuguese.

Lugard's form of indirect rule was initially successful in Northern Nigeria although discredited by some critics as unduly conservative[15] and was then extended after the war throughout much of British Africa, including the newly acquired German possessions of Tanganyika and the Cameroon. It was even adapted by the Belgians for their use in the Congo after 1920. Although conditions were nowhere else so optimal or the results so successful as in the Hausa-Fulani region of Nigeria, the British did try to follow the contours of local custom so that even newly devised institutions, like local councils, were in consonance with indigenous forms of organization. The egregious exception, however, was South Africa where the concept of 'native authority' was the means by which the white minority assured local administration of Africans now displaced by the policy of segregation to territorial reserves.

Throughout sub-Saharan Africa during the inter-war period, the chief became an administrative agent and not a 'native authority' and his traditional roles and powers were greatly weakened or curtailed. This shift in position, even in regions submitted to indirect rule, is easily explained. Most obviously, traditional functions were distended by new demands, such as the collection of taxes, the taking of censuses, or the recruitment of labour and military conscripts. Where there appeared to European eyes no satisfactory individuals in positions of traditional authority, other personnel, such as veterans, non-commissioned officers or clerks, were installed as chiefs. This was especially the case in French and Portuguese colonies where the local roles for the recruitment of personnel for chieftaincy positions were more often than not violated. Then, chiefs were sometimes endowed with political significance which had not previously been inherent in their office; on other occasions they were installed in acephalous societies where they previously had no administrative purpose. Examples of these two developments are found among the Igbo of Nigeria, the Gikuyu of Kenya and the Langi of northern Uganda.[16]

With the establishment of European administration, chiefs were manipulated as if they were administrative personnel who might be reposted

14. J. van Vollenhoven, 1920, p. 207.
15. For a recent assessment see S. Abubakar in O. Ikime (ed.), 1980.
16. On this subject see particularly R. Tignor, 1971; J. Tosh, 1973; A. E. Afigbo, 1972; W. R. Ochieng in B. A. Ogot (ed.), 1972; G. Muriuki in B. A. Ogot (ed.), 1972.

PLATE 13.3 *Indirect rule in action: the Prince of Wales receiving chiefs at Accra while on tour of the Gold Coast, 1925*

or removed to satisfy colonial needs. Chieftaincies were abolished where considered superfluous and created where considered colonially useful. Perhaps the most striking example of this process occurred in the Belgian Congo (now Zaire) where, after 1918, the reforms proposed by the colonial minister, Louis Franck, led to a drastic revision in the colonial order of things. The number of *chefferies* was reduced from 6095 in 1917 to 1212 in 1938. Furthermore, an entirely new administrative unit, called *le secteur*, was introduced for purposes of consolidation. Along similar lines the French in West Africa also created a new unit, a grouping of villages into a *canton*, which, in the words of one governor, 'is placed under the authority of an *indigenous administrative agent* who assumes the name of canton chief'.[17] In Libya the population was subjected to new administrative organization by a royal decree of 31 August 1929 which notably allowed for the division of the nomadic peoples of the colony into 'tribes' and 'subtribes' at the discretion of the governor and upon the advice of the regional commissioner. And even the British made such alterations in the eastern district of Nigeria when indirect rule was introduced there. Faced with an elaborate number of local rulers whose range of authority they were then unable to discern, the British introduced the principle of the warrant chief whose authority extended over districts of many thousands of people but derived directly from the warrant issued by the colonial government.[18]

Operating as a disruptive agent in connection with these factors was the local administrator. Whatever his intentions, he invariably became a surrogate chief. As Delavignette described the situation with satisfaction, the colonial administrator was not an administrator at all, but a commander and recognized as such by the African population under his control. His primary function, he asserted unequivocally, 'is to act as a chief'.[19] The reserved and unobtrusive role which Lugard had hoped the British Resident would generally play in Northern Nigeria was denied in their territories by the French and Portuguese administrators, both sets of whom were prominent in the exercise of local authority. While the administrators in Italian Somaliland came closest to the British in their relationship to the local chiefs, even among these two groups Lugard's dicta were necessarily modified by the exigencies of colonial rule and the personalities of the individuals exercising it. The truly subtle and empathetic rapport which Lugardian indirect rule actually required for success was seldom to be found among the colonial officers who served in Africa. More significantly, the new set of social requirements imposed by colonialism was quite alien to African custom and hence was incorporated into indigenous institutions only by a distortive process.

17. 'Programme d'action économique, politique et sociale', 1933, p. 185; quoted by J. Suret-Canale, 1971, p. 323. Italics in author's original.
18. For further details, see A. E. Afigbo, 1972.
19. R. Delavignette, 1946, p. 29.

Purposes and impositions of colonialism

Beyond the official rhetoric, the mundane purposes of colonization turned out to be quite limited. In their starkest form, they were the maintenance of order, the avoidance of heavy financial expenditure, and the establishment of a labour force, initially for porterage and later for the creation of roads and railways but also for commercial purposes. In general practice, these purposes were added to the functions of local rule and were fulfilled in three ways: redirection of systems of justice, use of forced labour, and the imposition of personal taxes. The latter two were the most disturbing of colonial institutions while the former was, perhaps, the most wisely reviewed of all by the Europeans.

The introduction of European judicial institutions was usually done with some attention to African customary law and to Muslim law where it also existed, as for instance, in Italian Somaliland; but the effects were modificatory none the less. As Lord Hailey has remarked, the basic concept of European law differed markedly from that of the African systems, for it was directed towards the punishment of the guilty and not the redress of the aggrieved.[20] Frequently, there were colonial attempts at a dyarchical judicial arrangement wherein civil litigation involving Africans was settled according to pre-colonial legal modes, while criminal law and litigation involving Europeans fell directly under colonial jurisdiction.

However, everywhere, with the noticeable exception of the Portuguese colonies, a court system was developed or reinforced according to African needs as perceived by the Europeans.[21] In the first decade of the century, there were particular attempts by the Italians in Somaliland and the Germans in East Africa to extend the judicial function of African chiefs or magistrates. In the same period, the most elaborate and successful of such efforts occurred on the other coast: Lugard's implementation of 'native courts'. Part of his tripodal 'native administration', the 'native court' was, in his mind, an instrument by which to 'inculcate a sense of responsibility, and evolve among a primitive community some sense of discipline and respect for authority'.[22] Presided over by Africans, and directed primarily to domestic affairs, these courts were to adhere as closely as possible to African customary law, modified only where basic customs were not in accordance with fundamental English norms. The Lugardian model was introduced into many British possessions and the mandated territories, and was also emulated by the Belgians in the Congo.

In direct contrast to this method was the French which tended to erode African authority, finally making the administrator the responsible judicial official. However, the most peculiar and inequitable element in the French

20. Lord Hailey, 1957, p. 591.
21. For a fascinating case study of this process, see O. Adewoye, 1977.
22. F. D. Lugard, 1929, p. 548.

system was the *indigénat*.[23] First employed in Algeria in the 1870s, this device was imported into French West Africa in the 1880s and remained institutionally operative there as well as in Algeria until the end of the Second World War. Regularized by a decree of 1924, it allowed any French administrator to impose a punishment of up to fifteen days gaol sentence and a fine for a series of infractions ranging from failure to pay taxes on time to displaying discourtesy to French officials.

More pervasive in effect than the legal systems were the personal taxes which all African males eventually encountered. Primarily designed as one means by which to make the colonial effort financially self-sustaining, they were also inspired by the notion that they would force the African into European economic enterprises and would extend the money economy. By the early twentieth century, these taxes were regularized as was no other colonial institution, having undergone what appears to be a clear cycle of development.[24] The 'hut' tax was an obvious form in the early years of domination and was also a source of considerable African contention and protest.[25] It was generally replaced by about the second decade of the twentieth century with a poll or capitation tax which remained the dominant form until the end of the colonial regime. Between the wars there were attempts to graduate this tax on a regional basis or on an assessment of the potential yield of the land. Lastly, there was the income tax, introduced in the 1920s into several British territories and the Belgian Congo, but then primarily affecting non-Africans who generally were the only ones with sufficient income to be required to pay it.

Within this general pattern there were many regional distinctions, the most prominent being that connected with Lugard's idea of 'native authority'. As he wrote in his *Dual Mandate*, the 'tax ... is, in a sense, the basis of the whole system, since it supplies the means to pay the Emir and all his officials'.[26] The institution through which the process worked was the 'native treasury', an idea originating with Sir Charles Temple, in service under Lugard in Northern Nigeria. Each native authority was to be returned a percentage of the taxes collected in his district. This amount was to form part of a 'native treasury' further enriched by various licensing fees and fines collected in the courts. From this sum, the emir or chief was to draw his own revenue and supply the salary of his subordinates. The remaining funds were to be used for public services and improvements. The arrangement, originally employed in the emirates, spread with indirect rule, not only to British possessions on both coasts but also to the Belgian Congo.

Of all the colonial devices, the tax system was the one which most obviously encouraged the bureaucratic development of colonial rule. It

23. For a recent detailed study, see A. I. Asiwaju, 1979.
24. Lord Hailey, 1957, p. 676.
25. See Chapter 6 above.
26. F. D. Lugard, 1929, p. 201.

assigned a common function to the administrator and the African chief who in assessing and collecting the tax, often in conjunction with local councils of elders or notables, reminded everyone of the regulatory power of the new system.[27] Furthermore after tax collectors as such, there soon appeared administrative agents who became part of the new colonial elite. The most striking and controversial among them were no doubt the *akidas* used by the Germans in East Africa. Swahili-speaking officials who served on the coast before European domination, they were used in redefined positions both to collect taxes and to recruit labour for the German administration. In 1936, special African clerks were appointed to collect taxes in Northern Rhodesia (now Zambia), another indication of this bureaucratic trend.

The introduction of money taxes was briefly accompanied by labour taxes, the most obvious expression of European attempts to enlist labour forcibly into the economic organization of the colonial effort. The *impôt de cueillette*, the tax by which wild rubber was harvested in the Congo Free State, was the most criticized of such taxes, but in duration the French *prestation*, a labour tax required of all males in French West and Equatorial Africa unless remitted by cash payment, was the longest; it was only abolished in 1944. Conversely, the Germans in the Cameroon allowed the capitation tax to be remitted by a labour 'payment'. And in parts of Uganda, the British continued the *luwalo*, a pre-colonial public-work tax of one month's labour, until 1938, when it was replaced by a money tax. Yet such taxes were the exception to forced labour devices employed by all of the colonial powers.

Consistently concerned with shortages of manpower for new projects and new employments which colonial rule supported, European administrators imposed their domination before the end of the century by a system of virtual impressment, frequently satisfying private as well as public purposes. It is true that such direct forced labour declined in the early twentieth century, because of the decreasing need for portage as well as the increasing concern with international opinion. But the uses, however modified, remained an integral part of colonial domination until the Second World War. At least this was the case with the French colonial governments which, as in West Africa still employed large numbers of Africans through *prestation* particularly on railway building until after the Second World War. Moreover, French colonial officials frequently sanctioned labour recruitment for commercial purposes, as on rubber plantations of Equatorial Africa or in the forests of the Ivory Coast.[28] Abuses at this time were still sufficient in intensity to arouse expressions of public

27. Lugard in particular extolled the virtues of personal taxation as marking 'the recognition of the principle that each individual in proportion to his means has an obligation to the State ...' ibid., p. 232.

28. The case of the Ivory Coast has been covered by Z. Semi-Bi, 1973, and R. P. Anouma, 1973.

indignation, most well marked in the celebrated commentary of André Gide in his *Voyage au Congo* (1927).

Yet the most oppressive forms of labour regulations were those found in German South West Africa and in the Union of South Africa. Union policies were, of course, extended to South West Africa when it became a mandated territory after the war, but German policy before then was strikingly similar in nature and severity to that devised in the Union. Pass laws were imposed, as were identity cards, both regulating the movement of Africans; Africans without labour contracts were subject to vagrancy laws; and labour contracts were designed to give the German employer an enormous advantage. In the Union, there were also pass laws and Acts against vagrancy, the penalty for which was required, if minimally paid, labour. The Native (Urban Areas) Act of 1923 and the Native Administration Act of 1927 reinforced previous pass laws, while other enactments, such as the Apprenticeship Act of 1922, effectively restricted the forms of employment an African might take.

Means of control and administration

Whatever the variety of theories and methods of colonial domination suggested and implemented in the period between the two world wars, an emergent pattern of bureaucratic rule is evident. By then domination had shifted from military to civil institutional control while direct force tended to be replaced by administrative persuasion. This shift, however, in no way denied the fact that the *ultima ratio* of colonial authority was displayed by European arms.

As its most ardent advocates were willing to remark, colonial rule was won by the sword and so maintained. With this dictum in mind, all the European powers utilized in their military establishments elements recruited from the indigenous population. Although organization and effectiveness varied both according to region and particular national purposes, such colonial troops primarily performed police functions in the inter-war era and were joined by newly created constabulary forces in this capacity. Yet because they were frequently made to serve in geographical regions culturally and ethnically unfamiliar to them, African soldiers were thus alienated from their own society and were often received with hostility by the local populations they forcefully encountered. As a result of this condition and, furthermore, of the European denial of command positions to Africans, the army never came to play the political role in the independence movements that its counterparts in Asia and the Near East did. In fact, the only colonial power which elaborated a significant military policy for the Africans under its domination was France which, from the first years of the twentieth century, considered sub-Saharan Africa a man-power reservoir essential to the maintenance of the French military posture in the world.

327

PLATE 13.4 *Forced labour: East African askaris collect labour for the civil administration, near Rumu river, April 1917, during the German East African campaign*

However, even in the inter-war period, labelled by contemporaries as one of 'colonial peace', military activities still punctuated African affairs in a severe manner. The professed European desire to keep Africa as militarily neutralized as possible was in fact never realized. The French introduced a law of conscription in 1919 whereby an African contingent of 10000 was to be annually obtained; the British developed a Sudan Defence Force, uniquely staffed by Sudanese as well as by British officers, but primarily directed to imperial strategic needs in the Near East as well as in East Africa. The *Force Publique* of the Belgian Congo, exhibiting the qualities both of occupation army and police force, was frequently used during this era to quell resistance expressed in the form of syncretistic religious movements.[29] On the scale of open warfare, events can be easily measured. The Italian campaign to subdue Libya in the 1920s and the Spanish and French effort to resolve the Rīf war in Morocco in the same period are obvious. But they are surpassed in scope by the rapacious war undertaken by Mussolini against the Ethiopians, an event with which the period here under consideration was tragically closed.

This account of military developments in Africa in the inter-war period does not seriously impair the assertion that divergent intentions of European colonial method and practice are those which, in retrospect, seem the most significant. There is little doubt that colonial bureaucratization did provide partial preparation for an unintended movement towards national independence. The configurations of a new political elite were slowly emerging, as lower-echelon clerks and appointed chiefs in various colonial services – but particularly the British – were learning to apply, if only modestly, Napoleon's imperative: 'careers open to talent'. Training schools, such as the Ecole William Ponty in Dakar, were undertaking the preparation of educators and administrators upon whom the colonial administration was more and more to depend. Principally in the urban regions, the 'wind of change' was slowly being generated.

Yet this was not what the European colonial administrators actually intended. Even when they emphasized 'native paramountcy', they did so with the thought that the welfare of the African populations could only be guaranteed and effectively structured socially and economically by them. Good government and independent government were, as Lord Cromer once remarked, opposing objectives in a colonial context. Thus the colonial system existed as an authoritarian one, and it was in no meaningful way calculated to confer political power upon the Africans it supposedly served. Its most common characteristic was paternalism, with shared responsibility at best only tolerated in areas of considerable white settlement. The history of the changing purposes and interpretation of 'native paramountcy' in Kenya is instructive in this matter. The White Paper of 1923 employed

29. Of the several studies of the historical development of the military in modern Africa, the best brief introduction, and the one the comments in this text have generally recapitulated, is J. S. Coleman and B. Belmont Jr in J. J. Johnson (ed.), 1962.

the concept as a device by which to stave off the demands of the Indian population for equitable representation in the affairs of the colony. Subsequent White Papers issued in 1927 and 1930 qualified the concept and contained concessions to the growing white residential population which was now allowed to join in the responsibilities of 'trusteeship'. Native paramountcy therefore did not really imply dominance of African interests, but only respect for them.

Even where parliamentary institutions were introduced to provide a degree of responsible colonial government, this arrangement was effected so that white preponderance was guaranteed. In Algeria, for instance, a two-college electoral system, sanctioned by the Jonnart Law of 1919, provided proportionately lower Arab participation than European in the *Délégations financières*, the incipient parliamentary body representing interest groups, not geographic areas. In South Africa, Africans enjoyed no role whatsoever in the parliamentary procedures that were developed there. The Representation of Natives Act of 1936 effectively removed the Africans from the Cape Colony electoral rolls and limited their political status throughout the Union to the election of a limited number of whites who were to represent 'native interests'. In these two major settler colonies, exactly as in all the other colonies in which residential Europeans were to be found, the demographic minority was in fact the political majority, thus precluding any resemblance to democratic government on the European model.

If the general political effects of the various colonial methods were historically more similar than divergent, distinctions in method were important in the preparation for the timing of colonial devolution. In large measure, colonial rule ultimately collapsed in Africa because of the declining ability – a combined financial, military, and moral condition – of Europeans to continue it in the face of African nationalist pressure. Yet within the terminal decade of colonialism, the pre-established methods of control were influential in determining the process of change. The administrative matters of identity and differentiation and of centralization and local autonomy then became effective determinants. The smoothest transmission of power, as will be seen in the concluding volume of this History, was that accomplished through the English 'Westminster system', the outgrowth of the colonial legislative councils through which methods of political opposition were developed, as is most evident in the independence of the Gold Coast as Ghana. The most radical change was that which occurred in French Algeria and, more recently, in the Portuguese settler colonies of Angola and Mozambique, where the assimilationist approach held that these areas were overseas extensions of the national state.

Diversity of colonial method was not as important historically as was the similarity in assessment of the colonial situation. Despite the pronouncements enshrined in the documents of the League of Nations, and in defiance of their weakened global positions as a result of the World

War, the European powers in Africa did not entertain thoughts of political devolution in the inter-war period. Egypt excepted, Africa was seen as the one continent in which colonialism would be of very long duration, and colonial methods were all designed to accommodate European interests and intentions. Therefore, the essential political activity was one of African adjustment to European objectives, regardless of whether the particular colonial practice followed was indirect or not.

Most important of all the historical developments of the inter-war period, the colonial system established the general administrative framework in which national government would be housed in the first decade of independence. This incipient regularization of political activity within a European arranged structure was the principal aspect of modernization that the Europeans introduced, but for their own purposes, to contemporary Africa at that time.

The colonial economy

W. RODNEY

Conquest and new production relations, 1880–c. 1910

From the late fifteenth century onwards, Africa participated in the Europe-oriented world economy as a peripheral and dependent sector. But, on the eve of the imposition of European colonial rule, there was no direct alien control of everyday economic activity on African soil. Such a situation came into being by a slow process after the loss of African sovereignty. The colonial economic system cannot be said to have reached its prime until the coming of the Second World War. The years 1880–1935, therefore, cover the laying of the foundations of production relations characteristic of colonialism. African opposition and resistance held prospective colonizers at bay until the second decade of this century and occasionally longer. Africans responded aggressively to the attempted destruction of their economic independence, as illustrated by some of the more famous anti-colonial resistances already discussed, such as the Hut Tax war in Sierra Leone, the Bailundu revolt in Angola, the Majī Majī wars in German East Africa and the Bambata rebellion in South Africa.

Africans witnessed the first physical evidence of a new economy in the form of road, rail and telegraph construction. Transport and communication lines were a prelude to conquest and they were logistically necessary in occupied areas so that the latter could serve as the staging points for further aggression. African rulers were sometimes hostile towards the Europeans building a transport and communications infrastructure. Their followers were told to pull down telegraph posts and tear up railway tracks, as in the Niger/Senegambia region when the French military presence was first manifest in the 1880s and 1890s.[1] However, few roads or railways were of purely military interest; and the same railways which facilitated conquest were used for the extraction of groundnuts, cotton and so on.

Coastal African economies were quickly reduced to dependent entities within the economies of the respective colonizing powers, while the interior peoples were usually the last to be brought into the network of produce

1. G. Ganier, 1965; see also Chapter 6.

collection, cash-crop cultivation and paid labour. Considerable expenditure was needed to provide certain African ports with deep berths and viable off-loading capacity;[2] but this was less onerous than the capital which had to be invested in arterial roads or railways penetrating the hinterland. Therefore, distance from the coast was one of the determinants of how early the colonial economy could be set in motion.

The most decisive variable affecting the implanting of the colonial economy was the extent to which various parts of Africa had already been participating in the world economy. This was partly because Europeans preferred jurisdiction over areas with which they were already familiar, and partly because pre-colonial foreign trade orientation caused African communities to be more susceptible to colonial economic innovations, such as the cultivation of crops specifically for sale to Europeans. The slaving zones from Senegal to Sierra Leone, from the Gold Coast (now Ghana) to Nigeria and from the Congo river to Angola were the stretches of coast-line first encroached upon by the European colonizers. In these localities, features of the colonial economy emerged before the formal advent of colonial rule, because of mutual African and European attempts to stimulate export commodities which served as 'legitimate' replacements to slaves. Rulers, professional traders and other sectors of the population in western Africa perceived advantages in maintaining the foreign trade nexus and access to imported goods. Of course, African propensity to trade with Europeans was not always restricted to the coast. Europeans knew that their trade with West Africa had its roots inland. Indeed, they overestimated the amount of wealth which could be readily made if they penetrated to these sources. This accounts for the commercial attention paid to the countryside above the Niger/Benue confluence during the 1880s and 1890s.

On the eastern side of the continent, the Indian Ocean trade was not exclusively directed towards European countries, nor was the long-distance trade out of East Africa controlled by Europeans or Afro-Europeans. The colonizers had to supplant the Arab, Swahili and Indian merchants. Experiences in East Africa underscored the premise that colonial activities first centred around parts of Africa which had a prior involvement in inter-continental exchange. The coastal area of greatest interest to Britain and Germany was that claimed by the Sultan of Zanzibar (now Tanzania), who was the foremost comprador for the supply of ivory, slaves and slave-grown cloves to Europeans, Arabs, Indians and Americans. Setting out from the Swahili coastal towns, European colonizers followed the Arab lead and sought the termini of the caravan routes in the interlacustrine region. By the mid 1880s, the Scramble was already taking place on Lake Victoria, on whose shores colonial enterprises were quickly grafted on to the already high level of African economic activity. When the British completed their railway from Mombasa to the Lake in 1902 (see Fig. 16.3), it attracted

2. R. G. Albion, 1959.

freight which had been part of the caravan traffic which previously had existed further south at Tanga and Bagamoyo. As a result of British competition, the Germans too began a coast–hinterland railway in 1905, and this faithfully traversed the slave and ivory route to Lake Tanganyika. Deep within Central Africa, it was also the Arab trading network which provided the European colonizers with their first economic base.

North Africa combined some of the features of East and West Africa, and displayed these in a heightened form. North African economies were as much part of a Mediterranean complex as they were part of the African trans-Saharan network. Prior experience with the European economy allowed segments of North African society to accommodate to the intensification of production for Europe and to the spread of European commodities in local markets. But the well-defined and exploitative ruling class was determined to defend state frontiers, even if willing to enter closer economic relations with Europeans. Therefore, colonial rule often advanced while maintaining North Africans in nominal authority, and the colonial economy was institutionalized before the complete subjugation of the indigenous polities.

The prelude to European colonization of Egypt goes back to the Napoleonic expedition of 1798. The European presence in the nineteenth century frustrated the economic innovations of Muḥammad ʿAlī. Long-staple cotton, introduced as a basis for industrialization, was by the 1840s the basis for integrating Egypt as a primary agricultural producer within the global capitalist system. After contributing to the failure of Egyptian industrialization, Britain and France sought control of Egypt's trade and entered the internal market in land and mortgages.[3] In Algeria, bitter resistance against the French was not yet over in the 1870s, but by then the country was already host to an entrenched settler agriculture, which was the principal feature of the Algerian colonial economy and which appeared in varying degrees in the rest of the Maghrib and in Libya. Tunisia entered the colonial epoch in 1881–2; while Morocco and Libya were partially annexed in 1912. The settler economy of the Maghrib was instituted at roughly thirty-year intervals – firstly in Algeria from 1860, then in Tunisia from 1890, and finally in Morocco from 1920.[4] Italian immigrants in Libya were fewer than their French counterparts in the Maghrib, and settler agriculture in Tripolitania had to await the complete defeat of the Libyan people by about 1931.

In spite of the broad span of years covering the starting-points of the colonial economies of respective North African territories, the conventionally assigned start of colonialism in the 1880s is still applicable. European powers reduced North African economies to colonial dependency mainly through the power of finance capital. North Africa entered the imperialist epoch when large amounts of capital were invested in the Suez

3. C. P. Issawi, 1963.
4. S. Amin, 1970, p. 256.

Canal and when loans were thrust upon the ruling class from Egypt to Morocco. This process was at its height by 1880, leading to the increasing subservience of the local regimes and ultimately to the assumption of sovereignty by one or other of the interested European nations. Therefore, while the colonial economy had a long and early period of genesis in North Africa, it cannot be said to have been definitively established until the 1890s when monopoly capital was to the fore in Europe. The same observations are applicable to Southern Africa.

By the time of imperialist partition, European settlement in South Africa involved tens of thousands of whites maintaining economic ties with Africans. African economic independence was undermined through the forcible alienation of land while African labour power was placed at the behest of the whites. During the nineteenth century, whites and blacks 'engaged in the formation of new economic and social bonds'.[5] These new bonds were at first colonial ones only in the sense that they bound together an alien minority and an indigenous majority in positions of super-ordination/subordination, but they soon became the type of colonial relations determined by the intrusion of large-scale capital due to the discovery of diamonds and gold.

The mining of diamonds and gold in South Africa could not have been carried on without modern technology and relatively heavy concentrations of capital. Neither the British government nor the mining monopolies which emerged from the 1870s had any intention of leaving mineral resources under the control of the Boers or of allowing priority to settler agricultural concerns with arable land, water, pasture and cattle, when the subsoil and African labour promised huge surpluses exportable to the metropolises. Boer social formations combined elements of the slave plantation, the feudal fief and the patriarchal community, in addition to capitalist commodity relations. After the Kimberley diamond finds (1870) and particularly after the Witwatersrand gold strike (1886), the bourgeoisie was determined to impose hegemony over all pre-capitalist social formations in South Africa, irrespective of race. The Anglo–Boer wars (1899–1902) were also anti-imperialist resistances, albeit in a perverse sense, since at the same time they sought the further entrenchment of settler colonialism. The defeat of Boer attempts at settler autonomy and the crushing of the African peoples of the region discussed in Chapter 9 marked the formation of a South African colonial economy which was unquestionably geared towards the transfer of raw materials, profits and other inputs to the capitalist metropolises.

Capital and coercion, *c.* 1900–*c.* 1920

African resistance helped substantially to dictate a slow pace of economic colonization for at least the three decades between 1880 and 1910. Besides,

5. C. W. de Kiewiet, 1965, p. 34.

immediate interest on the part of European monopoly capital was low. Africa commanded high priority during the mercantilist era of accumulation, but the relative obscurity of the nineteenth century persisted into the early years of colonialism, in spite of the increase in politico-economic control which followed upon partition and conquest. Viewed in terms of the global investment drive of monopoly capitalism up to the First World War, figures concerning the growth of the African colonial economy are unimpressive. The most relevant of these figures concerned imports and exports, since the import/export sector was the central feature of the colonial economy. The volume of goods imported into Africa rose sluggishly. With the exception of South Africa, import lists were not headed by machinery, plant or high-quality consumer items. Trade growth usually meant the extension of product lines characteristic of the mid nineteenth century, and those had not departed radically from the patterns of the slave trade era. Cotton piece-goods continued to dominate European exchanges with Africa, and in many places the import of cotton cloth never lost its priority throughout the period in question, although other items of domestic consumption, such as kitchen utensils, radios, bicycles and sewing machines were later to gain in popularity.

Production of export commodities within Africa advanced slowly and not always steadily. Natural rubber, for instance, enjoyed only a momentary prominence in West Africa during the 1880s. In East and Central Africa, the more substantial rubber industry fell into decay after an international crisis of prices in 1912–13; so that eventually only Liberia came to be identified with a product which was once highly touted by Europeans bent on the exploitation of Africa. The more usual performance graph of African staples in the colonial context comprised a first stage of insignificant quantities covering two decades of the present century, followed by a second stage of appreciable growth until 1930. Cotton, palm oil, coffee, groundnuts and cocoa illustrate such characteristics in the parts of the continent with which they are respectively associated.

Only small amounts of foreign capital were invested in African industry and agriculture during the early colonial period. South Africa was again the obvious exception, while to a lesser extent Algeria also attracted settler and mining capital. However, the case about capital scarcity can be over-stated,[6] since capital was not the only means of mobilizing labour and hence surplus in the African colonial economy. On the contrary, it was coercion which was principally responsible for bringing labour and cash crops to the market-place. In Europe, the decline of feudalism and the concomitant rise of capitalism witnessed the brutal destruction of peasant independence and the creation of a working class whose members had no alternative but to seek wage labour as a means of survival. In Africa, the autonomy of the indigenous village economy had to be destroyed even

6. S. H. Frankel, 1938.

more violently, since there were no internal social mechanisms transforming labour into a commodity. Such European funds as were available for investment in Africa had of course to enter into a relationship with African labour. But this capital was inadequate to induce labour through good wages and high prices; and from the African viewpoint, there was the inherent difficulty of making the traumatic leap from independent non-capitalist formations to quasi-capitalist formations in subjugation to the economic centres of imperialism. Therefore, African labour had to be recruited by the massive intervention of force – either nakedly or clothed by the laws of the new colonial regimes.

Undisguised forms of forced labour and barely disguised forms of slavery were prominent aspects of the entrenchment of the colonial economy in Africa. By the early years of this century, Portuguese 'contract labour' in São Tomé and the horrors of King Leopold's Congo Free State (now Zaire) were sufficiently scandalous that some reforms, or at least camouflage, were necessary to calm liberal opinion in Western Europe. Occasionally, the European working class joined African resisters to remedy such situation. The imperial German government succeeded in callously crushing African unrest in Cameroon, South West Africa (now Namibia) and German East Africa (now Tanzania) between 1904 and 1907; but thereafter Social Democrats intervened to reform the colonial order through legislation in the Reichstag. When the disposition of German colonies became an issue after 1918, Britain took the lead in arguing that Germany should be permanently deprived of its colonies because German colonialism was supposedly more coercive. Arguments were marshalled imputing the continuation of slavery and the generalized resort to flogging by German authorities. German response involved a defence against these charges and counter-allegations that the British (and the French) were guilty of such policies.[7] The reality is that the colonial mode of production incorporated an unusual amount of coercion both to recruit African labour and to maintain it at the point of production.

At the onset of colonial rule, private capital sometimes undertook policing and coercion on its own behalf. This was the case with the chartered and concession companies which were active in Southern and Central Africa and in Nigeria and German East Africa. At first glance, these companies appeared to be unchecked in the process of accumulation. However, they bore the cost of the armed interventions necessary for destroying African political independence and for laying the groundwork of the colonial economies. They were indeed unrestrained in their brutality, especially where labour recruitment was made more difficult by sparse population, as in French Congo (now Congo). But chartered companies could not cope with coercive state functions. European states had to assume direct responsibility for their colonial territories – usually during the 1890s –

7. H. Schnee, 1926.

and the locally established colonial state apparatus supervised the economy on behalf of private capitalists. The latter were usually compensated for relinquishing their political privileges, making it clear whose class interests were being advanced by the colonial regimes. Compensation was a means of financing these companies to place their enterprise on a more secure footing than had been the case when they were virtually in a state of war with the African people.

Metropolitan states and their colonial counterparts in Africa had to continue state coercion for economic exploitation, because the colonial economy had constantly to be hewn out in the face of opposition from Africans. In many places, African land had first to be seized before the settler-type socio-economic formations could flourish. The necessary infrastructure of roads and railways could be laid down only by government assistance, one aspect of which was the requisitioning of African labour. The use of taxation to build the money economy is a device which is too well known to require lengthy elaboration. Taxation undoubtedly provided the major constraint driving Africans initially into wage labour or cash-crop production; and subsequent increases in taxation deepened African involvement. Tax defaulters were at times used by private capital, but more usually by the state for the building and maintenance of administrative centres, roads and bridges.

Colonial states discriminated with regard to the types of force which they sanctioned in their colonies. Remnants of slavery were suppressed because they had become anachronistic. Whipping and physical abuse of Africans by European employers was frowned upon and usually legislated against by the second decade of the twentieth century. Colonial states, like any others, tried to retain a monopoly over legal forms of violence. At the same time, they sought to reassure European investors or settlers that the power of the state was unquestionably at their disposal. Thus, whipping under the orders of employers was merely replaced by judicial floggings, which were resorted to in far greater measure than was the case with workers in Europe. African labour codes remained backward throughout the 1930s; breach of contract was almost invariably treated not as a civil but as a criminal offence; and the unilateral termination of contract on the part of African workers continued to be regarded as 'desertion', with all of the militaristic implications of this term.

Some parts of Africa were more predisposed than others to a foreign-trade orientation, and some Africans had taken the initiative to establish colonial economic relations with Europeans. West Africans had been experimenting with new export lines since the early nineteenth century, while in contrast the population of German East Africa and the eastern Belgian Congo had turned to cotton and other export crops only when driven under the lash. The East African caravan traders had not brought as large a number of Africans into contact with European markets and European goods as was the case with West African pre-colonial trade.

Consequently, the local population had no strong initial inducement to withdraw a proportion of its labour from meeting its own needs. Even in West Africa, however, the colonial states often had to bring pressure to bear on cultivators to ensure that they joined the colonial economy and that they did so on terms which European capital dictated. The fact that partition took place against a background of prolonged and recurrent crisis in the capitalist economy was of significance in this context. For instance, Europeans were desirous of an extension of groundnut production in Senegal from 1883 onwards when falling prices obviously offered no inducement to Africans, and taxation had to provide the dynamic 'impetus'.[8] In areas where dependency was entrenched by pre-colonial trade, colonial economic relations spread more rapidly and the amount of force necessary for stimulating the colonial economy was reduced – although never entirely dispensed with.

The combination of European capital with coerced African labour registered a sizeable surplus in products destined for European consumption and export. Crops and minerals were exported and the profits expatriated because of the non-resident nature of the capital in the mining and plantation companies and the import/export houses. However, some of the accumulation was reinvested. This allowed Southern African capital to grow to massive proportions; and it speeded up monopolization among the West African commercial firms, enabling them to support, and integrate with manufacturing and distributing enterprises in Europe. In Algeria and South Africa and to a lesser extent in Tunisia, Kenya, Northern and Southern Rhodesia (now Zambia and Zimbabwe) and Nyasaland (now Malawi), the first flow of profits from the colonial economy also permitted higher living standards as well as greater economic viability for the white settlers.

African participation in the colonial economy, 1920–30

Coercion in economic relations was decisive in the formative years of the colonial economies in Africa; and it subsequently attained a prominence which it did not hold in the capitalist epicentres. At some point, each colonial economy became less dependent on external force and non-economic sanctions as the principal propellants. This turning-point was generally reached first in the British and German colonies, followed by the French and then the Belgian and Portuguese. Whenever it came, Africans contemplated the money economy as a fact of life – a new order which they could not reverse and which in many instances they were prepared to welcome. The new phase involved a choice between alternatives presented for earning a living and participating in the imposed economy of commodity production. Colonial Africa produced a wide range of agri-

8. M. A. Klein (ed.), 1968, p. 285.

cultural and mineral exports; but, for any African community, only a single option might have been locally available – perhaps tending vines on a European farm or growing an acre of cotton or descending daily into a mine shaft. Genuine alternatives were circumscribed by the ecology, and the policy of the given colonial administration. Nevertheless, Africans influenced the terms on which they were involved. They began by expressing their feelings on wage rates and prices; and ultimately they were drawn into discussing the variety of social and political questions which derived from and affected the colonial economy.

No precise date marks the onset of the above phase for the continent as a whole. It overlaps with conquest and with the period of ascendancy of coercive economic relations. In French Equatorial Africa and in the Portuguese territories, primitive coercion continued into the 1930s. The transition must be evaluated with reference to each colony and to geographic regions within the same colony. In several places, the colonial economy had been stabilized by the end of the first decade of the twentieth century. It was then interrupted by the First World War and restored thereafter at a higher level.

Mining dominated the post-war economies of Southern Africa, and came close to transforming the whole region into a single colonial economy. Firstly, the process of monopolization and cartelization assured the hegemony of large-scale capital in the then Union of South Africa, South West Africa and the Rhodesias. Secondly, the economic power of the mining centres was such that they required and were provided with a vast pool of labour which extended to areas where mining was not the principal economic activity – notably, the High Commission territories (Basutoland, now Lesotho; Bechuanaland, now Botswana; and Swaziland), Nyasaland, Mozambique and Angola. Collusion between the Portuguese and the regime in South Africa continued to ensure a regular and heavy flow of workers from Mozambique and Angola. This was reminiscent of slavery, but the paradoxical truth is that the trip to the mines became a highly desirable objective on the part of many Africans. Colonialism created great disparities within Southern Africa. Capital was introduced in heavy concentrations in a few spots, outside of which economic activity was at a low ebb. Wherever they resided, Africans fell under the obligation to meet taxes and they sought items of consumption which had to be purchased with cash. In this connection, the mines were often the only opportunity which presented itself.

The pattern of the colonial economies in the plantation sector had a great deal in common with that of the mining sector. Geographically the two overlapped in Southern Africa, and to some extent in the Belgian Congo and North Africa. Plantations combined large-scale capital with large quantities of labour. A powerful international firm controlled oil palm plantations in the Belgian Congo. Sisal plantations in German East Africa were dominated by big German firms backed by industrial and banking capital; and even when the industry became relatively decentralized under the British, sisal cultivation had still to be pursued with large acreages and a factory requiring significant capital investment. The state never left the side of the plantation owners, and gave them invaluable aid in procuring supplies of labour at the depressed wage rates which allowed for super-profits. Yet, when no viable alternative form of earning cash income existed in given parts of East, South and Central Africa, the plantation acted as an attraction to labour from far afield. Tanganyika had an influx from Nyasaland, Northern Rhodesia, Mozambique and Ruanda-Urundi (now Rwanda and Burundi). The British administration avoided regularizing labour supplies from Mozambique through treaty relations with the Portuguese government. Instead, they relied solely on the differential between Tanganyika and Mozambique, where the money economy was weak and where the persistence of blatant coercion for taxes and labour frightened Africans into crossing the frontier.

Wage-earners of all categories remained a tiny minority of the adult African population. Undoubtedly, cash-crop farming embraced the largest proportion of Africans – providing the basis for what has been termed the *économie de traite*, an economic system in which imported manufactured goods were directly exchanged for cash crops which were unprocessed or minimally processed.[9] Cash crops offered Africans slightly greater room for manoeuvre than wage labour. Occasionally, there was a choice between export crops. Food crops were grown for family consumption, sometimes for local cash sales and more rarely for export. African peasants used the limited flexibility in these circumstances to determine the nature and quantity of what they would plant or prepare for export. Prices were set by metropolitan agencies, but agricultural prices could be marginally affected where peasants switched from one crop to another or deployed stocks into a local market. In a few desperate instances, they turned to the technique of 'hold-up' of the sale of their produce, even though this meant serious loss to themselves.

Wherever there was a clash between peasant farming and hired labour, the African choice was almost invariably in favour of his own cultivation. Virtually all agricultural staples produced by peasants in Africa were associated with plantations elsewhere – notably, coffee in Latin America and palm oil in the East Indies. The strength of the African communities was responsible for the widespread incidence of peasant farms. Central Africa, with its low population density, was the arena for concession companies, infamous for forced labour. Such settled agriculture as was developed in Central Africa, continued with coercion over a rural proletariat, as on the sugar, sisal and cotton plantations of Mozambique and Angola, or it became capital-intensive, as in the Belgian Congo. It was possible for Lever Brothers to set up oil palm plantations in the Belgian

9. R. Dumont, 1966.

Congo from 1911. Their requests to have similar concessions in British West Africa were turned down, because the colonial administration correctly perceived that such a venture would necessitate the violent subjugation of thousands of inhabitants. Besides, the colonialists had early proof in West Africa of the success and viability of the African peasantry in producing an exportable surplus and lucrative returns to the European trading community. French persistence with settler agriculture in West Africa demonstrated its inferiority *vis-à-vis* African small-scale production. In East Africa, Nyasaland and Southern Rhodesia, the settler economy had to be subsidized and protected from African competition by legislation, without which it could not have secured enough labour. Where mining was merely a localized intrusion into an agricultural colonial economy, African choice was once more in favour of peasant production, giving rise, for example, to difficulties in the recruitment of local mine labour in Asante and the Western Province of the Gold Coast and Sukumaland (Tanganyika).

While it was still being forced on to some African communities, cash-crop farming was actively pursued by other Africans in the face of official indifference or hostility. They demanded the transport and marketing infrastructure, seizing the opportunity as soon as a railway line was completed. In many cases, they pioneered before the colonial governments had built bridges and feeder roads. Seed for new crops were taken from the colonial governments, from missionaries, from European farms and from Africans who were already engaged in cultivation. Cocoa and coffee are the two best known and most important of the cash crops whose extension relied mainly on African initiatives. Minor crops such as tea, tobacco and pyrethreum also bear out the same principle. Besides, Africans fought specifically for crops which were better money-earners than others. In the case of cocoa, this meant cultivating lands which were only marginally suitable. At other times, African preference precipitated a struggle against discriminatory colonial legislation. Thus, the latter part of the 1920s and the early 1930s saw a determined effort on the part of Africans in several highland areas of Tanganyika to cultivate *Arabica* coffee rather than hire their labour out or grow the less profitable *Robusta* variety. The Africans won literally by planting coffee trees faster than the colonial administration could destroy them.[10]

Where peasant cultivation established itself as the hegemonic form of the colonial economy, it functioned like mines and plantations in drawing labour resources from an area much wider than the actual zone of production. Senegambian groundnut farming attracted seasonal labour from the hinterland of the Senegal and Niger rivers; cocoa in the Gold Coast and in the Ivory Coast drew upon Upper Volta; while Ugandan coffee-growers turned to Ruanda-Urundi and Tanganyika to expand

10. W. Rodney, n.d.

output. Together, cash-crop farming and the wage labour of mines and agriculture accounted for the overwhelming majority of Africans who participated directly in the colonial economy. However, a host of other activities were generated or transformed by the new commodity relationships. It was rather late before the extensive forest reserves of the continent were seriously maximized, but an extractive timber industry arose early in Gabon and in varying degrees some such enterprise was pursued wherever forest reserves existed. The transportation network was a factor of more general significance. Thousands of Africans found wage employment at the ports on the trains, and – as road networks developed – as lorry drivers, especially when head porterage declined after the First World War.

As the colonial economy began to mature, hardly any sector of the African community could stand apart. In spite of their reputation for conservatism, all pastoral groups were drawn into the money economy by the 1920s, if not earlier. They sold meat for local consumption and occasionally for export along with hides. In the territories that were to become Somalia, this was the principal manifestation of the colonial economy. Fishing peoples were similarly affected. Trade in the traditional item of dried and smoked fish, like trade in meat and other foodstuffs, became dependent upon the cash of the main export earners, and sensitively reflected the seasonal buying power of peasants receiving their 'cocoa money', 'cotton money' and the like. Africans naturally exerted themselves to earn in a manner which was remunerative and congenial. Colonial administrations, missionaries and private companies employed junior clerks, artisans and (in the case of the first two) schoolteachers. The drive to obtain education was related to these job opportunities, especially since they were closely connected with the growing popularity of urban living. The drop-outs from primary schools or those who for one reason or another could not arrive at more prestigious paid employment filled the interstices of the colonial economy as domestic servants or as members of the police or army or by reaching out for forms of urban 'hustling' such as prostitution.

African reactions at the personal level remained fundamentally mere responses to they dynamic of the imposed colonial economy. They extended and strengthened that economy and confirmed the patterns of exploitation.

Wages were kept abysmally low. Upward trends were resisted; purchasing power was eroded partly because of the periodic inflations and partly because wages were depressed or allowed to lag behind commodity prices. Settlers and other resident Europeans and the managers of foreign enterprises combined to keep wages low and to keep labour semi-feudal through the issue of work-cards which severely limited the freedom to shift labour from one employer to another. Throughout the period in question, employers remained hostile to worker organizations which would have had an effect in raising the wage rate. The backward regime of task- or piece-work was widely pursued, and workers received no benefits for sickness, disability, unemployment and old age. Besides, the constant mobility of the largely migratory labour force, its low level of skill and the pervasiveness of racism all added to the disadvantages of the African worker in confronting the capitalists over wages and working conditions.

African peasants were up against the commercial system. The tendency of West African merchant firms to monopolize through 'pools' is well known, and trading companies throughout the continent guarded their interests by refusing to compete in such a way as to raise prices. Indeed, intermediaries such as the 'Asians' in East Africa and the Lebanese in West Africa also set prices and conditions among themselves so that the African peasant had little choice when he went to make his sales. The cash-crop farmer faced the prospect of being gypped at the weighing scales, in the processing stage (as with the cotton ginnery), in transportation, in the calculation of returns and in the repayment of loans or advances where applicable. African producers were also making retail purchases from the middlemen traders and the commercial firms. A fundamental inequality marked the exchange between the colonial economy and the metropolises. This unequal exchange was reflected in the disparity between the low remuneration Africans received and the relatively high cost of manufactured imports; and it also manifested itself in the low wage rate in the colonies as compared with the metropolises. Of course, unequal exchange was not a purely economic phenomenon. It derived from the asymmetry in political power and from the organizational and technological weaknesses of African producers.[11]

Africans were exploited by the colonial system irrespective of whether or not they produced an export surplus. Tax collection grew more and more far-reaching, and it was utilized not so much for services to the people as for building the state and economic infrastructure. The migrant labour of the mines, farms and plantations was secured at the expense of the previously autonomous village and local economies. Thereby, capital avoided the cost of production of labour. As in slavery, labour arrived fully formed from outside the capitalist system as such. Workers never received a living wage or any social benefits because they were part-time farmers, and throughout their working lives other members of their family remained self-supporting at the stagnant level which Europeans considered to be African subsistence. In the same way, cash crops which went into the local or export markets were generated as a surplus over and above peasant subsistence. For these reasons, it is misleading to conceptualize the colony as a 'dual economy' with distinct 'modern' and 'traditional' sectors.[12] The supposedly dynamic modern enclave and the backward traditional forms were dialectically interrelated and interdependent. Growth in the export sector was possible only because it could constantly

11. S. Amin, 1974; A. Emmanuel, 1972.
12. A. Mafeje, 1972; C. Meillassoux, 1972.

alienate value from the African communities in the form of land, labour, agricultural tribute and capital. The stagnation within these communities was induced rather than inherent. The 'traditional' no longer existed as such, with its labour drawn off and its rationale destroyed. Its agricultural production either dropped or failed to keep up with the growth of the population. In this way, isolated areas which registered no growth in capitalist terms were nevertheless affected by the presence of capitalism on the continent.

Dependence and repression, 1930–8

Colonial production relations were built within Africa over a span of years, during which the numerous self-sufficient African economies were either destroyed or transformed and subordinated. Their connections one with the other were broken, as in the case of the trans-Saharan trade and the commerce of the interlacustrine zone of East and Central Africa. Links previously existing between Africa and the rest of the world were also adversely affected, notably with regard to India and Arabia. A large number of discrete colonial economies came into being. Economic partition was not exactly the same as political partition, since stronger capitalist powers mulcted the colonies of weaker nations. Even Britain had to accept the penetration of United States capital into South Africa after the formation of the Anglo American Corporation in 1917. Nevertheless, the arbitrary political boundaries were generally taken to be the limits of the economies, each of which was small scale, artificial and separately oriented towards Europe. They lacked continental, regional or internal linkages. These were preconditions for external dependence – manifest in terms of capital, markets, technology, services and the decision-making process.

By definition, the colonial economy was an extension of that of the colonizing power. African economies were integrated first into that of their respective colonizer and secondly into the economies of the leading nations of the capitalist world. One of the most obvious connections was that of shipping. Only a handful of nations had maritime capitalists capable of operating during the era of imperialism. Portugal was almost completely out of the reckoning, while the United States considerably expanded on its nineteenth-century involvement in African trade. Competitive and monopolistic tendencies were juxtaposed in the shipping world. By subsidies and special shipping laws, countries sought to ensure that colonial commerce increased the tonnage of national shipping. Yet, early in the present century 'Conference lines' emerged as agencies for resolving competition and establishing monopolies over freight rates. Weaker nations had little or no representation within the Conference lines, while the Germans were major participants even after the loss of their African colonies.[13]

13. C. Leubuscher, 1963.

Banks were the pinnacle of early monopoly capitalism. They constituted the principal avenues for the export of African surplus, there being no obstacles to the free flow of capital funds out of the colonies. Private banks initially issued the specie in circulation in most colonies, until this became a central bank function with the establishment of statutory currency boards. The treasuries of the colonizing powers manipulated the currency reserves of the colonies in their own interests and ultimately in the interest of finance capital, since the investment of colonial reserves was made on the metropolitan money market. By underwriting marine insurance and by backing large capitalist ventures, banks retained hegemony over the colonial economy. They advanced credit notes to the white settlers and the non-African retail traders while for capitalist and above all pseudo-scientific racist reasons, they denied them to Africans. Colonial credit restriction ordinances sometimes confirmed this.

The workings of the colonial economy can be traced in large part through shipping companies and mining concerns. But for an understanding of why the exploitative institutions functioned as they did, one must analyse the economic structures of the colony as part of the global capitalist economy. Colonialism confined African colonies to the production of primary goods for export and in turn kept them dependent upon the developed capitalist countries for manufactures and technology. This rigid international division of labour could not be permanently maintained, and shifts towards processing and light manufacturing took place before the Second World War. Nevertheless, the period until 1935 came closer to illustrating the classic colonial international division of labour. Initiatives to crush oil seeds in Senegal were vigorously and for a long while successfully opposed by French manufacturers. In Tanganyika, a few sisal plantation capitalists were able to establish a rope-making factory in 1932, but as soon as the product reached the London market the outcry from British rope manufacturers was so great that the Colonial Office explicitly reasserted the principle that Africa must be confined to the production of export raw materials. With few exceptions, colonial production tended towards monoculture, with dependence on specialized markets in a few capitalist countries.

The international division of labour presented itself within the colonial economies as an ever-widening divergence between production and consumption. The bulk of the production within the growing money economy was never intended to meet local demand and consumption. Conversely, the variety of goods obtainable at the retail markets were increasingly of foreign origin. Local artisanship suffered heavily from European competition and manipulation, along lines already manifest in the pre-colonial period. As the colonial economy became firmly rooted in the 1920s, Africans were producing that which they did not consume and consuming that which they did not produce. In effect, domestic demand did not stimulate the maximization of domestic resources. As a further deleterious consequence, the colonizers wasted some African resources and ignored others, because their yardstick was the utility of the given resource to Europe rather than Africa. None of the major economic elements such as savings, investment, prices, incomes and output were correlated in response to domestic requirements. For these structural reasons, recent research by African economists and historians has challenged the old formulations of colonial development and has posited instead that colonialism produced economic dependence, lopsidedness and underdevelopment.[14]

The most significant event in the evolution of African economies in the inter-war period was the great depression of 1929–33. When this hit the interdependent capitalist economies, it necessarily struck at the dependent African colonial economies – boldly illumining their extent and character in the process.

Cyclical crises in the world economy since the nineteenth century had the effect of slowing growth in Africa and imposing hardships on Africans already attached to the money nexus. It was the severity of these tendencies which was new in 1930 when the repercussions were felt on the African continent. The depression entered via the most advanced sectors of capitalism in Africa – the mines, plantations and primary cash-crop areas. However, it spread through all the secondary and tertiary channels, causing hardships to Africans who sold food to workers or to other farmers and to pastoralists who found it uneconomical to part with their livestock at the prevailing prices. Africans specializing in trade were all quickly affected, even where the trade was in an indigenous product such as kola. The fact is that the supposedly traditional Hausa or Dyula traders were subjugated to the colonial economy. They were successful to the extent that they could wrestle with the new order and transform themselves – for example, by becoming lorry-owners – but they were defenceless when a major external factor such as the depression caused a contraction of the currency made available to their customers by cash-crop farming and wages.

Each participant in the colonial economy took steps to counter the effects of the depression. The initiative lay with the capitalist firms. Banks and commercial houses cut back on their operations, so that in cash-crop areas they maintained a presence in key centres like Dakar, Lagos and Nairobi, while branches up-country and in lesser capitals were closed. Above all, the export houses achieved economy at the expense of the peasants by slashing producer prices when the 1930 crop came to market. As employers, they retrenched workers and cut wages drastically. Except in the gold industry, which was avidly pursued, retrenchment was the major response of all major employers in various spheres of production. Wage labour had increased considerably after the First World War, but declined by 50% or more between 1931 and 1934. Meanwhile, although many settlers and small businesses went bankrupt, the principal beneficiaries of the colonial system continued to make reduced but substantial profits.

14. W. Rodney, 1972; J. Rweyemamu, 1974; E. A. Brett, 1973.

Africans reacted to the crisis by struggling against attempted European solutions. To deal with lowered wages, workers resorted to the strike weapon with greater frequency and in larger numbers, in spite of the non-existence or lack of development of trade unions. Relatively little has been written on the spontaneous struggle of the African working class before the coming of trade unions,[15] but business cycles and wars appear to have sharpened conflict, judging from unrest during the depression of 1920–1, during the major depression of 1929–33, and once more during the 1938 recession. Similarly, it could be no mere coincidence that farmers on the Gold Coast held up their cocoa and boycotted foreign stores in 1920–1 and again in 1930 and 1938. Foreign firms were determined that accumulation should continue under all circumstances, while workers and peasants in entrenched cash-crop environments tried to counter impoverishment and defended any small gains which might have been made in better years.

Another line of defence on the part of Africans was withdrawal from the money economy. Areas which had been recently brought into the money economy or which were only lightly touched were the first to retreat. The same phenomenon had previously occurred at the end of the First World War, leaving colonial governments with the task of re-establishing the colonial economy in some regions. Many Tanganyikan peasants, who had a much lower level of involvement in money exchanges than their brothers on the Gold Coast, simply sought to abandon cash-crop farming in the years after 1930. In this they were not very successful, because the power of the colonial state was brought in to tilt the scales against what was considered to be a reversion to barbarism. Campaigns to 'grow more crops' were instituted, and bureaucratic sanctions were thinly veiled forms of force for the expansion of acreages in the face of falling prices. This type of campaign was backed not merely by merchants but also by industrialists requiring raw material and by powerful metropolitan organizations such as the Empire Cotton Growing Association, which continued to be active in the years after the slump.

Most capital projects were suspended during the depression; and, where this was not so, the investment was associated with the expansion of cheap primary production and was undertaken with the use of forced labour, as with the French Office du Niger irrigation project. There was an overall revival of coercion in economic relations, indicating that the colonial economy had to be buttressed by non-economic means when in crisis. African labour and taxes kept the railways viable and maintained colonial revenues. Yet, the African masses suffered most from the cutback on already skimpy social services, such as medicine and education, and they had to pay more for these services. In the years of recovery after 1934, wages, prices and facilities for Africans remained retrenched in contrast to the return to high profit levels for private capital.

15. H. Deutschland, 1970.

Colonial governments granted minimum relief to Africans suffering from the depression. They suspended tax collection, and they subsidised prices, as the French did for groundnuts. They also tried to moderate the crudest forms of middleman exploitation. These measures arose out of necessity, since no money was circulating and since lower prices in one country forced desperate peasants to march long distances and smuggle their produce out through an area where there was some marginal advantage. As far as the middlemen were concerned, the governments needed to restrain them from cornering the reduced profit rather than let it be exported. However, in East Africa the 'Asian' merchants were essential for keeping the money economy intact and avoiding reversion to barter, just as their capital had been the original basis for the extension of specie and small-scale money exchanges throughout the region.[16] In the final analysis, therefore, the British administration co-operated to protect the interests of these retailers and produce buyers. Africans emerged from the depression subject to more bureaucratic controls (designed to increase production) and still entirely vulnerable to manipulation by the import/export firms and their local compradors.

The dependence illustrated by the great depression indicates the degree of change in the lives of Africans some fifty years after the coming of colonialism. The impact in the early years was often slight, but major transformation was wrought by colonialism as it advanced. Investigation into the economy has been given low priority both during the colonial economy and during the nationalist phase when there was greater commitment to the study of African history from an indigenous perspective. This shortcoming has inhibited discussion on the significance of the colonial experience, since many changes were economic, while others of a political, social or cultural nature had their basis in economic activity. Consequent upon the growth of the money economy, African society became more differentiated and new classes were formed. There was limited proletarianization in various parts of the continent, and there was widespread peasantization. The latter held within it the seeds of further differentiation. As in all peasant communities within a capitalist orbit, big peasants arose at the expense of small peasants and landless labourers. All of the cash-crop areas witnessed during the 1920s the emergence of big peasants owning land privately, employing labour and occasionally capable of new techniques. A second well-known stratum comprised the privileged few who received an education in the first years of colonialism, when certain skills were being introduced to make the colonial economy function. Finally, it is to be noted that the distribution networks were manned at the lowest levels by Africans, who achieved prominence in West and North Africa. Successful cash-crop farmers, African traders and the educated elite together created the embryonic petty bourgeoisie. They often had roots in the old possessor classes in quasi-feudal parts of Africa, and as such

16. J. S. Mangat, 1969.

were often pampered by the Europeans. But the more portentous fact was that, irrespective of colonial policy, the operation of the economy favoured the advance of these strata, who were economically and culturally part of the dependent colonial order.

15

The colonial economy of the former French, Belgian and Portuguese zones, 1914–35

C. COQUERY-VIDROVITCH

Both in their general configuration and from the standpoint of colonial policy, the French, Belgian and Portuguese colonies were similar in a number of ways.* They were colonies or federations of enormous geographical area, though in terms of population generally smaller than the average for British Africa, especially French Equatorial Africa (AEF) and Angola (see Fig. 15.1).[1] Mozambique and Ruanda-Urundi (now Rwanda and Burundi) served as reservoirs of labour for neighbouring Northern and Southern Rhodesia (now Zambia and Zimbabwe) and the Belgian Congo (now Zaire), in the same way that the Voltaic Zone (now Upper Volta) of French West Africa (AOF) supplied Mossi workers for the cocoa plantations of the Ivory Coast and the Gold Coast (now Ghana).[2]

Indeed, exploitation of these territories based on high investment was relatively recent. Not much capital had been risked there before the First World War, as Table 15.1 indicates.

In the economic field, the period was decisive; its beginning and end were marked by two profound traumas. The first – the World War – served to trigger off, despite the brief but acute crisis of 1921–2, an unprecedented colonial boom which in fact reflected the prosperity of the metropolitan countries during the 1920s. Although spectacular, this expansion was relatively short-lived, ending with the long slump which followed the collapse ushered in by the 1930 crisis. All this led to great disruption in economic as well as in social and ideological terms. By the end of the period, the relations of Francophone and Lusophone Africa with the outside world were transformed. The colonies, which on the whole had not been very dependent on the metropolitan countries, began from this time to

---

* Editor's note: this chapter was written in 1974 and revised in 1980.

1. In 1936, the population density was 4.2 per sq km in the Belgian Congo, 2.8 in French Black Africa, 2.4 in Angola, according to S. H. Frankel, 1938, pp. 170 and 202–3.

2. Mozambique and Ruanda-Urundi had population densities of 5.1 and 6.8 per sq km respectively in 1936. Account must also be taken in AOF of the difference between the semi-desert region of the Sahel and the more fertile coastal zone, where the high density of little Togo (14.4 per sq km) is a typical example. ibid.

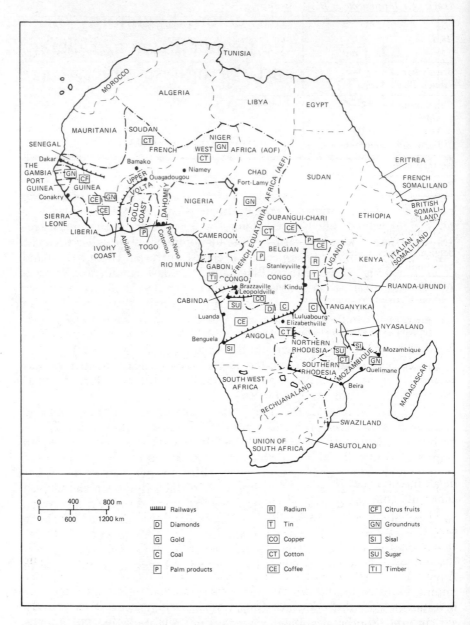

FIG. 15.1 *The resources of the French, Belgian and Portuguese colonies (after Grandidier, 1934)*

352

TABLE 15.1 *Investments in Black Africa (£mn)*

Area	Accumulated investments 1870–1913[1]	Accumulated investments 1914–36	% total investments in Black Africa, 1936
British Africa	695	421[2]	77
French Black Africa[3]	25	29.5	5.7
including:			
AOF		30.4[4]	2.5
AEF		21.2[4]	1.7[9]
Togo and Cameroon		18.6[4,5]	
German colonies	85		
Portuguese colonies		66.7	5.4
including:			
Angola	very little	31.9[4,6]	2.6
Mozambique		34.7[4,7]	2.8
Belgian colonies: Congo, Urundi	40	94.4[8]	11.7
TOTAL (Non-British territories)	at least 150	190	22.9

1. According to S. H. Frankel, 1938, pp. 149–59; G. Paish, 1909, 1910–11.
2. Excluding German investments in South West Africa (£126.5mn) and in Tanganyika (£33.5mn), S. H. Frankel, 1938, pp. 202–3.
3. Frankel's appraisal of the capital invested in French Black Africa is none the less clearly under-valued (perhaps by one-third) because it takes into account only the companies quoted on the Stock Exchange.
4. 1870–1936.
5. Including approximately £15.8mn of earlier German investments.
6. Including approximately £16mn of British capital.
7. £20mn of British capital.
8. Less the German investments in Ruanda-Urundi (£9mn).
9. AEF and Cameroon.

be an integral part of the western capitalist system in the framework of a coherent economic system of colonial exploitation.

The dominant trait of the period was the emphasis on the import of capital equipment which was as profitable to the metropolitan countries as it was sorely trying for the colonies. But there was a contrast between the mining countries (particularly the Belgian Congo; to a minor extent Angola and – as the outlet for the Rand – Mozambique), in which the mining industry or the railway infrastructure entailed a higher level of investment, and the other territories, which still remained exclusively agricultural. Another factor of diversity lay in the mode of exploitation; AEF and the Congo long remained countries exploited by monopoly companies, whereas AOF and little Ruanda-Urundi were subjected to the competitive system of the *économie de traite*, or the 'milking economy', that is, an economy based on the export of primary agricultural commodities produced by traditional means and the import of consumer goods. The Portuguese colonies, relatively well endowed, suffered chiefly from dependence on an 'underdeveloped' metropolis that was itself unable to finance their exploitation.

The financing of capital equipment

The accompanying graphs (see Fig. 15.2) reveal a remarkable similarity in foreign trade between the Belgian Congo and AOF amounting to approximately £20 million on the eve of the depression. On the other hand, the figures for Angola and AEF were four to five times lower. In 1930 the foreign trade of Angola, at 475 000 contos, represented something less than £5 million as against £4.3 million for AEF. By comparison, the trade of little Ruanda-Urundi seems almost non-existent. In 1930, it stood at B.frs 70 million, or only £360 000.

But all the graphs reveal one constant for the decade 1920–30, even though inflation tends to exaggerate the value of imported goods in relation to their volume (cf. the Ruanda-Urundi curves – the conversion into sterling having the advantage of cancelling the effects of continental inflation on the other figures). In all the territories an adverse trade balance – appearing at the turning-point of the First World War and culminating during the years of maximum economic euphoria of 1925–30 – reflected the emphasis placed on capital-goods investment. It is superfluous to point out the importance during this period of the transport infrastructure sector, especially ports, railways and roads. This was a new phenomenon linked with the introduction of motor transport. In the Belgian Congo, 65% of the accumulated investments in 1932 were in mines, transport and real estate or secondary agricultural or commercial undertakings related to the expansion of railways or mines. For the years 1927–30, goods imported for public works accounted on average for 47% of the special imports. In 1929, capital goods such as coal and coke, mineral oils, metal products, machines, ships and vehicles constituted nearly half of all imports,[3] as opposed to only a third in AOF. As a result, the cumulative capital invested in the Belgian Congo rose sharply from B.frs 1215 million before the war to more than 3000 million gold francs in 1935.[4] Already increasing rapidly between 1920 and 1924, it more than doubled between 1924 and 1929, bordering on the maximum of the inter-war period, before the abrupt drop during the depression. The annual capital subscribed by Belgian companies fell from B.frs 1400 million in 1929 to B.frs 276 million in 1932, that is, from about 30 million to 50 million gold francs.

3. F. Passelecq, 1932, Vol. I, pp. 417–20.
4. S. H. Frankel, 1938, p. 167.

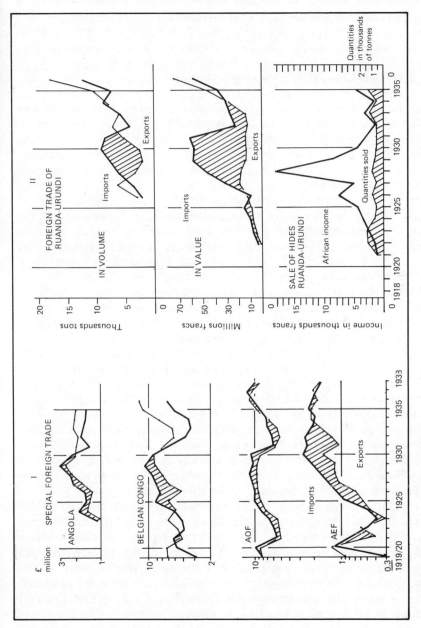

FIG. 15.2 Colonial foreign trade of former French, Belgian and Portuguese zones (after J. P. Chretien, 1970)

355

TABLE 15.2 *Evolution of capital invested in the Belgian Congo (1950 B.frs 'ooomn)*

1920	1924	1929	1933	1938
6.6	11	29.7	30.9	30

Source: J. P. Peemans, 1968, p. 383.

But the colonies were poor from the financial point of view. Despite the increase in customs revenue associated with the rise in foreign trade, and particularly the increase in head tax, they were in no position to take on the financing of expansion by themselves. Development of capital equipment went hand in hand with an intensive policy of borrowing from the metropolitan countries.

Paradoxically, the main effort was undertaken just at the time of the great depression. Started in the Belgian Congo during the euphoria of the last years of the decade, the policy of borrowing reached a peak there between 1928 and 1932. From 1931, AOF in turn began a serious effort at borrowing; the débâcle of the 1930s having convinced the government of the urgent need for a capital investment programme.

Whereas the public debt of the Belgian Congo amounted in 1909 to less than B.frs 250 million, the colony borrowed, especially after 1928, approximately B.frs 3500 million or nearly 600 million Belgian gold francs.[5] Despite the fact that it had a larger area and a larger population, AOF had to make do with a quarter of this amount after 1920, or only a third of the sum authorized by law. An amount of B.frs 630 million or approximately 120 million French gold francs out of the B.frs 1750 million of the time authorized between the two wars was actually paid-up in 1935. This was still only half the figure for AEF which, both more poverty-stricken and patterned more on the Belgian example, had begun a policy of borrowing for infrastructure projects earlier. The loans were spent almost entirely on the construction of the Congo–Océan railway, that is, approximately 300 million gold francs borrowed between 1920 and 1936, or virtually the whole of the amounts legally authorized.

The result was an increase in the external debt which became all the more alarming for budgetary equilibrium as the payments became heavier in the midst of the depression, precisely when export prices fell sharply. In 1933, the annual instalment of the Congolese debt (estimated at B.frs 298 million) represented nearly 88% of the budgetary receipts of the colony, or almost half its expenditure or nearly half the value of its exports. Much less heavy, the amounts payable by AOF (F.frs 40 million in 1933) amounted to more than a third of its general budget during the worst years of the depression but only 5 to 8% of the whole of the revenue of AOF including all budgets, general and territorial. Those of AEF then exceeded 80% (81% of the global budget in 1934). The Portuguese terri-

5. During the period, parity oscillated around the rate 100 Belgian francs = 70 French francs.

tories, on which there is little precise information, were also overwhelmed by debt. In 1936, Angola owed a total of almost 1 million contos which is equal to £8.7 million or 220 million French gold francs. This is distinctly more than the debt of AOF but was supported by only a seventh of the latter's exports,[6] but less than half of that of the Belgian Congo which had a similar colonial budget.

In general, the increase in the burden of instalments during the depression years was distinctly more rapid than in the most debt-ridden of the British territories; as indicated in Table 15.3.

TABLE 15.3 *Annual instalments on debts: comparative charges on various territories in 1928 and 1935, expressed as percentages*

	Belgian Congo			AOF			AEF		
	1928	1935	% rate of increase	1928	1935	% rate of increase	1928	1935	% rate of increase
Revenue	20.6	79.3	384	2.5	6.8	367	16.6	47.1	284
Exports (special)	9.5	26.8	282	1.5	6.9	460	17.2	46.6	271

Source: S. H. Frankel, 1938, p. 182, and C. Coquery-Vidrovitch, forthcoming.

Although difficult to make because of currency fluctuations, a comparison between the Belgian Congo and AOF shows the differences in the modes of exploitation. Considered more profitable, and in any case much more avid for capital, the Belgian Congo nevertheless presented obvious economic weaknesses. Her indebtedness was infinitely heavier than that of AOF while the volume of her export trade was somewhat less despite the importance of the mining industries. Above all, her budgetary revenues were substantially more limited owing to lower customs duties and a lighter taxation of the African population. The result was a more serious financial deficit at the time of the depression.

TABLE 15.4 *Some colonial statistics (F.frs mn)*

	AOF			Belgian Congo		
	1928	1935	Change %	1928	1935	Change %
Debt instalment	17.2	54.8	+218	87	225	+158
Ordinary budget receipts	723	593	−18	420	290	−21
Value of exports	1144	698	−39	915	850	−7
Customs revenues	213	142	−33	?	79	
Capitation tax	143	152	+6	75(?)	64	−15

6. S. H. Frankel, 1938, p. 371; J. Duffy, 1962, pp. 139 *et seq.*

This apparent inconsistency is accounted for, in fact, by the distortion of the level of exploitation. The Congo was reaching the stage of exploitation by capital, whereas AOF was still more or less at the stage of the 'milking economy'. On the eve of the depression, the commercial superiority of the French federation, more than half of which (52.7% in 1928) was still based on the export of Senegalese groundnuts, was proof of the profitability of a short-sighted commercial policy limited to the exploitation of the profit margins between imported goods sold at high prices to African producers, and the purchase at low prices of crops the production of which was left to the traditional sector (*économie de traite*). This colony was supposed to be self-sufficient, since the basis of colonization was a profit-yield to the metropolitan state; so it lived off customs duties drawn from expanding trade, and also off heavy taxation. Despite the depression, which brought business to a standstill and at the same time wiped out African revenues, the metropolitan state refused any subsidy in aid. In the same way, the last subsidy paid out to the wretched AEF – which received in all, from 1910 to 1934, F.frs 375 million – occurred in 1928, the metropolitan state resigning itself only to assuming the servicing of loans at the height of the depression to the value of F.frs 80 million in 1935.[7]

But the head tax continued to increase throughout the depression, or at least it scarcely receded: for AOF it was F.frs 156 million in 1929, F.frs 181 million in 1931, its lowest point being F.frs 153 million in 1935. Though France finally agreed to make efforts to invest in the African colonies, this was strictly a temporary measure which took the form of state-guaranteed loans payable after fifty years at a rate of 4–5.5%. In other words, the French colonies were still essentially required to pay for their own capital equipment. Of course AEF was so poverty-stricken that the metropolitan state finally took over its debt almost in its entirety. But in AOF the French share of expenses was reduced between 1931 and 1936 to only 16% of the total, allowing for servicing of the debt. In other words, it was indeed the labour of the inhabitants that was first used to develop the territory.

Since this archaic economy, that is, an economy that depended on taxation and plundering instead of production and investment, was fragile, the depression triggered off its bankruptcy. In 1934, the rapporteur of the colonial budget informed the French Chamber of Deputies that the colonies were at the end of their tether, and recommended the financing of capital equipment by the state. In the same year, the Economic Conference of Metropolitan and Overseas France was held to make the first attempt at setting up a programme of support. But this programme was in fact only carried out after the Second World War.[8]

Although the depression was sudden and severe in the Belgian Congo, with the value of exports falling by almost two-thirds, from B.frs 1511

7. A. Moeller, 1938, pp. 3–5.
8. C. Coquery-Vidrovitch and H. Moniot, 1974, pp. 407–9.

million to B.frs 658 million between 1930 and 1933, it was less pronounced in relative value and was more quickly overcome. This is evident from the fact that exports rose again to B.frs 1203 million in 1935. To be sure, the Belgian Congo still remained only moderately productive. Compared with the British colonies in Southern Africa, its mining yield was, to say the least, still very low. Although in 1935 this yield represented 62% of the total value of the Belgian Congo's exports, and, in the case of Angola 30%, these two territories together still exported a mere 6% of the total value of the mining products of black Africa.

TABLE 15.5 *Relative importance of the foreign trade (total of imports and exports) of various colonies (expressed as percentage of total trade of black Africa)*

	AOF	*Belgian Congo*	*Angola*
1928	5.9	4.7	1.3
1935	5.8	4.1	1.1

The Belgian colony, where economic activity was already of the capitalist type, nevertheless had the advantage of its technological advance and its policy of long-term investments. The grave budgetary crisis of the 1930s was due more to the reduction in the flow of investments than in the value of exports. The colony's own revenues, lower than in AOF, were compensated for by the great volume of private capital and the support of the state which, in addition to loans, made up the deficit through heavy subsidies. These amounted to B.frs 687 million between 1933 and 1937; not including a colonial lottery, the profits from which (B.frs 271 million) served to cover part of the deficits of 1934 and 1935 (B.frs 673 million, or 47% of regular expenditures). From 1914 to 1935, the Congo 'cost' Belgium, exclusive of loans, a total of 112.5 million gold francs, or nearly half the total metropolitan expenditure between 1908 and 1950.[9]

In short, even though, or rather because, it 'cost Belgium more', the Congo, unlike the French federations, was able to 'take off' as soon as industry recovered after the depression. Nevertheless, one must not exaggerate this phenomenon. The fact that, following the depression, exports everywhere again took the lead over imports, proved that the capital equipment of the preceding phase had only helped develop to a further stage a policy still basically centred on exploitation from outside rather than on the development of the territories for their own benefit.

The workers' burden

This period – falling between two difficult phases marked by increasing exploitation of the workers, the First World War and the depression – was hard on the Africans. At that time of colonial 'development', Africans

9. A. Moeller, 1938; see also J. Stengers, 1957, p. 394.

interested the colonizers only to the extent that they represented a commodity or an instrument of production. It was, moreover, to ensure their efficiency that the first measures for the protection of labour were taken. But the precarious living standard was vulnerable to the slightest upset, and collapsed with the depression. As a French administrator remarked, 'I have always noticed that whenever the budget of a native family was properly and regularly kept, it never managed to make ends meet. The life of a native is, in fact, a miracle.'[10]

Labour

Although forced labour was officially repudiated everywhere, the shortage of labour encouraged coercion, whether direct or imposed through the expedient of taxes that had to be paid.

Compulsory service and provision of crops

Everywhere, the use of unpaid labour was common. The French federations, after the war, officially sanctioned unpaid labour for projects of local or colonial interest. Initially set at seven days per year, labour demands soon rose to twelve days in AOF or fifteen days in AEF. The Decree of 6 October 1922, revised on 7 January 1925, provided for the possibility of individuals purchasing exemption at the rate of 50 centimes to two francs per day, according to the degree of penetration of the money economy.

The obligation, limited in itself, was the more unpopular because of the fact that the feeding of the workers, previously not even considered, remained the women's responsibility if the work was within a day's walking distance from the village. This labour obligation was in addition to forced (but paid) recruitment for railway work. From 1921 to 1932, 127 250 men representing a total absence of 138 125 years were recruited in AEF for building the Congo–Océan railway; probably some 20 000 lives were lost before 1928.[11] In AOF such labour obligations were accompanied by the system known as 'the second portion of the contingent', under which workers could be drafted for 'social and utilitarian' purposes from the half of the quota not called up for military service.[12] Finally, on the eve of the depression, porterage, although decreasing in most places, was still wreaking havoc in Ruanda, where compulsory free labour nevertheless declined from twenty-nine to thirteen days per year.[13]

The period was also characterized by the institution of compulsory

10. M. Urvoy, 1940.
11. G. Sautter, 1967.
12. Decree of 31 October 1926. This system was also used in Madagascar.
13. P. de Dekker, 1974. The annual number of days of labour required declined from fifteen in 1928 to thirteen in 1931. But in the Belgian Congo, compulsory free labour rose to 120 days a year during the Second World War. M. Merlier, 1962, p. 95.

cultivation of crops. The principle, which originated as early as the end of the nineteenth century in the Belgian Congo, was revived during the First World War, following a mission carried out in 1915 in Uganda and the Gold Coast with respect to cotton and cocoa respectively.[14] The compulsory cultivation of rice was introduced in the Eastern Province, and that of cotton spread from the Maniema and the Uele to the entire colony. In 1930, the 'state fields' covered more than a million hectares; as a result the Congo produced 15000 tonnes of rice and 30000 tonnes of cotton; some ten companies controlled 111 ginning mills. The innovation was particularly unpopular but was none the less adopted in the French federations. It was initiated in 1916 in connection with the 'war effort'. That it survived was due, from the start, to the artificial maintenance of prices by means of French subsidies. At the same time, by contrast, the government of Nyasaland (now Malawi) abandoned subsidies for cotton production, and they were also reduced in the Belgian Congo. In AEF at the instigation of the administrator Felix Eboué (1927–8), four companies were given a purchasing monopoly over vast 'protected zones' in exchange for minimum capital equipment.[15] This scheme followed the Belgian pattern of monopolies in the Congo which sprang from the decree of 1 August 1921.

The compulsory cultivation of cotton, started in the same period in AOF, was also one of the major ideas of the Office du Niger (1933). There again, specially developed village centres first established in 1937 were a lamentable failure, owing to the impossibility of solving the demographic problem and because of the low yields of an inferior cotton whose selling price fell from 1.25 francs in 1928 to 90 centimes in 1929, 70 centimes in 1931 and only 60 centimes from 1933 to 1936.

TABLE 15.6 *AOF cotton: average 5 years' exports (tonnes)*

1910–14	1915–19	1920–4	1925–9	1930–4	1935–9	1954
189	467	895	3500	2500	3900	1300

Source: San Marco, 1940.

Throughout the Portuguese colonies, the failure of the administrative authorities to ensure the distribution of seed or to provide technical instruction, explains the inefficiency of the system. It nevertheless prevailed in a particularly archaic form in the territory of the Mozambique Company, which was created in 1891 and enjoyed fifty-year sovereign rights over 160000 sq km. Thus, it was the only company in the world that was still exercising sovereign powers by 1930, and it also accounted for 11.6% of the colony's total trade from 1918 to 1927, controlling 6.5% of the territory and the labour of 4% of the population.[16]

14. F. Passelecq, 1932, Vol. I, p. 281.
15. C. Coquery-Vidrovitch, 1972, pp. 475–7.
16. E. Bohm, 1938, p. 155.

Results were not always too disappointing. It was at the turning-point of the great depression that large-scale production, still using the system of compulsory planting, was launched for the production of cocoa, and especially coffee in the Ivory Coast, Cameroon and Ruanda-Urundi. In the latter territory, the 'coffee programme', launched on an experimental basis in 1925 (with an obligation on each chief or sub-chief to cultivate a half-hectare), was systematized as soon as the first effects of the depression were felt.

TABLE 15.7 *Ruanda coffee exports (tonnes)*

1929	*1932*	*1935*	*1936*	*1937*
50	100	375	1150	2000

Source: G. Molitor, 1937.

The rapid take-off of speculative crop-raising can be explained first because the Africans were overwhelmed by their burdens and had no other remedy at the worst periods of the depression than to compensate for the drop in their income by increasing production, thereby offsetting the fall in money values. But at the end of the depression, the peasants, finally convinced of the profitability of their efforts, voluntarily took to producing the new crops. The spectacular nature of the take-off in AOF in 1936 is indicated in Table 15.8.

TABLE 15.8 *AOF exports (tonnes)*

	1935	*1936*
Coffee	5300	43500
Cocoa	6700	49700

Source: 'L'evolution des exportations de l'AOF de 1905 à 1957.' *Institut d'Emission de l'AOF et du Togo*, no. 36, July 1958.

This speculative crop-raising guaranteed the minimum of ready money required for the head tax and the satisfaction of primary consumption needs, both of which in turn led to the elimination of forced crop-cultivation.

In the circumstances, the role of institutions intended to aid producers, such as the Crédit Agricole (organized in 1931 in AOF, AEF and in the Cameroon) to guarantee short- and medium-term production operations while favouring the transformation to private property, was by no means negligible. Only farmers belonging to a legally recognized association (Société de Prévoyance, Association agricole, etc.) and owners of property registered in their own names (and not family inheritances) were eligible for aid.[17] In the same way, the Sociétés Indigènes de Prévoyance, whose

17. Decree of 26 June 1931. M. Desanti, 1940.

numbers in AOF increased fivefold in four years (from twenty-two in 1929 to 101 in 1933 and 104 in 1936), also played a role, though too often they interested the 'commandant de cercle' solely from the standpoint of the additional resources resulting from compulsory subscriptions. In Senegal in 1940, only two or three of them – in Sine-Saloum – were able to play a useful role.[18] Up to that time, compulsory labour, whether in the fields, the mines or on railway projects, remained the general rule.

The labour system and legislation

In French Africa, the administration controlled recruitment which in theory, after 1921 in AEF, could not exceed 'one-third of the able-bodied male population having reached adult age'. In Gabon, from 1926 onwards, with the increased exploitation of forests, the new owners were warned that they opened their logging sites 'at their own risk, in full awareness that they might not find the labour they needed on the spot'.[19]

In the Belgian Congo, recruiting was limited to 25% of the 'able-bodied adult males'. The limit was reduced to 10% in the middle of the decade because of the drying-up of the labour pool; but in general the official quota was very considerably exceeded.[20] In the Portuguese colonies, a subtle distinction was established between 'penal labour' reserved for convicts, and the labour – 'a moral and social obligation' – of men between 14 and 60 years of age, for at least six months per year.[21] The state was 'to have no scruples about obliging and if necessary forcing the Negro savages of Africa to work, that is, to improve themselves through labour in order to improve their means of existence, to civilize themselves'.[22]

The plague of recruiters was particularly prevalent in the Congo, where the state delegated its powers of recruiting to companies such as the Bourse du Travail du Katanga (BTK) a private agency recruiting for the mines in the rural zones. In 1926, to ease the labour shortage, the government awarded to the Union Minière du Haut Katanga (UMHK) the recruiting monopoly in Maniema (Eastern Province) and in Ruanda-Urundi.[23] Finally, in the Portuguese colonies, scandals broke out periodically, such as the scandal of forced and slave labour on the cocoa plantations of São Tomé and Principe at the turn of the twentieth century. These took between 2000 and 4000 'voluntary recruits' each year. In accordance with its policy of neo-slavery, Portugal rejected, in 1930, the 'Recommendation

18. M. Tupinier, 1940.
19. G. G. Antonetti, 1926, 1927.
20. M. Merlier, 1962, pp. 134–5. The notion of 'adult' was loose, as it designated any individual having 'reached normal adult development'. H. Leonard, 1934, p. 382.
21. Labour Code in 1911. *Le régime et l'organisation du travail des indigénes dans les colonies tropicales*, Brussels, 1929, pp. 224–315.
22. Recommendation of the Commission, incorporated into the Labour Code of 14 October 1914; cited by J. Duffy, 1962, p. 132.
23. B. Fetter, 1976, p. 90.

concerning the indirect coercion of Labour' proposed by the Geneva International Conference. In 1947, there was the famous protest of Henrique Galvão, the member of parliament for Angola. When he reported that 2 million Africans had been expatriated from the Portuguese colonies, he was arrested as a result in 1952.[24] In 1903, recruitment in Mozambique of miners for the Transvaal was entrusted to the Witwatersrand Native Labour Association (WNLA). In exchange for an agreement to reserve 47.5% of South African traffic for the Laurenço Marques railway, the Convention of 1928 authorized some 250 recruiters to enrol as many as 80000 Africans a year. The average between 1913 and 1930 was 50000 emigrants per year or a total of 900000 of whom 35000 died and only 740000 returned in satisfactory health. The hiring out of manpower thus constituted, with the transit of goods, the chief financial resource of the colony (two-thirds in 1928).[25] In addition to the sums received for emigration permits, which constituted 9.8% of budgetary receipts in 1928–9 and the 28% for railway taxes, one should also take into account the return customs duties paid (25%), and as part of the revenue collected through the head tax, the funds sent to families or brought back into the country.[26]

To a lesser degree, Ruanda-Urundi played an equivalent role for the Katanga mines. In 1930, 7300 labourers out of a total population of 350000 able-bodied adult males resided in the Congo, including more than 4000 in Katanga.[27] Also worthy of mention was the widespread phenomenon of voluntary emigration due to natural calamities. Some 25000 Ruandese emigrated to Uganda during the great famile of 1928–9. There was also the flight from forced labour comparable to that resorted to by the Mossi of Upper Volta, who found refuge in the Gold Coast.

All the colonial powers felt, at approximately the same time, the need for labour regulations. These had previously been purely formal, but their enforcement became essential as wage labour proliferated.[28] The regulations, which were similar everywhere, fixed the legal duration of the contract at three years maximum in the Congo and two years in the French and Portuguese colonies. However, the registration (subject to tax) of the contract in the labourer's 'livret' was not compulsory everywhere. Although from 1922 the administration of the French federations established an

24. E. Bohm, 1938, p. 124; J. Duffy, 1962, p. 185.
25. E. Bohm, 1938.
26. See tables in J. Cardozo, 1931, p. 29.
27. P. de Dekker, 1974.
28. In the Belgian Congo, a Decree of 1910 concerning 'all native workers' of the Congo or neighbouring colonies, employed by a 'civilized master' or 'subject to personal taxation' other than the per capita tax was amended in 1922. In AEF, a Decree of 1902 was resumed from 1907 to 1911, and completely revised in 1922, although it was not until 1935 that the first general Decree specifying how it was to be implemented was promulgated. In AOF, the first general Decree regrouping the local measures was promulgated only in 1928. In the Portuguese colonies, a Labour code of 1911 was revised in 1926, and again in 1928 (Salazar Code). H. Leonard, 1934.

authorized 'minimum wage', there was no inspection, and abuses flourished. It was not unusual for an African believing he had signed up for a year to find himself expatriated for two years or more; his wages were paid in goods not money, and the ration was often not what was originally agreed upon. Finally, very heavy fines were imposed for the least disobedience. Furthermore, in the name of the proclaimed freedom of labour, the hiring of day-labourers whose employment was not subject to any form of control remained prevalent for a long time.

The manpower crisis, particularly acute in the mines and on railway projects, caused a change of policy in the Belgian Congo. Until the 1920s, the pattern remained that of the South African mines, in which unskilled labour, recruited under short-term contracts of 6–9 months, was replaced as it was used up. Following an investigation in 1922, the UMHK undertook its reforms. The rapid increase in production – which doubled in the following two years – entailed a parallel increase in African personnel from 7500 to 14000. This was the origin of the famous Belgian 'paternalism'. The reorganization of the compounds was undertaken in 1926; within a year the cost of labour had increased by 40%, although wages no longer represented more than one fifth of the budget. In 1930, for the first time, the birth rate exceeded the death rate in the UMHK camps, which at the time offered the least unfavourable working conditions in Central Africa.[29] The success of the policy of stabilizing manpower in return for regularity of employment after 1928, and of providing leadership in all sectors of life (leisure activities, religion, schooling, etc.), was evident when, as a result of the depression, workers were retrenched from 16 000 to only 5000 between 1930 and 1932. This provoked successive revolts of the Northern Rhodesians against the repatriation policy, a series of riots by the labourers living outside the compounds, and the revolt of men from Ruanda-Urundi in 1932.

Taxation

Despite the progress achieved, the undeniable improvement in the economy had little effect on the living standards of Africans. To be sure, wage-earning became standard practice; the number of workers in the Congo increased tenfold within a decade, from 47 000 in 1917 to 427 000 in 1927, a figure only exceeded in 1937 after the great depression had waned.[30] However, this represented only a moderate percentage of the population: less than 20% of the 'able-bodied adult males' in the Congo of whom 2% in any case were Ruandese,[31] and, as late as 1950, still only 2% of the total population in French Africa.[32]

29. B. Fetter, 1976, p. 113.
30. Annual Reports on the administration of the Belgian Congo, 1919–1939.
31. 7300 workers out of 350000 able-bodied adult males. P. de Dekker, 1974.
32. T. Hodgkin, 1956, p. 118.

Despite the rising curve of employment, wages failed to keep pace. For, unlike the situation of Great Britain which remained faithful to its deflationary policy, the inflation of the 1920s was the dominant financial phenomenon in other European countries. By 1926, the French franc had lost four-fifths of its pre-war value and the Belgian franc a little more (parity of B.frs 100 for F.frs 87.60 in 1926, stabilized the following year at about B.frs 100 F.frs 71), to say nothing of the galloping inflation of the Portuguese escudo. Because of the metropolitan inflation which was felt in Africa through the rising cost of imported goods at a time when no change occurred in the prices paid for export produce, African real wages tended to fall.

The only effort that met with any success was the gradual substitution of payment in cash for payment in kind– imposed in the Belgian Congo from 1916 onwards and more slowly adopted in AEF. However, this led to cash payment of the tax, which was required of all able-bodied adults and which was from the beginning of the century considered to be the sign of the country's accession to a monetary economy and, by the same token, as the condition for its development.

This problem of taxation weighed more and more heavily on the purchasing power of Africans caught up in the cycle of colonial production. The completion of colonial penetration and the progress in administration, strengthened after the war, made it increasingly difficult for the populations to retaliate by fleeing or rebelling. Once they became more regular, tax receipts finally began to perform their functions as the chief source of finance for expansion. This, in turn, led, between the two wars, to a more rapid increase in the rate of the head tax than in pay for the workers.

The income of the peasants remained, in fact, ridiculously low, especially among those planting compulsory crops. Between 1928 and 1932, in the Belgian Congo, 700 000 cotton-planters each earned an average of B.frs 165 a year; rice-growers did only a little better (B.frs 170).[33] Results were even worse in AEF. By cultivating 20 acres of cotton a year (on the basis of the 200 days required by law), the Ubangi peasant earned in the same period only from F.frs 9.20 to F.frs 40, or hardly more than the amount of the tax.[34]

Although less beggarly, the remuneration of wage-earners hardly kept pace with inflation, although it tended to progress more rapidly in the zones where a monetary economy prevailed. The average monthly wage fell in the Middle Congo from B.frs 25.45 in 1912 – admittedly a peak year (B.frs 19.30 in 1913) – to B.frs 19.35 in 1920, and rose to about B.frs 30 only in 1929.[35] It was higher in the Gabonese forestry zones

33. M. Merlier, 1962, pp. 83–4.
34. San Marco, 1940.
35. Annual Reports, Moyen-Congo, Archives AEF, Aix-en-Provence, Dossier 4(2)D. Cf. C. Coquery-Vidrovitch, 1972, pp. 490–2.

366

(B.frs 40–50), where it was approximately equal to the average for the Belgian Congo (B.frs 60 per month).[36]

At best, in the most productive areas, there was a parallel rise in taxation, as for instance in Gabon, where the amount of work needed to pay the tax even tended to decrease throughout the decade – from 23 days just after the war to 18 days on the eve of the depression. By and large, nevertheless, the tax burden grew heavier, especially for the peasants and above all during the depression with the dismissal of workers and the collapse of the prices for tropical goods. In general, the burden of direct taxation on the African was far higher than his wages, and led him into debt and destitution – all the more so since taxes rose just at the moment when prices fell to their lowest level and dragged peasants' wages down with them. Cases studied in Guinea or the Ivory Coast show that during these hard years, the peasant had to pay more than he received, at least in the framework of the money economy. Despite the concurrent increase in speculative crops, all the evidence shows that poverty was acute. Peasants dipped into their meagre resources, gave up the last bits of silver they had saved with immense difficulty, and sold even their scanty family possessions.

Although comparisons between the territories with which we are concerned are difficult, certain similarities and certain differences in their evolution can be discerned. It was in the Portuguese colonies that the burden of the head tax remained consistently heaviest, since it corresponded officially to three months' labour, the tax being payable in labour. The corresponding daily wage was estimated as being 1 to 1.5% of its total. The head tax was also proportionately high in AOF. The average amount

TABLE 15.9 *Relative share of head tax in total receipts of colonial budgets*

	%						Frs mn		
Belgian Congo		AOF		AEF		Total amount of head tax			
Taxation of African population	Customs duties	Taxation of African population	Customs duties	Taxation of African population	Customs duties	Belgian Congo (B.frs)	AOF AEF (F.frs)		
1928			20	29.4	22.6	27.3	—	144	27
1931	21.2	21	28	18.4	22.5	30.9	115	181	38
1932	29	19.6	28.7	19.9	24.6	30.9	109	168	37
1934	22.5	18.9	27.1	21.1	19	30.3	82	154	41
1935	22.4	27.9	25.8	23.9		46.5	91	153	

Source: *Rapports annuels sur l'administration de la colonie du Congo belge, 1932 à 1938. Annuaires statistiques de l'AOF*, Vols. I, II, III, 1932–8, and of AEF, Vol. I, 1936–51.

36. In 1927, for example: B.frs 227 million for 315 000 workers, i.e. B.frs 720 a year or B.frs 60 a month (60 B.frs 1927 = 42.50 F.frs). In 1924, the UMHK paid between B.frs 30 and B.frs 45 for 30 days of effective work. B. Fetter, 1976.

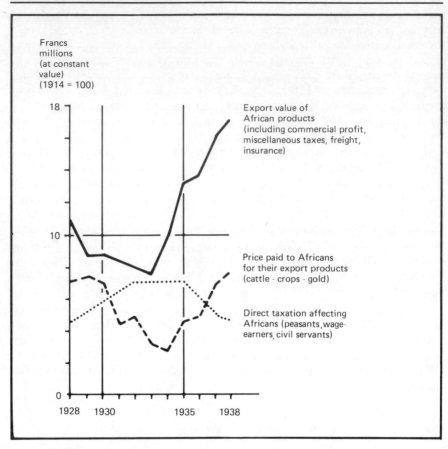

FIG. 15.3 *Approximate evaluation of African monetary possibilities in French Guinea, 1928–38 (after M. Trentadue, 1976)*

of the direct tax collected in 1915 per inhabitant was F.frs 2 in AOF, F.frs 1.55 in AEF, and B.frs 1.35 in the Belgian Congo. The more the country was obliged to live off its own resources, the heavier was the tax.

As a general rule, the colonial budgets were all funded in the same way: 25% from customs revenues and 25% from the head tax.[37] The tragedy was that, with the depression, the authorities tried to have the head tax

37. In AOF nearly half (43–45%) of the budget was funded, from 1928 to 1935, by the capitation tax plus customs duties. A third came from other taxation, especially indirect taxes (15–20%) – which also fell largely on the indigenous population (land tax; taxes on cattle; consumer and circulation taxes) and on the railways (13–16%) – the latter furthermore constantly showing a deficit. The remainder (only 21–24%, a percentage similar to that in the Belgian Congo) came from various public or private concerns (state property, licences, incomes, industrial plants). *Annuaires Statistiques* cited in source to Table 15.9.

make up the deficit in customs receipts, which everywhere had fallen to less than 20% in 1932. Nevertheless, once more, the Congolese taxes were the least oppressive; although, in 1931, the average tax per inhabitant was almost on a par with that levied by the French authorities (the average per inhabitant: F.frs 12.48 in AOF and F.frs 11 in AEF, as against B.frs 11.50 in the Congo or F.frs 8.30), the decrease during the depression was greater. The total receipts from the head tax in the Belgian Congo fell by 29%, as against 15% in AOF between 1931 and 1934, not to mention AEF, where it increased by 43% between 1929 and 1934.

The fact is that in French Africa, despite the reductions sometimes dramatically requested by the local administrators during the depression, lack of support from France obliged them to 'start down the path [of reductions] only with the greatest caution'.[38] In the Congo, on the other hand, if the situation, on the whole, was worse by the end of the period, the tax still remained less than a month's wages. Moreover, the work-time required in addition to cover basic needs (expressed by the purchase of *kitenge* or printed cloth), which had risen in some cases (for example in Kasai) to nearly five months, had on the whole declined since 1920, if not since before the war. However, it later rose to barely one month and a half.

TABLE 15.10 *Value of annual head tax in 3 rural regions, in relation to monthly wage (total monthly wage: 1912–33 = 100)*

	Tax					Tax + kitenge				
	1912	1920	1924	1928	1933	1912	1920	1924	1928	1933
Lower and Middle Congo	65	50	36	31	78	106	175	198	119	138
Kasai	75	37	41	22	59	175	482	291	143	135

Source: J. P. Peemans, 1968, p. 361. In AOF, on the other hand, the SCOA estimated that as late as 1940 taxes took half the yearly earning of the groundnut farmer. Report appended to the balance-sheet, Archives of the Company.

Here we find – although still in the embryonic stage – the effects of an earlier investment policy, which was to result in a more dynamic system of production, or one which, at least, tended to differ increasingly from the retarded type of exploitation in the French Sahel zone. For lack of any profitable produce, the Africans in this zone were still being squeezed in an attempt to avoid economic collapse.

The crises and their repercussions

The situation of the Africans, always precarious, became in 1930 as tragic as it had been at the beginning of the period.

38. Circular No. 68 from the Commission of the Republic in Cameroon, 19 September 1932, Archives Yaoundé, APA–10895/A.

Production

Despite the global scale of the hostilities, the First World War brought about an occasionally spectacular rise in production. With a few exceptions (as in the case of Gabon's *okoume* timber trade, wholly dependent upon the German market, which closed abruptly), the exports and profits of the expatriate firms showed an appreciable rise. The fact is that the 'war effort' was particularly severe in French-speaking Africa; a programme for 'intensifying production' was launched in 1915, and expanded in 1916–17.[39] Work camps were organized for the cultivation and harvesting of so-called strategic products (rubber, oil-yielding crops, timber, etc.). Most important of all, the French government temporarily guaranteed their purchase; it accordingly requisitioned 140000 tonnes of oilseeds in 1918, and almost 3 million tonnes in 1919. The production of certain commodities such as castor-oil and rubber, which then enjoyed a boom, collapsed once and for all when the First World War ended and the state ceased to buy them. On the whole, however, the war made clear the need to organize production (this was the role played by the Colonial Economic Conference in 1917) and served to launch the first large-scale speculative enterprise – cotton in Oubangui-Chari (now Central African Republic), timber in Gabon and Ivory Coast – in the early 1920s, after the violent but brief crisis of 1921–2.

It was for quite opposite reasons that the 1930 crisis, which triggered off the collapse in prices, led to a radical rethinking of production objectives and techniques, at least in the territories under French authority whose economy had up to then been an *économie de traite*.

The crisis was not one of overproduction. The extremely low yield meant that the products in question represented only a minimal proportion of international trade (for example, Senegal's groundnut exports represented 50% of the income of AOF, but only 5% of world production), and the protection of the colonial powers ensured rapid disposal thanks to a policy (albeit limited) of subsidies. These subsidies included export bonuses in AOF paid to expatriate firms to compensate for the fall in prices, and the underwriting of the national debt in AEF which had been driven to the verge of bankruptcy by the deficit in customs revenues.

Burdened by taxes which they were no longer able to meet (a high rate of taxation being maintained despite the collapse in prices and wages), Africans reacted to the fall in their incomes by stepping up production. As we have seen, it was at the height of the crisis that tropical plantation crops (coffee, cocoa, bananas, cotton) enjoyed a boom due solely to the production of small-scale indigenous planters. Despite the extremely low prices, the overall drop in export tonnage, which had been substantial in 1932, was rapidly reversed. The average of the inter-war years was exceeded for the first time in 1931, then again, definitively, from 1934. This was

39. Cf. circular of 13 February 1915, AEF cited in C. Coquery-Vidrovitch, 1972, p. 492. With regard to AOF, see M. Michel, 1982.

of course the consequence of the effort begun in the 1924–8 boom years, as well as of the policy of developing the transport infrastructure which had been vigorously pursued during the crisis from the loans provided to the French colonies in 1913.

However, as the allocation of these funds coincided with the period of deepest depression, it served essentially not to promote the expansion of the programmes but rather to correct – albeit only very partially – domestic deficit, particularly in Cameroon (where the work camps were discontinued) and in AOF, where more than half the operations continued to be financed by the federation's own, extremely reduced, resources. Moreover, this massive loan policy led to a sharp rise in the internal debt at the very moment when, due to the shortfall in customs revenues, the receipts of colonial budgets collapsed.

Thus, the manifest economic transformation brought about during the period was achieved and paid for by the peasantry, since the increase in the tax burden upon the producer occurred at the very moment when, as prices reached their lowest levels, the wages of rural workers declined correspondingly. Admittedly, the increase in tax receipts and the development of the wage-earning sector of the farming population, which gradually replaced forced labour, must be related to the expansion in speculative crop-farming. However, such farming served essentially to trigger off an incipient process of social differentiation through the emergence of a class of indigenous 'new rich', small-scale landowners and commercial entrepreneurs who made their money by exploiting the destitution and indebtedness of the majority. For example, it is significant that, throughout the years of crisis, savings rose steadily in African countries, whether measured in terms of the number of savings accounts or the value of deposits. This growth in savings was undoubtedly brought about by the 'comprador' lower middle classes, who were quick to understand, thanks to relatively favourable terms of trade, that their status depended on their quickly adopting the rules of the capitalist game.

On the other hand, for the mass of the poor small peasants, poverty appeared to be at its worst. The Africans dug into their meagre reserves, mortgaged their land and became share-croppers on the two-thirds and three-quarters system (the *abusa* of the Ivory Coast cocoa plantation area). There was no longer even any need to constrain them by strict compulsory work legislation. From 1931 onwards the shortage of money (whose use could no longer be avoided) became acute; and it was less and less possible for them to fall back on the traditional life of subsistence food cropping, which no longer even ensured survival. Strictly speaking, peasants no longer had the choice.[40]

40. For French Equatorial Africa see G. G. Reste, *Rapport économique au Min. des Col.*, Brazzaville, 24 June 1937, Archives Nationales, Section d'Outre-Mer, Paris (ANSOM), Fonds Guerut, 827. For AOF, see Report by E. Giscard d'Estaing to the Min. Col. on his mission to French West Africa, 1931–2, ANSOM, *Affaires politiques*, 539. Cf. C. Coquery-Vidrovitch, 1977 and (ed.) 1976.

Food shortage, famine and epidemic

A feature of the whole of this period was the acuteness of the food supply crises.

The war economy of the years 1915–18 had some very serious implications. The most harmful step was the requisitioning of foodstuffs for the home country just when the troops (only 10 000 men in AEF, but a little over 160 000 in AOF) were draining the countryside.

In Gabon, only a quarter of the compulsorily produced crops were left for local consumption. Even manioc (cassava) was exported from the Middle Congo and Oubangui–Chari: 210 tonnes in 1915 and 157 tonnes in 1917.[41] In AOF as a consequence of the decision to export local staple crops, the authorities emptied the reserve granaries which were already suffering from the succession of two years of semi-drought (1911–12) and one year of total aridity (1913). This drought had spread over the entire Sudan area, from Senegal to Wadai and Chad. From periodic shortages, the situation worsened to a devastating famine which claimed probably 250 000 to 300 000 victims,[42] alleviated only by the 4000 tonnes of cereals that the French Soudan (now Mali) had had neither the means nor the time to ship to France.[43]

TABLE 15.11 *AOF: exports of requisitioned food products ('000 tonnes)*

	1916	*1917*	*1918*	*1919*	*Total*
Maize	1.5	4.6			6
Millet	9.6	3.6	1.3	1.6	16.2
Paddy and rice		2.7			3
TOTAL	11.3[1]	11.1[2]	3.2[2]	3.3[2]	25.2

1. Including wood, cola and gonakié (variety of cola).
2. Plus beans.
Source: Annuaire du Gouvernement Général de l'AOF, 1917–21, Paris, 1921, p. 55.

In AEF where forced sales continued into the following decade in order to provision the Congo–Océan railway projects, famine, which had begun in 1918, spread to the northern half of the country (Woleu-Ntem) between 1922 and 1925; it probably reduced the Fang population by half, from 140 000 to 65 000 in 1933.[44]

The weakened populations then fell a prey to epidemics: renewed outbreaks of smallpox and especially the spread of Spanish influenza imported from Europe, from which perhaps one-tenth of the population of AEF perished.[45]

41. Cf. circular of 13 Feb. 1915, AEF; C. Coquery-Vidrovitch, 1972, p. 492.
42. J. Suret-Canale, 1964, pp. 169–72.
43. H. C. Cosnier, 1921, p. 253.
44. G. Sautter, 1966, pp. 859, 864, 871.
45. Huot, Marzin, Ricau, Grosfillez, David, 1921.

Though not always accompanied by such disastrous results, the famine problem resulting from food shortages caused by the colonial system was a recurrent feature of the period. It recurred, for example, in 1928–9 in Ruanda, the 'granary' of the Belgian Congo, following another drought,[46] and was indeed the sign of the fragility of countries exhausted by the *économie de traite* despite the rise in export figures.

There were situations of severe famine such as that in Niger in 1930, of which Zerma–Sonrai still have memories, followed by an invasion of locusts. But the colonial system did a great deal to aggravate the famine as the reports of the time, which are full of self-criticism, indicate. Exorbitant taxes (increasing in ten years from B.frs 1.25 to B.frs 7) encouraged the population to flee to the Gold Coast instead of raising crops. Forced labour was increased after 1927 by the installation of the administrative services at Niamey and by the extension of the railway. This completely disrupted the farm calendar though the precariousness of the rains made farming times particularly important. The supplies of millet, non-compulsory, depended entirely on the local chiefs. In 1931, the refusal of the administration to lower the head tax, and its insistence on collective payment, which forced the peasants to pay also for deserters and for deceased people, led to a situation in which, as one report put it, 'entire villages vanished ... and an age group was completely decimated'[47] with, in some areas, a mortality rate of over 50%.

Taken all round, however, the catastrophe was less spectacular. The famines were checked thanks to progress in transport facilities and the epidemics were halted by the first health campaign. But the fall in prices and loss of employment were everywhere cruelly felt. 'It was in the price paid to the producer that the decline made itself most heavily felt. The purchasing power of the natives was reduced to a greater extent than in any of the earlier crises.'[48]

It is revealing that, in Francophone Africa, large-scale urban immigration began precisely when the great crisis occurred. Notwithstanding the overall stagnation in population growth (in AOF 14.4 million inhabitants in 1931, as compared with 14.6 million in 1936), the towns and cities began to be swollen by the massive influx of destitute peasants, in spite of the fact that the urban employment situation was also critical. In 1936, for example, there were still no more than 167000 wage-earners in AOF, which was hardly more than 1% of the population. Nevertheless, between 1931 and 1936 the populations of Dakar and Abidjan increased by 71%, while that of Conakry doubled. Even more revealing is the case of an impoverished little town in the interior like Ouagadougou which, reversing its previous

46. This famine did not prevent the subsequent rise in exports of manioc, an increase from 239 to 2515 tonnes being registered from 1930 to 1934. P. de Dekker, 1974.

47. Quoted by F. Fuglestad, 1974, p. 25.

48. Société du Haut-Ogoué, Report to the General Assembly of Stockholders, 1930; Archives of the Company.

trend, increased its population by one-third over the same period.

The overall stagnation in population growth during this period is particularly indicative of the prevailing state of poverty. For social expenditure, was, by contrast, tending everywhere to rise: the parallel increase in expenditure on health care, and in the number of dispensaries and treatment facilities tended effectively to curb the traditional scourges (trypanosomiasis, venereal diseases, leprosy). By contrast, populations proved to be particularly vulnerable during the taxing period 1931–6 to epidemics ('sporadic illnesses': influenza, smallpox, etc.). It is extremely tempting to relate such increased morbidity to the state of profound distress and physical destitution in which a weakened and defenceless population found itself.[49]

The economic balance sheet

Because they were held under strict control by the administrative authorities, and because of their very limited participation in social and economic changes, the populations, at the end of the period, were in a perilous situation, while the system itself was in the throes of change.

The private sector

The period was indeed marked by the rise of powerful firms which had only just been founded at the turn of the century.

The Belgian Congo was at the forefront of this development. Just before the depression, the country numbered 278 industrial and commercial concerns, and agencies for thirty-six foreign companies – not counting a scattering of privately owned local businesses. In all, the number of establishments had increased by more than a third in three years, rising from 4500 in 1926 to 6000 in 1929.

TABLE 15.12 *Belgian companies operating in the Congo, 1929*

	Transport	*Banking*	*Mining*	*Agriculture, industry*	*Commerce (occasionally agriculture, industry)*	*Forestry (or forestry, agriculture)*
Number	23	24	27	125	88	9
Capital (frs mn)	2167	1037	951	1982	1196	105
Average capital per company	94	43	35	16	*14*	12

Source: F. Passelecq, 1932, p. 362.

49. Cf. C. Coquery-Vidrovitch, forthcoming.

From 1919 to 1930, the amount of capital invested had risen by 1000 million gold francs, and included 1000 million due to colonial issues. The government portfolio (estimated at 16000 million gold francs in 1928, of which the market value had fallen to 5000 million by September 1930 and been brought down to one-third of the assets held by the private sector) was then estimated at half the value of the Congolese securities held by private individuals.

But although the sectors covered were already diversified, the chief impetus was from mining and railway activities. Four principal companies (Société Générale, Empain, ComNiniére and Banque de Bruxelles), with more than 6000 million gold francs invested, accounted for nearly 75% of the capital.[50] The leading company, the Société Générale, was itself responsible for half of this, controlling three railway companies, three general companies, two banks, twelve mining companies, six plantations, three finance companies, eleven industrial and commercial companies and one real estate company, that is to say, almost all the mining production (copper, diamonds, radium and a good share of the gold), the entire cement industry and the most important hydroelectric installations.[51]

Its success was linked to the productive level of its mines, chief among which were the UMHK (copper), founded in 1906 by an agreement with the Comité Spécial du Katanga. The Comité itself had taken over from the Compagnie du Katanga (1891), which had been entrusted by the Congo Free State with the economic management of the area in 1900, and had begun operations with the arrival of the railway at Elisabethville (now Lubumbashi) in 1910, and Forminière (Kasai Diamonds) whose prospecting operations had started in 1907 and exploitation in 1914.

It contrasted with the relative inactivity of the other concessionaire companies, most of which had not assembled sufficient capital to exploit their excessively vast areas.

This was particularly true[52] of AEF, paralysed since 1900 by an unfortunate thirty-year concessionary scheme that had sold off the territory to some forty enormous monopoly companies, most of which had already collapsed by the eve of the First World War. Some of the few survivors had either been converted into strictly commercial companies such as the Société du Haut-Ogooué, in the eastern half of Gabon, the Compagnie Propriétaire du Kouilou Niara bought out by Lever Brothers in 1911; or into companies vaguely exploiting palm plantations that remained in a rudimentary state such as the Compagnie Française du Haut et du Bas-Congo. Others served to prolong belatedly an absurd regime of coercion and poverty in products that were unprofitable or even already condemned such as the Compagnie Forestière Sangha-Oubangui, with a capital of

50. S. H. Frankel, 1938, p. 292.

51. In addition, it had a large share in seven other companies, and was represented on the board of directors of about fifteen more. ibid., p. 294.

52. Cf. C. Coquery-Vidrovitch, 1972.

B.frs 12 million for a monopoly covering 17 million ha which had regrouped eleven former concessionaire companies of the Middle Congo and Oubangui-Chari, and imposed its monopoly over wild rubber harvesting until 1935. On the other hand, the exploitation of Oubangui diamonds, discovered in 1913, was not begun until the 1930s. The only boom had been that in Gabon of *okoume* wood, a raw material used in the plywood industry, which emerged during the First World War.

On the eve of the depression, the combined capital of 107 firms totalled a nominal B.frs 309 million which – in gold francs – had scarcely doubled since 1913, when private shareholder capital reached B.frs 70 million. The dominant role in capital investment was still played by the state – the sign of a country considered to be poor, where the private sector had long abandoned to the public authorities the burden of the enormous outlays for equipment.

It was a far cry from the success of a firm like Lever Brothers which, starting with the first palm oil purchased in the Belgian Congo (based on a concession of 750 000 ha from the SEDEC – Société des Huileries du Congo Belge, 1911), soon extended its oil plantation empire to the whole of West Africa (Gabon/Middle Congo, Nigeria, Cameroon). Unilever, finally founded in 1928 by the merging of the British firm with the German–Dutch margarine trust, developed, alongside the English empire of the United Africa Company, a whole series of French subsidiaries (Niger Français, Nosoco in Senegal, Compagnie Française de Côte d'Ivoire, etc.) which grew bigger around the time of the Second World War.[53]

AOF remained, in effect, the domain of commercial firms founded on agriculture for export. Even in this field, the lag was enormous compared with the Belgian Congo.

TABLE 15.13 *Investments in AOF concerns in 1943 (expressed as percentage)*

	Commerce	Plantations	Forestry	Mines
All enterprises	38	18	12.5	7.5
Companies only	42.8	11 to 12	11 to 12	8.8

Source: J. Dresch, 1952, pp. 232–41, based on the investigation carried out by the Ministry of Colonies in 1943, ANSOM, Affaires Economiques series, carton 52.

In 1938, the French federations numbered only some fifty commercial firms whose registered capital barely exceeded F.frs 600 million.[54] At the time, ten of them listed a capital of more than F.frs 20 million, among which only two accounted for a third of the whole: the Société Commerçiale de l'Ouest-Africain (SCOA) founded in 1906 with a capital of F.frs 125 million, and the Compagnie Française de l'Afrique Occidentale (CFAO)

53. M. Sherril, 1973, p. 48.
54. M. Tupinier, 1940.

founded since 1887, with F.frs 75 million.[55] But their investments, negligible before the war, scarcely exceeded an average of 10–20 million gold francs during the best years, even though at the end of the period they represented 10% of the total investment in French Africa.[56]

The reason was that trading, which consisted in collecting and routeing to the ports the products of the country, exported unprocessed or in a semi-refined state, and in distributing in exchange imported manufactured commodities consisting chiefly of consumer goods, required but little capital. Certainly the 1920s were the heyday of the *économie de traite*, and inflation was a source of major profit: from 1913 to 1920, the foreign trade of AOF rose from F.frs 277 to F.frs 1143 million. In five years the value of British cotton goods exported to Africa quadrupled and, taking into account the stability of the pound, increased by 800% in relation to French prices in 1914. Within a few years, SCOA and CFAO had spread over all of West Africa, and by 1924 they had more or less reached their final form (SCOA: 140 agencies, 145 in 1930, 250 in 1940; CFAO: 141 agencies, 191 in 1930, 411 in 1939). But they also operated in the British territories, where commerce was more active: oil palm products and tin from Nigeria for CFAO, and cocoa from the Gold Coast for SCOA which was soon to account for a third of that company's turnover.

The depression was felt severely, for the basis of prosperity was largely speculative and ill-equipped to resist the collapse of commodity prices since the diversification of activities had scarcely begun, industrialization was as yet virtually non-existent, and since the traditional trading economy still constituted the bulk of AOF activities.

As for the Portuguese colonies, they had as yet scarcely managed to choose between these various approaches. Mozambique found herself in a general state of mediocrity; she was still largely under the concessionaire regime in which, alongside the relatively efficient pillage by the Mozambique Company, or the rather good lands held as a sub-concession by the Zambezi Company, the Niassa Company had lost its monopoly in 1929, owing to its disastrous record.[57] Mozambique stood up to the depression very badly as is evident from the fact that the value of exports fell by half between 1929 and 1933. In Angola, the first attempt at mining operations was that of the Diamang group with Belgian and British capital. Since 1920, it had figured as the chief financial support of the colony, despite its still relatively limited contribution of £600000 sterling in 1929, or a quarter of the value of Angolan exports. Exempted from taxes and customs duties, the company, which had labour and the market at its exclusive disposal, was already forging its monopolistic empire.

55. In 1945, stock investments in the two firms represented 84% of the capital of the AOF commercial enterprises quoted on the French Stock Exchange, and 52% of that of all AOF enterprises. P. Valdant, 1946.

56. On the history of the two firms see C. Coquery-Vidrovitch, 1975.

57. E. Bohm, 1938, p. 155.

Capital equipment and production

With respect to capital equipment and production, the economic balance sheet still remained poor at the end of the period. The main achievement had been the railways; everywhere the state had replaced or largely financed the former private companies. The Belgian Congo network had expanded considerably. The investments in this field rose from 480 million gold francs in 1920 to 535 million in 1935 and the length of permanent way from 1940 km to 2410 km. In all, by 1934, the government had guaranteed railway capital to the amount of 2271 million gold francs. The corresponding charge amounted in 1934 to 103 million gold francs.[58] The programme had consisted essentially in making comprehensive the network around the mines, by linking Katanga to the Rhodesian system in 1918, to the Lower Congo in 1928 and towards Benguela after 1930. But the financial balance remained catastrophic (with an average yearly revenue of around 1%), except in the case of the Katanga railway, 85% of whose tonnage was in copper. The fact was that the railway was looked upon as a good speculation rather than as a public service. The goal was less a rise in traffic than a rise in profits, through exploitation of the excessively high rates, which were protected by the prohibition of rail/road competition,[59] which impeded production, particularly during the period when prices slumped. This was obviously to the advantage of the Portuguese colonies which, with 2348 km of railway in Angola and 1936 km in Mozambique by 1930, drew the greater part of their resources from their transit function, amounting to 80% of the total foreign commerce of Mozambique.[60]

In AEF the grandiose railway projects launched in 1913 including the Gabonese railway and the Congo–Chad link-up[61] finally resulted in the laborious construction, at great cost in men and money, of the Congo–Océan line (less than 500 km, 1922–34). The latter opened up the territory previously dependent on the Belgian Congo. On the other hand, AOF, which suffered from the poverty of its mineral resources, carried out only a few extension projects on a haphazard network of older sections of railway perpendicular to the coast and indicative of the archaic, fragmentary and extraverted character of the colony's exploitation. These extensions amounted to 550 km from 1921 to 1934, out of a total in operation of more than 3500 km.

58. S. H. Frankel, 1938, pp. 407, 414.

59. Each of the sectors enjoyed a monopoly. Cf. *Monopole des transports automobiles delimite entre 1928 et 1934*, Report No. 108 to the Belgian Senate, 1935, quoted by H. S. Frankel, 1938, pp. 409–11. The policy was similar to that of the British territories in which, as for example in the Gold Coast, the government at the same period forbade planters to ship their cocoa by truck, in order to guarantee the profits of the railway. G. B. Kay (ed.), 1972, p. 431.

60. According to the tables in S. H. Frankel, 1938, p. 369.

61. C. Coquery-Vidrovitch, 1972, p. 286.

More important as an innovation was the construction, in savanna country, of a road network which, by putting an end to the ravages of human porterage, transformed the conditions governing the collection and distribution of products. The beginning of the construction of the Oubangui network (AEF) dated from the war and, by 1926, 4200 km had been completed. However, only a few vehicles were seen using it and most of them were exclusively commercial. There were less than 1000 vehicles in 1930, 1500 in 1931 and only 2850 in 1945, 600 of which were for tourism.[62]

AOF, especially, made up for its railway deficiencies with roads. By 1937, 27000 km were open to 17229 vehicles, including nearly 10000 trucks and light trucks. Between 1926 and 1934 highway projects and port improvements absorbed almost as much capital as the railways, amounting to F.frs 475 million as against F.frs 520 million.[63]

Nevertheless, the infrastructure provided hardly had time to affect the volume of exports before the onset of the depression. To be sure, a certain number of territories offered a wide range of products: cotton, coffee, sugar cane, sisal and maize in Angola; coconuts, groundnuts and rice in Mozambique; wood in Gabon and the Ivory Coast; and bananas in Guinea. But exports continued to be based almost exclusively on minerals and oil-yielding plants. Few territories were as favourably situated as the Belgian Congo, whose improvement was based, at best, on two or three groups of products which, at least, were already partially processed. These were vegetable oil whose production increased from 2500 tonnes in 1914 to 9000 in 1921 and 65000 in 1930; and copper, which tripled between 1922 and 1931, from 43000 to 120000 tonnes before falling again the following year to 54000 tonnes, as a result of a reduction in production decided upon by international agreements.

TABLE 15.14 *Belgian Congo: value of exports (expressed as percentage)*

	1927	1928	1929	1930	1931	1932	1933	1934	1935
Minerals	61	61	60	67	70	60	54	59	62
Palm products, palm oil	20	19	17	14	11	17			12
Cotton	5	8	9	8	8	8			11
TOTAL	86	88	86	89	89	85			85

Source: S. H. Frankel, 1938, pp. 289–301.

Certainly, Angola seemed almost as well endowed potentially. However, Portuguese negligence left its haphazard agricultural production to the risks of the weather and of speculation, which led to its stagnation for ten years.[64]

As for AEF, it was just emerging from the Gabonese forestry monopoly,

62. ibid., p. 284.
63. *Annuaires statistiques de l'AOF*, op. cit. in source to Table 15.9.
64. S. H. Frankel, 1938, pp. 371–3.

which accounted for a little more than 400000 tonnes of its exports in 1930. Although the tonnage exported from Cameroon had tripled since 1923 (from 48000 to 124000 tonnes), exploitation of the country was barely getting under way by 1934 with F.frs 73 million in exports, of which nearly 60% consisted of cocoa and oil palm products. Finally, AOF, despite the slow emergence of a few new products, still depended for more than half its exports on Senegalese groundnuts, almost all of them leaving the country unprocessed.

TABLE 15.15 *AOF: value of exports (expressed as percentage)*

	1928	1929	1930	1931	1932	1933	1934	1935	1936
Peanuts	52.7	47	46	47	38	42	49	53	53
Palm products, palm oil	13	14	14	13	12	6.5	6	8	10
Wood	7.5	6	7.5	5.5	4.5	3	3	3	1.6
Cocoa	9	8	9.5	10	16	13	11	8	7.7
Coffee								0.3	0.3
Bananas				0.1	0.3	0.4	0.4	0.3	0.4
TOTAL	88.2	75	77	75.6	70.8	64.9	69.4	72.6	73

Source: 'L'évolution des exportations de l'AOF', op. cit. in source to Table 15.8.

Conclusion

In short, the economic balance sheet at the end of the inter-war period was a negative one, both from the colonizers' standpoint – with production slumping and insufficiently diversified – and from the African angle – with the populations poverty-stricken and distraught. Nevertheless, despite appearances, the available infrastructure and production facilities had profoundly altered the structure of the economy. In this respect, the crisis of 1930 drew attention to the need for a concerted policy directed by the state. It heralded the emergence of colonial planning, in which the international division of labour served to justify the organization of specialized, intensified production zones. In short, state capitalism as conceived by the industrial colonial powers (particularly France) was aimed a integrating the colonial world, which till then had remained relatively on the periphery, into the global system of the production and distribution of goods.

A further feature of the period was the reversal of the population trend. In the case of the French-speaking territories at least, it would appear that population decline was halted in the mid-1920s. The war had revealed both the reservoir of human resources that Africa represented and the dangers which threatened it, at the very time when the 'development' of the territories was generating an ever greater demand for labour. Admittedly, by the end of the 1930s the population explosion had not yet begun. The resumption of population growth none the less helped to speed up the process of recovery. Indeed, colonial exploitation soon resumed with renewed vigour, with the populations, by then on the way to becoming integrated into the modern economy, preparing to act otherwise than as passive or rebellious instruments of colonial law. Certainly Portuguese colonies, where Great Britain or the Union of South Africa were taking over capitalist development, remained wretchedly poor. Belgian paternalism was always ready to invest, but accompanied this with a systematic rejection of internal advancement for the Africans. France, for its part, had finally awoken to the need to contribute on a massive scale to investment in production, even if such investment did not bring immediate returns. As early as 1936, it fell to the Popular Front government to put forward a coherent colonial programme that was both modernist and reformist. Even though lack of funds prevented it from going very far in this direction, it introduced into the French federations the very first reforms that were finally to permit the formation of African trade unions and political parties.

16

The colonial economy:
the former British zones

M. H. Y. KANIKI

By the second decade of the present century the British had firmly established themselves in many parts of tropical Africa including Nigeria, Gold Coast (now Ghana), The Gambia, Sierra Leone, Kenya, Tanganyika (now Tanzania), Nyasaland (now Malawi), Uganda, Northern Rhodesia (now Zambia), Southern Rhodesia (now Zimbabwe) and South Africa (see Fig. 2.1) and the colonial economies were clearly taking shape. This chapter seeks to examine the nature and major characteristic of these economies.

The British, like other colonizers, did not develop a universal theory of colonialism which could embrace all aspects of life in all colonies. Nor did they develop anything near a universal practice of colonialism. Indeed this was impossible as colonialism was imposed on peoples with extremely diverse cultures and backgrounds, and living in widely differing environments. Much was left to the administrators to deal with situations depending on the local conditions. Even in the absence of a clear theory, however, a critical examination of colonial relations brings to light some fundamental assumptions which seem to have acted as guidelines for both the framers and implementers of colonial economic policies. First, the colonies were expected to provide raw materials (agricultural products and minerals) to feed the machines of the industrial imperial power. Second, the colonies had to import manufactured goods from the imperial power. These two assumptions divided the empire into two distinct economic camps – the colonies and the metropolis. Significantly there was very little reciprocity in the relationship. While in most cases the colonies had an obligation to export to Britain before they could consider any other buyer, even if such a buyer would pay higher prices, Britain had no obligation to import exclusively from any of her colonies. She operated through rational economic choices and bought from whoever sold at low prices. The colonized people were also at a disadvantage in the import trade. In some cases they had to buy expensive British manufactures as the colonial state apparatus, under pressure from Britain, raised customs duties for non-British goods. Third, the colonies had to be self-supporting. The colonized peoples had to raise revenue for the general administration and for whatever limited development projects that were undertaken.

All these guiding principles were made clear, explicitly or implicitly, to the colonial administrators. But there was an equally important assumption which seems to have been confused by some colonial administrators and other apologists of colonialism and this is the fact that the British, like other colonizers, went out to the colonies primarily, if not exclusively, to enrich themselves and promote their own interests. The development of the colonized was none of their business. Where there was 'development' in the colonies, it was by and large a by-product of activities intended to promote the interests of the colonizers. It would be meaningless to imagine the colonial state apparatus making important policy decisions without taking into account the interests of the unofficial representatives of imperialism. These unofficial agents operated especially through commercial firms, mining firms and banks. They represented group interests in the colonial legislatures and different committees, or acted as pressure groups. In the absence of well-organized African representation, as was the case in most colonies, white settlers and representatives of expatriate companies were able to obtain many concessions from the colonial governments at the expense of the local populations. Colonial policy and practice, in other words, were shaped by both political and economic determinants. As a matter of fact, in many cases, the unofficial elements affected the local population more directly than the administration did. They bought and collected agricultural products from the former and sold imported goods to them. They also employed indigenous labour. In both cases, there was very little government interference. Evidently the prices of exports and imports and the level of wages affected the people's day-to-day life more than the district commissioner's annual tax-collecting visit to the rural areas. Such a state of affairs was in no way a peculiarity of a few colonies. It was the normal reality of colonial economic relations. And since such relations are predominantly economic, colonial practice was conditioned by economic laws.[1]

Right from the early days of British effective occupation of Africa, the British government recognized the potential and importance of the economic forces of their new colonies in the promotion of British interests overseas. In 1895 the Prime Minister, Lord Salisbury, revealed this awareness to Parliament quite clearly:

> It is our business in all these new countries to make smooth the path for British commerce, British enterprise, the application of British capital, at a time when other paths, other outlets for the commercial energies of our race are being gradually closed by the commercial principles which are gaining more and more adhesion ...
>
> In a few years it will be our people that will be masters, it will be our commerce that will prevail, it will be our capital that will rule ...
>
> My Lords, this is a tremendous power, but it requires one condition.

1. J. S. Furnivall, 1948, p. 8.

You must enable it to get to the country where its work is to be done. You must open the path.[2]

Indeed, the path was open, and each colonial state apparatus created and maintained effective conditions for the 'orderly' running of economic activities in the colony. These included the maintenance of 'law and order' which facilitated effective exploitation of colonial resources, both human and material.

Ownership of the means of production

The basic and almost only means of production in the British dependencies in the period up to 1935 was land. British attitudes and policies towards land varied from region to region, and even, in each region, from colony to colony. It can be stated in general terms, however, that whereas Africans remained in practice in control of their lands in British West Africa, many of them were deprived of theirs in British East and Central Africa. There were, however, some important variations from colony to colony in each region.

In Uganda and to a lesser extent Tanganyika, most of the fertile land was owned by the indigenous population, the Africans. With a few exceptions, for example Buganda in Uganda, the Bukoba and Kilimanjaro areas in Tanganyika and Gikuyuland in Kenya, land did not acquire market value on a large scale, and it was held communally. Every member of the community had the right to land. In most cases it was labour, and not land, which was the scarcer means of production.

Foreigners, mostly British, secured and held concessions on land with mineral and timber resources, but such arrangements had little adverse effect on the local agricultural communities. In some cases, however, serious hardships were faced where mineral resources were located on rich arable land. With almost no exception, mineral wealth belonged to the British Crown or its agents and was disposed of in ways decided by the official and unofficial agents of imperialism.

In Kenya and Central Africa, as was the case in Tanganyika under the Germans, Africans owned some land, but substantial portions of the most fertile arable land were alienated for European settlers. The process of land alienation and its political and economic repercussions in Kenya and Southern Rhodesia have been well documented by M. P. K. Sorrenson[3] and Giovanni Arrighi.[4] It has been argued that British perception of economic activity in Kenya at the beginning of the twentieth century led them to look for economic agents from outside. Contrary to well-developed peasant agriculture found in Uganda (especially in Buganda)

2. Quoted by R. D. Wolff, 1974, pp. 134–5.
3. M. P. K. Sorrenson, 1968.
4. G. Arrighi, 1967.

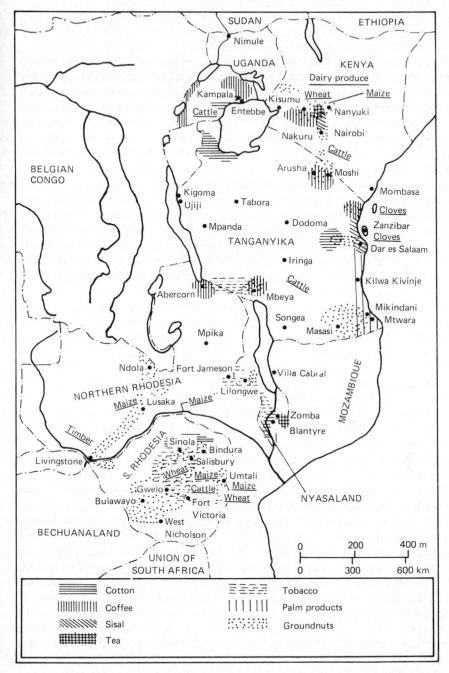

SUDAN · ETHIOPIA

Nimule

UGANDA · KENYA
Dairy produce
Kampala · Kisumu · Wheat · Maize
Cattle · Entebbe · Nanyuki
Nakuru · Nairobi

BELGIAN
CONGO

Arusha · Moshi
Cattle
Kigoma · Mombasa
Ujiji · Tabora
Cloves
Mpanda · Dodoma · Zanzibar
TANGANYIKA · Cloves
Dar es Salaam
Iringa

Cattle
Abercorn · Kilwa Kivinje
Mbeya
Mikindani
Songea · Mtwara
Masasi

Mpika

Ndola · Fort Jameson · Villa Cabral
NORTHERN RHODESIA
Lilongwe
Maize · Lusaka · Maize

Timber · Zomba
Sinola · Blantyre
Livingstone · Bindura
S. RHODESIA · Salisbury
Wheat · Maize · Umtali
Gwelo · Cattle · Maize
Bulawayo · Fort · Wheat
Victoria · NYASALAND
BECHUANALAND · West
Nicholson

MOZAMBIQUE

0   200   400 m
0   300   600 km

UNION OF
SOUTH AFRICA

	Cotton		Tobacco
	Coffee		Palm products
	Sisal		Groundnuts
	Tea		

FIG. 16.1 *East Africa: economic development in the former British zones, agricultural products*
(after R. Oliver and A. Atmore, 1972)

385

under the control of centralized political institutions, the argument goes, the economies of most communities in Kenya were too backward to be relied upon as a springboard for economic growth. Consequently, the argument concludes, white settlers were chosen to form the base of economic life of the dependency.[5] This line of thought offers only part, and the lesser part, of the explanation. There were many parts of the British Empire where indigenous economies were miserably undeveloped. The coastal regions of Kenya are a case in point. The fact that these regions were spared from settler colonization clearly indicates that the Kenya Highlands had something special to offer for European settlement. Evidently it was the temperate climate above other factors, which attracted the white settlers. The land occupied by settlers was mostly over 1400 m above sea level. Such areas were among those with the highest and most reliable levels of precipitation. In short, the alienated land was situated in the most favourable agricultural zones.

The beginning of land alienation in East Africa was discussed in Chapter 7. It took a dramatic trend especially in Kenya after 1909 and was carried out at give-away prices. In 1903 only about 2000 ha had been alienated to Europeans in Kenya. By 1914 the area alienated had risen to about 260 000 ha and to about 2 740 000 ha in 1930.[6] This was a very substantial chunk of the arable land, bearing in mind the fact that the Kenya Highlands (about 90 000 sq km) comprised less than 15% of Kenya's area and yet supported over 75% of the total population of the country until the 1930s. The chief losers were the Gikuyu, but the Nandi, Maasai, Kipsigis and others also lost land.

The availability of land, and the propaganda by the colonial authorities to popularize settler agriculture attracted many Europeans, both adventurers and genuine settlers. In 1903 there were only 596 Europeans in Kenya, two years later the number had reached 954 of whom 700 were South Africans;[7] by the end of March 1914 the number had risen to 5438 and by the end of December 1929 there were 16 663 Europeans in Kenya.[8] Many of the early settlers, especially until 1910, acquired land at little or no cost. Among them was Lord Delamere who came to be one of the leading landowners, at one time owning more than 400 000 ha.[9] The land bought between 1902 and 1915 was held on ninety-nine-year leases. In the latter year the administration changed terms of land leases in favour of the settlers who were by then an effective political force. The Crown Lands Ordinance of 1915 extended the duration of the leases from 99 years to 999 years. It also reduced the rents and the minimum value of the required improvements as stipulated in the 1902 ordinance.

5. R. D. Wolff, 1974, pp. 47–67.
6. ibid., pp. 57, 60.
7. ibid., pp. 54, 103.
8. ibid., p. 107.
9. E. J. Huxley, 1935, p. 287; M. P. K. Sorrenson, 1968, pp. 86ff.

Much of the alienated land was not put to any productive use. While Africans, who needed it badly, were refused access and right to it, Europeans made spectacular gains with it through speculation. By 1930 as much as 64.8% of the land available to Europeans was not 'in any form of agriculturally productive activity'.[10] Speculative profits were accompanied by the consolidation of holdings. By 1912 only five owners together held 20% of all land alienated to Europeans. At one time over 50% of all alienated land in the most fertile parts of the Rift Valley was owned by two syndicates and four individuals. It was also in this area that speculation went out of proportion. Farms which sold for half a shilling per acre in 1908 were resold for ten shillings per acre in 1912. Two years later the same land changed hands on the market at twenty shillings per acre.[11]

In Southern Rhodesia an even greater proportion of land was alienated to Europeans. Between 1890 and 1900 European entrepreneurs and adventurers poured into the country expecting to find a 'Second Rand', which was nowhere to be found. Only small and scattered mineral deposits were discovered. Many of the Europeans bought land from the British South Africa Company (BSAC), which ruled by Charter on behalf of the British Crown, and settled in Mashonaland as farmers. Then in 1894 each member of the Victoria and Salisbury columns recruited to crush the Ndebele was promised 6000 acres of farm land. Land alienation was extended to Matabeleland. Unlike the situation in Kenya, the European population increased very fast, and between 1900 and 1935 Southern Rhodesia had more Europeans than any other country in tropical Africa. By 1901 their number had reached 11 000. Within a decade the population had more than doubled to 23 000, and by 1926 there were more than 35 000 Europeans in Southern Rhodesia. Of this total, 29.9% were born in Rhodesia, 29.2% in the United Kingdom and 32.6% in South Africa. Until the 1930s the European population increased more through immigration than through births.

The increase in European population led to more alienation of land. Throughout the period 1900–35 Europeans held a disproportionate amount of land. By 1911 they had acquired about 7 700 000 ha; slightly less than the areas of the Native Reserves. Land alienation continued, and by 1925 Europeans owned about 12 500 000 ha which included nearly all land over 900 m within 40 km of the railways[12] where temperatures were mild and precipitation was adequate and reliable. In contrast, by 1925 Africans had purchased only some 18 000 ha of land outside the Native Reserves. This figure vividly illustrates their inability to compete with Europeans under the then prevailing circumstances. But up to this time, landownership did not have a rigid legal seal in favour of the white minority. It was the Land Apportionment Act, enacted in 1930 and enforced in April 1931, which

10. R. D. Wolff, 1974, p. 60.
11. ibid.
12. G. Kay, 1970, p. 50.

legally promoted the interests of the white minority at the expense of the black majority. The Act divided the country into four major categories.[13] Native Reserves (22.4%) were the areas within which land was held according to customary African laws; the Native Purchase Area was reserved for purchase as farms by individual Africans, and could be regarded as compensation for loss of the right to buy land elsewhere in Southern Rhodesia; the European Area (50.8%) consisted of existing European-owned land and a further 7700 ha all of which henceforward could be owned or occupied by Europeans only. 'All urban areas lay within the European Area.'[14] The Unassigned Area (18.4%) comprised 720 000 ha of poor inhospitable land, and was held by the government to be distributed in future among any of the other categories. Evidently, the Land Apportionment Act of 1930 introduced racial prejudice into the allocation of land, but did not reject the distribution of land between the races prior to 1925. Consequently it prevented the possibility of 'separate development' of the races within their respective area. The white minority were allocated such a large amount of land because by then Southern Rhodesia enjoyed internal self-government dominated by the whites. To them land served a double function; it was a factor of production as well as an object of speculation.

In Northern Rhodesia relatively less land was alienated to Europeans. The British South Africa Company, which ruled the dependency until 1924, had secured land rights over the entire territory except Barotseland, through treaties with local chiefs in the 1890s.[15] The company successfully encouraged white immigrants. Africans whose land was alienated were forced to move, at times with some compensation. By 1921, 714 out of a total European population of 3634 were engaged in agriculture.[16] During the mid-1930s land in Northern Rhodesia was divided roughly into three categories. Areas reserved especially for Africans totalled 28 740 000 ha and comprised Barotseland (14 970 000 ha) and the Native Reserves (13 760 000 ha). Land already allocated to Europeans was more than 3 430 000 ha, of which 2 225 000 ha were held by two companies and more than 1 200 000 ha in farms. The remaining 60 700 000 ha comprised forest and game reserves.[17]

In British West Africa (see Fig. 16.2), the British attempted even earlier than in East Africa to establish direct control over land, to create forest reserves and to offer land as concessions to European planters and concessionaires. As early as 1894, and again in 1897 the British introduced a Lands Bill in the Gold Coast which was to establish direct British control over lands which were said to be vacant. The reaction of the people, as has been pointed out already in Chapter 6, was the formation of the

13. ibid., p. 30.
14. ibid.
15. R. E. Baldwin, 1966, pp. 144–5.
16. ibid., pp. 41, 146.
17. ibid., p. 149.

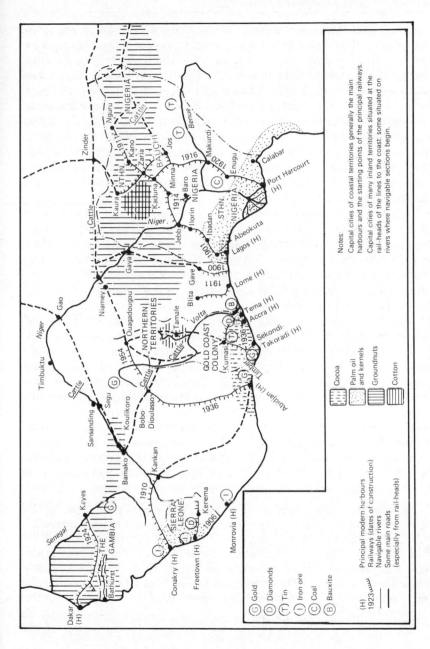

FIG. 16.2 *West Africa: economic development in the former British zones (after R. Oliver and A. Atmore, 1972)*

Within the map:

Notes:

Capital cities of coastal territories generally the main harbours and the starting points of the principal railways.

Capital cities of many inland territories situated at the rail-heads of the lines to the coast: some situated on rivers where navigable sections begin.

Legend:

| Cocoa |
| Palm oil and kernels |
| Groundnuts |
| Cotton |

G Gold
D Diamonds
T Tin
I Iron ore
C Coal
B Bauxite

(H) Principal modern harbours
1923 Railways (dates of construction)
Navigable rivers
Some main roads
(especially from rail-heads)

Map labels include:

Dakar (H), Keyes, Senegal, 1924, THE GAMBIA, Bathurst, Conakry (H), SIERRA LEONE, Freetown (H), 1906, Monrovia (H), Kerema, Kankan, Bamako, 1910, Koulikoro, Segu, Sansanding, Bobo Dioulasso, 1936, Timbuktu, Niger, Gao, Niamey, Ouagadougou, NORTHERN TERRITORIES, 1954, Cattle, Tamale, Volta, GOLD COAST COLONY, Kumasi, 1936, Abidjan (H), Takoradi (H), Sekondi, Accra (H), Tema (H), Blita, Gave, 1911, Lome (H), 1900, 1901, Lagos (H), Abeokuta, Ibadan, STHN. NIGERIA, Port Harcourt (H), Calabar, Enugu, 1920, Makurdi, 1916, Benue, Jos, Baro, NIGERIA, Minna, Kaduna, 1914, Ilorin, Jebb, Gaya, Niger, Kaura, Zaria, Kano, 1911, BAUCHI, NTHN. NIGERIA, Nguru, Cattle, Zinder, Cattle

389

Aborigines' Rights Protection Society in Cape Coast in 1897 by the educated elite and the traditional rulers to resist this proposed legislation. The Society sent a delegation to London in May 1898 which succeeded in persuading the Colonial Office to drop the Bill on the grounds that there were no vacant lands in the Gold Coast and that every piece of land was owned by one extended family or another. A move to introduce a similar Bill in Lagos in Nigeria in the 1910s was also checkmated by the Anti-Slavery and Aborigines' Rights Protection Society founded by the elite led by Herbert Macaulay and the traditional rulers. This Society did this by appealing to the Privy Council in London which ruled that land was the 'undisputed right of the community'.[18] As a result of these victories by the West Africans, the British abandoned the policy of direct control of land though in theory all lands in the conquered areas of British West Africa such as Benin in Nigeria and Asante in the Gold Coast or lands ceded to the British Crown such as Lagos were owned by the Crown while lands in the protectorates such as Northern Nigeria or the Northern Territories of the Gold Coast were held in trust by the Crown for the people.[19] However, rigorous campaigns were mounted by Europeans like W. H. Lever, the Liverpool soap and margarine tycoon, and societies such as the British Cotton Growing Association between 1906 and 1925 for the establishment of plantations in British West Africa, and indeed a few plantations were established in the Gold Coast, Southern Nigeria and Sierra Leone. These campaigns, however, failed and by 1930 only a relatively small proportion of land in British West Africa had been alienated for the use of the colonial rulers and other Europeans and most of this was for mining purposes.

It was neither a deliberate policy on the part of British colonial rulers which saved the land in British West Africa for the Africans during the inter-war period, nor was it because of the notorious reputation that West Africa had acquired as 'the White Man's Grave' by the late nineteenth century. As A. G. Hopkins has pointed out:

> The alleged unhealthiness of the tropics did not prevent the establishment of European plantations in the Belgian Congo, French Equatorial Africa, or Malaya, and it did not discourage serious applicants in West Africa either. Furthermore, the control of malaria and other tropical diseases was becoming more effective by the start of the twentieth century, and the so-called White Man's Grave was beginning to lose some of its unsavoury reputation.[20]

What then did prevent the wholesale alienation of land in British West Africa? The first answer was what Hopkins has termed 'a fortuitous geological fact', that West Africa was found to be not profusely rich in mineral

18. J. F. A. Ajayi and M. Crowder (eds), 1974, p. 576.
19. T. O. Elias, 1971, pp. 1–33.
20. A. G. Hopkins, 1973, p. 212.

deposits. The second was the failure of the move to establish plantations in West Africa. This failure was caused by a number of factors. The first was the vigorous opposition put up by the other British firms operating in these areas, which could not go in for the plantation system themselves. The second was the failure of the few plantations that were established owing to lack of capital and 'a considerable ignorance of tropical condition', shortage of labour and the shifts in world supply. The third and most important factor was the success of the West Africans themselves in meeting the demand for export crops such as cocoa, groundnuts and oil palm using their own simple methods on their small farms, which obviated the necessity of the plantation system in these areas. Another factor was the opposition that any attempt to seize any large areas or introduce large-scale forced labour for plantations would have generated among West Africans.[21] It was a combination of these factors that saved the people of British West Africa from the expropriation of their lands that was the fate of some of those in British East and Central Africa.

Production

The colonial economies under discussion were characterized by two major sectors – one producing mainly for the subsistence of the producers and for the home market, and the other producing essentially primary products for export. Production for subsistence had been well-developed long before colonial rule, and it received only negligible attention from the colonial authorities. Plantains, yams, cassava, rice and maize were produced by West African peasants with the very simple technology which the British met at the end of the nineteenth century. Things were not different in the production of bananas, maize, cassava, millet, and a variety of other crops in East and Central Africa. In an average year most families produced enough for home consumption and put a small amount into the exchange sector. But to both the official and unofficial agents of imperialism, the subsistence sector was of little interest as it did not directly promote the interests of international capital. Unlike the export sector, it did not earn the badly needed foreign currency with which to pay for imports, nor did it provide raw materials to feed the factories of the metropolis. No wonder, therefore, that this sector was neglected by the colonial authorities.

Cash crops

The export sector was basically concerned with the production of primary products – agricultural products and minerals. With the few exceptions of the areas where European settlers owned much land, the agricultural export sector in the former British dependencies of tropical Africa was

21. ibid., pp. 213–14.

PLATE 16.1 *Tea pickers at work on a plantation in Nyasaland (the Lujenda estates, Cholo)*

392

almost wholly in the hands of millions of unspecialized small producers. The family was the basic unit of production. It was only in the southern Gold Coast, and to some extent in western Nigeria, where a substantial proportion of farmers successfully organized their cocoa farms upon a capitalist basis.[22] The unspecialized producers could not take full advantage of market opportunities to maximize their profits during the boom years.[23] But since they were only partially integrated into the international capitalist system, they were neither fully exposed to adverse international economic conditions, which were far beyond their control, nor fully subjected to different forms of colonial exploitation. The main cash crops grown by small-scale farmers comprised cocoa from the Gold Coast and western Nigeria; palm oil and palm kernels from Nigeria, Sierra Leone and to a lesser extent, the Gold Coast; groundnuts from The Gambia and Northern Nigeria; cotton from Uganda, Nigeria and Tanganyika; and coffee from Uganda and Tanganyika (see Figs 16.1 and 16.2). The production of cloves in Zanzibar (now part of Tanzania), from where almost all British Empire requirements came, does not fit into this category. Clove plantations were worked by African labour but owned by Arabs.

Participation in the production of cash crops under the colonial situation did not give African producers any undue emotional shock. First, it did not involve any fundamental technological innovation. Second, many of these crops or similar ones had been grown and processed long before the colonial era.

In the case of the palm oil industry, it had served West Africans for centuries, and required few changes either in production or processing. Three crops – cocoa, coffee and cotton (in Buganda) – were new to the producers, but they all fitted easily into customary working cycles. Consequently the export sector expanded fast.[24] In the absence of any major technological innovation, this fast expansion can be attributed to increased inputs of land and labour.[25]

Contrary to what colonial historians would want us believe, the peasant export sector in the countries under consideration was established with little government initiative. As a matter of fact, in some cases advances were made despite discouraging official policies and practices. Even the Gold Coast cocoa industry, of which the British were greatly proud, was essentially developed with local initiative. Allan McPhee, one of the enthusiastic admirers of imperialist expansion into Africa, erroneously gave credit to the colonial administration for the success of the cocoa industry in the Gold Coast. To him 'there seems little doubt that the cocoa industry of the Gold Coast is a foster child of the Government'.[26] But recent

22. P. Hill, 1963.
23. H. Myint, 1968, pp. 50–2.
24. S. H. Frankel, 1938, p. 193.
25. See R. Szereszewski, 1965, *passim*.
26. A. McPhee, 1926, p. 41.

scholarship[27] has drawn attention to the limited nature of the government contribution to the formative stages of this industry. Indeed, on a number of occasions, agricultural experts, who were paid substantial salaries from the taxes of the agricultural producers, proved more ignorant than the producers, and their advice proved disastrous.[28] Despite the misguided activities of the Agricultural Department, the industry expanded. Starting from almost nothing in the early 1890s, by 1903 the farmers had put over 17 000 ha under cocoa. By 1928 there were 364 000 ha of cocoa.[29] Within two and a half decades cocoa replaced both rubber and palm oil to become the leading domestic export.[30] In 1934 the Gold Coast produced 40% of world output. Yet until this time the industry had benefited little from scientific research carried out in the country. As the West African Commission observed:

> It is ... extraordinary that until 1937 there was no single agricultural station in the cocoa belt proper at which research could be carried out on the requirements of the crop. It is difficult to see how any officer of the Department could be expected to offer correct advice on cultural or other treatments, as he had no opportunity to acquire knowledge under the local conditions.[31]

Real government contribution to peasant agriculture was limited to two related aspects: first, to the making and reinforcing of regulations governing the quality of produce, and, second, to introducing agricultural techniques to increase or preserve the productivity of both land and labour. In both cases there was only limited success, mainly due to the ignorance and presumptuous attitude of 'the experts'.[32]

In Kenya and the Rhodesias the production of cash crops increasingly passed into settler hands as the twentieth century advanced. During the first decade of the century African peasant producers in Kenya and Southern Rhodesia competed with white settlers quite effectively in producing most of the grain which fed the growing numbers of wage earners. Indeed until 1914 African farmers in Kenya contributed more to the cash and export sector than the settlers. This was the period when the settlers were struggling without much success to establish themselves. At this time, too, the impact of the political economy of colonialism was relatively small. Soon the settlers and planters discovered that they could participate effectively in the production of cash crops only if they acted through the

27. S. H. Hymer, in G. Ranis (ed.), 1971, pp. 129–79; also G. B. Kay (ed.), 1972, pp. 12–35.

28. G. B. Kay (ed.), 1972, pp. 13–15, 231.

29. S. La Anyane, 1963, pp. 40, 100.

30. In 1915 cocoa exceeded 50% of the value of domestic exports.

31. *The West African Commission, 1938–9* (London, Leverhulme Trust, 1943), para. 185, cited in G. B. Kay (ed.), 1972, p. 231.

32. For the West African experience see M. H. Y. Kaniki, 1972, pp. 63–7.

respective colonial administrations and systematically reduced the role of African producers to the minimum possible. But settler agriculture, inefficient as it was, required an ample supply of cheap labour. As one Kenya administrator assessed the situation in 1905, 'native labour is as necessary in the development of the land as are rain and sunshine'.[33] Accordingly a number of steps – mostly imported from South Africa – were taken to drive Africans to work for the white man. First, the land curtailment which had been going on was intensified. This step was aimed at denying the Africans alternative sources of cash income.

The case of Northern Rhodesia, where African producers tried to take advantage of the market created by mining labour during the 1920s, is particularly striking. During the early 1920s they sold a negligible quantity of maize to traders, but by 1927 they sold as much as 30 000 200 lb bags. In 1930 they contributed up to 50% of the marketed cattle and by 1935 they sold about 100 000 bags of maize.[34] These developments were not in the interest of the settlers who, by then, had formed an effective pressure group. They were not interested in lowering the price of agricultural products to the miners but rather in acquiring more land for expansion and gaining high prices for their products. In 1928–9, to promote settler interests the government established native reserves in the railway area and other places where Africans and Europeans were competing for the same land. Apart from lessening existing African market competition, this measure, more significantly, 'limited severely' potential African competition in commercial markets by reserving for European settlement a strip extending in most areas about 30 km on each side of the railway.[35] Such steps were taken quite deliberately. A European elected member of the Legislative Council expressed the feelings of the time in 1930, noting that 'the British Empire is *primarily* concerned with the furtherance of the interests of British subjects of British race *and only thereafter* with other British subjects, protected races, and the nationals of other countries, in that order.'[36]

Indeed the colonial administration was committed to promoting settler interests at the expense of the local population as is evident from a number of measures that were taken. First, in 1936 the Maize Control Ordinance was enacted. It established the Maize Control Board which was empowered to purchase and sell all maize at fixed prices. The market was divided into an internal pool and an export pool, with higher prices in the former. European producers were allocated three-quarters of the internal pool and Africans only one-quarter.[37] A year later African participation in the cattle

33. M. F. Hill, 1956, p. 7.
34. R. E. Baldwin, 1966, p. 150. European maize output for sale from 1930 to 1935 increased from 168 000 bags to 211 000 bags.
35. ibid.
36. ibid., p. 147. Emphasis added.
37. ibid., p. 152.

PLATE 16.2 *Breaking cocoa pods in the Gold Coast*

396

trade was also restricted by the Cattle Marketing and Control Ordinance which established the Cattle Control Board with power to fix minimum prices below which livestock sales were illegal, and to regulate exports and imports of cattle. Undoubtedly the ordinance was to some extent aimed at improving the quality of beef, but its 'main purpose' was 'to prevent the destruction by competition of a significant part of the European cattle industry'.[38]

Secondly, prices of agricultural products from peasants were badly deflated. In Southern Rhodesia this took place especially between 1908 and 1911 with grains. But even after the introduction of these two devices, most Africans were not attracted by wage employment on settler farms and plantations, mainly because of the hostile surroundings and conditions of work and the low wages. This state of affairs was not a peculiarity of Kenya and the Rhodesias since the rest of tropical Africa experienced the problem until the 1920s.[39]

Thirdly, taxation was introduced or increased, not only to raise revenue, but to drive Africans to serve the interests of international capitalism. The guiding principle here was stated vividly by the governor of Kenya in 1913:

> We consider that taxation is the only possible method of compelling the native to leave his reserve for the purpose of seeking work. Only in this way can the cost of living be increased for the native ... it is on this that the supply of labour and the price of labour depend. To raise the rate of wages would not increase, but would diminish the supply of labour.[40]

Fourthly, in many of the colonies forced labour was legalized. Africans were forced to provide work for a certain number of days in a year on public works and settler farms and plantations. This was done both during peace and war. Then, the notorious pass system, based on the South African experience, was introduced to regulate the supply of labour. It became effective in Kenya after July 1920. Every African adult male was required to carry a pass (*kipande*) on which the employer recorded, among other things, the kind of work performed, time worked and wages earned. Failure to carry, or loss of the *kipande* rendered Africans liable to a fine and/or imprisonment up to three months. The *kipande* greatly restricted the African's freedom of movement. A man could not leave his job of his own accord. The contractual relationship between employer and employee became subject to the force of criminal law, and the former right of withholding labour became a criminal offence. The African's determination to free himself from such bondage is evidenced by the thousands of prosecutions of 'deserters'.

Furthermore, Africans were forbidden to grow certain crops. In Kenya,

38. ibid., pp. 153–4.
39. E. J. Berg, 1965, pp. 394–412.
40. *East African Standard*, 8 February 1913.

for instance, Africans were forbidden to grow coffee, 'by far the most lucrative cash crop' in the country.[41] It was not until the 1950s that this European monopoly was shattered by Mau Mau.

The main result of all these steps was the proletarianization of the African peasantry, which appears to have taken place on a larger scale in Southern Rhodesia than in the other countries under discussion.[42] Thus African labour employed by Europeans at starvation wages produced cash crops for both the home market and for export. In Kenya, by 1927, between 83 700 and 117 000 Africans, or more than 50% of total wage labour, worked in commercial agriculture. The leading crops were maize, coffee, wheat and sisal. Maize occupied only 325 ha in 1905; by 1920 it occupied nearly 12 500 ha, and nine years later the area had risen to over 90 000 ha.[43] By the early 1920s the settlers had ousted African peasants from the production and trade of this important staple. The area under coffee also recorded a dramatic expansion, rising from 32 ha in 1905, reaching over 11 250 ha in 1920, and shooting up to nearly 39 000 ha ten years later.[44] In 1913 coffee and maize exports earned the country £64 991; in 1920 export of these two crops and sisal earned £566 556 and their value reached £2 429 655 in 1930, with coffee accounting for more than 50%.[45] These developments led to significant structural changes. In 1913, the exclusive African sector contributed 24% of the value of total domestic exports while the exclusive European sector contributed only 5%. Evidently by this time, African labour had made little impact on commercial agriculture. By 1932 the contribution of African areas had dropped to 9% while that of European areas had risen to 76%.[46] A dominant feature of the economy in colonial Kenya was established.

Settler farmers in Southern Rhodesia began to experiment with a number of crops like cotton, citrus fruit and tobacco, but only tobacco became well established and was the leading agricultural export from the 1910s (see Fig. 16.1). In 1927, the value of unmanufactured tobacco exports reached £1 254 000; its highest point between 1909 and 1937. This contribution was 19.9% of total domestic exports.[47] But tobacco was only one of the country's crops. For a long time cash products for the home market (especially maize and livestock products) were more valuable than the production of tobacco for export. For example, with the exception of three years (1926–8), the value of maize between 1920 and 1929 was over 50% of the total value of crops.[48] The expansion of maize exports was hampered

41. R. D. Wolff, 1974, p. 141.
42. G. Arrighi, 1970.
43. R. D. Wolff, 1974, p. 73.
44. ibid.
45. ibid., p. 54.
46. ibid., p. 137.
47. S. H. Frankel, 1938, pp. 231–2.
48. ibid., p. 239.

by high transport costs, as maize is a bulky and low-value commodity.

Settler agriculture in Southern Rhodesia, as was the case in Northern Rhodesia and Kenya, was established and developed with substantial government aid, which was given in the form of loans, research and technical advice. In 1938 the Director of Agriculture, himself a European, complained about the glaring lack of help to African producers, but he was ignored.[49]

In Southern Rhodesia, more than anywhere else in tropical Africa, settlers formed a powerful rural bourgeoisie and adopted a national characteristic through deep commitment to the economic advancement of the country.[50] As early as 1926 agriculture employed more Europeans (22.9% of the total employed) than any other sector.[51] It is noteworthy that in 1935 this sector employed 4305 Europeans, of whom 2733 were farm owners, while the number engaged in mining was 2899.[52]

Minerals

A number of the former British dependencies of tropical Africa were rich in a variety of mineral resources (see Figs. 16.2 and 16.3). Gold was mined in the Gold Coast, Southern Rhodesia, Tanganyika and Sierra Leone. Diamonds became an important industry in Sierra Leone and the Gold Coast. Copper mining was restricted to Northern Rhodesia, while iron-ore mining remained a speciality of Sierra Leone. Only Nigeria and Southern Rhodesia mined coal, an important source of power. Most territories had one or two minerals, only Southern Rhodesia and Sierra Leone had a variety. Starting with platinum and gold in 1929, by the mid-1930s Sierra Leone was mining, in addition, chrome ore, iron ore and diamonds.

The discovery of mineral deposits in the countries under discussion was not a fortuitous affair of the colonial period. Either minerals had been known and worked long before the colonial era, or deposits were found by men who were specifically searching for minerals. Before the colonial era both Southern Rhodesia and the Gold Coast, where the local population had mined and worked gold for generations, were noted for their potential mineral wealth rather than their agricultural prospects. In Nigeria, too, the local population had mined and worked tin for generations before the white men penetrated the interior. Thus in a number of cases prospecting during the colonial period started with locating areas where mining had been carried out by the local population. Expectations of growing rich overnight attracted many Europeans and much capital into Southern

49. *The Minutes of Proceedings at the First and Second Meetings of the Native Development Board*. Lusaka, 1938, pp. 12–17. I am grateful to Miss Maud Muntemba for this reference.
50. G. Arrighi, 1967, p. 20.
51. G. Kay, 1970, pp. 46–7.
52. S. H. Frankel, 1938, p. 238.

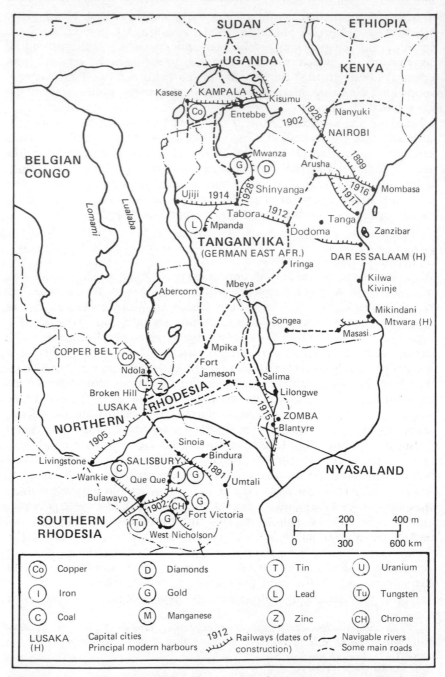

FIG. 16.3 *East Africa: economic development in the former British zones, minerals (after R. Oliver and A. Atmore, 1972)*

Rhodesia from the 1890s, but a 'Second Rand' was not found, only small deposits being located. The small miners, together with the settler farmers, came to form the rural bourgeoisie which began to exhibit strongly national characteristics, rather than becoming involved with large-scale international capitalism.

With the exception of a few cases, mineral resources were exploited with foreign capital. Two main reasons accounted for this feature. First, there were cases where capital on a scale beyond the ability of Africans was required, for example in copper mining in Northern Rhodesia and iron-ore mining in Sierra Leone. Second, and this had a wider applicability, the colonial administrations deliberately and systematically excluded Africans from benefiting from the mineral resources of their country. Soon after mineral deposits were found a series of legislative measures was introduced to give monopolies to imperialist interests. Even where Africans had been working minerals for generations, it became illegal for the African to be found in possession of minerals without a licence. No Africans were allowed to deal in diamond mining. The industry, both in Sierra Leone and the Gold Coast, was monopolized by the Consolidated African Selection Trust (CAST), a powerful multinational company engaged in mining a number of minerals. This monopoly was granted on the pretext that the diamonds market could not be controlled where a number of dealers were operating. Whatever the rationale, bowing to the pressure of international capital, the colonial administration viciously excluded the local population from this most lucrative industry of the day. The Sierra Leone Selection Trust (SLST) was given exclusive rights to prospect for, mine and dispose of all diamonds for 99 years beginning in 1933.[53] It was not until the 1950s, when it became impossible to police the extensive diamondiferous areas, that the government was forced to legalize African participation.[54]

But even in the cases where Africans could take mining licences from the beginning, a number of regulations and technicalities minimized African participation. In the Nigerian tin-mining industry, for instance, it was a crime for the mine owner, in his absence, to leave the mine under the charge of an African, regardless of his qualifications.[55] In Sierra Leone an African could not secure a mining licence unless he could read and understand the Mining Ordinance of 1927, which was written in English. Thus inability to read English disqualified an individual outright from participating in mining.[56] All the same, mining was established as a viable industry.

The export sector of the countries under discussion, comprising mainly

53. A copy of the Agreement is in Public Record Office, Kew (PRO), CO 267/644/22008/Part 1/1934.
54. H. L. Van der Laan, 1965.
55. E. G. Charle, 1964, p. 38.
56. Africans sidestepped this discrimination by establishing partnerships with those who could read English.

401

agricultural products and minerals, expanded fast. By 1914 all countries had experienced a decade of appreciable growth.

Minerals have been regarded as 'the touchstone of economic development in most of Africa',[57] and colonial administrators struggled feverishly in the effort to strike 'a lucky spot'. But clearly the contribution of minerals to colonial economies has been greatly exaggerated. It is true, as Table 16.1 shows, that minerals contributed substantially to the export sector of a few countries, especially the Rhodesias, the Gold Coast and Sierra Leone. In the Gold Coast minerals gained significance from the early years of this century. Between 1905 and 1909 minerals, mostly gold, contributed

TABLE 16.1 *Value of minerals as percentage of total domestic exports*

Country	1913	1929	1930	1931	1932	1933	1934	1935
Sierra Leone	a	a	a	4.0	7.4	21.5	44.7	52.0
Nigeria	8.4	13.1	9.3	11.0	6.7	9.1	17.6	15.7
Gold Coast	33.0	17.8	25.6	25.1	29.3	34.8	46.6	41.0
N. Rhodesia	26.7	28.9	29.4	51.2	85.7	86.8	84.2	72.0
S. Rhodesia	93.3	66.0	65.5	69.2	72.8	79.2	78.2	79.9
Kenya	a	10.0	7.0	8.0	8.0	9.0	7.0	6.0
Tanganyika	a	3.0	n	n	n	n	n	12.0

Note: a = negligible or small
      n = not available
Source: calculated from Annual Reports.

over 40% of the total value of domestic exports, and during eight of the nine subsequent years the proportion was over 30%. The proportion dropped to below 20% during the 1920s, but in 1935 it stood at 41%.[58] The case of Southern Rhodesia is even more striking. Between 1909 and 1913 minerals (mostly gold) contributed over 90% of domestic exports. For most of the subsequent years to 1935 the proportion was over 70%. In Northern Rhodesia, copper was mined from 1910, but it was not until the late 1920s when the mines came into full production that minerals made an appreciable impression on the export sector. From 1931 minerals contributed over 50% of the total value of domestic exports. The proportion increased considerably in subsequent years. In Sierra Leone mining started late, but by 1935 minerals contributed over 50% of domestic exports. In 1936 mineral exports in British dependencies of tropical Africa stood in the following order of importance: Northern Rhodesia, £5 094 000; Southern Rhodesia, £4 422 000; Gold Coast, £2 124 213 and Sierra Leone, £1 245 000. It is interesting to note that though minerals in Nigeria were important in their own right, they were relatively unimportant as a proportion (only 14%) of total exports, while the smaller amount mined in Sierra Leone accounted for 56% of that colony's exports.

The substantial contribution of minerals to the export sector could

57. S. H. Frankel, 1938, p. 210.
58. ibid., pp. 320–1.

mislead us into exaggerating their contribution to the general wealth. But the limited nature of African participation should guide our assessment. Mining was established with foreign capital, and profits accruing from the industry were repatriated to swell the pockets of shareholders abroad, or to develop economies outside Africa. For instance, when the Charter of the Niger Company was revoked in 1899, the company was compensated £150000 for its mining rights in the region where tin mining was later established. According to the same agreement, the company was to receive as much as 50% of all royalties from mining for ninety-nine years.[59] This was a very heavy price for the local population to pay, but the situation was even worse in the Rhodesias, where mining rights remained in the hands of the British South Africa Company until 1933 when they were purchased by the state for £2000000.[60] But even after this change the local population was rarely regarded, and even more rarely treated, as the beneficiaries of mining operations. As late as 1942, a high-ranking official in the British Colonial Office shamelessly placed on record that 'there is particularly little reason for reserving the value of the mineral product to the local inhabitants when those inhabitants have done nothing to develop it'.[61] But even where the colonial administrations nationalized minerals, as was the case in Sierra Leone, Kenya, Tanganyika and Uganda, little revenue, mainly from royalties and income tax, was realized. In Sierra Leone direct revenue from minerals in 1935 was £34100, which was only 5% of total revenue.[62]

Wages remained the only way by which the local population could have acquired a substantial portion of the proceeds from mining, but, as was the case in settler and plantation agriculture, they were kept so low that wage earners had to be subsidized by the peasant sector. Racial discrimination was an important guiding line in this issue.[63] European employees were paid many times the amount paid to African employees, even for similar tasks. Africans were rarely taught important skills which would increase their productivity and, subsequently, their incomes. In Southern Rhodesia where white skilled and semi-skilled workers dominated the labour market,[64] African workers were not even allowed to form trade unions. But even in the territories free from settler domination, it was not until the late 1930s that trade unions, an important feature of collective bargaining, were given legal recognition. With the exception of Southern Rhodesia where mining has 'provided a basis for much local industrial

59. P. Bower in M. Perham (ed.), 1948, p. 5.
60. ibid.
61. Dawe, Minute, PRO, CO 54028/42 J. A. Dawe was Assistant Under-Secretary at the Colonial Office.
62. M. H. Y. Kaniki, 1972, pp. 238, 239.
63. R. E. Baldwin, 1966, pp. 42, 82–99; P. Bower in M. Perham (ed.), 1948, p. 23; G. Arrighi, 1967, pp. 25–6; G. Kay, 1970, pp. 57–8.
64. G. Arrighi, 1967, pp. 20–1; G. Kay, 1970, pp. 57–8.

development'[65] and in contrast to the South African experience, where mining was the 'original creator and protector' of manufacturing,[66] the sector had few spin-off effects. And the few benefits were not without their costs. Damage was done to farmland; bush and economic trees were destroyed; the traditional way of life was interfered with and there was a general breakdown of law and order.

The export sectors of the countries under discussion had two major characteristics. First, exports, both agricultural products and minerals, left the countries unprocessed. Thus, most exports were of relatively low value. Second, there was a tendency towards monocultures. This made the economies of the countries which depended mostly on agricultural exports highly vulnerable. Only Nigeria, with three or so crops (cocoa, palm oil products and groundnuts), and Kenya developed somewhat diversified economies. The weakness of monoculture economics was vividly exposed during the great depression of 1929–34 by the panic and confusion displayed by colonial administrators.

Currency and banking

Like the other colonial powers, the British also introduced modern currencies into their colonies in place of the traditional system of barter, commodity currency, and currencies such as gold dust and cowries. This was mainly to encourage production and export of cash crops and the importation of European manufactures. Indeed, the colonial powers went out of their way to promote and encourage the adoption of modern money in three main ways. These, according to Hopkins, were 'by demonetising traditional currencies; by paying [the] expanding labour force in European coin; and by insisting on receiving taxes in cash rather than in kind'.[67] These methods proved very successful and by 1910 European currencies were widespread in West Africa. In the British colonies these consisted of a wide variety of English coins. In 1912, the West African Currency Board was established to supply currencies to British West Africa. In 1913, the Board issued its first coins of the denominations of 2s, 1s, 6d and 3d and three years later its first currency notes. In British East Africa, the British at first introduced the currency system operating in British India. In 1920, however, one currency board was established to issue coins and notes for the three colonies. It should be noted that all these currencies were linked with sterling in London.

One important consequence of the increasing use of currencies was the introduction of banking institutions in British Africa. In West Africa the first bank to start operations was the Bank of British West Africa in 1894, followed in 1926 by Barclays Bank (Dominion, Colonial and Overseas).

65. G. Kay, 1970, p. 24.
66. S. Patterson, 1957, p. 150.
67. A. G. Hopkins, 1973, p. 206.

These two banks completely dominated banking activities in British West Africa throughout the colonial period. In British East and Central Africa, the National Bank and the Grindlay's Bank also appeared and soon dominated the field. The operations of these banks impeded economic developments in the colonies in three main ways. First, the banks invested all their money in England, including the savings made by the Africans themselves. This meant that they promoted capital formation and therefore economic development of the rich metropolitan country at the expense of the poor colonies. Secondly, and more seriously, recent research has shown that in their lending policies, all the banks discriminated against African entrepreneurs and in favour of the British and Asian population.[68] Thirdly, since banking became the exclusive preserve of Europeans, Africans were denied the opportunity of acquiring training and experience in this vital field.

Marketing

Marketing was greatly neglected by the colonial administrators. The policy of laissez-faire was applied to varying degrees in all the countries under discussion. Cyril Ehrlich's generalization that this policy, 'contrary to popular myth, is practically the only untried Utopia'[69] could only be valid for the post-1940 period. Indeed, marketing boards are an affair of the late 1940s and 1950s. Most of the regulations until the mid-1930s dealt with only two major issues: trading licences and the quality of certain agricultural exports. Marketing co-operatives were recognized by law in Tanganyika in 1932, but nothing was done for five years. Being the champion of free trade till this period, Britain did not even restrict the operations of non-British commercial firms and individuals in her dependencies. Before the emergence of the United Africa Company (UAC) in 1929, for instance, the two leading French firms – the Compagnie Française de l'Afrique Occidentale (CFAO) and the Société Commerciale de l'Ouest-Africain (SCOA) – competed quite effectively with the British firms in the British dependencies of West Africa. During the mid-1920s each of these firms had more branches and 'factories' in Sierra Leone than any British firm.[70] Yet there were no safeguards to protect the local population. The main concern of the colonial administrations was to expand the export–import trade which could lead to increased revenue from customs duties.

Certainly, until the early 1930s, the tendency was to encourage whoever was likely to contribute in this respect. Thus Indian traders were not only allowed, but, to some extent, were also encouraged to patronize trade in East Africa, and to some extent in Central Africa. The Asian population in East Africa increased as follows: Uganda: 1910 – 2000; 1917 – 13026;

68. ibid., p. 209.
69. C. Ehrlich, 1973, p. 660.
70. See M. H. Y. Kaniki, 1972, pp. 58–60.

Tanganyika: 1913 – 18784; 1931 – 23422; Kenya: 1921 – 22800; 1931 – 26759. The 'dislike and distrust of the Levantine communities' in West Africa, which Professor Bauer noticed to be 'marked in official circles',[71] was a relatively recent development. Real hostility towards the Levantines, mostly Lebanese, came not from official circles but from the various European agents of commercial firms, and such hostility was in response to effective trade rivalry presented by the Levantines.[72] And where British firms appear to have been given preference, it was not because of their respectability, but because they could – with the blessing of the British government – act as effective pressure groups and influence colonial policy-makers.[73]

Still, Ehrlich's generalization that 'administrative attitudes, throughout British Africa, rarely encouraged indigenous commercial initiative'[74] is quite valid. But other factors stifled local initiatives. First of all, general official policy, as would be expected in a colonial situation, was geared primarily towards the advancement of imperialist interests. Consequently, the local population was not protected from the devouring jaws of gigantic firms. If anything, they were exposed for easy destruction. By the first decade of the twentieth century, following the construction of railways, European firms were squeezing African traders in two related ways. Through concentration of capital they undersold small, usually one-man, African firms. In this way the big indigenous West African merchants who emerged during the nineteenth century were pushed out of business. Then the big European firms extended their business from wholesale to retail sale. What T. J. Alldridge said of Sierra Leone in 1908 is applicable to many parts of the British empire:

> Formerly the large European firms were merchants pure and simple, in the old-fashioned sense of the term ... their business then was strictly wholesale; they imported their goods; they bought native produce and shipped it, but they never broke bulk. They sold their imported goods in the original packages; they dealt only in large quantities, and left the retail business entirely in the hands of the Sierra Leone traders ... All this is now changed. The middleman's occupation is no longer what it used to be, as the great firms of importers have gradually become their own middlemen, and, while continuing to be wholesale merchants, they have developed retail business on their own account.[75]

Secondly, in most cases African businessmen could not secure bank

71. P. T. Bauer, 1954, p. 148.
72. Slater to Amery, Confidential Dispatch, CO 267/607, 11 January 1925, Encls. 3 and 5.
73. C. Ehrlich, 1973, p. 652.
74. ibid.
75. T. J. Alldridge, 1910, pp. 73–4.

loans because they had no collateral. Furthermore, at times racial prejudice was also employed in this respect.

The role of the European commercial firms has been assessed by many scholars, most of whom agree on the significance of connecting Africa with markets in Western Europe and the Americas. The firm bought produce in and exported it from Africa. They also imported and sold a variety of manufactured goods, mostly textiles. McPhee, Bauer and Hopkins have rightly emphasized the firms' role in expanding the traders' frontier and the cash sector as a whole, but they say very little about the exploitative tendencies of these firms.[76] Traders – Europeans, Indians, Lebanese, and to a limited extent, Africans – appropriated the surplus generated by peasant production, especially through unequal exchange. They paid little for produce and charged relatively high prices for imported goods. The experience of Latin American peasants is quite relevant here.

> A further obstacle to the commercial development of the smallholders' economy is the marketing mechanism. On account of the contractual inferiority of the peasant, and the usual concentration of three commercial functions in the hands of single individuals (purchaser of produce, supplier of credit and vendor of consumption goods), any surpluses developed by the little economy tend to be transferred to the middleman rather than remain available for reinvestment.[77]

In settler-dominated areas, for example Southern Rhodesia, it 'became customary for European landowners to market their tenants' produce, and often that of neighbouring peasants as well',[78] a practice which minimized African competition and assured the settler of a semi-monopolistic position.

Occasionally African producers defended their interests collectively through hold-ups (refusals to deliver produce to market). There were several such hold-ups in the Gold Coast where cocoa farmers were substantially exposed to international market forces. The most serious cocoa hold-up, between October and December 1930, has been described as 'an economic strike for higher prices' and was 'directed against the large expatriate buying firms and their monopoly control' over the Gold Coast economy.[79] In addition to withholding their cocoa, Gold Coasters boycotted European goods. Arrests were made and fines imposed by chiefs to maintain the hold-up. The effectiveness of the movement threatened the very foundation of colonial economic relations, as the colonial government, like the expatriate firms, depended on the cocoa trade for its revenue. Evidently the movement was against the interests of both sides. Accordingly, the colonial administration broke the movement by force, fining

---

76. A. G. Hopkins, 1973, pp. 188–209; A. McPhee, 1926, pp. 32–105; P. T. Bauer, 1954.
77. S. Pearse in T. Shanin (ed.), 1971, p. 73.
78. G. Arrighi, 1970, p. 209.
79. S. Rhodie, 1968, p. 105.

and imprisoning chiefs who supported the hold-up.[80] During the 1937/8 cocoa season another big hold-up was staged against the most important cocoa exporting firms which had formed an agreement to buy cocoa at a fixed maximum price. This time, the hold-up was extended to Western Nigeria, and it ended only with the intervention of the British government. A commission of enquiry headed by Nowell[81] revealed that the marketing system, which involved thousands of intermediaries, was both inefficient and wasteful, and was disadvantageous to both the producers in West Africa and the consumers in Western Europe.

The United Africa Company (UAC), an amalgamation of many former British firms, was the most prominent and most powerful firm in West African trade after 1920. It alone handled nearly half of West Africa's overseas trade during the 1930s, and dominated British West Africa,[82] especially Nigeria. The Company's subsidiaries operated in East and Central Africa, but their role there was much smaller. Nor was there an equivalent of UAC in East and Central Africa.

Trade with Britain put African dependencies at a great disadvantage, as was the case during the great depression. In 1932 Imperial Preference was introduced in British dependencies. Imports from the British Empire had customs duties fixed at between 10 and 50% lower than the general level. But since trade between the dependencies was negligible, the intended beneficiary of the arrangement was obviously Britain. In September 1931 the Colonial Office dispatched a circular to officers administering dependencies asking them to help Britain and reminding them that:

> the interests of the United Kingdom and those of the Colonies and Dependencies are inseparably bound up with one another, that the perils which face the United Kingdom are perils which menace the whole Empire ... that any general collapse of British credit and decline in the exchange value of sterling must spell ruin for the colonies no less than for the United Kingdom.[83]

Despite the higher tariff on non-British goods, their importation, to the advantage of consumers in the dependencies, increased greatly. Canvas shoes and artificial silk and cotton clothing, all from Japan, featured prominently, and their prices were far below those of British goods which enjoyed protection. In 1934 the district officer of Dar es Salaam, Tanganyika, observed that 'practically every shop in the district'[84] was stocked with

80. ibid., pp. 109–15.

81. Great Britain, *Commission on Marketing West African Cocoa* (London: HMSO, 1938), p. 157 and *passim*.

82. A. G. Hopkins, 1973, p. 199.

83. *West African Mail and Trade Gazette*, 24 October 1931, p. 4; *Sierra Leone Royal Gazette*, 15 October 1931.

84. Dar es Salaam District Officer's Annual Report for 1934, p. 4, Tanzania National Archives, 54/4.

many Japanese goods. The development was especially important during this period of economic distress. As one colonial administrator in Tanganyika put it, probably with some exaggeration, 'the average African would now be reduced to wearing bark cloth if it were not for the fact that large quantities of cheap cotton goods from Japanese manufacture are exposed for sale in all the town and country shops'.[85] But the British Government's concern was the success of the British industry and not the welfare of the poor people in the dependencies. In 1934 a further attack was made on non-British goods by raising the tariff to 100%, as a general rule. In addition, a quota system was imposed on the importation of Japanese textiles. There were isolated protests against these measures but the colonized people had to pay high prices, thereby promoting imperialist interests at their own expense.

Infrastructure

One of the most important aspects of marketing is infrastructure. The construction of railways, roads, telegraph lines and harbours received the attention of the colonial administrations quite early on. Though these facilities helped in the general administration, their main task was to evacuate exports. No wonder therefore that the location and general direction of railways and roads took little account of the general welfare of the dependencies. Most railways ran directly from the coast to interior sources of cash crops or mineral deposits. Only a few lateral and inter-colonial links were established. Railways therefore served only limited areas, and, important as they have been, their role in 'opening up' the continent has certainly been exaggerated.[86] Only in Southern Rhodesia and South Africa were there more sophisticated railway networks, mainly intended to connect and serve the widely-scattered mining areas and settler farming regions. The cocoa belt of the southern Gold Coast, too, was well served by railways, while the Northern Territories with no export crops, were completely ignored. (See Figs 16.2, 16.3.)

Most of the railways were constructed, owned, and operated by governments or official agencies. Construction of the first railway in British West Africa took place in Sierra Leone during the 1890s. The first train started operating in the colony area in 1897, and by 1909 the main line, crossing the rich palm oil belt to Pendembu, in the east (365 km) had been completed. A branch line from Bubuyan to Makeni in the north (132 km) was opened in 1915. Soon after the work started in Sierra Leone, other dependencies followed her example with even better results. All major lines were built by 1920. In Tanganyika the British inherited the two railways constructed by the Germans earlier during the twentieth century.

Only in the Rhodesias and Sierra Leone did private capital contribute

85. ibid., for 1933, pp. 3–4.
86. A. McPhee, 1926, pp. 47–8, 108–15, 126–7.

to railway construction. The main railway running northwards through the Rhodesias was a continuation of the South African system and was constructed by the British South Africa Company. The line reached Bulawayo in October 1897 and crossed the Zambezi at the Victoria Falls in 1904. A number of branch lines were constructed by firms interested in promoting mining.[87] The main line reached Livingstone (then capital of Northern Rhodesia) in 1905 and Broken Hill the following year. It was finally extended to the Congo border by a new firm, the Rhodesia-Katanga Junction Railway and Mineral Company in 1909 (see Fig. 16.3). In Sierra Leone the Sierra Leone Development Company, which had been mining iron ore at Marampa since 1933, constructed an 83 km line between Marampa and their loading jetty at Pepel during the early 1930s. The line was exclusively for the company's use. Road construction was carried out by both the colonial administration and local authorities. African chiefs, where resources allowed, mobilized their people to integrate their economies with the wider world. But roads, as a rule, were meant to act as feeders, not as alternatives, to the railways which were official undertakings. Thus the taxpayer had to maintain expensive and inefficient systems.

The most important contribution of modern transport was the dramatic reduction of freight rates, which had two related results. First, human porterage was replaced by machinery, thereby releasing scarce human resources for other productive activities. Secondly, the decreased cost of transport increased the profit margins of producers and encouraged the expansion of the cash sector. Only rarely, however, did African producers benefit from this development. Commercial firms and others engaged in the export sector were too eager to benefit as well, and being more influential, they got the lion's share. In the settler regions, freight rates were manipulated in favour of Europeans, thereby forcing the African sector to subsidize settler agriculture.

The impact of railways was dramatic in Uganda and Nigeria. Before 1902, the year the Uganda Railway connected the landlocked territory with Mombasa through the Kenya highlands, transport costs added 150% to the price of most commodities from the coast. The arrival of the Lagos railway in Kano in 1911 had similar effects. It greatly accelerated the expansion of the groundnut industry. Exports increased from a previous maximum of 2000 tons to 50000 in 1916 and 117000 by 1929. In Northern Rhodesia, too, railways contributed substantially to the export sector, especially to the development of mining.[88] In most other countries, railways contributed relatively little, and for most of the period under consideration they were liabilities.[89] It should be emphasized that even though modern transportation was quite beneficial, it did not create an export economy out of nothing. 'Indeed ... modern transport was attracted primarily to

87. G. Kay, 1970, pp. 42, 44.
88. R. E. Baldwin, 1966, pp. 17–18, 171–2.
89. S. H. Frankel, 1938, *passim*.

regions which though still full of uncertainties, had already begun to demonstrate their economic potential'.[90]

Another part of the infrastructure which had been in existence in pre-colonial days but increased in efficiency and importance during the colonial period was shipping. In British West Africa, this field was by 1900 dominated by one single British firm, the Elder Dempster Line and Co Ltd which was an amalgamation in 1890 of all the British shipping companies operating on the west coast. In 1895, this line and the German shipping firm, the Woermann line, agreed not to compete between themselves and were therefore able to fix rates to the disadvantage of their patrons. In East and Southern Africa, shipping was dominated by the Union Castle Line.

South Africa, 1880–1935

Of the British African colonies and dependencies, so unique and so phenomenal and yet so notorious in their impact were the economic changes that occurred in South Africa during the period under review that they merit separate treatment here, however briefly.

By 1869, South Africa – consisting of the two British colonies of Cape Colony and Natal and the Boer or Afrikaner settler-colonies of Transvaal and Orange Free State – was economically as poor and as peripheral to the world capitalist economy as any of the other European colonies and settlements in Africa (see Fig. 27.1). This combined European population was only 260 000, about 20% of whom lived in the Cape Colony.[91] The Cape had the only town with a population of over 10 000 – Cape Town. There were only 3 km of railway by 1860 and no road for motor traffic. All transport was drawn by animals. Manufacturing was confined only to the making of wagons, furniture, shoes and the tanning of leather.[92] The exports of South Africa in 1860 consisted of primary products with wool as the leading one, followed by iron, hides and skins, all worth £2.5 million a year. As D. Hobart Houghton has concluded: 'The general character of the [Cape] Colony [by 1860] was that of a sparsely populated country largely engaged in pastoral farming and self-subsistence agriculture, too poor to advance rapidly by domestic capital formation, and lacking any exploitable resources to attract foreign capital'.[93] And the Cape Colony was economically the leading province of South Africa by then. Conditions in the other colonies, especially Transvaal and Orange Free State, were even worse.

Not only the economy but the society of South Africa underwent a revolutionary change during the last three decades of the nineteenth cen-

90. A. G. Hopkins, 1973, p. 198.
91. P. Curtin, S. Feierman, L. Thompson and J. Vansina, 1978, p. 329.
92. M. M. Cole, 1961, p. 396.
93. D. H. Houghton in M. Wilson and L. Thompson (eds), 1971, p. 4.

tury. This was primarily because of one single event, the discovery of minerals, first of diamonds in Griqualand in 1867 and Kimberley in 1870, and then of gold in Transvaal in 1886. Within five years of the discovery in Griqualand, more than £1.6 million-worth of diamonds was being annually exported. This had increased to more than £5 million by 1880, that is more than the total value of all the other exports of South Africa.[94] By 1899 De Beers Consolidated Mines Ltd had emerged 'to reorganize mining as a highly capitalized and concentrated modern industry, employing the latest scientific techniques, and establishing a world monopoly of sales through the London Diamond Syndicates'[95] and the value of diamonds exported continued to rise. By 1905, it was about £10 million and by 1910 over £15 million. Even more rapid was the growth of the gold mining industry after its discovery in 1886. By 1890 £10 million-worth of gold was being exported which made gold the leading South African export; this had risen to £25 million by 1905 and to between £45 and £50 million by 1910.

The effects of this mining boom in South Africa were truly phenomenal and all-embracing. Politically, the discovery of diamonds led first to the annexation of the Kimberley area, then Transvaal itself in 1877, and finally to the conquest of Zululand in 1879 after the humiliating defeat of the British at Isandhlwana. Both also contributed to the first Anglo–Boer war of 1881, which was won by the Boers. Similarly, the discovery of gold led to the annexation of all the African states south of the Limpopo river, the Jameson Raid of 1896, and finally the Second Boer War of 1899 which ultimately resulted in the creation of the Union of South Africa in 1910. Some aspects of these far-reaching political consequences and the reaction of Africans to them have been discussed in Chapter 9 above.

Secondly, the discovery led to the pouring in of capital and technical personnel from Britain, Europe and the United States. Indeed, the bulk of the investments in colonial Africa between 1880 and 1939 went to Southern Africa alone. According to P. Curtin and others, on the eve of the Second World War, 'outside per capita investment was estimated at £56 in South Africa, £38 in the two Rhodesias ... and £13 in the Belgian Congo, but not more than £10 anywhere else in tropical Africa'.[96] It was this investment that promoted not only the mining industry but, as we shall see presently, the infrastructure of South Africa. That South Africa should have led here is not surprising for, as Houghton has pointed out, Griqualand from being 'a forgotten no-man's-land inhabited by a few hundred Griqua under their chief Waterboer', thanks to the discovery of diamonds, 'suddenly became a focus of world interest'.[97] The discovery

94. See Fig. 2: 'Exports of South African Produce 1861–1910' in ibid., p. 18.
95. ibid., p. 13.
96. P. Curtin, S. Feierman, L. Thompson and J. Vansina, 1978, p. 500.
97. D. H. Houghton in M. Wilson and L. Thompson (eds), 1971, p. 11.

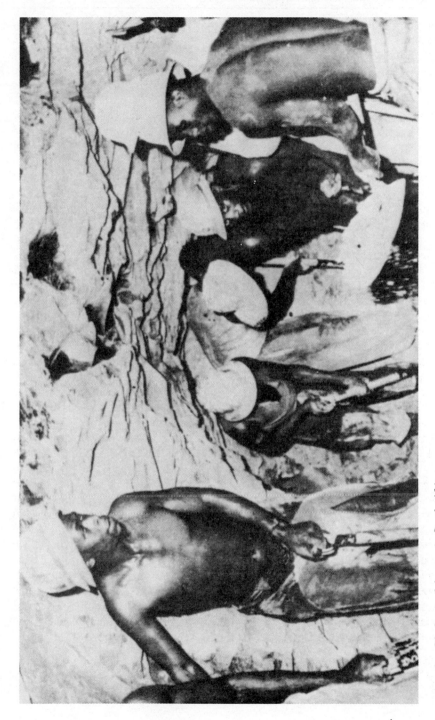

PLATE 16.3 *Black mine labourers in South Africa*

413

of gold did the same thing for the Transvaal and the areas south of the Limpopo river.

Equally revolutionary was the impact of the mining industry on the provision of infrastructure in South Africa. The huge distances between settlements and towns – Johannesburg is 1540 km from Cape Town – and the sparseness of the population had hitherto ruled out the construction of railways as a viable proposition. But the discovery of gold and diamonds made railways and roads not only necessary but also practical. It is not surprising then that railway construction began in the 1870s from different points – Cape Town, Port Elizabeth, East London and Durban – all leading first to the diamond fields and then after 1886 into the Transvaal. The length of railway line rose from 110 km by 1869 to 1700 km by 1889, 3300 km by 1899 and 4190 km by 1905 (see Fig. 16.4).[98] Side by side with railways went the construction of roads. By the end of the First World War, 75 000 km of provincial roads and many more of farm roads had been constructed.

The fourth important impact was in the field of labour and land, and with them came the growth of urban centres. The demand for labour created by the diamond- and gold-mining activities was virtually inexhaustible. It was partly to ensure the supply of labour and partly to safeguard even more the positions of the whites – especially the Afrikaners – that a whole series of pieces of legislation was passed, especially in the 1910s and 1920s, to compel the Africans to leave their farms and places of birth for the mining and other industrial centres. These Acts included the Natives' Land Act of 1913, the Mines and Works Act of 1911 and its amendment in 1926, the Apprenticeship Act of 1922, the Natives (Urban Areas) Act of 1923, the Native Administration Act of 1927 and finally the Native Service Contract Act of 1932. The most notorious of these Acts was the Natives' Land Act under which 88% of the land in South Africa was reserved for the exclusive use of whites who constituted only 20% of its population.[99] The remaining 12% was established as a series of 'native reserves' for the Africans. This Act also abolished squatting and the system of farming-on-the-half by which Africans were allowed to farm part of the land of a white man in return for which the latter received half of the Africans' produce. Thirdly, the Act prevented Africans from buying land outside the reserves from persons other than Africans except in the Cape Province and, in Transvaal and Orange Free State, except by the special dispensation of the governor-general. The Act thus struck at the very basis of African society and caused the immediate displacement of thousands of independent African pastoral and agricultural farmers from their traditional homes and lands and from the white-owned farms. Indeed it

98. ibid., p. 20.
99. P. Curtin, S. Feierman, L. Thompson and J. Vansina, 1978, p. 505; D. K. Fieldhouse, 1981, p. 75; F. Wilson, L. Kuper in M. Wilson and L. Thompson (eds), 1971, pp. 126–36, 436, 440.

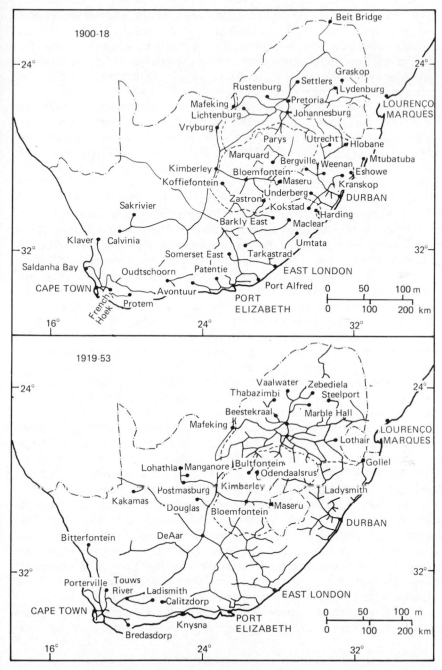

FIG. 16.4 *The growth of the railway network of South Africa, 1900–53 (after M. M. Cole, 1961)*

415

transformed them, in the words of Leo Kuper, into 'a landless and exploitable proletariat' – the worst form of economic dependence. The Act also introduced the principle of territorial segregation into South Africa. This Act remained unaltered until 1936, and by 1931 about 6 million Africans were occupying reserves totalling only 88 000 sq km while 1.8 million Europeans were occupying 1 140 000 sq km.[100]

The Mines and Works Act of 1911 and its amendment of 1926, and the Apprenticeship Act of 1922 also excluded Africans from many skilled occupations and laid down different scales of pay for skilled (largely white) labour and unskilled (largely African, Indian and Coloured) labour. In 1935, the white miner was receiving on the average eleven times what an African was receiving.[101] The Natives (Urban Areas) Act of 1923, the Native Administration Act of 1927 and the Native Service Contract Act of 1932 all also jointly regulated the movement, residence and employment of Africans in the interest of white workers. The Natives (Urban Areas) Act of 1923, for instance, introduced compulsory residential segregation of Africans so as to stop 'undesirable mixing', while the Civilised Labour Policy adopted in 1924 intensified the industrial colour bar by stipulating that non-white workers were to be replaced with poor whites.[102] Finally, the Native Labour Regulation Act of 1911 also made the breaking of contract by African labourers on mines and works a criminal offence.

The total effect of all these measures was to drive Africans from their homes and farms into the new mining and industrial centres and to keep them on European farms as wage earners. The number of labourers on the mines rose by leaps and bounds during the period under review. By 1906, the mines were employing 163 000 people – 18 000 whites, 94 000 Africans and 51 000 Chinese; by 1918 this number had risen to 291 000 of whom 32 000 were whites. By 1936 there were as many as 300 000 African mine labourers, about 40% of whom were from the Transkei and Ciskei Native Reserves, 25% from Portuguese Mozambique and nearly 15% from Basutoland. It should be noted from these figures that in spite of those Acts, not enough labour was being obtained from within South Africa and therefore African labourers had to be recruited in Mozambique, Basutoland and even Nyasaland and the Rhodesias, while from 1899 indentured Chinese had to be imported.[103] It should also be emphasized that partly as a result of the legislation described, most of the Africans employed were not permanent, but rather migrant or seasonal labourers. They were therefore compelled to spend their lives shifting back and forth between work on the white portions and the 'native reserves'.

Another important impact of the mining boom was on urbanization. Since the workers migrated into the new mining and industrial areas,

100. D. K. Fieldhouse, 1981, p. 75.
101. P. Curtin, S. Feierman, L. Thompson and J. Vansina, 1978, p. 502.
102. D. Welsh in M. Wilson and L. Thompson (eds), 1971, pp. 183–4.
103. D. H. Houghton in M. Wilson and L. Thompson (eds), 1971, pp. 15, 19–20.

completely new towns came into existence while some existing ones saw very rapid growth. Thus, Kimberley which was not in existence in 1866 had become a town with a population of 18 000 by 1877, while Johannesburg had grown from a small village into a large town with a population of 166 000 by 1900.[104] Existing towns like Cape Town and Port Elizabeth also saw very rapid expansion during the same period. The percentages of whites living in towns rose from 35.8% in 1890–1 to 65.2% in 1936 and that of Africans from 13% in 1904 to only 17.3% in 1936.[105]

Two other sectors of the South African economy also saw tremendous development, partly as a result of the mining boom. These were the agricultural and manufacturing sectors. The great increase in the population of South Africa and the new urban populations created new markets for both agricultural products and manufactured goods. These markets were further expanded by the acquisition of South West Africa by the Union of South Africa as a mandated territory after the First World War. The new infrastructure of roads and railways facilitated the transportation of these products and the farmers took advantage of these opportunities as well as of the Land Act of 1913. Between 1927 and 1937, the government also introduced a number of measures such as protective tariffs and the establishment of various marketing boards and extension of banking facilities to assist the white farmers at the expense of black farmers. The result was that not only were the white farmers producing enough for home consumption but they also began to export maize from 1907, meat and eggs after the First World War and sugar and dairy products from the late 1920s onwards.[106] But by now Africans had been virtually eliminated from commercialized farming and had become mere wage earners on these farms. To worsen their plight, their wages remained either static or were increased only very slowly. Between 1914 and 1934, the married African farm labourer's average wage increased from 6s to 10s a month to only 8s to 12s.[107] Furthermore, the average monthly wage for a white farm employee in the Cape rose from £2 18s 1d in 1866 to £19 7s 7d in 1952, while that of the non-white farmer increased from 12s 10d to only £2 7s 10d.[108] Thus, during the period under review, the economic gap between white and black widened and the living standard of the black in fact deteriorated.

Even more revolutionary were the changes that occurred in the manufacturing sector and this is all the more interesting since this did not occur, as we have seen already, in most other parts of colonial Africa. As Monica Cole has pointed out, 'The changed political conditions after the Anglo-Boer war encouraged industrial growth and the unification of the four

104. F. Wilson in M. Wilson and L. Thompson (eds), 1971, pp. 113–14.
105. D. Welsh in M. Wilson and L. Thompson (eds), 1971, p. 173.
106. F. Wilson in M. Wilson and L. Thompson (eds), 1971, pp. 132–6.
107. D. Welsh in M. Wilson and L. Thompson (eds), 1971, p. 158.
108. ibid.

provinces in 1910 aroused a surge of national feeling which expressed itself in a desire for industrial development and greater self-sufficiency.'[109] The whites therefore did begin to promote economic development and by 1912 a number of industries had been established. These included fruit preserving, jam making, brewing, soap making, candle making and small-scale engineering industries making windmills, pumps and water-boring drills, gates and fences; and boots, shoes and clothing.[110] The growth of this sector was particularly encouraged during the First World War with a view to diversifying the economy of the country and minimizing its dependence on the mining industry and also providing employment for the 'poor whites'. To promote that sector further, the government not only introduced protective tariffs in 1924 but also created the Board of Trade and Industries in 1921, the Electricity Supply Commission in 1923 and the South African Iron and Steel Corporation in 1928. That these efforts proved successful is evident from the number of people employed in this sector. By 1918, there were 124000 workers of whom 44000 were white; by 1928 this had increased to 141000. The manufacturing sector saw even more rapid growth after the depression of the 1920s and early 1930s. By 1939 its output in food, drink, tobacco, textiles and clothing, leather and footwear, chemicals, metals and engineering was worth about £75 million, making it the second leading contributor to national income with mining in the lead.[111]

It should be obvious from the above that unlike that of most colonies, the economy of South Africa definitely experienced a revolutionary development during the period between 1880 and 1935. By 1932, the gross national product was as high as £217 million and this rose to £320 million in 1937. It also became highly diversified unlike the economy of most other African countries depending, as it did, on mining, manufacturing and agriculture. By 1932, as many as 555000 people were employed in the mining, manufacturing and construction and railway sectors, a majority of whom were Coloured, Indian and African.[112] And all this was due primarily to the discovery of gold and diamonds and partly to the fact that the whites of South Africa were given virtually full control over their fate by the British during the period under review. But all this phenomenal development was achieved at the expense of the non-white peoples of Africa especially the Africans and the Coloureds. As the Native Economic Commission appointed in 1932 reported, while the phenomenon of the 'poor white' had completely disappeared by then, the condition of the non-whites had radically deteriorated. In the reserved areas overpopulation and poverty were widespread; this had caused mass migrations into the towns and mining centres where the Africans were underpaid, discriminated

109. M. M. Cole, 1961, p. 396.
110. ibid.
111. ibid., p. 399.
112. D. H. Houghton in M. Wilson and L. Thompson (eds), 1971, p. 35.

against and packed into slums and ghettos. What was even worse still, they were not allowed to settle permanently in these places with their families but most of them became temporary migrants moving between town and country, and thereby becoming 'men of two worlds', because, as Houghton puts it, 'they had close and inseparable ties both with their peasant society and with the modern industrial world'.[113] Displaced, landless, underpaid and discriminated against, the Africans of South Africa suffered far more economically and socially than Africans in any other part of Africa during the period under review.

Conclusion

By the mid-1930s British colonialism had been well entrenched by integrating the economy of tropical Africa into the world capitalist economy. The dependencies remained important sources of primary products with hardly any industrial sectors. Through participation in the cash sector, African peasants and workers experienced with the rest of the world some of the most serious economic adversities between 1929 and 1935. Neither the worker nor the peasant was a beneficiary of colonial economic relations, but the former experienced worse exploitation. The appropriation of the surplus by international capital is revealed by the backwardness and general poverty of the dependencies during the mid-1930s. Colonial administrators attempted, often feverishly, to arrest the increasing deterioration of soil fertility, especially in the native reserves where population pressure threatened land productivity, by restricting African cultivation. But European exploitation of different resources was nowhere restricted. No one suggested, for example, that minerals should not be mined because they could never be replaced.[114] And mining, generally considered to be a modern sector, contributed only marginally to industrial life. As a matter of fact, mining thrived on the peasant sector by paying workers starvation wages. The economic features which were established during the period under discussion have, in most cases, persisted to the post-independence era.

113. ibid., p. 35.
114. R. E. Baldwin, 1966, p. 160.

The colonial economy: North Africa

The economy of North Africa in the first quarter of the twentieth century did not develop at the same pace or pass through the same stages in all constituent countries (Tunisia, Algeria, Morocco, Libya, Egypt and Sudan), because they were not colonized at the same time (see Fig. 17.1).

Part I: the economy of Tunisia, Algeria and Morocco, 1919–35   A. KASSAB

The economy from the end of the First World War to the economic crisis of 1929

In 1919, Algeria had already been a French colony for eighty-nine years, Tunisia for thirty-eight and Morocco for only seven. But it is clear that on the morrow of the First World War the political, administrative, economic and financial institutions introduced by the French authorities were already well established, and that the process of dispossessing the *fallāḥīn* (peasants; sing. *fallaḥ*) and draining wealth away for the benefit of the metropolitan country (barely begun in Morocco) was already well under way in Algeria and Tunisia. The war had merely slowed the pace of this process: once hostilities ended it resumed at high speed.

The disruption of rural society by agricultural colonization

In Algeria the growth of settler estates stemmed mainly from a consistent policy of 'official colonization'. Land taken from the indigenous peoples was made up into lots by the authorities and allocated to European settlers, who were given every facility for setting themselves up (loans, implements, housing, etc.). Settlers' centres were built for them at public expense to provide essential services (shops, schools, hospitals, etc.).

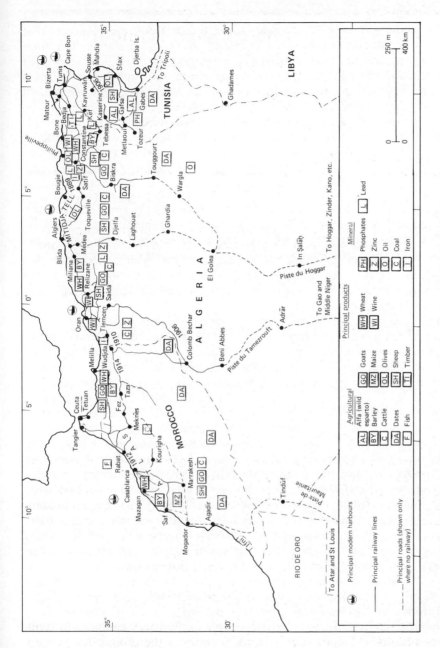

FIG. 17.1 *North-West Africa: economic development in the colonial period (after J. D. Fage, 1978)*

After the war, official colonization ran out of steam (only 70 000 ha of state land was allocated between 1921 and 1931), and private colonization took over. After a short slowing-down period (1918–20), the growth of colonization started again faster than ever, despite the increase in the price of land. This was due to land legislation of 4 August 1926, which simplified the inquiry procedure through which *'arsh* (communal) land could be alienated by replacing piecemeal with overall inquiry. Thanks to this legislation, several thousand hectares of *'arsh* land was acquired by settlers. In 1930 the 25 795 settler estates in Algeria had a total area of 2 334 000 ha.[1] They were mainly in the Tell, the best-watered area with the best land: i.e. the plains of Oran, Sīdī Abūl-Abbās, Mu'askar, the Mitidja, Skikda and Annāba and the plateaux of Constantine, Satīf, Guelma, etc. (see Fig. 17.2).

These estates were already extensive before the great economic crisis. The average area was 90 ha. Large estates of over 100 ha, which made up only 20.6% of the total number of European estates, accounted for 73.4% of the total area of settler land. 'The striking feature of European agriculture in the years 1920–30 was thus the increase in large and especially in very large estates.'[2]

In Tunisia the process of dispossessing the *fallāḥīn* had started as soon as the Protectorate was established in 1881. 'Colonization by capital' (1881–2), which had allowed big capitalist firms (Compagnie des Batignolles, Société Marseillaise de Crédit, Société Foncière de Tunisie, etc.) to gain control of nearly 430 000 ha, had been followed by 'official colonization' systematically organized by the Protectorate authorities, who were apprehensive about the 'Italian peril'.[3] The main aim of 'official colonization' was to increase the French population in Tunisia and promote 'colonization by Frenchmen'. Considerable sums of money were allocated to it. In addition to legislation tending to transfer Tunisian-occupied land into French hands – beylical decree of 13 November 1898 requiring the *ḥabūs* (pious foundations) administration to make at least 2000 ha of land available to the state each year; beylical decree of 22 July 1903 taking the mountain areas into state ownership, etc. – the Protectorate authorities gave settlers major financial help. There were subsidies for European farm credit bodies, settler co-operatives and farming unions, and interest-free setting-up loans repayable in twenty annual instalments for recipients of settler estates. At the same time the authorities developed at public expense the roads and railways in areas with substantial settler populations, built settler villages and improved the water and sewerage provision in country areas where there were settlers. In 1931 settler estates in Tunisia amounted to some 700 000 ha, as in Algeria mainly in the best-watered and most fertile parts of the country. Thus, in the Tell, there was nearly 400 000 ha of settler

1. C. R. Ageron, 1979.
2. ibid., p. 484.
3. In 1911 the Italian population was 86 000 against 46 000 Frenchmen.

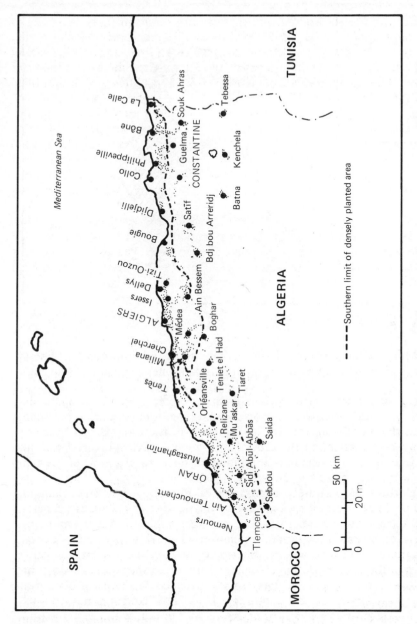

FIG. 17.2 *European grape-wine plantations in Algeria, c. 1930* (*after* Encyclopédie de l'Empire Français, *1946*)

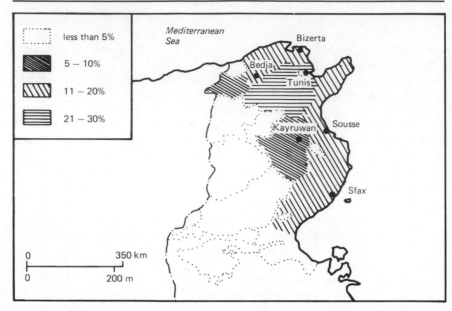

Legend:
- less than 5%
- 5 – 10%
- 11 – 20%
- 21 – 30%

Mediterranean Sea

Bizerta

Bedja

Tunis

Kayruwan

Sousse

Sfax

0 ————— 350 km

0 ————— 200 m

FIG. 17.3 *The extent of agricultural colonization in Tunisia in 1921 (after J. Poncet, 1952)*

land, while in the centre and south there were only 300 000 ha. These figures include both French estates and Italian ones (43 600 ha) (see Fig. 17.3).

Italian estates were typically small (under 10 ha); settlers from Sicily and Calabria were usually vine-growers, market gardeners and nurserymen living in the Tunis–Bizerta area on the coast of the Cape Bon peninsula. French settler estates, on the other hand, were on average very large: in the Abū Sālim area in the middle Medjerda, for example, 80% of French estates were over 500 ha in area.[4]

In Morocco agricultural colonization admittedly began later than in Algeria or Tunisia, but it took advantage of Algerian and Tunisian experience. Progress dated from 1918, and was very rapid from 1923 to 1930. The Protectorate administration, which wanted to bring about heavy European settlement throughout the Sherifian empire, likewise methodically organized official colonization. It made available to the settlers – 60% of whom came from Algeria – state land transferred in the form of settler estates of varying sizes, and communal land. This land was not granted free as in Algeria but sold at low prices, as in Tunisia, with the obligation to develop it and live on it, generous payment terms, ample installation and equipment loans, subsidies for land-clearing, mechanization, planting, etc., exemption from customs duties on imports of agricultural equipment, advances to agricultural friendly societies, and so on.

4. A. Kassab, 1979.

During the same period (1922–32), private colonization managed to take over more than 350 000 ha.[5] Most of the settler land belonged to Frenchmen; a small part of it was farmed by Spaniards, Belgians, Swiss and Italians. This land was mostly in the plains of Atlantic Morocco (Shāwiya, Dukkāla and 'Abda), the Sa'īs and eastern Morocco (plain of Trīffa). Estates of 100–500 ha represented 50% of all European farms.

The features of agricultural colonization

Despite considerable efforts by the authorities to increase the French rural population, official colonization did not manage to establish many French settlers in the countryside of North Africa. Apart from smallholders in vineyards and orchards (Italians in Tunisia, Spaniards in Morocco), European settlers did not constitute a real peasantry such as existed in France at that time. They were mainly large farmers owning enormous estates, a wide range of agricultural equipment and often impressive farm buildings. They had close links with the banks, the various agricultural credit bodies, the research institutes and the many administrative departments directly or indirectly concerned with colonization.

The agriculture they practised was essentially speculative and aimed at exporting their produce rather than selling it on the home market. Most settlers specialized in a single crop, such as vines, cereals or olives (in Tunisia). In the Oran area (Algeria) settler agricultural economy was almost wholly centred on vines, while in the high plains of Constantine and the plains of the Tunisian Tell cereal monoculture was the rule.

This specialization, applied to estates of several hundred hectares, made possible some rationalization of agricultural work and the systematic use of modern agricultural equipment. It was after the First World War that tractors, both tracked and wheeled, appeared in the North African countryside. They gradually became widespread, along with tractor-drawn equipment (ploughs with plough-shares, disc ploughs, multi-disc ploughs, cultivators, drills, etc.). After reaper-binders, combine harvesters also became widespread, bringing enormous savings in agricultural manpower. The new machinery also made it possible to apply dry-farming techniques to cereal land on the semi-arid fringes of the Tell, and to expand the growing of wheat, particularly soft wheat.

At the same time much effort was put into agricultural economics research in the research institutes of Tunis, Algiers, Rabat, etc.; and this provided the settlers with new varieties of cereals, fruit trees, tobacco, etc. suited to the soils and climates of North Africa.

This agriculture, with its sophisticated techniques, often reached a high level of productivity. Yields in all sectors increased continuously between 1919 and 1929; wine production in Tunisia made a great leap, rising from 498 148 hectolitres (hl) to 918 853 hl between 1920 and 1925; and in Algeria

5. In 1932 official colonization had alienated 202 000 ha.

average annual wine production, 6 853 000 hl in the years 1916–20, rose to 18 371 000 hl in the years 1931–5.[6] For wheat the increase in production was also spectacular. In particular soft wheat, an essentially European crop, increased remarkably not only in area cultivated but also in annual production.

Settler production of soft wheat in Morocco rose from 68 285 quintals in 1920 to 1 884 000 quintals in 1935. The Moroccan *fallāḥīn* obtained only 1 316 000 quintals from a larger area (222 815 ha).

Local markets could not absorb the increasing quantities of agricultural produce: in the case of wine (the overwhelming majority of the population being Muslim) almost the whole output had to be exported. Wheat production was also superabundant, especially in wet years.

This highly mechanized agriculture needed large investments, and was continually having to call on credit. Most settlers went heavily into debt between 1919 and 1930, not only to enlarge their holdings but also to equip themselves with farm machinery.

The agricultural sector

SOCIETY AFTER THE FIRST WORLD WAR

On the morrow of the First World War the majority (more than 80%) of the population of North Africa lived off the land in rural areas. The system of land tenure broadly comprised *mulk* land (private property), *'arsh* or communal land and, in Tunisia and Morocco, *ḥabūs* land (property in mortmain). The relative size of each category varied from one area to another: *mulk* land, for example, predominated in the settled areas around the towns and the well-watered plains of the Tell and the Sa'īs in Morocco; while *'arsh* land was mainly in the pastoral uplands, for instance among the Zā'er, who lived from seasonal grazing, and the semi-arid areas (the high plains of Algeria and Morocco and the high and low Tunisian steppe), where the way of life was based on the breeding of sheep, goats, camels and horses.

In areas of *mulk* land there was a whole hierarchy of landowners, the top consisting of a minority of large landowners who concentrated in their hands a major part of the arable and pasture land. These large landowners were particularly common in Morocco. In Algeria, too, despite the great growth of settler land, large Muslim holdings on the morrow of the First World War covered a sizeable area; but nowhere near as much as those of the large Moroccan landowners. 'Large estates were mainly in the *arrondissements* of Mustaghānim, Médea and Constantine. In the latter, there were 834 owners of more than 100 ha in 1914 and 1463 with an average of 185.4 ha in 1930. At that date the average was 263.7 ha in the *arrondissement* of Mustaghānim and 367.3 ha in that of Médea. Lastly, for

6. C. R. Ageron, 1979, p. 487.

Algeria as a whole the 1930 statistics give 7035 proprietors, i.e. 1.1% holding 21% of the Muslim areas.'[7]

In Tunisia also there was a landed aristocracy living in Tunis. Its land was mostly in the cereal-growing Tell (areas of Bedja, Mateur and the Kēf). This land was farmed by fifth sharecropping, the *khammāsāt*, practised throughout North Africa, which did not allow much development of techniques or methods of cultivation. The category of 'middling' or 'well-off' landowners was not insignificant: it is said to have accounted for 22.6% of Algerian proprietors and held 34.8% of the total Muslim area in 1930.[8]

Smallholdings were legion around the towns, in the fertile grain-growing plains such as those of the Sa'īs in Morocco and the middle Medjerda in Tunisia, in the mountains where there were settled farmers (Kabylia, Rīf and the western High Atlas) and in the oases.

Agricultural production and herd populations were liable to wide fluctuations because of the irregular rainfall; famines, though on the decrease, were still frequent. In addition usury still wrought havoc in the countryside, and only large farmers had access to the credit institutions set up by Europeans. But early on in Tunisia (1907) and later in Morocco (1922) *sociétés indigènes de prévoyance* (indigenous provident societies) were set up, mainly to make seed loans[9] to small *fallāḥīn*. The colonial authorities' financial help for settlers was incomparably bigger. Thus, between 1917 and 1929–30, for example, Moroccan *fallāḥīn*[10] obtained short-term loans through the *sociétés indigènes de prévoyance* amounting to 19 million Moroccan francs; whereas long-term loans alone given to settlers (about 4000 in number) between 1925 and 1930 by the Caisse des Prêts Immobilier (Property Loan Fund) set up in 1920 reached 140 million francs.[11]

CHANGES IN RURAL SOCIETY UNDER COLONIALISM

Nevertheless North African rural society perceptibly developed on contact with the colonial occupation. On the one hand, the big farmers took their cue from the settlers, and adopted with varying degrees of success their techniques and methods and even their crops (vines and soft wheat). On the other, a great many countryfolk working on settler farms or those of the big North African farmers became agricultural wage labourers, and were thus proletarianized: social inequalities became more entrenched after the First World War with the spread of agricultural mechanization. The

7. ibid., p. 59.
8. ibid.
9. The very limited cash credit was subject to such strict conditions (binding commitments, guarantees in the form of third-party sureties or liens on land, mortgages on title deeds, etc.) that only a minority of 'well-off' farmers could get it.
10. The rural population in 1926 was estimated at 5450000 (87.9% of the total population.
11. R. Hoffherr, 1932.

use of tractors and modern agricultural machinery gave the settlers and big indigenous farmers insatiable land hunger. To make their modern equipment profitable, whether they owned or hired it, they had continually to increase their output, and hence the size of their holdings; and this expansion was only possible, once the state land was used up, at the expense of the small and middling Muslim farmers, who were driven further and further back towards the mountainous areas or the foothills. In order to spread out also into the space used by the pastoral peoples of the steppes and take part of it for settlement, the colonial authorities set out by every possible means to sedentarize the peoples who lived in these areas and turn them into cereal-growing or orchard-farming peasants. In the Tunisian high steppes, for example, 'after the First World War, for every allocation of land to settlers there was a corresponding allocation intended to tie the local people to the land; and since 1922 many small plots of uniform size have been distributed to the occupants of certain communal or *ḥabūs* lands'.[12]

The consequence of this was the spread of settlement into areas where the indigenous peoples needed large areas of grazing for their cattle, and the start of a process of sedentarization that led to impoverishment and flight from the land.

The colonial character of the new ways of organizing the infrastructure

Mining

European settlement in the three countries of North Africa meant not only the seizure by settlers of much of the best land, but also the working of underground resources mainly for the benefit of foreign companies.

These resources were prospected very early and exploited quickly. In Algeria the first mines were opened in 1845; in Tunisia the phosphate deposits at Ḳafsa were already discovered by 1885–6 (only four years after the establishment of the Protectorate) and exploited from 1889 on.

In Morocco the first mining *ẓahīr* (decree) organizing mineral prospecting and working dated from 1914: it laid down the principle that 'the mine belongs to the first occupier', which led to abuses; the 1923 *ẓahīr*, intended to put a stop to the manoeuvres of speculators by redrafting the mining regulations, only delayed the systematic working of the country's mineral resources. Apart from the Khūribḳa phosphates worked since 1920, Morocco even in 1928 exported only some 8000 tonnes of ore. But prospectors and applicants for mining concessions fell on the country like a swarm of locusts: the number of search licences issued between 15 September and 1 January 1939 reached 3500, while prospecting licences numbered 400.

The discovery of the Djerāda coalfield in 1923 was to lead to another

12. J. Despois, 1961.

redrafting of Moroccan mining legislation. In that year the Bureau de Recherches et de Participations Minières (Mining Research and Joint Stock Bureau) was set up, specializing in the search for solid and liquid fuels; while the * zahīr* of 1 November 1929 simplified earlier mining regulations and protected the interests of the state. From that time onwards the prospecting and working of mineral resources grew faster. The Djerāda coal basin, and also the Khenīfra iron ore deposits and the Iminī manganese deposits, were systematically explored and prospected; the Awlī lead mine on the upper Mulūja, one of the largest in North Africa, was brought into production and quickly equipped. The manganese deposits at Abu 'Arafa, in south-eastern Morocco, were linked by rail to Wudjda in 1933, while the cobalt at Abū 'Azīz, the lead and zinc at Mibladen, the tin at Wulmīs and the molybdenum at Azzekūr, in the High Atlas, were all brought into production. On the eve of the economic crisis, Morocco was seemingly one of the North African countries richest in mineral resources. But it was phosphates above all that took pride of place, both in terms of tonnage produced and of quantities exported. Exports rose from 8232 tonnes in 1921 to 1 179 000 tonnes in 1930.

In Algeria and Tunisia deposits of phosphates (Kuwayf and Ḳafsa), iron ore (Benī Sāf, Wenza and Djarīsa), lead, zinc, etc., had already been brought into production before the First World War, and nearly the whole output was exported to France and other West European countries. This mineral wealth was exploited entirely by foreign companies, which provided the capital, the technicians, the managers and so on. The Société des Mines d'Aouli et Mibladen, for example, was under the control of the Société Penarroya-Maroc, which was associated with the Banque de l'Union Parisienne-Mirabaud and also with the Banque de Paris et des Pays-Bas, Kuhlamann and the Bureau Minier de la France d'Outre-Mer. The zinc and lead mines at Tūwaysit were owned by the Belgian Compagnie Royale Asturienne des Mines; and the American Morgan group was one of the biggest shareholders in the Zellīdja mine. In Tunisia the Djarīsa iron ore mines were under the control of the Compagnie Algérienne de Crédit et de Banque, representing the Banque de l'Union Parisienne. In Algeria likewise all the mineral wealth was in the hands of foreign, particularly French, capitalists.

Communication and ports

To link the various mineral deposits to the export ports, railways were built very early in Algeria (from 1844) and in the early years of the Protectorate in Tunisia and Morocco. By 1919 the main lines of the Algerian and Tunisian railways were already set up: they linked the large towns (mostly near the coast) with each other and the mines with the main export ports (Oran, Algiers, Annāba, Tunis, Sfax and Sousse). In Morocco railway development was slower because of a clause in the Franco-German treaty of 4 November 1913 prohibiting France from building any railways before the construction of the Tangiers–Fez line (see Fig. 17.1). It was not until April 1923 that the first line, Casablanca–Rabat, was inaugurated. Unlike most of the Tunisian and Algerian lines, the Moroccan network consisted mainly of standard-gauge track (1.44 m). But like that of the other North African countries it was manifestly colonial in character, with the main lines linking the towns and ports with the Atlantic coast and the axial lines serving the mines and the large towns in the interior (Fez, Meknès and Marrakesh). It was built and run entirely by foreign companies.

The road network was also planned to serve the big towns where most of the European population lived and those parts of the countryside where settler estates had been established. Most of the Algerian road network, for example, is in the northern Tell, where the European farms and the largest towns were concentrated.

The same was true of the port infrastructure, which was planned and developed essentially in order to open up the countries of North Africa to French and foreign manufactured goods and to export minerals and agricultural produce.

By 1919, whereas the Algerian and Tunisian port infrastructure had already been built, Morocco's had hardly been begun. It was not until 1917 that the fitting up of the port of Casablanca was completed. Traffic through this port grew rapidly and steadily, from 400 000 tonnes in 1920 to 2 220 000 tonnes (including 1 198 000 tonnes of phosphates) in 1927.[13] It handled over 80% of the total traffic through Moroccan ports. Traffic through Kenitra (formerly Port Lyautey), the second biggest port in Morocco, barely reached 191 000 tonnes in 1927.

The type of traffic through all the ports showed the colonial nature of the trade and the unequal relationships between the three countries of North Africa and France.

The iniquity of the customs and fiscal system

The customs system
Algeria being a colony, Algerian and French merchandise was reciprocally admitted duty-free into the other country. Foreign goods imported into either France or Algeria were likewise liable to the same tariffs; and under the flag monopoly French shipping had the exclusive right to sail between Algeria and French ports. Thus there was a true customs union between France and Algeria, 'one of the most perfect met with in the world of economics'.[14] But this union condemned Algeria to remain an exporter

13. The ports, like the railways, were built by means of a series of public loans floated by the Moroccan administration and guaranteed by the French government (1916 loan and 1920 loan of 290 million francs).

14. L. Bouis, 1946, Vol. II, p. 56.

of raw materials and agricultural produce and an importer of manufactured goods.

The customs system in Tunisia on the morrow of the First World War was governed by the acts of 19 July 1890 and 2 May 1898. The latter gave a preferential position to French manufactured products, especially metal goods, machinery, textiles, etc. Similar foreign goods, however, were not liable to duty under the French tariff, so that the Tunisian market was flooded with manufactured products from France and foreign countries. A partial customs union was introduced in 1928: Tunisian agricultural produce admitted free of duty was no longer subject to quotas, but French goods were given either complete exemption from duty or protection against similar foreign goods. Thus French goods could compete on the Tunisian market with those from other industrial countries, and sometimes even eliminate them, which had the effect of making imported goods dearer and paralysing Tunisian attempts at industrialization.

Commercial and customs relations between Morocco and foreign countries were even more iniquitous and unequal. The Act of Algeciras (1906) laid down the principle of strict economic equality between signatory countries on the Moroccan market. Wherever they came from and whatever bottoms they were carried in, goods entering Morocco were liable to a flat 10% *ad valorem* duty plus an additional 2.5% duty for the Caisse Spéciale des Travaux Publics (Special Fund for Public Works). This 'open door' system allowed the big exporting countries to flood Morocco with their manufactured goods and agricultural produce, with no *quid pro quo* except possibly the advantage of buying supplies at competitive prices during the fitting-out stage (1920–30). But with the beginning of the economic crisis Morocco felt the drawbacks of this system, which was 'a growing impediment to Moroccan prosperity as the country's activity began to move towards a comprehensive economy in which infant industries would require the necessary protection'.[15]

Morocco nevertheless had to have recourse to indirect protectionism restricting access for certain foreign foodstuffs. Thus the *ẓahīr* of 22 February 1921 made the entry of wheats, barley and their derivatives subject to licence; that of 4 June 1929 virtually banned foreign wheats and flours; but manufactured goods continued to pour into Morocco on the same terms as in the past.

The nature of North Africa's exports clearly demonstrated the nature of the North African economy and its customs system. Moroccan exports between 1920 and 1930, for example, consisted mainly of phosphates and cereals. The imbalance in the type of goods bought and sold by North Africa was responsible for the almost continual deficit on its balance of trade, imports by value being far higher than exports for all three countries (see Figs. 17.4, 17.5, 17.6). For example, the value of Tunisian

15. R. Hoffherr, 1932, p. 243.

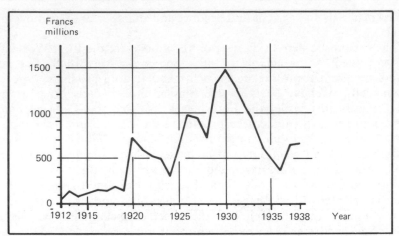

FIG. 17.4 *The Moroccan balance of trade deficit, 1912–38* (*after* Encyclopédie de l'Empire Français, *1946*)

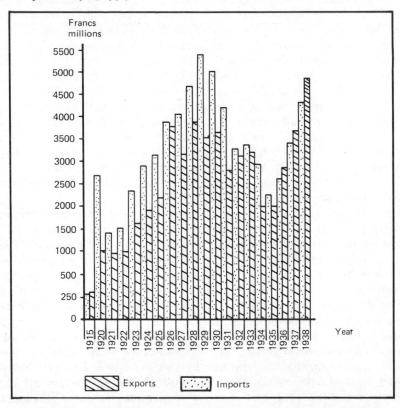

FIG. 17.5 *Global Algerian trade, 1915–38* (*after* Encyclopédie de l'Empire Français, *1946*)

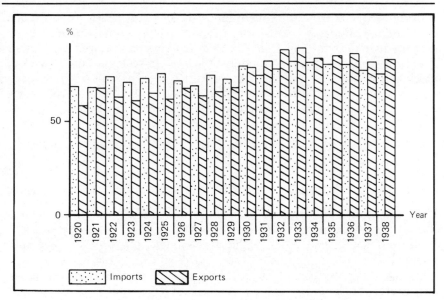

FIG. 17.6 *Trade with France as a percentage of global Algerian trade, 1920–38 (after Encyclopédie de l'Empire Français, 1946)*

imports reached 1984 million francs in 1929, whereas exports brought in only 1408 million francs.

Finally, the customs system was largely responsible for the ruin of the rural and urban craft industries.

The fiscal system

One of the first things the French authorities did when they took over North Africa was to reorganize the financial and fiscal system. They set up a Financial Administration whose first task was to draw up a budget and check expenditure. Budgetary strictness and discipline enabled them to balance receipts and expenditure, and this balance was frequently achieved between 1919 and 1930. But as a result of the crisis expenditure exceeded receipts; and in 1939 the Tunisian budget had a deficit of over 100 million French francs.

Revenue came mainly from customs duties and from taxes on land, agricultural produce (*tartīb* in Morocco) and consumption goods (indirect taxes), in short mainly from the indigenous population: 'spread over an organic mass of native taxpayers, the [fiscal] burden on the natives often became very heavy'.[16]

In addition, in order to purchase equipment, the three North African

16. ibid., p. 292.

countries had to borrow at frequent intervals. In 1930 Algeria owed France 2000 million francs,[17] while in 1932 Morocco's total indebtedness amounted to 1691 million francs.[18] The equipment acquired by dint of these loans benefited first and foremost the modern sectors of the economy, which was dominated by European concerns; yet the bulk of these loans was redeemed out of Muslim money. In 1931 the servicing of Morocco's public debt absorbed more than a third of the country's budget.

Tunisia, Algeria and Morocco during the great economic crisis (1930–5)

The crisis and the major sectors of the economy of North Africa

The crisis hit North Africa a little late. Its full effects were felt from 1932 onwards; but it came on earlier in Morocco than in Tunisia or Algeria,[19] the former being then right in the development phase of its economic potential.

One of the first sectors of the economy affected by the crisis was settler agriculture, which, as we have seen, was highly dependent on credit and foreign markets. Once prices collapsed and foreign outlets were shut off or became scarce, the mechanized but debt-ridden farmers could no longer honour their commitments to the various credit bodies to which they were indebted. Likewise with mining, which was totally dependent on foreign markets because mineral raw materials were hardly processed or used at all in the producer countries.

The domestic economy was also hit by the crisis, its contribution to the export of agricultural produce being affected by the slump and the fall in prices. So were the craft industries, which played an important role in the economy of the big towns in Morocco (Fez, Meknès and Marrakesh) and in Tunisia (Tunis, Kayruwān and Sfax) and whose foreign outlets were practically cut off.

The effects of the crisis on the settler economy

AGRICULTURE

The first European agricultural sector affected by the crisis was the one most dependent on foreign markets, especially the French market, namely the wine industry, whose exports (in Algeria, for example) represented 66% by value of all exports in 1933. The average selling price of a hectolitre of wine, which in 1927 reached 168 francs, fell to 108 francs in 1931 and 54 francs in 1934. The slump and superabundant harvests, especially the 1935 one, led to the accumulation of enormous stocks of wine in Algerian and Tunisian cellars. Now the wine industry, particularly in Algeria, was

17. C. R. Ageron, 1979, p. 414.
18. R. Hoffherr, 1932, p. 304.
19. J. Berque, 1970.

one of the cornerstones of the settler economy. In Tunisia it provided a living for 1372 European proprietors: 'hence the bankruptcy of the wine industry could mean the bankruptcy of a large part of the French rural colony on whose settlement such care had been lavished'.[20]

The crisis also affected the olive-oil industry, especially the Tunisian one, a third of whose annual output was exported, mainly to Italy but also to France. Now Italy subsidized its olive-oil producers, to encourage them to export at low prices and to protect its olive-oil industry; and in 1932 it imposed prohibitive duties on foreign oils. In 1935 it stopped its imports from France and the French empire in retaliation for the French embargo, adopted in pursuance of the League of Nations sanctions of 5 October 1935 following the Italian aggression against Ethiopia. The drop in exports and prices[21] admittedly hit Tunisian growers first; but it also hit the European planters in the Sfax area, who owned enormous estates and produced mainly for export. The quantity of oil exported, 409800

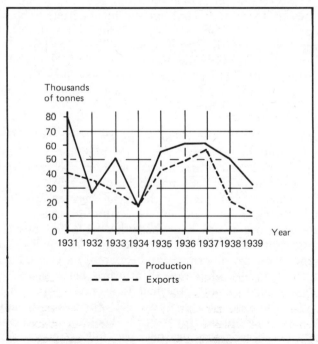

FIG. 17.7 *Production and export of Tunisian olive oil, 1931–9* (*after* Encyclopédie de l'Empire Français, *1946*)

20. J. Poncet, 1952, p. 300.
21. The price of oil, which reached more than 1000 francs a quintal in the years 1925–8, fell to 700 francs in 1930 and 300 francs in 1933.

quintals in 1930, fell to under 200 000 in 1936; 'this was another real disaster: it brought European planting to a halt, and marked the end of the expansion of French settlement in the Sfax area' (see Fig. 17.7).[22]

The third agricultural venture, essential both to *fallāḥīn* and settlers was cereal growing. Algerian settlers had over a million hectares of land under wheat in 1934; and in Morocco nearly 96% of the land farmed by Europeans was given over to cereal growing. But the settlers grew mostly soft wheat, intended for the French milling trade: in Tunisia, for example, nearly all the 160 000 ha under soft wheat belonged to Europeans. In this sector too a drop in prices went hand in hand with a fall in exports; the value of European exports of Tunisian wheat, 291 408 000 francs in 1931, fell to 60 845 000 francs in 1934.

THE CRISIS IN THE MINES

The increase in mineral prices on the world market became unsteady in 1927, and the downward trend in mineral exports emerged clearly in 1931. Shipments of Moroccan phosphate fell from 1 779 000 tonnes in 1930 to 900 731 tonnes in 1931; and Tunisian shipments from 3 600 000 tonnes bottomed out at 1 623 000 tonnes in 1932. While selling prices continued to fall, prime costs rose. In 1932 a tonne of Tunisian phosphate whose prime cost was 65.77 francs at the port of loading sold for 53.77 francs.[23] The same held good for other minerals (lead, zinc, iron, etc.).

The crisis led to the closure of a great many mines, especially those that were marginal or split up.

The disruption of the Muslim economy by the crisis

Given that the overwhelming majority of the population of North Africa made its living out of agriculture, it was mainly in the agricultural sector that the effects of the crisis were most painfully felt.

The main products disrupted by the crisis were cereals (particularly hard wheat and barley), wool and oil, especially in Tunisia.

All categories of producers, both those that were part of the domestic and foreign agricultural marketing networks and also small *fallāḥīn* living on a subsistence economy, felt the painful effects of the crisis. For Tunisian hard wheat, for example, while the fall in prices between 1928 and 1931 was only 20% of 1926 prices, it reached an average of 45% in 1932 and 60% in 1935 (the bottom of the depression).[24] For barley the fall in prices reached 75% of 1926 prices in 1935.[25] Wool, produced and largely marketed by stock-breeders of all categories, fell in 1935 to 60% of the 1926 price. The crisis likewise hit the craft industries, which were already

22. J. Poncet, 1952, p. 302.
23. Grand Council of Tunisia, Eleventh Session (November–December 1932). French Section, Report by Boissée, Director of the Chamber of Mining Interests, p. 29.
24. A. Nouschi, 1970.
25. H. el Annabi, 1975.

severely depressed by competition from imported manufactured goods. The Tunisian craft industries' share of Tunisian exports, for example, 3% in 1920–5, fell to 1.95% in 1930–5.[26]

It is not surprising, in these circumstances, that in the three North African countries the overall value of external trade fell steadily between 1931 and 1936. The value of Tunisian external trade fell in 1936 by nearly 40% compared with 1927–8. In Morocco the total value of external trade fell from 3 780 606 francs in 1929 to 1 750 518 francs in 1935. Algerian external trade also fell off markedly, from 9 983 000 francs in 1930 to 6 702 000 francs in 1936.

Social effects of the crisis

In the first place, the social effects were extremely serious. The debt-ridden settlers and North African farmers who could not honour their commitments were faced with bankruptcy. A great many of those who were not yet in debt had to take out loans and mortgage their possessions. The small and middling farmers, who did not have access to the banks or agricultural credit institutions, had to turn to moneylenders in the countryside or the towns in order to pay off their debts.

The crisis considerably sharpened social divisions by enabling financiers (often also moneylenders), big business men and rich owners of blocks of plots in the town and the country to increase their wealth inordinately. Property and farming became increasingly concentrated in the hands of a minority of big property owners from the country (and often too from the towns). In Algeria 'this world crisis, marked by a catastrophic drop in cereal and sheep prices, made life difficult, on the other hand, for proprietors of 50 to 100 ha, and aggravated the impoverishment of peasants on small parcels of land. Thus it is understandable that large areas were put up to auction and part of the land was bought up by the wealthiest people.'[27] The formation of many very large settler and Muslim estates dates from the time of the great crisis. With the farming crisis and natural calamities, drought and famine became commonplace in several parts of North Africa, particularly in the steppe areas. A considerable number of *fallāḥīn*, ruined, starving or pursued by tax collectors, flocked to the towns. One of the consequences of the great crisis was intensification of the flight from the countryside and the establishment or growth of shanty-towns[28] on the outskirts of the towns. Henceforth no town of any size escaped this phenomenon, which took on enormous proportions during and after the Second World War.

The economic depression led to the stoppage of building work and the closure of mines and workshops, and so brought about massive unemploy-

26. A. Kassab, 1976.
27. C. R. Ageron, 1979, p. 509.
28. For example, the shanty-towns of Ben Msīk at Casablanca, of Melāsīn and Djabal al-Aḥmar at Tunis, and so on.

ment among townspeople, craftsmen and workers in all occupations. 'By 1932 12% of workers in Algiers were unemployed ... [in 1935], 77% of building workers were out of work in Algiers'.[29]

Solutions to the crisis

Government intervention
A crisis of such proportions could not leave the authorities unconcerned; and the role of the state in the organization of the various sectors of the economy was considerably expanded as a result. The main measures taken by the colonial authorities and the government in France had to do with the agricultural sector; for most of the North African population made their living out of it, and the future of European settlement depended on it.

The steps taken to help the wine industry took the form for Tunisia in particular of increasing the quotas of wine admitted duty-free into the home country. The extension of new vineyards was forbidden throughout North Africa, and the pulling up of vines was encouraged by the making of grants.

As regards cereal growing, several measures were taken by the government to put it on its feet again. Stocks of hard wheat and soft wheat were built up, and stockpiling grants given; a minimum price was fixed for hard wheats and soft wheats, and the sale of stockpiled cereals was staggered; government-guaranteed warehouse warrants were issued, on which farmers could obtain bank loans of up to more than two-thirds of the value of the produce; and measures adopted in France to control, protect and regulate the cereals market were applied in the three North African countries.

Semi-governmental agencies (Office des Céréales, Office de l'Huile, and Office du Vin) were set up to apply these measures in the respective sectors.

To end the foreclosures and prosecutions directed against insolvent settlers and farmers, the Caisse des Prêts de Consolidation (Consolidation Loan Fund) (1932) was set up in Algeria and the Caisse Foncière (Land Fund) (1932) and the Caisse Tunisienne de Crédit et de Consolidation (Tunisian Credit and Consolidation Fund) (1934) in Tunisia. Days of grace, debt reductions and mortgage loans could also be granted to debtors threatened with expropriation.

The distress in the rural communities, and the resultant nationalist unrest, led the French authorities to investigate the lot of the North African *fallāḥīn*. From 1933 to 1935 a peasant policy was introduced in the three countries of North Africa.

The peasant policy
In Algeria the Act of 9 July 1933 established a Fonds Commun des Sociétés

29. C. R. Ageron, 1979, p. 43.

Indigènes de Prévoyance (Pool of Indigenous Provident Societies), which enabled the Administration to give loans and grants to Muslims alone through the Société Indigènes de Prévoyance. The Pool also helped, on the same basis as the Caisse des Prêts Agricoles (Agricultural Loans Fund), to get *fallāḥīn* out of debt by giving them consolidation loans. A 'social economy' department in the Directorate of Native Affairs instituted certain measures to modernize the production techniques of the *fallāḥīn*; it gave long-term loans for tree-planting, and made advances for the purchase of fertilizers, ploughs, etc. But all these measures, useful though they were, were nowhere near enough: the loans to farmers were frittered away 'among a myriad of *fallāḥīn*',[30] and the steps taken to modernize Muslim agriculture and stiffen up the *fallāḥīn* were not really persevered with.

In Tunisia and Morocco the state also set out to inject credit into the countryside, settle land-tenure problems and diversify the agricultural production systems of the *fallaḥīn*. But the legislation enacted was not backed up by large-scale campaigns to improve and expand the production methods of the herdsmen and *fallāḥīn* or enlarge the holdings of the poorest ones.

New trends in agriculture; the persistently colonial nature of the economic system

The economic crisis clearly showed the dangers of monoculture, the predominant system in particular among European farmers. The government promoted crop diversification by encouraging the extension of orchard farming and market gardening and developing irrigation.

The interruption of Spanish and Italian fruit exports to France because of the Spanish Civil War, and the application of sanctions against Italy by the League of Nations, laid the French market wide open to North African fruit production and contributed to a very rapid development of fruit-tree cultivation, particularly citrus fruits. Enormous orchards of orange trees, clementine trees and lemon trees were planted in the Mitidja in Algeria, on Cape Bon in Tunisia and in the Casablanca, Khenīfra, Meknès, Wudjda, etc. areas in Morocco. Semi-governmental bodies such as the Office Tunisien de Standardisation were set up to organize the packing, sale and export of the fruit.

The growth of market gardening and early vegetable and fruit gardening in the coastal plains was linked to that of irrigation and to the tapping of underground water and streams. In Morocco dams were built on the Wādī Baht (1934), on the Umm al-Rabī'a at Kasba-Zaydāniya, in the Tadla (1936) and on the Wādī Nafīs at Lalla Takerkust (1936). Irrigated areas were laid out in the Sīdī Sulajmān area, the plain of the Tadla, the plain of the Triffas, etc.

In Tunisia large olive groves were planted in the grain-growing areas of the Tell, particularly on the big settler estates.

30. ibid., p. 497.

439

Nevertheless the economy of North Africa remained essentially agricultural. There were only a few processing industries using as raw material either local agricultural produce, namely flour-mills, oil mills, distilleries, pasta factories, breweries and canneries, or minerals; these latter were given either an initial processing (e.g. lead smelters) or a more complex preparation (e.g. hyperphosphate and superphosphate plants) before being exported.

Firms, mostly small, were almost entirely in the hands of Europeans, and the number of workers in industry was not large: 40000[31] for the whole of Algeria in 1938. Despite the highly under-industrialized state of the country, the towns of North Africa were nevertheless growing very rapidly. The proportion of built-up area in Morocco, 7% at the beginning of the century, rose to over 15% in 1936. The population of the big commercial centres (Casablanca, Algiers and Tunis) rose by leaps and bounds. Casablanca, which had only 20000 inhabitants in 1900, had 257400 in 1936. With little industry, these towns with a superabundant tertiary sector acted as magnets for countryfolk in search of work.

On the eve of the Second World War the economy of North Africa was typically – as a colonial system – dualist and extraverted. The sectors of the economy in which North Africans predominated suffered from arrested development because of lack of finance, the survival of archaic practices, fragmentation of land holdings and the fact that they had been driven back to the marginal land. North Africans were in fact excluded from the modern sectors of the economy (banking, mining, processing industries and development project planning and implementation bodies). But these sectors themselves, dominated as they were by foreign capital, were closely dependent on outside decision-making centres and markets, whose options and fluctuations they could only more or less passively suffer.

Part II: Libya, Egypt and the Sudan
A. A. ABDUSSALAM and F. S. ABUSEDRA

Libya

During the colonial period, the economy of Tripoli evolved around two main activities, namely agriculture (including animal husbandry) and trade. Agriculture was carried out in the rural areas while trade was conducted in the cities. These two activities were the main occupation and source of income for most of the population. No attempt was made by the Turkish

31. C. R. Ageron, 1979.

rulers to change this situation. The Italians, however, tried to introduce some drastic changes in the economy. The first part of this section deals with the late years of the Ottoman rule, while the second part describes the economy under the Italian occupation.

The economy of Libya during Ottoman domination (1880–1911)

The economy was stagnant during the period of the Ottoman administration and economic activities were confined to agriculture, trade and small handicrafts. Agriculture remained traditional during the Ottoman rule. Animal-drawn wooden ploughs were used to till the soil. The main crops were wheat and barley. Other crops were dates, olive oil, citrus fruit and livestock. Agricultural production depended to a large extent on rainfall which varied from season to season. Huge numbers of livestock were raised in the plains of Cyrenaica and Tripoli. Some of these animals were exported to neighbouring countries. It was estimated that the total export of sheep in 1906 was about 500000. Export of livestock from Cyrenaica alone in 1908 was about 58000 head of cattle and 340000 head of sheep.

In the field of trade, due to the lack of paved roads and the absence of modern means of transportation, caravans were used not only to carry merchandise between local cities, but also between the main cities in Tripoli and other neighbouring countries in Africa. There were five main caravan routes, three going to the south, one to the east and the other to the west (see Fig. 17.8). One caravan route went from Tripoli to Kano (in Nigeria), passing through Ghadāmes, Ghāt, Air and Zinder. The second route went from Tripoli to Borno (in Nigeria) via Murzuk̦, Tadjarhī, Bilma, Nuigni and Kukawa. The third route went from Benghazi to Wadai (in Chad) by way of Awdjīla, Kufra and Tibesti. Other routes went from Benghazi to Sallūm (in Egypt) in the east and from Tripoli to Tunisia in the west.[32]

The caravan trade carried glassware, dresses, silk, spices and paper to Borno and Wadai and brought back commodities such as leather, ivory and ostrich feathers. But from the end of the nineteenth century, the caravan trade started to decline. The colonization of other African countries brought about new and cheaper routes. Modern and more efficient methods of transportation replaced the old ones. Consequently, the importance of the caravan trade slowly diminished. On the other hand, Tripoli and Benghazi, the main ports, did a brisk business with Europe and other neighbouring countries. The exports to these countries included cattle, sheep, wool, goat- and camel-hair, dates, barley, wheat and esparto grass. Imports included cotton and silk textiles, glass, firearms, rice, sugar, tea and coffee. The main trading partners were Italy, England, Malta, Egypt, Tunisia, France, Austria, Germany and Greece.

32. F. Coro, 1971.

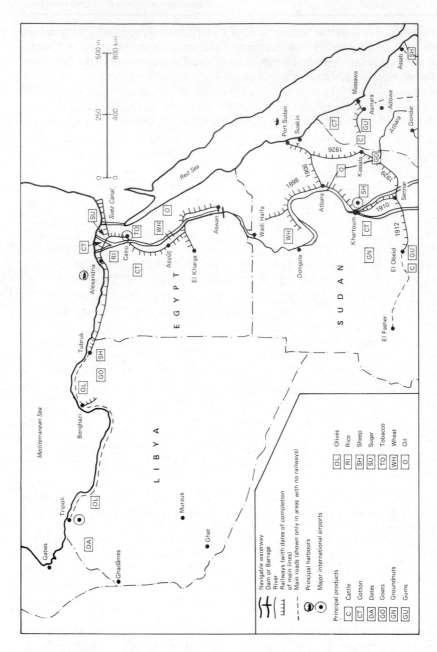

FIG. 17.8 *Libya, Egypt and Sudan: economic development in the colonial period (after J. D. Fage, 1978)*

Industry was carried out on a small scale and was confined to a few handicrafts. These small industries included textiles, mat-making, tanning, soap and some gold and silver works. By 1911, there were about 2000 looms for weaving cotton, 550 looms for weaving wool and about 120 looms for weaving silk.[33] These local industries produced national dress for both men and women. Tents and carpets were also home-made products. Some privately-owned small factories made fine ornaments, such as bracelets, rings and earrings. Other industries such as salt and tobacco were monopolized by the government.

Although the second Ottoman reign in Tripoli lasted for more than seventy years (1835–1911), little effort was made to develop the Libyan economy. There was no conscious policy to improve the economic infrastructure such as roads, ports and the educational system. Few technical schools were operating in the country at the time. The neglect of the economy could be attributed partly to the fact that Turkey was preoccupied by her own problems. She was at war with some of her neighbours, while also trying desperately to hold on to her possessions in Europe and to save the empire from disintegrating. As a result, little attempt was made to foster the economy of Libya. All that the Turkish administration seemed to care about was to collect taxes.

The tax system which was implemented in Tripoli during the Ottoman rule included a head tax on male adults, a tithe on agricultural products and an income tax. Other taxes included a real-estate tax, inheritance tax and a tax for exemption from military services which was levied on non-Muslim male adults; a tax on stamping gold and silver and customs duties were imposed on exported and imported goods.[34] Furthermore, the government gained sizeable revenues from monopolizing salt and tobacco. Those taxes added to the burden of the economy and contributed to its sluggish growth. They also precipitated several revolts which caused political instability and weakened Turkish control of the country.

The Libyan economy during the Italian occupation (1911–42)

The Italian interest in Libya began late in the nineteenth century. Like other European powers, Italy wanted to secure a foothold in North Africa. But it was not until early in the twentieth century that Italy embarked on her colonization policy. In the beginning, Italy wanted to accomplish this goal by peaceful means, and used the Banco di Roma as her Trojan Horse.

The Banco di Roma was the first Italian financial institution to operate in Libya. It opened for business in Tripoli in 1907. Soon afterwards, it opened several branches in other cities and widened the scope of its operations. Its activities were not confined to financial matters but also

33. ibid., p. 79.
34. A. J. Cachia, 1975, pp. 72 ff.

included business ventures in industry, agriculture and transportation. The bank established plants for processing olive oil, flour mills in Tripoli and a sheep farm in Cyrenaica. In addition, it inaugurated shipping lines between the major Libyan cities and the neighbouring countries, and also bought land and sent survey teams to explore the country's mineral resources. These activities and others aroused suspicion about its real role in Libya. Consequently, the bank's activities were restricted, if not frustrated, by the Turkish authorities.[35] The hostile attitude towards the Banco di Roma was one of the pretexts used by Italy to invade Libya in 1911 (see Chapter 5).

Economic policy during the period of Italian occupation

When Italy invaded Libya in 1911, she had a dream of making her new colony a source of raw materials for Italian industry, a market for Italian products and a means of solving Italy's population problem. The Italian intention was to make Libya an integral part of Italy and every effort was geared towards accomplishing this aim. The Italians invested heavily in agriculture, industry and infrastructure.

AGRICULTURAL SETTLEMENTS

The Italian agricultural programme in Libya passed through two distinct stages, namely private settlement and colonial settlement.

To encourage colonial settlement of Libya in the early stages of the Italian occupation, the Italian government granted large estates to wealthy Italians in order to develop them for agricultural purposes. These lands were either government lands or lands which were expropriated from their original owners. By 1929, about 58087 ha of land had been acquired. The estates were leased to Italian farmers for ninety years. At a later stage, these concessionaires were required to settle more Italian farmers with them, a matter which burdened both the original settlers and the government. The government subsidies to the private settlers amounted to £62 million, in addition to a loan of nearly £158 million from a savings fund.[36] Only about 2031 families were settled according to this plan, which was far below the Italian expectations.[37] Therefore, the Italian government embarked on a new settlement scheme with the aim of speeding up the settlement process but was not able to carry out any major development programme until the national resistance ended in 1932.

Shortly after the suppression of the national resistance (for details see Chapter 5 above), the Italian government set out to implement an ambitious development scheme encompassing certain parts of Libya, especially Al-Djabal al-Akhḍar (the Green Mountain). Its goal was to resettle about

35. F. Malgeri, 1970, pp. 17 ff.
36. M. M. Sharkasi, 1976, pp. 67–71.
37. ibid., p. 71.

300 000 Italians in a period of 25 years.[38] This job was entrusted to private and semi-public institutions which pooled together whatever resources they could muster from both the private and public sectors and channelled them to finance the new development plan. These institutions were the ENTE per la colonizzione delle Libia (ENTE), Instituto Nazionale della Providenza Sociale (INPS) and the Azienda Tabacci Italiani (ATI). The scheme included clearing land, providing water supply, erecting farm buildings and related facilities and providing stock and equipment to the settlers. The farmers, in turn, were to pay for the development expenses by handing over most of their produce to these institutions, the value of which was credited to their accounts.[39] After a certain period of time, the settlers would be able to own their farms. Up to 1936 the settlement project had cost about £800 million and only 85 000 Italians had been resettled.[40]

INDUSTRY

The Italians did not establish major industries in Libya but they did develop some of the small industries which already existed before the Italian invasion. A small tuna-processing plant was established in Tripoli and the capacity of the olive-oil processing plant was increased to 2200 tonnes annually.[41] The production of salt grew markedly, rising from about 14 000 tonnes annually in 1927 to an annual average of 50 000 tonnes in 1937.[42] Moreover, a second and bigger tobacco factory was established in Tripoli in 1923. Two shoe factories were also built, one in Tripoli in 1923 and the other in Benghazi in 1929. Food-processing plants and textile factories continued to produce on a larger scale. Other industries which were operating at the time included building materials, asphalt, gunpowder, fats and soap. During the period under study, there were about 789 factories, most of them in Tripoli. The local handicrafts industry continued to exist during the Italian occupation because of its character and the smallness of the market.

DEVELOPING THE INFRASTRUCTURE

Prior to the Italian occupation the infrastructure of Libya was grossly underdeveloped and the Italian government therefore had to invest massively in it. It built roads, railways, ports, a modern communication system, hydraulic works and public buildings. The investment expenditure in these areas amounted to 870 million lire for the period between 1913 and 1936.[43] The purpose of such massive investment in the infrastructure

38. ibid., p. 72.
39. J. Lindberg, 1952, p. 11.
40. M. M. Sharkasi, 1976, p. 72.
41. ibid., pp. 33–4.
42. ibid.
43. J. Lindberg, 1976, p. 46.

was to develop the economy to benefit Italy. The object was to provide jobs for the Italian population and to secure a potential market for Italian products.

This huge investment, however, was not without its cost to the Libyans. The Libyan population had been reduced by the war. Many people died fighting the Italian occupation. Others perished in concentration camps. Moreover, large groups migrated to neighbouring countries. Those who survived the concentration camps were herded, in semi-slave conditions, to build the coastal road and new agricultural development projects. The Italian aim was to drive out the local population to the marginal land in the interior and to resettle the surplus Italian population in the most fertile lands of Libya.

The Italians also reduced the number of livestock in Libya. For years the Libyan population in the interior had been dependent on sheep and camels for food, as a source of raw materials and as a means of transportation. Huge numbers of livestock were either killed or confiscated by the Italians. What remained of these animals was further reduced by starvation when they were moved from the pastoral land to inhospitable areas near the concentration camps. Table 17.1 shows the drastic decline in the number of animals during the period of the Italian occupation.

TABLE 17.1 *The number of animals in Libya, 1926, 1933*[44]

Year	Sheep	Goats	Cattle	Camels	Horses	Donkeys, mules
1926	800000	70000	10000	75000	14000	9000
1933	98000	25000	8700	2000	10000	5000

The Italians did not know the extent of the damage they had inflicted on the animal wealth of Libya until after the resistance ended in 1932. While they tried to encourage animal husbandry, it took years before the animal wealth could be restored to its original level. This was mainly because of the damage which had weakened the economic base and impoverished the population and reduced their ability to save.

Finally, to make things worse, the Italians did not train the Libyans in administration nor did they provide them with adequate education. As K. Folayan has pointed out, 'while the Italians (about 10% of the total population) had in 1939–40 eighty-one elementary schools for their children, the Libyans who constituted more than 85% of that population were given only ninety-seven schools'.[45] There were also seven secondary schools for the Italians and only three for the Libyans. Even in the police and military services no Libyan national could be promoted beyond the rank of sergeant. Only a handful of Libyans were permitted to assume relatively important

44. J. A. Allan, K. S. McLachland and E. T. Penrose (eds), 1973, p. 52.
45. K. Folayan, 1974, p. 7.

administrative jobs after 1934. The lack of trained personnel impeded economic development in Libya for many years to come.

Egypt

Muḥammad 'Alī's military defeat in 1840 marked the end of an important phase of Egypt's modern economic history. His system called for the simultaneous development of both agriculture and industry under the control and ownership of the state, and his schemes started the country on the road leading to an export-oriented economy.[46] The trend he had initiated was reinforced during the period between 1850 and 1920. All economic activities were geared to the cultivation and the export of cotton, thus converting Egypt into a highly specialized monocrop economy. During the 1920s, Egypt witnessed a trend towards industrialization, mainly by import substitution. The period under consideration was characterized by two main trends. The first was towards concentration on agriculture, especially cotton, for export. The second was towards industrialization. Several structural changes occurred to accommodate these trends. This section will discuss the factors that led to each phase.

Exported-oriented economy

The development of the infrastructure
The period under study witnessed an impressive infrastructural development of the country. This was, however, concentrated on activities related to cotton and its export. Major irrigation projects were undertaken. The Aswān dam, the largest in the world at that time, was completed in 1902 and made higher in 1907–10; the Delta barrage was reinforced and put into service, and so also were the Zifta, Asyūṭ and Esnā barrages. About 13 500 km of canals were dug during Ismā'īl's reign (1863–79). Thus the cultivated area rose from 4.76 million *feddāns* in 1881 to 5.66 million in 1911. It was also possible after the extension of the perennial irrigation to grow more than one crop. Therefore, the crop area increased to 7.71 million *feddāns* in 1911.[47] The bulk of the increase was used up by cotton not only because it was more profitable than other crops but also because of British encouragement since cotton was both a cash crop which enabled Egypt to pay her debts and a much-needed raw material for Lancashire. In other words, the British wanted and successfully kept Egypt as a source of cotton to supply their textile industry.[48] The size of the cotton crop increased from 3.12 million *ḳantārs* in 1879 to 7.66 million in 1913, a 140% increase during a period of twenty-four years.[49]

---

46. C. Issawi, 1963, p. 24.
47. C. Issawi, 1954, p. 34. *Feddān* = 0.56 ha.
48. ibid., p. 35.
49. *Ḳantār* of cotton = 45 kg.

448

PLATE 17.1 *The Aswān dam (Egypt) in 1937*

The need to move the cotton crop required an expansion of the transportation and the communication network, on which most effort was consequently concentrated (see Fig. 17.8). Railways connecting all major cities of the Delta, and from Cairo to Upper Egypt were completed. The first railway was opened in 1853 and by 1877 there were 1519 km of standard-gauge railways. These railways were more than doubled during the British occupation reaching 3200 km in 1909. In addition there were 1600 km of light railways. Harbour facilities at Alexandria were modernized and repeatedly enlarged and new ports at Suez and Port Said were built on the Suez Canal, which was opened for navigation in 1869. Such developments greatly facilitated the transformation of the agricultural sector from subsistence farming to the cultivation of cash crops on a large scale for export to international markets.

It is worthwhile to emphasize that the main economic impact of the British administration was largely felt in these fields of irrigation and transportation. The reconstruction of several barrages and the construction of the Aswān dam ensured Egypt perennial irrigation and increased the total crop area. However, it must be remembered that the British were trying to develop alternative sources for their cotton requirements. Instead of relying solely on the United States for the supply of cotton to their textile industry as was the case before the American Civil War, other sources were sought. Egypt had comparative advantages over other possible suppliers like India and Brazil. In other words, the main concern of the British was to secure a stable source of raw material for their textile industry. Hence, it was not surprising that most of the government capital expenditure was directed towards the promotion of the export sector. It was argued that a considerable investment in the irrigation network, despite Egypt's difficult financial situation, was necessary to increase the revenues to repay Egypt's foreign debts. Cotton was the main beneficiary of investment in public works. Other sectors that benefited were those related to the needs of the export sector.

Free-trade policy

One of the fundamental changes that characterized the phase under study was the government's belief in a free-trade policy. This belief was in contrast to Muḥammad 'Alī's approach which defended government intervention as a necessary step towards development. Lord Cromer, the British financial advisor and the senior British official in Egypt for twenty-four years, was a laissez-faire economist. He opposed granting protection through import duties to any infant industry. His negative attitude towards Egypt's textile companies is a good example. He argued that 'it would be detrimental to both English and Egyptian interests to afford any encouragement to the growth of a protected cotton industry in Egypt'.[50]

50. Quoted by C. Issawi, 1954, p. 37.

In any case, the Egyptian government was bound by international trade agreements that prevented it from protecting infant industries even if it had desired to do so. According to the Anglo-Turkish treaty of 1838, foreign traders could buy and sell anywhere within the Ottoman empire at a uniform duty of 8% *ad valorem* or less.[51] This treaty opened the empire to free trade, and foreign goods began to flood the unprotected Egyptian market. It has been argued that the treaty 'inhibited for more than a century any new attempt at industrialization by the state'.[52] These agreements expired on 16 February 1930, and Egypt regained her fiscal autonomy. This, as we shall see, enabled her to change the structure of customs duties in such a way as to protect the emerging domestic industry. This tariff reform brought about the import-substitution phase.

Investment pattern

The investment pattern that prevailed during this period favoured agriculture. Gross fixed-capital formation during the period 1880–1914 amounted to 15% of the gross domestic product (GDP). This is a high investment ratio when compared with other countries. However, most of the investment went to agriculture and urban building whereas the share of industry did not exceed 2.3% of all gross fixed-capital formation (GFCF). Most writers explain this pattern of capital accumulation in terms of relative profitability, arguing that investment in agriculture was more profitable and less risky than in industry. However, R. Mabro and S. Radwan have argued that other factors, mainly government policy, give a better explanation.[53]

Egyptian investors preferred land and property to investment in industrial projects because social prestige was bestowed on landowners. Being a member of the 'agrarian bourgeoisie' also gave privileges since this class was at the top of the social hierarchy. Hence, there was a clear trend towards concentration of large holdings of agricultural land. The number of large landowners (owning 50 *feddāns* or more) represented 15% of all landowners in 1897 and held 44% of total agricultural area. In 1913 the large landowners represented less than 1% of all owners, but held 44.2% of the agricultural land. Therefore, the size of the average large holding increased from 183 to 193 *feddāns* during the same period.[54] This development was important since investments by those owners was concentrated on land and resulted in a biased investment pattern. Moreover, foreigners enjoyed a fiscal and judicial immunity under the Capitulations which gave them the edge over Egyptian competitors when it came to industrial investment. However, not much interest was shown in the unprotected Egyptian market, and industrialization was negligible until the 1930s.

51. D. C. Mead, 1967, p. 15.
52. R. Mabro, and S. Radwan, 1976, p. 18.
53. ibid., p. 21.
54. ibid., p. 25.

It was also argued by the Egyptian administration that the encouragement of cotton and its export was necessary to increase the country's revenues and to enable Egypt to repay its debts. The accumulation of a huge public debt begun in 1858 was to finance the infrastructural projects as well as the extravagances of some of the monarchs. The law of liquidation of 1880 had fixed Egypt's public debt at £98.37 million and during the next twenty years a further £18.2 million was borrowed. Egypt's liabilities to foreigners had reached £E 8.5 million per annum by 1914.[55] Establishing export surplus was vital to meet those liabilities.

The American Civil War stimulated the production and export of cotton in Egypt. Output increased from a little over half a million *kantārs* in 1860 to over 2.1 million in 1865, to 4.1 million in 1890 and to 7.7 million in 1913. However, after the rapid increase in the price of cotton caused by the American Civil War, prices continued to fall until the end of the century and the rise in production was insufficient to offset the fall in prices. During the first decade of this century, cotton prices more than doubled, and the value of the crop rose to over three times what it had been at the beginning of the occupation. In 1916 cotton prices rose to an average of US $38 and again to US $90 per *kantār* in 1919; exports jumped to £E 88 million in 1920 and a large export surplus was built up.[56]

The financial achievement of the British administration was to ensure the proper collection and administration of the increased revenues accruing to the government out of this surplus. Fiscal reform in the form of reducing expenditure, except those considered remunerative like irrigation works, was undertaken. Increasing revenues from exports repaid all loans contracted during the occupation as well as reducing Ismāʿīl's debt by some £10 million by 1913.

The import-substitution phase

There is no doubt that the British administration carried out many reforms that benefited the Egyptian economy. The major achievements were in the financial field, irrigation works, and in efficient administration. However, it is equally true that the British administration's attitude towards the industrialization of Egypt was hostile while the free-trade policy resulted in deepening Egypt's concentration on cotton. But during the late 1920s, several important changes were introduced which mark the beginning of a new era when attention was directed towards industry. One of the important reasons for these changes was the great depression which resulted in a slump of international demand for raw materials, including cotton. This, in turn, was reflected in a severe deflation of all activities in the Egyptian economy. Therefore, the government policy of free trade came under increasing pressure and calls for government intervention grew

55. C. Issawi, 1963, p. 27.
56. ibid., p. 31.

stronger. In addition, Egypt's terms of trade deteriorated during the late 1920s. This added more thrust to the pressure to move out of cotton – which continued to form the bulk of the exports – into other items. This period also witnessed the emergence of a strong nationalist movement. The 1919 revolution marked the peak of the growth of the Egyptian nationalism which was reflected in the emergence of national entrepreneurs with new ideas regarding the future development of Egypt. Furthermore, while the increase in agricultural output during the final decades of the nineteenth century kept pace with population growth, this was not the case during the first part of the twentieth century; total output in agriculture grew by 30% while the growth of the population was close to 50%.[57] Egypt's population was outrunning the absorptive capacity of agriculture, and other sectors had therefore to be developed to find productive employment outlets and to raise the *per capita* income. Finally, owing to shortages of imports during the First World War, several new industries came into being and needed protection if they were to continue in the face of increasing foreign competition.

It was for all these reasons that, after the country had attained fiscal autonomy in 1930, the government imposed tariffs of 15 to 20% on a wide range of consumer goods likely to compete with domestic products. The following decades saw tariff protection extended to all competing foreign goods. A new phase of economic growth through import substitution had thus begun. Several indices showed the growth of industry. The first was the rise in industrial employment. In 1937, about 155 000 persons worked in manufacturing establishments employing ten persons or more as compared with 30 000 in 1916. Another index was the increase in industrial output. For example, sugar production increased from 79 000 tonnes in 1917 to 159 000 tonnes in 1939; cement output rose from 24 000 tonnes to 353 000 tonnes over the same period; and the production of mechanically woven cotton cloth increased from 7.2 million sq m in 1917 to 132.6 million sq m in 1939.[58] A third index was the high percentage of local requirements of certain industrial commodities which local production could satisfy by 1939, as shown in Table 17.2.

Another important development was the emergence of national enterprises during the 1920s. The first purely Egyptian-owned and -managed bank, Bank Miṣr, was founded in 1920. It pioneered the development of large-scale manufacturing firms. The bank managed to attract private capital away from the traditional investment channels; by 1940 the Miṣr group included twenty-one affiliated companies. It was estimated that the share of Bank Miṣr industrial companies amounted to 45% of the increase in the total paid-up capital of all joint-stock industrial companies during the 1922–38 period. Thus, Bank Miṣr gave a big push to the industrial development of Egypt during the inter-war period. Investment during the period

57. D. C. Mead, 1967, p. 16.
58. C. Issawi, 1963, p. 44.

TABLE 17.2 *Egypt: local production and local requirements of industrial goods, 1939*[59]

Commodity	% requirements produced locally	Commodity	% requirements produced locally
Sugar	100	Soap	90
Spirits	100	Furniture	80
Cigarettes	100	Matches	80
Salt	100	Beer	65
Milled flour	99	Vegetable oils	60
Cotton yarn	96	Caustic soda	50
Shoes	90	Cotton textiles	40
Cement	90		

showed an increasing participation of local capital. The successive cotton crises, the high profits expected at some branches of industry as shown by the profit made by foreigners engaged in local industry, and the establishment of national investment opportunities by Bank Miṣr and its companies changed the investment behaviour towards industrial projects.

In conclusion, the period under consideration witnessed several attempts at achieving economic development. After the failure of Muḥammad 'Alī's plan to carry on a forced programme of industrialization without having adequate infrastructure, the economy was led to specialization in one crop for export. This trend was reinforced under the British occupation which encouraged the expansion of cultivable land and cotton exports. There were three main arguments advanced to support this trend. One was that free trade and specialization according to comparative advantage would result in higher welfare. The second was that revenues were needed to pay for the accumulated public debt. The third was that international treaties limited Egypt's ability to provide protection to new industries. The result was an export-oriented economy. On the other hand, the first three decades of the twentieth century were characterized by structural transformation of the economy towards industrialization. This was due to several factors, namely, the successive agricultural crises resulting in the deterioration of Egypt's terms of trade, the emergence of national enterprises, the reattainment of fiscal autonomy and the change in government policy or attitude towards industry. Industry, therefore, grew rapidly towards the end of the period under review.

The Sudan

In the last part of the nineteenth century, the Sudan, as it has been seen already, witnessed the rise of a religious movement which sparked a revolt against the Turco–Egyptian rule of the Sudan and culminated in the establishment of the Mahdist state from 1881 to 1898. At about the same

59. M. M. el-Kammash, 1968, p. 41.

time, Egypt fell to the British, and, later on, the Sudan was reoccupied by Britain. Then, the Sudan came under Anglo-Egyptian rule. The first part of this section deals briefly with the situation under the Mahdist state, while the second part will highlight the major developments during the Anglo-Egyptian rule.

The Mahdist state (1881–98)

The Mahdist state set up its own type of administration as well as a judicial system. One of the outstanding achievements of the Mahdist administration was the establishment of a simple and practical tax system which was based on Islamic teachings. *Zakāt* comprised the bulk of the revenue. It was levied at the rate of 2.5% on money and at the rate of 10% on livestock and grain. Owing to the simplicity of this tax system and its adaptability to social conditions, it continued even after the fall of the Mahdist regime. The Mahdist administration encouraged both agriculture and trade because these activities were geared to support the army and equip it with arms and ammunition.

The Mahdist state was, however, short-lived. Several factors contributed to its downfall. First, the Mahdist movement suffered from internal strife due to power struggles after the Mahdī's death in 1885. Secondly, the process of consolidating the control over the whole country had strained the resources of the state. Moreover, the new state had to contend with several European colonial powers on its borders.[60] The Mahdist state wanted to expand northward towards Egypt, a move which proved to be disastrous because it prompted the British, who were in Egypt at that time, to occupy the Sudan.

Anglo-Egyptian rule

The Anglo-Egyptian conquest of the Sudan ended the brief period of national independence under the Mahdists. But fortunately, the colonial administration was not heavy-handed. British colonial policy in the Sudan was relatively mild and there was a conscious attempt to develop the country's economy. The main contribution of the British administration in the Sudan was the development of the infrastructure and the introduction of a modern agricultural system.

The development of the infrastructure
During the British colonial period in the Sudan, the British built railways, ports and dams, and advanced the educational system (see Fig. 17.8). The first railway was constructed during the period from 1896 to 1898 to be used for the military campaign. It was later extended to Atbara and was

60. P. M. Holt, 1970, pp, 204 ff.

used for transportation between the northern part of the Sudan and the Mediterranean via Egypt. When Port Sudan was built in 1906, a new railway was constructed to connect it with Atbara. Then in 1910 the main line was extended to Sennār. Another line was laid in 1924 between the Djazīra and the Red Sea. Steamboat services were also used to link the south with the north of the country. These modern and efficient means of transportation helped to convey agricultural products and considerably reduced transportation costs. The British administration also assisted in developing the educational system. Furthermore, measures were taken to improve the utilization of soil and water resources. A few pumping stations were built and several canals were dug for irrigation purposes.

Agricultural development

From the beginning the British realized the great agricultural potential of the Sudan. They started the experimental cultivation of cotton so that they could supplement the Egyptian production of this crop. When the first experiment in Zaydab in 1905 showed promising results, it was extended to the Djazīra plain between the Blue Nile and the White Nile, which contained the most fertile soil in the Sudan. An ambitious plan was drawn up for the Djazīra plain. The Sudan Plantation Syndicate, which was a private concern, was granted a concession to cultivate cotton in this area. The arrangement called for co-operation between the government, the syndicate and Sudanese tenants. The government rented the land from its owners and provided the basic capital expenditure for canalization and the pumping stations. The syndicate was responsible for minor expenditure and for managing the project. It also arranged for the transportation and marketing of the product. The tenants, on the other hand, were to undertake the cultivation. The proceeds of the sale were then to be divided between the three partners in the following manner: 40% to the tenants, 35% to the government and 25% to the syndicate. The shares of both the government and the syndicate were later changed to 38% and 22% respectively.[61]

The Djazīra plan envisaged the irrigation of about 200 000 ha on which cotton, millet and fodder were to be cultivated. But the plan was delayed because of the First World War. It was, however, revised in 1919 and was highlighted by the completion of the Sennār Dam in 1925.[62] The success of the Djazīra scheme stimulated the development of other related activities such as transportation, irrigation and ginning factories for cotton.

To finance these schemes, the existing tax system was supplemented by an agreement between Britain and Egypt by which the latter would provide the Sudan with financial aid and loans for development projects and budget purposes. The Egyptian contribution to the Sudanese budget amounted to £E 2.8 million for the period from 1899 to 1916, while the

61. W. N. Allan and R. J. Smith in J. D. Tothill (ed.), 1948, pp. 608–9. See also A. Gaitskell, 1959, p. 70.
62. A. Gaitskell, 1959, p. 94.

PLATE 17.2 *Djazīra irrigation scheme, Sudan: a farmer at work in a cotton field*

Egyptian loans to Sudan totalled about £E 5.4 million for the period from 1900 to 1910.[63] The Egyptian grants and loans were called for because taxes were light in the Sudan. The land tax ranged between 10 piastres and 100 piastres per *feddān*. The tithe remained part of the tax system in the Sudan during the British occupation. Other taxes were levied on trade and different types of industry.[64]

To stimulate land use, a quarter of the cultivable land was taxed after two years. Then, the whole land would be taxed after eight to ten years. Other taxes included a herd tax which was levied on an ethnic group as a whole. A poll tax of between 25 piastres and 80 piastres per head was collected. In 1912 property tax was introduced. Moreover, a boat tax was assessed on boats according to their capacity.

The impact of British colonial economic activities on the Sudan

Compared with those of the French and the Italians in the Maghrib and Tripoli respectively, British colonial economic activities in the Sudan were laudable to some extent. Land was not appropriated by foreigners nor was it concentrated in the hands of a few people as was the case in the other colonies. The Djazīra scheme also proved quite beneficial both to the British and to those people of the Sudan who were directly involved in it. The development of a modern transport system together with the construction of ports and irrigation facilities also helped the growth of a modern agricultural system in the Sudan. However, there is a negative side to this story. First, the infrastructure that was provided was totally inadequate and was clearly meant to promote the interests of Britain more than those of the Sudanese. It is most significant that not one single mile of motor road was constructed in the whole of the Sudan during the period under review while the railway was constructed initially to facilitate British military campaigns and later to promote their cotton and gum projects in Djazīra and the western areas respectively. As in most of the colonies, industrialization was completely neglected. However, the greatest indict ment against British colonialism in the Sudan is its total neglect of the Southern Sudan economically and socially. This neglect is undoubtedly one of the most important contributory factors to the creation of the southern problem in the Sudan, a problem which has still not been solved.

63. ibid., p. 35.
64. H. A. Tunley in J. D. Tothill (ed.), 1948.

The social repercussions of colonial rule: demographic aspects

J. C. CALDWELL

The years from the early 1880s to the mid-1930s mark the demographic divide in Africa. At the beginning of the period the continent's population was still sparse, at least by the standards of the Old World. More significantly it probably was not growing rapidly and evidenced a vulnerability to the kind of pressures, both internal and external, which were being increasingly applied. By about 1935, the population was undoubtedly growing because of increasing control over mortality, and the basis was laid for a doubling over the next third of a century which almost certainly hastened and consolidated independence.

Many indices can be used to illustrate the changes between the two dates, and some help to explain the demographic transition. In 1880 a European presence inland from the coast was largely restricted to Algeria, where a third of a million migrants, mainly from France, Spain, Italy and Malta, had consolidated the victory of the French army, and South Africa, where a similar number of Europeans, predominantly of Dutch and English extraction, now had a vanguard as far north as the Limpopo river. (See Fig. 1.1.) Elsewhere Europeans were beginning to exert control over Egypt and Tunisia, ruled some coastal populations in Senegal and the Gold Coast (now Ghana) and held such enclaves as The Gambia, Sierra Leone, Lagos, Libreville and parts of Angola and Mozambique. By 1935 European administations controlled almost the entire continent (see Fig. 12.2). The half century saw European medical science progressing from an ignorance of the cause of most of Africa's major diseases to an ability to contain or cure most of them; indeed the period ends just as the sulpha drugs were ushering in an era of chemotherapy of great significance for the continent. It also spans almost the whole railway-building age and a transition from a time when nearly all land transport was by human porterage to one where lorries were beginning to multiply on a growing network of dusty or muddy roads.

Population growth

Demographers have published tables of African population change with apparent assurance,[1] but the truth is that our most certain knowledge of nineteenth-century human numbers is provided by a retrospective view from the vantage of the post-Second World War censuses. If these had claimed twice as many people as they did, we probably would have adjusted our estimate of populations before the present century upwards by almost as much.

The much-quoted estimates for the nineteenth century are those of W. F. Willcox and A. M. Carr-Saunders, and these have recently been joined by those of J. D. Durand.[2] The first two at least were based on practically no evidence at all and have gained acceptance almost entirely by repetition and by the authority apparently derived from being close to each other.

In fact Willcox chose merely to repeat the estimate of a seventeenth-century Italian writer, B. Riccioli,[3] justifying the decision by saying that he was a 'learned Jesuit priest' who 'summarized the knowledge of his day', and assuming that there was no population growth between the seventeenth and mid-nineteenth centuries.[4] In fact Riccioli had been more influenced by the mystical quality of numbers than by solid demographic evidence, and had constructed a global estimate of a 1000 million people which he distributed between the continents in multiples of 100 million. In order to allow for the fact that Africa was demonstrably not uninhabited while permitting an estimate of a very large Asian population, there was little alternative but to allocate 100 million inhabitants to Africa. Willcox justified his use of these estimates by claiming that the population density of those parts of Africa not known to be growing fast in 1931 (that is excluding Egypt, Tunisia, northern Algeria, Sierra Leone, Liberia, The Gambia, South Africa and Northern Rhodesia (now Zambia)) was the same as Riccioli's figure for the whole continent.[5] This procedure is, however, meaningless: Willcox retained the countries with the least known populations at the time: there is no evidence that their populations were still stationary; there is no reason why their past densities should have been the same as the countries excluded. Willcox, arguing that there was no evidence of growth in Africa's population until recent times, retained the 100 million figure as his estimate of its population up to 1850.

Carr-Saunders' estimates are not in fact a separate series, but merely a commentary on those of Willcox, concerned less with the central estimates than with trends of sub-regional figures that may have been overlooked. Therefore he accepted the proposition that Willcox was probably right with regard to his population estimate for 1650, a mere three hundred

---

1. See United Nations, 1973, Table II. 4, p. 21.
2. W. F. Willcox, 1931; A. M. Carr-Saunders, 1936, pp. 17–45; J. D. Durand, 1967, pp. 136–59.
3. B. Riccioli, 1661, 1672, pp. 630–4.
4. W. F. Willcox, 1931, p. 45.
5. ibid., pp. 53–4.

years before his time and widespread census-taking on the continent, but argued that account had not been taken of the likelihood that the ravages of slavery had caused a diminution of numbers before 1800 but that this had been more than counterbalanced subsequently by relatively rapid population growth in North Africa.[6] Thus he concluded that a low of 90 million must have been reached by 1800 with a subsequent rise in population by one-third in the course of the nineteenth century.[7]

The thesis of population decline during all or part of the nineteenth century is frequently encountered but less frequently justified. One observer believed that it could mostly be accounted for by two facts: the lack of familiarity of Europeans with sparse farming populations and hence the conclusion that they were encountering areas of depopulation; and the desire of philanthropists to believe that they had brought assistance after a period of devastating disorder largely caused by their own people.[8] Another argued that overestimates of the populations had been made at the time of the major move forward by European powers in order to encourage investment in European companies participating in that movement.[9] Certainly it was easy to calculate large populations from the accounts of such explorers as H. M. Stanley, partly because the explorers tended to choose the highest figures and partly because they tended to follow rivers or paths that inevitably passed through areas of abnormally high density.

Durand's population series apparently represents a major change. For most of Africa's population, namely that found south of the Sahara, he made retrospective estimates supposedly employing United Nations figures for 1920.[10] But, as he then disregarded the 1920 figure when constructing his medium estimate on the grounds that it suggested an improbably high population growth rate (1.5 per cent per annum) between then and the 1950 United Nations figure which he accepted, the real basis for these reverse projections is the post-Second World War censuses. Even so, Durand gives no reason for rejecting the United Nations 1920–50 implied growth rate and the suspicion remains that the influence of Riccioli transmitted through Willcox and Carr-Saunders continued to be dominant. He concludes, with the appearance of trying to justify his approach, by observing: 'When the estimate for North Africa is added, this [the medium estimate] agrees approximately with Willcox's surmise that the population of all Africa was stationary at the level of about 100 million during this period [1750–1850]'.[11] Durand's estimates for North Africa are based on studies of population growth in Egypt and Algeria during the second half

6. A. M. Carr-Saunders, 1936, pp. 34–5.
7. ibid., p. 42.
8. R. R. Kuczynski, 1948–53, Vol. II, p. 120.
9. J. Suret-Canale, 1971, p. 37.
10. J. D. Durand, 1967, pp. 152–3.
11. ibid., p. 153.

of the nineteenth century and the early decades of the present one,[12] and his medium estimate is prepared to credit the area with an annual growth rate of 1.25 per cent between 1850 and 1920.

More revealing are Durand's low and high estimates, which for 1850 he places at 81 and 145 million respectively, thus providing a margin of error of about 30 per cent either way. Similar estimates for Asia and Latin America are made within margins of 10 per cent and for Europe within 4 per cent. Part of the explanation for the uncertainty about sub-Saharan Africa lies in the scarcity of written records. The possibility of uncertainty is illustrated by such facts, at the time of writing, as the debate as to the population of Nigeria, with contending figures 20 million apart, and great uncertainty about the magnitude of such considerable populations as that of Ethiopia.

Clearly no one knows what the population of Africa, more particularly sub-Saharan Africa, was during the period covered by this chapter. No one appears prepared to put it much under 100 million or over 150 million in 1880; by 1900 lower and upper estimates are narrowing to perhaps between 115 and 155 million; while it is now becoming clearer that by 1935 the 150 million mark had already been exceeded. Most of Africa had no real population counts during this period, and some of the censuses barely deserve that name. The 1911 census of Northern Nigeria was forwarded to London on a single sheet of paper.[13] R. R. Kuczynski devoted years to the writing of three large volumes[14] totalling almost 2500 pages meticulously examining pre-Second World War population information on all the British colonies and her two mandates in Africa. The world has an antiquarian fascination for the demographer but it would be wrong to suggest that it established much of significance about population levels or trends in the period covered here.

However, it is possible, and almost certainly more instructive, to say something from recent evidence about the nature of African population and then to look at the forces which must have shaped it in earlier times.

A fragile population emerging from near stability

Except in unusual periods, such as the present time when a scientific and technological revolution is changing the world, population growth rates must be relatively low, and hence average death rates must approximate average birth rates. This follows from the nature of exponential growth which over any sustained period yields enormous numbers from apparently low rates of increase. A growth rate as low as 0.5 per cent per annum (yielded by a birth rate only five points per thousand above the death rate) results in a fifteen-fold increase over a millennium. Even if Africa's

12. Especially C. V. Kiser, 1944, pp. 383–408; L. Chevalier, 1947.
13. C. K. Meek, 1925, p. 169.
14. R. R. Kuczynski, 1948–53; 1939.

population were as high as 150 million in 1900, it is highly improbable that the continent would have contained no more than 10 million people a thousand years earlier.

Thus it is possible to think of pre-modern death rates as having been within five points of the birth rate. Cautions should be added. This is an average over a very long period. The whole continent may have seen population oscillations over the last millennium, and almost certainly many individual societies have experienced disastrous population decline with subsequent recovery. It would, however, be surprising if recovery had ever been achieved by natural increase rates much over 1 per cent per annum in North Africa before the early nineteenth century or in sub-Saharan Africa before the end of the century. These are average birth and death rates. The evidence – much of it from pre-modern Europe – indicates that in most years births exceed deaths; mortality catches up during a relatively few years of horrendously high death rates resulting from such disasters as epidemics, famine and warfare.

Thus, if fertility levels have remained fairly constant in Africa, something can be learnt about both fertility and mortality in the past by studying recent fertility patterns. From the mid-1950s large-scale demographic surveys were carried out in greater numbers in Africa than anywhere else in the world.[15] The data were difficult to interpret, largely because the African populations had not been culturally attuned to regard the kind of information (particularly that about exact age) needed by demographers as important or quantifiable. However, the very difficulties produced new methods of analysis (to an extent that the challenge of African data has revolutionized methodology in demography) that have yielded much information on sub-Saharan Africa.[16]

The pattern revealed is one of greater variety than theoretical considerations of long-term population stability might have led one to anticipate (some of the variety may well be explained by defects in the data). Nevertheless, it is clear that in most sub-Saharan African populations women average 6.5–8 live births in a reproductive lifetime and the crude birth rate is close to 50 per thousand or even higher. The exception is a rectangle in middle Africa of over 5 million sq km embracing Gabon, Cameroon, the Congo Republic, Central African Republic and much of northern Zaire. Here average births per woman apparently do not rise above six and fall in some areas to below four, yielding a crude birth rate for the

15. See, for instance, the African predominance in the lists of fertility surveys in W. G. Duncan, 1973.
16. The methodology is described in W. Brass and A. J. Coale in W. Brass *et al.*, 1968, pp. 108–42; A. J. Coale and P. Demeny, 1967. Successive findings and interpretations are given in A. J. Coale and F. Lorimer in W. Brass *et al.*, 1968; and in A. J. Coale and E. van de Walle in W. Brass *et al.*, 1968; H. J. Page and A. J. Coale in S. H. Ominde and C. N. Ejiogu (eds), 1972; and in H. J. Page in J. C. Caldwell (ed.), 1975.

whole area which was certainly below 40 per thousand when the children surveyed were born – the 1940s to the early 1960s. Much of the explanation of the figures, if not the cause, rests on the number of women who have no children at all, which reaches two-fifths in some areas.

Confining our attention to the area outside the low fertility zone, we can hazard some reasonably good guesses about pre-modern sub-Saharan populations by employing stable population methods of analysis.[17] But first two problematic issues should be noted. One is the birth rate, which is most unlikely ever to have been higher than its present level. It may have remained constant, as the evidence of the age structure recorded over fifty years by the censuses of the Gold Coast and Ghana suggest.[18] On the other hand, improving health conditions may have reduced sterility and sub-fecundity, as has been suggested at least in the cases of Kenya and Mauritius.[19] If this has been the case, it is improbable that pre-modern fertility was less than 90 per cent of that now found and most unlikely that it was under 80 per cent. The other is the possibility that the population has not been stationary, but has been averaging a rate of growth of up to 0.5 per cent per annum for several centuries (for reasons which will be discussed below). The full range of possibilities allows us to describe a society where women averaged 5.5–7 live births yielding a birth rate of 42–50 per thousand, and where the expectation of life at birth was 20–30 years yielding a death rate of 38–50 per thousand and an infant mortality rate of 250–375 deaths per thousand live births. A medium assumption might be a situation where women averaged little more than six live births, where population growth averaged 0.33 per cent, where the expectation of life at birth was about 22.5 years (about the level of Rome at the end of the Republic)[20] and where the crude birth rate was about 48 per thousand, the crude death rate 45 per thousand and the infant mortality rate 300–350 per thousand. Tropical Africa's high birth rates, which are sustained by culture and religion, are undoubtedly a response to high death rates in what has long been one of the world's most disease-ridden regions.

This picture is not in any way surprising. Health conditions of this order have lingered on almost into our own time in remoter parts of the continent. Surveys in Mali in the late 1950s and Upper Volta in the early 1960s have

17. The tables used were the 'North' set in A. J. Coale and P. Demeny, 1966, pp. 220–435.

18. J. C. Caldwell in W. Birmingham, I. W. Neustadt and E. N. Omaboe (eds), 1967, p. 94.

19. The birth rate in Mauritius, having averaged below 40 per thousand all the century, rose from 33 per thousand in 1943 to 50 per thousand in 1950, the greatest rise occurring during and immediately after the antimalarial campaign; William Brass believes that birth rates in Kenya rose during the 1950s (personal communication); and D. J. van de Kaa believes that contemporary birth rates are rising in New Guinea in conditions of health and social change similar to those found in parts of Africa (D. J. van de Kaa, 1971).

20. L. I. Dublin, A. J. Lotka and M. Spiegelman, 1936, p. 42.

yielded adjusted data suggesting crude death rates of close to 40 per thousand and infant mortality rates of close to and even exceeding 300 per thousand.[21] However, this situation is incompatible with stability in the Middle Africa low fertility zone if the birth rates now claimed for that area are supposed to have persisted at that level from the past. Given the mortality levels described above (which is a conservative assumption in view of the fact that the health conditions of the forests of the west coast equatorial area have probably long been worse than elsewhere), the conclusion could be drawn that in the centuries past those areas averaging 5 births per woman had experienced population declines averaging over 0.5 per cent per annum, and those averaging 3.5 children declines of over 1.5 per cent per annum. This is inconceivable over any protracted period; the latter population would be halving every forty years, and both situations suggest much larger populations during the earlier years of European contact than has ever been suggested. The conclusion is inescapable that fertility has fallen in the area within comparatively recent times and probably within the period being described in this chapter.

The main aim here will be to examine those influences which may have caused long-term population change as well as those which may have had more dramatic short-term effects within the last century. It is commonly assumed that the major constraint on population numbers in traditional societies has been the availability of food. However, E. Boserup has argued that critical population densities do not lead to a Malthusian situation but to changes in the methods of cultivation: 'the low rates of population growth found (until recently) in pre-industrial communities cannot be explained as the result of insufficient food supplies due to overpopulation, and we must leave room for other factors in the explanation of demographic trends ... medical, biological, political, etc.'[22] The African past may well have been more complex than this and the ultimate bounds may have been those of food resources, even though infrequently brought into play. The land available for farming was that land not proscribed by other uses; for instance, the nearly deserted land between warring kingdoms had alternative employment as a no-man's land. In much of the continent little land appeared to be in use at any one time, either because slash-and-burn or savanna shifting cultivation meant that most land at any given time was fallow or because hunters and food gatherers needed huge areas for their support. Only occasionally did extreme famine conditions strike, caused by drought or locusts or by the disorganization arising from war or epidemic. The crisis was usually too sudden to allow any substantial temporary invasion of the fallow,[23] and in effect the limits of the carrying

21. P. Cantrelle, in J. C. Caldwell (ed.), 1975, p. 102.
22. E. Boserup, 1965, p. 14.
23. A good deal of this argument is based on a first-hand study of the Sahelian and Ethiopian drought of the early 1970s which was reported on in J. C. Caldwell, forthcoming.

capacity of the land were reached with resulting huge mortality and a drop in population numbers for decades. The pressure on the capacity of the system to produce food was usually – but not always – too short and sudden to produce the successive changes in methods of land use that Boserup describes. Such changes are most likely when population numbers push persistently against the food-producing capacity of the cultivation system either in a situation where the great peaks of mortality have been reduced by health measures or other actions or where luck or geographical conditions moderate those peaks. For decades subsequent to the crisis, populations remained well below the level at which they pressed on food supplies;[24] they grew, but only at a modest rate, because they were still subject to the ravages of fearful diseases. The rate of growth may have risen somewhat when the population was thinned out, because of the temporary reduction in the communicability of infectious disease,[25] but this is far from certain as the disaster may have led to such disorganization in the community (as, for example, an increased level of orphanage) as to tend to raise mortality from other causes.

The clashing forces of demographic change up to and beyond 1880

The clearest assault on the demographic balance was the slave trade. Although this chapter is concerned with a period which begins just as the Atlantic slave trade had been all but extinguished, it is important to discuss the magnitude of the trade and its lasting effects.

The story of how certain numbers became conventionally accepted as measuring the volume of tropical Africans shipped to the New World bears a remarkable resemblance to the origin of the population estimates with Riccioli. Curtin has demonstrated how nearly all modern historians have drawn indirectly on Kuczynski, who borrowed the estimates from W. E. B. Du Bois who took them from the unresearched surmises of Edward Dunbar, a mid nineteenth-century American publicist for a Mexican political cause.[26] Until some future researcher attempts an even more complete examination of the original sources, there is no alternative now to employing Curtin's own estimates which show a total of just over 9.5 million slaves reaching the New World with the following distribution by century: fifteenth century – 34 000 (0.4 per cent of the total); sixteenth century – 241 000 (2.5 per cent); seventeenth century – 1 341 000 (14.0 per cent); eighteenth century – 5 652 000 (59.1 per cent); and nineteenth century –

24. For a discussion of this type of pressure, see W. Allan, 1965.

25. As was apparently the case among seventeenth- and eighteenth-century settlers in North America in contrast to the position in the societies from which they came.

26. P. D. Curtin, 1969, pp. 3–8; the intermediate source of most of these estimates is R. R. Kuczynski, 1936, p. 12.

2 298 000 (24.0 per cent).[27] This movement, supplemented by a very small free movement across the Atlantic in the nineteenth century,[28] established in the Americas a population of at least partial African ancestry numbering by the time of writing many times the volume of transported slaves and clearly establishing Africa as second only to Europe as a source of settler population outside the continent of origin. The full historical significance of this has yet to be played out.

The export of slaves (calculated in the first place in terms of those landed in the Americas) can be worked out as an emigration rate, subject admittedly to the proviso that there is no real knowledge of the size of the base population from which they were drawn. For illustrative purposes here we will employ Durand's medium and low estimates[29] (the latter because it will be argued later that it may be closer to the truth than the new constant population estimates). Concentrating on four time periods, the sixteenth, seventeenth, eighteenth and first half of the nineteenth centuries, and calculating annual average rates per thousand base population, the medium estimate yields emigration rates rising to 0.5 in the eighteenth century and falling to 0.4 in the early nineteenth, while the low estimate for the same dates climbs to 0.9 only to fall to 0.6. For sub-Saharan Africa during these two periods, the medium estimate rates would be 0.6 and 0.4 and the low estimate rates 1.1 and 0.6. However, most slaves came from restricted parts of the Atlantic coast of Africa, mostly from Senegal to Angola, with the great majority originating from birthplaces within 500 km of the coast. Assuming these areas to have had about one-third of the sub-Saharan African population, we can calculate rates for the whole four time periods of 0.1, 0.6, 2.5 and 1.8 according to the medium estimates and 0.2, 0.8, 3.1 and 1.9 according to the low estimates. To these should be added extra deaths occasioned by slaving. The losses on the Atlantic voyage seem to have fallen from perhaps one-fifth in the earlier two centuries to about one-sixth and one-tenth in the eighteenth and nineteenth centuries respectively.[30] There were certainly very substantial losses of life in Africa too during capture and the march to the coast. Some of this additional mortality would have

27. Derived from tables on pp. 116, 119, 216 and 234 of P. D. Curtin, 1969. At the meeting of experts on the African Slave Trade held at Port-au-Prince, Haiti, under the auspices of UNESCO from 31 January to 4 February 1978, no agreement was arrived at on the exact number of slaves transported to the New World. It was generally believed that Curtin's figures were too low and that the correct figure was somewhere between 15 and 30 million. See Final Report of the meeting, Ref. CC-78/CONF.601/7, UNESCO, Paris, 17 July 1978, and J. E. Inikori, 'Slave Trade and the Atlantic Economies, 1451–1870.' Working paper presented to the meeting, CC-76/WS/22 Paris, 1 October 1976.

28. For instance the recruitment of 36 100 Africans into the British West Indies between 1841 and 1867. See G. W. Roberts, 1954, p. 235.

29. Constructing sixteenth- and seventeenth-century estimates by employing Durand's methods.

30. P. D. Curtin, 1969, pp. 275–86.

occurred in any case, because analyses of slave origins in West Africa make it clear that captives for sale became most plentiful when such internal wars as the Fulani conquests in Nigeria produced large numbers of refugees and prisoners;[31] but without doubt the existence of the market on the coast increased capricious violence producing victims of extra lawlessness or of the harsher implementation of customary law. Thus the rates calculated above probably should be increased by minimums of half for the sixteenth and seventeenth centuries, one-third for the eighteenth century and perhaps one-fifth for the nineteenth century.

This inflation of loss rates, even when applied to the low population estimates, does not produce total African levels for the eighteenth and nineteenth centuries above 1.3 and 0.7 respectively. This would be compensated by an average difference of one point between the birth and death rates (that is, an annual rate of natural increase of 0.1 per cent). When restricted to sub-Saharan Africa, the rates become 1.4 and 0.8 respectively; while a further restriction to one-third of this population yields levels of 4.2 and 2.9. These latter rates might well produce population decline or halt a tendency towards growth, in the absence of other substantial changes tending to move the balance of vital rates towards growth, for natural increase in pre-modern societies rarely seems to have averaged levels as high as 0.4 per cent for long periods. The area of certain population decline was the coast from Cabinda to Luanda and the country behind it during the eighteenth and early nineteenth centuries. The coast and its hinterland, even if we include much of what is now Angola and Zaire and even some of Zambia, could hardly have contained more than 4 million people and yet may have yielded well over a million slaves in the nineteenth century alone, suggesting loss rates (according to the formula employed above) of close to 1 per cent per annum, resulting almost certainly in declining population and the depopulation of some areas, especially in Angola.

What then were the lasting effects in 1880? External slavery was now minor: slaves from the southern Sudan would filter down the Nile and to Ethiopia, East Africa and perhaps the Middle East for a few more years; and *de facto* slavery would continue from Angola to the plantations of São Tomé and Principe until 1913. The trade of Zanzibar (now part of Tanzania) practically ceased after 1873 and had never been on the massive scale of the Atlantic trade although it had probably resulted in a movement of people away from the main routes inland, especially that west through Tabora. Within the continent there was still domestic slavery, as was evidenced by the 1904 report on French West Africa which showed almost a quarter of the population in some type of bondage,[32] but the demographic impact was probably slight. Although by 1880 the Atlantic trade was four centuries old, half the slaving had occurred since about 1770, first in

31. ibid., p. 260.
32. J. Suret-Canale, 1971, p. 66.

response to the American cotton boom and then to the growing demands from Brazil.

During this period of just over a century those successfully transported across the Atlantic plus those who had died during capture or subsequent transportation probably numbered about 6 million, of whom about 4.5 million may have been males and 1.5 million females.[33] The fraction of these persons who would otherwise have probably lived until 1880 is small: a quarter of a million at the most in view of the decline in numbers transported after 1840. However, a greater loss arises from the transportation of females. Even at the net reproduction levels of a stationary population, 1.5 million females would be succeeded by 3 million surviving children (thus reproducing numbers equal to themselves and their partners), and a small level of natural increase (0.3 per cent per annum) could raise this to 3.25 million by 1880 given that the bulk of the slaves were taken in the earlier part of the period. Thus a total deficit of 4 million persons would seem a reasonable estimate. This would be a small deficit for either Africa or sub-Saharan Africa taken as a whole: perhaps 4 or 5 per cent respectively and equivalent at a rate of natural increase of 0.5 per cent per annum to eight or ten years' growth. However, the position would have been very different for the main source area of slaves, where, if we employ the same assumption as used above (that is, that the area contained one-third of the sub-Saharan population) the deficit would have been 15 per cent or at least a generation's growth.

There are two debatable assumptions embodied in these calculations. The first is that the late eighteenth- and nineteenth-century populations were not bound by Malthusian limits, in that food supplies could be increased by extra cultivation or a change of food staples. If this were not so, then the population would normally have grown very little but would have expanded rapidly enough to fill the deficit left by slaving before slowing down, thus implying that the trade had very little impact on total numbers. On the other hand, some kind of Malthusian restraint has been assumed when considering the earlier half of all slaves transported, those taken in the three centuries before 1770. If such an assumption is not warranted (and if the sex ratios of slave cargoes remained much the same over the centuries), then we can assume a further deficit of 4 million persons if moderate natural increase had been confined to the period after 1770, and 5 million if it had not. The second assumption, much less debatable, is that the universality of female marriage in Africa, guaranteed even in areas of imbalance between the sexes by the practice of polygamy, means that the removal of large numbers of males had little effect on reproduction. It was in fact the African institutions of marriage which limited the wounds inflicted by the slave trade.

A subtler change has also been affecting the areas of slave origin, and

33. Employed sex ratios derived from P. D. Curtin, 1969, p. 41, fn. 37.

other areas beyond, for half a millennium and may well have had a greater demographic impact. That is changes in the sources of food brought about largely by external contact.

Some of Africa's densest population is now found in the wet tropics which extend around the coast of West Africa to the Congo basin and farther still to the East African highlands. Most of the area was originally covered by thick forest and much still is. It is now the home of two-fifths of the continent's population, but this was not always so. The most extraordinary feature of this vast region is that a very large proportion of the food is of a type that was unknown there five hundred years ago. A careful assessment of the scientific dietary studies in sub-Saharan Africa,[34] and other supporting information, shows that cassava (manioc) is now the most commonly used staple on the coast from the Ivory Coast to Angola and inland as far as the western ramparts of the East African highlands. In this area the most frequently used additional crop is maize, which becomes the dominant staple in Angola and in a vast area of East Africa stretching from Kenya to Lesotho and Natal. In Rwanda and Burundi the major staples are in order of importance beans, sweet potatoes, cassava and potatoes.

The neolithic revolution, according to some authorities though disputed by others, came to Africa by way of Egypt over six thousand years ago and reached the West African savanna about three thousand years ago.[35] The change to crop cultivation was surprisingly successful, resulting in the domestication of wild crops in Ethiopia and West Africa and even high neolithic cultures such as that of Nok in northern Nigeria. The invasion of wetter, tropical Africa by cultivated crops was less successful, although the locally domesticated yam was rain-tolerant and grew well enough on the forest margins as did the West African variety of rice. Early in the Christian era plants more suited to equatorial Africa, the banana (especially its large non-sweet variety, the plantain) and the Asian yam reached East Africa and slowly spread westward.[36] But the conquest of the forest was a long slow process and agriculture and population grew slowly within its confines, so slowly indeed that up to the fifteenth century the forested northerly part of the Congo basin seems to have been sparsely occupied by hunters and food-gatherers and considerable areas are still occupied by these people.[37]

In terms of demographic history, the important point is that the forest

34. M. P. Miracle in C. Gabel and N. R. Bennett (eds), 1967, pp. 201–25. Miracle convincingly demonstrated the inadequacy of the anthropological data employed by G. P. Murdock, 1960, and the value of painstaking sample surveys taken around the year by governmental organizations. With reservations induced by Miracle's criticism, Murdock has been used here as a supplementary source.
35. R. Oliver and J. D. Fage, 1962, p. 25; G. P. Murdock, 1960.
36. R. Hallett, 1970, pp. 16–17. See also C. O. Sauer, 1952, pp. 34–5.
37. D. F. McCall, 1964, pp. 142–3; D. W. Phillipson, 1977, pp. 220–30.

was the home of very few people five hundred years ago. The major exceptions were the fringes, the coast and the important inter-regional routes. For instance in Nigeria an example of the first is the lagoon area either side of Lagos, of the second is Old Oyo, and of the third is both Ife and Benin on the route which crosses the Niger at the lowest point where it is easily accessible and crossable before reaching the delta. Since then the movement into the forest has continued at an accelerating rate and is by no means complete. To take another Nigerian example, and a contemporary one, the opening up of the wet forest south of Ondo (and to the south-east of the massively crowded central Yorubaland) to intensive cultivation has largely been a product of the building of the road from Ijebu Ode to Benin in the early 1960s.

Without doubt, the peopling of the forest was sustained almost entirely by natural increase and not immigration. It is equally clear that the process accelerated during the nineteenth century and was proceeding at an un-precedented speed in the period covered by this study. Maize reached some parts of the northern Congo basin only after 1830 becoming the most important Zande crop around 1900. Maize was known in Kenya in the 1880s but until the end of the century it was important only on the coast,[38] while it became important in Uganda, Rwanda and Burundi only during the first decades of this century.[39] Cassava's great spurt was even later. In West Africa its spread was inhibited by inadequate knowledge of how to prepare it and remove all poisons until the Brazilians (Africans returning from Brazil whence they or their ancestors had been transported as slaves) came to the Guinea Coast in the nineteenth century and taught the preparation of gari (cassava meal), which 'seems to have spread from the Brazilian centers to most of the old yam-growing areas, but its expansion has been most rapid since about 1900.'[40] Cassava has been grown on any scale in Senegal only since 1900 and in Nigeria north of the Niger and Benue not until the 1920s.[41] All evidence points the same way. Asian rices have largely supplanted indigenous rice, especially in far West Africa, during the last century and the present one; while even the older varieties of cocoyam (taro) were supplemented during the nineteenth century by the introduction of new types from the Pacific.[42]

The food historian would note the revolutionary change in diet which has occurred. The demographer, however, must stress that much of sub-Saharan Africa has been subject to changes over five hundred years which could hardly fail to induce population growth and that these changes were still accelerating at the end of the nineteenth century, making a particularly strong impact on precisely the areas from which slaves had been taken.

38. M. P. Miracle, 1966, pp. 95–9.
39. M. P. Miracle in C. Gabel and N. R. Bennett (eds), 1967, pp. 219–20.
40. W. O. Jones, 1959, p. 79.
41. ibid., pp. 80–4.
42. B. F. Johnston, 1958, p. 26.

These were the major forces determining population change but there were undoubtedly others. Commerce was one, although whether such activities brought prosperity and the ability to buy food in times of need and perhaps some health care in the few places where it existed to a greater degree than it brought disease arising from increased contact with strangers is debatable. By 1880 cash crops included the cotton of Egypt, cloves in Zanzibar, sugar in Natal and an increasing area of groundnuts (peanuts) in Senegal, while in Algeria a European settler economy largely based on wheat and wine was being established. One aspect of trade almost certainly did have a deleterious effect on health, and that is the flow of strong alcoholic drink into the continent. There were two reasons for the trade: firstly that alcohol could be produced cheaply in Europe and sold for immense profits; secondly, in economies without widely accepted mediums of exchange, there were real problems about what goods would be accepted in return for the produce of Africa.[43] Mary Kingsley found the trade spirit pure and likely to do less harm than cannabis,[44] a view shared by a committee that investigated the liquor trade in 1909.[45] Spirits were distributed on a huge scale, frequently as wages. In 1894 half the total government revenue and 95 per cent of the customs duties of the Niger Coast Protectorate were derived from spirits; by 1894 the governmental income from this source totalled nearly £2 million.[46] Although the Brussels Act of 1892 tried unsuccessfully to limit the trade in the Congo (now Zaire), it was not successfully regulated in tropical Africa until the eve of the First World War.

Much the same doubts could be cast on another of the trade goods, guns. It was firearms that made it possible for a relatively small number of people to control a greater number of slaves, as Arab and Ethiopian experience in East Africa demonstrated. In the longer run, those areas most advanced in commercialization first developed a commercial, administrative and civil infrastructure: port facilities, roads, trading premises, cash cropping and eventually schools and health facilities and possibly declining mortality levels. In West Africa there was a tendency for those areas most involved in the slave trade to be ahead in such development; some of the trading acumen of the Igbo and the Asante almost certainly developed during the time of the trade. In North Africa drainage, refuse collection and other sanitary measures were demonstrably under way by mid-century in certain Egyptian and Algerian cities, motivated largely by the desire to protect the new European populations but doubtless affecting the indigenous population as well. In the 1840s the impact of such measures in Algiers was particularly great as the French strove to control cholera.[47]

43. See H. M. Stanley's remarks quoted in L. Middleton, 1936, p. 288.
44. M. H. Kingsley, 1897, pp. 662–8.
45. R. Schram, 1971, p. 115.
46. ibid., pp. 114–15.
47. J. R. Morrell, 1854, p. 87.

The impact of colonialism

One of the most common justifications for the European forward movement which began in the 1880s was that the new stable administrations reduced the mortality toll from inter-ethnic warfare and slaving raids. Lugard laid much stress on this, claiming that Nigeria's more deserted areas were evidence of periodic devastation.[48] Certainly there was some insecurity in pre-colonial Africa, as is evidenced by the defensive location of many villages from which 'downhill movements' of farmers to better agricultural locations occurred after their safety could be guaranteed.[49]

The claim of greater security was true in the long run but highly questionable during the first decades. African instability had been exacerbated by the European contact. In any case it was almost certainly exaggerated by both European administrators and missionaries, each seeking to justify the kind of new order that they had brought. The object of much of the raiding was not people but cattle and grain,[50] although without question the owners of such property ran risks in protecting it. What was less frequently emphasized by the new regimes was the heavy loss of life arising in parts of Africa from their intervention. The deaths were rarely a product of the original extension of administration, but rather of the suppression of subsequent revolts and of the ensuing punitive expeditions which apparently often inflicted most damage because of starvation resulting from the upsetting of the subsistence farming cycle. Examples include the thousands killed in Senegal in 1886 when opposing the building of a railway[51] and in the Ndebele war in Southern Rhodesia (now Zimbabwe) in 1893, the long-drawn-out suppression of the Batetela rebellion in the Congo Free State from 1895 to 1907, and a series of episodes in German South West Africa (now Namibia) between 1901 and 1906. Greater disasters racked Tanganyika (now Tanzania), where the Germans adopted a 'scorched earth' policy in the 1905–6 Majī Majī rebellion resulting perhaps in hundreds of thousands of deaths largely from starvation,[52] and where fighting between British and German forces throughout the First World War undoubtedly raised mortality levels again. More complex, but certainly arising indirectly out of the presence of Europeans, was the devastation caused in areas surrounding the Zulu nation after 1800 and in the Zulu Wars from 1879 until the last rebellion in 1906. Nor did occupation settle all internal disputes. Some were embittered because administrators or missionaries sided with one ethnic

48. F. D. Lugard, 1929, p. 66.
49. R. M. Prothero, 1965, pp. 39–40; R. M. Prothero in J. C. Caldwell and J. Okonjo (eds), 1968, p. 252.
50. W. M. Macmillan, 1938, pp. 47 ff.
51. P. Gaffarel, 1905, pp. 80–4.
52. See C. J. Martin, in K. M. Barbour and R. M. Prothero (eds), 1961, where estimates of up to half a million deaths are reported.

group. In parts of the continent the colonial peace allowed farming peoples to encroach upon the lands of nomads as occurred in the domains of both the Maasai and the Tuareg.

Certainly in some areas stable administrations apparently resulted in increasing populations in the nineteenth century, such as apparently occurred in Egypt from early in the century as Muḥammad ʿAlī extended irrigation and sanitation[53] and in Algeria after the French subjugated all opposition in 1879.[54] The necessity for such stability, especially as civilian instead of military administration became the rule around the turn of the century, arose out of the metropolitan powers' demand that their colonial administrations in Africa should be financially self-supporting.[55] Hence the increasing concentration on communications and export production.

Perhaps the major demographic problem in the years up to the First World War centres on the so-called 'labour question' and on the concessionaire schemes of Middle Africa.

In the late nineteenth century it was the central belief of colonizers that colonies should be profitable. Whether this could be achieved or not depended entirely on African labour. Profits depended on moving goods and this meant human porterage in most of tropical Africa, for the tsetse fly often prevented the use of draught animals and the lack of roads or railways prevented powered and wheeled vehicles being used. In Middle Africa the most profitable produce was at first ivory which entailed huge quantities of labour for carrying tusks. With the development of the pneumatic bicycle tyre in the late 1880s and the pneumatic car tyre in the 1890s a huge demand for rubber was created, which could not be met for a generation by plantation rubber (the first Malayan plantation came into production in 1910). In the meantime tropical Africa and South America met the demand from wild rubber, found in Africa mostly in vines and also needing great quantities of labour for its collection and initial processing..

The difficulty was that subsistence farmers had few needs and often felt that regular employment savoured of slavery[56] and that these tasks were women's work.[57] Europeans, frustrated by seeing large profits slipping away from them, had little sympathy with such attitudes: 'fear had to take the place of ambition or covetousness as the motive sentiment inducing them to labour'.[58] The solutions were primitive and often brutal. For government purposes forced labour was used, with the chiefs designating those who were to work. Individual and hut taxes were imposed, with, in some areas and more frequently in the earlier years of the system, the

53. C. V. Kiser, 1944, pp. 385 ff.
54. R. Oliver and J. D. Fage, 1962, p. 150.
55. ibid., pp. 204 ff.
56. J. C. Mitchell in K. M. Barbour and R. M. Prothero (eds), 1961.
57. R. Oliver and J. D. Fage, 1962, p. 202.
58. W. G. B. de Montmorency, 1906, p. 149.

possibility of commuting payment to labour. The Mossi of Upper Volta, following the introduction of taxation after the French conquest in 1896, at first attempted to increase production and trading, but soon the young men began to seek paid seasonal employment in the Gold Coast, only to find the taxes trebled between 1906 and 1910.[59] The system had a long history; it was being used as part of a new French approach to colonization in the 1920s when the Mossi were employed on the Ivory Coast railways and other projects designed to improve the infrastructure of French West Africa, although porterage petered out in the 1930s as lorries became more plentiful.[60] In addition Africans were recruited and conscripted into armies and police forces. In some areas labour was recruited from overseas, such as the importation of Indians to build the Mombasa–Uganda railway at the beginning of the present century and to cultivate sugar in Natal from as early as 1860. Everywhere there was movement of labour either to concentrate it in places where it was needed or because some African peoples were regarded as better or more willing workers either because of their longer contact with a commercial economy or because of age-old features of their specific cultures.

Much of this labour movement in the third of a century after 1880 was accompanied by appallingly high mortality. The labourers were often shifted to areas which exposed them to new diseases; but in addition Africans apparently immune to malaria in their home areas developed not only virulent malaria in distant areas but even blackwater fever.[61] Some of the migrant labourers did not observe the careful sanitary arrangements which exist widely in Africa, especially defecation in areas outside the village and away from streams[62] thereby polluting their water supplies and spreading dysentery and the newly introduced diseases of typhoid and paratyphoid fever. Certainly the conditions of the work camps encouraged the spread of venereal disease and diarrhoea. The workers, carrying within themselves the great load of worms and agents of diseases commonly found in tropical Africa, worked more strenuously at times than they had learnt was possible for them, and came down with sickness. Many of the labourers were weakened by hunger, partly because they were offered diets astonishingly different from their usual ones, but partly because porters and others were underfed apparently because Europeans either did not care or, in some unanalysed way, believed Africans lived off the land.[63] Little is known of the nineteenth-century death rates, but in 1915 the British Consul on São Tomé and Principe claimed a death

59. E. P. Skinner in H. Kuper (ed.), 1965, pp. 60–3.

60. M. L. Bates in V. Harlow and E. M. Chilver (eds), 1965, p. 625.

61. H. B. Thomas and R. Scott, 1935, p. 309.

62. R. H. Faulkingham, J. H. Belding, L. J. Faulkingham and P. F. Thorbahn, 1974, pp. 31–5; I. O. Orubuloye, n.d. p. 77.

63. R. R. Kuczynski, 1939, pp. 50–1; J. Suret-Canale, 1971, pp. 26 ff; E. P. Skinner in H. Kuper (ed.), 1965, p. 65.

rate of 100 per thousand among the indentured labourers there,[64] while a similar rate has been calculated for forced labour on the railway from Brazzaville to the sea in 1922.[65] The latter rate contrasts with one of 150 per thousand for the pre-First World War Cameroon railway.[66] The Mossi made a proverb out of the situation when they said that 'White Man's work eats people', and the French administration of Upper Volta intervened to have rations and wages improved during the 1920s for construction workers on the Ivory Coast railway so as to attempt to reduce the toll in lives.[67] Similarly bad conditions prevailed on those plantations which did exist, as is evidenced by the loss in 1902 of one-fifth of the workforce a year in Cameroon.[68]

The worst situation developed in Middle Africa, in the Congo Free State (later Belgian Congo and then Zaire), French Congo (later French Equatorial Africa) and German Cameroon, in almost exactly the area of the low fertility belt. From about 1890 concessionaires were given the whole produce of the land in vast areas of the Free State, while the system was supplemented by the creation of Leopold's Domaine Privé from 1892. Within a decade the system had spread to the other two areas and remained intact until almost the First World War. Indeed André Gide found substantial remnants in the late 1920s.[69]

Great similarities existed in each of the systems. The Africans discovered that they no longer owned even their accumulated ivory and that they had to kill elephants for more ivory and scour the forest for rubber. Some of the most callous riffraff of Europe drifted in to become agents for the concessionaires, and to an extraordinary degree they were permitted to utilize the apparatus of the colonial administration including its army, police and courts. Taxation and compulsory labour, although in theory limited, were reinterpreted by the agents to mean such continuous work that crop planting and, consequently, diet suffered very considerably. The population grew reluctant to toil collecting, and to hand over what had always been communally theirs. Imprisonment was an unsatisfactory punishment as it reduced the available labour. Instead, floggings, mutilation, the taking as hostages of women and children, the burning of villages and a considerable amount of killing were employed. Undoubtedly disease and famine followed the break-up of the village organization of labour and the flight of whole villages.[70] No one kept adequate population records

64. E. D. Morel, 1920, pp. 157–8.
65. R. R. Kuczynski, 1939, p. 162.
66. ibid., p. 61.
67. E. P. Skinner in H. Kuper (ed.), 1965, p. 65.
68. R. R. Kuczynski, 1939, p. 58.
69. A. Gide, 1930, *passim*.
70. Widely documented largely as a result of the debate in Europe during the period. See J. Suret-Canale, 1971; E. D. Morel, 1906; 1920; L. Middleton, 1936, and even Information and Public Relations Office, Belgian Congo and Ruanda-Urundi, *Belgian Congo*, Vol. I, Brussels, 1959.

but enormous declines in population were widely agreed upon. Probably the evidence for such declines was based upon exaggerated estimates of pre-partition populations, and from the evidence of vanished populations along the tracks and riverbanks from which the people had fled. But it is difficult to avoid the conclusion that population probably did decline in the region between 1890 and 1910 or even later (the theory that millions went to the nearest British territories receives little support from reports and censuses of those areas). It is more difficult, but perhaps not impossible, to imagine that the level of disease (venereal disease and other infections) generated during this period still resulted in a high level of female sterility half a century or more afterwards. It is also difficult to feel that the situation in this region is adequately covered by a recent United Nations' publication writing of 'cultural shock' and 'the processes of adjustment'.[71]

Eventually the colonial penetration was to lead to a great increase in population. This was partly due to the establishment of an economic base which is evidenced by many developments discussed in several of the chapters above. Some of the more spectacular of them were the development of palm-oil exports from the Niger delta, the discovery of diamonds and then gold in Southern Africa in the years from 1870 to 1900, the development of an indigenous cocoa-growing industry in the Gold Coast in the 1890s and the discovery of huge deposits of copper between the Congo and Northern Rhodesia (now Zambia) in the early years of the century.

However, the development which probably had the earliest impact on the mortality level was the penetration of the roads and railways. By the end of the 1920s most of the railway system had been built and roads were improving; by the late 1930s lorries in limited numbers were reaching almost every part of the continent. This system made it possible for food to be sent by governments or traders to famine areas. The very existence of a transport network together with a currency acceptable over great distances encouraged the production of a surplus of food for the market. From about 1920 famine deaths, relative to the size of the rainfall deficit, fell consistently, and the great mortality peaks, which kept up the average level of mortality, began to be under major attack. Until that time, even countries like Uganda could experience over a hundred thousand famine deaths in a single year, as it apparently did in 1918–19.[72]

Missionaries probably had a small but real impact on mortality, quite apart from the setting up of hospitals. One authority argues that 'their pupils imbibed ... at least some sense of mastery over the new conditions of life created by the colonial system'.[73]

Finally, what effect did *western* medicine have on Africa? The short answer is that, apart from emergency measures against certain epidemics,

71. United Nations, 1973, p. 31.
72. D. A. Low in V. Harlow and E. M. Chilver (eds), 1965, p. 110.
73. R. Oliver and J. D. Fage, 1962, p. 204.

the meagre services that did exist were concentrated mainly on saving Europeans until the First World War; thereafter services became progressively available for African labourers who were still justifiably regarded as the chief source of wealth in Africa, while mass medicine was hardly attempted before the middle of the present century. That little more could be attempted by the medical services is shown by the fact that as late as 1939 they were awarded an annual budget of only two shillings per head in the Gold Coast and five pence in Nigeria.[74]

The diseases to which the population were subject were awesome. As late as the 1930s, it was reported of conditions in Kampala that: 'Every patient attending for treatment is a latent or active subject of malaria, and harbours one or more varieties of helminths. From 50 to 80 per cent have or have had syphilis or yaws or both, and the same is true of gonorrhoea, while leprosy, spirillum fever and dysentery, among other diseases, are far from rare.'[75] The helminths included hookworm, *Ascaris* infections, schistosomiasis, filariasis and Guinea worm. To these must be added such epidemic diseases as yellow fever, smallpox and sleeping sickness (trypanosomiasis) and the new imports like tuberculosis and cholera. Until near the end of the nineteenth century, Europeans were far more likely to succumb to indigenous diseases, as is evidenced by the death rates early in the century among British West African forces which were nine times as great among the European as among the African soldiers.[76]

Europe was not medically well equipped for its African ventures. At the beginning of the nineteenth century Britain's expectation of life at birth was less than 40 years; while, by the end, those of Britain, France and Germany had reached about 47 years with death rates close to 20 per thousand and infant mortality rates near to 200.[77] Furthermore, the medical revolution was late in turning its attention to tropical disease. Although smallpox vaccination had been known since the eighteenth century (largely because the disease was not a specifically tropical one), even the methods of transmission of elephantiasis, malaria, and yellow fever were established only in 1877, 1897 and 1900 respectively. Apart from quinine, and a limited use of arsenical compounds against syphilis and yaws, the development of drugs and vaccines to combat tropical diseases really dates only from the 1920s. Nevertheless, tropical medical schools were established in Europe as early as 1897 in Liverpool and London, 1900 in Hamburg, 1901 in Brussels, followed later by Paris, Bordeaux and Marseilles, and in Africa by 1912 in Cape Town and 1918 in Dakar.

In tropical Africa governmental medicine was long a military concern

74. R. R. Kuczynski, 1948–53, Vol. I, p. 10.

75. H. B. Thomas and R. Scott, 1935, pp. 303–4.

76. Calculated from data in R. R. Kuczynski, 1948–53, Vol. I, p. 16, which yield crude death rates for European soldiers of 427 per thousand and for Africans of 46 per thousand.

77. N. Keyfitz and W. Flieger, 1959, pp. 32–6; L. I. Dublin, A. J. Lotka and M. Spiegelman, 1936, p. 61.

although small civilian hospitals began to appear in the 1890s. From 1840, when the first mission doctor arrived in Sierra Leone, there were across West Africa a scattering of medical missionaries including some Africans (mostly Sierra Leoneans). These services were concentrated very largely on saving the soldiers, administrators and missionaries, although some care was also extended to African troops, government workers and mission personnel. Real success was achieved only at the beginning of the present century, as is shown by the crude death rates for European officials in the Gold Coast which fell from a level of 76 per thousand in the last two decades of the nineteenth century to 31, 22 and 13 respectively in 1902, 1903 and 1904, and even taking age composition into account, compared favourably with levels in Britain from about 1912.[78] The explanation was held to be sanitary measures against malaria and yellow fever, improved methods of treating tropical diseases, and segregated living quarters. The sanitary measures must have had some impact on the relatively small number of Africans living in the chief administrative centres, especially in Lagos after the measures taken in the first years of the present century by Governor William McGregor and Dr Ronald Ross (who had identified the mechanism of malarial spread). The use of European methods to improve African health was relatively insignificant, partly because Europe offered more temptations after the First World War and partly because colonial powers cut back on health expenditures with the onset of the depression of the 1930s. In 1924 Nigeria had a theoretical medical establishment of one doctor for every 200 000 persons, but in fact only a quarter of these posts were filled. Indeed, by 1939 there was a lower ratio of doctors to population in the country than there had been in 1914.[79] Even these figures exaggerate the chance of an African receiving health care, for in the 1930s twelve hospitals met the needs of 4000 Europeans, while fifty-two hospitals catered for 40 million Africans.[80]

In the absence of many doctors, extensive treatment services really depended on whether rural clinics could be established providing adequate care with the services of medical auxiliaries and whether local self-help projects could be organized. In Nigeria, a dispensary was opened in Ibadan in 1904 and others followed in Yoruba towns in succeeding years.[81] By 1910 the Sierra Leonean government was awarding prizes to the chiefs of the two villages in each district which had shown the greatest improvement in sanitation.[82] By 1934 Uganda had hospitals in all major centres and eighty-eight sub-dispensaries in rural areas which recorded 1 378 545

78. R. R. Kuczynski, 1948–53, Vol. I, pp. 17–18.
79. ibid., pp. 9–10.
80. W. Rodney, 1972, p. 225.
81. R. Schram, 1971, p. 125.
82. Anon., 1910(a).

attendances during the year.[83] One should not exaggerate the significance of these changes: in many dispensaries drugs were few and attendants uncertain about what to do, as has remained the position in much of rural Africa until the time of writing. André Gide, visiting health facilities at Bétou on the Oubangui river in the late 1920s, commented scathingly that the only supplies received to combat the diseases of Middle Africa were iodine, boracic acid, and Glauber's salts.[84]

The major reduction in African mortality (certainly in the period covered by this chapter) has probably been achieved by attacking the periodic peaks in mortality caused by famine and epidemic disease. Some of this reduction may have merely been a compensation for an upturn in certain diseases caused by the European presence. Nearly all authorities before the First World War believed that the sleeping sickness epidemics found across tropical Africa at that time had largely been caused by European activities and often assumed that the new communications and disturbance of the bush had spread tsetse flies or brought them close to the villages.[85] Similarly the so-called syphilis epidemic in Uganda in the early years of the century was said to be a new phenomenon and was taken so seriously that the campaign against it resulted in the foundation of the Uganda Medical Service. In Cameroon it was said to be unknown in 1895 and widespread in 1905. The truth about African syphilis is probably more complex than this: the microbe causing it is so similar to yaws that it is difficult to imagine some form of syphilis not having a long history in the continent;[86] while there is clear evidence that virulent forms of syphilis spread from Southern Africa's mining areas, it appears that milder endemic syphilis may have long been widespread and may have been communicated by a form of vaccination in Uganda.[87]

With gathering momentum from the early years of the century, the campaigns against epidemic disease apparently gained some success. The British attacked sleeping sickness by keeping the tsetse fly away from people: preventing game from using waterholes in inhabited areas, clearing bush, and, more spectacularly, moving populations, as occurred from the foreshores of Lake Victoria. The French treated huge numbers of individual

83. H. B. Thomas and R. Scott, 1935, pp. 304–5.
84. A. Gide, 1930, p. 33.
85. Recent analyses have supported the original beliefs although differing slightly as to the reasons. In A. J. Duggan, 1962, it is argued that sleeping sickness was transmitted by the freer movement of peoples and their animas allowed by colonial administrations; while in J. Ford, 1971, this argument is taken further by suggesting that a whole range of new types of movements of people, domesticated animals and wild animals was made possible which fundamentally altered the ecological balance allowing, for a considerable period, major outbreaks of the disease.
86. F. Cartwright and M. D. Biddiss, 1972.
87. J. N. P. Davies, 1956, pp. 1041–55.

cases, especially noteworthy being the work of Dr E. Jamot using the arsenical compound, atoxy. One area of 124 000 people in the Cameroon, which was treated this way, was recorded in 1924 as having a crude death rate of 81 per thousand of which 36 points could be attributed to sleeping sickness; by 1930 the epidemic there was being beaten. In Uganda, where sleeping sickness was first identified in 1901, it was held to have caused over 200 000 deaths by 1906 when the large population transfers began; but by 1918 there was sufficient confidence that the disease was being contained to allow some people to move back to their old areas.[88] Outbreaks of bubonic plague were far from rare in the first third of the present century: in the first decade Egypt reported 6000 cases of whom half died;[89] almost 60 000 deaths had been recorded in Uganda up to 1932;[90] and there were outbreaks in Accra in 1908, Lagos in 1924 and more generally in Yoruba areas of Nigeria in 1925.[91] Control measures in British West Africa indicated that the disease could be contained; during the Accra outbreak the town had been sealed off and 35 000 doses of Haffkine's vaccine were administered. Yellow fever epidemics have occurred from Senegal to Sudan at unpredictable intervals. By 1927 a vaccine had been developed in the Rockefeller laboratories in Yaba on the outskirts of Lagos, but, as it was not used on a large scale until the Second World War, any success against the disease up until 1935 was due to the suppression of mosquitoes in urban areas and the use of mosquito netting. It is doubtful whether leprosy declined in this period; alepol oil was used in Nigeria from the early 1920s but by 1938 it was estimated that one per cent of the population still had the disease[92] (see Plate 18.1). Smallpox vaccination was on such a small scale that by the late 1930s a significant reduction of the disease had probably taken place only in the Gold Coast and southern Nigeria.[93] In contrast, contact with Europeans and participation in the First World War ensured that the influenza epidemic of 1918–19 swept through Africa probably resulting in the highest annual death rate this century, although the rise in death rates was probably not as great as in Asia, for many African populations were still protected by comparative isolation. Death rates were still enormous in the mines of Southern Africa in the early years of the present century; a 1907 commission reporting on the situation in Transvaal drew attention to death rates in the mines at the time of 71 per thousand for tropical Africans compared with 28 for Africans from the temperate south and 19 for whites, the rates having declined from 130, 35 and 20 respectively two years earlier.[94] In most of the continent

88. D. A. Low in V. Harlow and E. M. Chilver (eds), 1965, p. 111.
89. Anon., 1910(b).
90. H. B. Thomas and R. Scott, 1935, p. 309.
91. R. Schram, 1971, pp. 121–2, 196.
92. ibid., p. 231.
93. R. R. Kuczynski, 1948–53, Vol. I, pp. 11–12.

PLATE 18.1 *A mobile leprosy clinic at work in a small village north of Bangui, Oubangui-Chari*

481

little progress had been made against the greatest scourge of all, malaria, which weakened when it did not kill and explained many deaths attributed to other causes.

Demographic movements up to 1935

The attempt at this much more detailed analysis of probable countervailing demographic forces in Africa than underlay previous attempts at estimating change in overall population numbers, does not lead to any real conviction about trends. The key to change has undoubtedly been the levels and trends of mortality. We have no evidence that fertility changes have had much impact on the continent as a whole. Fertility may well have declined for a period in the low fertility zone of Middle Africa; the Princeton project believed that an analysis of fertility by age indicated that this had occurred during the period under examination here in parts of the northern Cameroon, Central African Republic, Gabon, Niger, Sudan and Zaire.[95] There may have been some increase in fertility in places because of improving female health, but such improvements, as we have seen, were not substantial before 1935; in any case the evidence we do possess from age structure data indicates surprising stability.[96] There may have been changes in the patterns of polygyny, but, although it has been widely believed that the institution depressed fertility, the evidence from tropical Africa suggests that there may have been little effect of this kind: women in polygynous unions may average fewer births than those in monogamous ones because of a greater tendency to add wives to subfertile marriages and because levirate marriage is the source of some wives in polygynous unions.[97]

There is unequivocal evidence of population growth during the first decades of the present century in those areas with adequate statistics, such as in Egypt where population may well have doubled between 1882 and 1937,[98] the Gold Coast, where the apparent growth of over one-third between the 1921 and 1931 censuses could not have been entirely an artefact of better census-taking,[99] and South Africa where both total and

94. Anon., 1911. However, see also Anon., 1913, where it was reported that questions in the South African Parliament had forced the Minister for Native Affairs to admit that the death rates of mine labourers had been systematically understated by excluding deaths in the residential compounds where as late as 1913 monthly deaths suggested annual rates of 200 per thousand or more.

95. W. Brass *et al.*, 1968, *passim*.

96. That is for Ghana between 1921 and 1960; J. C. Caldwell in W. Birmingham, I. W. Neustadt and E. N. Omaboe (eds), 1967, p.94; and for Northern Nigeria between the 1921 and 1952–3 censuses, C. K. Meek, 1925, p. 180, and E. van de Walle in Brass *et al.*, 1968.

97. See H. V. Musham, 1951, pp. 354–63; P. O. Ohadike, 1968; pp. 264–8.

98. C. V. Kiser, 1944, pp. 385 ff.

99. J. C. Caldwell in W. Birmingham, W. I. Neustadt and E. N. Omaboe (eds), 1967, pp. 20–3.

African numbers came close to doubling between the 1904 and 1936 censuses. But these were areas of unusual prosperity or administrative action, as is partly evidenced by the existence of censuses, and must be assumed to have had populations growing more rapidly than the continent as a whole.

Given all these disclaimers, and repeating that no one will ever know the population of Africa prior to the present century, the following trends appear to be more plausible than those suggested to date. Largely because of the invasion of the tropical forest by agriculturists, a growth rate of 0.25 per cent per annum for the whole continent (and probably 0.5 per cent in the forest) seems a reasonable guess for the period from 1500 to 1840, assuming that an accelerated rate of diet change in the eighteenth and early nineteenth centuries counterbalanced the ravages of the slave trade. With the decline of that trade, it is reasonable to suggest that the rate rose to a peak of 0.5 per cent around 1880 only to decline with the impact of the European partition and occupation of sub-Saharan Africa. Although population growth probably continued to falter in some areas until the First World War, increasing populations in parts of North and Southern Africa, and possibly the Gold Coast, may well have more than compensated for the onslaught on the Congo Free State and the French Congo by 1900, so that we can assume that continental population growth reached a low of about 0.25 per cent about the beginning of the century and thereafter continued to rise so that growth averaged 0.5 per cent up to 1920 and 1 per cent between that date and 1935. Projecting backwards from an assumed figure of 165 million in 1935,[100] we reach the following population estimates for various dates: 1500 – 47 million; 1840 – 104 million; 1880 – 120 million; 1900 – 129 million; 1920 – 142 million; 1935 – 165 million.

The essence of the projection is that it argues that the neolithic revolution has been slowly moving through sub-Saharan Africa for three thousand years bringing with it more intensive land use and denser settlement. In its suggestion of sustained population growth, it can be compared only with Durand's low estimates, and the two sets would probably come close to agreement about the population size around 1500. But it implies lower rates of growth in the nineteenth and twentieth centuries and during this period is much closer to his medium estimates. The projection suggests that Africa had a population of about 120 million when our period begins and that this grew by 37.5 per cent during the next fifty-five years to 165 million in 1935.

Population redistribution and urbanization

These fifty-five years witnessed a flow of population that was to do much

100. Derived from the United Nations estimates somewhat adjusted to accord with the new knowledge of population derived from the post-Second World War censuses.

to determine the nature of the new Africa. An addition of 45 million meant that everyone could not be fitted into exactly the same space as was occupied by their ancestors and the movement of people to unoccupied land speeded up. More significantly, from the 1890s in West Africa – earlier in Southern Africa and somewhat later in East Africa – labour migrants began to move great distances looking for paid employment. At first they were impelled by the need to pay taxes, but later the desire to purchase goods and to go to distant places became stronger; at first they were nearly all seasonal migrants but longer-term migration steadily assumed significance. By the late 1920s, almost 200 000 migrants a year were pouring from the savanna into the Gold Coast and Nigeria.[101] Governments put few restrictions on who moved, except in South Africa and Southern and Northern Rhodesia where the movement was restricted to temporary, adult males because of fears of settlement and pressures from white trade unions.[102]

Ultimately, a larger proportion of these migration streams flowed not to the plantations and mines but into the towns, thus eventually ensuring centres in most regions large enough to support national administrations and secondary industries. Africa had, of course, ancient cities in the lower Nile valley, and more recent ones in the Maghrib, savanna West Africa and Nigeria's Yorubaland and the central Gold Coast. Nevertheless, by 1880 only about one person in three hundred lived in centres with populations of over 100 000, compared with perhaps one in fifty in Asia and one in fifteen in Europe.[103]

The real change occurred in our period, especially in sub-Saharan Africa. In tropical Africa, if we exclude Nigeria, and list sixteen towns which were to be of major significance in the twentieth century, we can estimate a combined population in 1880 of about 80 000; by 1930 this had multiplied fivefold to over half a million (thus establishing a base for a multiplication of over ten times in the next forty years). By 1931 Dakar's population had grown to 54 000; Freetown had reached 44 000 but this was only a doubling of the population of half a century before; Accra was 60 000; Addis Ababa 65 000; Nairobi 48 000; and Dar es Salaam 25 000. In Nigeria the scale was different: Ibadan had a population of 400 000 but probably had 150 000 inhabitants at the beginning of the period; Lagos had perhaps doubled to 126 000; ten other Yoruba towns had a total population of almost half a million which may have been little more than they had had half a century earlier; while, in the north, Kano had probably doubled in the fifty years from 1880 to 89 000 and eleven other towns had in total increased from perhaps 150 000 to 200 000.[104] In the Sahel, the population

101. J. Suret-Canale, 1971, p. 246.
102. R. Oliver and J. D. Fage, 1962, pp. 219–20.
103. Calculated from P. M. Hauser in P. M. Hauser (ed.), 1957, pp. 53–95.
104. Most figures for Nigerian towns are from W. Bascom, 1959, pp. 29–43.

of the historic cities was undoubtedly declining partly because they had not become the main French administrative centres; by 1931, Timbuktu, Gao and Mopti had a combined population of only about 15 000. In North Africa, many of the historic towns had retained their importance; in our period Cairo, Alexandria and Algiers had all trebled their populations to over a million, about 600 000 and a quarter of a million respectively; by 1931 fourteen other old towns of the Maghrib had attained a total approaching one and a half million which represented at least a doubling in half a century and in Sudan, Khartoum-Omdurman had 159 000 people. By 1931 the fourteen largest towns of Southern Africa (South Africa, Rhodesia, Angola and Mozambique) had a total population of well over a million, perhaps a tenfold increase in the previous half century, and Johannesburg was approaching 400 000. In sub-Saharan Africa, people were pouring into the new ports, mining towns and administrative cities which took over the whole region and were doubling in size about every twenty years; in North Africa there were some new towns, but growth was mostly on older foundations and a doubling was taking place about every thirty-five years. In the half century these large towns had grown by about four million, and the regional balance had changed so that, of all people found in such centres, North Africa's proportion had fallen from three-quarters to less than three-fifths, Southern Africa had risen from one-fifteenth to a sixth, and tropical Africa from one-fifth to a quarter (while within tropical Africa, the fraction outside Nigeria had climbed from a quarter to a third).

A basis for the future

By 1935 Africa had successfully withstood the demographic shock of European colonization. Its births now far exceeded its deaths, and in many parts of the continent, especially in the growing towns, life was no longer very precarious. Admittedly its death rates were still very high – in the continent as a whole the death rate was probably still well over 30 per thousand and the expectation of life at birth barely more than 30 years – but it was the diseases of tropical Africa, more than any other factor, which had held the invader largely at bay and prevented Africa from becoming another Latin America. Even as it was, the white population of the continent had increased thirty times from 25 000 in 1800, found mostly in the Cape, to three-quarters of a million in 1880, of whom five-sixths were in South Africa, Algeria and Egypt. By 1935 it had multiplied again by five to 3.75 million, of whom half were in South Africa, a quarter in Algeria and a further fifth in the rest of North Africa. During the same period, Asians (almost entirely Indians except for a few small Chinese communities of which the largest was on the Rand) increased from about 50 000 to over a third of a million of whom over two-thirds were in South Africa. Change was coming but few perceived it clearly as is evident from a serious European appraisal of the racial numbers in Algeria in the 1920s: 'Most Frenchmen in Africa had little to fear of there ever being another serious effort to overthrow authority; for, as they point out, there are over eight hundred thousand Europeans to five and a half million natives who have little cohesion and could not do much more than indulge in sporadic outbreaks.'[105]

In 1935 Africa stood at the brink of rapid population growth, which would take its numbers – which had already grown according to our estimates from 120 million in 1880 to 165 million – to 200 million by the late 1940s, 300 million by the mid-1960s and inevitably to 400 million in the mid-1970s. Of the latter number, 50 million would be in cities with more than 100000 inhabitants, a far cry from the Africa of the partition of the 1880s with its debate about creating a labour force.

Finally, it is pertinent to ask whether these massive changes were largely or even entirely the result of the colonial penetration. Without doubt the upsetting of stable populations, leading in the Congo Free State and elsewhere in Middle Africa to an upsurge in the death rate, the slow reduction in mortality in other parts of the continent during the nineteenth century and generally in this century, and the accelerating nucleation of population in towns and on mining fields owed nearly everything to the industrial revolution and to increasing contact with people from industrial societies. Much of this process would have occurred even without colonial rule: the traders would have provoked trading centres into growth; European medical schools would have become interested in the problem of protecting the traders and others from tropical disease; missionaries would have laid the foundations of a hospital system.

Nevertheless, direct colonial rule certainly speeded up all these processes. Eventually, and certainly towards the end of our period, it helped to reduce the great peaks of mortality by increasingly and effectively importing and utilizing epidemic control technology and creating a modern transport system which could distribute food in areas of famine. The need for administrative centres provided a nucleus for new towns, and colonial administrations' guarantees of personal safety and investment security to the nationals of their metropolitan countries hastened the growth of commercial settlements, mining camps and plantations. Without colonial administrations European entrepreneurs might well have been even more rapacious and murderous than they were. Europeans usually justified the colonial penetration by pointing to these achievements. Yet the history of Latin America and China shows that in time most of these gains would have been achieved in any case; the growth of industrialization was irreversible and a *modus vivendi* with Africa and other developing areas, from which needed raw materials were secured, was essential.

105. G. Casserley, 1923, p. 50.

19

The social repercussions of colonial rule: the new social structures

A. E. AFIGBO

Change and continuity

In the rival mythologies of European imperialism and colonial nationalism, change was an innovation introduced by European rule into so-called traditional societies. To imperial apologists change, as applied to colonial peoples, suggests progress, a dramatic and beneficial linear transition from a static and barely productive traditional culture to a dynamic and limitless modernism. But to colonial nationalists the word primarily connotes 'disruption', the process by which unsympathetic and uncomprehending imperialists shattered the idyllic world of colonial peoples leaving in its place turmoil, instability and uncertainty.

These differing attitudes notwithstanding, the two rival mythologies would appear to subscribe to a number of common assumptions regarding change and traditional societies in the colonial situation. These include the belief that traditional societies were basically static, and therefore antithetical to modern values as a result of which the natural relationship between them was one of conflict; that new values, attitudes and structures necessarily displaced their traditional counterparts once they came into contact; and that in any given colony or even geographic region, traditional societies responded uniformly to the impact of European culture.

Recently, however, scholars have shown that for Africa the above assumptions are unfounded since the societies on which European rule was imposed were far from static. On the contrary they were the products of generations, or even centuries and millennia, of change. One can, in fact, assert that 'modernization in Africa has been a continuous process from earliest times'. Such ingredients as occupational specialization, urbanization, social mobility or even labour migration, usually associated with change and modernization, were operative in pre-colonial Africa.

Nor is the 'traditional–modern' polar model, with all its attendant implications of conflict and incompatibility, applicable to the entire spectrum of African experience of change under colonialism. There were manifold variations in the reaction of African cultures to western innovations. Not only were certain customs and beliefs discarded or modified, but some were retained at one level of society at the same time as new alternatives were being accepted at another level. Thus while human sacrifice, the slave trade and the killing of twins were discarded in societies where such practices had existed, and old and new ideas were amalgamated in the sphere of religion, the European ideal of monogamous marriage, accepted as part of an expected public image by sections of the westernized elite, exists side by side under the law with the institution of polygamy among the urban and rural masses. Today we have existing side by side in Africa indigenous and European architectural traditions; local ethnicity and nationalism; local and regional-locked economies and a notional money economy; rural and urban life; western bureaucratic institutions and traditional local authorities; Ku'ranic and Western schools.

Thus with ease many indigenous African institutions and ideas survived the impact of, or even blended with, alien European values. There is, for instance, the case of the Igbo who are often regarded as having massively embraced western ways. According to Sylvia Leith-Ross, an Igbo in the 1930s would – with disengaging facility – patronize holy communion and traditional magic and medicine, and plant 'side by side in the garden round his new cement and pan-roofed house the hibiscus of "civilization" and the *ogirisi* tree of pagan family rites'.[1] Margaret Read has shown how the Nguni integrated the Christian Church and western education into their society, using both as instruments for further ensuring the survival of their culture in the modern world. They see no contradiction, and have no difficulty, in combining Christian and traditional Nguni rites in marriage and funeral ceremonies.[2] Professor Fallers has also described some Ugandan groups as 'enthusiastically and successfully' accepting many elements of modernization – confining their influence, and adapting them to traditional culture and social structure. The point is that colonial Africans were probably not unaware of the elementary fact that accepting 'new forms [would] increase the range of alternatives'[3] available to them.

Any easy generalization on the response of African societies to the European impact is thus bound to be misleading. One must always bear in mind the territorial vastness of the continent, the rich diversity and variegation of African cultures, differences in individual and group temperaments and psychologies – and thus the fact that response to even similar stimuli was likely to vary not only from individual to individual or from society to society, but also from time to time within the same society and by the same individual. In Nigeria attention has usually been drawn to the differing responses of the Igbo, the Yoruba and the 'Hausa-Fulani' to indirect rule. In Kenya, the Gikuyu accepted western innovations, modifying these to suit themselves while many of their neighbours tended to adopt the opposite stance.

1. S. Leith-Ross, 1939, p. 293.
2. M. Read in V. Turner (ed.), 1971, p. 362.
3. J. R. Gusfield in J. L. Finkle and R. W. Gable (eds), 1971, p. 19.

One can, therefore, subscribe to the view that change as such was not new to colonial Africa and that there is no African society which was not affected to an appreciable extent by European contact or which simply withered before it. One must also concede that with colonial rule the ideology of change came to be consciously embraced by the rulers of Africa and their would-be friends. Even those colonial officials who were strongly committed to the policy and practice of indirect rule, with its emphasis on the preservation of traditional institutions and values, still recognized the need for change. Indeed under indirect rule indigenous institutions and rulers were expected to serve as media for introducing reform in measured doses and in ways acceptable to the colonial authority. Every colonial administration saw *change* as the only way of modernizing Africa and fitting her into the orbit of the West to the latter's advantage. The indigenous elites have patronized *change* as a way of getting Africa on to her feet and making her states equal members of the community of nations.

The main forces of change

The forces which played the leading part in changing the social structure and character of colonial Africa are easily catalogued. They were the very fact of colonial conquest with its attendant political settlement, western education, western Christianity, western economic forces and increased urbanization. Details of how most of these forces – especially those of military conquest, political conquest, consolidation and economic exploitation – penetrated Africa and gained a firm grip on her society have been given in other chapters of this volume. It remains to do the same briefly for urbanization and western education before passing on to an analysis of the social effects which all the forces working jointly produced.

In dealing with urbanization it is necessary to emphasize that this important force of change was not introduced into Africa by European rule. On the contrary it had been operating there – with all the opportunities it offered for occupational specialization, population aggregation, social mobility and so on – for centuries before the imposition of European colonialism. The coasts of North, East, West and Southern Africa, as well, for example, as inland areas such as the Sudanic belt and Yorubaland were all centres of ancient and continuing urban aggregation thanks to the catalytic impact of political consolidation and international trade. But it is undeniable that European rule gave urbanization in Africa a new impetus by strengthening those political and economic forces already working in that direction. The result was the rise of new urban centres in places, such as Igbo and Ibibio lands of Nigeria, which had not previously experienced urbanization, as well as the expansion of the old centres. This it did largely by creating improved means of communication, new political and administrative headquarters as well as new centres of trade, mineral

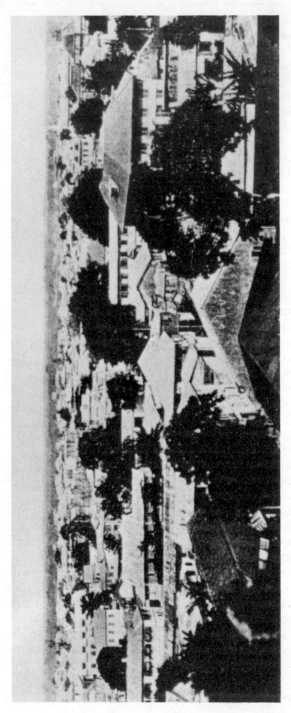

PLATE 19.1 *General view of Lagos, Nigeria, one of the chief ports of colonial West Africa*

and agricultural exploitation. In this regard it is noteworthy that between 1850 and 1950, for the continent the critical century of European contact and foreign rule, the annual growth rate of urban population of Africa was 3.9 per cent compared to the world average of 2.6 per cent. This throws much light on the growth rate of urbanization generally in colonial Africa. The new outburst of urban development and expansion invariably meant an increase in its catalytic role in social change.

Unlike urbanization, western education was brought to Africa by Europe, though not spread by her agencies alone. It is correct to say that the educational revolution in Africa was the work of three interest groups – Christian missions, colonial governments and local African initiative, in that order of importance. For the Christian missions the school was a key institution, being the most reliable means for membership recruitment, and for creating self-perpetuating congregations whose members would ensure the survival of Christianity in the event of withdrawal by the white missionaries. Education and evangelization were so closely linked that for many parts of Africa the pitching of the missionary tent was synonymous with the establishment of a school. Among the Nguni the opening of a school is said to have preceded the opening of a church in all cases.[4]

The colonial administrations, on their part, hoped through the school to raise the low-grade personnel they needed for staffing the bottom echelons of the colonial bureaucracy, to create such conditions – political, economic, social and moral – as would enable Europe to exploit as fully as possible what were regarded as the hitherto insufficiently tapped resources of Africa. To this end not only did colonial administrations erect and run essentially lay schools, they also supported the educational efforts of the missions by means of subventions. Furthermore, the political settlements they effected enabled the missions to penetrate the heart of the continent without fearing for the safety of their agents. The government lay schools were particularly important for the spread of western education in many Islamized parts of Africa where it was feared that unrestrained missionary activity would provoke violent reaction from Muslims.

With regard to local initiative, it is noteworthy that even before the onset of colonial rule, the rulers of Egypt and of the states of the Maghrib had introduced western education into their countries as part of an effort to bridge the technological gap between their societies and Europe. In black Africa local initiative also played some part in spreading education. From the 1920s Gikuyu cultural nationalists established and ran their own schools which, unlike mission schools, were sympathetic to Gikuyu culture. In Uganda and Southern Nigeria local rulers and elders joined with either the colonial administration or the missions to establish schools. In these places, too, some of the new elite established and ran schools, especially at the secondary level where the felt need for self-reliance at times led to

4. M. Read in V. Turner (ed.), 1971, p. 359.

the building of technical rather than grammar schools, independent of the colonial administration and the missions.

While it is easy to enumerate the forces making for social change in colonial Africa, it is less easy to catalogue the changes which each force brought about. In fact so pervasive was the influence of each of these forces that it would be pointless attempting to specify in all cases which force induced what change.

Military conquest and the establishment of the colonial administration, for instance, did not only challenge and defeat the old political and military lords, but also the monopolists of traditional religious and magical powers who were equally involved in the movement of resistance. Thus the loss of the war of resistance against the colonial powers could quite easily lead to a loss of faith in the old priests and gods and to a decision to embrace the supposedly superior faith of the conquerors. The success of the conquerors had other side effects as well. The old military classes, where they existed, could not continue, under the new dispensation, to live on militarism. Nor could the old political elite who had lived by ruling continue to do so unless they were recruited into the political service of the colony whether as 'native authorities' under indirect rule or as tax collectors and intelligence agents under the so-called direct rule. In other words, many of the old political, military, economic and religious elites had to embrace new professions either in place of or in addition to the old ones. Thus not all who seized the new economic opportunities offered by alien rule did so simply in response to the attractions of the new economic regime. Some who migrated to the new urban centres did so not just because of the lure of urbanism, but because the military conquest and the consequent political settlement made their positions in the rural areas obsolescent and untenable. The triumph of military and political force thus struck in many places at the roots of society and called on the different classes for appropriate adjustment.

So did the introduction of Christianity which sought to abolish traditional gods and beliefs. Wherever Christianity took root, for instance, many traditional priests and other manipulators of the supernatural had to take to other professions. Slaves obtained their freedom, thus forcing those who formerly depended on slave labour to do their own work for themselves or shift to dependence on wage labour. Lands hitherto reserved for gods and goblins were released either for arable use or for the siting of social institutions like the school, hospital and so on. The younger generations went to school where they learned new techniques which equipped them for employment in government, commercial firms or missions. And since these jobs were available for the most part in urban areas, it means that conversion to Christianity could also imply a predisposition to live in urban areas. Or to take another example, a man could go to the urban area in search of economic advancement while being still staunchly loyal to the traditional religion. In time, however, his physical separation from the shrines and religious rites of his home gods, as well as the economic, social and psychological pressures of the new environment could turn him into a Christian of sorts. These examples of how one social force usually produced a variegated impact could be multiplied many times.

The new social structures

Among the social effects of foreign rule on African society, the most immediately noticeable was the political one. Pre-existing African states, except for Liberia and, up to 1935, Ethiopia, lost most of their sovereignty and with it the right to participate in the affairs of the world community except indirectly through their new masters. Even their right to interact with their African neighbours, except at the most rudimentary and unofficial level, was severely limited if such neighbours now found themselves on the opposite sides of the line marking the boundary of a colony. For example, the Efik of Nigeria were severed from their traditional markets in the Cameroons, the Yoruba were prevented from taking a direct and open part in events in those parts of Dahomey (now Benin) which formerly formed part of their most celebrated empire, while the Bakongo of Angola could not interact to any significant extent with their kith and kin in either Gabon or the French Congo.

Furthermore, foreign rule transformed and simplified the political map of Africa. Where formerly there were countless rival sovereign states and communities with shifting and at times vague frontiers, we now had a few dozen colonies with fixed and clearly marked boundaries. Attempts were made in international boundary conventions and treaties to take into account the pre-existing political and economic zones. However, such other considerations as the claims of the rival powers, the lure of natural frontiers (hills, rivers, etc.) and of lines of longitude and latitude tended to carry more weight than African claims. As a result, closely related and sometimes previously politically united peoples at times found themselves on opposite sides of the agreed boundary lines.

If the more abiding claims of ethnic integrity were not always respected, neither were the more ephemeral claims of conquest states and empires to territorial integrity. The Sokoto caliphate and the Borno empire lost large tracts of territory by the time the boundaries of the Colony and Protectorate of Nigeria emerged. In the case of the 'peripatetic empires' of Samori Turé and Rabi ibn Fadlallah, these were simply parcelled out between adjoining colonies. The secondary empires of Msiri and Tippu Tib in Central Africa were similarly shared out among the Belgians, the Portuguese and the British. The imposed boundaries of the colonies fossilized under the dead hand of colonialism and international law to become the international boundaries of independent African states to which the liberties and rights of whole peoples are at times sacrificed. It is now impossible to contemplate a significant change in any one of these boundary lines without a major upheaval. Events in the Horn of Africa are beginning to suggest that these imaginary lines on the map of Africa are eternal.

Another aspect of the new political structure deserving mention was the imposition of an alien European bureaucratic administrative structure on the pre-existing African political systems. Between the European and African structures there existed a wide range of patterns of relationship. Taking our examples from the policies of the two leading colonial powers of the period (Britain and France) we discover there were even variations within each system. The French were less concerned than the British with maintaining intact the empires, kingdoms and chiefdoms they conquered and using their political systems in local administration. Therefore they tended to break up the old paramountcies, pensioning off their rulers, while the British made an effort to hitch the local rulers and their political systems to their wagon of imperial administration. This was the general pattern. But in Morocco the French made an effort to preserve the king and his political system and to use them in administration, while for nearly three decades in Asante in the Gold Coast (now Ghana), and for nearly two in Benin in Nigeria, the British sought to break the indigenous administrative systems of these two empires.[5]

However, we find that even in the Muslim emirates of Northern Nigeria where it would appear there was a harmony of interests between the colonial power and the emirs, the union between the European and indigenous administrative systems was never organic. The result was that in some aspects of the life of a colony such as the purely secular the two systems could work hand in hand, while in some others they would work independently and, sometimes, at cross purposes.

One other social impact of foreign rule which was noticeable quite early in the colonial period was the general depression of the status of Africans. Colonialism superimposed on the pre-existing class structure of the continent at least an extra layer of leaders and pacesetters. In East Africa where it encouraged Asian immigration, colonialism in fact superimposed two classes. In each colony Europeans had the monopoly of political, economic and educational power, except in East Africa where a fraction of the economic power fell into the hands of Asians. In this situation the Africans became the underprivileged and looked up to the Europeans, and at times to the Asians, for leadership and example.

This structure of social relationship was shored up with a bogus racial theory which sought to arrange the different branches of the human family in a hierarchical order of civilization with the Africans (the Negroes) occupying the bottom of the ladder while the Europeans (whites) occupied the top. In Southern Africa, in particular, where white settlers found themselves locked in conflict with numerically superior Bantu peoples, the racial theory was especially stringent, with the authority of the Holy

5. A. E. Afigbo in J. F. A. Ajayi and M. Crowder (eds), 1974.

Bible being wrongly used to reinforce the presumed social implications of pseudo-Darwinism. For the Negroes in particular the theory postulated a degree of cultural barrenness which made it necessary and possible to explain their history and social evolution in terms of the Hamitic impact.

In practical life the ascendancy of this racist theory led to a policy of denying Africans, no matter how well educated, equal rights and opportunities with the whites in the colonial service. In West Africa this meant a retreat from the liberal policies of the middle years of the nineteenth century which had made it possible for Africans to hold the same posts as the Europeans. The theory also led to a policy of segregating Africans from the Europeans in the urban areas. Not only were there European housing reserves, there were also European hospitals, European clubs and so on, distinct from those established specifically for the use of Africans. One effect of all this was to induce in the African a feeling of inferiority, a tendency to lose confidence in himself and his future – in short a state of mind which at times encouraged an uncritical imitation of European powers. Luckily, however, some African path-finders were nettled by it all into questioning the whole social and ideological façade of colonialism using facts from history and Christianity. By so doing they helped to prepare the way for post-Second World War radical nationalist thinking.

At the macro-level, then, colonial rule in Africa tended to transform racial distinctions into class divisions. A closer analysis, however, reveals that in no colony did all the Africans form one class. At first the pre-colonial class structure persisted, but in time the new forces of change occasioned a rearrangement of the structure, and the emergence of new classes.

Though pre-colonial Africa provided many avenues for people of ability to rise in social status through personal achievements, its class structure tended to give an undue weight to birth. This was so to the extent that not only political offices but also certain honoured professions like priesthood and smithing ran in families. Foreign rule was to bring about far-reaching changes in African social structure by simply laying emphasis on individual talent and achievement rather than birth, and by providing many openings for advancement which lay beyond the control of the traditional manipulators of African social structure and institutions. Furthermore, its desecration of many African institutions and systems tended to undermine the authority and respect of the old nobility and to erode the awe in which they were held.

Colonial legal and moral codes, by abolishing slavery and proclaiming the equality of all before secular and divine law offered even the most underprivileged in traditional society the opportunity to rise in status, each person according to his ability and destiny.

The anonymity of the urban centres reinforced the effects of the legal and moral revolution by providing for the ex-slaves and their like an arena of action where they could operate unencumbered by history. Similarly, the urban centres held out and still hold out an irresistible attraction to other classes of people in the rural areas. While some people went there to seek a fortune on their own volition, others did so in response to the tax and land policies of the colonial powers in the rural areas, especially in the settler colonies. Those immigrants who were well educated or highly skilled rose fast to become members of the new elite, or to hover on the fringe of that class as sub-elites. The less fortunate immigrants who had little or no education and who in addition were barely skilled or unskilled, sank to the bottom of the urban society to become the urban mass, also called the urban proletariat by some scholars. Many of these found themselves at the mercy of the employers of labour, while others learned some trade and established independent businesses of varying viability. They differed from their rural counterparts, the peasants, in that they did not derive their livelihood from the land, had a closer brush with modernizing influences and lived in slums.

Both the new elite and the urban proletariat were important as agents making for change in rural colonial society, but the former were indisputably the more important in the political, economic and social history of colonial Africa. Their greatest advantage over the traditional elite and the urban and rural masses lay in their literacy. The fact was that for the non-Muslim areas of Africa probably the most important single innovation of foreign rule was literacy. Even for the Islamized areas, the coming of literacy in the Roman script gave a new impetus to Muslim education. Literacy was for many African peoples a new magic, and was sought after as such and at all costs since it appeared to open the treasure house of the modern world. To know the amount of power, authority and influence which the first generation of African clerks, interpreters and teachers exercised is to have some idea of the spell which literacy cast over many African peoples. Literacy gave the elite access to the scientific and social thought of the western world, equipped them to enter into dialogue with the colonial powers over the destiny of Africa, and familiarized them with the social fashions of Europe which made their life style an example to be emulated by their less fortunate countrymen.

But not all those classified as belonging to the new elite in colonial Africa owed their membership of that class to education, nor did all those who owed it to education attain a uniform standard. As Professor Lucy Mair and a number of other scholars have shown, some gained entry into that class because they had made money from either large-scale farming or business and could help to finance the political agitation of their better educated but poorer brethren.[6] Some cotton and coffee farmers of Uganda, cocoa farmers of western Nigeria and the Gold Coast, coffee farmers of Ivory Coast and groundnut farmers of Senegal and The Gambia were able to gain membership of the new elite class on grounds of their success in that profession. Similarly, in West Africa especially, where many

6. L. Mair in V. Turner (ed.), 1971; P. C. Lloyd (ed.), 1966; M. Kilson in L. H. Gann and P. Duignan (eds), 1970.

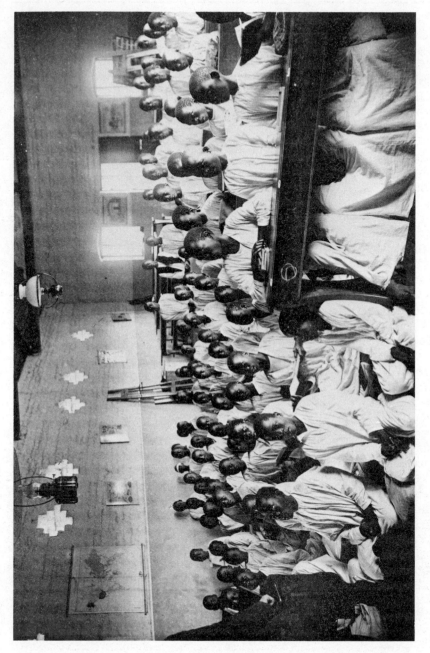

PLATE 19.2 *Seeking after literacy: a class at Mengo CMS High School, Uganda*

indifferently educated Africans were able to interpose themselves as middlemen between the primary producers and the big European commercial companies, commercial success also provided a ready passport to the new elite status. There were, however, others who qualified for consideration as members of the elite because they controlled mass organizations like labour unions and could give the better-educated elite the kind of mass support which they needed to convince the colonial powers that they spoke for the people. On the contrary, in East and Central Africa relatively few Africans gained admission into the elite group as a result of the deliberate policies pursued by the colonial rulers and the activities of the Indians and Portuguese and Greek petty traders. In fact, in many of these areas, the old central elite virtually disappeared.

It is largely this wide variation in their qualifications and background that makes it so difficult to define precisely in those terms who were the new elite of colonial Africa. One can thus justifiably argue that the issue of the rise of a new elite among any African people in the colonial era was largely a question of what amount and kind of educational and economic opportunities were available to the people and how far they put those opportunities to effective use. All the studies so far carried out on this aspect of the matter suggest that regions or colonies which witnessed the most intensive efforts in the propagation of western education and which offered Africans more opportunities for meaningful participation in trade and commercial agriculture produced the largest number of people of elite status.

In parts of Africa, especially among such chiefless peoples as the Igbo, Ibibio, Ogoja, Tiv, Idoma, Birom, Angas and Gwari of Nigeria where it was difficult to identify the traditional rulers and associate them with the work of the colonial government, many members of the new elite came from among those who in pre-colonial times would have been classified as commoners. Some were even of the servile class or were as yet unassimilated immigrants. This was because in such places it was members of these classes who first embraced western education, tried their hands at the new professions and moved to the urban centres while the traditional elite tended to stand back. But as soon as the benefits of western education and the new professions were demonstrated, members of the traditional elite also joined in. Some colonial powers, especially France and Britain, deliberately set out with varying results to encourage this belatedly awakened traditional elite group, for instance by establishing special schools for them. With the wealth they derived from their estates and/or their salaries as local authorities they were usually able to train their sons not only locally but also in higher institutions in Europe and America.

In some other parts of Africa, however, the traditional elite responded early to the call of western education and modern commercial ventures. In Egypt it was this class which took the lead in establishing western-type institutions. In Buganda this same class quickly recognized the advantages

PLATE 19.3 *Colonial cricket: producing the new elite*

of western education and commercial farming. In Ethiopia they reacted in a similar manner to western education, sending their children to Europe and America to be educated. In this way they were able to retain the leadership of their countries.

Thus the fact that the ranks of the new elite contained people from different strata of society makes it risky to talk in easy terms of conflict between the new elite and the traditional rulers. In Sierra Leone and Liberia where for much of the period the new elites were made up of people who were not indigenous to these territories, there was an understandable tendency for the elite communities of the coast to be in conflict and competition with the traditional societies of the interior. They were inclined to be contemptuous of the traditional leaders who in turn harboured an abiding suspicion of them. In the nineteenth-century Gold Coast and in Yorubaland (Nigeria), many of the founding members of the new elite group were – or at least believed they were – related by blood to the peoples of the interior.

Elsewhere in Africa where the first generation of new elites did not include repatriates such as slaves freed from slave-ships or returnees from the Americas, the ethnic and cultural tie was even closer. The result was that throughout the nineteenth century, and even during the early part of this century, the new and old elites built up a tradition of co-operation – the new elite being regarded as those who mediated between their indigenous societies and western culture. After all they had been enabled to learn the new techniques in order to help their people meet the problems posed by European presence. In the Gold Coast and in Egbaland (Nigeria) they had worked closely with the traditional elite in an effort to build a new society and ward off European rule. But these efforts had failed.

However, as colonial rule took deeper root, strains and stresses appeared in the relationship of the two groups. The new elites had wrongly hoped that Europe was out to modernize Africa and would use members of their group as the instruments for achieving that goal. But under colonial rule it was European bureaucrats who assumed the role which the new elites had cut out for themselves. And instead of taking the new elites into partnership, the administration tended to prefer the traditional rulers whom they relegated to the area of local government. This was particularly so in British-ruled Africa where a determined effort was made to preserve the old ruling families and to some extent in Belgian-ruled Africa after 1906. Even in the French territories where most of the great paramountcies were destroyed, the old ruling families at times survived in attenuated forms to be used at the village and district levels. And where people who had no traditional status were used in local government, they were often labelled 'chiefs' and assigned the same kind of functions as members of the traditional ruling families.

Because of their exclusion, the new elites went into open opposition against the colonial powers. In this open opposition the traditional rulers

PLATE 19.4 *The new elite and the colonial administrators: a garden party at Government House, Lagos, Nigeria*

could not join them. Their continued survival depended on the colonial power and this tied their hands. Also for the most part the traditional rulers were not sufficiently educated to participate meaningfully in the highfaluting debates of the new elites. In any case if they accepted the arguments of the new elites, they would be consigning themselves to second or even third place. Because they did not side with the new elites, the latter regarded them as the lackeys of imperialism. They in turn regarded the new elites as revolutionaries who wanted to destroy immemorial custom and turn the world upside down.

To make matters worse the two were driven by imperialist propaganda into engaging in a struggle over who spoke for the people. The new elites said they did. This the traditional rulers denied, claiming the honour for themselves. The colonial administration agreed with them. The kind of acrimony which this disagreement at times generated could be seen in the dispute between the chief of Akyem-Abuakwa in the Gold Coast, Nana Sir Ofori Atta and the leaders of the National Congress of British West Africa in the 1920s. It could also be seen in the same period in the quarrel between Harry Thuku's Young Kikuyu Association on the one hand, and the Kikuyu Association dominated by the traditional rulers on the other.[7]

Yet one cannot conclude from the foregoing that in the period 1880 to 1935 the normal relationship between the new elites and the traditional rulers was invariably one of conflict. The nature of the relationship varied both in place and time. In the French territories neither the new elites nor the traditional rulers flourished under alien rule. And when after the Second World War the stranglehold of colonial autocracy came to be progressively relaxed, those who emerged as the leaders of French African nationalism included traditional rulers and their descendants.

In the Gold Coast the leading political party until the ascendancy of Dr Kwame Nkrumah – the United Gold Coast Convention – represented some kind of rapprochement between the new and traditional elites. In places like Ethiopia, Egypt and Buganda where the traditional rulers had responded positively to western influences, no logical conflict developed between them and the new elites. It was the same in societies like that of the Igbo where the traditional elites had not the kind of stature that survived far into the colonial period. In any case the new elites were not all the 'uprooted natives' of imperialist mythology, nor were all the traditional rulers the obscurantist opponents of change of latter-day nationalist demagogy. Both groups had more in common than was often admitted in the evanescent heat of occasional debate.

The rise of new organizations

Apart from giving rise to the new structures discussed above, colonial rule

7. D. Kimble, 1963, pp. 389–96; K. J. King, 1971(b).

introduced other changes into the structure of African society. Here we have in mind the rise of new organizations which helped to mediate the adjustment of many individuals and their rural homes to the new demands and norms of colonial society. These new organizations have generally been described as 'voluntary' by social scientists. They are 'voluntary' in the sense that people are not born into them as they are born into lineages, villages or ethnic groups. But closer analysis would show that for some of them, especially the ethnic-based welfare or improvement associations, membership is not that voluntary since the practical alternative to membership is generally ostracism of a kind.

Africanists are agreed on the social conditions which brought these organizations into being. It has been found that they generally originated in the urban centres, although some of them – like the ethnic-based ones – in time established home branches. The fact was that, as Professor Wallerstein has aptly put it, migration from 'the traditional rural to the modern urban area' led to 'dislocation and disorientation for the individual'.[8] Since neither the traditional society nor the colonial administration had the means to step in and meet the new needs of such migrants, they had to evolve their own institutions, systems and norms for achieving meaningful existence in the strange and heady social world of the town.

The studies of Godfrey Wilson in East Africa have shown that there was a clear correlation between the pressure of colonial society and the formation of these organizations. Thus Kenyan Africans, whose traditional culture came under unusually severe pressure from colonial rule and settler aggressiveness, had stronger and much more numerous ethnic associations than Africans in neighbouring territories like Tanganyika and Uganda. There was thus an element of individual self-protection and self-stabilization in the formation of the associations. Furthermore, urban conditions of existence created opportunities that made it relatively easy to form such organizations since, as Thomas Hodgkin has put it, it provided 'physical centres ... where men and women, with particular interests in common, can collide with one another'.[9]

Though it has been correctly pointed out that it is difficult to group the different organizations into clear-cut categories, especially owing to their functional versatility, we shall here distinguish between three kinds. In the first group are those organizations which could be described as purely 'social', that is devoted to promoting conviviality and relaxation. These were made necessary by the absence from the towns of the traditional forms of amusement, relaxation and citizenship training – such as the masquerades, age-grade associations and traditional festivities. There was also the attraction of forms of modern European social life as advertised in the life of the European community in each colony. In this category

8. I. Wallerstein in J. S. Coleman and C. G. Rosberg (eds), 1970, p. 319.
9. T. Hodgkin, 1956, p. 84.

were the football clubs, Scout and Girl Guide movements, debating societies and alumni associations.

In the second group are the ethnic unions. These were an extension of rural ethnicity to the urban areas. There were different hierarchies of them – village, clan and ethnic unions. These had two main functions. One was to help the individual who had migrated newly to the town to adjust as smoothly as possible to the conditions of urban life. Thus when a migrant first reached the town, he usually made his first contacts with members of his village or clan union who would help to find him accommodation, to introduce him to employers of labour or master craftsmen to teach him modern skills. They also taught him how to comport himself in the city. Through such associations members got help when in difficulty. They could get loans to continue their business if they sustained crippling losses. Funeral, marriage and other expenses approved by the association could also be met with loans or donations from the group as the case may be.[10]

The other function of the ethnic unions was 'to provide a channel for progressive public opinion at home', especially through maintaining an organized link between the sons at home and the sons abroad. To do this they had to take an interest in the political and social development of their homes. At first this won the associations the opposition and obstruction of suspicious colonial officials. In south-eastern Nigeria, for instance, where by the 1930s the colonial power was still toiling to entrench the idea of native authorities, the formation of these unions caused uneasiness in official circles. Their activities became, on occasions, the object of secret intelligence inquiries.

In the third group were the trade unions which came into being largely for economic bargaining. For the most part modern urban centres grew up at vital commercial, mining and communication points which had openings for the employment of skilled and unskilled workers. In these towns, therefore, there soon came to be concentrations of people who earned their living mainly by means of salaried or wage employment. These men, especially those of them at the lowest rungs of the labour ladder, have at times been referred to rather inappropriately in Marxist-oriented analysis as proletarians. Apart from those who were bound by the wage nexus to the big employers of labour – the colonial government, the commercial and the mining firms, the missions, etc. – there were also the self-employed artisans who supplied certain of the needs of the urban population.

The life of these urban dwellers was tied to the vagaries of the world economy and market whose structure and behaviour they did not understand. To protect themselves in this unfamiliar economic world, those in waged or salaried employment formed trade unions for the purpose of

10. For a good analysis of the rise and function of a voluntary association of the ethnic-based type see M. Banton in I. Wallerstein (ed.), 1966, pp. 402–19.

effective negotiation with their employers for higher pay and better conditions of work. The self-employed craftsmen also formed craft guilds which helped to fix prices, standards, conditions of apprenticeship and so on. The trade unions and craft guilds also functioned at times as friendly societies, helping members in difficulty with money and advice, providing fitting funerals, educational facilities, scholarships and occasional feasts.

The years 1880–1935 saw something of the beginnings of these new organizations. Professor Kilson has shown that by 1937 there were all kinds of tradesmen's and workers' organizations in Nigeria, Sierra Leone, Kenya and elsewhere. But his study and others like those of Professor Kimble on Ghana, Professor Yesufu and Mr Ananaba on Nigeria, V. Thompson and R. Adloff on French Equatorial Africa and R. H. Bates on Zambia clearly show that the golden age of these organizations did not arrive until after the Second World War.[11]

The reasons for this were many. These associations depended to some extent on the spread of education, and the impact of this as of urbanism took time to manifest itself. Outside the coastal areas of West Africa, the Maghrib, Egypt and Kenya, this generally took more than three decades. While in South Africa where the conditions should have been ideal owing to an early industrial and communications revolution, the growing harshness of Boer nationalism and the opposition of other whites stifled African initiative. The rise of these associations also depended to some extent on the development of a capitalist economy, but colonial Africa is said to have only 'a rudimentary capitalist economy' which depended substantially on migrant workers – a species of labour which is said to be very resistant to trade union organization. And even after the Second World War there were very few wage earners in colonial Africa. In the 1950s their number was estimated at between 4 and 5 million. And finally there were the many prohibitions associated with the autocratic and exploitative colonial regimes which for the most part did not accord legal recognition to trade unions until the late 1930s or early 1940s.

As already mentioned, the social effects of foreign rule were far from uniform throughout the continent. With respect to the spread of education, the triumph of the new economic forces, the expansion of urbanization and therefore the rise of the new elites, West Africa would appear to have witnessed the greatest advances, followed by Egypt and the Maghrib, South Africa, East Africa and Central Africa. If, on the other hand, in this matter we compared the colonial blocks rather than geographical regions, we discover that greater changes took place in the British territories, followed by Belgian- and French-ruled Africa with Portuguese Africa limping far behind. And even among the British territories, there was also a differential impact. The British colonies where substantial transforma-

11. See, for example, M. Kilson in L. H. Gann and P. Duignan (eds), 1970; D. Kimble, 1963; T. M. Yesufu, 1962; W. Ananaba, 1969; V. Thompson and R. Adloff, 1960; R. H. Bates, 1971.

tions were registered included Egypt, Gold Coast, Nigeria, Uganda and Sierra Leone, with Kenya and the Rhodesias (now Zambia and Zimbabwe) coming after. And if we take individual colonies we discover that more changes took place in the southern than in the northern parts of Gold Coast and Nigeria. In Francophone Africa, on the other hand, the West African colonies would come first, followed by the North African colonies and then French Equatorial Africa. Within French West Africa, Senegal and Dahomey (now Benin) led the way with the other colonies lagging rather far behind.

The fact was that the spread and impact of the forces of change were controlled by more factors than any colonial government or African group was in a position to master completely. First there was the question of the length and extent of contact which the particular territory or geographic region had enjoyed with Europe by the time colonial rule was imposed. West and Southern Africa had maintained fairly regular contact with Europe from the sixteenth century. By the beginning of the nineteenth century, therefore, quasi-urban conditions of life had come into existence at several points along the coast – at St Louis, Banjul, Accra, Lagos, the Oil River's ports, Luanda, and at the Cape. These provided good stepping stones for the forces of western education, western Christianity and western commerce to penetrate the interior. The east coast of the continent, on the other hand, came under sustained European contact only from about the 1870s.

This difference in time factor is important in any attempt to account for the differential impact of the forces of change on the different regions and countries of Africa. That part of the nineteenth century which preceded the onset of European rule was the most liberal phase of Europe's relationship with Africa. Between the abolition of the slave trade and the imposition of colonial rule, Europe was by and large prepared to encourage the emergence of a group of Africans equipped to co-operate with her in the business of 'civilizing' the continent. This meant encouraging African initiative in education and commerce. As a result West Africa gained immensely through the application of this policy.

But with the imposition of colonial rule with its concomitant illiberal racial policies, all kinds of obstacles were placed in the way of free African participation in education and commerce. As a result those regions where the earlier liberal policies had not taken firm root before the dawn of alien rule, found themselves greatly handicapped. The colonial powers were by and large suspicious of the new African elites and sought to restrict their growth by slowing up the expansion of schools, while those who succeeded in graduating from the schools were frustrated through being denied fitting jobs in the colonial service. Also their scope for participation in the new commercial ventures was narrowed down to a minimum.

Equally important in helping to explain the differential impact of these forces was the presence or absence of white settlers. There were very few

European settlers in West Africa and this to some extent explains the relatively rapid progress of the West Africans in educational and economic matters. But settlers were present in force in Algeria, Kenya, the Rhodesias, South Africa and the Portuguese territories. In the Belgian Congo where there were fewer settlers, company rule was as illiberal and debilitating as settler influence. The interests of these settlers clashed with those of the Africans and they used their influence with the colonial administration to obstruct or stultify African development.

Finally, there was the question of differing African responses to foreign influences. In Nigeria the Igbo embraced Westernism much more enthusiastically than the Fulani did. In Kenya, the Gikuyu saw the advantages of western education long before their neighbours. Islamic cultural conservatism and resistance, especially in the Western Sudan, tended to hinder the spread of western influence, especially western education. In North Africa and Egypt, on the other hand, sections of the ruling elite sought to ensure the survival of Islamic culture through the introduction of western science and commerce. Their stand led to a fruitful marriage between Islamic culture and western scientific thought. Because the Western Sudanese Muslims failed to show comparable initiative in this matter, they found themselves unprepared to meet the challenges posed by colonial rule. As a result it was possible for the British and the French to determine what types of western influences to admit into the region and in what doses.

Religion in Africa during the colonial era

K. ASARE OPOKU

The imposition of European colonial rule on Africa was not merely the forceful establishment of European political, economic and social power on colonial possessions. It was also a cultural imposition and it used culture to buttress the political, economic and social superstructure which colonialism represented. It is the religious aspect of this cultural imposition of colonialism and the African response to it that this chapter deals with.

The state of African religious life on the eve of colonial rule

Traditional African religion in the pre-colonial period

Traditional African religion was, and still is, inextricably bound up with African culture. It was a pervasive force, and as Emmanuel Obiechina aptly puts it:

> There is hardly any important area of human experience which is not linked to the supernatural and the people's sense of religion and religious piety ... these ... are part and parcel of the ideological structure of traditional society, and so essential to a proper interpretation of experience in the traditional social context.[1]

This pervasiveness of religion through the total way of life of African peoples gave traditional religion a remarkable wholeness within the context of the culture out of which it originated.

It was based on a particular world view, which included not only the people's view of the supernatural but also their understanding of the nature of the universe, the nature of human beings and their place in the world, and the nature of God, who was known by various local names. Essentially a spirit, God had no images or physical representations and was acknowledged as the Creator and Sustainer of the world. Power, justice, beneficence and eternity were attributed to Him, and as the Source of all Power, God had power over life and death. He rewarded men but also

1. E. Obiechina, 1978, p. 208.

punished them when they went wrong and was in many ways likened to the Overlord of Society and was the Final Authority in all matters. On the whole, God was unlike human beings and was completely above His creation, but at the same time, He was involved in the affairs of men, sustaining creation and upholding the moral order. Human beings depended upon Him as a Power superior to them. God was therefore transcendent as well as immanent.

There was a hierarchy of spirits. Below God were the ancestral spirits, which were always treated with reverence and with awe, and then there were also the deities or gods who were believed to have the power of rewarding human beings or punishing them with misfortune, disease or even death. The divinities had their cults, priests and shrines and there were some among them which were associated with various features of the environment: but these palpable objects were the abodes of the gods and not the gods themselves.

In addition to these supernatural entities, there were other spirits or mystical powers which were recognized and reckoned with for their ability to aid or harm human beings. Included in these were agents of witchcraft, magic and sorcery. Finally, there were charms, amulets and talismans which were used for protective as well as offensive purposes.

The general conception of man was that he was a compound of immaterial and material substance. The immaterial part of man (the soul) survived him after death, while the material part (the body) disintegrated after death. Death therefore did not end life; it was an extension of life. The dead remained members of society and there was believed to be a community of the dead alongside the community of the living, and there was a symbiotic relationship between the two communities. Human society was an unbroken family made up of the dead, the living and the yet unborn.

With regard to man's relation to society, being human meant belonging to a community and that involved participating in the beliefs, ceremonies, rituals and festivals of that community[2] and membership of the community was emphasized more than a member's individuality. For society was based more on obligation than on individual rights and an individual assumed his rights in the exercise of his obligations, which made society a chain of interrelationships. Furthermore, human life was viewed and understood as a cycle of birth, puberty, marriage and procreation, death and the afterlife. An individual did not stay in one stage of existence for ever; he necessarily moved on to the next, and in order to make the transition smooth, special rites were performed to ensure that no breaks occurred, and movement and regeneration continued perpetually.[3]

African traditional religion was not only pervasive, it also bound men to the unseen powers and helped them to form correct relations with the non-human powers; it also bound men to their fellow human beings.

2. J. S. Mbiti, 1969, p. 2.
3. K. A. Opoku, 1978, pp. 10–11.

PLATE 20.1 *Makishie characters during an initiation ceremony in Zambia. The dancers represent ancestral spirits*

Religion acted as the cement which held societies together, providing them with support and stability. Furthermore, traditional religion helped men to understand and control events, to relieve doubt, anxiety and guilt.

But the situation was not static, for from generation to generation, changes occurred and each generation added to the religious and cultural heritage on the basis of its experience. There were no jealous gods that forbade the acceptance or addition of new gods or beliefs, and new cults and shrines appeared whilst others declined. Gods who proved powerful had their shrines spread far and wide, and it was not uncommon for defeated ethnic groups to adopt the gods of their conquerors. And since movement characterized life, changes which occurred were accepted as normal so long as they did not do violence to African values.

Islam in the pre-colonial period

In addition to traditional religion two guest religions – Islam and Christianity – were introduced, in pre-colonial times. The rise and spread of Islam in Africa has been dealt with in the earlier volumes. The greatest expansion of Islam in pre-colonial times took place in the nineteenth century, in part when Islamic militants who were dissatisfied with the intolerable accommodations Islam had made with traditional African religion declared holy wars aimed at firmly restoring the Islamic faith to its original purity. These *djihāds* led to the formation of theocratic states in which Islamic religion and law were imposed on the people, and this led to widespread conversions. These theocratic states extended across the Sudanic zone of West Africa from Senegal to what is now northern Nigeria, and included Futa Jallon, Futa Toro, the Sokoto caliphate and the Borno empire.[4]

In East Africa, Islam moved from the coast into the interior, but unlike their counterparts in West Africa, Muslims in East Africa appear to have been more interested in trade than in converting people to their faith. They concentrated on maintaining their trade links with the interior and perpetuating their economic spheres of influence. Some parts of East Africa had, however, adopted Islam over the centuries; and along the coast, a new culture developed, and it was out of the mixture of Bantu with Muslim culture that the Swahili culture was born. The Swahili language is today the *lingua franca* of most of East Africa.

Islam had made considerable advances before the arrival of the colonial powers. Among them may be mentioned the replacement in many parts of Africa of the traditional cycle of festivals with the Islamic calendar and the adoption of many Arabic loan words and concepts into African languages such as Hausa, Fula and Mandinka leading to their enrichment. Pilgrims returning from pilgrimages had adopted new fashions in dress

4. M. Last in J. F. A. Ajayi and M. Crowder (eds), 1974.

and together with the example of visiting and resident Muslim scholars and holy men in many parts of Africa, Arabic culture had begun to make a considerable impact on Africans. This impact also included Muslim architecture, titles, music and other aspects of Arabic culture, especially among the wealthier segments of the African population, notably in the Sudanic zone.

In spite of the advances Islam had made before the arrival of the colonial powers, the last decades of the nineteenth century witnessed the destruction of some of the theocratic states in West Africa and the weakening of Islamic trade and economic influence in East Africa. Nevertheless, colonial rule was to provide Islam with the opportunity for unprecedented expansion.

Christianity in pre-colonial Africa

Before the onset of colonial rule, Christianity – as has been shown in the earlier volumes – had been through three phases in its history on the African continent. Its first phase ended in the seventh century with the rise of Islam, leaving scattered Christian colonies in the deserts and parts of North Africa. Ethiopia remained firmly Christian from the fourth century onwards. The period of Portuguese explorations in the fifteenth century began the second phase; and this, too, was ended by the slave trade which followed on the heels of the explorations and lasted for nearly three centuries. The third phase, 1800–85, was sparked off by the rise of a tremendous missionary awakening in Europe towards the end of the eighteenth century, and the period from the 1840s marked a missionary thrust from the coast into the interior of Africa, whereas the period before that was marked by a concentration along the coast of Africa, largely in the European coastal enclaves and in Ethiopia and South Africa. The push into the hinterland was made possible by the geographical explorations which greatly increased European knowledge of the interior of Africa. Besides, great inspiration was derived by many missionaries from the exploration and ideas of David Livingstone, who made the results of his expeditions known through his prolific writings. His view that missionaries should establish centres of Christianity and civilization which would not only promote religion but also commerce and agriculture, came to be widely shared by many enthusiastic missionaries who penetrated far into the interior of Africa, following the old trade routes. Mention must also be made of the advances that were made in medical science in the nineteenth century which led to the control of many tropical diseases and thus made it easier for missionaries to settle in many parts of Africa.

The opportunity to live in the hinterland made missionaries more and more knowledgeable about Africa and this was to become a crucial factor during the last quarter of the nineteenth century when the Scramble for Africa began. As European nations increasingly became interested in the acquisition of African territories, the missionaries paved the way in some areas of Africa and served, quite consciously, as agents for European colonialism. Most missionaries were of the firm persuasion that if there was to be European intervention, then it should come from their own countries. As Roland Oliver wrote, 'They wished to ensure that the intervention would be carried out by their own countrymen or by the power most likely to offer the best opportunity for the work of their denominations.'[5]

Moreover, colonial government in Africa, most missionaries argued, would not only provide the much desired security and protection which would assist them in redressing the evils of the slave trade, but would also stimulate and guarantee the development of new economic opportunities for the Africans. Missionaries therefore enthusiastically encouraged European intervention as a morally justified undertaking, especially from the 1870s onwards.

African traditional religion and colonial rule

The establishment of colonial rule in Africa from 1885 onwards led to the spread of European influence far into the interior where formerly European influence had been concentrated along the coast. The entire European intervention during the colonial period was based on the assumption that to bring about development, African culture had to be modified if not destroyed altogether. Since African culture was so intricately intertwined with religion, it is easy to see how even a European colonial policy could clash violently with some of the tenets in African traditional religion which underpinned African society. And right from the very beginning, African traditional religion was faced with the challenge of survival and the need to strengthen itself.

Before the onset of colonial rule, the missionaries were the torch-bearers of western culture until about the beginning of the 1890s, and from the very beginning they expressed an uncompromising attitude towards African religion. They were bent not only on converting Africans to Christianity but also to western culture, which was believed to be thoroughly infused with, and profoundly informed by, Christianity. In fact, in the minds of most enthusiastic missionaries, there was no distinction between the two. But while making no distinction between their religion and culture, the missionaries endeavoured relentlessly to convert Africans to a way of life in which religion was separated from other aspects of life. The missionaries taught their converts that life could be separated into spiritual and secular spheres, a teaching which ran counter to the fundamental basis of African culture, namely the unity of religion and life. Missionary teaching thus attempted to attack the cement which held African societies together. The danger signals were picked up early by many perceptive African rulers,

5. R. Oliver and G. Mathew (eds), 1971, p. 69.

who initially resisted missionary penetration into their societies, seeing in it a challenge and a threat to traditional patterns of authority. Missionaries, and colonial administrators alike, preached against belief in spirits, supernatural forces and gods, witchcraft, sorcery, sacrifices and rituals, taboos and veneration of ancestors, and thus weakened the influence of African traditional and ritual leaders such as priests, priestesses, magicians, rainmakers and divine monarchs. The introduction of western medicine by the colonial administrators and their attack on 'pagan' customs also led to a weakening of the role of the traditional doctors and herbalists. The old order was thus severely threatened and attempts to defend and protect it came from many sectors of African society.

Even though the colonial administrators could be said to have been primarily interested in political, economic and social control of their colonies, matters pertaining to religion could not be isolated from their central concerns. What the missionaries taught was also shared by the colonial powers, and generally the colonial rulers adopted a hostile attitude towards certain religious practices and tried to abolish them while at the same time suppressing some cults. The colonial administrations sought to eradicate belief in witchcraft, and practices such as poison ordeals, meant to detect persons believed to be guilty or innocent of crimes whose detection was difficult, and 'carrying' the corpse to find out the person or persons believed to have caused the death by witchcraft or sorcery.

Africans responded to these attacks in many ways. In the first place, those who remained unconverted opposed colonial rule and defied missionary condemnation of their traditional ways by simply continuing to hold on to traditional beliefs and practising essential rites either openly or in secret. But for those who converted to Christianity and whose beliefs and attitudes were strongly influenced by the new dispensation, resistance was expressed by taking some of the traditional beliefs along with them into the new faith, and this resulted in a blending of ideas.

Africans used their religion as a weapon to resist colonial rule and its threat to their values, and often relied on magic and the intervention of their ancestors and gods in their fight against colonial oppression. In the first two decades of this century, the Igbo warriors of south-eastern Nigeria resorted to such means to defend themselves from alien invaders. The Esza people of Abakaliki Division, the Uzuakoli and the Aro may be cited as examples.[6] Some cults were clearly a focus for resistance to colonial rule, such as the Mwari in Southern Rhodesia (now Zimbabwe), or secret associations like the Poro in Sierra Leone and other parts of West Africa. War-charm movements also occurred in Madagascar and the Congo basin. In East Africa, especially Kenya, African prophets arose to provide spiritual reinvigoration[7] to resist colonialism, such as occurred in the Machakos

6. A. E. Afigbo, 1973.
7. The founding of independent churches alongside mission-founded churches under European control also served the same purpose of protest by Africans.

PLATE 20.2 *Members of a secret society in Sierra Leone*

District among the people of Kilungu in the early months of 1922 (see Chapter 26). One of the best-known movements which used both religion and magic to resist colonial rule and oppression was the Majī Majī movement in German East Africa during the first decade of the twentieth century.[8] (See Fig. 7.1.) Even though the movement failed, it served as a demonstration of the fact that unity could be achieved in African traditional religion in the face of European pressure and that African traditional religion was not a fragmentary force confined to limited localities. Besides, the movement provided the seed for African nationalism which was later to germinate and blossom into the struggle for independence and its final achievement in the 1960s.

Another cult similar to Majī Majī was the Nyabingi cult, which also covered a wide area and cut across ethnic and regional boundaries and was found in Ruanda (now Rwanda), north-western Tanganyika (now Tanzania) and Uganda. Like the followers of Majī Majī its adherents believed that the power of its medicines could neutralize the effect of European bullets, as well as believing in possession by the spirits of legendary ancestors. It began during the late nineteenth century and gathered momentum until it finally broke out in 1928 in revolt against European occupation in the Kigezi region of Uganda. (See Fig. 7.1.) As E. Hopkins put it, 'the movement succeeded in immobilizing the administrative efforts of three colonial powers for nearly two decades until its final suppression in 1928'.[9] The Germans, and the Belgians who took over Ruanda from them after the First World War, failed to suppress it, and even after the suppression of the 1928 uprising, the cult lingered on until it was finally suppressed in 1934.

Other cults gathered force against the European pressure by reviving aspects of traditional religion and combining them with ideas borrowed from Christianity. Such, for example, was the Mumbo cult which was used by the Gusii people, near Lake Victoria in Kenya, as the buttress of their revolt against British colonialism which began in 1900.[10] (See Fig. 7.1.)

In the Gold Coast (now Ghana), the British colonial administration adopted a hostile attitude towards certain religious practices, abolished some and endeavoured to suppress certain deities and cults. Thus the cult of Katawere, the tutelary deity of Akim Kotoku, was prohibited by the government in 1907.[11] Prior to this the German government had destroyed the shrines of the cult of Denteh of Kete-Krachi in the 1880s and the priest of Denteh had been imprisoned and executed by the government. The Krobo people were forced to abandon their settlements on the Krobo mountain by the British colonial administration which destroyed their

8. For details, see Chapter 7.
9. E. Hopkins in R. I. Rotberg and A. A. Mazrui (eds), 1970.
10. For details, see Chapter 7 above and Chapter 26 below.
11. H. Debrunner, 1967, p. 255.

settlements and suppressed the cult of their tutelary shrines of Kotoklo and Nadu.

Colonial administration attacked the belief in witchcraft, and sought to eradicate it through the passage of witchcraft ordinances, and the adoption of measures to stop African witchcraft eradication movements. In spite of the opposition to witchcraft by both missionaries and colonial administrators, the belief persisted among converts and non-converts alike, and Africans continued to resort to their own ways of dealing with it.

Some of the new cults which arose to protect people from witchcraft in West Africa may be mentioned, for example, *Aberewa* (Old Woman) cult in the Gold Coast which was suppressed by the administration in 1908. The most widespread of the witchcraft eradication movements was the Bamucapi cult of south-eastern and Central Africa which spread widely over Mozambique, Nyasaland (now Malawi), the Rhodesias (now Zimbabwe and Zambia), southern Tanganyika (now Tanzania), and Belgian Congo (now Zaire). (See Fig. 8.1.) Members of the cult drank a medicine which was believed to have the capacity to rid them of witchcraft or protect them from its effect.[12] The cult thrived in the early 1930s and borrowed ideas from both African traditional religion and Christianity.

As some Africans continued to use traditional methods of eradicating witchcraft, the colonial administration enacted witchcraft ordinances. In Uganda, for example, a Witchcraft Ordinance was passed in 1912; in 1921 it was revised, the punishment being made severer by increasing terms of imprisonment from one to five years and also making the possession of witchcraft articles in which the power of witchcraft is believed to reside a punishable offence.[13] But all these ordinances of the colonial governments and condemnation by missionaries and African converts proved to be limited deterrents to the belief in witchcraft.

Another attack on African traditional religion took the form of measures against initiation rites of boys and girls into adulthood. For the Africans, the initiation rituals were aimed at preparing the young boys and girls not only for adulthood but also for community and social life, and constituted a central and vital component of social, cultural and religious life.

In many parts of Africa, the initiation rites involved circumcision for boys and clitoridectomy for the girls, and this was the source of the greatest controversy. The missionaries found the rituals unacceptable to their taste and theology and often sought the assistance of the colonial administrations in their fight against them. The attack on these rituals amounted to an assault on the central significance in the conception of man and the organization of religious life, and the reaction of Africans to this attack was equally strong. It was especially in East Africa that the question of circumcision, especially clitoridectomy, provoked the sharpest reaction.

12. T. O. Ranger in D. B. Barrett (ed.), 1971, p. 132.
13. E. Hopkins in R. I. Rotberg and A. A. Mazrui (eds), 1970, p. 311.

The missionaries found clitoridectomy abhorrent and sought its total elimination from the life of their converts, but as far as circumcision was concerned, they were prepared to go along with it provided it was pruned of its 'pagan', 'demonic' and 'satanic' aspects.

In the diocese of Masasi in southern Tanganyika and in the Central Province of Kenya, we find examples of the most serious confrontation between Christian missions and African peoples on the matter of circumcision. (See Fig. 7.1.) In the former, a policy of adaptation was pursued, and it resulted in attempts to modify the *jando* (male circumcision) and the *malango* (female circumcision) by performing them under Christian auspices and eliminating whatever elements were thought or judged to be 'un-Christian'. This policy avoided a head-on collision between traditional initiation and Christian missions and practice, even though the Church omitted an essential element in the girls' initiation, namely, the elongation of the clitoris, and thus failed to give *malango* the type of respectability that traditional initiation otherwise commanded. The Church, however, recognised the need for its members to be at once Christians and fully initiated members of their communities, and this objective was achieved within the Church rather than in revolt against it.[14]

But in the case of the Central Province of Kenya, the missionary policy towards initiation resulted in a head-on collision. The Africans had already begun to feel pressure and to harbour resentment against the British colonial administration for setting vast stretches of their land aside for European settlers. This move also coincided with the activities of a number of missions, for example the Scottish Mission (in Ukambani in 1891 and Kikuyu in 1898), Bavaria Evangelical Lutheran Mission (in Ukambani, 1893), African Inland Mission (in Ukambani, 1896), Gospel Missionary Society (in Nairobi, 1897) and Church Missionary Society and African Inland Mission (in Nairobi, both in 1901), which began to speak against the cherished traditions of the Akamba, Meru, Tharaka, Maasai and other peoples, especially that of initiation using circumcision of both boys and girls. The European presence thus spelt a double pressure on their land and traditions.

What missionaries found particularly abhorrent was female initiation, and they vehemently spoke against it, and the Church of Scotland Mission, African Inland Church, and Gospel Missionary Society prohibited it in their churches in 1920 and 1921. Boys' circumcision among Christians was not as severely interfered with, but the missions required that it should be done in hospitals or private homes. As the pressure against clitoridectomy began to mount, the British colonial administration came to recognize it as a 'harmful' practice which 'education' would gradually bring to an end. But the Africans felt that both male and female initiation served a profoundly meaningful purpose in their communal life and that

14. T. O. Ranger in T. O. Ranger and I. Kimambo, 1972.

any sudden abolition or prohibition would greatly disrupt their psychological, social and religious security.

The African opposition to the negative attitude towards female circumcision came into the open in the early 1920s, beginning in 1923. For example, independent schools were established among the Gikuyu whose aim was to restore the practice and to provide education for those children who could not get admission into mission schools on account of the female circumcision issue. In 1929 a dance song, called *muthirigu*, which ridiculed missions and Christians who were opposed to female initiation, spread quickly among the Gikuyu but was banned by the British colonial administration the following year. Furthermore African opposition expressed itself in the secession of many members from the Protestant and Anglican churches among the Gikuyu, Embu and Meru peoples. An independent Church, the African Orthodox Church, arose in 1928, while in 1930 a prophetic movement sprang up among the Gikuyu, preaching God's impending judgement upon Europeans and missions, but was quickly banned by the colonial administration.

African protest continued to express itself in many forms, including disturbances, attacks on mission schools, attempts to prevent preachers from conducting services, and even the murder of a missionary at Kijabe. Combined with the African protest against the missionary attitude to female circumcision was also a growing nationalism which eventually resulted in political resistance against foreign rule.[15] Among the Akamba, Embu and Meru peoples, however, the issue of female initiation did not create the same degree of tension as it did among the Gikuyu, but out of this came independent schools and independent churches.

All these attacks against African traditional religion and African reactions to them on the whole greatly reinvigorated African traditional religion by the 1930s.

Islam and colonial rule

It would appear that Islam fared far better than traditional religion during the period of colonial rule. In the areas where Muslim rule was established before the arrival of the colonial power, Islamic law had provided territorial rather than ethnic uniformity and it commanded obedience to authority.[16] This was good for efficient administration and commerce and Muslims were also able to proselytize and make more converts.

The development of communications made it possible for Muslim agents to penetrate into areas which had not been open to them before, and with the trading routes being redirected from the desert to the coast in West Africa, the number of Muslims, which had been scanty along the coast in the early days of colonial rule, now began to increase. The steady

15. For further discussion, see F. B. Welbourn, 1961, pp. 135–43.
16. D. L. Wiedner, 1964, pp. 245–6.

increase in the number of Muslims in Sierra Leone from 1891 to 1931 is illustrative of this fact. Thus, whereas in 1891 Muslims formed 10 per cent of the population, they formed 12, 14, 19.5 and 26.2 per cent respectively in 1901, 1911, 1921 and 1931.[17]

The Muslim presence along the West African coast was also further increased by the Ahmadiyya Muslims who came as missionaries using the coastal sea routes. Although considered heretical by some, they were important in fostering an interest in western education among Muslims.

The attitude of colonial administrations towards Islam was mixed. While some felt that Islam was a more enlightened form of religion than traditional African religion, others regarded Muslim institutions as advanced social institutions and used them in the interest of the colonial administrations. Islamic law courts were therefore allowed to be set up, Muslim rulers were given greater authority in some areas,[18] and Muslims were employed by the colonial administrators in subordinate positions as guides, agents and clerks. This brought Muslims into close contact with African peoples, and as Trimingham observed, this familiarized the traditionalists, 'with the outward characteristic of Islam, enhanced the prestige of adherence to the favoured religion, and provided the Islamic agents with facilities for the exercise of propaganda and various forms of pressure'.[19]

Not all colonial administrations looked favourably upon Islam. The administration in the Belgian Congo was especially hostile to Islam and saw in it a threat to its 'Christianizing' and 'civilizing' mission. Only a few mosques were allowed to be built and there was a total ban on Muslim schools in the colony.[20]

Other Europeans, especially the French, attempted to impose European culture on their subjects, Muslim and non-Muslim alike, believing that they had an obligation to raise the standard of their colonial subjects by imparting to them the 'benefits' of French culture. Unlike the British whose policy towards the Muslim states was based on the belief that they could secure the co-operation of Muslim rulers, the French thought otherwise. They initially tried to limit the areas under Muslim control in their bid to conquer the bulk of the Western Sudan. They endeavoured to avoid the use of Arabic in official correspondence, and even openly helped those who did not accept Muslim proselytization such as the Bambara. Furthermore, the French took care to ensure that Muslim rulers would not be appointed to rule over non-Muslim peoples. To effectively oppose the spread of Islam and Islamic jurisprudence, they also tried to build up traditional religion and codify African customary law as a counterforce.[21]

17. J. S. Trimingham, 1962, p. 226.
18. In Northern Nigeria, for example, where the policy of indirect rule was first tried, the British government upheld the power of the Muslim rulers and colonial power was placed behind Islam as the official religion of Northern Nigeria.
19. J. S. Trimingham, 1962.
20. See N. S. Booth in N. S. Booth (ed.), 1977, p. 325.
21. See J. F. A. Ajayi, n.d.

PLATE 20.3 *Entrance façade of a mosque in northern Ghana*

But the French were more familiar with Islam than traditional African religion in spite of their fear and hostility to the former and when they did not succeed in their intentions they settled down to try to cope with Islam and established institutes to study and document Muslim life, beliefs, practices and institutions.[22]

Colonial powers were determined to break up large Muslim states and religious organizations and to foster rivalry and competition among them. Thus the British abolished the Sokoto caliphate in Northern Nigeria while the French openly encouraged the ethnic and dynastic rivalries which led to the disintegration of the Tukulor empire (see Fig. 6.2) and the proliferation of Sufi orders, and refused to recognize one Khalifa for all Muslim members of the Tijaniyya order in West Africa.

Both colonial powers in West Africa, Britain and France, were willing and anxious to guarantee freedom of worship to Muslims under certain conditions. They were anxious to see a West African Islam shorn of its international connections and universal aspects. What the colonial powers were particularly anxious to prevent was a pan-Islamic movement which constituted a threat to their power, and this fear became real when Turkey entered the First World War on the side of Germany and the Ottoman Sultan, as the Caliph of all Muslims, reportedly ordered a general revolt against the European unbelievers.

The colonial powers later came to encourage Islam and not merely to tolerate it as before. For they came to prefer to deal with Islamized Africans rather than with their Christianized counterparts. A French official is reported to have said in 1912 that 'Islamized Negroes are on the whole gentle people who are grateful for the security which our arms have brought them; they only think of living in peace in the shade of our power.'[23]

The modernizing influence of Islam was also appreciated by colonial powers who were said to have regarded it as a 'bridge between the narrow particularism of traditional society and the wider impulses and requirements of modern life and economic interests'.[24] Submissive Muslim leaders were therefore greatly encouraged and frequently received official favours such as national honours and awards. Mosques and Ḳu'ranic schools were built for them, and they were also helped to go on pilgrimages and study tours. But at the same time those Muslims who did not toe the colonial line and showed defiance were disciplined and often harassed.

But Muslims also opposed colonial rule on both religious and political grounds, and although colonial administrations, such as the French, succeeded in gaining a measure of Muslim support in their West African territories, there were large numbers of Muslims who were bent on preserving the purity of Islam and who could therefore not tolerate submission to a Christian infidel administration, and they sought to rid

22. ibid.; see also M. Crowder, 1968, pp. 359–61.
23. Quoted in J. F. A. Ajayi, n.d., p. 22.
24. ibid.

their countries of French colonialism. Such a desire led to the resurgence of Mahdism which was to end the rule of the unbeliever. The Mahdī, the equivalent of the Christian Messiah, was believed to be the one who would come into the world to establish a just government in accordance with Islamic dogma and finally rid society of the rule of unbelievers. Mahdism reared its head in many parts of the Sudanic zone of West Africa as an expression of anti-French sentiment in Upper Guinea, Mauritania and Senegal, especially from 1906 to the First World War.

Other Islamic movements which expressed an anti-French or anti-colonial posture were the Hamalliyya movement, founded by Shaykh Hamallah, which was active in Senegal, French Soudan, Mauritania and Niger and the Sanūsiyya brotherhood, founded by Muḥammad b. ʿAlī al-Sanūsī in Libya which became the force which led the Libyans against Italian colonialism. Between 1860 and 1901 the Sanūsiyya spread to Tunisia, Egypt, the central Sahara, central Sudan and Senegal.

The Sanūsiyya order had a tradition of opposition to foreign domination in Libya and developed not only as a religious order but also a political movement. It opposed Turkish rule even though it regarded the Sultan of Turkey as the Caliph of all Muslim lands. The only reason why the order did not take up arms against Turkey was the fact that their common religion of Islam held them together. But in the case of the Italians, there was no such common bond and the order resisted the Italian invasion with firmness, and led the Libyan resistance from 1911 to 1932. After the withdrawal of Turkish sovereignty from Libya in 1912, the Sanūsiyya order assumed full leadership and responsibility for Libyan liberation, and orders and proclamations for the direction of the resistance were issued in the name of 'al-Hakuma al-Sanūsiyya', the Sanūsiyya government. In the course of time, members of the order came to be recognized in other Muslim lands not only as liberators of Libya but also as 'Fighters of the Faith', 'Mujahidin'. K. Folayan has written that:

> The role of the Sanusiya Order in providing effective leadership for Libya's resistance movement makes it politically significant as a good example of a religious movement becoming the backbone of resistance to Western imperialism, and the Order actually had the longest record of such a resistance in Africa. In fact, the role of the Sanusiya did not end with the collapse of their military strength and the Italian occupation of Libya in 1932. Rather, right up to the year of Libya's political independence (1951) the Sanusiya continued to stand for Libya as the *effendiya* class has stood for Egyptian or Maghribi nationalism.[25]

Some of the most vigorous opponents of the French invasion of Upper

25. K. Folayan, 1973, p. 56.

Volta in the late nineteenth century were Muslims, most of whom were reported to have told local Mossi people that the whites would leave their country as soon as the blacks became Muslims.[26] Furthermore, the conquests of Samori in West Africa and Rabih in the Chad area in the last part of the nineteenth century brought them into conflict with Europeans and helped to identify Islam with opposition to colonial rule.

But Islam prospered under colonial rule as a result of the many advantages it had over Christianity imposed by missionaries, as well as from the disruption of traditional life which colonialism gave rise to. Islam was seen by many as an indigenous religion, spread by Africans, whose adherents did not separate themselves from the community but instead mixed with them. By contrast the Christians tended to create their own separate communities and followed an essentially European way of life. It is thus no mere accident that the Temne (Sierra Leone) word for both Christian and European is *poto*.[27] Besides, unlike mission-imposed Christianity, Islam was able to accommodate more African traditional social and religious institutions, such as magic, divination, polygamy, and communalism. Becoming Muslim did not therefore require the radical break with tradition which Christian missionaries insisted upon. 'It [Islam] placed more emphasis than Christianity on cohesion and less on competition and individual achievement.'[28] A further asset in favour of Islam was that with all the disruptions which colonial rule had brought in its wake, there was the need for a new basis for social integration, and Islam provided this basis since it possesses significant resources for those who had lost their traditional roots.

Commenting on the reasons for the 'explosion' of Islam during the period, N. S. Booth has written that:

> In some areas this may have been because Islam was seen as a way of resisting Western political and cultural domination while in others it was because colonial policies unintentionally favoured it. Perhaps in a complex way both the European hostility toward Islam and the European use of Muslims and Muslim institutions for their own purposes contributed to Islamic growth. Being Muslim could be a way of gaining advantages under the colonial system and at the same time expressing a certain distance from Western culture. It was a way of being part of a worldwide community which received grudging respect from Europeans while providing an alternative centre of loyalty and a basis for an independent dignity. The pressure of a new alien culture and religion tended to strengthen the sense of identity with a culture and religion that, although also originally alien, had become an accepted part of the local scene.[29]

26. N. S. Booth in N. S. Booth (ed.), 1977, p. 323.
27. J. Karefa-Smart and A. Karefa-Smart, 1959, p. 19.
28. R. W. Hull, 1980, p. 146.
29. N. S. Booth in N. S. Booth (ed.), 1977, p. 320.

But this acceptance has not resulted in the abandonment of the traditional world view altogether; in fact Islam, as well as Christianity, has come to supplement traditional beliefs and practices rather than supplant them. This is because the 'guest religions' have tended to be understood largely in terms of the fundamental notions which undergirded African traditional religion. Thus Islam means to most African Muslims one of the many ways of being religious, Islam complementing traditional religion and the latter making up for some of the deficiencies of Islam.

There are, however, some basic changes from the traditional outlook among African Muslims. The Islamic article of faith concerning the final Judgement and the separation of believers from non-believers in the future life differs sharply from traditional notions, where the emphasis is on community with one's dead forebears. Islam is seen as possessing a new source of power which is tapped for the achievement of wholeness of life, healing, and the improvement of life in the community.

Christianity in the colonial era

The imposition of colonial rule was to aid considerably the work of the Christian missionaries. In the first place, both colonial administrators and missionaries shared the same world view and sprang from the same culture. Secondly, the colonial administration was favourably disposed to the work of the missionaries and often subsidized mission schools. Thirdly, the imposition of colonial control over each territory ensured peace and order within which the missionaries assured themselves of the protection of colonial administrations. Fourthly, the introduction of efficient means of communications, and the establishment of a money economy gave impetus to trade and commerce and helped usher in a new way of life which was to prevail all over Africa and which was characterized by a breakdown of communalism in favour of individualism. On the whole, it may be said that Christian missions in Africa were the ally and adjunct of European imperialism and the activity of missionaries was part and parcel of the advance or penetration of the West into the non-Western world.

Christianity as the religion of the conqueror was regarded as containing the secret of the source of power of the white man. At least it provided access to education, employment, power and influence in the white man's world. The main thrust of missionary preaching was the particularity of Christianity, especially as it was understood and interpreted by European missionaries. Using the spoken word, or direct evangelization, schools and medical work, missionaries made many converts, and the late nineteenth century was marked by a phenomenal success of Christian missions. As a result of this, many Christian communities sprang up where before there had been none and many converts also took up the further evangelization of their peoples. The reduction of many African languages to writing as well as the teaching of European languages in schools, introduced literacy into many parts of Africa. With the reduction of African languages to writing, written literature in many African languages came into being.

The close association of Christianity and education cannot be over-emphasized, for it was through the innumerable schools established by missionaries that many Africans came into contact with Christianity, and in fact school was the church in many parts of Africa. The importance of schools for the missionary enterprise was expressed by Elias Shrenk as follows:

> If we had a nation with formal education, able to read and write, my plans for mission work would be different. But now I am convinced that the opening of schools is our main task. I have a low opinion of Christians who are not able to read their Bible. The smallest schoolchild is a missionary and establishes a relationship with the grown-ups, which would not exist without a school.[30]

The missionaries played quite an important role in the introduction of a money economy in Africa. Mission stations developed plantations in many parts of Africa and in addition to growing local foodstuffs and introducing new crops, they helped in the diffusion of commercial crops like cocoa, coffee, tobacco, cotton and sugar cane.

Above all, Christianity infused many new ideas. The ideas were not entirely new, and there were points of convergence between what the missionaries preached and what the Africans believed, such as the belief in God and obedience to His will as the final Judge and Creator of men.

The missionaries, however, had a negative attitude towards African religion and culture and were determined right from the start to stamp them out. The missionaries preached that the only God was the one whose nature and character had been revealed in the Bible, and that all other gods were mere illusions; that the Son of God, Jesus Christ, was the final revelation and the only Saviour of mankind, and that the Church was the sole dispenser of divine grace and that there was no salvation outside the Church. The European missionaries therefore felt it a divine duty to bring all peoples into the arena of salvation and grace.

Armed with the conviction of possessing the only truth, missionaries condemned all that was 'pagan'. They preached against all kinds of traditional practices – the pouring of libation, holding state offices, drumming and dancing, traditional ceremonies of the rites of passage, such as outdooring, girls' puberty rites and customs associated with deaths and burials. They also denied the existence of gods and witches and other supernatural powers which Africans believed in. On the whole, becoming a Christian meant, to a large extent, ceasing to be an African and using European culture as a point of reference. Thus Christianity had a dis-integrating effect on African culture.

The African response to the missionary endeavour expressed itself in

30. Quoted by H. Debrunner, 1967, p. 145.

three distinct ways: acceptance, rejection and adaptation. There is no doubt that many Africans readily accepted the new faith and that Christianity gained far more ground in Africa during the period under review than it had done in the previous two or three centuries. The first group of Africans to embrace Christianity would appear to be those who were regarded by the Africans as social outcasts, and the downtrodden such as lepers and others who suffered various forms of social disabilities in traditional African societies. Included in this category were those who had broken certain traditional taboos and were fleeing from persecution, and mothers who gave birth to twins in societies where there was a taboo against twin births. Such mothers found refuge for themselves and their children in mission stations. The social outcasts had nothing to lose by embracing Christianity: on the contrary, they gained hope, confidence and inspiration from the missionary teaching of equality and brotherhood, and also 'from the idea that one must not fatalistically accept his or her station in life as beyond human control'.[31]

The spread of Christianity during colonial times was not due exclusively to missionary initiative. African converts, catechists and ministers zealously spread Christianity, while some of the traditional rulers such as Lewanika and Lobengula, as we have seen already, gave every assistance to missionaries. The expansion of Christianity in Africa was largely due to the zeal of African converts, especially in the period after 1914. There were innumerable instances of African evangelists going outside their own ethnic groups to work as missionaries. For example, evangelists from Buganda took Christianity to other peoples like the Banyakare, Bakiga, Batoro, Bagisu and Langi, and Baganda evangelists went as far as Ruanda and the Belgian Congo (see Fig. 7.1). Famous among them was Canon Apolo Kivebulaya (1866–1933), who worked among the Pygmies as a missionary in the Belgian Congo (1896–9 and again 1915–33).[32] In West Africa, the Yoruba bishop, Samuel Ajayi Crowther, worked in the Niger valley. The itinerant Liberian prophet, William Wade Harris, travelled through the Ivory Coast and the Apolonia District of the Gold Coast between 1910 and 1915 and converted some 100000 people. When expelled from the Ivory Coast, he withdrew to the Gold Coast, and his activities in both places resulted in the establishment of the Eglise Harriste in the Ivory Coast and the Twelve Apostles Church in the Gold Coast.[33]

There were also those Africans already dealt with above who rejected the message of Christianity altogether and stuck to the religious and cultural traditions of their forefathers, seeing in them more meaning and significance than what the missionaries preached. Some of these participated in the persecution and ostracism of those who had become Christians but others also carried on the sacrifices and observances that were intended to keep

31. R. W. Hull, 1980, p. 143.
32. See A. Luck, 1963.
33. For details, see G. M. Haliburton, 1971.

PLATE 20.4 *William Wade Harris (c. 1865–1929), the Liberian-born West African evangelist*

528

human beings in harmony with the spiritual forces. Out of their ranks came the religious and cultural leaders as well as herbalists and it is they who have been largely responsible for upholding African values and for providing knowledge about traditional African cultures.

Separatist churches

Finally, there were those who chose to adapt the new religion by founding what has come to be known as separatist or independent churches, and this development represents the fourth stage in the history of Christianity in Africa. These churches were of two main types, namely, those which broke away from already existing independent churches and those which sprang up independently of any existing religious groups. In most instances, these churches sought to incorporate a larger measure of African beliefs and practices into Christian life than was permitted in churches under missionary control. They were an expression of the desire of Africans to find 'a place to feel at home', and include African ideas of worship in their Christian liturgies. An important causative factor was the translation of the Bible into many African languages and the Africans' reading and interpretation of the Christian Scripture. On the basis of their own understanding of Holy Scripture, Africans formed or founded their own churches, thus doing away with the monopoly over scriptural interpretation which had been in missionary hands for so long.

The breakaway churches, in part, represented the African reaction or adaptation to colonialism and were emancipatory in character. Especially in areas of European settlement, where political repression was intense, such churches proliferated and attracted African nationalists. The Ethiopian churches in South Africa, which emphasize African self-improvement and political rights, are a case in point. Nehemiah Tile broke away from the Methodist Mission Church in 1882 and two years later founded the Tembu Church,[34] one of the first independent churches ever to be formed in Africa. The second, which was the first to be called 'Ethiopian', was founded by a Wesleyan minister, Mangena M. Mokone, in 1892, again in South Africa. The 'Ethiopian' movement spread to other parts of Southern and East Africa.

In other areas of colonial Africa, breakaway churches often expressed open hostility to the colonial administration. John Chilembwe, for example, founded his Province Industrial Mission in Nyasaland, vehemently attacked the British colonial practice of taxation and military recruitment and eventually led an abortive armed resistance to the British colonial administration in 1915 before being captured and executed. Around this time, the Watchtower Movement began to grow and spread from Nyasaland to Southern Rhodesia among the Shona, becoming a religious movement with strong political overtones. The African Watchtower Movement which

34. See B. G. M. Sundkler, 1961, pp. 38–9.

PLATE 20.5 *The Reverend John Chilembwe (1860s/1870s–1915), churchman and leader of the 1915 rising in Nyasaland, pictured with his family*

530

spread in Central Africa and the Congo was a distinct body and traced its origins to the separatist Church movement in the area founded by Elliot Kamwana in northern Nyasaland in 1908. It became known as the Kitawala (Kingdom) or the Church of the Watch Tower, and in Northern Rhodesia its millennial preachers predicted the total collapse of colonialism and the end of the world.[35]

Similar developments took place in other parts of Africa, especially between the early years of the First World War. The example of William Wade Harris in West Africa has already been discussed. Simon Kimbangu founded his Eglise de Jésus-Christ sur la Terre par le Prophète Simon Kimbangu (EJCSK) in 1921 in the Belgian Congo. His followers refused to pay taxes to the Belgian colonial administration and declared their intention to withhold their labour in the face of the forced labour which the administration had introduced. These acts constituted a veritable threat to the administration and in order to avert a general uprising in the country, Simon Kimbangu was arrested and kept in prison until his death in 1951. But Kimbanguism continued to spread from its original base in the Lower Congo River.[36] The neo-Kimbanguist Mission des Noirs, founded by Simon-Pierre Mpadi, which became known as the 'Khakists', spread from the Lower Congo to the French Congo and Oubangui-Chari (now Central African Republic).

Similar in orientation to the movements founded by Kimbangu and Mpadi were those founded in Uganda by an ex-serviceman in the King's African Rifles, Ruben Spartas Mukasa, who dedicated his life to work for the redemption of all Africa at whatever personal cost. His African Progressive Association and the Christian Army for the Salvation of Africa, as well as a branch of the African Orthodox Church which he started, expressed the political and social purpose of all these movements. In Nyasaland, Jordan Nguma's Last Church of God and His Christ was of the same stamp as Mukasa's in Uganda.

Other churches, in the spirit of the Reformation, emphasised certain aspects of Christian theology which the mission-founded churches had neglected. The Zionist churches of South Africa emphasized possession by the Holy Spirit, healing and prophecy and spread widely in Southern and East Africa. The Dini ya Roho (Holy Ghost Church),[37] which grew up among the Abaluyia of Kenya and was founded by Jakobo Buluku and Daniel Sande in 1927, regarded baptism by the Holy Spirit, speaking in tongues, and the free confession of sins as a necessary prerequisite for full membership of the church. This same emphasis on the Holy Spirit also led Alfayo Odongo to found his Joroho (Holy Ghost) Church among the Luo of Kenya in 1932. Various African and Aladura churches in West Africa also emphasized possession by the Holy Spirit.

35. For further details, see Chapter 27 below.
36. ibid.
37. O. Odinga, 1967, p. 69.

PLATE 20.6 *Prophet Simon Kimbangu* (c. *1890–1951*), *founder of the Eglise de Jésus-Christ sur la Terre in the Belgian Congo*

Some churches had a narrower scope. In 1910, as we have seen already, the Nomiya Luo Mission was founded by John Owalo, among the Luo of Western Kenya, and the Church adopted circumcision and made it a condition for salvation. Even though the Luo did not have a tradition of circumcision, the Church adopted it in keeping with biblical precedent.[38] Other churches were set up specifically to accommodate those who had not been able to comply with the missionary churches' insistence on monogamy and had been expelled, as well as those who could not join the Church because they were already polygamous. An example of such a Church was the African National Church[39] which thrived in the Rungwe District of Tanganyika in the 1930s.

Indigenous Christianity

Besides these churches, another set arose which were not the product of anxiety alleviation or stress in society but rather derived their inspiration from a more positive ideology. From the earliest days of the process of presenting Christianity to Africans, some converts had accepted the new faith lock, stock, and barrel. Others, on the other hand, accepted it on the basis of what they already knew, and understood Christianity in terms of the basic underlying concepts of African traditional religion, relating the message of the Church to their enduring religious needs.

Thus Christianity did not come merely to supplant traditional religious beliefs and practices, rather it came to supplement them. In other words, some African Christians used certain aspects of Christianity to strengthen aspects of traditional beliefs that needed strengthening, and at the same time used traditional beliefs to strengthen aspects of Christianity where they were found wanting. Thus they came out with what they sincerely believed to be a meaningful religion, and their Christianity can be seen as an expression of the African way of being religious. This is why we have termed it indigenous Christianity.

Underlying indigenous Christianity is an expression of religious creativity and cultural integrity, and not a mere reaction, response or adaptation to outside stimuli, as some scholars are wont to assert. Usually, and with a few exceptions, the explanation for the emergence and proliferation of movements of indigenous Christianity has been derived from factors outside these movements themselves which has given them a functional reasonableness or a dysfunctional aberrant quality. Such interpretations may not be devoid of validity but they tend to overstress the role of outside factors in the emergence of these movements. Thus when they are called 'independent' churches, the underlying suggestion is that there is some more important reference point outside these churches.

Having taken the bold step of grafting Christianity on to the African

38. E. S. Atieno-Odhiambo, 1974, pp. 10–11.
39. T. O. Ranger, n.d., pp. 16–20.

tradition, the indigenous churches satisfy the spiritual hunger of their followers by portraying the Gospel in ways which are compatible with the traditional African world view, and are also comprehensible within the African view of things.

Forms of worship have been provided to satisfy the spiritual and emotional needs of members, thereby enabling Christianity, like traditional religion, to cover every area of human life and fulfil all human needs. Included in these is the concern for healing, whose centrality in both traditional religion and indigenous Christianity cannot be over-emphasized. Healing contributes to human wholeness and religion is essential in this respect. And in addition to healing, the religious needs of divining, prophesying and visioning are also fulfilled, for there is the firm belief that God reveals the future and the causes of misfortune through visions. While mission-founded churches deny the existence of evil forces such as witchcraft and sorcery, the indigenous churches recognize their existence and provide a Christian source of protection against these evil powers, firmly believing that Jesus Christ can effectively protect and heal.

The recognition of the reality of evil forces, such as witchcraft and sorcery, is an acceptance of the African world view and is reminiscent of the biblical world view which recognized demons, evil spirits, principalities and powers and the rulers of darkness in this world. To deny such powers, as the missionaries did, was to be western and not necessarily biblical, for the Bible recognizes these powers, but proclaims the power of God over them.

The emergence of these churches has provided the opportunity for the exercise of African leadership and ability in Christianity, and in these churches a truly African Christianity has been expressed. And with this development has come the beginning of an African Christian theology. These churches have cut across ethnic, and even international boundaries and have united many peoples in common faith and practice. At a time of tremendously radical and great changes in African life, these churches have provided religious or cultural shelter for many.

Examples of indigenous Christian churches that emerged in the colonial period and are still very much alive are the Apostolowa Fe Dedefia Habobo (Apostolic Revelation Society) in the Gold Coast; the Negro Church of Christ (Nigeria); l'Eglise des Banzie in Gabon; Dini ya Nsambwa (The Church of the Ancestors) in Kenya; as well as Calici ca Makolo (Church of the Ancestors) in Nyasaland; the original Church of the White Bird among the Zazuru of Southern Rhodesia; Church of Christ for the Union of the Bantu and Protection of Bantu Customs in South Africa; Eglise des Noirs in the Congo; and the Herero Church of South West Africa (now Namibia).[40] To these may be added those churches which stress the

40. For further details, see J. B. Webster, 1964; H. W. Turner, 1965 and 1967; R. L. Wishlade, 1965; V. E. W. Hayward (ed.), 1963; C. G. Baeta, 1962.

indigenous nature of their Christianity by either including the name of the dominant ethnic group or the adjective African in their titles. But for a detailed illustration, the example of the Musama Disco Christo Church of Ghana will be given.

The example of the Musama Disco Christo Church

In the light of the above consideration, the Musama Disco Christo (Army of the Cross of Christ) Church of the Gold Coast (Ghana)[41] merits consideration as an indigenous Christian Church. For, relative to the traditional Akan pattern of social organization, the founder of the church, Prophet Jemisimiham Jehu-Appiah, successfully adapted Christianity by reorganizing it on the Akan pattern and portrayed Christianity in terms which are comprehensible in the Akan view of things. The church began as a prayer group, the Faith Society, within the Methodist Church at Gomoa Oguan, in the Central Region of the Gold Coast in 1919. But when its leader, Catechist William Egyanka Appiah, and his followers were expelled from the Church, it was established as a full-blown Church in 1922.

The founder did not only found a Church and become its General Spiritual Head, but he also established a dynasty and became its progenitor with the title of *Akaboha* (King) I, and his son, the *Akasibeena* (Prince), and became, according to the constitution of the Church, 'entitled to hold this line of succession as a divine right, as ordered by the Holy Spirit'.[42] The wife of the founder, the Prophetess Natholomoa Jehu-Appiah, became the *Akatitibi* (Queenmother) of the Church; and the King and Queen therefore became the supreme authorities in the Musama Disco Christo Church. As a prophet and leader of a spiritual movement, Jemisimiham Jehu-Appiah laid down the foundation of his Church as an 'indigenous Christian church, founded to serve as our humble present – a "Myrrh" from Africa to Christ, which is our divine and precious gift, not caring whether others are offering Gold or Frankinsence'.[43]

The Church is organized on the traditional Akan state (*Oman*) structure based on military formation. At the head of the *Oman* is *Nana Akaboha*, who combines both spiritual and temporal power. The *Akaboha* has his wing and divisional chiefs, and the importance of the Akan state structure arises from the fact that it is tied up with the history and development of the Church, and the Church's sense of mission and destiny are reflected in the divisions.

The headquarters of the church, Mozano, functions as an *ahenkro*, capital town of an Akan traditional state. Here the *Akaboha* resides and

---

41. For further reading see K. A. Opoku in E. Fasholé-Luke, R. Gray, A. Hastings and G. Tasie (eds), 1978.
42. Constitution of the Musama Disco Christo Church, Mozano, 1959, p. 11.
43. ibid., p. ii.

PLATE 20.7 *Prophet M. Jehu-Appiah, Akaboha III, grandson and successor of the founder of the Musama Disco Christo Church (Gold Coast/Ghana) riding in a palanquin during the Church's annual Peace Festival*

all major decisions affecting the church emanate, and it is here that the annual festival, *Asomdwee Afe* (Peace Festival), is held. At an *ahenkro*, there are shrines and holy places where the faithful pray and receive healing.

Members of the Church are identified from others by their use of copper rings and copper crosses which serve as 'tribal marks'. The heavenly names which each member receives and which are peculiar to the Church also serve as 'tribal names'. The Church has its own language, *osor kasa* (heavenly language), which is used in salutations, greetings and entry into houses; and the names used in the Church are also from this language. Although it is not an extensive language it is enough to add distinction to the Church as an *oman* with its own language. Membership of the Church cuts across ethnic and status boundaries, and is largely determined by the needs of people who come to the Church to seek solutions to the problem of life. Like traditional religion:

> ... the Christianity practised in the *oman* of Musama is a religion of being and doing, and represents a rejection of missionary Christianity which was largely a religion of mental culture. It [the Christianity of the Musama Disco Christo Church] is a religion which is meant for day to day living and which provides satisfying answers to the problems of contemporary life. Unlike missionary Christianity which denied the existence of demons, witches and evil spirits, the Musama church recognizes the existence of such spirits but demonstrates the power of God over them.[44]

The Church draws heavily on Akan religion and culture in its search for satisfactory answers to the problems of contemporary life and combines elements of Methodism with a strong African polity. It represents a further extension of Christianity in Africa based, as it is, on the conviction that a Christian society can be built on the foundations of African culture.

Conclusion

The period of colonial rule in Africa from 1880 to 1935 saw not the destruction but rather the confirmation of religious pluralism in Africa. Orthodox Christianity and Islam also gained wide grounds during the period thanks to some of the activities of the colonial administrators. Traditional religion, as the host religion, formed the foundation upon which the new religions were based, although in the end many changes were made in its total outlook. Its institutional expression was greatly affected by the new colonial order but its world view has persisted even among professed Muslims and Christians. The fact of religious pluralism created rivalries, competition and even conflict in many parts of Africa, but at the same time the opportunity for inter-religious dialogue was created.

44. K. A. Opoku in E. Fasholé-Luke, R. Gray, A. Hastings and G. Tasie (eds), 1978, p. 121.

The weakening of traditional religion also meant a corresponding weakening of many of the traditional social and political institutions which depended on it for their vitality and sanction. Thus morality, the network of family relationships, communal cohesiveness and the institution of chieftaincy were considerably enfeebled though not completely overthrown.

This period saw the birth in Africa of indigenous churches, sometimes referred to as independent, separatist, breakaway, or Ethiopian churches. The causative factors were many but the colonial presence and the spread of literacy were crucial. However, whatever the reasons might be, this development marks the fourth stage in the history of Christianity in Africa, a period in which, under African leadership, a new brand of Christianity which is compatible with the African view of reality has come into being and has drawn thousands into its fold. These churches have provided an alternative resource to the time-honoured services of traditional herbalists and diviners for their members, although people in need may turn to them (traditional medical practitioners).

On the whole, the coming into existence of several religions side by side, instead of the erstwhile single, traditional religion, has brought about a ferment of ideas which has enriched religious life. All three religions have borrowed from one another in order to maintain their relevance to their African practitioners.

But traditional religion still continues to be relevant in the face of the mounting individualism, secularism, rootlessness, excessive exploitation of nature and even atheism, which have accompanied the impact of the West on Africa. The traditional religion offers an alternative perspective on universal human concerns, and is not detached from everyday life nor from nature. Its world view provides a refreshing counterpoint to the aridity which has engulfed much of the spiritual dimension of modern life.

21

The arts in Africa during the period of colonial rule

WOLE SOYINKA

In February 1976, at a police checkpoint between Ibadan and Lagos, Nigeria, a man was arrested for being in possession of antiquities, believed stolen. He had two sackfuls of bronze and wooden sculptures, all of which, he insisted, were his own property. The police later discovered that he was telling the truth. This man, a recent convert to Islam, lived and worked in Ibadan in a communal compound. The Yoruba deities whose carved figures were found on him were typically brought into the city by labour migrants where, in their temporary homes, they ministered to the spiritual needs of the displaced artisans, petty traders, city clerks and other workers. Later, however, the head of this compound was converted to Islam and he in turn began to convert his neighbours. After the suspect's own conversion, he was made to understand that his former religious symbols had to give way if the compound was to become a fitting habitation for the spirit of Allah. Unable to bear the thought of their physical destruction, he resolved to take them back to their original home, his village, where they are now reinstalled.

A common pattern of the movement of cultural forms and their concrete manifestations, the incident provides an apt model of survival, even renewal of cultural values in the face of religious and other more socially intensive forms of domination. What was true in 1976 can be seen as having been even more commonplace in that more dramatic period of external domination in Africa, when an entire people, its social organizations, and its economic and artistic patterns became subjugated to strategies for maximum exploitation by outside interests. The slave trade had intensified internecine warfare for over two centuries, leading to cultural devastation on an unprecedented scale. Punitive raids by colonial forces, missionary intolerance and lack of understanding – all these had thoroughly derailed the accustomed cultural directions of the continent. Different methods of foreign control or interaction with the African populace naturally evoked or created different cultural responses from the displaced African. Belgian and Portuguese colonialism, as well as British settler colonialism in East Africa, are easily recognized as the most ruthless on the continent. They created conditions for the truly displaced African in the most literal sense of the word. The Arabic dimension was unique in its own right, an ambivalent face of expansionism which none the less left strong cultural impressions on the landscape. Yet the reality that we extract from that period is the resilience and even increased vitality of the forms and values of the authentic cultures of the peoples.

African art

It is difficult to gauge the qualitative impact of imperial commerce on artistic productivity. Certain media remained obviously unaffected; for instance, the 'bead-paint' technique of the Cameroon artists or the art of religious sculpture among the Yoruba, the Baule, the Bakota, etc. Yet subtle transformations had begun to take place in other art media, both in form and content. While retaining much of its chromatic sensibilities, the Mbari mural art of the Igbo (Nigeria) had began to undergo 'pop' crudities at the hands of urban returnees, the result of sudden access to paints in all tints and textures. Formerly such mural art was controlled by the very nature and sparse range of dyes of local manufacture.

A feature of the annual festival of the Koumina canton in the Bobo-Dioulasso-Koumina department of French-administered Upper Volta was, significantly, arguments which raged between the 'traditionalists' and the 'modernists' on this very question of dyes. The former group of mask-makers preferred the old technique of natural dyes not merely for their visual and textural satisfaction, but from the feeling for an organic relationship which should exist between the materials of artistic production. The latter group found the use of imported dyes not merely convenient, but filled with a greater potential for variety. This harvest festival, incidentally, one which brought together the blacksmiths, weavers, dyers, carvers, dancers and griots of all the neighbouring cantons, especially the famous musician of Diagaso, the Kare, provides yet another example of the persistence of collective creativity even within the community-fragmenting grid system adopted by the colonial administrators for their workers. Just that once every year, at least on such an assertively massed scale, the scattered families poured into town with an artistic affirmation of their authentic world-view.

Local genius was hardly a match for factory productivity which began to flood African markets even at the early stages of the colonial venture. The loss of the integrative role of art of normal community development may be seen in a decline in the art of the *forowa* and the *kuduo*, finely worked containers of the Asante (Gold Coast – now Ghana) whose decorative motifs were, as is much the case in Africa, ideograms for traditional lessons, proverbs, moral counsels and vignettes of history. Like the goldweights which could be rightly said to have commenced a reduction in commercial utility, the *forowa* was still commonly used as a container for snuff, unguents, etc. But its production was now largely taken over

PLATE 21.1 *Wooden figures from a Yoruba shrine to the god Shango*

541

PLATE 21.2 *An Akan brass* kuduo *from Ghana*

by factories in Britain, which additionally could experiment with a variety of metals. Thus, Doran H. Ross[1] records a silver *forowa* stamped 'Birmingham,' 1926'. By contrast, there is no indication that canoe ornamentation underwent, during this same period, a similar attenuation in the aesthetic wedding of image and sentiment; together with motorized vehicles, which had begun to make their appearance by the second decade, and in woven cloth they continued to perpetuate that strategy of communal education which may be described as 'lessons in motion'.

African architecture

A more than cursory look at the layout, exterior and interior of some of the truly harmonious of traditional living-spaces would reveal the existence of an effective, sophisticated expression of the architectural genius of the indigene, one which contrasted vividly with the regimenting 'grid' planning into which Africans were being forced at this time, by Belgian and French (especially) forms of plantation slavery. An extensive description is deservedly provided by André Gide in his *Voyage au Congo* (1927):

> The Massas' hut, it is true, resembles no other; but it is not only strange; it is *beautiful*; and it is not its strangeness so much as its beauty that moves me. A beauty so perfect, so accomplished, that it seems natural. No ornament, no superfluity. The pure curve of its line, which is uninterrupted from base to summit, seems to have been arrived at mathematically by an ineluctable necessity; one instinctively realizes how exactly the resistance of the materials must have been calculated. A little farther north or south and the clay would be too much mixed with sand to allow of this easy spring, terminating in the circular opening that alone gives light to the inside of the hut, in the manner of Agrippa's Pantheon. On the outside a number of regular flutings give life and accent to these geometrical forms and afford a foothold by which the summit of the hut (often twenty to twenty-five feet high) can be reached; they enabled it to be built without the aid of scaffolding; this hut is made by hand like a vase; it is the work, not of a mason, but of a potter ...
>
> Inside the hut the coolness of the air seems delicious, when one comes in from the scorching outside. Above the door, like some huge keyhole, is a kind of columbarium shelf, where vases and household objects are arranged. The walls are smooth, polished, varnished. Opposite to the entrance is a kind of high drum made of earth, very prettily decorated with geometrical patterns in relief, painted white, red and black. These drums are the rice bins. Their earthen lids are luted with clay, and are so smooth that they resemble the skin of a drum. Fishing tackle, cords, and tools hang from pegs; sometimes too a sheaf of assagais or a shield of plaited rush. Here, in the dim

1. D. H. Ross, 1974, p. 45.

twilight of an Etruscan tomb, the family spend the hottest hours of the day; at night the cattle come in to join them – oxen, goats, and hens ... everything is in its proper place; everything is clean, exact, ordered. There is no communication with the outside as soon as the door is shut. One's home is one's castle.[2]

It would be futile to claim that all African housing of this period was capable of arousing such flights of lyricism in the traveller, yet one can only regret that little of the urban architecture of the time found it rewarding to borrow from the structural lessons of such traditional architecture.

The cities continued to be developed either as replicas or adaptations of European urban planning, or, as already stated, in rigid 'grid' forms which aided the depersonalization of the African, and his alienation from his communal sensibility. Nevertheless, it must be conceded that pockets of traditional housing were successfully inserted in the heart of the alien structures which rose all over the landscape. Tucked neatly away in the 'high-rising' centres of even the capital cities of the Belgian Congo (now Zaire), Senegal, the Gold Coast (Ghana), Nigeria, Angola, etc., are traditional compounds, overshadowed by the concrete edifices, which date back to the nineteenth century. They are usually centred on a communal well. A circular or rectangular veranda opens into the courtyard and a series of family residences are linked to a common roof and drainage systems which unite and flow into the open gutters on the main streets. Even where the houses consist of more than one floor, the spatiality and interplay of planes reveal the same liberating quality. The contribution of the Brazilian returnees to the continent was, in this respect, quite immense. Even in the minor cities of the African hinterland, isolated instances of an arrested development of traditional architecture from this period continue to create a sense of aesthetic loss in this most immediate of man's creative and utilitarian productions. The modern urban city in Africa constantly reminds one that the environment was never transformed on its own terms, but in the image of the colonizers, with all its alienating consequences, even in the urban-influenced production of other forms of art – the mural, sculpture, music, etc.

African music

The real music of the people of Africa continues to remind us that it remained undisplaced as the regenerative source of the continent's cultural will. The 'salons' played their dubious role in this; with few exceptions the fate of music on the West African coast was duplicated in those areas of Southern Africa with which the European world came increasingly in contact in the last quarter of the century. The pattern was the same: responsibility for the education of the 'natives' was left to the missionaries

2. A Gide, 1930, pp. 217–18.

who established schools and, with a mixture of cajolery, threats (backed by the fleeting presence of expeditionary forces), commercial lures, in addition to a variety of unassailable demonstrations of the superior advancement of the culture of the proselytizers, succeeded in filling their schools with eager to reluctant schoolchildren. The nature of missionary education which was provided for this harvest of children requires no reiteration but it must not be imagined that the process of cultural reorientation was applied to captive pupils alone. From the Cape to The Gambia the routine differed only in details:

> two Natal musicians, Mr. Ganney and Mr. A. E. Rollands, formed a Zulu choir of about 14 members who were trained to sing, instead of their own native songs, English glees, part-songs and ballads. They were considered good enough for a concert tour of South Africa and later a tour of England, where at least 5 of the members became detached from the choir and subsequently fell into disrepute by accepting the more attractive wages offered in the music-halls of London. Nothing further is known about the Zulu Choir of 1892, but it was the forerunner of many African choirs which in more recent years have given excellent renderings of European choral works.[3]

This event probably owed something to the fact that two years before, Durban's exotic musical appetite had been whetted by the invasion of a troupe of black singers from the United States who had delighted the audiences with their 'unaccompanied renderings of the old favourites, "My Old Kentucky Home", "Old black Joe", "Jingle bells" ... and the richness especially of genuine negro voices after so many poor imitations ...'[4]

The author was obviously unaware of the irony of this undertaking, for earlier, he had written the following on the musical career of yet another Durbanite:

> William Swift's musical activities extended to musical research, which took him in his spare time to Zulu kraals where he listened to native songs, afterwards playing them himself on a violin which he always took with him on his wanderings. Some of the twenty-four songs he had collected in this way he sang at concerts where they were crudely described as 'kaffir songs'.[5]

The 'kaffir songs' which Mr Swift rendered to elegant European gatherings in the salons of Durban were of course contemporaneously rendered in environments of the most profoundly contrasting physical, spiritual, economic and social significance. For the Kuyu people (Central Africa), similar songs would be an invocation of the life-force of the community, such as the rituals of planting and harvesting, death and fertility. (It may of course be safely assumed that few Europeans ever succeeded in collecting

3. G. S. Jackson, 1970, p. 117.
4. ibid.
5. ibid., p. 50.

the truly sacred songs of such peoples.) But the role and social function of music is what is of fundamental interest here, for it is through music, more than any form of art, that the *lived* cultural reality of the peoples is most readily grasped.[6] When the Kuyu, for example, performed their dusk-to-dawn sequence of song, dance and symbolic mime in the funeral ceremonies for a famed woman farmer, who was regarded as being exceptionally proficient in the cultivation of manioc (cassava), we are brought into a process of affirmation of life continuity, and even the practical evocation of economic survival for the living. The mime and lyric are consciously directed to transmitting her magical touch with plants to the living; an explosion of voice and motion simultaneously induced a catharsis for the entire community, purged them of their grief and strengthened them for the continuing struggle for survival. Such music went beyond mere 'song'.

But music did not minister only to the mysterious and the profound. Oratory, her twin-sister, has always, in any community, constituted a favourite medium of formal, social exchanges, including political arrangements and the administration of justice. Its role in warfare hardly requires emphasis. The combination of music and oratory in formal judicial structures may, however, be regarded as being yet another property of cultures in which music is not simply an isolated activity of society, but an integral one. The Idoma of north-eastern Nigeria employed a tradition of judicial processes which utilized a semi-choric pattern within a predominantly theatrical setting. Against a background of choric responses the contestants presented their cases like formal actors, moving out of the human, semicircular backcloth and merging into the mass again. Gestures were deliberately theatrical, fully measured even for incongruous effects. The process would last two days to a week. A litigation among the Watutsi involved similar theatricalities. A scene from the Bambala people described by A. P. Merriam provides a typical glimpse of the attitude of the people towards the colonial hovering presence, one which increasingly gathered all reins of social control in its hands. This reality of contemporary life was formalized in a variety of ways in the cultural repertory, but never allowed to dominate the actual operations of the idiom:

FIRST PARTY: I was in my house and would have liked to stay. But he has come and wants to discuss the matter in public. So I have left my house and that is why you see me here. (*sings*) 'I am like a cricket. I would like to sing, but the wall of earth that surrounds me prevents me. Someone has forced me to come out of my hole, so I will sing.' Let us debate the things, but slowly, slowly, otherwise we will have to go before the tribunal of the white people. You have forced me to come. When the sun has set, we shall still be here debating. (*sings*) 'I am like the dog that stays before the door until he gets a bone.'

6. J. H. Nketia, 1975, pp. 21–4.

OPPONENT: Nobody goes both ways at the same time. You have told this and that. One of the two must be wrong. That is why I am attacking you. (*sings*) 'A thief speaks with another thief. It is because you are bad that I attack you.'[7]

In spite of tendencies towards romanticization, racial extravagance and other forms of sentiment and bias, it is impossible to deny the larger truth of claims on behalf of music in the lives of the African peoples. According to a contemporary Shona musician:

> Much of African history has been handed down ... in song. [As you play *mbira* and sing] you can see the panoramic scenes of those bygone days and the vague dreamy figures of the past come into ... focus in the modern time ... You can almost see your ancestors limping towards the living world again ...[8]

What has been written about the griot in Malian, Senegalese, Gambian and Guinean societies, not merely as the leaven of social occasions, but as recorder, historian, cultural formalist of society, is more than applicable also to the Shona musician, whose instruments, the *mbira*, inspired the comments quoted above. The griot has been amply celebrated in the epic of a slave's descendant who returned from the United States in the last decade to trace his Gambian ancestry.[9] To move from the griot's home in the Western Sudan southwards to Central and Southern Africa is to encounter his counterpart and the epic of his survival in a phase of even greater violence and instability. Even for Southern Africa with its history of epic empire-building and its attendant warfare and violent subjugations, the five decades across the turn of the century were singularly insecure for the inhabitants and recorded numerous violent dispersals.

The *mbira* survived this culture-fragmenting process; indeed it succeeded in creating an identity of culture among its practitioners, with all its social structures of the religious and the secular. Part of the consequences of the violent movements of the Shona peoples between the Cape and Central Africa is that it is now difficult to say how much of their musical instrumentation – and indeed the social functions of their music – were carried into or came from the neighbouring countries of Mozambique, Northern Rhodesia (now Zambia), Tanganyika (now Tanzania), the Congos (now Zaire and Congo), and Uganda where the practice was widespread, into Southern Rhodesia (now Zimbabwe) where the majority of the Shona gradually became concentrated at the turn of the century. (See Fig. 8.1.) What is beyond dispute, however, is that the *mbira* culture became a unifying bond among the scattered peoples and survived their constant and intensive fragmentation.

Mbira music was considered by the Shona a gift of their great common

7. Collected by A. P. Merriam, quoted in R. Brandel, 1961, pp. 39–40.
8. E. Majuru, quoted by P. Berliner, 1978, p. 133.
9. A. Haley, 1976.

ancestral spirit Chaminuka who appears to have been a living person, a king in the early part of the nineteenth century. The music entered wholly into social life, penetrating it so thoroughly that it became indispensable to the various activities of healing, weddings, funerals, field labour, birth, initiations and a host of other social undertakings. The *mbira* instrument itself was held 'capable of projecting its sound to heaven and linking up with the world of spirits' and therefore, in effect, linked the activities and the thoughts of the living with the presence of their ancestors.

The performers were both settled and itinerant; they did not always wait upon invitations, although notable *mbira* players have been hired from distances of hundreds of miles either for their sheer artistic reputation, or because their style of playing was considered best suited to a desired end – usually the successful possession of a medium. It can be observed that a culturally cohesive community was maintained in this way, across geographical boundaries. The night-long *bira* ceremonies which moved early into the possession of the medium, thereafter into the purely social pleasures of dancing, singing, poetic (including comic) recitals and mimicry, have been aptly described as 'a long, communal journey through the night'. The possessed medium would also, on regaining normality, pronounce judgments on disputes, advise on matters of common interest – planting, harvesting, even politics.

A footnote to the internal evolution of musical cultures in Africa is happily provided by the ubiquitous *mbira*. The instrument itself, a plucked board which was set in its classic form within a gourd, has, naturally, a hundred variants. The principal form was the *mbira huru dzadzima* which was considered the '*mbira* of all ancestors', being the instrument of the great ancestor himself, Chaminuka. It was this form which the Shona brought into the Transvaal during the southward drive of the Ndebele towards the end of the nineteenth century, shortly before they again fled northwards as the Europeans commenced their own push into the interior. The same version was employed by the Venda and Lemba in South Africa, and the Karanga of the southern parts of Northern Rhodesia during the same period. Altogether, the *dzadzima* had enjoyed a prominence of at least half a century since it was first described and appeared in the drawing published by Charles and David Livingstone in 1865.

However, a rival cult, the *mashawe*, was introduced into Shonaland early in the twentieth century, using the *njira* version of the *mbira*. Within a decade this version had begun to gain ascendancy. With its frequent accompaniment of drums, even flutes, the *njira* began to attract preference especially for social occasions such as weddings, births, etc. Adherents of both schools even took their names from their instruments – the vaMbira for the *dzadzima*, the Njanja for the adherents of *njira*. This ethnic division became marked also in a geographical dispersal, affecting social usages in subtle variations but without breaking up the overall unity of the Mbira culture.

548

The diaries of missionaries and adventurers alike confirm also the *emotional* quality experienced by the *mbira* society. Such reports liken the sound of its playing to that of the zither, the harpsichord and the spinet.[10] The singing, from similar accounts, suggests something of the emotional ambiance of the Portuguese *fado* which, significantly, was the music of the homesick Portuguese colonists in South America; the experience of displacement would appear to produce recognizable musical correspondences in any language.

Unlike a number of other forms of African social music, *mbira* was no court art but a true music of the people, of the entire scattered communities. That its practitioners were so highly respected within the community and their work so valued is explained by the fact that they were regarded as the people's artistic medium with the other world. Moreover, they were accessible, professional and became a symbol of ethnic cohesion during a period of violent upheavals. And such was the mastery of the artists over their forms that in spite of the predictable early hostility, even the missions were eventually won over. In the 1920s, *mbira* instruments had begun to trickle into church orchestration in Southern Rhodesia. Experimental compositions, based on *mbira* melodies, had crept into the missions' seasonal festivals, and schoolchildren no longer faced certain expulsion for plucking the 'devil's instrument' at playtime.

In or out of the mission compound, however, the socially integrating role of music remained the strongest feature of cultural life on the continent. As spiritual medium or as social entertainer, as historian or even as court retainer ministering to a privileged class, the musician was a vital feature of the cultural devices.

The theatrical arts

The theatrical arts were, in most instances, an extension or elaboration of the musical; some of the examples already given above demonstrate quite effectively how difficult it is to draw the dividing line. However, as the theatrical arts evolved in the nineteenth century through contact with outside influences, they do offer, more specifically than in music, evidence of the processes of transposition from traditional to adaptive modes. The West African coast truly dramatizes the situation, shifting forms and localization under the double assault of Islamic structures and Christian evangelizing, the latter being in turn supported by the influence of returnee slaves in Sierra Leone and Liberia, who brought with them the entertainment forms of their countries of exile, their manners, values, costumes, and idioms.[11]

10. P. Berliner, 1978, p. 41.
11. J. H. Kopytoff, 1965, pp. 86–133; J. F. A. Ajayi, 1965, pp. 25–52; R. W. July, 1968, pp. 177–95.

Throughout the nineteenth century, theatrical professionalism was a way of life in the old Oyo empire in Nigeria, representing the evolution of secular theatre from masked representation during the funeral rites of a king. The disintegration of the empire under the assaults of the Fulani from the north, and the ravages of civil war with rebellious dependencies to the south, led simultaneously to the spread of the professional troupes to the south and across the borders to Dahomey (now Benin), and to its demise in its place of origin. The victorious Muslims banned most forms of theatrical performances, and most definitely the genre represented in festivals of the ancestors whose representation of human figures was anathema in the Muslim religion.

The disruption of political life in Oyo, where the troupes had enjoyed the protection of a stable monarchy, did not long enhance the further dissemination (and secularization) of theatre. For by then, the missionaries had begun their own northward drive from the first footholds on the coast, usually only a few steps ahead of arms-backed commercial companies.[12] They completed the task which Islam had begun by forbidding their adherents membership of any cult. These theatre companies were run like family guilds, with the familiar practice of trade secrets and initiatory rites; their material was also firmly rooted in the traditional – all of which qualified them for definition as devilish, sinister cults. The Christian missionaries, like the Muslims, did not content themselves with banning only the performances. Like the *mbira* in Southern Africa, instruments which were associated with such theatre arts were banished with equal vigour. A vacuum was thus created into which the returnee slaves' culture neatly stepped. The slave trade had been instrumental to the process of religious conversion on the west coast even as it proved detrimental to cultural life, as manifested, in the affected societies. The missionary compounds and spheres of influence, just as in Southern Africa, guaranteed some measure of safety, so did submission to the Muslim overlords: the price of safety was inevitable renunciation of authentic art. Now the cycle of cultural substitution began to close: having broken up the cultural life of the people, the slave era, now in its dying phase, brought back the sons of the land with a new culture in place of the old.[13]

Victory was not so simple, however. 'Pagan' theatre withstood the onslaught, not only preserving its forms but turning itself consciously into a base of resistance against Christian culture. So durable had it proved that it was to participate, in various forms, in experimentations which the colonial elite now embarked upon for a meaningful theatre. For now, as the century entered its last three decades, the west coast came under the creative influence of these returnee Christians, confident in the superiority of their acquired arts, eager to prove to the white colonials who now

12. E. A. Ayandele, 1966, pp. 29–70, 117–23.
13. J. F. A. Ajayi, 1965, pp. 126–65.

controlled their existence that the black man was capable not only of receiving, but of practising the refined arts of the European. There was only one fortunate complication: despite this conscious drive which made them cut themselves off culturally from the indigenous peoples of the hinterland, the latter remained 'comfortably and firmly attached to their own customs and institutions'.[14]

The direction of new (Euro-American) forms of theatrical activity followed an eastward pattern, initiated largely by expatriate life in Liberia, Senegal, and Sierra Leone. As it moved eastward, however, it received ever-increasing blood transfusions. The bastardized vaudeville of the 'Nova Scotians', a self-appellation of the returnees of Sierra Leone, did enjoy a long run along the coast. However, its arrival in the more easterly countries of the Gold Coast, Dahomey, and Nigeria, brought about its transformation both in form and content. It is not an exaggeration to claim that, by the first decade of the twentieth century, a completely new form of theatre had achieved distinct form in West Africa: the 'concert party'. Its progenitor was a 'genteel' breed which catered for the middle-class population of the capital cities along the west coast:[15] the robust, even bawdy slapstick with its generous lardings of stevedore songs which had been refined for concerts at which the colonial aristocracy of the administrative centres might be present.

'Academies' were formed for the performance of concerts which were modelled on the Victorian music hall or the American vaudeville. The Christian churches organized their own concerts, schools were drawn into the concert rage – prize-giving days, visit of the district officer, Queen Victoria's birthday, etc. The black missionaries refused to be outdone – the Reverend Samuel Ajayi Crowther was a famous example; a black prelate prominent in the patronage and encouragement of this form of the arts, while the Reverend James Johnson turned the famous Breadfruit Church in Lagos into a springboard for theatrical performances.[16] The Brazilian returnees added an exotic yet familiar flavour, their music finding a ready echo in the traditional melodies of the west coast and the Congo whose urban suppression had not occurred long enough for such melodies to be totally forgotten. Christmas and New Year at the turn of the century, and in the first decades of the twentieth, witnessed the streets of the capital cities of Freetown and Lagos transformed by mini-pageants reminiscent of Latin fiestas, of which the *caretta*, a kind of satyr masquerade,[17] appears to have been the most durable.

Cultural nationalism was, however, constantly at work countering a total

14. R. W. July, 1968.

15. B. Traoré, 1972, Ch. II; O. Ogunba and A. Irele (eds), 1978.

16. J. F. A. Ajayi, 1965, pp. 206–38; R. W. July, 1968, pp. 196–207; E. A. Ayandele, 1966, pp. 175–238.

17. The possibility also exists that the *caretta* was the Hispanicized form of the 'Gelede' masque, now reimported to its original home from South America.

PLATE 21.3 *Bishop Samuel Ajayi Crowther (1808–91), photographed while on a visit to Benin City, with three local Africans and their gods*

usurpation by imported forms.[18] Once again religion and its institutions provided the base. Unable to accept the excesses of the Christian cultural imperialism such as the embargo on African instruments and tunes in a 'universal' Church, the breakaway movements began. From 1882 to the early 1930s a proliferation of secessionist movements took place mostly inspired by a need to worship God in the cultural mode of their fore-fathers.[19] And now commenced also a unique 'operatic' tradition in West Africa, but especially Lagos, beginning with church cantatas and moving to the dramatization of biblical stories until it asserted its independence in secular stories and the development of professional touring troupes. The process is identical with the evolution of the Agbegijo Theatre – then temporarily effaced – from the sacred funeral rites of the Alafin of Oyo to court entertainment and, thereafter, independent existence and geographi-cal expansion. From the general concerts of classical music and English folk songs by the 'Academy' of the 1880s to the historical play *King Elejigbo* of the Egbe Ife Church Dramatic Society in 1902, a transformation of thought and sensibility had recognizably taken place even among the Westernized elite of Southern Nigeria. The Church did not take kindly to it. It closed its churchyards and schools to the evolving art. Alas, it only succeeded in accelerating the defiant erection of theatre halls, specifically designed for the performing arts. It was in reality a tussle between groups of colonial elites, fairly balanced in the matter of resources. By 1912 the secularization of theatrical entertainment was sufficiently complete for the colonial ad-ministration of Lagos to gazette a 'Theatre and Public Performance Regulations Ordinance' which required that performing groups obtain a licence before going before the public. In the climate of cultural nationalism which obtained in Lagos at that time, it is doubtful whether this ruse at political censorship would have worked; it is significant that the ordinance was never enacted.

The 'vaudeville' troupes prospered. Names of groups such as we encounter in 'Two Bobs and their Carolina Girl' of the Gold Coast tell us something of the inspiration of much of these. Teacher Yalley, a school-master, is credited with having begun the tradition of the 'vaudeville' variety act in the Gold Coast.[20] His pupil Bob Johnson and his 'Axim Trio' soon surpassed the master and became a familiar figure on the Gold Coast cultural landscape, and indeed along the west coast.[21] More important still, Bob Johnson's innovation must be credited with having given birth to the tradition of the 'concert party' of the Gold Coast, groups which specialize in variety routine – songs, jokes, dances, impersonations, comic scenes. But the most notable achievement in the sense of cultural

18. On cultural nationalism, with particular reference to Nigeria, see J. Hatch, 1971, Ch. XII; F. A. O. Schwarz Jnr, 1965, Chs I, II, IV.

19. B. C. Ray, 1976, Ch. VI; see also Chapter 20 above.

20. J. C. de Graft, 1976.

21. E. Sutherland, 1970.

continuity was their thrusting on to the forestage of contemporary repertoire a stock character from traditional lore – the wily trickster *Ananse* (the spider). This dramatic form quickly developed into a vehicle for social and political commentary, apart from its prolificity for pure comic situations.

By the mid-1930s, Bob Johnson had become sufficiently established to take his brand of vaudeville to other West African cities. West Africa in this decade could boast of a repertoire of shows displaying the most bizarre products of eclectic art in the history of theatre. Even cinema, an infant art, had by then left its mark on West African theatre – some of Bob Johnson's acts were adaptations of Charlie Chaplin's escapades, not omitting his costume and celebrated shuffle. And the thought of Empire Day celebration concerts at which songs like 'Mini the Moocher' formed part of the evening musical recitals, side by side with 'God's Gospel in our Heritage' and vignettes from the life of a Liberian stevedore, stretches the contemporary imagination, divorced today from the historical realities of colonial West Africa.

Again, another irony of colonial intentions. While Bob Johnson was preparing his first West African tour and Hubert Ogunde, later to become Nigeria's foremost 'concert party' leader was undergoing his aesthetic formation from the vying forces of a clergyman father and a grandmother priestess of the *osugbo* cult,[22] in Senegal, a European educationist, Charles Beart, was beginning to reverse the policy of European acculturation in a leading secondary school in Senegal. The extent of this development – including also an appreciation of the slow pace of such an evolution – will be better grasped by recalling the educational character of assimilationism, spelt in diverse ways by the publications of such dedicated African Francophiles as the Abbé Boilat, Paul Holle, etc. Boilat, in spite of proofs of extensive sociological research,[23] the result of his examination of the culture, philosophy, social structure, languages, etc., of the Bambara, Sarakole, Wolof, Serer, Tukulor and Moorish groups in Senegal, found no lessons to be drawn from African society for a modern cultural development, no future but to witness 'the fall of all those gross, if not dishonorable, ways known as *the custom of the country*'. If his addresses to the metropolitan centre of the French world did not become the cornerstone of French assimilationist policies, they undoubtedly played a key role in their formulation.

It was against this background, and ensuing decades of such conservatism, that the Ecole William Ponty was born and enjoyed a prolonged existence.[24] A famous teachers' college, it served Francophone Africa in the same way as did Achimota College in Anglophone West, and Makerere College in East Africa. They were all designed to provide a basic European education for would-be teachers and low-echelon civil servants. Such

22. See M. A. Fadipe, 1970, Chapter VII.
23. A. Boilat, 1853.
24. B. I. Obichere in J. L. Balans, C. Coulon and A. Ricard (eds), 1972, pp. 7–18.

554

cultural education as came into the curriculum of Ecole William Ponty was of necessity French – French plays, poetry, music, art, history, sociology. Beart, however, during his principalship embarked on a new orientation of the students' cultural instructions. From 1930 onwards the students received encouragement to return to their own societies for cultural directions. Assignments were given which resulted in the students' exploration of both the form and substance of indigeous art. Groups from every colonial territory represented at William Ponty were then expected to return from vacation, armed with a theatrical presentation based on their researches, the entire direction being left in the hands of the students themselves. Since the new theatrical sociology did not confine itself to the usual audiences of European officials and 'educated' Africans nor to Senegal alone, its influence spread widely through different social strata of Francophone Africa. Was it, however, an authentic development of the culture from which it derived?

The answer must be in the negative, though the experiment was not without its instructive value. It would be too much to expect that, at that period, the 'classic' model of French theatre could yield completely to the expression of traditional forms. The 'community' represented by William Ponty was an artificial one. It was distanced from the society whose cultural hoards it rifled both in qualitative thought and in cultural ends. The situation was of course not peculiar to William Ponty but was common to the other schools and institutions set up by the colonizer for the fulfilment of his own mission in Africa. Thus the theatre of William Ponty served the needs of exotic satisfaction for the community of French colonials. Even when it 'went to the people', and with their own material, it remained a curiosity that left the social life and authentic cultural awareness of the people untouched.

The literary renaissance in Egypt[25]

In the sphere of literary culture, Egypt and the Western Sudan provide instances in the first case of literary renaissance and in the second of both direct and indirect mutual assistance in the cultural penetration of Africa during the colonial period by basically contending interests.

Napoleon Bonaparte's occupation of Egypt, Muḥammad 'Alī's reforms in the military, social and economic fields, his sending of educational missions to Europe, especially France, and the establishment of a printing press in Bulaq in 1822 paved the way for the beginning of a new relationship between two worlds – the West and the Islamic East – and ushered in a new age in Egypt. This preparatory stage in Egypt's literary renaissance was accelerated during the reign of Khedive Ismā'īl (1863–79) and reached the

25. This section on the literary renaissance in Egypt (pp. 555–7) was contributed by Professor Y. A. Talib of the Department of Malay Studies, University of Singapore, Singapore (Ed.).

high road of decisive development from the latter half of the nineteenth century onwards.

The creation of a necessary environment for the flowering of a modern Arabic culture was brought about by several factors. The first was the continued migration from the 1870s onwards of largely Christian Libano-Syrian intellectuals[26] into Egypt escaping the autocratic rule of the Ottomans and imbued with ideas on politics, science and literature adopted from the West. Within Egypt itself, among the Muslims, a new elite group emerged, filled with the Islamic modernist views of Al-Afghani and 'Abduh. literary and intellectual renaissance'.[27] However, local literary output was Europe exposed to a programme of studies with a humanistic bias, providing several crops of writers with varied viewpoints and interests.

The economic development and transformation of the country as well as the establishment and founding of academies, learned societies, a national library in 1870, the secular universities, the reforming of existing religious ones (e.g. Al-Azhar) and the creation of a modern system of education 'gave birth to a public endowed with leisure, education and interest to form an audience. The result measured against the situation preceding it was a truly literary and intellectual renaissance.'[27] However, local literary output was still heavily reliant on the translation of European works, undertaken before the establishment of the British Protectorate over Egypt and continuing to flourish under it. In time, this gave way to adaptations and imitations and finally creative works of originality.

This cultural awakening coupled with the changing political climate of Egypt towards the end of the nineteenth century was reflected in the very extensive development of the press. By 1898, there were already 169 papers and journals in existence with their numbers increasing to 282 in 1913.[28] Under the influence of the eminent Muslim reformer Al-Afghani,[29] the periodical press was widely acclaimed as an educating or politicizing instru-

26. Among these émigrés, three personalities were largely responsible for acquainting their reading public with the main currents of eighteenth- and nineteenth-century French and British liberal and scientific thought – Farah Antun (1874–1922), founder of the review *Al-Jamiah*; Yagub Sarruf (1852–1927), editor of the widely read review *Al-Muqtataf* which served as an instrument for the popularization of Darwinian and Spencerian theories of evolution; and Jurji Zaidan, a prolific writer on a variety of subjects, and who especially through his review – *Al-Hilāl* – educated entire generations, not only in Egypt but equally in the Arab East.

Of the Muslim authors, Fathi Zaghlūl was the most prominent, who introduced western political thought and sociology through his translations of such works as Bentham's *Principles of Legislation*, Rousseau's *Social Contract* and Edmond Demolin's *A quoi tient la supériorité des Anglo-Saxons*, into Arabic. He had a worthy successor in the person of Lutfi Al-Sayyid, editor of the daily *Al-Jaridah* and 'Apostle of Liberalism and Utilitarianism in Egypt'. For details see J. M. Ahmed, 1960; A. Hourani, 1962.

27. N. Safran, 1961, p. 57.

28. M. Zwemer in J. R. Matt (ed.), 1914, p. 129.

29. See A. A. Kudsi-Zadeh, 1980, pp. 47–55.

ment. It became increasingly the preferred media of expression for a whole generation of literary personalities as well as intellectual leaders after the First World War. Thus, newspapers equally became vehicles for experimentation with new literary forms such as the short story, the drama, etc. The need to express and interpret the newly acquired foreign ideas led to the evolution of a 'neo-classical Arabic'.

But the controversy produced – whether to reform classical Arabic or to evolve a modern Arabic appropriate for contemporary Egyptian literature – became a bone of contention between two groups, the classicists and the modernists. The former were in favour of a 'recondite style, studded with obscurities and graced with literary allusion and erudite wit typical of courtly culture'. The latter whose members were primarily of Syrian-Lebanese migrant stock, adherents of the Christian faith, with a Western-educational background, opted for a 'simple direct language, accommodating colloquial and Arabised foreign words'.

Looming large in the ensuing cultural conflict was the question of values – Western ideals and norms versus traditional Islamic concepts. In its initial phase, this struggle of ideas was essentially given to an arduous acquisition of ideas from the West or merely being indifferent to it. Confrontations of opposing attitudes were in the form of cultural skirmishes and lacked 'coherent centres of gravitation'. However, in the first half of the twentieth century, the external cultural challenge as presented by the new conditions of life was keenly felt in all aspects of the traditional value system. The first and vital response to this challenge was concentrated on the issue of power – between a militant reformist Islam and a rational liberal movement.[30] Egypt's cultural and national identity were given various interpretations – the Pharaonic-Mediterranean by such literary figures as Tewfik al-Hakim, Mahmuh Taymur and Taha Husayn in their various social, literary and historical writings,[31] the Arabism of al-Kawakibi[32] as well as the underplaying of Egypt's African cultural dimensions by most members of the literati until the emergence of Nasserism.

This transformation of culture in Egypt under foreign rule during this period led to a greater political awareness that later found expression in the nascent nationalist movement.

Literary culture in the Western Sudan

It would appear that basically contending interests penetrated the Western Sudan zone of West Africa during the colonial period, the colonial or

30. Especially the violent controversies aroused by polemical works written by the western-oriented authors, e.g. Taha Husayn, *Fi'l-shi'r al-Jahili*, Cairo, 1926 (on pre-Islamic poetry), which questioned the foundations of the Islamic faith.

31. See notably, Taha Husayn, *The Future of Culture in Egypt*, Cairo, 1938 (English translation 1954).

32. As expressed in his work, *Umm al-gura*, Port Said, 1899.

European and the Muslim represented by the Dyula. The conditions for this resided in the social structure of the people of the Western Sudan. The traditional caste system of the Western Sudanese, which recognized the authority of skilled craft groups over the related materials and geographical territory of their craft and its practice, accorded to the *iman* or *alim* (Islamic intructor) a monopoly of authority over the province of literacy, writing and communication, and also indirectly over commercial relations that developed with European colonialism.

Historically, the *alim* was himself the agent of a unique community. This was a distinct, often dominant cultural unit scattered among the non-Muslim peoples of Western Sudan and was characterized by its religion and efficient commercial organization. They were called the Dyula. The Dyula's penetration into the countries of the Western Sudan had commerce for its basic end; their immigration into towns such as Bobo-Dioulasso, Kong, Bonduku, and so on, followed the trade patterns from gold sources in the Gold Coast, Upper Volta and other mines in the tropical belt, ending along the caravan trails of the Sahara.[33] Not only did they establish towns, they also created urban outposts which formed links from the major centres to the Sahara trails. The Dyula (a name which itself described their main occupation, trade) were, however, equally concerned with the preservation and promotion of their Islamic culture and served as the link for further Moorish and Arabic penetration into the rain-belts of the west coast. Records exist still of the 'sabbaticals' of the Dyula learned man, the *karamoko* – a higher state of achievement than the more common *alim* – who visited centres of learning in Cairo and left learned legal judgments in their courts (a returned compliment of the same order as that of William Amo, the Ghanaian ex-slave who delivered philosophical treatises at the universities of Wittenberg and Jena in Germany in the eighteenth century).[34]

And while admittedly the literary culture of Islam which penetrated areas of West Africa was largely conservative, rhetorical and stereotyped, its methodology consisting of learning by rote rather than by recognition, its content restricted essentially to Islamic exegesis and the Law (*hadith* and *fiqh*), the continuing movement of scholars between the west coast and North Africa and the Middle East right into the twentieth century, the valuable trade in manuscripts which flourished side by side with the more mundane material of Dyula commerce, testify to the more inquiring nature of Arabic scholarship among its African adherents. Historical writings owe as much to the Arabic scholars as to their counterparts of the Europeanized coastal towns or émigré products of Western literacy. For instance, a survey of the libraries of mallams of the west coast, largely around the Ivory Coast in 1920, revealed manuscripts which covered history,

33. For details about the Dyula see Y. Person, 1968–75, Volume I, pp. 95–122; Y. Person in M. Crowder (ed.), 1971, pp. 113–26.
34. For details, see W. Abraham (ed.), 1964; N. Lochner, 1958.

language (Arabic grammar), poetry, mathematics, logic, jurisprudence, etc.[35]

The existence of a literary culture, even of a tiny educated elite at the pyramidal tip of a non-literary mass has enormous consequences not merely for the majority group but for the alien culture from whose canons the literary equipment of that cone is derived. And most especially when that literary advantage is fostered in the proselytizing service of the alien culture. The experience of Islam was therefore different only in quality, not in results from the Euro-Christian incursion into the culture of the indigenous peoples. The event of *two* literacies from historically opposing cultures meeting on a 'passive' terrain provokes intensified devices from both groups, and more especially from the first arrival which sees its carefully nurtured field invested, literally on the eve of harvest. Both factions of course ignore, or are prepared to deny, the previous existence of authentic values of the contested ground, conveniently presuming it a cultural vacuum. The syncretic tolerance of African cultural systems naturally lent credence to this presumption and, ironically, of the two contestants, it was the culture which itself displayed some of this syncretic possibility – the Islamic – which lost the great element of its own orthodoxy – including the 'orthodoxies' of later schisms – in the seemingly accommodative passivity of the indigenous people.

We have already commented on some devices employed by the 'autochthones' against the mechanisms of cultural negation employed by European colonialism; the Islamic culture, in the proselytizing polity of the Dyula, was to encounter the same resistance. In some cases, the Dyula community became thoroughly assimilated into the local community. Such instances of total assimilation were rare, but I. Wilks, in his informative study,[36] points to one example – the Tagara of Jirapa in north-western Ghana. The process was insidious enough. As already discussed in the case of the funeral rites of the Koumina canton, the Africans retained their custodianship of land, both physically and ritualistically, so that while, in the towns, contacts with the French and Islamic 'civilizing' missions, demonstrated undeniable advantage for the converts, the seasonal 'commuting' between land and city itself displaced 'unsecured' groups and individuals. Such was the fate of the Dyula.

It should be recalled additionally that, as colonialism became an organized fact and industries mushroomed in the cities, migrants from the Islamic far north (Mali, Mauritania) joined the labour force of the southern city centres. This movement attracted the ministration of the *'ulamā'* or *karamoko* who soon became established within the city community. In keeping with the strategy of Islamic renewal or reinvigoration, the Dyula tried to maintain constant contact between the Muslim communities by dispatching the *'ulama'* to communities which had began to show evidence

35. I. Wilks in J. Goody (ed.), 1968.
36. ibid., p. 165.

of backsliding. This demand on their services overstretched the available custodians of the true way. Moreover, they were often unwilling to leave the ease of the cities with the built-up prestige – which came from recognition as 'leaders of thought' through their role as intermediaries between the migrant labour and the *toubab* (white man) as rudimentary accountants for the new middlemen of produce companies. To go and minister to some rural community of the Dyula became an imposition. Often it was not even the Dyula on behalf of whom the appeal was made. The value of literacy held a tremendous appeal to the non-Muslims and, frequently, the rural village, or perhaps a local chief or farmer would make an appeal to the local Dyula for an instructor. The local bright hope sometimes became a peripatetic scholar, moving from *'ulamā'* to *'ulamā'*. The prestige of the educated elite – largely Islamic – in these areas in the nineteenth century, was coveted by many. A good pupil could go up in grades, graduating to the *karamoko*, in possession of his own *isnad* or chain of learning, linking him backwards through illustrious, legendary scholars possibly to the Prophet himself. Cheik Hamidou Kane in his beautiful work, *Ambiguous Adventure*,[37] captures this atmosphere of the conquest of a 'pagan' type by the aesthetics of Islamic teaching in a locality of the Western Sudan.

Not all the West African Westernized authors at the time were prepared to see the Muslim cultural challenge as necessarily opposed to the true genius of the African or indeed as incompatible with the Christian values then feverishly expanding through missionary stations set up by black converts along the Niger, the Volta and the Senegal. For sociologists and educationists like the Abbé Boillat (or his gallant compatriot, the scholar-soldier Paul Holle), Arabic language and Islamic culture deserved study preferably in higher institutions in France where they would leave no contaminating influence on impressionable Africans. Bishop Samuel Ajayi Crowther of Nigeria went further and was prepared to have them studied and taught.[38] It might even lead, through the translation of the Bible and catechism into Arabic, to an amelioration of the 'grosser aspects' of Islamic beliefs and society.

The St Thomas-born West Indian, Edward Wilmot Blyden, who migrated and settled in Liberia, however, was of the firm conviction that Islamic culture was, of all the major civilizations of the world, best suited to the temperament and cultural realities of the African. Islam was for him only a component – albeit a major one – in the reformulation of an African culture for the African, with its own guaranteeing structures and institutions.[39] This forerunner of *négritude* believed in nothing less than a complete reorientation of African education from its Eurocentric bias to a more African-attuned direction. Muslim-Arabic civilization, which had impressed him with its 'literary cultivation and intellectual activity' was to

37. C. H. Kane, 1972.
38. R. W. July, 1968, pp. 188–9.
39. ibid., pp. 46–7, 218–19.

play a major role in this. Tracing the history of the black man backwards into antiquity, Blyden published his findings on the prior existence of a black civilization in Egypt, established Herodotus as a more worthwhile commentator than later European annotators who, apart from being 'not contemporary' to the events described, had prostituted their scholarship by racist preconceptions.[40]

But it was not merely history in antiquity which formed the main material of Blyden's fight for the African's cultural reorientation. Recent events in the history of the African, the extension of his culture and genius even into a disadvantaged environment in the 'New World' prompted Blyden to examine the history books and declare that the history of European figures such as Admiral Nelson be discarded for the history of black heroes such as Toussaint L'Ouverture. This was revolutionary, even dangerous talk; it meant the commencement of a new school of analysis of much in Africa's recent experience and went down even worse than his championing of the study of Arabic language and culture in West African systems of education, especially in Blyden's proposed university. Not surprisingly, such a university never became a reality in his lifetime, but the evidence we have today is that this West African 'returnee', versed thoroughly as he was in Western traditions, was the direct catalyst of the break-up of the Christian missionary monolith on the West African coast. For, on 2 January 1891, he gave a speech to a crowded audience in the assembly hall of the Breadfruit Church in Lagos, stressing the incompatibility of European ecclesiasticism with the society and traditions of the African. A few months later, again in Lagos, the first schism occurred in the 'orthodox' Breadfruit Church, giving birth to the United Native African Church, with consequences – as already described – for the cultural life of the African as the movement spread westwards and northwards of West Africa.[41]

Literature in European languages

Literary culture in European languages in West and Central Africa may be said to have constituted the highest force of colonial confrontation. Oral literature retained its place as a satirical outlet, so did mime, dance and innovations in masquerade forms to take note of and make commentaries on the colonial phenomenon. But it was the colonial language literatures in journalistic form and in poetry, drama and the novel, which mobilized the literary imagination in the service of anti-colonialism.[42] The West African coast, from Liberia to Lagos, nourished the pamphlet industry on a scale that is comparable to eighteenth-century England. So did Kenya although, in the East African case, this appeared to have been largely in the hands of the Asian community, as were most of the journals. The brief tract, cheaply

40. E. W. Blyden, 1887.
41. J. F. A. Ajayi, 1965, pp. 254–5; E. A. Ayandele, 1966, pp. 201–3.
42. See C. H. Kane, 1972; M. Beti, 1971; A. K. Armah, 1973; W. E. G. Sekyi, 1915.

printed and easily disseminated, launched tirades against foreign domination and exploitation, against acts of deceit by the colonial administration
and the ever-increasing encroachments on the life style and social dignity
of the peoples. Portuguese Luanda for its part obtained its first printing
press in 1841 and with it the commencement of active journalism in the
championing of the Africans' cause. It was a period remarked for its stylistic
consciousness – no matter in which colonial language. Racist accusations
against French colonialism from Ahmadou Dugay Cledor of Senegal reveal
meticulous prose in flights of indignation. Petitions to the British Colonial
Office became an art, a study in diplomatic prose.

The early 'parliamentarians' – the nominees, the *assimilés* of French
administration, the spokesmen of the masses approved by the British system
as members of the so-called legislative councils – utilized the tongue of the
alien ruler to destroy his illusions over what he had presumed were captive
colonial executives. Thus, despite his genuine gratitude, even obsequious
conduct towards British audiences and potential philanthropists, a William
Grant of the *West African Reporter* could write (or permit to appear) the
following searing indictment in his journal in 1882:

> It continues to be a standing blot upon the intercourse of Europeans
> with Africa, that every steamer that comes to the coast ... brings
> in large quantities of that which is comparatively worthless to be
> exchanged for that which is valuable and useful ... If the articles given
> were simply worthless but harmless gew-gaws in exchange for articles
> of value, the morality of the transaction would even be reprehensible,
> but how much more when the articles are not only of trifling value ...
> but often positively destructive. They take home that which builds
> them up in wealth, often leaving to the African that which im-
> poverishes and destroys him. It is a sad reflection that, in many cases,
> European commerce has left its African customer as naked as it found
> him ... they will never secure a footing in Africa for their ideas of
> civilization, until the commercial relations between the high-toned,
> enlightened European and the 'savage' African, are placed upon a more
> equitable basis. But so long as demijohn follows demijohn of rum ...
> no reinforcements of missionaries and no homilies from professional
> philanthropists, on the blessing of European civilization will avail
> anything.[43]

An ardent campaigner for Africa-oriented educational reforms, Grant,
deeply influenced by Blyden, sought an educational system which had the
university at its apex but only as an institution which was designed to
provide research and teaching in fields related to Africa, as opposed to the
'conventional literary education which emphasized European culture and
values'. You must, he wrote, 'educate him [the African] by himself'. The

43. Quoted by R. W. July, 1968, p. 142.

annals of the Aborigines Rights Protection Society of the Gold Coast in the 1910s and 1920s, notably the speeches of J. E. Casely Hayford, are filled with masterpieces of Victorian prose, spiced with devastating wit of classical precision. More than a few district officers touring their pacified territories underwent the startling experience of being welcomed to a 'loyal speech' and departing in fury at the 'smooth insolence' of practised black orators in English.

In 1911 Casely Hayford also published his *Ethiopia Unbound*,[44] one of Africa's earliest novels, an attempt in a mixture of styles, ranging from caustic sarcasm to passionate indictment of the greed and racial arrogance that went into the partitioning and colonization of Africa. Casely Hayford's writings throughout his life kept permanent vigil on the fate of the black continent, a refusal to the last to accept the act of colonization or accord it authority in his own thinking. *Ethiopia Unbound* curiously did not give birth to known imitators during this period and remained in an exclusive class of its own. By contrast, however, Africa did produce scholars and literate public figures of a differing school of thought, such as Bishop Samuel Ajayi Crowther of Nigeria and Bakary Dialo of Senegal. Like the Abbé Boillat, they defended European colonialism as a positive and laudable experience for Africa. For Crowther, a Protestant theologian weighed down by the horrors of his pagan origin and society, Christianity (of which colonialism was a mere agent or enforcer) represented, in the most primitive sense, a divine instrument for the salvation of a heathen continent. Bakary Dialo was, for his part, simply overwhelmed by the virtue of French culture.

The dilemma of the product of the colonial policy of culture substitution resided principally in this alienation, and it created a wrench in the creative personality of educated Africans. Even for the most radical anti-colonials, a manifest fascination with and preference for European culture as experienced in their society, and as encountered in the expanded intellectual horizons of the individual, was often discernible in their writings. The tragedy of the gifted poet from Madagascar, Jean-Joseph Rabéarivelo (??–1937) who committed suicide through his – it was believed – failure to resolve this internal wrench in his colonial psyche, was a dramatic example. This gave a discernible ambiguous quality to the writings of many articulate Africans in the early period of colonial affirmation. It facilitated the policy of cultural assimilation, especially in the French, Portuguese and Spanish territories, resulting in the deliberate withdrawal from, even denial of the authentic sources of African creative genius by the new elite. 'Primitivism', either in inspiration or in images or idiom conversion, became evidence of backsliding; it delayed the total act of re-baptism which alone guaranteed acceptance into the magical society of the European colonial officials abroad.

Exceptions, especially notable in the settler situation that turned the policy of *assimilado* into political art were poets like Silverio Ferriera,

44. J. E. C. Hayford, 1911.

Antonio José de Nascimento and Francisco Castelbranco, whose poetry from the turn of the century denounced the racial bigotry of the settlers. But simultaneously, both in Angola as in other Portuguese territories (as indeed in *all* colonial territories), an escapist form of response to the daily reality of humiliation did evolve. An example is found in the poetry of Caetano da Costa Alegre (São Tomé) whose sentimental love lyrics, glorifying the beauty of the black woman, were published after his death[45] and may be regarded as forerunner to the literary school of black self-reclamation that became celebrated in the movement called *négritude*.

The principal midwives of *négritude* were Aimé Césaire (Martinique), Léopold Senghor (Senegal) and Leon Damas (French Guiana); the cradle was France. *Négritude* produced a flowering of poetry,[46] not all of it 'propaganda' poetry in the manner of da Costa Alegre, but one which nevertheless owed its existence to the renewed consciousness of an African reality, a recovery of which was turned into a concrete programme by the group's persuasive *prise de conscience*. It was a revolt, to summarize it quite simply, a revolt against the successful assimilative strategy of French and Portuguese colonialism, products of which the initiators of the movement realized they were. But the genesis of the movement can be attributed with justification to the 'manifesto' in one issue of the journal *Légitime Défense*, published by three students from Martinique. In this manifesto, they rejected the 'bourgeois conventions' of European culture, rejected a number of European literary models and the false personality which they imposed on the black man. As substitutes, however – and the fact best defines the cyclic trap of the colonial artist-intellectual – they adopted Marx, Freud, Rimbaud, Breton and other European mentors.

Négritude, which rounds off the period under study, held undisputed sway in the formulation of creative sensibilities for the next two decades, and not merely among the Francophone colonial writers and intellectuals but the Lusophone, and even Anglophone. Among the most uncompromising opponents of *négritude* today – convinced Marxists who hold a view of history irreconcilable with the tenets of *négritude* – are some African leaders who gave *négritude* a new lease of life in their own struggle against Portugal's *assimilado* policies in the early 1950s. Thus, it is accurate to say that *négritude* was a historical phenomenon which was called into being by a particular set of circumstances and has since lost its affective hold as those circumstances disappeared, and as society became subjected to more comprehensive forms of analysis and radical prescriptions.

45. C. da C. Alegre, 1916.
46. L. Kesteloot, 1974; A. Irele, 1964, pp. 9–11; D. S. Blair, 1976.

African politics and nationalism, 1919–35

B. O. OLORUNTIMEHIN

We need a clear understanding of the nature of nationalism in Africa for a proper appreciation of the events that will be discussed in this chapter. A preliminary point to make is the distinction between the expression of nationalism in Europe from the nineteenth century and that in colonized Africa in the period between the two world wars. Nationalism in Europe has been the expression of the desire of communities which accepted the fact of common cultural identities, coupled with a common historical past, for an independent, sovereign existence in political organizations (states) of their own. The struggle was to ensure a coincidence between the cultural nation and the organization of its political life as a state. As the Greek, Italian and German examples illustrate, what emerged from the nationalist movements were, by and large, nation-states.

In Africa, the aspirations of the states and groups which fought against European empire builders and tried to prevent the establishment of the colonial system up to the outbreak of the First World War were in essence the same as those which imbued the nationalist movements in Europe. However, one feature of the war was that it ended with the imperial lords consolidating their positions *vis-à-vis* the defenders of African independence and sovereignty. In spite of the ferment of ideas which contributed to undermining imperialism as a system, colonial rule became a *de facto* situation to the extent that some authors have referred to the inter-war period as the 'golden age' of colonialism in Africa.

Most of the colonies that had been created were made up of several culturally and historically diverse nationality groups for whom, for the most part, the fact of subjection to a common alien ruler was the main base for unity. The colonial situation represented for all a new setting in which they had to forge new identities of alien rule. In such situations colonial boundaries which in nearly all cases incorporated many cultural nations under a common imperial administration were taken as given. The forging of new identities began with the acceptance of the essential African-ness of the various cultural nations. The units of the colonial administrations represented, in practically all cases, the territorial definitions of what the

Africans began to see as proto-states around which they sought to develop in their peoples a sense of common belonging.

Political and social developments in the colonial situation were a product of the interactions between the colonizer on the one hand, and the colonized on the other. In a sense, the orientations of African leadership elites were shaped partly by the form of colonial administration. Where the administrations were regional in structure and/or policy, as in the French colonial federations, the African leaders tended to adopt a regional outlook. Hence, champions of African nationalism in the inter-war period (*wanasiasa* as they are known in Swahili) have been referred to as being primarily pan-Africanists rather than nationalists in the European sense. The point was that nationalism was taking a reverse course to the expression of the same phenomenon in Europe. Contrary to what happened in Europe, the state was created before the cultural nations that would make it a meaningful political community were welded together. It is in this sense that one should take James Coleman's observation that:

> ... the drive behind African nationalism in many instances is not the consciousness of belonging to a distinct politico-cultural unit which is seeking to protect or assert itself, but rather it is the movement of racially-conscious modernists seeking to create new political and cultural nationalities out of the heterogenous people within the artificial boundaries imposed by the European master ...[1]

We must recognize that colonialism, as a system of relations, rests upon some kind of racialism, and that since development in a colonial situation is a product of interactions between the colonizer and the colonized, racial consciousness is basic to the growth of nationalism as a search for sovereignty and independence.

That African nationalists are regarded as 'modernists' is a reflection of the fact that they were operating within an externally defined setting which imposed alien systems of values, norms, and definitions of political and social developments to which they had to subscribe as a condition for success. That nationalism in Africa is a dynamic, ongoing phenomenon is clear from the extensive literature on themes like nation-building and irredentism. Probably an accurate word for this phenomenon in Africa – as E. S. Atieno-Odhiambo shows in Chapter 26 – is the Swahili word *siasa*.

In general, colonialism requires a social base for its survival. This is usually provided through a diffusion of the culture of the colonizer through education. Attainments within the educational system established for this purpose provide the yardsticks for raising a new group of elites among the colonized society. However, the diffusion of the imported culture of the colonizer almost invariably involves not only harmonious culture contacts, but also culture conflicts, which could find expression in violent reactions

1. J. S. Coleman in P. J. M. McEwan and R. B. Sutcliffe (eds), 1965, p. 177.

from the subject people. Apart from this, there is always the problem of conflict of interests as between the colonizer and the colonized, the former working to perpetuate control, the latter struggling for self-fulfilment either through accommodation within the colonial system or through the recovery of independence and sovereignty.

As M. Crowder has shown above (Chapter 12), the First World War raised the hopes of the emergent educated elites all over Africa for greater opportunities for their being identified with the processes of development in their respective communities. They expected to be absorbed and accepted as colleagues by the colonial rulers; but as the colonial situation became more and more of a reality they found their expectations checkmated or frustrated. Even where mass recruitment of European personnel during the war had led to job opportunities opening up for educated Africans, the realities of the post-war period soon caused disillusionment and discontent. Educated Africans not only found themselves placed in inferior positions *vis-à-vis* the European personnel of comparable training and experience with whom they served in the same colonial administrations, they were also kept in the background socially. Having been educated away from their indigenous milieu with the encouragement that the education they were getting would lift them into the European world, they were men who were largely alienated from the masses of their people in terms of orientation, life style, ambition and expectations of rewards in material and social terms.[2] The barriers which the illiberalism inherent in colonialism erected against them were, therefore, a source of resentment, bitterness and agitation against the colonial regimes.

The colonial regimes were no exception to the truism that every administration makes use of intermediary structures, largely for reasons of economy and effectiveness. The colonial governments made varied use, as R. F. Betts has shown above (Chapter 13) of traditional institutions and leadership elites to facilitate their control of the subject peoples. Indeed, in the search for such authority structures and personnel, the colonial officials often created new ones which they could understand and use. Such were the 'warrant chiefs' of South-eastern Nigeria, the native authorities among the Maasai in Tanganyika (now Tanzania), and in parts of Uganda outside Buganda, and most of the so-called chiefs (*chefs de paille*) under the French, Belgians and the Portuguese. But even then, the elites so recruited to sustain colonial rule were hardly any better treated than the Africans who were raised through education in the colonial system. Like the new educated elites, the 'traditional' rulers fell between two stools. Having lost the traditionality of their positions and roles in the eyes of their people, they were treated in most cases like mere instruments of control by the colonial masters and not as real partners. The loss of real power and social status and prestige was a source of discontent for many of them.

2. See Jean-Paul Sartre's preface to F. Fanon, 1967.

Only few of the colonial administrators seemed to have understood how to manage the uneasy relationship which existed between the 'traditional' and the new African elites on the one hand, and between these two sets of elites and the colonial regimes on the other. The few exceptions included, notably, General (later Marshal) Lyautey in Morocco, Sir Frederick (later Lord) Lugard in Northern Nigeria and Sir Gordon Guggisberg in the Gold Coast (now Ghana). Even for these, the general strategy consisted in dampening the aspirations of the new educated elite who were usually portrayed as ambitious upstarts. It was generally convenient to cultivate a conflict situation in relations between the two sets of African leadership elites, with the imperial master acting as the protector of 'traditional' leadership and systems of government. In such a situation neither set of elites was satisfied with the colonial regimes. In 1917, Governor-General Joost Van Vollenhoven highlighted the potentially explosive nature of the problem, especially in relation to the future of colonialism, in the following perceptive piece:

> The indigenous chiefs, those of yesterday whom we have preserved, or those of today whom we have created, complain of being humiliated. The 'interpreters', the various types of auxiliaries of the administration and of commerce, complain that they are 'instruments' and do not have the rank due to them as collaborators. There is among the whole of this badly payed and very wretched elite – as remote from indigenous society, from which it has been driven out, as it is from European society into which it is not admitted – a feeling of disillusionment, discontent and bitterness which it would prove dangerous to be unaware of.[3]

He offered the following prescription that could not have found favour then among colonial rulers; 'it is necessary that this elite should be recognized and given a better welcome by us. The reform which should be brought about is less in the letter of the law than in actual practice.'[4]

The adoption of the attitude being recommended would have been contrary to the ethos of imperialism, hence it went unheeded at the time. Instead, colonial authorities concentrated on consolidating their control and exploiting the human and material resources of their colonies. The absorbing problem was the solution to Europe's post-war problems of rehabilitation of the economy and the services. However, the international environment, with its streaks of liberalism being expressed on colonialism and colonial affairs,[5] made a change of attitude inevitable in the long run.

But colonialism did not affect only the educated elite and the traditional

3. Archives du Sénégal, Fonds Afrique Occidentale Française (ASAOF) 17G61/2, 1917, p. 10.
4. ASAOF, 17G61/2, 1917, p. 20.
5. See A. Sarraut, 1923; F. D. Lugard, 1929.

rulers. To see African nationalism in the inter-war period only as an elitist and urban phenomenon alone as has hitherto been done is wrong. Recent research is showing more and more that a great deal of discontent and anti-colonial feelings were aroused in the rural areas mainly as a result of the new economic and financial measures, the new system of administering justice and, above all, the economic depression of the 1930s. The protest migrations from, say, the Upper Volta and Ivory Coast into the Gold Coast in the 1920s, the waves of deposition by their subjects of chiefs, the symbol of colonialism in many parts of Africa, and of course the well-known and well-documented cocoa hold-ups in West Africa,[6] all this shows that resistance to colonialism in the inter-war period was not confined to the urban centres and the elites only but also found echoes in the rural areas and among the illiterate farmers and workers. Admittedly, research in this area of the extent of rural anti-colonial sentiments and activities, and above all, of the linkage, if any, between the elitist/urban and illiterate/ rural activities in the inter-war period is very much in the embryonic stage, and any synthesis therefore cannot be attempted in this chapter. The attention of future historians is very much drawn to this new but fascinating theme.

Another phenomenon of African nationalism and politics in the inter-war period was the concern with cultural revivalism. This was an inevitable reaction to the stark reality that colonialism was a negation of the culture of the colonized. Cultural revivalism was part of the struggle for the reassertion and preservation of self-identity, first as Africans and, secondly, as members of particular cultural nations. Pan-Arabism and pan-Islamism were perhaps the most striking examples; but the so-called 'nativistic' and religious movements, as well as 'Ethiopianism' belonged to the same genre of activities.

Furthermore, colonialism is total in scope, affecting or representing a potential threat to all aspects of life; therefore the movements against it as a system were necessarily all-embracing. As a security-oriented system, colonialism is normally threatened by all claims to fairness and equality in relations between the colonizer and the colonized, whether such claims were made by groups of workers, in Church organizations, within the colonial bureaucracy or through agitations for the provision of social amenities like schools or health facilities. The essential point is that colonialism embodies inequality based on racial discrimination and any call for equality in any area of human relations is tantamount to demanding the end of colonialism.

Intensity of variations in European influences in the form of ideas and institutions also influenced African reactions. The Africans in the areas which had experienced European dominance longest tended to be the most receptive to European political culture, and had the greatest expectations

6. P. Jenkins (ed.), 1975; B. O. Oloruntimehin, 1973(a).

that progress would be made towards the achievement of self-determination through such channels. As they had been the most exposed to European education, they were well equipped and willing to adopt the European model of political and social development. They tended, therefore, to be constitutional in their agitations for desired change. The existence of a forum for doing this in the colonial legislatures was an incentive.

In places like Egypt and the Anglo-Egyptian Sudan, Algeria (especially the three departments of Algiers, Constantine, and Oran), the French Protectorates of Morocco and Tunisia, and the coastal areas of British and French West Africa, African activities were characterized by constitutionalism, and the employment of techniques of exerting political pressures that were appropriate to Western European political processes. One reason for this was that the African nationalists were addressing themselves both to the immediate colonial authorities and to liberal political groups and opinions in the imperial metropolis.

The constitutional approach found an ever-widening social base as the groups of educated Africans expanded and as new economic and social groups emerged as part of the dynamics of the colonial economy and measures, especially educational institutions, which were adopted to ensure African manpower for the economic and social activities. The emergent labour force gradually became unionized in many colonies and added momentum to the expression of African nationalism through anti-colonial politics. As labour in the colonies exhibited all the malaise of a colonial situation, especially harsh exploitation based on racial discrimination and social injustice, labour relations automatically became political relations which were antagonistic as between the citizens of the colonizing country and the colonized Africans. The role of labour in the politics of African nationalism was to become very important from the Second World War onwards.[7]

The role of the different official ideologies enunciated by the colonial powers was another determinant. As John Peel says 'An ideology, like the ideals of the great religions, is a factor shaping behaviour even when uncompletely realised ...' and 'Development does not occur apart from men's interpretation of their situation and ideas for their future.'[8] The differences in the orientation and style of African nationalists derived in part from the fact that the various groups had different ideologies to guide their expectations and by which to assess their achievements. Hence, among African nationalists under French control in Algeria and Senegal, where the possibility of ending colonialism through the policy of 'assimilation' – by the attainment of French citizenship for individuals with full rights and responsibilities – had been demonstrated, the tendency was to continue to press for the extension, in scope and territorially, of the implementation of the policy. On the other hand, those in British territories,

7. G. Balandier and B. Dadie (eds), n.d., pp. 202–406; I. Davies, 1966.
8. J. D. Y. Peel, 1968.

with the hope of eventual independence as separate sovereign countries, though as members of the British Commonwealth, were understandably more explicitly concerned during the period under consideration with reforms and participation which would prepare them ultimately for independence. The difference was not as to the objective of freedom, which they all wanted, but rather as to method. The latter was dictated by the context of action as set by the dialectic relations between ideologies and actual colonial practices.[9]

Related to ideology as a factor is the settler factor. The settler factor showed in the relative intensity of colonization as a process, the frustration of the expectations of the colonized or lack of responsiveness to African claims. This factor explains the differences in tone and intensity in the expression of African nationalism as between settler-ridden Algeria on the one hand and, on the other, French territories which did not have Algeria's settler problem. The same happened as between settler-dominated Kenya, Southern Rhodesia (now Zimbabwe) and South Africa on the one hand, and other British colonies. The declaration of the paramountcy of African interests (otherwise known as the Devonshire declaration) of 1923 in respect of Africans in Kenya was, in essence, an expression of the same ideology as informed British colonial administration in other regions. The different experiences of these territories resulted from the settlers' firm determination to perpetuate the subjugation of the indigenous population by practising what has been described as 'ultracolonialism'.[10]

African nationalism and international developments

The situations which African nationalists found themselves in the inter-war years were essentially the same: deprivation of political and social liberties; exploitation of human and material resources to the benefit of the alien rulers; denial of facilities and services which could contribute to the political and social upliftment of the colonized societies or, when it became clear that changes could not be prevented, the pursuit of actions aimed at limiting and reorientating the course of development with the main objective of perpetuating colonial dominance.

As counter-currents to these situations created by the colonialists were the aspirations of the nationalists for the recovery of lost sovereignty and independence albeit within the context of the new colonial territorial structures in the northern parts of the continent and, in the rest, for the improvement in the economic and social status of their communities with a view to making the enjoyment of civil liberties meaningful. In the pursuit of their aspirations, African nationalists were aided by developments on the international scene. Such were, for example, the impact of the First

9. B. O. Oloruntimehin, 1971, pp. 33–50.
10. J. Duffy, 1962; W. Minter, 1972. Also see B. O. Oloruntimehin, 1972(b), pp. 289–312.

World War already referred to and discussed in Chapter 12 above, and the League of Nations' expression of the desirability of regarding the development of the colonized as a major objective of colonialism, and as a yardstick against which the performance of imperial masters, especially in the mandated territories, would be judged. The introduction of the idea of accountability to the international community in respect of the mandated territories served as a source of encouragement to some of the nationalists. On the political plane, international ideological movements like the Leninist anti-imperialist Communist International (Comintern) and other socialist movements, as well as the march towards independence in other continents of the world were also an incentive to African nationalists. So also was anti-imperialist pan-Africanism inspired by Sylvester Williams, Marcus Garvey, William Du Bois and other black American and Caribbean influences, which will be discussed later.[11]

An international congress which was convened under the auspices of the Comintern at Brussels in February 1927 resulted in the formation of the League against Imperialism and for National Independence (known simply as the League Against Imperialism). The Congress was attended by about 180 delegates from Western Europe, North, Central and South America, the Caribbean, Asia and Africa. The Congress brought together Communists, left-wing socialist groups like the Independent Labour Party, represented by its general secretary, Fenner Brockway (later Lord Brockway); radical socialist intellectuals and representatives of national movements in colonial territories. Participants from Africa included Messali Hadj and Hadjali Abdel-Kader (Maghrib); Mohamed Hafiz Bey Ramadan and Ibrahim Youssef (Egypt); Lamine Senghor (French West Africa); Jomo Kenyatta (Kenya); as well as J. T. Gumede and I. A. La Guma (South Africa). Also represented were members of the Inter-Colonial Union like Max Bloncoux, while Carlos Deambrosis Martins came from Haiti.[12]

There were also movements concerned with protecting the rights of man and citizenship and anti-slavery bodies which operated both in Europe and in several colonies in Africa. Movements which originated from America like Marcus Garvey's Universal Negro Improvement Association first launched in 1917 exerted influence in several colonies in Africa.

As a counter-current to all these forces which were working for the upliftment of the social and political status of colonized or oppressed groups, there was the spread and influence of illiberal and retrogressively racialist political doctrines which became institutionalized in fascist and Nazi regimes in Europe and in repressive autocracies in the colonies, especially the Italian ones. Even in European countries, like France, where liberal political doctrines prevailed, fascism and Nazism found adherents and this fact reflected on the thinking over the situation in the colonies.

11. See Chapter 29 below.
12. See I. Geiss, 1974; G. Padmore, 1956.

In general, industrial and commercial capitalists in Europe continued to see colonies as estates to be preserved at all costs.

The expression of African nationalism and politics

Much as the colonial and the general international environment were broadly the same, the actual expression of African nationalism and politics, phenomena neatly summed up by the Swahili word *siasa*, varied from place to place, even in territories under the same imperial master. The explanation for this lies partly in the fact that colonial territories were acquired in different ways, at different points in time, and therefore had different experiences of colonialism, lasting for varied lengths of time. Factors which conditioned the form and intensity of action by nationalists (*wanasiasa*) in the colonies included the type of leadership, the variations in the spread and intensity of European influences in the form of ideas and institutions; the number and significance of the settler (white) population; and, lastly, the colonial ideologies and practices.

In nearly all cases, the nationalist movements and the attendant colonial politics were led and dominated by the new western-educated elites who were the best equipped to understand the European political culture and therefore to react effectively to the colonial regimes on the terms enunciated by the latter. Sometimes, they co-operated actively with members of the 'traditional' leadership elites, even if there were tensions in their relations. Such co-operation features in territories like the Gold Coast with the Aborigines Rights Protection Society, in Southern Nigeria, Morocco, and among the Gikuyu of Kenya. In some cases, leadership remained within the ranks of the 'traditional' elites as in Libya and Morocco. In most cases, however, since those who represented or were recruited to represent traditional leadership elites were preferred by colonial regimes as instruments of control, the tendency was for the expression of nationalism to involve treating the traditional elites as accomplices and for them to be attacked as such.

Serving as channels for the expression of the aspirations and claims of African nationalism, and of specific grievances, were political parties and youth organizations. Political parties were meaningful in the few places where there were colonial legislatures. In Egypt, the bestowing of a parliament by the British who had unilaterally declared a sham independence in 1922, provided a purpose for the organization and operation of political parties. The constitutional situation made it possible for Sa'd Zaghlūl's Wafd Party and the Nationalist Party to play a very important role in the struggle for the restoration of full independence and sovereignty to Egypt.[13] The introduction of constitutional changes, though of less importance, in Nigeria and the Gold Coast in British West Africa, paved

13. See Chapter 23 below.

the way for the appearance and meaningful operation of political parties. Before such constitutional changes, the National Congress of British West Africa had been easily checkmated in its endeavours.[14] Thereafter the National Democratic Party of Nigeria was, for instance, able to make a more sustained impact on both the colonial authorities and the indigenous population. So also did political parties play important roles in Senegal where the General Council which, after 1920, became the Colonial Council, provided the forum.

Youth organizations, ethnic associations, old boys' associations and other movements dedicated to the achievement of civil liberties and the rights of man fulfilled an invaluable role in all the colonies irrespective of their constitutional situations. They were an unavoidable political and social force especially in areas where overt political activities were made impossible by the repressive nature of colonial rule. Youth organizations which acted as catalysts in the nationalist, anti-colonial politics and whose activities will be discussed in Chapter 25 below, included the Gold Coast Youth Conference which was founded in 1929; the Lagos (later Nigeria) Youth Movement, Young Egypt, Harry Thuku's Young Kikuyu Association founded in Kenya in 1921, the Sudan Graduates' Congress, the Young Gabonese (Jeune Gabonais), and Young Tunisians. Some of the movements were inter-regional while others were trans-territorial. The former included the North African Star under the leadership of Messali Hadj, the National Congress of British West Africa, the South Africa Congress and the West African Students' Union led by the Nigerian, Ladipo Solanke, which drew its membership from all of British West Africa.

Social organizations which contributed to the expression of African nationalism and anti-colonial politics included the several branches in Africa of Marcus Garvey's Universal Negro Improvement Association which had been founded in America in 1917. Such was the Nigerian Improvement Association (1920). We also have bodies like the League for the Rights of Man and Citizenship in Gabon (Ligue des Droits de l'Homme et du Citoyen); the Liga Africana at Luanda and Lorenço Marques in Portuguese Angola and Mozambique; André Matswa's Société Amicale des Originaires de l'Afrique Equatoriale Française with membership from Libreville, Bangui and Brazzaville; and La Ligue Universelle pour la Défense de la Race Nègre (1925), led by Tovalou Quenum (Dahomey, now Benin), Le Comité, then La Ligue de Défense de la Race Nègre, led by Kouyaté Garang (French Soudan, now Mali) and Lamine Senghor (Senegal).[15] There was also, at the international level, the Comité mondial contre la guerre et le fascisme and the various Pan-Africanist congresses organized by Sylvester Williams and William Du Bois. Trade unions and other working-class movements also became important agents in the fight

14. See Chapter 25 below.
15. I. Geiss, 1974; J. A. Langley, 1973.

against the colonial system though they became even more so after the Second World War.

Multifarious were the weapons that were fashioned during the inter-war period for the attack on the colonial system. Revolts and rebellions which were so common in the previous period were reduced to a minimum. Instead, newspapers, books, pamphlets, petitions, protest migrations, strikes, boycotts, the ballot box, the pulpit and the mosques became the stock-in-trade of the nationalists. The newspapers became a particularly vital organ for the dissemination of the views for these political and social organizations. The slowly expanding intelligentsia provided the audience and market which sustained an increasing number of newspapers and periodicals in the period. Apart from those published within Africa, a fair number also came from outside the continent serving as vehicles for transmission of the anti-colonial and anti-imperialist propaganda of inter-national movements. The appearance of these papers varied from daily, weekly, fortnightly to monthly. Others were published only when it was possible. A number of the newspapers and periodicals had been in existence before the First World War. Such were *al-Liwa*, an Arabic newspaper founded in 1900 to popularize Egyptian nationalist ideas, *La Démocratie du Sénégal*, and *The Lagos Weekly Record* founded in 1891. The majority were, however, founded in the inter-war period. Such were the *Times of Nigeria* (1921–30), *Daily Times* (from 1926), *Lagos Daily News* (1925–38), *Le Périscope Africain* (Dakar, 1929), *L'Ouest-Africain Français* (*Journal Républicain-Socialiste*), *Le Courrier de l'Ouest-Africain* (Dakar), the *African Morning Post*, *The Gold Coast Times* (Accra), *L'Action Tunisienne* (1932) and *La Presse Porto-Novienne* with sub-titles and a section in Yoruba. Newspapers in African languages, other than the Egyptian *al-Liwa*, included the Yoruba language paper, *Akede Eko* (Lagos, 1932 onwards) and *La Voix du Dahomey*. From outside Africa came communist-inspired and pan-African periodicals like the *Race Nègre*, *Negro World*, *La Voix des Nègres*, and *Vox Populi*, as well as *New Times and Ethiopia News*, the *Cri des Nègres*, *African Times and Orient Review*, *The Crusader*, and *New York Age* and *Coloured American*. Besides newspapers, plays, pamphlets, tracts and many books were written by some of the nationalist leaders in which the colonial system was subjected to sharp criticism and ridicule.

The newspapers served as media for diffusing nationalist and anti-colonial activities across frontiers. To that extent, they were a constant source of worry for colonial administrators as the various sedition laws of the mid-1930s and the attempts to establish iron curtains by legislation against certain publications show. The spread of the radio later made the repressive measures which colonial rulers adopted to screen away their colonies from external influences more difficult and less effective.

As has been emphasized, constitutionalism, and the use of newspapers and radio as media of expression, were dependent on the availability of legislative institutions in the colonies or the hope of having them, as well as the existence of a significant number of western-educated Africans who could make appropriate use of such institutions and organs of expression. Also, the approach of the western-educated African nationalists pre-supposed the acceptance of Western European models of political development such as nationalists without their experience could not appreciate. Uneven spread of education was, therefore, an important variable in the expression of African nationalism and anti-colonial politics. As European powers concentrated on making colonies pay for their administration and services, relatively little was done to spread western education and provide infrastructure for political and social development. In several areas of colonized Africa between the two world wars, primary schools were still few and far between and secondary education was a rarity. In British Central Africa, French Equatorial Africa, Soudan and Portuguese Angola, Mozambique and Guinea, there was practically no access to secondary education before the Second World War. In such areas, nationalists could hardly be expected to adopt a constitutional approach to the expression of their anti-colonialism.

It is in this context that one should seek to understand the role of traditionalist or 'nativistic' socio-religious movements in our period. Of particular relevance as we have seen already in some of the earlier chapters were the messianic movements which expressed indigenous ideologies as well as those which reflected Islamic and Christian ones. They were movements which were emancipatory in character, expressing what is essentially a universal phenomenon in situations in which communities had to express their dissatisfaction with their living conditions and a desire for regeneration. They represented an ideology competing against colonialism in so far as the latter represented a negation of indigenous culture and economic, social and psychological depression of the colonized. In the words of Lanternari, 'They reflect the anxieties and hopes of the groups that participate in them for a sudden and total transformation of their physical, social and psychological environment.'[16]

Prominent examples of such movements in our period, some of whose activities have been discussed in Chapter 20 above, were Ethiopianism in South and East Africa, and the movement spearheaded by millenarian preachers in Southern and Central Africa, notably the Kitawala (African and Congo Watch Tower) with large following in the Rhodesias, spreading to the Congo (now Zaire) and Nyasaland (now Malawi); the Kimbanguist movement (founded in the Belgian Congo by Simon Kimbangu) with following in Belgian and French Congo and the neo-Kimbanguist *Mission des Noirs* founded in the Lower Congo by Simon-Pierre Mpadi. Otherwise known as the Khakists, the movement had influence among the population of French Congo and Oubangui-Chari (now Central African Republic). Some of these movements were inspired by their acceptance of Christianity

16. V. Lanternari, 1974, p. 483.

but were disenchanted with the expression of the religion in the organized Church of the colonial societies. African nationalists who were anxious to preserve Africans against colonial oppression found the Church at best indifferent. They therefore broke away very much in the spirit of the Reformation which has been characteristic of the growth and spread of Christianity in many societies. Like the reformation movements in Europe and elsewhere, the churches and movements founded by African National-ists aimed at applying Christian ideologies like the ideas of the brotherhood of man and the essential oneness of believers, without distinction as to race or colour, to end discrimination and oppression.

That the spiritual was closely linked with the social and material situation was evident in the methods they adopted. While religion necessarily remained the medium of expression of African aspirations, the concrete actions taken included labour unrest and refusal to pay taxes. Like the movements founded by Kimbangu and Mpadi, Ruben Spartas Mukasa in Uganda founded the African Progressive Association, and the Christian Army for the Salvation of Africa. An ex-serviceman in the King's African Rifles, Mukasa gave expression to the unifying purpose of all these movements when he promised to work for the redemption of Africa at whatever personal risks. When he started a branch of the African Orthodox Church in Uganda, the political and social purpose was clear in his declaration that the Church was '. . . for all right-thinking Africans, men who wish to be free in their own house, not always being thought of as boys'. Mukasa's church spread to Kenya. Of the same stamp was Jordan Msuma's Last Church of God and His Christ in Nyasaland as were the various African and Aladura churches in West Africa.

Islam represented a counterpoise to colonial ideology as well as a forum for the expression of messianism. The Mahdī is for the Muslim as the Messiah is for the Christian. Mahdism haunted colonial authorities in North and West Africa, in the Sudan and Somaliland. The Sanūsiyya in Italian-dominated Libya, as we have seen already, presented perhaps the clearest example of the expression of African nationalism and anti-colonialism through Islam. Pan-Islamism, the religious side of the culture-bound pan-Arabism and the idea of the *Salafiya*, also played a prominent role in the nationalist and colonial politics in Egypt, the Maghrib and northern Anglo-Egyptian Sudan. The Sanūsiyya influence as an anti-colonial force spread to parts of West Africa. The colonial authorities found Islamic movements like the Hamalliyya, the Tijaniyya, and Mouridiyya a constant threat to the security of the colonial system.

These Islamic movements provided a strong link among adherents who found themselves under different colonial regimes. From the First World War on, as Crowder has shown above,[17] pan-Islamic ideology being disseminated from Turkey was a worrying issue to colonial authorities in

17. Chapter 12 above.

many parts of Africa. It was a problem colonial rulers sought to tackle through the exchange of information and inter-colonial co-operation.

Regardless of the degree of exposure to western influences experienced by the colonized African, a common base for the expression of African nationalism were the different forms of cultural movements. The point has been made about the resilience and continuing relevance of African cultures and institutions throughout Africa for the colonized. Even the most westernized of African educated elites were faced with the reality that they were essentially Africans whatever their degree of acculturation. Most of the youth movements already referred to, and as will be seen later, showed an awareness of the crucial importance of their culture to the preservation of their self-identity in spite of the inroads of Europe by way of the school system. The various Gikuyu associations were a good example. So also were the pan-African movements and the rather fluid concept of *négritude* which, as has been shown in Chapter 21 above, found expression from the early 1930s, as well as the so-called 'nativistic' and 'religious' movements already referred to.

All these expressions of African nationalism and anti-colonial politics constituted the antithesis in the dialectical relationship between the European colonizers and the colonized Africans. The general reactions of the colonial regimes in seeking to tighten control by the use of physical force and the imposition of legal disabilities were understandable in view of the fact that the period witnessed the expansion of autocracies and illiberal tendencies in Europe itself. But it was not just the opposition of the Africans which was making the colonial regimes insecure. The spread of European ideas and institutions proved a sore point for the colonizers. The general attempt to limit the quality and scope of education was predicated upon the fear that European education and political and social ideas were destructive of colonialism as a system of relations. It was the desire to avert the danger that was looming that explained the general denunciation of education in the humanities at all levels, and the preference for rural schools, vocational schools, and technically-orientated post-secondary institutions which were concerned with intermediate manpower, but not universities. The idea was to avoid the example of India where the spread of liberal education had been a major lever for the expansion of anti-colonial and nationalistic politics. This is the explanation for the orientation and scope of such colleges as the Ecole William Ponty in French West Africa, and the Yaba Higher College (Nigeria), Achimota College (Gold Coast), Gordon's College, Khartoum, and Makerere College in British East Africa.[18]

But the attempt to regulate the measure and type of social change that could take place in the colonies was itself another source of anti-colonial grievances that fuelled the nationalist movements. The world economic

18. B. O. Oloruntimehin, 1974; pp. 337–57; D. B. Abernethy, 1969, pp. 79–88.

crisis worsened the situation in two ways. It limited the resources available to the colonial regimes to be viable without any subvention from the metropolis. The general tendency was to keep the colonial regimes going by cutting down on expenditures on amenities and infrastructures that could benefit the colonized by the freezing of job opportunities regardless of the disruptive impact of unemployment on the societies. At the same time, the pauperizing exactions made against the colonized became greater with higher taxes, frequent use of cheap and forced labour, in a situation in which farmers were receiving diminishing returns for their raw materials while paying higher prices for imported European manufactures.

Finally one can point to the Italo-Abyssinian war which began in 1935, and the eventual Italian occupation of Ethiopia, as a major international event which furthered the feeling of alienation on the part of the colonized, especially the educated, against the colonial regimes. The tones of the Italian invasion, and of fascism and Nazism in general, emphasized the racialist nature of European colonialism in Africa. Those who had nursed hope in the League of Nations were sadly disappointed. The desire to protect the wounded pride of the African explains the resurgence of pan-African ideas and ideologies like *négritude* at this time. Equally important were international organizations in defence of the independence of Ethiopia, a country which symbolized the hope of the educated African for eventual independence.

The newspapers and periodicals, both local and foreign, naturally served as vehicles for the transmission of anti-colonial, anti-European nationalism. It was to checkmate this development that various repressive administrative and legislative measures were taken against the mass media, including the slowly-expanding radio services. Efforts were made to prevent or limit the circulation of literature, newspapers and periodicals, and radio sets even when these emanated from the home countries of the colonial administrators. The local press was in nearly all cases rigidly controlled through censorship and sedition laws. All these measures were taken to facilitate the operations of the colonial administrations, which became characterized by greater intolerance of nationalist aspirations, and deprivation of civil, personal liberties and rights.

In the inter-war period, colonialism and African nationalism existed in a dialectical relationship. African nationalism and anti-colonial activities did not achieve much success in the inter-war period but they did cause some concern among the colonial officials. All the repressive anti-colonial measures taken during the period reflect this concern. Their responses to the challenges posed by African nationalism amounted to wanting to screen off Africa from general currents of development in the world. Not only was this unrealistic and self-contradictory, the attempt acted as a catalyst that snowballed African nationalism and anti-colonialism to deeper and wider forms which, with the impact of the Second World War, soon led to the movement for the overthrow of the colonial system.

23

Politics and nationalism in North-East Africa, 1919–35

H. A. IBRAHIM

Introduction

Two forms of nationalism competed for supremacy in North-East Africa in the inter-war years – secular nationalism on the one side and religiously-inspired patriotism on the other. The continuing legacy of the Mahdī in the Sudan and of Sayyid Muḥammad in Somalia managed to fuse religion and patriotic sentiment the most directly. On the other hand, Egyptian nationalism in the inter-war years was getting more secular (see Fig. 4.1). But even in Egypt, Islamic modernism and nationalism interacted in the theatre of politics. After all, Saʿd Zaghlūl, the nationalist who dominated Egyptian politics for the first decade following the First World War, was influenced by Djamāl al-Dīn al-Afghānī, the stormy revolutionary pan-Islamist who had had a part in 'bringing about the first stirrings of national consciousness and discontent under Ismāʿīl'.[1] However, it would still be true to say that the movement which Zaghlūl led was basically a secular patriotic movement. The protests in southern Sudan were also basically secular: it was in northern Sudan and Somalia during those inter-war years that the religious factor was the more difficult to disentangle from the political.

In addition to the dialectic between religion and secularism in politics during these years, there was the dialectic between nationalism and economic problems. This period included some of the worst years of economic depression in the history of the modern world. By the end of the 1920s the imperial powers themselves were experiencing the pressures of a deepening recession, culminating in the Great Depression. The colonies of North-East Africa had been feeling the economic squeeze a decade or two before the Great Depression hit the industrialized world.

For North-East Africa yet another characteristic of the inter-war years was that they witnessed both a further expansion of imperialism, on one side, and a new militancy against imperialism on the other. The years between the two world wars were the years of Europe's last frontier – as new territory was annexed and colonial control was consolidated. This

1. A. Hourani, 1962, pp. 108–9; see also N. R. Keddie, 1968.

was imperialism's last territorial push in Africa. But the same years also witnessed the rise of anti-colonial militancy among the colonized peoples and the beginnings of effective political organization in pursuit of freedom and equality. In North-East Africa this was particularly marked in Egypt – but by no means exclusively there.

The First World War itself played a part in creating these contradictions. Of all the countries of this part of Africa, Egypt was perhaps the most directly affected by the war. After all, when Turkey entered the war on Germany's side, Britain had regarded it as a pretext not only for ending the Ottoman empire's residual suzerainty over Egypt but also for declaring Egypt a British protectorate, and for installing an alternative monarch of Britain's choosing. This declaration of a protectorate and the nature of the new monarchy together worked as a major catalyst for Egyptian nationalist resentment. This new militancy was deepened by the militarization of Suez, as half a million troops under British command were brought in to guard the canal.

Britain's role in the Sudan was also consolidated – generating in turn new forms of nationalist sentiment. European imperialism was indeed pushing for its last territorial frontier in Africa – but in that very process it was also stirring a new patriotic awakening among the indigenous peoples. However, it is worth bearing in mind that during these years Egyptian nationalism was still tainted by a form of expansionism of its own. The leaders of the new nationalist movement in Egypt still regarded the Sudan as an Egyptian dependency and sought to recover effective Egyptian sovereignty over it.

These, then, are the basic contextual contradictions of the inter-war years in North-East Africa – the dialectic between economic and political forces, the dialectic between religion and nationalism, the dialectic between the last frontier of imperialism and the new frontier of anti-colonialism, and the dialectic between local patriotism and local expansionism, especially in Egypto-Sudanese relations.

Let us now look at these developments in greater detail, country by country, bearing in mind that some of the economic problems unleashed on North-East Africa in this period played a major role in creating a responsive atmosphere for nationalist agitation and resentment among the people.

Egypt

The 1919 Revolution

Because of Britain's declaration of the protectorate in 1914, Egyptian nationalists felt the urgent necessity to form a united body to represent the nation in its forthcoming conflict with Britain. Consequently, in November 1918, Saʿd Zaghlūl, the distinguished Egyptian leader, and two of his colleagues formed al-Wafd al-Miṣrī, or the Egyptian Delegation.

PLATE 23.1 *Nationalism in Egypt: Zaghlūl Pasha (c. 1857–1927) speaks at a demonstration demanding the withdrawal of British troops, c. 1920*

582

The Wafd was militant in its approach to change. Its ultimate objectives were to win complete independence for Egypt, ensure Egyptian sovereignty over the Sudan and abolish the Capitulations which granted special privileges to foreigners resident in Egypt. Though the Wafd's constitution did not openly mention the last two objectives, this was apparently a tactical move to achieve freedom first and then turn to the two other issues.[2]

Zaghlūl and his colleagues represented not only the new Egyptian elite of modern administrators, lawyers and other secular professionals, but also a new group of landowners. Socially, they 'belonged to a native and relatively recent land-owning and professional class from the provinces'.[3] Their emergence was a signal that the older alien Turco-Egyptian and Albanian aristocracy had to hand over leadership to the long-suppressed professional elite.

The Wafd reverted to militant tactics to strengthen its leadership. It distributed leaflets, organized public meetings, and collected 'formal signed dispositions from all representative organisations in the country to the effect that the Wafd was the official representative of the Egyptian nation solely responsible and authorized to negotiate its future'.[4] Moreover, the Wafd mobilized a country-wide support for its position through effective articulation of the people's grievances and demands.

The unacceptable and humiliating unilateral British declaration of a protectorate over Egypt in December 1914 was thus forcefully dismissed by the Wafd as illegal and a war measure only. It advocated its immediate abolition in fulfilment of President Woodrow Wilson's doctrines and the Allies' promises of freedom for small nations.

Meanwhile, economic hardships were helping the nationalist cause. The many social and economic problems that beset the Egyptian society during the First World War created a widely-felt sense of deprivation among the masses. Though the British government had promised to undertake all the responsibilities for the War, the Egyptian Expeditionary Force was employed in defending the Suez Canal, and in Syria and Palestine. The peasants were forcefully recruited in large numbers to serve in the Allied labour and camel corps. Their grain and animals were requisitioned without adequate compensation. The sharp rise in the cost of living was particularly harmful to government employees and unskilled labourers because it was not accompanied by a proportionate increase in their wages. Landowners were unable to profit substantially from the rise in the price of cotton because Britain limited its acreage to allow for the increase of the cultivation of essential foodcrops, fixed its prices, and restricted its export. The Wafd repeatedly stressed Britain's responsibility for this injustice and persuaded the Egyptians to rally behind it to redress it. This energetic campaign led to the gradual alienation of all classes from Britain. By 1919 an inflammable

2. A. M. Ramaḍān, 1968, pp. 431–2.
3. P. J. Vatikiotis, 1969, p. 252.
4. ibid., p. 255.

state of discontent prevailed throughout the country.[5] Economic deprivation was setting the stage for a political response on a mass scale.

The failure of the British government to appreciate the strength and
dimensions of the sweeping new nationalist spirit, and its arrogant
insistence on the permanent status of the protectorate were serious errors
of judgement. Its subsequent stubborn refusal to allow Ḥusayn Rushdī,
the wartime prime minister, and Zaghlūl to present Egypt's case in the
Paris Peace Conference added fuel to an already explosive situation. But
the most dangerous of all British blunders was the arrest on 8 March 1919
of Zaghlūl and two of his colleagues, and their deportation to Malta. This
was the spark that led to the 1919 Revolution.

The immediate result of the Wafd's mobilization was a series of violent
demonstrations and massive strikes by transport workers, judges and
lawyers. Students from the al-Azhar university and secondary and
professional schools actively participated in the nationalist struggle. Soon
the provinces joined in the general protest, and attempted more daring
attacks upon railway and telephone communications. Frequent attacks
were also made on British military personnel, culminating in the murder
of eight British officers and men on a train from Aswān to Cairo at Deyrūt
on 18 March. In short, the country was brought to a standstill and Britain's
position in Egypt was seriously threatened. The Wafd now emerged as
the sole representative of the nation and Zaghlūl dominated the national
political scene until his death in 1927.

The 1919 Revolution is indeed a significant event in the history of
modern Egypt. For it mobilized, for the first time, all Egyptian classes
(peasants, workers, students, landowners and intellectuals) and religious
groups (both Copts and Muslims) against British colonialism. Leaders of
the Coptic community were, in fact, equally involved in the nationalist
bid for independence, and a few were selected as members of the Wafd's
central committee. This was one measure of the new secularism, as was
a new development, the participation of women in public demonstrations
against Britain.

This national upheaval forced Britain to inaugurate a policy of concilia-
tion with the nationalists. Lord Allenby, who was appointed a Special
High Commissioner, released Zaghlūl and his colleagues and allowed them
to go to Paris. The British government appointed a special mission, under
the chairmanship of Lord Milner, the Secretary of State for the Colonies,
to report on the causes of the 'disturbances', and the most suitable constitution for Egypt under the Protectorate. Though the Wafd had organized
a nation-wide effective boycott of the Milner Mission, its conclusion that
the unsatisfactory protectorate should be replaced by a treaty of alliance
negotiated with the nationalists was a triumph for the Wafd.

Britain was also forced to recognize the Wafd as the official spokesman

5. P. G. Elgood, 1928, p. 227.

of the nation. Milner went even further than this by inviting Zaghlūl for unofficial negotiations in London. The result was the Milner–Zaghlūl memorandum in 1920 which provided for an offensive and defensive alliance between the two countries, and, subject to the approval of the Capitulatory powers, the transfer of their rights in Egypt to Britain. The memorandum was, however, silent about the Sudan since, in Milner's view, her status was clearly defined by the Condominium Agreement.[6] Though these negotiations collapsed over the Wafd's insistence on complete independence and Egyptian sovereignty over the Sudan, this memorandum formed the starting-point for all subsequent negotiations.

The Declaration of Independence of 28 February 1922 was the most significant result of the 1919 Revolution. Under the pressure of the nationalists, Britain unilaterally abolished the protectorate and recognized Egypt's independence on condition that the *status quo* would be maintained in the following matters (usually called the Reserved Points) until the conclusion of an agreement with Egypt: the security of imperial communications, the defence of Egypt, the protection of minorities and foreign interests, and the Sudan.[7] Egypt's independence was formally declared on 15 March 1922, and Sultan Fu'ād assumed the title of Fu'ād I, King of Egypt. But was this a genuine case of decolonization? Or was Britain still guarding the new imperial frontier?

The Declaration of Independence gave the Egyptian government a freer hand in conducting its internal and external affairs. It restored the Ministry of Foreign Affairs abolished in 1914, and allowed Egypt to have diplomatic and consular representation. Moreover, the Declaration provided for constitutional rule in Egypt, a goal for which the nationalists had been struggling since 1883.[8] On its basis, the 1923 Constitution was enacted.

But this is only one side of the story. When compared with its militant ideology, the 1919 Revolution achieved only a limited success in both the political and constitutional fields. The independence granted by the Declaration was diluted by the Reserved Points, particularly by the reservation which provided for the continued British military occupation of Egypt. Moreover, foreigners continued to enjoy their extra-territorial privileges, while the Condominium Agreement dictated by Britain remained to provide the constitutional framework for the administration in the Sudan. Similarly, the 1923 Constitution did not establish a solid and secure foundation for constitutional rule in Egypt since it gave extensive powers to the monarchy, such as the right to select and appoint the prime minister, dismiss the cabinet, and dissolve parliament or postpone its sessions. This undermined parliamentary democracy in Egypt before it started.

This inability to achieve all the nation's aspirations was, in the main,

6. Milner, 1921, pp. 24–34.
7. J. Marlowe, 1965.
8. A. al-Rāf'ī, 1969, Vol. I, pp. 39–40.

PLATE 23.2 *Nationalism in Egypt: demonstration in support of King Fuʿād I, c. 1920*

586

the outcome of the progressive break-up of the national unity achieved in 1919. Owing to personal jealousies over the leadership of the Wafd and differences in outlook about the question of national independence, a serious split in the national front occurred in 1920 between the moderates led by 'Adlī Yakan, and the militants led by Zaghlūl. The former felt that the failure of the Egyptians to gain international support for their cause and their inability to continue the struggle by themselves made compromise with Britain inevitable. The militants, on the other hand, were so frustrated by Britain's stubbornness and impressed by the 1919[9] people's awakening that they advocated the continuation of the struggle until Britain yielded to all the nation's demands. The outcome of this controversy was the tragic division of the Wafd and the country at large into two rival groups: the Zaghlūlists and the 'Adlists. The Wafd therefore became a party representing the majority of the Egyptians rather than the united body that was speaking for the whole nation.

Britain's colonial diplomacy of 'divide and rule' made extensive use of this cleavage in the Wafd's ranks. Through manipulation and deception, colonial administrators encouraged the alienation of the 'Adlists from the Zaghlūlists. While suppressing the latter, Allenby accommodated the moderates and negotiated the Declaration of Independence with them. Though Zaghlūl described it as a 'national disaster',[10] and though the Wafd organized a violent campaign of protest against it, the Declaration continued to function as a transitional imperial frontier.

The era of negotiations, 1924–35

In the post-Declaration period, the nationalist struggle was predominantly focused on liberation from the crippling Reserved Points through a negotiated settlement with Britain. Four negotiations took place between 1924 and 1935. These were: the MacDonald–Zaghlūl negotiations in 1924, the Tharwāt–Chamberlain in 1927, the Maḥmūd–Henderson in 1929, and the Naḥḥās–Henderson in 1930.[11] But they all failed because Britain refused to make any concessions that might relax its occupation of Egypt or change the *status quo* in the Sudan. This intransigence was closely related to the British-inspired, if not created, rise of the Palace as a powerful anti-Wafdist centre of power.

Britain brought Fu'ād to power in 1922 to act as a buffer between her and the 'extremist' Wafd and to enforce her wishes. Though the ambitious and autocratic Fu'ād had supported the Wafd-led independence movement in 1919, he hoped to control it and use it 'for his own ends, a means of

9. The Paris Peace Conference recognized the British Protectorate over Egypt in May 1919.
10. A. al-Rāf'ī, 1969, Vol. I, p. 135.
11. H. A. Ibrāhīm, 1976, pp. 15–16.

increasing his stature and power'.[12] But he soon realized that Zaghlūl was following an independent path and suspected that he was planning to overthrow the monarchy and declare Egypt a republic. This led to the bitter enmity between the monarch and the Wafd that characterized Egyptian politics until 1952. Britain encouraged this hostility and exploited it for her own imperial interests.

To prevent the Wafd's accession to power, Fu'ād suspended the 1923 Constitution three times in less than seven years – in 1924, 1928 and 1930 – and in each case appointed his own prime minister. By the 1930 constitutional *coup d'état*, the Palace Premier, Ismā'īl Ṣidḳī, replaced the 1923 Constitution by a less democratic one. The main objective of the new electoral law was to keep the Wafd out of power.[13] During the greater part of the succeeding five years, Egypt, in fact, lived under anti-Wafdist governments. This frequent interference in the country's constitutional machinery prevented parliamentary government and its institutions from taking root in the political life of Egypt.

The various Palace governments that ruled Egypt before 1935, particularly that of Ṣidḳī (1930–3), took repressive measures against the Wafd. Its leaders were imprisoned, newspapers were banned and supporters were dismissed from their posts in the government and civil service. Besides their endorsement of these extreme measures, the colonial administrators occasionally took direct measures to humiliate the Wafd. For instance, Zaghlūl was not allowed on two occasions, in 1924 and 1926, to become prime minister, though his party had a majority in parliament.

This Palace–Residency suppressive campaign led to a gradual decline in the Wafd's popularity and erosion of its unity. Dissatisfied with what they called the 'uninspired leadership'[14] of Naḥḥās, Zaghlūl's successor, a group of Wafd leaders deserted the party in 1932. Being less able and willing to confront colonialism, the majority of the Wafd leaders therefore decided in the mid-1930s to strengthen themselves against the Palace by a deal with Britain.[15] To achieve this, they were bound to compromise on the nation's demands. The upshot of this weakness was the conclusion of the 1936 treaty that legalized British occupation of Egypt and maintained the British-dominated administration in the Sudan.

The Sudan

Sudanese resistance to British colonial rule expressed itself in the aftermath of the First World War in various activities and sentiments. The educated elite and the Mahdists, the religious nationalists, organized this opposition

12. E. Kedourie (ed.), 1970, pp. 90–1.
13. O. Tweedy, 1931, p. 198.
14. A. L. A. Marsot, 1977, p. 139.
15. H. A. Ibrāhīm, 1976, pp. 24–5.

in the northern Sudan while the protest movements in the southern Sudan were predominantly local in nature.

Young protest movements

The recently emergent educated elite played a distinctive role in the development of Sudanese politics during the period 1919–25. This group of men was mainly composed of students and 'graduates' of Gordon Memorial College and Khartoum Military College. They formed their own associations through which they conducted an active political campaign against colonialism. The earliest of these 'young' associations was the Graduates' Club of Omdurman formed in 1918. But in the immediate post-war years two clandestine associations of a more political nature were formed, namely, the League of Sudanese Union (LSU) in 1919, and, more importantly, the White Flag League (WFL), founded in May 1924 by 'Alī 'Abd al-Laṭīf, the most prominent nationalist leader at the time.

The Sudanese nationalist movement of the early 1920s has been dismissed by many British writers as unrepresentative and its proponents as mere agents and pawns of Egypt. But recent studies by Sudanese scholars have demonstrated that though tactically, culturally and ideologically closely connected with Egypt, this movement was indigenous and mainly concerned with the repudiation of British colonial rule. The programmes of both the LSU and WFL stressed and gave precedence to liberation from 'the slavery of the colonial master'. The originality of this movement is better seen in a telegram that 'Alī 'Abd al-Laṭīf and three of his colleagues sent to the governor-general on 15 May 1924. This important document spoke explicitly of a Sudanese *nation* and a right to self-determination, brushing aside British and *Egyptian* claims to decide, alone, the future of the Sudan.[16]

The call for unity with Egypt that the nationalists advocated was apparently more of a political slogan than a tenet of nationalist faith. It was largely an expedient calculated to gain the sympathy and support of Egypt, which was undergoing a national struggle herself. Moreover, this slogan of unity seems to have been forced on the nationalists by the refusal of Britain to concede the right of self-determination, and her policy of using local and religious leaders to perpetuate her rule. From this point, 'the idea of unity was the most, if not the only, leeway and counter-strategy for the nationalists'.[17] Once Britain, the common enemy, was expelled from the Sudan, the nationalists expected that Egypt could be persuaded to leave. The motto of 'The Sudan for the Sudanese' raised by the traditional and conservative leadership was dismissed by the educated as a British-inspired plot to exclude Egypt and dominate the Sudan.

Inspired by the example of the Wafd, Sudanese nationalists concept-

16. For the official translation of this telegram see H. Abdin, 1970, pp. 48–9.
17. ibid., p. 4.

PLATE 23.3 *University College, Khartoum, in 1953, with Gordon Memorial College in the background*

ualized and articulated local grievances into an ideology of opposition to alien rule. They did not, however, formulate their opposition in religious terms, but dwelled upon the economic and political grievances, always emphasizing the greed and foreignness of the colonizer. The 'Demands of the Nation' which 'Abd-al-Laṭīf wrote for al-Ḥaḍāra in 1922 was devoted entirely to criticism of the government.

The main technique used by the nationalists for the dissemination of their ideas and propaganda on a mass level was at first hand-outs. Leaflets were mailed to different addresses in the country. In November 1920 a 'Faithful Advisor' sent to hundreds of addresses copies of a famous circular letter in which he attacked British policy of 'divide and rule' in Egypt and the Sudan, and called upon the two nations to unite against British colonialism.[18] Leaflets were sometimes posted in public places and scattered on the streets. Moreover, the nationalists occasionally smuggled some material for publication in the sympathetic Egyptian press and organized plays and literary festivals.

By 1923, however, the nationalists had abandoned these ineffective clandestine methods of propaganda for more revolutionary tactics. They felt that open confrontation with the British colonial regime was the best way to broaden the nationalist base and mobilize popular support for its ideals. In this militancy, the nationalists were apparently consciously emulating the example of the Wafd in Egypt.[19] Like their counterparts in India, they also appealed over the heads of colonial officials in Khartoum to liberal opinion in Britain to support the Sudan's claim to self-determination.

This change in political orientation and tactics produced in 1924 violent political agitation in Khartoum and some provincial capitals and towns. The WFL organized a series of demonstrations and riots in Atbara, Port Sudan, El Obeid and Shendī (see Fig. 4.1), particularly after the arrest of its president, 'Abd al-Laṭīf, and two of his colleagues in July. The secular side of Sudanese nationalism was more pronounced in these riots.

The Sudanese military were particularly susceptible to the ideas and propaganda of the WFL. The cadets were incited to demonstrate in some northern and southern towns. Those of the Military School in Khartoum paraded in the streets of the town, with arms and ammunition.

The Sudanese officers, many of whom were of Dinka origin, resorted to arms against British colonialism. They planned and executed the important military revolt of November 1924 in Khartoum. The main political motive of this revolt was a gesture of solidarity and comradeship with the departing Egyptian battalions.[20] Sudanese troops marched from

18. M. Abd al-Rahim, 1969, pp. 102–3.
19. H. Abdin, 1970, p. 64.
20. Britain used the assassination of Sir Lee Stack, the Governor-General, in Cairo as a pretext to demand, *inter alia*, the immediate withdrawal of Egyptian troops from the Sudan.

591

their barracks to join the Egyptian units in Khartoum North. The possibility that they planned to act in concert with their Egyptian colleagues to bring off a *coup d'état* cannot be overlooked.

But the British troops fired on them *en route*. The result was a fierce battle that continued throughout the evening and night of 27–8 November, and claimed the life of more than a dozen Sudanese troops. A subsequent court martial executed three others and sentenced the rest of the participants to long terms of imprisonment.

The total collapse of this revolt marked the beginning of a decade during which the intelligentsia 'laid low nursing the wounds of the previous years and rethinking their plans and methods for the future'. Politically it was a decade of disillusionment and futility. The hostility of the colonial regime and its determination to suppress open political action forced the educated class to fall back on literary, religious and social activities 'as an alternative outlet and a means of regroupment'.[21] They formed small study groups in various towns and pioneered several newspapers and magazines. These short-lived but lively journals 'testify to the vigour and earnestness of that generation'.[22] The folklore of this period, particularly poetry, expressed resentment and bitterness towards the arrogance and authoritarianism of British officials.

The first nationalist movement of the early 1920s was thus not successful and the main reason for its failure was that it lacked popular support. This was mainly because it neither sought nor wished to ally itself with local and religious forces, the two reservoirs of mass following in the country. Nevertheless, it is significant because it emerged earlier than nationalist movements in other tropical African dependencies. Moreover, its ideological components survived the decade of political apathy. For its most important political slogan – the Unity of the Nile Valley – was picked up by the Ashiḳa and other Unionist parties in the 1940s.

Mahdist resistance to colonial rule

Mahdism was one of the early weapons that the Sudanese used in their struggle against colonialism outside the metropolitan province around Khartoum. Both the militants and the neo-Mahdists had, in their own ways, opposed colonial rule during this period.

Mahdist risings

Hardly a year passed during the first generation of Condominium rule (1899–1955) without a Mahdist rising against colonialism. Though this wave of millenarian movements had subsequently gradually died down in the sedentary parts of the Sudan, the Mahdists remained active in Dārfūr (see Fig. 4.1). Many assumed for themselves messianic prophecy and

21. H. Abdin, 1970, p. 98.
22. Abd al-Rahim, 1969, p. 113.

declared a *djihād* against the 'infidel' British rule. The most important of them was *faḳī* 'Abdullāh al-Sihaynī, the leader of the Nyāla revolt of 1921.

Like its predecessors, the Nyāla revolt aimed at the repudiation of the 'infidel' colonial rule and the restoration of the 'glorious' Mahdiyya in the Sudan. Beside this fundamental religious drive, the imposition of a centralized colonial administration, increase in the herd tax, and the over-estimation of the *'ushūr*, were all other factors that provoked the people in Dārfūr to join the revolt.[23]

Led by al-Sihaynī, a force of about five thousand warriors attacked Nyāla fort and the market on 26 September 1921. They gained control of the fort and set fire to a nearby building. Al-Sihaynī launched a second attack that could have driven the enemy into confusion had he not been seriously wounded. The colonial casualties in this round were forty-three killed and twenty-one wounded, while at least six hundred Sudanese died in action.

Though al-Sihaynī was publicly hanged on 4 October, his adherents continued the struggle. They concentrated a force of about five thousand men some 80 km from Nyāla. Faced with these dangerous developments, colonial officials sent a strong punitive force that toured southern Dārfūr. It arrested many people, burned their houses, seized their cattle and confiscated their property. By May 1922, this period of resistance in Dār Masalīt had ended.

The Nyāla revolt was certainly the most important revolt against colonialism in the Sudan before 1924. Unlike previous Mahdist movements, it 'nearly succeeded in its apparent immediate objective', and fully revived 'the old fear of a large-scale religiously-inspired revolt'.[24] Though the rising failed to destroy colonial rule, its limited success was taken as a warning.

Neo-Mahdism

Since 1914, Sayyid 'Abd al-Raḥmān, the posthumous son of the Mahdī, had felt that fanaticism would no longer work and that the interests of both the Sudanese nation and the Mahdist sect would best be served by co-operating with the British on the motto of the Sudan for the Sudanese. This constitutionalism did not really ring true, but was, in fact, dictated by political realities. For al-Sayyid clearly realized that an armed rising could only lead to total destruction.

Similarly al-Sayyid was shrewd enough to realize that political and religious agitation required financial backing. Consequently, he enlarged his agricultural and commercial enterprises until he had become a large landowner and a wealthy capitalist by 1935. Rather than giving a non-political outlet to his ambitions as the colonial officials had naïvely expected, 'Abd al-Raḥmān used this wealth to strengthen the Anṣār organization.

23. H. A. Ibrāhīm, 1979, pp. 459–60.
24. M. D. Daly, 1977, p. 144.

Through adroit manoeuvres and obstinate contest, he shrewdly by-passed colonial restrictions, consolidated his influence in traditional Mahdist centres in the west, and attracted fresh adherents and founded new spheres of influence. Seeing that political nationalism was beginning to supersede religion as the principal motive power in the east, al-Sayyid made special efforts in the 1930s to gain the support of the educated class.[25]

By 1935 neo-Mahdism had thus become an important anti-colonial political force. The potential unity that it achieved between a sizeable section of the intelligentsia and the traditional and religious elements became the nucleus for the Independence Front that had an overwhelming nationalist appeal in the 1950s. This Front played an important and unique role in achieving the independence of the nation in 1956.

Local protest movements in the southern Sudan

The African peoples of the southern Sudan continued their risings against British colonial rule during this period. This resistance was marked by three notable features. It was not always, or even usually, a response to obvious administrative oppression. Instead, its fundamental objective was to end British colonialism in this African region. Moreover, it now extended to groups whose earlier attitudes, though aloof and suspicious, had not been systematically hostile to colonial rule. Above all, it represented an enormous increase in the scale of activity in which the Dinka and Nuer, the two largest ethnic groups in this region, were particularly active. They ignored their usual local distinctions and concentrated their resistance under emergency leaders, some of whom were religious leaders – often charismatic 'prophets'. Of this major wave of resistance two risings deserve particular attention: the Aliab Dinka uprising (1919–20) and the Dinka revolt (1927–8). African traditional religion affected the nature of these revolts. But, in addition, neglect as much as oppression had stung the Aliab Dinka into open revolt in 1919.

The immediate cause of the first uprising was the malpractices of the Aliab's immediate colonial administrator, the *ma'mūr*, particularly his extortion of cattle and women. This uprising seemed to have been part of a master plan in which other southern Sudanese peoples were involved.[26] While the Bor Dinka were only with difficulty restrained from rising in support of the Aliab, the Mandari, a completely separate non-Dinka people, actually joined them in this uprising.[27]

The Aliab Dinka uprising began on 30 October 1919, when a force of about three thousand warriors attacked the police station at Minkamman south of Sobat river. The station itself was overwhelmed by the Aliab, though the *ma'mūr* managed to escape. Two days later, a group of Mandari

25. H. A. Ibrāhīm, 1977.
26. L. L. Mawut, 1978, p. 80.
27. G. N. Sanderson, 1980, pp. 4–5.

entered a telegraph linesmen's *zarība* at Mulla, killed three of its men and carried off their guns. On 2 November the Aliab struck again, attacking a resthouse and killing two policemen.[28] Although this Dinka assault was eventually repelled, the campaign proved very costly for the colonial rulers. Some colonial officials and many policemen died on the battlefield.

In this crisis of Dinka history, a very large part of the Dinka peoples found their charismatic leader in one Bul Yol, better known by his 'God-given' name of Ariendit. With his great skill in creating political organization, Prophet Ariendit had by 1921 mobilized the Dinka peoples against colonialism. His programme was simple and radical: an end to colonialism – in effect Dinka independence.[29] His militant supporters made various attacks on colonial positions, but they were dispersed in February–March 1922.

The Nuer peoples offered another formidable challenge to colonialism in the southern region. In spite of the successive punitive patrols of the British forces, they did not accept defeat. In their eyes they had lost a number of battles but had not lost the war. Their resistance, however, reached its climax in their revolt in 1927–8.

Led by the powerful and influential Prophet Garluark, the western Nuer refused to obey the orders of the administration. When Fergusson, the district commissioner of western Nuerland, arrived in December 1927 at Lake Jorr on an inspection tour, a crowd of several thousand Nuer warriors attacked his party. They killed him with eighteen of his people while the rest of the visiting party rushed away panic-stricken and escaped.

Simultaneously, the Nuer people in Lou country south of the Sobat river rose against colonialism. Their influential leader, Prophet Gwek Ngundeng, refused to see colonial officials including the Governor-General himself. He sent emissaries to all parts of the Lou country and neighbouring groups of Nuer with the message to prepare for war against the 'Turks'.[30] Knowing that Ngundeng could strike at any time, colonial officials took strong measures to suppress his movement.

The extreme and indiscriminate violence used against these risings led to huge death and destruction. Nevertheless, the gallant resistance of the Dinka and the Nuer impressed the British colonialists that violence alone would not work. It forced them to inaugurate by the early 1930s a new conciliatory and 'caring' policy towards the peoples of the southern Sudan.

Somaliland

The Somali people had for long had a deeply-rooted common sentiment of Somali nationality, accentuated by a virtually uniform national culture,

28. R. O. Collins, 1967, p. 77.
29. G. N. Sanderson, 1980, p. 22.
30. O. Digernes, 1978, p. 88.

and reinforced by a strong adherence to Islam.[31] Like both their predecessors and successors, the inter-war Somali nationalists appealed to this national identity in their struggle against Italian, British and French imperialism in the respective Somaliland territories (see Fig. 4.1).

Besides this underlying factor, there were other forces at work too. They related to the social innovations that colonialism had introduced into the Somali social fabric. Colonial forces had, in fact, destroyed the traditional social and political institutions and imposed their own. They introduced in all parts of Somalia a centralized system of administration that vested all effective powers in the hands of colonial administrators, and gave no Somali any position of command except at the very lowest level. Colonial appointed chiefs, known as *akils* in the British Protectorate and *capos* in Italian-ruled Somalia, operated in an advisory capacity only, and as vehicles for colonial directives to the people. This was indeed a wide departure from the traditional free local institutions and the nomadic way of life to which the Somali people were overwhelmingly dedicated. With their fierce sense of independence and traditional disdain for all foreign elements, especially white Christians, the Somali people were bound to resist this radical innovation.

Before the colonial era, the Somali were not subject to government imposts other than *qadi* fees and import and export duties. But the colonial powers campaigned to mobilize and exploit all Somali resources – human and material – using their newly-appointed chiefs who had no regard for traditional authority. Direct taxes were instituted for the first time in Somaliland. While in Italian Somalia this took the form of an annual hut tax, in the Protectorate the British imposed taxes on livestock. Moreover Somali labour was forcibly recruited for colonial enterprises. The French recruited 2000 Somali to work for them as manual labourers during the First World War. Of these, 400 were killed and another 1200 were wounded.[32] Italian administrators sent out frequent expeditions to provide the required labour for their plantations in Somalia. These Somali recruits were grouped according to their ethnic origins and forced to live in colonial villages on the consortiums. All this hardship and exploitation produced a widely-felt sense of resentment to colonialism.

Somali resistance to colonial rule during the period 1919–35 was thus a direct response to these social changes. It expressed itself in two types of protest movements: local and elitist.

Local protest movements

By and large, Somali resistance in the inter-war period in the European colonies and in the Ethiopian-occupied Ogaden was local in nature and at no time involved all Somali people. This was mainly due to the fact

31. I. M. Lewis, 1963, p. 147.
32. V. Thompson and R. Adloff, 1968, p. 10.

that the Somali did not constitute a single autonomous political unit. Instead they were divided into a number of large and often mutually hostile clans, themselves 'further split into a wide array of subsidiary kingship groups', each usually composed of a few thousand men only.[33]

These local risings are too many and too diverse to be enumerated here. But what they stood for could be seen from studying some of them.

The directive of the colonial administrators to all Somali chiefs and elders to surrender firearms and ammunition was rejected outright by Ḥādji Ḥasan of the Galjal Haya. He defiantly replied to the regional commissioner:

> I do not accept your order. We will not come to you at any cost because you have broken our pact. . . . The government has its law and we have ours. We accept no order other than our own. Our law is that of God and the Prophet. . . . If you come into our land to make war we will fight you in every way. . . . God has said: The few can defeat the many. The world is near its end; only 58 years remain. . . . We do not want to stay in this world, it is better to die following Muslim law. All Moslems are one.[34]

Though Ḥādji Ḥasan was captured, the spirit of resistance could not be killed. For the Bantu Eile people waged another rising near Bur Acuba.

Meanwhile, imperialism was pushing for a new frontier. The resistance to the Italian attempt to incorporate in their colony the two provinces of Obbia and Majerteyn (see Fig. 4.1), was another example of the determination of the Somali people to maintain the traditional and free social fabric of their society. Yūsuf 'Alī Kenadid, Sultan of Obbia, approached his counterpart in the Sultanate of Majerteyn for a united front against the invaders. But local differences prevented this.

Though Obbia was annexed in 1925 and the Italians pensioned Yūsuf off to Mogadishu,[35] a daring rising occurred at El Bur. It was led by 'Umar Samatar, a Majerteyn clansman appointed by the Italians as chief of the local population. Samatar seized El Bur's fort and entrenched his forces in its central building. The Italian forces that besieged him were in turn besieged by the surrounding population led by Herzi Gushan, Sultan 'Alī Yūsuf's district military commander. On 15 November the colonial forces retreated to Bud Bud, leaving behind thirty-eight dead among whom was the Italian Resident himself. On 30 November the Italians suffered another defeat in an ambush at Bot.[36] Samatar and some of his followers crossed the border to Ethiopia where they campaigned against Italian infiltration in the Ogaden and attacked border posts.

33. I. M. Lewis, 1963, p. 147.
34. Quoted by R. L. Hess, 1966, p. 151.
35. G. O. 'Isa, 1965, p. 172.
36. R. L. Hess, 1966, p. 154.

The Italians faced an even more serious resistance in the Midjurtayn Sultanate. Its reputable Sultan, 'Uthmān Maḥmūd, refused the inferior status assigned by the colonialists to himself and his people. In spite of colonial repression, his movement continued to thrive, and he held out against the invaders for almost two years. He was, however, arrested towards the end of 1927 to be treated in the same manner as his kinsman Yūsuf.[37] But the struggle continued under the leadership of his son and heir apparent, Herzi Bogor.

Supported by the traditional chiefs who urged an outright war, Herzi attacked the Italian bases at Ras Hafun, and early in December 1925 drove an Italian garrison out of Hordio. A second large attack six weeks later threatened Italian installations at Cape Guardafui. Herzi made another daring assault on Eil at the mouth of the Nogal.[38] Again the colonialists reacted in their predictable manner: making arrests and deporting leaders. As for Herzi he went to Ethiopia, but returned after several years to Mogadishu where he died of smallpox.

Meanwhile the ever-present memory of Sayyid Muḥammad's revolt entrenched the spirit of resistance in the hearts of many Somalis in the Protectorate. They remained active and alert to harass the colonial regime whenever they felt it to be weak. Some of the Sayyid Muḥammad's supporters, like Faraḥ 'Umar and Ḥādjdj Bashīr Yūsuf, continued the struggle.[39] Moreover, local risings, particularly in the west and along the eastern borders, were often waged against the British. The innovation of western education in the Protectorate was interpreted by religious leaders as an instrument for Christian missionary activities and consequently a threat to Islam. The attempts to foster such education in 1920 and 1935 aroused fierce resentment that culminated in two riots: at Burao in 1922 and Baro in 1936. On the latter occasion the newly-appointed British director of education was greeted with a shower of stones.[40]

Equally significant were the local risings against French colonialism. Both the Afar, and the Isa Somalis, the two main ethnic groups in French Somaliland, displayed a hostile attitude towards colonial administration. The Afar Sultanates of Tadjūra and Gobaad were particularly active in this respect. The French had in fact summarily deported the Sultan of Gobaad to Madagascar in 1931.[41]

The Sultan of Awṣa, who had for long opposed French penetration in the area, had his own grievances during the inter-war period. French control of the region between the coast and the Ethiopian frontier deprived him of the revenues he had formerly derived from the local people and the caravan trade. Hence Sultan Yayū ambushed and arrested Lippmann,

37. I. M. Lewis, 1965, p. 99.
38. R. L. Hess, 1966, p. 155.
39. G. O. 'Isa, 1965, p. 130.
40. I. M. Lewis, 1965, pp. 103–4.
41. V. Thompson and R. Adloff, 1968, p. 11.

the newly appointed French governor at Dikhil. His successor, Albert Bernard, and sixteen of his Somali troops were murdered at Morheito in 1935. The activism of the Sultan of Awṣa further increased after the Italian conquest of Ethiopia in 1935 and Rome's backing of Awṣa's territorial claims at the expense of France.[42]

The arbitrary colonial partition of Somali frontiers was done without consulting the clansmen concerned and with little or no account of clan distribution or grazing needs. The Gadabursi and Isa clans, for example, were divided between Britain and Ethiopia, and, in the case of the Isa, France also. Boundaries sometimes cut across many ethnic groups, and in several cases lands belonging to one group were allocated to new owners with no traditional claims to them. The outcome was agitation to get back lost lands or to be allowed to rejoin kinsmen in a different location. The Somali people had often resisted this colonial demarcation of the frontiers by force. The joint Anglo-Ethiopian commission that was sent in 1932 to fix the Protectorate's boundary, for example, encountered violent opposition from the clansmen in the area, and its officer in charge was killed.[43]

These local risings against colonial rule in Somaliland were limited in scope and nature. Since they were undertaken within the traditional framework of the Somali segmentary system, widespread co-operation was extremely difficult. The inherent rivalry between different clans, and their internal fights for water and grazing grounds were crippling disadvantages to Somali resistance.[44] Colonial administrators took advantage of this situation to play off one ethnic group against another, and to find for themselves agents and allies. The tough policy that they used against these risings was a further reason for their limitation. Nevertheless they provided an element of continuity with the former era and laid the foundation for further popular resistance to colonialism in Somaliland.

Elitist protest movements

Working in opposition to the government-appointed chiefs, who were becoming increasingly unpopular, the educated elite and the politically conscious Somali inside and outside the peninsula organized their own 'young' associations. Through these organizations the modern Somali nationalists – government officials, merchants, seamen and so on – conducted their political campaign.

Ḥādjdjī Farah ʿUmar, a former colonial official and a pioneer modern politician, became an active nationalist in 1920 in the Protectorate. He protested against the excesses of colonial administration, and campaigned for the improvement of economic facilities and the expansion of education. Significantly, he did not limit his activities to matters concerning British

42. ibid.
43. I. M. Lewis, 1965, pp. 106–7.
44. E. R. Turton, 1972, p. 124.

Somaliland alone but also took a wide interest in Somali affairs in general. The British exiled him to Aden, but, with the co-operation of the Somali community there, he founded the Somali Islamic Association. Though not a political organization as such, this association promoted Somali interests. Ḥādjdjī Faraḥ brought Somali national aspirations to the notice of the British public through articles in Aden newspapers, and petitions and letters addressed to the British government, press and members of parliament.

Significant among these 'young' activities were the clandestine meetings organized by junior colonial officials and the political clubs established by merchants in the main towns of the Protectorate in the mid-1930s. These, however, did not attempt a large-scale organization, but were limited to select membership.[45] Nevertheless, they played a role in articulating people's grievances, and in promoting political consciousness in towns and urban centres. In French Somaliland, too, some interest in politics was displayed by the Seamen's Union established in Djibuti in 1931. This organization's range of interest was not limited strictly to sailors' affairs, but included national matters such as 'the Somali representation in government and their share in the territory's economy'.[46]

From these tentative beginnings the Somali National League (SNL), the most important 'young' association in the inter-war years, emerged in 1935. From its inception the SNL had been a 'Pan-Somali organization striving to break down all traditional resistance to a national patriotism'.[47] The SNL continued to exist under various titles, and in 1951 it emerged as a fully-fledged political party in the British Protectorate.[48]

These elitist associations have, however, played a limited role in mass mobilization against colonialism. We should remember that the intelligentsia, the only people capable of organizing and sustaining a modern political movement, were very limited in number since Western education during the inter-war period was virtually ignored in all parts of Somaliland. Furthermore, colonial authorities took prompt steps to penalize the activists among the educated elite, for instance dismissal from government service and posting to remote areas. Nevertheless the limited awareness founded by these associations developed into a stronger political consciousness in the years after the Second World War.

In this connection one has to mention the invention in about 1920 of an indigenous alphabet for the Somali language, the 'Osmania Alphabet', so named after its inventor 'Uthmān Yūsuf Kenadid. Both the conservative religious leaders, who favoured Arabic as a medium for writing Somali,

45. S. Touval, 1963, p. 65.
46. ibid., p. 70.
47. I. M. Lewis, 1961, p. 286.
48. I. M. Lewis, 1963, pp. 148–9. For the programme of this party which stressed Somali nationhood, see ibid., p. 149.

and the Italian colonialists opposed its use.[49] Nevertheless, it gained restricted currency and was later heralded by the nationalists 'as a symbol of Somali achievement'.[50]

Conclusion

We have narrated the basic facts about political change in North-East Africa in the years between 1919 and 1935. But it is important to place those basic events within the wider dialectical contexts we mentioned earlier.

In parts of North-East Africa, there was an interplay between religion and nationalism. In Egypt during these inter-war years, the trend was discernibly in the direction of secular nationalism, but in Somalia and northern Sudan the trend was less clear since religion was more politicized there. In southern Sudan, nationalism was still at the level of basic localized protest but conditioned sometimes by indigenous religious symbols.

We should also note that the inter-war years witnessed severe economic problems in this region even before the Great Depression began in the industrialized world. The tensions generated by regional and global economic dislocations helped to make the political climate in North-East Africa, especially in Egypt, more responsive to the trumpet call of patriotism. One of the few benefits of economic hardship can sometimes be the activation of a sense of patriotic duty and commitment. Egypt's economic suffering and exploitation helped to arouse nationalist sentiment.

Thirdly, these inter-war years witnessed both new imperial expansion and new anti-colonial militancy. As we indicated, European imperialism was pushing for its last territorial frontier, while African nationalism entered a new phase of articulation. Egypt had become a protectorate from 1914, and even after formal 'independence' in 1922, it remained an unwilling British vassal. On the other hand, the astonishing (if short-lived) unity Egypt achieved in 1919 did extract significant concessions from imperial Britain.

What should not be tactfully overlooked in this period was Egypt's own role in relation to the Sudan. Egyptian nationalism under Saʿd Zaghlūl and subsequent Wafd leaders included a romanticized notion of Egyptian sovereignty over the Sudan, which was thought of as going back a millennium.

And yet even Egypt's expansionist role had liberating functions. Pro-Egyptian sentiment in the Sudan was often simultaneously anti-British. It also provided the basis of solidarity among Egyptian and Sudanese nationalists – helping them to create their own myth of 'the Unity of the Nile Valley' in order to combat Lord Salisbury's earlier imperial myth of the conquest of the Nile.

49. R. al-Barāwī, 1973, p. 77.
50. I. M. Lewis, 1965, p. 115.

In Somalia and the Sudan the nationalist struggle was not yet strong enough to achieve substantial results. But the Egyptian struggle had a demonstrable impact on its neighbours. The seeds of liberation were indeed being sown in the Nile Valley and the Horn of Africa in these inter-war years.

Politics and nationalism in the Maghrib and the Sahara, 1919–35

J. BERQUE

After the First World War: an upsurge of nationalism and colonialist reaction

The political historian on the look-out for signs of what is somewhat inaccurately called 'nationalism'[1] at first finds explicit evidence of it only in Tunisia. In Algeria he notes a growing malaise, but is puzzled by its ambiguity. In Morocco the birth of a nationalist party dated only from some ten years after the end of the First World War, and even then had a formidable traditional past to contend with. In Libya, the people were still preoccupied with the problem of maintaining their sovereignty and independence in the face of the aggressive imperialism of Italy, and as it was seen in Chapter 5, this struggle continued until the 1930s. Libya is therefore not dealt with in this chapter.

Open war and passive resistance

The 'dissidence' or *sība* of the Berbers, then practically general in Morocco, was clearly a continuation of a pre-colonial phenomenon. But it was no longer the same as it had been under Mulāy Ḥasan,[2] when it could easily accommodate itself to the official fiction which saw it as a fairly harmless game akin to refusal to pay taxes. The penetration of the French into the Middle Atlas region, at the time of which we are speaking, encountered more difficulty than that of the sultans,[3] despite the fact that it was still effected in the name of the 'legal government' or *Makhzen*. But the *Makhzen* was from now onwards that of the Christians – the *Makhzen al-Naṣāra* – and aroused more dangerous reactions than the old ethnic unrest. The defence of the nation took the form of xenophobia and holy war, and resistance spread over all the High and Middle Atlas. Towards

1. At this point it would be more appropriate to speak of 'patriotism'; cf. M. Lacheraf, 1963, p. 69. And as Anouar Abdel Malek has suggested, *'nationalitaire'* ('nationalitarian' – pro-nationality) would be more correct in this context than *'nationaliste'* (pro-nation).
2. Cf. Al-Nāṣirī, 1907, pp. 277 ff (trans. Eugène Fumey).
3. See A. Guillaume, 1946, p. 47.

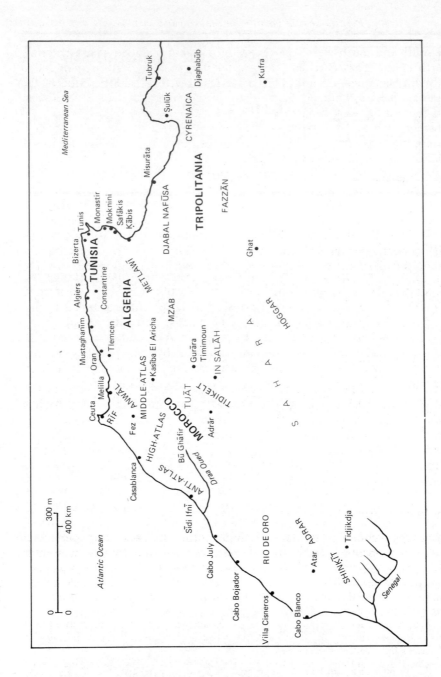

FIG. 24·1 *Politics and nationalism in the Maghrib and the Sahara, 1919–35*

604

the south and south-west, it encountered a strong continental substratum.[4] North of the Tāza corridor, the greater part of the coastal region ceded to Spain remained unsubdued. Far to the east, on the other side of the Algerian Sahara,[5] independent organizations functioned in Tripolitania, and the Sanūsī were able to consolidate their position in the oases.[6] To consider such a widespread phenomenon as mere unruly conservatism is certainly to underrate it. In my opinion the main impetus behind it was a tradition of communal liberty.

Parallel to this war-like continuity, there prevailed over the rest of the Maghrib the exact opposite, in the form of growing stability and the establishment of civilian government. It is very likely that the behaviour of many people concealed different kinds of opposition. This took various forms, including loyalist protest and passive resistance. But, as one unusually perspicacious governor wrote, 'one cannot speak of passiveness among the natives'.[7] He had observed that 'certain grievances, everywhere the same, commanded such unanimity that on these particular subjects a public opinion could be said to exist'. As soon as the occasion presented itself, this public opinion took the form of opposition. Its swift transformation into political action alarmed the rulers during the brief electoral career of the Emir Khālid.[8] A former captain in the French army, grandson of the great ʿAbd al-Ḳādir, Khālid enjoyed a short period of popularity. In the name of his 'Muslim personality' he extolled the honour of Algeria and emphasized her claims to France's gratitude for all the soldiers she had supplied. Khālid's party, which defeated the moderates in the Algiers town council election, seemed to the authorities so dangerous that they annulled the election. The emir then won a second and a third election, but was finally obliged to leave Algeria (1923). In metropolitan France, he remained active for a while, though his objectives might no longer have been restricted to France and the Maghrib.[9]

The constitutional quarrel in Tunisia

During the second part of the nineteenth century, Tunisia had experienced a reformist upsurge which was in some respects in advance of similar

4. The areas later known as the Algero-Moroccan Marches, the north of present-day Mauritania and the western part of the Sahara, known as the Rio de Oro, were still the scene of communal raids or *rezzous*, while at the same time attempts at organization were being made by the successors of the great religious reformer, Māʾ al-ʿAynayn.

5. Where, until his accidental death, General Laperrine worked energetically to rally the Tawārik, who during the First World War had been roused by Sanūsī propaganda and various independent movements.

6. The Italians did not succeed in reducing the 'Misurata Republic' until 1923, when they had to resume the fight in Cyrenaica against the Sanūsī and their supporters.

7. M. Violette, 1931, p. 396.

8. M. Kaddache, 1970, pp. 65 ff.

9. A. K. Saʿdallāh, 1969, pp. 420 ff.

movements in Egypt and Turkey.[10] The failure of these attempts had not lessened their appeal for the enlightened bourgeoisie, which was inclined to look to the East rather than to the West for its models. Ottoman nostalgia was now replaced by hope in the principles enunciated by Woodrow Wilson, and nationalism, as in the case of the Egyptian Wafd Party, changed its tune. Shaykh 'Abd al-'Azīz al-Tha'ālibī (Taalbi) and his friends decided to plead their cause before public opinion in metropolitan France, especially the socialist sector. Their pamphlet, *La Tunisie martyre* (The Martyrdom of Tunisia) (1920), presented a vigorous analysis of colonial deterioration. By founding the 'constitutionalist' or Destūrian party (February 1920) they intended to restore Tunisia to her independent existence.

Their argument was not without logic. The Protectorate had interrupted the renewal of an Arabo–Mediterranean nation. But strangely enough, as against the opinion of eminent French jurists,[11] the only response was the invocation of the power of the Bey three-quarters of a century after it had itself begun to fix its own constitutional limits. True, there had been indigenous representation on the Consultative Conference in Tunis since 1907. It was made up of nominated members, and like the French section had only fiscal powers. At the end of 1920, reform was requested by the majority of the French and by almost half the indigenous members; elective representation and an extension of powers were demanded. But the Destūr, going back on its original radical proposals (June 1920), published a reformist manifesto which 'played into the Protectorate's hands' (December 1921). Bey Nāṣir's quasi-ultimatum of 3 April 1922 was countered by intimidation.[12] But in the following year, various beylical decrees and Resident-General's orders (June 1922)[13] set up caïdal, regional and central representation by election at various levels.[14] A Ministry of Justice, entrusted to the son of the reformer Khayruddīn, had already been created. These were scanty results for a campaign which had managed to win over both local sovereigns and the French Chamber. Shaykh al-Tha'ālibī had served several months in prison. His release did not contribute to the unity of his party: it broke up into two groups, not equally active. In a colonial context, as Maître Guellati's experience showed, moderation is always suspect. But the radicalism of Shaykh al-Tha'ālibī and Maître Al-Ṣāfī (Essafi), for lack of even minor successes, was in danger of becoming perilously isolated, moribund and divorced from the course of events. 'Now that the first excitement was over, the Destour tended to bury itself

10. See J. Karoui, 1973.

11. C. A. Julien, 1972, p. 67; R. Le Tourneau, 1962, pp. 65 ff. These two books provide a sustained account of the events which the present chapter tries to interpret, and references to them could be multiplied.

12. C. A. Julien, 1972, p. 69.

13. On the context of these measures see R. Balek, 1922, pp. 240 ff.

14. The Italians, by setting up an 'Arab Parliament' in Cyrenaica (30 April 1921), had taken an initiative intended to go beyond what was demanded, but which failed to have the hoped-for pacifying effect.

in the subconscious, and to take on the purely theoretical colour of the *djihād* that slumbers there ...'[15]

Popular communities

The rural Maghrib consisted for the most part of an aggregate of traditional communities. The administration of Morocco openly depended on them, and institutionalized the chieftaincies. But beneath this official network, less docile traditional institutions with an even more turbulent potential could be discerned. French policy had long exploited particularism and local loyalties. The Senatus Consultum of 1863 had proposed the splitting up of the Algerian people into *duwārī*, or territorial divisions. The application of the law of 1884 had even given these divisions a communal significance similar to that existing in France.[16] In 1919, both the energy of the Berber resistance on the one hand, and, on the other, a development of public opinion that was already evident everywhere else, in their different ways emerged from popular democracy: this upthrust was archaic and defensive in the case of the Berbers, and frustrated and apparently repressed in the case of the rest, but for both the essential organ of expression was the *djemāʿa*.[17] For the French to take this rising social force into account and make it the principle and objective of an ultimate rapprochement was by no means absurd, and might in the long run have led to the emancipation of rural Algeria and its penetration by the metropolitan political system.

This was no doubt the ultimate aim of the law of 4 February 1919, known as the Jonnart Law, and of the two decrees putting it into effect. It gave Algerians who possessed certain qualifications (such as having served in the army, being able to read and write French, owning some land in the rural areas, etc.) the right to take part in electing the communal assembly of the *duwār-commune*, and some municipal offices, including that of the mayor.[18] Nearly half a million Muslims made up this primary electorate; among them were about a hundred thousand with the right to vote for departmental and central assemblies. But this did not end inequality. In the town councils, for example, the Muslims' representatives found themselves limited to a minority of a third of the membership. Although this prevented the Algerian masses from carrying the day,[19] the enlarging of the electoral college at the lowest level, and the fact that Algerian representatives were now able to take part in the choice of a

15. R. Balek, 1922, p. 286.
16. J. Berque, 1970, pp. 137 ff.
17. The heads of families of a community, and the 'collective' which ran it.
18. C. R. Ageron, 1966.
19. Even if, through naturalization, they managed to elect the mayor. This happened at Mekla, in Kabylia, where, flying in the face of all good faith, the administrative tribunal annulled the election.

mayor, struck the conservatives as subversive, though the timidity of these measures fell far below what had been asked for.[20]

The first responses of the workers

The heavy concentration of wage labourers in Tunisia, such as that in the Metlawī mines, for example, showed for a long time little sign of protest. As in Algeria, industrialization was not advanced enough, and the social context was too authoritarian, for the energy of the proletarian masses to manifest itself to begin with other than through a small avant-garde group educated in the ways of European trade unionism.

But in tunisia, the early action of Muḥammad 'Alī[21] and the analysis offered by Ṭahār al-Ḥaddād[22] had some effect on class organization. The adventurous life of the former had brought him into contact with German socialism and made him a friend of Enver Pasha, probably the man with the clearest sense at that time of the ways in which the leading ideas of the West might combine with the nationalist upsurge of the Islamic peoples. Al-Ḥaddād supplemented the foreign experience of Muḥammad 'Alī with an examination of the domestic problem. He discussed both the subject of the workers and that of women, showing a clear grasp of the nature of each question. The dockers, first of Tunis and then of Bizerta, the cement-workers of Ḥammām Līf, and others gave a practical response to Ḥaddād's dual drive.

At Bizerta, on 12 October 1924, nine regional unions became affiliated: they had the support of the French Communist Party (PCF), but were strongly criticized by the French section of the Workers' International (the SFIO), which was worried by the new group's nationalist affinities. The Destūr dissociated itself from what it considered to be a compromising collusion. But it joined, on a reformist basis, a coalition which in February 1925 brought together, in addition to the Destūr, the indigenous section of the Grand Conseil, the socialist party, and the French General Confederation of Labour (CGT). The complexity of these alliances and controversies, with their quarrels and reconciliations and changes of position, tend to obscure the spontaneity equally characteristic of such movements. At the same time, sectarian and ideological rivalries fore-shadowed a conflict of options. French socialism, at the Tours Conference, had split over both party policy and the unions. The semi-colonial proletariat seeking its own aims was thus exposed to a variety of conflicting influences. A number of different options took shape, which were to have different outcomes – for example, those of the Algerians, 'Amar Uzagān and Ben 'Alī Būkurt, and that of the Tunisian Mokhtār 'Ayārī. What place,

20. But C. A. Julien, 1972, p. 377, is probably right in thinking that the effect of this legislation on Algerian public opinion was probably not negligible.
21. P. Mamet, 1964; A. B. Hermasi, 1966.
22. T. al-Ḥaddād, 1927.

for example, would forthcoming trends of events accord to national identity, up till then defined in terms of Islam? Would national identity be swallowed up in the general aspirations of the proletariat?

The North African scene was not yet ready to provide clear-cut answers.[23] It was rather in Paris, among the émigrés from the Maghrib, that the Etoile nord-africaine was founded in 1924. Among its founders was an active member of the French Communist Party (PCF), 'Abd al-Ḳādir Ḥādj 'Alī. The new organization was set up in a revolutionary and anti-colonialist spirit rather than with any preoccupation with the problems of the working class as such. At first it enjoyed the patronage of the Emir Khālid.

The prevailing system and mounting opposition

The 1920s saw expanding communications in the Maghrib. Towns began to grow because of the influx of newcomers from the country. A new generation came of age, which had not known what life was like before the war.[24] Everything called out for change. The authority of colonialism and the authority of tradition, in varying combinations, called each other into question. These developments worried the colonial rulers, who tried to neutralize them by cunning or coercion. Yet more often, however, it was inertia that governed colonial practice, though one section of opinion in metropolitan France denounced abuse and inefficiency, and saw them as a source of danger.

It was true that the acceleration of events observable immediately after the First World War had slackened off both in Algeria and in Tunisia. The simultaneous departure in 1923 of al-Tha'ālibī and Khālid, the two principal leaders, seemed to have weakened the opposition. But in Morocco the authorities had to face other kinds of difficulty which were considered more pressing.

An anticipation of future events: the Rīf Republic

To describe as a 'revolt' the national struggle which the Rīf leader Muḥammad ben 'Abd al-Khaṭṭābī ('Abdel Karīm) brought to a resounding climax in 1925–6, and to treat it as a mere episode, is to underrate the

---

23. Repression was always on the alert. In Tunisia, for example, the experiment of the Confédération Générale des Travailleurs Tunisiens (CGTT) seems to have failed because of the arrest of its organizers and the banishment of their leader, Muḥammad 'Alī. It was not until some years later (in 1937) that Tunisian trade unionism, recognized as legal on 16 September 1932, resumed independent activity in the context of the events of the Popular Front. But after the second CGTT with Belḳāsim al-Ḳanāwī, it succumbed for the second time to political repression (1938).

24. For Tunisia see F. b. 'Ashūr, 1956. For Algeria, T. al-Madanī, 1963, pp. 92 ff., 353 ff. See also, A. Berque, 1947, pp. 123 ff.

PLATE 24.1 '*Abdel Karīm (1882–1963)*, ķādī *of Mellila, leader of Moroccan resistance to Spanish imperialism during the Rīf war, 1921–6*

PLATE 24.2 *The Rīf war: Spanish troops display heads of* '*Abdel Karīm's soldiers*

610

significance of facts which we now recognize as the forerunners of much later developments.[25]

The Rīf had never given up the struggle. 'Abdel Karīm's military talent had inflicted on Spain (at Anwāl, July 1921) one of the most famous disasters of the colonial wars.[26] The Spaniards suffered an equally murderous defeat in November 1924, when they had to evacuate Shafshāwīn in order to consolidate their front.

'Abdel Karīm, the son of a *ḳāḍī* (judge) of the Spanish Protectorate, and thus born and brought up in a situation of compromise, had studied for a time at the religious university of Ḳarāwiyyīn at Fez, where he probably first came into contact with Islamic modernism.[27] It was no less as a Muslim reformer than as a political leader that he established a position for himself among his contemporaries. As well as possessing military skill, he had an open-mindedness and political dexterity which enabled him to play a more influential part internationally than the Libyans who may to a certain extent be regarded as his counterparts – Sulajmān al-Bārūnī, Ramḍān Shatīwī, and especially 'Umar al-Mukhtār.[28] The metamorphosis he brought about in his own clan, the Benī Warighīl, and in the neighbouring communities, was a lasting one. He led these groups, ridden by clan vendettas, back to Islamic law, banning collective oaths and membership of brotherhoods, and forbidding married women to dance. The *ichbrawn* – little watchtowers in every village which from time immemorial had been the symbol of the aggressiveness of relations between neighbouring communities – were destroyed.[29] Even before the victory at Anwāl, a meeting at al-Kāma between Benī Warighīl, Temsamān, Benī Tūzīn and Ruḳḳūya produced a 'crystallization of the Rīfian state structure'.[30] The 'Rīfian Republican Nation', proclaimed according to some on 18 January 1923 and according to others on 1 February, was thus an attempt to reform the traditional state without destroying its positive aspects, such as certain practices facilitating group consultation and co-operation.

This reforming impulse should be related to other attempts of a similar kind which were then being made all over the Islamic-Mediterranean area:

25. For all we know, all the possibilities have not yet been realized although on the military plane 'Abdel Karīm's activity undoubtedly foreshadowed what happened after 1954.

26. This disaster was rightly described as 'the battle of Omdurman in reverse', the reference being to the battle in 1898 in which Kitchener crushed the Mahdist state. See A. Youssoufi, n.d., p. 113.

27. It is to be noted, however, that he later violently attacked Shaykh Būsha Ib-al-Dukkālī, who was chiefly responsible for introducing modernism into Morocco.

28. A. al-Misurātī, 1964, gives a lively account of the events of this period from the point of view of a Libyan patriot.

29. Unpublished communication by D. Hart, at the Conference on the Fiftieth Anniversary of the Rīf Republic in Paris in 1973.

30. A. Youssoufi, n.d., and in a communication to the Conference mentioned in note 29.

in Tripolitania; the Egyptian Delta; Mesopotamia, at Raḳḳa on the Euphrates, and so on.[31] Specialist studies will be needed to determine whether or not these were symptoms of nationalism. From the point of view of the colonial powers, their simultaneous occurrence was all the more dangerous in view of the fact that 'Abdel Karīm had established relations with the PCF, which actually called a strike in his support.[32] During this strike which occurred on 12 October 1925, many French workers demonstrated against the colonial war in Morocco. There was also a strong campaign of the masses at the national level against the war, organized by the PCF, the Young Communists, the CGTU (the CGT Unifié), ARAC (Association Republicaine des Anciens Combattants), etc. From the spring of 1926 onwards, the Third Republic resorted to disproportionate force to bring 'Abdel Karīm to heel.[33] But the rest of Morocco did not react.[34] Nevertheless, the military solution, which enabled Spain to establish itself effectively in its own zone, did not wipe out the significance of the 'Abdel Karīm experiment.

Contemporary accounts of the situation

In 1901 Algeria had been granted a regime known as the Délégations financières, a kind of internal political autonomy that was dominated almost until the end of colonial rule by the representatives of the white settlers. When this little agrarian parliament refused in 1927 to sanction the governor-general's wretched estimates for social welfare and school meals, it was to all intents and purposes signing its own death warrant. Maurice Violette pointed this out in a book prophetically entitled *L'Algérie vivra-t-elle?* (Will Algeria survive?); the solution he proposed was of course extremely orthodox, not to say Jacobin.[35] But the book represents an appreciable step forward, in that it suggests extending the representational reform of 1919.[36] Later, Violette went further to advocate that a minority of educated Algerians should be given the right to elect deputies to the French Parliament, without losing their other voting rights, based on their 'personal status'.

This status, which the French settlers used to emphasize their own different position, provided successive French governments with a useful excuse for not granting full French citizenship to Algerians. Reference to this status was probably, on both sides, no more than a pretext – a pretext

31. J. Berque, communication to Conference mentioned in note 29.
32. R. Gallisot, communication to Conference mentioned in note 29.
33. 'Abdel Karīm surrendered to the French authorities on 26 May 1926.
34. Despite a few individual gestures, people's hopes and sympathies remained stifled. A few youths in Fez forged a tract supposed to be by the Rīf leader thanking the notables of the country for their solidarity.
35. M. Violette took care to proclaim himself opposed to the extreme Left.
36. M. Violette, 1931, pp. 474 ff.

for one side to refuse, and a pretext for the other side to reject. But the proclaimed desire of most Algerians, who took the notion of assimilation literally, to become part of the French commonwealth, is striking. It cannot be dismissed out of hand as a deceit, but it should be interpreted at different levels, of which the most fundamental was probably the desire for emancipation. This semantic complexity is evident in the articles published by Ferhāt ʿAbbās between 1922 and 1927, which he brought out in 1931 under the title *Le Jeune Algérien* (The Young Algerian).[37]

These articles have certainly dated. But we must not forget that his arguments, his compassion for suffering, and the generosity of his hope, though they may not have constituted a political ultimatum, nevertheless provided a moral and conceptual framework for a possible political goal. Colonization was denounced as 'power without thought, brain without soul'. Islam's right to respect emerged as self-evident, though this had long been obscured. The preface to the articles, written long afterwards in 1930, made a careful distinction between the two aspects of the problem: the French and the Algerian. For the French, 'colonization is simply a military and economic venture defended thereafter by the appropriate administrative regime'. For the Algerians, by contrast, it is:

> a veritable revolution, overthrowing a whole ancient world of beliefs and ideas and an immemorial way of life. It confronts a whole people with sudden change. An entire nation, without any preparation, finds itself forced to adapt or perish. This situation is bound to lead to a moral and physical disequilibrium, the barrenness of which is not far from total disintegration.[38]

One would look in vain in the scientific writings of the period – in the works of L. Milliot, Augustin Bernard, R. Maunier, or even E. F. Gautier – for such a good definition of social change. Even the impressive historical synthesis of C. A. Julien, which was published at the time and played a recognized role in arousing North African awareness, could not improve on this inside view.

This view also gave rise to the 'Book of Algeria', the *Kitāb al-Djazāʾir* (1931), by Tawfīḳ al-Madanī. Its first page, illustrated by the miniaturist Rāsim, bears the triple device of the 'Ulamā', and the book as a whole, while describing the troubles of the Algerians and claiming their right to be an Arab nation, avoids polemics and aims at objectivity. It is still an indispensable contemporary document. The chapter on Algerian music[39] brings out essential values, and this part of the book also has pertinent remarks about the obstacles in the way of the Arabic press[40] and the signs

37. Ferhāt ʿAbbās took up the same themes retrospectively; see F. Abbās, 1962, pp. 113 ff.
38. F. Abbās, 1931, p. 9.
39. T. al-Madanī, 1963, pp. 339 ff.
40. ibid., pp. 343 ff.

of a literary renaissance.[41] The list of writers and poets provides a useful inventory for further studies, though it should be noted that it omits the 'Young Algerians', who were anxious to be regarded as French; and among these was Ferhāt 'Abbās.

Islamic reformism

As has been said, the book has the device of the 'Ulamā' on the flyleaf. Nowadays, emphasis is rightly put on the national aims of this association as well as on its religious objectives. The programme of Shaykh 'Abd al-Ḥamīd ben Bādīs,[42] though it is aimed at being free of circumstantial implications, was perhaps really more political than the other projects then in the forefront, compromised as these were by administrative manoeuvres at the bottom and by political intrigue at the top. The most spectacular attempts were far from being the most effective: for example, Dr Bendjellūl's venture at Constantine, or the egalitarian claims of the 'Elus'.[43] The Shaykh, while taking care not to defy French sovereignty, insisted on an 'intellectual and moral reform', and in so doing raised the question of identity, touched on the impulses of the majority, and echoed similar movements in the Middle East. He thus appealed to a model which compared well with that of western democracy. Above all he addressed himself to clearly existing signs of social dispersion and moral deterioration. Claiming Algeria as his homeland or *waṭan* (but not openly as a 'state' or *dawla*), Islam as his religion, and Arabic as his language, he combined tactical subtlety with foreknowledge of the role that culture could play in decolonization.

Another, less well-known aspect is the geographical one. As the *nasabs* (lines of descent) show, the leadership of the movement included several provincial names: not only those of the Constantine aristocracy, like Ben Bādīs, but also Tébessa, Mīla and Sīdī 'Oḳba.[44] Not content with having established the 'Circle for Progress' over the central plateau, especially Algiers and other urban areas, the movement also aimed at covering 'the unknown country'. Shaykh Bashīr al-Ibrāhīmī stirred Tlemcen to its depths, and attempts of this kind grew more and more numerous, in the form of sermons, and the activities of friendly societies and mutual benefit associations.

The resulting proliferation of centres of the movement is often recorded

41. ibid., pp. 353 ff.

42. A. al-M. Murtāḍ, 1971, pp. 54 ff., 115 ff., 179 ff. See also A. Merad, 1967.

43. A term used at the time for the members of a Federation formed on 11 September 1927 by various Muslim notables elected to the different Algerian assemblies. Mostefa Lacheraf distinguished carefully between the actions of these politicians and those of the 'Ulamā', though he is critical of the latter. See M. Lacheraf, 1965, pp. 188 ff.

44. Shaykhs al-Arabī al-Tebessī, Mubārak al-Mīlī and Ṭayyib al-'Oḳbī (a celebrated orator), were among the most famous members of the Ulemas' Association, founded in 1931.

only in terms of theological controversies which are almost incomprehensible to outsiders. But all these stirrings, whether under the aegis of the Ulemas or of some rival such as Shaykh Ben 'Alīwa at Mostagānem,[45] or arising out of ineradicable differences, as at Le Mzāb,[46] represented the first contact with a worldwide problem for communities which up till then had been quite cut off, and which the administration had been unable to arouse except perhaps against themselves. Shaykh Ben Bādīs and his friends set an example by giving North African Islam a doctrinal shake-up which had not been attempted for centuries: their commentaries on the Ḳu'rān, for example, were a cultural exploit if ever there was one.[47] They were even so bold as to distinguish between transcendental invariables and circumstantial variables in religion.[48] Detailed monographs are needed to study the relationships between the most important tendencies and the various social factors involved, and to distinguish the roles played by different social and age groups, economic strata, individuals, and moral attitudes. Such studies would without doubt reveal that the period was a turning-point in the social history of Algeria.

Three challenges to imperialism, and the reactions

Strange as it may seem today, the celebration of the centenary of the French landing in Algeria[49] did not call forth the open rebuke that we in this age of decolonization tend to attribute retrospectively to the colonized.[50] To the many Algerians who were then concerned with the claim for justice and equality, the festivities, which seemed likely to attract the interest of democratic elements in metropolitan France, brought first a renewal of hope, though this was swiftly followed by disillusion. The Muslim dignitaries of the regime – elected members, *caïds* and *bachagas* – vied shamelessly with one another in flattering the French,[51] thus discrediting what remained of the authority of the traditional aristocracy

45. A. Berque, 1936. There is no doubt that the ferment of Algerian Islam went far beyond the activities of the 'Ulamā'.

46. We may refer here to scholars such as Shaykhs Bayād' and At'fiyech. See M. A. Dabbūr, 1971.

47. Shaykhs Ben Bādīs and Ben 'Ashūr were probably the first modern North Africans after Shaykh Abū Rās of Mascara (end of eighteenth century) to apply themselves to this formidable task, though a Moroccan scholar as famous as Shaykh Ibn al-Khayyāṭ advised against it. See the latter's lithographed pamphlet on the subject, published in Fez.

48. According to a rather extraordinary passage in a funeral address given by Shaykh Ibrāhīmī by the grave of Professor Moḥammed Ben Sheben, *Shihāb*, May 1928.

49. There is a whole contemporary literature on the subject, most of it exasperatingly official in tone; but fortunately some scientific accounts stand out from the rest.

50. Some adverse propaganda was organized in certain towns in collaboration with the PCF. See A. Ouzegane, 1962, pp. 171 ff. and *passim*. The teachers' union, and Benhādj, a socialist militant, also had the courage to protest. See M. Kaddache, 1970, p. 193.

51. See M. Kaddache, 1970, p. 192, for some rather painful examples.

and of the inveterate profiteers of the policy of compromise. The paean of praise that arose to the glory of the settlers, now raised to the power of myth, set the seal on a policy from which France would rarely be able to free itself except by fits and starts. More serious still, the regime simply passed over its own weaknesses. This was all very well as far as the hypothesis of sovereignty was concerned, since the balance of forces was so staggeringly unequal that almost no one challenged the theory openly. But that very responsibility which should have been its corollary was exercised by officials with little generosity and even less lucidity. Is this painting too sombre a picture? Let us admit that there were brighter patches. The intention was that everything should be done with as little coercion as possible. There was undoubtedly to be exploitation but it was to be legal, softened with cultural prestige, enveloped in a republican aura, sparing of violence, and even permitting itself to invoke the liberties of bourgeois democracy. By a paradox which is difficult for us to understand now, this apogee of imperialism was also the apogee of liberalism in manners. It is for this reason that French North Africa presents historians with a much less tormented situation than that, for example, of British Egypt at the same point.

But this apparent good humour, and its corollary, acceptance, were not put to good use. This can be seen in the provocatively triumphant tone of the celebrations in Algiers, and, more characteristically still, in the Eucharistic Congress held at Carthage from 7 to 11 May 1930, which was seen by the young people of Tunisia as a crusade against Islam in North Africa.[52] However that might be, such a gathering was not in tune with the ideas towards which many people in the Maghrib still looked for hope and understanding: the great principles of the Revolution, the Jaurès tradition, the myth of progress.

In Morocco the Berber *zahīr* (royal proclamation) of 16 May 1930,[53] which incorporated Berber customary law into the French colonial judicial system, provided middle-class youth with an opportunity to appraise the position and with a first springboard for mass action. It was regarded as an attack on Islam and an attempt to divide the country, carried out in contempt of the undertakings of 1912. Though intended as a local and localizing measure, it had repercussions throughout the Muslim world, while on the spot it brought out into the open an opposition hitherto limited to small clandestine groups in two or three large towns.

In the three months[54] from 20 June to 30 September 1930, there were more than a hundred and twenty incidents. Most of them occurred in mosques, the dogmatic setting for the *laṭīf*, the Muslim prayer in distress.

52. J. Berque, 1970, pp. 253 ff.
53. ibid., pp. 250 ff.
54. Special number, May–June 1933, of the review *Maghreb*, which appeared under the patronage of such varied celebrities as Bergery, Renaudel, and the Spanish philosopher Ortega y Gasset.

These imprecations were considered such a threat to public order that the authorities met it with summonses, imprisonment, and beatings. A delegation from the town of Fez went to the capital, and on 31 August three of its members were imprisoned, among them 'Allāl al-Fāsī, 'a young scholar from Karāwiyyīn',[55] and Bel Ḥasan al-Wazzānī, 'graduate of the School of Social and Political Sciences in Paris'. The pair represented an almost symbolic combination of the two driving forces of resistance – orthodox tradition and modernity – and, appropriately enough, repression played the role of catalyst. The number of arrests rose to 150. Many shops closed, as before, in protest. Despite the official ban, the *laṭif* rang out again from the mosques. There were clashes in the streets. The spell of the Protectorate was well and truly broken, if one interprets it as the sort of hypnosis through which technical superiority and the prestige of Lyautey had so long held the country in their grip.

In Paris, three years later, the review *Maghreb* devoted a special number to these incidents. Jean Longuet and other well-known Frenchmen, and particularly several young Moroccans, put forward a set of coherent arguments. The French sympathizers, though they rightly saw the 'Berber *ẓahīr*' of 1930 as a classic colonialist propaganda trick, had some difficulty, in view of their own anti-clericalism, in explaining the apparently religious aspect of many of the Berber reactions. 'Everyone must be aware that in the East and in all Muslim countries, religion and nationality intermingle', said the French leader writer. Less complacently, one of the Moroccan contributors to the review wrote: 'In our country we are ready to grant the Berbers what is generally refused to the Bretons in France. But we want it to be in the context of Islam, which for us is not only a religion but above all a civilization.' He thus brought out the cultural factor in the debate, an element modestly passed over by many, both friends and adversaries.

Towards confrontation

Out of the twenty years between the two world wars, half thus went by without any progress in the relations between France and the Maghrib. Of course, the economic situation was scarcely favourable. Hardly was the immediate post-war depression over than the world slump loomed ahead. It reached the Maghrib in 1932, accentuating the generally depressed state of the economy that had reappeared in 1925 and was to last for a whole decade. This embittered relations between capital and labour, that is between the French settlers and the Algerians. Progress in mechanization,

55. A member of an old family, already well known as a poet and scholar, he now discovered he had gifts as a speaker and organizer. He produced an impressive amount of work, among which the most directly related to the present subject are *al-Ḥarakāt al-Istiḳlāliyya fi'l-Maghreb*, Cairo, 1948, and *Al-Naḳd al-dhātī*, Cairo, 1956. On him, see A. Gaudio, 1972, and El Alamī, 1972.

planning, co-operatives, and even the unionization of public servants, enabled the French element to strengthen its stranglehold on the colony. The regime showed itself incapable of moderating the damaging effect of this stranglehold upon those it ruled. The connection between economic deterioration, which aggravated inequality, and political demands, is plain, but needs working out in more detail.[56] It seems to me that social change and the desire for a restored collective identity were even stronger factors than inequality in the awakening of North Africa. At all events, various motives combined to produce an aspiration which largely overrode party groupings. The Waṭaniyyīn or Moroccan 'Patriots' were then for the most part members of the bourgeois intelligentsia. The Etoile nord-Africaine had scarcely established itself in Algeria. The Destūr was still imprisoned in unreality. The PCF did not back up its radical theories with enough support on the spot.[57] Most drives for action remained implicit. Political expression was to be found in clubs, committees, groups without a name, or even just in the spreading of attitudes, rather than in political parties as such.

The administration, though unable to understand these nuances of expression, was very good at exploiting personal interests and rivalries. But it played down political protest. It had superiority of means on its side, as well as continuity, and even an apparent consensus. But it was oblivious of the forces which were gathering beneath the seemingly normal surface. If there happened to be an outburst, the government blamed 'trouble-makers', local or abroad, or the 'Reds', an attitude which excused both ultra-conservatism and repression.

New tactics, and obstructions to action

It was not all or nothing – far from it – but a deliberately temporal or even secular foothold on the political scene that Bourguiba[58] and his friends Baḥrī Ḳīḳa Ṭahār Ṣafār and Dr Maṭarī, among others, aimed at. They defended the conformist president of the Tunisian Co-operative, because by so doing they were able to rally public opinion. They went so far as to support a measure prescribed by the Resident, but which seemed to them to serve their cause 'objectively', as we might say (the proposal was that the budget provision for French officials should be reduced).[59] As

56. Attempts have already been made, without any great success. See J. Berque, 1970, pp. 101 ff. See also A. Nouschi, 1962, pp. 31 ff. As far as I know, this analysis, which is of great importance especially for its appraisal of the role played by social change during the period, has not yet been pressed far enough.

57. Apart from the positions it took up over the Rīf war, the PCF generally confined itself to anti-colonialism pure and simple, in Algeria itself and right up till the Popular Front. Thereafter the idea of a 'nation in the making' seemed to prevail.

58. See especially A. Bourguiba, 1954, *passim*.

59. ibid., pp. 10, 35 ff.

PLATE 24.3 *Habib Bourguiba (b. 1903), leader of the Neo-Destūr Party (Tunisia)*

regards the Great Mosque and the Tunis bourgeoisie, which provided many recruits for the Destūr, they did not conceal their criticism or their sarcasm. It was already apparent that the whole movement would be coloured by the fact that the men of the Sāḥel had become militant, and politicizing the country districts[60] was to be one of the aims of the Neo-Destūr. It was not by chance that the split which brought it into being took place at a vividly rural congress held at Ḳaṣr Hilāl (12 and 13 May 1933).[61] Meanwhile clashes with the Residency became more and more violent, for example at Monastīr and Moknīn. Obnoxious decrees were introduced to legalize repression, and Bourguiba, who applied that adjective to them, was imprisoned with his friends in the south (3 September 1934).[62] But even though he was 'down' he still went on pleading the cause.

In Algeria the administration tried to limit the spreading influence of the 'Ulamā', mustering against them both the religious brotherhoods and the official clergy, the latter of extremely low standard.[63] The authorities, seeing the people flock to hear the new preachers, whom they instinctively recognized as presenting a necessary updating of Islam, decided to forbid them to preach in the mosques. On 16 February 1933 the 'Michel Circular' – named after the official who drew it up – and three supporting decrees, set up an official monopoly to this effect.[64] Not only believers but also trade unionists and militants of the extreme Left took part in the demonstration that followed – a coalition which might have proved effective. Admittedly there occurred at that point a kind of 'divorce' between the Communist and nationalist tendencies,[65] which was far from healed by the reunification of the CGT and the CGTU in 1935. After several years of clandestine activity, the Etoile nord-africaine resumed open activity in Algeria itself in June 1933.[66] Mesalī Ḥādj, its president, had been using the word independence since 1927. And now, amidst the growing uneasiness, there was an anti-Jewish riot at Constantine in August 1934.[67] Whether this was a plot, a mere explosion, a diversion, or the result of provocation was not clear. But, whatever it was, it was a street outbreak which frightened all the politicians by its violence. Yet at the next elections, in January 1935, the opposition list of Dr Bendjellūl carried the day in Constantine: this showed in which direction the sympathies of the majority were tending. Although the victor was a convinced assimilationist,[68] he

60. Or 'restoring' them *vis-à-vis* the city. The same morphological effect has been noted, *mutatis mutandis*, in the action of the 'Ulamā' in Algeria.

61. J. Berque, 1970, pp. 289 ff., partly based on recollections by M. Bourguiba.

62. A. Bourguiba, 1954, pp. 70 ff.

63. A. Berque, 1951.

64. Complete text in A. Nouschi, 1962, p. 69.

65. An Algerian Communist Party was formed in July 1938.

66. A. Ouzegane, 1962, pp. 84 ff.

67. A. Nouschi, 1962, pp. 74 ff.

68. See his preface to A. Kessous, 1935.

aroused the prevailing powers to a fury of preventive measures. Clearly, what mattered in this vague radicalization of public life in Algeria was not the theory expressed but what it suggested or actually provoked.

In Morocco, the settlers, embittered by the slump and irritated by such few limits as the administration imposed upon them, issued an ultimatum. This development, full of symbolic significance, occurred on the same day as the disorders in Paris on 6 February 1934. The same period saw in Morocco the rise of a nationalist press. The Moroccan Action Committee, in which 'Allāl al-Fāsī was beginning to stand out as a leading figure, put forward a 'Reform Plan' on 1 December 1934, which if adopted would have developed its real significance and object in the course of the Protectorate.[69] In the Spanish zone, opposition was already being expressed more openly through Torrès and Nāṣirī;[70] it established contacts up country,[71] and almost compromised the future Moḥammed V in a demonstration in Fez on 10 May 1934.

The introduction of the Plan coincided with the wiping out of the last centre of dissidence in the south.[72] Henceforth, history was to take quite a different course from the archaic, almost legendary one that had been prolonged beyond its natural span by Lyauteyism and the Ministry for Native Affairs. The coincidence had a bearing outside Morocco itself. The cessation of the *barūd* was also potentially the end of the 'Arab bureaux'.[73] In Algeria and Tunisia, too, social change, which weakened old solidarities, also created new ones. The streets of the large towns and even village market places became the scene of mass action which class and party ideology were able to organize across traditional groupings. In all three countries of French North Africa, and especially in Algeria, where Régnier, the Minister, carried out a showy inquiry, the government's only answer to these material and intellectual developments was to manipulate elections[74] and bring its repressive arsenal up to date.[75]

This refusal of the administration to act cannot be explained entirely

69. For a detailed analysis see R. Le Tourneau, 1962, pp. 189 ff.

70. R. Rêzette, 1955, pp. 83 ff.

71. By using the distribution networks of retailers in Fez. These contacts reached as far as the mountains and the Sūs, where militants as well known as Mukhtār al-Sūsī were recruited.

72. Merebbī Rebbo was reduced by a combined operation on the part of French troops from Algeria and Morocco. Tindūf was finally occupied in 1934.

73. *Barūd* meaning 'powder' and thence 'fight', came to be used by the army in Africa to mean the warlike and even desperate resistance engaged in by peoples whose honour had been slighted by 'pacification'. The 'Arab bureaux' created a century earlier by Lamoricière, had been the French administration's characteristic method for ruling the different traditional groupings. No parallel existed in the towns, and even in rural districts of the Maghrib this method became out of date as things progressed.

74. J. Menaut, 1935.

75. As well as the 'décrets superscélérats' in Tunisia, there was the Decree of 30 March 1935 in Algeria, and the *dahir* of 29 June 1935 in Morocco.

by the mounting dangers beyond the Rhine and the arguments this lent to the conservatives in France. The attitudes which the three parties concerned – metropolitan France, the colonialists, and the nationalist movement – had taken up, enjoined the first two to defend a *status quo* which the third was not yet in a position to challenge seriously. In return for the slavish allegiance which forbade Europeans in North Africa any originality, metropolitan France gave them her unconditional support. Those in Algeria, for example, who called themselves 'Algerians', carried particularism far enough to get super-profits out of it, but not far enough to risk finding themselves alone, face to face, as a 'dominion' or under some other arrangement, with the Muslim majority. Algeria was France, as they said, but France without democracy. The situation was to all intents and purposes the same in Tunisia and Morocco.

Provisional conclusions

Not everything has emerged into the daylight about the period we have just been examining. Every so often, narrative history comes up against the stumbling-block of secret history. Future studies will shed more light on people, circumstances and decisions which at present are still enigmatic. But we are also obliged to reserve for the future certain judgements concerning social history. Is there a close connection between the fluctuations of the economy and those of political tension? It would seem that ethnic, or rather cultural dualism, is better able to explain the attitudes involved than class stratification. And since the conflict concerns a far wider area than the Maghrib, events in North Africa are probably affected more deeply, though more indirectly, by relevant events in the East than by French policy, which nevertheless seems to occupy the foreground. Perhaps one day we shall be able to bring all these variables together in one general diagram, or at least give each of them its appropriate weight in relation to the others.

Science, ideology and action, in the period we are concerned with, tended to subscribe to a Eurocentric view of things: this applies both to the French Left and to most North African theories of that time. This only brings out more clearly those movements which, despite the difficulties this entailed, were able to avoid this distortion. Events after the Second World War were largely to justify them.

But it is only too easy for the historian to set up as the prophet of what actually happens. Nowadays we know the aftermath, or, if you like, the consequences, of the situations described in this chapter. Could those consequences have been different? In particular, might the reformism expressed by respectable men in all three countries of French North Africa have proceeded to its logical conclusion – the establishment, in an up-to-date form, of solidarity between those three countries and France? It is easy now to answer no, but we should avoid such an easy solution.

When we raise one of the possibilities unrealized by the actual course of events, we do not merely reproach the authorities at the time with errors and abuses which probably helped to prevent things from taking their course. At the same time we challenge ourselves as to the true significance of words and deeds at the time. We hope to have suggested that the situation in the Maghrib at the period we have been concerned with is, more than many others, to be interpreted in terms of a kind of underground movement, where what was implicit – and even what was hidden – was more important than what was explicit.

An approach to bourgeois democracy; international socialism; the reaffirmation of a separate identity – we know now that of these three alternatives it was the third which prevailed. Yet at the time it was not unequivocal, but left the alternative open between two rival camps – Islamic and secular; westernizing and pan-Arab; moderate and revolutionary. In 1935 no one could have said which of the two tendencies would prevail, nor even if either would prevail over the colonial set-up. What we may conclude is that history probably left in suspense other possibilities which might have come – perhaps may still come – to govern in other forms other phases of the future.

Politics and nationalism in West Africa, 1919–35

25

A. ADU BOAHEN

As indicated in Chapters 6 and 12, resistance to colonialism in most parts of West Africa died down during the First World War. Indeed, as M. Crowder has shown,[1] except in parts of the Ivory Coast, Niger, the Gold Coast (now Ghana) and the eastern parts of Nigeria, most West Africans showed loyalty to their colonial rulers during the war and some of the traditional rulers even voluntarily contributed men and resources in the form of money to the imperial war effort. However, after the war, African reactions to colonialism were resumed with even greater vigour and determination. Indeed, if the period from 1919 to 1935 has been described as the high noon of colonialism in West Africa, it was also the period that saw African resistance to colonialism and nationalist activities in West Africa at its peak.

African nationalism and political activities in West Africa during this period were shaped by a number of factors. These were the impact of the First World War, the colonial situation itself, an increase in the number of the educated and professional elite as well as the working class, especially in the urban centres, the general economic conditions of the 1920s and 1930s, the socio-economic changes in the rural areas caused by the spread of the cultivation of cash crops, and finally, the diffusion of pan-Africanism and pan-Africanist activities into West Africa. Crowder (Chapter 12) has discussed in detail the impact of the First World War on Africa and on nationalist activities. Suffice it to state here first and foremost that the forced conscription of many Africans aroused a great deal of anger especially in the former French African areas. Secondly, the war proved to the African that the white man was after all not a superman and could therefore be resisted. Thirdly, after the war, 'loyalist' West Africans were expecting rewards for their loyalty in the form of more concessions and more participation in the running of their own affairs, a feeling which was very much strengthened by the principles of liberal democracy and self-determination enunciated by President Woodrow Wilson of the United

1. See Chapter 12 above.

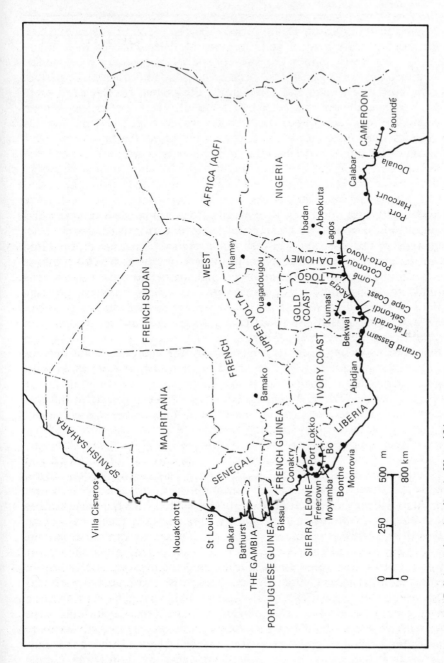

FIG. 25.1 *Politics and nationalism in West Africa, 1919-35*

States and Prime Minister David Lloyd George of Great Britain. All these factors undoubtedly made a good number of West Africans more ready than before to participate in the anti-colonial and resistance movements.

The colonial system itself also became consolidated during the period, and the authoritarianism and racialism of the system became even more evident. It was during this period that the alliance between the African traditional rulers and the colonial masters was strengthened and various ordinances were introduced which greatly increased the powers of these rulers and virtually eliminated the new educated elite and professional groups from participation in the administration of their own countries.

What made this factor all the more explosive was the fact that the period saw a substantial increase in the size of this educated elite and the professional group, following the spread of western education locally and the education of more and more people overseas. In the rural areas also, the spread of the cultivation of cash crops such as cocoa and groundnuts led to the emergence of an increasing number of young men and women who became even richer than the traditional rulers and therefore resented not only the non-traditional and authoritarian powers conferred on their chiefs but their elimination from the new state councils of the so-called native authorities. All these social changes definitely shaped nationalism and political activities in West Africa.

But even more important as a factor were the economic conditions of the inter-war period. Indeed, the first thing to note in connection with nationalist politics in English-speaking West Africa during the inter-war period is the way in which the commercial crises and changes in the colonial economy affected the initiatives and reactions of the colonial elite of lawyers and merchants, the sub-elite of teachers and civil servants, and the workers. For the 'economic revolution' in West Africa not only introduced a monetary economy and expanded commerce, it also introduced certain social and economic values among African enterpreneurs and social classes, notably the lawyer-merchant class. Although the position of these classes, particularly the small traders, had begun to change with the development of the colonial economy in the 1890s, it was in reality the First World War and its attendant economic crises which had a more immediate and significant impact on their status. It had been already apparent during the stagnation of the 1880s and the 1890s that the growing sophistication of commerce, expansion of markets, and competition from extra-territorial firms meant that the African businessmen would either have to be more efficient, or play a secondary role in the colonial economy. The First World War, with its economic controls, discriminatory export duties, currency shortages and loss of shipping, created a growing awareness among educated Africans in business and in the professions, that the cosmopolitan days of harmony were over and that the era of the combine and of monopoly capitalism had arrived.

In Sierra Leone, the frustration of the educated classes and the African traders, and the unemployed in the big towns was given open expression in the riots of 1919 in which protests against the price of rice took the form of attacks on Syrian and Lebanese traders, and in the workers' strike that same year. Though directed against the Levantines (who were accused of creating scarcity by hoarding essential commodities, and of elbowing out local middlemen), these riots were in fact a violent and uncoordinated protest against what were believed to be injustices arising from the management of the colonial economy. The looting and the riots spread from Freetown to Moyamba, Kangahun (25–26 July 1919), Mano, Boia, Makump, Bo, Bonthe, Mange and Port Lokko. The situation was so serious that troops had to be brought in from the Gold Coast. In addition to the riots, the technical staff and labourers on the railway and in the public works department went on strike, demanding the same war bonus paid to the government clerical staff, and complaining of low wages and rising food prices.[2] In The Gambia, too, rising prices had their social and political effects, leading to sporadic outbursts of looting and petty theft, as well as a seamen's strike for better wages, and to the formation of unions, notably the Gambia Native Defensive Union.

The 1921 slump also led to more agitation from West African merchants, a few of whom were financially ruined. The issue of paper currency and shortage of silver did not improve matters either, and the European merchants were accused of hoarding the currency notes and charging high prices. According to one Gold Coast newspaper, 'The kings, chiefs, and all classes will soon be paupers' unless West Africans got together to protect themselves against the wily manoeuvres of combine magnates. In general, then, all these economic hardships led the West African press to advocate the formation of the National Congress of British West Africa (NCBWA), and the abolition of the Crown Colony system of administration to enable Africans to have more say in the running of the economy and more representation in the administrative and legislative bodies.

The final background factor was the launching of the pan-Africanist movement, and, in particular, the activities of Dr W. E. B. Du Bois and Marcus Garvey especially in the 1920s. These themes are discussed in great detail in Chapter 29. But it should be mentioned here that the various Pan-African Congresses organized by Du Bois – in Paris in 1919, in London, Brussels and Paris in 1921, in London and Lisbon in 1922 and in New York in 1927 which were attended by participants from West Africa – not only internationalized nationalist activities and struggle against colonialism in Africa in general and in West Africa in particular, but also very much strengthened the consciousness of blacks throughout the world of their common plight as a downtrodden and oppressed race and won more converts to the nationalist cause in West Africa.

Against this background, let us examine the organizations and move-

2. Public Record Office, Kew, CO 267/582/45278; also *Sierra Leone Weekly News*, 19 July 1919, p. 8.

ments that were formed during the inter-war period for the articulation of nationalist grievances and demands first in British West Africa and then in Francophone West Africa.

Politics and nationalism in British West Africa

Youth Leagues and Movements

The most common of these organizations were ethnic unions and youth movements or associations. The inter-war period certainly saw the formation of an increasing number, indeed a host, of ethnic, welfare, literary, old boys', voluntary and youth associations, clubs, societies and movements in many countries in West Africa. Numerous Igbo unions were formed in the cities of Nigeria such as Ibadan, Abeokuta and Lagos. In the Colony and Asante regions of the Gold Coast alone, there were as many as fifty such clubs and associations by 1930, most of them formed between 1925 and 1930.[3] Examples of these clubs were the Achimota Discussion Group, the Literary and Social Club and the Eureka Club of Cape Coast, the Optimum Club and the Literary and Social Clubs of Sekondi, the Young Peoples' Club, the Cosmos Club and Rodger Club of Accra, the Anum Improvement Society, the Ewe League, the Asante Kotoko Society of Kumasi and the Bekwai Kotoko Union. It was some of these clubs and associations that J. B. Danquah organized into the Youth Conference Movement which held its first meeting in Accra in 1929. In the Gold Coast and Sierra Leone, I. T. A. Wallace Johnson founded his Youth League and the West African Youth League, while in 1934 the Nigerian Youth Movement was formed which, as a recent Nigerian scholar has shown, 'embraced almost all the young intellectuals of the period – H. O. Davies, Nnamdi Azikiwe, Dr Vaughan, Dr Kofo Abayomi, Obafemi Awolowo'.[4]

All these clubs and associations were led either by the missionary educated elite or the young lawyers, doctors and businessmen. Though the aim of these leaders was to wrest political leadership from the old conservative nationalist leaders of the Congress stamp to be discussed below, none of them – with the sole exception of the West African Youth League – made any radical demands in spite of the deteriorating economic conditions of the 1920s and 1930s. Their demands were confined to more educational facilities and of a higher quality, university education, higher wages and salaries, equitable representation on the legislative and executive councils, abolition of racial discrimination, admission into the higher grades of the civil service, the provision of economic opportunities for Africans and better relations between the colonial administration and the Africans.

3. K. O. Hagan, 1968.
4. G. O. Olusanya in O. Ikime (ed.), 1980, p. 558.

Such certainly were the demands made by the Gold Coast Youth Conference at its first meeting in Accra organized by Danquah in 1929.

The demands made by the Nigerian Youth Movement (NYM) were similar. It advocated an African majority in the legislative council, and called for the progressive representation of all Nigerians in it. The NYM Charter also demanded universal suffrage, criticized both the practice of Indirect Rule and the representation of European commercial and economic interests in the legislative council, and pressed for the gradual Nigerianization of the civil service. In the economic sphere, like the Gold Coast Youth Conference, it called for equal African participation in the economy. It even provided the outline of a five-year development plan, in which priority would be given to manufacturing, banking, textiles and transport. It also proposed to set up co-operative societies which would help Nigerians buy up some industries; agricultural banks were also to be established to help modernize agriculture and improve the standard of living of the peasantry. It condemned the monopoly of extra-territorial firms, and urged the introduction of social welfare programmes for the benefit of Nigerian workers. On the socio-cultural side, the NYM Charter called for a state-financed mass education and primary school education programme; health and adult education programmes were also recommended as responsibilities of local and central government authorities.

The West African Youth League, the only radical one among these movements, was led by I. T. A. Wallace Johnson, a Sierra Leonean trade unionist who had studied in Moscow in 1931–2 (see Plate 25.1). He returned to West Africa with the aim of creating a new political force based on wage labourers and the unemployed in the urban areas for the overthrow of the colonial system. He founded the Youth League in the Gold Coast by organizing the workers and arousing them against the colonial system by his near-seditious and violent articles and by his skilful manipulation of local grievances, especially the unemployment situation, rising food prices and the frustration caused by reduced value of cocoa exports since 1929. Because of his efforts to mobilize these elements and use them in radicalizing local politics, the colonial administration came to see him as a dangerous radical paid by the communists to organize the colonial youth, and therefore deported him to Sierra Leone. In Sierra Leone, he established branches of the Youth League in Freetown and Bo, and started a newspaper, *The Sentinel*, which agitated against bad labour conditions and the Education Ordinance.

Apart from newspaper campaigns and petitions, these youth movements took part in local elections and also resorted to strike actions. Thus, they were involved in the demonstrations, riots and strike in Freetown in Sierra Leone (1926–31), and in Bathurst (now Banjul) in The Gambia (1929). In Accra, the Youth Movement led by Kojo Thompson, an Accra barrister and the Nigerian newspaper editor, Nnamdi Azikiwe, participated in the Accra municipal elections under the umbrella of the Mambii Party against

PLATE 25.1 *I.T.A. Wallace Johnson (1894–1965), Sierra Leonean journalist, trade unionist, pan–Africanist and nationalist politician, addressing a political meeting*

the older and more conservative nationalists like Dr F. V. Nanka-Bruce, while the Youth League took part in the Cape Coast local elections. The Nigerian Youth Movement backed by Azikiwe's *West African Pilot* also mounted a vigorous and successful campaign against Herbert Macaulay's conservative Nigerian National Democratic Party which had dominated Lagos politics since its foundation in 1923.

However, the youth movements did not achieve much. Their electoral successes of the 1930s failed to dislodge the conservative leadership nor did their detailed economic programmes prove capable of implementation under a semi-Crown Colony system of administration. However, though much of the activity of the youth movements apart from some electoral successes in the urban areas did not yield any substantial political gains, the political style of the post-1945 nationalist movement in British West Africa owed much to the experience some of the leaders had gained in the youth movements.

Political parties

In addition to these youth movements, a number of political parties were formed to agitate for reforms. The best known of these was the Nigeria National Democratic Party formed in Nigeria by Herbert Macaulay in 1923. The aims of the party were stated to be:

> To secure the safety or welfare of the people of the Colony and Protectorate of Nigeria as an integral part of the British Imperial Commonwealth and to carry the banner of 'Right, Truth, Liberty and Justice' to the empyrean heights of Democracy until the realization of its ambitious goal of 'A Government of the People, by the People, for the People' ... and, at the same time, to maintain an attitude of unswerving loyalty to the Throne and Person of His Majesty the King Emperor, by being strictly constitutional in the adoption of its methods and general procedure.[5]

Among its programme were the nomination and election of the Lagos members of the Legislative Council, achievement of municipal status and complete local self-government for Lagos, the development of higher education and the introduction of compulsory education throughout Nigeria, Africanization of the civil service, free and fair trade in Nigeria and equal treatment for traders and producers of Nigeria, and, finally, the economic development of the natural resources of Nigeria under controlled private enterprise. The Party employed the usual methods to achieve its aims – participating in elections in Lagos which it won in 1923, 1928 and 1933, holding mass meetings and sending deputations to the governor as it did in 1930 'to discuss such national matters as the trade depression

5. Quoted by J. S. Coleman, 1958, p. 198.

and the appointment and deposition of chiefs'.[6] This party dominated the politics of Lagos until its defeat by the Nigerian Youth Movement in the Lagos elections of 1938.

Trade unions

Another vehicle for the articulation of anti-colonial sentiments and nationalist grievances was the trade union movement. While many trade unions were formed in Southern and Central Africa beginning with the first of them, the Industrial Workers and Commercial Union formed by Clements Kadalie in 1919 in South Africa, and its branch formed in Southern Rhodesia in 1927, it would appear that the French government did not allow trade union activities in West Africa until 1937 while the British did not officially tolerate them until 1932 in The Gambia, 1939 in Sierra Leone and Nigeria, and 1941 in the Gold Coast.[7] But even though trade union activities were not allowed or encouraged officially during this period, a number of them did emerge mainly as a result of the high cost of living. They included the Railway Workers Union of Sierra Leone, the Nigerian Mechanics Union formed in 1919 and the Gambia Native Defence Union. The typical weapons of these unions were strikes, boycotts and hold-ups. The first series of strikes occurred among the railway and mine workers. Thus a railway strike occurred in Sierra Leone in 1919 and again in 1926. The workers of the Ashanti Goldfields went on strike at Obuasi in the Gold Coast in 1924 while the Enugu coal mine strike occurred in 1925 and the Dakar-St Louis Railway strike in 1925.[8] All these strikes were for higher wages and better conditions of service.

Inter-territorial movements and international movements: the National Congress of British West Africa

The associations, parties and movements that we have been discussing so far were local or territorial in organization and outlook. But what differentiates the political movements of the inter-war period from those immediately before and after the period were the formation of an inter-territorial movement in British West Africa and of international movements in the metropolitan capitals of the colonial ruler. The first was the National Congress of British West Africa in West Africa and the second was the West African Students Union formed in London.

Undoubtedly, the National Congress of British West Africa (NCBWA) was the most interesting of the nationalist movements that emerged in West Africa in the inter-war period.[9] It was founded through the efforts

6. ibid., p. 199.
7. M. Crowder, 1968, pp. 351–2.
8. ibid., p. 352.
9. For details, see J. A. Langley, 1973.

of J. E. Casely Hayford, a Gold Coast lawyer and intellectual and Dr Akiwande Savage of Nigeria, and, throughout, its leadership was dominated not by the traditional rulers but by professional men such as lawyers, doctors and businessmen. The leading spirit of the movement was undoubtedly Casely Hayford whose idealism, political vision and faith in the unity of African peoples enabled the NCBWA to survive from 1920 to 1930, and injected a flavour of pan-Africanism into West African politics matched only by Kwame Nkrumah's efforts twenty-five years later.

As I have shown elsewhere in my analysis of the social and occupational background of the NCBWA leaders,[10] this leadership had inherited the acquisitive individualism of Western liberal democracy, particularly some of its Victorian tenets such as laissez-faire, the idea that knowledge meant power, belief in progress and the natural harmony of interests as well as the belief that 'ordered liberty' and property went hand in hand. Moreover, for most of the leaders, 'British West Africa' existed as a more important entity than the Gold Coast, Sierra Leone, or Nigeria. This identification of the parts with the whole was to continue till the depression of 1929 and the 1930s when a narrower conception of nationality became dominant.[11] The educated West African urban 'middle class', from the Sierra Leonean diaspora of the nineteenth century to the late 1930s, had more in common, and communicated more easily with their counterparts along the coastal towns, than with their brethren in their own hinterland.

Having been told that they had no history worth taking seriously, and conscious of the fact that their own socio–economic group had limited opportunities in the colonial system, it is perhaps not surprising that the nationalist intelligentsia came to prefer a visionary 'West African nationality' to a political system in which they had no voice and which, in any case, was alien and therefore, in their view, oppressive. Gold Coast newspapers never tired of denouncing alien rule. As one of the editorials observed: 'The introduction of the British system of government in place of the one existing before was an encroachment which no self-respecting nation would allow'.

In spite of all the objection to 'alien rule', however, there was never any mention of severing relations with the colonial power; alien rule was bad but there were good reasons for consenting to it; it was better to demand more opportunities for a particular social group and make moderate demands than to do away with alien rule completely; and one could still

10. ibid., Chapter IV.
11. For example, the *Gold Coast Leader* 26 September 1928 asserted: 'The idea of a Gold Coast Nation is a fundamental one'. *Sierra Leone Weekly News*, 27 October 1928 also declared, 'whatever may be said to the contrary, Sierra Leone is our country ...' It is interesting to learn, however, that between 1918 and 1929 no really considerable body of evidence is to be discovered in the newspapers to suggest that the press did not consistently view matters from a wider West African point of view rather than from the point of view of individual colonies. W. D. Edmund, 1951, p. 113.

be 'free', 'under the Union Jack'. Even Herbert Macaulay, regarded by the administration as the gadfly of Lagos politics, could speak sincerely about the 'manifold blessings of Pax-Britannica'. The National Congress of British West Africa also declared:

> That the policy of the Congress shall be to maintain strictly and in-violate the connection of the British West African Dependencies with the British Empire, and to maintain unreservedly all and every right of free citizenship of the Empire and the fundamental principle that taxation goes with effective representation ... to aid in the development of the political institutions of British West Africa under the Union Jack ... and, in time, to ensure within her borders the Government of the people by the people for the people; to ensure equal opportunity for all, to preserve the lands of the people for the people.[12]

Finally, the leaders also saw themselves as the only class of people who, by virtue of their social and occupational status, were qualified to control by constitutional means what hysterical American racists like Lothrop Stoddard and Madison Grant called 'the rising tide of colour against white supremacy'.

It is important to clarify the attitudes of the leaders of this movement in order to emphasize the fact that, in spite of all the race rhetoric, they were essentially co-operationists with exceedingly limited political objectives, a sub-elite whose interests generally coincided with, and were in fact protected by, the foreign rulers they were agitating against. Although they claimed to speak in the name of 'the people', the interests of the nationalist petit-bourgeoisie were not identical with those of the people; in fact, it was the contradictions within the colonial system itself that they sought to harmonize in order to protect and expand their own interests without upsetting the system; hence their constitutionalism and their recognition of the benefits of British colonial rule. Their pan-Africanism apart, their main objective was the acquisition of representative institutions to protect their socio-economic interests and to enhance their opportunities in colonial society.[13]

The NCBWA held its first conference at Accra from 11 to 29 March 1920. Attended by delegates from Nigeria, the Gold Coast, Sierra Leone and The Gambia, it attracted wide attention in Africa, London and as far afield as the West Indies.[14] The 'Humble Petition' in which the Conference embedded its resolutions declared its members' 'unfeigned loyalty and devotion to the throne and person of His Majesty the King-Emperor'. Their recommendations presupposed not the destruction but the modification of the existing structures of government. Constitutional

12. The constitution of the National Congress of British West Africa. Also the Resolutions of the Conference of Africans of British West Africa, Accra, 1920, p. 9.
13. See E. J. Hobsbawm, 1964; pp. 176–7 and the useful essay by M. Kilson, 1958.
14. *Gold Coast Times*, 15 September 1931, p. 11; *West African Nationhood*, 9 April 1931.

changes advocated included the reconstitution of the West African legislative councils so that half of the members be nominated by the Crown,
and the other half be elected by the people, with the addition of part-elected
assemblies to control taxation. They condemned the rigid colonial policy
of appointing only Europeans to senior official posts. They asked for
municipal institutions, and for the establishment of a West African
university along the lines proposed in 1872 by E. W. Blyden with the
support of the Governor of Sierra Leone, John Pope-Hennessy.

They complained of the post-war fiscal and economic controls and the
growing power of extra-territorial firms. It is interesting to note that in
their desperation, the conference, influenced by the merchants, and by
the approaches of Garvey's Universal Negro Improvement Association
(UNIA) through the Reverend Patriarch J. G. Campbell, resolved:

> That this Conference, being of the opinion that trade competition
> in the British West African dependencies should be free from restric-
> tion, views with great dissatisfaction the passing of the Palm Kernels
> Export Duty Ordinance ... That, in view of the difficulties hereto
> experienced in the matter of space on British bottoms by legitimate
> African traders and shippers, this Conference welcomes competition
> in the shipping line with particular reference to the 'Black Star Line'.

Legal reforms were proposed, especially the establishment of a West
African Court of Appeal. The conference also resolved to set up a West
African Press Union in recognition of 'the important part the Press plays
in National Development'; a committee of experienced journalists was to
look into the problem of better co-ordination of the press policy of the
English-speaking West African press. It was also proposed to start an
official organ of the NCBWA, under the editorship of Casely Hayford,
and financed by the Congress Inaugural Fund, to be called the *British
West African National Review*.

Sanitary and medical reforms were also thoroughly dealt with and highly
technical papers were read by Dr H. C. Bankole-Bright of Sierra Leone;
delegates also dealt with residential segregation of races and the position
of African doctors in government service. The eternal and important land
question was also discussed, with the conference tartly declaring: 'That
in the opinion of this Conference the principle of Trusteeship with respect
to the lands of the people of British West Africa has been overdone, and
that it is proper to declare that the average British West African is quite
capable of controlling and looking after his own interests in the land.'

They condemned the right assumed by the European powers of
exchanging or partitioning countries between them without reference to,
or regard for, the wishes of the people, which they declared to be tantamount to a species of slavery. Specifically, they denounced the partitioning
of Togoland between the English and the French governments and the
handing over of the Cameroons to the French government without con-

635

sulting or regarding the wishes of the peoples in the matter, and respectfully desired an assurance from His Majesty's Government that under no circumstances whatsoever would it be a consenting party to the integrity of any of the four British West African colonies being disturbed. Finally, the Conference resolved itself into a National Congress of British West Africa, and determined to represent its views to London.

A delegation in which The Gambia, Sierra Leone, the Gold Coast and Nigeria were represented, went to London in 1920 to petition His Majesty's Government to grant elective representation to the four colonies (see Plate 25.2). Casely Hayford of the Gold Coast led the delegation. The delegation also petitioned various parliamentary groups and humanitarian organizations. It also had the support and understanding of the Liverpool Chamber of Commerce, Albert Cartwright, the editor of *West Africa*, and some influential public personalities. However, because of the opposition of Sir Hugh Clifford, Governor-General of Nigeria, Gordon Guggisberg (Governor of the Gold Coast), as well as the opposition of some of the Gold Coast chiefs led by Nana Sir Ofori Atta and, above all, because of the negative attitude of the Colonial Office during Viscount Milner's tenure of office as Secretary of State, the NCBWA petition was rejected, principally on the grounds that the NCBWA leadership did not represent the majority of the people in the four West African territories.

The Congress met again in Freetown (January–February 1923), Bathurst (December 1925–January 1926) and Lagos (1930) though most of the agitational politics of the movement was conducted by the individual territorial committees set up in The Gambia, Sierra Leone, Gold Coast and Nigeria. The Freetown session, fully supported by the Freetown social elite, ratified the constitution of the movement, and laid down the functions of the president, general secretary, executive council, financial secretary and the central executive committee. The Freetown session also recommended the creation of a journal for the movement, to be called the *British West African Review*, which would report on all the activities of the various territorial branches. The general secretary, who was based at Sekondi (Gold Coast) would receive quarterly reports from the secretary of each territorial committee. Significantly, the NCBWA constitution ratified in Freetown, also dealt with inter-West African economic co-operation, urging the NCBWA branches to educate public opinion, especially African businessmen and entrepreneurs, as to the ways and means of developing West Africa economically.

The Bathurst session, which was held from 24 December 1925 to 10 January 1926, recalling the rejection of the local committee's petitions for elective representation since 1920, resolved that 'constitution is best that makes provision for the effective and efficient expression of public opinion', that the time had arrived for the elective system of representation to be fully applied to the Colony of The Gambia, and finally that the various sections of the NCBWA should seriously consider the question of British

PLATE 25.2 *The deputation of the National Congress of British West Africa that visited London in 1920: left to right, seated, Dr H. C. Bankole-Bright (Sierra Leone), T. Hutton Mills (Gold Coast), Chief Oluwa (Nigeria), J. E. Casely Hayford (Gold Coast), H. Van Hein (Gold Coast); standing, J. Egerton Shyngle (Nigeria), H. M. Jones (The Gambia), Herbert Macaulay (Nigeria), T. M. Oluwa (Nigeria), F. W. Dove (Sierra Leone), E. F. Small (The Gambia)*

637

West African Federation with a Governor-General and in due course representations made to His Majesty's Government to take it into deep and sympathetic consideration.

The Bathurst session also advocated the establishment of national schools, compulsory education in all urban areas, industrial and agricultural education for the rural areas, the establishment of agricultural banks and co-operatives, and called for the 'commercial and economic independence' of West Africa, as well as the creation of a West African Appelate Court and the appointment of Africans to higher posts in the judiciary. It is noteworthy that the Gambia Women's Auxiliary Committee of the Gambia section of the NCBWA movement participated in the deliberations of the Bathurst session. With the support of Herbert Macaulay's Nigerian National Democratic Party and the efforts of energetic members of the Lagos branch such as J. C. Zizer, Reverend W. B. Euba and E. M. E. Agbebi, the Fourth Session was finally held in Lagos in 1930.

What did the NCBWA achieve? Though it continued its activities throughout the 1920s, its main achievement was the introduction of new Constitutions in Nigeria in 1923, Sierra Leone in 1924 and the Gold Coast in 1925 in which the principle of elective representation was conceded. It used to be thought that this change was introduced on the initiative of Sir Hugh Clifford, the then Governor of Nigeria.[15] It has, however, now been established beyond doubt by the present author that this concession was granted as a result of the persistent pressure exerted on their respective administrations by the various branches of the NCBWA.[16] The NCBWA also succeeded in developing a feeling of unity and common political destiny among the British West African political leadership. Apart from these, it did not succeed in achieving economic independence nor the unification of the four British colonies nor any other amelioration or weakening of the colonial system. On the contrary, by the 1930s, colonialism was even more firmly entrenched than it was in the 1920s.

Rural politics or rural mass nationalism in the inter-war period

In the youth movements, NCBWA and trade unions, we have been dealing with nationalism and politics as seen in the urban centres in former British West Africa and led by the educated and professional elite. But as recent research has been revealing – and future research in other countries in West Africa will confirm or reject or modify these conclusions – African nationalist activities were not confined to the urban centres only but were evident in the rural areas; in the various paramountcies, states and communities, and here the principal actors were the commoners and farmers, both literate and illiterate on the one hand, and the traditional rulers on the other. The latter were seen at times acting in co-operation with their

15. See J. A. Langley, 1973, Chapter IV.
16. ibid., pp. 243–5.

subjects against the colonial system and at times being attacked by their subjects as agents of the same system. Another aspect of this theme which is still very much in the dark is the linkage there was, if any, between rural and urban politics and how or whether one influenced the other.

Let me illustrate this theme from the results of the limited research that has been conducted so far in Ghana.[17] The inter-war period was characterized in the Gold Coast, as in the other British colonies in West Africa, by the establishment and consolidation of the system of indirect rule in the rural areas through the introduction of a number of ordinances and acts – the Native Jurisdiction Amendment Ordinance of 1910, the Guggisberg Constitution of 1925, the Native Administration Ordinance of 1927 and the Native Administration Revenue Bill of 1931. All these measures which gave the traditional rulers powers to collect revenue and to impose court fines as were unknown before, were, according to Stone, 'an attempt to make the chiefs a living part of the machinery of (colonial) government'. Economically, the era saw the alternation of periods of boom with those of recession and inflation – the latter in 1915–17, 1929–30 and the second half of the 1930s. It also saw the spread of the cocoa industry into the rural areas especially of Akuapem and Akyem Abuakwa which led to the emergence of an increasing number of rich young farmers and long-distance traders. Socially, the period also saw the spread of elementary education into the rural areas and while some of the products of these schools drifted into the urban centres, others stayed behind and took to either farming or petty trading. With all these changes in their socio-economic status, these rural people began to demand a corresponding change in their political status and especially representation on the state and provincial councils, a demand which the ordinances mentioned above made steadily impossible. The principal objectives of the rural folk, then, were to acquire representation on these councils and, above all, to curb the increasing powers of their traditional rulers and the district commissioners and abolition or reduction of some of the fines and taxes being imposed by them.

As recent research in Ghana has shown, two main instruments were fashioned in these areas for the attainment of these ends, namely the traditional instrument of the *asafo* companies, i.e. permanent organizations in Akan-speaking societies of commoners for military and social purposes outside the control of the traditional rulers or political elite, and new associations such as the Cocoa Farmers Association and the Gold Coast Federation of Cocoa Farmers formed in 1910 and 1928 respectively. The methods that these bodies employed were petitions and cocoa hold-ups. The most interesting of the *asafo* companies that emerged in the rural areas was the Kwahu *asafo* company.[18]

In 1915, the Kwahu *asafo*, made up of commoners from all parts of

17. See R. Addo-Fening, 1975; J. Simensen, 1975(a) and R. L. Stone, 1975.
18. J. Simensen, 1974 and 1975(b).

Kwahu assembled at Abetifi, summoned the Omanhene of Kwahu to the meeting and forced him to sign a document which they had already prepared consisting of rules 'regulating political and economic affairs in the state'. In 1917, this document was formally ratified by the Kwahu State Council and became known later as the Magna Carta.

In this document, fees and fines being imposed by the traditional rulers were reduced and regulations for their imposition were laid down; the Okwahuman Council was also to be made a truly representative body of chiefs and commoners and failure to attend was to be made punishable by fine. Even more interesting and comprehensive were the regulations about socio-economic activities. Trade in foodstuffs was to be centralized in certain towns, a detailed list of market prices and trade fees was to be drawn up, the export of fish and game from Kwahu was prohibited and rules governing marriages, family responsibilities in debt cases, funerals, adultery by chiefs, etc., were laid down. As J. Simensen has concluded, 'this Charter is probably the most detailed documentation that we have from the early period of colonial rule in the Gold Coast of an attempt by commoners to curtail the authority of the traditional elite and assert their own influence more effectively in the fields of jurisdiction and legislation.'[19]

The second method adopted by the commoners of the rural areas was the destoolment (deposition) of their traditional rulers, and this became quite a common feature of rural politics in the Gold Coast in the inter-war period. Between 1910 and 1944, there were at least thirty-three depositions of divisional chiefs in Akyem Abuakwa alone. The charges usually ranged from abuse of power, improper sale of land, extortionate fines, enforcement of levies to compulsory labour imposed by the colonial administration.

The most interesting and most significant of these depositions were those that occurred in 1932, when all the *asafo* companies in Akyem Abuakwa combined to depose all the main divisional chiefs of the state and went on to prefer deposition charges against the Omanhene himself, Nana Sir Ofori Atta. It is interesting to note that the action of the *asafo* was precipitated by the decision of the Akyem Abuakwa State Council to approve the Native Administration Revenue measure proposed by the Colonial administration which was to give the council power to impose a levy on its subjects. As Simensen has shown, the list of charges preferred against the Omanhene show 'an increased awareness of the commoners that many of their troubles arose from the fact that the chiefs were being integrated into the administrative structure of the Colonial Government, and thereby removed from popular control'.[20] Thus the action of the *asafo* was directed as much against the colonial administration as it was against the traditional rulers. It is significant that it was only the timely intervention of the colonial rulers that saved Ofori Atta himself, though he conceded some of the

19. J. Simensen, 1975(a), pp. 37–8.
20. J. Simensen, 1974.

demands by, for instance, admitting three members of the Akyem Abuakwa Scholars Union to the State Council in 1933.

The other method that the rural folk adopted was the use of cocoa hold-ups. Thus in 1921–2, 1930–1 and again in 1937–8, the cocoa farmers, led by John Kwame Ayew and Winifried Tete-Ansa, both educated men, refused to sell their cocoa until better prices were paid.[21] The 1937–8 hold-up, which had the support of some of the traditional rulers including the paramount chief of Akyem Abuakwa, Nana Sir Ofori Atta, was particularly widespread, and has been described by Hopkins as 'the last and most significant demonstration of rural discontent before World War II'. There were similar rural activities in such areas as Akyem Abuakwa, Akuapem and Akyem Swedru.

From research done so far, it would appear that there was no formal linkage between the urban and rural movements though there were contacts on an individual basis, for example, between J. B. Danquah and the commoners in Akyem Abuakwa, and between Kobina Sekyi, a Cape Coast lawyer and nationalist, and the commoners in Denkyira and Anyan Abaasa.[22]

It seems evident from the Gold Coast case then, that politics and nationalist activities in the inter-war period were not confined to the urban areas alone but were in evidence in the rural areas which involved the commoners and farmers. There is no doubt that research in other countries will confirm the conclusion so far arrived at in Ghana.

The outcome of nationalist activities in British West Africa

The question then is why did the nationalist movement in British West Africa have so limited an impact on the people and the colonial governments? The first and most important answer is that neither the NCBWA nor the youth movements ever commanded a mass following nor did any significant linkage occur between urban and rural politics. The leaders could therefore be written off by the colonial rulers as being unrepresentative of the people, a strategy which, in fact, both Sir Hugh Clifford and the Colonial Office pursued. Clifford described the NCBWA leadership as a 'self-appointed congregation of African gentlemen, vainly and erroneously hankering after constitutions and modes of government which were unsuitable and unworkable in Africa'.

Secondly, in spite of all the rhetoric, neither the leaders of the NCBWA nor those of the youth movements were prepared to use any radical methods to achieve their objectives. It used to be thought that an entirely new style of radical politics developed in West Africa during the inter-war period. But it is quite clear from both the objectives and methods of the nationalist

21. A. G. Hopkins, 1966(b).
22. R. Stone, 1975.

groups and associations, that despite the economic depressions, no such revolutionary development in anti-colonial politics took place. As has been shown, the nationalist politics of the inter-war period should be seen as a transitional period during which both chiefs and intelligentsia participated in agitational politics, and as the formative period for some of the leaders of the nationalist movements after 1945. There were certainly elements of radicalism in the mid-1930s but in general, these movements were moderate nationalist movements, conducting their politics within the colonial framework. Political independence was decidedly not on their programme.

Thirdly, there was a great deal of conflict among the leaders of the movements which greatly impeded their activities. In all the colonies, conflicts occurred between the conservatives and the moderates, and between both of them and the old traditional elite of kings. Such, indeed, was the conflict between the leaders of the NCBWA and those of the Aborigines Rights' Protection Society, and between the leaders of both on the one hand and the traditional rulers led by Nana Sir Ofori Atta in the Gold Coast on the other. These conflicts greatly weakened the nationalist movement in that country. Similarly, it was largely because of the internal dissensions and personality conflicts in the Lagos branch of the NCBWA and the opposition of Sir Kitoyi Ajasa's *Nigerian Pioneer* and the Lagos conservatives that the fourth session of the NCBWA could not take place in Lagos until 1930. Fourthly, it would appear that the limited elective representation granted between 1923 and 1925 had the effect of politically anaesthetizing the nationalist movements. Finally, and undoubtedly, the death of Casely Hayford in 1930 constituted the final *coup de grâce* for nationalist activities in British West Africa in general and in the Gold Coast in particular in the inter-war years.

For all these reasons, then, by the end of the period under review, politics and nationalism in British West Africa were at their lowest ebb, and it needed two events to ginger them up again, the Ethiopian crisis of 1935 and the Second World War of 1939–45, discussion of both of which belongs to the last volume of this work.

Political activities in Francophone West Africa, 1919–35

There are still some gaps in our knowledge of African political activities in the French West African colonies during the inter-war period. However, from the rather limited evidence available now, it would appear that there was a relative lack of political activity which would seem to stem from France's more restrictive attitude towards African political activities and organizations, and to the absence of a vigorous African press in French West Africa, comparable to the African newspapers in Sierra Leone, the Gold Coast and Nigeria. However, like the activities in British West Africa, those in French West Africa had their local as well as their international aspects. Indeed, as I have shown elsewhere,[23] a good deal of Francophone African political activity took place in Paris between 1924 and 1936. However, as most of these political groups were radical and aligned to radical French political parties and trade unions, the impact of their anti-colonial agitation on the French authorities was limited. Among these groups were the Ligue Universelle pour la défense de la Race Noire, founded in Paris by a Dahomean lawyer and nationalist, Prince Kojo Tovalou Houénou, in 1924. This movement agitated against conditions in Dahomey (now Benin) and the French colonies in general and had strong connections with Garvey's UNIA in the United States. Another group was the Comité de la défense de la Race Nègre, which succeeded Houénou's Ligue and was led by a Senegalese Communist, Lamine Senghor, until his death in 1927 when the Comité was renamed the Ligue de la défense de la Race Nègre under the leadership of another Francophone West African Marxist, Tiémoho Garan-Kouyaté of Soudan. Interesting as these movements were, however, they did not operate in West Africa, although as will be seen later, some of their anti-colonial publications as well as those of their left-wing allies in France, did find their way into some of the French West African colonies. Similarly, French humanitarian organizations such as the Ligue des Droits de l'Homme (similar to the British Anti-Slavery Society) had branches in some of the French colonies, and as there was little or no organized African political activity, these branches were used by the Africans as instruments of protest against the colonial administration.

Politics and nationalism in Senegal

Perhaps the two most interesting French West African colonies where there was some African political activity in the inter-war period are Senegal and Dahomey. In Senegal the four *communes* had been electing deputies to the French Chamber of Deputies since the nineteenth century. Although the Africans in the urban areas were regarded as *citoyens* by virtue of the decree of 1833, they were represented by *métis* or Creole delegates until Blaise Diagne became Senegal's first black African Deputy in 1914. Diagne represented Senegal in the Chamber of Deputies from 1914 to 1934, was High Commissioner of African Troops during the First World War, President of the Commission of Colonies in the Chamber of Deputies, and was instrumental in convening the 1919 Pan-African Congress in Paris, although he later fell out with the black American leaders of the movement.[24]

Diagne was also the first Senegalese politician to form a political organization. This was the Republican Socialist Party, which he founded

23. For a more detailed treatment of this subject, see J. A. Langley, 1973, pp. 286–325.
24. For a general background to the interaction of French and Senegalese politics between 1919 and 1940, and for the details about the career of Blaise Diagne, see G. W. Johnson, 1966; T. Hodgkin, 1954; M. Crowder, 1962; M. Boulegue, 1965.

in 1914 to unite the various ethnic groups in Dakar and St-Louis. Diagne, after almost twenty years' absence from Senegal, offered himself as a candidate in 1914, at a time when more Senegalese were coming into the urban areas and the groundnut economy was developing. This was also a time when, with the political demise of the traditional chiefs, the *marabouts* (leaders of Islamic orders) were becoming a new political and social force in the rural areas. Young Senegalese clerks and school teachers in the urban areas were also becoming restive. The latter group had its origins in the Jeunes Sénégalais, which discussed politics and culture, demanded more jobs and better salaries and educational opportunities. It was later renamed the Parti des Jeunes Sénégalais, with a journal, *La Démocratie*. It participated in the 1914 elections, although it could not field a candidate.

Blaise Diagne was able in 1914 to gain the support of the *grands marabouts* in the urban areas, as well as the political sponsorship of the Jeunes Sénégalais and some liberal-minded Frenchmen. Although a Serer, he was able to appeal to the other ethnic groups in Dakar and St-Louis such as the Lebou and the Wollof. In fact, the Wollof language was extensively used during his electoral campaign. Instead of appealing to race, Diagne spoke of the political representation of Senegalese Africans, the political awakening of the Africans, and of 'rational evolution, not brutal revolution' in the colonies.[25] Throughout the campaign, Diagne emphasized the importance of maintaining the right of citizenship and the right to vote by the African in the four *communes*, while his European and *métis* opponents (who had dominated the politics of the *communes* since 1900 and had come to regard the electoral seats as their personal or family fiefs) largely ignored this issue and dismissed Diagne as a candidate of no consequence. In fact, even some of the Africans, especially the Lebou, opposed Diagne in the beginning.

Diagne, however, not only campaigned for the electoral rights of the Africans, he also advocated official recognition of Ku'ranic law and custom. He also called for more commercial concessions to the Africans, the creation of a Colonial Council to manage the finances of the French colonies, the establishment of a medical school in Dakar, the right to organize trade unions, and compensation to the Lebou for lands taken from them through French military conquest. Largely through his energetic campaign, the secret ballot and the political support of the Muslim groups in the rural areas, Diagne emerged victorious in the 1914 elections, and became the first African deputy to the French Chamber of Deputies in July 1914. His electoral victory was in itself a revolution in the participation and organization of the Africans in Senegalese politics. The African voters had become a significant political factor and not electoral fodder of the *colons* and *métis*.

Blaise Diagne did not seek independence from France; he advocated

25. Quoted in G. W. Johnson, 1966, p. 246.

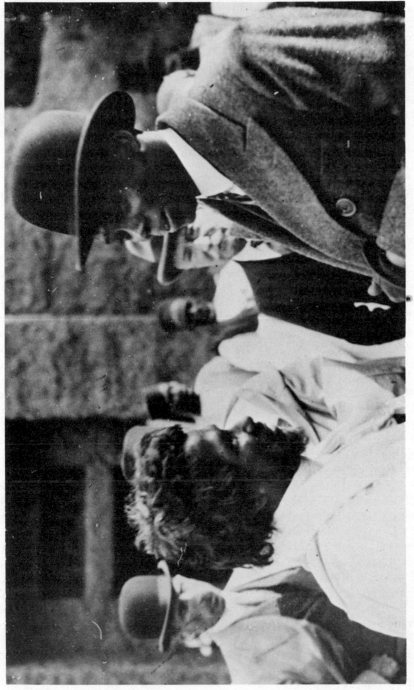

PLATE 25.3 *Blaise Diagne (1872–1934), the first African to be elected as a Deputy to the French National Assembly for Senegal, greeting his constituents after the May 1914 elections in Dakar*

645

equality and dignity, and control of the administration and municipal institutions by the Senegalese Africans. He remained faithful to this programme of evolution ('diagnisme') until his death in 1934. M'Galandou Diouf who succeeded him did not deviate from this policy either, although the radical intellectuals mentioned earlier came to regard the Blaise Diagne of the 1920s and 1930s as conservative and even anti-African. Nevertheless, his political awakening of Senegal did lay the foundation for the Senegalese politicians and nationalists of the 1940s and 1950s.

Politics and nationalism in Dahomey

In Dahomey, apart from the usual African protest through the local branch of the Ligue des Droits de l'Homme, which was perhaps the only permissible forum of 'political' activity, 'politics' was largely a question of conflicts within the religious groups and the interaction of these conflicts with chieftaincy and succession disputes. This was, in fact, part of the origin of the 1923 Porto Novo incidents. Because of their education and socialization, however, the African intelligentsia did not necessarily participate in chieftaincy politics or divide along ethnic lines. The most significant Dahomean political activist during this period, who combined participation in chieftaincy politics (he supported the Sognigbe faction of the Porto Novo Muslim community against the Jose Paraiso group of Yoruba Muslims) with anti-colonial agitation was Louis Hunkanrin.[26] Hunkanrin was educated in Senegal, worked for some time in Dahomey and returned to Senegal in 1913. He wrote critical articles against colonial maladministration in Dahomey in French and Senegalese newspapers, and assisted Blaise Diagne during the latter's election campaign in 1914. Through Blaise Diagne, Hunkanrin was given a job in Paris, but got involved with radical political groups there and was sent back to Dahomey in 1921. While in Paris he started a newspaper called *Le Messager Dahoméen* which condemned colonial abuses in Dahomey and was later taken over by the Union Inter-Coloniale whose radical pro-communist journal *Le Paris* was at one time edited by the Vietnamese revolutionary Ho Chi Minh. Through these radical groups, Tovalou Houénou's *Ligue Le Paria* and Garvey's *Negro World* began to reach Dahomey.

Back in Dahomey, Hunkanrin revived the local branch of the Ligue des Droits de l'Homme as well as a branch of the Comité Franco-Musulman. Through colleagues in these local branches, radical and communist newspapers from France and the United States reached Dahomean intellectuals, and petitions and grievances against the local administrations were sent to Paris. In Gabon, too, a similar body had existed since 1919. Laurent Antchouey, a young Gabonese who had studied in Senegal, revived a branch of the Ligue in Libreville in 1925, after returning from France

26. M. Crowder, G. W. Johnson in J. F. A. Ajayi and M. Crowder (eds), 1974, pp. 511; 565–7.

where he had edited two journals *L'Echo Gabonais* and *La Voix Africaine*.

In February–March 1923, partly because of increased taxes and lower price for palm kernel following the depressions of 1919 and 1920–1, and the subsequent price inflation and shortage of metal coins, workers in private firms went on strike and public meetings were organized by Hunkanrin's friends in the Comité Franco-Musulman and in the Ligue.[27] The army had to be called out to break up meetings, and the Africans reacted by mounting a passive resistance movement which lasted from 13 February to early March. There were also strikes in Whydah. Some of the chiefs even requested fellow chiefs to resist the new taxes. The colonial administration countered by arresting the leaders of the resistance, calling for more troops from Togo and Ivory Coast, and declaring a state of emergency which lasted until June 1923. With the arrest and exile of nearly all the leaders of the protest movement, including Hunkanrin, nationalist agitation in Dahomey came to an end, and a period of political quiescence as in the other French West African territories followed.

The major difference between conservative and radical French West African nationalists (and the conservatives were certainly in the majority during this period) was that the conservatives, led by Blaise Diagne, were satisfied with the 'symbolic representation' and gradual evolution of France's colonial subjects, with selected *évolués* representing the African population, whereas Kouyaté, Senghor, Houénou and the few radical African intellectuals who expected greater changes in the colonies after the First World War, stood for significantly increased African representation through radical and ideologically articulate political groups which could operate either in France or in the colonies. This latter group also advocated the right to form trade unions in the colonies, as well as the possibility of some form of autonomy within the French empire. It was only when the radicals were frustrated beyond measure by Blaise Diagne and the French authorities that their radicalism came to assume autonomy and political independence from France as a goal. This was clearly not characteristic of the general political evolution of the French West African territories, and it is, therefore, not surprising that this radicalism was short-lived, and that the pattern of colonial politics in French West Africa followed the style and concept of Blaise Diagne and M'Galandou Diouf up to the constitutional changes of the post-1945 period.

Apart from the demonstrations and riots in Porto Novo in 1923, which stemmed from rivalry between Muslim and government-supported factions among the traditional groups, imposition of taxes, and deterioration in the palm kernel trade, and which was exploited by a group of nationalist intellectuals, nationalist movements organized along the lines of the NCBWA or Macaulay's Nigerian National Democratic Party scarcely figured in French West Africa during this period.

27. J. A. Ballard, 1965; R. Buell, 1928, Vol. II, pp. 16–17.

Politics and nationalism in East Africa, 1919–35

26

E. S. ATIENO-ODHIAMBO

The Kiswahili word *siasa* provides a useful umbrella for the two key words in the title of this chapter. *Siasa* includes opposition, complaint, agitation, activism. It embraces actions by organized groups as well as the spontaneous actions of spirited individuals. The practitioners of *siasa* are referred to as *wanasiasa* (singular: *mwanasiasa*). The British colonial authorities however referred to *siasa* as 'agitation', and to the *wanasiasa* as 'agitators'. But beyond this apparent British simplicity lay significant diversity at the levels of organizational scale, and with regard to areas of *concern*. Recent scholarship[1] has usefully drawn attention to the various levels of concern, and therefore the various arenas of activity, that the *wanasiasa* indulged in. This categorization is an improvement on John Lonsdale's earlier historiographical designation[2] of East African politics in the inter-war years as being essentially activism with a local focus. For, granted that the grounds for political activity lay in the local grievances of the masses and of certain individuals among the masses, the arenas for their articulation varied: from the chiefs' *baraza* in the location to the files of the Secretary of State for the Colonies in London; also from the licensed political rally to the defiant mass meetings on hilltops and armed rehearsals for war in the forests. Thus one local issue could be presented at two or more levels at the same time, the initiative for action depending on the perception of the articulators as to what level would be most responsive to the given pressure at the given time. *Siasa*, then, represents a collective consciousness about colonial wrongs at a specific location in a given time. The term simultaneously captures the consciousness of clans, of nationalities, of social classes. The political activities that are the concern of this chapter, then, were the activities arising from concrete group consciousness. They were mass activities. Each movement required a leadership, but the masses were the movement while the leadership was the vanguard. The assumption in the rest of this chapter is therefore that behind each movement and each leader, there lined up the masses.[3] And depending on the levels and arenas

1. D. A. Low and J. M. Lonsdale in D. A. Low and A. Smith (eds), 1976, pp. 40–8.
2. J. M. Lonsdale, 1968(a).
3. ibid.

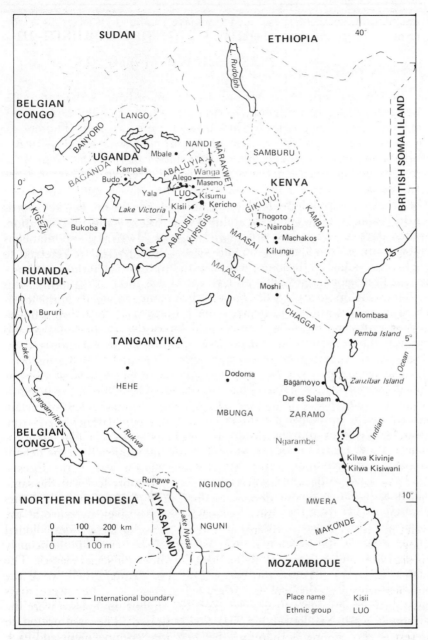

SUDAN

ETHIOPIA

40°

BELGIAN
CONGO

L. Rudolph

BANYORO

LANGO

NANDI

SAMBURU

BRITISH SOMALILAND

UGANDA

Mbale •

MARAKWET

BAGANDA

Kampala

ABALUYIA

Wanga

KENYA

0°

Budo •

Alego •

Maseno

Yala •

LUO

Kisumu •

• Kericho

KIGEZI

Bukoba •

Kisii •

ABAGUSII

KIPSIGIS

GIKUYU

Thogoto
•

KAMBA

• Nairobi

• Machakos

Lake Victoria

MAASAI

Kilungu

RUANDA-
URUNDI

MAASAI

Moshi •

• Bururi

CHAGGA

• Mombasa

Pemba Island

5°

Lake Tanganyika

TANGANYIKA

Dodoma
•

Bagamoyo •

Zanzibar Island

HEHE

Dar es Salaam •

Indian Ocean

L. Rukwa

MBUNGA

ZARAMO

BELGIAN
CONGO

Ngarambe
•

Kilwa Kivinje
Kilwa Kisiwani

NORTHERN RHODESIA

Rungwe •

NGINDO

MWERA

10°

NYASALAND

Lake Nyasa

NGUNI

MAKONDE

| 0 | 100 | 200 km |
| 0 | 100 m | |

MOZAMBIQUE

—·—·— International boundary

Place name   Kisii

Ethnic group   LUO

FIG. 26.1 *Politics and nationalism in East Africa, 1919–35*

of articulation, some of these activities have qualified in latter days for description as acts of nationalism.

Religious protest movements

One of the weapons that East Africans used from early on in their struggle against colonialism was religion. Resistance called for mobilization, and in many regions religious leadership arose to fulfil this role. The era of primary resistance was also the era of the prophets. While the Africans lost the actual wars in the battlefield, the mood of resistance remained entrenched in the hearts of the many. The followers of the *Orkoiyot* in Nandi remained active and watchful and the Nandi were repeatedly mobilized by this prophetic leadership to resist the abuses of colonialism over the years.[4] Similarly colonial archives from Kenya are full of references to witch doctors and *laibons* creating trouble in Marakwet, Kericho and Samburu. In western Uganda the followers of the Nyabingi cult in Kigezi were being watched all through these years. Thus these traditional religious resistance movements provided an element of continuity with the former era. But as the first decade wore on into the second, colonialism appeared to be gaining in strength; to many, indeed, it appeared as if the worst of the evils had come to earth. The colonial forces dug in, restructured or destroyed the known social and political institutions, and imposed their own structures over the various communities. It appeared that colonized Africans needed a new spiritual reinvigoration in order to stand up against colonialism in its many forms. This spiritual need was filled in two ways: first by the emergence of a new generation of African prophets, and secondly by the founding of African independent churches alongside the European Christian churches, with a view to providing 'a place to feel at home' for the many Africans who had accepted Christianity but found it intolerable to live under missionary patronage.[5]

Although not sufficiently covered in the existing historical writing, substantial initiative was displayed by those African prophets who arose and offered relief from the stresses which colonialism had introduced into the social fabric. These religious innovations were protest movements. Starting from the second decade, these activities were to continue throughout the 1920s and 1930s, and were to be joined by many more after the Second World War. What they stood for can be seen by two studies from the Kamba and the Abagusii of Kenya.

The Kamba had been in contact with the colonizing forces from the early 1800s when Kamba traders were plying to the coast.[6] In their wake came the missionaries in the 1840s, and later on the more determined efforts at Christianization by the end of the nineteenth century and into the

4. P. K. arap Magut in B. G. McIntosh (ed.), 1969.
5. F. B. Welbourn and B. A. Ogot, 1966.
6. J. F. Munro, 1975.

twentieth century. But Christianity, like Islam, made little impression on the mass of the Kamba. What made visible inroads into Kamba society was colonialism as a political and an economic force. During the first two decades of this century, the colonial situation produced a widely-felt sense of deprivation and frustration among the Kamba masses as the colonial authorities campaigned to appropriate Kamba resources in the form of taxes, land and labour, using their newly appointed chiefs who had very little regard for traditional authority. The pre-capitalist social institutions for conflict resolution were rendered irrelevant for the purposes of restraining these chiefs and their policemen. As the masses got more and more disillusioned they resorted to religious movements for succour and as vehicles for protest. These movements manifested themselves in prophets and spanned the period between 1910 and 1922. A widespread cult, *Kathambi* or *Ngai*, had emerged in Machakos district between 1901 and 1911, promising an imminent millennium. For a time the cult's leadership frightened the British authorities, who responded by instituting reforms in the political system. But these were not considered enough, and although the main wave of millenarianism cooled down, there were still elements in Kamba society that were not reconciled to the colonial situation. Compulsory recruitment into the Carrier Corps in the First World War years, plus the widespread inability of the colonial authorities to deal with the many social and economic problems that beset the Kamba masses after the war, served to increase the numbers of those who would answer to the clarion-call for a millenarian resolution to the tensions in society.

Such a call came with the emergence of Ndonye wa Kauti, who began to preach a prophetic message to the people of Kilungu in Machakos district in the early months of 1922. Ndonye's movement grew in response to the local expressions of the worldwide economic crisis of the 1920–1 period. As a result of this crisis, many Kamba found it more and more difficult to acquire enough money to pay their taxes. In addition, the prices of their surpluses were declining while at the same time the burden of taxation rose up from three to eight rupees per head in 1920. The currency reforms of 1921–2, converting the rupee first to the paper florin and then to the shilling coin, led to losses in cash sales. To crown it all, a drought decimated Kamba production during these years, and yet there were not enough employment opportunities to absorb the surplus male labour. It was in these impecunious circumstances that Ndonye wa Kauti offered a millenarian and messianic solution to the cash shortage. He claimed to be a prophet, asserting his ability to foretell the coming of rain, and invited women to dance a religious step (*Kilumi*) at his home. He also stated that God, *Ngai*, appeared to him in a dream and announced that he, Ndonye, had been selected to lead the people in a New Age about to come on this earth. At the onset of this new era, Europeans would be driven out, following which the earth would be as good as it was before colonialism, with plentiful water, and no taxes. When Ndonye had built a sanctuary as instructed by God, He would send him books, clothes, rifles and a telegraph line. 'The telegraph line', Ndonye prophesied, 'will provide a means of communication between us. As soon as all these articles have been sent to me by God, I shall take complete charge of the whole country.' But take charge he would not, for the district commissioner arrested him before the sanctuary was completed, and deported him to Siyu along the Kenya coast. Ndonye was never to return again, for like many activists before and after him, he died in exile. And with his departure the movement collapsed, an indication that in this as in other movements, the role of the mobilizer was crucial.

Not so easy to suppress was the Mumbo cult, a movement contemporaneous with Ndonye wa Kauti's prophetism which outlasted Ndonye. This movement was rooted in the resentment of colonial authority which the Luo and the Abagusii shared. This resentment dated back to the wars of occupation the British had inflicted on the Abagusii in 1904 and 1908, and on the Luo of Alego in 1908–10.[7] But it was further ingrained because of the British coercion of these people to yield compulsory labour for road construction and for the settler farms. There was, in addition, the hated hut tax which weighed particularly heavily on those who were polygamous. The paternalism of the missionaries further fuelled this mood of resentment. As in Ukambani, the Abagusii began to look for new categories of thought that would hold forth promise for a better world view. They found this in the Luo Mumbo cult, a traditional lake spirit cult which was at the height of its influence in the nineteenth century. This cult found revitalization into a political movement for resistance to the white man's presence in the second decade of this century. In an epiphany in 1913 this Mumbo spirit addressed one Onyango Dunde of the Seje clan in Alego as follows:

> I have chosen you to be my mouth-piece. Go out and tell all Africans – and more especially the people of Alego that from henceforth I am their God. Those whom I choose personally and also who acknowledge me will be forever in plenty. Their crops will grow of themselves, and there will be no more need to work. I will cause cattle, sheep and goats to come out of the lake in great numbers to those who believe in me, but all unbelievers and their families and cattle will die out.
>
> The Christian religion is rotten and so is its practice of making its believers wear clothes. My followers must let their hair grow and never wash. All Europeans are your enemies but the time is shortly coming when they will disappear from our country.

As in Ukambani, the message was one of denunciation of the European

7. J. M. Lonsdale, 1977.

and a repudiation of his way of life. Because the message was succinct, but more particularly, because it was such a harmonious blend of a restatement of the validity of a traditional religious cult together with a consciousness of the more recent political happenings, the movement spread very quickly from Alego in Siaya District to South Nyanza, making its début in Gusii in 1914 through the agency of another Luo prophet, Mosi wuod Auma, who was reportedly 'promising cures of all evils' and predicting 'the early departure from Kisii of all white men after which the native would possess their land in peace'.

The message about the imminent departure of the white men assumed a fortuitous reality when in 1914 the Germans attacked the British stockade at Kisii township. The Africans saw the prophecy as fulfilling itself, and joined in the rampage by plundering colonial and missionary centres in the district. When reprisal came it was brutal, about 150 Abagusii being killed in the British effort at the suppression of the revolt. But it did not deter the adherents, who continued with their activities in the inter-war years, in spite of frequent arrests and the predictable deportations of the leaders. And in the process of entrenching itself further, the Mumbo cult intermeshed in Gusiiland with the more indigenous cult of Sakawa. Sakawa was a nineteenth-century Gusii prophet whose return was fixed by the Abagusii foretellers for some time in the middle of 1921. A prophetess, Bonairiri, began marshalling up an organization to prepare people for the return of Sakawa. The colonial administration's response was to break up this movement using the Abuse of Opiate Ordinance. This did not deter the followers, who continued through 1921 and 1922 to preach both Sakawaism and Mumboism. Repressed by the colonial administration, these movements continued to thrive in Gusiiland throughout our period. Persecuted, deported, forbidden in the district, the Mumboites continued to preach and sing their recalcitrant refrain:

> Sabaye Laesi, Sabaye
> Wuriande you are going
> George you are going
> Sabaye Laesi, Sabaye.[8]

But as is well known, 'George' (the white man) did not go, and the kingdom of Mumbo did not come. Yet the spirit of resistance could not be killed. It simply went underground, surfacing later in the 1950s to gall the British administration in Gusii yet again.

Equally significant, and the second strand of religious resistance, was the emergence of Christian independent churches. As we have seen in Chapters 12 and 20, some of these churches played the role of protest movements against European patronage in the missionary churches; all of them had the aim of going beyond the missionary churches and offering

8. B. A. Ogot and W. R. Ochieng in B. A. Ogot (ed.), 1972(a), p. 173.

solutions which they believed to be positively good for the communities they served. Yet having stated this common purpose of the independent churches, it is important also to identify the many varieties that emerged in East Africa in this period. Some were 'Ethiopian' churches in that they emphasized, as K. Asare Opoku has pointed out already, African self-improvement and political rights. Yet others belonged to the 'Zionist' school, with their emphasis upon possession by the Holy Spirit, upon healing, and upon prophecy. More than this there were differences between the independent churches with regard to doctrine, ritual, organization and aspirations. These differences are best identified as the narrative on independency flows.

The earliest independent African Church in this region, the Nomiya Luo Church, founded in 1910 by John Owalo, a former Church Missionary Society adherent who had been converted in turn first to Islam and then to Roman Catholicism, has already been dealt with in Chapter 7 of this volume.[9] It may be recalled that he had a vision in which he was taken to Heaven, and of this place it has been written that:

> It is a beautiful place; and all the nations of the earth wanted to enter in but the Angels closed the gate. When all the Nations of the earth had gathered at the gate of heaven, the Angels let the Jews in first, then secondly the Arabs. After them went in John Owalo, the Angel Gabriel and the Angel Rafael, all three entering together. The White races attempted to enter in after them, but the Angels closed the gate on their face and chased the White men away, kicking them.

Owalo's heavenly vision, apart from its pointedly anti-white testimony, was in part a synthesis of his diverse religious experience and background. This synthesis was further carried into the practices of his new Church, whose ever-increasing adherents were enjoined to practise circumcision and to observe the Ten Commandments; and who were also enjoined not to smoke, drink beer or dance. In essence then, as Ogot has observed,[10] Owalo was not rejecting alien religions: he merely wanted the Africans to accept them on their own terms.

Equally exciting was the message the Watchtower Church delivered to the Africans in Central Africa and southern Tanganyika (now Tanzania) in the years during and after the First World War: the world was in its last age; the great empires and nations of Europe were the instruments of Satan; so too were the historic churches. All these were to be overthrown in one last great struggle. The world would then become the inheritance of the true believers. This message was to be easily received in Northern Rhodesia (now Zambia), where Hanoc Sindano preached, from 1917 onwards, against the authority of the colonial chiefs, colonial administra-

9. See Chapter 7 above and also O. Odinga, 1967, pp. 68–9; B. A. Ogot, 1974(b), pp. 262–3.

10. B. A. Ogot, 1974(b), pp. 262–3.

tors, and missionaries. By 1919 the movement had entered Tanganyika, and caught on substantially in the Kasanga, Mambwe, Ufipa and Mbozi areas. Matters came to a head in 1923 when the British accused the Church's leaders of vilifying the missionary churches; seventeen men were arrested and gaoled. This did not deter the followers and the religion continued to spread throughout the colonial period. Like Mumboism, it was a religion of the masses.

The Watchtower movement was an attempt to provide solutions to the problems of colonized rural peoples. By rejecting the authority of the chiefs, the missionaries and British officials, and setting up new villages for the believers, the adherents sought to create new societies where they could feel at home. Like the Nomiya Church, it sought to create whole and whole-some societies to replace those which had been destroyed by colonialism.

But some of the churches were started with a narrower scope than the two discussed above. These latter movements would be identified through their concern with single issues. For example, the African National Church that thrived in the Rungwe district of Tanganyika from the 1930s onward was set up specifically as a Christian Church that would accommodate those who had been expelled from the missionary churches because they had 'reneged' into polygamy, and to embrace those who had not joined these mission churches because they were already polygamous.[11] Likewise, the Dini ya Roho (Holy Ghost Church) was founded among the Abaluyia of Kenya in 1927 as a breakaway from the Friends African Mission.[12] The followers of Dini ya Roho insisted that in order to count oneself fully a Christian one had to accept 'baptism by the Holy Spirit', speaking in tongues, and the free confession of sins. This emphasis on 'baptism by the Holy Spirit' also led Alfayo Odongo Mango to found his Joroho (Holy Ghost) Church[13] among the Luo in 1932. But though founded as a result of a specific grievance, each religion would then evolve its own specific doctrine, ritual, and organization 'in the struggle', in response to the specific historical experience of each faith.

Although regarded by many colonial authorities merely as 'impulsive negative retorts',[14] these religious protest movements were a testimony to the strength and vitality of the African spirit, and in a fundamental way laid the foundations for the mass nationalist movements of later years. Although not often honoured in the annals of nationalism, they were, as it were, the 'illegitimate uncles' of African nationalism. And the basis of their support was the people, the rural masses.

11. T. O. Ranger, n.d., pp. 16–20.
12. O. Odinga, 1967, p. 69.
13. B. A. Ogot in K. J. King and A. Salim (eds), 1971.
14. J. S. Coleman quoted in J. M. Lonsdale, 1968(b), p. 12.

PLATE 26.1 *The Reverend Alfayo Odongo Mango, founder of the Joroho (Holy Ghost) Church among the Luo (Kenya) in 1932*

656

The Young Associations

Much prominence has been given in the recent historiography to the educated elites, the *Asomi* or *Josomo*, in the development of African politics during these years.[15] This newly emergent group consisted of those few men (and hardly any women) who had attended the missionary schools like Maseno, Budo, Thogoto and Zanzibar, subsequently becoming teachers, catechists, clerks and artisans. Working in opposition to the colonial-appointed chiefs, and to the local administration, these people organized 'Young' Associations as protest movements through which to conduct their political campaigns. These associations therefore had a mass following. The doyen of them was the Young Baganda Association, which excelled in its opposition to the chiefs and the Kabaka of Buganda. Equally prominent was the Young Kavirondo Association in mobilizing peasants in Nyanza. As well, there was the Kikuyu Central Association, which was noted for its persistence and organizational ability during these years. To their fortunes we must now turn.

The Young Baganda Association, for example, emerged as a result of the basic tensions in Ganda society during the time. Generally it can be said that political competition in Buganda was very intense during the first three decades of this century. Certain factors were contributory to this intensity. The first was a legal creation of the British colonialists and the Protestant Baganda chiefs, namely the Buganda Agreement of 1900. This Agreement, whose economic aspects have already been discussed in Chapter 7 above, established, *inter alia*, a treaty relationship between the British and the Baganda ruling class. It was through this agreement that Buganda enjoyed more autonomy than was available in other areas of East Africa. The Buganda Agreement gave external protection to the Baganda; for that reason political activity in Buganda assumed an introspective form and the issues that were raised were those of specific pertinence and consequence to Ganda society. The internal dynamic for this activity were the chiefs. Beneficiaries from the Agreement, having been awarded substantial personal and official estates, these overlords were to bear the brunt of criticism from both the traditional clan-heads (the *bataka*), the peasants (*bakopi*), and the 'young' men. As the Kabaka of Buganda was the biggest individual beneficiary of the Agreement, the questioning eyes, tongues and pens of the 'young' men did not spare him. There was, indeed, cause for political discord in this community, for the Agreement and its consequence, the creation of new social classes in society, left many groups – the Muslims, the Catholics, the *bataka* and the *bakopi* – dissatisfied. And the demeanour of the newly created chiefs left a lot to be desired. They were, in the years after 1918, becoming increasingly unpopular. Being colonial bureaucrats and not traditional leaders, they were willing to flout the patron–client

15. A. M. Karani, 1974; B. E. Kipkorir, 1969; G. P. McGregor, 1967; I. N. Kimambo and A. J. Temu (eds), 1969, Ch. VI.

relationships that had obtained in Buganda in favour of their new masters. Moreover, as agents of colonialism they were regarded as agents of sometimes undesirable changes in, and interference with, the traditional ways of life. For example, they were meant to enforce health and sanitation regulations which were unpopular with the peasants. Those members of the western-educated elite who were not co-opted by the hierarchy exploited these grievances to the full.

Leading in this revolt were the young men,[16] the most pre-eminent of whom was Z. K. Sentongo, an articulate pamphleteer who organized the immigrant Baganda Community in Nairobi. In 1919 he founded the Young Baganda Association, whose aims were

1. to improve Uganda in every way;
2. to give a helping hand to deserved [*sic*] Muganda who may be in distress;
3. to settle the best way to enable us to get and maintain our education.

In their many testimonies and writings, these leaders complained about the chiefs in Buganda, accusing them of imprisoning the people without trial by jury. Their other grievance was economic: they wanted the many restrictions which had been imposed on the cotton trade by the Uganda Protectorate government to be removed. Thirdly, they made a characteristic demand as new men: they asked for an improvement in the education facilities then existing, calling for the introduction of government schools, expansion in the education facilities for girls, and a higher institution of learning in Buganda.

But if this was a modest beginning, the Young Baganda Association was to become more intransigent in the following three years. By 1921 it had become racialist and anti-Asian. The Asians served as a convenient scapegoat for the economic grievances of the period. Writing in the *Uganda Herald* in that year, Sentongo accused the Asians of being the immediate exploiters of the Africans. 'Who but the Indians are exploiting us? – and in turn smuggling our hard earned money into India for their own benefit – robbing us doubly? The Indian effort is only to blind the natives' he concluded. By 1922 the Young Baganda Association had become anti-monarchical as well, attacking the chiefs and the Kabaka, and suggesting that Uganda should be a republic. In that year Yowasi Paito, Joswa Naluma and Yusufu Mukasa, the three of them medical assistants at Namirembe Hospital and all of them old boys of Budo High School, wrote a letter attacking the Kabaka Daudi Chwa on grounds of personal immorality, for failure to run the *Lubiri* (palace) properly, and for supporting the chiefs. 'The Kabaka is worthless', they wrote. They concluded by asking for a constitution for Buganda. Obviously neither the chiefs nor the Kabaka would let them get away with all this. A campaign was mounted to discredit these elements. For a start, the *Lukiko* passed a law making it illegal to

16. D. A. Low, 1971, p. 53–5.

abuse the Kabaka, arguing that this was against traditional custom. Offenders were to face gaol sentences, and the three letter writers fell victim to this law, all of them being imprisoned in July 1922 for the letter they had written. Furthermore Kabaka Daudi Chwa himself wrote pamphlets in the following years aimed at arousing popular support for himself by attacking the young intelligentsia. He accused them of 'foreignization'.[17] This two-pronged attack, coupled with the fact that some of the Association's supporters were co-opted by being offered minor chiefly positions, undermined the solidarity of the organization which steadily fizzled out.

The Kavirondo Taxpayers Welfare Association[18] is a classic product of the missionary impact. Its parent body, which was subverted by missionary effort, was the Young Kavirondo Association, which had been founded in the latter half of 1921 by the alumni of Maseno School in Nyanza. The issue at stake was the change of status of the colonial territory in 1920 from the British East Africa Protectorate to a Crown Colony – the Kenya Colony and Protectorate. The Association's leaders read into the transformation an ominous attempt by the British to change the status of Africans and possibly to expose the lands of western Kenya to European settlement. This territorial concern was married with the local grievances to precipitate a strike at Maseno School. Jonathan Okwiri, Jeremiah Awori, Reuben Omulo and Simeon Nyende as teachers took part in this. Very soon, word was spread that there would be a public meeting at Lundha to discuss the grievances of the Luo and the Abaluyia people.

This meeting was held on 23 December 1921. The outcome was the setting up of the Young Kavirondo Association (YKA) with Jonathan Okwiri as chairman, Benjamin Owuor Gumba as secretary and Simeon Nyende as treasurer. More importantly, resolutions were passed calling for, among other things, the establishment of a separate legislature for Nyanza as an autonomous administrative unit with an elected African president; for the election of paramount chiefs for Central and South Nyanza; the abolition of the infamous *kipande* (identity card); the reduction of hut tax and poll tax with a view to excluding women from taxation; an increase in wages; the revocation of the Crown Colony status and reversion to Protectorate status; the granting of individual title-deeds to land; the abolition of forced labour, and the dissolution of the labour camps at Yala, Rabuor, Nyahera and Pap Onditi; and the building of a government school in Central Nyanza. Following this, a delegation went to see the provincial commissioner with these resolutions. Subsequently the delegation asked to see the governor so as to present these resolutions to him in person. The commissioner would not oblige the first time nor the second, but as tensions were running high the governor finally came to meet the petitioners at Nyahera on 8 July 1922. None of the requests were immediately granted; but the one lesson that emerged from this experience

17. ibid., pp. 104–8.
18. M. Okaro-Kojwang, in B. G. McIntosh (ed.), 1969.

of confrontation was that this nascent elite had demonstrated impressive ability at mass mobilization. This was because they were articulating local mass grievances. There was a need therefore to contain them. The option chosen was that of colonial patronage, through an agreeable missionary, Archdeacon Owen. In 1923 the leaders of the Young Kavirondo Association felt that he would be a good go-between for them. Owen on his part found opportunity to patronize these people and make of them 'law-abiding' citizens. In July 1923 they handed the presidency of their movement, YKA or *Piny Owacho* as it was more popularly known, to Archdeacon Owen.

Owen proceeded immediately to make this organization respectable by subverting it. He thus shifted the basis of its support from the masses to the elites. There was a shift in emphasis away from political agitation towards new demands for better houses, better food, better clothing, better education and better hygiene. Members were often required to chant in ritual fashion the pledge not to dirty water in springs, to kill so many rats a week, to plant two hundred trees a year, not to mix cow's urine with milk (a traditional delicacy), to build latrines, to make one bed for each hut in the village, not to get drunk, and not to encourage marriage for girls before the age of sixteen. In other words, Owen removed the mass political sting from this Association, which from then on took on the impotent title of Kavirondo Taxpayers Welfare Association (KTWA). Owen encouraged and organized the now muted leadership, whenever there was a political grievance, to write memoranda to the authorities. These were often accurate and stung the colonial administration, but precisely because they were so elitist and so formalized, they were effete. During the period, the memorandum became the basic tool for the struggle, so much so that these leaders were referred to as Jo-Memorandum.[19]

The Association was rendered even more effete by its split into Luo and Abaluyia factions in 1931. The Luo wing of the Association limped on under Owen's leadership until 1944, its firebrand approach having been stifled by Owen's intervention and by the siphoning off of the radical leadership into respectable roles: Jonathan Okwiri and Odindo both became chiefs, Simeon Nyende was appointed to the Local Native Council and Apindi was the Nyanza representative before the Joint Select Committee into the Closer Union in East Africa. Recalcitrants there were, like Aduwo Nyandoje and John Paul Olola. The latter, a man from Alego location, was particularly active from 1927 onwards in the Kisumu Chamber of Commerce. But these efforts were towards petty-bourgeois economic grievances and were a far cry from the comprehensive mass political programmes of the early 1920s. And yet, in spite of all this, the KTWA did serve as an inspiration to a neighbouring area.

The neighbouring area was eastern Uganda, where Erisa Masaba founded the Bugishu Welfare Association in the early 1920s. The associa-

19. O. Odinga, 1967, pp. 61–94.

tion aimed at getting rid of Baganda agents and instituting local leadership, in addition to pledging itself to 'working for the uplift of the Bagishu', and keeping a close watch on the Kenya settlers, in case the latter might encroach upon their lands in the Mount Elgon areas. Also contemporaneous with Masaba's organization and broadly pursuing the same goals was the Young Bagwere Association, set up to resist Baganda acquisition of the lands around Mbale township, and also to teach the members to 'learn to teach properly and to plant our crops properly'.

More intractable during the period was the Kikuyu Central Association (KCA), a movement that articulated Gikuyu rural grievances, beginning from 1924. Its headquarters was at Kahuhia in Muranga where it was launched under the leadership of Joseph Kang'ethe and James Beauttah. As to what it stood for, Beauttah has remarked that, 'Our main goal in the KCA was to get back the land Europeans had taken from us.'[20]

But who were its members? The KCA was a body representing those elements among the Gikuyu who did not fully accept the ideas and practice of European dominance. They were more militant in their approach to change than the establishment chiefs and mission boys. In a word, the KCA stood for dissent. And what did its members dissent from? It is difficult to put it succinctly as the KCA leaders were never able to articulate their objectives with any precision. But in general terms they were protesting against the excesses of the colonial situation in so far as these manifested themselves in Gikuyu society. The racial indignities which the Gikuyu suffered as a result of the cultural arrogance of the white rulers coupled with the many resented policies and actions of the colonial administration came in for constant rapping.

Something of their attitudes may be garnished from the list of grievances the KCA leadership presented to the governor when the latter visited Muranga in 1925. They protested against the Crown Lands Ordinance of 1915 which had made all Africans tenants at will of the Crown. They also requested the release of Harry Thuku, and asked for an appointment of a paramount chief 'with judicial powers for trying our cases, one who should be well educated and to be elected by the majority of our people'. The petition also dealt with the local problems that the colonial administration created for the people, such as the compulsory rebuilding of sanitary huts to prevent plague and the banning of the growing of cotton and coffee by Africans. Finally, it put forward programmes for improvement, asking the administration to expand the training facilities for hospital orderlies, for the building of a high school, and for the setting up of a school for girls. These requests made little impression on the colonial authorities.

But official scorn did not deter these leaders. By 1927 something of a rapprochement was made with the Kiambu politicians, when Jomo

20. J. Spencer, 1971, p. 94.

PLATE 26.2 *Harry Thuku (1895–1970), a founder and leader of the East African Association, the pioneer nationalist organization in Kenya*

PLATE 26.3 *Jomo Kenyatta (1890s–1978), Kenyan nationalist and first President of independent Kenya, 1963–78*

662

Kenyatta was asked by the Association to take over the post of general secretary, a job which he took up the following year.

The fortunes of the KCA improved in the following two years for reasons both local and international. Kenyatta's efforts as party secretary led to a cultural revival. In his efforts to build up grass-roots support for the Association, Kenyatta appealed to the Gikuyu through *Mwigwithania*, a Gikuyu-language newspaper he founded, to be proud of their cultural heritage. The pages of the monthly *Mwigwithania* were full of riddles, proverbs and stories which encouraged the readers to think of themselves as Gikuyu. This paper also narrated the day-to-day activities of the KCA in detail, thus bringing it to the attention of the readers. This cultural revival was to be intensified when a major quarrel broke out within the churches of Gikuyuland the following year. The issue at stake was clitoridectomy which has already been discussed in Chapter 20 above.

This was also the decade of Kenyatta in London. Beginning with the petition and evidence of the Kikuyu Central Association to the Hilton Young Commission in 1928, the Gikuyu placed their land grievances at the centre of their problems. Kenyatta was part of the KCA delegation that gave evidence to this commission. The gist of their grievance was captured in this statement of evidence, which noted that, 'We have tried for many years to make the government give us title deeds for our land but we have not got them and we cannot know whether it is our land or whether it is Crown Land.'[21] This concern with security of tenure in the African 'reserves' was reiterated by Kenyatta when in 1929 the KCA sent him to London to articulate their demands. In London, Kenyatta summarized the KCA's aims as being the security of their lands; increased educational facilities of a practical nature; the abolition of the hut tax for women, and elected representation to the Legislative Council. This theme was to be pursued with particular vigour two years later when the Africans were invited to submit evidence before the Kenya Land Commission – a body set up as a result of a parliamentary recommendation in 1931 that African land problems should be looked into. The KCA took an active part in helping the Gikuyu lineages (*mbari*) to prepare their evidence. And when the report came out, the KCA marshalled all the Gikuyu political groups to draft a unanimous memorandum of rejection and protest. Because these protests went unheeded, the question of land assumed the central place in Gikuyu politics that it did, leading to the Mau Mau war two decades later.

These 'young' associations did not succeed, and yet it would be unfair to state that they failed. Although the system regularly undermined their effectiveness by co-opting some of the leadership while detaining others, their lasting legacy is that they articulated the grievances of the Africans against the colonial system using methods like pamphleteering and abilities

21. C. G. Rosberg and J. Nottingham, 1966, p. 94.

like the capacity to speak the English language and Kiswahili to expose the basic evils of colonialism.

Segmentary associations

Too many and too diverse to be enumerated were the segmentary associations formed specifically to deal with the issue of boundaries. Colonial regimes did indeed fix the territorial boundaries of Kenya, Uganda, Tanganyika, Zanzibar and Somaliland in the period before 1933. But in their attempts to organize the internal administration in the territories, the colonial masters created provincial, district, locational and country, and sub-location and sub-country boundaries that cut across many ethnic groups, clans and lineages. In many instances, lands belonging to one group were allocated to new owners with no traditional claims to these areas. In both instances, the outcome was agitation: agitation to get back lost lands; or to be allowed to rejoin clansmen in a different sub-location; or to be given a distinct administrative boundary through the creation of a sub-location specifically catering for one clan or sub-clan group. The scale of contention was local, but the intensity and persistence of these segmentary agitations were such that the colonial administration could not ignore them. Besides, many of the 'new men' found roles to play in these internecine quarrels: preparing evidence, litigating in the courts, writing memoranda to district commissioners, to the colonial governor, or even to the British Secretary of State for the Colonies. The potential for segmentary violence was always great in these conflicts, and sometimes the feuds ended tragically.

The Ugenya Kager Luo Clan (South Bank of River Nzoia) Association,[22] which was set up by the Luo-speaking Kager clansmen in 1932 with a view to recovering 'lost territory' from their Wanga neighbours, represents this type of conflict on a minute scale. By contrast, the more famous Mubende Banyoro Committee[23] persistently sought the return of the 'lost counties' of Huyaga, Bugangaizi, Buwekula, Buruli and Rugonjo by the Baganda to the kingdom of Bunyoro in Uganda. But by and large it was not possible for the colonizers to satisfy the demands emanating from segmentary associations. And precisely because these demands could not be satisfied, these associations provided avenues for the practice of the politics of local focus. And because of their persistence the British dismissed all of this activity as *fitina* – small-scale strongheadedness. But factionalism, after all, is the very stuff of village politics.

22. B. A. Ogot in K. J. King and A. Salim (eds), 1971.
23. J. B. Kyeyune, 1970.

Improvement associations and trade unionism

Of minor political significance during this period were the many commercial associations formed by the African farmers and businessmen. Quite often they set out with specific aims but because of the day-to-day annoyances of the colonial situation, they very soon found themselves acting as vehicles of protest against all and sundry that was wrong with the colonial system within their areas. Their daily activities thus became a matter of contest between the mass leadership and the local representatives of the colonial administration. A case in point was the Kilimanjaro Native Planters (Coffee) Association (KNPA) which was founded in 1925 'to protect and promote the interests of the Native Coffee Growers on the mountain'.[24] Partly as a result of the fears of European settlers about organized African lobbying, and also as a result of the personality clashes between the leader, Joseph Merinyo, and the various British administrative officials and African chiefs, this organization found itself pushed to take up other matters like land registration, land alienation and use, closer union with Kenya, political rights, and representation in the Central Legislative Council and the Moshi District Water Board. At the local level, the posture the union took often appeared calculated to oppose chiefly authority. This was in fact the case, and in this respect it was similar to the many local protest movements in East Africa in the mid-1920s. Their existence was an indication that a new generation of elites had emerged outside the official chiefly elite that had been set up by the colonial authorities fifteen or twenty years earlier. These new individuals were active not only among the Chagga and Gikuyu but also among the Langi,[25] the Kamba[26] and the Haya.[27] Their emergence was a signal that one age-group ought to hand over authority in the local community to the other.

Basically what they were saying was that the colonial chiefs should not necessarily see themselves as the only vehicles of social change; the new elites felt that they should also be co-opted into this process. Thus when the Bukoba Bahaya Union was formed in 1924 part of its ambition was to advise the people, 'to civilize them'. The government clerks and local traders in Bukoba who formed it – Clemens Kiiza, Suedi Kangasheki, Ludovic Kaitaba and Herbert Rugizibwa – stated that the organization was launched 'for the establishment of an institution for the development of our country and for the seeking of a system for the simple way to civilization to our mutual advantage'. The two avenues open for the attainment of this 'civilization' were through literacy education, and the planting of coffee. Throughout the 1920s and 1930s this organization championed these causes, and in the process regularly clashed with both those colonial and

24. S. G. Rogers, 1972 and 1974.
25. J. Tosh, 1973 and 1978.
26. J. F. Munro, 1975, Chapters 7 and 8.
27. G. Hyden, 1969, Chapters 4 and 5.

chiefly authorities which they considered to be standing in the way of progress. In retrospect, this Union was merely another African trading association like the Kisumu Native Chamber of Commerce, associations set up to try to wrest a little of the privileges that the Asian Associations of the period enjoyed. In East African historiography they have been described as 'improvement' associations[28] led by 'modern' men.[29] Among these men have been counted Hugh Martin Kayamba, Francis Lwamugira and the Harry Thuku of the late 1930s. Their contribution to the political awareness of the African is being debated by historians of East Africa. On the one hand are those scholars who emphasize their vision for the African people.[30] On the other hand there are those who regard these modernizers as primarily self-seekers and would deny them any legitimate role in African political radicalism.[31] On the whole, the improvers set off primarily to defend their own and their class interests; and therefore it is difficult to accord them a leadership role in the politics of mass activism.[32] Espousing popular causes was to be the task of these elites only in the years after the Second World War. The history of trade unionism clearly illustrated this lack of linkage between the modernizers and the masses.

Resistance among employed labour, as opposed to trade unionism proper, came early to East Africa. One of the first challenges the colonial authorities faced was how to force the Africans to work for them in the settler farms and in the newly created sectors of employment like the Kenya-Uganda Railways, the Central line in Tanganyika, and the public works departments. The colonial rulers solved this by passing legislation that would create a 'contract of service' enforceable by penal sanctions, any infringement of which was a criminal offence punishable by fine and/or imprisonment. Supplementing this legislation, particularly in Kenya, was the process whereby all liable African male labour was registered under the Native Registration Ordinance, the infamous ordinance that introduced the hated *kipande* to the Africans. But all this did not deter workers from striking.[33] The first known African strike in Kenya took place in Mombasa in 1902 when fifty police constables downed their batons, followed, in 1908, by a strike of African railway workers at Mazeras. In the same year, African rickshaw pullers went on strike in Nairobi. Four years later, African boatmen in Mombasa went on strike followed by the railway workers in Nairobi. And so on. These single industry strikes did not involve the exercise of forming trade unions, which in any case could have been considered illegal then. But they did represent the idea that action could be taken with regard

28. J. Iliffe, 1969, pp. 123–61; 1979, pp. 405–35.
29. J. Iliffe (ed.), 1973.
30. J. Iliffe (ed.), 1973; K. K. Janmohamed, 1974.
31. See E. S. Atieno-Odhiambo, 1973, a review of J. Iliffe (ed.), 1973.
32. E. S. Atieno-Odhiambo in B. A. Ogot (ed.), 1975, pp. 218–22.
33. M. Singh, 1969, p. 45.

to labour grievances, and were part and parcel of the growing African awareness that was characteristic of the years before 1919.

This awareness was to mature into full-scale political consciousness in the years after the war. The economic problems and the hardship faced by the Africans in the 1919–22 period led to an appreciation that there was a linkage between labour and the overall political economy in which the Africans operated. The 'young men' who were to take up the political leadership in these years were by and large urban Africans, and the plight of the labouring masses did not escape their notice. Thus the labour grievances were often part of their memoranda and rhetoric. For example, at the founding of the Young Kikuyu Association on 11 June 1921, labour matters featured prominently. Harry Thuku's summary of the proceedings of the day attests to this. He wrote to the newspapers:

> A meeting of the Young Kikuyu Association was held at Pangani village ... on Tuesday when the subject was the native wages reduction. It was ... suggested and carried out [that] in order to show the native grievances to the Government in the matter of wages reduction ... [the Association should be] in the position of writing to the Hon. Chief Native Commissioner, asking him to lay the matter before H. E. the Governor.[34]

This memorandum was duly sent to the chief native commissioner. It asked the colonial administration to desist from reducing the wages and to enjoin the settlers to do likewise; denounced forced labour; opposed the registration system; and complained of the high rates of hut tax, among other things. The description that fits this organization (as well as its successor the East African Association) is that it was 'a political association as well as a general workers union'. This description can also be well applied to the contemporary Young Kavirondo Association which likewise argued against compulsory labour, and is a fair summary of those organizations that were involved in the struggle by African workers during this period. Recurrently in the 1920s African political activity in Kenya would touch on the labour question, arguing against forced labour and demanding higher wages and the abolition of tax for women. These demands, for instance, formed part of the African presentation to the Ormsby-Gore Commission in 1924. Likewise African leaders raised these issues in the memorandum that the Kikuyu Central Association presented to the Hilton Young Commission in 1928.

But what of direct trade union organization? The colonial administration tolerated staff associations rather than trade unions as such, provided the staff associations took on a welfare mantle rather than pursuing direct union activities. The hope was that the emergent skilled African workers would form their own exclusive elitist clubs. This thinking guided the British into permitting the founding of the Tanganyika Civil Servants Union

34. Quoted in ibid., p. 11.

(TCSU) in 1922 and the Kenya African Civil Service Association sometime before 1933. The Tanganyika Territory African Civil Service Association[35] was founded by Martin Kayamba 'to promote social and educational development among its members' and 'to foster the welfare of its members in the various Government Departments'. It was partly a trade union and partly a social club whose activities included sports and evening classes. This organization was renowned for its open elitism and was largely concerned with elitist privileges. Although Kayamba had hoped to build a countrywide organization, his Association seems to have faded out in the late 1920s as the obsequious Kayamba found more favour with his masters and moved higher up the ladder of colonial administration. Its achievements, therefore, were limited even while it lasted.

The exact origins of the Kenya African Civil Service Association are obscure, but it did submit an important memorandum to the Commission of Inquiry into the Administration of Justice in Kenya, Uganda and Tanganyika Territory in Criminal Matters, which was set up in 1933.[36] The authors of this memorandum were one Newland Gibson, who was the General Secretary of the Association, Ishmael Ithongo, H. G. Shadrack and Albert Awino. This memorandum touched on important matters related to the legal system. It requested that all the laws of the country should be translated into Kiswahili, asked for an assessor jury in all criminal trials, and the repeal of the *kipande* system. The memorandum also criticized the provisions of the Vagrancy Ordinance, the Collective Punishment Ordinance, and urged the abolition of payment of tax by widows, the unemployed and those over 50 years of age. Apart from this memorandum there is a dearth of information as to what else the Association did. Equally little is known about the Kenya African Teachers Union, which was formed in 1934 under the leadership of Eliud Mathu and James Gichuru.

But generally it can be stated that these elite associations were a pale reflection of the reality of the overall labour situation, which was characterized throughout our period by the recurrent resort to strikes in the factories, ports and workshops and also in the settler farms. Given the official disapproval of trade unionism, and the lack of a communication network among the vast unskilled workers and labouring masses, these individual strikes at the site of work were the logical avenues of expression. That so little is known about them, particularly with reference to Uganda and Tanganyika, is perhaps the limitation of the scholar rather than the subject of study. But it cannot be overemphasized that the feeling of deprivation was recurrent among African labour.

35. J. Iliffe (ed.), 1973, p. 73.
36. M. Singh, 1969, pp. 24–45.

Efforts at territorial politics

This narrative has so far been concerned with the politics of local concern articulated at various levels. When it comes to the question of African attempts at territorial politics, the experience is one of failure, or alternatively of lack of serious effort. In a sense that is not derogatory since very few Africans regarded themselves as Tanganyikans or Kenyans in the inter-war years. Political consciousness had not matured to embrace the boundaries of the colonial state. Exceptions there were – men like Jomo Kenyatta, Akiiki Nyabongo, and Mbiyu Koinange, who had the rare opportunity of travelling to Europe and the United States and interacting with others who saw the colonial situation in an imperial perspective. While in Britain from 1930 onwards, Kenyatta certainly widened his horizons to embrace not only the African cause but the plight of the black man in general. Similarly Mbiyu Koinange's American education, and more so his relations with Dr Ralph Bunche, widened his perspectives. By 1933 he was writing memorandum to the Colonial Office against injustices being meted out to his father Chief Koinange and generally to the Kenya Africans. But these men were few; what is more, they were away from home, and therefore did not have the opportunity to organize the local masses.

In this context, Harry Thuku's East African Association stood out as a unique body in the early 1920s in the sense that it did, at least on paper, set its sights on encompassing the whole colonial territory of Kenya and beyond. The East African Association was founded in 1921 in Nairobi by Harry Thuku, Jesse Kariuki, Job Muchuchu and Abdullah Tarrara.[37] Africans from other territories were also prominent, including the indomitable Z. K. Sentongo of the Young Baganda Association and an unnamed Nyasa man from Nyasaland (now Malawi). It was certainly trans-ethnic, and its name reflects its Kenya-wide concern. But its membership was predominantly Gikuyu. It was given life and direction by Harry Thuku, a clerk working in the Treasury.

Thuku was one of a number of young Gikuyu then living in Nairobi who felt the need to organize themselves into a body that would rival the chiefly-dominated Kikuyu Association. It has been suggested that these young Gikuyu men were modelling themselves on the Young Baganda Association. More importantly, Thuku and the young men in Nairobi felt that there was a need for a Kenya-wide African organization. As he wrote to the *East African Standard* in 1921, it was felt 'that unless the young people of this country form an Association the Native in Kenya will always remain voiceless.' This quest for solidarity is what led Thuku to fraternize with the Kamba, Luo and Ganda young men then living in Nairobi. Thus, on 1 July 1921, they formally launched the East African Association. The organization passed resolutions on the subject of *kipande*, forced labour,

37. K. J. King, 1971(b).

excessive African taxation, and education. Thuku cabled these resolutions directly to the Colonial Office in London. The Indian politicians, A. M. Jevanjee and B. M. Desai, played a supportive role, helping Thuku in the drafting of the memorandum to the British government and printing broadsheets for the Association. These connections with the Asians caused much furore among the settlers at the time. Recent research has, however, conclusively demonstrated that Thuku was no pawn in Indian hands, and there the issue must for the moment lie.

Of more importance for this analysis were the efforts by Thuku to involve non-Gikuyu in his Association at this time. His contacts in Nairobi naturally led him to attempts at propagating his Association among the Kamba. But if the Kamba in Nairobi were enthusiastic, the rural Kamba were not. When Thuku had a public meeting with Chief Mathendu at Iveti in Machakos, the elders rebuffed his overtures, refused to sign the papers he had presented, and advised him to return to the Gikuyu 'with whom the Akamba had little in common.'[38] The situation was different in Nyanza, where Thuku's Association found a corresponding body in the Young Kavirondo Association. By December 1921 the leaders of the latter group were in touch with Thuku and had assured him that they were 'struggling' with him for the country, and had contributed financially to his funds. The relationship was one of equals, and the Young Kavirondo Association was in no way subordinate to Thuku's organization.[39] It is also important to stress that the two associations were only in touch: their relations were in no way close, and there is no substantial evidence that one influenced the other. The link-man between these two organizations was James Beauttah, then a member of Thuku's Association employed at Maseno. In his own words:

> There was a large school there [at Maseno] with well-educated African teachers, most of whom were interested in politics and who wanted to learn about the EAA. It was the only group I knew of outside Nairobi which was concerned with Nationalism. *I connected these two groups*; these future Luo politicians and the supporters of the EAA. These people ... were enthusiastic and contributed 90 rupees to send to Nairobi to support the movement. They wanted to join with the Kikuyu and the coastal people, and I think I was the one that got them interested.[40]

The proximity of Maasai country to Nairobi, and the tribulations the Maasai had experienced at the hands of the British in the first two decades with regard to their land, made western-educated Maasai elites natural allies in any protest movement taking place in town in the early 1920s. All these Maasai elites had variously had education at Thogoto, or at the

38. J. F. Munro, 1975, p. 126.
39. M. Okaro-Kojwang in B. G. McIntosh (ed.), 1969, p. 120.
40. Quoted in J. Spencer, 1971, p. 10 (emphasis added).

African Inland Mission schools in Kijabe and Siyiapei. They became the supporters of Harry Thuku among the Maasai.[41] Among them were Maitei Ole Mootian and Molonket Ole Sempele. There is little evidence that they organized a political movement in the Maasai countryside, as they were, by and large, urban workers. Their influence among the rural Maasai was to come after 1923 when they were posted back to their districts. It is from this home base that they were to organize support for the later Kikuyu Central Association.

It was the personal touch that Thuku lent to his Association which led him to associate with the Baganda. Of special interest to him was the Kampala-based Young Baganda Association, whose secretary, Joseph Kamulegeya, corresponded with Thuku on a number of issues. Kamulegeya introduced Thuku to the Black American world, and Thuku wrote to Dr W. E. B. Du Bois, Marcus Garvey and the Tuskegee Institute for black American aid missions to East Africa. No lasting associations were created however, although Garvey's paper, the *Negro World*, was sent to Thuku.[42] All this was fine on paper. But the colonial administration was upset by Thuku's populist assertions. On 14 March 1922 he was arrested, the intention being to deport him. While in confinement at the police station in Nairobi, his followers and the general African populace in Nairobi who were apparently on strike from work as well, picketed the police compound. The inevitable in this kind of colonial confrontation followed; the policemen after a while lost their nerve and fired into the crowd, killing twenty-one Africans. The date was 16 March 1922.

Following this incident, Thuku was deported to Kismayu and his Association went into disarray. Politics in the Gikuyu countryside from this time on took a more ethnic dimension. The new organization that emerged was the Kikuyu Central Association. British gunpowder put an end to any pretensions that the Nairobi Africans had entertained on multi-ethnic political organization in the inter-war years.

Prospects in Tanganyika were not much better than in the other territories, as the example of the Tanganyika African Association reveals. The Tanganyika African Association (TAA) was founded in Dar es Salaam in 1929. Under the leadership of Cecil Matola, Kleist Sykes, Mzee Bin Sudi and Ramadhan Ali, the Association stated its aim as being 'to safeguard the interests of Africans, not only in this territory but in the whole of Africa'.[43] In practice, however, the influence of the TAA did not extend beyond Dar es Salaam in the subsequent six years unless some member was transferred to work upcountry, as happened in 1933 when Mack Makeja was posted to Dodoma and founded a branch there. Moreover, even within Dar es Salaam, its achievements were limited to building a club house; it also unsuccessfully petitioned the government for the appointment of

41. K. J. King, 1971(a).
42. K. J. King, 1971(b).
43. G. G. Hajivayanis, A. C. Mtowa and J. Iliffe in J. Iliffe (ed.), 1973, p. 235.

an African town magistrate. Internal rifts denuded its membership in the years of 1931 and 1932 and it was not until 1934 that the Zanzibar branch took the initiative in reviving the Association. Apart from the fact of colonial repression, a legitimate conclusion can be drawn, namely, that in the inter-war period, there were politically no Kenyans, or Ugandans, or Tanganyikans.

Conclusion

This chapter has attempted to narrate the extent, nature and limitations of African politics and nationalism in East Africa in the period between 1919 and 1935 through examining the various forms of activism. The main actors were the masses, while the main organizers of politics, *siasa*, during these years were the 'young' men, people who had benefited from the introduction of missionary education in the first two decades of the century, and were competent to articulate African grievances before the colonial authorities. They largely concerned themselves with local grievances, agitating against those ills that colonialism had brought in its train. These people operated at various levels, ranging from the locational *baraza* or public meeting to sending petitions to the colonial governors or the Secretary of State for the Colonies in London. Their attempts at political organization were often thwarted by the colonial power, and none of the associations succeeded in all their aims. But while they lasted, these organizations were a reminder to the colonial authorities that 'the African voice' could be heard through channels other than the structure of the colonial administration. Yet there were many areas of African grievances which did not coalesce into formal organizations; no trade unions emerged during this period because few of the leaders attempted to organize such movement. This chapter notes the limitations of African activity in the period: because of their primarily local focus, they failed to organize effective territorial political movements.

Politics and nationalism in Central and Southern Africa, 1919–35

A. B. DAVIDSON, A. ISAACMAN and R. PÉLISSIER

Deep differences have always marked African political life in such widely differing countries as Angola, Bechuanaland (now Botswana), Belgian Congo (now Zaire), Northern Rhodesia (now Zambia), Basutoland (now Lesotho), Nyasaland (now Malawi), Mozambique, Swaziland, Southern Rhodesia (now Zimbabwe), South West Africa (now Namibia), and the Union of South Africa (now Republic of South Africa). These differences, still apparent now, were considerable in the period between 1919 and 1935. One reason for these differences was that these countries were parts of different colonial empires – the British, Portuguese or Belgian. Another was their different political status, with some being colonies, others protectorates and one a dominion. Last, but not least, great variations existed at the economic level, in turn generating distinct patterns of social differentiation. And yet, the emergence of the new anti-colonial movements in Southern and Central Africa reveal distinctly specific features compared with East and West Africa. This chapter examines the changing nature of popular protest in Southern and Central Africa with particular attention being given to South Africa, the Belgian Congo, and the former Portuguese colonies.[1]

The economic and political setting in Southern Africa and the Belgian Congo: an overview

The specific features of Southern Africa stem both from the character of colonial-capitalist penetration and from the ethnic stratification of societies which was more complex than elsewhere in Africa. Nowhere did the 'European sector' develop so rapidly, dwarfing the 'traditional' African economy. This economic pattern and the complexity of ethnic stratification

1. A. B. Davidson was primarily responsible for the discussion on the economic and political setting in Southern Africa and the Belgian Congo, and the section on popular resistance in South Africa and the neighbouring territories. A. Isaacman wrote the sections on Mozambique and the Belgian Congo and, together with R. Pélissier, the overview of the economic and political setting in Angola and Mozambique. R. Pélissier also wrote the section on Angola.

are attributable to the ways in which colonization proceeded, which in turn was determined by the natural conditions and the vast natural wealth of that part of Africa.

By 1919 the historical tenor of economic life in most of Southern Africa had been upset to a greater degree than in other parts of the continent. Millions of people had been drawn into the sphere of capitalist exploitation. By the middle of the 1920s more than 200000 migrant workers, recruited from as far away as Northern Rhodesia and Nyasaland, were employed in the South African mines.[2] Upwards of 60000 labourers worked in the copper, tin, diamond and gold mines of the Congo.[3]

Because of the development of European farming and large-scale expropriation of land from the peasants in a number of Southern African countries, African participation in the production of export crops and in trade was thwarted except in sectors of forced production such as cotton in the Congo.[4] Similarly, the road was barred to the emergence of a large stratum of African capitalist farmers and merchants, which is a feature of many other colonies where there were much fewer white settlers. Loss of land, strangulation of the peasantry, proletarianization and urbanization were thus processes that went faster and deeper in most Southern African countries than in other parts of Africa.[5]

A permanent and numerically significant proletarian body of African and non-European descent was, it has been seen in Chapter 16, forming more rapidly in a number of Southern African countries. Its more advanced contingents were represented by workers in the industrial cities and ports. Most of the African labour in mining and in the cities was initially recruited from seasonal workers. Yet an increasing number of people came to depend on the seasonal occupation for their livelihood, and, over time, a process of labour stabilization occurred. As a result, the emergence of an African urban proletariat was more advanced there than in most parts of West and East Africa. There were even more seasonal workers in white-owned farms, with land expropriation rapidly swelling the ranks of the rural proletariat.

The emerging intelligentsia went a long way to determine the sense of national and political identity. The development of the intelligentsia was determined by the specific character of European colonization and relative access to education. The social 'ceiling' for Africans in the south was far lower than in West Africa where, in the absence of a permanent body of white settlers, Africans found it easier to become clerks or secure a job in the civil service. In Southern Africa, whites had monopolized all the employment opportunities that might have been open to educated

2. For statistics on the composition of the South African mine labour force see Centro de Estudos dos Africanos, 1977, 24c.

3. C. Perrings, 1979, pp. 56, 84, 176.

4. B. Jewsiewicki in M. A. Klein (ed.), 1980.

5. C. Bundy, 1979; G. Arrighi, 1970; I. R. Phimister and C. van Onselen, 1978.

Africans, be they in the administration, the economic sector, the church or other spheres of life.

By the same token, the intelligentsia in Southern Africa was from its inception closer to the people. This was due to the fact that, in these regions, it derived from the midst of the indigenous population and was not initially recruited, as was sometimes the case in some West African countries, from repatriated 'freed' slaves or their descendants. The regime of cruel race discrimination, of which Africans in Southern Africa were victims without exception, inevitably tended to bring the intelligentsia closer to the people. African intellectuals there found it more difficult to play the role of inter-mediaries.

Another crucial distinguishing feature of anti-colonial protest in Southern Africa lies in the fact that opposition to the colonial order was recruited, not only from among Africans, but from among the sizeable non-African populations – the 'coloured people', Indians and progressive whites. Consequently, Africans were the main but not the sole anti-colonial force, and this left its imprint on the whole character of the struggle.[6]

A further circumstance that contributed to the general features of the anti-colonial movements in Southern Africa was their internationalist ties. In Southern Africa both the trade union movement and early nationalist activities received substantial assistance from abroad, while Belgian socialists and communists vigorously criticized repressive colonial policies in the Belgian Congo. Finally, because Southern Africa was more closely linked to the world capitalist economy, there were more contacts with the outside world with the result that worldwide changes were more keenly felt there. The period between 1919 and 1935 saw many such changes. One could mention the impact of the October Revolution of 1917 in Russia and the revolutionary upsurge in the wake of the First World War lasting until 1923, the beginning of the crisis in the colonial system, the world economic crisis of 1929–33, and, towards the end of the period considered in this volume, the echoes of the Italian–Ethiopian war which began in 1935.

Popular protest, nationalism and politics in South Africa and the surrounding territories

Opposition to colonial rule and capitalist exploitation in South Africa took four principal forms. The first was peasant protest. Often sporadic, isolated and largely with low visibility, various expressions of peasant protest were nevertheless widespread during the period under examination. In addition, many peasants and urban dwellers articulated their opposition to the

6. Even in this explicitly racist environment, the colonial regime had to rely on loyalist chiefs and African police who became part of the state apparatus. This alliance undercuts any analysis of resistance which views events exclusively through the prism of race without reference to class and ethnic factors.

culturally arrogant and racist system through the medium of the independent churches which flourished in South Africa. Still others joined the African National Congress – the oldest nationalist organization on the continent. By the 1920s an embryonic African working-class movement had also emerged – symbolized by the meteoric growth of the Industrial and Commercial Workers Union under the leadership of Clements Kadalie.

In response to increased impoverishment and economic uncertainty which accompanied the transformation of much of the rural South African area from a peasant economy to a labour reserve, peasants engaged in a number of actions to minimize or eliminate increasing political and economic pressures. Most forms of resistance were designed to protect their land and livestock, and to protest against increased taxation and labour demands. Often these were individual acts such as flight, tax evasion, violation of registration laws and attacks on loyalist chiefs and police.[7] In other cases, they represented more coherent and organized forms of opposition such as the anti-dipping campaign.

The state's effort to enforce more stringent cattle and sheep dipping regulations and increase dipping fees provoked widespread peasant opposition throughout the Transkei in the period from 1913 to 1917. While many peasants acknowledged the necessity to protect their herds from East Coast fever, they objected to the excessive taxation at a time of severe pressures on the rural economy. Opposition to dipping took a variety of forms. In Pondoland the peasants initially refused to pay the tax. In Fingoland they organized boycotts and refused to allow anyone to participate in the dipping programme. The most militant action occurred in East Griqualand, where dipping tanks were dynamited and destroyed, and protesters attacked police who tried to disrupt their campaign. From the perspective of rural political organizing, what is most significant is the scale of opposition and the inability of loyalist chiefs to control the activities of their militant peasant subjects.[8] Four years later, rural women in the Transkei organized a series of boycotts against European merchants to protest against price manipulation and their refusal to provide basic commodities on credit. By 1922 their movement had spread to Northeastern Province and East Griqualand where state officials and traders alike complained about the 'feminist' agitators. The protesters picketed rural shops, and – despite threats from the authorities – they forcibly blocked prospective customers from entering the stores. Ultimately state intervention and threats from loyalist chiefs undercut the boycott.[9]

7. W. Beinart and C. Bundy in M. A. Klein (ed.), 1980; A. T. Nzula, I. I. Potekhin and A. Z. Zusmanovich, 1979, pp. 104–6; E. Roux, 1964, pp. 88–120; A. B. Davidson, 1972. Here and elsewhere materials are drawn from the collective work entitled the *History of African National Liberation Struggle*, Contemporary Period (Istoriya Natziionalno-osvoboditelno borby navodor Afriku V novelschee Vremia) which appeared in Russian in the Nauka of Moscow edition.

8. W. Beinart and C. Bundy in M. A. Klein (ed.), 1980, pp. 280–4.

9. Quoted in ibid., pp. 286–7.

Peasant uprisings surfaced periodically in South West Africa where the South African government only began to effectively consolidate its power after the First World War. Thereafter the government of Jan Smuts cruelly put down the Bondelswart people, one of the Nama cattle-raising peoples living in the south. Unrest among the Bondelswart people had been prompted by a rise in taxes. In May 1922 a punitive military operation was launched against them involving 400 troops armed with machine guns and aircraft. Perhaps for the first time in history, African dwellings became targets of air raids. About 100 Africans were killed and over 150 gaoled.[10]

Three years later an equally cruel treatment was meted out to the 'coloured community' on the Rehoboth river in the central part of the country. In protest against the violations of an agreement signed by the colonial authorities with the community during German rule, the community refused to comply with the new demands of the authorities. The community's counsel filed a complaint about illegal treatment on the part of the authorities with the League of Nations. In April 1925 the village was surrounded by troops, as aircraft appeared in the sky above. The villagers offered to 'surrender' and about 640 of them were taken prisoner.[11] The question of the Bondelswarts and Rehobothers was discussed at the League of Nations because South West Africa was a mandated territory. However, no measures were taken to prevent similar brutalities in the future. On the contrary, when in 1932 the people of Ukuabi in Ovamboland (in the north of the country) rebelled, planes and armoured cars were used against them.

Most of the peasant rebellions were spontaneous and narrow in character. Some of the earliest of the broader-based, more organized movements owed much to the Afro-Christian churches and sects. The peasants provided the social base for these movements, although city-dwellers often took an active part in them.

The Afro-Christian churches, or 'independent native churches' are a curious phenomenon. It may seem odd at first sight that people drew ideological inspiration for their struggle against European conquerors from the very religion those conquerors imposed on them. Yet this was precisely the case and is accounted for by various reasons. The first was the character of the old African religions. 'The local traditional religions of tropical and southern Africa – the cults of the early states – were local in character and tended to separate rather than unite', wrote Dr B. I. Sharevskaya, a Moscow student of African religions.[12] Christianity with its idea that all men are the children of God made it possible for the new converts to identify with a community larger than an ethnic group. Unity on a new basis was possible only in a milieu which marked a departure from the old forms of unity and saw no way of returning to them. The new

10. E. Roux, 1964, pp. 143–4.
11. R. First, 1963, pp. 101–5.
12. B. I. Sharevskaya, 1968, pp. 215–16.

converts were in just such a milieu. These were, as a rule, people whose break with tradition and prevailing custom was most complete. No wonder anti-colonial protest was accompanied by disenchantment with those who had brought the new faith to them, a disenchantment with the Europeans as genuine Christians and with racial discrimination in the established churches. There was also a wish to assert themselves and their values in this faith and to discard everything associated with the white man who, in their eyes, turned out to be an oppressor, deceiver and an epitome of all evil.

The ideology of these churches had much in common. There was, in the first place, the idea that, in the true teaching of Christ, blacks are equal in everything, and that the European missionaries were distorting the Bible. Messianism was a feature of Afro-Christian churches, with their belief in the second advent of the Saviour – this time a black one. The second advent, the adherents of these churches and sects believed, would usher in a thousand-year rule of good and justice, while colonialists would be driven out of Africa.[13]

Independent churches, both of the Zionist and Ethiopian varieties, were particularly widespread in South Africa and represented an important form of dissent. Their numbers spread rapidly. In 1918 there were seventy-six; by 1932 the number had increased to 320; and a decade later there were more than 800.[14] From the standpoint of social movements, the separatist Ethiopian churches, with their elected officials, flags, charters and paramilitary organizations, represented the assertion, within the framework of the Church, of the claim for African self-government. Similarly, the Zionist churches were often led by charismatic anti-European prophets who held out an apocalyptic vision and the hope of a reconstructed society free of oppression and white rule.[15]

Despite close state surveillance, independent churches periodically engaged in explicit insurgent activities. As early as 1884 Nehemiah Tile, a Methodist preacher, had urged his adherents in Tembuland to disregard state officials.[16] In 1921 an Ethiopian sect known as the Israelites under the leadership of Enoch Mgijima forcibly resisted removal from a squatter settlement in Queenstown. The Israelites contended that the New Testament, a fiction of the white man's, must be disregarded and that if they worshipped the ancient Hebraic forms, Jehovah would ultimately liberate them from the yoke of oppression. Even as a large police and military force approached, the Israelites, armed only with swords and spears, remained defiant. 'Jehovah tells us that we are not to allow you to burn our huts, or drive away our people from Ntabelanga, or allow you to arrest

13. T. Hodgkin, 1956, pp. 93–112.
14. B. G. M. Sundkler, 1961, p. 76.
15. ibid.; T. Hodgkin, 1956, pp. 99–100.
16. E. Roux, 1964, p. 78.

PLATE 27.1 *Isaiah Shembe (1870–1931), founder of the Nazarite Baptist Church, a Zionist African Church in South Africa*

679

the men you wish to arrest.'[17] The soldiers, armed with machine guns, killed 163 Israelites and wounded 129.

Other militant independent churches combined an apocalyptic vision with an abridged form of Garveyism. The most important was the Wellington movement named after its founder, Wellington Butelezi, which flourished from the early 1920s until the mid-1930s. He assured his followers in the Transkei that American blacks in aeroplanes would come to their aid and help to liberate them. After this liberation, Butelezi proclaimed, taxes and dipping fees would be abolished and clothing would be distributed to all the people. When state officials became aware of his radical vision and militant rhetoric, they deported him and arrested several of his lieutenants. Nevertheless, his influence persisted and a whole series of separatist schools and churches were organized to spread his word. In the early 1930s a number of militant adherents refused to pay dipping taxes and on occasion attacked state officials.[18]

By the latter half of the 1930s Afro-Christian movements had passed their prime as vehicles of anti-colonial struggle. In most Southern African countries, that role was passing to more developed forms of organization and struggle.

Besides the older forms of peasant rebellions and the Afro-Christian Church movements, the period 1919–35 also saw the emergence – in Southern Africa as well as elsewhere in the continent – of new forms of African political organization not based on ethnic communities. These were the elitist and working-class organizations. The first, and by far the most important, of these new elitist organizations in Southern Africa was the African National Congress (ANC), founded in 1912.[19] The ANC was a major organization which united politically-active Africans, and was originally set up as an African organization for all the countries of Southern Africa which were part of the British Empire. Its constitutional congress was attended by representatives from Rhodesia, Basutoland, Bechuanaland, and Swaziland (see Fig. 27.1). Later, national organizations sprang up in each of these countries which, as a rule, were under heavy ANC influence. Many national organizations in Southern, Central and even East Africa borrowed not only the name of the ANC but, to varying degrees and at different stages, also its structure, programme and rules, methods, strengths and weaknesses. The ANC was followed, twenty, thirty or forty years later, by the setting up of the African National Congress of Southern Rhodesia and the African National Congress of Northern Rhodesia, as well as similar organizations in Nyasaland, Tanganyika, Kenya, Uganda and Basutoland.

Its precept and example were followed so closely because the ANC was

17. Quoted in ibid., pp. 136–7. For a detailed discussion of the Israelites, see R. Edgar, forthcoming.
18. W. Beinart and C. Bundy in M. A. Klein (ed.), 1980, pp. 280–4.
19. For the early history of the African National Congress, see E. Roux, 1964, pp. 74–6; H. J. Simons and R. E. Simons, 1969, pp. 132–6; G. M. Gerhart, 1978, pp. 21–39.

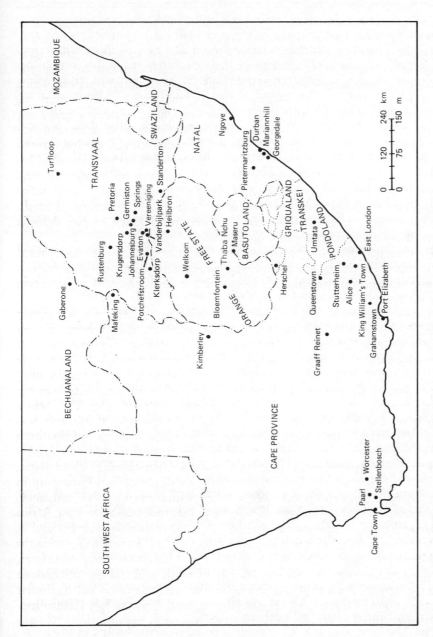

FIG. 27.1 *Politics and nationalism in South Africa, 1919–35 (after G. M. Gerhart, 1978)*

681

formed at a time when most African countries had hardly any intelligentsia or working class not to speak of African political organizations. As the intelligentsia and the working class emerged, the eyes of those who came out for consolidation of Africans in their countries inevitably turned to the organizations which existed in the Union of South Africa. An important factor contributing to the spread of this influence was the migration of labour to the Union of South Africa which gradually affected the countries of Southern and Central Africa namely, Mozambique, Nyasaland, Southern Rhodesia, Basutoland, Bechuanaland, and Swaziland. Returning to their villages they brought with them not only the occupational miners' diseases, but also knowledge of the wider world: other places, other peoples and new forms of unity in the struggle for their rights.

By the beginning of the inter-war period the ANC had behind it seven years of stormy activity. However, its formative period did not end until 1925, when it adopted, at its annual conference, the name of African National Congress. (Previously, it was called the South African Native National Congress.) In the same year the anthem and flag of the Congress were adopted. The anthem was called *Nkosi Sikelel' iAfrika* ('Lord, Bless Africa') and the tricolour flag – black, green and gold – symbolized the people (black), the green fields and veld (green) and the country's main wealth (gold).[20] Between 1919 and 1935, the ANC experienced various degrees of successful political organizing. In 1926 it initiated a mass campaign against a new series of racist Bills, which the government of the then South African Prime Minister, J. Hertzog, tried to put through. In February 1926 the ANC called a national convention in Bloemfontein which sharply condemned all racial segregation, demanded constitutionally guaranteed equality of all citizens irrespective of skin colour and decided to boycott puppet 'native conferences' being called by the government.

At the end of the same year – together with a number of other African organizations, as well as with the African Political Organization (APO) which was the major political organization of the 'Coloured people', and the South African Indian Congress, which had been set up shortly after the First World War (as an amalgamation of pre-existing Natal and Transvaal organizations) – the ANC called the First Non-European Convention in Kimberley. The participants in the convention rejected 'any policy of differentiation on grounds of colour or race'. They condemned the racist practices in the country, sharply opposed the new Hertzog legislation and called for 'closer cooperation among the non-European sections of South Africa'. That marked a breakthrough, an early step towards creating a united anti-racist front in Southern Africa.[21]

The ANC was also active outside the country, contributing to the long-standing participation of South Africans in the pan-African movement. Sol T. Plaatje, one of the ANC founding fathers and leaders, attended

20. M. Benson, 1966, p. 46.
21. A. Lemumo (pseudonym of Michael Marmel), 1971, pp. 60–1.

the Pan-African Congress of 1919 in Paris and in February 1927, ANC President J. J. Gamede visited the Soviet Union.

However, the late 1920s and early 1930s saw a decline in the activities of the ANC. Leadership was then in the hands of moderates who feared communist influence. It was not until the mid-1930s that there was a resurgence of activity in connection with the preparation for the All-African Convention to protest against Hertzog's legislation. The convention, held in Bloemfontein in December 1935, launched a massive campaign against the land and election rights bills. A delegation of the convention met Hertzog to present the grievances of the African people.[22] Yet the convention failed to agree on a programme and a single plan of action.

In neighbouring Southern African countries, the emergence of African political organizations proceeded in much the same direction, although it did not go as far as in South Africa. As a rule, there were initially 'native associations', 'native conventions' and 'welfare societies' which dealt with local matters first but gradually expanded the range of their activities. They became the vehicles of their communities' day-to-day needs, and collected and presented complaints, requests and grievances to the colonial authorities. Step by step, they involved the population in political activity and evolved into political organizations or contributed to the setting up of such organizations.

In Nyasaland, the first 'native association' sprang up on the eve of the First World War, and from the late 1920s such associations mushroomed throughout the country. In 1933 alone, fifteen were formed in the major cities – Zomba, Blantyre, Limo, Lilongwe, Fort Johnston, Karonga and Chiradzulu. In Northern Rhodesia, the first 'welfare association' was set up in 1923 and was directly modelled on similar organizations in Nyasaland. Among its founders was David Kaunda, the father of Kenneth Kaunda.[23] In 1930 a similar association was formed in Livingstone, the protectorate's administrative centre. Its founders were two civil service employees, Isaac Nyirenda and Edward Tembo (both of Nyasaland extraction). It had a membership of 350 and enjoyed the support of the Tonga chiefs. In the ensuing period, associations arose in many places, particularly in the Copper Belt towns and along the railway track; in Lusaka, Mazabuka, Broken Hill, Ndola, Choma, Luanshya, Chinsali, Abercorn, Kasama, Fort Jameson and other cities and villages.[24]

In Southern Rhodesia, too, political organizations of a new character came to be formed in the early post-war years. Set up in January 1923, the Rhodesian Bantu Voters Association sought greater voting rights for Africans and the return of seized lands. Its activity was confined to the Bulawayo area and several districts in Matebeleland. There was a welfare

22. ibid., pp. 74–5.
23. H. S. Meebelo, 1971, pp. 235–43.
24. R. I. Rotberg, 1966, pp. 115–34.

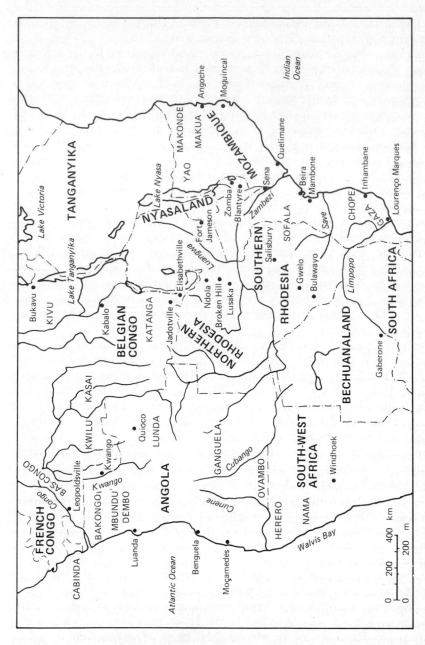

FIG. 27.2 *Politics and nationalism in Central Africa, 1919–35*

684

society in Gwelo and a Rhodesian native organization in Mashonaland.[25]

In the British protectorates of Basutoland, Bechuanaland and Swaziland, which were closely linked with the Union of South Africa, anti-colonial forces had close ANC associations. Among ANC founders was a Sotho, Maama Seiso, and a Tswana, Joshua Molema, and the several honorary presidents of the ANC elected at its constitutional conference including the supreme Basutoland ruler Letsie II and chiefs of the main Tswana peoples. The ANC newspaper, *Abantu Batho*, was largely financed from the funds made available by the Swaziland supreme ruler. The most active organization in Basutoland was *Lekhotla la Bafo* ('League of the Poor'), which played an important role there throughout the inter-war period. The social base of Lekhotla la Bafo was provided by peasants, many of whom were seasonal miners in Transvaal. The organization was headed by two brothers, Maphutseng and Josiel Lefela, who had formed links with the ANC.[26]

The adherents of the Lekhotla la Bafo considered that the British had violated the protectorate agreement with Moshoeshoe and had therefore forfeited any legal claim to Basutoland. Partly because of its very radical stand and partly because from 1928 it began to draw closer to the Communist Party of South Africa, it scared the ANC leaders. The British authorities ordered the chiefs to ban the League meetings. But in August 1928 Lekhotla la Bafo staged a protest demonstration in Maseru against the ban. That was the first mass demonstration in Basutoland history and it was attended by several thousand people. When ANC President Gumede returned from his trip to the Soviet Union, Lekhotla la Bafo invited him to address a rally in Basutoland. Subsequently, the organization was for a number of years alleged to be 'an instrument of Moscow' and was persecuted. Still, it continued its activities.[27]

The social base of all these early political organizations in Southern Africa was not broad. Often it consisted of the members of the educated elite who had become professionals. The associations and societies did not often have a clear action programme, and were short-lived. Yet they paved the way for other organizations, more numerous, durable and effective.

Working-class movements in the industrial areas provided another new form of anti-colonial struggle. People who took part in the early strikes and the workers' unions which sprang up about the same time, could only be called workers with reservations. The lives of most of them were still heavily anchored in the rural life, at least spiritually, and often economically as well. They had no sense of their identity as proletarians. Even so, the African proletarian movement traces its origins to those early actions. The earliest mass protest occurred in 1918–20 in the Union of South Africa.

25. T. O. Ranger, 1970, pp. 95–109.
26. E. Roux, 1964, p. 212.
27. ibid., pp. 212–13.

The strikes took place in the Transvaal mines, but the strikers were seasonal workers who came from many countries of Southern and Central Africa.[28] The first mass movement occurred in early 1918 with the boycott of the company shops through which the mine owners sold food and manufactured goods to workers. The boycott was staged by the miners in the eastern part of the Witwatersrand, a mining area in Transvaal.

The next strike took place in Johannesburg and involved African sewage and garbage collectors. The strikers were fewer in number but better organized. Members of the Industrial Workers of Africa, set up in 1917 among Johannesburg municipal service employees, probably took part in the strike. The strike was quelled and its participants were put on trial, of whom 152 were sentenced to two months of forced labour. However, the 'bucket strike' had shown that the labour of any group of African workers was essential for the normal life of the continent's largest industrial centre. The city streets were overflowing with rubbish and sewage, and there was a threat of epidemics erupting.

The strike triggered off a wider movement. During the meetings protesting against the arrests and unjust sentences, the idea emerged of calling a general strike of African workers on 1 July 1918. The strike was also to be in support of a demand for raising the daily wages of African workers by one shilling. The African National Congress went along with the idea although with some reservations. Faced with this pressure, the authorities repealed their sentences on the strikers and Prime Minister Louis Botha received an African delegation led by the Zulu Saul Msane, the leader of the Transvaal ANC chapter, and heard their grievances. The general strike was called off. However, on 1 July 15 000 Africans working in three mines downed their tools. Police forced them into the mines after a fierce clash in which workers used axes, picks and lengths of metal pipe as their weapons. In the ensuing repressions, Africans and Europeans found themselves together in the same dock on charges of inciting the strike. These were D. S. Letanka, Vice-President of the Transvaal ANC, L. T. Mwabaza, Director of the *Abantu Batho* newspaper, N. D. Ngojo, H. Kraai and A. Cetyiwe, three members of the Industrial Workers of Africa, and three white socialist leaders of the South African International Socialist League formed in 1915: S. P. Bunting, H. C. Hanscombe and T. P. Tinker. In the course of the trial, the prosecutor, basing himself on reports by several police agents who had infiltrated the Industrial Workers of Africa, accused Bunting, Hanscombe and Tinker of provoking the Johannesburg and the mine strikes.

In February 1920, a new strike swept twenty-two mines in Transvaal in which 71 000 African workers took part. They advanced a number of demands: a major pay rise (from 2 shillings to 5–10 shillings a day), an

28. There were smaller industrial protests of mine workers dating back to the beginning of the twentieth century. See P. Warwick in E. Webster (ed.), 1978; S. Moroney in E. Webster (ed.), 1978.

opportunity to get more responsible and better-paying jobs, major improvements in the running of company shops, and the easing of the colour bar. The strikers displayed remarkable unity. One can only wonder how these people of different ethnic groups, speaking a babble of tongues, were able to achieve such a high degree of unanimity. Troops and police were used to put down the strike.[29] The strike was the largest in African history until 1946, when an even larger strike took place, also in Transvaal.

In Rhodesia, the first mass working-class action was recorded in May 1935, in the Copper Belt mines in Northern Rhodesia. Miners demanded higher wages and a cut in taxes and protested against poor working conditions and various forms of racial discrimination. The protest was not entirely spontaneous and the manner in which the strikers acted indicated the presence among them of a group which tried to give organized leadership to the movement. Leaflets calling for strike action were distributed. They were written in the Chibemba language, which was the mother tongue of most of the miners. The strike started at Muflira mine on 22 May and was quelled the next day by troops. However, on 26 May the strike spread to Nkana mine, and on 28 May the Luanshya mine was strike-bound. Twenty-eight strikers were killed or wounded in clashes with the troops and arrests were made among the workers. The strike had repercussions well beyond the Copper Belt since it attracted, along with neighbouring Katanga, many seasonal workers from other parts of Africa.[30]

As the African proletarian movement was mounting, the militancy of the white industrial proletariat was waning. The armed uprising of white miners in Transvaal early in 1922 was the last major action by white workers in South Africa. As the African proletariat increased, white workers came increasingly to be appointed as overseers and evolved into a workers' aristocracy. On the crest of the wave of industrial action which swept Southern Africa in the early post-war years, the largest African proletarian organization was formed. The 1920s saw it reach its peak and decline. The Industrial and Commercial Workers' Union of Africa (ICU) was born in January 1919 in Cape Town during a strike of African and Coloured dock workers. The first constituent meeting was attended by less than thirty people. But five years later, in 1924, it had a membership of 30000. By 1927 it had grown to 100000 (its leader even claimed a figure of 250000), with affiliates far beyond the Union of South Africa in Southern Rhodesia and other countries. The ICU sought to unite the most diverse trades: municipal service workers, builders, railwaymen, miners, seamen, farm labourers, factory, port and transport workers, as well as people engaged

29. For a discussion of these strikes see P. L. Bonner in B. Bozzoli (ed.), 1979; E. Roux, 1964, pp. 132–4; H. J. Simons and R. E. Simons, 1969, pp. 220–43.

30. R. I. Rotberg, 1966, pp. 161–8. Smaller strikes date back to the beginning of the twentieth century.

in trade and the services. The ICU had Coloured as well as African workers among its members.[31]

The Preamble to the ICU Constitution reveals a strong influence of socialist ideas:

> Whereas the interests of the workers and those of the employers are opposed to each other, the former living by selling their labour, receiving for it only part of the wealth they produce, and the latter living by exploiting the labour of the workers; depriving the workers of a part of the product of their labour in the form of profit, no peace can be between the two classes, a struggle must always obtain about the division of the products of human labour until the workers through their industrial organizations take from the capitalist class the means of production, to be owned and controlled by the workers for the benefit of all, instead of for the profit of a few. Under such a system he who does not work, neither shall he eat. The basis of remuneration shall be the principle, from every man according to his abilities, to every man according to his needs.

The ICU set itself numerous and diverse tasks. It promised its members that it would seek higher wages, better working conditions, pensions, sick and unemployment allowances and protection of the workers' rights. The ICU proclaimed the whole of the African continent to be the field of its activity.

The founder and leader of the Union, Clements Kadalie (*c.* 1896–1951), was a seasonal worker who came to South Africa from Nyasaland, where he had completed a missionary school education which enabled him to become a schoolteacher. The ICU reached the peak of its influence in the mid-1920s, but suffered a sharp decline at the turn of the 1920s and 1930s because it found itself split into three factions.[32]

Socialist influence was also felt in an earlier African proletarian organization – the above-mentioned Industrial Workers of Africa. The International Socialist League had played no small role in its formation and activities. The League, set up by South African white socialists and working-class activists, was gradually coming to realize the need for proletarian solidarity, irrespective of the colour of the skin. That became particularly evident in 1918–20 in its appeals to black and white workers. During the strike of Transvaal African miners in February 1920, socialists were distributing a leaflet among white miners written by one of the League's leaders, S. P. Bunting (1873–1936) entitled 'Don't Scab!' It read in part:

> White workers! Do you hear the new army of labour coming? The

31. For an analysis of the ICU, see P. Bonner in E. Webster (ed.), 1978; C. Kadalie, 1970; S. W. Johns in R. I. Rotberg and A. Mazrui (eds), 1970; K. Luckhardt and B. Wall, 1980, pp. 39–46.

32. C. Kadalie, 1970, pp. 52–3, 61–2.

Native Workers are beginning to wake up.... White workers! Do not repel them! ... Be on the side of labour, even Native labour against our common capitalist masters.[33]

In an earlier leaflet addressed to African workers entitled 'To the Bantu Workers', the socialists wrote: 'No matter though you are different in colour you are one in kind with the workers of the world. All those who work for wages are becoming one great brotherhood of labour.'[34]

Another leaflet issued in 1918–19 in several languages including English, Zulu and Sotho, was addressed to 'Workers of South Africa, Black as Well as White' and contained the following appeal: 'The way to get ready is to combine in the workshops. Combine as workers, no matter what colour. Remember that an injury to one is an injury to all, be he black or white.'[35] At the time these appeals were hardly expected to be implemented. Workers, black as well as white, were yet numerically too small and too unsophisticated. Still, it is important to know that even in these years, such ideas were proclaimed on African soil.

The International Socialist League and several other South African socialist organizations merged and at a congress in Cape Town in 1921 proclaimed the formation of the Communist Party of South Africa, the first Communist Party on the African continent. The party set out its goals in a manifesto adopted by the first congress. It sought to combine the idea of radical social transformation with genuine internationalism that marked the thinking of the more progressive members on the international task of bringing nearer the time 'when the class war shall have been forever stamped out, when mankind shall no longer cower under the bludgeon of the oppressor, when the necessaries and amenities of life, the comfort and the culture, the honour and the power, shall be to him who toils not him who exploits, when none shall be called master and none servant, but all shall be fellow workers in common.'[36]

Admittedly, South African communists were unable to come up immediately with a comprehensive programme that would address itself to all the specific and complex problems of Southern Africa, and initially they might have relied too heavily on European experience. This, in the context of South Africa, is understandable. It is accounted for by the membership of the Communist Party which initially consisted only of whites, the profound impact of the west European, notably British, working-class movement and the real complexities of the South African situation. However, by the early 1930s, Africans formed the majority of party membership and its general secretary was a Zulu, Albert Nzula (1905–34). National liberation became the focus of the Party's effort.

33. E. Roux, 1944, pp. 46–8.
34. See Union of South Africa, 1922, pp. 288–9.
35. See *The International*, Johannesburg, 25 April 1919.
36. A. Lemumo, 1971, pp. 117–20.

Popular opposition to colonial rule in the Belgian Congo

Increased state control, a tightening web of racist regulations, an elaborate patronage policy and a wave of epidemics undercut the effectiveness of social protest in the Belgian Congo.[37] Nevertheless, popular opposition continued, although on a smaller scale, and took different forms than it had in the preceding period.

Peasant opposition in the Congo, often sporadic and barely visible, took a variety of forms all of which were designed to avoid or minimize the disruptive impact of the colonial capitalist system on their way of life. Tax evasion continued with great frequency in the years immediately following the First World War. Thousands of Congolese peasants fled across the open borders to the adjacent regions of Angola and the French Congo, while others disappeared into the bush just prior to the arrival of state tax officials. The Angolan border was particularly attractive because the Portuguese colonial presence was so minimal and because of historic ties that united the Bakongo living on both sides of the frontier. Many members of the rural population used a similar strategy to avoid working on state projects, mines and European plantations. As one elder who was ordered to work on the Katanga railway line recalled, 'We just escaped from our village ... Nobody knew where we had gone, not even the white people at the boma. We left our village at night time and headed for the Luapula. At the river some good fishermen helped us to cross.'[38] Still other peasants refused to cultivate the obligatory cotton or rice or planted less than the required amounts.[39]

As the state apparatus extended into the more remote areas and a network of loyalist chiefs was created, however, possibilities of remaining outside the colonial-capitalist system diminished substantially. Increased state hegemony is reflected by the 400% increase in taxes extracted between 1917 and 1924 and by the dramatic rise in the number of peasants compelled to cultivate cotton.[40] As of 1935 it was estimated that more than 900 000 peasants were enmeshed in the cotton regime.

Given this shifting balance of power, it is hardly surprising that direct confrontations which had frequently occurred in the period preceding the

37. For a general overview of the colonial period, see B. Jewsiewicki, forthcoming; J. Stengers, 1974, pp. 391–440. A discussion of insurgent activities is complicated because until recently most historians have assumed that this was a period of quietism and have, therefore, focused on the post-Second World War era. There is also an economic tendency in the literature in general which tends to reduce peasants to mere producers of surplus value whose own history lacked any meaning or significance within the colonial-capitalist context. Such an interpretation denies them the dignity of historical agents who played a role in shaping their own destinies and instead casts them as either impotent or impassive victims.

38. Quoted in C. Perrings, 1979, p. 153.
39. B. Jewsiewicki in M. A. Klein (ed.), 1980, pp. 62–8.
40. B. Fetter, 1976, p. 83; B. Jewsiewicki in M. A. Klein (ed.), 1980.

First World War almost disappeared. Occasionally, alienated peasants attacked the symbols of oppression – loyalist chiefs, African police and tax collectors. Far more hazardous were peasant revolts which were reported in the Bas-Congo in the period between 1920 and 1922, in the Kwango area a decade later,[41] and among Pende peasants and workers in Kwilu in 1931 (see Fig. 27.2). A sharp increase in taxes, a 50% reduction in the price peasants received for their commodities and the decision of Unilever to lower wages on its plantations fuelled the popular discontent that led to the major uprising in 1931. The insurgents gained additional adherents when a 'prophet', Matemu-a-Kenenia, revealed that the ancestors had instructed Africans to kill or destroy all white animals and objects in the land as well as all symbols of European rule as a prelude to divine intervention and the end of white domination. The movement attracted widespread support, but it was immediately suppressed, and more than 400 Pende and one European lost their lives in the process.[42]

Other religious–political movements attracted even larger peasant followings, which may be partly due to the fact that the colonial authorities had imposed a strict ban on political organizations. Their appeal also reflected the growing sense of anxiety and frustration brought on by the economic uncertainties of the 1921 recession and the depression a decade later.

The largest of these movements was Kimbanguism, named after Simon Kimbangu, a Bakongo peasant. A catechist, he proclaimed that he had been touched by God which gave him the power to cure the sick, combat witchcraft and resurrect the dead. To his followers, who were proud to have a black Messiah, he declared in 1921 that he was an emissary of God, a prophet and the son of God. Kimbangu's divine quality was symbolized in his Bakongo name, Gunza, 'All together'.[43]

Kimbangu also proclaimed in a general but vague way that he was to deliver Africans from the yoke of colonial oppression. His anti-colonial rhetoric, his growing popularity and the militancy of some of his followers convinced the Belgian administrators that Kimbangu had to be eliminated. On 14 September 1921, he was arrested and condemned to death. Subsequently he was deported to Katanga where he died a martyr thirty years later.[44]

Although Kimbangu himself was not revolutionary, his followers made his movement strongly anti-European rather than simply religious. With its slogan, 'Congo to the Congolese', the movement provided an outlet for spontaneous popular protest against colonial rule. The Kimbanguists exhorted the people not to work for the Europeans, not to grow the export crops imposed by the colonial administration, not to pay taxes and levies,

41. A. T. Nzula, I. I. Potekhin and A. Z. Zusmanovich, 1979, pp. 108–11.
42. ibid.; E. Bustin, 1975, pp. 119–20.
43. G. Balandier in P. Van den Berghe (ed.), 1965, pp. 443–60.
44. ibid., p. 450.

not to send their children to missionary schools, and generally to disobey the Belgians.[45] Their hymns are replete with references to Kimbangu's heroic deeds and, according to Belgian officials, they held out the hope that Kimbangu and his disciples would 'return to bring white domination to an end'.[46]

For over two decades there were periodic revivals of Kimbanguism, generally at times of severe tension and economic stress. In both towns and villages his adherents actively participated in the struggle against colonialism, and their propaganda efforts even affected the strikes of railway, white-collar and oil-mill workers in the lower Zaire from 1921 to 1925. Although cruelly repressed, the Kimbanguists were undaunted. In 1921 alone, at the dawn of the movement, 37000 people were evicted from Bas-Congo but they continued their activities and recruited new adherents in the places to which they were exiled. Various offshoots of Kimbanguism, themselves often loosely connected, sprang up throughout the Congo, where Kimbanguists established links with Afro-Christian churches of Nigeria and Uganda and with the opponents of French colonialism in the French Congo.

Another major independent Church movement – the African Watchtower, known more commonly in the Congo as Kitawala – appeared at about the same time that Kimbangu began his activities. Its initial bases of support seem to have been in Northern Rhodesia, Nyasaland and Tanganyika, and by 1923 preachers from eastern Northern Rhodesia and western Tanganyika had begun to attract a large following in Katanga province, primarily in areas adjacent to the Union Minière recruiting stations.[47] Under the forceful leadership of Tomo Nyirenda, known also as Mwana Lesa – the son of God – the Kitawala movement, whose name in Swahili signifies 'a means of ruling', adopted an explicit anti-colonial posture. Along with militant slogans such as 'Africa for the Africans' and 'Equality of the Races', Nyirenda and his principal lieutenants urged their followers to assassinate Europeans and their African allies, especially loyalist chiefs.

By 1926 the Kitawala movement was firmly entrenched in southern Katanga which had suffered from a number of epidemics and where the deleterious effects of labour recruitment were most acutely felt. It also extended its influence into the mining areas of Kasai and Kivu, and miners returning home after their contracts brought Kitawala into the eastern and equatorial regions. Fearing Nyirenda's increased influence and growing ties with several dissident chiefs, the colonial authorities dispatched a military force in 1926 to capture him. Nyirenda fled to Northern Rhodesia

45. *A History of Africa*, Moscow, 1968, pp. 391–2.
46. G. Balandier in P. Van den Berghe (ed.), 1965, p. 450.
47. The most important analysis of the Kitawala movement in the Congo is J. Higginson, forthcoming. Much of the discussion on Kitawala is drawn from this article.

where British authorities detained and ultimately executed him.[48]

As in the case of Kimbanguism, the elimination of the prophet did not diminish popular support for Kitawala. In the rural areas Kitawala priests organized protests against taxation and fanned hostility to appointed chiefs. One offshoot, led by Mumba Napoleon Jacob, began to make major inroads among labourers in Elizabethville (Lumumbashi), and railway workers and miners employed by Union Minière. Kitawala adherents helped to organize the 1931 Elizabethville boycott and five years later played an important part in the labour unrest at the Union Minière factory at Jadotville. During the Jadotville strike, an outspoken Kitawala member used religious scriptures to attack the injustices of racial wage differentiation. 'It stands out clearly from this book,' he proclaimed, Bible in hand, 'that all men are equal. God did not create the white man to rule over the black ... It is not just that the black man who does the work should remain in poverty and misery and that the wages of the whites should be so much higher than those of the blacks.'[49] In the aftermath of Jadotville the state unsuccessfully renewed its efforts to smash Kitawala which subsequently played an important role in the Elizabethville strike of 1941.[50]

The fact that strikes only began in the 1930s suggests that the formation of an African working class and an incipient working-class movement developed at a mucn slower rate in the Belgian Congo than in South Africa. The discovery of copper, tin and uranium in Katanga, of diamonds in Kasai and of gold in Kilo Moto precipitated the growth of an industrial working class. By the 1920s over 60000 labourers were involved in mineral extraction.

As in other parts of the continent, the initial response of Africans to the lower wages and harsh working conditions of the mines was desertion. Large numbers of peasants fled from Katanga and Kasai provinces to avoid the agents working for the Bourse du Travail de Katanga (BTK), the industrial labour bureau that recruited and distributed workers within Katanga. Still others escaped shortly after their arrival at the mines. As early as 1914 desertion had become such a serious problem that the BTK introduced a pass system and a finger-printing bureau to trace 'fugitives'.[51] Despite such coercive tactics, desertion continued to be prevalent. In 1918,

48. ibid.

49. Quoted in C. Perrings, 1977, p. 50.

50. J. Higginson, forthcoming. Kimbanguism and Kitawala were not the only religious-political movements in the Congo. Muvungu, Lukusu, Mpewe and other sects which were active in the Bandundu province told Africans not to work for the Belgians but rather to prepare for the time when the Belgians would be driven out. These were the sentiments advocated in the 1930s by the 'Talking Serpent' (or 'Man-Serpent') sect in the Bandundu and western Kasai provinces. The 'Black Mission' and Tunzi in Lower Zaire and the 'Leopard People' movements opposed forced cultivation of export crops in Upper Zaire.

51. C. Perrings, 1979, p. 153.

for example, at the Star and Liksai copper mines, the desertion rate was 74 and 66.5% respectively. Although desertion declined somewhat in the 1920s, it continued to run at between 20 and 35% up until the Great Depression, when the lack of alternative sources of income made such a strategy counterproductive.[52]

While thousands fled from the mines, others in Katanga began to organize, albeit in the most tentative and sporadic fashion, in order to improve the conditions of their employment. In 1921, a large number of miners at Luishi, for example, walked off the job and proceeded to Elizabethville to complain to government officials of ill-treatment and poor rations. Two years later a similar work stoppage occurred at the Kakontwe mines.[53]

The Depression created new economic uncertainties. Jobs disappeared, wages dropped and working conditions deteriorated, as mining interests sought to minimize costs. Despite threats to workers that they would be dismissed, however, work stoppages and labour 'riots' erupted at the Union Minière mines of Kipushi, Ruashi and Mswenu Ditu in 1931, temporarily paralysing operations.[54] In the same year workers organized a boycott in Elizabethville to protest against the high prices charged for basic commodities by the Union Minière company stores and independent European merchants. Before it ended, the boycott spread to surrounding regions and gained the support of construction workers, carpenters, and bricklayers – suggesting a growing labour consciousness.[55] The district commissioner of Haut-Katanga bemoaned this new militancy. 'The Negroes, animated by unbounded haughtiness,' he noted contemptuously, 'are becoming more and more refractory, no longer obeying passively, they discuss the orders they are given and talk back, sometimes insolently.'[56]

The growing militancy was also reflected in a number of strikes between 1935 and 1937 involving both miners and other segments of the working class in Katanga. Employees protesting against low salaries and racial discrimination closed down the Union Minière factory at Jadotville and the tin mines at Manon and Mwanza. Railway workers at Niemba and Kabala employed by the Chemin de Fer du Grand Lacs also went on strike, as did labourers at the government-owned cotton mill at Niemba.[57] Although the leaders were arrested and the strikes repressed, insurgency sentiment and underground networks grew stronger as did a sense of collective self-confidence. All this set the stage for the great strike of 1941 in which several thousand African workers walked off their jobs at tin and copper mines throughout Katanga province. Their objective transcended narrow

52. ibid., p. 171; B. Fetter, 1974, p. 208.
53. C. Perrings, 1979, pp. 213–35.
54. J. Higginson, forthcoming, pp. 8–10.
55. ibid., pp. 9–10.
56. Quoted in B. Fetter, 1974, p. 217.
57. J. Higginson, forthcoming, pp. 10–13.

economic concerns. 'They did not try to hide their purpose,' noted one European observer. 'It was to drive the whites from the country and replace the blue flag of Belgium with the black flag of Kitawala in order to signal a change in the regime.'[58]

As in the case of a working-class movement, political associations and nationalist parties developed much more slowly in the Belgian Congo than in South Africa. Indeed, explicit nationalist organizations, such as the Association de Bakongo (ABAKO), did not emerge until the late 1950s.[59] During this period, however, closed associations, known as Mbeni, proliferated. These were brought back to the Belgian colony by African servicemen who had been stationed in German East Africa during the First World War. The Mbeni were essentially dance societies which also provided a self-help network for members. The leaders often had military titles patterned on the European military which created the impression that they possessed a certain measure of European power. Although not primarily anti-colonial, their songs and dances often ridiculed European officials and expressed deep-seated popular resentment against colonial rule. Moreover, Africans who were considered as supporters of the Europeans were barred from joining the Mbeni societies and those closely associated with the Europeans could not hold leadership positions.[60]

Their explicit criticisms of colonialism and their attacks on loyalists concerned Belgian officials who were anxious to stifle all forms of social protest. A 1923 government sub-commission concluded that the Mbeni associations were becoming radicalized and were open to communist infiltration, and three years later all African urban associations, including the Mbeni societies, were placed under direct supervision by the colonial regime. The government also encouraged the Benedictine missionaries to organize competing associations, whose members engaged in gang warfare with the Mbeni societies. Government harassment, gang warfare, rivalries among and within Mbeni societies, and the urban dislocation created by the Depression combined to reduce the influence and significance of these societies by the mid-1930s.[61]

The economic and political setting in Angola and Mozambique: an overview

Despite the distance separating them and the diversity of their peoples and economies, the colonial societies of Angola and Mozambique shared more in common with each other than with their immediate neighbours. The specific character of Portuguese colonialism and, to a measure, the

58. Quoted in ibid., p. 60.
59. See, for example, H. Weiss, 1967; C. Young, 1965.
60. B. Fetter, 1974, pp. 210–15.
61. ibid. For a general study of the development and spread of Mbeni societies throughout Central and East Africa, see T. O. Ranger, 1975.

popular opposition which it generated, stem from four sets of factors – the initial weakness of the colonial state, the progressively authoritarian nature of the colonial regime, the lack of Portuguese capital and a concomitant dependence upon forced labour and the policy of assimilation.

By the eve of the First World War appreciable areas of both Angola and Mozambique remained outside Lisbon's effective control. Whereas the colonial administration was well entrenched in the coastal urban enclaves such as Luanda, Benguela, Beira and Lourenço Marques and their hinterlands, throughout vast interior regions the colonial presence was nominal and often depended on an alliance with local chiefs and African police whose loyalty was problematical.

In Angola, for example, as late as 1914, the Ovambo in the south remained effectively independent while revolts smouldered in the adjacent region of Ganguela until 1917 and the Lunda homelands of Quioco were only occupied in 1920. To the north opposition in the Congo region continued until 1915 while Dembo insurgents defied the colonial state until 1918.[62]

Portugal's position in Mozambique was only slightly better. Several northern sultanates and Yao chieftaincies had effectively defied the colonial regime until 1914 and the Makonde highlands remained outside the sphere of colonial rule as late as 1921. Moreover, during the First World War when German forces from neighbouring Tanganyika invaded northern Mozambique, they were greeted as liberators by a number of Makua chieftaincies which had suffered under the extremely harsh rule of the Niassa Company. Even in the southern half of the colony, where the colonial state was most firmly entrenched, officials feared a massive uprising (see Fig. 27.2).[63]

In the aftermath of the war, Lisbon intensified the autocratic nature of its rule. The initial 'enlightened' policies of the republican government (1912–26) gave way to more repressive, although not necessarily more efficient, programmes. Inefficient and corrupt, the republican government was finally brought down by a conservative alliance of bankers, industrialists, the church hierarchy and the military in 1926 paving the way for the fascist government of António Salazar. To ensure social harmony and perpetual colonial rule which Salazar's ultra-nationalist corporate ideology envisaged, the colonial regimes, like the government in Portugal, employed a vast array of instruments of oppression. Censorship, informers, secret police and the military were used to repress any opposition – black or white – which surfaced.

The third common feature was the particular character of economic exploitation in Angola and Mozambique which was shaped by the impoverishment of the mother country. Throughout the period under

62. For a detailed discussion of these revolts, see R. Pélissier, 1977.
63. For a discussion of African resistance during this period, see A. Isaacman, 1976; M. D. D. Newitt, 1981, pp. 57–64.

examination, Portugal's ability to extract resources from her African colonies depended on the mobilization and control of unfree labour because her own economy, which was both archaic and on the verge of bankruptcy, lacked the capacity to export the fixed capital necessary for development. An 1899 government commission, whose task it was to analyse the prospects for development in Angola and Mozambique, had been unequivocal on this last point:

> We need native labour, we need it in order to better the conditions of these labourers, we need it for the economy of Europe and for the progress of Africa. Our tropical Africa will not grow without the Africans. The capital needed to exploit it, and it so needs to be exploited, lies in the procurement of labour for exploitation. Abundant, cheap, solid labour ... and this given the circumstances, will never be supplied by European immigrants.[64]

The state had also introduced a series of tax laws designed to force many African agriculturalists off their land and create the beginnings of a semi-proletariat. While the tax laws did provide the colonial administration with a new source of revenue, they failed to generate a cheap labour force on the scale anticipated by the colonial regime. Many peasants were able to circumvent the labour requirement by cultivating new or additional cash crops to pay their taxes. Others in Mozambique opted to work in the mines and plantations of neighbouring South Africa and Rhodesia at wages that were 200–300% higher than those that the under-capitalized Portuguese firms and planters offered.

Since the nascent capitalist sectors in Angola and Mozambique were unable to attract workers, either with these tax 'incentives' or through competitive wages, the colonial state, as has been amply demonstrated in Chapter 15 above, had to resort to undisguised coercion as early as the first native labour code was introduced. The legal basis for forced labour which was to continue under varying guises until 1961, was delineated in Article 1:

> All native inhabitants of the Portuguese overseas are subject to the moral and legal obligations to seek to acquire through work, those things which they lack to subsist and to improve their own social conditions. They have full liberty to choose the means through which to comply with this obligation, but if they do not comply in some way, the public authorities may force them to comply.[65]

And force them they did. Local administrators had complete discretion to determine who was 'idle', and virtually all *chefes des posto* supplemented their modest salaries through gifts and favours from European planters, merchants, factory owners and farmers in return for African labour. As a result, the rural areas were transformed into large labour reserves. When

64. Quoted in J. M. da Silva Cunha, 1949, p. 144.
65. ibid., p. 151.

workers were needed to work on settler estates, to build roads, expand the ports of Luanda, Lourenço Marques and Beira, lay railway lines, serve as domestic servants or for any other private or public tasks, local administrators did not hesitate to use their control and their power to satisfy labour demands. Women, though legally exempt from forced labour, often suffered a similar fate. An American sociologist visiting Angola and Mozambique in 1924 observed that:

> women, even pregnant or with a nursling, are taken for road work by Cipaes. In out-of-the-way places the Government builds little barracks to house them. No pay nor food. According to the circumscription the term is from one week to five but a woman may be called out again in the same year. Others in the village bring food to them, in some cases a day's journey away. Girls as young as fifteen are taken and some are made to submit sexually to those in charge. They work under a black foreman who uses a stick. They begin work at six, stop an hour at noon, and work till sunset. There are some miscarriages from heavy work.[66]

After 1926 peasants especially in Mozambique were also compelled to cultivate cotton and sell it at deflated prices to European concessionaire companies. Failure to do so was tantamount to a crime and was treated accordingly.[67]

The final distinguishing feature was the policy of assimilation which the colonial regime pursued in an effort to co-opt the nascent African bourgeoisie by providing them with a veneer of Portuguese culture and exemption from some of the most flagrant colonial abuses. Formalized under the *regime do indigenato*, this policy insured that the overwhelming majority of Angolans and Mozambicans would be frozen into a subordinate race, culture and class position. Under this legislation, Africans were divided into two groups. The tiny majority who could read and write Portuguese, had rejected 'tribal customs', and were gainfully employed in the capitalist sectors could be classified as *assimilados* or *não indigenas*. In principle, at least, they enjoyed all the rights and responsibilities of Portuguese citizens. Although it was theoretically possible for any African to change his legal status, the constraints imposed by the colonial-capitalist system – including the lack of schools, the limited opportunities for paid employment and the culturally arrogant assumption of state officials – effectively precluded this, thereby denying 99% of the African population the minimal rights of citizenship.[68]

66. E. A. Ross, 1925, p. 40.
67. A. Isaacman, M. Stephen, Y. Adam, M. J. Homen, E. Macamo and A. Pililão, 1980.
68. The illusion of assimilation and the corresponding ideology of Lusotropicalism is powerfully presented in G. J. Bender, 1978.

Popular opposition to colonial rule in Angola

Regarded as nonentities by the Europeans, subject to corporal punishment, and sometimes to arbitrary and venal treatment at the hands of the colonial authorities, to the demands of labour-recruiters and the collusion between government officials and resident Portuguese, Africans became outcasts in their own countries. They did, however, have several means of escaping the pressures that were brought to bear on them.

The first form of resistance consisted of taking up arms, but this was steadily abandoned from the end of the First World War since it was ultimately and hopelessly doomed to failure. There were fewer and fewer leaders, most weapons had been confiscated and gunpowder was, with a few exceptions, no longer available on the open market. The second alternative was to go into hiding. When the situation became intolerable, entire villages abandoned their fields and moved to areas furthest from the reach of the colonial authorities. Peasant flight was particularly common in the northern and eastern regions which remained effectively outside Lisbon's control. Such withdrawal could go on for years without being detected.

The third solution was even more radical for it was to all intents and purposes final. There is widespread evidence of massive clandestine emigration into the Belgian Congo, Northern Rhodesia and even South West Africa. Often members of the rural population travelled great distances through harsh terrain with young children on their backs to free themselves from the tyranny of Portuguese colonial rule. If they were caught by the colonial authorities or the local African police, the men were beaten and imprisoned and the women sexually abused.

The fourth type of resistance to colonial rule were the religious or messianic cults founded by Africans in reaction to the colonial religion. There appears to have been little local initiative behind this metaphysical revolt of the Angolans since most of the independent churches came primarily from the Belgian Congo, spilling over into the Bakongo region of northern Angola.

Unlike the situation in the Belgian Congo, the independent churches had a relatively small following and a short life span. The revolt of the Mafulu in 1918 is sometimes cited as the first Angolan messianic protest to have led to armed revolt.[69] Followers of Simon Kimbangu gained a number of adherents among the Bakongo living inside the Angolan border. The colonial state, fearing its popular appeal and the resurgence of Bakongo nationalism, made a serious effort to suppress Kimbanguism in 1921 and 1922. Despite their efforts an underground network continued to operate and – as in the Belgian Congo – Kimbangu acquired an aura of martyrdom after his arrest.[70]

69. See R. Pélissier, 1977; W. G. Clarence-Smith, 1979, pp. 88–9.
70. A. Margarido in R. Chilcote (ed.), 1972, pp. 37–9; R. Pélissier, 1978, pp. 165–7.

Other more obscure sects surfaced such as Maiaigni, which was detected in the Cabinda enclave in 1930 and the short-lived Cassongola movement among the Mbundu between 1924 and 1930. Kitawala also spread from the Belgian Congo and Northern Rhodesia into eastern Angola around 1932. Two years later a prophetess from the Congo linked to Kimbanguism attracted a following in the region of the Pombo, and in 1936 the Mayangi or Nlenvo sect – operating near the Congolese border – forbade all its members from fraternizing with whites. Although the data are extremely fragmentary, these religious expressions of protest seem to have had a minimal impact. Only in the 1950s with the advent of Tokoism did an independent Church attract a large permanent following. And Tokoism exhibited contradictory tendencies portraying white colonialists as evil yet preaching passivity.[71]

While most of these protests were rurally based, assimilated intellectuals and journalists in Luanda and Lisbon spoke out against the abuses of colonialism and reaffirmed their Angolan identity. Indeed, a very rich tradition of literary protest dates back to the middle of the previous century. The best known of these proto-nationalists were the canon Antonio José de Nacimento (1838–1902), the lawyer and journalist José de Fontes Pereira (1838–91), the writer Joaquim Dias Cordeiro da Matta (1857–94) and possibly the members of an association formed in connection with a virulently anti-colonial work entitled *Voz d'Angola clamando no deserto* published in Lisbon in 1901.[72] The collapse of the monarchy (October 1910) and the advent of the Republican government was welcomed by the *assimilados* and considerably raised their hopes, for they were acutely aware that their own status had deteriorated and that clandestine slavery continued to exist in their homeland. But even during this wave of liberalism, the incipient nationalist feeling among the more educated Africans could be expressed more openly in Portugal than in Angola.

The Liga Ultramarina had been organized in Lisbon in 1910 and was followed shortly thereafter by the Liga Colonial. Two years later, African expatriates living in Lisbon from all the colonies founded the Junta de Defensa dos Direitos de Africa. In Angola itself, Liga Angolana, a small association of Angolan civil servants, gained formal recognition from Governor-General Norton de Matos in 1913. Almost immediately a split in this association led to the emergence of Gremio Africano. The proliferation of these organizations notwithstanding, all lacked a substantial following and had extremely limited influence.

Of far greater potential importance than the formation of any of these associations was the Cuanza Norte 'conspiracy' of 1916–17 which momentarily linked a number of alienated intellectuals with Mbundu peasants living in the Luanda hinterland. It was led by António de Assis

71. A. Margarido in R. Chilcote (ed.), 1972.

72. For a discussion of this tradition of literary protest, see D. L. Wheeler in R. Chilcote (ed.), 1972.

Júnior (1887–1960), a lawyer, novelist and journalist.[73] He vigorously condemned colonial oppression and the preferential treatment given to the settler community which he described as 'still composed mainly of men who do not know from whence they came nor where they are going, men motivated simply by the desire to get all they can, to acquire and grab'.[74] Fearing a growing alliance between *assimilados* and peasants, and concerned about the rash of uprisings, the colonial state acted swiftly. António de Assis Júnior was arrested and narrowly escaped being deported.

In Lisbon, the Junta de Defensa dos Direitos de Africa, led mainly by mulattos from São Tomé, had very little power. A dissident offshoot of the Junta founded the Liga Africana in 1919, to which the Liga Angolana de Luanda was affiliated. The Junta de Defensa was reorganized as the Partido Nacional Africano in 1921, to avoid being taken over by left-wing elements. *Mutatis mutandis*, these two metropolitan groups represented the two pan-Africanist trends that prevailed in Portugal at the time, the Liga Africana opting for the reformism of Dr Du Bois, and the Partido Nacional Africano more sympathetic to the philosophy of Marcus Garvey.[75]

The return of the High Commissioner Norton de Matos in 1921, an unyielding opponent of the Liga Angolana and the Gremio Africano, left both organizations extremely vulnerable. In 1922 he formally clamped down on the two associations. He ordered that António de Assis Júnior be arrested, that several influential members of the Liga Angolana be deported, and finally that the Liga Angolana be formally dissolved. He also banned 'nativist' newspapers and curtailed promotion opportunities for *assimilado* civil servants. After this blow, organized nationalism in Angola went underground. There subsequently appeared sporadic protests against compulsory labour in the Luanda-Malange corridor between 1922 and 1925. The state took the opportunity provided by these protests to smash the last vestiges of intellectual dissidence.[76]

Conditions became so difficult in Angola that African associations adopted a policy of co-operation with the government. The Partido Nacional Africano went as far as to defend Portugal at the League of Nations against charges of forced labour. Thus when the military dictatorship was set up in Lisbon in 1926, followed by the Salazar regime, it found that the will to resist on the part of Angolan intellectuals had already been broken. 'Purged' of its hard-line elements, the Liga Angolana was allowed to reappear in 1929–30 under the name of the Liga Nacional Africana. The Gremio Africano, which had succumbed to the torrent of restrictions in the 1920s, also re-emerged as the Associação dos Naturais de Angola

73. A. de Assis Júnior, 1917.
74. Quoted in D. L. Wheeler in R. Chilcote (ed.), 1972, p. 81.
75. For a discussion of events surrounding this split, see E. A. Friedland, 1979, pp. 119–20.
76. R. Pélissier, 1978, p. 233.

(ANANGOLA). Sapped of their vital force and rendered politically impotent, the two organizations were induced to pursue purely social aims.

Their collapse coincided with the decline in Portugal of the two 'parties' claiming to be pan-Africanist. In 1931 they merged and became the Movimento Nacionalista Africano (nationalist in the sense of the Portuguese nation), and eventually petered out, caught in the implacable stranglehold of Dr Oliveira Salazar. Watched by the police, in danger of losing their jobs, the local leaders of the Liga Nacional Africana and the ANANGOLA suspended their activities for over twenty years (approximately 1925–45). Inevitably, the decline of the *assimilados'* political role meant that socially, too, they were degraded especially with the arrival of an increasing number of white settlers.

The latter tried on many occasions to rise up against metropolitan rule (especially in 1924–5), and subsequently against the dictatorial regime (notably in 1930), but these attempts only indirectly affected the oppressed African population.[77] Africans had become foreigners in their own country and their only apparent function in the eyes of the Europeans was their productive capacity. In those circumstances, the few strikes in which they took part in the ports (1928) or the railways (1933) were no more than flashes in the pan, and came to nothing, for there was no lasting unity between white labourers and black unskilled workers. Moreover, black workers lacked the support of the African soldiers enrolled in the colonial army, and could not look to an alliance with the *assimilados* who had been reduced to silence by the authorities.

Popular opposition to colonial rule in Mozambique

The mode of popular protest in Mozambique was similar to that in Angola though it varied somewhat in scale and intensity. There were fewer armed insurrections and the literary tradition and connections with the pan-Africanist movement were less well developed. The number of documented examples of peasant and worker opposition, on the other hand, is appreciably greater in Mozambique than in Angola and independent churches were far more numerous and politically significant.

Peasant opposition posed a recurring challenge to the colonial-capitalist system. To be sure, not all, or perhaps even most, peasants resisted. Divided from each other by space, ethnicity, religion, primordial kinship affiliations, the tyranny of their work schedule and a host of other factors, individual peasants were relatively powerless to mount large-scale opposition which lends itself to detailed historical analysis. Their actions tended to be isolated, diffused and sporadic, their limited aims and systemic importance hard to measure and easy to ignore. Yet, acting within the serious constraints imposed by the colonial-capitalist system, Mozambican peasants

77. A different interpretation is advanced by E. Sik, 1964, Vol. II, pp. 314–15.

were able to varying degrees to minimize the disruptive effects of Portuguese domination. For them the central arena of struggle was against the appropriation of their labour and its products.

As in the early years of the colonial period, tax evasion recurred with great regularity throughout all of rural Mozambique. Peasants developed a variety of different strategies to reduce or avoid the annual payments. Peasants commonly falsified their age or marital status, thereby reducing their financial burdens. Many young adults claimed to be minors, sometimes temporarily residing in pre-puberty huts when the revenue officials arrived. Husbands often hid their junior wives or claimed that they were either sisters-in-law or wives of friends who had gone away to work. In southern Mozambique, where hut taxes were the dominant form of retribution, extended families gathered together in one hut which they claimed to be their exclusive domicile.[78] Even after they were assessed many peasants continued this duplicity in an effort to postpone, or even avoid, paying the taxes. As late as 1928 one frustrated Portuguese official in the central part of the colony noted:

> The village headmen and peasants belonging to the populations of Mambos Cussarara, Chuau, and Capanga are engaged in an incredible campaign of passive resistance. When they are called to bring their taxes they come without any money and negotiate long postponement which they invariably exceed, necessitating the use of sepais to bring in the fumos each of whom only brings in a small percentage of the taxes from their respective villages, and thus it takes many months, often an infinite period, before the obligations are liquidated.[79]

Other members of the rural population hid in the interior. Official reports indicate that women often claimed that their husbands were dead when, in fact, 'they temporarily fled returning to the village shortly after the tax collectors or census officials had left.'[80] Africans living close to international frontiers moved back and forth avoiding all tax obligations.

Thousands of rural Mozambicans compelled to grow cotton or to work on settler farms, plantations and state public work projects contested the amount of labour they were expected to provide to the colonial-capitalist system. In the most extreme action they withheld their labour entirely by fleeing to neighbouring colonies. Flight was both arduous and dangerous. Nevertheless, by 1919, it was estimated that more than 100000 northern Mozambicans had resettled in Nyasaland alone.[81] Even in the south where the state exercised greater control, colonial officials

78. J. Nunes, 1928, p. 116.
79. Arquivo de Tete, Documentos Diversos, Circumscrição Civil da Maravia, 'Relatório do Administração Referenate ao Anno de 1928'; Documento no. 8, Manoel Arnaldo Ribeiro to Administrator Manoel Alves, Vianna, undated.
80. J. Nunes, 1928, p. 116.
81. L. Vail, 1976, p. 402.

acknowledged that 'Africans fleeing the province of Sul de Save because of cotton is not something new ... it was reported that many natives abandoned their lands after setting fire to their huts.'[82]

Other deserters reluctant to break all links with their families and traditional homelands fled to sparsely populated backwater areas. In at least a few instances they created permanent refugee communities, primarily in rugged mountainous zones or in the coastal swamps, where the difficult topography served as a natural barrier against Portuguese penetration. Several of these refugee communities were able to maintain their independence for a number of years, surviving both the harsh environmental conditions and armed colonial intervention.[83]

The covert withholding of a portion of their labour probably represented the most widespread expression of defiance by cotton-producing peasants and rural workers. This strategy was both less risky than desertion and, at least for the peasants, provided them with additional opportunities to work their gardens. According to official reports peasants, for example, rarely planted their cotton fields at the designated time, cultivated the minimum acreage, weeded their plants the required number of times or burned their field after the harvest.[84] European planters in southern Mozambique bitterly complained about the 'docility' of their grossly underpaid labourers, rejecting the proposition of one of their members that 'if you contract to pay a pound a month you get pretty fair men.'[85] The governor of Inhambane echoed their sentiments, deploring the reluctance of the Nguni men to perform agricultural tasks which they claimed to be 'women's work'.[86]

Given the factors which tended to divide both the peasantry and migrant workers and frustrate any sense of class solidarity, it is hardly surprising that rural resistance rarely took a collective form. Occasionally, however, rural dissatisfaction was incorporated in a more radical mode of protest. From 1917 to 1921 peasants throughout the Zambezi valley, angered by forced labour, increased taxation, mandatory cotton production, sexual abuses and military conscription, joined in a rebellion directed by descendants of the Barue royal family and Shona spirit mediums. Their objective, which they momentarily accomplished, was to liberate their homelands and dismantle the oppressive colonial system.[87] During the next two decades there was also a series of localized peasant uprisings in Erati,

82. Quoted in A. Isaacman, M. Stephen, Y. Adam, M. J. Homen, E. Macamo and A. Pililão, 1980, p. 596.

83. ibid., pp. 597–9.

84. ibid.

85. E. A. Ross, 1925, p. 50.

86. Districto de Inhambane, *Relatório do Governador 1913–1915*, Lourenço Marques, 1916, p. 41.

87. A. Isaacman, 1976, pp. 156–85.

Moguincal, and Angoch in northern Mozambique precipitated by taxation and forced labour (see Fig. 27.2).[88]

Where fear or coercion prevented overt opposition, peasants and rural workers often manifested their hostility through cultural symbols which were unintelligible to the colonial officials. The Chope, living in southern Mozambique, for example, developed an entire repertoire of songs denouncing the colonial regime in general and the hated tax official in particular:

> We are still angry; its always the same story
> The oldest daughter must pay the tax
> Natanele tells the white man to leave him alone
> Natanele tells the white man to leave me be
> You, the elders must discuss our affairs
> For the man the whites appointed is the son of a nobody
> The Chope have lost the right to their own land
> Let me tell you about it....[89]

The work songs of labourers employed by Sena Sugar Estates were even more explicitly hostile, often depicting the European overseers in the most unflattering sexual terms.[90] To the north the Makua and Makonde artists ridiculed state officials – both African and European – in highly stylized carvings which distorted their features and eliminated their humanity.[91]

Urban workers like their rural counterparts initially engaged in individual and sporadic actions to escape or minimize the new capitalist economic order. They fled before the labour recruiters arrived at their villages, deserted in large numbers, 'loafed' and, on occasion, engaged in sabotage of machinery or raw materials. Although such actions continued to be a dominant mode of protest for *chibalo* (forced labour), by the second decade of the twentieth century urban wage earners had begun to shift their tactics and organize within the new system in order to improve their conditions of employment.

Several factors militated against the organized efforts of Mozambican workers during this period. First, their numbers were extremely small. Mozambique's retarded capitalist sectors employed relatively few permanent labourers. Moreover, the state explicitly prohibited the formation of African unions, and the white labour movement, with a few noticeable exceptions, remained hostile, embracing the racial and cultural prejudices which were part of the official state ideology.[92] Thus, small in number,

88. J. A. G. de Melo Branquinho, 1966, pp. 81–3, 108, 114, 193.

89. Quoted in E. Mondlane, 1969, p. 103.

90. See L. Vail and L. White, 1980, pp. 339–58.

91. The best collection of these carvings is to be found in the Museum de Nampula in the city of Nampula.

92. For an important examination of the white working-class movement see J. Capela, forthcoming.

isolated from the larger working-class movement, and facing a hostile alliance of state and capital, African workers were clearly in an unenviable position.

Nevertheless, as early as 1911, a small group headed by Francisco Domingos Campos, Alfredo de Oliveira Guimares, Agostinho José Mathias, attempted to organize the União Africano to include all African workers in Lourenço Marques. For them the issues were clear cut. Black workers had to organize if they were to survive. They specifically warned against the divisive tendencies of ethnicism and the danger posed if those workers in better-paying jobs did not unite with common day-labourers. 'In our association there are no distinctions', their pamphlets proudly proclaimed. On the point of working-class struggle and solidarity they were equally unequivocal. Despite their eloquence and the power of their critiques, strong opposition from the colonial-capitalist state and the white trade union movement, plus the apparent lack of unity among African workers, undercut União Africano even before it got started.[93]

Despite this initial setback there were a number of sporadic attempts to organize African workers in Lourenço Marques. Strikes and work stoppages were reported by employees of the Merchants Association in 1913, tram workers in 1917, railroad technicians in 1918, and employees at an engineering firm in 1919.[94]

As in many other parts of Africa, port workers were the most militant and relatively best organized sector in the labour force. During the first two decades of the twentieth century Lourenço Marques had grown into a major centre of international commerce, linking the Transvaal and Swaziland as well as southern Mozambique to the larger world economy. Despite the strategic economic importance of the port and the state's effort to prevent any dislocation of traffic, there were seven major strikes between 1918 and 1921 precipitated by the refusal of the shipping and forwarding companies to increase African wages to keep up with the spiralling rate of inflation. Between 1918 and 1920, for example, the prices of such basic staples as rice, beans, potatoes, and soap had doubled and in the latter year a kilogram of rice cost three cents – equal to the average daily salary of most port workers.[95]

The strikes at the port followed a broad pattern. Disgruntled workers, organized through informal grass-roots networks, refused to work unless their wages were adjusted. They gathered in front of the main entrance to the port demanding better salaries and working conditions. The colonial governor sent in troops to smash the demonstration and arrest the leaders. At the same time *chibalo* workers were used as strike breakers to keep the port going. Quickly the strikes were broken. Even where the employers agreed to pay increases, they often reneged upon them as in the case

93. *Os Simples*, 24 June 1911.
94. J. Penvenne, n.d.
95. Other non-essential commodites increased at an even higher rate.

of the 1919 strike. Nevertheless, despite these reversals and the rise to power of a fascist government, strikes continued after 1926, though less frequently.[96]

Perhaps the most bitter port confrontation was the Quinhenta strike in 1933. Port officials and handling companies, suffering the effects of the world depression, decided to reduce the already low wages of wharf workers by between 10 and 30%. This cutback represented five times the amount gained in the 1921 strike. When the announcement was made, workers walked off the job and refused to return after lunch, leaving the port paralysed. Leaders of the strike vowed that they would not return until the cuts were rescinded. Faced with a paralysed port, employers agreed to the demands and port workers returned only to find themselves locked in the port and surrounded by police who forced them to unload all the ships. Thereafter, it was announced that the cuts would not be restored. One Lourenço Marques newspaper captured the anger and frustration on the wharf. 'Workers with empty bellies faced their boss, who, with his full belly, answered them with empty promises.'[97]

As in other parts of Southern and Central Africa, independent churches offered another institutional framework for workers and peasants to vent their hostility against the new social order and the hypocrisy of the established Christian churches. A secret government report noted that the popularity of the separatist churches was due 'both to the racial discrimination within the larger society and the insensitivity of the European missionaries with regard to the natives'.[98] As early as 1918 there were seventy-six separatist churches known to be operating in Mozambique. Twenty years later the number had jumped to more than 380.[99] Membership ranged from a mere handful of adherents to more than 10 000 in the case of the Missão Christa Ethiopia whose network extended throughout four provinces.

Virtually all the independent churches traced their origin to the Zionist and Ethiopian movements in neighbouring South Africa and Rhodesia. Disgruntled and alienated Mozambican migrant labourers, primarily working in the mines, found refuge in these churches and when they returned home either organized branches or formed autonomous sects modelled after their South African and Rhodesian counterparts. Samuel Belize, the moving force behind the powerful African Methodist Episcopal Church, previously had a long association with a black off-shoot of the Wesleyan Mission in South Africa, and Sebastião Peidade de Sousa modelled the

96. See, for example, J. Penvenne, forthcoming. Ms Penvenne is currently completing her doctoral dissertation on the making of the working class in Lourenço Marques which should add an extremely valuable dimension to our knowledge of Mozambican labour history.

97. Quoted in J. Penvenne, forthcoming, p. 20.

98. J. A. G. de Melo Branquinho, 1966, p. 77.

99. ibid., pp. 73–80.

Missão Christa Ethiopia after the Ethiopian Church to which he belonged in Durban.[100] In other cases, the reputation of a particular apostolic leader provided a sufficient incentive for Mozambicans to join his flock. Because most of the migrant labourers came from the southern half of the colony, the independent churches enjoyed their greatest support in the districts of Lourenço Marques, Gaza, Inhambane and Sofala.

From the standpoint of social movements the Ethiopian churches in Mozambique are of particular interest because they often acted as relatively autonomous institutions in which Mozambicans could elect their own officials, have their own budgets, constitution, flag and even para-military organizations. In short, they represented an arena of 'free space', within an enclosed authoritarian system, in which oppressed workers and peasants could enjoy a modicum of self-rule and racial and cultural dignity. The Zionist churches, on the other hand, derived much of their appeal from their apocalyptic vision of divine intervention and the destruction of the oppressive colonial order.

In terms of explicit anti-colonial action, Mozambican independent churches ran the gamut from radicalism to quietism. According to confidential government reports, the Methodist Episcopalian Church, based primarily in Gaza and Manica districts, was a centre of subversive activities. Government infiltrators reported that the Church fostered anti-white sentiment and explicitly attacked the oppressive colonial regime in its services and at clandestine meetings. Moreover, its officials reputedly maintained links with the African National Congress.[101] Other government inquiries found evidence that the Methodist Episcopalian Church advocated revolt and that its members attacked colonial authorities and loyalist chiefs on several occasions. The sect was subsequently accused of helping to organize a major peasant uprising in Mambone in 1952. Such insurgent activities, however, seem to have been the exception. Most independent churches did not adopt an explicitly anti-colonial programme, choosing instead to limit their opposition to verbal criticism and, in some cases, an apocalyptic vision.[102]

There are also tantalizing suggestions of Islamic revisionist movements in northern Mozambique whose Muslim population had historically opposed colonial rule. In the 1920s Islamic holy men protested against the abuses of forced labour, low wages, and land appropriation in the area of Quilemane. A number of Muslim chiefs and their followers were also involved in uprisings in the early 1930s but the exact cause of the revolts remains unknown.[103]

Urban intellectual protest, although not as deeply rooted in Mozambique as in Angola, nevertheless became an important forum for reformist dis-

100. ibid.; E. Moreira, 1936, pp. 28–9; H. I. F. de Freitas, 1956–7.
101. H. I. F. de Freitas, 1956–7, Vol. II, pp. 32–5.
102. ibid., p. 134.
103. J. A. G. de Melo Branquinho, 1966, pp. 56, 81, 108.

course. The first, somewhat tentative, call for change came in 1908 with the publication of the Lourenço Marques newspaper, *O Africano*, the official organ of Gremio Africano (African Union) – a social and civil group founded by the *grande familias* of colour two years earlier. Despite their relatively privileged position and their self-conscious sense of importance, the leading families of Gremio Africano took as their mandate the responsibility to speak for the oppressed Africans. Indeed, the masthead of *O Africano* boldly proclaimed that it was 'Devoted to the defense of the native population of Mozambique'. Its successor, *O Brado Africano* (The African Voice), pursued a similar objective as the self-defined guardian of African peasants and workers. On the occasion of its seventh anniversary, *O Brado Africano* proudly proclaimed that 'the Africans have in *Brado Africano* their best defense, indeed, their only weapon against the injustices which fall upon them.[104]

In their news stories and commentaries both journals highlighted four recurring abuses – *chibalo*, the poor working conditions of free African labour, the preferential treatment given to white immigrants, and the lack of educational opportunities – which to the editors symbolized the very essence of colonial oppression. Throughout this period editorials vigorously denounced and carefully documented the abuses inherent in the system of *chibalo*. They protested against the brutal methods used by African *sepais* to recruit forced labour, the low wages and poor working conditions of the *chibalo* labourers and the arbitrary and capricious actions of the European overseers. The editors were particularly incensed by the common practice of seizing 'African women to repair and construct roads, not even supplying them with food nor paying them a salary', while 'forcing them during the rainy season to sleep in mud-huts, beside the road, like slaves'.[105]

The newspapers also unleashed a broadside attack on the conditions of employment of free African workers. They deplored the fact that peasants and nominally free agricultural workers were compelled to work on European estates 'from sunrise until sunset earning hardly a shilling a month', that Mozambicans working in the South African mines are 'denied the right to select their own employers ... and die like flies in the mines', that African workers are arrested and beaten if they lack proper identification, and that the state used *chibalo* labourers to break strikes and drive down wages of free workers.[106] The informal colour bar conventions, which froze Africans in the lowest paying jobs while reserving the most desirable employment for Europeans, was also the target of several editorials.

The protest against the colour bar represented part of a more generalized

104. *O Brado Africano*, 24 December 1926.
105. ibid., 28 February 1925.
106. ibid.; *O Brado Africano*, 13 December 1924; 30 July 1927; J. Penvenne, 1978, p. 10.

hostility towards state policies which favoured white immigrants while ignoring the needs of the indigenous population. In one scathing commentary, *O Africano* questioned the colonial regime's logic in underwriting the expensive white 'riff-raff' who contributed nothing to the colony.

> The common Portuguese, who is known as *mumadji* [common Portuguese immigrant] among the African population, always leaves Portugal with the fixed intention of a short stay in the land of the blacks to gather enough savings; and then to save it all to return to Portugal, settle in and enjoy the wealth which he managed to accumulate, with God knows what sacrifices over 2, 3 or 4 years.
>
> Are they aware there [in Portugal] of the deprivations that those men suffer in order to save that 300 or 400 000 reis? It is a poem of pain and misery. A veritable madness that some of them live through in an effort to fill their suitcases – with those paltry pieces of metal. Gold Fever!
>
> They live in pig-sties, without light, without air, some 4 or 5 together in order to cut costs. They customarily eat three persons from the same meal, because it costs less. In a squalid dinner of soups or stews, which are more accurately puddles of warm water in which some five beans swim hopelessly in search of company ...[107]

Although the tone of the editorials in both newspapers was cautious and reformist, appealing to the goodwill and sense of justice of the colonial government, mounting frustrations produced outbursts of anger and even implicit threats to the system. This somewhat more defiant tone surfaced with greater regularity in the period immediately after the Salazar regime (1928–68) imposed its authoritarian rule, smashing any illusion of reform and generating a sense of despair even among the most privileged members of the African and mulatto community. A ringing editorial in *Brado Africano*, entitled 'Enough', represents the clearest expression of their rage:

> We are fed up to the teeth.
> Fed up with supporting you, with suffering the terrible consequences of your follies, your demands, with the squandering misuse of your authority.
> We can no longer stand the pernicious effects of your political and administrative decisions.
> We are no longer willing to make greater and greater useless sacrifices ...
> Enough ...[108]

Yet for all their criticism of colonial abuses and their self-defined role as guardians of oppressed Africans, the *grande familias* lived in a social and cultural milieu which was totally apart from that of the workers and

107. Quoted in J. Penvenne, 1979, p. 10.
108. *O Brado Africano*, 27 February 1931. The English translation is taken from J. Duffy, 1959, p. 305.

peasants who returned to their shanty towns, barracks and villages after a hard day's labour. Moreover, as members of a nascent colonial bourgeoisie, they had very different class interests which often placed them at odds with their less privileged counterparts and precluded a more radical critique of colonial-capitalism. Intense rivalries between mulatto and African segments of the colonial elite further reduced the influence of Gremio Africano and helped precipitate its demise.[109]

By the early 1930s these animosities had grown progressively worse providing the colonial regime with an opportunity to shatter the last vestiges of unity. Appealing to the discontent of the African membership, state officials convinced several of them to break away and organize the Institutio Negrophilio in 1932. As an additional incentive, the colonial administration provided office space, furniture, books and generous funding while a prominent Portuguese businessman, Paulo Gil dos Santos, offered several leaders of the new organization employment as labour recruiters. Four years later the Salazar regime imposed extremely stringent censorship laws which effectively silenced *O Brado Africano*.

During this period a small number of Mozambican intellectuals, living in Portugal, helped to form organizations which were linked to the larger pan-African movement. The most important were the Liga Africana and the Partido Nacional Africano. Liga Africana maintained close ties with W. E. B. Du Bois' Pan-African Congress, while the latter expressed greater sympathy for Garveyism. Neither, however, had any substantial following in the colony and their actions were largely symbolic.[110]

Conclusion

To sum up, the Africans of the countries of Southern and Central Africa stood up to colonialism and made a substantial contribution to the preparation of the liberation movement on the African continent which followed after 1935. The most advanced forms of anti-colonial protest in that period were observed in the Union of South Africa where industrial development and the accompanying process of urbanization involved Africans in the capitalist economy earlier than in the other African countries. Nationalists and political organizations set up in the Union of South Africa were used as models in many countries of Southern, Central and East Africa.

109. Interview with Luis Bernardo Honwana, 3 and 4 October 1981; R. Hamilton, 1975, pp. 164–7.

110. E. A. Friedland, 1979, pp. 119–21.

28

Ethiopia and Liberia, 1914–35: two independent African states in the colonial era

M. B. AKPAN *based on contributions* *from* A. B. JONES *and* R. PANKHURST

His Majesty's Government will join with the United States Government in making representations in the strongest terms to the Liberian Government to induce that Government to lay before the forthcoming meeting of the Council of the League of Nations a request for the appointment of a Governing Commission [over Liberia] ... His Majesty's Government will also exert strong pressure on the Liberian Government to persuade them to apply for a loan under the League auspices.[1] (British Foreign Office, London, to British Ambassador in Washington, DC; January 1931.)

I do not want agreements unless they give me everything, including the head of the Emperor [Haile Sellassie] ... Even if I am given everything I prefer to avenge Adowa. I am prepared.[2] (Benito Mussolini, Italian Fascist leader, August 1935.)

On the surface, it would appear that the matters in dispute between Ethiopia and Italy could have only academic interests for Liberia. But a more profound consideration of the implications inherent in the facts surrounding the dispute would convince the most unthinking mind that the situation is of the highest significance to a State situated as is Liberia. Should the League of Nations be unable to assert its moral influence in the maintenance of international decency, decorum and security, then the smaller States in the World will become, as in fact they have always been, the prey of imperialistic Adventurers.[3] (Edwin J. Barclay, President of Liberia, December 1935.)

The quotations above convey the force of European imperialism against Liberia and Ethiopia during many of the inter-war years, and the bond that continued to bind Liberians and Ethiopians as Africans and victims of European aggression. This chapter discusses, in comparative terms, this aggression, the responses of Liberia and Ethiopia to it, and other political, economic and social developments that occurred in both countries during the period 1915–35.

1. R. E. Anderson, 1952, pp. 110–11.
2. E. M. Robertson, 1977, pp. 160–2.
3. E. J. Barclay, 1935(b), p. 15.

Liberia and Ethiopia: socio-cultural developments, 1915–35

During this period, Liberia and Ethiopia encountered grave problems of national integration and survival resulting partly from vast expansion during the previous century and the increased disparateness of their peoples and cultures. What major cultural and social changes occurred in both countries during this period?

Of Liberia's population, the Americo-Liberians as a group remained politically and economically dominant. Since the late nineteenth century their number had reportedly declined owing to a higher death than birth rate, and the virtual cessation of immigration of blacks from America. The situation led to increased intermarriage and liaison, mostly between Americo-Liberian men and indigenous African women (many of whom were educated in the Liberian schools), and a corresponding increase of Liberians with mixed Americo-Liberian/indigenous African parentage. Invariably, such Liberians and indigenous African youths apprenticed to or adopted by Americo-Liberian families became assimilated to the Americo-Liberian socio-cultural milieu.[4]

The decline in the Americo-Liberian population probably also intensified their practice of in-group marriages, and correspondingly the extended family system that had developed among them since the late nineteenth century. Thus throughout our period, established families like the Shermans; the Barclays, Colemans, Coopers, Dennises, Grimeses and Morrises; the Greens, Grigsbys, Rosses, Witherspoons and Worrells; the Brewers, Dossens, Gibsons and Tubmans, mentioned in Chapter 11 of this volume, continued to provide most of Liberia's political and economic leadership.[5] Indeed by the 1920s it became the practice for these families to allocate, through some mutual agreement, legislative seats, ministerial posts, and other high public positions and patronage many months before formal elections to the legislature took place.[6]

As for the indigenous Liberians, the gradual expansion of schools and Christian missionary work throughout Liberia somewhat increased their literacy, modernization, and assimilation of some aspects of the Americo-Liberian culture. Indigenous Liberians thus assimilated were regarded as 'civilized' (or 'semi-civilized') by the Americo-Liberians who granted a comparatively few of them political and civil rights on an equal footing with themselves. A few of those thus favoured rose to prominent public or political positions, like Dr Benjamin W. Payne, a Bassa man trained

---

4. C. L. Simpson, 1961, pp. 84, 88; H. A. Jones, 1962, p. 153.
5. United States National Archives (USNA), Records of the Department of State relating to the Internal Affairs of Liberia (RDSL), 1909–29, 4/88, US State Department Memorandum, 16 June 1924.
6. USNA, RDSL, 1909–29, 4, Clarke to US Secretary of State, Monrovia.

PLATE 28.1 *Didwo Twe, Kru Senator, Liberia, one of the few indigenous Liberians to attain high public office*

in medicine in the United States, who held a Cabinet position as Secretary of Public Instruction for most of the 1910s and 1920s; Henry Too Wesley, a Grebo man, who was Liberia's Vice-President in the early 1920s; Didwo Twe, a Kru Senator (Plate 28.1); and Momolu Massaquoi, a Vai man, who was at various times in the 1920s Acting Secretary of the Interior and Liberia's Consul in Germany.[7]

Nevertheless, even the favoured educated Africans – let alone the mass of unenfranchised and largely oppressed indigenous Liberians – were more or less dissatisfied with 'Americo-Liberian rule' – as they rightly termed the Liberian government. As a rule the educated indigenous Liberians sought to reform Liberia's socio-political system to secure a better deal for the indigenous Liberians. Only rarely, as in 1930, during the forced labour crisis in Liberia, did some of the leading educated indigenous Liberians actively seek to overthrow the Americo-Liberians and supplant them in the government.[8]

Acculturation was, however, not unidirectional. Over the years the Americo-Liberians had themselves adapted many aspects of indigenous Liberian culture which they had earlier abhorred or decried as superstitious or heathenish, such as belief in the efficacy of magic, witchcraft and 'native medicine'; initiation into the *poro*; and the practice of pawning persons to meet a debt or other obligation.[9] The degree of such Africanization was, however, too limited to blur the main social, economic, political and cultural distinctions between the Americo-Liberians as a group, and the indigenous Liberians, by the terminal date of this study in 1935.

As was the case with Liberia, a major consequence of Ethiopia's vast expansion under Menelik was to exacerbate the ethnic diversity of Ethiopia's population. Prominent among the peoples incorporated into Ethiopia by 1914 through this expansion were the Oromo who numbered at least as many as the Amhara–Tigreans and were dispersed over almost one half of Ethiopia's territory; the Gurage; Sidama; and Beni Shanguls.[10]

The Amhara–Tigreans as a group retained their economic, political and military dominance over the rest of Ethiopia during our period, a position comparable to that of the Americo-Liberian oligarchy in Liberia. Unlike the Americo-Liberian minority, however, the Amhara–Tigreans were variously estimated at between 33 and 40% of Ethiopia's population.[11] Although they constituted a privileged group, actual economic and political

7. R. L. Buell, 1947, p. 751.
8. See below.
9. Liberian National Archives (LNA), Grand Bassa County File (uncatalogued), Smith to King, Lower Buchanan, 14 November 1924.
ibid., Russell to King, Lower Buchanan, 5 May 1928.
ibid., Harris (for Banks) to King, North Harlandville, 6 August 1928.
10. E. Ullendorff, 1960, pp. 30–44; R. Greenfield, 1965, pp. 98–108; G. W. B. Huntingford, 1969, pp. 35–7.
11. E. Ullendorff, 1960, p. 31; G. W. B. Huntingford, 1969, p. 23.

power and high status were concentrated in some Ethiopian noble families mostly from whom the holders of high public office or titles like (in order of precedence) *negus, betwoded, ras, dajazmach,* and *fitawrari* were recruited. It was largely through these noblemen (and the armies they commanded) that Menelik had expanded Ethiopia by conquest. Thereafter he occupied the conquered territories with 'garrison settlements' in much the same manner as did colonialists from Europe in other parts of Africa.[12] Hence many of these noblemen and their descendants, as well as descendants of the garrison settlements, government officials, 'and even Christian clergy not infrequently adopt[ed] the worst possible type of "colonial" approach' or racial attitude towards other Ethiopians 'of slightly different ethnic groupings'.[13] They prided themselves, for example, on being Ethiopia's empire-builders – the 'men who with their knowledge served the country and the Emperor and who handed Ethiopia down' through the ages to posterity.[14]

Much the same 'colonial approach' was manifested by the Americo-Liberians in perceiving themselves as Liberia's nation-builders. As President William V. S. Tubman put it in May 1951, the African repatriates to Liberia, schooled in the hardship and lash of slavery in the New World:

> Brought here the civilization, education and religion that were to be imparted to the natives and with these it was hoped that the two elements would build a great solidified and united nation ... From them, feeble as they were, everything that is here has sprung forth and grown, including state buildings, colleges, school houses, churches and expanding economy, industry, embassies, legations, consulates, roads, bridges, et cetera.[15]

The self-image of nation- or empire-builder was comparable to the European colonial self-image of the 'White Man's Burden' which posits, erroneously, that whatever advances are found in the economic, technological, political and cultural development of Africa – or in 'civilization' in its broad meaning – were introduced through European colonization of Africa.[16]

Among the non-Amhara–Tigreans (that is, the Oromo, Sidama, Gurage, and so on), a significant social and cultural development in the first half of the twentieth century has been increased 'Amharization', despite resistance by Muslim, traditional, and other influences. This increased Amharization owed much to forced Christianization following Menelik's conquests and the imposition of imperial administration, Christian education in Ethiopian schools, and the prestige of Amharic as Ethiopia's national

12. R. Greenfield, 1965, pp. 48–9, 119, 136, 460–2.
13. ibid., pp. 105–6.
14. Quoted in ibid., p. 107.
15. W. V. S. Tubman, May 1951, in E. R. Townsend (ed.), 1959, pp. 98–9.
16. L. H. Gann and P. Duignan, 1967, Chapters 15 and 22.

language, as well as the activities of traders and Coptic priests from Amhara and Tigre, and increasing urbanization which attracted labour migrants from other parts into the orbit of Amharic culture.[17] Manifestations of Amharization during our period included to a greater or lesser extent, the use of the Amharic language, dress and calendar; changes in religious beliefs; modifications in political institutions and structures, and in the system of land tenure.[18] However, as in Liberia, acculturation was not uni-directional. Some of the Amhara–Tigrean settlers in the more isolated garrison settlements were eventually assimilated by the local population.[19]

Furthermore, Ethiopian society segmented into various classes and groups. These included slaves; peasants;[20] nascent intellectuals and commercial bourgeoisie who supported the Regent, Tafari Makonnen (later Emperor Haile Sellassie), and favoured reforms and a strong central government;[21] and a conservative group comprising most of the great nobles and high clergy of Ethiopia's Coptic Church. This group, which supported Empress Zauditu and favoured regional autonomy, constituted the bulwark of Ethiopia's socio-cultural system.[22]

Thus, in both Liberia and Ethiopia, ethnic and cultural pluralism and social inequality posed serious threats to social stability and harmony, or produced actual conflicts during our period (some of which are examined in this chapter).

Political development

Liberia

In both Liberia and Ethiopia during our period, strains and stresses occurred in the political system and processes in three main spheres: within the core, on the periphery, and between the core and periphery.

As regards Liberia's core, throughout the 1910s, the True Whig Party firmly held the reins of power with minimum challenge from a formal opposition party. This situation changed somewhat in the 1920s when the People's Party, organized in 1922 under the leadership of ex-President Daniel B. Howard, seriously challenged the ruling True Whig Party. Even so, there was no question, considering Liberia's largely corrupt political culture and the overwhelming political leverage wielded by the ruling party, that the People's Party could unseat the True Whig Party solely through the constitutional means of the ballot box.

Indeed, since the 1890s, formal opposition had become very weak and

17. W. A. Shack, 1969, pp. 8, 48, 138–9.
18. G. W. B. Huntingford, 1969, pp. 27–9, 55–8, 68; W. A. Shack, 1969, p. 202.
19. W. A. Shack, 1969, p. 25.
20. R. V. Vivo, 1978, pp. 38–9.
21. R. V. Vivo, 1978, p. 37; R. Greenfield, 1965, p. 147.
22. R. Greenfield, 1965, pp. 151–2; R. V. Vivo, 1978, pp. 36–8.

sporadic, organized mostly on an *ad hoc* basis, becoming a party only when national elections were being held. This lack of continuity was manifested in the variety of names which such parties bore: the Union Party, during the elections of May 1897 and 1899; the People's Party, in May 1901; the National Union True Whig Party, in May 1911; the People's Party in May 1921, 1927, and 1931; and the United True Whig Party, in May 1935. Furthermore, the opposition parties contested for only a limited number of the seats in the Legislature. At the elections of 1897, 1903 and 1905, it fielded no candidates for the presidency or vice-presidency, only for the House and Senate. At the elections of 1907 and 1919, the True Whig Party was the only party in the field. Whereas most of the True Whig candidates won with large majorities, only a few of the opposition candidates won.[23]

Thus, excepting the 1920s and early 1930s when the People's Party seriously challenged the True Whig Party, Liberia had gradually evolved during the twentieth century into a virtual one-party state – one of the earliest African countries to do so.

Various factors contributed to this position. The decline, since the late nineteenth century, of agriculture and trade which had provided many Liberians with means of livelihood, made the Liberian government the main employer of labour as well as the source of income and high social status for most Liberians.[24] Increasingly, therefore, it was important that prospective as well as incumbent holders of public or political office should support the government which was tantamount to supporting the ruling True Whig Party. Secondly, during the period 1915–35, perhaps even more than before, gross corruption and malpractices were resorted to in Liberia's public system and political processes. The keen competition between the True Whig and People's parties in the 1920s and early 1930s particularly exacerbated election malpractices, mostly by the ruling True Whig Party. At the elections of May 1927, for instance, President King allegedly polled 235 000 votes, and his People's Party opponent, T. J. R. Faulkner, 9000 votes, whereas there were not more than 10 000 individuals entitled to vote throughout Liberia in that year.[25]

Thirdly, as in the nineteenth century, the ruling and opposition parties were divided mainly by clashes of personalities or disagreements over the sharing of the social surplus and not by any marked ideological or policy differences. In 1911, for instance, the People's Party was organized by

23. USNA, DUSM 14/88, Lyon to Hay; Monrovia, 13 January 1905; ibid., Lyon to Adee, Monrovia, 8 May 1905; USNA, DUSM(NF) 405/112, Lyon to Secretary of State, Monrovia, 20 May 1907; T. J. R. Faulkner, 1927; 'Janus', 'The Defeat of ex-President C. D. B. King, at the National Election on 7 May 1935 – And why', in LNA, material in unlabelled file.

24. American Colonization Society Ms. (ACS), *Liberian Letters*, 28, Stevens to Wilson, Monrovia, 1 May 1901.

25. T. J. R. Faulkner, 1927.

a splinter group of the True Whig Party as a consequence of Liberia's Vice-President Jerome J. Dossen of Maryland losing his bid for nomination as True Whig presidential candidate to Daniel B. Howard, the National Chairman of the party. Similarly in 1927, many True Whigs joined the People's Party not primarily because they favoured that party's programmes, but because they opposed President King's bid for a 'third term'.[26] In the absence of major ideological or policy differences among Liberians, politics became largely a matter of collaboration or competition between the leading, mostly Americo-Liberian, families in the ruling or opposition parties to control the social surplus.

Finally, had the political base of Liberia been broadened to bring in the indigenous Liberians, things would have been different. But apart from Too Wesley, Twe, and a few others already referred to, no such political developments took place. Liberia's political system therefore remained basically conservative, serving mainly the interests of the Americo-Liberian elite and perpetuating its political ascendancy.

Ethiopia

The political situation in Ethiopia during our period contrasted with that of Liberia in certain important respects, notably the nature and range of political power and privilege. However, regarding the more fundamental issues of the structure of the political system, the extent of political change, class structure and interests, and foreign imperialist intervention, Ethiopia had much in common with Liberia.

Menelik's last years were difficult times for Ethiopia. During his protracted illness, the Emperor appointed his grandson, Lij Iyasu – a boy of twelve – as his successor in mid-1908.[27] Later in that year, when he became paralysed and lost the power of speech, Menelik appointed his former general, Ras Tasamma, as Regent. Tasamma died in 1911, whereupon the Ethiopian Council of State declared that Iyasu was old enough to act for himself with their guidance. Up to Menelik's death in December 1913, the power vacuum created by his illness exacerbated political intriguing by factions of the Ethiopian nobility and encouraged European colonial powers to meddle in Ethiopian affairs.[28]

Lij Iyasu, son of Ras Mikael, the ruler of Wallo, was impetuous by nature. Besides possessing little of his grandfather's statecraft, he lacked a power base outside Wallo, and Menelik's old courtiers, predominantly from Shoa, resented him. Gradually opposition crystallized against some aspects of his domestic policies, especially his friendship with the Muslim population and his foreign policies which centred on support for Germany,

26. Anon., *Confidential Diary of Liberian Events 1926–9* (kept in Executive Mansion) (MS).

27. R. Pankhurst, 1976.

28. R. Greenfield, 1965, pp. 131–2.

Austria–Hungary and Turkey on the outbreak of the First World War in 1914. It is not surprising, then, that the nobles, the Church dignitaries and possibly the Allied delegations in Addis Ababa colluded to depose him in September 1916 and to keep him a prisoner from 1921 till his death in 1935.[29] Menelik's daughter, Zawditu, was thereupon proclaimed Empress, and Tafari, son of the deceased Emperor's cousin Ras Makonnen, Regent and heir to the throne. Empress Zawditu's coronation, on 11 February 1917, was followed by a regime of dual authority in which power was shared between the Empress and the Regent, each with a palace, a distinct group of followers and often conflicting policies.

The advent of Tafari as Regent was an event of importance in that he was a resolute leader desirous of resuming Menelik's policy of modernization, as well as of persevering in the late Emperor's efforts to maintain Ethiopia's independence. Tafari Makonnen's disposition to a strongly personal style of administration partly enabled him to gradually extend his power, during his regency, over several crucial areas of the public sector, viz: his lieutenants at court, the provinces, the army, the Church and Empress Zawditu. On 7 October 1928, Tafari was crowned Negus, and assumed complete control of the government. The coronation earned him further resentment and opposition by Zawditu and her supporters. In March 1930, Zawditu's husband, Ras Gugsa Wolie, rebelled, but was defeated with the aid of the Regent's tiny air force. On the following day, Zawditu passed away, and Tafari assumed the imperial title as Emperor Haile Sellassie I (Plate 28.2). His coronation took place on 2 November 1930.[30]

Having thus strengthened his political position, Haile Sellassie moved on to further modernize Ethiopia's political system by promulgating a written constitution in 1931, and increasing the authority of the central government at the expense of the old nobility.[31] The constitution provided for a bicameral Parliament with a nominated Senate and a Chamber of Deputies likewise nominated 'until the people are in a position to elect'.

Since Haile Sellassie regarded the 1931 Constitution as a landmark in Ethiopia's political history, we may ask to what extent it changed Ethiopia's political system and, more importantly, what political development occurred during our period. As in Liberia's case, though some political changes did take place, they were neither fundamental nor structural. Political changes were reflected in the gradual strengthening of the Regent's (and then the Emperor's) power at the expense of the old nobility and the Church – that is, in increased centralization; the increased application of achieved criteria in public appointments coupled with the elimination of the most conservative of the Ethiopian nobility; the explicit recognition

29. ibid., pp. 136–46.
30. E. Waugh, 1931; L. Mosley, 1964, pp. 151–63. For a chronological listing of some of the principal events of the reign, see S. P. Petrides, 1964, pp. 157–9.
31. R. Greenfield, 1965, p. 168.

PLATE 28.2 *Haile Sellassie I, Emperor of Ethiopia, 1930–74*

of the need for modernization by some Ethiopian leaders including Haile Sellassie; and the formal promulgation of a Constitution.

As for political development involving fundamental normative, institutional and other structural changes in Ethiopia's political culture, there was hardly any during our period. Rather – in spite of increased political centralization – social separatism, cultural regionalism, and ethnic chauvinism among the Oromo, Sidama, Tigreans and Gurage, for example, remained the dominant characteristics of the Ethiopian empire and were serious hindrances to national integration.[32]

Secondly, the Constitution of 1931 was far from being a radical innovation and had little immediate impact on Ethiopia's political culture. The constitution left Haile Sellassie's absolute powers intact and largely retained the privileged position of the nobility. Haile Sellassie appointed the members of the Senate from that class, while, in turn, the nobles and the 'local shums' (chiefs) in turn appointed the Chamber of Deputies.[33] Given hardly any initiative in legislation or policy-making, and convened and dissolved at will by the emperor, the Parliament merely rubber-stamped matters placed before it by the emperor.[34] By the time of the Italian invasion, Parliament was almost defunct.[35] Similarly, the ministers were allowed hardly any initiative or independence of action. They were appointed from outside Parliament and were directly responsible to Haile Sellassie.[36]

In all this Ethiopia differed markedly from Liberia. For, although the Liberian Constitution granted the Liberian president wide constitutional powers, these were far from absolute. The Liberian Legislature was politically active while the Ethiopian Parliament was docile and complacent. The most striking contrast was perhaps the absence of political parties in Ethiopia, attributed to factors like the historically dominant position of the emperor in Ethiopian affairs, and the lack of economic development or a westernized elite that could significantly modify Ethiopia's conservatism.[37]

Thus during our period, Liberia and Ethiopia had more common features than differences in the fundamental determinants of political culture like their conservatism; inegalitarian and ascriptive social norms; lack of national integration, economic development, or firm commitment to radical social change; and more importantly, their tenuous political independence amid unfriendly, covetous, imperialist European powers.

32. E. M. Robertson, 1977, pp. 31–3.
33. ibid., p. 169.
34. Quoted in ibid., from J. E. Baum, 1928.
35. ibid.
36. ibid.
37. R. L. Hess and G. Loewenberg in P. J. M. McEwan (ed.), 1968, pp. 199–201.

Economic and social change in Liberia and Ethiopia, 1915–35

Liberia

In many respects, the years 1915–35 were trying times economically for most Liberians and the Liberian government. The decline as from the late nineteenth century of Liberian trade and agriculture, Liberia's leading sectors, drastically curtailed government revenue (derived mostly from customs duties), and deprived many Liberians of their principal means of livelihood.

Partly to repay Liberia's mounting debts, including the English loan of 1870, and partly to carry out internal development, the Liberian government secured a loan of $500000 in 1906 at 6% interest from some English financiers. But the new loan provided hardly any relief and was cancelled in 1912 when a new loan of $1700000 was secured to redeem it from certain European banks at 5% interest. Liberia's revenues were then split into 'assigned revenue', made up primarily of the customs duties, which was to be used exclusively to pay interest and the sinking fund on the loan of 1912; and the 'internal revenue', made up of various internal fees, fines, and taxes raised by the Liberian government (including the hut tax levied on the indigenous Liberians) which the Liberian government was to use for its essential services including payment of the salaries of government employees. The collection and management of the 'assigned revenue' were entrusted to an 'International Receivership' made up of an American as a 'General Receiver of Customs', assisted by French, German, and British Receivers.

In actual fact, the proceeds from the 'assigned revenue' fell after the outbreak of the First World War largely as a result of the contraction of trade which followed the withdrawal of the Germans who had controlled about three-quarters of the Liberian trade.[38] Furthermore, as the price of coffee, Liberia's principal export, and other Liberian products like cocoa, ivory, palm oil and kernels, and piassava fell drastically in the world market,[39] planters drastically cut production, so that Liberia's exports, and, correspondingly, the customs revenue, declined the more. Thus as from 1916, the annual interest and sinking fund on the loan of 1912 could not be met regularly or in full.[40] Arrears of payment therefore accumulated,

---

38. A. Sharpe, 1920, p. 302; USNA, RDSL 1909–29, 4, Young to US War Department, Monrovia, 7 October 1915.

39. USNA, RDSL 1909–29, 5, Bundy, 'Quarterly Diplomatic Report', Monrovia 2 August 1919; ibid., 4, C. Young, 'Memo of Major Charles Young on Conditions in Liberia', Monrovia, 7 October 1915.

40. D. E. Howard, 1916; USNA, RDSL 1909–29, 4, 'Memo of Major Charles Young ...' op. cit. in note 39.

amounting to $178657 by 30 September 1918. At the same time, the 'internal revenue' hardly sufficed – largely owing to corrupt practices by Liberian officials – to meet the Liberian government's essential services, like payment of the salaries of government employees, which had already been severely cut.

Thus, faced with bankruptcy, the Liberian government first borrowed constantly and extensively from the Bank of British West Africa during 1917–18.[41] Then, as from late 1918 to 1921, it tried, in vain, to raise a loan of $5 000 000 from the United States government.[42] The failure of this attempt forced the Liberian government to introduce several measures designed to stimulate trade and increase revenue from it. These included an upward revision of the tariff, the reopening of the Liberian hinterland to foreign traders (closed to foreigners since the outbreak of the First World War), and the raising of port and harbour dues.[43] Simultaneously, the Liberian government welcomed plans by the Universal Negro Improvement Association, an American-based nationalist movement of New World blacks led by the Jamaican, Marcus Garvey, to bring capital and black immigrants to Liberia to develop her resources. But those plans never materialized.[44]

Fortunately for Liberia, as from late 1923, the performance of the Liberian economy gradually improved. By selling German property confiscated during the First World War, the Liberian government realized about $154 000.[45] Moreover, the fiscal measures introduced in December 1922, particularly the new tariff, were beginning to pay off.[46] As Liberia's foreign trade began to revive, especially after the Germans re-entered it in 1922, and the Liberian hinterland was reopened to foreign traders, exports rose, and the balance of trade began to shift in Liberia's favour. During the first nine months of 1923, for example, the value of exports exceeded that of the corresponding period for 1922 by $169 000.[47]

Just as Liberian government finances thus began to recover, even brighter prospects for the Liberian economy became foreseeable when in 1926 the American, Harvey S. Firestone obtained from the Liberian government the right to lease for ninety-nine years up to one million acres in Liberia to grow and export rubber, and Liberia secured a loan of $5 000 000 from the Finance Corporation of America to develop infrastructure including roads, hospitals and schools, as well as to pay her debts.[48] The loan, which

41. R. C. Bannermann, 1920; R. L. Buell, 1947, p. 26.

42. R. C. Bannermann, 1920; F. Starr, 1925, p. 113; C. D. B. King, 1924, pp. 2–3.

43. R. L. Buell, 1928, Vol. II, pp. 769–70; USNA, RDSL 1909–29, 8.882/032/43, Bur to American Minister Resident, Monrovia, 1 February 1923.

44. M. B. Akpan, 1973(a).

45. R. L. Buell, 1928, Vol. II, p. 767.

46. C. D. B. King, 1924, p. 9.

47. C. D. B. King, 1923, p. 7.

48. A. G. Jones, n.d.

PLATE 28.3 *Rubber in Liberia: the labour force of a plantation*

received United States government support, greatly increased the influence of Firestone and the United States in Liberia.

As for rubber production, Firestone's investment in two vast rubber plantations had a modest though not insignificant impact on the Liberian economy in the short run, particularly in employment. First, Firestone became the largest employer of labour in Liberia[49] (see Plate 28.3). However, most of the Liberian employees were unskilled or semi-skilled, doing mainly clearing and planting or working as artisans and mechanics. Secondly, Firestone built several health clinics and schools for its Liberian (and American) employees, and distributed rubber seedlings to Liberians wishing to plant rubber.[50] However, for several decades to come, Firestone's rubber production remained largely an enclave activity. It had few spread effects over, or linkages with, the largely undeveloped, peasant economy of Liberia, particularly rice production in which over 80% of the indigenous Liberians were engaged. Only in 1935, when substantial exports of rubber commenced, did rubber emerge as Liberia's major export commodity (and remained so till 1961 when iron ore superseded it).[51]

The year 1935 was significant in two other respects. Exploration confirmed the presence of iron ore in Bomi Hill, although actual mining and production came much later – in 1951.[52] It also marked the end of the dominance of Britain and Europe as Liberia's principal trade partners, and their replacement as from 1936 by the United States – thanks to increased exports of Liberian rubber, mostly to America.[53] It should however be noted that as the prices of Liberia's major products – palm oil, palm kernel, piassava, coffee, cocoa, and kola nuts – fell in the world market from the outset of the depression, the volume and value of Liberia's trade declined as well. And throughout the 1930s the balance of trade was against Liberia.[54] European firms had dominated Liberia's import–export business since the late nineteenth century. As from the 1920s an increasing number of Lebanese and Syrian traders joined them and by the end of our period in 1935 controlled much of Liberia's retail trade.[55]

In these more or less bleak economic circumstances throughout our period (1915–35), the Liberian government was left with perennially meagre funds after continuous debt payments and could not effect economic or social development of Liberia to any extent. Its road-building programme, begun by President Arthur Barclay, was intensified but mostly with forced, unpaid indigenous Liberian labour (see Fig. 28.1). The labourers also pro-

49. C. D. B. King, 1928, p. 8.
50. C. M. Wilson, 1971, pp. 137–8.
51. Liberia Trading and Development Bank Ltd, 1968, pp. 76–7.
52. R. W. Clower, G. Dalton, M. Harwitz and A. A. Walters, 1966, pp. 197–201.
53. Republic of Liberia, 1941, pp. 36–40.
54. Republic of Liberia, 1940, pp. 8, 11.
55. Z. B. H. Roberts, 1934, pp. 6–7.

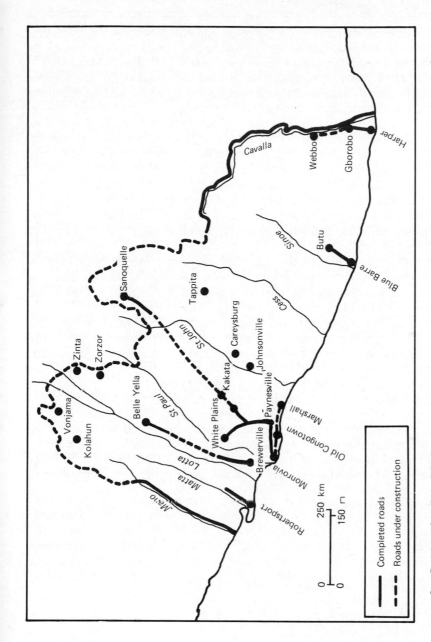

FIG. 28.1 *Position of roads in Liberia, 1925*

Completed roads

Roads under construction

250 km

150

0

0

Cavalla

Webbo

Gborobo

Harper

Sinoe

Butu

Blue Barre

Sanoquelle

Tappita

Cess

Careysburg

Johnsonville

St John

Zinta

Zorzor

Kakata

Belle Yella

St Paul

White Plains

Paynesville

Marshall

Vonjama

Kolahun

Brewerville

Old Congotown

Monrovia

Lotta

Matta

Mano

Robertsport

vided the hoes, matchets and other equipment for the work.[56] During the 1920s the Liberian government – for the first time in Liberia's history – established several elementary schools in the remote Liberian hinterland.[57] Late in 1930 the government also started the Booker T. Washington Agricultural and Industrial Institution to train junior and middle-level technical and agricultural manpower.[58] In 1934 it commenced a much-needed Teachers Training College at Monrovia.[59] Existing institutions like the Liberia College and the College of West Africa were reportedly doing well.[60] In August 1927, the central government at Monrovia established radio communication with the Liberian coast and with the United States by building several radio stations which greatly supplemented the existing inefficient Liberian coastal telephone service.[61] In 1924 the government built a hospital at Monrovia. In 1927 it purchased and erected an electric power plant at Monrovia which supplied electricity and light to the town.[62]

American missionary bodies – as they had done since Liberia's foundation – contributed by establishing schools, hospitals, as well as churches, manned by devotees like the physician and ethnographer, Dr George W. Harley, and Mrs Harley of the Methodist Mission at Ganta.[63]

However, any significant expansion of education was inhibited as much by inadequate government revenue as by the Liberian government's traditional caution in opening the Liberian hinterland to missionaries, traders or other foreigners, some of whom might exert influence on the indigenous Liberians 'subversive to the Liberian Government'.[64]

More invidiously, the Liberian government's penury and inability to pay salaries to public officers in full or on time partly encouraged them to practise corruption and exploitation like filching government funds or extorting from the indigenous Liberian population. The most notorious malpractice – the forced shipment of indigenous Liberians to Fernando Po by some prominent Americo-Liberians to labour for Spanish planters there – became a matter of international concern with grave implications for Liberia's sovereignty.[65]

56. League of Nations, 1930, pp. 147–70.
57. C. D. B. King, 1922, pp. 23–4; 1924, pp. 5–6.
58. C. M. Wilson, 1971, p. 154; F. Starr, 1925, pp. 128–9.
59. E. J. Barclay, 1934, pp. 2–4.
60. ibid.
61. C. D. B. King, 1927, pp. 33–6.
62. A. D. B. Henries, 1963, pp. 90–1.
63. C. M. Wilson, 1971, p. 154.
64. USNA, RDSL, 1909–29, 882/00/705, Critchlow to Garvey, Monrovia, 24 June 1921.
65. See below for discussion of the forced labour crisis in Liberia.

Ethiopia

The imposition of feudal levies and the increased exploitation of peasant and slave labour in the far-flung provinces conquered by Menelik placed substantial funds in the coffers of the Ethiopian government. However, Ethiopia, like Liberia, was not undergoing any significant economic development. Such economic and social changes as did occur during our period were too limited to alter significantly Ethiopia's essentially feudal economy and conservative socio-economic fabric.

The principal initiator of economic and social change was the Regent, Tafari Makonnen. One of his first reforms was the extension of Menelik's ministerial system by the establishment in 1922 of a Ministry of Commerce and a Department of Public Works. In 1923, he set up the Berhanena Salam, or 'Light and Peace', printing press, which was purchased in Germany and supervised by Gabra Krestos Takla Haymanot who had been educated by Swedish missionaries in Eritrea. This press printed a newspaper of the same name, founded in 1925, as well as religious and educational books, and contributed significantly to the development of Amharic literature.[66]

Reform of Ethiopia's slavery impinged on both Ethiopia's internal stability and Ethiopia's relations with foreign powers. Hence it proved problematic. Tafari, much preoccupied with international relations, was quick to appreciate the advantages which the League of Nations and its system of collective security seemed to offer. He applied for Ethiopia to join the organization at its founding in 1919. However, though France gave its support, Britain contended that Ethiopia would not be able to fulfil its obligations as a member-state, especially those concerning the abolition of slavery. Bitter attacks on Ethiopian slavery appeared in the *Westminster Gazette* and other British newspapers, and suggestions were made that European powers or the League of Nations should intervene.

Tafari was probably more concerned with the diplomatic than the humanitarian side of the slavery question. He issued an edict in July 1922 reiterating the old prohibition on the sale of slaves, meted out stiff punishments to slave traders, and assured the British government of his willingness to protect and educate such slaves as might be freed at sea. On 15 September 1924, he issued a proclamation rendering slave raiding punishable by death.[67] The Regent's more incisive approach to slavery facilitated Ethiopia's entry into the League which, though still resisted by Britain, received support from Italy and France, both of whom hoped thereby to gain influence in Addis Ababa. Ethiopia, accordingly, became a member on 23 September 1923, when the Regent signed a declaration adhering to the principal international conventions for the suppression of slavery.

66. C. F. Rey, 1927, pp. 28–9.
67. C. Sandford, 1946, p. 58.

Almost immediately after issuing the anti-slavery decree, the Regent, accompanied by two of the principal noblemen, Ras Haylu Takla Haymanot of Gojam and Ras Seyoum Mangasha of Tigre, left for Palestine, Egypt, France, Belgium, Holland, Sweden, Italy, the United Kingdom, Switzerland and Greece. He met the French President, Raymond Poincaré, the Italian dictator, Benito Mussolini, and the British Prime Minister, Ramsay Macdonald, and urged them to grant Ethiopia a port in one of their nearby colonial territories. This diplomatic move, which ran counter to the interests of the three colonial powers in keeping Ethiopia isolated, was, however, fruitless. Tafari returned with only a few vague promises – and the crown of Emperor Tewodros, returned by the British who had looted it sixty-six years earlier.

As far as Ethiopia's internal affairs were concerned, however, the visit has been compared with Peter the Great's stay in Western Europe,[68] since it was very significant in awakening Ethiopian society to the outside world and the need to adopt foreign inventions and develop Ethiopia's manpower. The Regent and Ras Haylu purchased several motor cars and thereby set a fashion among the Ethiopian nobility. Consequently the number of vehicles in Addis Ababa rapidly increased to several hundred.[69] Increasing numbers of Ethiopian youths were sent abroad for study, mainly to Lebanon, Egypt, France, the United Kingdom and the United States.

A new hospital, the Bet Sayda, was founded by the Regent in 1924, and run by a Swede, Dr Kurt Hanner.[70] A couple of years later, Tafari, despite opposition from the traditionalists, opened the country's second modern educational establishment, the Tafari Makonnen School, run by a French headmaster; its curriculum included French, English, Amharic, Arabic and scientific and other subjects. Tafari's opening speech referred to the 'crying need' for education without which the country could not maintain its independence, and called on his compatriots to found schools, as the time for mere lip-service to patriotism had passed.[71] Other developments of this period included the engaging, in 1925, of Belgian officers to train the Regent's bodyguard, the grant to two Greeks, in 1927, of a concession to build a road from Gore to Gambela on the western frontier, and the purchase, from France and Germany, in 1929, of the first aeroplanes, the coming of which had hitherto been prevented by the conservatism of some of the nobility.

After his coronation, Haile Sellassie continued his modernization work, and was assisted by three foreign advisers, General Virgin, a Swede, in foreign affairs; E. A. Colson, an American, in finance; and M. Auberson, a Swiss, in legal matters.[72] Development was, however, seriously affected

68. R. Greenfield, 1965, p. 157.
69. R. Pankhurst, 1968, pp. 290–1.
70. L. Farago, 1935, pp. 132–3.
71. R. Pankhurst, 1962(b), pp. 266–7.
72. G. L. Steer, 1936, pp. 28–9.

by the world economic depression, which led to a fall in exports and a decline in foreign investment possibilities. A law was nevertheless proclaimed in 1930 for the survey and registration of land, and in the same year, a Ministry of Education was established. The year 1931 witnessed three significant developments. The first was the promulgation of the written Constitution which has already been discussed. The second was the replacement of the old Bank of Abyssinia, a foreign-owned private company, by a national bank, the Bank of Ethiopia. The third was the passing of a supplementary law for the gradual eradication of slavery, which laid down that all slaves should be freed on the death of their master, and envisaged the day 'when slavery shall have completely disappeared'.[73]

Efforts were also made to improve communications. A Ministry of Public Works was set up in 1932 and road-building was restarted. A temporary radio station was put into operation in 1933, and replaced by a more powerful one, erected by an Italian company, in 1935. Several new schools were opened, the best of which were run by the government, though there were also some educational activities by missionaries, particularly in the provinces. By 1935, Addis Ababa had fourteen government schools, with thirty foreign teachers and some four thousand students. Provincial education was also initiated by the establishment of government schools at Dessie, Gondar, Jijiga, Lakamti, Dire Dawa, Harar, Asba Tafari, Ambo, Jimma, Dabra Marqoa, Makalle and Salale, while a military college was founded in 1934 at Holeta, near Addis Ababa, and run by Swedish officers.[74] The number of students studying abroad rose to several hundred. There were also activities in the medical field, mainly by missionaries, notably the United Presbyterian Church of North America, the Seventh Adventist Mission, and the Italian Catholic Mission, all of which operated hospitals in Addis Ababa, while the Sudan Interior Mission ran a leprosarium at Akaki.[75] Other developments included the creation of a small civil service, partly formed with students returning from abroad, which received salaries instead of the revenues from fiefs, and the increasing replacement of tribute in kind by taxes in cash. A decree to curtail labour services from the peasant was enacted in 1934, and legislation for the reform of the land tax in 1935. Efforts at modernization were, however, by then overshadowed by the impending threat of Italian Fascist invasion.[76]

Thus the period between 1915 and 1935 witnessed a wider spread and a greater degree of economic and social change in Liberia and Ethiopia than before. However, this change did not amount to much and both countries therefore remained economically backward and socially undeveloped. Finally, investment by foreign nationals and firms in commercial, agricultural and mining enterprises was greater in Liberia than in Ethiopia;

73. A. L. Gardiner, 1933, p. 202.
74. E. Virgin, 1936, pp. 117–24; A. Zervos, 1936, pp. 223–32.
75. A. Zervos, 1936, pp. 255–7.
76. R. Pankhurst, 1968, pp. 177–9.

and while it aided the processes of modernization, it also led to greater foreign control of the Liberian economy than was the case in Ethiopia.

Foreign intervention in Liberia and Ethiopia, 1915–35

Liberia

Foreign intervention in Liberia and Ethiopia, already discussed in Chapter 11, persisted during the period 1915–35. As in the era of the Scramble and partition, the grounds for intervention were provided as much by events and circumstances within Liberia and Ethiopia as by those in Europe and America.

First, the Liberian government's penury and perennial indebtedness partly led to increased foreign control of Liberia's financial administration by the International Receivership, the Bank of British West Africa, and Firestone interests supported by the United States government. The Liberian economy was also dominated by European, American and Lebanese firms. Secondly, Liberia's unfavourable economic, social and administrative conditions became a major issue in the bitter political rivalry between the True Whig and People's parties and attracted considerable international attention. Within Liberia, Faulkner, the opposition leader, wooed the support of the indigenous Liberians by denouncing the use of forced labour for public works, forced recruitment of labour for export abroad, maladministration of the Liberian hinterland and national election malpractices.[77] He also travelled to Europe and America, following his second election defeat in 1927, both to gain international support, and to discredit the True Whig administration of President King.[78]

It was in January 1930 during Faulkner's visit to the United States that the influential *New York Times* reported on maladministration in Liberia. Simultaneously, it reported favourably on Faulkner as a 'progressive-minded citizen'.[79] Earlier, too, in 1929, the British press had carried several editorials highly critical of the Liberian government. More importantly, the reports in both the American and British press and other reports by foreign missionaries and visitors accused the Liberian government and certain influential Americo-Liberians of practising slavery, recruiting forced and indentured labour, and exporting or selling migrant labour to European colonies especially to the Spanish island-colony of Fernando Po.[80]

Britain spearheaded the foreign attack, condemning the exports and demanding, as in 1907–9, that to ameliorate the unfavourable conditions

77. T. J. R. Faulkner, 1926.
78. A. G. Jones, n.d.
79. R. E. Anderson, 1952, p. 98.
80. A. G. Jones, n.d.

in Liberia, her government should be placed under European control.[81] The United States similarly berated Liberia about 'the so-called "export" of labour from Liberia to Fernando Po ... which seems hardly distinguishable from organized slave trade'. She went on to hint that the governments of the world might have to consider 'some effective and affirmative action'[82] to terminate the situation!

Rather indiscreetly, perhaps, President King not only denied the charges but also appealed to the League of Nations for an investigation. The League accordingly appointed a fact-finding Commission to Liberia comprising a British dentist, Dr Cuthbert Christy, as Chairman; a black American sociology professor, Dr Charles S. Johnson; and Liberia's ex-president, Arthur Barclay. The Commission conducted an inquiry for four months only, and neither visited Fernando Po nor levied any charges against Spain. In the end it filed its Report on 8 September 1930. The Report showed that while no form of organized slave trading existed, labour was wastefully and forcibly recruited for public works, private use and for export with the collaboration of the Liberian Frontier Force and high government officials.[83] The Report also examined Americo-Liberian/indigenous Liberian relations and the general administration of the Liberian government, both of which it found unsatisfactory.[84] Hence it recommended to the League that Liberia should be placed under a 'capable and warmhearted white administration'.[85]

In view of the largely deplorable internal conditions in Liberia, most of the Commission's findings and recommendations were fair and reasonable in many respects. However, had the Commission made an objective study of contemporary European colonial policies, it would have been less harsh on the Liberian government's errors of omission or commission and perhaps less ready to endorse 'white administration' of Liberia, since the European colonial regimes were equally, if not more, brutal than Liberia in some of their policies towards their colonial subjects, including the use of forced labour for public works.[86]

Reacting to the Christy Report, the League of Nations pressed Liberia to abolish slavery and the export of labour to Fernando Po, to reorganize the Liberian government, and to institute basic reforms to give equal opportunities for all Liberians. On its own part the United States government expressed 'profound shock' at the 'shocking suppression of the natives' revealed in the Report. It urged that in order not to strain traditional United States–Liberian relations, the Liberian government must promptly abolish 'the twin scourges of slavery and forced labor' and carry out 'a compre-

81. ibid.
82. Republic of Liberia, 1930, p. 1.
83. J. G. Liebenow, 1969, pp. 64–70; League of Nations, 1930, pp. 168–70.
84. E. J. Yancy, 1934, pp. 201–20.
85. J. G. Liebenow, 1969, pp. 64–70.
86. A. G. Jones, n.d.

hensive system of reforms ...'[87] This statement led to the institution of impeachment proceedings by the Liberian Legislature against Vice-President Allen Yancy (who was a labour recruiting agent) and President King (Plate 28.4), both of whom resigned in early December 1930 before the passage of the Bill of impeachment.[88]

Thus prompted, the new administration of Edwin J. Barclay, who succeeded President King, decided to implement the recommendations of the League. Accordingly, the Liberian Legislature passed several Acts between December 1930 and May 1931 which abolished the export of labour, pawning and domestic slavery; substituted voluntary communal labour on public works for forced labour; reopened the entire Liberian hinterland to foreign traders, and reorganized the hinterland administration into three provinces with provincial and subordinate district commissioners and paramount chiefs.[89]

In spite of those reforms – which, of course, the Liberian government could not effectively or willingly implement in their entirety – Britain and the United States refused to recognize the Barclay administration and conducted their affairs in Liberia through their respective chargés d'affaires. Britain in particular persistently attacked Liberia and initiated certain measures to terminate her independence. Less than two months after Barclay became President, Britain requested the United States to make a joint representation 'in the strongest terms' to the Liberian government to urge it to petition the League of Nations to appoint a Governing Commission which the Christy Report had recommended.[90]

The joint representation urging 'that the Government of Liberia should be committed for a time to an International Governing Commission' which would carry out the necessary reforms was made to President Barclay on 21 January 1931 by the envoys of Britain, the United States and Germany (persuaded by Britain to join in the movement). Barclay and his Cabinet promptly and rightly rejected the urging since they considered 'that acceptance thereof would not only be a violation of the Constitution of the Republic, but would also be tantamount to a surrender of its sovereignty and autonomy'.[91] Barclay and his Cabinet, however, went on to express readiness to seek and accept assistance from the League of Nations, particularly in the form of experts in such fields as economics, judicial organization, public health, and 'native' administration.[92]

Accordingly, the League commissioned another fact-finding mission, this time consisting of representatives of eight nations – Britain, France, Germany, Italy, Spain, Venezuela, Poland and Liberia – charged with the

87. Republic of Liberia, 1931(a), pp. 2–3.
88. A. G. Jones, n.d.
89. Republic of Liberia, 1931(a), pp. 11–12; 1931(b); E. J. Barclay, 1934.
90. R. E. Anderson, 1952, pp. 110–11; A. G. Jones, n.d.
91. E. J. Barclay, 1931, p. 37.
92. ibid., p. 38.

PLATE 28.4 *President C. D. B. King of Liberia*

responsibility to end slavery and forced labour, and to give technical assistance to Liberia. The United States was requested to send a representative
although it was not a member of the League. Once again a Briton, Lord
Robert Cecil, was appointed chairman of the new commission. A small
committee of three persons headed by a French lawyer, Henri Brunot,
was also appointed to advise the mission on the financial and administrative
reforms necessary in Liberia to make the League's assistance successful.
The Committee subsequently visited Liberia during June and July 1931
to investigate conditions, collect data and make a report.

Like its predecessor, this second commission drew up elaborate plans
for the improvement of Liberia's internal administration, finances, and
public health. In January 1932 the Brunot Commission also presented its
Report to the League. Its recommendations were similar in many respects
to those of the Christy Commission but less unfavourable to Liberia on
the whole. Traditional African communal labour was to replace forced
labour for public works; the indigenous Liberians were to be granted an
undisputed ownership of their lands, the authority and dignity of the
African chiefs were to be upheld by the Liberian government, and the
education of the indigenous Liberians and the means of communication
with the Liberian hinterland were to be improved. The hinterland was
to be divided into three provinces to be administered by foreign provincial
and deputy commissioners under whom would be Liberian county super-
intendents and district commissioners. The commission also suggested that
for Liberia's finances to improve reasonably, Firestone would have to
modify the terms of the loan agreement of 1926.[93]

This intervention in Liberian affairs by the League significantly increased the opposition to the Liberian Government of many indigenous
Liberians, particularly the Kru, Grebo and Vai. Many of them believed
that the 'white men' would soon take over the Liberian government from
the Americo-Liberians; hence they ceased to pay taxes or perform forced
labour on public projects like road building. Simultaneously, some of them
revived intra-ethnic conflicts over disputed boundaries, farmlands and
chieftainships.

To maintain peace and order, President Barclay sent a detachment of
the Liberian Frontier Force to the Kru and Grebo districts in May 1931
with specific instructions to its Americo-Liberian commander, Colonel T.
Elwood Davis, that the detachment was 'a patrol in force and not a punitive
expedition'.[94] However, in the course of the patrol, fighting broke out
between the detachment and the Kru of Sasstown led by their paramount
chief, Juah Nimley, which provided fresh grounds for external intervention
in Liberian affairs. Several biased reports to the League, including
that of Rydings, the British chargé d'affaires in Monrovia,[95] portrayed

93. B. N. Azikiwe, 1934, p. 165.
94. E. J. Barclay, 1931, p. 8.
95. J. Rydings, 1932.

the detachment as a punitive expedition and charged it with wanton destruction of the lives and property of the Kru people.

Predictably, the United States and British governments reacted to these reports by demanding that the Liberian government should put an end to the so-called military reprisals against the Kru 'pending the conclusion of an arrangement between the League, the United States and Liberia for the future administration of the country'.[96] The Liberian government on its own part promptly protested to the League against this fresh threat by America and Britain against Liberia's sovereignty.[97] In addition, President Barclay sent a fact-finding commission of three men led by Winthrop A. Travell, an American employed in Liberia's fiscal service, to ascertain the situation on the Kru coast.

The commission's subsequent findings largely refuted the charges of wanton destruction made against the Frontier Force detachment.[98] And, fortunately for Liberia, the League reacted not by imposing a foreign administration over Liberia as America and Britain had mooted, but by sending a representative, Dr Melville D. Mackenzie, a British physician, to assist the Liberian government in pacifying the Kru.

Furthermore, on the receipt of the Brunot Report, the League's Liberia Committee drew up the 'General Principles of the Plan of Assistance' to Liberia. These were adopted on 27 September 1932 by the Committee and accepted by the Liberian Government on condition that the negotiations it was to carry out with Firestone were successful. The financial negotiations took place in London in June 1933 and resulted in a report presented by Mr Lighthart, the League expert on finance who had participated in them. On the basis of the 'General Principles' and the Lighthart Report, the League's Liberia Committee drew up a 'Protocol' embodying the proposed plan of assistance and reforms. These included the employment of foreign 'specialists' as provincial and deputy commissioners; a 'Chief Adviser' to the Liberian government appointed by the Council of the League with the agreement of the Liberian President, who would serve as liaison between the Liberian Government and the League; and two medical officers for hospital and health work in the Republic.

If implemented, the recommendations of the League Committee could have effected the radical changes in Liberia which the Americo-Liberian leaders as a rule feared. They could also have severely encroached on Liberia's sovereignty and considerably drained Liberia's finances considering the wide powers of the 'Chief Adviser' and the high salaries of the foreign specialists. Not surprisingly, therefore, President Barclay, while

96. E. J. Barclay, 1932, pp. 2–4.
97. ibid., pp. 7–8.
98. ibid., pp. 9–14. The other members of the Travell Mission were two Liberians: Dr F. A. K. Russell of Sinoe and Dr J. F. B. Coleman of Montserrado. Actually the commission made a majority report (Russell and Coleman), and a minority report (Travell) which was apparently the one the Liberian government accepted.

accepting the plan of assistance as embodied in the League's Liberia Committee 'Protocol', made some reservations about the powers of the 'Chief Adviser' and the expense which the implementation of the plan would involve. The League Committee, however, refused to revise the plan and withdrew it when Liberia – in spite of renewed threats of foreign intervention from the British and American governments – refused to accept it in its entirety.[99]

The Liberian government then drew up a 'Three Year Development Plan' of internal reforms in Liberia, including modifications to the Loan Agreement of 1926 already demanded by the Liberian government.[100] This plan won the support of the American government under President Franklin D. Roosevelt and formed the basis of the negotiations between Firestone, the United States and the Liberian government in 1935, during which the necessary modifications to the loan were made. The most important innovation was the principle 'that the cost of Government should be the first charge upon the revenues of the country, and not as heretofore when the cost of Government was borne out of the residue remaining after the cost of the fiscal administration and interest and sinking fund had been paid'.[101] The basic annual 'cost of Government' was fixed at \$450000, which was duly set aside annually from government revenue to meet the essential needs of government in the first place before Liberia's debt payments should be made. The interest on the loan was also reduced from 7 to 5%.[102]

Not surprisingly, as Liberia's relations with Firestone thus improved, Liberian–United States relations correspondingly improved, culminating in United States' recognition of the Barclay administration on 11 June 1935.[103] Britain followed suit on 16 December 1936,[104] by which event the crisis of Liberia's independence could be said to be formally over!

It is significant to note that although hard-pressed by the powers in the League, Liberia had not been without her vocal defenders and sympathizers. Most of them were individual Africans and black Americans or black religious, business or intellectual organizations who rightly argued that internal conditions in the European colonies in Africa were in many respects as bad as those in Liberia. Hence they strongly argued that Liberia's independence should not be sacrificed for the sake of the white man's economic interests exemplified by Firestone. Nor, they argued, should the double standard of condemning Liberia but turning a blind eye to white oppression in the colonies go unchallenged. Such individuals and organizations included Professor W. E. B. Du Bois; Mordecai Johnson, President

99. E. J. Barclay, 1934, pp. 2–4.
100. E. J. Barclay, 1934; R. L. Buell, 1947, pp. 41–4.
101. E. J. Barclay, 1935(a), p. 3.
102. ibid.
103. E. J. Barclay, 1935(b), p. 14.
104. E. J. Barclay, 1937, p. 14.

of Howard University; Nnamdi Azikiwe, a Nigerian journalist; the Lott Carey Baptist Foreign Mission Society, the A.M.E. Church; the National Association for the Advancement of Coloured People (NAACP), and a section of the Black press like the Baltimore *Afro-American*. Their exertions for Liberia's cause perhaps influenced but did not radically affect the United States government's policy towards Liberia in respect of the forced labour crisis.[105]

Ethiopia

Even more persistent and far more serious in its consequences was foreign intervention in the internal affairs of Ethiopia during the period under review. The Tripartite Convention of 1906 which divided Ethiopia into British, French and Italian spheres of interest was an indication that European imperialist intervention would sooner or later recur in Ethiopia. Menelik's death in 1913, the accession of Lij Iyasu and the events of the First World War spurred Italy in particular to revive her imperial designs against Ethiopia as from 1913. Thus between 1913 and 1919 the Italian Colonial Ministry vigorously sponsored the implementation of a 'minimum' or a 'maximum' programme of Italian colonization in Africa. Either programme sought particularly to give Italy control of the Red Sea and to make Ethiopia 'the exclusive sphere of influence of Italy'.[106] However, British and French imperial ambitions in North-East Africa conflicted with the Italian programme. In the end, the crucial Versailles Peace Treaty left the Italian programme largely unrealized.[107]

In spite of Italy's colonial ambitions in Ethiopia and the painful memories of Adowa, which many Italians wished to avenge, actual relations between Ethiopia and Italy were remarkably good during the Tafari Makonnen regency. Italy supported Ethiopia's entry into the League of Nations in 1923, and was one of the countries visited by Tafari during his epoch-making trip abroad in 1923.[108] Notwithstanding the friction during 1925–6 over Italy's continued claim to a sphere of influence in Ethiopia, a twenty-year treaty of friendship and arbitration was signed between the two countries on 2 August 1928 and reinforced by a convention granting Italy the right to construct a road from Assab to Dessie while Ethiopia was to be given a free zone at the port. These plans, however, were not implemented, for Italian policy began to switch from peaceful penetration to military intervention.

The change in Fascist policy occurred in 1930 when Marshal De Bono, the Italian Minister of the Colonies, urged the Italian Council of Ministers to increase his budget for 'expansion beyond the confines of the Father-

105. A. G. Jones, n.d.
106. R. L. Hess, 1963, pp. 105–8.
107. W. R. Louis, 1963(a).
108. R. Pankhurst, 1976.

land'.[109] In 1932, he visited Eritrea, and in 1933 held secret talks with Mussolini, at which he suggested the invasion of Ethiopia. Mussolini readily agreed and ordered him 'to go full speed ahead' and to be 'ready as soon as possible'. Steps were accordingly taken to improve the land, sea and air communications of the Italian colonies of Eritrea and Somalia, while Fascist agents began to foment political subversion in Ethiopia.[110] The secrecy surrounding Italy's intentions was abandoned on 18 March 1934 when Mussolini, addressing the Fascist Party, demanded that the 'satisfied' nations with colonies should abstain from blocking the 'cultural, political and economic expansion of Fascist Italy'.

Mussolini's pretext for invasion was the Wal Wal incident of 1934. An Anglo-Ethiopian boundary commission which had been demarcating the frontier between Ethiopia and British Somaliland arrived on 23 November at the wells of Wal Wal, 160 km on the Ethiopian side of the un-demarcated frontier with Italian Somaliland, which it found occupied by an Italian force. The commission's British chief, Colonel Clifford, protested to the Italians that their presence prevented his men from moving freely in Ethiopian territory, but withdrew to avoid an 'international incident'. The Ethiopians, on the other hand, stayed their ground, and the two armies faced each other until 5 December when a shot of indeterminate origin precipitated a clash, after which the Ethiopians, who were weakly armed, retired. Ethiopia invoked the treaty of friendship and arbitration of 1928, while Italy, rejecting arbitration, demanded an apology, Ethiopia's recognition of Italian sovereignty over Wal Wal, and an indemnity of 200 000 Maria Theresa dollars.[111] Britain and France, anxious to avoid a conflagration, urged Ethiopia to agree, but Haile Sellassie, fearing to encourage Italy to further expansion, refused, and took the matter to the League of Nations on 14 December. Realizing that Ethiopia was unwilling to capitulate, Mussolini gave secret orders on 30 December to prepare for an invasion, which required considerable preparation on account of Ethiopia's size and mountainous terrain.

The League appointed a committee to study the dispute, but Mussolini, who was now almost ready to strike, took little interest in the proceedings. The League's committee came out with compromise proposals which, in an effort to satisfy Italy, proposed placing Ethiopia under international control so as to prevent her from endangering the adjacent Italian colonies as Mussolini claimed. The Duce, however, no longer had any need for compromises. On 2 October, he ordered mobilization, and on the following day the Italian army, commanded by De Bono, crossed the Ethiopian frontier from Eritrea, without declaration of war, and Italian aircraft

109. St Antony's College, University of Oxford, captured Italian documents 112809.
110. E. de Bono, 1937, pp. 12–13, 15.
111. R. Cimmaruta, 1936; A. de La Pradelle, 1936, pp. 149–60; G. W. Baer, 1967, pp. 45–61.

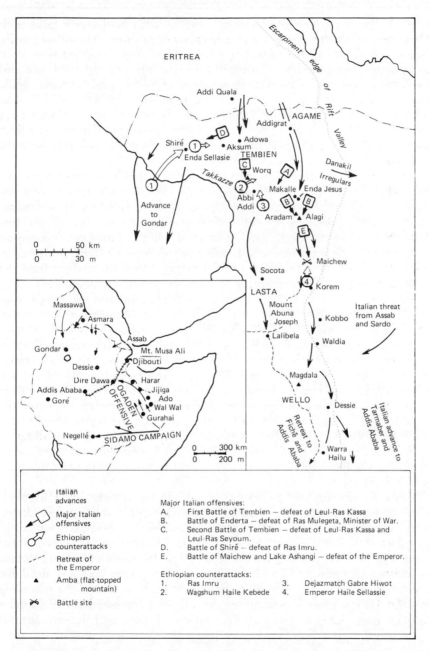

ERITREA

Addi Quala

AGAME

Escarpment edge of Rift Valley

Addigrat

Shiré
Enda Sellasie
Aksum
Adowa
TEMBIEN
Worq

Danakil
Irregulars

Makalle
Enda Jesus

Advance
to
Gondar

Takkazze

Abbi
Addi

Aradam
Alagi

| 0 | 50 km |
| 0 | 30 m |

Socota

Maichew

LASTA

Korem

Mount
Abuna
Joseph

Kobbo

Italian threat
from Assab
and Sardo

Lalibela

Waldia

Massawa

Asmara

Assab

Gondar

Mt. Musa Ali

Dessie

Djibouti

Magdala

Dire Dawa
Harar

Addis Ababa
Goré

Jijiga
Ado
Wal Wal
Gurahai

WELLO

Dessie

Negellé
SIDAMO CAMPAIGN

OGADEN OFFENSIVE

| 0 | 300 km |
| 0 | 200 m |

Retreat to
Fiché and
Addis Ababa

Italian advance to
Tarmaber and
Addis Ababa

Warra
Hailu

Italian
advances

Major Italian
offensives

Ethiopian
counterattacks

Retreat of
the Emperor

Amba (flat-topped
mountain)

Battle site

Major Italian offensives:
A. First Battle of Tembien — defeat of Leul-Ras Kassa
B. Battle of Enderta — defeat of Ras Mulegeta, Minister of War.
C. Second Battle of Tembien — defeat of Leul-Ras Kassa and
   Leul-Ras Seyoum.
D. Battle of Shiré — defeat of Ras Imru.
E. Battle of Maichew and Lake Ashangi — defeat of the Emperor.

Ethiopian counterattacks:
1. Ras Imru   3. Dejazmatch Gabre Hiwot
2. Wagshum Haile Kebede   4. Emperor Haile Sellassie

FIG. 28.2 *The Italian Fascist invasion of Ethiopia: the northern campaign (main map); the invasion as a whole (inset) (adapted from R. Greenfield, 1975)*

bombed Adowa. A force from Italian Somaliland also attacked from the south (see Fig. 28.2).

The invasion, despite its long preparation, provoked world consternation. The League Assembly met on 9 October and decided by fifty votes against one (Italy) with three abstentions (Albania, Austria and Hungary) that Italy was the aggressor and had violated the League Covenant.[112]

Despite this near-unanimous condemnation, the League, dominated by the colonial powers of France and Britain, was reluctant to offend Mussolini by resort to immediate and total sanctions as advocated by the Soviet Union. Instead, the League set up a Coordinating Committee which proposed only limited economic sanctions comprising four separate embargoes. These sanctions, which were applicable only to Member States, covered: (1) the export of arms and munitions to Italy; (2) loans and credits to Italy; (3) the import of all goods from Italy; and (4) the export to Italy of certain raw materials, including rubber, bauxite, aluminium, iron ore and scrap iron. The first of these sanctions was imposed on 11 October and the remainder on 18 November.[113] These prohibitions, described by Lord Keynes as 'comparatively mild economic sanctions',[114] proved totally ineffective. The fact, as Winston Churchill noted, was that these were 'not real sanctions to paralyse the aggressor, but merely such half-hearted sanctions as the aggressor would tolerate'.[115]

Undeterred by such ineffective measures, and spurred on by repeated telegrams from the Duce who wanted a quick victory before the League realized the need for more resolute action, the Italian army occupied Adowa on 6 October and Makalle on 8 November. Ethiopian resistance then obliged the invaders to halt. De Bono was thereupon recalled and replaced on 16 November by Marshal Badoglio, who, faced with a strong Ethiopian counter-offensive, also found it impossible to advance for many weeks. In the hope of breaking Ethiopian morale, Mussolini then insisted that his troops use poison gas.[116]

The failure of the League's limited sanctions led to demands that they be extended, above all to oil which was of crucial importance as Mussolini later admitted when he told Hitler that if it had been introduced, he 'would have had to withdraw from Abyssinia within a week'.[117] Britain and France were, however, resolutely opposed to this as they believed that Mussolini would interpret it as an act of war. The British and French foreign ministers, Hoare and Laval, therefore met in Paris on 7 December to devise a new compromise. It had two main principles: first, an 'exchange of territories' whereby Ethiopia would cede to Italy the Ogaden and a large

112. S. Heald (ed.), 1937, pp. 192–3.
113. ibid., pp. 193–4, 203–7. See also L. Villari, 1943, pp. 151–219.
114. *New Statesman and Nation*, 28 November 1935.
115. W. S. Churchill, 1948, pp. 172–3.
116. A. del Boca, 1969.
117. P. Aloisi, 1957, p. 324.

742

part of Tigre in exchange for a port on either the Red Sea or the Gulf of Aden; second, Italy would be given a 'zone of economic expansion and colonization' in the greater part of Ethiopia south of Addis Ababa; this area was to remain part of Ethiopia, but Italy was to have exclusive economic rights therein. News of this plan, which was a criminal surrender to the condemned aggressor and a total abandonment of the League, leaked to the French press, and created a storm of indignation in many countries, particularly in Britain where Hoare was obliged to resign on 18 December.[118]

Ethiopia at the close of 1935 was thus in the forefront of world news and the centre of international excitement and indignation.[119] A British Foreign Secretary had fallen for what was considered as Britain's betrayal, while in Ethiopia's rugged mountains a powerful Fascist army using the most modern weapons of war, including poison gas, was temporarily halted by the heroism of Ethiopia's relatively poorly-armed warriors.[120] It was a case of David and Goliath re-enacted in the greatest colonial war ever fought on the continent of Africa. Though the Ethiopian army was soon to be defeated, much fierce fighting lay ahead before the Italians occupied Addis Ababa on 6 May 1936. This was followed by five long years of Italian Fascist usurpation, during four of which the Ethiopian patriots were to fight on alone.[121]

The Duce's invasion evoked instant reaction in and around Africa.[122] In August 1935, a group of Africans and persons of African descent in London founded the International African Friends of Abyssinia, whose committee included C. L. R. James of the West Indies, Dr P. McD. Millard of British Guiana, Marcus Garvey's wife Amy Ashwood Garvey, Mohammed Said of Somaliland, and Dr J. B. Danquah of the Gold Coast. The Society's aim, as stated by its secretary, Jomo Kenyatta, was 'to assist by all means in their power in the maintenance of the territorial integrity and political independence of Abyssinia'.[123]

The subsequent outbreak of fighting, which placed Ethiopia in the headlines of every newspaper, made a deep impact on African thinking. Kwame Nkrumah, then a student passing through England, recalled that when he saw posters declaring 'Mussolini invades Ethiopia' he was seized by emotion, and added:

> At that moment it was almost as if the whole of London had suddenly declared war on me personally. For the next few minutes I could

118. S. Heald (ed.), 1937, pp. 316–413.
119. For a recent account of the Italo-Ethiopian crisis, see F. Hardie, 1974.
120. On the war see Haile Sellassie, 1936; G. L. Steer, 1936; E. de Bono, 1937; P. Badoglio, 1937; R. Graziani, 1938; R. Greenfield, 1965, pp. 196–266; A. J. Barker, 1968; A. del Boca, 1969; G. Rochet, 1971; F. Bandini, 1971.
121. R. Pankhurst, 1970.
122. W. R. Scott, 1966 and 1972, pp. 132–8; R. Ross, 1972.
123. *New Times and Ethiopia News*, 30 January 1954; R. Makonnen, 1973, pp. 112–20. See also S. K. B. Asante, 1977.

do nothing but glare at each impassive face wondering if these people could possibly realise the wickedness of colonialism, and praying that the day might come when I could play my part in bringing about the downfall of such a system. My nationalism surged to the fore; I was ready to go through hell itself, if need be, in order to achieve my object.[124]

Similar sentiments were aroused all over Africa. The Nigerian intellectual, Nnamdi Azikiwe, devoted much space to Ethiopia's struggle in his newspapers, the *West African Pilot* and the *Comet*, and later recalled in his influential work, *Renascent Africa*, which has been called 'a Bible for Africans', the excitement aroused in a typical school in the Gold Coast when students heard how 'black soldiers, aided by the invisible hand of God were outwitting and overthrowing their enemies'.

Ethiopia, the first foreign victim of Italian Fascism, and the rallying point for advocates of collective security, was thus at the end of 1935 the burning symbol of Africa's awakening from colonial rule.

The outcome for Liberia and Ethiopia of the European imperialist intervention

By the end of 1936 Liberia had survived foreign intervention with her sovereignty intact, whereas Ethiopia had succumbed to it and her sovereignty had been terminated – albeit temporarily. What was responsible for this difference?

The internal situation in Liberia and Ethiopia up to the time of the Italian invasion on 3 October 1935, though of great historical significance, was largely irrelevant in the determination of the final outcome of the foreign intervention. Indeed, the situation in both countries did not differ in any significant respects. The central governments of both had internal opponents who sought to exploit the situation of foreign intervention for their own purposes by allying with the foreign powers, notably the opposition People's Party in Liberia, and feudal nobles like Leul-Ras Hailu and Dejazmatch Haile Sellassie Gugsa.[125]

Both countries, although not lacking in ardent patriots ready to defend the Fatherland at the cost of their lives, were militarily very weak compared with the military might of their potential or actual foreign aggressors. The Liberian militia of all able-bodied men – mostly Americo-Liberians – was largely irregularly trained and lacked arms. The Frontier Force, Liberia's standing army, was similarly poorly trained and armed, and irregularly and poorly paid and provisioned. In September 1920, for instance, arrears of salaries due to both the officers and men of the Force amounted to $90 689.52, which greatly lowered their morale.[126] Discipline and training

124. K. Nkrumah, 1957, p. 22.
125. R. Greenfield, 1965, pp. 192–4.
126. Republic of Liberia, 1920, p. 9.

of the Force was reported to be so unsatisfactory that it was 'extremely difficult to get an order carried out either in letter or spirit'.[127] The Force numbered altogether 821 men in November 1917, 767 in December 1920, and 744 in December 1925. In 1935 a Liberian author described Liberia as 'not more than an infant' in matters of self-defence: she had no navy or air fleet.[128]

As for Ethiopia, her armed forces consisted of feudal levies of the governors and shums, the troops of the central government, and Haile Sellassie's own standing army.[129] Only the last was trained and armed in the modern manner. The others were 'men who lack all training other than that afforded by their natural aptitude for warfare and their traditions'.[130]

Quite clearly, neither Liberia nor Ethiopia was in a position to match the might of a European invasion. The crucial difference in the survival of Liberia and the non-survival of Ethiopia would be that whereas one faced a determined, European military intervention, the other did not.

Following from this, one might ask why the intervention occurred in the one and not in the other country. In answering this question, it is important to bear in mind that up to the end of 1935, neither Liberia nor Ethiopia enjoyed any uncompromising sympathy, support or protection from the foreign powers within or outside the League of Nations, or of the League itself. In spite of its acknowledged, traditional friendship with Liberia, the United States demonstrated numerous times over during the forced labour crisis that it toed the line of the European colonial powers who had designs on Liberia's sovereignty, particularly in supporting the plan for an international governing commission over Liberia.

The great diplomatic competence of the Liberian Government, particularly of Liberia's brilliant intellectual President, Edwin J. Barclay, and Liberia's negotiator in Geneva and Secretary of State, Louis A. Grimes, should also be taken into account. By silencing local opposition by force or persuasion, and by most doggedly holding to the principle of self-determination for Liberia, the Liberian leaders promoted the cause of their country's sovereignty. However, since Ethiopian leaders including Haile Sellassie were also competent in diplomacy and ardent guardians of their country's sovereignty, the survival of Liberia seems to dwell ultimately in the fact that Ethiopia had a mad, blood-thirsty imperial power as a neighbour who was bent on territorial aggrandizement and above all on avenging Adowa, and therefore on actually attacking Ethiopia. On the other hand, Britain and France already possessed expansive colonial territories in Africa and had no Adowa to avenge and they therefore had no compelling motivation to attack and conquer Liberia in the same manner that Italy attacked and conquered Ethiopia.

127. Major M. Staten, 1925.
128. E. J. Yancy, 1934, pp. 93–9.
129. R. Greenfield, 1965, pp. 194–5, 199–201.
130. E. Virgin, quoted in ibid., p. 194.

Africa and the New World

R. D. RALSTON
with sections on Latin America and the
Caribbean by ALBUQUERQUE MOURÃO

Substantial African expatriate communities or influences have affected such diverse regions of the world as classical Greece and Rome; Portugal (since the fifteenth century); the Caribbean; the United States (since the seventeenth century); Britain (since the eighteenth century); Canada (particularly after the American War of Independence); Brazil (particularly since the eighteenth century); Saudi Arabia; India; and, occasionally, Turkey. Meanwhile, variations on the African diaspora have been represented in the coming and going of African traders, sailors, interpreters, educators and African students in the Americas, and in the resettlement of black North Americans, Afro-Brazilians and Afro-Cubans in Africa. Linkages between what became the two principal spheres of the black world – Africa and the Americas – were maintained over time through exchanges of personnel, cultural materials, and political ideology. The purpose of this chapter is to delineate the interactions between Africans and peoples of African descent in the Americas during the colonial period of African history.

African and American black linkages during the period 1880–1935 consisted essentially of five types of activities: (1) back-to-Africa movements or black emigration – mostly from North America, but also from the Caribbean and Brazil – into parts of Africa (mostly West Africa, but also South Africa and the Horn); (2) American evangelism featuring Afro-American missionaries as 'gospel conductors' in Africa; (3) a renewed Middle Passage in the form of a stream of African students matriculating at American black schools and universities; (4) several varieties of pan-Africanist activities, including conferences, organizations and educational, literary or commercial activities which put Africans in touch with the black world of the Americas and which helped to influence events in colonial Africa; and (5) persistence and transformation of African cultural values in Latin America and the Caribbean. These five themes will be discussed in turn in the five divisions of this chapter.

Back-to-Africa movements

Despite a discernible shift in black sentiment away from Liberian emigration apparent among North American blacks during the first half of the
nineteenth century, Afro-Americans continued to display an interest in
African emigration in the late nineteenth and early twentieth centuries.
Indeed, if anything, the emigration tradition championed earlier by blacks
like Daniel Coker, Lott Cary, John B. Russwurm, Paul Cuffee, Henry
H. Garnet and Martin R. Delany, was continued and enlarged upon in
the last quarter of the nineteenth century. In 1878, for example, the South
Carolina-Liberian Exodus Joint Stock Steamship Company brought 206
black immigrants to Liberia. In 1881, Henry H. Garnet was appointed
resident minister and consul-general to Liberia, fulfilling his own earlier
convictions; and in 1889, the St Thomas-born West Indian pan-Africanist,
Dr Edward W. Blyden, visited the United States from Liberia on behalf
of the American Colonization Society (ACS) to help generate black support
for emigration. Moreover, between 1880 and 1900, Bishop Henry NcNeal
Turner laboured to combine the two traditions long dominant in the modern
history of African/Afro-American interaction: African emigration and
Christian evangelism. Similarly, widespread interaction between Africans
and American blacks occurred because of the return of thousands of
Brazilian blacks to West Africa until the time of the official abolition of
slavery in Brazil (1888). Upon resettlement in or near their previous homes
in Nigeria, Dahomey (now Benin), Togo and the Gold Coast (now Ghana),
the Afro-Brazilians' technical and commercial competence and political
aspirations seem to have broadly affected the social, economic and political
conditions there. Possibly because of the absence of differentiation of themselves as a corporate community of settlers in their regions – such as was
the case in Liberia – there were subsequently little differentiation between
the social and political goals of indigenous Africans and Afro-Brazilians.

Liberia – although founded by American whites through the ACS long
before the period of the Scramble – occupies a special place in any consideration of immigration between different spheres of the black world.
Partly as a result of Blyden's efforts to muster support for ACS programmes,
a bill to aid black emigrants was debated in the United States Senate in
1889. Also, by 1892 black applications to the ACS for passage to Liberia
had increased rapidly and several hundred black farmers from Arkansas
and Oklahoma arrived in New York hoping to be transported to Africa.
Moreover, in 1893, when he visited Liberia, Bishop Turner glowingly
reported that 'one thing the Black man has here [in Liberia] . . . is Manhood,
freedom; and the fullest liberty; he feels like a Lord and walks the same
way'.[1] And again in 1896 he asserted: 'I believe two or three million of
us should return to the land of our ancestors and establish our own nations,

1. L. Davis, 1974, p. 3.

civilizations, laws, customs, style of manufacture … and cease to be grumblers, chronic complainers and a menace to the white man's country he claims and is bound to dominate'.[2] Through Bishop Turner's efforts, over 300 Afro-Americans emigrated to Liberia in March 1896. Even the young W. E. B. Du Bois – later to be an opponent of emigration as a solution to black Americans' problems – endorsed Turner's emigration idea as a commendable alternative to 'the humiliating experience of begging for justice and recognition' in the United States.[3]

While in Liberia, Bishop Turner advised what he called American 'black capitalists' that 'if they would start trading with Liberia they would be worth millions in a few years'. Few responded, although a group did organize the African Development Society in 1899, the chief objective of which was to encourage Afro-Americans to buy land and settle in East Central Africa. The Society would sell shares or land rights offered by African petitioners but only to Afro-American or African purchasers.[4] Bishop Turner also later served as an adviser to the International Migration Society (IMS) of Alabama, which sent about 500 emigrants to Africa before it became defunct in 1900. Some of the 500 remained in Liberia; others returned to the United States. Those who remained fared reasonably well; evidently more than a few of them prospered. On the other hand, those who returned told horror stories of poor land, inadequate food and poor living conditions. These stories reduced the likelihood of any large-scale Afro-American emigration movement, even though prospects for blacks in the United States were declining from 1895 to 1900. Nevertheless, numerous Afro-Americans evidently continued to give serious consideration to African emigration, just as others in the United States and the Caribbean simply moved away from overt discriminatory practices into other regions near by.

After the turn of the twentieth century, the back-to-Africa baton was picked up by others. For example, one Captain Dean, early in the twentieth century, hoped to engineer the settlement of American blacks in South Africa to fashion a powerful black state there. After the briefest sojourn meant to arrange for this settlement, however, white authorities expelled Dean from the Cape for what were termed 'provocative activities'. And in 1914, Chief Alfred C. Sam, a Gold Coast African, turned up in Oklahoma, persuaded about sixty black farmers that Africa offered them greater opportunities and sailed with them to Saltpond in the Gold Coast. Finding Chief Sam's claims to be exaggerated and encountering restrictions from the Gold Coast officials which inhibited the entry of American immigrants, most of the Oklahomans eventually returned to the United States. But no one made so deep an impression as an advocate of emigration on Africans and

2. ibid., p. 5.
3. ibid.
4. A. C. Hill and M. Kilson (eds), 1971, pp. 192–4.

American blacks alike as did Marcus Garvey who was born in Jamaica in 1887.

Because of his general appeal to black pride, Garvey focused the attention of millions of American blacks on Africa in the period following the First World War. Dr Du Bois later observed that 'within a few years [of Garvey's rise], news of his movement, of his promises and plans, reached Europe and Asia, and penetrated every corner of Africa'.[5] His travels in the Caribbean, Central and South America and a two-year sojourn in Britain persuaded Garvey that the uniform plight of blacks required a militant self-help programme. Two specific aspects of his London experience affected his thinking; the reading of Booker T. Washington's *Up From Slavery* (1899), because of which he later said he was 'doomed' to become a race leader,[6] and his encounter with the Egyptian intellectual Duse Muhammed Ali, a staunch critic of Britain and American African policies in his book *In the Land of the Pharaohs* (1911). Duse himself had earlier travelled and worked briefly as a stage actor and political activist in the United States before settling in London.

After returning to Jamaica, in 1914 Garvey founded his project designed to advance African emigration and related programmes and called it the Universal Negro Improvement and Conservation Association and African Communities League (later simply the UNIA). At the age of 28, Garvey went to the United States attracted by Washington's work, fired by Duse's example, and armed with a programme of race redemption: the establishment of industrial and agricultural schools for blacks in Jamaica, a Black Star fleet of ships for commerce between blacks in Africa and the Americas, and, most of all, a 'central nation for the race'. Liberia, long a focus of Afro-American emigrationism, became the lodestone for Garvey's emigration schemes.

Garvey sent an emissary to Liberia in May 1920, who laid out the aims of the Association: transfer of UNIA headquarters to Liberia, financial aid to Liberia for constructing schools and hospitals, liquidation of Liberia's debts, and the settlement of American blacks in Liberia, who would help to develop agriculture and natural resources.[7] The Liberian government enthusiastically granted UNIA's initial request for land outside Monrovia and Garvey in turn sent a group of technicians to survey the site and erect buildings for between 20 000 and 30 000 families whom he hoped to send over the course of two years beginning about 1924. But when Garvey's technicians arrived in Maryland County in May 1924, they were arrested, detained, and in July 1924, deported. It was not long before the Liberian government proscribed the UNIA altogether, thus guaranteeing the failure of the Garvey colonization scheme in Liberia.

Meanwhile, in another venue on the other side of the African continent,

5. W. E. B. Du Bois, 1968, p. 277.
6. A. J. Garvey (ed.), 1923–5, Vol. I, p. 126.
7. See M. B. Akpan, 1973(a); F. Chalk, 1967, pp. 135–42.

PLATE 29.1 *Marcus Garvey (1887–1940), founder and leader of the Universal Negro Improvement Association*

Garvey sent a small mission of skilled technicians in the late 1920s to investigate the possibilities of American black emigration to Ethiopia. The mission, however, encountered less enthusiasm than was anticipated. By the 1930s, there existed a tiny Afro-American community residing in Ethiopia. Some had come as a result of Garvey's appeals, but many of them came because of other factors. Recent, as well as earlier scholarship, reveals a good deal about Afro-American and Ethiopian relationships,[8] but the subject remains an underworked one in African–American relations.

A black rabbi, Arnold Ford, from Barbados (via New York) emigrated to Ethiopia in 1930 and entertained in the Tambourine Club with Negro spirituals before it was 'closed down by the government for discriminating against local Ethiopian clients'.[9] While in Harlem, Ford became attracted to Garvey's message. It seems, therefore, that although the UNIA deputation failed to establish organizational links with the Horn of Africa as with Liberia, it did succeed in orienting a number of prospective American black emigrants towards service there. Possibly more individual Garveyites emigrated to Ethiopia than to Liberia. For despite its greater inaccessibility, Ethiopia's antiquity and grandeur might have 'exercised a stronger pull than the bourgeois' – and to Garvey's mind – 'anti-African politics of the Americo-Liberian ruling elite'.[10] Thus, when Garvey broke openly with the Liberian government, evidently many of his adherents looked fondly toward this new horizon.

However, while some American blacks who emigrated to Ethiopia in and after the 1920s were motivated generally by Garvey, the immediate trigger for their actions might have been a chance meeting with Ethiopian students or contact with the occasional Ethiopian delegation that went to New York in the late 1920s 'to solicit trained Negro Colonists for Africa'.[11] Moreover, Ford, like Bishop Turner, believed that American blacks bore a special redemptive role *vis-à-vis* Africa based on their years of suffering and exile. Ford himself answered such a call by a delegation of Fälasa (black Ethiopian Jews) and left for Ethiopia in 1930 where he evidently remained until his death during the time of the Italian–Ethiopian War (1935–6).[12] The majority of the American emigrants Ford encountered in Ethiopia when he arrived there were Jamaicans, and, occasionally, other Afro-Caribbean folk. A recent account suggests that 'the West Indians appear to have been more prepared than some of the Americans to make what adjustments were necessary to living in Ethiopia' although both groups suffered discrimination from time to time.[13]

8. See, for example, C. Coon, 1936; K. J. King, 1972, pp. 81–7; W. R. Scott, 1971.
9. C. Coon, 1936, p. 137.
10. K. J. King, 1972, p. 82.
11. ibid.
12. But for slightly different chronology see H. Brotz, 1970, p. 12 and W. R. Scott, 1971.
13. K. J. King, 1972, p. 82.

Of course, even before Garvey's time, other American blacks had emigrated to Ethiopia, but as individual settlers. For example, in the 1890s Benito Sylvain, a Haitian, brought to the Court of Menelik II a plan for a 'Pan-Negro' organization. Clearly, however, the largest waves of American black immigrants came in the late 1920s and early 1930s, that is, after Garvey's break with the Liberians and through the time of the Emperor's accession, with the greatest numbers of these responding to meetings with Ethiopian travellers. In the period immediately following the restoration of Haile Sellassie in 1941, a new trickle of Afro-Americans (possibly twenty) came to Ethiopia. The period, however, falls beyond the scope of this chapter. Suffice it to say that the numbers of black immigrants from the Americas to Ethiopia peaked during activities associated with Garvey, Ford and the Emperor and were not equalled before or after that era.[14]

The Afro-Brazilians

Contacts between Brazil and the west coast of Africa were facilitated by the establishment of regular mixed cargo and passenger lines, which thus replaced the slave ships. The British African Company and the African Steam-Ship Company, to mention but two, regularly plied between the ports of Bahía de Todos os Santos and Lagos. According to the *Weekly Times* of 11 October 1890, the steamer *Biaffra* returned to Lagos after its maiden voyage with 110 passengers and 400 tons of merchandise on board. At that time the volume of trade between the two coasts was quite considerable. According to Pierre Verger,[15] exports from Brazil 'consisted mainly of cigars, tobacco and rum', and imports took the form of 'local fabrics, woven from European cotton, cola nuts and palm oil'. Over the five years from 1881 to 1885 the average annual value of imports and exports was £19 084 and £11 259 sterling respectively.

Trade between the two seaboards, apart from its importance as such, led to the emergence of an African bourgeoisie made up of former slaves from Brazil and Cuba. This movement began at the end of the eighteenth century,[16] and became more marked after the revolt of the 'Malês' (Muslim slaves) in 1835. These bands of emigrants settled particularly in the coastal cities of Nigeria and Dahomey and, to a lesser extent, in Togo and the Gold Coast (see Fig. 29.1). They formed communities in these coastal areas, thus avoiding going inland with the exception of those who joined the Yoruba and Hausa groups and settled not only in Lagos but also in inland towns such as Abeokuta.[17] A large number of emigrants had been *negros de ganho* in Brazil, in other words, slaves living in the cities who plied their trades (as masons, carpenters, caulkers, and so on) quite freely

14. See W. R. Scott, 1971.
15. P. Verger, 1968, p. 623.
16. C. W. Newbury, 1961, pp. 36–7.
17. L. D. Turner, 1942, p. 65.

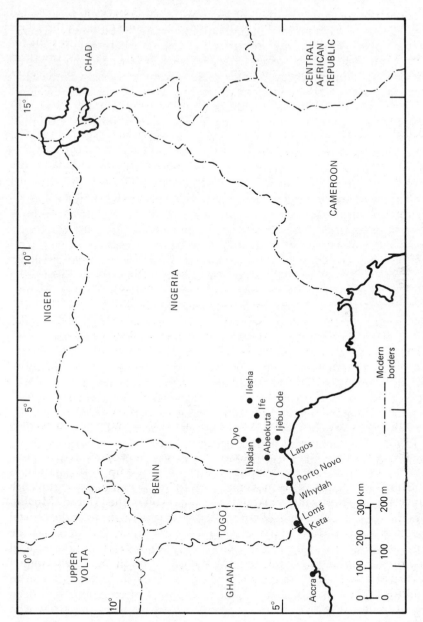

FIG. 29.1 *Afro-Brazilians in West Africa in the eighteenth and nineteenth centuries*

753

and shared their earnings with their masters. Bringing with them their technical know-how, a few outstanding builders created residential districts in Porto Novo, Whydah and in particular Lagos, where the Brazilian Quarter[18] was built. Here, to this day, in what is now Tinubu Square and in Campos Square, storeyed houses reminiscent of those of Bahia can be found, as well as large buildings such as the Catholic cathedral of Lagos or the mosque erected in the town centre. The style of these storeyed houses is to be seen in a few buildings in inland areas inhabited by the Yoruba. In Whydah as in Porto Novo, a type of building developed which, whether built in the grand manner or in more simple style, followed very closely the plan of the 'Casa-Grande' type of structure characteristic of the sugar mills or plantations of colonial Brazil.

In Dahomey some of the children who attended the schools of the English and French missionaries were used as assistants by the colonial administration, on account of their educational attainments. This group acquired a special status by virtue of its members' religion, housing and clothing and the fact that they engaged in the Atlantic trade and served in the colonial administration. However, they were not wholly accepted by European society[19] and were not always on good terms with the autochthonous African population owing to their habits and life styles.

Such groups gradually lost their specifically Afro-Brazilian characteristics for, although they had brought with them books from Brazil, such as the *Compêndio de Doutrina Christã* and *O Fabulista da Mocidadem*,[20] little by little, in schools, the language of instruction came to be exclusively that of the French or English colonizers. Furthermore, the descendants of the Yoruba, in order to become more integrated in local society, went back to using Yoruba names and some began to attend services in the African churches which derived from mission Protestantism.

In Lagos, the community maintained its identity, for instance, taking to the streets on feast days to perform folk dances, following in this the example of the Aurora Relief Society which, in 1900[21] continued to be identified with a small middle-class group. With time, however, this group lost its distinguishing features. Portuguese, once considered a commercial language, was supplanted by English in Nigeria and French in Dahomey.[22] A few forms of resistance were recorded, as for instance the appearance in 1920 of the newspaper *Le Guide du Dahomey* in Porto Novo[23] which, until 1922, published criticism of the French colonial administration.

18. D. Araedon in S. O. Biobaku (ed.), 1976, pp. 40–1.

19. J. M. Turner, 1975, Ch. V.

20. Bouche to Planque, Porto-Novo, 25 January 1869, Societ delle Missione Africane Archives, Rome, entry No. 21.150, Heading No. 12/80200 (11/082) (letter from Father Bouche to his superior, Father Planque).

21. *Lagos Standard*, 8 January 1896 and 2 May 1900.

22. M. C. da Cunha, 1976, p. 33.

23. J. A. Ballard, 1965, p. 16.

Another paper, *La Voix du Dahomey*,[24] published at a later date by the descendants of Afro-Brazilians, lamented the difficulty of engaging in foreign trade, as had been the practice before the establishment of the French administration.

In the Gold Coast the Afro-Brazilians, although established as a separate group on account of their more or less Westernized habits and known for that reason as the *Tabon*, gradually forsook their specifically Brazilian traditions, while retaining other cultural traits such as the beating of drums on the occasion of such festivities as the two-day-long annual procession through the old streets of Accra.[25] When the Tabon settled in the country, they had to sign a pact of vassalage with a Ga chief of Accra. They abandoned the use of the Portuguese language very early on, although a mixture of Ga, English and Portuguese is to be found in their songs. The rapid integration of the Tabon in the Gold Coast contrasts with the rather slow one of the Afro-Brazilians of Lagos, Abeokuta, Porto Novo, Whydah and other less important coastal towns in Nigeria, Dahomey and Togo.

In Lagos, alongside the Brazilian community, an Afro-Cuban community came into being, composed of the smaller number of individuals who had returned from Cuba.

Black American evangelism in Africa

One of the means by which African–American black interchanges were nurtured in the colonial period, short of mass migrations, was the coming of black missionaries to 'elevate' Africa by Christian evangelism. In the main, evangelization took the form of American black missionaries working, first, in the service of mainstream, predominantly white denominations. For example, the Presbyterian Church sponsored black missionaries in French Cameroon as early as 1896. And the Reverend William H. Sheppard, a black graduate of Hampton Institute, Virginia, prodded the Southern Presbyterian Church into undertaking missionary work in the Congo in the 1890s, where he represented the Church and quickly found that his mission was attracting converts by 'the hundreds' and expanding 'until it was one of the most important stations of Christianity'.[26] Meanwhile, at the turn of the twentieth century, the Seventh-Day Adventists dispatched three black missionaries to Nyasaland (now Malawi), and as a result of a five-year tour sent three young African adherents, including Daniel Sharpe Malekebu, to the American black schools for education. (Not only were some of the 'white church' evangelists black, but some white missionaries were placed in Afro-American schools to prepare for African service.) But black church organizations of their own volition and in their own right

24. C. Tardits, 1958, p. 39.
25. J. M. Turner, 1975, p. 23.
26. C. Clendenen, R. Collins and P. Duignan, 1966, p. 63.

soon became the bellwether in, arguably, the most effective missionary enterprises in Africa.

Indeed, Afro-Americans in the nineteenth century were exhorted to assume a special stance toward the 'redemption' of African societies. Bishop Turner, for one, boldly argued that 'God brought the Negro to America and Christianized him so that he might go back to Africa and redeem that land'.[27] Others alluded to the future political greatness of Africa as well as divine mission as compelling reasons for New World blacks to act. For example, in a 1902 speech, blacks were told, 'if the Negro American will but feel his responsibility, face his opportunity and undertake the evangelization of Africa in God's name, unborn millions ... of Africa's sons will witness a transformed continent'.[28]

Earlier, in 1884, the African Methodist Episcopal (AME) Church sponsored a major symposium on the question: 'What Should be the Policy of Colored Americans Toward Africa?'. In August 1893, African and other participants from the United States and Europe attended an American Missionary Association 'World Congress on Africa', held in conjunction with the Chicago World Fair of that year. The week-long Congress was intended to promote interest in Afro-American missionary work in Africa, and also in the rights of 'Africans in America'.

At the Congress, Bishop Turner renewed his advocacy of black emigration to Liberia. Indeed, at least one Liberian (Momolu Massaquoi) attended and participated in the proceedings. At a subsequent conference in December 1895 on 'Africa and the American Negro', in Atlanta's Gammon Theological Seminary, at least one African delegate (Etna Holderness of Liberia) participated. The Gammon meetings once again emphasized American black obligations to help Christianize all of Africa: 'There ought to be, and there must be, an unbroken line of Christian workers stretching from the Cape of Good Hope to Egypt ... thence Sierra Leone and Liberia; thence onward ... to the Sudan and the Congo State'.[29]

American blacks responded in varying ways to this type of call. For example, in 1930, in a fit of exuberance, an AME bishop purchased a farm of several thousand acres of land in South Africa with the intention of settling members of the Church on it in an AME colony. On the other hand, black churches in the United States became apprehensive over news reports carried in the black press in January 1926 to the effect that all missionaries were being deported from Liberia.

At a more substantial level, however, the AME and African Methodist Episcopal Zion (AME Zion) churches and the National Baptist Convention (NBC) all deployed black missionaries in Africa throughout the colonial period. Early stations of the NBC were set up in Liberia in 1883, building on the still earlier work of Lott Carey. The AME Zion Church also put

27. M. M. Ponton, 1917, p. 77.
28. I. G. Penn and J. W. E. Bowen (eds), 1902, p. 310.
29. J. W. E. Bowen (ed.), 1896, p. 205.

down roots in Liberia in 1878 and in the Gold Coast in 1896. Bishop John Bryan Small, of the Caribbean, subsequently organized two annual AME Zion conferences in the Gold Coast and consequently lured J. E. K. Aggrey and Franck Osam-Pinanko into Afro-American churches and, ultimately into the service of the AME Zion Church. In 1930, AME Zion missionaries went to work in Nigeria, responding to a request from African churches there to affiliate with Zion. Meanwhile, the AME Church sponsored missions in several African venues, including Sierra Leone in 1886 (building on Daniel Coker's earlier evangelism), in Liberia in the 1890s (via a personal visit from Henry Turner), and in South Africa in 1896. Because of its longevity, something more must be said about the evolution of AME mission work in Africa, and particularly about the area of the Church's greatest impact – Southern Africa.

Many American blacks who responded to the call of their churches in the later nineteenth century went to Southern Africa as missionaries and with profound effect. A veritable alliance between the schismatic, independent African or 'Ethiopian' Church and the AME Church was completed in 1896, opening a momentous decade in South African black and American black history. Although the AME–Ethiopianist union was short-lived, the AME Church on the strength of its early penetration remained strong in South Africa for the next fifty years.

Formed out of dissident elements of the Wesleyan Church and other 'religious malcontents', the Ethiopian or black separatist Church movement struggled to sustain itself over its first few years. It was only saved, however, by the fortuitous intervention of an African student at Wilberforce University. Charlotte Manye – one of several Southern Africans who arrived at Wilberforce and Lincoln universities in 1895, as part of a so-called 'Zulu Choir' – wrote a letter to her sister in South Africa using AME Church stationery. The letter triggered the interest of leaders of the Ethiopianist movement in securing more information about AME; they requested and received copies of the AME Church discipline, hymn books, and liturgy. However, particular interest was shown in possibilities of higher education for Africans in the United States. This fortuitous train of events led to the dispatch of an Ethiopianist delegation, headed by Reverend James Mata Dwane, to the United States in 1896, and culminated in the formal absorption of the 'Ethiopian' Church by the AME and the formal entry of the AME Church into the foreign missionary field.

Specifically, Dwane pressed Afro-Americans to come to South Africa and to push the educational mission of the AME Church, arguing that South Africa offered 'educated and consecrated American Negroes their greatest field of usefulness'.[30] For the time being, however, it would be necessary for the mother Church to help out by training African youth in American educational institutions. Bishop Turner responded by placing

30. J. M. Dwane, 1897.

a cryptic notice of advice in his paper, *The Voice of Missions*: 'Take Notice, Wilberforce. South Africa coming'.

Nevertheless, Dwane and the African leadership considered it the logical outcome of the Afro-American connection that it should be turned into a development of indigenous schools similar to the ones African students were then attending in the United States. He believed that teachers and preachers in the quantity required by the African population should come from that school, thereby breaking the total reliance for missionary and teaching personnel on overseas schools. In the meantime, Turner visited South Africa in 1898, consecrated Dwane as AME vicar-bishop and proclaimed the intention of the Church to build an AME College second to none among 'previous missionary educational endeavors'. Dwane, in turn, talked of establishing 'The Turner Normal School at Queenstown' or 'The Wilberforce of the Dark Continent'.

Turner devoted the entire issue of *Voice of Missions* for March 1899 to publicity for the South African College Campaign. In one article portraying the redemption of Africa as the 'American Negro's Burden', the specifications of the College took shape: it would be a school for Africans, taught by Africans, founded and supported by the AME missionary department. The founding faculty would come from African students already studying at Wilberforce University, Morris Brown College, Howard University, and the Medical Department of Central State College at Nashville, Tennessee.

The issue of non-African direction and dominance in the Church movement proved, however, unendurable for Dwane. In 1899, he seceded from the AME–'Ethiopian' union and thus created a schism within the ranks of the black Church in South Africa. Trying to retrieve its missionary foothold in South Africa, the AME General Conference in 1900 appointed Levi Coppin as the first Resident Bishop. The Church, moreover, was aided in its work by Charlotte Manye, the Sotho student who had triggered the AME–Ethiopian affiliation in the first place. Manye returned from her American studies in 1901 and immediately picked up the South African College idea – by founding an AME mission school among the Pedi in the Eastern Cape. By 1908, Charlotte Manye Maxeke and her spouse had obtained enough money from the Missionary Department to buy land in Transvaal, build a hall (named after Bishop Coppin) and to move the school (now named Wilberforce Institution) to its permanent location at Evaton.

Meanwhile in Nyasaland, John Chilembwe, a young Yao NBC convert wrote uncertainly in 1905 to his parent Church that 'the mission work chiefly depends upon your help'. With a trace of despair, he continued in sentiments expressed just ten years before he led an ill-fated rebellion against the British in Nyasaland: 'here in British Central Africa it is not like it is in South Africa where the people can do something themselves for missions ... I do not know what the future events of this work will be.'[31] Chilembwe had travelled to America in 1897 for study at the all-

31. J. Chilembwe, 1905.

black Virginia Theological Seminary, trained as a minister, and had returned to Nyasaland around 1900 under the auspices of the National Baptist
Convention. He worked to set up a mission – about which he wrote the
above lament – along lines he had observed among American blacks: 'an
industrial mission in which Africans were trained in the arts and crafts
as well as taught Christianity'.[32]

Bishop Coppin assessed black American Church efforts in Africa in an
address to the 1916 AME General Conference. He noted that:

> The home church has built, and assisted in building churches and
> school houses in Africa, West and South. Many students have been
> trained in our schools at home, largely or wholly at the expense of
> the Church ... [because] we have not been indifferent to the call
> to duty by our kindred beyond the seas; to recognize the debt we
> owe to the foreign field in general and to Africa in particular ... for
> the redemption of Africa where millions are yet in darkness, and to
> grasp the outstretched hand of Ethiopia.[33]

Notwithstanding the resistance by white South African political and
church authorities, the AME connections sown by Turner, deepened by
Dwane, and given firm institutional grounding by the Coppins and the
Maxekes produced a veritable cornucopia of African students matriculating
at American schools. Similarly, in British Central Africa, and West Africa,
African students were encouraged and often subsidized by American black
churches. The latter student sojourns set the stage for a major new phase
in African and Afro-American interaction in the colonial period, one which
had great consequences for subsequent African nationalist movements in
the mid-twentieth century. Indeed, the period of missionary-generated
contacts, in which black American church leaders played the role of
mentors, was gradually changed to one in which the level, interaction
and nature of American interests in black America was increasingly
determined by African initiatives.

Religious interactions between Brazil and the African coast

In matters of religion, and with regard more specifically to evangelism,
we cannot compare the influence of the North American blacks with that
of the Afro-Brazilians. While the former were directly or indirectly involved
in the work of spreading the Gospel, the latter were never committed to
proselytizing work. Several of them, after arriving in Lagos, succeeded
in making their way to their countries of origin. Reference is made in
a few historical documents to Muslim Afro-Brazilians passing through
Lagos on their way to Hausa country. Verger[34] mentions the activity of

32. G. Shepperson and T. Price, 1958, p. 113.
33. Quoted in AME Church *Episcopal Handbook*, 1963.
34. P. Verger, 1968, pp. 617–18.

the English consul in Lagos, Benjamin Campbell, who, in 1858, issued passports to Afro-Brazilians expressing a desire to travel to their homelands. In Lagos, on the edge of the Brazilian Quarter, a central mosque was erected by craftsmen from Brazil (Plate 29.5).

Furthermore, the Catholics[35] built their first church, the Holy Cross Church, started in 1879, in Lagos, and sent their children to the schools of the French and English missionaries who were beginning to use English and French for their teaching.

Thanks to the religious influence exercised intermittently by Portuguese-speaking priests from the island of São Tomé, the community was guided and assisted during its initial period by a freed slave known as Father Antonio.[36] The sons of Afro-Brazilians living in the Brazilian Quarter who had attended the missionary schools began to work as schoolteachers and catechists in the schools and missions that the priests of the African Mission Society were establishing in the region, without forgetting other activities such as work for the colonial administration.[37] These catechists were working for the missions, which were of European origin, and not for any educational missionary ventures originating in Brazil or resulting from an initiative of the Afro-Brazilian community of Lagos. In fact, the language of instruction was English and sometimes French.

For the Afro-Brazilians their Catholicism was a distinguishing feature which conferred a special social status, making them the first nucleus of an African bourgeoisie in Lagos.

A large number of Afro-Brazilians who had returned to Africa, although they professed to be Catholics, had never abandoned their traditional African religious beliefs. Thus, when they returned to their homeland, their religious practices were invigorated and assumed a more or less syncretic form, with the formal aspects of Catholicism resulting from religious life in Brazil such as the Catholic Saints being set alongside the African divinities of the Yoruba pantheon which they continued to worship. 'What struck the Catholic missionaries when they landed on the coast of Africa was the parity of the respect shown by the Brazilian Africans for the religion they had acquired in South America and that handed down to them by their forefathers ...'. Father Lafite added that 'the Brazilians were Christians only in so far as they had been baptized, which did not prevent them from invoking the negro divinities ...'. The Brazilians and other converts put their trust in the social benefits resulting from their *status* as Christians rather than in a whole-hearted acceptance of the teachings of the Church.[38]

In contrast with what occurred in the United States where conversions took place at a deeper level, with several North American blacks becoming

35. J. F. A. Ajayi, 1965, pp. 199–200, 202.
36. P. Verger, 1968, p. 618.
37. M. C. da Cunha, 1976, p. 32.
38. P. Verger, 1968, p. 601.

propagators of the Christian faith, the Afro-Brazilians stood by their African religious beliefs.

Thus, Afro-Brazilians living in the Brazilian Quarter and forming a middle-class nucleus which remained a cohesive and distinct social group thanks partly to the Catholic religion, subscribed to the cult of the household *orixas* ('gods') and consulted *babalaos ifa* (diviners).[39] What is more, African religions still exerted their influence on Brazil from across the Atlantic. Nina Rodrigues[40] points out that at the beginning of the twentieth century, sailing boats from Lagos transported Yoruba – and English-speaking Nago merchants who brought with them kola nuts, cowrie shells, Yoruba jèje (juju) cult objects, soap, 'sarongs from the coast', and so on. In 1888, out of £8237 worth of goods exported from Brazil, pam oil represented only £2600; the remainder was made up essentially of religious or cult objects, especially 'coast sarongs' (£3367), for which there was considerable demand in Brazil, kola nuts of two kinds (£1525), 'straw from the coast', black soap, cowrie shells, 'oris', gourds and 'rosary beads'. African cult objects and articles used in Afro-Brazilian religious ceremonies never ceased to be imported into Brazil and gradually came to be much sought after, consequently acquiring great value as the numbers of those practising Afro-Brazilian syncretism increased.

The educational impact of the Americas

When African students lived in America during the colonial period, they created the context for a different relationship between Africans and Afro-Americans and between African students themselves drawn from all over the African continent. On their return home, they also inspired thousands of their compatriots to enrol in American schools between 1880 and the Second World War. The number of African students in the United States was thereby increased and the time during which Africans as a group were in contact with American blacks was prolonged. The names of such American-educated colonial African students are legion and include recent heads of state (such as Nnamdi Azikiwe, Kwame Nkrumah, and Kamuzu Banda) as well as earlier nationalist or community leaders such as A. B. Xuma, John Dube, Marshall and Charlotte Maxeke, J. E. K. Aggrey, Pixley Ka Izaka Seme, D. S. Malekebu, Franck Osam-Pinanko, Peter Koinange, Ndabaningi Sithole, Eduardo Mondlane and John Chilembwe. In time, the expanding pipeline of Africans booking passages to America surpassed substantially the flow of black missionaries in the opposite direction. What began as an American evangelistic foray into Africa for spiritual redemption, in other words, eventually helped build springboards for an educational, technical and political revolution.

It may be possible to deduce the impact of American educational

39. M. C. da Cunha, 1976, p. 33.
40. N. Rodrigues, 1976, p. 105.

PLATE 29.2 *J. E. K. Aggrey (1875–1921), Gold Coast educationist*

experience on colonial Africans and anti-colonial processes by examining brief biographies of some of the individual African students. J. E. K. Aggrey, for example, went to the United States from the Gold Coast in 1898 under the direct influence of an American-educated AME Zion Bishop from Barbados. Aggrey was steered to Livingstone College in Salisbury, North Carolina, the chief educational institution of the AME Zion Church, with the apparent understanding that he would return directly to Africa in the service of the Church. Upon taking a baccalaureate and a divinity degree, however, Aggrey accepted employment in the AME Zion publishing house in Charlotte, became correspondent for one or two black newspapers, conducted free classes for black teachers in the vicinity, was ordained a Church elder, and was offered a pastorate by two black churches. According to his biographer, this pastoral work was 'one of the most important incidents in Aggrey's American experiences', because 'it took him out of an academic atmosphere and introduced him to the activities of the life led by the American Negro'.[41] Moreover, his connections with black America had already been deepened when he married, in 1904, a young Afro-American woman, possibly a descendant of Frederick Douglass. After twenty-two years work in black America, Aggrey returned to Africa on two separate occasions as a member of the Phelps-Stokes Commission, but died in 1927 shortly after accepting the post of assistant vice-principal of the newly created Achimota College in Ghana. Among the scores of young Africans on whom his impact was felt were Nnamdi Azikiwe, Kwame Nkrumah, and Kamuzu Banda, all of whom later matriculated at American black schools.

While in the United States, John Chilembwe from Nyasaland was exposed to a growing black race-consciousness. Chilembwe was a student in Virginia during the time of the race riots in Wilmington, North Carolina, in 1898. Also he seems to have travelled back to Africa in the company of Reverend Charles S. Morris, an 'Ethiopia-minded' Afro-American Baptist and an eyewitness to the Wilmington disorders. George Shepperson and Thomas Price, in an admirable study, assessed the effects of Chilembwe's experiences in a race-conscious America, noting that the manner of post-Reconstruction black adjustment to discriminatory legislation 'offered him a pattern of strategy and tactics from which he could draw lessons for his own reactions to the less distinguished but nonetheless effective discriminations against Africans in his own land'. Shepperson and Price do not argue that Chilembwe derived the very idea of African schools, 'independent of Government and European missions', from Afro-American institutions; only that 'it is not unreasonable to suppose that his conception of them was influenced by his experiences in the United States'.[42]

Although no evidence is available to reveal the nature of his reading

41. E. Smith, 1929, p. 85.
42. G. Shepperson and T. Price, 1958, pp. 97–8.

while in the United States, Chilembwe lived in America at the time when the speaking and writing of Bishop Turner and Booker T. Washington were already newsworthy items and those of Du Bois and militant black newspapermen, such as T. Thomas Fortune, were becoming so. Moreover, the Commission set up to investigate the Nyasaland Rising of 1915 alleged that much incendiary literature from black America was a factor motivating Chilembwe's adherents in that revolt.

Meanwhile, the Reverend D. S. Malekebu, also from Nyasaland returned in 1926 to British Central Africa after studying in the United States. His absence had not been nearly so protracted as Aggrey's nor was his return so cataclysmic as Chilembwe's, but his emergence as a community leader during the colonial period was equally noteworthy. Malekebu had studied at the National Training School in Durham, North Carolina, at the Moody Bible Institute in Chicago, and then took a medical degree at Meharry Medical School in 1917. Upon his return to Nyasaland, in the company of his wife, Flora Ethelwyn, a Spelman College graduate from the Congo, he reopened Chilembwe's Providence Industrial Mission which the Nyasaland Protectorate Government razed to the ground in the aftermath of the abortive rebellion of 1915. Moreover, Malekebu founded the Chiradzulu Native Association, and got appointed to the Local District Council. In short, his construction of a church and a hospital, reconstruction of the Chilembwe mission, and his broad-based community work attracted glowing reports.

Nnamdi Azikiwe – who like Kamuzu Banda was prompted to journey to America by the ubiquitous James Aggrey and by the mood in the United States associated with Marcus Garvey – enrolled first at a black preparatory school in West Virginia in 1925. When he attended Howard University a few years later, Azikiwe studied and worked closely with such black scholars as Ralph Bunche, and particularly, Alain Locke and William Leo Hansberry on such subjects as Afro-American and pre-colonial African history.

Professor Locke became a personal tutor for Azikiwe who, in turn, worked as Locke's personal secretary. Published in 1925, Locke's *The New Negro* must have had an enormous impact on the studious Azikiwe, for the book was a model of comparative study of black societies and cultures, and included evocative contributions by a kaleidoscope of Harlem Renaissance writers and scholars: Jean Toomer, Countee Cullen, James Weldon Johnson, the Jamaican Claude McKay, Langston Hughes, the black Puerto Rican emigrant Arthur A. Schomburg, E. Franklin Frazier, and W. E. B. Du Bois. Furthermore, contact with the West Indian law student, George Padmore, evidently influenced Azikiwe while a student at Howard; Padmore spoke to a student rally about political choices in the 1928 United States elections. Padmore later contributed political analyses to the pages of Azikiwe's *African Morning Post*, published in the Gold Coast in the 1930s.

In an address before the Howard University Board of Trustees in 1954,

PLATE 29.3 *Nnamdi Azikiwe (b. 1904), Nigerian journalist, pan-Africanist and politician*

a short time before he became Premier of Eastern Nigeria, Azikiwe told of his student days at Howard: 'Here at the Hilltop, I learned the rudiments of the humanities, the anatomy of the social sciences, and the grammar of politics'.[43] Professor Hansberry was on hand when Azikiwe was elevated to Governor-General of Nigeria in 1960. At that time, Hansberry paid tribute to Azikiwe as the 'most illustrious of my former students … one who perceived most clearly the greatness of Africa's past, who demonstrated the great potentialities of the African present'.[44] Implicit in his praise of Azikiwe was surely something of Hansberry's disappointment at the unreceptive and often hostile climate in which his own work in African history was carried out among Afro-American faculty and student body at Howard.

When he transferred to Lincoln University in 1930, Azikiwe continued his interest in black history and race relations, exhibited a determination to secure the appointment of blacks to the all-white faculty and criticized 'the conventional ambitions of his fellow students and the apparent middle class aims of the institution …'.[45] He thought it 'an enormity that a college for Negroes should have persisted for 86 years before a Negro was appointed to the faculty'.[46] The university authorities grew disenchanted with Azikiwe's protest activities (which were publicized not only on campus, but in the black *Philadelphia Tribune* and in Baltimore Afro-American newspapers). Consequently, the school refused to recommend Azikiwe for a renewal of his student visa; in effect, such a refusal assured the termination of his American sojourn. Azikiwe departed for Africa in 1934. By the time Kwame Nkrumah enrolled at Lincoln in 1935, at the tail end of the period considered here, a number of reforms pressed for by Azikiwe had been instituted.

While travelling in West and Southern Africa with the Phelps-Stokes Commission and while lecturing in the Gold Coast as part of his Achimota appointment, Aggrey and several others in similar ways reached across many African communities and prompted dozens of African youth to seek an American rather than a British education. Azikiwe, Banda and Nkrumah became the three most well-known of those touched by Aggrey. The experiences of these men also illustrate the pan-African or pan-black aspects of their American days. Yet these aspects of African interaction with blacks of the diaspora do not wholly explain the activities of the American-educated Africans on their return home. Nor are they adequately explained in currently available scholarship. What appears to have occurred, particularly among Africans in British colonies, was an altered perspective of the American-educated African colliding with an inhospitable colonial

43. B. N. Azikiwe, 1961, p. 13.
44. K. A. B. Jones-Quartey, 1965, p. 76.
45. Horace Mann Bond Papers, Lincoln University (Pennsylvania).
46. H. M. Bond, in J. A. Davis (ed.), 1958, p. 257.

reception (which was prompted by educational experiences completely outside the colonial orbit).[47]

American education, however, was not universally or categorically opposed or disdained in the African colonies. Indications are that industrial or vocational training was welcomed by the colonial entrepreneur since it enabled him to secure well-trained artisans to drive motor lorries, build his houses, and manage his mechanical or electrical plant. Government officials and white missionaries encouraged this kind of training for different reasons: government officials because they believed that the commercial and economic development of the territory would be advanced, missionaries because they believed that Booker T. Washington's 'practical education' approach built character and would help to raise the general moral standard of African life.

That the Afro-American component of the experience of those Africans who studied in the United States contributed to the distinctiveness of those experiences may be seen in the following two examples. The Reverend John Dube, later first President-General of the African National Congress (1912–17), who was sometimes referred to as the 'Booker T. Washington of South Africa', in a talk in New York City, explicitly affirmed the value for him of Washington's Tuskegee model. Indeed, Dube founded an 'indigenous Tuskegee' in Zululand to train the mind, the hand, and the heart of Zulu youth in the Washington manner. Obstacles hindering Dube's efforts were formidable. They included problems in fund-raising because of South African suspicions of 'disturbing influences' emanating from the 'Ethiopian' activities of Bishops Turner, Dwane, and Coppin.

After his own nine-year stay in the United States, Azikiwe returned in 1934 not to his native Nigeria, but to the Gold Coast where he settled temporarily after being refused positions in Nigeria (as a teacher at Kings College, Lagos) and in the Liberian diplomatic service. President Barclay of Liberia rejected Azikiwe's application with the curt reminder that he was not a Liberian and, therefore, knew rather less than required about the republic to discharge the duties in question. With characteristic zeal, however, Azikiwe set out to make himself such an authority on Liberia that even the Americo-Liberian citizenry would be envious. By the end of 1931, he was knowledgeable enough on the subject to read a paper on Liberia at the annual Conference of the Association for the Study of Negro Life and History. In the paper, he came to Liberia's defence and condemned Western critics. In 1934 he published his book *Liberia in World Politics*.

Pan-Africanism: political and cultural aspects

Besides these educational exchanges, a series of pan-Africanist organizations and conferences, as well as commercial and literary or cultural activities

47. See R. D. Ralston, forthcoming, for development of this argument.

put Africans in touch with American blacks and helped to influence events in colonial Africa. The activities of four persons dominated the development of formal, organized pan-Africanism during the colonial period. The first was Booker T. Washington, founder and principal of Tuskegee Institute, the educational model for many African and Caribbean communities. The second was Dr W. E. B. Du Bois who, as editor of the magazine *The Crisis* and 'father' of the pan-African Congress movement, *per se*, made Africa a subsidiary activity of the National Association for the Advancement of Colored People (NAACP). Marcus Garvey, who used his UNIA not only to forge an emigrationist movement but to promote organizational or political solidarity between all peoples of African descent was the third, and the last was Aimé Césaire who (in concert with other Caribbean blacks such as Léon Damas of Cayenne, Dr Jean Price-Mars of Haiti, and the Senegalese poet-politician Léopold Senghor) propounded a cultural variant of pan-Africanism of black group-consciousness, called *négritude*, largely within the Francophone black world.

While the pan-Africanist interest, involvement, and impact of Washington and Tuskegee on Africa and on enrolled and aspiring African students were considerable, those aspects of Washington's work are not well known. The reputation and resources of Tuskegee, however, were brought to Africa by African and American alumni and, often, by numerous African visitors to Tuskegee or correspondents with Washington who had never been matriculated students. Consequently, through the media of numerous international conferences, visitations, and technical missions, many Africans were touched by the 'Tuskegee Spirit' or drew upon Tuskegee's and other American black resources.

In keynoting the pan-Africanist 'International Conference on the Negro', convened at Tuskegee in the spring of 1912, Washington stressed the theme of an exchange of techniques and resources between blacks in Africa and America. 'The object of calling this Conference at Tuskegee', he declared, 'is to afford an opportunity for studying the methods employed in helping the Negro of the United States, with a view of deciding to what extent Tuskegee and Hampton methods may be applied to conditions ... in Africa'.[48] Among those attending the 1912 Conference were delegates from the Gold Coast (J. E. Casely Hayford, author of the influential *Ethiopia Unbound* published the year before, and a representative of the Aborigines Rights Protection Society), British East Africa, Liberia (F. E. T. Johnson), Nigeria, Ruanda (now Rwanda), Portuguese East Africa (now Mozambique), and South Africa (Rev. Isaiah Sishuba, of the Ethiopian Church, Queenstown).

Although African interest in Tuskegee was fired by the 1912 Conference, the repatriation of African students and news of earlier Tuskegee projects had already kindled much interest. For example, a Tuskegee mission to

48. *The Tuskegee Student*, 1912.

Togoland (now Togo) had arrived in 1901 at the invitation of the German colonial government; the mission was designed to improve African methods of cotton cultivation. Success of the mission led to further invitations for missions to Tanganyika (now Tanzania), Zanzibar and Sudan; and to Washington being invited to set up shop in South Africa.

Related Tuskegee/Washington pan-Africanist activities included meetings of the Negro Business League in 1908, at which Washington showed his appreciation of pan-Africanism for African/Afro-American interchange. As he introduced five Liberian envoys who were seeking American financial assistance, Washington emphasized that 'they are here in the United States on an official visit, not merely as envoys of their land, but as representatives of the entire Negro race ...'.[49] Although little real commerce resulted between Africans and Afro-Americans, the African Union Company (a shipping line founded in 1913 by Washington's aide Emmett Scott) was meant to promote the trading of African products on the world market. Evidently, this idea of a shipping line to Africa particularly attracted Garvey to Washington.

The meeting of African and American blacks at Tuskegee as well as Tuskegee projects caused the spreading of the 'Tuskegee Spirit' in an almost geometric progression. The work in Nigeria of a graduate of the Phelps Hall Bible Training School at Tuskegee provides a very small example of this. In a letter to the faculty, he reported that 'I have put before my people the plan of establishing a school like Tuskegee and they gladly consented. One of them has given 50 acres of land and $1000 to start with right away'; he continued, 'I am starting to build two or three houses and then begin at once to preach the Tuskegee spirit'.[50]

John Dube and D. D. T. Jabavu were two of the long list of African notables who passed over common ground provided in Tuskegee. Dube, during his years in the United States as a student at Oberlin and in New York, became associated with both Atlanta educator, John Hope, and Booker T. Washington at Tuskegee. Dube returned to South Africa in 1899, and established Ohlange Institute, openly patterned after Tuskegee. Subsequently, Jabavu, then a student at the University of London, spent about six weeks in 1913 at Tuskegee, observing agricultural techniques, *en route* to other black institutions in the South.

In addition, a series of annual graduation exercises, called 'African Rhetoricals' were organized at Tuskegee to respond to specific African agenda needs such as the raising of funds to support a Tuskegee Chapel in Liberia. The exercises usually featured African and Afro-American students at the Institute in speech and song. In the exercises of 1916, speeches ranged from 'The Development of the Cocoa Industry on the Gold Coast', and the 'Possibilities of the Development of Agriculture in

49. *Liberian Bulletin*, 1908, pp. 64–5.
50. *Southern Letter*, 1917.

South Africa' by A. B. Xuma,[51] to 'Religion and Social Life in Madagascar'.

Pan-Africanism as an organized political movement also became an important linkage between colonial Africans and American blacks. In 1900, Henry Sylvester Williams, a Trinidadian lawyer, organized in London the first of a series of pan-African conferences to which delegates went from the United States, the Caribbean, South America and Africa. Moreover, Williams, admitted as an 'advocate of the Supreme Court in the colony of the Cape of Good Hope' to practise law in South Africa from 1903–4, participated in various African political protest activities. Williams is also known to have become involved in the Diamond Jubilee Celebration of Liberian independence, when, at the behest of President Barclay, he took up in 1907 the cause of New World emigration to Liberia.

Unquestionably, however, it was the three Pan-African Congresses, following Williams' conference, convened by W. E. B. Du Bois in various European capitals (Paris, 1919; London, Brussels and Paris, 1921; London and Lisbon, 1923) which dominated the organized pan-Africanist movement. Du Bois himself, in turn, dominated these next three Congresses. He convened the first in Paris in 1919, while in France to cover the Paris Peace Conference for *The Crisis*, to collect information for a proposed 'History of the American Negro in The Great War'; and to lobby for the political rights of 'the Darker races living within the U.S. as well as throughout the rest of the world'.[52] Among the resolutions adopted at the Paris Congress in 1919 was a resolution calling for self-determination for Africans.

At the second Pan-African Congress convened in 1921, Du Bois attended in the company of Walter White; the Afro-American artist Henry O. Tanner; Jessie R. Fauset, a black editorial writer for *The Crisis* and the most prolific of the Harlem Renaissance novelists; Afro-American concert singer Roland Hayes; and Blaise Diagne from Senegal. The 1923 Congress drew attendance from America, the Caribbean and Africa. Besides Du Bois, Rayford Logan and AME Bishop Vernon of the United States, Chief Amoah III of the Gold Coast and Kamba Simango of Portuguese East Africa attended and helped to formulate several substantive resolutions plus a general call for 'the development of Africa for the benefit of Africans'.[53] The Congress also called for representation on the League of Nations Mandates Commission, 'an institute to study the Negro problem', the restoration or improvement of black rights throughout the black world, and a freeing of Abyssinia, Haiti and Liberia from 'the grip of economic monopoly and usury at the hands of money-masters of the world'.[54] Du Bois personally took the resolutions to Geneva to place them before the League.

51. A. B. Xuma is the subject of a biography being prepared by the author.
52. *The Crisis*, 1921, pp. 119–20.
53. *The Crisis*, 1924, p. 120.
54. ibid., p. 121.

Possibly because of the statement of concern for Liberia, President Coolidge asked Du Bois to represent the United States at the inauguration of the Liberian president in 1923. While in Liberia, on what was his first visit to Africa, Du Bois may have spoken out against Garvey's brand of emigrationist pan-Africanism, for not long afterwards the Liberians rejected the UNIA plan.

However, despite sectarian criticism of himself and of the UNIA, Garvey became the focus of much pan-Africanist interest in the United States, the Caribbean, West Africa, East Africa, Central Africa and, most of all, Southern Africa between 1916 and the mid-1930s. Indeed, by the end of the First World War, Garvey's militant newspaper, *The Negro World* – under the editorship of Hubert Harrison, a Caribbean journalist living in New York – struck a responsive chord among the black masses in New York, throughout North America, and in Africa. Garvey's message to all was: organize, buy black, support the Black Star Steamship Line (which could take black emigrants to Africa and bring back raw materials), and help drive whites out of Africa. He stressed that:

> We are the descendants of a suffering people. We are the descendants of a people determined to suffer no longer ... We do not desire what has belonged to others, though others have always sought to deprive us of that which belonged to us ... The other races have countries of their own and it is time for the 400,000,000 Negroes [of the world] to claim Africa for themselves.[55]

Whereas Du Bois was a greater pan-African force among black intellectuals outside Africa, and Washington was better known among rural artisan classes, Garvey's influence fell equally upon the submerged black masses of all strata both outside and inside Africa. Garvey received much of his own pan-Africanist inspiration from the Egyptian intellectual, Duse Muhammad Ali, while in England in 1912 and from reading, also in London, Washington's autobiography, *Up From Slavery*.

Initially organized around the idea of setting up a Tuskegee-type school in Jamaica, Garvey's UNIA became the organizational link between large numbers of Africans and American blacks outside Africa, and, through *The Negro World*, achieved substantial pan-African effect within Africa. Between 1920 and 1938, eight UNIA conventions were held. The first five, with Garvey in charge, were held in New York City in August of each year from 1920 to 1924, the next two, following Garvey's deportation from the United States, took place in Jamaica in 1929 and 1934, and the eighth and last, in Canada, in 1938.

Beginning with the first convention, Garvey advocated the creation of special schools to teach technical education to blacks in Africa and the Americas, the development of 'economic opportunities in agriculture,

55. Quoted in E. D. Cronon, 1962, p. 65.

industry, and commerce' in order to promote commerce between blacks, the launching of the Black Star Steamship Line to facilitate that commerce, and the establishment of a daily newspaper 'in several large cities of the world to shape sentiment in favour of the entire Negro race', especially in London, Paris, Berlin, Cape Town, New York, Washington, DC, the Gold Coast and the Caribbean. For Garvey the implementation of this programme, potentially, could unify 'every unit of the Negro race throughout the world into one organized body'.[56] Contemporaries felt that Garvey's message literally 'reverberated inside Africa' and that 'from his narrow vantage point in Harlem [he] became a world figure'.[57]

In 1917, J. E. Casely Hayford, the Gold Coast intellectual, used the general impetus from Garveyism to found the National Congress of British West Africa, the inaugural session of which was held in Accra in March 1920. Elsewhere, Jomo Kenyatta remembered that in 1921 'Kenya nationalists, unable to read, would gather round a reader of *The Negro World*, and listen to an article 2 or 3 times ... [and] then ... run various ways through the forest, carefully to repeat the whole story ... to Africans hungry for some doctrine which lifted them from the servile consciousness in which Africa lived'.[58] Garvey himself wrote editorials and long articles for *The Negro World*, as it secured a readership much larger than its actual circulation of about 200000.

In Nyasaland, the establishment of auxiliaries of the UNIA was resisted by colonial authorities as well as some African leaders, such as Clements Kadalie, founder of the Industrial and Commercial Workers' Union.[59] Notwithstanding the socialist Kadalie's apparent opposition to the 'Africa for the Africans' posture of the UNIA, Garvey possibly directly contacted African students, including Nyasalanders, then studying in the United States. Consequently, the British Colonial Office conducted an intensive investigation of Nyasaland students, for example the activities of Dr D. S. Malekebu as a medical student in the 1920s at the black Meharry Medical College. Moreover, upon his return to Africa, Malekebu initially was denied entry to Nyasaland and therefore went for a time to Liberia. In part, fear of a re-emergence of the revolutionary spectre of John Chilembwe caused British colonial authorities to reject a proposed 'tour of Nyasaland and other areas of East Africa by Garvey and some of his associates' in the 1920s. Because of the possibility that Garvey's influence might spread via more informal means, such as the return of migrant workers from South Africa[60] and his vaunted newspaper, the authorities effectively banned *The Negro World* by 1922. Authorities may have felt particularly provoked because of such articles in the paper as a later one referring to Kamuzu

56. A. C. Hill and M. Kilson (eds), 1971, p. 241.
57. J. H. Clarke, 1964, p. 15.
58. C. L. R. James, 1963, p. 396.
59. S. W. Johns in R. I. Rotberg and A. A. Mazrui (eds), 1970.
60. For references to South African branches of the UNIA, see *The Negro World*, 1927.

Banda, then a recent graduate of the University of Chicago, as 'heir apparent to the chieftaincy of 25 000 African natives in Nyasaland'.[61]

Garvey's widow, Amy Jacques Garvey, has explained how meanwhile Garvey's influence truly travelled in mysterious ways: 'From other parts of Africa, [besides Liberia] both Seamen and Students have been indoctrinated in Garveyism in England, France, and the USA and on their return home, quietly and secretly spread the gospel of Unity and Freedom; some have become leaders, others have created dedicated followers by their teaching and inspired faith'.[62] Garvey's influence became apparent in the area of mission schools attended by Azikiwe. Kwame Nkrumah later confided that no literature had made a greater impact on him while a student in the United States than Garvey's *Philosophy and Opinions* (1923).

While Garvey and Du Bois were stirring the black world politically during the first three decades of the twentieth century, a broadly influential Africa-oriented cultural efflorescence was taking place. The reaffirmation of black culture took hold in Europe, the Caribbean and West Africa, particularly, led by the French-language African and Caribbean students in Paris who were drawn into the Pan-African Congress movement, the programmes of the UNIA and the general excitement of the Harlem Renaissance.

In short, the interaction between Francophone Caribbean blacks (such as Aimé Césaire of Martinique, whose famous poem *Cahier d'un Retour au Pays Natal* was published in 1939) and West African intellectuals (such as the Senegalese poet-politician Léopold Senghor) forged the *négritude* movement. Based on a belief in a common cultural heritage among all African and African-descended peoples, the *négritude* writers tried to re-link the spheres of the black world.

The concept of *négritude* was strongly influenced by the black experience overseas, and by the writings and intellectual vigour of the Harlem Renaissance. In turn, the Renaissance movement was fuelled by a rising cultural identification with Africa. Countee Cullen wondered poetically 'What is Africa to Me?' in his poem called 'Heritage', while Langston Hughes in his poem 'The Negro Speaks of Rivers' mentions how he built his hut near the Congo and it lulled him to sleep.[63] Both greatly influenced Senghor and the *négritude* writers.

But it was another Jamaican, Claude McKay, whose poetry helped to unify cultural and political pan-Africanism, when he insisted through the vehicle of his poetry that blacks should acknowledge, and protest against their common suffering and assert their dignity. Particularly telling was a defiant McKay poem, later used without credit by Winston Churchill during the Battle of Britain, called 'If We Must Die'. McKay, like Garvey and thousands of African students, began his sojourn in the United States

61. *The Negro World*, 1932, p. 8.
62. A. J. Garvey, 1963, p. 258.
63. Quoted in C. H. Rollins, 1970, p. 19.

because of an interest in Tuskegee, but soon left and joined the millions of blacks who turned up in New York in the 1920s.

Occasionally, colonial African interaction with black America was expressed in popular literature and thought in a symbolic form. Various African communities occasionally focused their millennial dreams of deliverance from colonial subjugation on American black populations. For example, in the millennial penumbra surrounding the disastrous Xhosa cattle sacrifice of the mid-nineteenth century, Africans widely believed that traditional lands and property and relatives would be returned via black intervention from across the seas. Again in 1910, during the time of the formation of the Union of South Africa, newspaper accounts told of an African bishop named Msiqinya who claimed to be a messiah from black America. The theme was repeated in 1921 when Enoch Mjigima, a Garveyite and leader of a group calling itself the Black Israelites, established contact with the Afro-American Church of God and Saints of Christ during the Bulhoek rebellion and in the Wellington prophecy (see Chapter 27). Mjigima at the time had corresponded with Garvey and wished to set up a branch of the UNIA in South Africa.

One of two lurid, fictionalized versions of the Afro-American millennial theme in the early twentieth century was a novel called *Prester John* (1910). Written by a white man, the novel portrayed an overseas-educated African clergyman leading an enormous revolt against the whites. It created an immediate sensation in Southern Africa. For some, it was the blueprint followed by Chilembwe in the Nyasaland Revolt five years later. A second novel entitled *Bayete!* appeared in 1923 and dramatized the prospect of Afro-American influences in Southern Africa, playing upon the fear of Afro-American influences held by South African whites.

Amidst the scare over the two prophetic movements (Msiqinya and Mjigima/Wellington) and the two millennial novels (*Prester John* and *Bayete!*) came two apparent reifications of the Afro-American messianic theme in the form of the emergence of the Garvey movement and the Phelps-Stokes visit to Southern Africa of James Aggrey. Although he was a Fante from the Gold Coast, Aggrey was widely perceived as the advance guard of the black invasion emphasized so strongly in African, Cape Coloured, and white oral traditions. A contemporary account validated the popular beliefs:

> To understand the fervid reception accorded to Aggrey in the Transkei and the effectiveness of his speeches over, at least, many minds, it is necessary to remember that there, as elsewhere on the African continent, a number of inhabitants were looking to America for redemption from their troubles. Aggrey was supposed by some to be the herald of an invading band of Negroes – they thought all Americans were Negroes – who would drive the Whites of South Africa into the sea.[64]

64. E. Smith, 1929, p. 181.

In short, Aggrey's appearance seemingly dovetailed with Garvey's boast of resettling millions of American blacks in Africa and defeating colonialism there, and thereby, kindled long-standing hopes and fears.

During the period under consideration a few black Brazilians in Brazil were actively involved in the struggle to secure the emancipation of slaves (1888).[65] These included Luis da Gama (1830–85), André Reboucas (1838–98) and José do Patrocínio (1853–1905). Among studies relating to the African contribution in Brazil, mention should be made of the work by Manuel Raimundo Querino (1851–1923) who lived in São Salvador da Bahía and whose many publications included *O Africano como colonizador e costumes africanos no Brasil*. Solano Trinidade (1908–73)[66] brought the concept of pan-Africanism and *négritude* into Brazilian poetry. Mention can also be made of the role of the Afro-Brazilian press, with the launching of the newspaper *O Menelick* in 1915, in São Paulo, and many others, such as *Getulino* (1923–26) in Campinas, *O Clarim da Alvorada* (1924–32) in São Paulo, founded by José Correia Leite and Jayme de Aguiar, and, later, *A Voz da Raca* (1933–7), the organ of a political movement known as the Negro-Brazilian Front.

The persistence and transformation of African cultural values in Latin America and the Caribbean

Several authors[67] draw attention to the African presence in American and the Caribbean countries, which they assess in terms of the percentage of descendants of Africans in the total population of each country. Three main groups can be identified on the basis of this criterion.

The first group consists of countries where the majority of the population is black. This is true of Haiti, Jamaica, Trinidad and Tobago, and Barbados, for example. The second group comprises countries where the proportion of the population of African origin is insignificant in demographic terms. This is the case in Argentina, Chile, Uruguay, Paraguay and Bolivia, among others. The third group includes Brazil and Cuba, where blacks have played a key role in the economy,[68] have exercised considerable cultural influence, and where the ethnic configuration is largely the result of cross-breeding.

Finally, mention should be made of two other groups of countries. The first consists of countries such as Colombia, Panama and Nicaragua, which contain small, somewhat tightly-knit population groups of African origin. The second group consists of those countries which have groups of African origin which have not undergone an integration process in the New World, such as Surinam where the Bonis, the Djukas, the Saramacas and the Akwas

65. D. B. Porter, 1978; S. M. Couceiro, 1974; H. L. Alves, 1976.
66. M. Andrade, 1959, pp. 97–9.
67. For example, L. B. Rout Jr, 1976.
68. J. H. Rodrigues, 1964, Vol. I, p. 51.

are found, and Jamaica, Santo Domingo and even Haiti and Cuba, the home of the maroons. Living in the forest, groups in Suriname and in French Guiana have retained more or less intact their fundamental cultural values and a certain social organization. The maroons were communities of run-away slaves who took refuge in the mountains of those countries, thus cutting themselves off from contact with the colonizers. At least a good portion of these communities succeeded in maintaining themselves isolated from the former colonizers. Later on, in Suriname, French Guiana and, to a certain extent, in Jamaica, they held themselves aloof from what could be called the 'national community'.

From the demographic standpoint, the composition of the population of each country should be carefully checked with reference to three main groups: the population of African origin, that of European origin and, lastly, that of local origin – the 'Amerindians'. The demographic survival of each group as such and the result of cross-breeding between several different groups, as the case may be, should also be considered.

The distribution of each group by social category, regardless of other indicators such as schooling, should then be studied, and this will provide a basis for analysing changes in the position of the population of African origin. This approach was used by Octavio Ianni and Fernando Henrique Cardoso[69] to study the process by which former slaves entered the free labour market and, subsequently, their integration into the urban economy.

This type of analysis makes it possible to evaluate the extent to which the population of African origin is integrated in the economic systems and societies of South America. However, it leaves on one side the continuing prestige of African cultural values in the New World, although of course one may hold the view that this can only be measured by using a racial criterion or that it is not an important variable.

Here there are two conflicting schools of thought. The position taken by M. J. Herskovits[70] regarding the 'reinterpretation' of African culture as reflected in continuing cultural elements, provoked the black North American sociologist, E. Franklin Frazier[71] to draw attention to the central problem of integration in society as a whole. As Frazier saw it, Herskovits' theory could lead to the conclusion that the persistence of African cultural values might be regarded as evidence supporting the racialist argument that blacks cannot be assimilated. In the United States, on account of various factors including the work of the Protestant churches, the former slaves lost most of their traditional African cultural values and became part of the Anglo-Saxon cultural world.

The parallel between North America and South America and the Caribbean in terms of the African presence and particularly of African cultural values is not conclusive, for the situations were very different in

69. O. Ianni, 1962; F. H. Cardoso, 1962.
70. M. J. Herskovits, 1941, 1948, 1966(a), 1966(b), 1966(c).
71. E. F. Frazier, 1949.

view of the different ways in which the former slaves became 'integrated' in those regions, even from one country to another.

From the cultural standpoint, whereas in the United States conversion to the Protestant religion led to the forsaking of cultural traditions and to the emergence of a new outlook, in Latin America and the Caribbean African cultural values persisted to varying degrees or underwent a process of transformation.

Methodologically, two forms of presence should be distinguished: the cultural presence of Africa and the Negro presence in the physical sense. Evidence may be found of either form of presence, or of both simultaneously, depending on the situation and the type of colonial process involved.

The problem of colour distinctions arises in different ways, for, according to Roger Bastide, 'whether the colour line is institutionalized, as in the United States, or not, the result is the same. The Blacks live or tend to live in a separate world, in a world apart. They feel "different" from others and they are forced – or prefer (the reasons matter less to us than the consequences) – to "keep themselves to themselves" '.[72]

Historical analysis reveals that, through the years, rather than the dichotomy between 'African culture' and 'black culture' being accentuated, as the result of a series of social changes, what occurred was cultural transformation in varying degrees according to the situation. In Haiti, for example, where the black population is in the majority, a characteristically African religion was influenced by the structural realities of Haitian society and the role of the half-castes, and underwent a series of changes set in motion by new 'gods' that met the requirements of the new situation. In the neighbouring islands, as a result of Protestant mission work, a 'black culture' had already taken shape in various movements such as that of the Rastafarians (a Messianic wave of reaction against the white overlord in which African imagery was thinly veiled, Haile Sellassie being cast as Messiah). On the other hand, in Jamaica, with the Sasabonsan cult, of Asante origin, elements of 'African culture' persisted during that historical period, subsequently vanishing to give way to spirit-based cults involving a large dose of magic, as was the case in 1894 of the 'Jamaica Baptist Free Church', a sect founded by Bedward.

In those parts of the Americas exposed to the teachings of Catholicism, a form of syncretism based on the co-existence of European and African cultural features arose. In such situations being a Catholic did not involve radical changes as was the case in situations where Protestantism was dominant.

A feature of this syncretism was observance of Catholic feast days and saints' days, together with recourse to the *orixas* and to voodoo. Thus, the feast days of the gods coincided with the dates of the Catholic saints'

72. R. Bastide, 1967, p. 199.

days. Bastide asserts that syncretism is no more than a white mask for Negro gods. The values of the two religions interpenetrate in varying degrees. In Brazil, for instance, a series of Catholic sacraments, such as baptism, are repeated not only for ritualistic purposes but also to give the individual additional strength. This acculturation of values of European origin marks even the forms closest to the African sources, such as *candomblé, macumba* and other cults, some of which are close to, or even characterized by, magic. In the case of *macumba*, attention should be drawn to the presence of Amerindian values, the acculturation here being of a threefold variety.

Examples of syncretism involving Amerindian culture can be seen in the West Indies, particularly in Honduras, where a mestizo people has emerged as the result of interbreeding between Amerindian women and Africans referred to as black Caribs.[73] These Africans were the descendants of the Igbo and Efik and, subsequently, of the Fante, Asante, Fon and Congo.

The 'African societies' gradually turned into 'black societies', varying in the strength of their connection with Africa and in their integration in society as a whole, in the sense of gaining full citizenship.

From the social standpoint, integration in society as a whole was keyed to the following variables: the type of society of the white colonizer; the form of land exploration; the religion of the colonizer – Protestant or Catholic; the percentage of Amerindians in the population and the degree of integration in the economic process imposed by the regime of the colonizer, either during the colonial period proper or following the attainment of independence by the Americas.

The forms of resistance already noted during the colonial period, when small numbers of fugitive slaves including half-castes banded together and attempted to live outside the system imposed by the colonizer, emerged in the late eighteenth century. These groups maintained the values typical of African societies. The isolation or integration of these 'runaways' in terms of the national society varied in the nineteenth century with the degree of development of the country concerned and with the stage reached in the socio-economic evolution from a world characterized by the rural values of an economy centred on plantations, farms and sugar mills to forms more closely resembling the type of economy existing at the end of the century and at the beginning of the twentieth century.

The integration of blacks into rural society varied according to the requirements of agriculture, the shortage or availability of labour and the size of the contingents of migrants from Europe, some of these contingents arriving for the express purpose of finding work within the labour system, as in Brazil in the coffee plantations. This integration is revealed in a variety of ways, encompassing the songs of African religious groups in Cuba and

73. R. Coelho, 1964.

PLATES 29.4(a)–(d) *Examples of the influence of Yoruba religion on the peoples of African descent of Bahia in Brazil*

(a)

(c)   (d)

(b)

PLATE 29.5 *Central Mosque, Lagos, showing the Brazilian influence on architecture*

779

Brazil, the rhythm of African instruments[74] which were effectively incorporated in the musical culture, the art of African cooking, the utilization of certain African techniques as, for example, in Haiti, the use of agricultural implements such as the hoe among others, and the transmission of religious values and philosophies of life. Despite the break imposed by the practice of slavery, African culture survived and, what is more, created a new culture.

Conclusions

What were the effects of colonial African and American black interaction? Only African populations of certain regions were initially involved in interaction with American and Caribbean blacks. Those regions involved early in our period were the ones which became the focus of American black emigration or evangelism, particularly West Africa, South Africa, and the Horn. Peoples of other regions became involved because of the penetration of their region by pan-Africanist projects, American black writings, folklore, and the like, or more importantly, because of the initiatives of school leavers who went, in growing numbers from all over the African continent, to America for higher education.

Perspectives were undoubtedly affected by direct and substantial interaction of Africans within a particular black environment or set of influences. Exactly how much is anybody's guess. The effect of colonial African experience with American blacks appears, nevertheless, unique and vital in terms of subsequent social and political activities. For some, the American black component within African nationalist ideology and strategies emerging during the colonial period was striking and unequivocal. In the view of others, for example some African students, interactions within American black arenas were disappointing and unrewarding. The caustic assessment of one such visitor illustrates the latter point: 'One of the things I had decided to find out during my stay in America was the condition of the descendants of former slaves brought here from Africa ... I feel safe in saying that, so far as economic and material progress are concerned the Negro in America is on the average ahead of the West African, but when it comes to integrity and genuine manhood, the American Negro is far below him.'[75]

Another view was that many Afro-American missionaries who viewed Africans as 'poor heathen savages' must bear some of the responsibility for perpetuating a distorted and pernicious picture of Africa and Africans in the minds of their fellow American blacks. In other words, in their sedulous campaign to recruit American black workers for foreign missions, missionary churches undoubtedly succumbed occasionally to the tempta-

74. F. Ortiz, 1950.
75. A. E. Ani-Okokon, 1927, p. 10.

tion of portraying an exotic, erotic and socially inferior Africa much in need of great sacrifice, hard work, and alien redemption.

In broad pan-Africanist terms, however, the evidence seems clear that African political and ideological visions were expanded and technical expertise was improved because of colonial African interactions with American blacks. The much-heralded black emigration schemes trumpeted by Garvey, whose ubiquitous publications reached deep into Africa, were only one example of a *leitmotif* which brought American blacks within the world view of African peoples. The themes of African redemption through American black missionaries were another.

Africans themselves, however, created the context of their next interaction with American blacks as they matriculated at American, largely Afro-American, schools and attended pan-African conferences and the like. Consequently, many Africans underwent a technical-educational-political experience alien to their colonial world. When they re-entered their own worlds, many felt driven to resolve questions of ideology, cultural definition, educational values, political power, and pan-African unity or consciousness, guided by new perspectives.

Viewed against such an historical backdrop, the numerous pan-African conferences, Tuskegean educational and technical projects, the *négritude* movement and the occasional focus on American blacks in African millennial dreams, all illustrate the consistency of the pan-African theme among American and Caribbean blacks. They also show the variability of African responses to the New World overtures and ultimately the shaping by Africans themselves of these overtures to fit African specifications.

In sum, the populations of the African diaspora and the motive characterizing the many interactions between persons of the first and second black worlds included two visions. One was a vision of the union of religious forces among black populations in Africa and America or the reconstruction of Africa through importation of American and Antillean black technical expertise, initiated at the behest of American blacks. Another reflected the transformation of Africans from predicate to subject during the colonial period. The latter was a vision of the spiritual redemption, social reconstruction, and political reformation of African communities through the repatriation of *African* personnel and the energizing of *African* resources. Because of this vision, Africans had been educated in American schools, or sent to participate in technical and commercial activities; others were touched by American black writings or by anti-colonial ventures organized among blacks of the diaspora. This latter vision seemed not so much to discard as simply to vindicate and to reorientate to an African perspective the idealism implied in the earlier vision.

Colonialism in Africa: its impact and significance

30

A. ADU BOAHEN

By 1935, as is evident from the earlier chapters of this volume, colonialism had been firmly fastened on Africa like a steel grid, and it looked as if it was going to remain there forever. However, colonialism proved just as ephemeral as any other institution created and maintained by force. Within a matter of only some forty-five years from 1935, the colonial system had been uprooted from over 90% of Africa and confined only to that part of the continent south of the Limpopo River. That is to say, colonialism lasted in most parts of Africa for under a hundred years, indeed from the 1880s to the 1960s. In the history of a people and a whole continent, this is a very brief span indeed. How and why this incredible feat of the uprooting of colonialism was accomplished, or, to quote the words of Margery Perham, why this 'astonishingly rapid emancipation since 1950'[1] form two of the main themes of the concluding volume of this History. In the concluding chapter of this volume, however, we would like to address ourselves to two main questions. First, what legacies did colonialism bequeath to Africa, or what impact did it make on Africa? The second question is, in view of this impact or balance sheet, what is the significance of colonialism for Africa? Does it constitute a revolutionary or important episode in the history of the continent? Was it a major break with the past of the continent, or was it, after all, a mere passing event which did not constitute a break in the history of the continent? Or as L. H. Gann and Peter Duignan have posed the same question, what is 'the place of the colonial era within the wider context of African history'?[2]

The colonial impact

Probably nothing has become as controversial a subject as the impact of colonialism on Africa. To some writers on Africa such as Gann, Duignan, Perham and P. C. Lloyd, its impact was on balance either a blessing or at worst not harmful for Africa.

1. M. Perham, 1961, p. 24.
2. 'Epilogue' in L. H. Gann and P. Duignan (eds), 1970, p. 526.

Lloyd, for instance, has no hesitation about the beneficial nature of the colonial impact. 'It is easy to cavil today,' he states:

> at the slow rate of economic development during the half-century of colonial rule ... Nevertheless, the difference between the condition of African society at the end of the nineteenth century and at the end of the Second World War is staggering. The colonial powers provided the infrastructure on which progress in the 'independence' period has depended: a fairly efficient administrative machine, reaching down to villages in the most remote areas; a network of roads and railways; and basic services in health and education. West African exports of primary products brought considerable wealth to the people.[3]

In her Reith Lectures in 1961, Margery Perham also argued: that, 'The critics of colonialism are mainly interested in to-day and to-morrow but we must remind them that our vanishing empire has left behind it a large heritage of history which is loaded with bequests good, bad and indifferent. This neither they nor we can easily discard.'[4] It is interesting to note that another English historian, D. K. Fieldhouse, has arrived at the same conclusion in a book published as recently as 1981: 'It would thus appear that colonialism deserves neither the praise nor the blame it has often been given for, if it did relatively little to overcome the causes of poverty in the colonies, neither did it make them poor for the first time. Empire had very significant economic effects, some good, some bad ...'[5]

Finally, Gann and Duignan, who have devoted themselves virtually to the defence of colonialism in Africa, concluded in 1967 that 'the imperial system stands out as one of the most powerful engines for cultural diffusion in the history of Africa; its credit balance by far outweighs its debit account'.[6] And in their introduction to the first volume of the five-volume work entitled *Colonialism in Africa* which they jointly edited, they again concluded: 'We do not share the widely-held assumption that equates colonialism with exploitation ... We accordingly interpret European imperialism in Africa as an engine of cultural transformation as well as of political domination.'[7]

Others, mainly African, black and Marxist scholars and especially the development and underdevelopment theorists, have contended that the beneficial effect of colonialism in Africa was virtually nil. The black Guyanese historian, Walter Rodney, has taken a particularly extreme position. As he contends: 'The argument suggests that, on the one hand, there was exploitation and oppression, but, on the other hand, colonial

3. P. C. Lloyd, 1972, pp. 80–1.
4. M. Perham, 1961, p. 24.
5. D. K. Fieldhouse, 1981, p. 105.
6. L. H. Gann and P. Duignan, 1967, p. 382.
7. 'Introduction' in L. H. Gann and P. Duignan (eds), 1969, pp. 22, 23.

783

governments did much for the benefit of Africans and they developed Africa. It is our contention that this is completely false. Colonialism had only one hand – it was a one-armed bandit.'[8]

Such are the two main opposing assessments of colonialism in Africa. From the available evidence, however, it would appear that a much more balanced assessment is necessary and this is what is attempted here. As will be shown below, the impact of colonialism was positive as well as negative. However, it should be emphasized right from the beginning that most of the positive effects were not deliberately calculated. They were, by and large, rather accidental by-products of activities or measures intended to promote the interests of the colonizers, as M. H. Y. Kaniki and A. E. Afigbo have pointed out above (Chapters 16 and 19), or were the outcome of changes which were inherent in the colonial system itself; or, to borrow Ali Mazrui's phrase, the positive effects were 'by default, by the iron law of unintended consequences'.[9] On the negative side, it should also be pointed out that there could indeed be reasons, good, bad or indifferent, why certain things were not done – for instance, why, as Fieldhouse has striven hard to show, forced labour was used, industrialization was not promoted, agriculture was not diversified or why medical services were inadequate,[10] but from the point of view of the colonized African, they were negative effects all the same. Let us begin, then, by drawing up the balance sheet in the political field beginning first with the positive and then the negative aspects.

The impact in the political field

The first positive political impact was the establishment of a greater degree of continuous peace and stability following the consolidation of colonialism in Africa than before. The nineteenth century, as seen already, was the century of the Mfecane and the activities of the Swahili-Arab and Nyamwezi traders such as Tippu Tip and Msiri in Central and Southern Africa, of the Fulani *djihāds* and the rise of the Tukulor and Mandingo empires in the Western Sudan, of the disintegration of the Oyo and Asante empires in West Africa; and all this caused a great deal of instability and insecurity. But, then, conditions in Europe during the same period were not so very different either. This was the period of the Napoleonic wars, the 'intellectual' revolutions, the German and Italian wars of unification, the Polish and Hungarian uprisings and the imperial rivalries culminating in the First World War. In Africa, while it should be admitted that the first two or three decades of the colonial era, that is from 1880 to the 1910s even intensified this state of instability, violence and disorder and, as Caldwell has shown, caused wholesale and unpardonable destruction

8. W. Rodney, 1972, p. 223.
9. A. A. Mazrui, 1980, p. 41.
10. D. K. Fieldhouse, 1981, pp. 67–8, 71–4, 88–92.

and loss of population – the population of Belgian Congo was reduced by half during the first forty years of colonial rule, the Herero by four-fifths, the Namo by half and that of Libya by 750000[11] – not even the anti-colonial and Marxist schools would deny the fact that after the colonial occupation and the establishment of various administrative machineries, such wars of expansion and liberation came to an end, and most parts of Africa especially from the end of the First World War onwards enjoyed a great degree of continuous peace and security. Such conditions were definite assets since they greatly facilitated normal economic activities and social and physical mobility in each colony, which greatly accelerated the pace of modernization through the diffusion of new ideas, new techniques, new tastes and new fashions.

The second positive political impact is the very geo-political appearance of the modern independent states of Africa. The colonial partition and conquest definitely resulted, as A. E. Afigbo has pointed out above (Chapter 19), in a revolutionary reshaping of the political face of Africa. In place of the hundreds of independent clan and lineage groups, city-states, king-doms and empires, without any clearly marked boundaries, were now established fifty new states with, in most cases, fixed boundaries, and it is rather significant that the boundaries of the states as laid down during the colonial era have not undergone any changes since independence.

Thirdly, the colonial system also introduced into most parts of Africa two new institutions which again rather significantly have been maintained since independence, namely, a new judicial system and a new bureaucracy or civil service. There is no doubt that in practically all the independent states except the Muslim ones, the higher courts of judicature introduced by the colonial rulers have been retained; in the former British colonies not only in form (including, despite the climate, even the wigs and gowns), but also in content and ethos.

The machineries introduced for the administration of the colonies also steadily led, though in many areas rather belatedly, to the emergence of a civil service whose membership and influence increased with the years. The importance of this particular legacy varied from one colonial system to the other. There is no doubt that the British bequeathed a better trained, numerically larger and more experienced bureaucracy to her colonies than the French, while the record of the Belgians and the Portuguese is the worst in this respect.

The final positive impact of colonialism was the birth not only of a new type of African nationalism, but also of pan-Africanism. The former, as we have seen, was the fostering of a sense of identity and consciousness among the various classes or ethnic groups inhabiting each of the new states, or, as in the French West African colonies, a cluster of them; while the latter was a sense of identity of black men the world over. The vehicles for the articulation of the former were, as B. O. Oloruntimehin has shown

11. B. Davidson, 1964(b), p. 37; 1978(b), p. 150.

above (Chapter 22), various movements, political parties, youth leagues and associations, religious sects and newspapers, while those of the latter were the various Pan-African Congresses discussed by R. D. Ralston above (Chapter 29). But important as this legacy was, it is a typical example of the accidental by-products rather than deliberate creations of the colonial presence. No colonial ruler ever set out to create and nurture African nationalism.

But if there were positive effects, even greater were the negative ones. In the first place, important as the development of nationalism was, not only was it an accidental by-product, but it was not the result of a positive feeling of identity with or commitment or loyalty to the new nation-state, but a negative one generated by a sense of anger, frustration and humiliation caused by some of the oppressive, discriminatory, humiliating and exploitative measures introduced by the colonial rulers. With the overthrow of colonialism, then, that feeling was bound to lose, and indeed has lost, its momentum and the problem that has faced the rulers of independent African states has been how to replace this negative response with a positive and enduring feeling of nationalism.

Secondly, while admitting that the new geo-political set-up that emerged was an asset even though an accidental one, it nevertheless created far more problems than it solved. Though, as both A. E. Afigbo and G. N. Uzoigwe have shown (Chapters 2 and 19), the boundaries of the states that emerged were not as arbitrary as is generally believed, there is no doubt that many of the states that emerged were artificial creations, and this artificiality has created a number of problems that are bound to bedevil the future development of the continent. The first of these is the fact that some of these boundaries cut across pre-existing ethnic groups, states and kingdoms and this has caused widespread social disruption and displacement. The Bakongo are, for instance, found divided by the boundaries of Angola, Belgian Congo (now Zaire), French Congo (now Congo) and Gabon. Today, some of the Ewe live in Ghana, some in Togo and some in Benin; the Somali are shared among Ethiopia, Kenya, Somalia and Djibouti; the Senufo are found in Mali, Ivory Coast and Upper Volta. The examples can be multiplied. One important consequence of this situation has been the chronic border disputes that have plagued the relations between some independent African states – such as those between Sudan and Uganda; between Somalia and Ethiopia; between Kenya and Somalia; between Ghana and Togo; and between Nigeria and Cameroon. Secondly, because of the arbitrary nature of these boundaries, each African nation-state is made up of a medley of peoples with different cultures, traditions of origin and language. The problems of nation-building posed by such a medley of peoples have not proved to be easily soluble.

Another outcome of the artificiality and arbitrariness of the colonial divisions was that the states that emerged were of different sizes with unequal natural resources and economic potentialities. While some of the states that emerged from the partition are giants such as Sudan, Nigeria and Algeria, others were midgets like The Gambia, Lesotho, Togo and Burundi. While Sudan and Zaire have areas of 2.5 million sq km and 2.4 million sq km respectively, the area of The Gambia is only 10 350 sq km, that of Lesotho 29 200 sq km and that of Burundi 28 800 sq km. Unfortunately, there are far more states of small or medium size than the other way round.[12] Secondly, and worse still, while some states have very long stretches of sea coast, others such as Mali, Upper Volta, Niger, Chad, Zambia, Uganda, Malawi, are landlocked. Thirdly, while some states have very rich natural resources such as Ghana, Zambia, Zaire, Ivory Coast and Nigeria, others such as Chad, Niger and Upper Volta have not been so fortunate. Finally, while some such as The Gambia, have borders with only one other state to police, others have four or more and Zaire as many as ten, a situation which poses serious problems of ensuring national security and checking smuggling. The problems of development posed by the lack of or limited natural resources, limited fertile land and lack of access to the sea for those independent African states which inherited these unfortunate legacies can be readily imagined.

Another important but negative political impact of colonialism was the weakening of the indigenous systems of government. In the first place, as S. Abubakar has recently pointed out and as is evident from many of the chapters above, most of the African states were acquired as a result of the conquest and deposition or exile of the then rulers which 'certainly brought into disrepute the whole business of chieftaincy, especially during the period before the First World War'.[13] Some of the colonial powers, such as the French as we have seen already, also abolished some of the traditional monarchies and ruling families altogether, appointed people as chiefs who had no right to such posts and turned all of them into administrative officers. The British and the Belgians retained the traditional rulers and their institutions and even, as R. F. Betts has shown (Chapter 13), created some where they did not exist and tried to administer the colonies through them. However, the colonial officials on the spot became, in effect, dictators instead of advisers to these traditional rulers and used them also to enforce some of the measures deemed obnoxious by their subjects such as forced labour, direct taxes and compulsory recruitment of men for the colonial armies. This manipulation of the institution of chieftaincy resulted in loss of prestige and respect of the traditional rulers in the eyes of their subjects. The colonial records, as recent research into rural politics in the inter-war years in Ghana has shown,[14] are full of revolts and rebellions by the young men against their chiefs and even their destoolment. Besides, the colonial system of administering justice in which subjects could appeal to the colonial courts further weakened not only the authority but also

12. A. A. Mazrui, 1980, p. 90.
13. S. Abubakar in O. Ikime (ed.), 1980, p. 451.
14. P. Jenkins (ed.), 1975.

the financial resources of the traditional rulers.[15] Furthermore, the spread of the Christian religion undermined the spiritual basis of the authority of the kings. In all these ways, then, the colonial system, in accordance with its own interests, at times weakened or even destroyed the traditional rulers and at times allied with them and used them. But in both cases, the colonial system finally diminished their authority.

Another negative impact of colonialism in the political field was the mentality that it created among Africans that government and all public property belonged not to the people but rather to the white colonial rulers and could and should therefore be taken advantage of at the least opportunity. This mentality is evident from the Ghanaian saying that *Oburoni ade see a, egu po mu*, or, *aban wotwuu no adze wonnsua no* meaning that if the white man's property gets damaged, it should simply be dumped into the sea, or government should be dragged on the ground rather than carried aloft. Both sayings imply that nobody should be concerned with what happens to government property. This mentality was the direct product of the remote and esoteric nature of the colonial administration and the elimination of an overwhelming majority of Africans, both educated and uneducated, from the decision-making process. It is important to note that this mentality is still with most Africans even after decades of independence and is part of the explanation for the reckless way in which government property is handled in many independent African countries.

A product of colonialism and one which is often ignored by most historians, but which has turned out to be of crucial and fundamental importance, was, as is evident from R. E. Betts' contribution (Chapter 13), a full-time or standing army. As has been amply demonstrated, most traditional African states south of the Sahara did not have standing armies. In the whole of western Africa, it was only Dahomey that had a standing army with its unique female wing, the famous Amazons. In most cases, there was not a dichotomy between civilians and soldiers. Rather, all adult males, including even members of the ruling aristocracy, became soldiers in times of war and civilians in times of peace. Thus, one of the most novel institutions introduced by each colonial ruler was the professional army. These armies were originally created, most of them in the 1880s and 1890s, first for the conquest and occupation of Africa, then for the maintenance of colonial control, and, finally, for the prosecution of global wars and the suppression of independence movements in Africa. After the overthrow of the colonial rulers, these armies were not disbanded but were taken over by the new independent African rulers and they have turned out to be the most problematic of the products of colonialism since, as W. Gutteridge has admitted, the armed forces have 'operated in the longer term against the stability of the ex-colonies'.[16] Indeed, as will be seen

15. R. Addo-Fening, 1980, pp. 509–15.
16. W. Gutteridge, 1975.

in the next volume, as a result of their repeated and often unnecessary and unjustifiable interventions in the politics of independent African states, those armies have become the heaviest of the millstones round the necks of African governments and peoples.

The final and probably the most important negative impact of colonialism was the loss of African sovereignty and independence and with them the right of Africans to shape their own destiny or deal directly with the outside world. As early as the sixteenth and seventeenth centuries, the states of Africa such as Benin and the Congo could send embassies and missions to the courts of European kings. Even until as late as the 1890s, as we have seen already, some African states could deal with their European counterparts as equals. The Asantehene, the King of Matabeleland and the Queen of Madagascar sent diplomatic missions to the Queen of England in the 1890s. Colonialism put an end to this and thereby deprived African states of the opportunity of acquiring experience in the conduct of international relations and diplomacy.

But the loss of independence and sovereignty meant far more to Africans than this. It meant, above all, the loss of their right to control their own destiny, plan their own development, manage their economy, determine their own strategies and priorities, borrow freely from the outside world at large the latest and most appropriate technology, and generally manage or even mismanage their own affairs and derive inspiration and a sense of fulfilment from their successes, and lessons and experience from their failures. In short, colonialism deprived Africans of one of the most fundamental and inalienable rights of a people, the right of liberty.

Moreover, as Rodney has shown, the seventy-year period of colonialism in Africa was the very period which witnessed tremendous and decisive developments and changes in both the capitalist and socialist countries. It was that period, for instance, that saw the entry of Europe into the nuclear age and the age of the aeroplane and the motor vehicle. Had Africa been in control of her own destiny, she could have benefited from or even been part of these phenomenal changes. But colonialism completely isolated and insulated her from these changes and kept her in a position of dependency. It is clearly in this loss of independence and sovereignty, in this denial of the fundamental right to liberty and in this political isolation imposed on Africa by colonialism that we see another of the most pernicious political impacts of colonialism on Africa.

The impact in the economic field

The impact in the political field, then, was important though of mixed blessing. Equally and even more so was the impact in the economic field. The first and most obvious and profound of the positive impacts here, as is evident from many of the chapters above, was the provision of an infrastructure of motor roads, railways, the telegraph, the telephone and in some cases even airports. These did not exist in pre-colonial Africa where, as J. C. Caldwell has shown, until the colonial era, 'nearly all land transport was by human porterage' (Chapter 18). This basic infrastructure had been completed in Africa by the 1930s and not many new miles of, say, railways have been built since then. This particular development is more than of economic interest since it facilitated movement not only of goods, new cash crops and troops but also of peoples and this latter factor helped to minimize parochialism, regionalism and ethnocentricism.

Equally important and significant was the impact of colonialism on the primary sector of the economy. As is obvious from above, every effort was made to develop or exploit some of the rich natural resources of the continent, and this was attended by some significant successes. It was during the colonial period that the full mineral potential of Africa was realized and the mining industry definitely boomed, while the cultivation of cash crops such as cocoa, coffee, tobacco, groundnuts, sisal and rubber spread. It was certainly during the colonial period that Ghana became the world's leading producer of cocoa while by 1950 farm crops were accounting for 50% of the gross domestic product of French West Africa. It should be emphasized, as M. H. Y. Kaniki has done above (Chapter 16), that in West Africa these cash crops were produced by the Africans themselves, clear evidence of their willingness and ability to adapt and respond to the right incentives. As J. Forbes Munro has shown, most of these fundamental economic changes took place during the two decades from the mid-1890s to 1914 'when the infrastructural foundations of most contemporary national economies were laid down by colonial governments and commerce between Africa and the rest of the world grew at an historically unprecedented rate'.[17]

This economic revolution had some far-reaching consequences. The first one was commercialization of land which made it a real asset. Before the colonial era, there is absolutely no doubt that huge tracts of land in many parts of Africa were not only underpopulated but also under-utilized. The introduction and spread of cash crops and the mining industries put an end to all this. Indeed, such was the pace of the utilization of virgin forests that, in many parts of Africa, the colonial administration created forest reserves to prevent further encroachment. Secondly, the economic revolution led to an increase in the purchasing power of some Africans and with it an increase in their demand for consumer goods. Thirdly, the growing of cash crops by Africans enabled individuals of whatever social status, especially in the rural areas, to acquire wealth.

Another significant revolutionary impact of colonialism in many parts of the continent was the introduction of the money economy. As W. Rodney has pointed out above (Chapter 14), every sector of the African community including even the pastoral groups, who were noted for their conservatism,

17. J. F. Munro, 1976, p. 86.

had been drawn into the money economy by the 1920s.[18] Again, the effects of this shift were very significant. In the first place, even by the 1930s, a new standard of wealth had been introduced which was based not only on the number of sheep or cows or yams one possessed but on actual cash. Secondly, people were engaged in activities not for subsistence alone but also to earn money which, in turn, led, as will be seen later, to the emergence of a new class of wage earners and salaried groups. Thirdly, the introduction of the money economy led to the commencement of banking activities in Africa, which have become another significant feature of the economy of independent African states.

The introduction of currency and with it banking activities and the tremendous expansion in the volume of trade between colonial Africa and Europe in turn led to what A. G. Hopkins has described as the completion of 'the integration of West Africa into the economy of the industrial world' through 'the creation of conditions which gave Europeans and Africans both the means and the incentive to expand and diversify legitimate commerce'.[19] This was true of the other parts of Africa also, and so by 1935, the economy of Africa had become inextricably tied to that of the world in general and to that of the capitalist economy of the colonial powers in particular. The years after 1935 merely deepened this link and not even independence has fundamentally altered this relationship.

Was the colonial impact on Africa in the economic field, then, such a very enviable one? Far from it, and most of the present-day developmental problems facing African countries can be traced to this.

In the first place, as M. H. Y. Kaniki has pointed out above (Chapter 16), the infrastructure that was provided by colonialism was not as adequate nor as useful as it could have been. Most of the roads and railways were constructed not to open up the country but merely to connect the areas having mineral deposits and potentialities for the production of cash crops with the sea or, to quote Fieldhouse, 'to link internal areas of production to the world commodity market',[20] and there were hardly any feeder or branch roads. Nor were they meant to facilitate inter-African travel and communication. Such infrastructure as was provided was meant, then, to facilitate the exploitation of the resources of the colonies and to link them with the metropolitan countries but not to promote the over all economic development of Africa nor to promote inter-African contacts. In the second place, such economic growth as occurred in the colonies was based on the natural resources of the area and this meant therefore that areas not naturally endowed were totally neglected. This led to sharp economic differences in the same colony. These differences, in turn, accentuated and exacerbated regional differences and sentiments which have been a great impediment in the way of nation-building in independent Africa.

18. See Chapter 14 above.
19. A. G. Hopkins, 1973, p. 235.
20. D. K. Fieldhouse, 1981, p. 67.

As an eminent economist has pointed out, 'tribal differences might disappear easily in the modern world if all tribes were equal economically. Where they are vastly unequal, tribal difference is called in to add protection to economic interest.'[21]

Thirdly, a typical feature of the colonial economy was the total and deliberate negligence or discouragement of industrialization and the processing of locally produced raw materials and agricultural products in most of the colonies. As Fieldhouse has pointed out, 'Probably no colonial government had a department of industry before 1945'.[22] Simple and basic items such as matches, candles, cigarettes, edible oil, even lime and orange juice all of which could easily have been produced in Africa were imported. All African states were, therefore, in accordance with the workings of the colonial capitalist economy, turned into markets for the consumption of manufactured goods from the metropolitan countries and producers of raw materials for export. It is this total neglect of industrialization by the colonial powers and their mercantile and mining companies which should be chalked up as one of the most unpardonable indictments against colonialism. It also provides the strongest justification for the view that the colonial period was the era of the economic exploitation rather than the development of Africa. One of the important effects of this neglect of industrialization was that, to a greater extent even than in the political field, few Africans were trained to take over from the Europeans.

Fourthly, not only was industrialization neglected but such industries and crafts as had existed in Africa in pre-colonial times were almost destroyed. It should be emphasized that Africa's pre-colonial industries produced all that Africans needed including building materials, soap, beads, iron tools, pottery and above all cloth. Had these manufacturers been encouraged and promoted through the modernization of productive techniques, as was done in India between 1920 and 1945,[23] Africa could not only have increased her output but could have steadily improved her technology. But these crafts and industries were all virtually killed as a result of the importation of cheap commodities produced on a mass basis into Africa. African technological development was thereby halted and was never resumed until after independence.

Fifthly, even though agricultural crops came to constitute the main source of income for most African states, no attempts were made to diversify the agricultural economy of the colonies. On the contrary, as has been shown in some of the earlier chapters, by 1935, the production of only single or at best two cash crops had become the rule – cocoa in the Gold Coast, groundnuts in Senegal and The Gambia, cotton in Sudan, coffee and cotton in Uganda, coffee and sisal in Tanganyika, etc. The period after the Second World War did not see any improvement in this area

21. W. A. Lewis, 1965, pp. 24–5.
22. D. K. Fieldhouse, 1981, p. 68.
23. ibid., pp. 92–5.

hence most African states, on the attainment of independence, found themselves saddled with monocrop economies and were therefore highly sensitive to the prevailing international trade conditions. Colonialism did indeed complete the integration of African economies into the world international economic order but in a very disadvantageous and exploitative manner and this has not been altered ever since.

The heavy reliance on cash crops had another disastrous effect, which was the negligence of the internal sector of the economy of Africa. The economy of Africa had always been divided, as M. H. Y. Kaniki has pointed out above (Chapter 16), into two major sectors – the internal sector which produced both for the subsistence of producers and for the home market and the export sector which catered for the long-distance and caravan trade. Both sectors were given equal emphasis in pre-colonial times with the result that neither food nor fish was imported to feed anyone. However, because of the concentration on the production of cash crops during the colonial era, the internal sector was virtually neglected and Africans were in fact compelled to ignore the production of food for their own consumption in favour of the production of cash crops for export even where, as Fieldhouse has observed, it was uneconomic to do so.[24] Food therefore had to be imported which the ordinary people had to buy, usually at high prices, to feed themselves. This, for instance, was what happened in The Gambia where the Gambians were made to abandon the cultivation of rice in favour of the production of groundnuts, and rice therefore had to be imported.[25] In Guinea, Africans in the Futa Jallon area were compelled to produce rubber which led to a shortage of rice in 1911. Rice therefore had to be imported and bought with the money earned from rubber. Egypt, which for centuries exported grains and foodstuffs, was compelled to import maize and wheat from the beginning of the twentieth century onwards owing to her excessive concentration on the production of cotton for export. The same thing happened in the Gold Coast where cocoa production was so much emphasized that foodstuffs had to be imported. This is evident from the lament of A. W. Cardinall, one of the sympathetic colonial officials in the 1930s, that the country could have itself produced half 'the fresh fish, rice, maize, and other meal, beans, salted and fresh meat, edible oils, spices and fresh vegetables [imported], or in other words would have saved 200000 pounds'.[26] It was this neglect of food production coupled with forced labour which caused so much malnutrition, severe famine and epidemics in some parts of Africa during the early colonial days, especially in the areas of French Africa, as C. Coquery-Vidrovitch has pointed out above (Chapter 15). Thus, under the colonial system, Africans were in most cases made to produce what they did not consume and to consume what they did not produce,

24. ibid., p. 88.
25. W. Rodney, 1972, pp. 257–8.
26. Quoted by M. Crowder, 1968, p. 348.

clear evidence of the lopsided and exploitive nature of the colonial economy.

In those parts of Africa where Africans were not allowed to grow cash crops such as Kenya and Southern Rhodesia (now Zimbabwe), as Colin Leys has shown, 'within the space of a generation they had effectively been converted from independent peasants, producing cash crops for the new markets, into peasants dependent on agricultural wage-labour'.[27]

Sixthly, the commercialization of land already referred to led to the illegal sale of communal lands by unscrupulous family-heads and to increasing litigation over land which caused widespread poverty especially among the ruling houses. In East, Central and Southern Africa, as has been shown in many of the earlier chapters, it also led to large-scale appropriation of land by Europeans. In South Africa 89% of land was reserved for whites who constitute 21% of the population, 37% of land in Southern Rhodesia for only 5.2%, 7% of Kenya for less than 10% of the population, 3% in Northern Rhodesia (now Zambia) for only 2½% of the population, and all these lands were the most fertile in each country.[28] Such appropriation could not but cause much bitterness, anger and frustration and constituted the fundamental cause of the serious explosion that occurred in Kenya known as Mau Mau.

The colonial presence also led, as has been pointed out above, to the appearance on the African scene of an increasing number of expatriate banking, shipping and trading firms and companies, and from the 1910s onwards their amalgamation and consolidation into fewer and fewer oligopolies. Since it was these trading companies that controlled the export as well as the import trade and fixed the prices not only of imported commodities but also of the exports produced by the Africans, the huge profits that accrued from these activities went to the companies and not to the Africans. Moreover, there was hardly any tax on profits nor were there any regulations compelling the companies to invest part of their profits locally or to pay higher rents for concessions. Neither the local colonial administrations nor the African landowners therefore benefited directly from their activities. The other consequence of this development was of course the elimination of Africans from the most profitable and important sectors of the economy altogether. The African merchant princes of the second half of the nineteenth century therefore virtually disappeared from the scene while their descendants merely had to become the employees of the expatriate firms and companies in order to survive. Here again, as in the industrial field, the emergence of a class of Africans with business experience and managerial skills was prevented.

Colonialism, as Rodney has pointed out, also virtually put a stop to inter-African trade. Before the colonial era, a great deal of trading went on between African states and long-distance and caravan trading activities were a very common feature of the economies of Africa. But with the

27. C. Leys, 1975, p. 31.
28. M. J. Herskovits, 1962, pp. 147–50; A. Sampson, 1960, pp. 46–7.

establishment of colonialism, such inter-African short- and long-distance trade was discouraged if not banned altogether as, in the words of Rodney, 'the arbitrary political boundaries of each colony were generally taken to mean the limit of the economies',[29] and as the flow of trade from each colony was reoriented towards the metropolitan country. The elimination of much of this age-long inter-African trade and commercial relations thus prevented the strengthening of old links and the development of new ones that could have proved of benefit to Africans. For the same reason, Africa was also prevented from developing direct trading links with other parts of the world such as India and China.

Finally, whatever economic growth was achieved during the colonial period was done at a phenomenal and unjustifiable cost to the African – what with forced labour, migrant labour (which, says Davidson, 'probably did more to dismantle pre-colonial cultures and economies than most other aspects of the colonial experience put together'),[30] compulsory cultivation of certain crops, compulsory seizure of land, forced movements of populations with the consequential dislocation of family life, the pass system, the high mortality rate in the mines and on the plantations, the brutality with which African resistance and protest movements generated by these measures were suppressed, etc. Above all, the monetary policies pursued by the colonial powers towards their colonies – tying their currencies to those of the colonial powers, introducing tariffs and keeping all foreign exchange earnings in the metropolitan capitals – while ensuring stable and fully convertible currencies, led to the freezing of colonial assets in the metropolitan capitals instead of their being realized and invested in the colonies. The repatriation of savings and deposits of Africans by the banks and the discrimination practised against Africans in the granting of loans further impeded African development.

From the above, it can be safely concluded, in spite of the protestations of Gann and Duignan, that the colonial period was a period of ruthless economic exploitation rather than of economic development in Africa, and that the impact of colonialism in Africa in the economic field is easily the bleakest of all.

The impact in the social field

Finally, what is the record of colonialism in the social field? The first important beneficial social effect was the overall increase of the population of Africa during the colonial period by about 37.5%, as J. C. Caldwell has shown (Chapter 18), after its decline during the first two or three decades of colonialism. This increase, according to Caldwell, was due to the establishment of an economic base, the spread of roads and railways which ensured the rushing of food to famine areas, and the campaigns

29. See Chapter 14 above.
30. B. Davidson, 1978(b), p. 113.

launched against epidemic diseases such as sleeping sickness, bubonic plague and yellow fever.

Closely connected with this and the second social impact of colonialism was urbanization. As A. E. Afigbo has emphasized (Chapter 19), urbanization was of course not unknown in pre-colonial Africa. The kingdoms and empires of Africa had such capitals or political centres as Kumbi Saleh, Benin, Ile-Ife, Kumasi, Gao and Great Zimbabwe; such commercial centres as Kano, Jenne, Sofala and Malindi, and such educational centres as Timbuktu, Cairo and Fez. But there is no doubt that as a result of colonialism, the pace of urbanization was greatly accelerated. Completely new towns such as Abidjan in Ivory Coast, Takoradi in the Gold Coast, Port Harcourt and Enugu in Nigeria, Nairobi in Kenya, Salisbury (now Harare) in Southern Rhodesia, Lusaka in Northern Rhodesia and Luluabourg in the Kasai Province of the Belgian Congo (now Zaire) came into existence.

Moreover, as Caldwell has shown above (Chapter 18), the population of both the already existing towns and those of the new ones grew by leaps and bounds during the colonial era. The population of Nairobi, founded in 1896 as a transit depot for the construction of the Uganda Railway, increased from a mere handful to 13145 in 1927 and to over 25000 by 1940. The population of Casablanca rose from 2026 in 1910 to 250000 in 1936; that of Accra in the Gold Coast from 17892 in 1901 to 135926 in 1948; that of Lagos from 74000 in 1914 to 230000 in 1950, that of Dakar from 19800 in 1916 to 92000 in 1936, and to 132000 in 1945; and finally that of Abidjan from only 800 in 1910 to 10000 in 1914, and to 127000 by 1955. It is quite clear from these figures that this rapid growth of urban population in Africa took place after the First World War, and especially during the period 1919 and 1945, which has been described as the heyday of colonialism in Africa. Moreover, these towns grew so rapidly during this period simply because they were either the new capitals or administrative centres of the colonial regimes – for instance Abidjan, Niamey, Nairobi, Salisbury and Lusaka; or the new harbours, railway termini or crossroads such as Takoradi, Port Harcourt, Bamako and Bulawayo or the new mining and commercial centres such as Obuasi, Jos, Luluabourg, Kimberley and Johannesburg.

There was undoubtedly also an improvement in the quality of life particularly for those living in the urban centres. This, as Caldwell has shown (Chapter 18), was the product of the provision of hospitals, dispensaries, pipe-borne water, sanitary facilities, better housing and the abolition of such practices as domestic slavery by the colonial rulers as well as the increase in employment opportunities.

The spread of Christianity, Islam and western education was another important impact of colonialism. There is no doubt that taking advantage of the peace and order as well as the patronage and in some areas the positive encouragement provided by colonialism, Christian missionaries and Muslim clerics pushed their activities further and further inland. As

K. Asare Opoku has shown (Chapter 20), Christianity and Islam gained far more ground during the colonial period than had been the case during the previous three or four centuries put together. It was during this period that Christianity gained a firm foothold in East and Central Africa at times following or at times being followed by the flag and trade. Islam also spread rapidly in West and East Africa as a result of the general improvement of communications during the colonial period and the patronage of both the French and the British rulers. It should be emphasized, as Opoku has done, that these gains were not made at the expense of traditional religion. What colonialism did, then, was to strengthen and perpetuate religious pluralism in Africa and thereby enrich her religious life.

Closely associated with the spread of Christianity was that of western education. As has been shown in many of the chapters above, the Christian missions were mainly responsible for this. It should, however, be borne in mind that they could operate mainly because of the grants they received from the colonial administrations. Certainly, by the end of the colonial regime, there were relatively few areas without at least elementary schools. The spread of western education had far-reaching social effects among which was an increase in the number of the westernized educated African elite, an elite which now constitutes the ruling oligarchy and the backbone of the civil service of African states.

Another important colonial impact, a mixed blessing as will be shown later, was of course the provision of a *lingua franca* for each colony or set of colonies. In all the colonies, the mother tongue of the colonial power, either in its pure or pidgin form, became the official and business language and in many cases the main means of communication between the numerous linguistic groups that constitute the population of each colony. It is significant that except in North Africa, Tanzania, Kenya and Madagascar, these languages have remained the official languages even to this very day.

The final beneficial social impact was the new social structure that colonialism introduced into some parts of Africa or whose development it accelerated in other parts. As A. E. Afigbo has pointed out (Chapter 19), though the traditional social structure allowed for social mobility, its class structure appeared to give undue weight to birth. The new colonial order on the other hand, emphasized individual merit and achievement rather than birth. This change together with the abolition of slavery, the introduction of western education, Christianity and Islam, the expansion of cash-crop agriculture which facilitated the acquisition of wealth in some areas and the many other avenues for advancement that the new colonial order introduced, radically altered the traditional social structure. Thus, by the 1930s, in place of the pre-colonial social classes of the traditional ruling aristocracy, the ordinary people, domestic slaves and a relatively small educated elite, had emerged a new society that had become more sharply divided than before into urban and rural dwellers, each of which was differently stratified. The urban dwellers had become divided into three main sub-groups: the elite or as others call them the administrative-clerical-professional bourgeoisie; the non-elite or, as Lloyd prefers to call them, the sub-elite, and the urban proletariat. The elite was subdivided into three groups: the bureaucratic elite of civil servants, the professional elite of doctors, lawyers, architects, surveyors, professors, etc., and the commercial elite of managers of the expatriate firms and companies and private traders and businessmen. The sub-elite consisted of brokers, middlemen, clerks, teachers, nurses and junior civil servants, while the urban proletariat consisted of the wage-earners, store assistants, drivers, mechanics, messengers, tailors, bricklayers, etc. In the rural areas, there emerged for the first time in many parts of Africa new classes, namely, a rural proletariat of landless Africans, and peasants. The former consisted of those Africans especially in East and Southern Africa, whose lands had been alienated by the Europeans but who were not allowed to reside permanently in the urban and industrial centres and were therefore compelled to spend their lives shunting between the urban and rural areas, mainly as migrant labourers. The peasants were those described by John Iliffe as people who 'live in small communities, cultivate land they own or control, rely chiefly on family labour, and produce their own subsistence while also supplying larger economic systems which include non-peasants'.[31] Some members of the latter class became quite wealthy through the production of cash crops for sale which led to the development of what has been described as rural capitalism. Iliffe has described this 'peasantization' as 'a once-for-all transformation comparable in impact to industrialisation'. It should be emphasized that since mobility within this new structure was based more on individual effort and attainment rather than on ascription, it was a considerable improvement on the traditional social structure.

But if colonialism did have some positive social impact, it did have some negative, indeed some seriously negative ones too. The first of these was the creation and widening of the gap between the urban centres and rural areas that developed during the colonial period. The phenomenal growth of the population of the urban centres that we noted above was not the result of the natural increase of the urban population but rather of what has been described as 'push-pull forces',[32] the continuous pull of young men and women to the urban centres by the need for education and employment and the push from the rural areas, as C. Coquery-Vidrovitch has shown above (Chapter 15), by famine, epidemic, poverty and taxation. Moreover, since the Europeans tended to live in the urban centres, all those facilities that improved the quality of life enumerated above were established only in those areas. The rural areas were therefore virtually neglected, which, in turn, accentuated the drift from one to the other. A huge gap exists even today between urban and rural areas in Africa

31. J. Iliffe, 1979, p. 273–4.
32. F. Wilson in M. Wilson and L. Thompson (eds), 1971, p. 132.

and there is no doubt that it was the colonial system that originated and widened this gap.

Nor did the migrants find the urban centres the safe and rich haven that they had expected. In no town were the Africans accepted as equals and fully integrated. Moreover, nowhere did a majority of them find jobs or decent accommodation. Most of them found themselves crowded into the suburbs and the shanty towns in which unemployment, juvenile delinquency, drunkenness, prostitution, crime and corruption became their lot. Colonialism did not only impoverish rural life, but it also bastardized urban life. It is not surprising then that members of this group became the storm-troopers of the nationalist movements after the Second World War.

A second serious social legacy has been the European and Asiatic settler problem. Though there were European settlers in the North African states and in South Africa before the colonial era, there is no doubt that not only did the number of these people increase but European and Asiatic settlers were also introduced into East and Central Africa and parts of West Africa during the colonial days. As M. H. Y. Kaniki has shown above (Chapter 16), the number of Europeans in Kenya rose from only 596 in 1903 to 954 in 1905, to 5438 in 1914 and to 16663 in 1929; that in Southern Rhodesia increased from 11000 in 1901 to over 35000 by 1926,[33] and that in Algeria from 344000 in 1876 to 946000 in 1936. But in many areas in East, Central and North Africa, what made their presence so inimical to Africans was that the Europeans came to occupy most of the fertile lands, while the Asiatics monopolized the retail and wholesale trade. In West Africa, too, the Asiatics – Syrian, Lebanese and Indians – whose population increased from only 28 in 1897 to 276 in 1900, 1910 in 1909, 3000 in 1929 and to 6000 by 1935 also drove out their African competitors. By 1935, this European and Asiatic problem had assumed very serious proportions for Africa and it has not been entirely resolved to this day.

Furthermore, though colonialism did introduce some social services as has been pointed out already, it must be emphasized that not only were these services grossly inadequate and unevenly distributed in each colony, but they were all by and large meant primarily for the benefit of the few white settlers and administrators, hence their concentration in the towns. Rodney has shown that in Nigeria in the 1930s whereas there were twelve modern hospitals for 4000 Europeans in the country, there were only fifty-two for Africans numbering over 40 million.[34] In Tanganyika by 1920, the ratio of beds to population was approximately 1:10 for the European Hospital and 1:400–500 for the African Hospital in Dar es Salaam.[35]

In the field of education, what was provided during the colonial days was grossly inadequate, unevenly distributed and badly orientated and therefore not as beneficial as it could have been for Africa. Five different

33. See Chapter 16 above.
34. W. Rodney, 1972, p. 223.
35. D. E. Ferguson in M. H. Y. Kaniki (ed.), 1980, p. 326.

types of educational institutions were established under colonial rule: primary, secondary, teacher-training, technical and university. But while many primary schools had been established by 1860 in British West Africa, it was not until 1876 that the first secondary schools, Mfantsipim and the Methodist High School, were established in the Gold Coast and Nigeria respectively, both by the Wesleyan Missionary Society, while the British colonial administration did not establish its first secondary school (Achimota College) in the Gold Coast until 1927. In the Italian colony of Libya, as it has been pointed out already, there were only three secondary schools for the Libyans by 1940, two in Tripoli and one in Benghazi. It was not until after the Second World War that technical schools and university colleges were established in most parts of Africa. And significantly, only one university college each was established in the Gold Coast in 1947, in Nigeria in 1948, in Uganda in 1950, in Senegal and Madagascar in 1950, in Salisbury in 1953, in Congo Leopoldville in 1954 and Elizabethville in 1956. In other words, university and technical education was not introduced into Africa until towards the end of the colonial era.

Moreover, nowhere and at no level did the facilities provided meet the demand nor were they evenly distributed. As even Lloyd admits, as late as the mid-1930s, 'government expenditure everywhere remained low, amounting in the mid-1930s to only 4% of total revenue in Nigeria and the French territories, and 7% in Ghana'.[36] Nor were these schools and institutions properly distributed in each colony. Most of the post-primary institutions were found in the main urban centres and in some countries most of the secondary schools were found in one town. In the Gold Coast for example about 80% of the secondary schools were found in Cape Coast. In Uganda, by 1920, there were 328 elementary schools in Buganda and only 34, 24 and practically none in the Western, Eastern and Northern provinces respectively.[37] Facilities for education were so inadequate and so unevenly distributed, because the colonial powers did not aim at promoting education for its own sake or for the sake of the Africans, but rather, to quote one African scholar, 'to produce Africans who would be more productive for the [colonial] system'.[38]

Besides its grossly inadequate nature numerically and its uneven distribution, the curricula provided by all these institutions were determined by the colonial rulers and were closely modelled on, if not carbon copies of, those of the metropolitan countries and therefore irrelevant to the needs of the continent. No less an authority than the Governor of the Gold Coast from 1919 to 1927, Sir Gordon Guggisberg, testified in 1920: 'One of the greatest mistakes of the education in the past has been this, that it has taught the African to become a European instead of remaining African. This is entirely wrong and the Government recognizes it. In future, our

36. P. C. Lloyd, 1972, p. 79.
37. T. B. Kabwegyere, 1974, p. 179.
38. ibid., p. 110.

education will aim at making an African remain an African and taking interest in his own country.'[39]

But though Guggisberg did establish Achimota College to make good this promise, not much was achieved since education in the country continued to be controlled by the Christian missions whose primary aim was to produce people who could read the Bible in English or in the vernacular as well as teachers and priests.

The impact of this inadequate, lopsided and wrongly orientated education on African societies has been profound and almost permanent. First, it left Africa with a huge illiteracy problem, a problem whose solution will take a long time. Secondly, the educated elite that was produced was by and large an alienated elite, an elite that adored European culture and civilization and looked down on African culture, that had new tastes in food, drink, clothing, music, dance and even games, an elite so brilliantly lampooned by the radical Ghanaian scholar and nationalist, Kobina Sekyi in his play *The Blinkards*. Another gap thereby came to exist between this elite and the rest of the masses which has still not been bridged. Moreover, though the membership of this elite increased in the 1940s and 1950s with the increase in educational facilities and the establishment of university colleges, it nevertheless remained extremely small throughout the colonial era. However, since the elite came to include the wealthiest people and since they came to occupy the highest posts available both during and after the colonial era, they came to wield power and influence totally out of proportion to their number and relations between them on the one hand and the traditional elite on the other became strained during the colonial days and have never really been healed ever since.

Furthermore, the explanation of phenomena such as death, rainfall and sickness in natural and scientific terms also struck at the very roots of African religious beliefs, sanctions and taboos and thereby shook the foundations of African societies bringing in its trail a sense of uncertainty, frustration and insecurity – an atmosphere so brilliantly captured by Chinua Achebe in his novel *Things Fall Apart*. This sense of insecurity and frustration, often heightened by the series of economic crises that occurred, especially in the 1920s and 1930s and after the war, led, especially in the towns, to a high incidence of crime, divorce, delinquency and violence. It was this same situation that partly accounts in the religious field for the rise of the millenarian and Ethiopian or syncretic churches that have already been discussed.

The neglect of technical and industrial education and the emphasis on liberal and clerical training and the consequent love for white-collar jobs also created among the educated folk disdain for manual labour and agricultural work which is still with us. Furthermore, the uneven nature of the distribution of educational facilities prevented a uniform process of

39. Quoted by R. Addo-Fening, 1980.

modernization in each colony, which further accentuated differences and tensions between ethnic groups and regions. These have remained in many areas and underlie some of the civil wars and rivalries that have occurred in some independent African states. The neglect of higher education and technical training also compelled some Africans who could afford to do so, to send their children to the metropolitan countries as well as to the United States, and it was such people who, partly from their varying experiences of racial discrimination and, even more important still, their deeper appreciation of the evil nature of the colonial system, became on their return, as will be shown in the next volume, the most bitter critics of the system and the leaders of the anti-colonial or nationalist movements.

Beneficial as the *lingua franca* which was promoted through the educational system was, it had the regrettable consequence of preventing the development of some of the indigenous languages into national languages or *lingua franca*. Twi, Hausa and Swahili could easily have been developed as the national languages of the Gold Coast, Nigeria and the three British East African colonies respectively. In fact, as Kabwegyere has shown, an attempt was made by the colonial administrators of British East Africa to develop Swahili into a *lingua franca* in the 1930s and 1940s but this attempt was countermanded by the Colonial Office. The reason given for this merits quotation:

> ... The development of a *lingua franca* has very little connection with immediate expediency, being essentially concerned with enduring values and hence with a penetration which however gradual shall steadily become co-extensive with the country. Applying this criterion neither Swahili nor Ganda nor any other vernacular has admissible claims.[40]

And this advice went on to add that only English should be recognized 'as the inevitable *lingua franca* of the future, a fact which general and education policy should admit without delay'. It is doubtful if any of the other colonial powers even ever considered this possibility. With the departure of the colonial powers, who could have been credited with some objectivity in this exercise and who also had the power to enforce any such language policy, and with the unfortunate upsurge and hardening of ethnic and regional sentiments since independence in many African countries, the question of an indigenous *lingua franca* has become an extremely sensitive one, and it is not surprising that only a few African governments have been able to touch it so far.

Another highly regrettable social impact of colonialism was the deterioration that it caused in the status of the woman in Africa. This is a new theme which needs further research but there does not appear to be any doubt that women were inhibited from joining most of the activities intro-

40. Quoted by T. B. Kabwegyere, 1974, p. 218.

duced or intensified by colonialism such as Western education, cash-crop farming in some parts of Africa, many of the professions and job opportunities such as law, medicine, mining, etc. Nor were they, partly as a result of this exclusion, given any place in the new colonial political set-up. Even in matrilineal societies, partly because of the spread of Islam and partly because of the new emphasis on individual achievement, some families began to move towards the patrilineal system.[41] The colonial world, as Iliffe has pointed out, was indeed a man's world and women were not encouraged to play any meaningful role in it.

Moreover, as a result of colonialism, the African himself was looked down upon, humiliated, and discriminated against both overtly and covertly. Indeed, as A. E. Afigbo has contended above (Chapter 19), one of the social impacts of colonialism 'was the general depression of the status of Africans'. Ali Mazrui also emphasized this legacy of humiliation imposed on the African by the triple sins of the slave trade, apartheid and colonialism in his recent Reith Lectures. 'Africans,' he said, 'are not necessarily the most brutalized of peoples, but they are almost certainly the most humiliated in modern history'.[42] Thus, although, as has been pointed out above, the members of the educated elite admired European culture and went out of their way to identify with it, yet they were never accepted as the equal of their European counterparts, they were barred from the societies of the Europeans and were prevented from living in the European quarters of the towns, parts which Sembene Ousmane has called 'the Vatican' in his novel *God's Bits of Wood*.[43]

Instead of growing weaker with the progress of colonial rule, this discrimination, which was propped up by the bogus racial theories and the Social Darwinist ideas of the day, grew in intensity, culminating in South Africa in the inhuman and bogus philosophy of apartheid. The educated elite therefore became disgruntled and bitter and it is not surprising that they were the first to develop a strong consciousness of the iniquities and exploitative and discriminatory nature of the colonial system and increasingly questioned the moral and legal basis for its continued existence. It was this very class produced by the colonial and missionary presence that was to lead the campaign for the overthrow of the colonial system. Some historians such as M. H. Y. Kaniki have concluded that 'colonialism ... produced its own grave-diggers', while Robin Maugham has maintained that 'on the tombstone of the British Empire' [in which this racial discrimination was most overt] 'may be written "Lost by snobbery".'[44] Both conclusions are unexceptionable. This racial discrimination also created in some Africans a deep sense of inferiority which Afigbo has defined above

41. J. Iliffe, 1979, p. 300.
42. A. A. Mazrui, 1980, pp. 23–45.
43. S. Ousmane, 1962, p. 162.
44. M. H. Y. Kaniki, 1980 (a) in M. H. Y. Kaniki (ed.), 1980, p. 10; R. F. R. Maugham, 1961, p. 84.

quite succintly as 'a tendency to lose confidence in himself and his future –
in short, a state of mind which at times encouraged an uncritical imitation
of [and one may add subservience to] European powers' (Chapter 19).
This feeling of inferiority has not entirely disappeared even after two
decades of independence.

Even worse still was the impact of colonialism in the cultural field.
Indeed, as it was declared at the Second Congress of Negro Writers and
Artists in Rome in March–April 1959, 'among the sins of colonialism, one
of the most pernicious because it was for a long time accepted by the
West without discussion, was the concept of peoples without culture'.[45]
But this should not surprise us. As P. Curtin and others have pointed
out, 'The European movement into Africa coincided with the nineteenth-
and twentieth-century peak of racism and cultural chauvinism in Europe
itself'.[46] The Europeans who moved into Africa during this period,
especially between 1900 and 1945 – missionaries, traders, administrators,
settlers, engineers and miners alike – were generally imbued with this spirit
and therefore condemned everything African – African music, art, dance,
names, religion, marriage, systems of inheritance, etc. To be admitted into
a Church, an African had not only to be baptized but had to change his
name and renounce a whole range of traditional practices. Even the wearing
of African dress was banned or discouraged in certain areas and those
educated people who insisted on wearing African clothes were branded
as having 'gone native'. Throughout the colonial period, therefore, African
art, music, dancing and even history were all not only ignored but even
positively discouraged or denied. Those were the days when Professor A.
P. Newton could write 'Africa has practically no history before the coming
of Europeans ... [since] history only begins when men take to writing',[47]
and Sir Reginald Coupland could endorse five years later the view that
until the nineteenth century:

> the main body of the Africans, the Negro peoples who remained in
> their tropical homeland between the Sahara and the Limpopo, had
> had ... no history. They had stayed, for untold centuries, sunk in
> barbarism. Such, it might almost seem, had been nature's decree ...
> So they remained stagnant, neither going forward nor going back.
> Nowhere in the world, save perhaps in some miasmic swamps of South
> America or in some derelict Pacific Islands, was human life so stagnant.
> The heart of Africa was scarcely beating.[48]

Such views were not nature's decree but rather products of the fertile
imagination of these chauvinist European historians; Africa's heart was

45. Anon., 1959, p. 3.
46. P. Curtin, S. Feierman, L. Thompson, J. Vansina, 1978, p. 484.
47. A. P. Newton, 1923, p. 267.
48. R. Coupland, 1928, p. 3.

beating except that the Europeans were then too deafened by their own prejudices, preconceptions, arrogance and jingoism to hear it.

It should be quite obvious from the above analysis that those scholars who are of the opinion that colonialism was an unmitigated disaster for Africa and that it caused nothing but underdevelopment and backwardness have overstated their case. Equally guilty of overstatement are those colonial apologists, such as Gann, Duignan and Lloyd who see colonialism as an unqualified blessing for Africa as well as those like Perham and Fieldhouse who see the record as a balanced one. A more accurate judgement in this writer's opinion is not that colonialism did not do anything positive for Africa, it indeed did. But Europeans did make huge profits in Africa through mining companies, trading houses, banks, shipping lines, plantations and concession companies. Moreover governments held substantial foreign reserves from the colonies in metropolitan countries which must have provided some of the capital for metropolitan development. Finally, metropolitan industries benefited from cheap raw materials obtained from the colonies and profits made from the export of manufactured goods. When all this is compared with what the African owners of the land, peasant agriculturalists and mine labourers obtained, and the fact that whatever infrastructural and social facilities that were provided had to be paid for by the colonies themselves, one cannot but marvel at the raw deal which colonialism thrust on Africans. Moreover, whatever colonialism did for Africans in Africa, given its opportunities, its resources and the power and influence it wielded in Africa at the time, it could and should have done far more than it did. As even Lloyd admits: 'So much more might perhaps have been done had the development of backward territories been seen by the industrial nations as a first priority'.[49] It is precisely because colonial rulers not only did not see the development of Africans as their *first* priority, but did not see it as a *priority at all* that they stand condemned. It is for these two reasons that the colonial era will go down in history as a period of growth without development, one of the ruthless exploitation of the resources of Africa, and on balance of the pauperization and humiliation of the peoples of Africa.

The significance of colonialism for Africa

This leads us on, then, to the second question posed at the beginning of the chapter, namely, the real significance of colonialism for Africa. Does it constitute a break with Africa's past or was it just a mere episode in its history, an episode which is of limited importance and which did not affect the course of African development? Here again, conflicting answers have been given to this question. To some historians, indeed a very large number, including the Marxist and the development and anti-development

49. P. C. Lloyd, 1972, p. 80.

theorists but for very different reasons, though colonialism was a short interlude, it nevertheless was of great significance for Africa and left an indelible impression on Africa. As R. Oliver and N. Atmore contend: 'Measured on the time-scale of history, the colonial period was but an interlude of comparatively short duration. But it was an interlude that radically changed the direction and momentum of African history.'[50] Gann and Duignan also regard the colonial era 'as most decisive for the future of Africa'.[51] The answer of the Marxists and the underdevelopment theorists is neatly summed up in the title of Rodney's book, namely, *How Europe Underdeveloped Africa*. On the other hand, there are others who regard the colonial impact as skin-deep and that colonialism did not constitute any break with the African past. In a series of publications,[52] J. F. A. Ajayi has consistently maintained that the impact of colonialism on Africa has been exaggerated, that colonialism 'represents only an episode in a long and eventful history', and did not cause any break in continuity, that Africans retained some control over their own destinies and 'to the extent to which Africans retained initiative, the ability of Europeans to make entirely new departures in African history was limited'. Hopkins has also maintained that the 'colonial era has ceased to be regarded as the sole substance of African history and there are sound reasons for thinking that colonial rule itself had a less dramatic and a less pervasive economic impact than was once supposed'. He has insisted that colonialism did 'not create modernity out of backwardness by suddenly disrupting a traditional state of low-level equilibrium' and that 'the main function of the new rulers was to give impetus to a process of economic development which was already under way'.[53]

To this author, there is really no simple yes or no answer to this question since the impact of colonialism varied from area to area and from theme to theme. There is no doubt that in the economic field, the colonial impact was by and large decisive and fundamental and affected both the rural and urban areas. In virtually all parts of Africa, the money economy had become the rule rather than the exception by the end of the colonial period and status even in the rural areas was being assessed not only in terms of birth and number of wives and children but also in terms of cash and the quantity of cash crops that one was producing each season. Furthermore, with the introduction of cash crops, land assumed a value that it had not had in pre-colonial days while individual effort and achievement came to be regarded far more than the communalism of the traditional order. The African economy also became integrated deeper into the world

50. R. Oliver and A. Atmore, 1972, p. 275.

51. 'Introduction' in L. H. Gann and P. Duignan (eds), 1969, p. 23.

52. J. F. A. Ajayi in L. H. Gann and P. Duignan (eds), 1969; M. Crowder and J. F. A. Ajayi in J. F. A. Ajayi and M. Crowder (eds), 1974; J. F. A. Ajayi in T. O. Ranger (ed.), 1968(c).

53. A. G. Hopkins, 1973, pp. 167, 206, 235.

economy in general and the capitalist economy in particular than before and this had effects that can probably never be undone. Unfortunately, this integration was effected in a very disadvantageous and exploitative manner for Africa and not even twenty years of independence have fundamentally altered the situation which has now become known as neo-colonialism.

But granting all this, is Perham correct in her assessment that the main impact of colonialism was to confront Africa with twentieth-century Europe?[54] or should we uphold the view of Hopkins here? There is every reason to reject Perham's view in favour of that of Hopkins. It should be emphasized that apart from the infrastructural changes – the motor roads, railways, the telephone and the telegraph – introduced by colonialism, all the other economic changes – the introduction of cash crops as well as a money economy and the consequent break-down in the traditional communalism of life, the integration of the economy of Africa into the world economic system and urbanization – were all going on before the colonial era. What colonialism did, as both Caldwell and Afigbo have rightly emphasized (Chapters 18 and 19) and as Hopkins has contended, was to greatly accelerate the pace of this change and thereby hasten and intensify rather than begin the confrontation between Africa and Europe. But colonialism not only accelerated the pace of change but did so in a way which sought to deny the Africans themselves, who were most intimately affected, any meaningful and beneficial role. Furthermore, and this is where I part company with Hopkins, so rapid and so deep was this change that not only was the impact on the Africans really traumatic but it ended up landing the economy of Africa on a course – and a very unhealthy and exploitative one – from which it could not and has not deviated. It is in these respects and not in its confrontation with twentieth-century Europe that the full impact of colonialism in the economic field should be seen.

Fundamental and destined to be lasting and felt by all members of the society, also, was the impact of colonialism in the political field. As we have already seen, the very physical appearance of the independent states of Africa is the creation of colonialism. With the adoption of the principle of the sanctity of national boundaries by the Organization of African Unity, this appearance is not likely to be altered. Secondly, even though independence has been regained, there is no doubt that there has been a fundamental and permanent shift in the source of political power and authority. In pre-colonial days, power was exercised by the traditional elite of kings, queens, family, clan and religious heads. But colonial rulers were compelled to restore African independence and sovereignty, as will be seen in the next volume, not to the traditional ruling elite but to the new elite or members of the upper and lower middle classes, the creation of the colonial

54. M. Perham, 1961.

system, and this situation is never going to be reversed. If anything, the chances of African traditional regal institutions being abolished altogether, as for example they have been in Guinea, are much greater than their retention let alone their rehabilitation. Thirdly, it was colonialism that gave birth to African nationalism which was the product of the sense of anger, resentment, bitterness, frustration and alienation generated by the colonial system. Fourthly, one colonial legacy which again has already played such a decisive role in the politics of post-colonial Africa is the army. This institution is not likely to be abolished and, as will be seen in the next volume, it has already changed the course of the history of many an African country, and it seems as if it has not completed its political innings yet. 'The man on horseback', to borrow Finer's phrase,[55] is going to be with us for a long time and will serve as a constant reminder, if ever we need one, of the colonial episode. Finally, it appears that the judicial and political institutions – the courts, parliaments, regional and district commissioners, etc. – are going to be retained even though some modifications and adaptations have been and will continue to be made. Probably more than in the economic field, then, the impact of colonialism in the political field was really fundamental and in many respects has proved of lasting consequence.

On the other hand, in the cultural and social field, the impact of colonialism was relatively neither profound nor permanent. Such changes as were introduced in the cultural field, such racial discrimination as was practised, and such condemnation of African culture as was preached even in the heyday of colonialism, were all confined primarily to the coastal areas and the urban centres, and never penetrated into the rural areas where life ran gaily on very much as before. African dance, art, music and traditional religious systems held their own and such borrowings and adaptations as were made by Africans were not only selective but also, to borrow M. J. Herskovits' terminology, 'additive' and not necessarily 'substitutive'.[56] Thus, in the rural areas and even to some extent in the urban ones, new beliefs, new gods, new utensils, new artefacts and new objects were added to the old ones. Certainly, in these areas, many Christians did and still do retain their belief in their traditional gods. Indeed, in the field of religion, if anything, it was the European religion that was rather Africanized as is obvious from the rituals, hymns, music and even doctrines of some of the syncretic and millenarian churches and not the other way round. What is even more important, the ground that was lost even in the urban centres in the field of culture has virtually been regained. Today, African art, music and dance are not only taught in educational institutions of all kinds but are now in boom in Africa and gaining recognition in Europe. Thus, as far as the cultural field is concerned, colonialism was certainly a mere episode and its impact skin-deep and very ephemeral.

55. S. E. Finer, 1962.
56. M. J. Herskovits, 1962, p. 379.

Finally, in the social field, the significance of colonialism here is clearly a mixed one. On the one hand, the foreign or colonial *linguae francae* are going to be retained for a very long time if not for ever. Secondly, the new classes created by colonialism and 'founded on western criteria of schooling and civilization, instead of on the African criteria of wealth and prestige'[57] are bound to remain and in fact increase in complexity. Already, two new groups have been added since independence. One is the political elite made up of the leading members of the political parties that have been mushrooming in Africa and who have become the prime ministers, presidents, ministers, ambassadors, etc. The other is the military elite made up of present and ex-officers of the armed forces of each independent state. The members of these elite groups are definitely different from the people of the rural areas in terms of their dress, life style, tastes and status. Now, had these elite groups constituted a good percentage of the population of Africa, one would have accepted their formation as yet another crucial and fundamental change introduced by colonialism. But as indicated already, the urban or elitist groups constituted by the end of the colonial era only a small fraction of the population, at most about 20%. The remaining people were the rural dwellers who remained predominantly illiterate and maintained their traditional beliefs, values and standards. Indeed, such civilization or socialization that colonialism introduced was essentially an urban phenomenon, and did not really affect the rural people, and, since the latter constitute the overwhelming majority of the population of every African state, we can safely and reasonably conclude that the colonial impact here, interesting as it is, was extremely limited.

In conclusion, then, though there is no doubt that colonialism was a mere chapter in the numerous chapters of the long history of the continent, a mere episode or interlude in the many faceted and variegated experiences of the peoples of Africa, lasting as it did no more than eighty years anywhere, it is nonetheless an extremely important episode politically, economically and even socially. It marks a clear watershed in the history of Africa and the subsequent development of Africa, and therefore its history has been and will continue to be very much influenced by the colonial impact on Africa, and destined to take a course different from what it would have taken had there not been any colonial interlude. The most expedient course of action for African leaders to embark upon today, then, is not to write off colonialism but rather to be conversant with its impact, and to try to redress its shortcomings and its failures.

57. C. D. Moore and A. Dunbar, 1969, p. 125.

Members of the International Scientific Committee for the Drafting of a General History of Africa

The dates cited below refer to dates of membership.

Professor J. F. A. Ajayi
(Nigeria), from 1971
Editor Volume VI

Professor F. A. Albuquerque Mourao
(Brazil), from 1975

Professor A. A. Boahen
(Ghana), from 1971
Editor Volume VII

H. E. Boubou Hama
(Niger), 1971–8 (resigned)

H. E. M. Bull
(Zambia), from 1971

Professor D. Chanaiwa
(Zimbabwe), from 1975

Professor P. D. Curtin
(USA), from 1975

Professor J. Devisse
(France), from 1971

Professor M. Difuila
(Angola), from 1978

Professor H. Djait
(Tunisia), from 1975

Professor Cheikh Anta Diop
(Senegal), from 1971

Professor J. D. Fage
(UK), 1971–81 (resigned)

H. E. M. El Fasi
(Morocco), from 1971
Editor Volume III

Professor J. L. Franco
(Cuba), from 1971

The late Mr M. H. I. Galaal
(Somalia), 1971–81; deceased 1981

Professor Dr V. L. Grottanelli
(Italy), from 1971

Professor E. Haberland
(Federal Republic of Germany), from 1971

Dr Aklilu Habte
(Ethiopia), from 1971

H. E. A. Hampate Ba
(Mali), 1971–8 (resigned)

Dr I. S. El-Hareir
(Libya), from 1978

Dr I. Hrbek
(Czechoslovakia), from 1971
Assistant Editor Volume III

Dr A. Jones
(Liberia), from 1971

The late Abbé Alexis Kagame
(Rwanda), 1971–81; deceased 1981

Professor I. N. Kimambo
(Tanzania), from 1971

Professor J. Ki-Zerbo
(Upper Volta), from 1971
Editor Volume I

M. D. Laya
(Niger), from 1979

Dr A. Letnev
(USSR), from 1971

Dr G. Mokhtar
(Egypt), from 1971
Editor Volume II

Professor P. Mutibwa
(Uganda), from 1975

Professor D. T. Niane
(Senegal), from 1971
Editor Volume IV

Biographies of Authors

CHAPTER 1   A. Adu Boahen (Ghana); specialist in West African colonial history; author of numerous publications and articles on African history; Professor and Head of the Department of History, University of Ghana.

CHAPTER 2   G. N. Uzoigwe (Nigeria); specialist in East African history, with emphasis on the former Bunyoro kingdom in Uganda; author of several works and articles on African history; Professor of History, the University of Michigan, Ann Arbor.

CHAPTER 3   T. O. Ranger (UK); specialist in African resistance and nationalist movements; author and editor of numerous works and articles in this field; former professor of History of the Universities of Dar es Salaam and UCLA; Professor of Modern History, University of Manchester.

CHAPTER 4   H. A. Ibrahim (Sudan); specialist in the nineteenth- and twentieth-century history of Egypt and the Sudan; published several studies; Lecturer in History, the University of Khartoum.

Abbas I. Ali (Sudan); specialist in the nineteenth-century history of the Sudan and East African history; author of works and articles in these fields; former Head of the Department of History, the University of Khartoum; deceased.

CHAPTER 5   A. Laroui (Morocco); specialist in the history of the Maghrib; author of works and articles on the nineteenth-century history of North Africa; Professor of Modern and Contemporary History at the University of Rabat, Morocco.

CHAPTER 6   M. Gueye (Senegal); specialist in nineteenth- and twentieth-century West African history; author of several works on the slave trade and French colonization; Lecturer in History at the Faculté des Lettres, the University of Dakar, Senegal.

A. Adu Boahen.

CHAPTER 7   H. A. Mwanzi (Kenya); specialist in East African history; author of several works and articles, mainly on the Kipsigi of Kenya; Senior Lecturer in History, the University of Nairobi.

CHAPTER 8   A. Isaacman (USA); specialist in African history; author of several works and articles; Professor of History, the University of Minnesota.

J. Vansina (Belgium); specialist in African history; author of numerous works and articles on pre-colonial history of Africa; Professor of History, the University of Wisconsin, Madison.

CHAPTER 9   D. Chanaiwa (Zimbabwe); specialist in the eighteenth- and nineteenth-century history of Southern Africa; author of numerous works and articles on the history of Southern Africa; formerly Professor of History, California State University, Northridge; Director, Department of Employment and Employment Development, Harare.

CHAPTER 10   M. Esoavelomandroso (Madagascar); specialist in the eighteenth- and nineteenth-century history of Madagascar; Professor of History, Faculté des Lettres, the University of Antananarivo.

CHAPTER 11   M. B. Akpan (Nigeria); specialist in West African economic history; author of several works and articles on West African history; Senior Lecturer, the University of Calabar, Nigeria.

A. B. Jones (Liberia); historian and specialist in the nineteenth-century West Africa; former Ambassador and Permanent Delegate of Liberia to the United Nations.

R. Pankhurst (UK), specialist in Ethiopian history; author of numerous works and articles on the history of Ethiopia; former director of the Institute of Ethiopian Studies, the University of Ethiopia.

CHAPTER 12   M. Crowder (UK); specialist in West African history; author of numerous works and articles on West African history; held professorship at various Universities; editor of *History Today*; currently Visiting Professor at the University of Botswana.

CHAPTER 13   R. F. Betts (USA); specialist in nineteenth- and twentieth-century European colonialism in Africa; author of several works and articles on African history; Professor of History at the University of Kentucky.

A. I. Asiwaju (Nigeria); specialist in West African history; author of different works and articles on this region; Professor of History at the University of Lagos.

CHAPTER 14   W. Rodney (Guyana); specialist in West African economic history; author of several works and articles on West African slave trade; former Professor of History at the University of Dar es Salaam, Tanzania and the West Indies; deceased.

CHAPTER 15   C. Coquery-Vidrovitch (France); specialist in socio-economic history of Africa; has published several works and articles on the subject; at present Professor of History, Université de Paris VII.

CHAPTER 16   M. H. Y. Kaniki (Tanzania); specialist in West African economic history; has published several works and articles on the subject; formerly Associate Professor of History, University of Dar es Salaam; currently Professor of History, the University of Zambia, Lusaka.

CHAPTER 17   A. Kassab (Tunisia); specialist in economic geography; has published several studies related to this field; Chief Editor of *La Revue Tunisienne de Geographie*.

A. A. Abdussalam (Libya); specialist in Libyan economic history; author of several works on this subject; Assistant Professor of Economics, the University of Garyounis, Benghazi, Libya.

F. S. Abusedra (Egypt); specialist in economic history; Assistant Professor of Economics, the University of Garyounis, Benghazi, Libya.

CHAPTER 18   J. C. Caldwell (Australia); specialist in demography; author of several works on population in tropical Africa; Professor of Demography and Head of the Department of Demography, Research School of Social Sciences, Australian National University.

CHAPTER 19   A. E. Afigbo (Nigeria), specialist in West African history; author of several works and scientific articles on Nigerian history; former Director of the Institute of African Studies, the University of Nigeria (Nsukka).

CHAPTER 20   K. Asare Opoku (Ghana), specialist in African religions; author of several books and articles on various aspects of African religions; Senior Research Fellow in Religion and Ethics, Institute of African Studies, the University of Ghana.

CHAPTER 21   W. Soyinka (Nigeria); specialist in African drama, literature and philosophy; author of numerous works in this area; formerly Professor at the University of Legon, Ghana and currently Professor of Drama at the University of Ife.

CHAPTER 22   B. O. Oloruntimehin (Nigeria); specialist in former French West Africa since the nineteenth-century; published a number of books and several articles related to this area; Professor of History, the University of Ife.

CHAPTER 23   H. A. Ibrahim.

CHAPTER 24   J. Berque (France); specialist in social history of contemporary Islam; author of several works on Egyptian and Maghrib history; former Professor at the Collège de France.

CHAPTER 25   A. Adu Boahen.

CHAPTER 26   E. S. Atieno-Odhiambo (Kenya); specialist in political history of East Africa; author of several works and articles on the rise of nationalism in East and Central Africa; Senior Lecturer in History, the University of Nairobi, Kenya.

CHAPTER 27   A. B. Davidson (UK), specialist in African history; published a number of works on Africa; Professor at the Institute of General History, USSR Academy of Sciences, Moscow.

R. Pélissier (France); specialist in resistance movements in nineteenth- and twentieth-century African history; author of several works and articles; Researcher.

A. Isaacman.

CHAPTER 28   M. B. Akpan, A. B. Jones and R. Pankhurst.

CHAPTER 29   R. D. Ralston (USA); specialist in nineteenth- and twentieth-century African history; author of several articles on relationship between Africa and the New World; Assistant Professor of History, Afro-American Studies Department, the University of Wisconsin, Madison.

F. A. Alburquerque Mourão (Brazil); specialist in African history; author of several works and articles on Afro-Brazilian history; Professor of History and Director of the Centro de Estudos Africanos, the University of São Paulo, Brazil.

CHAPTER 30   A. Adu Boahen.

Editorial Assistant   Y. Kwarteng (Ghana); specialist in journalism and communication; his MA thesis is on 'The development of journalism in West Africa since 1957'.

814

Bibliography

The publishers wish to point out that while every effort has been made to ensure that the details in this Bibliography are correct, some errors may occur as a result of the complexity and the international nature of the work.

Abbreviations and list of periodicals

AA   African Affairs, London, Royal African Society
AEH   African Economic History, Madison, Wisconsin
AESC   Annales: économies, sociétés, civilisations, Paris
Africa   Africa, International African Institute, London
African Arts   African Arts, University of California, Los Angeles, African Studies Center
African Literature Today   African Literature Today, London, Heinemann
AHR   American Historical Review, Washington DC, American Historical Association
AM   Archives Marocaines
Annuaire Médical et Pharmaceutique Colonial, Paris
AQ   African Quarterly, New Delhi
BIFAN   Bulletin de l'Institut Fondamental d'Afrique Noire, Dakar
BSGL   Boletim da Sociedade de Geografia de Lisboa, Lisbon
BUP   Boston University Press
BUPAH   Boston University Papers in African History, Boston University, African Studies Center
Bulletin des juridictions indigènes et du droit coutumier congolais
BWHO   Bulletin of the World Health Organization, Geneva
CEA   Cahiers d'Études Africaines, Paris, Mouton
CHJ   Calabar Historical Journal, University of Calabar
CJAS   Canadian Journal of African Studies, Canadian Association of African Studies, Department of Geography, Carleton University, Ottawa
CSSH   Comparative Studies in Society and History, Cambridge, CUP
CUP   Cambridge University Press
Cultura   Cultura, Brasilia
EAJ   East Africa Journal, East African Institute of Social & Cultural Affairs, Nairobi
EALB   East African Literature Bureau, Nairobi
EAPH   East African Publishing House, Nairobi
EDCC   Economic Development and Cultural Change, New York
EHA   Études d'Histoire Africaine, Kinshasa
EHR   Economic History Review, Cambridge, Economic History Society
Encounter   Encounter, London
EC   Études Congolaises
EO   Ethiopia Observer, Addis Ababa
ES   Economy and Society, London, Routledge & Kegan Paul
Genève-Afrique, Geneva
GJ   Geographical Journal, London, Royal Geographical Society
GR   Geographical Review, New York, American Geographical Society
HA   Horn of Africa
Hadith   Hadith, Nairobi
HJ   Historical Journal, Cambridge, CUP
HMSO   Her/His Majesty's Stationery Office, London
HUP   Harvard University Press
IAI   International African Institute, London
IFAN   Institut Fondamental de l'Afrique Noire
IJAHS   International Journal of African Historical Studies, Boston, Boston University, African Studies Center
IL   International Law
IRCBM   Institut Royal Colonial Belge, Mémoires, Brussels

IUP   Ibadan University Press
JAH   Journal of African History, Cambridge, CUP
JAS   Journal of African Studies, University of California, Los Angeles, African Studies Center
JAf. S   Journal of the African Society (later *African Affairs*)
JCAHA   Journal of the Central African Historical Association
JDS   Journal of Development Studies, Institute of Development Studies, University of Sussex
JES   Journal of Ethiopian Studies, Addis Ababa
JHMAS   Journal of the History of Medicine and Allied Sciences, New York
JHSN   Journal of the Historical Society of Nigeria, Ibadan
JMAS   Journal of Modern African Studies, Cambridge, CUP
JNH   Journal of Negro History, Washington DC
Journal Officiel de l'A.E.F., Brazzaville
JP   Journal of Politics, Gainesville, Florida
JSAS   Journal of Southern African Studies, London, OUP
KHR   Kenya Historical Review, Nairobi
Kongo-Oversee   Kongo-Oversee
The Lancet   The Lancet, London
Le Matériel Colonial, Paris
LSJ   Liberian Studies Journal, Newark, Delaware, University of Delaware
Marchés Coloniaux, Paris
MARSOM   Mémoires de l'Academie Royale des Sciences d'Outre-Mer, Brussels
MBAB   Mitteilungen der Basler Afrika Bibliographien, Basel
MMFQ   Millbank Memorial Fund Quarterly, London
MIT   Massachusetts Institute of Technology
MUP   Michigan University Press
The Muslim World   The Muslim World, Hartford, Connecticut
Nigeria Magazine   Nigeria Magazine, Lagos
NJESS   Nigerian Journal of Economic and Social Studies, Ibadan
NUP   Northwestern University Press
Odu   Odu, Ife, University of Ife Press
Omaly sy Anio   Omaly sy Anio, Antananarivo
Optima   Optima, Johannesburg
OUP   Oxford University Press
PA   *Présence Africaine*, Paris
PAPS   Proceedings of the American Philosophical Society, Philadelphia
Practical Anthropology   Practical Anthropology
PP   Past & Present, Oxford
PS   Population Studies, London
PUF   Presses Universitaires Françaises
PUP   Princeton University Press
RA   Revue Africaine, Journal des Travaux de la Société Historique Algérienne, Algiers
Research Review   Research Review, University of Ghana, Legon, Institute of African Studies
RFHOM   Revue Française d'Histoire d'Outre-Mer, Paris
RIIA   Royal Institute of International Affairs, London
RLJ   Rhodes-Livingstone Journal (now *African Social Research*), Lusaka
RM   Revue Marocaine,
R Med.   Revue de la Mediterranée, Algiers
ROMM   Revue de l'Occident Musulman et de la Mediterranée, Aix-en-Provence
RPC   Recherche Pedagogique et Culture
RSEHA   Revue Sémitique d'Épigraphie et d'Histoire Ancienne, Paris
RSSJ   Royal Statistical Society Journal, London
SNR   Sudan Notes & Records, Khartoum
SOAS   School of Oriental and African Studies, University of London
SR   Sociological Review, Manchester
SUP   Stanford University Press
Tarikh   Tarikh, Ibadan, Longman
THSG   Transactions of the Historical Society of Ghana, Legon
TJH   Transafrican Journal of History, Nairobi
TRSTMH   Transactions of the Royal Society of Tropical Medicine and Hygiene, London
Transition   Transition, Kampala (later Accra)

816

Ufahamu *Ufahamu*, Journal of the African Activist Association, Los Angeles
UJ *Uganda Journal*, Uganda Society, Kampala
UP University Press
West Africa *West Africa*, London
WUP Witwatersrand University Press
Yale Review *Yale Review*, New Haven
YUP Yale University Press

Bibliography

Abbās, F. (1931) *Le jeune Algérien* (Paris: Éditions de la Jeune Parque).
Abbās, F. (1962) *Le nuit coloniale* (Paris: Julliard).
'Abd al-Halim, M. O. (1975) 'Islam in Somalia, 1800–1920' (MA thesis: University of Khartoum).
'Abd al-Raḥīm, M. (1969) *Imperialism and Nationalism in the Sudan: a Study in Constitutional and Political Development, 1899–1956* (Oxford: Clarendon Press).
Abdin, H. (1970) 'The growth of nationalist movements in the Sudan' (PhD thesis: University of Wisconsin).
Abernethy, D. B. (1969) *The Political Dilemma of Popular Education: an African Case* (Stanford: SUP).
Abraham, W. E. (1964) 'The life and times of Anton Wilhelm Amo', *THSG*, VII, pp. 60–81.
Abubakar, S. (1980) 'The northern provinces under colonial rule' in O. Ikime (ed.) *Groundwork of Nigerian History*, pp. 447–81.
Abū Salīm, M. I. (1969) *Manshūrāt al-Mahdiyya* (Khartoum).
Abū Salīm, M. I. (1970) *Al-Haraka al-fikriyya fil Mahdiyya* (Khartoum).
Addo-Fening, R. (1975) 'The Asamankese dispute, 1919–1934', *MBAB*, XII, pp. 61–89.
Addo-Fening, R. (1980) 'Akyem Abuakwa, *c.* 1874–1943: a study of the impact of missionary activities and colonial rule on a traditional state' (PhD thesis: University of Ghana).
Adeleye, R. A. (1971) *Power and Diplomacy in Northern Nigeria, 1804–1906: the Sokoto Caliphate and its Enemies* (London: Longman).
Adewoye, O. (1977) *The Judicial System in Southern Nigeria, 1854–1954: Law and Justice in a Dependency* (London: Longman).
Adimola, A. B. (1954) 'The Lamogi rebellion 1911–12', *UJ*, XVIII, 2, pp. 166–77.
Afigbo, A. E. (1972) *The Warrant Chiefs: Indirect Rule in Southeastern Nigeria, 1891–1929* (London: Longman).
Afigbo, A. E. (1973) 'Patterns of Igbo resistance to British conquest', *Tarikh*, IV, 3, pp. 14–23.
Afigbo, A. E. (1974) 'The establishment of colonial rule, 1900–1918' in J. F.A. Ajayi and M. Crowder (eds) *History of West Africa*, Vol. II, pp. 424–83.
Ageron, C.-R. (1966) 'Enquête sur les origines de nationalisme algérien. L'Emir Khaled, petit-fils d'Abd El-Kader, fut-il le premier nationaliste algérien', *ROMM*, II, pp. 9–49.
Ageron, C.-R. (1978a) *France coloniale ou parti coloniale?* (Paris: PUF).
Ageron, C.-R. (1978b) *Politiques coloniales au Maghreb* (Paris: PUF).
Ageron, C.-R. (1979) *Histoire de l'Algérie contemporaine, 1830–1973* (Paris: PUF).
Ahmed, J. M. (1960) *The Intellectual Origins of Egyptian Nationalism* (London: OUP).
Ajayi, J. F. A. (n.d.) 'The impact of colonialism on Afro-Arab cultural relations in West Africa' (unpublished paper).
Ajayi J. F. A. (1965) *Christian Missions in Nigeria, 1841–1891: The Making of a New Elite* (London: Longman).
Ajayi, J. F. A. (1968) 'The continuity of African institutions under colonialism' in T. O. Ranger (ed.) *Emerging Themes of African History*, pp. 189–200.
Ajayi, J. F. A. (1969) 'Colonialism: an episode in African history' in L. H. Gann and P. Duignan (eds) *Colonialism in Africa*, Vol. I, *The History and Politics of Colonialism, 1870–1914*, pp. 497–509.
Ajayi, J. F. A. and Crowder, M. (eds) (1974) *History of West Africa*, Vol. II (London: Longman).
Akpan, M. B. (1973a) 'Liberia and the Universal Negro Improvement Association: the background to the abortion of Garvey's scheme for African colonization', *JAH*, XIV, 1, pp. 105–27.
Akpan, M. B. (1973b) 'Black imperialism: Americo-Liberian rule over the African peoples of Liberia, 1841–1964', *CJAS*, VII, 2, pp. 217–36.
Akpan, M. B. (1975) 'The Liberian economy in the nineteenth century: government finances', *LSJ*, VI, 2, pp. 129–61.
Akpan, M. B. (1976) 'Liberia and the origins of the Scramble for West Africa', *CHJ*, I, 2, pp. 61–75.

Akpan, M. B. (forthcoming) 'Native administration and Gola–Bandi resistance in north-western Liberia, 1905–19', *THSG*.
Al-Ashḥāb, M. T. (1947) *Barqa al-'Arabiyya* (Cairo: Matba't al Hawwari).
Al-Barāwī, R. (1973) *Al-Sūmāl al-Jadīd* (Cairo).
Al-Ḥaddād, T. (1927) *Al-Ummal 'al Tunisiyin* (no further details available).
Al-Ḥaṣan, M. A. (1964) *Ta 'rīkh Dārfūr al-Siyāsī* (Khartoum).
Al-Ḳaddāl, M. S. (1973) *Al-Mahdiyya wal Habasha* (Khartoum).
Al-Madanī, T. (1963) *Kitāb Al-Jazā'ir* (Blida).
Al-Masada, M. G. al-Dīn (1974) *Danshuwāi* (Cairo).
Al-Misurātī, A. (1964) *Sa'dūn al Batal* (Beirut).
Al-Murshidī, M. (1958) *Al-Thawra Al-'Urābīyya* (Cairo).
Al-Nāṣirī (1907) *Kitābal-Istiqqā* (tr. by E. Fumey in *AM*, X, p. 227).
Al-Rafʿī, A. (1966) *Al-Thawra al-'Urabīyya wal Iḥtilāl al-Ingilīzi* (Cairo).
Al-Rafʿī, A. (1969) *Fi Aqab Al-Thawra Al-Misriyya*, Vol. I (Cairo: 3rd edn).
Al-Sayyid, A. L. (1968) *Egypt and Cromer: a Study in Anglo-Egyptian Relations* (London: John Murray).
Al-Sūsī, M. (1961) *Al Ma'sul*, Vol. XX (Casablanca).
Al-Tillisi, K. (1973) *Mujam Ma'arik Al-j-Jihad Filibiya* (Beirut: Dar al-Thaqafa, 2nd edn).
Al-Zawi, Al-T. A. (1973) *Jihad al-Abtal* (Beirut: Dar al-Fath, 3rd edn).
Albion, R. G. (1959) *Seaports South of the Sahara: the Achievement of an American Steamship Service* (New York: Appleton-Century-Crofts).
Alegre, C. da C. (1916) *Versos Lisbon Livraria* (Ferin).
Allan, J. A., McLachland, K. S. and Penrose, E. T. (eds) (1973) *Libya, Agriculture and Economic Development* (London: Frank Cass).
Allan, W. (1965) *The African Husbandman* (London: Oliver & Boyd).
Allan, W. N. and Smith, R. J. (1948) 'Irrigation in the Sudan' in J. D. Tothill (ed.) *Agriculture in the Sudan*, pp. 593–632.
Alldridge, T. J. (1910) *A Transformed Colony, Sierra Leone, as it was, and as it is, its Progress, Peoples, Native Customs and Undeveloped Wealth* (London: Seeley).
Aloisi, P. (1957) *Journal, 25 juillet 1932–14 juin 1936* (Paris: Plon).
Alves, H. L. (1976) *Bibliografia afro-brasileira; estudos sobre o negro* (São Paulo: Edições H).
Amin, S. (1970) *The Maghreb in the Modern World: Algeria, Tunisia, Morocco* (Harmondsworth: Penguin).
Amin, S. (1972) 'Underdevelopment and dependence in Black Africa: origins and contemporary forms', *JMAS*, X, 4, pp. 503–24.
Amin, S. (1974) *Accumulation on a World Scale: a Critique of the Theory of Underdevelopment* (New York: Monthly Review Press).
Ananaba, W. (1969) *The Trade Union Movement in Nigeria* (London: C. Hurst).
Anderson, R. E. (1952) *Liberia: America's African Friend* (Chapel Hill: University of North Carolina Press).
Andrade, M. (1959) *Antologia da Poesia Negra de Expressão Portuguesa* (Paris: Pierre Jean Oswald).
Anene, J. C. (1970) *The International Boundaries of Nigeria, 1885–1960: the Framework of an Emergent African Nation* (London: Longman).
Ani-Okokon, A. E. (1927) 'A West African in the US: some reflections and observations', *Missionary Seer*, XXVIII, 6.
Anon. (1910a) 'Health and sanitation in Sierra Leone', *The Lancet*, 1 October 1910 (Vol. II), p. 1053.
Anon. (1910b) 'The Egyptian Public Health Department', *The Lancet*, 29 October 1910 (Vol. II), p. 1298.
Anon. (1911) 'The Transvaal Mining Commission', *The Lancet*, 11 March 1911 (Vol. I), p. 688.
Anon. (1913) 'Notes from South Africa', *The Lancet*, 14 June 1913 (Vol. I), p. 1702.
Anon. (1959) 'The policy of our culture' [Editorial], *PA*, XXIV–XXV, pp. 3–5.
Anouma, R. P. (1973) 'L'impôt de capitation, le système des prestations et des corvées en Côte d'Ivoire de 1901–1930' (thèse de doctorat de 3e cycle: University of Aix-en-Provence).
Antonetti, G. G. (1926, 1927) articles in *Journal Officiel de l'A.E.F.*, I June 1926, 1 December 1927.
Anyane, S. L. (1963) *Ghana Agriculture: its Economic Development from Early Times to the Middle of the Twentieth Century* (London: OUP).
Araedon, D. (1976) 'Architecture' in S. O. Biobaku (ed.) *The Living Culture of Nigeria*, pp. 38–44.
Arap Magut, P. K. (1969) 'The rise and fall of the Nandi Orkoiyot' in B. G. McIntosh (ed.) *Ngano: Studies in Traditional and Modern East African History*, pp. 95–108.
Arap Ng'eny, S. K. (1970) 'Nandi resistance to the establishment of British administration, 1893–1906', *Hadith*, II, pp. 104–26.

818

Armah, A. K. (1973) *Two Thousand Seasons* (Nairobi: EAPH; London: Heinemann 1979).
Arrighi, G. (1967) *The Political Economy of Rhodesia* (The Hague: Mouton).
Arrighi, G. (1970) 'Labour supplies in historical perspective: a study of the proletarianization of the African peasantry in Rhodesia', *JDS*, VI, 3, pp. 197–234.
Asante, S. K. B. (1977) *Pan-African Protest: West Africa and the Italo-Ethiopian Crisis, 1939–1941* (London: Longman).
Ashe, R. P. (1894) *Chronicles of Uganda* (London: Hodder & Stoughton).
Ashur, F.b. (1956) *Al-H'arakāt al-adahīya w'al-firkiya fī* (Tunis).
Asiwaju, A. I. (1976a) *Western Yorubaland under European Rule, 1889–1945: a Comparative Analysis of French and British Colonialism* (London: Longman).
Asiwaju, A. I. (1976b) 'Migrations as revolt: the example of the Ivory Coast and the Upper Volta before 1945', *JAH*, XVII, 4, pp. 577–94.
Asiwaju, A. I. (1979) 'Control through coercion: a study of the indigénat regime in French West African administration, 1887–1946', *BIFAN*, (B) XLI, 1, pp. 35–71.
Assis, A. de, Jr (1917) *Relatório dos Acontecimentos da Dala Tando a Lucala* (Luanda).
Atanda, J. A. (1969) 'The Iseyin-Okeiho rising of 1916: an example of socio-political conflict in colonial Nigeria', *JHSN*, IV, 4, pp. 487–514.
Atieno-Odhiambo, E. S. (1973) 'Review of J. Iliffe (ed.) *Modern Tanzanians*', *TJH*, III, 1 & 2, pp. 153–4.
Atieno-Odhiambo, E. S. (1974) '"Seek ye first the economic kingdom": the early history of the Luo Thrift and Trading Corporation, LUTATCO, 1945–1956' in B. A. Ogot (ed.) *Hadith*, V, *Economic and Social History of East Africa*, pp. 218–56.
Ayache, A. (1956) *Le Maroc: bilan d'une colonisation* (Paris: Éd. Sociales).
Ayache, S. and Richard, C. (1978) 'Une dissidence protestante malgache: l'église Tranozozoro', *Omaly sy Anio*, VI–VIII, pp. 133–82.
Ayandele, E. A. (1966) *The Missionary Impact on Modern Nigeria, 1842–1914: a Political and Social Analysis* (London: Longman).
Azikiwe, B. N. (1934) *Liberia in World Politics* (London: A. H. Stockwell).
Azikiwe, B. N. (1961) *Zik: a Selection from the Speeches of Nnamdi Azikiwe* (Cambridge: CUP).

Baden-Powell, R. S. S. (1897) *The Matabele Campaign, 1896: being a Narrative of the Campaign in Suppressing the Native Rising in Matabeleland and Mashonaland* (London: Methuen).
Badoglio, P. (1937) *The War in Abyssinia* (London: Methuen).
Baer, G. (1962) *A History of Land Ownership in Modern Egypt, 1800–1950* (London: OUP).
Baer, G. W. (1967) *The Coming of the Italo-Ethiopian War* (Cambridge, Mass: HUP).
Baeta, C. G. (1962) *Prophetism in Ghana: a Study of Some 'Spiritual' Churches* (London: SCM Press).
Baeta, C. G. (ed.) (1968) *Christianity in Tropical Africa* (London: OUP).
Balandier, G. (1965) 'Messianism and nationalism in Black Africa' in P. Van den Berghe (ed.) *Africa: Social Problems of Change and Conflict*.
Balandier, G. and Dadie, B. (eds) (n.d.) *Le travail en Afrique noire* (Paris: Présence Africaine).
Balans, J. L., Coulon, C. and Ricard, A. (eds) (1972) *Problèmes et perspectives de l'éducation dans un état du tiers-monde: le cas du Sénégal* (Bordeaux: Centre d'Etude d'Afrique Noire).
Baldwin, R. E. (1966) *Economic Development and Export Growth: a Study of Northern Rhodesia, 1920–1960* (Berkeley: University of California Press).
Balek, R. (1922) *La Tunisie après la Guerre (1919–21): problèmes politiques* (Paris: Comité de l'Afrique Française).
Ballard, J. A. (1965) 'The Porto Novo incidents of 1923: politics in the colonial era', *Odu*, II, 1, pp. 52–75.
Bandini, F. (1971) *Gli Italiani in Africa: Storia delle guerre coloniali, 1882–1943* (Milan: Longanesi).
Banks, A. (1975) *A Military Atlas of the First World War* (London: Heinemann).
Bannermann, R. C. (1920) 'Report on Conditions in Liberia', 2 October 1920 (New York).
Banton, M. (1966) 'Adaptation and integration in the social system of Temne immigrants in Freetown' in I. Wallerstein (ed.) *Social Change: The Colonial Situation*, pp. 402–19.
Barbar, A. M. (1980) 'The Tarābulus (Libyan) resistance to the Italian invasions, 1911–1920' (PhD thesis: University of Wisconsin).
Barbour, K. M. and Prothero, R. M. (eds) (1961) *Essays on African Population* (London: Routledge & Kegan Paul).
Barbour, N. (ed.) (1959) *A Survey of North West Africa (The Maghreb)* (London: OUP).
Barclay, E. J. (1931) *Annual Message*, 22 December (Monrovia).
Barclay, E. J. (1932) *Annual Message*, 24 October (Monrovia).

819

Barclay, E. J. (1934) *Annual Report of the Department of State to the Fourth Session of the Thirty-Seventh Legislature* (Monrovia).
Barclay, E. J. (1935a) *Special Message delivered before the Extraordinary Session of the Liberian Legislature*, 29 May (Monrovia).
Barclay, E. J. (1935b) *Annual Message*, 19 December (Monrovia).
Barclay, E. J. (1937) *Annual Message*, 29 October (Monrovia).
Barker, A. J. (1968) *The Civilization Mission: a History of the Italo-Ethiopian War of 1935–1936* (London: OUP).
Barrett, D. B. (ed.) (1971) *African Initiatives in Religion* (Nairobi: EAPH).
Bascom, W. (1959) 'Urbanism as a traditional African pattern', *SR*, VII, pp. 29–53.
Basso, L. (1972) 'An analysis of classical theories of imperialism' in N. Chomsky *et al. Spheres of Influence in the Age of Imperialism*, pp. 111–44.
Bastide, R. (1967) *Les Ameriques noires: les civilisations africaines dans le Nouveau Monde* (Paris: Payot).
Bates, M. L. (1965) 'Tanganyika: changes in African life, 1918–1945' in V. Harlow and E. M. Chilver (eds) *History of East Africa*, Vol. II, pp. 625–38.
Bates, R. H. (1971) *Unions, Parties and Political Development: a Study of Mineworkers in Zambia* (New Haven: YUP).
Bauer, P. T. (1954) *West African Trade: a Study of Competition, Oligopoly and Monopoly in a Changing Society* (Cambridge: CUP).
Bauer, R. A. and Bauer, A. H. (1942) 'Day to day resistance to slavery', *JNH*, XXVII, 4, pp. 388–419.
Baum, J. E. (1928) *Savage Abyssinia* (London: Cassell).
Beach, D. (1971) 'Resistance and collaboration in the Shona country' (London: SOAS unpublished seminar paper).
Beach, D. (1979) '"Chimurenga": the Shona rising of 1896–97', *JAH*, XX, 3, pp. 395–420.
Beer, G. L. (1923) *African Questions at the Paris Peace Conference* (New York: Macmillan).
Beinart, W. and Bundy, C. (1980) 'State intervention and rural resistance: the Transkei, 1900–1965' in M. Klein (ed.) *Peasants in Africa*, pp. 271–315.
Bender, G. J. (1978) *Angola under the Portuguese: the Myth and the Reality* (London: Heinemann).
Benians, E. A., Butler, J. and Carrington, C. E. (eds) (1959) *The Cambridge History of the British Empire*, Vol. III, *The Empire–Commonwealth 1870–1919* (Cambridge: CUP).
Bennett, G. (ed.) (1953) *The Concept of Empire: Burke to Attlee, 1774–1947* (London: Adam & Charles Black).
Bennett, G. (1963) *Kenya, a Political History: the Colonial Period* (London: OUP).
Benson, M. (1966) *South Africa: the Struggle for a Birthright* (Harmondsworth: Penguin).
Benz, E. (ed.) (1965) *Messianische Kirchen, Sekten und Bewengungen im heutigen Afrika* (Leiden: Brill).
Berg, E. J. (1965) 'The development of a labour force in sub-Saharan Africa', *EDCC*, XIII, pp. 394–412.
Berkeley, G. F. (1902) *The Campaign of Adowa and the Rise of Menelik* (London: Constable).
Berliner, P. (1978) *The Soul of Mbira* (Berkeley: University of California Press).
Bernard, A. and Lacroix, L. N. E. (1921) *La pénétration saharienne, 1830–1906* (Algiers).
Berque, A. (1936) 'Un mystique moderniste: le Cheikh Benalioua', *RA*, LXXIX, pp. 691–776.
Berque, A. (1947) 'Les intellectuels algériens', *RA*, XCI, pp. 123–51, 261–76.
Berque, A. (1951) 'Les capteurs du divan: marabouts et ulemas', *R. Med.*, X, 43, pp. 286–302; XI, 44, pp. 417–29.
Berque, J. (1970) *Le Maghreb entre deux guerres* (Paris: Éd. du Seuil, 2nd edn).
Bervin, A. (1969) *Benito Sylvain, apôtre du relèvement social des noirs* (Port-au-Prince: La Phalange).
Beti, M. (1971) *The Poor Christ of Bomba* (London: Heinemann).
Betts, R. F. (ed.) (1972) *The Scramble for Africa: Causes and Dimensions of Empire* (London: D. C. Heath, 2nd edn).
Bidwell, R. (1973) *Morocco under Colonial Rule: French Administration of Tribal Areas, 1912–1956* (London: Frank Cass).
Biobaku, S. O. (ed.) (1976) *The Living Culture of Nigeria* (London: Thomas Nelson).
Birmingham, W., Neustadt, I. and Omaboe E. N. (eds) (1967) *A Study of Contemporary Ghana*, Vol. II (London: Allen & Unwin).
Bittremieux, L. (1936) 'Brief van Musiri (Geschiedenis van een Negerkonig uit Katanga) door Zijn zoon en apvolger Mukanda-bantu (Met het relaas der groote daden van den Schrijver) Uit het Kisanga Vertaald', *Kongo–Oversee*, III, pp. 69–83, 252–91.
Blair, D. S. (1976) *African Literature in French* (Cambridge: CUP).
Blaug, M. (1961) 'Economic imperialism revisited', *Yale Review*, L, pp. 335–49.
Bley, H. (1968) *Kolonialherrschaft und Sozialstruktur in Deutsch-Südwestafrika 1894–1914* (Hamburg: Leibnez-Verlag).
Bley, H. (1971) *South West Africa under German Rule, 1894–1914* (London: Heinemann).

Blyden, E. W. (1864) 'The call of Providence to the descendants of Africa', *The African Repository*, XL, p. 358.

Blyden, E. W. (1887) *Christianity, Islam and the Negro Race* (London: W. B. Whittingham).

Boahen, A. A. (1966) *Topics in West African History* (London: Longman).

Boahen, A. A. (1974) 'Politics in Ghana, 1800–1874' in J. F. A. Ajayi and M. Crowder (eds) *History of West Africa*, Vol. II, pp. 167–261.

Boahen, A. A. (1977) 'Prempeh in Exile', *Research Review*, VIII, 3, pp. 3–20.

Boavida, A. A. (1967) *Angola: cinco séculos de exploração portuguêsa* (Rio de Janeiro: Civilizacão Brasileira).

Bohannan, P. and Curtin, P. (1971) *Africa and Africans* (New York: Natural History Press, rev. edn).

Bohm, E. (1938) *La mise en valeur des colonies portugaises* (Paris).

Boilat, Abbé (1853) *Esquisses Sénégalaises* (Paris: P. Bertrand).

Boiteau, P. (1958) *Contribution à l'histoire de la nation malgache* (Paris: Éd. Sociales).

Bond, H. M. 'Forming African youth: a philosophy of education' in J. A. Davis (ed.) *Africa Seen by American Negroes*, pp. 247–61.

Bonner, P. L. (1978) 'The decline and fall of the ICU: a case of self-destruction?' in E. Webster (ed.) *Essays in Southern African Labour History*, pp. 114–20.

Bonner, P. L. (1979) 'The 1920 Black mineworkers' strike: a preliminary account' in B. Bozzoli (ed.) *Labour, Townships and Protest: Studies in the Social History of the Witwatersrand*.

Bony, J. (1980) 'La Côte d'Ivoire sous la colonisation française et le prélude à l'émancipation, 1920–47 – Genèse d'une nation' (PhD thesis: University of Paris I).

Booth, N. S. (1977) 'Islam in Africa', in N. S. Booth (ed.) *African Religions: a Symposium* (New York: Nok Publishers).

Booth, N. S. (ed.) (1977) *African Religions: a Symposium* (New York: Nok Publishers).

Boserup, E. (1965) *The Conditions of Agricultural Growth* (Chicago: Aldine).

Botelho, J. J. T. (1934) *História Militar e Política dos Portugueses em Moçambique*, 2 vols (Lisbon).

Bouis, L. (1946) 'Algérie et Sahara: le regime douanier' in *Encyclopédie de l'Empire Française* (Paris).

Boulegue, M. (1965) 'La presse au Sénégal avant 1939: bibliographie', *BIFAN* (B) XXVII, pp. 715–754.

Bourguiba, A. (1954) *La Tunisie et la France: vingt-cinq ans de lutte pour une coopération libre* (Paris: Julliard).

Bowen, J. W. E. (1896) *Africa and the American Negro: Addresses and Proceedings of the Congress on Africa* (Miami: Mnemosyne Publishers, 1969 edn).

Bower, P. (1948) 'The mining industry' in M. Perham (ed.) *Mining, Commerce and Finance in Nigeria*, pp. 1–42.

Boyes, J. (n.d.) *My Abyssinian Journey* (Nairobi: W. Boyd).

Bozzoli, B. (ed.) (1979) *Labour, Townships and Protest: Studies in the Social History of the Witwatersrand* (Johannesburg).

Brandel, R. (1961) *The Music of Central Africa* (The Hague: Martinus Nijhoff).

Branquinho, J. A. G. de M. (1966) *Prospecção das Forças Tradicionas* (Nampula).

Brass, W. *et al.* (1968) *The Demography of Tropical Africa* (Princeton: PUP).

Brass, W. and Coale, A. J. (1968) 'Methods of analysis and estimation' in W. Brass *et al. The Demography of Tropical Africa*, pp. 88–139.

Brett, E. A. (1973) *Colonialism and Underdevelopment in East Africa* (New York: Nok Publishers).

Brotz, H. (1970) *The Black Jews of Harlem: Negro Nationalism and the Dilemmas of Negro Leadership* (New York: Schocken).

Brown, M. (1978) *Madagascar Rediscovered: a History from Early Times to Independence* (London: Damien Tunnacliffe).

Brunschwig, H. (1966) *French Colonialism, 1871–1914: Myths and Realities* (New York: Praeger).

Brunschwig, H. (1974) 'De la résistance Africaine à l'impérialisme Européen', *JAH*, XV, 1, pp. 47–64.

Buell, R. L. (1928) *The Native Problem in Africa*, 2 vols (New York: Macmillan).

Buell, R. L. (1947) *Liberia: a Century of Survival, 1847–1947* (Philadelphia: University of Pennsylvania Press).

Bundy, C. (1979) *The Rise and Fall of the South African Peasantry* (Berkeley: University of California Press; London: Heinemann).

Burns, A. C. (1957) *In Defence of Colonies: British Colonial Territories in International Affairs* (London: Allen & Unwin).

Bustin, E. (1975) *Lunda under Belgian Rule* (Cambridge Mass: HUP).

Cachia, A. J. (1975) *Libya under the Second Ottoman Occupation (1835–1911)* (Tripoli: Dar al Farjeni).

Caldwell, J. C. (1967) 'Population change' in W. Birmingham, I. Neustadt and E. N. Omaboe (eds) *A Study of Contemporary Ghana*, Vol. II, pp. 78–110.

Caldwell, J. C. (ed.) (1975) *Population Growth and Socio-Economic Change in West Africa* (New York: Columbia UP).
Caldwell, J. C. (forthcoming) *The African Drought and its Demographic Implications*.
Caldwell, J. C. and Okonjo, J. (eds) (1968) *The Population of Tropical Africa* (London: Longman).
Cantrelle, P. 'Mortality; levels, patterns and trends' in J. C. Caldwell (ed.) (1975) *Population Growth and Socio-Economic Change in West Africa*, pp. 98-118.
Capela, J. (forthcoming) *O Movimento Operário em Lourenço Marques, 1910-1927*.
Cardoso, F. H. (1962) *Capitalismo e escravidâd no Brasil meridional* (São Paulo: Difusão Europeia do Livro).
Cardozo, J. (1931) *Finances et crédit pan José Cardoso ...* (Lourenço Marques).
Carr-Saunders, A. M. (1936) *World Population: Past Growth and Present Trends* (Oxford: Clarendon Press).
Cartwright, F. and Biddiss, M. D. (1972) *Disease and History* (London: Rupert Hart-Davies).
Casserley, G. (1923) *Algeria Today* (London: T. Werner Laurie).
Cecil, G. (1932) *Life of Robert Marquis of Salisbury*, Vol. IV (London: Hodder & Stoughton).
Centro de Estudos dos Africanos (1977) *The Mozambique Miners* (Maputo).
Chaine, M. (1913) 'Histoire du règne de Iohannes IV, roi d'Ethiopie (1868-1889)', *RSEHA*, XXI, pp. 178-91.
Chalmers, J. A. (1877) *Tiyo Soga: a Page of South African Mission Work* (London: Hodder & Stoughton).
Chalk, F. (1967) 'Du Bois and Garvey confront Liberia', *CJAS*, I, 2, pp. 135-42.
Chanaiwa, D. (1974) 'The Shona and the British South Africa Company in Southern Rhodesia, 1890-1896', *AQ*, XIV, 3 & 4.
Chanaiwa, D. (1980) 'African humanism in South Africa' in A. Mugomba and M. Nyaggah (eds) *Independence Without Freedom. The Political Economy of Colonial Education in Southern Africa*, pp. 9-39.
Chapus, G. S. (1961) *Manuel de l'histoire de Madagascar* (Paris: Larose).
Charle, E. G. (1964) 'An appraisal of British imperial policy with respect to the extraction of mineral resources in Nigeria', *NJESS*, VI, 1, pp. 37-42.
Chester, E. W. (1974) *Clash of Titans* (New York: Orbis).
Chevalier, L. (1947) *Le problème demographique nord-africaine* (Paris: PUF).
Chilcote, R. (ed.) (1972) *Protest and Resistance in Angola and Brazil* (Berkeley: University of California Press).
Chilembwe, J. 'Letter', *Mission Herald*, IX, 9 April 1905.
Chinweizu (1975) *The West and the Rest of Us: White Predators, Black Slavers and the African Elite* (New York: Vintage Books).
Chomsky, N. *et al.* (1972) *Spheres of Influence in the Age of Imperialism* (Nottingham: Spokesman Books).
Chrétien, J. P. (1970) 'Une revolte au Burundi en 1934', *AESC*, XV, 6, pp. 1678-1717.
Churchill, W. S. (1948) *The Gathering Storm* (London: Cassell).
Cimmaruta, R. (1936) *Ual Ual* (Milan: Mondadori).
Clapham, C. (1977) 'Ethiopia' in R. Lemarchand (ed.) *African Kingships in Perspective: Political Change and Modernization in Monarchical Settings*, pp. 35-63.
Clarence-Smith, W. G. (1979) *Slaves, Peasants and Capitalists in Southern Angola, 1840-1926* (Cambridge: CUP).
Clarence-Smith, W. G. and Moorsom, R. (1975) 'Underdevelopment and class formation in Ovamboland, 1845-1915', *JAH*, XVI, 3, pp. 365-81.
Clarke, J. H. (1964) *Harlem USA* (Berlin: Seven Seas Publishers).
Clendenen, C., Collins, R. and Duignan, P. (1966) *Americans in Africa, 1865-1900* (Stanford: Hoover Institution Press).
Clower, R. W., Dalton, G., Harwitz, M. and Walters, A. A. (1966) *Growth Without Development. An Economic Survey of Liberia* (Evanston: NUP).
Coale, A. J. and Demeny, P. (1966) *Regional Model Life Tables and Stable Populations* (Princeton: PUP).
Coale, A. J. and Demeny, P. (1967) *Population Studies* (New York: UN).
Coale, A. J. and Lorimer, F. (1968) 'Summary of estimates of fertility and mortality' in W. Brass *et al. The Demography of Tropical Africa*, pp. 151-67.
Coale, A. J. and van de Walle, E. (1968) 'Appendix: notes on areas for which estimates were made but not subject to a detailed study' in W. Brass *et al. The Demography of Tropical Africa*, pp. 168-82.

Cobbing, J. (1974) 'Ndebele religion in the nineteenth century' (unpublished paper).

Cobbing, J. (1977) 'The absent priesthood: another look at the Rhodesian risings of 1896–1897', *JAH*, XVIII, 1, pp. 61–84.

Coelho, R. (1964) *Os Karibes Negros de Honduras* (São Paulo: Separata da Revista du Museu Paulista, n.s. 15).

Coelho, T. (ed.) (1898) *Dezoito annos em Africa* (Lisbon).

Cole, M. M. (1961) *South Africa* (London: Methuen).

Coleman, J. S. (1958) *Nigeria: Background to Nationalism* (Berkeley and Los Angeles: University of California Press).

Coleman, J. S. (1965) 'Nationalism in tropical Africa' in P. J. M. McEwan and R. B. Sutcliffe (eds) *The Study of Africa*, pp. 156–83.

Coleman, J. S. and Belmont, B., Jr (1962) 'The role of the military in sub-Saharan Africa' in J. J. Johnson (ed.) *The Role of the Military in Under-developed Countries*, pp. 359–405.

Coleman, J. S. and Rosberg, C. G. (eds) (1970) *Political Parties and National Integration in Tropical Africa* (Berkeley and Los Angeles: University of California Press).

Collins, R. O. (1967) 'The Aliab Dinka uprising and its suppression', *SNR*, XLVIII, pp. 77–89.

Confer, C. V. (1966) *France and Algeria: the Problem of Civil and Political Reform, 1870–1920* (New York: Syracuse UP).

Coon, C. (1936) *Measuring Ethiopia and Flight into Arabia* (London: Jonathan Cape).

Coquery-Vidrovitch, C. (1972) *Le Congo français au temps des grandes compagnies concessionnaires, 1898–1930* (Paris & The Hague: Mouton).

Coquery-Vidrovitch, C. (1975) 'L'impact des intérêts coloniaux: SCOA et CFAO dans l'ouest africain, 1910–1965', *JAH*, XVI, 4, pp. 595–621.

Coquery-Vidrovitch, C. (ed.) (1976) 'L'Afrique et la crise de 1930 (1924–1938)', *RFHOM* (special number), LXIII, 232–3, pp. 375–776.

Coquery-Vidrovitch, C. (1977) 'Mutations de l'impérialisme colonial français dans les années 30', *AEH*, IV, pp. 103–52.

Coquery-Vidrovitch, C. (forthcoming) 'French Black Africa' in A. D. Roberts (ed.) *Cambridge History of Africa*, Vol. VII.

Coquery-Vidrovitch, C. and Moniot, H. (1974) *L'Afrique noire de 1800 à nos jours* (Paris: PUF).

Cornevin, R. (1962) *Histoire du Togo* (Paris: Berger-Levrault).

Coro, F. (1971) *Settantasei Anni di Dominazione Turca in Libia, 1835–1911* (Tripoli: Stabilimento Poligrafico Editorial, Plinio Maggi).

Cosnier, H. C. (1921) *L'ouest africain français, ses ressources agricoles, son organisation économique* (Paris: Larose).

Cosnier, H. C. (1922) *L'Afrique du nord: son avenir agricole et économique* (Paris: Larose).

Couceiro, S. M. (1974) *Bibliografi sobre o negro brasileiro* (São Paulo: Centro de Estudos Africano/Universidade de São Paulo).

Coupland, R. (1928) *Kirk on the Zambezi* (Oxford: Clarendon Press).

Coutinho, J. A. (1904) *A Campanha do Barue em 1902* (Lisbon).

Cronon, E. D. (1962) *Black Moses: The Story of Marcus Garvey and the Universal Negro Improvement Association* (Madison: University of Wisconsin Press).

Crowder, M. (1962) *Senegal: a Study in French Assimilation Policy* (London: OUP).

Crowder, M. (1964) 'Indirect rule: French and British style', *Africa*, XXXIV, 3, pp. 197–205.

Crowder, M. (1968) *West Africa under Colonial Rule* (London: Hutchinson).

Crowder, M. (ed.) (1971) *West African Resistance* (London: Hutchinson).

Crowder, M. (1973) *Revolt in Bussa: a Study of British 'Native Administration' in Nigerian Borgu: 1902–35* (London: Faber).

Crowder, M. (1974) 'The 1914–1918 European War and West Africa' in J. F. A. Ajayi and M. Crowder (eds) *History of West Africa*, Vol. II, pp. 484–513.

Crowder, M. (1977a) *Colonial West Africa* (London: Frank Cass).

Crowder, M. (1977b) 'Introduction' [to 'Protest against colonial rule in West Africa'], *Tarikh*, V, 3, pp. 1–5.

Crowder, M. (1977c) 'The Borgu revolts of 1915–17', *Tarikh*, V, 3, pp. 18–30.

Crowder, M. (1977d) 'Blaise Diagne and the recruitment of African troops for the 1914–18 War' in M. Crowder, *Colonial West Africa*, pp. 104–21.

Crowder, M. and Ajayi, J. F. A. (1974) 'West Africa 1919–1939: the colonial situation' in J. F. A. Ajayi and M. Crowder (eds) *History of West Africa*, Vol. II, pp. 514–41.

Crowder, M. and Ikime, O. (eds) (1970) *West African Chiefs: Their Changing Status under Colonial Rule and Independence* (New York: Africana Publishing Corp.).

Crowe, S. E. (1942) *The Berlin West African Conference, 1884–1885* (London: Longmans Green).

Crummey, D. (1969) 'Tēwodros as reformer and modernizer', *JAH*, X, 3, pp. 457–69.

Cudsi, A. S. (1969) 'Sudanese resistance to British rule, 1900–1920' (MA thesis: University of Khartoum).
Cunha, J. M. da Silva (1949) *O trabalho indigesa: estudo do directo colonial* (Lisbon).
Curtin, P. D. (1969) *The African Slave Trade: a Census* (Madison: University of Wisconsin Press).
Curtin, P. D., Feierman, S., Thompson, L. and Vansina, J. (1978) *African History* (London: Longman).

da Cunha, M. C. (1976) 'Brasileiros Nagós em Lagos no século XIX', *Cultura*, October–December 1976 (Brasilia: Ministerio da Educacao e Cultura).
Dabbūr, M. A. (1971) *Nahd 'at al Jazā'ir al-Hadītha Fīthawratī-Hāx'l-Mubāraka* (Algiers).
Dachs, A. J. (1972) 'Politics of collaboration: imperialism in practice' in B. Pachai (ed.) *The Early History of Malawi*, pp. 283–92.
Daly, M. D. (1977) 'The Governor-Generalship of Sir Lee Stack, 1917–24' (PhD thesis: University of London).
Darwin, C. (1859) *On the Origin of Species by Means of Natural Selection, or the Preservation of Favoured Races in the Struggle for Life* (London: John Murray).
Davidson, A. B. (1968) 'African resistance and rebellion against the imposition of colonial rule' in T. O. Ranger (ed.) *Emerging Themes of African History*, pp. 177–88.
Davidson, A. B. (1972) *South Africa, the Birth of a Protest* (Moscow: African Institute).
Davidson, B. (1964a) *The African Past* (London: Longman).
Davidson, B. (1964b) *Which Way Africa?* (Harmondsworth: Penguin).
Davidson, B. (1978a) *Discovering Africa's Past* (London: Longman).
Davidson, B. (1978b) *Africa in Modern History* (London: Allen Lane).
Davies, I. (1966) *African Trade Unions* (Harmondsworth: Penguin).
Davies, J. N. P. (1956) 'The history of syphilis in Buganda', *BWHO*, XV, pp. 1041–55.
Davis, J. A. (ed.) (1958) *Africa Seen by American Negroes* (cover title) [*Africa From the Point of View of American Negro Scholars* – title page title] (Paris: Présence Africaine).
Davis, L. (1974) 'Black images of Liberia, 1877–1914' (unpublished paper prepared for the Sixth Annual Liberian Studies Conference, Madison, Wisconsin, 26–27 April 1974).
de Bono, E. (1937) *Anno XIII: The Conquest of an Empire* (London).
de Castro, L. (1915) *Nella terra dei Negus, pagine raccolte in Abissinia* (Milan: Fratelli Treves).
de Dekker, P. (1974) 'Mutations sociales, politiques et économiques au Rwanda entre les deux guerres' (Master's dissertation: University of Paris VII).
de Freitas, H. I. F. (1956–7) *Seitas Religiosas Genticicas*, 3 vols (Lourenço Marques).
de Graft, J. C. (1976) 'Roots in African drama and theatre', *African Literature Today*, VIII, pp. 1–25.
de Kiewiet, C. W. (1965) *The Imperial Factor in South Africa. A Study in Politics and Economics* (London: Frank Cass).
de Montmorency, W. G. B. [Viscount Mountmorres] (1906) *The Congo Independent State: a Report on a Voyage of Enquiry* (London: Williams & Norgate).
Debrunner, H. (1967) *A History of Christianity in Ghana* (Accra: Waterville Publishing).
Dejaco, A. (1972) *Di mal d'Africa si muore* (Rome).
del Boca, A. (1969) *The Ethiopian War, 1935–1941* (Chicago: Chicago UP).
de la Pradelle, A. (1936) *Le conflit Italo-Ethiopien* (Paris).
Delavignette, R. (1946) *Service Africaine* (Paris: Gallimard, 8th edn).
Denoon, D. (1972) *Southern Africa since 1800* (London: Longman).
Desanti, M. (1940) 'La propriété en Afrique noire' (paper presented to Conférences à l'Ecole Coloniale).
Deschamps, H. (1960) *Histoire de Madagascar* (Paris: Berger-Levrault).
Deschamps, H. (1962) *Madagascar, Camores, Terres Australes* (Paris: Berger-Levrault).
Deschamps, H. (1963) 'Et maintenant, Lord Lugard?', *Africa*, XXXII, 4, pp. 293–306.
Despois, J. (1961) *La Tunisie* (Paris: A. Colin).
Deutschland, H. (1970) *Trailblazers, Struggles and Organizations of African Workers before 1945* (Berlin: Tribune).
Digernes, O. (1978) 'Appearance and reality in the Southern Sudan. A study in British administration of the Nuer, 1900–1930' (PhD thesis: University of Bergen).
Dike, K. O. (1956) *Trade and Politics in the Niger Delta, 1830–1885* (Oxford: Clarendon Press).
Downes, W. D. (1919) *With the Nigerians in German East Africa* (London: Methuen).
Dresch, J. (1952) 'Les investissements en Afrique noire', *PA*, XIII, pp. 232–41.
Dreschler, H. (1966) *Südwestafrika unter deutscher Kolonialherrschaft* (Berlin).
Du Bois, W. E. B. (1968) *Dusk of Dawn. An Essay Towards an Autobiography of a Race Concept* (New York: Schocken Books).

Dublin, Louis I., Lotka, A. J. and Spiegelman, M. (1936) *Length of Life: a Study of the Life Table* (New York: Roland Press).
Duffy, J. (1959) *Portuguese Africa* (London: OUP).
Duffy, J. (1962) *Portugal in Africa* (Harmondsworth: Penguin).
Duffy, J. (1967) *A Question of Slavery* (Oxford: Clarendon Press).
Duggan, A. J. (1962) 'A survey of sleeping sickness in Northern Nigeria from the earliest times to the present day', *TRSTMH*, LVI, 1962, pp. 439–80.
Dumont, R. (1966) *False Start in Africa* (London: André Deutsch).
Dunbar, A. R. (1965) *A History of Bunyoro-Kitara* (London: OUP).
Duncan, W. G. (1973) *The Nature and Content of Fertility Surveys Conducted throughout the World since 1960* (The Hague).
Duperray, A. (1978) 'Les Gourounsi de Haute-Volta: conquête et colonisation, 1896–1933' (Thèse de 3e cycle: University of Paris).
Durand, J. D. (1967) 'The modern expansion of world population', *PAPS*, CXI, 3, pp. 136–59.
Dwane, J. M. (1897) Article in *Voice of Missions*, July 1897 (no further details available).

Easton, S. C. (1964) *The Rise and Fall of Western Colonialism* (London: Pall Mall).
Echenberg, M. J. (1975) 'Paying the blood tax: military conscription in French West Africa, 1914–1929', *CJAS*, IX, 2, pp. 171–92.
Edgar, R. (forthcoming) 'Enoch Mgijima, the Israelites and the background to the Bulhoek massacre', *IJAHS*.
Edmund, W. D. (1951) 'The newspaper press in British West Africa, 1918–1939' (MA thesis: University of Bristol).
Eggeling, W. J. (1948) 'Another Photograph of Mumia', *UJ*, XII, 2, pp. 197–9.
Eggeling, W. J. (1950) 'Death of Mumia', *UJ*, XIV, 1, p. 105.
Ehrlich, C. (1957) 'Cotton and the Uganda economy, 1903–1909', *UJ*, XXI, 2, pp. 162–75.
Ehrlich, C. (1973) 'Building and caretaking: economic policy in British tropical Africa, 1890–1960', *EHR*, XXIV, 4, pp. 649–67.
El-Alami, (1972) *Allal El Fasi, patriarche du nationalisme marocain* (Rabat).
El-Annabi, H. (1975) 'La crise de 1929 et ses conséquences en Tunisie' (Dissertation for Certificat d'Aptitude à la Recherche: Tunis).
El-Hareir, I. (1981) 'Mawaqif Khalida li umar al-Mukhtar' in *Umar Al-Mukhtar* (Tripoli: Libyan Study Centre).
El-Kammash, M. M. (1968) *Economic Development and Planning in Egypt* (New York: Praeger).
Elgood, P. G. (1928) *The Transit of Egypt* (London: Arnold).
Elias, T. O. (1971) *Nigerian Land Law* (London: Sweet & Maxwell).
Eliot, C. (1905) *The East African Protectorate* (London: Arnold).
Ellis, S. (1980a) 'The political elite of Imerina and the revolt of the *Menalamba*. The creation of a colonial myth in Madagascar, 1895–1898', *JAH*, XXI, 2, pp. 219–34.
Ellis, S. (1980b) 'Resistance or collaboration: the Menalamba in the Kingdom of Imerina, 1895–1899' (DPhil. thesis: University of Oxford).
Emmanuel, A. (1972) *Unequal Exchange: a Study of the Imperialism of Trade* (New York: Monthly Review Press).
Encyclopédie de l'empire française (1946) 2 vols (Paris).
Esoavelomandroso, F. (1977a) 'Politique des races et enseignement colonial jusqu'en 1940', *Omaly sy Anio*, V–VI, pp. 245–56.
Esoavelomandroso, F. (1977b) *L'attitude malgache face au traité de 1885 (d'après le Journal de Rainilaiarivony)* (Antananarivo: Collection Etudes Historiques).
Esoavelomandroso, F. (1979) 'Rainilairivony and the defense of Malagasy independence at the end of the nineteenth century' in R. K. Kent (ed.) *Madagascar in History, Essays from the 1970s*, pp. 228–51.
Esoavelomandroso, F. (1980) 'Une étude récente sur les Menalamba: compte rendu de la thèse de Stephen Ellis (Les Menalamba dans le royaume d'Imerina: résistance ou collaboration)', *Omaly sy Anio*, XI.
Esoavelomandroso, F. (1981) 'Differentes lectures de l'histoire. Quelques réflexions sur la VVS', *RPC*, L, pp. 100–111.
Esoavelomandroso, M. (1975) 'Le mythe d'Andriba', *Omaly sy Anio*, I–II, pp. 43–73.
Esoavelomandroso, M. (1979) *La province maritime orientale du Royaume de Madagascar à la fin du XIXe siècle (1882–1895)* (Antananarivo: F.T.).
Esoavelomandroso, M. (1981) 'L'opposition de l'Ambongo à la pénétration française en 1899', paper presented to Colloque International d'Histoire Malgache at Majunga (13–18 April 1981).
Evans-Pritchard, E. E. (1949) *The Sanusi of Cyrenaica* Oxford: Clarendon Press).

Fadipe, M. A. (1970) *The Sociology of the Yoruba* (Ibadan: IUP).

Fage, J. D. (1967) 'British and German colonial rule: a synthesis and summary' in P. Gifford and W. R. Louis (eds) *Britain and Germany in Africa: Imperial Rivalry and Colonial Rule*, pp. 691–706.

Fage, J. D. (1978) *An Atlas of African History* (London: Arnold, 2nd edn).

Fanon, F. (1967) *The Wretched of the Earth* (Harmondsworth: Penguin).

Farago, L. (1935) *Abyssinia on the Eve* (London: Putnam).

Farrant, L. (1975) *Tippu Tip and the East African Slave Trade* (London: Hamilton).

Fashole-Luke, E., Gray, R., Hastings, A. and Tasie, G. (eds) (1978) *Christianity in Independent Africa* (London: Rex Collings).

Faulkingham, R. H., Balding, J. H., Faulkingham, L. J. and Thorbahn, P. F. (1974) 'The demographic effects of drought in the West African Sahel' (paper presented to Annual Meeting of the Population Association of America).

Faulkner, T. J. R. (1926) *Programme of the People's Party* (Monrovia).

Faulkner, T. J. R. (1927) *An Appeal to Reason: to the Public* (Monrovia).

Fendall, C. P. (1921) *The East African Force, 1915–1919* (London: H. F. Witherby).

Ferguson, D. E. (1980) 'The political economy of health and medicine in colonial Tanganyika' in M. H. Y. Kaniki (ed.) *Tanzania under Colonial Rule*, pp. 307–43.

Fernandes Júnior, J. (1955) 'Narração do Distrito de Tete' (Makanga: unpublished Ms).

Fetter, B. (1974) 'African associations in Elisabethville, 1910–1935: their origins and development', *EHA*, VI, pp. 205–23.

Fetter, B. (1976) *The Creation of Elisabethville, 1910–1940* (Stanford: Hoover Institution Press).

Fidel, C. (1926) *Les colonies allemandes: études historiques et renseignements statistiques* (Tonnerre: C. Puyfagès).

Fieldhouse, D. K. (1961) 'Imperialism: an historical revision', *EHR*, XIV, 2, pp. 187–209.

Fieldhouse, D. K. (1981) *Colonialism 1870–1945: an Introduction* (London: Weidenfeld & Nicolson).

Fika, A. M. (1978) *The Kano Civil War and British Over-rule, 1882–1940* (Ibadan: OUP).

Finer, S. F. (1962) *The Man on Horseback* (London: Pall Mall).

Finkle, J. L. and Gable, R. W. (eds) (1971) *Political Development and Social Change* (New York: John Wiley, 2nd edn).

First, R. (1963) *South West Africa* (Harmondsworth: Penguin).

Fischer, F. (1967) *Germany's Aims in the First World War* (New York: W. W. Norton).

Flament, F. *et al.* (1952) 'La force publique de sa naissance à 1914. Participation des militaires à l'histoire des premières années du Congo', *IRCBM*, XXVII, pp. 1–585.

Ford, J. (1971) *The Role of Trypanosomiases in African Ecology: a Study of the Tsetse Fly Problem* (Oxford: Clarendon Press).

Folayan, K. (1973) 'The resistance movement in Libya', *Tarikh*, IV, 3, pp. 46–56.

Folayan, K. (1974) 'Italian colonial rule in Libya', *Tarikh*, IV, 4, pp. 1–10.

Frankel, S. H. (1938) *Capital Investment in Africa* (London: OUP).

Frazier, E. F. (1949) *The Negro in the United States* (New York: Macmillan).

Fremigacci, J. (1980) 'Madagascar de 1905 à 1940' (unpublished Ms).

Friedland, E. A. (1979) 'Mozambican nationalist resistance, 1920–1940' *TJH*, VIII, pp. 117–28.

Fugelstad, F. (1974) 'La grande famine de 1931 dans l'ouest nigérien', *RFHOM*, LXI, 222, pp. 18–33.

Furnivall, J. S. (1948) *Colonial Policy and Practice* (Cambridge: CUP).

Fynn, J. K. (1971) 'Ghana-Asante (Ashanti)' in M. Crowder (ed.) *West African Resistance*, pp. 19–52.

Gabel, C. and Bennett, N. R. (eds) (1967) *Reconstructing African Culture History* (Boston: BUP).

Gaffarel, P. (1905) *Histoire de l'expansion coloniale de la France depuis 1870 jusqu'en 1905* (Marseilles: Balatier).

Gaitskell, A. (1959) *Gezira: a Story of Development in the Sudan* (London: Faber).

Galbraith, J. S. (1961) 'Myths of the "Little England" era', *AHR*, LXVII, 1, pp. 34–48.

Gallagher, J. and Robinson, R. (1953) 'The imperialism of free trade', *EHR*, VI, 1, pp. 1–15.

Ganier, G. (1965) 'Lat Dyor et le chemin de fer de l'arachide, 1876–1886', *BIFAN* (B), XXVII, 1 & 2, pp. 223–81.

Gann, L. H. (1964) *A History of Northern Rhodesia: Early Days to 1953* (London: Chatto & Windus).

Gann, L. H. and Duignan, P. (1967) *Burden of Empire* (London: Pall Mall).

Gann, L. H. and Duignan, P. (eds) (1969) *Colonialism in Africa, 1870–1960* Vol. I, *The History and Politics of Colonialism 1870–1914* (Cambridge: CUP).

Gann, L. H. and Duignan, P. (eds) (1970) *Colonialism in Africa 1870–1960* Vol. II, *The History and Politics of Colonialism 1914–1960* (Cambridge: CUP).

826

Gardiner, A. L. (1933) 'The law of slavery in Abyssinia', *IL*, XV.
Garvey, A. J. (ed.) (1923–5) *Philosophy and Opinions of Marcus Garvey* (London: Frank Cass: 1967 edn).
Garvey, A. J. (1963) *Garvey and Garveyism* (Kingston: United Printers).
Gaudio, A. (1972) *Abd el-Fasi, or the History of the Istiqlal* (no further details available).
Gautier, E. F. (1910) *La conquête du Sahara* (Paris: A. Colin).
Geiss, I. (1974) *The Pan-African Movement* (London: Methuen).
Gerhart, G. M. (1978) *Black Power in South Africa* (Berkeley: University of California Press).
Gibson, G. W. and Russell, A. F. (1883) *Memorandum and Protest of the Government of Liberia against the Action of the British Authorities in the North Western Territories of the Republic* (Monrovia).
Gide, A. (1930) *Travels in the Congo* (New York and London: Knopf).
Gifford, P. and Louis, W. R. (eds) (1967) *Britain and Germany in Africa: Imperial Rivalry and Colonial Rule* (New Haven & London: YUP).
Gifford, P. and Louis, W. R. (eds) (1971) *France and Britain in Africa* (New Haven & London: YUP).
Giglio, C. (1968) *L'articolo XVII de Trattato di Ucciali* (Como: Cairoli).
Gilkes, P. (1975) *The Dying Lion: Feudalism and Modernization in Ethiopia* (London: Julian Friedmann).
Gleichen, E. (1898) *With the Mission to Menelik, 1897* (London: Arnold).
Gluckman, M. (1963) *Order and Rebellion in Tropical Africa* (London: Cohen & West).
Goodfellow, C. F. (1966) *Great Britain and South African Confederation, 1870–1881* (Cape Town: OUP).
Goody, J. (ed.) (1968) *Literacy in Traditional Societies* (Cambridge: CUP).
Grandidier, G. (1934) *Atlas des colonies françaises* (Paris: Soc. d'éditions géographiques, maritimes et coloniales).
Gray, J. M. (1948) 'Early treaties in Uganda', *UJ*, XII, 1, pp. 25–42.
Graziani, R. (1938) *Il Fronte Sud* (Milan: Montadori).
Graziani, R. (1976) *Verso al-Fezzan* (Cairo: Maktabat Saigh).
Graziani, R. (1980) *Cyrenaica Pacificata* (Benghazi: al-Andalus).
Greenfield, R. (1965) *Ethiopia: a New Political History* (New York: Praeger).
Groves, C. P. (1969) 'Missionary and humanitarian aspects of imperialism from 1870 to 1914' in L. H. Gann and P. Duignan (eds) *Colonialism in Africa 1870–1960*, Vol. I, pp. 462–96.
Guillaume, A. (1946) *Les Berbères marocains et la pacification de l'Atlas central (1912–1933)* (Paris: Julliard).
Gusfield, J. R. (1971) 'Tradition and modernity: misplaced polarities in the study of social change' in J. L. Finkle and R. W. Gable (eds) *Political Development and Social Change*.
Gutteridge, W. (1975) *Military Regimes in Africa* (London: Methuen).
Gwassa, G. C. K. (1972) 'African methods of warfare during the Maji Maji war' in B. A. Ogot (ed.) *War and Society in Africa*, pp. 123–48.
Gwassa, G. C. K. (1972) 'Kinjitile and the ideology of Maji Maji' in T. O. Ranger and I. N. Kimambo (eds) *The Historical Study of African Religion*, pp. 202–17.
Gwassa, G. C. K. and Iliffe, J. (eds) (1968) *Records of the Maji Maji Rising* (Dar es Salaam: Historical Association of Tanzania, Paper No. 4).

Hafkin, N. J. (1971) 'Sheikhs, slaves and sovereignty' (paper presented to the Conference of the African Studies Association of the USA, November 1971).
Hafkin, N. J. (1973) 'Trade, society and politics in northern Mozambique' (PhD thesis: University of Boston).
Hagan, K. O. (1968) 'The development of adult literacy and adult education and their influence in social change in Ghana, 1901–57' (B.Litt. thesis: University of Oxford).
Haile Sellassie (1936) 'La vérité sur la guerre Italo-Ethiopienne', *Vu* (Paris), July 1936.
Hailey, Lord (1938 and rev. edn, 1957) *An African Survey* (London: OUP).
Hajivayanis, G. G., Mtowa, A. C. and Iliffe, J. (1973), 'The politicians: Ali Mponda and Hassan Suleiman' in J. Iliffe (ed.) *Modern Tanzanians*.
Haley, A. (1976) *Roots* (New York: Doubleday).
Haliburton, G. M. (1971) *The Prophet Harris* (London: Longman).
Hall, R. (1965) *Zambia* (London: Pall Mall Press).
Hallett, R. (1970) *Africa to 1875: a Modern History* (Ann Arbor: MUP).
Hamilton, A. (1911) *Somaliland* (Westport: Negro Universities Press, 1970 edn).
Hamilton, R. (1975) *Voices from an Empire: a History of Afro-Portuguese Literature* (Minneapolis: University of Minnesota Press).

827

Hammond, R. J. (1969) 'Uneconomic imperialism: Portugal in Africa before 1910' in L. H. Gann and P. Duignan (eds) *Colonialism in Africa 1870–1960*, Vol. I, pp. 352–82.

Hamza, M. M. (1972) *Ḥiṣār wa Soqut al Khrṭūm* (Khartoum).

Hancock, W. K. (1962) *Smuts: the Sanguine Years, 1870–1919* (Cambridge: CUP).

Hardie, F. (1974) *The Abyssinian Crisis* (London: Batsford).

Hardy, G. (1930) *Vue générale de l'histoire d'Afrique* (Paris: A. Colin, 2nd edn).

Hargreaves, J. D. (1963) *Prelude to the Partition of West Africa* (London: Macmillan).

Hargreaves, J. D. (1969) 'West African states and the European conquest' in L. H. Gann and P. Duignan (eds) *Colonialism in Africa 1870–1960*, Vol. I, pp. 199–219.

Harlow, V. and Chilver, E. M. (1965) *History of East Africa*, Vol. II (Oxford: Clarendon Press).

Harmand, J. (1910) *Domination et colonisation* (Paris: Flammarion).

Harms, R. (1975) 'The end of red rubber: a reassessment', *JAH*, XVI, 1, pp. 73–88.

Hatch, J. (1971) *Nigeria: a History* (London: Secker & Warburg).

Hatton, P. H. S. (1966) 'The Gambia, the Colonial Office, and the opening months of the First World War', *JAH*, VII, 1, pp. 123–31.

Hauser, P. M. (1957) 'World and Asian urbanization in relation to economic development and social change' in P. M. Hauser (ed.) *Urbanization in Asia and the Far East*, pp. 53–95.

Hauser, P. M. (ed.) (1957) *Urbanization in Asia and the Far East* (Calcutta: UNESCO).

Hayes, C. J. H. (1941) *A Generation of Materialism, 1871–1900* (New York: Harper & Row).

Hayford, J. E. C. (1911) *Ethiopia Unbound: Studies in Race Emancipation* (London: C. E. M. Phillips).

Haykal, M. H. (n.d.) *Tarājim Misrtyya wa Gharbiyya* (Cairo).

Hayward, V. E. W. (ed.) (1963) *African Independent Church Movements* (London: Edinburgh House Press).

Heald, S. (ed.) (1937) *Documents on International Affairs, 1935*, Vol. II (London: RIIA).

Heimer, F.-W. (ed.) (1973) *Social Change in Angola* (Munich: Weltforum Verlag).

Henries, A. D. B. (1965) *Presidents of the First African Republic* (London: Macmillan).

Hermasi, A. B. (1966) 'Mouvement ouvrier et société coloniale' (unpublished thesis).

Herskovits, M. (1941) *The Myth of the Negro Past* (New York: Harper).

Herskovits, M. J. (1948) *Man and His Works: the Science of Cultural Anthropology* (New York: Knopf).

Herskovits, M. J. (1962) *The Human Factor in Changing Africa* (New York: Knopf).

Herskovits, M. J. (1966a) *The New World Negro. Selected Papers in Afroamerican Studies* (Bloomington: Indiana UP).

Herskovits, M. J. (1966b) 'Problem, method and theory in Afroamerican studies' in M. J. Herskovits, *The New World Negro*, pp. 43–61.

Herskovits, M. J. (1966c) 'Some psychological implications of Afroamerican studies' in M. J. Herskovits, *The New World Negro*, pp. 145–55.

Hertslet, E. (1896 and 1909) *The Map of Africa by Treaty*, 3 vols (London: HMSO 2nd and 3rd edns).

Heseltine, N. (1971) *Madagascar* (London: Pall Mall).

Hess, R. L. (1963) 'Italy and Africa: colonial ambitions in the First World War', *JAH*, IV, 1, pp. 105–126.

Hess, R. L. (1966) *Italian Colonialism in Somalia* (Chicago: Chicago UP).

Hess, R. L. and Loewenberg, G. (1968) 'The Ethiopian no-party state' in P. J. M. McEwan (ed.) *Twentieth Century Africa*, pp. 198–205.

Higginson, J. (forthcoming) 'Labourers into His harvest, lambs among wolves: African Watchtower and the spectre of colonial revolt in Katanga, 1923–1941'.

Hill, A. C. and Kilson, M. (eds) (1971) *Apropos of Africa: Sentiments of Negro American Leaders on Africa from the 1800s to the 1950s* (New York: Anchor).

Hill, M. F. (1956) *Planters' Progress: the Story of Coffee in Kenya* (Nairobi: Coffee Board of Kenya).

Hill, P. (1963) *The Migrant Cocoa-Farmers of Southern Ghana* (Cambridge: CUP).

Himmelfarb, G. (1960) 'John Buchan: an untimely appreciation', *Encounter*, LXXXIV, pp. 46–53.

Hinsley, F. H. (1959a) 'International rivalry in the colonial sphere, 1869–1885' in E. A. Benians, J. Butler and C. E. Carrington (eds) *The Cambridge History of the British Empire*, Vol. III, pp. 95–126.

Hinsley, F. H. (1959b) 'International rivalry, 1885–1895' in E. A. Benians, J. Butler and C. E. Carrington (eds) *The Cambridge History of the British Empire*, Vol. III, pp. 255–92.

Hinsley, F. H. (1962) (ed.) *The New Cambridge Modern History*, Vol. XI, *Material Progress and World-wide Problems, 1870–98* (Cambridge: CUP).

Hobsbawm, E. J. (1964) *The Age of Revolution* (London: Weidenfeld & Nicolson).

Hobsbawm, E. J. (1969) *Bandits* (London: Weidenfeld & Nicolson).

Hobson, J. A. (1902) *Imperialism: a Study* (Ann Arbor: MUP, 1965 edn).

Hodgkin, T. (1954) 'Background to AOF (3): African reactions to French rule', *West Africa*, No. 1925 (16 January 1954), pp. 31–2.

Hodgkin, T. (1956) *Nationalism in Colonial Africa* (London: F. Muller).
Hoffherr, R. (1932) *L'économie marocaine* (Paris: Recueil Sirey).
Holt, P. M. (ed.) (1968) *Political and Social Change in Modern Egypt* (London: OUP).
Holt, P. M. (1970) *The Mahdist State in the Sudan, 1881–1898* (Oxford: Clarendon Press, 2nd edn).
Hopkins, A. G. (1966a) 'The Lagos strike of 1897', *PP*, XXXV, 1966, pp. 133–55.
Hopkins, A. G. (1966b) 'Economic aspects of political movements in Nigeria and in the Gold Coast, 1918–1939', *JAH*, VII, 1, pp. 133–52.
Hopkins, A. G. (1968) 'Economic imperialism in West Africa: Lagos 1880–1892', *EHR*, pp. 580–606.
Hopkins, A. G. (1973) *An Economic History of West Africa* (London: Longman).
Hopkins, E. (1970) 'The Nyabingi cult of southwestern Uganda' in R. I. Rotberg and A. A. Mazrui (eds) *Protest and Power in Black Africa*, pp. 258–336.
Hordern, R. C. (1941) *Official History of the War. Military Operations: East Africa* (London: HMSO).
Houghton, D. H. (1971) 'Economic development, 1865–1965' in M. Wilson and L. Thompson (eds) *The Oxford History of South Africa*, Vol. II, pp. 1–48.
Hourani, A. (1962) *Arabic Thought in the Liberal Age, 1789–1939* (Oxford: Clarendon Press).
Howard, D. E. [President of Liberia] (1916) *Annual Message, 19 September 1919* (Monrovia: Republic of Liberia).
Howitt, W. (1969) *Colonization and Christianity* (New York: Negro Universities Press).
Huberich, C. H. (1947) *The Political and Legislative History of Liberia*, 2 vols (New York: Central Book Co.).
Hull, R. W. (1980) *Modern Africa: Change and Continuity* (Englewood Cliffs: Prentice Hall).
Huntingford, G. W. B. (1969) *The Galla of Ethiopia: the Kingdom of Kafa and Janhero* (London: IAI).
Huot, Marzin, Ricau, Grosfillez, David, Drs (1921) 'L'épidémie d'influenza de 1918–19 dans les colonies françaises', *Annuaire Médical et Pharmaceutique Colonial*, XIX.
Huxley, E. J. (1935) *White Man's Country: Lord Delamere and the Making of Kenya*, 2 vols (London: Macmillan).
Hyam, R. (1972) *The Failure of South African Expansion, 1908–1948* (London: Longman).
Hyden, G. (1969) *Political Development in Rural Tanzania* (Nairobi: EAPH).
Hymer, S. (1971) 'The political economy of the Gold Coast and Ghana' in G. Ranis (ed.) *Government and Economic Development*, pp. 129–80.

Ianni, O. (1962) *As Metamorfoses do Escravo* (São Paulo: Difusão Européia do Livro).
Ibrahim, H. A. (1974) 'The policy of the Condominium government towards the Mahdist political prisoners, 1898–1932', *SNR*, LV, pp. 33–45.
Ibrahim, H. A. (1976) *The 1936 Anglo-Egyptian Treaty* (Khartoum: Khartoum UP).
Ibrahim, H. A. (1977) 'The development of economic and political neo-Mahdism', *SNR*, LVIII.
Ibrahim, H. A. (1979) 'Mahdist risings against the Condominium government in the Sudan 1900–1927', *IJAHS*, XII, 3, pp. 440–71.
Ibrahim, M. A. (1969) 'Hamlat al-Amir Mahmūd Wad Ahmad ila al-Shamāl 1315/1897–98' (MA thesis: University of Khartoum).
Ikime, O. (1971) 'Nigeria–Ebrohimi' in M. Crowder (ed.) *West African Resistance*, pp. 205 32.
Ikime, O. (1973) 'Colonial conquest and African resistance in the Niger delta states', *Tarikh* IV, 3, pp. 1–13.
Ikime, O. (ed.) (1980) *Groundwork of Nigerian History* (Ibadan: Heinemann).
Iliffe, J. (1967) 'The organization of the Maji Maji rebellion', *JAH*, VIII, 4, pp. 495–512.
Iliffe, J. (1968) 'The Herero and Nama risings' in G. Kibodya (ed.) *Aspects of South African History* (Dar es Salaam: EAPH).
Iliffe, J. (1969) *Tanganyika under German Rule, 1905–1912* (Cambridge: CUP).
Iliffe, J. (ed.) (1973) *Modern Tanzanians* (Nairobi: EAPH).
Iliffe, J. (1979) *A Modern History of Tanganyika* (Cambridge: CUP).
Ingham, K. (1958) *The Making of Modern Uganda* (London: Allen & Unwin).
Irele, A. (1964) 'A defence of negritude. A propos of Black Orpheus by Jean-Paul Sartre', *Transition*, III, 13, pp. 9–11.
'Isa, G. O. (1965) *Ta'rīkh al-Ṣumāl* (Cairo).
Isaacman, A. (1972) *Mozambique: the Africanization of a European Institution: the Zambesi Prazos, 1750–1902* (Madison: University of Wisconsin Press).
Isaacman, A. (1973) 'Madzi-Manga, Mhondoro and the use of oral traditions a chapter in Barue religious and political history', *JAH*, XIV, 3, pp. 395–409.
Isaacman, A. (1976) *Anti-Colonial Activity in the Zambesi Valley, 1850–1921* (Berkeley: University of California Press).

Isaacman, A. (1977) 'Social banditry in Zimbabwe (Rhodesia) and Mozambique, 1894–1907: an expression of early peasant protest', *JSAS*, IV, 1, pp. 1–30.
Isaacman, A. and Isaacman, B. (1976) *The Tradition of Resistance in Mozambique: the Zambesi Valley, 1850–1921* (London: Heinemann).
Isaacman, A. and Isaacman, B. (1977) 'Resistance and collaboration in Southern and Central Africa, *c.* 1850–1920', *IJAHS*, X, 1, pp. 31–62.
Isaacman, A., Stephen, M., Adam, Y., Homen, M. J., Macamo, E. and Pililão, A. (1980) '"Cotton is the mother of poverty": peasant resistance to forced cotton production in Mozambique, 1938–1961', *IJAHS*, XIII, 4, pp. 581–615.
Isichei, E. (1977) *History of West Africa since 1800* (London: Macmillan).
Issawi, C. P. (1954) *Egypt at Mid-Century* (London: OUP).
Issawi, C. P. (1963) *Egypt in Revolution: an Economic Analysis* (London: OUP).

Jabavu, D. D. T. (1920) *The Black Problem* (Cape Town: Lovedale Press).
Jackson, G. S. (1970) *Music in Durban, 1860–1900* (Johannesburg: WUP).
Jackson, R. D. (1970) 'Resistance to the German invasion of the Tanganyikan coast, 1885–1891' in R. I. Rotberg and A. A. Mazrui (eds) *Protest and Power in Black Africa*, pp. 37–79.
Jacob, G. (1966) 'Des "Temps Malgaches" à la colonisation française: 1883–1896' (Draft Chapter XIX of *Histoire de Madagascar*: Tananarive).
Jacob, G. (1977) 'Influences occidentales en Imerina et déséquilibres économiques avant la conquête française', *Omaly sy Anio*, V–VI, pp. 223–31.
Jacob, G. (1979) 'Sur les origines de l'insurrection du sud-est de novembre–décembre 1904' (typescript ms., to be published in Actes du Colloque International d'Histoire Malgache).
James, C. L. R. (1963) *Black Jacobins: Toussaint L'Ouverture and the San Domingo Revolution* (New York: Vintage Books; reissued London: Allison & Busby 1982).
Janmohamed, K. K. (1974) 'Review of J. Iliffe (ed.) *Modern Tanzanians*', *KHR*, II, 2, pp. 335–7.
Jardine, D. (1923) *The Mad Mullah of Somaliland* (London: H. Jenkins).
Jenkins, P. (ed.) (1975) *Akyem Abuakwa and the Politics of the Inter-War Period in Ghana*, *MBAB*, XII.
Jewsiewicki, B. (1980) 'African peasants in the totalitarian system of the Belgian Congo' in M. Klein (ed.) *Peasants in Africa*, pp. 45–75.
Jewsiewicki, B. (forthcoming) 'Belgian Congo and Ruanda–Urundi, 1908–1940' in A. D. Roberts (ed.) *Cambridge History of Africa*, Vol. VII.
Johns, S. W. (1970) 'Trade unionism, political pressure group or mass movement? The Industrial and Commercial Workers' Union of South Africa' in R. I. Rotberg and A. A. Mazrui (eds) *Protest and Power in Black Africa*, pp. 695–754.
Johnson, G. W. (1966) 'The ascendancy of Blaise Diagne and the beginning of African politics in Senegal', *Africa*, XXXVI, 3, pp. 235–53.
Johnson, G. W. (1974) 'African political activity in French West Africa, 1900–1940' in J. F. A. Ajayi and M. Crowder (eds) *History of West Africa*, Vol. II, pp. 542–67.
Johnson, J. J. (ed.) (1962) *The Role of the Military in Under-developed Countries* (Princeton: PUP).
Johnston, B. F. (1958) *Staple Food Economies of Western Tropical Africa* (Stanford: SUP).
Johnston, H. H. (1899 and 1913) *A History of the Colonization of Africa by Alien Races* (Cambridge: CUP).
Jones, A. G. (n.d.) 'The Republic of Liberia, 1915-1935' (Ms prepared for *UNESCO General History of Africa*).
Jones, H. A. (1962) 'The struggle for political and cultural unification in Liberia, 1847–1930' (PhD thesis: Northwestern University).
Jones, W. O. (1959) *Manioc in Africa* (Stanford: SUP).
Jones-Quartey, K. A. B. (1965) *A Life of Azikiwe* (Harmondsworth: Penguin).
Julien, C. A. (1972) *L'Afrique du nord en marche* (Paris: Julliard, 3rd edn).
July, R. W. (1968) *The Origins of Modern African Thought* (London: Faber).
Justinard, L. V. (1951) *Un grand chef berbère: le caid Goundaf* (Casablanca: Ed. Atlantides).

Kabwegyere, T. B. (1974) *The Politics of State Formation* (Nairobi: EAPH).
Kadalie, C. (1970) *My Life and the ICU: the Autobiography of a Black Trade Unionist in South Africa* (London: Frank Cass).
Kaddache, M. (1970) *La vie politique à Alger de 1919 à 1939* (Algiers: SNED).
Kane, C. H. (1972) *Ambiguous Adventure* (London: Heinemann).
Kaniki, M. H. Y. (1972) 'The economic and social history of Sierra Leone, 1929–1939' (PhD thesis: University of Birmingham).

Kaniki, M. H. Y. (ed.) (1980) *Tanzania under Colonial Rule* (London: Longman).
Kaniki, M. H. Y. (1980a) 'Introduction' in M. H. Y. Kaniki (ed.) *Tanzania under Colonial Rule*, pp. 3–10.
Kanya-Forstner, A. S. (1971) 'Mali–Tukulor' in M. Crowder (ed.) *West African Resistance*, pp. 53–79.
Karani, A. M. (1974) 'The history of Maseno School, 1906–1962, its alumni and the local society' (MA thesis: University of Nairobi).
Karefa-Smart, J. and Karefa-Smart, A. (1959) *The Halting Kingdom: Christianity and the African Revolution* (New York: Friendship Press).
Karoui, J. (1973) 'La régence de Tunis à la veille du protectorat français: débats pour une nouvelle organisation, 1857–1877' (unpublished thesis).
Kassab, A. (1976) *Histoire de la Tunisie: l'époque contemporaine* (Tunis: STD).
Kassab, A. (1979) *L'evolution de la vie rurale dans les régions de la moyenne Medjerda et de Beja-Mateur* (Tunis: Pubn of the University of Tunis).
Kay, G. (1970) *Rhodesia: a Human Geography* (London: University of London Press).
Kay, G. B. (ed.) (1972) *The Political Economy of Colonialism in Ghana: Documents 1900–1960* (Cambridge: CUP).
Keddie, N. R. (1968) *An Islamic Response to Imperialism: Political and Religious Writings of Sayyīd Jamāl ad-Dīn 'Al-Afghani'* (Berkeley: University of California Press).
Kedourie, E. (ed.) (1970) *Nationalism in Asia and Africa* (London: Weidenfeld & Nicolson).
Keltie, J. S. (1893) *The Partition of Africa* (London: E. Stanford).
Kent, R. K. (ed.) (1979) *Madagascar in History, Essays from the 1970s* (Berkeley: Foundation for Malagasy Studies).
Kerr, W. M. (1886) *The Far Interior*, 2 vols (London: Sampson Low).
Kessous, A. (1935) *La vérité sur le malaise algérien* (Bône).
Kesteloot, L. (1974) *Black Writers in French. A Literary History of Negritude* (Philadelphia: Temple UP).
Keyfitz, N. and Flieger, W. (1959) *World Population: an Analysis of Vital Data* (Chicago: Chicago UP).
Kibodya, G. (ed.) (1968) *Aspects of South African History* (Dar es Salaam: EAPH).
Killingray, D. (1978) 'Repercussions of World War I in the Gold Coast', *JAH*, XIX, 1, pp. 39–59.
Kilson, M. (1958) 'Nationalism and social classes in British West Africa', *JP*, XX, pp. 368–87.
Kilson, M. (1970) 'Emergent elites of Black Africa, 1900–1960' in L. H. Gann and P. Duignan (eds) *Colonialism in Africa 1870–1960*, Vol. II, pp. 351–98.
Kimambo, I. N. (1970) 'The economic history of the Kamba', *Hadith*, II, pp. 79–103.
Kimambo, I. N. and Temu, A. J. (eds) (1969) *A History of Tanzania* (Nairobi: EAPH).
Kimba, I. (1979) 'Guerres et sociétés: les populations du Niger occidental au 19ème siècle et leurs réactions face à la colonisation, 1896–1906' (thèse de doctorat de 3e cycle; University of Paris).
Kimble, D. (1963) *A Political History of Ghana. The Rise of Gold Coast Nationalism 1850–1928* (Oxford: Clarendon Press).
King, C. D. B. [President of Liberia] (1922) *Annual Message* (Monrovia: Government of Liberia).
King, C. D. B. (1923) *Annual Message* (Monrovia: Government of Liberia).
King, C. D. B. (1924) *Inaugural Address* (Monrovia: Government of Liberia).
King, C. D. B. (1927) *Annual Message* (Monrovia: Government of Liberia).
King, C. D. B. (1928) *Annual Message* (Monrovia: Government of Liberia).
King, K. J. (1971a) 'The Kenya Maasai and the protest phenomenon, 1900–1960', *JAH*, XII, 1, pp. 117–37.
King, K. J. (1971b) 'The nationalism of Harry Thuku', *TJH*, I, 1, pp. 39–59.
King, K. J. (1972) 'Some notes on Arnold J. Ford and New World Black attitudes to Ethiopia', *JES*, X, 1, pp. 81–7.
King, K. J. and Salim, A. (eds) (1971) *Kenya Historical Biographies* (Nairobi: EAPH).
Kingsley, M. H. (1897) *Travels in West Africa: Congo français, Corisco and Cameroons* (London: Macmillan).
Kipkorir, B. E. (1969) 'The Alliance High School and the origins of the Kenyan African elite, 1926–1962' (PhD thesis: University of Cambridge).
Kiser, C. V. (1944) 'The demographic position of Egypt', *MMFQ*, XXII, 4.
Klein, M. A. (ed.) (1968) *Islam and Imperialism in Senegal: Sine-Saloum, 1847–1914* (Stanford: SUP).
Klein, M. A. (ed.) (1980) *Peasants in Africa* (Beverly Hills: Sage).
Koerner, F. (1968) 'Les débuts du nationalisme malgache 1913–40' (contribution to forthcoming *Manuel d'Histoire de Madagascar*).
Koffi, S. (1976) 'Les Agni-Diabé, histoire et société' (thèse de doctorat de 3e cycle: University of Paris I).

Kopytoff, J. H. (1965) *A Preface to Modern Nigeria: the 'Sierra-Leoneans' in Yoruba 1830–1890* (Madison: University of Wisconsin Press).
Krishnamurty, B. S. (1972) 'Economic policy: land and labour in Nyasaland, 1890–1914' in B. Pachai (ed.) *The Early History of Malawi*, pp. 384–404.
Kuczynski, R. R. (1936) *Population Movements* (Oxford: Clarendon Press).
Kuczynski, R. R. (1939) *The Cameroons and Togoland: a Demographic Study* (London: OUP).
Kuczynski, R. R. (1948–53) *Demographic Survey of the British Colonial Empire*, 3 vols (London: OUP).
Kudsi-Zadeh, A. A. (1980) 'The emergence of political journalism in Egypt', *The Muslim World*, LXX, 1, pp. 47–55.
Kuper, H. (ed.) (1965) *Urbanization and Migration in West Africa* (Berkeley: University of California Press).
Kuper, L. (1971) 'African nationalism in South Africa, 1910–1964' in M. Wilson and L. Thompson (eds), *The Oxford History of South Africa*, Vol. II, pp. 424–76.
Kuran, E. (1970) *La politique ottamane face à l'occupation d'Alger par les Français* (Tunis).
Kyeyune, J. B. (1970) 'The Mubende Banyoro Committee and the struggle to reunite Bunyoro, 1916–1965' (BA diss. (History): Makerere University).

Lacheraf, M. (1965) *L'Algerie: nation et société* (Paris: Maspero).
Langer, W. L. (1935) *The Diplomacy of Imperialism 1890–1902*, Vol. II (New York: Knopf).
Langley, J. A. (n.d.) 'The last stand in West Africa: resistance to British rule in West Africa, 1879–1939' (unpublished paper).
Langley, J. A. (1973) *Pan-Africanism and Nationalism in West Africa 1900–1945. A Study in Ideology and Social Classes* (Oxford: Clarendon Press).
Lanternari, V. (1974) 'Nativistic and socio-religious movements: a reconsideration', *CSSH*, XVI, 4, pp. 483–503.
Last, M. (1967) *The Sokoto Caliphate* (London: Longman).
Last, M. (1974) 'Reform in West Africa: the jihād movements of the nineteenth century' in J. F. A. Ajayi and M. Crowder (eds) *History of West Africa*, Vol. II, pp. 1–29.
League of Nations (1930) *Report of the International Commission of Inquiry into the Existence of Slavery and Forced Labour in Liberia* (Monrovia).
Leith-Ross, S. (1939) *African Women: a study of the Ibo of Nigeria* (London: Routledge & Kegan Paul).
Lejeune-Choquet, A. (1906) *Histoire militaire du Congo* (Brussels: Castaigne).
Lemarchand, R. (ed.) (1977) *African Kingships in Perspective: Political Change and Modernization in Monarchical Settings* (London: Frank Cass).
Lemumo, A. (1971) *Fifty Fighting Years: the Communist Party of South Africa* (London).
Lenin, V. I. (1916) *Imperialism: the Highest Stage of Capitalism* (Peking: Foreign Language Press, 1975 edn).
Leonard, H. (1934) *Le contrat de travail au Congo Belge et au Ruanda–Urundi (entre indigènes et maîtres civilisés)* (Brussels: Larcier).
Le Tourneau, R. (1962) *Evolution politique de l'Afrique du nord musulmane (1920–1961)* (Paris: A. Colin).
Leubuscher, C. (1963) *The West African Shipping Trade, 1909–1959* (Leyden: Sythoff).
Levine, D. N. (1974) *Greater Ethiopia: the Evolution of a Multi-ethnic Society* (Chicago: Chicago UP).
Lewis, I. M. (1961) *A Pastoral Democracy* (London: OUP).
Lewis, I. M. (1963) 'Pan-Africanism and pan-Somalism', *JMAS*, I, 2, pp. 147–61.
Lewis, I. M. (1965) *The Modern History of Somaliland: from nation to state* (London: Longman).
Lewis, W. A. (1965) *Politics in West Africa* (London: Allen & Unwin).
Leys, C. (1975) *Underdevelopment in Kenya. The Political Economy of Neo-colonialism, 1964–1971* (London: Heinemann).
Liebenow, J. G. (1969) *Liberia: the Evolution of Privilege* (Ithaca: Cornell UP).
Lindberg, J. (1952) *A General Economic Appraisal of Libya* (New York: UN).
Linden, I. (1972) 'The Maseko Ngoni at Domwe, 1870–1900' in B. Pachai (ed.) *The Early History of Malawi*, pp. 237–51.
Lindley, M. F. (1926) *The Acquisition and Government of Backward Territory in International Law* (London: Longmans Green).
Ling, D. L. (1967) *Tunisia: from protectorate to republic* (Bloomington: Indiana UP).
Little, T. (1958) *Egypt* (London: Ernest Benn).
Lloyd, P. C. (ed.) (1966) *The New Elites of Tropical Africa* (London: OUP).
Lloyd, P. C. (1972) *Africa in Social Change* (Harmondsworth: Penguin, rev. edn).
Lochner, N. (1958) 'Anton Wilhelm Amo: a Ghana scholar in eighteenth century Germany', *THSG*, III, 3, pp. 169–79.

Lonsdale, J. M. (1968a) 'Some origins of nationalism in East Africa', *JAH*, IX, 1, pp. 119–46.
Lonsdale, J. M. (1968b) 'Emergence of African nations: a historiographical analysis', *AA*, LXVII, 226, pp. 11–28.
Lonsdale, J. M. (1977) 'The politics of conquest: the British in western Kenya, 1894–1908', *HJ*, XX, 4, pp. 841–70.
Louis, W. R. (1963a) 'The United States and the African peace settlement of 1919: the pilgrimage of George Louis Beer', *JAH*, IV, 3, pp. 413–33.
Louis, W. R. (1963b) *Ruanda–Urundi, 1884–1919* (Oxford: Clarendon Press).
Louis, W. R. (ed.) (1976) *Imperialism: the Robinson and Gallagher Controversy* (New York: Franklin Watts).
Low, D. A. (1965) 'Uganda: the establishment of the Protectorate, 1894–1919' in V. Harlow and E. M. Chilver (eds) *History of East Africa*, Vol. II, pp. 57–120.
Low, D. A. (1971) *The Mind of Buganda* (London: Heinemann).
Low, D. A. and Lonsdale, J. M. (1976) 'Introduction: towards the new order 1945–63' in D. A. Low and A. Smith (eds) *History of East Africa*, Vol. III, pp. 1–63.
Low, D. A. and Smith, A. (eds) (1976) *History of East Africa*, Vol. III (Oxford: Clarendon Press).
Luck, A. (1963) *African Saint: the Story of Apolo Kivebulayo* (London: SCM Press).
Luckhardt, K. and Wall, B. (1980) *Organise or Starve! The History of the South African Congress of Trade Unions* (London: Lawrence & Wishart).
Lugard, F. D. (1893) *The Rise of Our East African Empire* (London: Blackwood).
Lugard, F. D. (1919) *Political Memoranda* (London: Frank Cass, 1970 edn).
Lugard, F. D. (1929) *The Dual Mandate in British Tropical Africa* (London: Frank Cass, 1965 edn).
Lynch, H. R. (1967) *Edward Wilmot Blyden: Pan-Negro Patriot* (London: OUP).

Mabona, M. A. (1974) 'The interpretation and development of different religions in the eastern Cape' (unpublished seminar paper: SOAS London).
Mabro, R. and Radwan, S. (1976) *The Industrialization of Egypt 1939–1973: Policy and Performance* (Oxford: Clarendon Press).
McCall, D. F. (1964) *Africa in Time Perspective* (London: OUP).
McCracken, J. (1972) 'Religion and politics in northern Ngoniland, 1881–1904' in B. Pachai (ed.) *The Early History of Malawi*, pp. 215–36.
McEwan, P. J. M. (ed.) (1968) *Twentieth Century Africa* (London: OUP).
McEwan, P. J. M. and Sutcliffe, R. B. (eds) (1965) *The Study of Africa* (London: Methuen).
McGregor, G. P. (1967) *King's College Budo: the First Sixty Years* (Nariobi: OUP).
McIntosh, B. G. (ed.) (1969) *Ngano: Studies in Traditional and Modern East African History* (Nairobi: EAPH).
Mackenzie, J. (1887) *Austral Africa* (London: Low, Marston, Searle & Rivington).
Macmillan, W. M. (1938) *Africa Emergent* (London: Faber).
Macmillan, W. M. (1963) *Bantu, Boer and Briton* (Oxford: Clarendon Press).
McPhee, A. (1926) *The Economic Revolution in British West Africa* (London: Frank Cass, 1971 edn).
Mafeje, A. (1972) 'The fallacy of dual economies', *EAJ*, IX, 2.
Mair, L. (1971) 'New elites in East and West Africa' in V. Turner (ed.) *Colonialism in Africa, 1870–1960*, Vol. III, pp. 167–92.
Makonnen, R. (1973) *Pan-Africanism from Within* (Nairobi: OUP).
Malgeri, F. (1970) *La Guerra Libica* (Rome: Edizione de Storia e Litteratura).
Maltese, P. (1968) *La Terra Promessa* (Milan: Sugareditore).
Mamet, P. (1964) 'Les expériences syndicales en Tunisie, 1881–1956' (unpublished thesis).
Mangat, J. S. (1969) *History of the Asians in East Africa* (London: OUP).
Marais, J. S. (1957) *The Cape Coloured People, 1852–1932* (Johannesburg: WUP).
Marcum, J. (1969) *The Angolan Revolution* (Cambridge, Mass: MIT Press).
Marcus, H. G. (1969) 'Imperialism and expansionism in Ethiopia from 1865 to 1900' in L. H. Gann and P. Duignan (eds) *Colonialism in Africa, 1870–1960*, Vol. I, pp. 420–61.
Marcus, H. G. (1975) *The Life and Times of Menelik II: Ethiopia 1844–1913* (Oxford: Clarendon Press).
Margarido, A. (1972) 'The Tokoist church and Portuguese colonialism in Angola', in R. Chilcote (ed.) *Protest and Resistance in Angola and Brazil*, pp. 29–52.
Marks, S. (1970) *Reluctant Rebellion: the 1906–1908 Disturbances in Natal* (Oxford: Clarendon Press).
Marks, S. (1972) 'Khoisan resistance to the Dutch in the seventeenth and eighteenth centuries', *JAH*, XIII, 1, pp. 55–80.
Marlowe, J. (1965) *Anglo-Egyptian Relations* (London: Cresset Press, 2nd edn).
Marsot, A. L. A. (1977) *Egypt's Liberal Experiment, 1922–1936* (Berkeley and Los Angeles: University of California Press).

833

Martin, C. J. (1961) 'Population census estimates and methods in British East Africa' in K. M. Barbour and R. M. Prothero (eds) *Essays on African Population*, pp. 49–62.

Martin, R. E. R. (1897) *Report on the Native Administration of the British South African Company* (London: HMSO).

Mashingaidze, E. (1974) 'Christianity and the Mhondero cult' (paper presented to the Conference on the Historical Study of Eastern African Religions, Limuru, June 1974).

Mason, P. (1958) *The Birth of a Dilemma* (London: OUP).

Matsebula, J. S. M. (1972) *A History of Swaziland* (Cape Town: Longman).

Matson, A. T. (1970) 'Nandi traditions on raiding', *Hadith* II, pp. 61–78.

Matt, J. R. (ed.) (1914) *Muslim World Today* (London).

Maugham, R. F. R. (1961) *The Slaves of Timbuctu* (London: Longman).

Maunier, R. (1949) *The Sociology of Colonies*, 2 vols (London: Routledge & Kegan Paul).

Mawut, L. L. (1978) 'The Dinka resistance to Condominium rule, 1902–1932' (MA thesis: University of Khartoum).

Mazrui, A. A. (1980) *The African Condition* (London: Heinemann).

Mbiti, J. S. (1969) *African Religions and Philosophy* (London: Heinemann).

Mead, D. C. (1967) *Growth and Structural Change in the Egyptian Economy* (Homewood: Richard D. Irwin Inc.).

Meebelo, H. S. (1971) *Reaction to Colonialism: a Prelude to the Politics of Independence in Northern Zambia, 1893–1939* (Manchester: Manchester UP).

Meek, C. K. (1925) *The Northern Tribes of Nigeria*, 2 vols (London: OUP).

Meillassoux, C. (1972) 'From reproduction to production. A Marxist approach to economic anthropology', *ES*, I, 1, pp. 93–105.

Menaut, J. (1935) 'Les raisons d'un décret', *Afrique Française*, August 1935.

Mérab, E. (1921–9) *Impressions d'Ethiopie, l'Abyssinie sous Ménélik II, par le docteur Mérab*, 3 vols (Paris: Libert & Leroux).

Merad, A. (1967) *Le reformisme musulman en Algérie de 1925 à 1940. Essai d'histoire religieuse et sociale* (Paris: Mouton).

Merlier, M. (1962) *Le Congo de la colonisation belge à l'indépendance* (Paris: Maspero).

Michel, M. (1982) 'L'Appel à l'Afrique—Contribution et réaction à l'effort de guerre en AOF, 1914–1919' (thèse de doct. d'état: University of Paris).

Middleton, L. (1936) *The Rape of Africa* (London: Robert Hale).

Milner, Lord (1921) *Report of the Special Mission to Egypt* (London: HMSO).

Minter, W. (1972) *Portuguese Africa and the West* (Harmondsworth: Penguin).

Miracle, M. P. (1966) *Maize in Tropical Africa* (Madison: University of Wisconsin Press).

Miracle, M. P. (1967) 'Murdock's classification of African food economies' in C. Gabel and N. R. Bennett (eds) *Reconstructing African Culture History*, pp. 201–25.

Mitchell, J. C. (1961) 'Wage labour and African population movements in Central Africa' in K. M. Barbour and R. M. Prothero (eds) *Essays on African Population*, pp. 193–248.

Mitchell, P. (1954) *African Afterthought* (London: Hutchinson).

Moberly, F. J. (ed.) (1931) *History of the Great War. Military operations: Togoland, Kamerun, 1914–1916* (London: HMSO).

Moeller, A. (1938) *Les finances publiques du Congo belge et du Ruanda–Urundi* (Brussels: Larcier).

Moffat, R. U. (1969) *John Moffat, C.M.G. , Missionary* (New York: Negro Universities Press).

Molema, S. M. (1920) *The Bantu Past and Present* (Edinburgh: W. Green & Sons).

Molitor, G. (1937) 'L'introduction et le développement de la culture du caféier arabica chez les indigènes du Ruanda–Urundi', *Le Matériel Colonial*, March, pp. 156–75.

Mondlane, E. (1969) *The Struggle for Mozambique* (Harmondsworth: Penguin).

Moore, C. D. and Dunbar, A. (1969) *Africa Yesterday and Today* (New York: Praeger).

Moreira, E. (1936) *Portuguese East Africa: a Study of its Religious Needs* (London: World Dominion Press).

Morel, E. D. (1906) *Red Rubber* (London: T. Fisher Unwin).

Morel, E. D. (1920) *The Blackman's Burden* (Manchester: National Labour Press).

Moroney, S. (1978) 'Mine worker protest on the Witwatersrand, 1901–1912' in E. Webster (ed.) *Essays in Southern African Labour History*, pp. 32–46.

Morrell, J. R. (1854) *Algeria: the Topography and History, Political, Social and Natural of French Africa* (London: Nathaniel Cook).

Mosley, L. (1963) *Duel for Kilimanjaro. An Account of the East African Campaign, 1914–1918* (London: Weidenfeld & Nicolson).

Mosley, L. (1964) *Haile Selassie: the Conquering Lion* (London: Weidenfeld & Nicolson).

834

Moulaert, G. (1945) *Souvenirs d'Afrique: 1902–1919* (Brussels: Dessart).

Mourão, F. A. A. (1977) *La présence de la culture Africaine et la dynamique du processus social brésilien* (Lagos: Collaquium).

Muffett, D. J. M. (1971) 'Nigeria – Sokoto Caliphate' in M. Crowder (ed.) *West African Resistance*, pp. 269–99.

Mugomba, A. and Nyaggah, M. (eds) (1980) *Independence Without Freedom. The Political Economy of Colonial Education in Southern Africa* (Santa Barbara & Oxford: ABC—Clio Press).

Mungeam, G. H. (1970) 'Masai and Kikuyu responses to the establishment of British administration in East Africa Protectorate', *JAH*, XI, 1, pp. 127–43.

Munongo, A. (1948) 'Lettere de Mwenda II Mukundabantu', *Bulletin des juridictions indigènes et du droit coutumier congolais*, XVI, pp. 199–229, 231–44.

Munro, J. F. (1975) *Colonial Rule and the Kamba* (Oxford: Clarendon Press).

Munro, J. F. (1976) *Africa and the International Economy, 1800–1960* (London: Dent).

Murdock, G. P. (1960) 'Staple subsistence crops of Africa', *GR*, I, 4, pp. 523–40.

Muriuki, G. (1972) 'Background to politics and nationalism in central Kenya' in B. A. Ogot (ed.) *Politics and Nationalism in Colonial Kenya*, pp. 1–17.

Muriuki, G. (1974) *A History of the Kikuyu, 1500–1900* (Nairobi: OUP).

Murtād, A. al-M. (1971) *Mahd'at al-adab al-'arabi al-mu'āsir fi'l-Jazā-ir* (no further details available).

Musham, H. V. (1951) 'Fertility and reproduction of the Beduin', *PS*, IV, 4, pp. 354–63.

Mutibwa, P. M. (1974) *The Malagasy and the Europeans: Madagascar's Foreign Relations 1861–1895* (London: Longman).

Mwanzi, H. A. (1977) *A History of the Kipsigis* (no further details available).

Myint, H. (1968) *The Economics of the Developing Countries* (London: Hutchinson, 3rd edn).

Nevinson, H. W. (1906) *A Modern Slavery* (London & New York: Harper).

Newbury, C. W. (1961) *The Western Slave Coast and its Rulers. European Trade and Administration among the Yoruba and Adja-speaking Peoples of South-western Nigeria, Southern Dahomey and Togo* (Oxford: Clarendon Press).

Newbury, C. W. and Kanya-Forstner, A. S. (1969) 'French policy and the origins of the Scramble for West Africa', *JAH*, X, 2, pp. 253–76.

Newitt, M. D. D. (1972a) 'The early history of the Sultanate of Angoche', *JAH*, XIII, 3, pp. 397–406.

Newitt, M. D. D. (1972b) 'Angoche, the slave trade and the Portuguese, c. 1844–1910', *JAH*, XIII, 4, pp. 659–72.

Newitt, M. D. D. (1973) *Portuguese Settlement on the Zambezi* (London: Longman).

Newitt, M. D. D. (1981) *Portugal in Africa. The Last Hundred Years* (London: C. Hurst).

Newton, A. P. (1923) 'Africa and historical research', *JAf.S*, XXII, 88, pp. 266–77.

Niege, J. L. (1968) *L'imperialisme colonial italien de 1870 à nos jours* (Paris).

Nketia, J. H. K. (1975) *The Music of Africa* (London: Gollancz).

Nkrumah, K. (1957) *Ghana: the Autobiography of Kwame Nkrumah* (London: Nelson).

Nouschi, A. (1962) *La naissance du nationalisme algérien (1914–1954)* (Paris: Éd. de Minuit).

Nouschi, A. (1970) 'La crise de 1930 en Tunisie et les débuts du Néo-Destour', *ROMM*, VIII, pp. 113–23.

Nunes, J. (1928) 'Apontamentos para o estudo da Questão da Mao d'Obra no Districto de Inhambane', *BSGL*, XLVIII.

Nzula, A. T., Potekhin, I. I. and Zusmanovich, A. Z. (1979) *Forced Labour in Colonial Africa* (London: Zed Press).

Obichere, B. I. (1971) *West African States and European Expansion: the Dahomey-Niger Hinterland, 1885–1898* (New Haven: YUP).

Obichere, B. I. (1972) 'L'education coloniale au Sénégal: analyse structurale' in J. L. Balans, C. Coulon and A. Ricard (eds) *Problèmes et perspectives de l'education dans un état du tiers-monde: la cas du Sénégal*, pp. 7–18.

Obiechina, E. (1978) *Culture, Tradition and Society in the West African Novel* (Cambridge: CUP).

O'Brien, P. (1968) 'The long-term growth of agricultural production in Egypt: 1821–1962' in P. M. Holt (ed.) *Political and Social Change in Modern Egypt*, pp. 162–95.

Ochieng, W. R. (1972) 'Colonial chiefs' in B. A. Ogot (ed.) *Politics and Nationalism in Colonial Kenya*, pp. 46–70.

Ochieng, W. R. (1977) *The Second Word: More Essays on Kenya History* (Nairobi: EALB).

Odinga, O. (1967) *Not Yet Uhuru* (Nairobi: Heinemann; London: Heinemann 1968).

Ogot, B. A. (1963) 'British administration in the central Nyanza district of Kenya, 1900–1960', *JAH*, IV, 2, pp. 249–73.

Ogot, B. A. (1971) 'Reverend Alfayo Odongo Mango, 1870–1934' in K. J. King and A. Salim (eds) *Kenya Historical Biographies*, pp. 90–112.

Ogot, B. A. (1972a) (ed.) *War and Society in Africa* (London: Frank Cass).

Ogot, B. A. (1972b) (ed.) *Politics and Nationalism in Colonial Kenya* (Nairobi: EAPH).

Ogot, B. A. (1974a) 'A community of their own' (paper presented to the Conference on the Historical Study of Eastern African Religions, Limuru, June 1974).

Ogot, B. A. (1974b) 'Kenya under the British, 1895 to 1963' in B. A. Ogot (ed.) (1974) *Zamani: a Survey of East African History*, pp. 249–94.

Ogot, B. A. (ed.) (1974) *Zamani: a Survey of East African History* (Nairobi: EAPH, 2nd edn).

Ogot, B. A. (ed.) (1975) *Hadith, V (Economic and Social History of East Africa)* (Nairobi: EALB).

Ogot, B. A. and Ochieng, W. R. (1972) 'Mumboism: an anti-colonial movement' in B. A. Ogot (ed.) *War and Society in Africa*, pp. 149–77.

Ogunba, O. and Irele, A. (eds) (1978) *Drama of Africa* (Ibadan: Ibadan UP).

Ohadike, P. O. (1968) 'Patterns and variations in fertility and family formation, a study of urban Africans in Lagos, Nigeria' (PhD thesis: Australian National University).

Okaro-Kojwang, M. (1969) 'Origins and establishment of the Kavirondo Taxpayers' Welfare Association' in B. G. McIntosh (ed.) *Ngano: Studies in Traditional and Modern East African History*, pp. 111–28.

Oliver, R. (1951) 'Some factors in the British occupation of East Africa, 1884–1894', *UJ*, XV, 1, pp. 49–64.

Oliver, R. (1965) *The Missionary Factor in East Africa* (London: Longman).

Oliver, R. and Atmore, A. (1972) *Africa since 1800* (Cambridge: CUP, 2nd edn).

Oliver, R. and Fage, J. D. (1962 and 1970) *A Short History of Africa* (Harmondsworth: Penguin, 1st and 2nd edns).

Oliver, R. and Mathew, G. (eds) (1971) *History of East Africa: A Century of Change, 1870–1970*, Vol. I (London: Allen & Unwin).

Oloruntimehin, B. O. (1971) 'Constitutional developments and the achievement of independence in French West Africa, 1914–1960', *Tarikh*, III, 4.

Oloruntimehin, B. O. (1972a) *The Segu Tokolor Empire* (London: Longman).

Oloruntimehin, B. O. (1972b) 'Theories and realities in the administration of colonial French West Africa from 1890 to the First World War', *JHSN*, VI, 3, pp. 289–312.

Oloruntimehin, B. O. (1973a) 'French colonisation and African resistance in West Africa up to the First World War', *Genève' Afrique*, XII, 1, pp. 17ff.

Oloruntimehin, B. O. (1973b) 'French colonisation and African resistance in West Africa up to the First World War', *Tarikh*, IV, 3, pp. 24–34.

Oloruntimehin, B. O. (1974) 'The culture content of alien domination and its impact on contemporary Francophone West Africa', *Symposium Leo Frobenius* (Final Report of international symposium organized by German and Cameroon Commissions for UNESCO, 3–7 December 1973, Yaoundé) (Cologne: Deutsche – UNESCO – Kommission; Pullach/Munich: Verlag Dokumentation).

Olusanya, G. O. (1980) 'The nationalist movements in Nigeria' in O. Ikime (ed.) *Groundwork of Nigerian History*, pp. 545–69.

Ominde, S. H. and Ejiogu, C. N. (eds) (1972) *Population Growth and Economic Development in Africa* (London: Heinemann).

Omu, F. I. A. (1968) 'The Nigerian press and the Great War', *Nigeria Magazine*, XCVI, pp. 44–9.

Omu, F. I. A. (1978) *Press and Politics in Nigeria, 1880–1957* (London: Longman).

Opoku, K. A. (1978) *West African Traditional Religion* (Singapore: FEP).

Opoku, K. A. (1978) 'Changes within Christianity: the case of the Musama Disco Christo Church' in E. Fashole Luke, R. Gray, A. Hastings and G. Tasie (eds) *Christianity in Independent Africa*, pp. 111–21.

d'Orleans, H. P. M. (1898) *Une visite à l'empereur Ménélick: Notes et Impressions de Route* (Paris: Librairie Dentu).

Ortiz, F. (1950) *La Africanía de la Música Folklórica de Cuba* (Havana).

Orubuloye, I. O. (n.d.) 'Differentials in the provision of health services and the effects of mortality levels in western Nigeria: a study of Ido and Isinbode communities in Eati Division' (MA thesis: University of Ibadan).

Osuntokun, J. (1975) 'Nigeria's colonial government and the Islamic insurgency in French West Africa, 1914–1918' *CEA*, XV, 1, pp. 85–93.

Osuntokun, J. (1977) 'West African armed revolts during the First World War', *Tarikh*, V, 3, pp. 6–17.

Osuntokun, J. (1978) *Nigeria in the First World War* (London: Longman).

Ousmane, S. (1970) *God's Bits of Wood* (London: Heinemann).
Ouzegane, A. (1962) *Le meilleur combat* (Paris: Julliard).
Owen, R. and Sutcliffe, B. (eds) (1972) *Studies in the Theory of Imperialism* (London: Longman).

Pachai, B. (ed.) (1972) *The Early History of Malawi* (London: Longman).
Padmore, G. (1956) *Pan-Africanism or Communism?* (London: Dobson).
Page, H. J. (1975) 'Fertility patterns: levels and trends' in J. C. Caldwell (ed.) *Population Growth and Socio-Economic Change in West Africa*, pp. 29–57.
Page, H. J. and Coale, A. J. (1972) 'Fertility and child mortality south of the Sahara' in S. H. Ominde and C. N. Ejiogu (eds) *Population Growth and Economic Development in Africa*, pp. 51–66.
Paish, G. (1909) 'Great Britain's capital investments in other lands', *RSSJ*, LXXI, pp. 465–80.
Paish, G. (1910–11) 'Great Britain's capital investments in individual colonial and foreign countries' *RSSJ*, LXXIV, pp. 167–87.
Palley, C. (1966) *The Constitutional History and Law of Southern Rhodesia, 1888–1965* (Oxford: Clarendon Press).
Pankhurst, R. (1962a) 'The foundation and early growth of Addis Ababa to 1935', *EO*, VI, 1.
Pankhurst, R. (1962b) 'The foundations of education, printing, newspapers, book production, libraries and literacy in Ethiopia', *EO*, VI, 3, pp. 266–79.
Pankhurst, R. (1964) 'Italian settlement policy in Eritrea and its repercussions 1880–1896', *BUPAH*, I, pp. 119–56.
Pankhurst, R. (1966) 'The great Ethiopian famine of 1888–1892: a new assessment', *JHMAS*, XXI, 2, pp. 271–94.
Pankhurst, R. (1967) 'Emperor Theodore of Ethiopia: a nineteenth century visionary', *Tarikh*, I, 4, pp. 15–25.
Pankhurst, R. (1968) *Economic History of Ethiopia, 1800–1935* (Addis Ababa: Haile Sellassie I UP).
Pankhurst, R. (1970) 'The Ethiopian patriots: the lone struggle', *EO*, XIII, 1, pp. 40–56.
Pankhurst, R. (1972) 'W. H. Ellis-Guillaume Enrique Ellesio: the first black American Ethiopicist?' *EO*, XV, 2, pp. 89–121.
Pankhurst, R. (1976) 'Ethiopia: 1914–35' (Ms. prepared for *UNESCO General History of Africa*).
Passelecq, F. (1932) *L'essor économique belge. Expansion coloniale, étude documentaire sur l'armature économique de la colonisation belge au Congo* (Brussels: Dcsmct-Verteneuil).
Patterson, S. (1957) *The Last Trek: a Study of the Boer People and Their Afrikaner Nation* (London: Routledge & Kegan Paul).
Pearse, S. (1971) 'Metropolis and peasant: the expansion of the urban-industrial complex and the changing rural structure' in T. Shanin (ed.) *Peasants and Peasant Societies*, pp. 69–80.
Peel, J. D. Y. (1968) *Aladura: a Religious Movement Among the Yoruba* (London: OUP).
Peemans, J.-P. (1968) *Diffusion du progrès économique et convergence des prix* (Louvain: Éd. Nauwelaerts).
Pélissier, R. (1969) 'Campagnes militaires au sud-Angola, 1885–1915', *CEA*, IX, pp. 54–123.
Pélissier, R. (1977) *Les guerres grises: résistance et révoltes en Angola (1845–1941)* (Orgeval: Ed. Pélissier).
Pélissier, R. (1978) *La colonie du minotaure: nationalismes et révoltes en Angola (1926–1961)* (Orgeval: Éd. Pélissier).
Penn, I. G. and Bowen, J. W. E. (eds) (1902) *The United Negro: his Problems and his Progress* (Atlanta: D. F. Luther Publishing).
Penvenne, J. (n.d.) 'Preliminary chronology of labour resistance in Lourenço Marques' (unpublished paper).
Penvenne, J. (1978) 'The impact of forced labour on the development of an African working class: Lourenço Marques, 1870–1902' (paper presented at the Conference of the African Studies Association of the United States).
Penvenne, J. (1979) 'Attitudes toward race and work in Mozambique: Lourenço Marques, 1900–1974' (African Studies Center, Boston University: Working Paper No. 6).
Penvenne, J. (forthcoming) 'Labour struggles at the port of Lourenço Marques, Mozambique, 1900–1943'.
Perham, M. (1934) 'A restatement of indirect rule', *Africa*, VII, 3, pp. 321–34.
Perham, M. (ed.) (1948) *Mining, Commerce and Finance in Nigeria* (London: Faber).
Perham, M. (1960a) 'Psychology of African nationalism', *Optima*, X, 1, pp. 27–36.
Perham, M. (1960b) *Lugard: the Years of Authority, 1898–1945* (London: Collins).
Perham, M. (1961) *The Colonial Reckoning* (London: Collins).
Perham, M. and Bull, M. (eds) (1963) *The Diaries of Lord Lugard*, Vol. I (Evanston: NUP).

837

Perrings, C. (1977) 'Consciousness, conflict and proletarianization: an assessment of the 1935 mine-workers' strike on the Northern Rhodesian Copperbelt', *JSAS*, IV, 1, pp. 31–51.
Perrings, C. (1979) *Black Mineworkers in Central Africa. Industrial Strategies and the Evolution of an African Proletariat in the Copperbelt, 1911–1941* (London: Heinemann).
Person, Y. (1960) 'Soixante ans d'évolution en pays Kissi', *CEA*, I, pp. 86–112.
Person, Y. (1968–75) *Samori: une révolution Dyula*, 3 vols (Paris: Mém. de l'IFAN).
Person, Y. (1969) 'Guinea-Samori' in M. Crowder (ed.) *West African Resistance*, pp. 111–43.
Peters, C. [K.] (1902) *The Eldorado of the Ancients* (London: Arthur Pearson).
Petrides, S. P. (1964) *Le livre d'or de la dynastie salomonienne d'Ethiopie* (Paris: Plon).
Phillip, J. (1828) *Researches in South Africa* (London: Duncan).
Phillipson, D. W. (1977) *The Later Prehistory of Eastern and Southern Africa* London: Heinemann).
Phimister, I. R. and van Onselen, C. (1978) *Studies in the History of African Mine Labour in Colonial Zimbabwe* (Gwelo: Mambo Press).
Plaatje, S. T. (1916) *Native Life in South Africa* (London: King and Sons, 2nd edn; reissued Johannesburg: Ravan Press 1982).
Plancquaert, M. (1932) 'Les Jaga et les Bayaka du Kwango. Contribution historico-ethnique', *IRCBM*, III, 1, pp. 1–184.
Poncet, J. (1952) *La colonisation et l'agriculture européene en Tunisie depuis 1881* (Paris: Mouton).
Ponton, M. M. (1917) *Life and Times of Henry M. Turner* (Atlanta: A. B. Caldwell).
Portal, G. L. (1892) *My Mission to Abyssinia* (London: Arnold).
Porter, D. B. (1978) *Afro-Braziliana* (Boston: G. K. Hall).
Potocki, J. (1900) *Sport in Somaliland: being an Account of a Hunting Trip in that Region* (London: R. Ward).
Price, R. S. (1973) *Maroon Societies: Rebel Slave Communities in the Americas* (New York).
Prothero, R. M. (1965) *Migrants and Malaria* (London: Longmans).
Prothero, R. M. (1968) 'Migration in tropical Africa' in J. C. Caldwell and J. Okonjo (eds) *The Population of Tropical Africa*, pp. 250–73.

Rabearimanana, L. (1980) *La presse d'opinion à Madagascar de 1947 à 1956* (Antananarivo: Librairie Mixte).
Ralston, R. D. (forthcoming) *African Nationalism in Embryo: Influence of American Study Sojourns in Metamorphosis of African Colonial Leadership.*
Ramaḍān, A. M. (1968) *'Tatawura al-Ḥaraka al-Waṭaniyya fī Miṣr 1919–1936* (Cairo).
Ranger, T. O. (n.d.) *The African Churches of Tanzania* (Nairobi: EAPH).
Ranger, T. O. (1965) 'The "Ethiopia" episode in Barotseland, 1900–1905', *RLJ*, XXXVII, pp. 26–41.
Ranger, T. O. (1967) *Revolt in Southern Rhodesia, 1896–1897* (London: Heinemann).
Ranger, T. O. (1968a) 'Connexions between "primary resistance" movements and modern mass nationalism in East and Central Africa', *JAH*, IX, 3, pp. 437–53; IX, 4, pp. 631–41.
Ranger, T. O. (ed.) (1968b) *Aspects of Central African History* (London: Heinemann).
Ranger, T. O. (ed.) (1968c) *Emerging Themes of African History* (Nairobi: EAPH).
Ranger, T. O. (1969) 'African reactions to the imposition of colonial rule in East and Central Africa' in L. H. Gann and P. Duignan (eds) *Colonialism in Africa, 1870–1960*, Vol. I, pp. 293–324.
Ranger, T. O. (1970) *The African Voice in Southern Rhodesia* (London: Heinemann).
Ranger, T. O. (1971) 'Christian independency in Tanzania', in D. B. Barrett (ed.) *African Initiatives in Religion*, pp. 122–45.
Ranger, T. O. (1972) 'Missionary adaptation of African religious institutions: the Masasi case' in T. O. Ranger and I. N. Kimambo (eds), *The Historical Study of African Religion*, pp. 221–52.
Ranger, T. O. (1975) *Dance and Society in Eastern Africa* (London: Heinemann).
Ranger, T. O. and Kimambo, I. N. (eds) (1972) *The Historical Study of African Religion* (London: Heinemann).
Ranis, G. (ed.) (1971) *Government and Economic Development* (New Haven: YUP).
Rathbone, R. (1978) 'World War I and Africa: introduction', *JAH*, XIX, 1, pp. 1–9.
Raum, O. P. (1965) 'From tribal prophets to sect leaders' in E. Benz (ed) *Messianische Kirchen, Sekten und Bewegungen im hautigen Afrika.*
Ray, B. C. (1976) *African Religions: Symbol, Ritual and Continuity* (Englewood Cliffs: Prentice Hall).
Read, M. (1971) 'The Ngoni and Western education' in V. Turner (ed.) *Colonialism in Africa, 1870–1960*, Vol. III, pp. 346–92.
Republic of Liberia (1920) *Report of the Secretary of the Treasury for the Fiscal Year ended October 1, 1919 to September 1920* (Monrovia: Department of the Treasury).
Republic of Liberia (1930) *Report of the Department of State, 30 November 1930* (Monrovia: Department of State).

Republic of Liberia (1931a) *Annual Report of the Department of State, December 1931* (Monrovia: Department of State).
Republic of Liberia (1931b) *Administrative Regulations Governing the Interior* (Monrovia: Department of the Interior).
Republic of Liberia (1934) *Annual Report of the Department of State to the Fourth Session of the Thirty-seventh Legislature* (Monrovia: Department of State).
Republic of Liberia (1940) *Bureau of Statistics: Annual Report 1939* (Monrovia: Bureau of Statistics).
Republic of Liberia (1941) *Import, Export and Shipping Statistics, 1940* (Monrovia: Bureau of Revenues).
Rey, C. F. (1927) *In the Country of the Blue Nile* (London: Duckworth).
Rezette, R. (1955) *Les partis politiques marocains* (Paris: A. Colin).
Rhodie, S. (1968) 'The Gold Coast cocoa hold-up of 1930–31' *THSG*, IX, pp. 105–18.
Riccioli, B. (1661, 1672) *Geographiae et Hydrographiae Reformatae* (Bologna & Venice).
Rigby, P. (1974) 'Prophets, diviners and prophetism: the recent history of Kiganda religion' (paper presented to the Conference on the Historical Study of Eastern African Religions, Limuru, June 1974).
Roberts, A. D. (1974) *A History of the Bemba: political growth and change in north-eastern Zambia before 1900* (Madison: Wisconsin UP).
Roberts, A. D. (ed.) (forthcoming) *Cambridge History of Africa*, Vol. VII (Cambridge: CUP).
Roberts, G. W. (1954) 'Immigration of Africans into the British Caribbean', *PS*, VII, 3, pp. 235–62.
Roberts, S. H. (1929) *The History of French Colonial Policy, 1870–1925*, 2 vols (London: Frank Cass, 1963 edn).
Roberts, Z. B. H. (1934) 'Supplement' to the *Liberian Crisis*, July–August 1934 (Monrovia).
Robertson, E. M. (1977) *Mussolini as Empire-builder: Europe and Africa, 1932–6* (London: Macmillan).
Robinson, R. (1972) 'Non-European foundations of European imperialism: sketch for a theory of collaboration' in R. Owen and B. Sutcliffe (eds) *Studies in the Theory of Imperialism*, pp. 117–142.
Robinson, R. and Gallagher, J. (1961) *Africa and the Victorians: the official mind of imperialism* (London: Macmillan).
Robinson, R. E. and Gallagher, J. (1962) 'The partition of Africa' in F. H. Hinsley (ed.) *The New Cambridge Modern History* Vol. XI, pp. 593–640.
Rochet, G. (1971) *Militari e Politici nelle Preparazione delle Campagna d'Ethiopia* (Milan).
Rodd, J. R. (1923) *Diplomatic Memories: 1894–1901, Egypt and Abyssinia* (London: Arnold).
Rodney, W. (n.d.) 'Political economy of colonial Tanzania, 1890–1934' (seminar paper: Department of History, University of Dar es Salaam).
Rodney, W. (1971a) 'The year 1895 in southern Mozambique: African resistance to the imposition of European colonial rule', *JHSN*, V, 4, pp. 509–36.
Rodney, W. (1971b) 'Resistance and accommodation in Ovimbundu/Portuguese relations' (seminar paper: Department of History, University of Dar es Salaam).
Rodney, W. (1972) *How Europe Underdeveloped Africa* (Dar es Salaam: Tanzania Publishing House).
Rodrigues, J. H. (1964) *Brasil e Africa outro Horizonte* (Rio de Janeiro: Civilicacão Brasileira).
Rodrigues, N. (1976) *Os Africanos no Brasil* (São Paulo: Ed. Nacional).
Rogers, S. G. (1972) 'A history of Chaga politics, 1916–1952' (PhD thesis: University of Dar es Salaam).
Rogers, S. G. (1974) 'The Kilimanjaro Native Planters Association: administrative responses to Chagga initiatives in the 1920s', *TJH*, IV, 1 & 2, pp. 94–114.
Rollins, C. H. (1970) *Black Troubadour: Langston Hughes* (New York: Rand McNally).
Rosberg, C. G. and Nottingham, J. (1966) *The Myth of Mau Mau: Nationalism in Kenya* (Nairobi: EAPH).
Rose, J. H. (1905) *The Development of European Nations, 1870–1900* (London: Constable).
Rosen, F. (1907) *Eine deutsche Gesandschaft in Abessinien* (Leipzig: Von Veit).
Ross, D. (1971) 'Dahomey' in M. Crowder (ed.) *West African Resistance*, pp. 144–69.
Ross, D. H. (1974) 'Ghanaian forowa', *African Arts*, VIII, 1, 1974, pp. 40–49.
Ross, E. A. (1925) *Report on Employment of Native Labor in Portuguese Africa* (New York: Abbott Press).
Ross, R. (1972) 'Black Americans and Italo-Ethiopian Relief 1935–1936', *EO*, XV, 2, pp. 122–31.
Rossetti, C. (1910) *Storia Diplomatic dell'Ethiopia* (Turin).
Rossini, C. C. (1935) *Italia ed Ethiopia dal Tractato d'Uccialli alla Battaglia di Adua* (Rome).
Rotberg, R. I. (1965) *Christian Missionaries and the Creation of Northern Rhodesia, 1880–1924* (Princeton: PUP).
Rotberg, R. I. (1966) *The Rise of Nationalism in Central Africa: the Making of Malawi and Zambia, 1873–1964* (Cambridge, Mass: HUP).
Rotberg, R. I. and Mazrui, A. A. (eds) (1970) *Protest and Power in Black Africa* (New York: OUP).

839

Rout, L. B. (1976) *The African Experience in Spanish America, 1502–Present Day* (Cambridge: CUP).
Roux, E. (1944) *S. P. Bunting: a Political Biography* (Cape Town: privately published).
Roux, E. (1964) *Time Longer than Rope* (Madison: Wisconsin UP, 2nd edn).
Rubenson, S. (1964) *Wichale XVII: the Attempt to Establish a Protectorate over Ethiopia* (Addis Ababa: Haile Sellassie I University).
Rweyemanu, J. (1974) *Underdevelopment and Industrialization in Tanzania: a Study in Perverse Capitalist Industrial Development* (London & Nairobi: OUP).
Rydings, J. (1932) *Report of Mission to the Kru Coast* (Monrovia), April.

Sabrī, A. al-M. (1969) *Muḥammad Farīd* (Cairo).
Sa'dallah, A. K. (1969) *Al-H'araka At Wat'anīya Al-Jazāi'rīya 1900–1930* (Beirut).
Safran, N. (1961) *Egypt in Search of Political Community: an Analysis of the Intellectual and Political Evolution of Egypt, 1804–1952* (Cambridge, Mass: Harvard University Center for Middle Eastern Studies).
Saint-Martin, Y. (1972) *L'empire toucouleur et la France, un demi-siècle de relations diplomatiques (1846–1893)* (Dakar).
Salifou, A. (1973) *Kaoussan ou la révolte Sénoussiste* (Niamey: Centre Nigérien de Recherches en Sciences Humaines).
Samkange, S. (1967) *On Trial for My Country* (London: Heinemann).
Sampson, A. (1960) *Commonsense about Africa* (London: Gollancz).
Sanderson, G. N. (1980) 'Aspects of resistance to British rule in the Southern Sudan, 1900–1928' (unpublished ms).
Sandford, C. (1946) *Ethiopia under Haile Selassie* (London: Dent).
San Marco (1940) 'Le problème des cultures obligatoires dans la production des produits d'exportation' (paper presented to Conférences à l'Ecole Coloniale).
Sarraut, A. (1923) *La mise en valeur des colonies françaises* (Paris: Payot).
Sauer, C. O. (1952) *Agricultural Origins and Dispersals* (New York: American Geographical Society).
Sautter, G. (1966) *De l'Atlantique au fleuve Congo, une géographie du souspeuplement: République Gabonaise, République du Congo*, 2 vols (Paris & The Hague: Mouton).
Sautter, G. (1967) 'Notes sur la construction du chemin de fer Congo–Océan (1921–1934)', *CEA*, VII, 26, pp. 219–99.
Schlemmer, B. (1980) 'Conquête et colonisation du Menabe: une analyse de la politique Galliéni' in *Changements sociaux dans l'ouest malgache* (Paris: Mém. de l'ORSTOM, no. 90), pp. 109–31.
Schnee, H. (1919) *Deutsch-Ostafrika in Weltkriege* (Leipzig: Quelle & Meyer).
Schnee, H. (1926) *German Colonization Past and Future* (London: Allen & Unwin).
Schoffeleers, M. (ed.) (forthcoming) *Guardians of the Land*.
Schoffeleers, M. (forthcoming) 'An organizational model of the Mwari shrines' in M. Schoffeleers (ed.) *Guardians of the Land*.
Schram, R. (1971) *A History of the Nigerian Health Service* (Ibadan: Ibadan UP).
Schumpeter, J. (1955) *Imperialism and Social Classes* (Cleveland & New York: World Publishing).
Schwarz, F. A. O. (1965) *Nigeria: the Tribes, the Nation, or the Race, the Politics of Independence* (Cambridge, Mass: MIT Press).
Scott, W. R. (1966) 'The American Negro and the Italo-Ethiopian crisis, 1934–1936' (MA thesis: Harvard University).
Scott, W. R. (1971) 'A study of Afro-American and Ethiopian relations, 1896–1941' (PhD thesis: Princeton University).
Scott, W. R. (1972) 'Malaku E. Bayen: Ethiopian emissary to Black America, 1936–1941', *EO*, XV, 2, pp. 132–8.
Segal, R. and First, R. (1967) *South West Africa: Travesty of Trust* (London: André Deutsch).
Sekyi, W. E. G. (1915) *The Blinkards* (London: Heinemann, 1974 edn).
Sellassie, G. (1930–32) *Chronique du règne de Ménélik II, roi des rois d'Ethiopie* (Paris: Maisonneuve).
Selous, F. C. (1896) *Sunshine and Storm in Rhodesia* (London: Rowland Ward).
Semi-Bi, Z. (1973) 'La politique coloniale des travaux publics en Côte d'Ivoire, 1900–1940' (thèse de doctorat de 3e cycle: University of Paris VII).
Shack, W. A. (1969) *The Gurage: a People of the Ensete Culture* (London: OUP).
Shanin, T. (ed.) (1971) *Peasants and Peasant Societies* (Harmondsworth: Penguin).
Sharevskaya, B. I. (1968) 'Natzionalno osvoboditelnoe dvizeheniye religia v tropitchescoi Afrike' [National liberation movements and religion in tropical Africa], *Voprosi nauchnogo atiesma*, No. 5 (Moscow).
Sharkasi, M. M. (1976) *Lamahaton Ani Al Awda'a Al Iqtisadia fi Libya Athna'a Al Ahd Al Italy* (Tunisia: Addar al Arabia Lil Kitab).

840

Sharpe, A. (1920) 'The hinterland of Liberia', *GJ*, LV, 4, pp. 289–304.
Sheikh-Abdi, A. (1978) 'Sayyīd Mohamed Abdille Hassan and the current conflict in the Horn', *HA*, I, 2.
Shepperson, G. (1968) 'Ethiopianism: past and present' in C. G. Baeta (ed.) *Christianity in Tropical Africa*, pp. 249–68.
Shepperson, G. and Price, T. (1958) *Independent African: John Chilembwe and the Origins, Setting and Significance of the Nyasaland Native Uprising of 1915* (Edinburgh: Edinburgh UP).
Sheriff, A. M. H. (1980) 'Tanzanian societies at the time of the partition' in M. H. Y. Kaniki (ed.) (1980) *Tanzania under Colonial Rule*, pp. 11–50.
Sherrill, M. (1973) *Unilever et l'Afrique* (Brussels: Cahiers du CEDAF, no. 4).
Shibayka, M. (1965) *Ta'rīkh Shu'aūb Wādī Al-Nīl* (Beirut).
Shibayka, M. (1978) *Al-Sudān wal Thawra al-Mahdiyya*, Vol. I (Khartoum).
Shibeika, M. (1952) *British Policy in the Sudan, 1882–1902* (London: OUP).
Shouqair, N. (1967) *Gurafiat wa Ta'rīkh al-Sūdān* (Beirut).
Shufeldt, R. W. *World Cruise: Liberia and the Liberian Boundary Dispute* (Washington DC: Naval Historical Foundation Collection, Ms Division).
Sik, E. (1964) *The History of Black Africa*, Vol. II (Budapest: Akadémiai Kiadó).
Silberman, L. (n.d.) *The Mad Mullah: Hero of Somali Nationalism* (London).
Simensen, J. (1974) 'Rural mass action in the context of anti-colonial protest: the Asafo movement of Akim Abuakwa, Ghana', *CJAS*, VIII, 1, pp. 25–41.
Simensen, J. (1975a) 'Nationalism from below: the Akyem Abuakwa example', *MBAB*, XII, pp. 31–57.
Simensen, J. (1975b) 'The Asafo of Kwahu, Ghana: a mass movement for local reform under colonial rule', *IJAHS*, VIII, 3, pp. 383–406.
Simons, H. J. and Simons, R. E. (1969) *Class and Colour in South Africa, 1850–1950* (Harmondsworth: Penguin).
Simpson, C. L. (1961) *The Memoirs of C. L. Simpson* (London: Diplomatic Press).
Singh, M. (1969) *History of Kenya's Trade Union Movement to 1952* (Nairobi: EAPH).
Skinner, E. P. (1964) *The Mossi of the Upper Volta. The Political Development of a Sudanese People* (Stanford: SUP).
Skinner, E. P. (1965) 'Labour migration among the Mossi of the Upper Volta' in H. Kuper (ed.) *Urbanization and Migration in West Africa*, pp. 60–84.
Skinner, R. P. (1906) *Abyssinia of to-day; an Account of the First Mission sent by the American Government to the Court of the King of Kings (1903–4)* (London: Arnold).
Slade, R. (1962) *King Leopold's Congo. Aspects of the Development of Race Relations in the Congo Independent State* (London: OUP).
Smith, C. B. (1973) 'The Giriama rising, 1914; focus for political development in the Kenyan hinterland, 1850–1963' (PhD thesis: University of California, Los Angeles).
Smith, E. (1929) *Aggrey of Africa: a Study in Black and White* (London: SCM Press).
Smith, H. M. (1926) *Frank, Bishop of Zanzibar: Life of Frank Weston, D.D. 1871–1924* (London: SPCK).
Smith, R. (1971) 'Yoruba–Ijebu' in M. Crowder (ed.) *West African Resistance*, pp. 170–204.
Sorrenson, M. P. K. (1968) *The Origins of European Settlement in Kenya* (Nairobi: OUP).
Spacensky, A. (1970) *Madagascar, cinquante ans de vie politique: de Ralaimongo à Tsiranana* (Paris: Nouvelles Editions Latines).
Spencer, J. (1971) 'James Beauttah: Kenya patriot' (seminar paper: Department of History: University of Nairobi).
Spillman, G. (1968) *Souvenirs d'un colonialiste* (Paris: Presse de la Cité).
Starr, F. (1925) 'Liberia after the World War', *JNH*, X, 2, pp. 113–30.
Staten, M. (1925) *Annual Report of the Liberian Frontier Force for Fiscal Year 1924–1925* (Monrovia: Republic of Liberia).
Steer, G. L. (1936) *Caesar in Abyssinia* (London: Hodder & Stoughton).
Steinhart, E. (n.d.) 'Anti-colonial resistance and nationalism, the Nyangire rebellion' (unpublished paper).
Stengers, J. (1957) *Combien le Congo a-t-il coûté à la Belgique?* (Brussels: ARSC).
Stengers, J. (1962) 'L'imperialisme colonial de la fin du XIXe siècle: mythe ou réalite', *JAH*, III, 2, pp. 469–91.
Stengers, J. (1969) 'The Congo Free State and the Belgian Congo before 1914' in L. H. Gann and P. Duignan (eds) *Colonialism in Africa 1870–1960*, Vol. I, pp. 261–92.
Stengers, J. (1974) 'La Belgique et le Congo, politique coloniale et decolonisation' in *Histoire de la Belgique Contemporaine, 1914–1970* (Brussels).

Stevens, R. P. (1967) *Lesotho, Botswana, and Swaziland* (New York: Praeger).
Stokes, E. (1966a) 'Barotseland: the survival of an African state' in E. Stokes and R. Brown (eds) *The Zambezian Past: Studies in Central African history*, pp. 261–301.
Stokes, E. (1966b) 'Malawi: political systems and the introduction of colonial rule, 1891–1896' in E. Stokes and R. Brown (eds) *The Zambezian Past: Studies in Central African history*, pp. 352–75.
Stokes, E. and Brown, R. (eds) (1966) *The Zambezian Past: Studies in Central African history* (Manchester: Manchester UP).
Stone, R. L. (1975) 'Rural politics in Ghana in the inter-war period: some comparisons between Akyem-Abuakwa and the states of the Central Province', *MBAB*, XII, pp. 117–41.
Storme, M. (1961) 'Het ontstaan van de Kasai missie', *MARSOM*, XXIV, 3.
Summers, A. and Johnson, R. W. (1978) 'World War I conscription and social change in Guinea', *JAH*, XIX, 1, pp. 25–38.
Sundkler, B. G. M. (1961) *Bantu Prophets in South Africa* (London: OUP, 2nd edn).
Suret-Canale, J. (1964) *L'Afrique noire, l'ère coloniale, 1900–1945* (Paris: Éd. Sociales).
Suret-Canale, J. (1971) *French Colonialism in Tropical Africa, 1900–1945* (London: C. Hurst).
Suret-Canale, J. (1977) 'Strike movements as part of the anticolonial struggle in French West Africa', *Tarikh*, V, 3, pp. 44–61.
Sutcliffe, B. (1972) 'Imperialism and industrialisation in the Third World' in R. Owen and B. Sutcliffe (eds) *Studies in the Theory of Imperialism*, pp. 171–92.
Sutherland, E. (1970) *The Original Bob: the Story of Bob Johnson, Ghana's Ace Comedian* (Accra: Anowuo Educational Publications).
Szereszewski, R. (1965) *Structural Change in the Economy of Ghana, 1891–1911* (London: Weidenfeld & Nicolson).

Tandia, A. K. (1973) 'Bakel et la pénétration française au Soudan' (DES thesis: Faculty of Letters, University of Dakar).
Tangri, R. (1967) 'Early Asian protest in East African Protectorate', *African Quarterly*, LXXII.
Tangri, R. (1968) 'African reaction and resistance to the early colonial situation in Malawi', *JCAHA*, XXV.
Tardits, C. (1958) *Porto-Novo* (Paris & The Hague: Mouton).
Temu, A. J. (1980) 'Tanzanian societies and colonial invasion, 1875–1907' in M. H. Y. Kaniki (ed.) (1980) *Tanzania under Colonial Rule*, pp. 86–127.
Thomas, H. B. and Scott, R. (1935) *Uganda* (London: OUP).
Thomas, R. G. (1975) 'Military recruitment in the Gold Coast during the First World War', *CEA*, XI, 57, pp. 57–83.
Thompson, V. and Adloff, R. (1960) *The Emerging States of Equatorial Africa* (Stanford: SUP).
Thompson, V. and Adloff, R. (1968) *Djibouti and the Horn of Africa* (Stanford: SUP).
Thornton, J. (1973) 'The state in African historiography: a reassessment' *Ufahamu*, IV, 2, pp. 113–26.
Tignor, R. (1971) 'Colonial chiefs in chiefless societies', *JMAS*, IX, 3, 339–59.
Tosh, J. (1973) 'Colonial chiefs in a stateless society: a case-study from northern Uganda', *JAH*, XIV, 4, pp. 473–90.
Tosh, J. (1978) *Clan Leaders and Colonial Chiefs in Lango: the Political History of an East African Stateless Society, c. 1800–1939* (Oxford: Clarendon Press).
Tothill, J. D. (ed.) (1948) *Agriculture in the Sudan* (London: OUP).
Touval, S. (1963) *Somali Nationalism* (Cambridge, Mass: HUP).
Touval, S. (1966) 'Treaties, borders and the partition of Africa', *JAH*, VII, 2, pp. 279–92.
Townsend, E. R. (ed.) (1959) *President Tubman of Liberia Speaks* (London: Consolidated Co. Ltd).
Traoré, B. (1972) *The Black African Theatre and its Social Functions* (Ibadan: UP).
Trentadue, M. (1976) 'La société guinéene dans la crise de 1930: fiscalité et pouvoir d'achat', *RFHOM*, LXIII, 232–3, pp. 628–39.
Trimingham, J. S. (1962) *History of Islam in West Africa* (London: OUP).
Tunley, H. A. (1948) 'Revenue from land and crops' in J. D. Tothill (ed.) *Agriculture in the Sudan*, pp. 198–209.
Tupinier, M. (1940) 'L'influence du commerce sur la mise en valeur de l'AOF' (paper presented to Conférences à L'École Coloniale).
Turner, H. W. (1965) 'Pagan features in West African independent churches', *Practical Anthropology*, July–August 1965, pp. 145–51.
Turner, H. W. (1967) *History of an African Independent Church* (Oxford: Clarendon Press).
Turner, J. M. (1975) 'Les Bresiliens' (PhD thesis: Boston University).
Turner, L. D. (1942) 'Some contacts of Brazilian ex-slaves with Nigeria, West Africa', *JNH*, XXVII, 1, pp. 55–67.

Turner, V. (ed.) (1971) *Colonialism in Africa 1870–1960*, Vol. III, *Profiles of Change: African Society and Colonial Rule* (Cambridge: CUP).

Turton, E. R. (1972) 'Somali resistance to colonial rule and the development of Somali political activity in Kenya, 1893–1960', *JAH*, XIII, 1, pp. 119–43.

Tweedy, O. (1931) *Cairo to Persia and Back* (London: Jarrolds).

Ullendorff, E. (1960) *The Ethiopians* (London: OUP).

Union of South Africa (1922) *Report on the Martial Law Enquiry* (Pretoria: Judicial Commission).

Union of South Africa (1924) *Union of South Africa and the Great War* (Pretoria).

United Nations (Department of Economic and Social Affairs) (1973) *The Determination and Consequences of Population Trends: News Summary of Findings on Interaction of Demographic, Economic and Social Factors* (New York).

Urvoy, M. (1940) 'Le rôle économique du Commandant de cercle' (paper presented to Conférences à l'Ecole Coloniale) (reproduced copy).

Uzoigwe, G. N. (1973) 'The slave trade and African societies', *THSG*, XIV, 2, pp. 187–212.

Uzoigwe, G. N. (1974) *Britain and the Conquest of Africa: the Age of Salisbury* (Ann Arbor: MUP).

Uzoigwe, G. N. (1976a) 'Spheres of influence and the doctrine of the hinterland in the partition of Africa', *JAS*, III, 2, pp. 183–203.

Uzoigwe, G. N. (1976b) 'The Mombasa–Victoria railway, 1890–1902', *KHR*, IV, 1.

Uzoigwe, G. N. (1977) 'The Victorians and East Africa, 1882–1900', *TJH*, V, 2, pp. 32–65.

Vail, L. (1976) 'Mozambique's chartered companies: the rule of the feeble', *JAH*, XVII, 3, pp. 389–46.

Vail, L. and White, L. (1980) *Capitalism and Colonialism in Mozambique: a Study of Quelimane District* (London: Heinemann).

Valdant, P. (1946) Article in *Marchés Coloniaux*, 19, p. 269.

Van de Kaa, D. J. (1971) 'The demography of Papua and New Guinea's indigenous population' (PhD thesis: Australian National University).

Van de Walle, E. (1968) 'Fertility in Nigeria' in W. Brass *et al.*, *The Demography of Tropical Africa*, pp. 515–27.

Van den Berghe, P. (ed.) (1965) *Africa: Social Problems of Change and Conflict* (San Francisco: Chandler).

Van der Laan, H. L. (1965) *The Sierra Leone Diamonds, 1952–1961* (London: OUP).

Van Onselen, C. (1973) 'Worker consciousness in black miners: Southern Rhodesia, 1900–1920', *JAH*, XIV, 2, pp. 237–55.

Van Velsen, J. (1966) 'Some early pressure groups in Malawi' in E. Stokes and R. Brown (eds) *The Zambezian Past: Studies in Central African history*, pp. 376–412.

Van Vollenhoven, J. V. (1920) 'Circulaire au sujet des chefs indigènes' in *Une âme de chef* (Paris: Dieval).

Vansina, J. (1966) *Kingdoms of the Savanna* (Madison: University of Wisconsin Press).

Vansina, J. (1969) 'Du royaume Kuba au territoire des Bakuba', *EC*, XII, 2, pp. 3–54.

Vatcher, W. H. (1965) *White Lager: the Rise of Afrikaner Nationalism* (London: Pall Mall).

Vatikiotis, P. J. (1969) *The Modern History of Egypt* (London: Weidenfeld & Nicolson).

Verger, P. (1968) *Flux et reflux de la traite des nègres entre le Golfe du Bénin et Bahia de Todos os Santos du 17e au 19e siècle* (Paris: Mouton).

Vidal, H. (1970) *La séparation des eglises et de l'état à Madagascar (1861–1968)* (Paris: ICDJ).

Villari, L. (1943) *Storia diplomatica del conflitto Italo-ethiopico* (Bologna: Zanichelli).

Violette, M. (1931) *L'Algérie, vivra-t-elle?* (Paris).

Virgin, E. (1936) *The Abyssinia I Knew* (London: Macmillan).

Vivo, R. V. (1978) *Ethiopia: The Unknown Revolution* (Cuba: Social Science Publishers).

Von Lettow-Vorbeck, P. E. (n.d.) *My Reminiscences of East Africa* (London: Hurst & Blackett).

Wallerstein, I. (1970a) 'Voluntary associations' in J. S. Coleman and C. G. Rosberg (eds) *Political Parties and National Integration in Tropical Africa*, pp. 318–39.

Wallerstein, I. (1970b) 'The colonial era in Africa: changes in the social structure' in L. H. Gann and P. Duignan (eds) *Colonialism in Africa 1870–1960*, Vol. II, pp. 399–421.

Warhurst, P. (1962) *Anglo-Portuguese Relations in South-Central Africa, 1890–1900* (London: Longman).

Warwick, P. (1978) 'Black industrial protest on the Witwatersrand, 1901–1902' in E. Webster (ed.) *Essays in Southern African Labour History*, pp. 20–31.

Waugh, E. (1931) *Remote People* (London: Duckworth).

Webster, E. (ed.) (1978) *Essays in Southern African Labour History* (Johannesburg: Ravan Press).

843

Webster, J. B. (1964) *The African Churches among the Yoruba, 188–1922* (Oxford: Clarendon Press).
Webster, J. B. and Boahen, A. A. (1967) *The Revolutionary Years: West Africa since 1800* (London: Longman).
Weiskel, T. C. (1980) *French Colonial Rule and the Baule Peoples, 1889–1911* (Oxford: Clarendon Press).
Weiss, H. (1967) *Political Protest in the Congo* (Princeton: PUP).
Welbourn, F. B. (1961) *East African Rebels* (London: SCM Press).
Welbourn, F. B. and Ogot, B. A. (1966) *A Place to Feel at Home: a Study of Two Independent Churches in Kenya* (London: OUP).
Welch, C. E. (1966) *Dream of Unity: Pan-Africanism and Political Unification in West Africa* (Ithaca: Cornell UP).
Welsh, D. (1971) 'The growth of towns' in M. Wilson and L. Thompson (eds) *The Oxford History of South Africa*, Vol. II, pp. 172–243.
Wheeler, D. L. (1963) 'The Portuguese in Angola, 1863–1891' (PhD thesis: Boston University).
Wheeler, D. L. (1968) 'Gungunyane the negotiator: a study in African diplomacy', *JAH*, IX, 4, pp. 585–602.
Wheeler, D. L. (1972) 'Origins of African nationalism in Angola: assimilado protest writings, 1859–1929' in R. Chilcote (ed.) *Protest and Resistance in Angola and Brazil*, pp. 67–87.
Wheeler, D. L. and Christensen, C. D. (1972) 'To rise with one mind: the Bailundu war of 1902' in F.-W. Heimer (ed.) *Social Change in Angola*, pp. 53–92.
Wheeler, D. L. and Pélissier, R. (1971) *Angola* (New York: Praeger).
Wiedner, D. L. (1964) *A History of Africa South of the Sahara* (New York: Vintage Books).
Wiese, C. (1891) 'A Labour Question em Nossa Casa', *BSGL*, X, p. 241.
Wilks, I. (1968) 'The transmission of Islamic learning in the Western Sudan' in J. Goody (ed.) *Literacy in Traditional Societies*, pp. 161–97.
Wilks, I. (1975) *Asante in the Nineteenth Century* (Cambridge: CUP).
Willcox, W. F. (1931) 'Increase in the population of the earth and of the continents since 1650', *International Migrations*, Vol. II, *Interpretations* (New York: National Bureau of Economic Research).
Wilson, C. M. (1971) *Liberia: Black Africa in Microcosm* (New York: Harper & Row).
Wilson, F. (1971) 'Farming, 1866–1966' in M. Wilson and L. Thompson (eds) *The Oxford History of South Africa*, Vol. II, pp. 104–71.
Wilson, M. and Thompson, L. (eds) (1971) *The Oxford History of South Africa*. Vol. II (Oxford: Clarendon Press).
Wishlade, R. L. (1965) *Sectarianism in Southern Nyasaland* (London: OUP).
Wolff, R. D. (1974) *The Economics of Colonialism: Britain and Kenya, 1870–1930* (New Haven & London: YUP).
Work, E. (1936) *Ethiopia: a pawn in European diplomacy* (New York).
Wright, J. (1969) *Libya* (New York: 1969).
Wylde, A. B. (1901) *Modern Abyssinia* (London: Methuen).

Xavier, A. A. C. (1889) *Estudos Coloniales* (Nova Goa).

Yancy, E. J. (1934) *Historical Lights of Liberia's Yesterday and Today* (New York: Doubleday Doran).
Yapé, G. (1977) 'Histoire du Bas-Sassendra de 1893–1920' (thèse de doctorat de 3e cycle: University of Paris).
Yesufu, T. M. (1962) *An Introduction to Industrial Relations in Nigeria* (Oxford: OUP).
Young, C. (1965) *Politics in the Congo: Decolonization and Independence* (Princeton: PUP).
Youssoufi, A. (n.d.) 'La résistance marocaine à la prévarication étrangère' (unpublished memoir).

Zayid, M. Y. (1965) *Egypt's Struggle for Independence* (Beirut: Khayats).
Zayid, M. Y. (1968) 'The origins of the Liberia Constitutionalist Party in Egypt' in P. M. Holt (ed.) *Political and Social Change in Modern Egypt*, pp. 334–46.
Zervos, A. (1936) *L'empire d'Ethiopie* (Alexandria).
Ziadeh, N. A. (1962) *Origins of Nationalism in Tunisia* (Beirut: American University of Beirut, Faculty of Arts Pubns, Oriental Ser.).
Zulfu, I. H. (1976) *Shikān Ta'rīkh Askarī Liḥamlat Al-Ganarāl Hicks* (Abu Dhabi).
Zwemer, M. (1914) 'Present-day journalism in the world of Islam' in J. R. Matt (ed.) *Muslim World Today* (London).

Index

Index